1996

COLLECTOR'S
mart magazine

Price Guide to
LIMITED EDITION
COLLECTIBLES

Published by

**krause
publications**

700 E. State Street • Iola, WI 54990-0001
Telephone: 715/445-2214

Please call or write for our free catalog of collectible publications.
Our toll-free number to place an order or obtain a free catalog is 800-258-0929
or please use our regular business telephone 715-445-2214
for editorial comment and further information.

Library of Congress Catalog Number: 95-77317
ISBN: 0-87341-408-X
Printed in the United States of America

Acknowledgements:

Special thanks to Dean Genth, Jay Brown, Meredith Good, Ken Armke, Susan K.
Elliott, Clara Johnson Scroggins and Betty Hodges for their contributions to this book.

Cover Photograph Credits:

Front cover: Friendship Hits the Spot Precious Moments figurine by Sam Butcher,
courtesy Enesco Corp., Itasca, Ill.; *Ndeko/Zaire* doll by Wendy Lawton, courtesy Lawton
Doll Co., Turlock, Calif.; *Lights of Home* plate by Terry Redlin, courtesy Hadley House,
Bloomington, Minn.; *Puppy Love* print by Sandra Kuck, courtesy V.F. Fine Arts, Houston,
Texas; *Starship Enterprise* ornament, courtesy Brent Frankenhoff; Hallmark, St. Louis,
Mo.; *Ada's Bed and Boarding House* cottage, courtesy Terry Tomsyck, Department 56,
Eden Prairie, Minn.

Back cover: The Lovebirds figurine, courtesy Swarovski Silver Crystal, Cranston,
R.I.; and *The Tuck Box Tearoom* print by Marty Bell, courtesy Marty Bell Fine Art,
Chatsworth, Calif.

Table of Contents

How to Use This Price Guide

Information used in this price guide was obtained from various manufacturers, publishers, producers, retailers and other secondary market sources.

Because secondary market prices can vary from region to region—and even within a given locale—values listed in this price guide are just that: *guides* to help collectors, insurance agents, appraisers and others determine the "going" or "asking" price. These values reflect the most often asked-for or sold-for prices. This guide is not published to determine exact pricing information on collectibles and should not be taken as such.

YR	NAME	LIMIT	ISSUE	TREND
① SCHMID			③	
② LOWELL DAVIS			L. DAVIS FARM SET	
85	MAIN HOUSE	CL	42.50	125.00
④	⑤	⑥	⑦	⑧

How to Read the Price Guide

① Manufacturer or Publisher

② Artist

③ Series

④ Year of Production or Publication

⑤ Name of Piece

⑥ Edition Size or Status of Piece

⑦ Issue price

⑧ Quote price at time of this publication

**These abbreviations will be used to indicate edition size or status of a piece:

CL = Closed

FD = Firing Days
    (limited to a certain number of firing days)

OP = Open

RT = Retired

SO = Sold Out

ST = Set
    (two or more items issued together with one price)

SU = Suspended

TL = Time Limited

UD = Undisclosed

YR = Year of issue
    (limited to calendar year of issue)

* = Unknown

Collectibles are listed alphabetically by category (Bells, Cottages, Dolls, etc.); alphabetically by company (Anri, Cybis, etc.); chronologically by year of issue; and alphabetically by title within each issue year.

Note: A range quote is given when a title may be found with several different trademarks (i.e., Hummel figurines) or when one price would not be an accurate reflection on the status of a piece.

Introduction

Welcome collectors, retailers and secondary market devotees to the comprehensive *1996 Price Guide to Limited Edition Collectibles*. We've taken all that we've learned through our experience with *Collector's mart* magazine and combined it with the sagacity of secondary market experts to create a resource of more than 35,000 prices covering the broad spectrum of limited edition collectibles.

Our goal for the *1996 Price Guide to Limited Edition Collectibles* was a simple one: to provide an accurate and comprehensive source for secondary market values. Along the way we found the secondary market to be a strange and exciting phenomena which is ever-changing.

The term "secondary market" is often confusing to collectors. It basically refers to collectibles which are sold out at the retail level and available only through a "secondary" market source. These sources provide a service in which the buying, selling and trading of limited edition art is made available to consumers. Prices are determined by a cross-section of dealers from various regions across the United States. How are those trends (or prices) established? Simple: the law of supply and demand.

We've divided this book into categories that make it easy for you to find information relevant to the items you collect: cottages, dolls, figurines, ornaments, plates, prints and steins. An introduction precedes each section and summarizes many of the trends occurring in today's marketplace.

Items within the listings are arranged alphabetically first by company name, then by series name and then by the artist's last name. They are further organized chronologically by the year in which the collectible was issued, and then alphabetically by the title of the piece. Folios marking each section make flipping through the book quick and easy. A full index will help you locate items for which you may not have the necessary information.

It goes without saying that our staff could have never completed this book without the help of our distinguished panel of secondary market specialists. Within their respective fields these experts have provided us with prices and trends; filled in missing information regarding series and artists; and prepared overviews of the various categories.

Dean Genth, owner of three Hallmark stores and highly regarded in many areas of collectibles, has compiled and provided updates for our vast and varied "Figurine" category.

Meredith B. Good, who owns and operates The Baggage Car, a secondary market brokerage dealing exclusively in ornaments, is recognized by many as the most proficient expert in the area of Hallmark Keepsakes. She has supplied us with current information for our "Ornament" section.

The "Print" portion was updated by Jay Brown, owner of Gallery One. Brown deals in limited edition prints by the industry's leading artists. His firm has successfully served print collectors for more than two decades.

Both our "Cottage" and "Stein" sections were cultivated under the auspices of Ken Armke Sr., who operates Opa's Haus Inc. (OHI), a firm specializing in the import and production of collectible steins. OHI also operates a comprehensive secondary market exchange which deals in both steins and cottages.

We turned to hobby experts Clara Johnson Scroggins, Susan K. Elliott and Betty Hodges to write introductions to the sections of their respective fields of expertise. Ms. Scroggins is considered to have the largest ornament collection of its kind numbering more than 200,000 items from every maker imaginable. She is a regular contributor to *Collector's mart* magazine, has authored several books for Hallmark and appears at speaking engagements across the country.

Susan K. Elliott has plate collecting in her bloodline and has been involved in the industry for more than 20 years. She served as editor for *Plate Collector* magazine and is a regular contributor to *Collector's mart*. She currently serves as executive director of the National Association of Limited Edition Dealers (NALED).

Betty Hodges has 25 years' experience in the area of collectible dolls and has served as a consultant to doll artists. She frequently writes for doll manufacturers and is a regular columnist for *Collector's mart*.

Even with all the information we've gleaned through our market experts and by studying auction reports and exchange service publications, we still strive for more accurate prices. That's where you can help. If you have information on prices realized for limited edition collectibles, please send them to us so that we may update our records. Send prices to: Mary Sieber, 700 E. State St., Iola, WI 54990. We hope you'll find this volume useful and wish you many happy days of collecting.

Bells

Bells—one of the very oldest forms of art—harken back centuries to ancient civilizations long gone. They are steeped in mystery, surrounded by legends of special powers ranging from thwarting demons to invoking curses and lifting spells.

In general, bells were most often used as a signal, marking significant points of ritual, calling to worship, tolling the hours, announcing events, rejoicing, warning and mourning. Their power was at one time extremely significant to many religions. Bells have also been treasured as patriotic symbols and war trophies.

Most cultures today have turned these once utilitarian objects into works of art with respect to shape, materials and ornamentation. Created of porcelain, wood, metal, china, crystal and other materials, the melodious chimers are a double joy for those who collect them because they are both lovely to hear *and* see.

The hobby of collecting limited edition bells rocketed to its zenith in the 1970s, especially during the United States' Bicentennial when a multitude of special bells were produced to commemorate the historic occasion. Unfortunately, the bell market became saturated, and as a result, the hobby settled into a quieter pastime.

Today, many special Bicentennial bells, as well as Lladró porcelain and Waterford crystal bells and Jan Hagara Christmas bells, which are no longer produced, remain popular and do well on the secondary market. Bells produced by Pairpoint still rank high on collectors' lists as well.

YR NAME	LIMIT	ISSUE	QUOTE

BELLS

ANRI
J. FERRANDIZ — ANRI WOODEN CHRISTMAS BELLS

YR NAME	LIMIT	ISSUE	QUOTE
76 CHRISTMAS	YR	6.00	50.00
77 CHRISTMAS	YR	7.00	42.00
78 CHRISTMAS	YR	10.00	40.00
79 CHRISTMAS	YR	13.00	30.00
80 THE CHRISTMAS KING	YR	17.50	18.50
81 LIGHTING THE WAY	YR	18.50	18.50
82 CARING	YR	18.50	18.50
83 BEHOLD	YR	18.50	18.50
85 NATURE'S DREAM	YR	18.50	18.50

J. FERRANDIZ — JUAN FERRANDIZ MUSICAL CHRISTMAS BELLS

YR NAME	LIMIT	ISSUE	QUOTE
76 CHRISTMAS	YR	25.00	80.00
77 CHRISTMAS	YR	25.00	80.00
78 CHRISTMAS	YR	35.00	75.00
79 CHRISTMAS	YR	47.50	60.00
80 LITTLE DRUMMER BOY	YR	60.00	63.00
81 THE GOOD SHEPHERD BOY	YR	63.00	63.00
82 SPREADING THE WORD	YR	63.00	63.00
83 COMPANIONS	YR	63.00	63.00
84 WITH LOVE	YR	55.00	55.00

ARTAFFECTS
R. SAUBER — BELLS

YR NAME	LIMIT	ISSUE	QUOTE
87 MOTHERHOOD BELL	*	25.00	25.00
87 NEWBORN BELL	*	25.00	25.00
87 SWEET SIXTEEN BELL	*	25.00	25.00
87 THE WEDDING BELL (GOLD)	*	25.00	25.00
87 THE WEDDING BELL (SILVER)	*	25.00	25.00
87 THE WEDDING BELL (WHITE)	*	25.00	25.00

R. SAUBER — BRIDE BELLES FIGURINE BELLS

YR NAME	LIMIT	ISSUE	QUOTE
88 CAROLINE	*	27.50	27.50
88 ELIZABETH	*	27.50	27.50
88 EMILY	*	27.50	27.50
88 GROOM	*	27.50	27.50
88 JACQUELINE	*	27.50	27.50
88 LAURA	*	27.50	27.50
88 MEREDITH	*	27.50	27.50
88 REBECCA	*	27.50	27.50
88 SARAH	*	27.50	27.50

G. PERILLO — INDIAN BRAVE ANNUAL BELL

YR NAME	LIMIT	ISSUE	QUOTE
89 CHRISTMAS POW-WOW	YR	24.50	33.00
90 INDIAN BRAVE	YR	24.50	24.50
91 INDIAN BRAVE	YR	24.50	24.50

G. PERILLO — INDIAN PRINCESS ANNUAL BELL

YR NAME	LIMIT	ISSUE	QUOTE
89 THE LITTLE PRINCESS	YR	24.50	30.00
90 INDIAN PRINCESS	YR	24.50	24.50

ARTISTS OF THE WORLD
T. DEGRAZIA — DEGRAZIA BELLS

YR NAME	LIMIT	ISSUE	QUOTE
80 FESTIVAL OF LIGHTS	5000	40.00	95.00
80 LOS NINOS	7500	40.00	85.00

BING & GRONDAHL
E. JENSEN — ANNUAL CHRISTMAS BELL

YR NAME	LIMIT	ISSUE	QUOTE
83 CHRISTMAS IN THE OLD TOWN	YR	45.00	45.00
84 THE CHRISTMAS LETTER	YR	45.00	45.00
85 CHRISTMAS EVE AT THE FARMHOUSE	YR	45.00	45.00
86 SILENT NIGHT, HOLY NIGHT	YR	45.00	45.00
87 THE SNOWMAN'S CHRISTMAS EVE	YR	47.50	47.50
88 THE OLD POET'S CHRISTMAS	YR	49.50	49.50
89 CHRISTMAS ANCHORAGE	YR	52.00	52.00
90 CHANGING OF THE GUARDS	YR	55.00	55.00
91 THE COPENHAGEN STOCK EXCHANGE AT XMAS	YR	59.50	59.50
92 CHRISTMAS AT THE RECTORY	YR	62.50	62.50
93 FATHER CHRISTMAS IN COPENHAGEN	YR	62.50	62.50
80 CHRISTMAS IN THE WOODS	YR	39.50	39.50
81 CHRISTMAS PEACE	YR	42.50	42.50
82 THE CHRISTMAS TREE	YR	45.00	45.00

J. WOODSON — CHRISTMAS IN AMERICA BELL

YR NAME	LIMIT	ISSUE	QUOTE
88 CHRISTMAS EVE IN WILLIAMSBURG	YR	27.50	100.00
89 CHRISTMAS EVE AT THE WHITE HOUSE	YR	29.00	75.00
90 CHRISTMAS EVE AT THE CAPITOL	YR	30.00	30.00
91 INDEPENDENCE HALL	YR	35.00	35.00

YR	NAME	LIMIT	ISSUE	QUOTE
91	INDEPENDENCE HALL	YR	35.00	35.00
92	CHRISTMAS IN SAN FRANCISCO	YR	37.50	37.50
93	COMING HOME FOR CHRISTMAS	YR	37.50	37.50

C.U.I./CAROLINA COLLECTION
J. HARRIS
STERLING CLASSIC

YR	NAME	LIMIT	ISSUE	QUOTE
91	BARN OWL	10,000	100.00	100.00
91	CAMBERWELL BEAUTY	10,000	100.00	100.00
91	CLOUDED YELLOW	10,000	100.00	100.00
91	KINGFISHER	10,000	100.00	100.00
91	LARGE BLUE	10,000	100.00	100.00
91	MOUSE	10,000	100.00	100.00
91	PEACOCK	10,000	100.00	100.00
91	SMALL TORTOISESHELL	10,000	100.00	100.00
91	SWALLOWTAIL	10,000	100.00	100.00

CROWN & ROSE
J. BERGDAHL
12 DAYS OF CHRISTMAS

YR	NAME	LIMIT	ISSUE	QUOTE
82	FIVE GOLDEN RINGS	7500	75.00	78.00
83	SIX GEESE A' LAYING	7500	75.00	78.00
84	SEVEN SWANS A' SWIMMING	7500	78.00	78.00
78	PARTRIDGE IN A PEAR TREE	7500	50.00	300.00
79	TWO TURTLE DOVES	7500	55.00	78.00
80	THREE FRENCH HENS	7500	60.00	78.00
81	FOUR CALLING BIRDS	7500	70.00	78.00

DANBURY MINT
N. ROCKWELL
THE NORMAN ROCKWELL COMMEMORATIVE BELL

YR	NAME	LIMIT	ISSUE	QUOTE
79	TRIPLE SELF-PORTRAIT	*	29.50	35.00

N. ROCKWELL
THE WONDERFUL WORLD OF NORMAN ROCKWELL

YR	NAME	LIMIT	ISSUE	QUOTE
79	BABY-SITTER	*	27.50	29.50
79	BACK TO SCHOOL	*	27.50	29.50
79	BATTER UP	*	27.50	29.50
79	FRIEND IN NEED	*	27.50	29.50
79	GRAMPS AT THE REINS	*	27.50	29.50
79	GRANDPA'S GIRL	*	27.50	29.50
79	LEAPFROG	*	27.50	29.50
79	PUPPY IN THE POCKET	*	27.50	29.50

N. ROCKWELL
VARIOUS

YR	NAME	LIMIT	ISSUE	QUOTE
75	DOCTOR AND DOLL	*	27.50	54.00
76	FREEDOM FROM WANT	*	27.50	44.00
76	GRANDPA SNOWMAN	*	27.50	44.00
76	NO SWIMMING	*	27.50	44.00
76	SAYING GRACE	*	27.50	44.00
76	THE DISCOVERY	*	27.50	44.00
77	KNUCKLES DOWN	*	27.50	40.00
77	PUPPY LOVE	*	27.50	40.00
77	SANTA'S MAIL	*	27.50	40.00
77	THE REMEDY	*	27.50	40.00
77	THE RUNAWAY	*	27.50	40.00
77	TOM SAWYER	*	27.50	40.00

DAVE GROSSMAN CREATIONS
ROCKWELL INSPIRED
NORMAN ROCKWELL COLLECTION

YR	NAME	LIMIT	ISSUE	QUOTE
75	FACES OF CHRISTMAS NRB-75	RT	12.50	35.00
76	BEN FRANKLIN (BICENTENNIAL)	RT	12.50	25.00
76	DRUM FOR TOMMY NRB-76	RT	12.00	30.00
80	LEAPFROG NRB-90	RT	50.00	50.00

ENESCO
KINKA
KINKA BELLS

YR	NAME	LIMIT	ISSUE	QUOTE
89	EASTER..FILLED W/HOPE & BLESSINGS 116610	OP	22.50	22.50
89	YOUR LOVE IS SPECIAL TO ME 116580	OP	22.50	22.50
90	CHRISTMAS IS A TIME OF LOVE 119962	YR	25.00	25.00
91	LIFE IS ONE JOYOUS STEP/ANOTHER 121320	YR	22.50	22.50
91	MAY THE GLOW OF GOD'S LOVE 120596	YR	22.50	22.50

M. ATTWELL
MEMORIES OF YESTERDAY

YR	NAME	LIMIT	ISSUE	QUOTE
90	HERE COMES BRIDE/GOD BLESS HER 523100	OP	25.00	25.00

S. BUTCHER
PRECIOUS MOMENTS ANNUAL BELLS

YR	NAME	LIMIT	ISSUE	QUOTE
80	LET THE HEAVENS REJOICE E-5622	YR	17.00	190.00-225.00
82	I'LL PLAY MY DRUM FOR HIM E-2358	YR	17.00	55.00-65.00
83	SURROUNDED WITH JOY E-0522	YR	18.00	50.00-60.00
84	WISHING YOU A MERRY CHRISTMAS E-5393	YR	19.00	45.00-50.00
85	GOD SENT HIS LOVE 15873	YR	19.00	35.00-42.00
85	WISHING YOU A COZY CHRISTMAS 102318	YR	20.00	35.00-40.00
86	LOVE IS THE BEST GIFT OF ALL 109835	YR	22.50	30.00-40.00
88	OH HOLY NIGHT 522821	YR	25.00	35.00-40.00
88	TIME TO WISH/MERRY CHRISTMAS 115304	YR	25.00	38.00-42.00

YR	NAME	LIMIT	ISSUE	QUOTE
89	ONCE UPON A HOLY NIGHT 523828	YR	25.00	35.00-37.50
90	MAY YOUR CHRISTMAS BE MERRY 524182	YR	25.00	32.00-35.00
92	BUT THE GREATEST OF THESE/LOVE 527726	YR	25.00	25.00-30.00
S. BUTCHER		**PRECIOUS MOMENTS COLLECTION**		
92	WISHING YOU/SWEETEST CHRISTMAS530174	YR	25.00	30.00-35.00
S. BUTCHER		**PRECIOUS MOMENTS VARIOUS BELLS**		
80	GOD UNDERSTANDS E-5211	RT	17.00	45.00-60.00
80	JESUS IS BORN E-5623	SU	17.00	35.00-50.00
80	JESUS LOVES ME E-5208	SU	17.00	40.00-55.00
80	JESUS LOVES ME E-5209	SU	15.00	42.00-60.00
80	PRAYER CHANGES THINGS E-5210	SU	18.00	40.00-55.00
80	WE HAVE SEEN HIS STAR E-5620	SU	17.00	35.00-50.00
81	MOTHER SEW DEAR E-7181	SU	17.00	35.00-52.00
81	THE LORD BLESS YOU AND KEEP YOU E-7175	SU	17.00	35.00-45.00
81	THE LORD BLESS YOU AND KEEP YOU E-7176	SU	17.00	40.00-55.00
81	THE PURR-FECT GRANDMA E-7183	SU	17.00	35.00-52.50
82	THE LORD BLESS YOU AND KEEP YOU E-7179	SU	22.50	35.00-55.00

FENTON ART GLASS
* *

			CHRISTMAS LIMITED EDITION	
93	BELL 7463SD	2500	39.50	39.50
93	BELL 7463TV	2500	30.00	30.00
93	BELL 7465GQ	2500	39.50	39.50
94	BELL 7463VG	1000	35.00	35.00
94	BELL 7463VP	1000	39.00	39.50
94	BELL 7465VK	1000	48.50	48.50
95	BELL 2967TH	900	39.50	39.50
95	BELL 7463TP	900	39.50	39.50
95	BELL 7667TQ	900	45.00	45.00
95	EGG 5145TQ	900	39.50	39.50
* *			**CHRISTMAS SERIES**	
93	BELL 7668HT	3500	39.50	39.50
94	BELL 7463VS	2500	45.00	45.00
95	BELL 7668VT	2500	45.00	45.00
* *			**HISTORICAL COLLECTION**	
93	BELL 3645RV	OP	17.50	17.50
94	BELL 9667SS	OP	25.00	25.00
94	BELL 9667ST	OP	35.00	35.00
95	BELL 9667JE	OP	35.00	35.00
* *			**MARY GREGORY**	
93	BELL 7463RQ	YR	49.00	49.00
94	BELL 7463RY	YR	49.00	49.00
95	BELL 7463RG	YR	49.00	49.00

GOEBEL INC.
MI HUMMEL

			M.I. HUMMEL ANNIVERSARY BELL	
85	ANNIVERSARY BELL HUM-730	CL	*	500.00-1000.00
M.I. HUMMEL			**M.I. HUMMEL ANNUAL BELLS**	
78	LET'S SING HUM-700	CL	50.00	75.00-100.00
79	FAREWELL HUM-701	CL	70.00	50.00-75.00
80	THOUGHTFUL HUM-702	CL	85.00	50.00-75.00
81	IN TUNE HUM-703	CL	85.00	75.00-100.00
82	SHE LOVES ME HUM-704	CL	85.00	100.00-125.00
83	KNIT ONE HUM-705	CL	90.00	100.00-125.00
84	MOUNTAINEER HUM-706	CL	90.00	100.00-125.00
85	SWEET SONG HUM-707	CL	90.00	100.00-125.00
86	SING ALONG HUM-708	CL	100.00	150.00-200.00
87	WITH LOVING GREETINGS HUM-709	CL	110.00	175.00-300.00
88	BUSY STUDENT HUM-710	CL	120.00	150.00-200.00
89	LATEST NEWS HUM-711	CL	135.00	150.00-200.00
90	WHAT'S NEW? HUM-712	CL	140.00	150.00-200.00
91	FAVORITE PET HUM-713	CL	150.00	150.00-200.00
92	WHISTLER'S DUET HUM-714	CL	160.00	175.00-225.00
93	CELESTRIAL MUSICIAN HUM-779	CL	50.00	55.00
MI HUMMEL			**M.I. HUMMEL CHRISTMAS BELL**	
89	CHRISTMAS BELL HUM-775	CL	35.00	60.00-70.00
90	CHRISTMAS BELL HUM-776	CL	37.50	60.00-70.00
91	CHRISTMAS BELL HUM-778	45	39.50	60.00-70.00
93	CHRISTMAS BELL HUM-780	CL	50.00	50.00-60.00
94	CHRISTMAS BELL HUM-781	OP	55.00	55.00
MI HUMMEL			**M.I. HUMMEL CHRISTMAS BELLS**	
92	CHRISTMAS BELL HUM-778	CL	45.00	60.00-70.00

GORHAM
CURRIER & IVES

			CURRIER & IVES MINI BELLS	
76	CHRISTMAS SLEIGH RIDE	YR	9.95	35.00
77	AMERICAN HOMESTEAD	YR	9.95	25.00
78	YULE LOGS	YR	12.95	20.00

YR	NAME	LIMIT	ISSUE	QUOTE
79	SLEIGH RIDE	YR	14.95	20.00
80	CHRISTMAS IN THE COUNTRY	YR	14.95	20.00
81	CHRISTMAS TREE	YR	14.95	17.50
82	CHRISTMAS VISITATION	YR	16.50	17.50
83	WINTER WONDERLAND	YR	16.50	17.50
84	HITCHING UP	YR	16.50	17.50
85	SKATERS' HOLIDAY	YR	17.50	17.50
86	CENTRAL PARK IN WINTER	YR	17.50	17.50
87	EARLY WINTER	YR	19.00	19.00

N. ROCKWELL — **MINI BELLS**

YR	NAME	LIMIT	ISSUE	QUOTE
81	TINY TIM	YR	19.75	19.75
82	PLANNING CHRISTMAS VISIT	YR	20.00	20.00

N. ROCKWELL — **VARIOUS**

YR	NAME	LIMIT	ISSUE	QUOTE
75	SANTA'S HELPERS	YR	19.50	30.00
75	SWEET SONG SO YOUNG	YR	19.50	50.00
75	TAVERN SIGN PAINTER	YR	19.50	30.00
76	FLOWERS IN TENDER BLOOM	YR	19.50	40.00
76	SNOW SCULPTURE	YR	19.50	45.00
77	CHILLING CHORE (CHRISTMAS)	YR	19.50	35.00
77	FONDLY DO WE REMEMBER	YR	19.50	55.00
78	GAILY SHARING VINTAGE TIMES	YR	22.50	22.50
78	GAY BLADES (CHRISTMAS)	YR	22.50	22.50
79	A BOY MEETS HIS DOG (CHRISTMAS)	YR	24.50	30.00
79	BEGUILING BUTTERCUP	YR	24.50	26.50
80	CHILLY RECEPTION (CHRISTMAS)	YR	27.50	27.50
80	FLYING HIGH	YR	27.50	27.50
81	SKI SKILLS (CHRISTMAS)	YR	27.50	27.50
81	SWEET SERENADE	YR	27.50	27.50
82	COAL SEASON'S COMING	YR	29.50	29.50
82	YOUNG MANS FANCY	YR	29.50	29.50
83	CHRISTMAS MEDLEY	YR	29.50	29.50
83	THE MILKMAID	YR	29.50	29.50
84	MARRIAGE LICENSE	OP	32.50	32.50
84	TINY TIM	YR	29.50	29.50
84	YARN SPINNER	5000	32.50	32.50
84	YOUNG LOVE	YR	29.50	29.50
85	YULETIDE REFLECTIONS	5000	32.50	32.50
86	HOME FOR THE HOLIDAYS	5000	32.50	32.50
86	ON TOP OF THE WORLD	5000	32.50	32.50
87	MERRY CHRISTMAS GRANDMA	5000	32.50	32.50
87	THE ARTIST	5000	32.50	32.50
88	THE HOMECOMING	15,000	37.50	37.50

HALLMARK KEEPSAKE ORNAMENTS

R. CHAD — **DICKENS CAROLER BELL**

YR	NAME	LIMIT	ISSUE	QUOTE
90	MR. ASHBOURNE 2175QX505-6	YR	21.75	54.50
91	MRS. BEAUMONT 2175QX503-9	YR	21.75	49.50
92	LORD CHADWICK 2175QX455-4	YR	21.75	49.50
93	LADY DAPHNE 2175QX550-5	YR	21.75	49.50

HAMILTON GIFTS

M. HUMPHREY — **BELLS**

YR	NAME	LIMIT	ISSUE	QUOTE
92	HOLLIES 996095	OP	22.50	22.50
92	SARAH 999385	OP	22.50	22.50
92	SUSANNA 999377	OP	22.50	22.50

HAMPSHIRE PEWTER CO.

* — **TWELVE DAYS OF CHRISTMAS**

YR	NAME	LIMIT	ISSUE	QUOTE
93	PARTRIDGE IN A PEAR TREE	500	65.00	70.00
94	TWO TURTLEDOVES	500	65.00	68.00

JAN HAGARA COLLECTABLES

J. HAGARA — **VICTORIAN CHILDREN**

YR	NAME	LIMIT	ISSUE	QUOTE
86	BETSY	TL	25.00	75.00
86	JENNY	TL	25.00	75.00
86	JILL	YR	35.00	100.00
86	JIMMY	TL	25.00	75.00
86	JODY	TL	25.00	75.00
86	LISA	TL	25.00	75.00
86	LYDIA	TL	25.00	75.00
87	HOLLY	YR	35.00	35.00
88	MARIE	YR	35.00	35.00

KAISER

K. BAUER — **KAISER CHRISTMAS BELLS**

YR	NAME	LIMIT	ISSUE	QUOTE
80	SLEIGH RIDE AT CHRISTMAS	15,000	60.00	60.00
81	SNOWMAN	15,000	60.00	60.00
79	ESKIMO CHRISTMAS	15,000	60.00	60.00

YR	NAME	LIMIT	ISSUE	QUOTE
78	THE NATIVITY	15,000	60.00	60.00

K. BAUER — KAISER TREE ORNAMENT BELLS

YR	NAME	LIMIT	ISSUE	QUOTE
79	THE CAROLERS	YR	27.50	44.00
80	HOLIDAY SNOWMAN	YR	30.00	44.00
81	CHRISTMAS AT HOME	YR	30.00	44.00
82	CHRISTMAS IN THE CITY	YR	30.00	44.00

KIRK STIEFF
*

				BELL
92	SANTA'S WORKSHOP CHRISTMAS BELL	3000	40.00	40.00

K. STIEFF — CHRISTMAS BELLS

90	SILVER BELLS	YR	29.00	29.00
91	HERALD ANGEL	YR	29.00	29.00

* — MUSICAL BELLS

92	ANNUAL BELL 1992	YR	30.00	30.00
77	ANNUAL BELL 1977	CL	17.95	40.00-120.00
78	ANNUAL BELL 1978	CL	17.95	70.00
79	ANNUAL BELL 1979	CL	17.95	50.00
80	ANNUAL BELL 1980	CL	19.95	50.00
81	ANNUAL BELL 1981	CL	19.95	60.00
82	ANNUAL BELL 1982	CL	19.95	60.00-120.00
83	ANNUAL BELL 1983	CL	19.95	50.00
84	ANNUAL BELL 1984	CL	19.95	35.00
85	ANNUAL BELL 1985	CL	19.95	40.00
86	ANNUAL BELL 1986	CL	19.95	40.00
87	ANNUAL BELL 1987	CL	19.95	30.00
88	ANNUAL BELL 1988	CL	22.50	35.00
89	ANNUAL BELL 1989	CL	25.00	25.00
90	ANNUAL BELL 1990	CL	27.00	27.00
91	ANNUAL BELL 1991	CL	28.00	28.00

D. BACORN — NUTCRACKER SUITE MUSICAL BELL

86	NUTCRACKER	OP	29.95	29.95
87	CLARA	OP	29.95	29.95

LANCE CORP.
P.W. BASTON — HUDSON PEWTER BICENTENNIAL BELLS

74	BENJAMIN FRANKLIN	CL	*	75.00-100.00
74	GEORGE WASHINGTON	CL	*	75.00-100.00
74	JAMES MADISON	CL	*	75.00-100.00
74	JOHN ADAMS	CL	*	75.00-100.00
74	THOMAS JEFFERSON	CL	*	75.00-100.00

LENOX CHINA/CRYSTAL COLLECTION
* — ANNUAL CRYSTAL CHRISTMAS BELL

81	PARTRIDGE IN A PEAR TREE	15,000	55.00	55.00
82	HOLY FAMILY	15,000	55.00	55.00
83	THREE WISE MEN	15,000	55.00	55.00
84	DOVE	15,000	57.00	57.00
85	SANTA CLAUS	15,000	57.00	57.00
86	DASHING THROUGH THE SNOW	15,000	64.00	64.00
87	HERALDING ANGEL	15,000	76.00	76.00
91	CELESTIAL HARPIST	15,000	75.00	75.00

* — BIRD BELLS

91	BLUEBIRD	OP	57.00	57.00
91	CHICKADEE	OP	57.00	57.00
91	HUMMINGBIRD	OP	57.00	57.00
92	ROBIN BELL	OP	57.00	57.00

* — CAROUSEL BELL

92	CAROUSEL HORSE	OP	45.00	45.00

* — SONGS OF CHRISTMAS

91	WE WISH YOU A MERRY CHRISTMAS	YR	49.00	49.00
92	DECK THE HALLS	YR	49.00	49.00

LINCOLN MINT BELLS
N. ROCKWELL — LINCOLN BELLS

75	DOWNHILL DARING	*	25.00	70.00

LLADRO
* — ANNUAL CHRISTMAS BELLS

87	CHRISTMAS BELL L5458M	YR	29.50	117.00-130.00
88	CHRISTMAS BELL L5525M	YR	32.50	75.00-100.00
89	CHRISTMAS BELL L5616M	YR	32.50	52.00-195.00
90	CHRISTMAS BELL L5641M	YR	35.00	124.00-156.00
91	CHRISTMAS BELL L5803M	YR	37.50	98.50-130.00

* — LLADRO CHRISTMAS BELL

92	CHRISTMAS BELL L5913M	YR	37.50	70.00

YR NAME	LIMIT	ISSUE	QUOTE

MUSEUM COLLECTIONS INC.
N. ROCKWELL — COLLECTORS BELLS

YR NAME	LIMIT	ISSUE	QUOTE
82 25TH ANNIVERSARY	OP	45.00	45.00
82 50TH ANNIVERSARY	OP	45.00	45.00
82 FOR A GOOD BOY	OP	45.00	45.00
82 WEDDING/ANNIVERSARY	OP	45.00	45.00

PICKARD
*

CHRISTMAS CAROL BELL SERIES

YR NAME	LIMIT	ISSUE	QUOTE
77 THE FIRST NOEL	3000	75.00	75.00
78 O LITTLE TOWN OF BETHLEHEM	3000	75.00	75.00
79 SILENT NIGHT	3000	80.00	80.00
80 HARK! THE HERALD ANGELS SING	3000	80.00	80.00

RECO INTERNATIONAL
J. MCCLELLAND — JOYOUS MOMENTS

YR NAME	LIMIT	ISSUE	QUOTE
80 I LOVE YOU	5000	25.00	25.00
81 SEA ECHOES	5000	25.00	25.00
82 TALK TO ME	5000	25.00	25.00

S. KUCK — SPECIAL OCCASIONS

YR NAME	LIMIT	ISSUE	QUOTE
89 THE WEDDING	OP	15.00	15.00

C. MICARELLI — SPECIAL OCCASIONS-WEDDING

YR NAME	LIMIT	ISSUE	QUOTE
91 FROM THIS DAY FORWARD	OP	15.00	15.00
91 TO HAVE AND TO HOLD	OP	15.00	15.00

S. KUCK — THE RECO BELL COLLECTION

YR NAME	LIMIT	ISSUE	QUOTE
88 CHARITY	OP	15.00	15.00
88 GRACE	OP	15.00	15.00
88 PEACE	OP	15.00	15.00

REED & BARTON
*

NOEL MUSICAL BELLS

YR NAME	LIMIT	ISSUE	QUOTE
80 1980 BELL	YR	20.00	50.00
81 1981 BELL	YR	22.50	45.00
82 1982 BELL	YR	22.50	35.00
83 1983 BELL	YR	22.50	45.00
84 1984 BELL	YR	22.50	50.00
85 1985 BELL	YR	25.00	40.00
86 1986 BELL	YR	25.00	35.50
87 1987 BELL	YR	25.00	30.50
88 1988 BELL	YR	25.00	27.50
89 1989 BELL	YR	25.00	27.50
90 1990 BELL	YR	27.50	27.50
91 1991 BELL	YR	30.00	30.00
92 1992 BELL	YR	30.00	30.00

*

YULETIDE BELL

YR NAME	LIMIT	ISSUE	QUOTE
81 YULETIDE HOLIDAY	YR	14.00	14.00
82 LITTLE SHEPHERD	YR	14.00	14.00
83 PERFECT ANGEL	YR	15.00	15.00
84 DRUMMER BOY	YR	15.00	15.00
85 CAROLER	YR	16.50	16.50
86 NIGHT BEFORE CHRISTMAS	YR	16.50	16.50
87 JOLLY ST. NICK	YR	16.50	16.50
88 CHRISTMAS MORNING	YR	16.50	16.50
89 THE BELL RINGER	YR	16.50	16.50
90 THE WREATH BEARER	YR	18.50	18.50
91 A SPECIAL GIFT	YR	22.50	22.50
92 MY SPECIAL FRIEND	YR	22.50	22.50

RIVER SHORE
N. ROCKWELL — NORMAN ROCKWELL SINGLE ISSUES

YR NAME	LIMIT	ISSUE	QUOTE
81 GRANDPA'S GUARDIAN	7000	45.00	45.00
81 LOOKING OUT TO SEA	7000	45.00	95.00
81 SPRING FLOWERS	347	175.00	175.00

N. ROCKWELL — ROCKWELL CHILDREN SERIES I

YR NAME	LIMIT	ISSUE	QUOTE
77 FIRST DAY OF SCHOOL	7500	30.00	75.00
77 FLOWERS FOR MOTHER	7500	30.00	60.00
77 FOOTBALL HERO	7500	30.00	75.00
77 SCHOOL PLAY	7500	30.00	75.00

N. ROCKWELL — ROCKWELL CHILDREN SERIES II

YR NAME	LIMIT	ISSUE	QUOTE
78 DRESSING UP	15,000	35.00	50.00
78 FIVE CENTS A GLASS	15,000	35.00	40.00
78 FUTURE ALL AMERICAN	15,000	35.00	52.00
78 GARDEN GIRL	15,000	35.00	40.00

ROMAN INC.
E. SIMONETTI — ANNUAL FONTANINI CHRISTMAS CRYSTAL BELL

YR NAME	LIMIT	ISSUE	QUOTE
91 1991 BELL	YR	30.00	30.00
92 1992 BELL	YR	30.00	30.00

YR	NAME	LIMIT	ISSUE	QUOTE
I. SPENCER			**ANNUAL NATIVITY BELL**	
90	NATIVITY	YR	15.00	15.00
91	FLIGHT INTO EGYPT	YR	15.00	15.00
92	GLORIA IN EXCELSIS DEO	YR	15.00	15.00
93	THREE KINGS OF ORIENT	YR	15.00	15.00
F. HOOK			**FRANCES HOOK BELLS**	
85	BEACH BUDDIES	15,000	25.00	27.50-30.00
86	SOUNDS OF THE SEA	15,000	25.00	28.00
87	BEAR HUG	15,000	25.00	27.50
R. FERRUZZI		**THE MASTERPIECE COLLECTION**		
82	MADONNA OF THE STREETS	OP	25.00	25.00
79	ADORATION	OP	20.00	20.00
80	MADONNA WITH GRAPES	OP	25.00	25.00
81	THE HOLY FAMILY	OP	25.00	25.00

ROYAL COPENHAGEN

YR	NAME	LIMIT	ISSUE	QUOTE
S. VESTERGAARD			**CHRISTMAS**	
92	THE QUEEN'S CARRIAGE	YR	69.50	69.50
93	CHRISTMAS GUESTS	YR	69.50	69.50

SANDSTONE CREATIONS

YR	NAME	LIMIT	ISSUE	QUOTE
T. DEGRAZIA			**A FANTASY EDITION**	
*	PARTY TIME	7500	40.00	40.00
*	WEE THREE	7500	40.00	40.00
80	LITTLE PRAYER	7500	40.00	40.00
81	FLOWER VENDOR	7500	40.00	40.00

SCHMID

YR	NAME	LIMIT	ISSUE	QUOTE
L. DAVIS			**DAVIS BELLS**	
91	BLOSSOM	OP	75.00	400.00-650.00
91	CARUSO	OP	75.00	165.00-390.00
91	KATE	OP	75.00	500.00-650.00
91	OLE BLUE & LEAD	OP	75.00	185.00-390.00
91	WILBUR	OP	75.00	250.00-325.00
91	WILLY	OP	75.00	200.00-390.00
*			**DISNEY ANNUALS**	
85	SNOW BIZ	10,000	16.50	16.50
86	TREE FOR TWO	10,000	16.50	16.50
87	MERRY MOUSE MEDLEY	10,000	17.50	17.50
88	WARM WINTER RIDE	10,000	19.50	19.50
89	MERRY MICKEY CLAUS	10,000	23.00	23.00
90	HOLLY JOLLY CHRISTMAS	10,000	26.50	26.50
91	MICKEY & MINNIE'S ROCKIN' CHRISTMAS	10,000	26.50	26.50
L. DAVIS			**LOWELL DAVIS MINI BELL**	
92	NEW DAY	YR	10.00	10.00
M.I. HUMMEL			**M.I. HUMMEL CHRISTMAS BELL**	
92	SWEET BLESSINGS	5000	65.00	65.00
M.I. HUMMEL			**M.I. HUMMEL CHRISTMAS BELLS**	
72	ANGEL WITH FLUTE	YR	20.00	75.00
73	NATIVITY	YR	15.00	80.00
74	THE GUARDIAN ANGEL	YR	17.50	45.00
75	THE CHRISTMAS CHILD	YR	22.50	45.00
76	SACRED JOURNEY	YR	22.50	25.00
77	HERALD ANGEL	YR	22.50	50.00
78	HEAVENLY TRIO	YR	27.50	40.00
79	STARLIGHT ANGEL	YR	38.00	45.00
80	PARADE INTO TOYLAND	YR	45.00	55.00
81	A TIME TO REMEMBER	YR	45.00	55.00
82	ANGELIC PROCESSION	YR	45.00	50.00
83	ANGELIC MESSENGER	YR	45.00	55.00
84	A GIFT FROM HEAVEN	YR	45.00	75.00
85	HEAVENLY LIGHT	YR	45.00	75.00
86	TELL THE HEAVENS	YR	45.00	45.00
87	ANGELIC GIFTS	YR	47.50	47.50
88	CHEERFUL CHERUBS	YR	52.50	52.50
89	ANGELIC MUSICIAN	YR	53.00	53.00
90	ANGEL'S LIGHT	YR	53.00	53.00
91	MESSAGE FROM ABOVE	1500	58.00	58.00
M.I. HUMMEL		**M.I. HUMMEL MOTHER'S DAY BELLS**		
76	DEVOTION FOR MOTHERS	YR	22.50	55.00
77	MOONLIGHT RETURN	YR	22.50	45.00
78	AFTERNOON STROLL	YR	27.50	45.00
79	CHERUB'S GIFT	YR	38.00	45.00
80	MOTHER'S LITTLE HELPER	YR	45.00	45.00
81	PLAYTIME	YR	45.00	45.00
82	THE FLOWER BASKET	YR	45.00	45.00
83	SPRING BOUQUET	YR	45.00	45.00
84	A JOY TO SHARE	YR	45.00	45.00

YR	NAME	LIMIT	ISSUE	QUOTE
	C. SCHULZ		**PEANUTS ANNUAL BELLS**	
79	A SPECIAL LETTER	10,000	15.00	25.00
80	WAITING FOR SANTA	10,000	15.00	25.00
81	MISSION FOR MOM	10,000	17.50	20.00
82	PERFECT PERFORMANCE	10,000	18.50	18.50
83	PEANUTS IN CONCERT	10,000	12.50	12.50
84	SNOOPY & THE BEAGLE SCOUTS	10,000	12.50	12.50
	C. SCHULZ		**PEANUTS CHRISTMAS BELLS**	
75	WOODSTOCK, SANTA CLAUS	YR	10.00	25.00
76	WOODSTOCK'S CHRISTMAS	YR	10.00	25.00
77	DECK THE DOGHOUSE	YR	10.00	20.00
78	FILLING THE STOCKING	YR	13.00	15.00
	C. SCHULZ		**PEANUTS MOTHER'S DAY BELLS**	
73	MOM?	YR	5.00	15.00
74	SNOOPY/WOODSTOCK/PARADE	YR	5.00	15.00
76	LINUS AND SNOOPY	YR	10.00	15.00
77	DEAR MOM	YR	10.00	15.00
78	THOUGHTS THAT COUNT	YR	13.00	15.00
	C. SCHULZ		**PEANUTS SPECIAL EDITION BELL**	
76	BICENTENNIAL	YR	10.00	20.00
	L. DAVIS		**RFD BELL**	
80	BLOSSOM	RT	65.00	450.00-550.00
80	CARUSO	RT	65.00	350.00
80	KATE	RT	65.00	450.00-470.00
80	OLE BLUE & LEAD	RT	65.00	255.00
80	WILBUR	RT	65.00	375.00-400.00
80	WILLY	RT	65.00	395.00

SWAROVSKI AMERICA

	*		**EXQUISITE ACCENTS**	
81	LARGE DINNER BELL 7467	CL	*	110.00
87	MEDIUM DINNER BELL 7467	OP	*	85.00
87	SMALL DINNER BELL 7467	OP	*	65.00

TOWLE SILVERSMITHS

	*		**SILVERPLATED CHRISTMAS BALL BELL**	
79	1979 BALL BELL	10,000	14.50	14.50
80	1980 BALL BELL	10,000	20.00	20.00
81	1981 BALL BELL	10,000	20.00	20.00
82	1982 BALL BELL	5000	24.00	24.00
83	1983 BALL BELL	3500	25.00	25.00
84	1984 BALL BELL	4000	20.00	20.00
85	1985 BALL BELL	4500	25.00	25.00
86	1986 BALL BELL	2500	32.00	32.00
	*		**SILVERPLATED CHRISTMAS BELL**	
80	1980 SILVERPLATED BELL	10,000	17.50	17.50
81	1981 SILVERPLATED BELL	5000	20.00	20.00
82	1982 SILVERPLATED BELL	5000	24.00	24.00
83	1983 SILVERPLATED BELL	3500	24.00	24.00
84	1984 SILVERPLATED BELL	5000	20.00	20.00
85	1985 SILVERPLATED BELL	4500	30.00	30.00
86	1986 SILVERPLATED BELL	4500	30.00	30.00
87	1987 SILVERPLATED BELL	4500	30.00	30.00
88	1988 SILVERPLATED BELL	2500	32.00	32.00
89	1989 SILVERPLATED BELL	4500	34.00	34.00
91	1991 SILVERPLATED BELL	*	20.00	20.00
	*		**SILVERPLATED CHRISTMAS MUSICAL BELL**	
81	1981 MUSICAL BELL	20,000	27.50	27.50
82	1982 MUSICAL BELL	10,000	27.50	27.50
83	1983 MUSICAL BELL	2500	27.50	27.50
84	1984 MUSICAL BELL	4500	25.00	25.00
85	1985 MUSICAL BELL	4000	30.00	30.00
86	1986 MUSICAL BELL	4000	32.00	32.00
87	1987 MUSICAL BELL	4000	32.00	32.00
88	1988 MUSICAL BELL	3500	34.00	34.00
89	1989 MUSICAL BELL	4000	35.00	35.00
90	1990 MUSICAL BELL	*	27.50	27.50
91	1991 MUSICAL BELL	*	27.50	27.50

WATERFORD WEDGWOOD USA

	*		**NEW YEAR BELLS**	
79	PENGUINS	YR	40.00	40.00
80	POLAR BEARS	YR	50.00	50.00
81	MOOSE	YR	55.00	55.00
82	FUR SEALS	YR	60.00	60.00
83	IBEX	YR	64.00	64.00
84	PUFFIN	YR	64.00	64.00
85	ERMINE	YR	64.00	64.00

Cottages

Ken Armke

One of the most popular limited edition collectibles today is the miniature architectural structure, more commonly referred to as the "cottage." The giants in the industry—Department 56, David Winter and Lilliput Lane—still rank high among collectors as their favorite collectible lines.

Due to the popularity of these enduring cottage lines over the past decade or more, many individual collections harbor items of substantial value in today's secondary marketplace. It is not that unusual, for instance, for a Department 56 lighted house, originally purchased for under $35, to have a value more than ten times that amount today.

Nearly everyone knows that certain collectible cottages, once retired, can accelerate in value. However, because the secondary marketing as we know it today is so new, no one knows what will happen to the values over the long run. A question frequently encountered by professionals in the field is: Should I try to sell my valuable possession now, or should I hold on to it even longer in hopes that it appreciates further in value?

No one can adequately answer such an inquiry because: A) it would take a working crystal ball, and B) the concept as practiced today is so new that nothing has been tried and proven over a long term. The best we can do is go back about five years. What have cottages done in this half-decade?

Let's begin with Department 56. What follows is the mid-1990 value, then the mid-1995 value.

Barley Bree Farm/Barn: $165-195 then, $390-500 today

Candle Shop: $100-130 then, $390-500 today

Chesterton Manor: $1,700-1,850 then, $1,825-2,100 today

Dickens' Village Original Set/7: $775-850 then, $1,100-1,300 today

Green Gate: $400-460 then, $300-330 today

Lighthouse (Snow Village): $250-275 then, $550-600 today

Mill: $5,500-6,000 then, $5,000-5,500 today

Public House: $600-650 then, $700-750 today

Smythe Woolen Mill (NEV): $975-1,050 then, $1,050-1,250 today

Village Church: $90-125 then, $160-200 today

What about David Winter cottages during the same period?

Black Bess Inn: $200-260 then, $100-125 today

Fairytale Castle: $225-260 then, $260-325 today

The Grange: $1,450-1,600 then, $900-2,050 today

Tythe Barn: $1,800-2,100 then, $1,450-1,600 today

Woodcutter's Cottage: $275-325 then, $320-360 today

And, finally, a sampling from the Lilliput Lane line.

Acorn Cottage: $60-85 then, $60-85 today

Castle Street: $375-400 then, $425-500 today

Dale Head: $140-190 then, $90-125 today

Red Lion Inn: $250-350 then, $350-450 today

Thatcher's Rest: $200-300 then, $250-300 today

What have we proven with this exercise? Only that with regards to collectible cottages, especially where financial speculation is involved, nothing has been proven.

KEN ARMKE SR., president of Opa's Haus Inc. (OHI), initiated one of the first comprehensive secondary market exchanges covering architectural miniatures. His company has since become a primary source for cottages available on the secondary market.

YR	NAME	LIMIT	ISSUE	QUOTE

COTTAGES

AMAZEE GIFTS
S. MEYERS — CENTURYVILLE

YR	NAME	LIMIT	ISSUE	QUOTE
94	CATHEDRAL	6500	70.00	70.00
94	CENTURY B&O	7000	56.00	56.00
94	CRANES EYE POINT	RT	50.00	55.00
94	GOTHIC CHURCH	10,000	60.00	60.00
94	MR. JON JOHNSON	10,000	50.00	50.00
94	MR. LYLE I. WILSON	12,500	50.00	50.00
94	MS. HILDA GRANT	RT	50.00	55.00
94	MS. MARY THOMPSON	10,000	50.00	50.00
94	POGGY POINT	5000	50.00	50.00
94	RICHARD AND JAN SMITH	10,000	50.00	50.00
94	SCHOOLHOUSE	12,000	56.00	56.00
94	VILLAGE CHURCH	12,500	60.00	60.00

S. MEYERS — EVERGREEN VILLAGE

YR	NAME	LIMIT	ISSUE	QUOTE
94	CANDYMAKER'S COTTAGE	10,000	36.00	36.00
94	CARPENTER'S COTTAGE	8,500	36.00	36.00
94	COBBLER'S COTTAGE	8,500	36.00	36.00
94	COTTAGE POINT LIGHTHOUSE	6500	36.00	36.00
94	EVERGREEN VILLAGE CHURCH	10,000	50.00	50.00
94	TRAIN CONDUCTOR'S COTTAGE	10,000	36.00	36.00

BAND CREATIONS
AMERICA'S COVERED BRIDGES

YR	NAME	LIMIT	ISSUE	QUOTE
95	BRIDGE AT THE GREEN	OP	30.00	30.00
95	CEDAR CREEK BRIDGE	OP	30.00	30.00
95	CHISELVILLE BRIDGE	OP	30.00	30.00
95	ELIZABETHAN BRIDGE	OP	30.00	30.00
95	HUMPBACK BRIDGE	OP	30.00	30.00
95	KNOX BRIDGE	OP	30.00	30.00
95	NARROWS BRIDGE	OP	30.00	30.00
95	ROBERTS BRIDGE	OP	30.00	30.00
95	ROBYVILLE BRIDGE	OP	30.00	30.00
95	ROSEMAN BRIDGE	OP	30.00	30.00
95	SHIMENAK BRIDGE	OP	30.00	30.00
95	THOMPSON MILL BRIDGE	OP	30.00	30.00
95	WAWONA BRIDGE	OP	30.00	30.00

BRANDYWINE WOODCRAFTS
M. WHITING — ACCESSORIES

YR	NAME	LIMIT	ISSUE	QUOTE
94	ELM TREE W/BENCHES	OP	16.00	20.00
94	LAMP W/BARBER POLE	OP	10.50	13.00

M. WHITING — COUNTRY LANE

YR	NAME	LIMIT	ISSUE	QUOTE
95	BERRY FARM	OP	30.00	35.00
95	COUNTRY SCHOOL	OP	30.00	35.00
95	DAIRY FARM	OP	30.00	34.00
95	FARM HOUSE	OP	30.00	35.00
95	THE GENERAL STORE	OP	30.00	35.00

M. WHITING — CUSTOM COLLECTION

YR	NAME	LIMIT	ISSUE	QUOTE
94	SMITHFIELD CLERK'S OFFICE	OP	9.00	10.00

M. WHITING — HOMETOWN IX

YR	NAME	LIMIT	ISSUE	QUOTE
94	BED & BREAKFAST	OP	29.00	34.00
94	CAFE/DELI	OP	29.00	34.00
94	HOMETOWN BANK	OP	29.00	34.00
94	HOMETOWN GAZETTE	OP	29.00	34.00
94	TEDDYS & TOYS	OP	29.00	34.00

M. WHITING — HOMETOWN VI

YR	NAME	LIMIT	ISSUE	QUOTE
93	COUNTRY CHURCH	OP	24.00	30.00
93	DINER	OP	24.00	30.00
93	GENERAL STORE	OP	24.00	30.00
93	PUBLIC SCHOOL	OP	24.00	30.00
93	TRAIN STATION	OP	24.00	30.00

M. WHITING — HOMETOWN VII

YR	NAME	LIMIT	ISSUE	QUOTE
93	CANDY SHOP	OP	24.00	30.00
93	DRESS SHO	OP	24.00	30.00
93	FLOWER SHOP	OP	24.00	30.00
93	PET SHOP	OP	24.00	30.00
93	POST OFFICE	OP	24.00	30.00
93	QUILT SHOP	OP	24.00	30.00

M. WHITING — HOMETOWN VIII

YR	NAME	LIMIT	ISSUE	QUOTE
94	BARBER SHOP	OP	28.00	32.00
94	COUNTRY DOCTOR	OP	28.00	32.00
94	COUNTRY STORE	OP	28.00	32.00
94	FIRE COMPANY	OP	28.00	32.00

YR	NAME	LIMIT	ISSUE	QUOTE
94	SEWING SHOP	OP	26.00	30.00
M. WHITING				**HOMETOWN X**
95	BRICK CHURCH	OP	29.00	32.00
95	GENERAL HOSPITAL	OP	29.00	32.00
95	POLICE STATION	OP	29.00	32.00
95	THE DOLL SHOPPE	OP	29.00	32.00
95	THE GIFT BOX	OP	29.00	32.00
M. WHITING				**NORTH POLE COLLECTION**
93	CANDY CANE FACTORY	OP	24.00	30.00
93	ELF CLUB	OP	24.00	30.00
93	TEDDY BEAR FACTORY	OP	24.00	30.00
93	TOWN CHRISTMAS TREE	OP	20.00	25.00
94	POST OFFICE	OP	25.00	30.00
94	TOWN HALL	OP	25.00	30.00
M. WHITING				**TREASURED TIMES**
94	HALLOWEEN HOUSE	750	32.00	40.00
94	HAPPY BIRTHDAY HOUSE	750	32.00	40.00
94	MOTHER'S DAY HOUSE	750	32.00	40.00
94	NEW BABY BOY HOUSE	750	32.00	40.00
94	NEW BABY GIRL HOUSE	750	32.00	40.00
94	VALENTINE'S DAY HOUSE	750	32.00	40.00
M. WHITING				**WILLIAMSBURG COLLECTION**
93	CAMPBELL'S TAVERN	OP	28.00	32.00
93	KINGS ARM TAVERN	OP	25.00	30.00
M. WHITING				**YORKTOWN COLLECTION**
93	DIGGES HOUSE	OP	22.00	27.00

CAVANAUGH GROUP

			COCA-COLA BRAND TOWN SQ. COLLECTION	
92	CANDLER'S DRUG	RT	39.99	100.00
92	DEE'S BOARDING HOUSE	RT	39.99	400.00
92	DICK'S LUNCHEONETTE	RT	39.99	75.00
92	GILBERT'S GROCERY	RT	39.99	150.00
92	HOWARD OIL	RT	39.99	150.00
92	TRAIN DEPOT	RT	39.99	250.00
93	CITY HALL	RT	39.99	50.00
93	JACOB'S PHARMACY	5000	25.00	300.00
93	MOONEY'S ANTIQUE BARN	RT	39.99	50.00
93	ROUTE 93 COVERED BRIDGE	OP	19.99	20.00
93	T. TAYLOR'S EMPORIUM	RT	39.99	50.00
93	TICK TOCK DINER, THE	OP	39.99	40.00
94	FLYING "A" SERIES STATION	OP	39.99	40.00
94	MCMAHON'S GENERAL STORE	OP	39.99	40.00
94	PLAZA DRUGS	OP	39.99	40.00
94	STATION #14 FIREHOUSE	OP	39.99	40.00
94	STRAND THEATRE	OP	39.99	40.00
94	TOWN GAZEBO	OP	19.99	20.00
95	COCA-COLA BOTTLING WORKS	OP	39.99	40.00
95	GRIST MILL	OP	39.99	40.00
95	JENNY'S SWEET SHOP	OP	39.99	40.00
95	LIGHTHOUSE POINT SNACK BAR	OP	39.99	40.00

DEPARTMENT 56

				*
*	BETSY TROTWOOD'S COTTAGE	*	*	95.00-100.00
*				**ALPINE VILLAGE COLLECTION**
86	ALPINE VILLAGE 6540-4 (SET OF 5)	OP	150.00	185.00
87	ALPINE CHURCH 6541-2	RT	32.00	235.00-325.00
87	JOSEF ENGEL FARMHOUSE 5952-8	RT	33.00	830
88	GRIST MILL 5953-6	OP	42.00	45.00
90	BAHNOF 5615-4	RT	42.00	70.00-100.00
91	ST. NIKOLAUS KIRCHE 5617-0	OP	37.50	37.50
93	SPORT LADEN 5612-0	OP	50.00	50.00
*				**BACHMAN'S**
87	HOME TOWN BOARDING HOUSE 670-0	SU	34.00	275.00
87	HOME TOWN CHURCH 671-8	SU	40.00	300.00
88	HOME TOWN DRUGSTORE 672-6	SU	40.00	675.00
*				**CHRISTMAS IN THE CITY**
87	BAKERY	RT	37.00	100.00-125.00
87	CHRISTMAS IN THE CITY 6512-9 (SET OF 3)	RT	112.00	450.00
87	PALACE THEATRE 5963-3	RT	45.00	1000.00-1200.00
87	SUTTON PLACE BROWNSTONES 5961-7	RT	80.00	850.00-1000.00
87	THE CATHEDRAL 5962-5	RT	60.00	325.00-400.00
87	TOWER RESTAURANT	RT	37.00	165.00-225.00
87	TOY SHOP & PET STORE	RT	37.00	180.00-300.00
88	CITY HALL 5969-2	RT	65.00	150.00-200.00
88	HANK'S MARKET 5970-6	RT	40.00	85.00-100.00

O'Donovan's Castle *is an impressive issue created by David Winter for John Hine Studios.*

Collectors purchasing David Winter's Birthstone Wishing Well *were given a choice of gemstones to signify the month in which they were born.*

Blossom Cottage *is represenative of the romantic English cottages sculpted by David Winter.*

Hogmanay *was created by David Winter for John Hine Studios.*

Pudding Cottage *by David Winter was issued in 1991 by John Hine Studios.*

Cherry Hill School *was sculpted by Moe Wideman as part of the "American Collection" for John Hine Studios.*

YR	NAME	LIMIT	ISSUE	QUOTE
88	THE CHOCOLATE SHOPPE 5968-4	RT	40.00	90.00-120.00
88	VARIETY STORE 5972-2	RT	45.00	150.00-200.00
89	5607 PARK AVENUE TOWNHOUSE 5977-3	RT	48.00	80.00-100.00
89	5609 PARK AVENUE TOWNHOUSE 5978-1	RT	48.00	85.00-100.00
89	DOROTHY'S DRESS SHOP 5974-9	12,500	70.00	375.00-400.00
89	RITZ HOTEL 5973-0	RT	55.00	85.00-100.00
90	RED BRICK FIRE STATION 5536-0	OP	55.00	55.00
90	THE DOCTOR'S OFFICE 5544-1	RT	60.00	105.00-125.00
90	WONG'S IN CHINATOWN 5537-9	RT	55.00	85.00-100.00
91	"LITTLE ITALY" RISTORANTE 5538-7	OP	50.00	50.00
91	ALL SAINTS CORNER CHURCH 5542-5	OP	96.00	96.00
91	ARTS ACADEMY 5543-3	RT	45.00	70.00-90.00
91	CATHEDRAL CHURCH OF ST. MARK 5549-2	17,500	120.00	120.00
91	HOLLYDALE'S DEPARTMENT STORE 5534-4	OP	75.00	75.00
92	CATHEDRAL CHURCH OF ST. MARKS 5549-2	3,024	120.00	2800.00-6000.00
94	CITY BROKERAGE HOUSE	OP	48.00	48
*			**DICKENS' VILLAGE COLLECTION**	
84	ABEL BEESLEY BUTCHER 6515-3	RT	25.00	90.00-110.00
84	BEAN AND SON SMITHY SHOP 6515-3	RT	25.00	170.00-200.00
84	CANDLE SHOP 6515-3	RT	25.00	390.00-500.00
84	CROWNTREE INN 6515-3	RT	25.00	320.00-360.00
84	GOLDEN SWAN BAKER 6515-3	RT	25.00	200.00-230.00
84	GREEN GROCER 6515-3	RT	25.00	180.00-220.00
84	JONES & CO. BRUSH/BASKET SHOP 6515-3	RT	25.00	265.00-385.00
84	THE ORIGINAL SHOPS 6515-3 (SET OF 7)	RT	175.00	1325.00-1500.00
85	DICKENS' COTTAGES 6518-8 (SET OF 3)	RT	75.00	900.00-1200.00
85	DICKENS' VILLAGE CHURCH (CREAM) 6516-1	RT	35.00	235.00-300.00
85	DICKENS' VILLAGE CHURCH (DARK) 6516-1	RT	35.00	165.00-230.00
85	DICKENS' VILLAGE CHURCH (GREEN) 6516-1	RT	35.00	350.00
85	DICKENS' VILLAGE CHURCH (TAN) 6516-1	RT	35.00	170.00
85	DICKENS' VILLAGE MILL 6519-6	2,500	35.00	4875.00-5725.00
85	STONE COTTAGE 6518-8	RT	25.00	488.00-663.00
85	THATCHED COTTAGE 6518-8	RT	25.00	210.00
85	TUDOR COTTAGE 6518-8	RT	25.00	455.00-535.00
86	BLYTHE POND MILL HOUSE 6508-0	RT	37.00	350.00-520.00
86	BY THE POND MILL HOUSE 6508-0	RT	37.00	156.00-195.00
86	CHADBURY STATION & TRAIN 6528-5	RT	65.00	455.00-500.00
86	CHRISTMAS/COTTAGES 6500-5 (SET OF 3)	OP	75.00	90.00
86	COTTAGE TOY SHOP 6507-2	RT	27.00	371.00-377.00
86	DICKENS' LANE SHOPS 6507-2 (SET OF 3)	RT	80.00	748.00
86	NORMAN CHURCH 6502-1	3,500	40.00	3120.00-3250.00
86	THOMAS KERSEY COFFEE HOUSE 6507-2	RT	27.00	156.00-190.00
86	TUTTLE'S PUB 6507-2	RT	27.00	312.00-371.00
87	BARLEY BREE FARMHOUSE 5900-5 (SET OF 2)	RT	60.00	390.00-500.00
87	BRICK ABBEY 6549-8	RT	33.00	442.00-468.00
87	CHESTERTON MANOR HOUSE 6568-4	7,500	45.00	1825.00-2100.00
87	KENILWORTH CASTLE 5916-1	RT	70.00	480.00
87	THE OLD CURIOUSITY SHOP 5905-6	OP	32.00	37.50
88	BOOTER AND COBBLER 5924-2	RT	32.00	91.00-130.00
88	C. FLETCHER PUBLIC HOUSE 5904-8	12,500	35.00	700.00-750.00
88	COBBLESTONE SHOPS 5924-2 (SET OF 3)	RT	95.00	377.00-384.00
88	COUNTING HOUSE OF S. THIMBLETON 5902-1	RT	32.00	91.00-117.00
88	IVY GLEN CHURCH 5927-7	RT	35.00	98.00-111.00
88	MERCHANT SHOPS 5926-9 (SET OF 5)	RT	150.00	260.00-285.00
88	MERMAID FISH SHOPPE	RT	32.50	65.00-85.00
88	NICHOLAS NICKLEBY 5925-0 (SET OF 2)	RT	72.00	170.00-220.00
88	NICKOLAS NICKLEBY COTTAGE 5925-0	RT	36.00	90.00
88	T. WELLS FRUIT & SPICE SHOP 5924-2	RT	32.00	59.00-156.00
88	THE WOOL SHOP 5924-2	RT	32.00	195.00-247.00
88	WACKFORD SQUEERS BOARDING SCHOOL 5925-0	RT	36.00	91.00-111.00
89	COBLES POLICE STATION 5583-2	RT	37.50	111.00-130.00
89	DAVID COPPERFIELD 5550-6 (SET OF 3)	RT	125.00	125.00-315.00
89	GREEN GATE COTTAGE 5586-7	RT	65.00	300.00-330.00
89	KNOTTINGHILL CHURCH 5582-4	OP	50.00	50.00
89	PEGGOTTY'S SEASIDE COTTAGE (TAN) 5550-6	RT	42.00	143.00-156.00
89	RUTH MARION SCOTCH WOOLENS 5585-9	17,500	65.00	455.00-494.00
89	THE FLAT OF EBENEZER SCROOGE 5587-5	OP	37.50	37.50
89	THEATRE ROYAL 5584-0	RT	45.00	72.00-85.00
89	VICTORIA STATION 5574-3	OP	100.00	110
90	BISHOPS OAST HOUSE 5567-0	RT	45.00	78.00-91.00
90	KINGS ROAD 5568-9 (SET OF 2)	OP	72.00	75.00
91	ASHBURY INN 5555-7	OP	55.00	55.00
91	FAGIN'S HIDE-A-WAY 5552-2	OP	68.00	68.00
91	NEPHEW FRED'S FLAT 5557-3	RT	35.00	65.00-98.00
91	OLIVER TWIST 5553-0 (SET OF 2)	RT	75.00	143.00-150.00
92	BLUEBIRD SEED AND BULB 5642-1	OP	48.00	48.00

YR	NAME	LIMIT	ISSUE	QUOTE
92	CROWN & CRICKET 5750-9	YR	100.00	195.00-202.00
92	OLD MICHAEL CHURCH 5562-0	OP	42.00	42.00
92	STONEY BROOK TOWN HALL 5466-8	OP	42.00	42.00
92	YANKEE JUD BELL CASTING 5643-0	OP	44.00	44.00
93	A. BIELER FARM 5648-0 SET OF 2	OP	92.00	92.00
93	BLUE STAR ICE CO. 5647-2	OP	45.00	45.00
93	GREAT DENTON MILL 5812-2	OP	50.00	50.00
93	KINGFORD'S BREW HOUSE 5811-4	OP	45.00	45.00
93	PUMP LANE SHOPPES 5808-4 SET OF 3	OP	112.00	112.00
93	THE PIED BULL INN 5751-7	YR	100.00	150.00
94	ARLINGTON FALLS CHURCH 5651-0	OP	40.00	40.00
94	BOARDING & LODGING SCHOOL 5810-6	OP	48.00	48
94	BOARDING & LODGING SCHOOL 5809-2	YR	48.00	225.00-275.00
94	BOARDING & LODGING SCHOOL 5810-6	OP	48.00	48.00
94	DEDLOCK ARMS 5752-5	RT	100.00	100.00
94	DEDLOCK INN 5752-5	OP	100.00	180.00-200.00
94	GIGGELSWICK MUTTON & HAM 5822-0	OP	48.00	48.00
94	GIGGLESWICK MUTTEN & HAM 5822-0	OP	48.00	48
94	POSTERN (10TH ANNIVERSARY PIECE)	RT	17.50	36.00-46.00
94	WHITTLEBOURNE CHURCH 5821-1	OP	85.00	85
94	WHITTLESBOURNE CHURCH 5821-1	OP	85.00	85.00
*	**EVENT PIECE-HERITAGE VILLAGE COLLECTION ACCESSORY**			
92	GATE HOUSE 5530-1	YR	22.50	52.00-98.00
*	**LITTLE TOWN OF BETHLEHEM**			
87	LITTLE TOWN/BETHLEHEM 5975-7 (SET OF 12)	OP	150.00	150.00
*	**MEADOWLAND**			
79	ASPEN TREES 5052-6	RT	16.00	32.00
79	COUNTRYSIDE CHURCH 5051-8	RT	25.00	100.00
79	SHEEP 5053-4	RT	12.00	24.00
79	THATCHED COTTAGE 5050-0	RT	30.00	250.00-275.00
*	**NEW ENGLAND VILLAGE**			
86	APOTHECARY SHOP 6530-7	RT	24.00	98.00-163.00
86	BRICK TOWN HALL 6530-7	RT	24.00	254.00-260.00
86	GENERAL STORE 6530-7	RT	24.00	377.00-423.00
86	JACOB ADAMS FARMHOUSE & BARN 6538-2	RT	65.00	507.00-585.00
86	LIVERY STABLE & BOOT SHOP 6530-7	RT	24.00	176.00
86	NATHANIEL BINGHAM FABRICS 6530-7	RT	24.00	156.00-169.00
86	NEW ENGLAND 6530-7 (ORIGINAL SET OF 7)	RT	170.00	950.00
86	RED SCHOOLHOUSE 6530-7	RT	24.00	325.00
86	STEEPLE CHURCH 6530-7	RT	24.00	117.00-130.00
86	STEEPLE CHURCH 6539-0	RT	30.00	91.00-104.00
87	CRAGGY COVE LIGHTHOUSE 5930-7	RT	35.00	85.00-110.00
87	SMYTHE WOOLEN MILL 6543-1	RT	42.00	1050.00-1250.00
87	TIMBER KNOLL LOG CABIN 6544-7	RT	28.00	130.00-163.00
87	WESTON TRAIN STATION 5931-5	RT	42.00	228.00-325.00
88	ADA'S BED & BOARDING HOUSE 5940-4 (1)	RT	36.00	124.00-150.00
88	ANNE SHAW TOYS 5939-0	RT	27.00	163.00-215.00
88	BEN'S BARBERSHOP 5939-0	RT	27.00	75.00
88	CHERRY LANE SHOPS 5939-0 (SET OF 3)	RT	80.00	254.00-390.00
88	OLD NORTH CHURCH 5932-3	OP	40.00	98.00-124.00
88	OTIS HAYES BUTCHER SHOP 5939-0	RT	27.00	65.00
89	BERKSHIRE HOUSE (ORIG BLUE) 5942-0	RT	40.00	163.00-169.00
89	JANNES MULLET AMISH BARN 5944-7	RT	48.00	98.00-111.00
89	JANNES MULLET AMISH FARM HOUSE 5943-9	RT	32.00	144.00-250.00
90	CAPTAIN'S COTTAGE 5947-1	OP	40.00	40.00
90	SHINGLE CREEK HOUSE 5946-3	RT	37.50	40.00
90	SLEEPY HOLLOW 5954-4 (SET OF 3)	RT	96.00	163.00-176.00
91	MCGREBE-CUTTERS & SLEIGHS 5640-5	OP	45.00	45.00
*	**NORTH POLE COLLECTION**			
90	NORTH POLE 5601-4 (SET OF 2)	OP	70.00	75.00
90	SANTA'S WORKSHOP 5600-6	RT	72.00	299.00-423.00
91	NEENEE'S DOLLS & TOYS 5620-0	OP	36.00	37.50
91	NORTH POLE SHOPS 5621-9 (SET OF 2)	OP	75.00	75.00
91	TASSY'S MITTENS/HASSEL'S WOOLIES 5622-7	OP	50.00	50.00
92	ELFIE'S SLEDS & SKATES 5625-1	OP	48.00	48.00
92	OBBIE'S BOOKS & LETRINKA'S CANDY 5624-3	OP	70.00	70.00
92	POST OFFICE 5623-5	OP	45.00	45.00
93	NORTH POLE CHAPEL	OP	45.00	45.00
93	NORTH POLE EXPRESS DEPOT 5627-8	OP	48.00	48.00
93	SANTA'S LOOKOUT TOWER 5629-4	OP	45.00	45.00
93	SANTA'S WOODWORKS 5628-6	OP	42.00	42.00
*	**RETIRED HERITAGE VILLAGE COLLECTION ACCESSORIES**			
84	CAROLERS 6526-9 (SET OF 3)	RT	10.00	26.00-98.00
85	VILLAGE TRAIN 6527-7 (SET OF 3)	RT	12.00	273.00-488.00
86	CHRISTMAS CAROL FIGS. 6501-3 (SET OF 3)	RT	12.50	104.00
86	COVERED WOODEN BRIDGE	RT	10.00	25.00-65.00

YR	NAME	LIMIT	ISSUE	QUOTE
86	LIGHTED TREE W/CHILDREN & LADDER 6510-2	RT	35.00	228.00-260.00
86	NEW ENGLAND WINTER SET 6532-3 (SET OF 5)	RT	18.00	55.00-65.00
86	SLEIGHRIDE 6511-0	RT	19.50	65.00-85.00
87	BLACKSMITH 5934-0	RT	20.00	65.00-78.00
87	CITY PEOPLE 5965-0 (SET OF 5)	RT	27.50	52.00-65.00
87	CITY WORKERS 5967-6 (SET OF 4)	RT	15.00	34.00-39.00
87	DOVER COACH 6590-0	RT	18.00	72.00-104.00
87	FARM PEOPLE & ANIMALS 5901-3 (SET OF 5)	RT	24.00	98.00-104.00
87	MAPLE SUGARING SHED 6589-7 (SET OF 3)	RT	19.00	190.00-200.00
87	OX SLED 5901-1	RT	20.00	117.00-130.00
87	SHOPKEEPERS 5966-8 (SET OF 4)	RT	15.00	21.00-39.00
87	SILO AND HAY SHED 5901-1	RT	18.00	163.00-189.00
87	SKATING POND 6545-5	RT	24.00	85.00-91.00
87	STONE BRIDGE 6546-3	RT	12.00	85.00-91.00
87	VILLAGE WELL/CROSS 6547-1 (SET OF 2)	RT	13.00	143.00-150.00
88	CHILDE POND & SKATERS 5903-0 (SET OF 4)	RT	30.00	85.00-91.00
88	CITY BUS & MILK TRUCK 5983-8 (SET OF 2)	RT	15.00	26.00-34.00
88	CITY NEWSSTAND 5971-4 (SET OF 4)	RT	25.00	39.00-59.00
88	FEZZIWIG AND FRIENDS 5928-5 (SET OF 3)	RT	12.50	65.00-85.00
88	NICHOLAS NICKLEBY 5929-3 (SET OF 4)	RT	20.00	39.00-46.00
88	SALVATION ARMY BAND 5985-4 (SET OF 6)	RT	24.00	52.00-65.00
88	VILLAGE HARVEST PEOPLE 5941-2 (SET OF 4)	RT	27.50	34.00-46.00
88	VILLAGE TRAIN TRESTLE 5981-1	RT	17.00	59.00-98.00
88	WOODCUTTER AND SON 5986 (SET OF 2)	RT	10.00	39.00-46.00
89	CONSTABLES 5579-4 (SET OF 3)	RT	17.50	46.00-65.00
89	FARM ANIMALS 5945-5 (SET OF 4)	RT	15.00	59.00
89	ORGAN GRINDER 5957-9 (SET OF 3)	RT	21.00	29.00-46.00
89	RIVER STREET ICE HOUSE CART 5959-5	RT	20.00	52.00-78.00
*	**THE ORIGINAL SNOW VILLAGE COLLECTION**			
76	COUNTRY CHURCH 5004-7	RT	18.00	423.00
76	GABLED COTTAGE 5002-1	RT	20.00	475.00
76	MOUNTAIN LODGE 5001-3	RT	20.00	618.00
76	SMALL CHALET 5006-2	RT	15.00	455.00-514.00
76	STEEPLED CHURCH 5005-4	RT	25.00	813.00
76	THE INN 5003-9	RT	20.00	500.00
77	MANSION 5008-8	RT	30.00	650.00-715.00
77	STONE CHURCH, 10 IN. 5009-6	RT	35.00	1300.00
77	VICTORIAN HOUSE 5007-0	RT	30.00	501.00
78	CAPE COD 5013-8	RT	20.00	449.00-455.00
78	GENERAL STORE 5012-0	RT	25.00	514.00-683.00
78	HOMESTEAD 5011-2	RT	30.00	195.00-293.00
78	NANTUCKET 5014-6	RT	25.00	228.00-306.00
78	SKATING RINK & DUCK POND 5015-3 (SET)	RT	16.00	715.00
78	SMALL DOUBLE TREES 5016-1	RT	13.50	52.00-65.00
79	ADOBE HOUSE 5066-6	RT	18.00	2000.00
79	BROWNSTONE 5056-7	RT	36.00	660.00-925.00
79	COUNTRYSIDE CHURCH 5058-3	RT	27.50	260.00-384.00
79	GIANT TREES 5065-8	RT	20.00	260.00
79	KNOB HILL 5055-9	RT	30.00	488.00-553.00
79	LOG CABIN 5057-5	RT	22.00	520.00
79	MISSION CHURCH 5062-5	RT	30.00	950.00
79	MOBILE HOME 5063-3	RT	18.00	1625.00
79	SCHOOL HOUSE 5060-9	RT	30.00	260.00-455.00
79	STONE CHURCH, 8.5 IN. 5059-1	RT	22.00	1300.00
79	TUDOR HOUSE	RT	25.00	394.00-501.00
79	VICTORIAN 5054-2	RT	30.00	325.00-371.00
80	CATHEDRAL CHURCH 5067-4	RT	36.00	825.00
80	COLONIAL FARM HOUSE 5070-9	RT	30.00	364.00-377.00
80	STONE MILL HOUSE 5068-2	RT	30.00	618.00-780.00
80	TOWN CHURCH 5071-7	RT	33.00	260.00-293.00
80	TRAIN STATION WITH 3 CARS 5085-6	RT	100.00	325.00-390.00
81	BAKERY 5077-6	RT	30.00	195.00-280.00
81	BARN 5074-1	RT	32.00	455.00-559.00
81	CORNER STORE 5076-8	RT	30.00	260.00
81	ENGLISH CHURCH 5078-4	RT	30.00	375.00
81	ENGLISH COTTAGE 5073-3	RT	25.00	423.00
81	LARGE SINGLE TREE 5080-6	RT	17.00	59.00-65.00
81	WOODEN CLAPBOARD 5072-5	RT	32.00	364.00-377.00
82	BANK 5024-5	RT	32.00	650.00-1105.00
82	CARRIAGE HOUSE 5021-0	RT	28.00	364.00
82	CENTENNIAL HOUSE 5020-2	RT	32.00	423.00-533.00
82	FLOWER SHOP 5082-2	RT	25.00	488.00-553.00
82	GABLED HOUSE 5081-4	RT	30.00	429.00
82	NEW STONE CHURCH 5083-0	RT	32.00	390.00-429.00
82	PIONEER CHURCH 5022-9	RT	30.00	345.00-442.00
82	SKATING POND 5017-2	RT	25.00	390.00

Convent in the Woods *by Lilliput Lane received "Best Collectible" at the 16th International Collectible Exposition in South Bend, Indiana.*

Ship Inn *was created by the artists of Lilliput Lane.*

Pussy Willow *was exclusive to members of the Lilliput Lane Collector's Club.*

The Old Vicarage at Christmas *is one of the few Lilliput Lane cottages to be designed with snow.*

Honeysuckle Cottage, *introduced in 1992, was the Lilliput Lane 10th anniversary special.*

Home Sweet Home *is the creation of artist Ray Day. The piece is produced by Lilliput Lane.*

YR	NAME	LIMIT	ISSUE	QUOTE
82	STREET CAR 5019-9	RT	16.00	520.00
82	SWISS CHALET 5023-7	RT	28.00	553.00-715.00
83	CHATEAU 5084-9	RT	35.00	585.00
83	ENGLISH TUDOR 5033-4	RT	30.00	384.00-423.00
83	FIRE STATION 5032-6	RT	32.00	650.00-676.00
83	GINGERBREAD HOUSE 5025-3	RT	24.00	579.00
83	GOTHIC CHURCH 5028-8	RT	36.00	351.00
83	GOVERNOR'S MANSION 5003-2	RT	32.00	293.00
83	GROCERY 5001-6	RT	35.00	390.00
83	PARSONAGE 5029-6	RT	35.00	390.00-416.00
83	TOWN HALL 5000-8	RT	32.00	260.00
83	TURN OF THE CENTURY 5004-0	RT	36.00	221.00-260.00
83	VICTORIAN COTTAGE 5002-4	RT	35.00	442.00-455.00
83	VILLAGE CHURCH 5026-1	RT	30.00	160.00-200.00
83	WOODEN CHURCH 5031-8	RT	30.00	488.00-520.00
84	BAYPORT 5015-6	RT	30.00	228.00
84	CONGREGATIONAL CHURCH 5034-2	RT	28.00	475.00-510.00
84	DELTA HOUSE 5012-1	RT	32.00	358.00-449.00
84	GALENA HOUSE 5009-1	RT	32.00	228.00-358.00
84	HAVERSHAM HOUSE 5008-3	RT	37.00	228.00-241.00
84	MAIN STREET HOUSE 5005-9	RT	27.00	250.00
84	NEW SCHOOL HOUSE 5037-7	RT	35.00	260.00-306.00
84	PARISH CHURCH 5039-3	RT	32.00	345.00
84	RIVER ROAD HOUSE 5010-5	RT	36.00	98.00-254.00
84	STRATFORD HOUSE 5007-5	RT	28.00	293.00
84	SUMMIT HOUSE 5036-9	RT	28.00	375.00
84	TRINITY CHURCH 5035-0	RT	32.00	358.00
85	CHURCH OF THE OPEN DOOR 5048-2	RT	34.00	98.00-117.00
85	DEPOT AND TRAIN WITH TWO TRAINS 5051-2	RT	65.00	130.00-143.00
85	DUPLEX 5050-4	RT	35.00	124.00
85	PLANTATION HOUSE 5047-4-6	RT	37.00	91.00-98.00
85	RIDGEWOOD 5052-0	RT	35.00	176.00-189.00
85	SPRUCE PLACE 50499-0	RT	33.00	260.00
85	STUCCO BUNGALOW 2045-8	RT	30.00	416.00-455.00
85	WILLIAMSBURG HOUSE 5046-6	RT	37.00	91.00-98.00
86	2101 MAPLE 5043-1	RT	32.00	416.00
86	ALL SAINTS CHURCH 5070-9	OP	38.00	60.00-90.00
86	APOTHECARY 5076-8	RT	34.00	117.00
86	BAKERY 5077-6	RT	35.00	91.00-104.00
86	BEACON HILL HOUSE 5065-2	RT	31.00	163.00-260.00
86	CARRIAGE HOUSE 5071-7	RT	29.00	78.00-130.00
86	HIGHLAND PARK HOUSE 5063-6	RT	35.00	124.00-260.00
86	LINCOLN PARK DUPLEX 5060-1	RT	33.00	156.00-163.00
86	MICKEY'S DINER 5078-4	RT	22.00	546.00-553.00
86	PACIFIC HEIGHTS HOUSE 5066-0	RT	33.00	98.00-195.00
86	RAMSEY HILL HOUSE 5067-9	RT	36.00	91.00-195.00
86	SAINT JAMES CHURCH 5068-7	RT	37.00	215.00-221.00
86	SONOMA HOUSE 5062-8	RT	33.00	156.00-260.00
86	TOY SHOP 5073-3	RT	36.00	91.00-260.00
86	TWIN PEAKS 5042-3	RT	32.00	325.00
86	WAVERLY PLACE 5041-5	RT	35.00	300.00
87	CATHEDRAL CHURCH 5019-9	RT	50.00	98.00-104.00
87	CUMBERLAND HOUSE 5024-5	OP	42.00	44.00
87	FARM HOUSE 5089-0	RT	40.00	91.00-163.00
87	FIRE STATION NO. 2 5091-1	RT	40.00	195.00-254.00
87	JEFFERSON SCHOOL 5082-2	OP	36.00	208.00
87	LIGHTHOUSE 5030-0	RT	36.00	550.00-600.00
87	RED BARN 5081-4	RT	38.00	104.00-117.00
87	SNOW VILLAGE FACTORY 5013-0	RT	45.00	130.00-280.00
87	SNOW VILLAGE RESORT LODGE 5092-0	RT	55.00	163.00-195.00
87	SPRINGFIELD HOUSE 5027-0	RT	40.00	72.00-98.00
87	ST. ANTHONY HOTEL & POST OFFICE 5006-7	RT	40.00	163.00-260.00
88	COBBLESTONE ANTIQUE SHOP 5123-3	RT	36.00	117.00-195.00
88	CORNER CAFE 5124-1	RT	37.00	111.00-176.00
88	HOME SWEET HOME/HOUSE & WINDMILL 5126-8	RT	60.00	98.00-111.00
88	KENWOOD HOUSE 5054-7	RT	50.00	104.00-163.00
88	MAPLE RIDGE INN 5121-7	RT	55.00	91.00-104.00
88	PALOS VERDES 5141-1	RT	37.50	72.00-104.00
88	REDEEMER CHURCH 5127-6	RT	42.00	65.00-85.00
88	SERVICE STATION 5128-4	RT	37.50	358.00-514.00
88	SINGLE CAR GARAGE 5125-0	RT	22.00	39.00-59.00
88	STONEHURST HOUSE 5140-3	OP	37.50	37.50
88	VILLAGE MARKET 5044-0	RT	39.00	85.00-195.00
88	VILLAGE STATION AND TRAIN 5122-5	RT	65.00	104.00-124.00
89	COLONIAL CHURCH 5119-5	RT	60.00	91.00-117.00
89	COURTHOUSE 5144-6	RT	65.00	254.00

YR	NAME	LIMIT	ISSUE	QUOTE
89	DOCTOR'S HOUSE 5143-8	RT	56.00	195.00
89	J. YOUNG'S GRANARY 5149-7	RT	45.00	85.00-98.00
89	JINGLE BELLE HOUSEBOAT 5114-4	RT	42.00	104.00-111.00
89	NORTH CREEK COTTAGE 5120-9	RT	45.00	91.00-98.00
89	PARAMOUNT THEATER 5142-0	RT	42.00	85.00-104.00
89	PINEWOOD LOG CABIN 5150-0	OP	37.50	37.50
89	VILLAGE WARMING HOUSE 5145-4	RT	42.00	78.00-85.00
90	56 FLAVORS ICE CREAM PARLOR 5151-9	RT	42.00	104.00-117.00
90	MAINSTREET HARDWARE STORE 5153-5	RT	42.00	72.00-228.00
90	MORNINGSIDE HOUSE 5152-7	RT	45.00	46.00-65.00
90	PRAIRIE HOUSE 5156-0	RT	42.00	65.00-91.00
90	QUEEN ANNE VICTORIAN 5157-8	OP	48.00	48.00
90	SPANISH MISSION CHURCH 5155-1	RT	42.00	85.00-98.00
90	VILLAGE REALTY 5154-3	RT	42.00	65.00
91	DOUBLE BUNGALOW 5407-0	RT	45.00	45.00
91	FINKLEA'S FINERY: COSTUME SHOP 5405-4	RT	45.00	65.00
91	GOTHIC FARMHOUSE 5404-6	OP	48.00	48.00
91	HONEYMOONER MOTEL 5401-1	RT	42.00	91.00-104.00
91	JACK'S CORNER BARBER SHOP 5406-2	RT	42.00	42.00
91	OAK GROVE TUDOR 5400-3	RT	42.00	42.00
91	SOUTHERN COLONIAL 5403-8	RT	48.00	48.00
91	THE CHRISTMAS SHOP 5097-0	OP	37.50	37.50
91	VILLAGE GREENHOUSE 5402-0	OP	35.00	35.00
92	GRANDMA'S HOUSE 5420-8	OP	42.00	42.00
92	GRANDMA'S HOUSE 5420-8	OP	42.00	42.00
92	POST OFFICE 5422-4	OP	35.00	35.00
92	POST OFFICE 5422-4	OP	35.00	35.00
92	ST. LUKE'S CHURCH 5421-6	RT	45.00	45.00
92	ST. LUKE'S CHURCH 5421-6	RT	45.00	45.00
93	DAIRY BARN 5446-1	OP	55.00	55.00
93	DINAH'S DRIVE-IN 5447-0	OP	45.00	45.00
93	HUNTING LODGE 5445-3	OP	50.00	50.00
93	MOUNT OLIVET CHURCH 5442-9	OP	65.00	65.00
93	NANTUCKET RENOVATION 5441-0	YR	55.00	100
93	SNOWY HILLS HOSPITAL 5448-8	OP	48.00	48.00
93	VILLAGE PUBLIC LIBRARY 5443-7	OP	55.00	55.00
93	WOODBURY HOUSE 5444-7	OP	45.00	45.00
94	FISHERMAN'S NOOK BASS CABIN 5461-5	OP	*	
94	FISHERMAN'S NOOK CABINS (SET/2) 5461-5	OP	50.00	50.00
94	FISHERMAN'S NOOK RESORT 5460-7	OP	75.00	75.00
94	FISHERMAN'S NOOK TROUT CABIN 5461-5	OP	*	
94	THE ORIGINAL SNOW VILLAGE STARTER SET	OP	49.99	50.00

* THE ORIGINAL SNOW VILLAGE COLLECTION ACCESSORIES-RETIRED

79	CAROLERS 5064-1	RT	12.00	117.00-130.00
80	CERAMIC CAR 5069-0	RT	5.00	46.00-65.00
81	CERAMIC SLEIGH 5079-2	RT	5.00	52.00-72.00
82	SNOWMAN WITH BROOM 5018-0	RT	3.00	21.00
83	MONKS-A-CAROLING 6459-9	RT	6.00	65.00-91.00
84	MONKS-A-CAROLING 5040-7	RT	6.00	26.00-39.00
84	SCOTTIE WITH TREE 5038-5	RT	3.00	115.00
85	FAMILY MOM/KIDS, GOOSE/GIRL 5057-1	RT	11.00	39.00-65.00
85	SANTA/MAILBOX 5059-8	RT	11.00	34.00-65.00
85	SINGING NUNS 5053-9	RT	6.00	75.00
85	SNOW KIDS SLED & SKIS 5056-3	RT	11.00	46.00-59.00
86	GIRL/SNOWMAN BOY 5095-4	RT	11.00	35.00
86	KIDS AROUND THE TREE 5094-6	RT	15.00	34.00-98.00
86	SHOPPING GIRLS WITH PACKAGES 5096-2	RT	11.00	34.00-39.00
87	3 NUNS WITH SONGBOOKS	RT	6.00	130.00
87	CAROLING FAMILY 5105-5 (SET OF 3)	RT	25.00	26.00-39.00
87	CHILDREN IN BAND 5104-7	RT	15.00	26.00-33.00
87	CHRISTMAS CHILDREN 5107-1 (SET OF 4)	RT	20.00	26.00-34.00
87	FOR SALE SIGN 5108-0	RT	3.50	16.00-21.00
87	PRAYING MONKS 5103-9	RT	6.00	46.00-65.00
87	SNOW KIDS 5113-6 (SET OF 4)	RT	20.00	52.00-65.00
88	APPLE GIRL/NEWSPAPER BOY 5129-2	RT	11.00	21.00-26.00
88	HAYRIDE 5117-9	RT	30.00	59.00
88	SCHOOL BUS/SNOW PLOW 5137-3 (SET OF 2)	RT	16.00	85.00
88	SCHOOL CHILDREN 5118-7 (SET OF 3)	RT	15.00	21.00-29.00
88	SISAL TREE LOT 8183-3	RT	45.00	72.00-91.00
88	WATER TOWER 5133-0	RT	20.00	65.00
88	WOODSMAN AND BOY 5130-6 (SET OF 2)	RT	13.00	39.00
88	WOODY STATION WAGON 5136-5	RT	6.50	23.00-34.00
89	CALLING ALL CARS 5174-8 (SET OF 2)	CL	15.00	34.00
89	KIDS TREE HOUSE 5168-3	CL	25.00	52.00-78.00
89	MAILBOX 5179-9	RT	3.50	21.00-46.00
89	SKATE FASTER MOM 5170-5	CL	13.00	30.00

YR	NAME	LIMIT	ISSUE	QUOTE
89	SPECIAL DELIVERY 5148-9 (SET OF 2)	RT	16.00	39.00-65.00
89	STATUE OF MARK TWAIN 5173-0	CL	15.00	39.00-46.00
89	THROUGH THE WOODS 5172-1 (SET OF 2)	CL	18.00	34.00
*			**VILLAGE CCP MINIATURES**	
86	CHURCH 6564-1	CL	22.50	100.00-125.00
86	ESTATE 6564-1	CL	22.50	100.00-300.00
86	VICTORIAN MINIATURES 6563-3 (SET OF 5)	CL	65.00	*
86	VICTORIAN MINIATURES 6564-1 (SET OF 2)	CL	45.00	300.00
86	WILLIAMSBURG HOUSE, BLUE 6566-8	CL	10.00	60.00
86	WILLIAMSBURG HOUSE, BROWN BRICK 6566-8	CL	10.00	40.00
86	WILLIAMSBURG HOUSE, BROWN CLPBD 6566-8	CL	10.00	40.00
86	WILLIAMSBURG HOUSE, RED 6566-8	CL	10.00	60.00
86	WILLIAMSBURG HOUSE, WHITE 6566-8	CL	10.00	40.00
86	WILLIAMSBURG SNOWHOUSE 6566-8 (SET OF 6)	CL	60.00	500.00
87	ABEL BEESLEY BUTCHER 6558-7	CL	12.00	39.00
87	BARLEY BREE FARMHOUSE 6562-5	CL	15.00	52.00
87	BEAN AND SON SMITHY SHOP 6558-7	CL	12.00	39.00
87	BLYTHE POND MILL HOUSE 6560-9	CL	16.00	36.00-45.00
87	BRICK ABBEY 6562-5	CL	15.00	50.00-75.00
87	CANDLE SHOP 6558-7	CL	12.00	46.00
87	CHESTERTON MANOR HOUSE 6562-5	CL	15.00	32.00-39.00
87	CHRISTMAS CAROL 6561-7 (SET OF 3)	CL	30.00	78.00
87	COTTAGE OF BOB CRATCHIT/TINY TIM 6561-7	CL	10.00	26.00
87	COTTAGE TOY SHOP 6591-9	CL	10.00	46.00-59.00
87	CROWNTREE INN 6558-7	CL	12.00	39.00
87	DICKENS VILLAGE CHURCH 6560-9	CL	16.00	32.00-49.00
87	DICKENS' CHADBURY STATION & TRAIN 6592-7	CL	27.50	59.00-72.00
87	DICKENS' COTTAGES 6559-5 (SET OF 3)	CL	30.00	175.00
87	DICKENS' LANE SHOPS 6591-9 (SET OF 3)	CL	30.00	111.00-137.00
87	DICKENS' VILLAGE 6558-7 (SET OF 7)	CL	72.00	195.00-319.00
87	DICKENS' VILLAGE 6560-9 (SET OF 3)	CL	48.00	*
87	DICKENS' VILLAGE 6562-5 (SET OF 4)	CL	60.00	*
87	FEZZIWIG'S WAREHOUSE 6561-7	CL	10.00	46.00-65.00
87	GOLDEN SWAN BAKER 6558-7	CL	12.00	40.00-46.00
87	GREEN GROCER 6558-7	CL	12.00	39.00
87	JONES & CO BRUSH & BASKET SHOP 6558-7	CL	12.00	40.00
87	LITTLE TOWN/BETHLEHEM 5976-5 (SET OF 12)	CL	85.00	130.00
87	NORMAN CHURCH 6560-9	CL	16.00	104.00-182.00
87	SCROOGE & MARLEY'S COUNTINGHOUSE 6561-7	CL	10.00	46.00
87	STONE COTTAGE 6559-5	CL	10.00	169.00
87	THATCHED COTTAGE 6559-5	CL	10.00	98.00-169.00
87	THE OLD CURIOSITY SHOP 6562-5	CL	15.00	59.00
87	THOMAS KERSEY COFFEE HOUSE 6591-9	CL	10.00	59.00
87	TUDOR COTTAGE 6559-5	CL	10.00	100.00-150.00
87	TUTTLE'S PUB 6591-9	CL	10.00	39.00-59.00
88	APOTHECARY SHOP 5935-8	CL	10.50	26.00
88	BRICK TOWN HALL 5935-8	CL	10.50	40.00
88	CRAGGY COVE LIGHTHOUSE 5937-4	CL	14.50	124.00
88	DICKENS' KENILWORTH CASTLE 6565-0	CL	30.00	85.00-91.00
88	GENERAL STORE 5935-8	CL	10.50	59.00
88	JACOB ADAMS BARN 5937-4	CL	14.50	46.00
88	JACOB ADAMS FARMHOUSE 5937-4	CL	14.50	42.00-50.00
88	LIVERY STABLE & BOOT SHOP 5935-8	CL	10.50	34.00
88	MAPLE SUGARING SHED 5937-4	CL	14.50	32.00-48.00
88	NATHANIEL BINGHAM FABRICS 5935-8	CL	10.50	59.00
88	NEW ENGLAND VILLAGE 5935-8 (SET OF 7)	CL	72.00	275.00-300.00
88	NEW ENGLAND VILLAGE 5937-4 (SET OF 6)	CL	85.00	*
88	RED SCHOOLHOUSE 5935-8	CL	10.50	98.00
88	SMYTHE WOLLEN MILL 5937-4	CL	14.50	189.00
88	STEEPLE CHURCH 5935-8	CL	10.50	40.00-120.00
88	TIMBER KNOLL LOG CABIN 5937-4	CL	14.50	30.00-42.00

ENESCO

**			**PRECIOUS MOMENTS**	
88	THERE'S A CHRISTIAN WELCOME HERE 523011	OP	45.00	45.00-115.00
**			**SUGAR TOWN**	
92	'94 SUGAR TOWN HOUSE COLL. SET 531773	OP	189.00	189.00-207.00
92	LIGHTED CHAPEL 529621	OP	85.00	85.00-90.00

JAN'S ORIGINALS

J. BENSON

		BATESBURG, SOUTH CAROLINA SERIES		
94	1ST BAPTIST CHURCH	500	48.00	48.00

J. BENSON

		CHARLESTON, SOUTH CAROLINA SERIES		
92	CITADEL BARRACKS, THE	1000	50.00	50.00
92	ST. PHILIPS CHURCH	1000	48.00	60.00
93	MIDDLETON PLANTATION	1000	50.00	50.00
93	RAINBOW ROW	*	65.00	65.00

YR	NAME	LIMIT	ISSUE	QUOTE
94	CHARLESTON HORSE CARR. CO.	1000	20.00	20.00
94	DOCK STREET THEATRE	1000	48.00	48.00
94	GAZEBO AT THE BATTERY	1000	20.00	20.00
94	PINEAPPLE FOUNTAIN	1000	20.00	20.00
95	CHARLESTON OLD FIREHOUSE	1000	50.00	50.00
95	CITADEL CHAPEL, THE	1000	52.00	52.00
95	PORGY & BESS CATFISH ROW	1000	50.00	50.00
J. BENSON		**GEORGIA OR SOUTH CAROLINA SERIES**		
93	COLLEGE OF CHARLESTON	1000	50.00	50.00
93	NO. 2 MEETING ST. INN	1000	48.00	48.00
93	PINK HOUSE, THE	1000	42.00	42.00
93	ST. MICHAEL'S CHURCH	1000	48.00	48.00
94	HOUSE OF CHARLESTON	1000	48.00	48.00
94	MARKET HALL	1000	48.00	48.00
94	MORRIS ISLAND LIGHTHOUSE	1000	46.00	46.00
94	RUTLEDGE HOUSE, THE	1000	48.00	48.00
J. BENSON				**GEORGIA SERIES**
92	SWAN HOUSE, THE	1000	52.00	60.00
94	WREN'S NEST, THE	1000	52.00	52.00
95	LI'L CUMBERLAND LIGHTHOUSE	1000	48.00	48.00
J. BENSON		**LEESVILLE, SOUTH CAROLINA SERIES**		
94	UNITED METHODIST CHURCH	500	48.00	48.00
J. BENSON		**LEESVILLE/BATESBURG, SOUTH CAROLINA SERIES**		
95	PRESBYTERIAN CHURCH	500	48.00	48.00
J. BENSON		**SOUTH CAROLINA SERIES**		
94	L. B. HAYNES CHAPEL	500	48.00	48.00
94	ST. JOHN'S UNITED METHODIST CHURCH	500	48.00	48.00

JEFFREY SCOTT CO.

				LIGHTHOUSE POINT
94	ADMIRALTY HEAD	15,000	25.00	28.00
94	BOSTON HARBOR	15,000	20.00	22.00
94	CAPE HATTERAS	15,000	20.00	22.00
94	CHICAGO HARBOR	15,000	20.00	22.00
94	KEY WEST	15,000	22.50	25.00
94	OLD MACKINAC POINT	15,000	22.50	25.00
94	POINT VICENTE	15,000	20.00	22.00
94	PORTLAND BREAKWATER	15,000	20.00	22.00
94	SPLIT ROCK	15,000	22.50	25.00
94	ST. AUGUSTINE	15,000	25.00	28.00
94	ST. SIMONS	15,000	25.00	28.00
94	WEST QUODDY HEAD	15,000	22.50	25.00

JOHN HINE STUDIOS LTD.

D. WINTER				*
*	BLACKSMITH COTTAGE	*	*	450.00-510.00
*	BOTTLE KILN	*	*	50.00-75.00
*	CANDLEMAKERS	*	*	85.00-100.00
*	COBBLER'S	*	*	40.00-60.00
*	HAYBARN	*	*	300.00-400.00
*	HOME GUARD	*	*	80.00-100.00
*	OLD CURIOSITY SHOP	*	*	1300.00-1700.00
*	PAVILION	*	*	65.00-90.00
*	THE COAL SHED	*	*	100.00-130.00
92	AUDREY'S TEA ROOM	RT	*	
M. WIDEMAN				**AMERICAN COLLECTION**
89	BAND STAND	OP	90.00	100.00
89	BARBER SHOP	OP	40.00	44.00
89	CAJUN COTTAGE	OP	50.00	70.00
89	CALIFORNIA WINERY	OP	180.00	230.00
89	CHERRY HILL SCHOOL	RT	45.00	70.00
89	COLONIAL WELLHOUSE	RT	15.00	30.00-35.00
89	DOG HOUSE	OP	10.00	30.00
89	FORTY-NINER CABIN	OP	50.00	70.00
89	GARCONNIERE	RT	25.00	40.00-45.00
89	HACIENDA	OP	51.00	56.00
89	HAUNTED HOUSE	OP	100.00	110.00
89	HAWAIIAN GRASS HUT	OP	45.00	50.00
89	KING WILLIAM TAVERN	RT	99.00	160.00-175.00
89	NEW ENGLAND LIGHTHOUSE	RT	99.00	125.00
89	OCTAGONAL HOUSE	OP	40.00	55.00
89	OXBOW SALOON	OP	90.00	125.00
89	PLANTATION HOUSE	RT	119.00	160.00-175.00
89	PRAIRIE FORGE	OP	65.00	90.00
89	RAILHEAD INN	OP	250.00	295.00
89	SEASIDE COTTAGE	OP	225.00	275.00
89	SIERRA MINE	OP	120.00	150.00

YR	NAME	LIMIT	ISSUE	QUOTE
89	SOD HOUSE	OP	40.00	55.00
89	STAR COTTAGE	OP	30.00	45.00
89	SWEETHEART COTTAGE	OP	45.00	70.00
89	THE BLOCKHOUSE	RT	25.00	32.00-36.00
89	THE GINGERBREAD HOUSE	RT	60.00	72.00-80.00
89	THE KISSING BRIDGE	RT	50.00	56.00-60.00
89	THE LOG CABIN	RT	45.00	56.00-60.00
89	THE MAPLE SUGAR SHACK	OP	50.00	56.00-60.00
89	THE MISSION	OP	99.00	110.00
89	THE NEW ENGLAND CHURCH	RT	79.00	96.00
89	THE OLD MILL	OP	100.00	115.00
89	THE OPERA HOUSE	RT	89.00	100.00
89	THE OUT HOUSE	RT	15.00	24.00
89	THE PACIFIC LIGHTHOUSE	RT	89.00	105.00
89	THE RIVER BELL	OP	99.00	110.00
89	TOBACCONIST	OP	45.00	48.00
89	TOWN HALL	RT	129.00	125.00
89	TREE HOUSE	OP	45.00	50.00
89	WISTERIA	RT	15.00	28.00
91	CHURCH IN THE DALE	RT	130.00	144.00
91	DESERT STORM TENT	RT	75.00	75.00
91	FIRE STATION	OP	160.00	176.00
91	JOE'S SERVICE STATION	OP	90.00	100.00
91	MILK HOUSE	OP	20.00	22.00
91	MO AT WORK	RT	35.00	35.00
91	MOE'S DINER	RT	100.00	300.00
91	PAUL REVERE'S HOUSE	RT	90.00	90.00
92	GRAIN ELEVATOR	OP	110.00	110.00
92	NEWSSTAND	OP	30.00	30.00
92	TELEPHONE BOOTH	OP	16.00	16.00
92	TOPPER'S DRIVE-IN	OP	120.00	120.00
92	VILLAGE MERCANTILE	OP	60.00	60.00

D. WINTER — **BRITISH TRADITIONS**

YR	NAME	LIMIT	ISSUE	QUOTE
90	BLOSSOM COTTAGE	RT	59.00	64.00
90	BULL & BUSH	OP	37.50	42.00
90	BURN'S READING ROOM	RT	31.00	34.00
90	GROUSE MOOR LODGE	RT	48.00	52.00
90	GUY FAWKES	OP	31.00	34.00
90	HARVEST BARN	RT	31.00	34.00
90	KNIGHT'S CASTLE	RT	59.00	64.00
90	PUDDING COTTAGE	RT	78.00	86.00
90	ST. ANNE'S WELL	RT	48.00	52.00
90	STAFFORDSHIRE VICARAGE	RT	48.00	52.00
90	STONECUTTERS COTTAGE	RT	48.00	52.00
90	THE BOAT HOUSE	OP	37.50	42.00

* — **BUGABOOS**

YR	NAME	LIMIT	ISSUE	QUOTE
89	ARNOLD	CL	45.00	45.00
89	BERYL	CL	45.00	45.00
89	EDNA	CL	45.00	45.00
89	ENID	CL	45.00	45.00
89	GERALD	CL	45.00	45.00
89	LIZZIE	CL	45.00	45.00
89	OSCAR	CL	45.00	45.00
89	WESLEY	CL	45.00	45.00
89	WILBUR	CL	45.00	45.00

D. WINTER — **COLLECTORS GUILD EXCLUSIVES**

YR	NAME	LIMIT	ISSUE	QUOTE
87	ROBIN HOOD'S HIDEAWAY	RT	54.00	375.00-400.00
87	THE VILLAGE SCENE	CL	*	220.00-250.00
88	BLACK BESS INN	CL	60.00	100.00-125.00
88	QUEEN ELIZABETH SLEPT HERE	RT	183.00	300.00-350.00
88	THE PAVILLION	CL	52.00	65.00-90.00
89	COAL SHED	OP	112.00	100.00-130.00
89	HOMEGUARD	OP	105.00	80.00-100.00
89	STREET SCENE	CL	*	110.00-130.00
90	CARTWRIGHTS COTTAGE	RT	45.00	50.00-70.00
90	PLUCKED DUCK	RT	*	50.00-70.00
90	THE COBBLERS	OP	40.00	40.00-60.00
90	THE POTTERY	OP	40.00	60.00-75.00
91	PERSHORE MILL	OP	*	50.00-60.00
91	TOMFOOL'S COTTAGE	OP	100.00	90.00-120.00
91	WILL O' THE WISP	OP	120.00	120.00-150.00
92	IRISH WATER MILL	OP	*	50.00-70.00
92	THE BEEKEEPER'S	OP	65.00	85.00-100.00
92	THE CANDLEMAKER'S	OP	65.00	85.00-100.00

D. WINTER — **DAVID WINTER CAMEOS**

YR	NAME	LIMIT	ISSUE	QUOTE
92	BARLEY MALT KILN	OP	12.50	12.50

Ruth Marion Scotch Woolens *was limited to 17,500 pieces and is part of Department 56's Dickens' Village.*

Ada's Bed and Boarding House, *from Department 56's New England Village, was issued in several colors before it was retired in 1991.*

New England Village's Timber Knoll Log Cabin *was closed by Department 56 in 1990.*

Cobles Police Station *was not embraced by Department 56 collectors who chose to believe that no crime existed in their miniature town. The piece was issued in 1990 and retired in 1991.*

Otis Hayes Butcher Shop, *a 1988 addition to New England Village, is from the "Cherry Lane Shops" set of three produced by Department 56.*

Apothecary Shop *was issued with the original seven in Department 56's New England Village set.*

YR	NAME	LIMIT	ISSUE	QUOTE
92	BROOKLET BRIDGE	OP	12.50	12.50
92	BUCKINGHAMSHIRE BULL PEN	RT	*	
92	GREENWOOD WAGON	OP	12.50	12.50
92	LYCH GATE	OP	12.50	12.50
92	MARKET DAY	OP	12.50	12.50
92	ONE MAN JAIL	OP	12.50	12.50
92	PENNY WISHING WELL	OP	12.50	12.50
92	POULTRY ARK	OP	12.50	12.50
92	SADDLE STEPS	OP	12.50	12.50
92	THE POTTING SHED	OP	12.50	12.50
92	THE PRIVY	OP	12.50	12.50
92	WELSH PIG PEN	OP	12.50	12.50
D. WINTER			**DAVID WINTER COTTAGES**	
80	LITTLE MARKET	OP	28.90	50.00
80	MARKET STREET	OP	48.80	80.00
80	ROSE COTTAGE	OP	28.90	50.00
80	THE WINE MERCHANT	OP	28.90	50.00
81	SINGLE OAST	OP	22.00	250.00-500.00
81	STRATFORD HOUSE	OP	74.80	118.00
81	THE VILLAGE	OP	362.00	520.00-550.00
81	TRIPLE OAST	RT	59.90	520.00-800.00
82	COTSWOLD COTTAGE	OP	22.00	400.00-500.00
82	DROVER'S COTTAGE	OP	22.00	30.00
82	IVY COTTAGE	OP	22.00	40.00-60.00
82	SUSSEX COTTAGE	OP	22.00	90.00-100.00
82	THE DOWER HOUSE	OP	22.00	40.00-60.00
82	THE VILLAGE SHOP	OP	22.00	30.00
83	FISHERMAN'S WHARF	OP	31.40	54.00
83	HERTFORD COURT	OP	87.00	130.00-140.00
83	PILGRAM'S REST	OP	48.80	65.00-90.00
83	THE BAKEHOUSE	OP	31.40	45.00-70.00
83	THE BOTHY	OP	31.40	54.00
83	THE GREEN DRAGON INN	OP	31.40	54.00
84	SNOW COTTAGE	OP	74.80	100.00-120.00
84	THE CHAPEL	OP	48.80	70.00-100.00
84	THE PARSONAGE	OP	390.00	510.00-650.00
85	BLACKFRIARS GRANGE	RT	24.10	38.00
85	CRAFTSMAN COTTAGES	OP	24.10	38.00
85	KENT COTTAGE	OP	48.80	90.00-100.00
85	MEADOWBANK COTTAGES	OP	24.10	38.00
85	SHIREHALL	OP	24.10	37.00
85	ST. GEORGE'S CHURCH	OP	24.10	42.00
85	THE APOTHOCARY SHOP	OP	24.10	42.00
85	THE COOPER'S COTTAGE	OP	57.90	65.00-80.00
85	THE HOGS HEAD TAVERN	OP	24.10	42.00
85	THE SCHOOLHOUSE	OP	24.10	42.00
85	THE VICARAGE	OP	24.10	38.00
85	YEOMAN'S FARMHOUSE	OP	24.10	38.00
87	DEVON COMBE	RT	73.00	106.00
87	DEVON CREAMERY	OP	62.90	94.00
87	SMUGGLER'S CREEK	OP	390.00	490.00
87	TAMAR COTTAGE	OP	43.30	70.00
87	THERE WAS A CROOKED HOUSE	OP	96.90	144.00
88	COAL MINER'S ROW	OP	90.00	106.00
88	CORNISH ENGINE HOUSE	OP	120.00	144.00
88	CORNISH HARBOUR	OP	120.00	144.00
88	DERBYSHIRE COTTON MILL	RT	65.00	80.00
88	GUNSMITHS	OP	78.00	94.00
88	JOHN BENBOW'S FARMHOUSE	OP	78.00	105.00-130.00
88	LACEMAKER'S COTTAGE	OP	120.00	130.00
88	LOCK KEEPERS COTTAGES	OP	65.00	80.00
88	WINDMILL	OP	37.50	50.00
91	CASTLE IN THE AIR	OP	675.00	675.00
91	INGLENOOK COTTAGE	OP	60.00	66.00
91	MOONLIGHT HAVEN	OP	120.00	132.00
91	THE PRINTERS AND THE BOOKBINDERS	OP	120.00	120.00
91	THE WEAVER'S LODGINGS	OP	65.00	72.00
92	BIRTHSTONE WISHING WELL	OP	40.00	40.00
92	MAD BARON FOURTHRITE'S FOLLY	*	275.00	165.00-200.00
92	SCROOGE'S SCHOOL	OP	160.00	105.00-130.00
92	SCROOGE'S SCHOOL	YR	160.00	130.00-230.00
D. WINTER			**DAVID WINTER RETIRED COTTAGES**	
80	COACHING INN	RT	165.00	3770.00-3850.00
80	DOVE COTTAGE	RT	60.00	2000.00-2400.00
80	LITTLE FORGE	RT	40.00	1700.00-2000.00
80	LITTLE MILL	RT	40.00	1150.00-1200.00

Weston Train Station *was out for a full year before Department 56 finally issued a train. The piece was retired in 1989.*

Guilford Lodge *from the "Gatehouse Collection" was produced in a limited edition of 400 by Patrick Gates for J.P. Editions.*

School Days *is from the "American Landmarks" collection by Lilliput Lane.*

Jacob Adams Farmhouse & Barn *are from the Dickens' Village produced by Department 56.*

YR	NAME	LIMIT	ISSUE	QUOTE
80	LITTLE MILL-REMODLED	RT	40.00	*
80	MILL HOUSE	RT	50.00	1100.00-2800.00
80	MILL HOUSE-REMODLED	RT	40.00	1950.00-2350.00
80	QUAYSIDE	RT	60.00	1825.00-2000.00
80	THE FORGE	RT	60.00	1950.00-2350.00
80	THREE DUCKS INN	RT	60.00	1700.00-1950.00
81	CASTLE KEEP	RT	30.00	2400.00
81	CHINCHESTER CROSS	RT	50.00	4680.00
81	DOUBLE OAST	RT	60.00	2800.00
81	ST. PAUL'S CATHEDRAL	RT	40.00	2200.00-2400.00
81	THE OLD CURIOSITY SHOP	RT	40.00	1300.00-1700.00
81	TUDOR MANOR HOUSE	RT	48.80	50.00-70.00
81	TYTHE BARN	RT	39.30	1450.00-1600.00
82	BLACKSMITH'S COTTAGE	RT	22.00	450.00-510.00
82	BROOKSIDE HAMLET	RT	74.80	65.00-85.00
82	CORNISH COTTAGE	RT	30.00	875.00-1075.00
82	COTSWOLD VILLAGE	RT	59.90	425.00
82	FAIRYTALE CASTLE	RT	115.40	260.00-325.00
82	MINER'S COTTAGE	RT	22.00	160.00-200.00
82	MOORLAND COTTAGE	RT	22.00	260.00-325.00
82	SABRINA'S COTTAGE	RT	30.00	2100.00-3250.00
82	THE HAYBARN	RT	22.00	260.00-350.00
82	THE HOUSE ON TOP	RT	92.30	350.00-390.00
82	WILLIAM SHAKESPEARE'S BIRTHPLACE (LARGE)	RT	60.00	1625.00-1825.00
83	CORNISH TIN MINE	RT	22.00	50.00-60.00
83	THE ALMS HOUSES	RT	59.90	390.00-425.00
83	THE COTTON MILL	RT	41.30	580.00-720.00
83	WOODCUTTER'S COTTAGE	RT	87.00	320.00-360.00
84	CASTLE GATE	RT	154.90	210.00-250.00
84	HOUSE OF THE MASTER MASON	RT	74.80	210.00-260.00
84	SPINNER'S COTTAGE	RT	28.90	35.00-50.00
84	TOLLKEEPER'S COTTAGE	RT	87.00	115.00-130.00
85	HERMIT'S HUMBLE HOME	RT	87.00	215.00-250.00
85	SQUIRES HALL	RT	92.30	75.00-100.00
85	SUFFOLK HOUSE	RT	48.80	50.00-70.00
86	CROFTER'S COTTAGE	RT	51.00	40.00-60.00
86	FALSTAFF'S MANOR	RT	242.00	325.00-350.00
87	EBENEZER SCROOGE'S COUNTING HOUSE	RT	96.00	200.00-230.00
87	ORCHARD COTTAGE	RT	91.30	90.00-110.00
88	BOTTLE KILNS	RT	78.00	50.00-70.00
88	HOGMANAY	RT	100.00	90.00-110.00
88	JIM'LL FIXIT	RT	350.00	2800.00-3500.00
88	THE GRANGE	RT	120.00	900.00-2050.00
89	A CHRISTMAS CAROL	RT	135.00	100.00-130.00
90	MR. FEZZIWIG'S EMPORIUM	RT	135.00	75.00-90.00
91	FRED'S HOME	CL	145.00	105.00-125.00
92	AUDREY'S TEA ROOM	RT	90.00	100.00-120.00
92	AUDREY'S TEA SHOP	RT	90.00	275.00-375.00
D. WINTER	**DAVID WINTER RETIRED COTTAGES-TINY SERIES**			
80	ANN HATHAWAY'S COTTAGE	RT	*	650.00-850.00
80	COTSWOLD FARMHOUSE	RT	*	450.00-650.00
80	CROWN INN	RT	*	650.00-850.00
80	ST. NICHOLAS' CHURCH	RT	*	910.00
80	SULGRAVE MANOR	RT	*	650.00-850.00
80	WILLIAM SHAKESPEARE'S BIRTHPLACE	RT	*	650.00-850.00
J. KING				**FATHER CHRISTMAS**
88	FALLING	OP	70.00	70.00
88	FEET	OP	70.00	70.00
88	STANDING	OP	70.00	70.00
M. COOPER				**GREAT BRITISH PUBS**
89	BLACK SWAN	RT	79.50	85.00-350.00
89	BLUE BELL	RT	57.50	57.50
89	COACH & HORSES	RT	79.50	79.50
89	DICKENS INN	RT	100.00	100.00
89	DIRTY DUCK	RT	25.00	25.00
89	FALKLAND ARMS	RT	25.00	25.00
89	GEORGE & PILGRIMS	RT	25.00	25.00
89	GEORGE SOMERSET	RT	100.00	100.00
89	GRENADIER	RT	25.00	25.00
89	HAWKESHEAD	RT	*	900.00
89	JAMAICA INN	RT	39.50	39.50
89	KING'S ARMS	RT	28.00	28.00
89	LYGON ARMS	RT	35.00	35.00
89	MONTAGUE ARMS	RT	57.50	57.50
89	OLD BRIDGE HOUSE	RT	37.50	37.50
89	OLD BULL INN	RT	87.50	87.50

YR	NAME	LIMIT	ISSUE	QUOTE
89	SHERLOCK HOLMES	RT	100.00	100.00
89	SMITH'S ARMS	RT	28.00	28.00
89	SUFFOLK BULL	RT	35.00	35.00
89	THE BELL	RT	79.50	85.00-350.00
89	THE CROWN INN	RT	79.50	79.50
89	THE EAGLE	RT	35.00	35.00
89	THE FALSTAFF	RT	35.00	35.00
89	THE FEATHERS	RT	200.00	200.00
89	THE GEORGE	RT	57.50	57.50
89	THE GREEN MAN	RT	*	*
89	THE LION	RT	57.50	57.50
89	THE PLOUGH	RT	28.00	28.00
89	THE SWAN	RT	35.00	35.00
89	WHEATSHEAF	RT	35.00	35.00
89	WHITE HORSE	RT	39.50	39.50
89	WHITE TOWER	RT	35.00	35.00
89	YE GRAPES	RT	87.50	87.50
89	YE OLD SPOTTED HORSE	RT	79.50	79.50
D. WINTER				**IRISH COLLECTION**
92	FOGARTYS	RT	75.00	75.00
92	IRISH ROUND TOWER	OP	65.00	65.00
92	MURPHYS	OP	100.00	100.00
92	O'DONOVAN'S CASTLE	OP	145.00	145.00
92	ONLY A SPAN APART	OP	80.00	125.00
92	SECRET SHEBEEN	OP	70.00	60.00-80.00
C. LAWRENCE				**MUSHROOMS**
89	ROYAL BANK OF MUSHLAND	2500	235.00	235.00-350.00
89	THE COBBLERS	2500	265.00	265.00-375.00
89	THE CONSTABLES	2500	200.00	200.00
89	THE ELDERS OF MUSHROOM	2500	175.00	175.00-225.00
89	THE GIFT SHOP	2500	350.00	420.00-525.00
89	THE MINISTRY	2500	185.00	185.00-300.00
89	THE MUSH HOSPITAL FOR MALINGERERS	2500	250.00	250.00-400.00
89	THE PRINCESS PALACE	750	600.00	730.00-950.00
D. WINTER				**SCOTTISH COLLECTION**
89	GATEKEEPER'S	OP	65.00	60.00-100.00
89	GILLIE'S COTTAGE	OP	65.00	80.00
89	HOUSE ON THE LOCH	RT	65.00	80.00
89	MACBETH'S CASTLE	OP	200.00	244.00
89	OLD DISTILLERY	OP	450.00	750.00-800.00
89	SCOTTISH CROFTER (REMOLDED)	OP	42.00	54.00
D. WINTER				**THE IRISH COLLECTION**
92	FOGARTYS	OP	*	
92	IRISH ROUND TOWER	OP	*	
92	ONLY A SPAN APART	OP	*	
92	SECRET SHEBEEN	OP	*	
J. HERBERT				**THE SHOEMAKER'S DREAM**
91	BABY BOOTY (BLUE)	OP	45.00	45.00
91	BABY BOOTY (PINK)	OP	45.00	45.00
91	CASTLE BOOT	OP	55.00	55.00
91	RIVER SHOE COTTAGE	OP	55.00	55.00
91	ROSIE'S COTTAGE	OP	40.00	40.00
91	SHOEMAKER'S PALACE	OP	50.00	50.00
91	TAVERN BOOT	OP	55.00	55.00
91	THE CHAPEL	OP	55.00	55.00
91	THE CLOCKTOWER BOOT	OP	60.00	60.00
91	THE CROOKED BOOT	OP	35.00	35.00
91	THE GATE LODGE	OP	65.00	65.00
91	THE JESTER BOOT	OP	29.00	29.00
91	WATERMILL BOOT	OP	60.00	60.00
91	WINDMILL BOOT	OP	65.00	65.00
92	CHRISTMAS BOOT	OP	55.00	55.00
92	CLOWN BOOT	OP	45.00	45.00
92	THE GOLF SHOE	OP	35.00	35.00
92	THE SPORTS SHOE	OP	35.00	35.00
92	UPSIDE DOWN BOOT	OP	45.00	45.00
92	WISHING WELL SHOE	OP	32.00	32.00
D. WINTER				**THE WELSH COLLECTION**
93	TYDDYN SIRIOL	RT	*	
93	Y DDRAIGG GOCH	RT	*	

JP EDITIONS

P. GATES				**CASTLES OF ENGLAND**
93	HEVER CASTLE	250	350.00	1000.00
93	SCOTNEY CASTLE	250	350.00	1100.00
P. GATES				**CASTLES OF GREAT BRITAIN**
94	GRAIGIEVAR CASTLE	400	390.00	410.00

YR	NAME	LIMIT	ISSUE	QUOTE
	P. GATES		**CASTLES OF WALES**	
94	CALDICOT CASTLE	400	380.00	400.00
94	CASTELL COCH	400	420.00	600.00
	P. GATES		**GATE HOUSE COLLECTION**	
94	GUILDFORD LODGE	400	420.00	440.00
	P. GATES		**GREAT ENGLISH HOMES**	
94	GAINSBOROUGH HALL	450	420.00	440.00
	P. GATES		**UNIVERSITY BUILDINGS**	
93	GATE OF HONOUR	250	295.00	600.00
93	RADCLIFFE CAMERA	250	295.00	900.00

LILLIPUT LANE LTD.
*

YR	NAME	LIMIT	ISSUE	QUOTE
*	ANNE HATHAWAY	*	*	78.00-98.00
*	BURNSIDE COTTAGE	*	*	625.00-660.00
*	GARDNER'S COTTAGE	*	*	140.00-170.00
			A YEAR IN AN ENGLISH GARDEN	
95	SPRING GLORY	*	120.00	120.00
95	SUMMER IMPRESSIONS	*	120.00	120.00
	D. TATE		**AMERICAN COLLECTION**	
84	ADOBE CHURCH	RT	22.50	390.00-650.00
84	ADOBE VILLAGE	RT	60.00	1950.00
84	CAPE COD	RT	22.50	260.00
84	COUNTRY CHURCH	RT	95.00	80.00-120.00
84	COVERED BRIDGE	RT	22.50	2000.00
84	FORGE BARN	RT	22.50	475.00-550.00
84	GENERAL STORE	RT	22.50	650.00-750.00
84	GRIST MILL	RT	22.50	500.00
84	LIGHTHOUSE	RT	22.50	785.00-795.00
84	LOG CABIN	RT	22.50	750.00-975.00
84	MIDWEST BARN	RT	22.50	290.00-377.00
84	SAN FRANCISCO HOUSE	RT	22.50	375.00
84	WALLACE STATION	RT	22.50	785.00-1035.00
	R. DAY		**AMERICAN LANDMARK SERIES**	
89	COUNTRYSIDE BARN	RT	75.00	180.00
89	FALLS MILL	RT	130.00	225.00
89	MAIL POUCH BARN	RT	75.00	240.00
90	COUNTRY CHURCH	RT	82.50	160.00
90	COVERED MEMORIES	RT	110.00	250.00
90	GREAT POINT LIGHT	OP	50.00	200.00-260.00
90	HOMETOWN DEPOT	RT	68.00	95.00
90	PEPSI COLA BARN	RT	87.00	175.00-275.00
90	PIONEER BARN	RT	30.00	99.00-110.00
90	RIVERSIDE CHAPEL	RT	82.50	130.00
90	ROADSIDE COOLERS	RT	75.00	190.00
90	SIGN OF THE TIMES	OP	33.70	50.00-65.00
91	FIRE HOUSE 1	OP	100.00	100.00
91	RAMBLING ROSE	OP	60.00	60.00
91	SCHOOL DAYS	OP	75.00	75.00
91	VICTORIANA	2500	295.00	385.00-440.00
92	16.9 CENTS PER GALLON	OP	150.00	150.00
92	GOLD MINERS' CLAIM	OP	110.00	110.00
92	HOME SWEET HOME	OP	120.00	120.00
92	SMALL TOWN LIBRARY	OP	130.00	130.00
92	WINNIE'S PLACE	2000	395.00	395.00
	D. TATE		**AMERICAN LANDMARKS**	
92	16.9 CENTS PER GALLON	OP	150.00	150.00
92	GOLD MINER'S CLAIM	OP	110.00	110.00
92	WINNIE'S PLACE	2000	395.00	395.00
			ANNIVERSARY SPECIAL	
93	COTMAN COTTAGE	RT	220.00	350.00
94	WATERMEADOWS	RT	189.00	200.00
95	GERTRUDE'S GARDEN	*	192.00	192.00
92	HONEYSUCKLE COTTAGE 1992	TL	195.00	130.00-175.00
			BLAISE HAMLET CLASSICS	
90	DIAL COTTAGE	RT	110.00	135.00
93	CIRCULAR COTTAGE	RT	95.00	100.00
93	DIAL COTTAGE	RT	95.00	100.00
93	DIAMOND COTTAGE	RT	95.00	100.00
93	DOUBLE COTTAGE	RT	95.00	100.00
93	JASMINE COTTAGE	RT	95.00	100.00
93	OAK COTTAGE	RT	95.00	100.00
93	ROSE COTTAGE	RT	95.00	100.00
93	SWEET BRIAR COTTAGE	RT	95.00	100.00
93	VINE COTTAGE	RT	95.00	100.00
	D. TATE		**BLAISE HAMLET COLLECTION**	
89	CIRCULAR COTTAGE	RT	110.00	135.00

Department 56's Smythe Woolen Mill, *from the New England Village, was issued in 1987 and is limited to 7,500 pieces.*

Berkshire House *was added to the Department 56 New England Village line in 1989.*

Nathaniel Bingham Fabrics, *also referred to as the Post Office because the mail came into and went out of the shop, was a 1986 New England Village issue from Department 56.*

The Red Schoolhouse *was issued with the original set of seven pieces which comprised Department 56's New England Village.*

Department 56 issued the General Store *with their original set of seven New England Village pieces.*

The Brick Town Hall *was an original issue packaged with the set of seven starter New England Village pieces manufacturerd by Department 56.*

YR	NAME	LIMIT	ISSUE	QUOTE
89	DIAMOND COTTAGE	RT	110.00	135.00
89	OAK COTTAGE	RT	110.00	135.00
90	SWEETBRIAR COTTAGE	RT	110.00	135.00
90	VINE COTTAGE	OP	110.00	127.50
91	DOUBLE COTTAGE	OP	200.00	200.00
91	JASMINE COTTAGE	OP	140.00	140.00
91	ROSE COTTAGE	OP	140.00	140.00
*				**CHRISTMAS**
92	CHESTNUT COTTAGE	OP	46.50	46.50
92	CRANBERRY COTTAGE	OP	46.50	46.50
92	HIGHLAND LODGE	YR	180.00	220.00-250.00
92	HOLLYTREE HOUSE	OP	46.50	46.50
88	DEER PARK HALL	RT	120.00	170.00-200.00
89	ST. NICHOLAS CHURCH	RT	130.00	125.00-150.00
90	YULETIDE INN	RT	145.00	165.00-210.00
91	THE OLD VICARAGE AT CHRISTMAS	RT	180.00	165.00-210.00
92	CHESTNUT COTTAGE	OP	46.50	46.50
92	CRANBERRY COTTAGE	OP	46.50	46.50
92	HOLLYTREE HOUSE	OP	46.50	46.50
				CHRISTMAS LODGE
93	EAMONT LODGE	RT	185.00	250.00
94	SNOWDON LODGE	RT	175.00	200.00
95	KERRY LODGE	*	160.00	160.00
92	HIGHLAND LODGE	OP	180.00	180.00
D. SIMPSON			**COUNTRYSIDE SCENE PLAQUES**	
89	BOTTLE KILN	RT	49.50	49.50
89	CORNISH TIN MINE	RT	49.50	49.50
89	COUNTRY INN	RT	49.50	49.50
89	CUMBRIAN FARMHOUSE	RT	49.50	49.50
89	LIGHTHOUSE	RT	49.50	49.50
89	NORFOLK WINDMILL	RT	49.50	49.50
89	OASTHOUSE	RT	49.50	49.50
89	OLD SMITTY	RT	49.50	49.50
89	PARISH CHURCH	RT	49.50	49.50
89	POST OFFICE	RT	49.50	49.50
89	VILLAGE SCHOOL	RT	49.50	49.50
89	WATERMILL	RT	49.50	49.50
D. TATE			**DUTCH COLLECTION**	
91	AAN DE AMSTEL	OP	79.00	79.00
91	BEGIJNHOF	OP	55.00	55.00
91	BLOEMENMARKT	OP	79.00	79.00
91	DE BRANDERIJ	OP	72.50	72.50
91	DE DIAMANTAIR	OP	79.00	79.00
91	DE PEPERMOLEN	OP	55.00	55.00
91	DE WOLHANDELAAR	OP	72.50	72.50
91	DE ZIJDEWEVER	OP	79.00	79.00
91	REMBRANT VAN RIJN	OP	120.00	120.00
91	ROZENGRACHT	OP	72.50	72.50
*				**ENGLISH COTTAGES**
86	GULLIVER	RT	65.00	230.00
87	CLOCKMAKERS COTTAGE	RT	40.00	255.00
87	STREET SCENE #1	RT	40.00	350.00
87	STREET SCENE #10	RT	45.00	290.00
87	STREET SCENE #2	RT	45.00	350.00
87	STREET SCENE #3	RT	45.00	350.00
87	STREET SCENE #4	RT	45.00	290.00
87	STREET SCENE #5	RT	40.00	290.00
87	STREET SCENE #6	RT	40.00	290.00
87	STREET SCENE #7	RT	40.00	290.00
87	STREET SCENE #8	RT	40.00	290.00
87	STREET SCENE #9	RT	45.00	290.00
89	CHILTERN MILL	RT	87.50	110.00
92	DERWENT-LE-DALE	OP	75.00	75.00
92	FINCHINGFIELDS	OP	82.50	82.50
92	GRANTCHESTER MEADOWS	OP	275.00	275.00
92	HIGH GHYLL FARM	OP	360.00	360.00
92	THE CHOCOLATE HOUSE	OP	130.00	130.00
92	THE NUTSHELL	OP	75.00	75.00
92	WEDDING BELLS	OP	75.00	75.00
92	WHEYSIDE COTTAGE	OP	46.50	46.50
94	LEONORA'S SEARET	RT 2500	350.00	500.00
94	SAXHAM ST. EDMUNDS	RT 4500	1550.00	1650.00
95	CHERRY BLOSSOM	*	128.00	128.00
95	CHIPPING COOMBE	3000	525.00	525.00
95	DUCKDOWN	*	95.00	95.00
95	PIPIT TELL	*	64.00	64.00

There are three versions of the
Steeple Church (New England
Village). The first were issued by
Department 56 in 1986.

Ben's Barber Shop *was issued along*
with Otis Hayes Butcher Shop *and*
Anne Shaw Toys *in a set designed for*
the New England Village produced by
Department 56.

The Wool Shop *was one of three*
issues in the "Cobblestone Shops"
set of three starter pieces for
Department 56's Dickens' Village.

The Counting House & Silas
Thimbleton Barrister *(Dickens'*
Village) was only issued from
1988-90. Department 56 retired
the piece after only two years.

YR	NAME	LIMIT	ISSUE	QUOTE
95	THE RUSTLINGS	*	128.00	128.00
87	FOUR SEASONS	OP	70.00	80.00-100.00
87	SADDLERS INN	RT	50.00	50.00-75.00
87	SECRET GARDEN	RT	145.00	200.00-300.00
86	COBBLERS COTTAGE	RT	42.00	40.00-65.00
88	SHIP INN	RT	210.00	215.00
86	TUDOR COURT	RT	260.00	280.00-300.00
87	BEACON HEIGHTS	RT	125.00	130.00-165.00
87	GABLES, THE	RT	145.00	115.00-150.00
82	ACORN COTTAGE	RT	40.00	60.00-85.00
82	APRIL COTTAGE	RT	*	50.00-75.00
82	BRIDGE HOUSE	RT	15.95	35.00-50.00
82	DALE HOUSE (MINI)	RT	25.00	1300.00
82	DRAPERS	RT	15.95	325.00
82	HONEYSUCKLE	RT	45.00	130.00-160.00
82	LAKESIDE HOUSE	RT	40.00	1000.00-1100.00
82	OAK LODGE	RT	40.00	75.00-100.00
82	OLD MINE	RT	15.95	2500.00
82	STONE COTTAGE	RT	40.00	350.00-400.00
82	SUSSEX MILL	RT	25.00	470.00
83	ANNE HATHAWAY'S	RT	40.00	50.00-75.00
83	CASTLE STREET	RT	130.00	425.00-500.00
83	COACH HOUSE (MINI)	RT	100.00	1040.00-1950.00
83	COOPERS	RT	15.00	360.00-400.00
83	HOLLY COTTAGE	RT	42.50	40.00-60.00
83	MILLERS	RT	15.00	120.00-170.00
83	MINERS COTTAGE	RT	15.00	490.00-600.00
83	RED LION INN	RT	125.00	350.00-450.00
83	THATCHERS REST	RT	185.00	250.00-300.00
83	THE OLD POST OFFICE	RT	35.00	800.00-1000.00
83	TOLL HOUSE	RT	15.00	85.00-130.00
83	TROUTBECK FARM	RT	125.00	228.00-450.00
83	TUCK HOUSE	RT	35.00	1105.00-1625.00
83	WARWICK HALL	RT	185.00	2500.00
83	WILLIAM SHAKESPEARE	RT	130.00	100.00-130.00
83	WOODCUTTERS	RT	15.00	125.00-175.00
84	CLIBURN SCHOOL	RT	22.50	7150.00
84	DALE FARM	RT	30.00	1175.00-1400.00
84	DOVE COTTAGE	RT	35.00	65.00-100.00
84	TINTAGEL	RT	39.50	150.00-200.00
85	BERMUDA COTTAGE	OP	29.00	325.00
85	BRONTE PARSONAGE	RT	72.00	110.00-125.00
85	BURNS COTTAGE	RT	35.00	90.00-130.00
85	CLARE COTTAGE	OP	30.00	45.00-65.00
85	FISHERMANS COTTAGE	RT	30.00	60.00-100.00
85	KENTISH OAST	RT	55.00	70.00-85.00
85	MORETON MANOR	RT	55.00	65.00-100.00
85	OLD CURIOSITY SHOP	RT	62.50	90.00-120.00
85	OSTLERS KEEP	RT	55.00	70.00-100.00
85	SAWYER GILL	RT	30.00	45.00-70.00
85	ST. MARY'S	RT	40.00	110.00-130.00
85	WATERMILL	OP	40.00	40.00-55.00
86	BAY VIEW	RT	39.50	80.00-100.00
86	DALE HEAD	RT	75.00	90.00-125.00
86	FARRIERS	RT	40.00	65.00-85.00
86	SCROLL ON THE WALL	RT	55.00	130.00-165.00
86	SEVEN DWARF'S COTTAGE	RT	*	780.00
86	SPRING BANK	RT	42.00	65.00-85.00
86	THREE FEATHERS	RT	115.00	165.00-195.00
87	CLOVER COTTAGE	RT	27.50	26.00-35.00
87	HOLME DYKE	RT	50.00	75.00-100.00
87	INGLEWOOD	RT	27.50	40.00
87	IZAAK WALTON'S COTTAGE	RT	75.00	60.00-120.00
87	KEEPERS LODGE	RT	75.00	100.00-130.00
87	MAGPIE COTTAGE	RT	70.00	65.00-90.00
87	RIVERVIEW	RT	27.50	35.00
87	RYDAL VIEW	RT	220.00	225.00-260.00
87	STONEYBECK	RT	45.00	60.00-80.00
87	SUMMER HAZE	OP	90.00	100.00-120.00
87	TANNER'S COTTAGE	RT	27.50	40.00-50.00
87	WEALDEN HOUSE	RT	125.00	130.00-170.00
88	BREDON HOUSE	RT	145.00	130.00-170.00
88	BROOKBANK	RT	58.00	65.00-85.00
88	CROWN INN	RT	120.00	165.00-200.00
88	PARGETTER'S RETREAT	RT	75.00	65.00-100.00
88	RISING SUN	RT	58.00	85.00-110.00

YR	NAME	LIMIT	ISSUE	QUOTE
88	ROYAL OAK	RT	145.00	175.00-225.00
88	SAXON COTTAGE	RT	245.00	230.00-260.00
88	SMALLEST INN	RT	42.50	65.00-85.00
88	ST. MARK'S CHURCH	RT	75.00	80.00-130.00
88	SWAN INN	RT	120.00	130.00-160.00
88	SWIFT HOLLOW	RT	75.00	80.00-120.00
89	ANNE HATHAWAY'S COTTAGE	OP	130.00	150.00
89	ASH NOOK	OP	47.50	65.00
89	BEEHIVE COTTAGE	RT	72.50	65.00-85.00
89	BUTTERWICK	OP	52.50	60.00-80.00
89	CHINE COT	OP	36.00	40.00
89	FIVEWAYS	OP	42.50	40.00
89	GREENSTED CHURCH	OP	72.50	90.00
89	HELMERE	OP	65.00	80.00
89	MAYFLOWER HOUSE	RT	87.50	195.00
89	ST. LAWRENCE CHURCH	OP	110.00	130.00
89	ST. PETER'S COVE	CL	1375.00	1300.00-1625.00
89	TANGLEWOOD LODGE	RT	97.00	120.00-150.00
89	THE BRIARY	OP	47.50	65.00-85.00
89	TITMOUSE COTTAGE	OP	92.50	105.00-130.00
89	VICTORIA COTTAGE	RT	52.50	50.00-65.00
89	WIGHT COTTAGE	RT	52.50	65.00
89	WILLIAM SHAKESPEARE'S	OP	130.00	100.00-130.00
90	BRAMBLE COTTAGE	RT	55.00	70.00
90	BUTTERCUP COTTAGE	RT	40.00	50.00-75.00
90	CHERRY COTTAGE	OP	33.50	40.00
90	CHILTERN MILL	OP	87.50	165.00
90	CONVENT IN THE WOODS	OP	175.00	210.00
90	MRS. PINKERTON'S POST OFFICE	OP	72.50	90.00-100.00
90	OLDE YORK TOLL	RT	82.50	125.00
90	OTTER REACH	OP	33.50	40.00
90	PERIWINKLE COTTAGE	OP	165.00	230.00
90	ROBIN'S GATE	OP	33.50	40.00
90	ROWAN LODGE	RT	50.00	115.00-125.00
90	RUNSWICK HOUSE	OP	62.50	75.00
90	STRAWBERRY COTTAGE	OP	36.00	42.50
90	SULGRAVE MANOR	RT	120.00	140.00
90	THE KING'S ARMS	OP	450.00	525.00
91	ANNE OF CLEVES	OP	360.00	360.00
91	ARMADA HOUSE	OP	175.00	175.00
91	BRIDGE HOUSE 1991	OP	25.00	35.00-50.00
91	CHATSWORTH VIEW	OP	250.00	250.00
91	DAISY COTTAGE	OP	37.50	37.50
91	DOVETAILS	OP	90.00	90.00
91	FARTHING LODGE	OP	37.50	40.00-60.00
91	HOPCROFT COTTAGE	OP	120.00	120.00
91	JOHN BARLEYCORN COTTAGE	RT	130.00	150.00
91	LACE LANE	OP	90.00	125.00
91	LAPWORTH LOCK	RT	82.50	100.00
91	MICKLEGATE ANTIQUES	OP	90.00	110.00
91	MOONLIGHT COVE	OP	82.50	82.50
91	OLD SHOP AT BIGNOR	RT	215.00	220.00
91	PARADISE LODGE	OP	130.00	130.00
91	PEAR TREE HOUSE	OP	82.50	100.00
91	PRIMROSE HILL	OP	46.50	46.50
91	SAXHAM ST. EDMUNDS	RT	1550.00	1375.00-1625.00
91	THE FLOWER SELLERS	OP	110.00	110.00
91	THE PRIEST'S HOUSE	RT	180.00	195.00
91	TILLERS GREEN	OP	60.00	60.00
91	VILLAGE SCHOOL	OP	120.00	120.00
91	WELLINGTON LODGE	OP	55.00	55.00
91	WITHAM DELPH	RT	110.00	120.00
92	BOW COTTAGE	RT	128.00	135.00
92	DERWENT-LE-DALE	OP	75.00	75.00
92	FINCHINGFIELDS	OP	90.00	90.00
92	GRANNY SMITHS	OP	60.00	60.00
92	GRANTCHESTER MEADOWS	OP	275.00	275.00
92	HIGH GHYLL FARM	OP	360.00	360.00
92	HONEYSUCKLE COTTAGE (10TH ANNIVERSARY)	OP	195.00	130.00-175.00
92	OAKWOOD SMITHY	OP	450.00	450.00
92	PIXIE HOUSE	OP	55.00	55.00
92	PUFFIN ROW	OP	127.50	127.50
92	RUSTIC ROOF HOUSE	OP	110.00	110.00
92	THE CHOCOLATE HOUSE	OP	130.00	130.00
92	THE NUTSHELL	OP	75.00	75.00
92	WEDDING BELLS	OP	75.00	75.00

YR	NAME	LIMIT	ISSUE	QUOTE
			ENGLISH TEA ROOM COLLECTION	
95	BARGATE COTTAGE	*	160.00	160.00
95	GRANDMA BATTY'S	*	120.00	120.00
D. TATE			**FRAMED ENGLISH PLAQUES**	
90	ASHDOWN HALL	RT	59.50	59.50
90	BATTLEVIEW	RT	59.50	59.50
90	CAT SLIDE COTTAGE	RT	59.50	59.50
90	COOMBE COT	RT	59.50	59.50
90	FELL VIEW	RT	59.50	59.50
90	FLINT FIELDS	RT	59.50	59.50
90	HUNTINGTON HOUSE	RT	59.50	59.50
90	JUBILEE LODGE	RT	59.50	59.50
90	STOWSIDE	RT	59.50	59.50
90	TREVAN COVE	RT	59.50	59.50
D. TATE			**FRAMED IRISH PLAQUES**	
90	BALLYTEAG HOUSE	RT	59.50	59.50
90	CROCKUNA CROFT	RT	59.50	59.50
90	PEARSES COTTAGES	RT	59.50	59.50
90	SHANNONS BANK	RT	59.50	59.50
D. TATE			**FRAMED SCOTTISH PLAQUES**	
90	BARRA BLACK HOUSE	RT	59.50	59.50
90	FIFE NESS	RT	59.50	59.50
90	KYLE POINT	RT	59.50	59.50
90	PRESTON OAT MILL	RT	59.50	59.50
D. TATE			**FRENCH COLLECTION**	
91	L'AUBERGE D'ARMORIQUE	OP	220.00	220.00
91	LA BERGERIE DU PERIGORD	OP	230.00	230.00
91	LA CABANE DU GARDIAN	OP	55.00	55.00
91	LA CHAUMIERE DU VERGER	OP	120.00	120.00
91	LA MASELLE DE NADAILLAC	OP	130.00	130.00
91	LA PORTE SCHOENENBERG	OP	75.00	75.00
91	LE MANOIR DE CHAMPFLEURI	OP	265.00	265.00
91	LE MAS DU VIGNERON	OP	120.00	120.00
91	LE PETITE MONTMARTRE	OP	130.00	130.00
91	LOCMARIA	OP	65.00	65.00
D. TATE			**GERMAN COLLECTION**	
87	DAS GEBIRGSKIRCHLEIN	OP	120.00	120.00
87	HAUS IM RHEINLAND	OP	220.00	145.00
87	JAGHUTTE	OP	82.50	82.50
87	MEERSBURGER WEINSTUBE	OP	82.50	82.50
87	MOSELHAUS	OP	140.00	140.00
87	NURNBERGER BURGERHAUS	OP	140.00	140.00
87	SCHWARZWALDHAUS	OP	140.00	140.00
88	DAS RATHAUS	OP	140.00	150.00
88	DER FAMILIENSCHREIN	RT	52.50	90.00
88	DIE KLEINEBACKEREI	RT	68.00	80.00
92	ALTE SCHMIEDE	OP	175.00	175.00
92	DER BUCHERWURM	OP	140.00	140.00
92	ROSENGARTENHAUS	OP	120.00	120.00
92	STRANDVOGTHAUS	OP	120.00	120.00
D. TATE			**GUILD COLLECTION**	
92	THE GREENGROCERS	OP	120.00	120.00
			IRISH COTTAGES	
87	DONEGAL COTTAGE	RT	29.00	30.00
89	BALLYKERNE CROFT	OP	75.00	110.00-125.00
89	DONEGEL COTTAGE	OP	29.00	35.00-40.00
89	HEGARTY'S HOME	RT	68.00	110.00
89	KENNEDY HOMESTEAD	OP	33.50	40.00
89	KILMORE QUAY	RT	68.00	130.00-155.00
89	LIMERICK HOUSE	RT	110.00	130.00
89	MAGILLIGANS	OP	33.50	40.00
89	O'LACEY'S STORE	OP	68.00	79.00
89	PAT COHEN'S BAR	OP	110.00	130.00
89	QUIET COTTAGE	RT	72.50	130.00
89	ST. COLUMBIA'S SCHOOL	OP	47.50	55.00
89	ST. KEVIN'S SCHOOL	OP	55.00	65.00
89	ST. PATRICK'S CHURCH	OP	185.00	255.00-280.00
89	THOOR BALLYLEE	RT	105.00	120.00
D. SIMPSON			**LAKELAND BRIDGE PLAQUES**	
89	AIRA FORCE	RT	35.00	35.00
89	ASHNESS BRIDGE	RT	35.00	35.00
89	BIRKS BRIDGE	RT	35.00	35.00
89	BRIDGE HOUSE	RT	35.00	35.00
89	HARTSOP PACKHORSE	RT	35.00	35.00
89	STOCKLEY BRIDGE	RT	35.00	35.00

Kenilworth Castle (*Dickens' Village*) was available for $40 to collectors who were purchasing $100 worth of Department 56 merchandise.

Anne Shaw Toys *was issued with the "Cherry Lane Shops" for Department 56's New England Village.*

Shown here is the Alpine Church *with caramel trim. Earlier issues were trimmed in cream. The church was issued in 1987 and retired in 1991.*

C. Fletcher Public House (*Dickens' Village*) was the fourth limited edition to be produced by Department 56.

YR	NAME	LIMIT	ISSUE	QUOTE
			LAKELAND	**CHRISTMAS**
95	LANGDALE COTTAGE	*	48.00	48.00
95	PATTERDALE COTTAGE	*	48.00	48.00
95	RYDAL COTTAGE	*	44.75	44.75
		LILLIPUT	**LANE COLLECTORS**	**CLUB**
95	PORLOCK DOWN		135.00	135.00
95	THIMBLE COTTAGE	*	*	0.00
86	CRENDON MANOR	RT	285.00	1000.00-1100.00
86	PACKHORSE BRIDGE	RT	*	435.00-515.00
87	LITTLE LOST DOG	RT	*	240.00-250.00
87	YEW TREE FARM	RT	160.00	145.00-185.00
88	WISHING WELL	RT	*	100.00-120.00
89	WENLOCK RISE	RT	175.00	190.00-220.00
90	BRIDLE WAY	RT	100.00	150.00-180.00
90	COZY CORNER	RT	*	35.00-50.00
90	DOVECOT	RT	50.00	100.00-120.00
90	LAVENDER COTTAGE	RT	50.00	85.00-100.00
91	GARDENERS COTTAGE	TL	120.00	130.00-160.00
91	PUDDLEBROOK	TL	*	40.00-55.00
91	WREN COTTAGE	RT	13.95	100.00
92	FORGET-ME-NOT	TL	130.00	170.00-190.00
92	PUSSY WILLOW	TL	*	35.00-50.00
D. SIMPSON			**LONDON**	**PLAQUES**
89	BIG BEN	RT	39.50	39.50
89	BUCKINGHAM PALACE	RT	39.50	39.50
89	PICCADILLY CIRCUS	RT	39.50	39.50
89	TOWER BRIDGE	RT	39.50	39.50
89	TOWER OF LONDON	RT	39.50	39.50
89	TRAFALGAR SQUARE	RT	39.50	39.50
D. TATE			**SCOTTISH**	**COTTAGES**
82	THE CROFT (WITHOUT SHEEP)	RT	29.00	1170.00-1300.00
84	THE CROFT (RENOVATED)	RT	36.00	65.00-80.00
85	PRESTON MILL	RT	45.00	70.00-155.00
87	EAST NEUK	RT	29.00	40.00
87	PRESTON MILL (RENOVATED)	OP	62.50	72.50
89	BLAIR ATHOLL	SO	275.00	390.00-450.00
89	CARRICK HOUSE	OP	47.50	65.00
89	CLAYPOTTS CASTLE	OP	72.50	85.00
89	CRAIGIEVAR CASTLE	RT	185.00	215.00-375.00
89	CULLODEN COTTAGE	OP	36.00	42.50
89	INVERLOCHIE HAME	OP	47.50	65.00
89	JOHN KNOX HOUSE	RT	68.00	250.00
89	KENMORE COTTAGE	OP	87.00	85.00
89	STOCKWELL TENEMENT	OP	62.50	90.00
90	CAWDOR CASTLE	SO	295.00	450.00-660.00
90	ELLEAN DONAN	OP	145.00	170.00
90	FISHERMANS BOTHY	OP	36.00	42.50
90	GLENLOCHIE LODGE	RT	110.00	180.00
90	HEBRIDEAN HAME	RT	55.00	65.00-80.00
90	KINLOCHNESS	OP	79.00	110.00-130.00
90	KIRKBRAE COTTAGE	OP	55.00	65.00
92	CULROSS HOUSE	OP	90.00	90.00
92	DUART CASTLE	3000	450.00	630.00-715.00
92	ERISKAY CROFT	OP	50.00	50.00
92	MAIR HAVEN	OP	46.50	46.50
85	7 ST. ANDREWS SQUARE	RT	15.95	120.00-170.00
D. TATE			**SPECIAL EVENT**	**COLLECTION**
89	COMMEMORATIVE MEDALLION-1989 SOUTH BEND	CL	*	105.00
90	ROWAN LODGE 1990-SOUTH BEND	CL	*	120.00-125.00
91	GAMEKEEPERS COTTAGE-1991 SOUTH BEND	CL	*	115.00-145.00
92	ASHBERRY COTTAGE-1992 SOUTH BEND	CL	*	260.00-390.00
		STUDLEY	**ROYAL**	**COLLECTION**
95	FOUNTAIN'S ABBEY	3500	395.00	395.00
D. TATE			**UNFRAMED**	**PLAQUES**
89	LARGE LOWER BROCKHAMPTON	RT	120.00	120.00
89	LARGE SOMERSET SPRINGTIME	RT	130.00	130.00
89	MEDIUM COBBLE COMBE COTTAGE	RT	68.00	68.00
89	MEDIUM WISHING WELL	RT	75.00	75.00
89	SMALL STONEY WALL LEA	RT	47.50	47.50
89	SMALL WOODSIDE FARM	RT	47.50	47.50
*			**WELSH**	**COLLECTION**
92	ST. GOVAN'S CHAPEL	OP	75.00	75.00
84	HERMITAGE	RT	30.00	234.00-299.00
86	BRECON BACH	OP	42.00	35.00-65.00
87	RENOVATED HERMITAGE	RT	42.50	50.00-60.00
91	BRO DAWEL	OP	37.50	37.50

YR	NAME	LIMIT	ISSUE	QUOTE
91	TUDOR MERCHANT	OP	90.00	90.00
91	UGLY HOUSE	OP	55.00	55.00
92	ST. GOVAN'S CHAPEL	OP	75.00	75.00

MICHAEL'S LTD.
B. BAKER

			DEJA VU COLLECTION	
93	AMERICAN CLASSIC	500	99.00	110.00
93	JAMES RIVER PLANTATION	500	108.00	120.00
94	HILL TOP MANSION	1200	100.00	110.00
94	PAINTED LADIES	1200	125.00	135.00
94	WHITE POINT	700	97.00	105.00

MIDWEST OF CANNON FALLS

			COTTONTAIL LANE	
94	PORCELAIN LIGHTED GARDEN VALLEY CHAPEL	3000	43.00	275.00
95	PORCELAIN LIGHTED ROSEBUD MANOR	3500	45.00	45.00

PACIFIC RIM
P. SEBERN

			BRISTOL TOWNSHIP	
90	BEDFORD MANOR	OP	30.00	30.00
90	BLACK SWAN MILLINERY	OP	30.00	30.00
90	BRISTOL BOOKS	OP	35.00	35.00
90	COVENTRY HOUSE	OP	30.00	30.00
90	GEO. STRAITH GROCER	OP	25.00	25.00
90	HIGH GATE MILL	OP	40.00	40.00
90	IRON HORSE LIVERY	RT	30.00	35.00
90	MAPS & CHARTS	OP	25.00	25.00
90	QUEEN'S ROAD CHURCH	OP	40.00	40.00
90	SILVERSMITH	OP	30.00	30.00
90	SOUTHWICK CHURCH	OP	30.00	30.00
90	TRINITY CHURCH	RT	30.00	35.00
90	VIOLIN SHOP	OP	30.00	30.00
90	WEXFORD MANOR	OP	25.00	25.00
91	BRIDGESTONE CHURCH	RT	30.00	35.00
91	ELMSTONE HOUSE	RT	30.00	35.00
91	FLOWER SHOP	OP	30.00	30.00
91	HARDWICKE HOUSE	RT	30.00	35.00
91	KILBY COTTAGE	RT	30.00	35.00
91	PEBBLESWORTH INN	OP	40.00	40.00
93	CHESTERFIELD HOUSE	OP	30.00	30.00
93	FOXDOWN MANOR	OP	30.00	30.00
94	SHOTWICK INN & SURGERY	OP	35.00	35.00
94	SURREY ROAD CHURCH	OP	40.00	40.00
95	KING'S GATE SCHOOL	OP	30.00	30.00

P. SEBERN

			BRISTOL WATERFRONT	
92	ADMIRALTY SHIPPING	OP	30.00	30.00
92	AVON FISH CO.	OP	30.00	30.00
92	CHANDLER	OP	30.00	30.00
92	CUSTOMS HOUSE	OP	40.00	40.00
92	HAWKE EXPORTS	OP	40.00	40.00
92	QUARTER DECK INN	OP	40.00	40.00
92	REGENT WAREHOUSE	OP	40.00	40.00
93	BRISTOL POINT LIGHTHOUSE	OP	45.00	45.00
93	LOWER QUAY CHAPEL	OP	40.00	40.00
93	RUSTY KNIGHT INN	OP	35.00	35.00
94	BRISTOL TATTLER	OP	40.00	40.00
94	PORTSHEAD LIGHTHOUSE	OP	30.00	30.00
95	BRISTOL CHANNEL LIGHTHOUSE	OP	30.00	30.00
			BUNNY TOES	
94	SWEETHEARTS	OP	50.00	50.00

SHELIA'S COLLECTIBLES
S. THOMPSON

			ACCESSORIES	
93	APPLE TREE	OP	12.00	12.00
93	DOGWOOD TREE	OP	12.00	12.00
94	AMISH QUILT LINE	1500	18.00	35.00
94	FORMAL GARDEN	1500	18.00	30.00
94	SUNRISE AT 80 MEETING	1500	18.00	30.00
94	VICTORIAN ARBOR	1500	18.00	35.00

S. THOMPSON

			AMERICAN BARNS	
94	PENNSYLVANIA DUTCH BARN	OP	18.00	18.00
94	ROCK CITY BARN	OP	18.00	18.00

S. THOMPSON

			AMERICAN GOTHIC	
93	GOTHIC REVIVAL COTTAGE	2500	20.00	20.00
93	MELE HOUSE	2500	20.00	20.00
93	PERKINS HOUSE	2500	20.00	20.00
93	ROSE ARBOR	2500	14.00	14.00
93	ROSELAND COTTAGE	2500	20.00	20.00

YR	NAME	LIMIT	ISSUE	QUOTE
S. THOMPSON				**AMISH**
93	AMISH BARN	OP	17.00	17.00
93	AMISH BUGGY	OP	12.00	12.00
93	AMISH HOME	OP	17.00	17.00
93	AMISH SCHOOL	OP	15.00	15.00
93	COVERED BRIDGE	OP	16.00	16.00
S. THOMPSON				**CHARLESTON**
93	ASHE HOUSE	OP	16.00	16.00
93	CITADEL	OP	16.00	16.00
93	CITY HALL	1300	15.00	50.00
93	COLLEGE OF CHARLESTON	OP	16.00	16.00
93	DRAYTON HOUSE	OP	18.00	18.00
93	JOHN RUTLEDGE HOME	OP	16.00	16.00
93	SINGLE SIDE PORCH	OP	16.00	16.00
S. THOMPSON				**COLLECTORS SOCIETY**
93	ANNE PEACOCK HOUSE		16.00	16.00
93	SUSAN B. ANTHONY		*	
94	IVY GREEN		*	
94	SEASVIEW COTTAGE		17.00	17.00
S. THOMPSON				**GHOST HOUSE SERIES**
94	INSIDE-OUTSIDE HOUSE	OP	18.00	18.00
94	PIRATE'S HOUSE	OP	18.00	18.00
S. THOMPSON				**INVENTOR SERIES**
93	FORD MOTOR COMPANY	OP	17.00	17.00
93	MENTO PARK LABORATORY	OP	16.00	16.00
93	NOAH WEBSTER HOUSE	OP	15.00	15.00
93	WRIGHT CYCLE SHOP	OP	17.00	17.00
S. THOMPSON				**JAZZY NEW ORLEANS**
94	BEAUREGARD KEYS	OP	18.00	18.00
94	GALLIER HOUSE	OP	18.00	18.00
94	LABRANCHE BUILD	OP	18.00	18.00
94	LEPRETRE HOUSE	OP	18.00	18.00
S. THOMPSON				**LIGHTHOUSES**
93	ASSATEAGUE ISLAND LIGHT	OP	17.00	17.00
93	CHARLESTON LIGHT	OP	15.00	15.00
93	NEW LONDON LEDGE LIGHT	OP	17.00	17.00
93	ROUND ISLAND LIGHT	OP	17.00	17.00
93	THOMAS POINT LIGHT	OP	17.00	17.00
S. THOMPSON				**MAIL ORDER VICTORIANS**
94	BREHAUT HOUSE	3300	24.00	24.00
94	GOELLER HOUSE	3300	24.00	24.00
94	HENDERSON HOUSE	3300	24.00	24.00
94	TRTMAN HOUSE	3300	24.00	24.00
S. THOMPSON				**MARTHA'S VINEYARD**
93	ALICE'S WONDERLAND	OP	16.00	16.00
93	CAMPGROUND COTTAGE	OP	16.00	16.00
93	GINGERBREAD COTTAGE	OP	16.00	16.00
93	WOOD VALENTINE	OP	16.00	16.00
S. THOMPSON				**OLD FASHIONED CHRISTMAS**
94	CONWAY SCENIC RAILROAD STATION	OP	18.00	18.00
94	DWIGHT HOUSE	OP	18.00	18.00
94	GENERAL MERCHANDISE	OP	18.00	18.00
94	OLD FIRST CHURCH	OP	18.00	18.00
S. THOMPSON				**PAINTED LADIES III**
93	GREEN STOCKTON	OP	16.00	16.00
93	LINDA LEE	OP	16.00	16.00
93	PINK STOCKTON	OP	16.00	16.00
93	TAN STOCKTON	OP	16.00	16.00
S. THOMPSON				**RAINBOW ROW**
93	AURORA RAINBOW ROW	OP	13.00	13.00
93	BLUE RAINBOW ROW	OP	13.00	13.00
93	CREAM RAINBOW ROW	OP	13.00	13.00
93	GRAY RAINBOW ROW	OP	13.00	13.00
93	GREEN RAINBOW ROW	OP	13.00	13.00
93	LAVENDER RAINBOW ROW	OP	13.00	13.00
93	OFF-WHITE RAINBOW ROW	OP	13.00	13.00
93	PINK RAINBOW ROW	OP	13.00	13.00
93	YELLOW RAINBOW ROW	OP	13.00	13.00
S. THOMPSON				**SAVANNAH**
93	CHESTNUT HOUSE	OP	18.00	18.00
93	OWENS THOMAS HOUSE	OP	16.00	16.00
S. THOMPSON				**VICTORIAN SPRINGTIME**
93	HEFFRON HOUSE	OP	17.00	17.00
93	JACOBSEN HOUSE	OP	17.00	17.00
93	RALSTON HOSUE	OP	17.00	17.00
93	SESSIONS HOUSE	OP	17.00	17.00

This festive and whimsical Christmas Boot *was the inspiration of Jon Herbert. The line of Boot Houses is produced by John Hine Studios.*

Audrey's Tea Room *was only issued for a limited time due to the mold being broken in a highway accident. The piece was created by David Winter for John Hine Studios.*

Fred's Home *is David Winter's special Christmas piece for 1991.*

Clown Boot *makes an impressive residence for those tiny enough to enjoy it. This piece by Jon Herbert also makes an equally impressive collectible (John Hine Studios).*

YR	NAME	LIMIT	ISSUE	QUOTE

SJS DESIGNS
S. STENTIFORD — **IVY ROSE COLLECTION**

YR	NAME	LIMIT	ISSUE	QUOTE
93	IVY POINT LIGHTHOUSE	2000	27.00	32.00
93	MELMACKER'S LOBSTER POT CAFE	2000	27.00	32.00
93	THE PERIWINKLE COTTAGE	2000	27.00	32.00
93	THE SEAFLOWER INN	2000	32.00	38.00
93	VALERIE ELIZABETH'S BEACH HOUSE	2000	25.00	30.00
94	ANTIQUES BARN	2000	28.00	33.00
94	AUNTIE GEN'S	2000	27.00	32.00
94	DARRELL'S COTTAGE	2000	27.00	32.00
94	DOROTHEA'S HOUSE	2000	29.00	34.00
94	GOG'S ANIMAL BARN	2000	30.00	35.00
94	INA'S FARMHOUSE	2000	30.00	35.00
94	LINDA IRENE'S	2000	28.00	33.00
94	MARY ELLEN'S	2000	27.00	32.00
94	MISS MARGARET'S	2000	29.00	34.00
94	POLICE STATION	2000	24.00	29.00
94	THE FARMER'S MARKET	2000	27.00	33.00
94	THE SUNFLOWER COTTAGE	2000	25.00	30.00
94	TOWN PHARMACY	2000	28.00	33.00

SPENCER COLLIN LIGHTHOUSES
C. COLLIN

YR	NAME	LIMIT	ISSUE	QUOTE
84	PORTSMOUTH LIGHTHOUSE	CL	18.00	18.00
93	ANNISQUAM HARBOR LIGHTHOUSE	2000	46.00	46.00
93	CAPE MAY LIGHTHOUSE	OP	79.00	79.00
93	FORT GRATIOT LIGHTHOUSE	2000	52.00	52.00
93	JUPITER INLET LIGHTHOUSE	2000	84.00	84.00
93	MARSHALL POINT LIGHTHOUSE	2000	46.00	46.00
93	NEW LONDON LEDGE LIGHTHOUSE	2000	120.00	120.00
93	PEGGY'S POINT LIGHTHOUSE	OP	38.00	38.00
93	PONCE INLET LIGHTHOUSE	2000	86.00	86.00
93	SAND ISLAND LIGHTHOUSE	OP	66.00	66.00
93	SPLIT ROCK LIGHTHOUSE	OP	110.00	110.00
93	ST. SIMONS ISLAND LIGHTHOUSE	2000	116.00	116.00
94	POINT ISABEL LIGHTHOUSE	2000	52.00	52.00

C. COLLIN — **ADMIRAL'S LIGHTS--FLAG QUARTER SERIES**

YR	NAME	LIMIT	ISSUE	QUOTE
94	YERBA BUENA LIGHTHOUSE	3000	90.00	90.00

C. COLLIN — **ADMIRAL'S LIGHTS--FLAG QUARTERS SERIES**

YR	NAME	LIMIT	ISSUE	QUOTE
94	ALKI POINT LIGHTHOUSE	3000	70.00	70.00
94	DIAMOND HEAD LIGHTHOUSE	3000	124.00	124.00
94	HOSPITAL POINT LIGHTHOUSE	3000	68.00	68.00

C. COLLIN — **COMMEMORATIVE STAMP SERIES**

YR	NAME	LIMIT	ISSUE	QUOTE
89	CAPE HATTERAS LIGHTHOUSE	RT	70.00	70.00

C. COLLIN — **TRADEMARK SERIES**

YR	NAME	LIMIT	ISSUE	QUOTE
94	10TH ANNIVERSARY LIGHTHOUSE	CL	100.00	100.00

WB STUDIOS
R. KAY — **LIGHTED SNOWHOUSE**

YR	NAME	LIMIT	ISSUE	QUOTE
93	ESTATE HOUSE	1000	900.00	1000.00
92	GREENHOUSE W/WALKWAY	2000	490.00	525
94	RAMBLING ROSE	500	660.00	700.00

Dolls

Betty Hodges

Doll collecting is a growing field, ranking second in popularity among hobbyists in the United States. There are more dolls available today than ever before. They abound in the marketplace, and are so delectable that one can scarcely ignore them.

As with all buying, your own personal tastes play an important role in collecting. There are unknown factors behind every doll purchase. Why one appeals to you and another does not goes back to some dim reference point. Sometimes there is a special feeling connected with a certain doll, and before you know it, you've acquired it!

Childhood dolls are often the start of a collection. Collectors will go out of their way to acquire a doll they fondly remember from their early years. But no matter how you start collecting, the doll industry continues to proliferate, allowing you to add new creations to your collection at any given time.

No one can guess which dolls produced today will increase in value tomorrow. Through the years, some contemporary dolls have become quite valuable while others have not. The dolls of the early 1900s remain very desirable. Many of these dolls were played with sparingly. It is often said that Sunday afternoon was the only time children were allowed to handle these dolls.

Despite the era in which they grew up, many collectors feel their childhood dolls are as sacrosanct as the ones made decades earlier. These dolls are quite different from their older cousins but still have the same allure. Bakelite dolls made in the 1930s were omnipresent, but unfortunately have not worn well. Dolls composed of wood and cloth show the timeworn caress of those little hands which played with them.

Limited edition dolls are a new factor in the equation. Putting a production limit on the number of dolls made adds to their desirability. The doll that catches your eye may not be available for very long. This initial limit on the supply can increase the demand for the doll, oftentimes making the doll more valuable over the years.

Today's dolls have myriad diverse characteristics. The collector's desire to add more dolls to his or her collection grows increasingly, and makers fall over themselves to produce them.

There are two definite audiences for dolls produced today—children and adults. The number of dolls bought and kept by adults is unprecedented in the doll world. These dolls are genuine collectibles, which will be cherished. They retain their beauty indefinitely.

Keep accurate records when you acquire your dolls; include the producer's name and the exact outfit the doll is wearing. Take pictures of each doll. Should you ever decide to sell your collection, these details will be essential.

Your personal taste is the key to your collection. Do you know which dolls will become valuable? Probably not, but this should not reduce the enjoyment you get from this hobby.

BETTY HODGES has 25 years of experience in the doll market. A consultant to doll artists, she has supervised dealer booths in international toy and trade markets and edits a doll manufacturers newsletter.

YR	NAME	LIMIT	ISSUE	QUOTE

DOLLS

ANNALEE MOBILITEE

YR	NAME	LIMIT	ISSUE	QUOTE
92	SAILOR KID W/BOAT	1	*	900.00
91	10 IN CONDUCTOR DOLL (MUSIC)	383	129.50	129.50
91	10 IN EASTER PARADE GIRL BUNNY	5,101	38.95	100.00
91	10 IN. ANNALEE COLLECTOR DOLL	588	149.95	300.00
91	10 IN. AVIATOR FROG (WWI)	2,110	19.95	275.00
91	10 IN. BEAR IN NIGHTSHIRT	2,774	32.95	75.00
91	10 IN. BEAR IN VELOUR SANTA SUIT	3,711	32.95	75.00
91	10 IN. BEAR W/SNOWBALL, KNIT HAT	3,121	29.95	75.00
91	10 IN. BLACK CAT	6,267	21.95	100.00
91	10 IN. BOB CRATCHET & 5 IN. TINY TIM	639	99.95	300.00
91	10 IN. BRIDE BEAR	2,977	39.95	75.00
91	10 IN. CHRISTMAS ELF	16,567	15.95	40.00
91	10 IN. CHRISTOPHER COLUMBUS	1,132	119.50	400.00
91	10 IN. COUNTRY BOY BUNNY	1,844	42.95	125.00
91	10 IN. COUNTRY GIRL BUNNY	2,044	34.95	90.00
91	10 IN. DOE	6,541	20.95	75.00
91	10 IN. EASTER PARADE BOY BUNNY	4,195	37.95	90.00
91	10 IN. GINGERBREAD BOY	10,453	22.45	22.45
91	10 IN. GIRL W/BASKET	3,592	37.95	100.00
91	10 IN. GROOM BEAR	2,745	39.95	75.00
91	10 IN. HOBO CLOWN	2,368	25.45	25.45
91	10 IN. HUSKIE W/5 IN. PUPPY	2,860	54.95	150.00
91	10 IN. IN.TINSEL IN. THE ELF	17,070	20.45	50.00
91	10 IN. INDIAN MAN	2,719	32.95	65.00
91	10 IN. INDIAN WOMAN	2,779	32.95	75.00
91	10 IN. JACOB MARLEY	598	89.95	175.00
91	10 IN. KITTEN ON SLED	3,810	35.95	90.00
91	10 IN. KITTEN W/KNIT MITTENS	4,124	33.95	75.00
91	10 IN. MAN SKATER	4,881	45.95	125.00
91	10 IN. MARTHA CRATCHET W/PLUM	2,136	59.95	175.00
91	10 IN. MUSIC CONDUCTOR DOLL	*	139.50	375.00
91	10 IN. NATIVITY ANGEL	2,112	59.95	150.00
91	10 IN. NATIVITY SET	658	149.95	149.95
91	10 IN. PILGRIM MAN W/BASKET	2,374	44.95	75.00
91	10 IN. PILGRIM WOMAN W/TURKEY	2,502	44.95	75.00
91	10 IN. REINDEER W/CAP & BELL	10,300	22.45	75.00
91	10 IN. SANTA FEEDING REINDEER	2.618	79.95	200.00
91	10 IN. SANTA ON ROCKING HORSE	2.398	49.95	150.00
91	10 IN. SANTA PIG	2,685	31.95	75.00
91	10 IN. SANTA PLAYING W/TRAIN	1,525	49.95	250.00
91	10 IN. SANTA W/REINDEER GOLFING	2,462	79.95	150.00
91	10 IN. SCROOGE	592	89.95	200.00
91	10 IN. SHEPHERD BOY & LAMB	591	89.95	89.95
91	10 IN. SKATING BUNNY	6,027	43.95	150.00
91	10 IN. SNOWY OWL	3,163	25.95	50.00
91	10 IN. SPRING ELF	4,060	15.95	35.00
91	10 IN. SUMMER SANTA	1.926	59.95	225.00
91	10 IN. THE SPIRIT OF '76	1,080	175.00	500.00
91	10 IN. TWO WISE MEN W/BRASS	476	109.95	109.95
91	10 IN. VICTORY SKI DOLL	1,192	49.50	400.00
91	10 IN. WISE MAN W/CAMEL	650	109.95	400.00
91	10 IN. WOMAN SKATER	4,975	45.95	125.00
91	12 IN. BASKET COUPLE	2,028	96.95	200.00
91	12 IN. BAT	3,113	29.95	50.00
91	12 IN. CHRISTMAS SWAN	674	63.95	225.00
91	12 IN. DRUMMER BOY	3,298	39.95	75.00
91	12 IN. EASTER DUCK W/WATERING	1,407	49.95	250.00
91	12 IN. PILGRIM BOY MOUSE	1,980	42.95	42.95
91	12 IN. PILGRIM GIRL MOUSE	1,978	42.95	42.95
91	12 IN. PJ KID W/BLONDE HAIR	2,726	29.95	50.00
91	12 IN. PJ KID W/BROWN HAIR	2,307	29.95	50.00
91	12 IN. SANTA DUCK	1,187	53.45	250.00
91	12 IN. SANTA W/POT BELLED STOVE	5,887	59.95	100.00
91	12 IN. SANTA'S HELPER PAINTING	5,274	35.95	75.00
91	12 IN. SANTA'S POSTMAN	6,980	35.95	50.00
91	12 IN. SCARECROW	2,330	40.95	100.00
91	12 IN. SPIDER	5,194	32.95	125.00
91	12 IN. SPRING SWAN	615	49.95	225.00
91	12 IN. TREE TOP ANGEL	2,589	42.45	125.00
91	12 IN. TUCKERED COUPLE	2,574	89.95	89.95
91	12 IN. VELOUR MRS. SANTA	3,677	49.95	100.00
91	12 IN. VELOUR SANTA W/TOYBAG	3,517	49.95	75.00

YR	NAME	LIMIT	ISSUE	QUOTE
91	15 IN. HOBO CLOWN	1,295	47.95	150.00
91	18 IN. ANGLE W/INSTRUMENT	1,009	55.45	225.00
91	18 IN. BUNNY KID W/BUNNY	2,859	49.95	75.00
91	18 IN. CHET SANTA	4,511	46.95	125.00
91	18 IN. CHOIR BOY	3,120	57.95	175.00
91	18 IN. CHOIR GIRL	2,188	57.95	175.00
91	18 IN. DAY-AFTER-CHRISTMAS SANTA	2,263	79.45	200.00
91	18 IN. EASTER PARADE BOY BUNNY	2,056	62.45	125.00
91	18 IN. EASTER PARADE GIRL BUNNY	2,254	62.45	125.00
91	18 IN. GINGERBREAD BOY	3,966	50.95	65.00
91	18 IN. MRS. SANTA W/PRESENTS	5,497	49.95	100.00
91	18 IN. MRS. SANTA W/TRAY	5,143	49.95	125.00
91	18 IN. MRS. SANTA W/TRAY	*	49.95	49.95
91	18 IN. NAUGHTY KID	547	74.95	100.00
91	18 IN. PJ KID	1,307	39.45	100.00
91	18 IN. PJ KID HANGING STOCKING	1,396	46.95	100.00
91	18 IN. PJ KID IN 2 FT. STOCKING	1,589	61.95	100.00
91	18 IN. PUMPKIN COSTUME KID	1,317	74.45	115.00
91	18 IN. REINDEER W/CHRISTMAS	4,053	52.95	150.00
91	18 IN. SANTA W/CARDHOLDER	8,056	59.95	125.00
91	18 IN. SANTA W/GIFT LIST	6,334	43.95	80.00
91	18 IN. SANTA W/STOCKING	4,466	47.95	90.00
91	18 IN. SNOWMAN W/BROOM	4,218	43.45	150.00
91	18 IN. SNOWY OWL	965	65.95	175.00
91	18 IN. THORNY THE GHOST	1,270	51.95	150.00
91	18 IN. TRICK OR TREAT BUNNY KID	625	49.95	90.00
91	18 IN. WITHC	2,033	63.95	150.00
91	22 IN. CHRISTMAS STOCKING	4,993	18.45	55.00
91	22 IN. RED CHRISTMAS ELF	3,679	34.95	75.00
91	3 IN. EATER BABY IN POND LILY	3,720	14.95	175.00
91	30 IN. MR. & MRS. TUCKERED	644	291.45	600.00
91	30 IN. MRS. SANTA W/CARDHOLDER	1,483	119.95	150.00
91	30 IN. SANTA W/LIGHTED TREE	509	189.95	200.00
91	30 IN. VELOUR MRS. SANTA W/MUFF	755	160.45	200.00
91	30 IN. VELOUR SANTA W/PIPE & BAG	1,221	160.45	200.00
91	36 IN. REINDEER (ANIMATED)	134	339.95	875.00
91	36 IN. REINDEER W/CARDHOLDER	879	148.45	300.00
91	5 IN. ANGEL	9,844	22.95	50.00
91	5 IN. BABY SWAN	3,168	13.95	50.00
91	5 IN. CHRISTMAS DRAGON	4,125	23.95	75.00
91	5 IN. DUCK ON FLEXIBLE FLYER	3,822	25.95	50.00
91	5 IN. EASTER PARADE BOY DUCK	4,261	21.95	85.00
91	5 IN. EASTER PARADE GIRL DUCK	5,105	23.95	85.00
91	5 IN. ELF (WORKSHOP)	16.359	13.45	25.00
91	5 IN. FAWN	13,027	14.45	25.00
91	5 IN. FLUFFY YELLOW CHICK	6,979	15.95	50.00
91	5 IN. LAMB	4,302	15.95	45.00
91	5 IN. LEPRECHAUN	6,384	15.95	35.00
91	5 IN. SAILOR DUCK	2,241	21.95	75.00
91	5 IN. SPRING LAMB	6,709	16.95	45.00
91	5 IN. TRIM-A-TREE ELF	10,108	12.95	25.00
91	5 IN. WINTER DUCK IN INNER TUBE	2.992	23.95	75.00
91	7 IN. ANGEL ON SLED W/CLOUD	2,313	29.95	50.00
91	7 IN. ANGEL W/MUSICAL INSTRUMENT	5,879	19.95	50.00
91	7 IN. ARTIST BUNNY W/BRUSH	5,346	20.95	90.00
91	7 IN. BAKER MOUSE	6,895	25.95	150.00
91	7 IN. BEN FRANKLIN MOUSE	5,029	29.95	150.00
91	7 IN. BUNNY KID	3,827	23.45	65.00
91	7 IN. CAROLLER BOY	5,010	22.95	50.00
91	7 IN. CAROLLER BOY MOUSE W/MUSIC	7,281	15.45	50.00
91	7 IN. CAROLLER GIRL	5,135	22.95	75.00
91	7 IN. CHRISTMAS GNOME	15,503	17.95	35.00
91	7 IN. COUNTRY BOY BUNNY	3,199	28.95	75.00
91	7 IN. COUNTRY BOY BUNNY	4,421	20.45	75.00
91	7 IN. COUNTRY GIRL BUNNY	3,805	20.45	100.00
91	7 IN. DISNEY COLLECTION	300	80.00	300.00
91	7 IN. DRAGON KID	1,116	31.95	175.00
91	7 IN. DUMMMER BOY	7,031	22.45	75.00
91	7 IN. EARTH DAY MOUSE	5,863	299.95	150.00
91	7 IN. EASTER PARADE BOY	7,043	20.95	50.00
91	7 IN. EASTER PARADE DRESS-UP BOY	*	27.45	27.45
91	7 IN. EASTER PARADE GIRL	9,120	18.95	50.00
91	7 IN. FLYING ANGEL W/MISTLETOE	6,003	18.95	50.00
91	7 IN. GHOST KID W/PUMPKIN	1,982	24.45	75.00
91	7 IN. GNOME W/MUSHROOM	5,007	29.95	80.00
91	7 IN. INDIAN BOY	3,371	29.95	60.00

YR	NAME	LIMIT	ISSUE	QUOTE
91	7 IN. INDIAN GIRL	2,777	22.95	60.00
91	7 IN. MOUSE IN BOX	5,526	19.95	40.00
91	7 IN. MOUSE IN SANTA'S HAT	9,742	17.95	50.00
91	7 IN. MOUSE W/CANDY CANE	5,206	17.95	50.00
91	7 IN. MOUSE W/CHRISTMAS STOCKING	6,543	17.95	50.00
91	7 IN. MOUSE W/MAILBAG	14,546	25.95	55.00
91	7 IN. MOUSE W/PRESENTS	8,075	17.95	50.00
91	7 IN. MOUSE W/SNOWBALL	6,805	17.95	40.00
91	7 IN. MOUSE W/TENNIS RACQUET	5,674	21.95	40.00
91	7 IN. MR. TUCKERED MOUSE	12,413	19.95	40.00
91	7 IN. MRS. SANTA HANGING MERRY	11,769	27.95	65.00
91	7 IN. MRS. SANTA W/PRESENTS	8,060	26.45	75.00
91	7 IN. MRS. TUCKERED MOUSE	13.266	19.95	40.00
91	7 IN. PILGRIM KIDS W/BASKET	2,672	53.95	125.00
91	7 IN. PILGRIM MICE SET W/BASKET	2,721	42.45	75.00
91	7 IN. PUMPKIN KID	3,517	27.45	50.00
91	7 IN. RITZ SNOWMAN	10,309	26.95	60.00
91	7 IN. SANTA BRINGING HOME	8,604	27.95	70.00
91	7 IN. SANTA IN TUB W/RUBBER	5,373	33.95	250.00
91	7 IN. SANTA W/GIFTLIST & TOY BAG	8,886	22.45	50.00
91	7 IN. SANTA W/MAILBAG & LETTERS	12,156	27.95	50.00
91	7 IN. SANTA W/SLEIGH	3,407	39.95	90.00
91	7 IN. SECRETARY MOUSE	6,364	29.95	100.00
91	7 IN. SHERIFF MOUSE (D.S)	1,191	49.50	200.00
91	7 IN. SKELETON COSTUME KID	2,596	24.45	55.00
91	7 IN. SLEDDING MOUSE	5,950	20.95	50.00
91	7 IN. SNOWMAN W/PIPE	7,401	23.95	75.00
91	7 IN. SWEETHEART BOY MOUSE	7,865	19.95	50.00
91	7 IN. SWEETHEART GIRL MOUSE	7,865	18.95	50.00
91	7 IN. TRICK OR TREAT BUNNY KID	2,187	25.95	100.00
91	7 IN. TWO IN A TENT MICE	*	34.95	80.00
91	7 IN. VELOUR MRS. SANTA W/COAT	5,808	27.45	50.00
91	7 IN. VELOUR SANTA W/COAT & PIPE	*	27.45	50.00
91	7 IN. VIDEO MOUSE	4,978	25.95	150.00
91	7 IN. WAITER MOUSE	4,573	25.95	150.00
91	7 IN. WITCH KID	3,311	27.45	100.00
91	7 IN. WORKSHOP MOUSE	12,536	21.95	100.00
91	7 IN. WORKSHOP SANTA	3,872	26.95	75.00
91	DESERT MOUSE HEAD PIN	9,141	7.95	35.00
91	LARGE PUMPKIN	1,872	48.95	125.00
91	LARGE TURKEY	1,132	57.95	95.00
91	RED CROSS NURSE MOUSE HEAD	8,572	7.95	25.00
91	SANTA W/PRESENTS	7,863	22.95	50.00
91	SMALL TURKEY	2,586	34.95	75.00
91	SMALL TURKEY W/7 IN. INDIAN GIRL	1,658	57.45	95.00
92	10 IN ANNALEE PITCHER	1,283	35.95	35.95
92	10 IN CHRISTMAS EVE BOB	1,681	69.95	69.95
92	10 IN. ANNALEE BASEBALL PLAYER	5,760	29.95	250.00
92	10 IN. BEAR IN NIGHTSHIRT	3,434	33.95	75.00
92	10 IN. BEAR IN VELOUR SANTA SUIT	3,938	32.95	75.00
92	10 IN. BEAR W/SNOWBALL, KNIT HAT	3,826	29.95	75.00
92	10 IN. BLACK CAT	4,101	25.95	100.00
92	10 IN. CHRISTMAS ELF	18,130	15.95	40.00
92	10 IN. CHRISTMAS EVE SCROOGE	1,722	59.95	199.00
92	10 IN. COUNTRY BOY BUNNY	2,395	34.95	85.00
92	10 IN. COUNTRY GIRL BUNNY	2,577	34.95	90.00
92	10 IN. DOE	2,096	20.95	70.00
92	10 IN. EASTER PARADE BOY BUNNY	3,902	38.95	90.00
92	10 IN. EASTER PARADE GIRL BUNNY	4,832	38.95	90.00
92	10 IN. FATHER TIME	1,796	54.95	100.00
92	10 IN. FISHING SANTA IN BOAT	1,582	99.95	175.00
92	10 IN. FROG IN BOAT	3,231	31.95	31.95
92	10 IN. GINGERBREAD BOY	7,361	22.45	22.45
92	10 IN. IN.TINSEL IN. THE ELF	9,967	20.45	50.00
92	10 IN. INDIAN MAN	1,834	34.45	65.00
92	10 IN. INDIAN WOMAN	1,816	32.95	75.00
92	10 IN. JACOB MARLEY	672	89.95	175.00
92	10 IN. KITTEN W/KNIT MITTENS	4,004	33.95	75.00
92	10 IN. MAN SKATER	2,688	45.95	125.00
92	10 IN. MARTHA CRATCHET W/PLUM	784	59.95	200.00
92	10 IN. MRS. BEAR IN NIGHTSHIRT	4,661	38.95	100.00
92	10 IN. PILGRIM MAN W/BASKET	1,803	44.95	75.00
92	10 IN. PILGRIM WOMAN W/TURKEY	1,904	44.95	75.00
92	10 IN. REINDEER W/CAP & BELL	10,650	22.95	75.00
92	10 IN. SANTA AT WORKBENCH	2,209	69.95	150.00
92	10 IN. SAVING SANTA	1,605	59.95	150.00

YR	NAME	LIMIT	ISSUE	QUOTE
92	10 IN. SKATING BUNNY	4,005	43.95	115.00
92	10 IN. SNOW QUEEN	4,390	38.95	90.00
92	10 IN. SNOWY OWL	2,634	25.95	50.00
92	10 IN. TENNIS SANTA	2,115	49.95	150.00
92	10 IN. UNCLE SAM FOLK HERO	1,034	87.50	87.50
92	10 IN. WOMAN SKATER	2,754	45.95	125.00
92	12 IN .BASKET COUPLE	1	600.00	600.00
92	12 IN .BAT	2,107	31.95	31.95
92	12 IN. CHEF SANTA	3,353	44.95	90.00
92	12 IN. DRUMMER BOY	3,316	39.95	75.00
92	12 IN. MRS. SANTA W/POINSETTA	3,463	49.95	100.00
92	12 IN. PILGRIM BOY MOUSE	1,449	42.95	42.95
92	12 IN. PILGRIM GIRL MOUSE	1,474	42.95	42.95
92	12 IN. PJ BOY	7,526	29.95	75.00
92	12 IN. PJ GIRL	7,903	29.95	75.00
92	12 IN. SANTA W/POT BELLY STOVE	1,818	61.95	100.00
92	12 IN. SANTA'S PAINTING HELPER	2,737	38.95	75.00
92	12 IN. SANTA'S POSTMAN	3,650	39.95	50.00
92	12 IN. SCARECROW	1,873	41.95	100.00
92	12 IN. SNOWMAN	5,457	41.95	75.00
92	12 IN. SPIDER	3,461	38.95	100.00
92	12 IN. TALL NORTH POLE W/SNOW	2,511	8.95	8.95
92	12 IN. TUCKERED COUPLE	1,827	89.95	89.95
92	12 IN. VELOUR MRS. SANTA	2,160	49.95	75.00
92	12 IN. VELOUR SANTA W/TOYBAG	2,284	49.95	75.00
92	18 IN. BUNNY KID W/BUNNY	2,117	49.95	75.00
92	18 IN. CHEF SANTA	5,314	47.95	100.00
92	18 IN. COUNTRY BOY BUNNY	1,501	54.95	135.00
92	18 IN. EASTER PARADE BOY BUNNY	1,695	65.45	100.00
92	18 IN. EASTER PARADE GIRL BUNNY	1,918	65.45	100.00
92	18 IN. GINGERBREAD BOY	2,969	50.95	50.95
92	18 IN. GIRL BUNNY W/FLOWERS	1,501	54.95	125.00
92	18 IN. MRS. SANTA W/POINSETTA	6,790	53.95	125.00
92	18 IN. MRS. SANTA W/PRESENTS	4,314	52.95	125.00
92	18 IN. REINDEER W/CHRISTMAS	3,441	52.95	150.00
92	18 IN. REINDEER W/NORTH POLE	2,755	63.95	160.00
92	18 IN. SANTA W/BANNER	6,871	52.95	125.00
92	18 IN. SANTA W/CARDHOLDER	4,260	59.95	100.00
92	18 IN. SANTA W/GIFT LIST	4,447	45.95	110.00
92	18 IN. SANTA W/STOCKING	3,859	49.95	75.00
92	18 IN. SANTA W/TRAY	3,955	52.95	125.00
92	18 IN. SNOWMAN W/BROOM	4,405	46.95	100.00
92	18 IN. SNOWY OWL	740	65.95	175.00
92	18 IN. WITCH	1,369	63.95	150.00
92	18 IN. WITCH W/STAND	2,760	65.95	125.00
92	22 IN. CHRISTMAS STOCKING	6,128	18.45	55.00
92	22 IN. RED CHRISTMAS ELF	4,066	34.95	75.00
92	30 IN. MRS. SANTA W/CARDHOLDER	1,380	119.95	150.00
92	30 IN. OUTDOOR SANTA	1,724	99.95	150.00
92	30 IN. SANTA W/BANNER	1,654	119.95	119.95
92	30 IN. SANTA W/NORTH POLE	1,674	109.95	995.00
92	30 IN. VELOUR MRS. SANTA W/MUFF	576	160.45	200.00
92	30 IN. VELOUR SANTA W/PIPE & BAG	548	160.45	200.00
92	32 IN. STOCKING W/REMOVEABLE 10 IN.	2,052	27.95	75.00
92	36 IN. REINDEER W/CARDHOLDER	1,219	148.45	300.00
92	5 IN. CHRISTMAS DRAGON	3,132	23.95	75.00
92	5 IN. CHRISTMAS LAMB	10,104	19.95	65.00
92	5 IN. DUCK ON FLEXIBLE FLYER	3,124	25.95	65.00
92	5 IN. EASTER PARADE BOY DUCK	3,370	21.95	75.00
92	5 IN. EASTER PARADE GIRL DUCK	4,468	23.95	75.00
92	5 IN. ELF (WORKSHOP)	13,825	13.45	25.00
92	5 IN. EQUESTRIENNE W/10 IN. HORSE	1,063	74.95	150.00
92	5 IN. FAWN	10,939	14.45	25.00
92	5 IN. FLUFFY YELLOW CHICK	4,342	17.95	50.00
92	5 IN. LEPRECHAUN	4,705	15.95	35.00
92	5 IN. RAINCOAT DUCK	5,397	26.95	65.00
92	5 IN. SPRING LAMB	5,053	17.95	45.00
92	5 IN. TRIM-A-TREE ELF	11,985	12.95	25.00
92	7 IN. ANGEL ON MOON	2,885	39.95	70.00
92	7 IN. ANGEL W/MUSICAL INSTRUMENT	6,347	19.95	50.00
92	7 IN. ARTIST BUNNY W/BRUSH	4,493	20.95	55.00
92	7 IN. BABY NEW YEAR	6,254	26.95	50.00
92	7 IN. BALLERINA KID	4,553	27.95	65.00
92	7 IN. BALLERINA ON MUSIC BOX	2,718	41.95	90.00
92	7 IN. BEACH KID W/BOAT	3,817	29.95	65.00
92	7 IN. BIRTHDAY GIRL MOUSE	*	23.95	23.95

YR	NAME	LIMIT	ISSUE	QUOTE
92	7 IN. BRIDE BUNNY	5,929	22.95	60.00
92	7 IN. BUNNY IN SLEEPER-GREEN	6,338	19.95	70.00
92	7 IN. BUNNY IN SLEEPER-YELLOW	6,338	19.95	70.00
92	7 IN. CAROLLER BOY	4,606	22.95	50.00
92	7 IN. CAROLLER GIRL	4,913	22.95	75.00
92	7 IN. CAROLLER MOUSE W/BIG HAT	18,789	19.95	50.00
92	7 IN. CHAMPAIGN MOUSE IN GLASS	9,553	25.95	65.00
92	7 IN. CHEF SANTA	11,297	28.95	60.00
92	7 IN. CHRISTMAS GNOME	9,102	18.95	35.00
92	7 IN. COUNTRY BOY BUNNY	3,993	20.45	75.00
92	7 IN. COUNTRY GIRL BUNNY	3,937	20.45	80.00
92	7 IN. DESERT STORM MOUSE	3,114	29.95	90.00
92	7 IN. DEVIL KID	6,076	23.95	60.00
92	7 IN. DISNEY COLLECTION	300	59.95	400.00
92	7 IN. DRACULA KID	5,637	25.95	25.95
92	7 IN. DRUMMER BOY	7,297	22.45	75.00
92	7 IN. EASTER PARADE BOY BUNNY	6,668	20.95	50.00
92	7 IN. EASTER PARADE GIRL BUNNY	9,314	20.95	50.00
92	7 IN. FISHING MOUSE	6,145	31.95	50.00
92	7 IN. FLYING ANGEL W/MISTLETOE	6,457	18.95	50.00
92	7 IN. GNOME W/MUSHROOM	1.691	35.95	75.00
92	7 IN. GROOM BUNNY	5,578	22.95	55.00
92	7 IN. INDIAN BOY	2,315	29.95	60.00
92	7 IN. INDIAN GIRL	2,297	22.95	60.00
92	7 IN. KID W/KITE	3,850	29.95	65.00
92	7 IN. LADY BUG KID	4,970	29.95	75.00
92	7 IN. MOUSE IN BOX	4,994	19.95	40.00
92	7 IN. MOUSE IN CORNUCOPIA	7,833	22.95	40.00
92	7 IN. MOUSE IN SANTA'S HAT	10,941	17.95	50.00
92	7 IN. MOUSE ON CHEESE	14,923	25.95	60.00
92	7 IN. MOUSE W/MAILBAG	8,000	25.95	55.00
92	7 IN. MOUSE W/NORTH POLE	10,089	21.95	50.00
92	7 IN. MOUSE W/PRESENTS	*	17.95	50.00
92	7 IN. MOUSE W/SNOWBALL	7,095	17.95	40.00
92	7 IN. MOUSE W/TENNIS RACQUET	4,110	21.95	40.00
92	7 IN. MR. TUCKERED MOUSE	7,533	19.95	40.00
92	7 IN. MRS. SANTA CANDLEHOLDER	9,595	25.95	65.00
92	7 IN. MRS. SANTA HANGING MERRY	6,411	27.95	65.00
92	7 IN. MRS. SANTA W/POINSETTA	11,484	29.95	75.00
92	7 IN. MRS. SANTA W/PRESENTS	7,124	27.95	65.00
92	7 IN. MRS. TUCKERED MOUSE	8,321	19.95	40.00
92	7 IN. PILGRIM KID W/BASKET	2,303	53.95	125.00
92	7 IN. PILGRIM MICE SET W/BASKET	2,364	42.45	75.00
92	7 IN. PIRATE KID	5,412	23.95	50.00
92	7 IN. PUMPKIN KID	3,619	27.45	50.00
92	7 IN. RED CROSS NURSE MOUSE	*	29.95	75.00
92	7 IN. RITZ SNOWMAN	6,037	26.95	60.00
92	7 IN. SANTA BRINGING HOME	5,921	27.95	70.00
92	7 IN. SANTA CARDHOLDER	9,831	25.95	65.00
92	7 IN. SANTA IN CHIMNEY	8,119	33.95	85.00
92	7 IN. SANTA ON 18 IN. MOON	4,157	46.95	100.00
92	7 IN. SANTA SKUNK	6,753	27.95	75.00
92	7 IN. SANTA W/GIFT LIST & TOY BAG	7,815	23.95	50.00
92	7 IN. SANTA W/MAILBAG & LETTERS	7,493	27.95	50.00
92	7 IN. SANTA W/PRESENTS	6,594	23.95	50.00
92	7 IN. SCARECROW KID	4,595	27.95	50.00
92	7 IN. SHERIFF MOUSE (D.S.)	283	49.50	150.00
92	7 IN. SKATEBOARD KID	3,894	29.95	75.00
92	7 IN. SLEDDING MOUSE	6,247	20.95	50.00
92	7 IN. SNOWMAN W/PIPE	7,779	23.95	55.00
92	7 IN. SPRING CHICKEN W/BOAT	2,753	34.95	34.95
92	7 IN. SPRING SKUNK	1,590	22.95	55.00
92	7 IN. SWEETHEART BOY MOUSE	5,723	19.95	50.00
92	7 IN. SWEETHEART GIRL MOUSE	6,522	18.95	50.00
92	7 IN. TWO IN A TENT MICE	2,910	34.95	80.00
92	7 IN. VELOUR MRS. SANTA W/COAT	5,289	27.45	50.00
92	7 IN. VELOUR SANTA W/COAT & PIPE	5,140	27.45	50.00
92	7 IN. WITCH KID	3,592	27.95	100.00
92	7 IN. WORKSHOP MOUSE	6,618	21.95	100.00
92	DESERT MOUSE HEAD PIN	991	8.95	35.00
92	LARGE FLOWER	2,526	18.95	18.95
92	LARGE PUMPKIN	2,469	48.95	125.00
92	MINI SANTA WREATH	2,140	23.95	65.00
92	NURSE MOUSE HEAD PIN	1,615	8.95	8.95
92	PINK FLOWER PICK	6,611	5.95	20.00
92	RED CROSS NURSE MOUSE HEAD	*	8.95	25.00

YR	NAME	LIMIT	ISSUE	QUOTE
92	SUN HEAD FLORAL PLANTER PICK	5,419	5.95	20.00
92	SUN MAGNET	7,133	6.45	15.00
92	SUN PIN	6,395	5.95	25.00
92	YELLOW FLOWER PICK	6,165	5.95	20.00
92	5 IN. ANGEL	7,967	22.95	50.00
93	10 IN. ANGEL BEAR	OP	32.95	32.95
93	10 IN. BEAR IN NIGHTSHIRT W/CANDLE	OP	33.95	33.95
93	10 IN. CATCHER	OP	38.50	38.50
93	10 IN. CHRISTA MCAULIFFE/SKATER	OP	35.95	35.95
93	10 IN. CHRISTMAS ELF	OP	15.95	15.95
93	10 IN. CHRISTMAS EVE BOB CRATCHET	OP	69.95	69.95
93	10 IN. CHRISTMAS EVE SCROOGE	OP	59.95	59.95
93	10 IN. COUNTRY BOY BUNNY W/VEG.	OP	34.95	34.95
93	10 IN. COUNTRY GIRL BUNNY W. VEG.	OP	34.95	34.95
93	10 IN. DOE	OP	20.95	20.95
93	10 IN. EASTER PARADE BOY BUNNY	5,139	38.95	38.95
93	10 IN. EASTER PARADE GIRL BUNNY	6,590	38.95	38.95
93	10 IN. FARMER W/ROOSTER	1	1000.00	1000.00
93	10 IN. FATHER TIME	OP	54.95	54.95
93	10 IN. FROG IN BOAT	OP	35.95	35.95
93	10 IN. GINGERBREAD BOY	OP	22.45	22.45
93	10 IN. HEADLESS HORSEMAN W/PUMPKIN/HORSE	OP	56.95	56.95-825.00
93	10 IN. KITTEN W/ORNAMENT	OP	33.95	33.95
93	10 IN. MRS. BEAR IN NIGHTSHIRT W/CANDLE	OP	38.95	38.95
93	10 IN. SANTA'S HELPER BEAR	OP	33.95	33.95
93	10 IN. SKATING PENQUIN	OP	34.95	34.95-525.00
93	10 IN. SNOW QUEEN TREE TOPPER	OP	29.95	29.95
93	10 IN. SNOWY OWL	OP	25.95	25.95
93	10 IN. ST. NICK TREE TOP	OP	29.95	29.95
93	10 IN. WINTER ELF	OP	16.95	16.95
93	12 IN. BOY PILGRIM W/BASKET	OP	44.95	44.95
93	12 IN. CHEF SANTA	OP	44.95	44.95
93	12 IN. DRUMMER BOY	OP	39.95	39.95
93	12 IN. GIRL PILGRIM W/PIE	OP	44.95	44.95
93	12 IN. INDIAN BOY	OP	35.95	35.95
93	12 IN. MRS. SANTA W/POINSETTA	OP	49.95	49.95
93	12 IN. PJ BOY	OP	29.95	29.95
93	12 IN. PJ GIRL	OP	29.95	29.95
93	12 IN. SANTA IN CHIMNEY	OP	69.95	69.95
93	12 IN. SANTA'S POSTMAN W/CDHLDR MAILBAG	OP	40.95	40.95
93	12 IN. SCARECROW	OP	41.95	41.95
93	12 IN. SNOWMAN	OP	41.95	41.95
93	12 IN. TUCKERED COUPLE	OP	89.95	89.95
93	14 IN. LG. USABLE PUMPKIN W/TOP	OP	49.95	49.95
93	14 IN. WREATH W/10 IN. WINTER ELF	OP	25.95	25.95
93	14" GRAPEVINE WREATH W/7" E.P.GIRL BUNNY	OP	31.95	31.95
93	18 IN. CHEF SANTA	OP	47.95	47.95
93	18 IN. COUNTRY BOY BUNNY W/VEG.	OP	54.95	54.95
93	18 IN. COUNTRY GIRL BUNNY W/VEG.	OP	54.95	54.95
93	18 IN. EASTER PARADE BOY BUNN	OP	65.45	65.45
93	18 IN. EASTER PARADE GIRL BUNNY	OP	65.45	65.45
93	18 IN. MAN SKATER (BRN. HAIR)	OP	44.95	44.95
93	18 IN. MRS. OUTDOOR SANTA	OP	49.95	49.95
93	18 IN. MRS. SANTA W/POINSETTA	OP	53.95	53.95
93	18 IN. REINDEER W/CHRISTMAS SADDLEBAGS	OP	52.95	52.95
93	18 IN. SANTA IN SLEIGH	OP	74.95	74.95
93	18 IN. SANTA ON TOBOGGAN	OP	69.95	69.95
93	18 IN. SANTA W/BANNER	OP	52.95	52.95
93	18 IN. SANTA W/GIFT LIST & TOYBAG	OP	45.95	45.95
93	18 IN. SANTA W/LIGHTS	5,441	54.95	54.95
93	18 IN. SNOWMAN W/BROOM	OP	47.95	47.95
93	18 IN. VICTORIAN MRS. SANTA	OP	64.95	64.95
93	18 IN. VICTORIAN SANTA	OP	64.95	64.95
93	18 IN. WITCH W/STAND	OP	65.95	65.95
93	18 IN. WOMAN SKATER (BLONDE)	OP	44.95	44.95
93	22 IN. CHRISTMAS ELF	OP	34.95	34.95
93	22 IN. CHRISTMAS STOCKING	OP	18.45	18.45
93	3 IN. BABY JESUS IN MANGER/BLONDE	OP	16.95	16.95
93	3 IN. FISHING SANTA IN BOAT	OP	24.95	24.95
93	3 IN. SANTA PIN IN CARD	OP	16.95	16.95
93	30 IN. MRS. SANTA W/CARDHOLDER	OP	119.95	119.95
93	30 IN. SANTA W/NORTH POLE	OP	129.95	129.95
93	30 IN. WITCH KID	OP	149.95	149.95
93	36 IN. REINDEER W/CDHLDR SADDLEBAGS	OP	148.45	148.45
93	5 IN. BABY JESUS IN MANGER W/BABY	OP	25.95	25.95
93	5 IN. BLACK CHRISTMAS LAMB	OP	19.95	19.95

"Hush My Baby" sings the chubby-cheeked Suzy *created by artist Bette Ball. Suzy is from the "Victoria Ashlea Originals" collection by Goebel.*

Molly *has learned not to put all her chicks in one basket. Her producer is* Roman.

Yolanda Bello *is able to capture all of the elements that make babies so special. Lisa is from "Yolanda's Picture-Perfect Babies" collection by the Ashton-Drake Galleries.*

Here comes the bride. Jennifer *is produced by the Ashton-Drake Galleries.*

Lee Middleton pays tribute to the season of joy with her 1991 Christmas Angel.

YR	NAME	LIMIT	ISSUE	QUOTE
93	5 IN. CHRISTMAS LAMB WHITE FLEECE	OP	19.95	19.95
93	5 IN. DUCK ON FLEXIBLE FLYER SLED	2,923	25.95	25.95
93	5 IN. EASTER PARADE BOY DUCK	OP	21.95	21.95
93	5 IN. EASTER PARADE GIRL DUCK	OP	23.95	23.95
93	5 IN. FAWN	OP	14.95	14.95
93	5 IN. LEPRECHAUN W/POT 'O GOLD	8,775	15.95	15.95
93	5 IN. RAINCOAT DUCK	OP	22.45	22.45
93	5 IN. TRIM-A-TREE ELF	OP	12.95	12.95
93	7 IN. ANGEL (BLACK HAIR)	OP	22.95	22.95
93	7 IN. ANGEL (BLONDE HAIR)	OP	22.95	22.95
93	7 IN. ANGEL (BROWN HAIR)	OP	22.95	22.95
93	7 IN. ANGEL MOUSE	OP	21.95	21.95
93	7 IN. ANGEL W/MUSICAL INSTRUMENT	OP	19.95	19.95
93	7 IN. ARTIST BUNNY W/BRUSH & PALETTE	OP	20.95	20.95
93	7 IN. BABY NEW YEAR (BLONDE)	4,127	26.95	26.95
93	7 IN. BALLERINA KID (BLONDE)	OP	27.95	27.95
93	7 IN. BALLERINA ON MUSIC BOX	OP	41.95	41.95
93	7 IN. BIRTHDAY GIRL MOUSE	OP	23.95	23.95
93	7 IN. BOY BUILDING SNOWMAN	OP	21.95	21.95-450.00
93	7 IN. BOY BUNNY W/ VEGETABLE	5,200	20.45	20.45
93	7 IN. BRIDE BUNNY	4,529	22.95	22.95
93	7 IN. BUNNY IN SLIPPER/GREEN	2,550	19.95	19.95
93	7 IN. BUNNY IN SLIPPER/YELLOW	OP	19.95	19.95
93	7 IN. BUTTERFLY KID	OP	27.95	27.95
93	7 IN. CAROLLER MOUSE W/BIG HAT & TREE	OP	19.95	19.95
93	7 IN. CHAMPAGNE MOUSE	6,985	25.95	25.95
93	7 IN. CHEF SANTA	OP	28.95	28.95
93	7 IN. CHOIR BOY	OP	25.95	25.95
93	7 IN. CHOIR GIRL	OP	25.95	25.95
93	7 IN. CHRISTMAS GNOME	OP	18.95	18.95
93	7 IN. COUNTRY GIRL BUNNY W/VEG.	5,621	20.45	20.45
93	7 IN. DEVIL KID	OP	23.95	23.95
93	7 IN. DRACULA KID	OP	25.95	25.95
93	7 IN. DRUMMER BOY	OP	22.45	22.45
93	7 IN. EASTER PARADE BOY BUNNY	OP	20.95	20.95
93	7 IN. EASTER PARADE GIRL BUNNY	OP	20.95	20.95
93	7 IN. FACTORY IN THE WOODS MOUSE	8,226	29.95	29.95-550.00
93	7 IN. FLYING ANGEL W/MISTLETOE	OP	18.95	18.95
93	7 IN. GHOST MOUSE	7,803	25.95	25.95
93	7 IN. GIRL EATING TURKEY	OP	38.95	38.95-525.00
93	7 IN. GROOM BUNNY	3,887	22.95	22.95
93	7 IN. INDIAN BOY (BLACK HAIR)	OP	29.95	29.95
93	7 IN. INDIAN GIRL (BLK. PONY TAILS)	OP	22.95	22.95
93	7 IN. LADY BUG KID	OP	29.95	29.95
93	7 IN. LOGO KID (DOLL SOCIETY)	OP	27.50	27.50
93	7 IN. MOUSE IN CORNUCOPIA	OP	23.95	23.95
93	7 IN. MOUSE IN SANTA'S HAT	OP	17.95	17.95
93	7 IN. MOUSE ON CHEESE	OP	26.95	26.95
93	7 IN. MOUSE W/MAILBAG & LETTERS	OP	25.95	25.95
93	7 IN. MOUSE W/NORTH POLE	OP	21.95	21.95
93	7 IN. MOUSE W/SNOWBALL	OP	17.95	17.95
93	7 IN. MR. TUCKERED MOUSE	7,059	19.95	19.95
93	7 IN. MRS. SANTA CANDLEHOLDER	OP	25.95	25.95
93	7 IN. MRS. SANTA W/POINSETTIA	OP	29.95	29.95
93	7 IN. MRS. SANTA W/PRESENTS	OP	27.95	27.95
93	7 IN. MRS. TUCKERED MOUSE	OP	19.95	19.95
93	7 IN. PILGRIM BOY HUGGING FAWN	OP	40.95	40.95
93	7 IN. PILGRIM GIRL W/PIE	OP	25.95	25.95
93	7 IN. PILGRIM MICE SET W/BASKET	OP	46.95	46.95
93	7 IN. PINK FLOWER KID	OP	25.95	25.95
93	7 IN. PIRATE KID	OP	23.95	23.95
93	7 IN. RITZ SNOWMAN	OP	26.95	26.95
93	7 IN. SANTA BRINGING HOME CHRISTMAS TREE	OP	27.95	27.95
93	7 IN. SANTA CANDLEHOLDER	OP	25.95	25.95
93	7 IN. SANTA IN CHIMNEY	OP	34.95	34.95
93	7 IN. SANTA SKIING	OP	27.95	27.95
93	7 IN. SANTA SKUNK	OP	27.95	27.95
93	7 IN. SANTA W/DOVE	1	1250.00	1250.00
93	7 IN. SANTA W/LIGHTS	OP	29.95	29.95
93	7 IN. SANTA W/MAILBAG & LETTERS	OP	27.95	27.95
93	7 IN. SANTA W/PRESENTS	6,996	23.95	23.95
93	7 IN. SANTA W/SLEIGH	OP	39.95	39.95
93	7 IN. SCARECROW KID	OP	27.95	27.95
93	7 IN. SNOWMAN (MRS. RITZ)	OP	25.95	25.95
93	7 IN. SNOWMAN ON TOBOGGAN	OP	29.95	29.95
93	7 IN. SNOWMAN W/PIPE	OP	23.95	23.95

YR	NAME	LIMIT	ISSUE	QUOTE
93	7 IN. SPRING CHICKEN W/BOAT	OP	34.95	34.95
93	7 IN. SPRING ROOSTER	OP	34.95	34.95
93	7 IN. SPRING SKUNK	OP	22.95	22.95
93	7 IN. ST. PATRICK'S DAY MOUSE	OP	25.95	25.95
93	7 IN. SWEETHEART BOY MOUSE	OP	19.95	19.95
93	7 IN. SWEETHEART GIRL MOUSE	OP	18.95	18.95
93	7 IN. VICTORIAN MRS. SANTA	OP	29.95	29.95
93	7 IN. VICTORIAN SANTA	OP	29.95	29.95
93	7 IN. VICTORIAN SANTA IN SLEIGH	OP	49.95	49.95-500.00
93	7 IN. WHITE MOUSE IN SLIPPER	OP	24.95	24.95
93	7 IN. WHITE MOUSE ON TOBOGGAN	OP	29.95	29.95
93	7 IN. WHITE MOUSE W/PRESENT	OP	21.95	21.95
93	7 IN. WHITE SKATING MOUSE	OP	24.95	24.95
93	7 IN. WITCH MOUSE	OP	25.95	25.95
93	7 IN. WIZARD MOUSE	OP	27.95	27.95
93	7 IN. YELLOW FLOWER KID	OP	25.95	25.95
93	7 IN.FLOWER KID/YELLOW	OP	27.95	27.95
93	7" MRS. SANTA HANGING "MERRY XMAS" SIGN	OP	27.95	27.95
93	8 IN. BOY TURKEY	OP	34.95	34.95
93	8 IN. GIRL TURKEY	OP	34.95	34.95
93	BLUE FLOWER PICK	OP	7.95	7.95
93	CHRISTMAS CHICKEN	OP	34.95	34.95
93	LARGE FLOWER W/FACE	OP	20.95	20.95-250.00
93	SANTA NAPKIN RINGS SET OF 4	OP	39.95	39.95
93	SM. CHRISTMAS DOVE	OP	25.95	25.95-375.00
93	SUN PIN	OP	5.95	5.95
94	10 IN. ANGEL BEAR	3.377	34.50	34.50
94	10 IN. BALLERINA BEAR	1	1100.00	1100.00
94	10 IN. BASKETBALL PLAYER, BLACK	2,012	31.95	31.95
94	10 IN. BASKETBALL PLAYER, WHITE	3,699	31.95	31.95
94	10 IN. BOSTON BRUINS HKY PLAYER	OP	47.50	47.50
94	10 IN. CATCHER	3,440	38.50	38.50
94	10 IN. CTY. GIRL BEAR	1	925.00	925.00
94	10 IN. DOE	4,319	21.95	21.95
94	10 IN. EASTER PARADE BOY BUNNY	4,527	39.95	39.95
94	10 IN. EASTER PARADE GIRL BUNNY	5,550	39.95	39.95
94	10 IN. EASTER PARADE SHOPPER OSTRICH	2,368	33.50	33.50-450.00
94	10 IN. GINGERBREAD BOY	5,182	23.50	23.50
94	10 IN. GREEN CHRISTMAS ELF	6,719	16.95	16.95
94	10 IN. HEADLESS HORSEMAN W/PUMPKIN	1,593	56.95	56.95
94	10 IN. HOBO CLOWN	6,826	30.95	30.95
94	10 IN. KITTEN W/ORNAMENT	6,550	34.95	34.95
94	10 IN. LG. FLOWER W/FACE	1,807	20.95	20.95
94	10 IN. MRS. SANTA "LAST M IN. MENDING"	5,751	47.95	47.95-650.00
94	10 IN. OLD WORLD CAROLLER MAN	5,549	27.95	27.95
94	10 IN. OLD WORLD CAROLLER WOMAN	5,595	27.95	27.95
94	10 IN. OLD WORLD SANTA W/SKIS	4,331	49.95	49.95
94	10 IN. OLD WORLD SKATERS ON MUSIC BOX	1,660	119.95	119.95
94	10 IN. RED CHRISTMAS ELF	9,079	16.95	16.95
94	10 IN. RED COAT	1,000	79.95	79.95
94	10 IN. REINDEER W/CAP & BELL	10,319	23.95	23.95
94	10 IN. SKATING PENQUIN	3,573	34.95	34.95
94	10 IN. SOCCER PLAYER	5,751	34.95	34.95
94	10 IN. TREE TOP ANGEL	3,794	29.95	29.95
94	10 IN. WHITE CHRISTMAS ELF, WHITE	4,492	16.95	16.95
94	10 IN. WHITE ST. NICHOLAS	5,560	43.95	43.95
94	10 IN. WINDOW SHOPPER OSTRICH	3,637	37.95	37.95
94	10 IN. WINTER ELF	8,504	17.50	17.50
94	12 IN. BOY PILGRIM W/BASKET	2,132	45.95	45.95
94	12 IN. CHEF SANTA	1,519	45.95	45.95
94	12 IN. DEVIL KID	2,610	39.95	39.95
94	12 IN. DRUMMER BOY	3,792	39.95	39.95
94	12 IN. GIRL CAT KID	3,176	35.95	35.95
94	12 IN. GIRL PILGRIM W/PIE	2,140	45.95	45.95
94	12 IN. GIRL SCARECROW	3,978	47.95	47.95
94	12 IN. IN.50S STYLE IN. BEAN NOSE SANTA	OP	119.50	119.50
94	12 IN. MRS. SANTA CARDHOLDER	4,443	39.95	39.95
94	12 IN. SANTA IN CHIMNEY	668	69.95	69.95
94	12" N. POLE W.POLE W/RD. RIBBON WRAP ARD	1,561	9.50	9.50
94	14 IN. GRAPEVINE WREATH W/GIRL BUNNY	2,505	34.95	34.95
94	14 IN. LG. USABLE PUMPKIN W/TOP	2,486	49.95	49.95
94	17 IN. TEE-PEE	1,838	37.95	37.95
94	18 IN. CHEF SANTA	2,888	49.95	49.95
94	18 IN. COUNTRY BOY BUNNY W/HOE	1,260	56.95	56.95
94	18 IN. COUNTRY GIRL BUNNY W/BASKET	1,549	56.95	56.95
94	18 IN. EASTER PARADE BOY BUNNY	2,019	65.50	65.50

YR	NAME	LIMIT	ISSUE	QUOTE
94	18 IN. EASTER PARADE GIRL BUNNY	2,299	65.50	65.50
94	18 IN. INDOOR SANTA W/LIGHTS	3,785	56.95	56.95
94	18 IN. MR. FUR SANTA ON STAND	4,546	45.95	45.95
94	18 IN. MR. OLD WORLD SANTA	OP	51.95	51.95
94	18 IN. MRS. OLD WORLD SANTA	5,278	49.95	49.95
94	18 IN. MRS. OUTDOOR SANTA	3,614	49.95	49.95
94	18 IN. MRS. SANTA CARDHOLDER	4,312	52.95	52.95
94	18 IN. MRS. SANTA W/POINSETTIA	2,992	55.95	55.95
94	18 IN. MUSICAL MRS. SANTA	1,498	59.95	59.95
94	18 IN. MUSICAL SANTA/GIFT LIST	1,316	59.95	59.95
94	18 IN. OLD WORLD REINDEER W/BELLS	5,201	59.95	59.95
94	18 IN. PJ KID W/2 XMAS STOCKINGS	2,428	59.95	59.95
94	18 IN. REINDEER W/CHRISTMAS SADDLEBAGS	3,235	54.95	54.95
94	18 IN. SANTA IN SLEIGH	1,140	77.95	77.95
94	18 IN. SANTA ON TOBAGGAN	1,499	69.95	69.95
94	18 IN. SANTA W/CDHLDR SACK	4,899	54.95	54.95
94	18 IN. SNOWMAN W/BROOM	4,092	49.95	49.95
94	18 IN. WITCH	1,823	67.95	67.95
94	22 IN. CHRISTMAS ELF, BLACK HAIR	3,606	34.95	34.95
94	22 IN. CHRISTMAS STOCKING	6,796	18.95	18.95
94	24 IN. TURKEY	1,116	99.95	99.95
94	3 IN. BABY JESUS IN MANGER	2,631	17.50	17.50
94	3 IN. FISHING SANTA IN BOAT	3,048	24.95	24.95
94	3 IN. SPRING PIXI PICK CHIL	3,557	10.95	10.95
94	3 IN. SUN PICK PAINTED SUN FACE	1,883	5.95	5.95
94	3 IN. SUN PIN	7,346	5.95	5.95
94	30 IN. CTY. GIRL BUNNY W/BASKET	722	119.95	119.95
94	30 IN. MR. OLD WORLD SANTA	1,453	124.95	124.95
94	30 IN. MRS. OLD WORLD SANTA	1,410	124.95	124.95
94	30 IN. MRS. SANTA W/CDHLDR SKIRT	1,141	119.95	119.95
94	30 IN. OUTDOOR SANTA W/TOY BAG	1,019	125.95	125.95
94	30 IN. SANTA W/CDHOLDR SACK	1,148	119.95	119.95
94	30 IN. SANTA W/N.POLE SUIT	643	131.95	131.95
94	30 IN. SNOWMAN	1,782	119.95	119.95
94	30 IN. WITCH KID	722	149.95	149.95
94	36 IN. REINDEER W/CDHLDR SADDLEBAGS	902	154.50	154.50
94	5 IN. BABY JESUS IN MANGER	1,726	26.95	26.95
94	5 IN. BLACK CHRISTMAS LAMB	4,713	19.95	19.95
94	5 IN. CHRISTMAS LAMB/WHITE	6,024	19.95	19.95
94	5 IN. DUCK/FLEXIBLE FLYER SLED	3,186	26.95	26.95
94	5 IN. EASTER PARADE BOY DUCK	3,678	22.95	22.95
94	5 IN. EASTER PARADE GIRL DUCK	4,697	24.95	24.95
94	5 IN. ELF (WORKSHOP)	9,416	13.95	13.95
94	5 IN. FAWN	8,700	14.95	14.95
94	5 IN. GOLD FALL ELF	6,153	14.50	14.50
94	5 IN. GREEN CHRISTMAS ELF	8,834	13.95	13.95
94	5 IN. GREEN SPRING ELF	3,261	13.95	13.95
94	5 IN. HALLOWEEN ELF, BLACK	4,624	14.95	14.95
94	5 IN. HALLOWEEN ELF, ORANGE	4,544	14.95	14.95
94	5 IN. LEPRECHAUN W/POT 'O GOLD	7,410	17.95	17.95
94	5 IN. OLD WORLD CAROLLER BOY	7,611	19.95	19.95
94	5 IN. OLD WORLD CAROLLER GIRL	7,817	19.95	19.95
94	5 IN. OLD WORLD SANTA W/9 IN. WREATH	2,330	32.95	32.95
94	5 IN. ORANGE FALL ELF	6,280	14.50	14.50
94	5 IN. RAINCOAT DUCK	2,410	27.95	27.95
94	5 IN. RED CHRISTMAS ELF	11,911	13.95	13.95
94	5 IN. SPRING ELF W/6 IN. WREATH	1,704	17.95	17.95
94	5 IN. WHITE CHRISTMAS ELF, WHITE	8,038	13.95	13.95
94	5 IN. WINTER ELF	10,769	13.95	13.95
94	5 IN. YELLOW SPRING ELF	3.932	13.95	13.95
94	7 IN. ANGEL MOUSE	10.343	22.95	22.95
94	7 IN. ANGEL W/MUSCIAL INSTRUMENT	4,302	20.95	20.95
94	7 IN. ANGEL, BLACK HAIR	2,877	23.95	23.95
94	7 IN. ANGEL, BLONDE HAIR	4,584	23.95	23.95
94	7 IN. ANGEL, BROWN HAIR	3,362	23.95	23.95
94	7 IN. ARTIST BUNNY W/BRUSH/PALETTE	4,303	21.95	21.95
94	7 IN. AUCTION TIMES MOUSE	5,962	29.95	29.95
94	7 IN. BABY BUNNY W/BOTTLE	6,588	19.95	19.95
94	7 IN. BIRTHDAY GIRL MOUSE	3,777	23.95	23.95
94	7 IN. BRIDE MOUSE	4.674	22.95	22.95-400.00
94	7 IN. BUTTERFLY KID, BLK BODY	2,226	28.95	28.95
94	7 IN. CANDY KISS KID	1	2250.00	2250.00
94	7 IN. CHAMPAGNE MOUSE	6.360	26.95	26.95
94	7 IN. CHEERLEADER GIRL	4,568	26.95	26.95-650.00
94	7 IN. CHEF SANTA	5,618	29.95	29.95
94	7 IN. CHOIR BOY	2,873	26.95	26.95

YR	NAME	LIMIT	ISSUE	QUOTE
94	7 IN. CHOIR BOY W/BLACK EYE	2,912	26.95	26.95
94	7 IN. CHOIR GIRL, BLONDE HAIR	3,424	26.95	26.95
94	7 IN. CHRISTA MCAULIFFE SNOWBD KID	OP	39.95	39.95
94	7 IN. CLOWN MOUSE	1	1050.00	1050.00
94	7 IN. COCKTAIL MOUSE	1	1100.00	1100.00
94	7 IN. COUNTRY BOY BUNNY W/HOE	4,842	21.50	21.50
94	7 IN. COUNTRY GIRL BUNNY W/BASKET	6,083	21.50	21.50
94	7 IN. DRACULA KID, BLACK HAIR	2,126	26.95	26.95
94	7 IN. DRUMMER BOY	6,817	23.95	23.95
94	7 IN. EASTER PARADE BOY BUNNY	9,937	21.95	21.95
94	7 IN. EASTER PARAGE GIRL BUNNY	13,186	21.95	21.95
94	7 IN. FLYING ANGEL	7,237	19.95	19.95
94	7 IN. FOOTBALL MOUSE	5,998	29.95	29.95
94	7 IN. GHOST MOUSE	4,698	26.95	26.95
94	7 IN. GIRL BLDG A SNOWMAN	13,459	23.95	23.95
94	7 IN. GIRL W/TEDDY BEAR	4,712	26.95	26.95
94	7 IN. GRADUATION BOY MOUSE	3,769	22.95	22.95
94	7 IN. GROOM MOUSE	OP	22.95	22.95
94	7 IN. HABITAT MOUSE	5,011	29.95	29.95
94	7 IN. HERSHEY KID	9,698	37.50	37.50
94	7 IN. HOT SHOT BUSINESS GIRL	OP	*	700.00
94	7 IN. INDIAN BOY, BLACK HAIR	2,848	30.95	30.95
94	7 IN. INDIAN GIRL, BLACK PONY TAILS	2,892	22.95	22.95
94	7 IN. JAIL HOUSE MOUSE	3,309	25.95	25.95
94	7 IN. LARGE CABBAGE	778	14.95	14.95
94	7 IN. LOGO KID (DOLL SOCIETY)	OP	27.50	27.50
94	7 IN. MISSISSIPPI LEVEE MOUSE	3,012	29.95	29.95
94	7 IN. MOUSE IN CORNUCOPIA	6,467	24.95	24.95
94	7 IN. MOUSE IN SANTA'S HAT	11,641	18.50	18.50
94	7 IN. MOUSE W/SNOWBALL	8,745	18.50	18.50
94	7 IN. MR. OLD WORLD SANTA	9,620	27.95	27.95
94	7 IN. MRS. OLD WORLD SANTA	9,439	27.95	27.95
94	7 IN. MRS. SANTA CARDHOLDER	4,443	39.95	39.95
94	7 IN. MRS. SANTA W/FUR-TRIM	8,848	22.50	22.50
94	7 IN. MRS. SANTA W/POINSETTA	5,397	30.95	30.95
94	7 IN. MRS. SANTA W/PRESENTS	5,923	28.95	28.95
94	7 IN. NAUGHTY ANGEL	8,380	22.95	22.95
94	7 IN. PILGRIM BOY HUGGING FAWN	2,004	41.95	41.95
94	7 IN. PILGRIM GIRL W/PIE BLONDE HAIR	2,984	26.95	26.95
94	7 IN. PILGRIM MICE SET W/BSKT	2,873	46.95	46.95
94	7 IN. POLICEMAN MOUSE	4,788	27.95	27.95
94	7 IN. RITZ SNOWMAN	4,903	27.95	27.95
94	7 IN. SANTA IN CHIMNEY	3,255	35.95	35.95
94	7 IN. SANTA W/DOVE	1	1250.00	1250.00
94	7 IN. SANTA W/LIGHTS	4,678	30.75	30.75
94	7 IN. SANTA W/PRESENTS	5,586	24.95	24.95
94	7 IN. SANTA W/RD. FUR TRIM SUIT	8,922	19.95	19.95
94	7 IN. SANTA W/SLEIGH	3,301	39.95	39.95
94	7 IN. SANTA W/SNOWSHOES & TREE	8,582	28.95	28.95
94	7 IN. SANTA W/TREE & SLED	8,865	28.95	28.95
94	7 IN. SCOTTISH LAD	3.995	29.95	29.95-675.00
94	7 IN. SMALL CHRISTMAS DOVE	3,125	26.95	26.95
94	7 IN. SNOWMAN (MRS. RITZ)	5.344	26.95	26.95
94	7 IN. SNOWMAN W/PIPE	6,179	25.95	25.95
94	7 IN. ST. PATRICK'S DAY MOUSE	4,746	26.95	26.95
94	7 IN. SWEETHEART BOY MOUSE	4,424	19.95	19.95
94	7 IN. THANKSGIVING BOY	1,881	39.95	39.95-650.00
94	7 IN. VALENTINE GIRL KID W/CARD	6,220	24.95	24.95-750.00
94	7 IN. VICTORIAN SANTA IN SLEIGH	1,179	49.95	49.95
94	7 IN. WHITE MOUSE IN SLIPPER	5,838	25.95	25.95
94	7 IN. WHITE MOUSE ON TOBOGGAN	6,575	29.95	29.95
94	7 IN. WHITE MOUSE W/PRESENT	8.170	22.95	22.95
94	7 IN. WHITE SKATING MOUSE	11,452	25.95	25.95
94	7 IN. WITCH MOUSE	5,336	26.95	26.95
94	7 IN. WIZARD MOUSE	3,892	28.95	28.95
94	7 IN. YELLOW FLOWER KID	OP	28.95	28.95
94	7 IN. YELLOW FLOWER KID, BLONDE	2,303	26.95	26.95
94	7 IN.MARBLES KID/RED TANK TOP	OP	27.50	27.50
94	8 IN. BOY TURKEY	2,852	34.95	34.95
94	8 IN. EAR OF CORN	1,342	9.95	9.95
94	8 IN. GIRL TURKEY	2,174	34.95	34.95
94	SET OF 3 LG. PEA PDS & CARROTTS	1,377	14.95	14.95
94	SET OF 3 RD. TOMATOES 2 IN.	805	9.95	9.95
94	SMALL PEA PODS & CARROTTS (3)	1,342	12.50	12.50
94	TREE SKIRT 4' DIAMETER	2,269	24.95	24.95
94	TREE TOP STAR W/ 3 IN. ANGEL	6,424	20.95	20.95-300.00

YR	NAME	LIMIT	ISSUE	QUOTE
A. THORNDIKE				**ANGELS**
56	10 IN. BABY ANGEL	*	5.50	550.00
60	12 IN. BIG ANGEL ON CLOUD	*	9.95	350.00
60	7 IN. BABY ANGEL	*	*	300.00
60	7 IN. BABY ANGEL W/BLUE WINGS	*	*	300.00
60	7 IN. BABY ANGEL WITH STAR ON LEG	*	*	300.00
63	5 IN. BABY WITH ANGEL HALO	*	2.00	300.00
63	7 IN. BABY ANGEL ON CLOUD	*	2.45	300.00
64	7 IN. SAT. NITE ANGEL W/BLANKET	*	2.95	250.00
64	7 IN. ANGEL IN A BLANKET	*	2.45	300.00
66	7 IN. ANGEL, WHITE WINGS	*	*	225.00
68	5 IN. BABY ANGEL ON CLOUD	*	2.95	300.00
71	7 IN. ANGEL WITH PAPER WINGS	608	3.00	325.00
76	7 IN. MISTLETOE ANGEL	17,540	6.00	80.00
78	7 IN. TREE TOP ANGEL WITH WREATH	8613	6.50	100.00
82	7 IN. ANGEL WITH TEARDROP	3092	12.95	200.00
84	7 IN. ANGEL ON STAR	772	32.95	200.00
84	7 IN. NAUGHTY ANGEL	4528	14.95	75.00
85	12 IN. NAUGHTY ANGEL	1393	36.95	125.00
86	12 IN. NAUGHTY ANGEL WITH SLINGSHOT	*	36.95	225.00
A. THORNDIKE			**ASSORTED ANIMALS**	
67	12 IN. FANCY NANCY CAT CHRISTMAS	*	6.95	700.00
67	12 IN. LAURA MAY CAT	*	6.95	850.00
67	36 IN. CHRISTMAS CAT	*	12.00	350.00
68	12 IN. ICE PACK CAT	*	6.95	500.00
68	12 IN. TESSIE TAR CAT	*	6.95	450.00
68	6 IN. MYRTLE TURTLE	*	3.95	700.00
70	7 IN. BLUE MONKEY	293	*	250.00
70	7 IN. MONKEY	293	4.95	525.00
71	7 IN. YELLOW KITTEN	103	4.50	575.00
72	10 IN. DONKEY	861	5.95	175.00
72	12 IN. CAT WITH MOUSE	*	13.00	450.00
72	16 IN. ELEPHANT	230	12.95	285.00
72	30 IN. ELECTION DONKEY	120	23.95	350.00
72	36 IN. ELECTION ELEPHANT	113	*	550.00
73	12 IN. GIRL NIGHTSHIRT MONKEY	*	7.50	300.00
75	18 IN. HORSE	221	17.00	200.00
76	10 IN. DONKEY	1202	5.95	175.00
76	10 IN. ELEPHANT	1223	5.95	225.00
76	10 IN. VOTE DONKEY	1202	5.95	225.00
76	15 IN. ROOSTER	485	13.50	1050.00
76	18 IN. ELEPHANT	285	16.95	425.00
76	18 IN. VOTE 76 DONKEY	285	16.95	300.00
76	36 IN. ELECTION DONKEY	119	*	650.00
76	36 IN. HORSE	27	48.00	500.00
76	8 IN. ELECTION ELEPHANT	1223	*	175.00
76	8 IN. ROOSTER	1094	5.50	250.00
77	15 IN. PURPLE ROOSTER	548	5.48	450.00
77	8 IN. ROOSTER	1642	6.00	400.00
77	8 IN. ROOSTER	1642	5.95	300.00
81	12 IN. BOY MONKEY WITH TRAPEZE	1800	23.95	300.00
81	12 IN. GIRL MONKEY WITH TRAPEZE	857	23.95	200.00
81	14 IN. DRAGON WITH BUSHBOY	1257	28.95	650.00
81	18 IN. CAT W/MOUSE & MISTLETOE	18,995	46.95	150.00
81	18 IN. ESCORT FOX	*	28.50	350.00
81	18 IN. FOXY LADY	*	28.50	350.00
81	29 IN. DRAGON WITH BUSHBOY	75	63.95	1050.00
81	29 IN. DRAGON WITH BUSHBOY	76	69.95	1050.00
81	7 IN. ESCORT FOX	*	12.50	250.00
81	7 IN. FOXY LADY	*	12.50	250.00
81	7 IN. MONKEY WITH BANANA TRAPEZE	3075	*	125.00
82	12 IN. BOY SKUNK	935	27.95	225.00
82	12 IN. GIRL SKUNK	936	27.95	225.00
82	12 IN. SKUNK WITH SNOWBALL	1304	*	225.00
82	5 IN. DRAGON WITH BUSHBOY	1066	17.95	475.00
82	7 IN. SANTA FOX W/BAG	3622	12.95	400.00
83	24 IN. STORK WITH BABY	858	36.95	175.00
83	5 IN. DRAGON WITH WINGS & BABY	199	22.50	900.00
83	5 IN. DRAGON WITH WINGS & BABY	199	22.50	300.00
85	12 IN. JAZZ CAT	2622	*	250.00
85	15 IN. JAZZ CAT	2622	31.95	250.00
85	18 IN. VALENTINE CAT WITH HEART	2129	34.95	225.00
85	8 IN. ELEPHANT-REPUBLICAN	*	4.95	225.00
86	10 IN. CHRISTMAS PANDA W/TOYBAG	4397	18.95	150.00
86	10 IN. KITTEN W/YARN & BASKET	3917	27.95	125.00
86	18 IN. VALENTINE CAT	*	*	125.00

YR	NAME	LIMIT	ISSUE	QUOTE
87	10 IN. BRIDE & GROOM CAT	727	*	200.00
87	10 IN. GROOM CAT (PAIR)	762	35.95	*
87	24 IN. CHRISTMAS GOOSE WITH BASKET	*	54.95	150.00
88	10 IN. STORK W/3 IN. BABY	500	49.95	145.00
A. THORNDIKE				**BUNNIES**
65	12 IN. NIPSY-TIPSY HARE	*	7.50	700.00
65	7 IN. DUMB BUNNY	*	3.95	400.00
66	7 IN. YUM YUM BUNNY	*	3.95	525.00
67	12 IN. YUM YUM BUNNY	*	9.95	550.00
69	7 IN. BUNNY W/OVERSIZED CARROT	*	4.95	400.00
70	18 IN. BUNNY W/BUTTERFLY	258	10.95	500.00
70	18 IN. GIRL BUNNY WITH EGG	1727	15.95	150.00
70	29 IN. GIRL BUNNY	*	22.00	250.00
70	7 IN. BUNNY W/BUTTERFLY	1264	4.95	150.00
70	7 IN. YELLOW BUNNY	*	3.95	300.00
71	18 IN. PETER BUNNY	219	10.95	425.00
71	30 IN. WHITE BUNNY WITH CARROT	172	*	165.00
72	29 IN. EASTER PARADE MOM BUNNY	508	35.00	250.00
72	30 IN. BOY BUNNY	237	25.00	225.00
72	30 IN. GIRL BUNNY	223	25.00	225.00
72	7 IN. BALLERINA BUNNY	4700	4.00	100.00
72	7 IN. BUNNY (WITH BANDANA)	1615	3.95	150.00
73	7 IN. BUNNY ON BOX	795	5.50	125.00
73	7 IN. WHITE BUNNY	1600	5.50	125.00
76	18 IN. EASTER PARADE BOY BUNNY	791	13.50	300.00
76	18 IN. GIRL BUNNY WITH EGG	789	13.50	375.00
77	18 IN. EASTER PARADE BOY BUNNY	1567	13.50	150.00
77	29 IN. EASTER PARADE POP BUNNY	477	35.00	250.00
77	29 IN. MECHANICAL SEE-SAW BUNNY	*	300.00	900.00
77	29 IN. POP BUNNY WITH BASKET	*	11.50	400.00
77	7 IN. BUNNY W/EGG	2442	5.95	125.00
77	7 IN. BUNNY WITH BUTTERFLY	2721	6.00	125.00
78	29 IN. E.P. MOM & POP BUNNIES (PAIR)	529	36.95	400.00
78	7 IN. ARTIST BUNNY	4217	7.50	250.00
78	7 IN. BUNNIES WITH BASKET	2253	*	150.00
79	18 IN. ARTIST BUNNY	1064	15.95	275.00
79	29 IN. E.P. MOM BUNNY	662	42.95	200.00
80	18 IN. C.G. BUNNY W/BASKET	3964	19.95	150.00
80	7 IN. BALLERINA BUNNY	*	8.95	175.00
81	18 IN. COUNTRY BOY BUNNY WITH CARROT	1998	23.95	275.00
81	7 IN. COUNTRY BUNNIES	7940	*	185.00
81	8 IN. GIRL BBQ BUNNY	2596	9.95	250.00
82	4 FT. BOY BUNNY	186	190.00	450.00
82	7 IN. BALLERINA BUNNY	4179	9.95	100.00
82	7 IN. EASTER PARADE BOY BUNNY	RT	11.95	50.00
83	29 IN. EASTER PARADE GIRL BUNNY	*	71.95	200.00
83	5 IN. BUNNY ON MUSIC BOX	*	29.95	375.00
83	5 IN. COUNTRY GIRL BUNNY	5163	*	50.00
83	5 IN. FLOPPY-EAR BOY BUNNY WITH BASKET	*	11.50	55.00
83	7 IN. COUNTRY BOY BUNNY WITH BUTTERFLY	*	12.50	100.00
83	7 IN. E.P. BOY BUNNY	*	12.50	50.00
83	7 IN. E.P. GIRL BUNNY	RT	12.50	50.00
84	18 IN. COUNTRY GIRL BUNNY WITH BASKET	1481	31.95	300.00
84	5 IN. COUNTRY BUNNIES WITH BASKET	1110	*	150.00
84	5 IN. FLOPPY EAR GIRL BUNNY	2594	11.50	75.00
84	5 IN. GIRL BUNNY	2594	11.50	65.00
84	7 IN. COUNTRY BUNNIES WITH BASKET	2345	25.95	75.00
84	7 IN. E.P. BOY BUNNY	5989	12.95	35.00
84	7 IN. TWO BUNNIES WITH BUSHEL BASKET	2339	25.95	75.00
84	7 IN. VALENTINE BUNNY	5602	13.95	125.00
85	18 IN. COUNTRY BOY BUNNY W/WATERING CAN	2355	46.95	*
85	7 IN. BOY BUNNY WITH CARROT	3273	14.95	55.00
85	7 IN. VALENTINE BUNNY	5602	13.95	125.00
86	18 IN. C.B. BUNNY W/WHEELBARROW	1224	46.95	75.00
86	18 IN. C.G. BUNNY W/FLOWERS	1205	41.50	75.00
86	30 IN. BOY BUNNY WITH WHEELBARROW	252	119.50	200.00
86	7 IN. BOY BUNNY WITH CARROT	2949	15.50	95.00
86	7 IN. BUNNY WITH EGG	2233	16.95	55.00
86	7 IN. VALENTINE BUNNY	*	14.50	125.00
87	18 IN. VICTORIAN COUNTRY BOY BUNNY	1394	49.95	350.00
87	18 IN. VICTORIAN COUNTRY GIRL BUNNY-PAIR	1492	49.95	*
88	18 IN. COUNTRY MOM BUNNY W/BABY	1800	68.95	140.00
88	7 IN. BUNNIES ON MUSIC BOX MAYPOLE	5602	13.95	75.00
88	7 IN. BUNNY WITH SLED	3050	21.95	45.00
90	18 IN. STRAWBERRY BUNNY	2365	59.95	200.00
90	30 IN. STRAWBERRY BUNNY	582	135.95	300.00

YR	NAME	LIMIT	ISSUE	QUOTE
A. THORNDIKE			**CHRISTMAS ANIMALS**	
73	7 IN. CHRISTMAS PANDA	1094	8.95	350.00
80	10 IN. SANTA FROG	7631	9.95	125.00
80	18 IN. SANTA FROG	2126	25.00	145.00
81	12 IN. SANTA MONKEY	1800	24.00	250.00
81	18 IN. CAT W/7 IN. MOUSE & MISTLETOE	10,999	46.95	140.00
81	7 IN. SANTA MONKEY	4606	10.00	200.00
82	18 IN. SANTA FOX	1499	29.95	575.00
82	22 IN. CHRISTMAS GIRAFFE WITH ELF	448	44.00	500.00
82	7 IN. SANTA FOX	3726	12.95	250.00
84	5 IN. DUCK IN SANTA HAT	2371	12.95	75.00
85	10 IN. PANDA WITH TOY BAG	1904	20.00	100.00
85	18 IN. CHRISTMAS PANDA	2207	43.95	100.00
A. THORNDIKE			**CLOWNS**	
70	10 IN. CLOWN	2362	4.00	125.00
70	18 IN. CLOWN	542	5.00	250.00
71	10 IN. CLOWN	708	2.00	200.00
76	10 IN. CLOWN	2285	5.50	100.00
76	18 IN. CLOWN	916	13.50	200.00
76	30 IN. CLOWN	466	30.00	650.00
77	10 IN. CLOWN	4784	6.00	125.00
77	18 IN. CLOWN	2343	13.50	475.00
78	10 IN. CLOWN	4020	6.50	175.00
78	18 IN. CLOWN	4000	13.95	225.00
80	10 IN. CLOWN	8136	12.50	75.00
80	18 IN. CLOWN	3192	24.95	125.00
80	18 IN. CLOWN WITH BALLOON	3192	24.95	100.00
80	4 FT. CLOWN	224	150.00	900.00
80	42 IN. CLOWN WITH STAND	224	84.95	600.00
81	10 IN. CLOWN	6479	12.95	100.00
81	10 IN. CLOWN	6479	9.95	125.00
81	18 IN. CLOWN	2742	24.95	200.00
84	10 IN. CLOWN	6383	13.95	95.00
84	18 IN. CLOWN	*	32.95	150.00
84	30 IN. CLOWN	381	165.00	325.00
84	30 IN. CLOWN	387	69.95	400.00
85	18 IN. CLOWN	2275	36.95	200.00
85	18 IN. CLOWN WITH BALLOON	1485	36.95	150.00
86	10 IN. CLOWN	3897	15.50	75.00
86	BALLOONING CLOWN	2700	16.95	110.00
87	10 IN. CLOWN	*	17.95	55.00
90	30 IN. CLOWN WITH STAND	530	99.95	150.00
A. THORNDIKE			**COLLECTORS EDITION**	
93	10 IN. GARDENING SUMMER SANTA	OP	69.95	69.95-550.00
93	10 IN. MRS. SKATING SANTA	OP	49.95	49.95-700.00
93	10 IN. SANTA W/FIREPLACE AND 3 IN. CHILD	OP	89.95	89.95-500.00
93	10 IN. SANTA W/TOBOGGAN	OP	59.95	375.00
93	10 IN. SKATING SANTA	OP	49.95	49.95-500.00
93	10 IN. TOBOGGAN SANTA	OP	59.95	59.95-375.00
A. THORNDIKE			**COMMEMORATIVE**	
66	10 IN. CENTRAL GAS CO. ELF	*	*	350.00
66	5 IN. NEW HAMPTON SCHOOL BABY	300	*	200.00
81	7 IN. I'M LATE BUNNY	*	*	575.00
			DOLL SOCIETY	
91	7 IN. LOGO KID	26,516	19.50	125.00
92	7 IN. LOGO KID	17,524	24.95	75.00
A. THORNDIKE			**DOLL SOCIETY-ANIMALS**	
85	10 IN. PENGUIN, #178	3000	30.00	225.00
86	10 IN. UNICORN, #268	3000	36.50	350.00
87	7 IN. KANGAROO	3000	37.50	*
88	5 IN. OWL	3000	37.50	*
89	7 IN. POLAR BEAR CUB, CURRENT ITEM	3000	37.50	*
90	7 IN. CHICKEN, CURRENT ITEM	3000	37.50	*
A. THORNDIKE			**DOLL SOCIETY-FOLK HEROES**	
84	JOHNNY APPLESEED, #627	1500	80.00	900.00
84	ROBIN HOOD	1500	80.00	*
85	ANNIE OAKLEY, #185	1500	95.00	700.00
86	MARK TWAIN, #467	2500	119.50	500.00
87	BEN FRANKLIN, #1776	2500	119.50	525.00
88	SHERLOCK HOLMES, #391	2500	119.50	500.00
89	ABRAHAM LINCOLN, CURRENT ITEM	2500	119.50	175.00
90	BETSY ROSS, CURRENT ITEM	2500	119.50	119.50
A. THORNDIKE			**DOLL SOCIETY-LOGO KIDS**	
85	7 IN. LOGO KID	3562	*	250.00
86	7 IN. LOGO KID	6271	*	175.00
87	7 IN. LOGO KID	11,000	*	150.00

YR	NAME	LIMIT	ISSUE	QUOTE
88	7 IN. LOGO KID	*	*	100.00
89	7 IN. LOGO KID	*	*	*
90	7 IN. LOGO KID,	*	*	*
A. THORNDIKE				**DUCKS**
75	5 IN. BABY DUCK	1333	4.00	135.00
76	8 IN. WHITE DUCK	3265	4.95	225.00
82	12 IN. DUCK WITH KERCHIEF	5861	26.95	125.00
83	5 IN. E.P. BOY DUCK	5133	*	50.00
83	5 IN. E.P. GIRL DUCK	5577	*	50.00
83	5 IN. SWEETHEART DUCK	1530	*	40.00
84	5 IN. PILOT DUCKLING	4396	14.95	150.00
85	12 IN. DUCK WITH RAINCOAT	*	*	275.00
86	5 IN. DUCK WITH RAINCOAT	5029	*	200.00
87	12 IN. DUCK ON SLED	300	*	500.00
A. THORNDIKE		**ELVES/GNOMES/WOODSPRITES/LEPRECHAUNS**		
54	10 IN. ELF	*	*	275.00
57	10 IN. HOLLY ELF	*	*	500.00
57	10 IN. MR. HOLLY ELF	*	*	1600.00
57	9 IN. ELF WITH MUSICAL INSTRUMENT	*	3.50	550.00
59	10 IN. ELF WITH INSTRUMENT	*	3.50	400.00
59	10 IN. GREEN WOODSPRITE	*	6.95	350.00
60	5 IN. ELF	*	*	200.00
62	5 IN. ELF W/FEATHER HAIR	*	9.00	300.00
63	10 IN. CHRISTMAS ELF W/TINSEL	*	*	250.00
63	10 IN. ELF SKIER	*	*	350.00
63	10 IN. WHITE WOODSPRITE	*	*	325.00
63	10 IN. YELLOW WOODSPRITE	*	*	275.00
63	18 IN. FRIAR BOTTLE COVER	*	3.00	350.00
63	24 IN. WOODSPRITE	*	5.45	125.00
63	5 IN. CHRISTMAS ELF	*	3.00	200.00
64	10 IN. IMP SKIER	*	4.00	350.00
64	18 IN. WOODSPRITE	*	6.00	325.00
64	22 IN. WOODSPRITE	*	5.95	325.00
65	5 IN. GREEN GNOME	*	*	125.00
67	10 IN. ELF WITH ROUND BOX	*	2.50	350.00
67	10 IN. ELF WITH SKIS	48	3.00	350.00
67	10 IN. WORKSHOP ELF	*	*	175.00
67	12 IN. GNOME W/PJ SUIT	*	*	425.00
67	7 IN. GNOME W/PJ SUIT	*	2.50	250.00
69	10 IN. WHITE ELF WITH PRESENTS	*	*	180.00
70	10 IN. CASUALTY ELF	991	2.25	300.00
70	10 IN. ELF SKIER	597	*	200.00
71	10 IN. ELF SKIER	*	*	100.00
71	5 IN. GNOME WITH CANDLE	*	3.00	300.00
71	7 IN. THREE GNOMES W/LARGE CANDLE	80	11.95	700.00
72	10 IN. ROBIN HOOD ELF	*	2.50	175.00
72	18 IN. LEPRECHAUN	1372	*	200.00
74	22 IN. WORKSHOP ELF	1404	10.45	125.00
74	22 IN. WORKSHOP ELF WITH APRON	1404	10.95	882.00
77	18 IN. WHITE ELF	2600	*	150.00
77	22 IN. JACK FROST ELF	2600	11.95	400.00
78	12 IN. CHRISTMAS GNOME	10,140	*	125.00
78	12 IN. GNOME	10,140	9.50	175.00
79	18 IN. GNOME	9048	16.95	350.00
79	29 IN. GNOME	1762	47.95	400.00
80	7 IN. GNOME	13,238	9.50	150.00
81	10 IN. ELF ON BUTTERFLY	1625	24.95	300.00
81	10 IN. JACK FROST WITH SNOWFLAKE	5950	31.95	175.00
82	10 IN. ELF ON BUTTERFLY	882	*	275.00
82	10 IN. JACK FROST WITH SNOWFLAKE	2289	13.50	250.00
83	10 IN. BALLOONING ELVES	7395	59.95	200.00
83	10 IN. WORKSHOP ELF	*	*	75.00
A. THORNDIKE				**FOLK HERO**
93	10 IN. PONY EXPRESS RIDER	OP	97.50	97.50-1800.00
A. THORNDIKE				**FROGS**
69	10 IN. BRIDE & GROOM FROGS COURTIN'	*	7.95	550.00
69	42 IN. FROG	30	29.95	700.00
71	10 IN. BRIDE & GROOM FROGS ON BIKE	13	17.50	625.00
71	10 IN. FROG W/INSTRUMENT	233	3.95	200.00
71	18 IN. FROG W/BASS VIOLA	224	11.95	1350.00
74	10 IN. WILLIE WOG GOIN' FISHING	*	5.50	200.00
79	10 IN. BOY FROG	5642	8.50	125.00
79	18 IN. GIRL FROG	2338	18.95	225.00
80	10 IN. BOY FROG	4185	9.50	125.00
80	10 IN. BRIDE FROG	1653	14.95	150.00
80	10 IN. GIRL FROG	421	9.50	125.00

YR	NAME	LIMIT	ISSUE	QUOTE
80	10 IN. GROOM FROG	1611	14.95	150.00
80	18 IN. BOY FROG	1285	23.00	150.00
80	18 IN. SANTA FROG	2126	25.00	225.00
80	42 IN. FROG	202	89.95	500.00
80	42 IN. SANTA FROG	206	100.00	700.00
81	10 IN. BRIDE FROG	1239	14.95	150.00
81	10 IN. GROOM FROG	2061	14.95	150.00
81	18 IN. GIRL FROG	666	24.00	225.00
A. THORNDIKE				**HUMANS**
50	10 IN. BOY & GIRL SKIERS	*	15.00	1250.00
50	10 IN. FROGMAN (GIRL DIVER)	*	9.95	3800.00
50	10 IN. GIRL GOLFER	*	*	475.00
50	20 IN. BOY & GIRL CALYPSO DANCERS	*	*	800.00
53	GIRL WATER SKIER	*	10.00	200.00
54	10 IN. COUNTRY GIRL	*	8.95	1000.00
54	10 IN. SAKES FIFTH AVE. SKIER	50	9.95	1500.00
55	10 IN. BOY SWIMMER	*	*	550.00
55	7 IN. BOY SKIER	*	*	1250.00
56	10 IN. FISHING GIRL	*	*	425.00
56	10 IN. WATER SKIER GIRL	*	9.95	800.00
57	10 IN. BOY BUILDING BOAT	*	*	925.00
57	10 IN. BOY SQUARE DANCER	*	9.95	475.00
57	10 IN. BOY WITH STRAW HAT	*	*	500.00
57	10 IN. CASUALTY SKI GROUP	*	35.00	3100.00
57	10 IN. CASUALTY TOBOGGAN GROUP	*	35.00	900.00
57	10 IN. FOURTH OF JULY DOLL	*	10.00	1600.00
57	10 IN. GIRL SKIER	*	*	1000.00
57	10 IN. GIRL SQUARE DANCER	*	9.95	475.00
57	10 IN. SKIER	*	15.00	1500.00
57	10 IN. SKIER WITH LEG IN CAST	*	35.00	1950.00
57	10 IN. THANKSGIVING DOLL	*	*	600.00
57	10 IN. VALENTINE DOLL	*	*	925.00
57	10 IN. VALENTINE DOLL	*	10.00	900.00
58	10 IN. SPRING DOLL	*	10.00	3500.00
59	10 IN. ARCHITECT	*	*	700.00
59	10 IN. BOY & GIRL IN FISHING BOAT	*	17.00	1000.00
59	10 IN. BOY & GIRL ON BIKE	*	*	575.00
59	10 IN. BOY GOLFER	*	10.00	325.00
59	10 IN. BOY GOLFER	*	*	475.00
59	10 IN. BOY SKIER	*	*	800.00
59	10 IN. BOY SQUARE DANCER	*	10.00	475.00
59	10 IN. DENTIST	*	10.00	600.00
59	10 IN. FOOTBALL PLAYER	*	10.00	600.00
59	10 IN. GIRL SKIER	*	*	825.00
59	10 IN. GIRL SQUARE DANCER	*	10.00	475.00
59	10 IN. GIRL SWIMMER	*	*	550.00
59	10 IN. TEXAS OIL MAN	*	16.00	1550.00
59	7 IN. GIRL SKIER	*	*	675.00
60	10 IN. BATHING GIRL	*	3.95	300.00
60	10 IN. GIRL SKI DOLL	*	*	450.00
60	10 IN. GIRL SKIER	*	*	400.00
60	33 IN. BOY & GIRL ON TANDEM BIKE	*	*	3500.00
63	10 IN. GIRL WATERSKIER	*	7.50	450.00
63	18 IN. FRIAR	*	*	400.00
63	22 IN. BELLHOP (RED)	*	*	700.00
64	10 IN. GENDARME	*	4.00	450.00
64	10 IN. MONK (GREEN)	*	3.00	275.00
64	10 IN. MONK WITH CAP	*	3.00	275.00
65	10 IN. BACK TO SCHOOL, BOY & GIRL	*	19.90	525.00
65	10 IN. MONK WITH CHRISTMAS TREE PLANTING	*	3.00	275.00
66	10 IN. BOY GO-GO DANCER	*	10.00	275.00
66	10 IN. GO-GO BOY & GIRL	*	3.95	500.00
67	10 IN. MONK	*	*	200.00
67	10 IN. SURFER BOY	*	9.95	400.00
67	10 IN. SURFER GIRL	*	9.95	400.00
67	18 IN. MONK W/PLANT	*	7.50	400.00
67	18 IN. NUN	296	8.00	525.00
68	10 IN. BOY WITH BEACHBALL	*	5.95	375.00
68	7 IN. FAT FANNY	*	5.95	375.00
68	7 IN. FAT FANNY	*	6.00	375.01
69	10 IN. NUN ON SKIS	1551	4.50	300.00
69	22 IN. GIRL GO-GO DANCER	*	10.00	300.00
70	10 IN. MONK WITH SKIS	406	4.00	350.00
71	10 IN. CHOIR GIRL	925	3.95	250.00
71	10 IN. NUN ON SKIS	617	4.00	300.00
74	10 IN. LAD & LASS	453	*	300.00

YR	NAME	LIMIT	ISSUE	QUOTE
75	10 IN. CAROLER BOY	*	*	275.00
75	18 IN. LAD	206	11.95	175.00
75	18 IN. LASS	224	11.95	95.00
76	10 IN. COUNTRY GIRL IN TIRE SWING	357	*	200.00
76	10 IN. DRUMMER BOY	*	6.00	200.00
76	10 IN. UNCLE SAM	1095	5.95	325.00
76	18 IN. CHOIR BOY	*	*	500.00
76	18 IN. DRUMMER BOY	402	13.50	400.00
76	18 IN. UNCLE SAM	245	17.00	425.00
76	18 IN. YANKEE DOODLE DANDY	153	*	425.00
76	25 IN. YANKEE DOODLE DANDY/30 IN. HORSE	41	77.50	1600.00
77	8 IN. DRUMMER BOY	6522	6.00	100.00
78	10 IN. BOY PILGRIM	3465	7.00	325.00
81	10 IN. BOY ON RAFT	*	*	200.00
81	18 IN. MONK W/JUG	494	*	290.00
82	10 IN. MONK	6968	12.95	130.00
83	16 IN. MONK WITH JUG	*	27.95	200.00
84	10 IN. AEROBIC DANCER	4875	17.95	150.00
84	10 IN. AEROBIC DANCER	4785	*	75.00
84	10 IN. DOWNHILL SKIER	3535	31.95	75.00
84	16 IN. MONK WITH JUG	1767	34.95	200.00
84	18 IN. AEROBIC DANCER	622	35.95	175.00
84	18 IN. BOB CRATCHET	1819	49.95	250.00
84	18 IN. MARTHA CRATCHET	1751	35.95	350.00
84	18 IN. MONK WITH JUG	1821	34.95	295.00
84	30 IN. MONK	432	78.50	300.00
84	32 IN. MONK WITH GARLAND	416	78.50	600.00
84	8 IN. MONK WITH JUG	3502	17.95	95.00
85	10 IN. BRIDE	318	*	125.00
85	10 IN. CROSS COUNTRY SKIER	1150	*	75.00
85	10 IN. GROOM	264	*	125.00
87	10 IN. HUCK FINN, #690	1200	102.95	400.00
87	18 IN. BOTTLECOVER MONK	718	29.95	105.00
87	3 IN. BRIDE & GROOM	1250	38.95	135.00
87	5 IN. MONK	*	13.95	50.00
89	10 IN. MERLIN	3565	69.95	300.00

A. THORNDIKE

YR	NAME	LIMIT	ISSUE	KIDS/BABIES
50	9 IN. CHOIR BOY	*	*	400.00
54	5 IN. SNO BUNNY (KID)	*	*	300.00
54	5 IN. SNO-BUNNY CHILD	*	2.95	350.00
54	8 IN. BOY SKIER	*	*	550.00
56	7 IN. BABY ANGEL WITH FEATHER HAIR	*	3.95	325.00
57	10 IN. BOY & GIRL IN BOAT	*	17.50	900.00
57	10 IN. BOY SKIER	*	16.00	800.00
57	10 IN. EASTER HOLIDAY DOLL	*	10.00	800.00
60	7 IN. BABY IN STOCKING	*	*	275.00
60	7 IN. BABY WITH BOW	*	1.50	125.00
60	7 IN. BABY WITH PINK BOW	*	*	450.00
62	10 IN. SKEEPLE (BOY)	*	9.00	425.00
63	5 IN. BABY	*	*	300.00
63	5 IN. BABY WITH SANTA HAT	*	2.50	175.00
63	7 IN. SATURDAY NIGHT BABY	*	2.95	350.00
64	18 IN. P.J. BOY & GIRL	*	7.00	525.00
65	10 IN. FISHING BOY	*	7.95	300.00
65	10 IN. FISHING GIRL	*	9.95	400.00
65	7 IN. DRESDEN CHINA BABIES, 2	*	*	525.00
67	10 IN. SURFER BOY	*	4.95	300.00
67	7 IN. GARDEN CLUB BABY	*	2.95	350.00
68	5 IN. BABY IN SANTA CAP	*	2.00	150.00
68	5 IN. BABY IN SANTA HAT	*	3.00	225.00
68	7 IN. BABY I'M READING	*	*	375.00
68	7 IN. BABY VAIN JANE	*	2.50	300.00
69	18 IN. SANTA KID	*	7.45	250.00
69	25 IN. COUNTRY BOY	70	7.00	500.00
69	25 IN. COUNTRY GIRL (PAIR)	69	7.00	*
69	7 IN. CHRISTMAS BABY ON 3 HOT BOXES	*	3.00	400.00
70	10 IN. CHOIR BOY	3517	4.50	150.00
70	10 IN. CHOIR GIRL	7245	5.00	225.00
70	18 IN. PATCHWORK KID	496	7.50	250.00
70	7 IN. TREASURE BABY	*	3.95	200.00
71	10 IN. CHOIR BOY	904	3.95	175.00
71	18 IN. CHOIR GIRL	424	7.95	400.00
71	18 IN. SANTA FUR KID	1191	7.95	400.00
71	7 IN. BABY BUNTING IN BASKET	195	3.95	350.00
75	10 IN. LAD & LASS	162	12.00	249.00
75	10 IN. LAD ON BICYCLE	453	6.00	300.00

YR	NAME	LIMIT	ISSUE	QUOTE
75	10 IN. LASS	558	6.00	300.00
75	18 IN. LAD & LASS ON BIKE	206	24.00	275.00
75	25 IN. LASS WITH BASKET OF FLOWERS	92	28.95	450.00
76	10 IN. BOY IN TIRE SWING	358	6.95	200.00
76	10 IN. GIRL IN TIRE SWING	357	6.95	225.00
76	10 IN. LASS W/PLANTER BASKET	313	6.95	200.00
78	18 IN. CANDY GIRL	1333	14.95	375.00
80	10 IN. BOY ON RAFT	1087	28.95	300.00
80	7 IN. BABY IN BASSINETTE	*	*	125.00
81	18 IN. BOY ON SLED	*	12.50	200.00
81	7 IN. NAUGHTY ANGEL	12,359	10.95	90.00
82	18 IN. GIRL P.J. KID	5389	25.50	125.00
82	7 IN. I'M A 10 BABY	2159	12.95	125.00
83	7 IN. FISHING BOY	*	12.95	125.00
84	18 IN. BOY ON SLED	2205	29.95	150.00
84	18 IN. CANDY BOY	1350	29.95	300.00
84	18 IN. CANDY GIRL	1333	29.95	125.00
84	18 IN. GIRL ON SLED	2328	29.95	150.00
84	7 IN. BASEBALL KID	2079	13.00	200.00
84	7 IN. BOY WITH FIRECRACKER	1893	19.95	140.00
84	7 IN. COUNTRY GIRL WITH BASKET	715	16.95	250.00
84	7 IN. CUPID IN HEART	2445	32.95	150.00
84	7 IN. CUPID KID	6808	14.95	150.00
84	7 IN. JOGGER KID	*	17.95	85.00
85	12 IN. KID W/SLED	4707	31.50	115.00
85	7 IN. BASEBALL KID	1225	*	75.00
85	7 IN. BASEBALL KID	1221	16.95	425.00
85	7 IN. BIRTHDAY GIRL	1017	18.95	75.00
85	7 IN. DRESSUP BOY	1174	18.95	225.00
85	7 IN. DRESSUP GIRL	1536	18.95	425.00
85	7 IN. HAPPY BIRTHDAY BOY	937	19.00	100.00
85	7 IN. HOCKEY PLAYER KID	1578	18.95	125.00
85	7 IN. JOGGER KID	654	17.95	85.00
85	7 IN. KID WITH KITE	1084	17.95	75.00
86	7 IN. CUPID IN HOT AIR BALLOON	391	54.95	175.00
86	7 IN. SKIING KID	8057	18.45	75.00
87	3 IN. BABY WITCH	*	13.95	55.00
87	3 IN. CUPID IN HEART BALLOON	1715	38.95	175.00
87	7 IN. BABY W/BLANKET & SWEATER	7836	21.95	60.00
87	7 IN. BOY GRADUATE	2034	*	80.00
87	7 IN. GIRL GRADUATE	2438	19.95	80.00
87	7 IN. INDIAN BOY	*	19.95	60.00
		LIMITED ONE YEAR RUN		
92	7 IN. BIRTHDAY MOUSE	9,592	23.95	75.00
92	7 IN. GOLFER MOUSE	7,435	26.95	75.00
92	7 IN. GREEN THUMB MOUSE	5,995	25.95	75.00
93	10 IN. DOCTOR BEAR	YR	35.95	35.95-600.00
93	7 IN. ARAB BOY	YR	35.95	35.95
93	7 IN. BAR MITZVAH BOY	YR	27.95	27.95
93	7 IN. BASEBALL MOUSE	6,261	25.95	25.95-525.00
93	7 IN. BASKETBALL BOY	YR	25.95	25.95-550.00
93	7 IN. BEDTIME KID	YR	25.95	25.95-450.00
93	7 IN. BIRTHDAY MOUSE	5,550	23.95	23.95
93	7 IN. FIREMAN MOUSE	YR	25.95	25.95-425.00
93	7 IN. FISHING BOY	YR	29.95	29.95-500.00
93	7 IN. HOT SHOT BUSINESSMAN KID	YR	36.95	36.95-600.00
93	7 IN. JUMP ROPE GIRL	YR	25.95	25.95-500.00
A. THORNDIKE				**MICE**
64	12 IN. GEORGE & SHEILA-BRIDE/GROOM MOUSE	*	12.95	600.00
64	7 IN. CHRISTMAS MOUSE	*	3.95	450.00
64	7 IN. BRIDE & GROOM MICE	*	2.75	750.00
65	7 IN. EEK, PEEK, SQUEEK MOUSE	*	3.95	500.00
65	7 IN. LAWYER MOUSE	*	6.95	425.00
66	7 IN. MOUSE WITH CANDLE	*	*	225.00
67	7 IN. CONDUCTOR MOUSE	*	3.95	300.00
67	7 IN. MIGUEL THE MOUSE	*	3.95	400.00
67	7 IN. MR. SANTA MOUSE	*	3.95	300.00
67	7 IN. MRS. HOLLY MOUSE	*	3.95	150.00
67	7 IN. SANTA MOUSE	*	2.00	250.00
68	7 IN. MR. HOLLY MOUSE	*	3.95	250.00
68	7 IN. NIGHTSHIRT BOY MOUSE	*	3.95	200.00
69	12 IN. NIGHTSHIRT MOUSE	*	*	225.00
70	7 IN. ARCHITECT MOUSE	2051	3.95	375.00
70	7 IN. ARCHITECT MOUSE	205	3.95	350.00
70	7 IN. BOXING MOUSE	321	3.95	400.00
70	7 IN. CARPENTER MOUSE	307	3.95	300.00

Daintily dressed for her first day of school, Sandy sports the nautical attire befitting a true sailor. Designed by artist Karen Kennedy, Sandy is from the "Victoria Ashlea Originals" collection by Goebel.

Blonde-haired and blue-eyed, Margot is an all-American beauty. Produced by Goebel, she plays the tune "Playmates."

The dramatic dark hair and intense eyes of Holly are sure to steal the hearts of collectors. She is second in the "Gifts of the Garden" series by Gorham.

Terry, by doll designer Bette Ball, is music to the hearts of collectors. She plays the tune "Fly Me to the Moon." Produced by Goebel.

YR	NAME	LIMIT	ISSUE	QUOTE
70	7 IN. NIGHTSHIRT GIRL MOUSE	*	3.95	175.00
70	7 IN. PLUMBER MOUSE	196	3.95	350.00
70	7 IN. PROFESSOR MOUSE	248	3.95	225.00
70	7 IN. SHERIFF MOUSE	11	3.95	500.00
71	7 IN. ARTIST MOUSE	422	3.95	175.00
71	7 IN. BASEBALL MOUSE	553	4.00	150.00
71	7 IN. CHEF MOUSE	*	*	75.00
71	7 IN. MOUSE WITH INNER TUBE	267	4.00	200.00
71	7 IN. SKI MOUSE	1326	3.95	175.00
72	7 IN. BAR-BE-QUE MOUSE	907	3.95	225.00
72	7 IN. CHRISTMAS MOUSE	2793	3.95	425.00
72	7 IN. DIAPER MOUSE, IT'S A BOY	2293	4.50	175.00
72	7 IN. DIAPER MOUSE, IT'S A GIRL	2293	4.50	225.00
72	7 IN. GIRL GOLFER MOUSE	*	3.95	100.00
72	7 IN. HOUSEWIFE MOUSE	1768	3.95	250.00
72	7 IN. PREGNANT MOUSE	820	5.50	100.00
72	7 IN. YACHTSMAN MOUSE	1130	3.95	250.00
73	12 IN. NIGHTSHIRT MOUSE	122	7.50	350.00
73	7 IN. FIREMAN MOUSE	557	4.50	200.00
73	7 IN. FOOTBALL MOUSE	944	4.50	150.00
73	7 IN. GOLFER MOUSE	*	5.00	55.00
73	7 IN. PAINTER MOUSE	*	4.50	275.00
73	7 IN. SKIING MOUSE	2774	4.00	175.00
73	7 IN. WAITER MOUSE	*	4.00	250.00
74	12 IN. RETIRED GRANDMA MOUSE	1135	13.50	300.00
74	12 IN. RETIRED GRANDPA MOUSE (PAIR)	1103	13.50	*
74	7 IN. ARTIST MOUSE	397	5.50	110.00
74	7 IN. CARPENTER MOUSE	551	5.50	175.00
74	7 IN. COWBOY MOUSE	394	5.50	150.00
74	7 IN. DOCTOR MOUSE	720	5.50	200.00
74	7 IN. HOCKEY MOUSE	687	7.95	200.00
74	7 IN. HUNTER MOUSE W/BIRD	690	5.50	300.00
74	7 IN. HUNTER MOUSE WITH 10 IN. DEER	1282	11.50	175.00
74	7 IN. PAINTER MOUSE	*	4.00	175.00
74	7 IN. PREGNANT MOUSE	820	*	200.00
74	7 IN. SEAMSTRESS MOUSE	387	4.00	175.00
74	7 IN. SECRETARY MOUSE	364	4.00	150.00
74	7 IN. VACATION MOUSE	*	*	175.00
75	7 IN. BEAUTICIAN MOUSE	1349	4.00	300.00
75	7 IN. BICYCLIST MOUSE	1561	5.50	125.00
75	7 IN. BOUQUET GIRL MOUSE	*	3.95	300.00
75	7 IN. CHRISTMAS MOUSE IN SANTA'S MITTEN	3959	5.95	150.00
75	7 IN. FISHERMAN MOUSE	1343	5.50	200.00
75	7 IN. GOIN' FISHIN' MOUSE	4507	5.95	125.00
75	7 IN. HOUSEWIFE MOUSE	1632	5.50	250.00
75	7 IN. PREGNANT MOUSE	879	5.50	150.00
75	7 IN. RETIRED GRANDPA MOUSE	793	5.50	95.00
75	7 IN. SKI MOUSE	5219	5.50	200.00
75	7 IN. TWO IN TENT MICE	914	*	85.00
76	12 IN. COLONIAL BOY & GIRL MOUSE	*	26.90	900.00
76	12 IN. COLONIAL BOY MOUSE	838	13.50	400.00
76	12 IN. COLONIAL GIRL MOUSE	691	13.50	350.00
76	12 IN. GIRL MOUSE WITH PLUM PUDDING	1482	13.50	400.00
76	7 IN. BIRTHDAY GIRL MOUSE	732	5.50	250.00
76	7 IN. CARD PLAYING GIRL MOUSE	2878	5.95	175.00
76	7 IN. COLONIAL BOY MOUSE	5457	*	200.00
76	7 IN. COLONIAL GIRL MOUSE	5457	5.50	225.00
76	7 IN. GARDENER MOUSE	1255	5.50	225.00
76	7 IN. MR. HOLLY MOUSE	2774	5.50	125.00
76	7 IN. MRS. HOLLY MOUSE	3078	5.50	125.00
76	7 IN. NURSE MOUSE	5164	5.95	250.00
77	29 IN. MRS. SANTA MOUSE	571	49.95	450.00
77	29 IN. MRS. SANTA MOUSE WITH MUFF	571	49.95	500.00
77	7 IN. BASEBALL MOUSE	1634	6.00	100.00
77	7 IN. BEAUTICIAN MOUSE	1521	5.50	250.00
77	7 IN. BINGO MOUSE	1221	6.00	150.00
77	7 IN. DIET TIME MOUSE	1478	6.00	200.00
77	7 IN. GROOM MOUSE	1211	6.95	50.00
77	7 IN. HOBO MOUSE	1004	5.95	250.00
77	7 IN. MR. NIGHTSHIRT MOUSE	309	49.95	650.00
77	7 IN. SWEETHEART MOUSE	3323	5.50	100.00
77	7 IN. VACATIONER MOUSE	1040	6.00	175.00
78	29 IN. CAROLER MOUSE	658	50.00	750.00
78	7 IN. AIRPLANE PILOT MOUSE	2308	6.95	375.00
78	7 IN. C.B. MOUSE	2396	6.95	75.00
78	7 IN. DOCTOR MOUSE	816	6.95	75.00

YR	NAME	LIMIT	ISSUE	QUOTE
78	7 IN. DOCTOR MOUSE	2028	6.95	100.00
78	7 IN. FIREMAN MOUSE	*	6.95	200.00
78	7 IN. GARDENER MOUSE	*	7.00	75.00
78	7 IN. GIRL GOLFER MOUSE	2215	6.95	100.00
78	7 IN. GROOM MOUSE	2952	9.50	85.00
78	7 IN. GROOM MOUSE	*	14.50	125.00
78	7 IN. NIGHTSHIRT MOUSE	6444	7.95	75.00
78	7 IN. POLICEMAN MOUSE	RT	7.00	150.00
78	7 IN. SKATEBOARD MOUSE	3733	7.95	300.00
78	7 IN. TEACHER MOUSE	2249	5.50	100.00
79	12 IN. MRS. SANTA MOUSE	7210	*	125.00
79	12 IN. NIGHTSHIRT MOUSE WITH CANDLE	5739	16.00	225.00
79	12 IN. SANTA MOUSE	*	*	125.00
79	7 IN. BOY GOLFER MOUSE	2743	7.95	100.00
79	7 IN. C.B. MOUSE	1039	7.95	100.00
79	7 IN. CARPENTER MOUSE	2024	6.95	175.00
79	7 IN. CHIMNEY SWEEP MOUSE	6331	7.95	275.00
79	7 IN. FIREMAN MOUSE	1773	6.95	200.00
79	7 IN. FISHING MOUSE	3053	7.95	150.00
79	7 IN. GARDENER MOUSE	1939	7.95	375.00
79	7 IN. GIRL GOLFER MOUSE	2316	7.95	90.00
79	7 IN. MRS. SANTA MOUSE WITH HOLLY	*	7.95	50.00
79	7 IN. PREGNANT MOUSE	1856	7.95	225.00
79	7 IN. QUILTING MOUSE	213	*	150.00
79	7 IN. SANTA MOUSE	12,649	7.95	100.00
79	7 IN. SKATEBOARD MOUSE	1821	6.00	300.00
79	7 IN. SWIMMER MOUSE	3640	9.50	225.00
80	7 IN. BACKPACKER MOUSE	1008	9.95	375.00
80	7 IN. BOY DISCO MOUSE	363	9.50	150.00
80	7 IN. BRIDE & GROOM MICE	2418	9.50	175.00
80	7 IN. CARD PLAYING GIRL MOUSE	1826	9.50	125.00
80	7 IN. DISCO BOY MOUSE	363	9.50	150.00
80	7 IN. DISCO GIRL MOUSE	*	9.50	325.00
80	7 IN. FISHING MOUSE	*	7.50	150.00
80	7 IN. GIRL DISCO MOUSE	915	9.50	150.00
80	7 IN. GREENTHUMB MOUSE	1869	9.50	60.00
80	7 IN. MOUSE WITH CHIMNEY	4452	*	75.00
80	7 IN. PILOT MOUSE	2011	9.95	100.00
80	7 IN. SKATING MOUSE	3369	10.95	100.00
80	7 IN. VOLLEYBALL MOUSE	915	9.50	75.00
81	12 IN. WITCH MOUSE ON BROOM	1049	34.95	160.00
81	7 IN. AIRPLANE PILOT MOUSE	1910	9.95	325.00
81	7 IN. BACKPACKER MOUSE	1008	9.95	100.00
81	7 IN. BASEBALL MOUSE	2380	*	100.00
81	7 IN. CARD PLAYING GIRL MOUSE	863	9.95	125.00
81	7 IN. ICESKATER MOUSE	1429	9.95	150.00
81	7 IN. JOGGER MOUSE	1783	9.95	65.00
81	7 IN. NURSE MOUSE	3222	11.95	50.00
81	7 IN. WITCH MOUSE ON BROOM WITH MOON	1585+	24.95	200.00
81	7 IN. WOODCHOPPER MOUSE	2121	11.00	75.00
82	12 IN. NIGHTSHIRT MOUSE	2319	25.95	125.00
82	12 IN. PILGRIM BOY MOUSE	2151	27.95	175.00
82	12 IN. PILGRIM GIRL MOUSE	2017	27.95	175.00
82	7 IN. BRIDE MOUSE	3681	10.95	50.00
82	7 IN. CHEERLEADER MOUSE	3441	10.95	150.00
82	7 IN. COWBOY MOUSE	3776	28.95	60.00
82	7 IN. FOOTBALL MOUSE	2164	10.50	200.00
82	7 IN. GIRL TENNIS MOUSE	2443	10.95	135.00
82	7 IN. GRADUATE BOY MOUSE	4971	12.00	100.00
82	7 IN. GRADUATE GIRL MOUSE	3563	10.95	85.00
82	7 IN. GROOM MOUSE	3406	10.95	50.00
82	7 IN. MOUSE WITH STRAWBERRY	*	11.95	75.00
82	7 IN. MRS. A.M. MOUSE	2184	11.95	80.00
82	7 IN. SWEETHEART MOUSE	4110	11.00	75.00
82	7 IN. WINDSURFER MOUSE	4114	13.95	250.00
82	7 IN. WITCH MOUSE ON BROOM	2798	12.95	75.00
82	7 IN. WOODCHOPPER MOUSE	1910	11.95	75.00
83	12 IN. BRIDE MOUSE	854	31.95	200.00
83	12 IN. GROOM MOUSE	826	31.95	200.00
83	7 IN. COWBOY MOUSE	1794	12.95	150.00
83	7 IN. COWGIRL MOUSE	1517	12.95	150.00
83	7 IN. EQUESTRIAN MOUSE	*	12.95	200.00
83	7 IN. QUILTING MOUSE	2786	11.95	75.00
83	7 IN. WINDSURFER MOUSE	2352	13.95	125.00
83	7.IN. CHEERLEADER MOUSE	2025	11.95	200.00
84	12 IN. DEVIL MOUSE	1118	29.95	145.00

YR	NAME	LIMIT	ISSUE	QUOTE
84	7 IN. ANGEL MOUSE	2093	14.95	150.00
84	7 IN. BOWLING MOUSE	1472	13.95	75.00
84	7 IN. DEVIL MOUSE	3571	12.95	3571.00
84	7 IN. DEVIL MOUSE	3571	13.95	100.00
84	7 IN. HOCKEYPLAYER MOUSE	1525	5.50	200.00
84	7 IN. MOUSE WITH STRAWBERRY	1776	11.95	75.00
84	7 IN. MOUSE WITH WREATH	*	12.95	55.00
84	7 IN. MRS. RETIRED MOUSE	1356	13.95	95.00
84	7 IN. NIGHTSHIRT MOUSE	*	11.95	150.00
84	7 IN. TEACHER MOUSE	3023	13.95	225.00
84	7 IN. TEACHER MOUSE	3150	13.95	75.00
84	7 IN. TEACHER MOUSE, GIRL	5064	13.95	200.00
85	12 IN. INDIAN BOY MOUSE	*	34.50	100.00
85	7 IN. BOY GOLFER MOUSE	2099	14.95	75.00
85	7 IN. BRIDE & GROOM MICE	2963	13.95	170.00
85	7 IN. GET-WELL MOUSE	1425	14.95	75.00
85	7 IN. GIRL TENNIS MOUSE	1947	14.95	75.00
85	7 IN. GRADUATE GIRL MOUSE	2884	13.95	100.00
85	7 IN. GRADUATION MOUSE	1999	14.00	75.00
85	7 IN. HIKER MOUSE	1781	13.95	275.00
86	7 IN. BALLERINA MOUSE	*	*	200.00
86	7 IN. BIRTHDAY GIRL MOUSE	3724	14.95	125.00
86	7 IN. BOATING MOUSE	2320	16.95	55.00
86	7 IN. INDIAN GIRL MOUSE WITH PAPOOSE	6992	24.95	115.00
86	7 IN. MOUSE WITH WHEELBORROW	2037	16.95	75.00
86	7 IN. SWEETHEART MOUSE	6271	12.95	100.00
86	7 IN. TENNIS MOUSE	1947	15.95	100.00
86	7 IN. TENNIS MOUSE	1947	15.95	75.00
86	7 IN. WITCH MOUSE IN PUMPKIN BALLOON	868	77.95	275.00
87	7 IN. BABY MOUSE	2500	13.95	80.00
87	7 IN. BARBEQUE MOUSE	1798	17.95	85.00
87	7 IN. BICYCLIST BOY MOUSE	1507	19.95	175.00
87	7 IN. BRIDE MOUSE	1801	14.50	55.00
87	7 IN. GRADUATION BOY MOUSE	*	19.95	85.00
87	7 IN. GROOM MOUSE	1800	14.50	55.00
89	12 IN. TRICK OR TREAT MOUSE	*	39.95	225.00
89	7 IN. BUSINESS MAN MOUSE	5085	21.95	150.00
89	7 IN. KNITTING MOUSE	5115	19.95	150.00
89	7 IN. SWEETHEART MOUSE	*	16.95	35.00
89	7 IN. TACKEY TOURIST MOUSE	5116	*	100.00
90	7 IN. ARTIST MOUSE	7285	*	90.00
90	7 IN. MAUI MOUSE	7220	*	100.00
90	7 IN. SAILOR MOUSE	6838	23.95	100.00
91	7 IN. DESERT STORM MOURSE	37,475	29.95	90.00
91	7 IN. RED CROSS NURSE MOUSE	8,305	29.95	75.00

A. THORNDIKE **MISCELLANEOUS**

YR	NAME	LIMIT	ISSUE	QUOTE
70	14 IN. SPRING MUSHROOM	*	*	450.00
76	10 IN. SCARECROW	2341	6.00	200.00
76	10 IN. SCARECROW	2341	5.95	120.00
76	18 IN. SCARECROW	916	13.50	250.00
76	42 IN. SCARECROW	134	62.00	375.00
77	10 IN. SCARECROW	4879	5.95	225.00
77	18 IN. SCARECROW	*	13.50	175.00
81	18 IN. BUTTERFLY WITH 10 IN. ELF	2517	27.95	400.00
82	22 IN. SUN	838	*	200.00
83	18 IN. GINGERBREAD MAN	5027	28.95	250.00
83	18 IN. SCARECROW	3150	32.95	175.00
83	18 IN. SCARECROW	2300	28.95	150.00
83	18 IN. SCARECROW	3896	32.95	200.00
83	22 IN. SUN	*	*	75.00
84	10 IN. GINGERBREAD MAN	4615	15.95	200.00
84	10 IN. SCARECROW	3008	15.95	125.00
85	10 IN. SCARECROW	2930	15.95	325.00
85	CHRISTMAS TREE SKIRT	1332	24.95	110.00
86	LARGE PUMPKIN WITH 7 IN. WITCH M.	668	77.95	250.00
87	CARROT	2503	9.95	300.00

A. THORNDIKE **PIGS**

YR	NAME	LIMIT	ISSUE	QUOTE
69	4 IN. PIG-BUBBLE TIME W/CHAMPAGNE GLASS	*	4.95	275.00
79	14 IN. FATHER PIG	1500	18.95	150.00
79	14 IN. MOM PIG	1807	18.95	150.00
80	4 IN. PIG	1615	8.50	100.00
81	3 IN. PIG	3435	7.95	100.00
81	4 IN. PIG	3194	7.95	100.00
81	8 IN. BOY BBQ PIG	1159	11.95	100.00
81	8 IN. BOY BBQ PIG	4072	10.50	200.00
81	8 IN. GIRL BBQ PIG (PAIR)	3854	10.50	*

YR	NAME	LIMIT	ISSUE	QUOTE
82	8 IN. BALLERINA PIG	1058	12.95	250.00
82	8 IN. BOY BBQ PIG	1044	11.95	55.00
88	10 IN. EASTER PARADE BOY PIG	3005	24.50	180.00
88	10 IN. EASTER PARADE GIRL PIG (PAIR)	3400	24.50	*

A. THORNDIKE — **REINDEER**

YR	NAME	LIMIT	ISSUE	QUOTE
65	10 IN. REINDEER	*	4.95	550.00
68	36 IN. RED NOSED REINDEER	*	*	300.00
69	10 IN. REINDEER WITH RED NOSE	*	4.95	350.00
70	10 IN. REINDEER WITH HAT	144	5.00	175.00
71	10 IN. RED NOSED REINDEER	1588	4.95	225.00
71	36 IN. REINDEER WITH TWO 18 IN. GNOMES	624	38.00	700.00
75	10 IN. RED NOSED REINDEER	4854	*	100.00
78	18 IN. REINDEER	*	18.00	125.00
78	18 IN. REINDEER	5134	9.00	125.00
78	36 IN. REINDEER WITH SADDLEBAGS	594	58.00	175.00
81	5 IN. MINIATURE REINDEER	9080	11.50	120.00
83	18 IN. FAWN	1444	32.95	225.00
83	18 IN. FAWN	*	33.00	200.00
84	18 IN. FAWN WITH WREATH	1444	32.95	225.00
85	10 IN. REINDEER WITH BELL	6398	13.95	55.00

A. THORNDIKE — **SANTAS**

YR	NAME	LIMIT	ISSUE	QUOTE
54	26 IN. BEAN NOSE SANTA	*	19.95	700.00
56	12 IN. SANTA WITH BEAN NOSE	*	20.00	1000.00
59	7 IN. SANTA WITH FUR TRIM SUIT	*	2.95	225.00
60	7 IN. MR. AND MRS. TUCKERED	*	*	500.00
65	12 IN. SANTA	*	5.00	125.00
65	18 IN. SANTA	*	9.00	150.00
65	26 IN. MRS. SANTA WITH APRON	*	14.95	1000.00
65	7 IN. MR. AND MRS. SANTA	*	5.95	325.00
66	29 IN. MR. OUTDOOR SANTA	*	17.00	350.00
67	7 IN. SANTA WITH TOY BAG	*	3.95	275.00
68	18 IN. MR. INDOOR SANTA	*	7.50	225.00
68	18 IN. MRS. INDOOR SANTA	*	7.50	250.00
68	29 IN. MR. SANTA WITH VEST & SACK	*	16.00	500.00
68	7 IN. MR. & MRS. SANTA TUCKERED	*	3.00	200.00
70	10 IN. XMAS MUSHROOM-7 IN. SANTA & DEER	*	11.00	600.00
70	7 IN. SANTA WITH 10 IN. XMAS MUSHROOM	*	7.00	125.00
71	18 IN. MRS. SANTA WITH CARDHOLDER	1563	8.00	200.00
71	7 IN. MR. & MRS. SANTA WITH BASKET	3403	5.95	150.00
72	18 IN. MR. SANTA WITH SACK	850	*	150.00
72	29 IN. SANTA WITH CARDHOLDER SACK	686	24.95	150.00
72	7 IN. MR. & MRS. TUCKERED	1187	6.50	375.00
72	7 IN. MRS. SANTA WITH APRON AND CAP	8867	5.50	50.00
72	7 IN. SANTA WITH MUSHROOM	540	*	275.00
73	18 IN. MRS. SANTA	3700	7.00	150.00
73	18 IN. MRS. SANTA WITH CARDHOLDER	3900	14.95	150.00
73	7 IN. MR. & MRS. SANTA-WICKER LOVESEAT	3973	10.95	250.00
73	7 IN. SANTA MAILMAN	3276	5.00	200.00
74	29 IN. MRS. SANTA WITH CARDHOLDER	*	28.95	200.00
74	7 IN. BLACK SANTA	1157	5.50	225.00
74	7 IN. SANTA IN SKI BOB	704	4.95	450.00
75	18 IN. MRS. SANTA WITH PLUM PUDDING	*	12.00	300.00
78	7 IN. SANTA WITH DEER AND TREE	5813	18.50	400.00
78	18 IN. MR. SANTA WITH CARDHOLDER	*	*	75.00
79	29 IN. MOTORIZED MR. & MRS. SANTA	136	400.00	1600.00
79	7 IN. C.B. SANTA	2206	7.95	75.00
79	7 IN. SANTA WITH MISTLETOE	*	7.95	50.00
80	7 IN. SANTA WITH STOCKING	17,665	9.95	75.00
81	10 IN. BALLOONING SANTA	1737	39.95	325.00
81	7 IN. CROSS-COUNTRY SKI SANTA	5180	10.95	100.00
81	7 IN. SANTA WITH MISTLETOE	*	10.50	40.00
81	7 IN. SANTA WITH POT BELLY	*	11.95	75.00
82	5 IN. MRS. SANTA WITH GIFT BOX	7566	10.95	75.00
82	5 IN. SANTA WITH DEER	3072	20.00	235.00
82	7 IN. SANTA WREATH CENTERPIECE	1150	*	150.00
84	7 IN. SANTA ON A MOON	*	*	150.00
86	18 IN. MRS. VICTORIAN SANTA	2000	*	200.00
86	7 IN. VICTORIAN SANTA W/SLEIGH & DEER	6820	44.00	200.00
87	10 IN. COLLECTOR SANTA TRIMMING TREE	*	130.00	250.00
87	18 IN. MR. VICTORIAN SANTA	2150	57.50	200.00
87	18 IN. WORKSHOP SANTA	980	*	600.00
87	30 IN. MR. VICTORIAN SANTA	450	150.00	350.00
87	30 IN. MRS. VICTORIAN SANTA	425	150.00	350.00
87	7 IN. VICTORIAN MR. & MRS. SANTA	*	23.95	200.00
88	30 IN. VICTORIAN MRS. SANTA WITH TRAY	*	119.95	360.00

YR	NAME	LIMIT	ISSUE	QUOTE
A. THORNDIKE				**SNOWMEN**
71	29 IN. SNOWMAN WITH BROOM	1075	19.95	200.00
71	7 IN. SNOWMAN	1917	3.95	275.00
78	10 IN. SNOWMAN	9701	6.95	175.00
78	18 IN. SNOWMAN	3971	79.95	250.00
79	10 IN. SNOWMAN	12,888	7.95	100.00
79	29 IN. SNOWMAN	917	42.95	400.00
83	7 IN. SNOWMAN	15,980	12.95	75.00
84	30 IN. SNOWGIRL	685	79.50	475.00
84	30 IN. SNOWGIRL AND BOY	685	79.95	475.00
84	30 IN. SNOWMAN	956	79.50	475.00
84	4 IN. SNOWMAN	*	169.95	350.00
A. THORNDIKE				**WORKSHOP**
93	5 IN. ELF	OP	13.45	13.45

ANRI
*

YR	NAME	LIMIT	ISSUE	QUOTE
				DISNEY DOLLS
89	MICKEY MOUSE, 14 IN.	2500	850.00	895.00
89	MINNIE MOUSE, 14 IN.	2500	850.00	895.00
89	PINOCCHIO, 14 IN.	2500	850.00	895.00
90	DAISY DUCK, 14 IN.	2500	895.00	895.00
90	DONALD DUCK, 14 IN.	2500	895.00	895.00
J. FERRANDIZ				**FERRANDIZ DOLLS**
89	GABRIEL, 14 IN.	1000	550.00	575.00
89	MARIA, 14 IN.	1000	550.00	575.00
90	MARGARITE, 14 IN.	1000	575.00	595.00
90	PHILIPE, 14 IN.	1000	575.00	595.00
91	CARMEN, 14 IN.	1000	730.00	730.00
91	FERNANDO, 14 IN.	1000	730.00	730.00
91	JUANITA, 7 IN.	1500	300.00	300.00
91	MIGUEL, 7 IN.	1500	300.00	300.00
S. KAY				**SARAH KAY DOLLS**
88	BRIDE AND GROOM MATCHING SETS	*	1300.00	1350.00
88	BRIDE TO LOVE AND TO CHERISH	750	750.00	775.00
88	CHARLOTTE (BLUE)	1000	550.00	575.00
88	EMILY, 14 IN.	750	500.00	500.00
88	GROOM WITH THIS RING DOLL	750	550.00	575.00
88	JENNIFER, 14 IN.	750	500.00	500.00
88	KATHERINE, 14 IN.	750	500.00	500.00
88	MARTHA, 14 IN.	750	500.00	500.00
88	RACHAEL, 14 IN.	750	500.00	500.00
88	REBECCA, 14 IN.	750	500.00	500.00
88	VICTORIA, 14 IN.	750	500.00	500.00
89	ELEANOR (FLORAL)	1000	550.00	575.00
89	ELIZABETH (PATCHWORK)	1000	550.00	575.00
89	HELEN (BROWN)	1000	550.00	575.00
89	HENRY	1000	550.00	575.00
89	MARY (RED)	1000	550.00	575.00
90	CHRISTINA, 14 IN.	1000	575.00	595.00
90	FAITH, 14IN.	1000	575.00	595.00
90	POLLY, 14 IN.	1000	575.00	595.00
90	SOPHIE, 14 IN.	1000	575.00	595.00
91	ANNIE, 7 IN.	1500	300.00	300.00
91	JANINE, 14 IN.	1500	750.00	750.00
91	JESSICA, 7 IN.	1500	300.00	300.00
91	JULIE, 7 IN.	1500	300.00	300.00
91	MICHELLE, 7 IN.	1500	300.00	300.00
91	PATRICIA, 14 IN.	1500	730.00	730.00
91	PEGGY, 7 IN.	1500	300.00	300.00
91	SUSAN, 7 IN.	1500	300.00	300.00

ARTAFFECTS

YR	NAME	LIMIT	ISSUE	QUOTE
G. PERILLO				**ART DOLL COLLECTION**
86	MORNING STAR, 17 1/2 IN.	1000	250.00	250.00
88	SUNFLOWER, 12 IN.	2500	175.00	175.00
90	LITTLE DOVE	5000	175.00	175.00
90	STRAIGHT ARROW	5000	175.00	175.00
92	BRAVE AND FREE		111.00	111.00

ASHTON-DRAKE GALLERIES

YR	NAME	LIMIT	ISSUE	QUOTE
*	CHEN	*	1.15	115.00-220.00
94	MY LITTLE BALLERINA		59.95	65.00
J. SINGER			**A CHILD'S GARDEN OF VERSES**	
91	THE LAND OF NOD	TL	79.00	79.00
J. GOOD-KRUGER				**BABY TALK**
94	BYE, BYE!	*	49.95	55.00

YR NAME	LIMIT	ISSUE	QUOTE
G. RADEMANN		**BEAUTIFUL DREAMERS**	
92 KATRINA	CL	89.00	89.00
92 NICOLETTE	YR	89.95	89.95
M. TRETTER		**CAUGHT IN THE ACT**	
92 STEVIE, CATCH ME IF YOU CAN	YR	49.95	49.95
Y. BELLO		**CHRISTMAS MEMORIES**	
94 JOSHUA		59.95	65.00
D. EFFNER		**DIANNA EFFNER'S MOTHER GOOSE**	
90 MARY, MARY, QUITE CONTRARY	CL	78.00	94.00
91 THE LITTLE GIRL WITH THE CURL (GOOD)	CL	79.00	79.00
91 THE LITTLE GIRL WITH THE CURL (HORRID	CL	79.00	79.00
P. COFFER		**DOWN THE GARDEN PATH**	
91 ANGELICA	YR	85.00	85.00
91 ROSEMARY	TL	79.00	79.00
L. DI LEO		**ELVIS: LIFETIME OF A LEGEND**	
92 '68 COMEBACK	YR	99.95	99.95
T. MENZENBACH		**FROM THE HEART**	
92 CAROLIN	CL	79.95	79.95
92 ERIK	YR	79.95	79.95
K. HIPPENSTEEL		**GROWING YOUNG MINDS**	
91 ALEX	TL	79.00	79.00
K. HIPPENSTEEL		**HAPPINESS IS...**	
91 PATRICIA (MY FIRST TOOTH)	CL	69.00	69.00
92 CRYSTAL	YR	69.95	69.95
K. B.-HIPPENSTEEL		**HAPPY THOUGHTS**	
94 BUBBLE UP WITH JOY	*	59.95	65.00
C. MCCLURE		**HEAVENLY INSPIRATIONS**	
92 EVERY CLOUD HAS A SILVER LINING	YR	59.95	59.95
H. HUNT		**HOLY HUNT'S BONNET BABIES**	
91 MISSY (GRANDMA'S LITTLE GIRL)	CL	69.00	69.00
92 SUSIE (SOMEBODY LOVES ME)	YR	69.00	69.00
F. WICK		**INTERNATIONAL SPIRIT OF CHRISTMAS**	
89 AMERICAN SANTA	CL	125.00	125.00
J. IBAROLLE		**LITTLE HOUSE ON THE PRAIRIE**	
92 LAURA	YR	79.95	79.95
94 MA INGALLS		85.00	90.00
W. LAWTON		**LITTLE WOMEN**	
94 AMY	*	59.95	65.00
94 BETH	*	59.95	65.00
94 MEG	*	59.95	65.00
		LITTLE WORDS OF WISDOM	
94 A FRIEND IN NEED IS A FRIEND INDEED	CL	59.95	65.00
94 TOMORROW IS ANOTHER DAY		59.95	65.00
Y. BELLO		**MOMENTS TO REMEMBER**	
91 JUSTIN	CL	75.00	75.00
92 JILL	YR	69.00	69.00
J. GOODYEAR		**MY CLOSEST FRIENDS**	
92 BOO BEAR (EVIE)	CL	79.00	78.00
92 ME/BLANKIE (STEFFIE)	CL	79.00	79.00
92 MY SECRET PAL (ROBBIE)	YR	85.00	85.00
H. HUNT		**NEW BONNET BABIES**	
91 GRANDMA'S LITTLE GIRL	TL	69.00	69.00
YOLANA BELLO		**PICTURE PERFECT BABIES**	
87 SARAH 14"	CL	58.00	225.00
88 AMANDA 12"	CL	63.00	110.00
91 EMILY	CL	63.00	63.00
YOLANDA BELLO		**PICTURE PREFECT BABIES**	
89 JESSICA	CL	63.00	200.00
K. B.-HIPPENSTEEL		**SOMEONE TO WATCH OVER ME**	
94 ANGEL LULLABY	*	24.95	30.00
94 ANGEL NIGHT-NIGHT	*	24.95	30.00
S. KREY		**TOGETHER FOREVER**	
94 COURTNEY	*	59.95	65.00
94 KIM	*	59.95	65.00
94 KIRSTEN	*	59.95	65.00
C. MCCLURE		**VICTORIAN NURSURY HEIRLOOM**	
94 VICTORIAN LULLABY	*	129.95	140.00
S. SHERWOOD		**WINTERFEST**	
91 BRIAN	TL	89.00	89.00
92 MICHELLE	YR	89.95	89.95
Y. BELLO		**YOLANDA'S LULLABY BABIES**	
91 CHRISTY (ROCK-A-BYE)	CL	69.00	69.00
92 JOEY (TWINKLE, TWINKLE)	YR	69.00	69.00
YOLANDA BELLO		**YOLANDA'S PICTURE PERFECT BABIES**	
85 JASON	CL	48.00	800.00-1380.00
86 HEATHER	CL	48.00	275.00-385.00

YR	NAME	LIMIT	ISSUE	QUOTE
87	JENNIFER	CL	58.00	275.00-360.00
87	MATTHEW	CL	58.00	150.00-360.00
90	LISA	CL	63.00	83.00
90	MICHAEL	CL	63.00	94.00-105.00
91	DANIELLE	CL	69.00	69.00
Y. BELLO		**YOLANDA'S PRECIOUS PLAYMATES**		
92	DAVID	CL	69.95	69.95
M. STAUBER		**YOUR HEART'S DESIRE**		
91	JULIA	CL	99.00	99.00

AVONLEA TRADITIONS INC.

			ANNE OF GREEN GABLES	
89	ARRIVING AT THE STATION	OP	260.00	260.00
90	DIANA BARRY	OP	260.00	260.00
90	PUFFED SLEEVES	OP	260.00	260.00
90	SCHOOL DAYS	OP	260.00	260.00

DEPARTMENT 56

			HERITAGE VILLAGE DOLL COLLECTION	
*				
87	CHRISTMAS CAROL DOLLS 1000-6 (SET OF 4)	250	1500.00	1500.00
87	CHRISTMAS CAROL DOLLS 5907-2 (SET OF 4)	OP	250.00	250.00
88	CHRISTMAS CAROL DOLLS 1001-4 (SET OF 4)	350	800.00	800.00
88	MR. & MRS. FEZZIWIG 5594-8 (SET OF 2)	OP	172.00	172.00
*			**SNOWBABIES DOLLS**	
88	ALISON & DUNCAN 7730-5	RT	200.00	750.00

DIANNA EFFNER PORCELAIN DOLLS
EMMY CHEN

94	BENJAMIN	25	325.00	350.00
94	HEATHER	25	350.00	375.00
93	BEDTIME JENNY	50	375.00	400.00
93	BIRTHDAY JENNY	50	375.00	400.00
93	DOLLY	50	95.00	110.00
93	EVERYDAY JENNY	CL	375.00	400.00
93	TINY (BOY OR GIRL)	50	250.00	275.00
94	KAYLA	50	450.00	475.00
93	SHEN	50	475.00	500.00

DOLLS BY JERRI
J. MCCLOUD

			DOLLS BY JERRI	
*	BOY	1000	350.00	395.00
*	DENISE	1000	380.00	525.00
*	GINA	1000	350.00	475.00
*	GOLDILOCKS	1000	370.00	500.00
*	JAMIE	800	380.00	450.00
*	LAURA	1000	350.00	425.00
*	LITTLE BO PEEP	1000	340.00	400.00
*	LITTLE MISS MUFFET	1000	340.00	400.00
*	MEGAN	750	420.00	550.00
*	MEREDITH	750	430.00	600.00
*	UNCLE REMUS	500	290.00	400.00
82	BABY DAVID	538	290.00	2000.00
84	CLARA	1000	320.00	1900.00
84	EMILY	1000	330.00	3500.00
85	BRIDE	1000	350.00	350.00
85	CANDY	1000	340.00	2000.00
85	MISS NANNY	1000	160.00	250.00
85	SCOTTY	1000	340.00	2000.00
85	UNCLE JOE	1000	160.00	250.00
86	ALFALFA	1000	350.00	350.00
86	ALLISON	1000	350.00	450.00
86	AMBER	1000	350.00	875.00
86	ANNABELLE	300	600.00	600.00
86	ASHLEY	1000	350.00	450.00
86	AUDREY	300	550.00	550.00
86	BRIDGETTE	300	500.00	500.00
86	CANE	1000	350.00	1200.00
86	CHARLOTTE	1000	330.00	450.00
86	CLOWN-DAVID, 3 YEARS OLD	1000	340.00	450.00
86	DANIELLE	1000	350.00	450.00
86	DAVID, 2 YEARS OLD	1000	330.00	550.00
86	DAVID-MAGICIAN	1000	350.00	350.00
86	ELIZABETH	1000	340.00	340.00
86	HELENJEAN	1000	350.00	450.00
86	JACQUELINE	300	500.00	500.00
86	JOY	1000	350.00	350.00
86	LUCIANNA	300	500.00	500.00
86	MARY BETH	1000	350.00	350.00

YR	NAME	LIMIT	ISSUE	QUOTE
86	NOBODY	1000	350.00	450.00
86	PRINCESS AND THE UNICORN	1000	370.00	370.00
86	SAMANTHA	1000	350.00	500.00
86	SOMEBODY	1000	350.00	500.00
86	TAMMY	1000	350.00	900.00
86	THE FOOL	1000	350.00	350.00
86	YVONNE	300	500.00	500.00
88	HOLLY	1000	350.00	800.00
89	GOOSE GIRL, GUILD	CL	300.00	700.00
89	LAURA LEE	1000	370.00	500.00

DYNASTY DOLL

			ANNA COLLECTION	
*				
92	POCAHONTAS	3500	95.00	95.00
92	COMMUNION GIRL	YR	125.00	125.00
*			ANNUAL	
89	AMBER	YR	90.00	90.00
90	MARCELLA	YR	90.00	90.00
91	BUTTERFLY PRINCESS	YR	110.00	110.00

LEE PO NAN — BALLERINA SERIES

91	MASHA-NUTCRACKER	7500	190.00	190.00
*			CHRISTMAS	
87	MERRIE	3500	60.00	60.00
88	NOEL	3500	80.00	80.00
90	FAITH	5000	110.00	110.00
91	JOY	5000	125.00	125.00

EDNA HIBEL STUDIOS

E. HIBEL — CHILD'S FANTASY

85	JENNY'S LADY JENNIFER	800	395.00	850.00-1105.00

E. HIBEL — WAX DOLL COLLECTION

86	WAX DOLL	12	2500.00	3000.00-3400.00

EDWIN M. KNOWLES

J. GOOD-KRUGER — AMISH BLESSINGS

90	REBECCAH	TL	68.00	68.00
90	REBECCAH	TL	68.00	68.00
91	ADAM	CL	75.00	75.00
91	RACHEL	CL	69.00	69.00
91	RACHEL AT PRAYER	TL	69.00	69.00
92	ELI	YR	79.95	79.95
92	RUTH	YR	75.00	75.00

K. HIPPENSTEEL — BABY BOOK TREASURES

90	ELIZABETH'S HOMECOMING	CL	58.00	80.00
91	CATHERINE'S CHRISTENING	TL	58.00	58.00
91	CHRISTOPHER'S FIRST SMILE	TL	63.00	63.00

K. HIPPENSTEEL — BORN TO BE FAMOUS

90	FLORENCE NIGHTINGALE	TL	87.00	87.00
90	LITTLE SHERLOCK	CL	87.00	95.00-130.00
91	LITTLE DAVEY CROCKETT	CL	92.00	92.00
92	LITTLE CHRISTOPHER COLUMBUS	YR	95.00	95.00

Y. BELLO — CHILDREN OF MOTHER GOOSE

87	LITTLE BO PEEP	CL	58.00	200.00-250.00
87	MARY HAD A LITTLE LAMB	CL	58.00	250.00
88	LITTLE JACK HORNER	CL	63.00	100.00-200.00
89	MISS MUFFET	CL	63.00	78.00-100.00

C. MCCLURE — CINDY'S PLAYHOUSE PETS

88	MEAGAN	TL	87.00	175.00
89	RYAN	TL	83.00	83.00
89	SHELLY	TL	87.00	87.00
91	SAMANTHA	TL	89.00	89.00

D. EFFNER — HEROINES FROM THE FAIRY TALE FORESTS

88	LITTLE RED RIDING HOOD	CL	68.00	150.00-200.00
89	GOLDILOCKS	CL	68.00	75.00-85.00
90	SNOW WHITE	TL	73.00	73.00
91	RAPUNZEL	TL	79.00	79.00
92	CINDERELLA	CL	79.00	79.00

K. HIPPENSTEEL — INTERNATIONAL FESTIVAL OF TOYS AND TOTS

88	CHEN, A LITTLE BOY OF CHINA	CL	78.00	175.00-350.00
89	NATASHA	CL	78.00	100.00
90	MOLLY	TL	83.00	83.00
91	HANS	TL	83.00	83.00

FANGEL INSPIRED — MAUDE FANGEL'S COVER BABIES

90	BENJAMIN'S BALL	TL	73.00	73.00
90	PEEK-A-BOO PETER	TL	73.00	73.00

J. GOODYEAR — MY CLOSEST FRIEND

91	BOO BEAR 'N ME	TL	78.00	78.00
91	ME AND MY BLANKIE	TL	79.00	79.00

YR NAME	LIMIT	ISSUE	QUOTE
STEVENS/ SIEGEL		**PARADE OF AMERICAN FASHION**	
87 THE GLAMOUR OF THE GIBSON GIRL	CL	77.00	195.00-225.00
87 THE SOUTHERN BELLE	CL	77.00	175.00-195.00
90 VICTORIAN LADY	TL	82.00	82.00
91 ROMANTIC LADY	TL	85.00	85.00
S. KREY		**POLLY'S TEA PARTY**	
90 POLLY	TL	78.00	78.00
91 LIZZIE	TL	79.00	79.00
92 ANNIE	TL	83.00	83.00
M. TRETTER		**THE LITTLEST CLOWNS**	
91 BUBBLES	TL	65.00	65.00
91 SMOOCH	CL	69.00	69.00
91 SPARKLES	TL	63.00	63.00
92 DAISY	TL	69.95	69.95
M. OLDENBURG		**YESTERDAY'S DREAMS**	
90 ANDY	TL	68.00	68.00
91 JANEY	TL	69.00	69.00
Y. BELLO		**YOLANDA'S PICTURE-PERFECT BABIES**	
85 JASON	CL	48.00	900.00-1500.00
86 HEATHER	CL	48.00	480.00-600.00
87 JENNIFER	CL	58.00	355.00-500.00
88 AMANDA	CL	63.00	165.00
88 MATTHEW	CL	58.00	260.00-300.00
89 JESSICA	TL	63.00	63.00
89 SARAH	CL	58.00	105.00
90 LISA	TL	63.00	63.00
90 MICHAEL	TL	63.00	175.00
91 DANIELLE	TL	69.00	69.00
91 EMILY	TL	63.00	63.00

ELKE'S ORIGINALS

E. HUTCHENS		**ELKE HUTCHENS**	
89 ANNABELLE	250	575.00	1295.00
90 AUBRA	250	575.00	1295.00
90 AURORA	250	595.00	1295.00
90 KRICKET	500	575.00	1000.00
90 LITTLE LIEBCHEN	250	475.00	1000.00
90 VICTORIA	500	645.00	645.00
91 ALICIA	250	595.00	1295.00
91 BELLINDA	400	595.00	800.00-1000.00
91 BRAELYN	400	595.00	1150.00-1500.00
91 BRIANNA	400	595.00	1000.00
92 BETHANY	400	595.00	1000.00
92 CECILIA	435	635.00	950.00
92 CHERIE	435	635.00	635.00

ENESCO

S. BUTCHER		**JACK-IN-THE BOXES**	
91 MAY YOU/OLD FASHIONED CHRISTMAS 417777	YR	200.00	200.00
S. BUTCHER		**JACK-IN-THE BOXES/4 SEASONS**	
90 AUTUMN'S PRAISE 408751	YR	200.00	149.00
90 SUMMER'S JOY 408743	YR	200.00	149.00
90 VOICE OF SPRING 408735	YR	200.00	149.00
90 WINTER'S SONG 408778	YR	200.00	149.00
KINKA		**KINKA LIMITED EDITION DOLL**	
91 WISHING YOU CLOUDLESS SKIES 408573	2500	120.00	120.00
M. ATTWELL		**MEMORIES OF YESTERDAY**	
90 HILARY JACK-IN-THE-BOX 376027	3750	175.00	175.00
90 HILARY, 11 IN. 376019	2500	100.00	100.00
		PRECIOUS MOMENTS	
83 MOTHER SEW DEAR E2850	RT	350.00	225.00-275.00
S. BUTCHER		**PRECIOUS MOMENTS DOLLS**	
80 DEBBIE, 18 IN. E-6214G	SU	175.00	220.00-250.00
81 CUBBY, 18 IN. E-7267B	5000	200.00	450.00-1000.00
81 MIKEY, 18 IN. E-6214B	SU	175.00	220.00-250.00
81 TAMMY, 18 IN. E-7267G	5000	300.00	550.00-1000.00
83 KATIE LYNNE, 16 IN. E-0539	SU	150.00	175.00-200.00
83 KRISTY, 12 IN. E-2851	SU	150.00	170.00
84 AARON, 12 IN. 12424	SU	135.00	125.00-135.00
84 AUTUMN'S PRAISE 408808	LE	150.00	130.00-150.00
84 MOTHER SEW DEAR, 16 IN. E-2850	RT	350.00	289.00
84 SUMMER'S JOY 408794	LE	150.00	130.00-150.00
84 THE VOICE OF SPRING 408786	LE	150.00	135.00-150.00
84 TIMMY, 12 IN. E-5397	SU	125.00	150.00-160.00
84 WINTER'S SONG 408816	LE	150.00	130.00-150.00
85 BETHANY, 12 IN. 12432	SU	135.00	135.00-140.00
85 BONG BONG, 13 IN. 100455	12,000	150.00	225.00-245.00

YR	NAME	LIMIT	ISSUE	QUOTE
85	CANDY, 13 IN. 100463	12,000	150.00	250.00-265.00
85	CONNIE, 12 IN. 102253	7,500	160.00	190.00-200.00
85	P.D., 7 IN. 12475	SU	50.00	70.00-80.00
85	TRISH, 7 IN. 12483	SU	50.00	70.00-80.00
86	ANGIE, THE ANGEL OF MERCY 12491	12,500	160.00	180.00-210.00
90	MAY YOU/OLD FASHIONED CHRISTMAS 417785	LE	150.00	150.00
90	THE EYES OF THE LORD ARE UPON YOU 429570	LE	65.00	65.00-75.00
90	THE EYES OF THE LORD ARE UPON YOU 429589	LE	65.00	65.00-80.00
90	YOU HAVE TOUCHED SO MANY HEARTS 427527	LE	90.00	80.00-90.00

S. BUTCHER PRECIOUS MOMENTS-JACK-IN-THE BOXES

YR	NAME	LIMIT	ISSUE	QUOTE
91	YOU HAVE TOUCHED SO MANY HEARTS 422282	YR	175.00	175.00

GEORGETOWN COLLECTION INC.

L. MASON   AMERICAN DIARY DOLLS

YR	NAME	LIMIT	ISSUE	QUOTE
90	JENNIE COOPER	100-DAY	129.25	129.25
91	BRIDGET QUINN	100-DAY	129.25	129.25
91	CHRISTINA MEROVINA	100-DAY	129.25	129.25
91	MANY STARS	100-DAY	129.25	129.25
92	RACHEL WILLIAMS	100-DAY	129.25	129.25

T. DEHETRE   BABY KISSES

YR	NAME	LIMIT	ISSUE	QUOTE
92	MICHELLE	100-DAY	118.60	118.60

B. DEVAL   FAERIE PRINCESS

YR	NAME	LIMIT	ISSUE	QUOTE
89	FAERIE PRINCES	CL	248.00	248.00

V. WALKER   KINDERGARTEN KIDS

YR	NAME	LIMIT	ISSUE	QUOTE
92	NIKKI	100-DAY	129.00	129.00

T. DEHETRE   LET'S PLAY

YR	NAME	LIMIT	ISSUE	QUOTE
92	EENTSY WEENTSY WILLIE	100-DAY	118.60	118.60
92	PEEK-A-B00 BECKIE	100-DAY	118.60	118.60

B. DEVAL   LITTLE LOVES

YR	NAME	LIMIT	ISSUE	QUOTE
88	EMMA	CL	139.20	139.20
89	KATIE	CL	139.20	139.20
89	MEGAN	CL	138.20	160.00
90	LAURA	CL	139.20	139.20

P. THOMPSON   MISS ASHLEY

YR	NAME	LIMIT	ISSUE	QUOTE
89	MISS ASHLEY	CL	228.00	228.00

T. DEHETRE   NURSERY BABIES

YR	NAME	LIMIT	ISSUE	QUOTE
90	BABY BUNTING	CL	118.20	118.20
90	PATTY CAKE	100-DAY	118.20	118.20
91	DIDDLE, DIDDLE	100-DAY	118.20	118.20
91	LITTLE GIRL	100-DAY	118.20	118.20
91	THIS LITTLE PIGGY	100-DAY	118.20	118.20

B. DEVAL   SMALL WONDERS

YR	NAME	LIMIT	ISSUE	QUOTE
90	COREY	100-DAY	97.60	97.60
91	ABBEY	100-DAY	97.60	97.60
92	SARAH	100-DAY	97.60	97.60

L. MASON   SUGAR & SPICE

YR	NAME	LIMIT	ISSUE	QUOTE
91	LITTLE SWEETHEART	100-DAY	118.25	118.25
91	RED HOT PEPPER	100-DAY	118.25	118.25
92	LITTLE SUNSHINE	100-DAY	141.10	141.10

P. COFFER   TANSIE

YR	NAME	LIMIT	ISSUE	QUOTE
88	TANSIE	CL	81.00	81.00

GOEBEL INC.

B. BALL

YR	NAME	LIMIT	ISSUE	QUOTE
93	ANGEL SWEETIE	1000	49.50	49.50
93	BILLIE BUMPS	500	150.00	150.00
93	CORY	1000	135.00	135.00
93	DOLLY DINGLE	1000	115.00	115.00

B. BALL   80TH ANNIVERSARY ISSUE

YR	NAME	LIMIT	ISSUE	QUOTE
93	DAISY DUMPLING	500	124.50	124.50
93	DIMPLES DUMPLING	500	150.00	150.00
93	DOLLY DINGLE	500	155.00	155.00
93	SNUGGLES SNOOKS	1500	65.00	65.00
93	TICKLEY TINGLE	500	129.00	129.00

B. BALL   AMERICANA SERIES

YR	NAME	LIMIT	ISSUE	QUOTE
93	CLARA	1000	235.00	235.00
93	RITA	500	475.00	475.00
93	ROSEMARIE	1000	220.00	220.00

B. BALL   ANNUAL TREE TOP ANGEL

YR	NAME	LIMIT	ISSUE	QUOTE
93	TREETOP ANGEL-6TH	1000	69.50	69.50

B. BALL   BEST DRESSED TODDLER

YR	NAME	LIMIT	ISSUE	QUOTE
93	BUFFY	1000	245.00	245.00
93	JOSEPHINE	1000	159.75	159.75

K. KENNEDY   BIRTHSTONE DOLLS

YR	NAME	LIMIT	ISSUE	QUOTE
94	APRIL/DIAMOND	2500	29.50	29.50
94	AUGUST/PERIDOT	2500	29.50	29.50
94	DECEMBER/ZIRCON	2500	29.50	29.50

YR	NAME	LIMIT	ISSUE	QUOTE
94	FEBRUARY/AMETHYST	2500	29.50	29.50
94	JANUARY/GARNET	2500	29.50	29.50
94	JULY/RUBY	2500	29.50	29.50
94	JUNE/LIGHT AMETHYST	2500	29.50	29.50
94	MARCH/AQUAMARINE	2500	29.50	29.50
94	MAY/EMERALD	2500	29.50	29.50
94	NOVEMBER/TOPAZ	2500	29.50	29.50
94	OCTOBER/ROSE STONE	2500	29.50	29.50
94	SEPTEMBER/SAPPHIRE	2500	29.50	29.50

K. KENNEDY   **CHERUBS COLLECTION**

YR	NAME	LIMIT	ISSUE	QUOTE
94	CHEERY CHERUB	500	169.50	169.50

B. BALL   **DOLLY DINGLE'S TRIP AROUND THE WORLD**

YR	NAME	LIMIT	ISSUE	QUOTE
94	DOLLY DINGLE	500	129.00	129.00

B. BALL   **FOUR SEASONS**

YR	NAME	LIMIT	ISSUE	QUOTE
94	BARBARA	500	299.25	299.25

B. BALL   **HOLIDAY DOLLS**

YR	NAME	LIMIT	ISSUE	QUOTE
94	CANDY CORN	2000	89.00	89.00
94	SANTA CLAWS	500	145.00	145.00

B. BALL   **INVITATION TO A PARTY**

YR	NAME	LIMIT	ISSUE	QUOTE
94	VANESSA	1000	124.50	124.50

M.I. HUMMEL   **M.I. HUMMEL DOLLS**

YR	NAME	LIMIT	ISSUE	QUOTE
*	ANDERL 1718	CL	*	100.00-200.00
*	BABY 1101 A-H	CL	*	100.00-200.00
*	BABY 1102 A-H	CL	*	100.00-200.00
*	BERTL 1503	CL	*	150.00-250.00
*	BERTL 1603	CL	*	150.00-200.00
*	BERTL 1703	CL	*	150.00-200.00
*	BRIEFTRAGER 1720	CL	*	150.00-200.00
*	CHRISTL 1715	CL	*	100.00-200.00
*	FELIX 1608	CL	*	150.00-200.00
*	FELIX 1708	CL	*	150.00-200.00
*	FRANZL 1812	CL	*	100.00-200.00
*	GANSELIESL 1717	CL	*	150.00-200.00
*	GRETL 1501	CL	*	150.00-250.00
*	GRETL 1601	CL	*	150.00-200.00
*	GRETL 1701	CL	*	150.00-200.00
*	HANSL 1504	CL	*	150.00-250.00
*	HANSL 1604	CL	*	150.00-200.00
*	HANSL 1704	CL	*	150.00-200.00
*	JACKL 1714	CL	*	100.00-200.00
*	JACKL 1806	CL	*	100.00-250.00
*	KONDITOR 1723	CL	*	150.00-200.00
*	MARIANDL 1713	CL	*	100.00-200.00
*	MARIANDL 1805	CL	*	100.00-250.00
*	MAX 1506	CL	*	150.00-250.00
*	MAX 1606	CL	*	150.00-200.00
*	MAX 1706	CL	*	150.00-200.00
*	MIRZL 1811	CL	*	100.00-200.00
*	NACHWACHTER 1719	CL	*	150.00-200.00
*	PETERLE 1710	CL	*	100.00-200.00
*	PETERLE 1810	CL	*	100.00-200.00
*	PUPPENMETTERCHEN 1725	CL	*	150.00-200.00
*	RADI-BUB 1724	CL	*	150.00-200.00
*	ROSL 1709	CL	*	100.00-200.00
*	ROSL 1801	CL	*	100.00-250.00
*	ROSL 1809	CL	*	100.00-200.00
*	RUDI 1802	CL	*	100.00-250.00
*	SCHORSCHL 1716	CL	*	100.00-200.00
*	SCHUSTERBUB	CL	*	150.00-200.00
*	SEPPL 1502	CL	*	150.00-250.00
*	SEPPL 1602	CL	*	150.00-200.00
*	SEPPL 1702	CL	*	150.00-200.00
*	SEPPPL 1804	CL	*	100.00-250.00
*	SKIHASERL 1722	CL	*	150.00-200.00
*	STRICKLIESL 1505	CL	*	150.00-250.00
*	STRICKLIESL 1605	CL	*	150.00-200.00
*	STRICKLIESL 1705	CL	*	150.00-200.00
*	VRONI 1803	CL	*	100.00-200.00
*	WANDERBUB 1507	CL	*	150.00-250.00
*	WANDERBUB 1607	CL	*	150.00-200.00
*	WANDERBUB 1707	CL	*	150.00-200.00
64	CHIMNEY SWEEP 1908	CL	55.00	100.00-150.00
64	FOR FATHER 1917	CL	55.00	100.00-150.00
64	GOOSE GIRL 1914	CL	55.00	100.00-150.00
64	GRETEL 1901	CL	55.00	100.00-150.00
64	HANSEL 1902	CL	55.00	100.00-150.00

Beautiful baby Caroline *is part of the "From the Heart" collection by the Ashton-Drake Galleries.*

Heather *has eyes shining bright with anticipation of her Sunday stroll. The doll, by designer Bette Ball, plays the tune "Let Me Be Your Teddy Bear."*

Among the "Parade of American Fashion," The Romantic Lady *dazzles collectors with the grace and beauty of a Southern belle. Produced by Ashton-Drake Galleries.*

Good things come in threes! Sheldon, Dacy *and* Brianna *are the work of artist Jan Hagara.*

YR	NAME	LIMIT	ISSUE	QUOTE
64	LITTLE KNITTER 1905	CL	55.00	100.00-150.00
64	LOST STOCKING 1926	CL	55.00	100.00-150.00
64	MERRY WANDERER 1906	CL	55.00	100.00-150.00
64	MERRY WANDERER 1925	CL	55.00	100.00-150.00
64	ON SECRET PATH 1928	CL	55.00	100.00-150.00
64	ROSA-BLUE BABY 1904/B	CL	45.00	75.00-100.00
64	ROSA-PINK BABY 1904/P	CL	45.00	75.00-100.00
64	SCHOOL BOY 1910	CL	55.00	100.00-150.00
64	SCHOOL GIRL 1909	CL	55.00	100.00-150.00
64	VISITING AN INVALID 1927	CL	55.00	100.00-150.00
M.I. HUMMEL		**M.I. HUMMEL PORCELAIN DOLLS**		
84	BIRTHDAY SERENADE/BOY	CL	225.00	250.00-300.00
84	BIRTHDAY SERENADE/GIRL	CL	225.00	250.00-300.00
84	ON HOLIDAY	CL	225.00	250.00-300.00
84	POSTMAN	CL	225.00	250.00-300.00
85	CARNIVAL	CL	225.00	250.00-300.00
85	EASTER GREETINGS	CL	225.00	250.00-300.00
85	LOST SHEEP	CL	225.00	275.00-358.00
85	SIGNS OF SPRING	CL	225.00	250.00-300.00
B. BALL		**MUSEUM COLLECTION**		
94	MASAKO	500	145.00	145.00
B. BALL		**NANA'S DARLINGS**		
94	COLLEEN	1000	195.00	195.00
94	MONIQUE	1000	195.00	195.00
B. BALL		**PARTY TIME**		
93	SCARLETT	1000	259.50	259.50
B. BALL		**PERFECT PETS**		
93	BOBBI SOCKS	1000	119.25	119.25
93	LIL' HONEYSUCKLE	500	124.50	124.50
93	PENNY PUSS	1000	200.00	200.00
93	SNOWFLAKE	250	129.00	129.00
93	WHISPURR	1000	150.00	150.00
94	CATSANOVA	500	129.00	129.00
R. KENNEDY		**RED HEADS**		
93	GINGER MUFFIN	500	220.00	220.00
94	CARROT TOP	500	129.00	129.00
94	SHARON & DARREN O'HAIR	500	99.00	99.00
K. KENNEDY		**SITTING PRETTY**		
94	SOMMER	500	139.50	139.50
B. BALL		**STERLING SERIES**		
93	TAYLOR	1000	215.00	215.00
K. KENNEDY		**STOLEN KISSES**		
93	KISSES	500	225.00	225.00
B. BALL		**SWEET ROMANTICS**		
94	DEIDRE	500	179.50	179.50
K. KENNEDY		**TINY TOT CLOWNS**		
94	BETH	2000	45.00	45.00
94	JULIE	2000	45.00	45.00
94	KAYLEE	2000	45.00	45.00
94	LESLIE	2000	45.00	45.00
94	NADINE	2000	45.00	45.00
94	SHANNON	2000	45.00	45.00
B. BALL		**VICTORIA ASHLEA ORIGINALS**		
*	CHARITY-912244	CL	70.00	70.00
82	CHARLEEN-912094	CL	65.00	65.00
82	CLOWN JOLLY-912181	CL	70.00	70.00
82	HOLLY-901233	CL	160.00	200.00
82	MARIE-901232	CL	100.00	100.00
82	TRUDY-901232	CL	100.00	100.00
84	AMELIA-933006	CL	100.00	100.00
84	BARBARA-901108	CL	57.00	110.00
84	CLAUDE-901032	CL	110.00	225.00
84	CLAUDETTE-901033	CL	110.00	225.00
84	CLOWN-901136	CL	90.00	120.00
84	DEBORAH-901107	CL	220.00	400.00
84	DIANA-901119	CL	55.00	135.00
84	HENRIETTA-901036	CL	100.00	200.00
84	JAMIE-912061	CL	65.00	100.00
84	JEANNIE-901062	CL	200.00	550.00
84	LAURA-901106	CL	300.00	575.00
84	SABINA-901155	CL	75.00	*
84	SHEILA-912060	CL	75.00	135.00
84	STEPHANIE-933012	CL	115.00	115.00
84	TOBIE-912023	CL	30.00	30.00
84	VICTORIA-901068	CL	200.00	1500.00
85	ADELE-901172	CL	155.00	275.00

YR	NAME	LIMIT	ISSUE	QUOTE
85	CHAUNCEY-912085	CL	75.00	110.00
85	CLAIRE-901158	1000	115.00	160.00
85	CLOWN CASEY-912078	CL	40.00	40.00
85	CLOWN CHRISTIE-912084	CL	60.00	90.00
85	CLOWN JODY-912079	CL	100.00	150.00
85	DOROTHY-901157	CL	130.00	275.00
85	GARNET-901183	CL	160.00	295.00
85	LYNN-912144	CL	90.00	135.00
85	MARY-912126	CL	60.00	90.00
85	MICHELLE-912066	CL	100.00	225.00
85	MILLIE-912135	CL	70.00	125.00
85	PHYLLIS-912067	CL	60.00	60.00
85	ROSALIND-912087	CL	145.00	225.00
85	ROXANNE-901174	CL	155.00	275.00
86	ASHLEY-912147	CL	125.00	125.00
86	BABY BROCK BEIGE DRESS-912103	CL	60.00	60.00
86	BABY COURTNEY-912124	CL	120.00	120.00
86	BABY LAUREN PINK-912086	CL	120.00	120.00
86	CAT/KITTY CHEERFUL GR DR-901179	2500	60.00	60.00
86	CLOWN CALYPSO-912104	CL	70.00	70.00
86	CLOWN CAT CADWALADER-912132	CL	55.00	55.00
86	CLOWN CHRISTABEL-912095	CL	100.00	150.00
86	CLOWN CLARABELLA-912096	CL	80.00	80.00
86	CLOWN CLARISSA-912123	CL	75.00	110.00
86	CLOWN CYD-912093	CL	70.00	70.00
86	CLOWN KITTEN CLEO-912133	CL	50.00	50.00
86	CLOWN LOLLIPOP-912127	CL	125.00	225.00
86	GINA-901176	500	300.00	300.00
86	GIRL FROG FREDA-912105	CL	20.00	20.00
86	GOOGLEY GERMAN ASTRID-912109	CL	60.00	60.00
86	PATTY ACRTIC FLOWER PRINT-901185	1000	140.00	140.00
86	PEPPER RUST DR/APPR-901184	CL	125.00	200.00
87	ALICE-901212	CL	120.00	160.00
87	AMANDA POUTY-901209	CL	150.00	215.00
87	BABY DOLL-912184	CL	75.00	75.00
87	BABY LINDSAY-912190	CL	80.00	80.00
87	BONNIE POUTY-901207	2500	100.00	100.00
87	BRIDE ALLISON-901218	1500	180.00	180.00
87	CAROLINE-912191	CL	80.00	80.00
87	CATANOVA-901227	CL	75.00	75.00
87	CATLIN-901228	1500	260.00	260.00
87	CHRISTINE-912168	CL	75.00	75.00
87	CLEMENTINE-901226	CL	75.00	75.00
87	CLOWN CHAMPAGNE-912180	CL	95.00	95.00
87	DOMINIQUE-901219	CL	170.00	225.00
87	DOREEN-912198	2000	75.00	75.00
87	JACQUELINE-912192	CL	80.00	80.00
87	JESSICA-912195	CL	120.00	135.00
87	JOY-912155	CL	50.00	50.00
87	JULIA-912174	CL	80.00	80.00
87	KITTLE CAT-912167	CL	55.00	55.00
87	KITTY CUDDLES-901201	CL	65.00	65.00
87	LILLIAN-901199	CL	85.00	100.00
87	MEGAN-912148	CL	70.00	70.00
87	MICHELLE-901222	CL	90.00	90.00
87	NICOLE-901225	CL	575.00	575.00
87	SARAH-901220	1500	350.00	350.00
87	SOPHIA-912173	CL	40.00	40.00
87	SUZANNE-901201	CL	65.00	65.00
87	TASHA-901221	CL	115.00	130.00
87	TIFFANY POUTY-901211	CL	120.00	160.00
88	AMANDA-912246	1000	180.00	180.00
88	ANGELICA-912204	CL	150.00	150.00
88	ANNE-912213	CL	130.00	150.00
88	APRIL-901239	1000	225.00	225.00
88	ASHLEY-901235	CL	110.00	110.00
88	BABY DARYL-912200	CL	85.00	85.00
88	BABY JENNIFER-912210	CL	75.00	75.00
88	BABY KATIE-912222	5000	70.00	70.00
88	BERNICE-901245	CL	90.00	90.00
88	BETTY DOLL-912220	1000	90.00	90.00
88	BRANDON-901234	1500	90.00	90.00
88	BRITTANY-912207	CL	130.00	145.00
88	CAMPBELL KID/BOY-758701	CL	13.80	13.80
88	CAMPBELL KID/GIRL-758700	CL	13.80	13.80
88	CAT MAUDE-901247	2500	85.00	85.00

YR	NAME	LIMIT	ISSUE	QUOTE
88	CATHERINE-901242	500	240.00	240.00
88	CHRISTINA-901229	CL	350.00	400.00
88	CLOWN COTTON CANDY-912199	CL	67.00	67.00
88	CRYSTAL-912226	2000	75.00	75.00
88	DIANA-912218	1000	270.00	270.00
88	ELIZABETH-901214	1500	90.00	90.00
88	ELLEN-901246	CL	100.00	100.00
88	ERIN-901241	1000	170.00	170.00
88	HEATHER-912247	1000	135.00	135.00
88	JENNIFER-901248	CL	150.00	150.00
88	JENNIFER-912221	CL	80.00	80.00
88	JESSE-912231	1000	110.00	110.00
88	KAREN-912205	CL	200.00	250.00
88	LAURA-912225	CL	135.00	135.00
88	LAUREN-912212	CL	110.00	110.00
88	MARITTA SPANISH-912224	CL	140.00	140.00
88	MELISSA-901230	CL	350.00	400.00
88	MELISSA-912208	CL	125.00	125.00
88	PAULETTE-901244	CL	90.00	90.00
88	POLLY-912206	CL	100.00	125.00
88	RENAE-912245	CL	120.00	120.00
88	SARAH W/PILLOW-912219	1500	105.00	105.00
88	STEPHANIE-912238	CL	200.00	200.00
88	SUSAN-901242	CL	100.00	100.00
88	WHITNEY BLK-912232	1000	62.50	62.50
89	ALEXA-912214	1500	195.00	195.00
89	ALEXANDRIA-912273	500	275.00	275.00
89	ASHLEA-901250	1000	550.00	550.00
89	DIANA BRIDE-912277	1000	180.00	180.00
89	EMILY-912303	1000	150.00	150.00
89	HOLLY-901254	1000	180.00	180.00
89	HOPE BABY W/PILLOW-912292	1000	110.00	110.00
89	JINGLES-912271	CL	60.00	60.00
89	LICORICE-912290	1000	75.00	75.00
89	LINDSEY-901263	1500	100.00	100.00
89	LISA-912275	CL	160.00	160.00
89	LONI-912276	1200	125.00	125.00
89	MARGOT-912269	CL	110.00	110.00
89	MARIA-912265	CL	90.00	90.00
89	MEGAN-901260	2000	120.00	120.00
89	MERRY-912249	1000	200.00	200.00
89	MISSY-912283	1000	100.00	100.00
89	NANCY-912266	CL	110.00	110.00
89	PAMELA-912302	1000	95.00	95.00
89	REBECCA-901258	1000	250.00	250.00
89	SARA-912279	1000	175.00	175.00
89	SIGRID-912282	2000	145.00	145.00
89	SUZANNE-912286	2000	120.00	120.00
89	SUZY-912295	1000	110.00	110.00
89	TERRY-912281	2000	145.00	145.00
89	VALERIE-901255	1000	175.00	175.00
89	VANESSA-912272	CL	110.00	110.00
90	AMY-901262	1000	110.00	110.00
90	ANNABELLE-912278	2000	200.00	200.00
90	BETTINA-912310	1000	100.00	100.00
90	FLUFFER-912293	1000	135.00	135.00
90	HEATHER-912322	2000	150.00	150.00
90	HEIDI-901266	2000	150.00	150.00
90	HELGA-912337	1000	325.00	325.00
90	JILLIAN-912323	2000	150.00	150.00
90	JUSTINE-901256	1500	200.00	200.00
90	KELLY-912331	1000	95.00	95.00
90	KIMBERLY-912341	1000	140.00	140.00
90	MATTHEW-901251	2000	100.00	100.00
90	MRS. KATZ-912301	1000	140.00	140.00
90	PAULA-912316	2500	100.00	100.00
90	PRISCILLA-912300	1000	185.00	185.00
90	REBECCA-901258	1000	250.00	250.00
90	ROBIN-912321	2000	160.00	160.00
90	SAMANTHA-912314	2000	185.00	185.00
90	SHEENA-912338	1000	115.00	1151.00
90	STEPHANIE-912312	2000	150.00	150.00
90	SUSIE-912328	2000	115.00	115.00
90	TRACIE-912315	2500	125.00	125.00
92	ALICIA-912388	500	135.00	135.00
92	ALLISON-912358	1000	160.00	160.00

YR	NAME	LIMIT	ISSUE	QUOTE
92	ANGELICA-912339	1000	145.00	145.00
92	ASHLEY-911004	2000	99.00	99.00
92	BETSY-912390	500	150.00	150.00
92	CINDY-912384	1000	185.00	185.00
92	HILARY-912353	1000	130.00	130.00
92	HOLLEY BELLE-912380	500	125.00	125.00
92	KELLY-912361	1000	160.00	160.00
92	MARJORIE-912357	1000	180.00	180.00
92	TAMIKA-912382	500	185.00	185.00
92	TRUDIE-912391	500	135.00	135.00
88	GOLDILOCKS-912234	1500	65.00	65.00
88	MOLLY-912211	1000	75.00	75.00
88	MORGAN-912239	1000	75.00	75.00
88	SANDY-901240	1000	115.00	115.00
88	SNOW WHITE-912235	CL	65.00	65.00
89	CANDACE-912288	1500	70.00	70.00
89	CLAUDIA-901257	1000	225.00	225.00
89	JIMMY W/PILLOW-912291	1000	165.00	165.00
89	JOY-912290	1500	110.00	110.00
89	KRISTIN-912285	1000	90.00	90.00
89	MARISSA-901252	CL	225.00	225.00
89	MELANIE-912284	2000	135.00	135.00
89	MELINDA-912309	1000	70.00	70.00
89	PINKY CLOWN-912268	1000	70.00	70.00
89	TAMMY-912265	CL	110.00	110.00
90	ALICE-912296	1500	65.00	65.00
90	AMIE-912313	1000	150.00	150.00
90	ANGELA-912324	2000	130.00	130.00
90	ANNETTE-912333	1500	85.00	85.00
90	APRIL BIRTHSTONE DOLL-912253	5000	25.00	25.00
90	AUGUST BIRTHSTONE DOLL-912257	5000	25.00	25.00
90	BARYSHNICAT-912298	CL	25.00	25.00
90	BRANDY-912304	1000	150.00	150.00
90	CAROLYN-901261	1000	200.00	200.00
90	DEBRA-912319	2000	120.00	120.00
90	DECEMBER BIRTHSTONE DOLL-912261	5000	25.00	25.00
90	FEBRUARY BIRTHSTONE DOLL-912251	5000	25.00	25.00
90	GIGI-912306	1000	15.00	150.00
90	GINNY-912287	1000	140.00	140.00
90	HELENE-901249	CL	160.00	160.00
90	JACQUELINE-912329	2000	136.00	136.00
90	JANUARY BIRTHSTONE DOLL-212250	5000	25.00	25.00
90	JOANNE-912307	1000	150.00	150.00
90	JULIA-912334	1500	85.00	85.00
90	JULY BIRTHSTONE DOLL-912256	5000	25.00	25.00
90	JUNE BIRTHSTONE DOLL-912255	5000	25.00	25.00
90	MARCH BIRTHSTONE DOLL-912252	5000	25.00	25.00
90	MARSHMALLOW-912294	1000	75.00	75.00
90	MAY BIRTHSTONE DOLL-912254	5000	25.00	25.00
90	MONICA-912336	1000	100.00	100.00
90	MONIQUE-912335	1500	85.00	85.00
90	NOVEMBER BIRTHSTONE DOLL-912260	5000	25.00	25.00
90	OCTOBER BIRTHSTONE DOLL-912259	5000	25.00	25.00
90	PENNY-912325	2000	130.00	130.00
90	SEPTEMBER BIRTHSTONE DOLL-912258	5000	25.00	25.00
90	SHERI-912305	1500	115.00	115.00
90	TASHA-912299	CL	25.00	25.00
90	TIFFANY-912326	2000	180.00	180.00
92	BRITTANY-912365	1000	140.00	140.00
92	CAROL-912387	1000	140.00	140.00
92	CASSANDRA-912355	1000	165.00	165.00
92	DENISE-912362	1000	145.00	145.00
92	DOTTIE-912393	1000	160.00	160.00
92	IRIS-912389	500	165.00	165.00
92	JENNY-912374	1000	150.00	150.00
92	KRIS-912345	1000	160.00	160.00
92	LAUREN-912363	1000	190.00	190.00
92	MARGARET-912354	1000	150.00	150.00
92	MICHELLE-912381	500	175.00	175.00
92	NOELLE-912360	1000	165.00	165.00
92	SHERISE-912383	500	145.00	145.00
92	SUSAN-912346	1000	325.00	325.00
92	TONI-912367	1000	120.00	120.00
92	TULIP-912385	500	145.00	145.00
92	WENDY-912330	1000	125.00	125.00

YR	NAME	LIMIT	ISSUE	QUOTE
E. WOODHOUSE			**VICTORIA'S JUBILEE**	
92	VICTORIA'S JUBILEE	YR	295.00	295.00

GORHAM

YR	NAME	LIMIT	ISSUE	QUOTE
B. PORT		**BEVERLY PORT DESIGNER COLLECTION**		
87	CHRISTOPHER PAUL BEARKIN, 10 IN.	2500	95.00	150.00
87	KRISTOBEAR KRINGLE, 17 IN.	2500	200.00	295.00
87	MOLLY MELINDA BEARKIN, 10 IN.	2500	95.00	150.00
87	SILVER BELL, 17 IN.	2500	175.00	275.00
87	TEDWARD JONATHAN BEARKIN, 10 IN.	2500	95.00	150.00
87	TEDWINA KIMELINA BEARKIN, 10 IN.	2500	95.00	150.00
88	BAERY MAB, 9 1/2 IN.	2500	110.00	150.00
88	HOLLYBEARY KRINGLE, 15 IN.	2500	350.00	395.00
88	MISS EMILY, 18 IN.	2500	350.00	450.00
88	T.R., 28 1/2 IN.	1000	400.00	600.00
88	THE AMAZING CALLIOPE MERRIWEATHER 17 IN.	2500	275.00	425.00
88	THEODORE B. BEAR, 14 IN.	2500	175.00	195.00
B. GERARDI			**BONNETS & BOWS**	
88	ALICIA	2500	385.00	800.00
88	ALLESSANDRA	2500	195.00	335.75-436.78
88	ANNEMARIE	2500	195.00	335.75-436.48
88	BELINDA	2500	195.00	335.75-436.48
88	BETHANY	2500	385.00	1350.00
88	BETTINA	2500	285.00	420.75-546.98
88	ELLIE	2500	285.00	420.75-546.98
88	FRANCIE	1000	625.00	760.75-988.98
88	JESSE	1000	525.00	795.00
88	LISETTE	2500	285.00	420.75-546.98
D. VALENZA			**BRIDE DOLLS**	
93	VICTORIAN BRIDE	9500	295.00	295.00
C. SHAFER			**CAROUSEL DOLLS**	
93	RIBBONS AND ROSES	OP	95.00	95.00
L. DILEO		**CELEBRATIONS OF CHILDHOOD**		
92	HAPPY BIRTHDAY AMY	OP	160.00	160.00
D. VALENZA			**CHILDHOOD MEMORIES**	
91	AMANDA	OP	98.00	98.00
91	JENNIFER	OP	98.00	98.00
91	JESSICA	OP	98.00	98.00
91	KIMBERLY	OP	98.00	98.00
S. STONE AIKEN			**CHILDREN OF CHRISTMAS**	
89	CLARA, 16 IN.	YR	325.00	675.00
90	NATALIE, 16 IN.	YR	350.00	335.75-436.48
91	EMILY, 16 IN.	1500	375.00	375.00
92	VIRGINIA	1500	375.00	375.00
R./L. SCHRUBBE			**CHILDREN WITH PETS**	
93	PLAY BALL	OP	98.00	98.00
S. STONE AIKEN			**DAYDREAMER DOLLS**	
92	HEATHER'S DAYDREAM	OP	119.00	119.00
R. SCHRUBBE			**DAYS OF THE WEEK**	
92	FRIDAY'S CHILD	OP	98.00	98.00
92	MONDAY'S CHILD	OP	98.00	98.00
92	SATURDAY'S CHILD	OP	98.00	98.00
92	SUNDAY'S CHILD	OP	98.00	98.00
92	THURSDAY'S CHILD	OP	98.00	98.00
92	TUESDAY'S CHILD	OP	98.00	98.00
92	WEDNESDAY'S CHILD	OP	98.00	98.00
J. PILALLIS			**DOLLIE AND ME**	
91	DOLLIE'S FIRST STEPS	OP	160.00	160.00
*			**DOLLS OF THE MONTH**	
91	MISS APRIL	OP	79.00	79.00
91	MISS AUGUST	OP	79.00	79.00
91	MISS DECEMBER	OP	79.00	79.00
91	MISS FEBRUARY	OP	79.00	79.00
91	MISS JANUARY	OP	79.00	79.00
91	MISS JULY	OP	79.00	79.00
91	MISS JUNE	OP	79.00	79.00
91	MISS MARCH	OP	79.00	79.00
91	MISS MAY	OP	79.00	79.00
91	MISS NOVEMBER	OP	79.00	79.00
91	MISS OCTOBER	OP	79.00	79.00
91	MISS SEPTEMBER	OP	79.00	79.00
YOUNG/ GERARDI			**GIFT OF DREAMS**	
91	CHRISTINA (CHRISTMAS)	500	695.00	695.00
91	ELIZABETH	1000	495.00	495.00
91	KATHERINE	1000	495.00	495.00
91	MELISSA	1000	495.00	495.00
91	SAMANTHA	1000	495.00	495.00

YR NAME	LIMIT	ISSUE	QUOTE
S. STONE AIKEN		**GIFTS OF THE GARDEN**	
91 ALISA	2500	125.00	125.00
91 DEBORAH	2500	125.00	125.00
91 HOLLY (CHRISTMAS)	YR	150.00	150.00
91 IRENE	2500	125.00	125.00
91 JOELLE (CHRISTMAS)	YR	150.00	195.00
91 LAUREN	2500	125.00	125.00
91 MARIA	2500	125.00	125.00
91 PRISCILLA	2500	125.00	125.00
91 VALERIE	2500	125.00	125.00
AIKEN/ MATTHEWS		**GORHAM BABY DOLL COLLECTION**	
87 CHRISTENING DAY	CL	245.00	245.00
87 LESLIE	CL	245.00	285.00
87 MATTHEW	CL	245.00	285.00
*		**GORHAM DOLLS**	
82 BABY IN WHITE DRESS, 18 IN.	CL	250.00	375.00-400.00
82 M. ANTON, 12 IN.	CL	125.00	150.00-200.00
82 MLLE. MARSELLA, 12 IN.	CL	125.00	275.00-345.00
82 MLLE. YVONNE, 12 IN.	CL	125.00	375.00-450.00
81 ALEXANDRIA, 18 IN.	CL	200.00	550.00-600.00
81 CECILE, 16 IN.	CL	200.00	875.00-950.00
81 CHRISTINA, 16 IN.	CL	200.00	425.00-475.00
81 CHRISTOPHER, 19 IN.	CL	200.00	850.00
81 DANIELLE, 14 IN.	CL	150.00	300.00-350.00
81 ELENA, 14 IN.	CL	150.00	650.00-750.00
81 JILIAN, 16 IN.	CL	200.00	425.00-475.00
81 MELINDA, 14 IN.	CL	150.00	300.00-350.00
81 ROSEMOND, 18 IN.	CL	250.00	525.00-625.00
81 STEPHANIE, 18 IN.	CL	200.00	2050.00-2150.00
82 BABY IN APRICOT DRESS, 16 IN.	CL	175.00	325.00-350.00
82 BABY IN BLUE DRESS, 12 IN.	CL	150.00	300.00-350.00
82 BENJAMIN, 18 IN.	CL	200.00	400.00-550.00
82 CORRINE, 18 IN.	CL	250.00	500.00-525.00
82 CORRINE, 21 IN.	CL	250.00	500.00-525.00
82 ELLICE, 18 IN.	CL	200.00	400.00-550.00
82 JEREMY, 23 IN.	CL	300.00	625.00-750.00
82 KRISTIN, 23 IN.	CL	300.00	575.00-625.00
82 MELANIE, 23 IN.	CL	300.00	625.00-725.00
82 MLLE. JEANETTE, 12 IN.	CL	125.00	195.00-225.00
82 MLLE. LUCILLE, 12 IN.	CL	125.00	350.00-450.00
82 MLLE. MONIQUE, 12 IN.	CL	125.00	250.00-305.00
83 JENNIFER, 19 IN. BRIDAL DOLL	CL	325.00	725.00-750.00
85 ALEXANDER, 19 IN.	CL	275.00	350.00-425.00
85 AMELIA, 19 IN.	CL	275.00	350.00-425.00
85 GABRIELLE, 19 IN.	CL	225.00	350.00-375.00
85 LINDA, 19 IN.	CL	275.00	403.75-524.88
85 NANETTE, 19 IN.	CL	275.00	340.00-442.00
85 ODETTE, 19 IN.	CL	250.00	382.50-497.25
86 ALISSA	CL	245.00	350.00-375.00
86 EMILY, 14 IN.	CL	175.00	318.75-414.38
86 FLEUR, 19 IN.	CL	300.00	350.00-375.00
86 JESSICA	CL	195.00	350.00-400.00
86 JULIA, 16 IN.	CL	225.00	350.00-375.00
86 LAUREN, 14 IN.	CL	175.00	325.00-375.00
86 MEREDITH	CL	295.00	280.00-425.00
87 JULIET	CL	325.00	335.75-436.48
*		**HOLLY HOBBIE**	
83 BLUE GIRL, 14 IN.	CL	80.00	325.00
83 BLUE GIRL, 18 IN.	CL	115.00	395.00
83 CHRISTMAS MORNING, 14 IN.	CL	80.00	275.00
83 HEATHER, 14 IN.	CL	80.00	275.00
83 LITTLE AMY, 14 IN.	CL	80.00	275.00
83 ROBBIE, 14 IN.	CL	80.00	275.00
83 SUNDAY'S BEST, 18 IN.	CL	115.00	350.00
83 SWEET VALENTINE, 16 IN.	CL	100.00	350.00
83 YESTERDAY'S MEMORIES, 18 IN.	CL	125.00	450.00
*		**HOLLY HOBBIE CHILDHOOD MEMORIES**	
85 BEST FRIENDS	CL	45.00	125.00
85 CHRISTMAS WISHES	CL	45.00	125.00
85 FIRST DAY OF SCHOOL	CL	45.00	125.00
85 MOTHER'S HELPER	CL	45.00	125.00
*		**HOLLY HOBBIE FOR ALL SEASONS**	
84 FALL HOLLY, 12 IN.	CL	42.50	165.75-215.48
84 SPRING HOLLY, 12 IN.	CL	42.50	195.00
84 SUMMER HOLLY, 12 IN.	CL	42.50	165.75-215.48
84 WINTER HOLLY, 12 IN.	CL	42.50	195.00

YR NAME	LIMIT	ISSUE	QUOTE
B. GERARDI		**JOYFUL YEARS**	
89 KATRINA	1000	295.00	295.00
89 WILLIAM	1000	295.00	295.00
KEZI		**KEZI DOLL FOR ALL SEASONS**	
85 ADRIENNE, 16 IN.	CL	135.00	500.00
85 AMBER, 16 IN.	CL	135.00	500.00
85 ARIEL, 16 IN.	CL	135.00	500.00
85 AUBREY, 16 IN.	CL	135.00	500.00
KEZI		**KEZI GOLDEN GIFTS**	
84 CHARITY, 16 IN.	CL	85.00	175.00
84 FAITH, 18 IN.	CL	95.00	195.00
84 FELICITY, 18 IN.	CL	95.00	195.00
84 GRACE, 16 IN.	CL	85.00	175.00
84 HOPE, 16 IN.	CL	85.00	175.00
84 MERRIE, 16 IN.	CL	85.00	175.00
84 PATIENCE, 18 IN.	CL	95.00	195.00
84 PRUDENCE, 18 IN.	CL	85.00	175.00
R./L. SCHRUBBE		**KIDS WITH STUFFED TOYS**	
93 TARA AND TEDDY	OP	119.00	119.00
S. STONE AIKEN		**LEGENDARY HEROINES**	
91 GUINEVERE	1500	245.00	245.00
91 JANE EYRE	1500	245.00	245.00
91 JULIET	1500	245.00	245.00
91 LARA	1500	245.00	245.00
S. STONE AIKEN		**LES BELLES BEBES COLLECTION**	
91 CHERIE	1500	375.00	318.75-414.38
91 DESIREE	1500	375.00	318.75-414.38
93 CAMILLE	1500	375.00	375.00
S. STONE AIKEN		**LIMITED EDITION DOLLS**	
82 ALLISON, 19 IN.	1000	300.00	4700.00-4900.00
83 ASHLEY, 19 IN.	2500	350.00	800.00-1200.00
84 HOLLY (CHRISTMAS), 19 IN.	2500	300.00	850.00-875.00
84 NICOLE, 19 IN.	2500	350.00	600.00-1000.00
85 JOY (CHRISTMAS), 19 IN.	2500	350.00	650.00-900.00
85 LYDIA, 19 IN.	1500	550.00	900.00-1800.00
86 NOEL (CHRISTMAS), 19 IN.	2500	400.00	600.00-800.00
87 JACQUELINE, 19 IN.	1500	500.00	550.00-750.00
87 MERRIE (CHRISTMAS), 19 IN.	2500	500.00	600.00-650.00
88 ANDREW, 19 IN.	1000	475.00	600.00-650.00
88 CHRISTA (CHRISTMAS), 19 IN.	2500	550.00	900.00-1500.00
90 AMEY (10TH ANNIVERSARY EDITION)	CL	650.00	1100.00
S. STONE AIKEN		**LIMITED EDITION SISTER SET**	
88 KATELIN	ST	*	*
88 KATHLEEN	1000	550.00	750.00
S. STONE AIKEN		**LITTLE WOMEN**	
83 AMY, 16 IN.	CL	225.00	575.00
83 BETH, 16 IN.	CL	225.00	575.00
83 JO, 19 IN.	CL	275.00	675.00
83 MEG, 19 IN.	CL	275.00	695.00
L. DI LEO		**LITTLEST ANGEL DOLLS**	
92 MERRIEL	OP	49.50	49.50
93 NOELLE	OP	49.50	49.50
L. GORDON		**PILLOW BABY DOLLS**	
93 BABY IN BLUE	OP	39.00	39.00
93 BABY IN PINK	OP	39.00	39.00
93 BABY IN YELLOW	OP	39.00	39.00
S. STONE AIKEN		**PRECIOUS AS PEARLS**	
86 COLETTE	2500	400.00	1275.00-1657.50
87 CHARLOTTE	2500	425.00	795.00
88 CHLOE	2500	525.00	925.00
89 CASSANDRA	1500	525.00	1105.00-1436.50
R./L. SCHRUBBE		**PUPPY LOVE DOLLS**	
92 KATIE AND KYLE	OP	*	225.00-225.00
*		**RAGGEDY ANN & ANDY**	
93 RAGGEDY ANN & ANDY	9500	119.00	119.00
B. GERARDI		**SMALL WONDERS**	
88 MADELINE	1000	365.00	310.25-403.33
88 MARGUERITE	1000	425.00	361.25-469.63
88 PATINA	1000	265.00	265.00
S. STONE AIKEN		**SOUTHERN BELLES**	
85 AMANDA, 19 IN.	CL	300.00	1232.50-1602.25
86 VERONICA, 19 IN.	CL	325.00	750.00
87 RACHEL, 19 IN.	CL	375.00	675.00
88 CASSIE, 19 IN.	CL	500.00	625.00
E. WORRELL		**SPECIAL MOMENTS**	
91 BABY'S FIRST CHRISTMAS	OP	125.00	125.00

YR	NAME	LIMIT	ISSUE	QUOTE
92	BABY'S CHRISTENING	OP	135.00	135.00
92	BABY'S FIRST BIRTHDAY	OP	135.00	135.00
92	BABY'S FIRST STEPS	OP	135.00	135.00
S. NAPPO			**THE FRIENDSHIP DOLLS**	
91	ANGELA-THE ITALIAN TRAVELER	OP	98.00	98.00
91	MEAGAN-THE IRISH TRAVELER	OP	98.00	98.00
91	PEGGY-THE AMERICAN TRAVELER	OP	98.00	98.00
91	KINUKO-THE JAPANESE TRAVELER	OP	98.00	98.00
L. DI LEO			**TIMES TO TREASURE**	
93	CRADLETIME	OP	195.00	195.00
93	PLAYTIME	OP	195.00	195.00
92	BEDTIME	OP	195.00	195.00
92	STORYTIME	OP	195.00	195.00
P. VALENTINE			**VALENTINE LADIES**	
87	ANNABELLA	2500	145.00	395.00
87	ELIZABETH	2500	145.00	450.00
87	JANE	2500	145.00	350.00
87	LEE ANN	2500	145.00	325.00
87	MARIANNA	2500	160.00	400.00
87	PATRICE	2500	145.00	325.00
87	REBECCA	2500	145.00	325.00
87	ROSANNE	2500	145.00	325.00
87	SYLVIA	2500	160.00	395.00
88	FELICIA	2500	225.00	335.75-436.48
88	JUDITH ANNE	2500	195.00	325.00
88	MARIA THERESA	2500	225.00	425.00
88	PRICILLA	2500	195.00	325.00
89	JULIANNA	2500	225.00	275.00
89	ROSE	2500	225.00	275.00
B. GERARDI			**VICTORIAN CAMEO COLLECTION**	
90	VICTORIA	1500	375.00	375.00
91	ALEXANDRA	1500	375.00	375.00
S. STONE AIKEN			**VICTORIAN CHILDREN**	
92	SARAH'S TEA TIME	1000	495.00	495.00
J. PILLALIS			**VICTORIAN FLOWER DOLLS**	
93	ROSE	OP	98.00	98.00

H & G STUDIOS

YR	NAME	LIMIT	ISSUE	QUOTE
B. BURKE			**BIRTHDAY PARTY**	
90	SUZIE	500	695.00	695.00
B. BURKE			**BRENDA BURKE DOLLS**	
89	ADELAINE	25	1795.00	3600.00
89	ALEXANDRA	125	995.00	2000.00
89	ALICIA	125	895.00	1800.00
89	AMANDA	25	1995.00	6000.00
89	ANGELICA	50	1495.00	3000.00
89	ARABELLE	500	695.00	990.00
89	BEATRICE	85	2395.00	2395.00
89	BETHANY	45	2995.00	2995.00
89	BRITTANY	75	2695.00	2695.00
90	BELINDA	12	3695.00	3695.00
91	CHARLOTTE	20	2395.00	2395.00
91	CLARISSA	15	3595.00	3595.00
91	SLEIGH RIDE	20	3695.00	3695.00
91	TENDER LOVE	25	3295.00	3295.00
92	DOROTHEA	500	395.00	395.00
B. BURKE			**CHILDHOOD MEMORIES**	
89	EARLY DAYS	95	2595.00	2595.00
91	PLAYTIME	35	2795.00	2795.00
B. BURKE			**DANCING THROUGH THE AGES**	
90	MINUET	95	2495.00	2495.00
B. BURKE			**THE FOUR SEASONS**	
90	SPRING	125	1995.00	1995.00

HAMILTON COLLECTION

YR	NAME	LIMIT	ISSUE	QUOTE
A. WILLIAMS			**ABBIE WILLIAMS DOLL COLLECTION**	
92	MOLLY	2500	155.00	155.00
B. PARKER			**BABY PORTRAIT DOLLS**	
91	MELISSA	OP	135.00	135.00
92	BETHANY	OP	135.00	135.00
92	JANNA	OP	135.00	135.00
C. BEATH ORAN			**BELLES OF THE COUNTRYSIDE**	
92	ERIN	OP	135.00	135.00
*			**BRIDE DOLLS**	
91	PORTRAIT OF INNOCENCE	OP	195.00	195.00
9P	PORTRAIT OF LOVELINESS	OP	195.00	195.00

YR	NAME	LIMIT	ISSUE	QUOTE
C. WOODIE		**CENTRAL PARK SKATERS**		
91	CENTRAL PARK SKATERS	OP	245.00	245.00
C.W. DERRICK		**CONNIE WALSER DERRICK BABY DOLL**		
90	JESSICA	OP	155.00	250.00
91	AMANDA	OP	155.00	155.00
91	ANDREW	OP	155.00	155.00
91	SARA	OP	155.00	155.00
K. MCKEE		**DOLLS BY KAY MCKEE**		
92	SHY VIOLET	OP	135.00	135.00
A. ELEKFY		**DOLLS OF AMERICA'S COLONIAL HERITAGE**		
86	KATRINA	OP	55.00	55.00
86	NICOLE	OP	55.00	55.00
87	COLLEEN	OP	55.00	55.00
87	MARIA	OP	55.00	55.00
87	PRISCILLA	OP	55.00	55.00
88	GRETCHEN	OP	55.00	55.00
H. KISH		**HELEN KISH DOLLS**		
91	ASHLEY	OP	135.00	135.00
92	ELIZABETH	OP	135.00	135.00
92	HANNAH	OP	135.00	135.00
*		**I LOVE LUCY**		
90	LUCY	OP	95.00	95.00
91	RICKY	OP	95.00	95.00
C. WOODIE		**INTERNATIONAL CHILDREN**		
91	ANASTASIA	OP	49.50	49.50
91	ANGELINA	OP	49.50	49.50
91	ANGELINA	OP	49.50	49.50
91	MIKO	OP	49.50	49.50
92	LIAN	OP	49.50	49.50
92	LISA	OP	49.50	49.50
92	MONIQUE	OP	49.50	49.50
J. ESTEBAN		**J. ESTEBAN DOLLS**		
91	REBECCA	OP	155.00	155.00
92	EMILY	OP	155.00	155.00
J. ZIDJUNAS		**JANE ZIDJUNAS PARTY DOLLS**		
91	KELLY	OP	135.00	135.00
92	KATIE	OP	135.00	135.00
J. ZIDJUNAS		**JANE ZIDJUNAS TODDLER DOLLS**		
91	JENNIFER	OP	135.00	135.00
91	MEGAN	OP	135.00	135.00
92	AMY	OP	135.00	135.00
92	KIMBERLY	OP	135.00	135.00
L. COBABE		**LAURA COBABE DOLLS**		
92	AMBER	OP	195.00	195.00
*		**MAUD HUMPHREY BOGART DOLLS**		
92	PLAYING BRIDESMAID	CL	195.00	195.00
B. PARKER		**PARKER-LEVI TODDLERS**		
92	COURTNEY	OP	135.00	135.00
P. PARKINS		**PARKINS TREASURES**		
92	TIFFANY	OP	55.00	55.00
J. ESTEBAN		**PICNIC IN THE PARK**		
92	EMILY	OP	155.00	155.00
92	VICTORIA	OP	155.00	155.00
*		**RUSSIAN CZANNA DOLLS**		
91	ALEXANDRA	4950	295.00	295.00
T. MURAKAMI		**SONGS OF THE SEASONS HAKATA DOLL COLLECTION**		
85	AUTUMN SONG MAIDEN	9800	75.00	75.00
85	SPRING SONG MAIDEN	9800	75.00	75.00
85	SUMMER SONG MAIDEN	9800	75.00	75.00
85	WINTER SONG MAIDEN	9800	75.00	75.00
E. DAUB		**STAR TREK DOLL COLLECTION**		
88	CAPTAIN KIRK	OP	75.00	75.00
88	MR. SPOCK	OP	75.00	75.00
89	DR. MCCOY	OP	75.00	75.00
89	SCOTTY	OP	75.00	75.00
90	CHEKOV	OP	75.00	75.00
90	SULU	OP	75.00	75.00
91	UHURA	OP	75.00	75.00
L. DI LEO		**STORYBOOK DOLLS**		
91	ALICE IN WONDERLAND	OP	75.00	75.00
*		**THE ANTIQUE DOLL COLLECTION**		
89	NICOLE	OP	195.00	195.00
90	COLETTE	OP	195.00	195.00
91	KATRINA	OP	195.00	195.00
91	LISETTE	OP	195.00	195.00

YR	NAME	LIMIT	ISSUE	QUOTE
B.P. GUTMANN		THE BESSIE PEASE GUTMANN DOLL COLLECTION		
89	HE WON'T BITE	OP	135.00	135.00
89	LOVE IS BLIND	OP	135.00	135.00
91	FIRST DANCING LESSON	OP	195.00	195.00
91	GOOD MORNING	OP	195.00	195.00
91	LOVE AT FIRST SIGHT	OP	195.00	195.00
91	VIRGINIA	OP	135.00	135.00
M. HUMPHREY		THE MAUD HUMPHREY BOGART DOLL COLLECTION		
89	PLAYING BRIDE	OP	135.00	135.00
90	FIRST PARTY	OP	135.00	135.00
90	THE FIRST LESSON	OP	135.00	135.00
91	LITTLE CAPTIVE	OP	135.00	135.00
91	SEAMSTRESS	OP	135.00	135.00
*		THE ROYAL BEAUTY DOLLS		
91	CHEN MAI	OP	195.00	195.00
D. SCHURIG		YEAR ROUND FUN		
92	ALISON	OP	95.00	95.00
D. ZOLAN		ZOLAN DOLLS		
91	A CHRISTMAS PRAYER	OP	95.00	95.00

HAMILTON GIFTS

M. HUMPHREY		MAUD HUMPHREY BOGART PORCELAIN DOLLS		
91	MY FIRST PARTY H5686	OP	135.00	135.00
91	PLAYING BRIDE H5618	OP	135.00	135.00
91	SARAH H5617	OP	37.00	37.00
91	SUSANNA H5648	OP	37.00	37.00

J.S. PERRY ORIGINALS

J. ZOOK				
94	CHRISTMAS NOELLE	500	224.00	246.00

JAN HAGARA COLLECTABLES

J. HAGARA			VICTORIAN CHILDREN	
*	ADRIANNE	*	*	198.00
*	AMANDA	*	*	225.00-250.00
*	AMY	*	*	125.00
*	ANN MARIE	*	*	420.00
*	ASHLEY	*	*	125.00
*	BONNIE	*	*	450.00
*	CLARA	*	*	475.00
*	CRISTINA	*	*	100.00
*	DACY	*	*	490.00
*	JESSICA	*	*	650.00
*	JIMMY		*	150.00-250.00
*	JODY	*	*	450.00
*	MATTIE	*	*	400.00
*	MEG	*	*	195.00
*	MICHAEL	*	*	650.00
*	PAIGE	*	*	1200.00
*	SHARICE	*	*	200.00
*	SHELDON	*	*	490.00
*	SHELLEY	*	*	450.00
*	TINA	*	*	420.00
*	TRACY	*	*	125.00-150.00

JOHANNES ZOOK ORIGINALS

J. ZOOK				
93	ADRIANNE	500	198.00	240.00
93	ALYSSA	500	204.00	286.00
93	ANGEL GABRIEL	1000	250.00	303.00
93	BREANNA	500	190.00	230.00
93	BROOKE	1000	170.00	206.00
93	CALVIN CLOWN	500	198.00	240.00
93	CANDY CANE	*	164.00	198.00
93	CHRISTMAS CAROL	500	226.00	273.00
93	CLAIRE	1000	194.00	235.00
93	CODY	1000	194.00	235.00
93	COLLETTE	500	198.00	240.00
93	DEANNE	100	170.00	206.00
93	DENISE	250	198.00	240.00
93	DIANNA	100	170.00	206.00
93	FRANCESCA	250	220.00	266.00
93	JASMINE	250	252.00	305.00
93	JOEY	500	198.00	240.00
93	KANIKA	1000	220.00	266.00
93	LITTLE MISS MUFFET	500	188.00	227.00
93	MARISSA	1000	170.00	206.00
93	MEREDITH	500	216.00	261.00

YR	NAME	LIMIT	ISSUE	QUOTE
93	MONIKA	500	198.00	240.00
93	ROCKY	500	172.00	208.00
93	ROXANNE	500	172.00	208.00
93	SISSY	500	272.00	329.00
93	TOOTH FAIRY	500	198.00	240.00
93	VALERIE	500	240.00	290.00
94	ANALISSA	350	210.00	231.00
94	ANNETTE	100	230.00	253.00
94	ANNIE	25	148.00	163.00
94	BABY ELF	250	198.00	218.00
94	CHERRY	100	114.00	125.00
94	COOKIE	350	170.00	187.00
94	CORY	350	170.00	187.00
94	COWBOY	25	172.00	189.00
94	CYNTHIA	100	194.00	213.00
94	DANIEL BOONE	500	250.00	275.00
94	EMMY	500	220.00	242.00
94	GOOD NIGHT KISS	500	158.00	174.00
94	GWEN	125	198.00	218.00
94	KAREEM	500	198.00	218.00
94	KATRINA	500	198.00	218.00
94	KAYLA	1000	198.00	218.00
94	LITTLE FEATHER	100	280.00	308.00
94	MELINDA	1000	190.00	209.00
94	MERCEDES	1000	218.00	240.00
94	NURSE BETTE	500	184.00	202.00
94	POLLYANNA	500	198.00	218.00
94	SHARON	1000	190.00	209.00
94	SHAYNA	1000	190.00	209.00
94	SHELLY	100	198.00	218.00
94	SOPHIE	500	198.00	218.00
94	STARR	25	150.00	165.00
94	TRISHA	500	198.00	218.00
J. ZOOK				**AMISH SERIES**
93	JACOB	500	158.00	191.00
J. ZOOK			**CHILDREN OF THE NATION**	
94	AMERICA	500	188.00	207.00
J. ZOOK				**HALLOWEEN SERIES**
93	TOMMY TURTLE	150	300.00	363.00
94	DONIE DINOSAUR	150	250.00	275.00
94	HERBIE HOLSTEIN	150	250.00	275.00
J. ZOOK				**STORYBOOK SERIES**
93	LITTLE RED RIDING HOOD	1000	244.00	295.00
94	GOLDILOCKS & BABY BEAR	350	254.00	279.00

KAISER

YR	NAME	LIMIT	ISSUE	QUOTE
*				**DOLLS**
90	AMANDA, 17 IN.	1000	74.00	82.00
90	AMY, 19 IN.	1000	98.00	106.00
90	ANN, 24 IN.	1000	128.00	138.00
90	ASHLEY, 19 IN.	1000	98.00	106.00
90	ELIZABETH, 19 IN.	1000	98.00	106.00
90	HEATHER, 22 IN.	1000	116.00	126.00
90	JENNIFER, 22 IN.	1000	116.00	126.00
90	JESSICA, 22 IN.	1000	116.00	126.00
90	JILL, 24 IN.	1000	128.00	138.00
90	KELLY, 19 IN.	1000	98.00	106.00
90	KRISTY, 24 IN.	1000	128.00	138.00
90	LAURA, 24 IN.	1000	128.00	138.00
90	NEWBORN/CHRISTENING DRESS, 17 IN.	1000	74.00	82.00
90	NICOLE, 17 IN.	1000	74.00	82.00
90	SARAH, 22 IN.	1000	116.00	126.00
90	SUSAN, 17 IN.	1000	74.00	82.00

KURT S. ADLER/SANTA'S WORLD

YR	NAME	LIMIT	ISSUE	QUOTE
* KSA/SMITHSONIAN			**MUSEUM CAROUSEL**	
87	ANTIQUE CAROUSEL BUNNY, THE S3027/12	RT	14.50	14.50
87	ANTIQUE CAROUSEL GOAT, THE S3027/1	RT	14.50	14.50
88	ANTIQUE CAROUSEL GIRAFFE, THE S3027/4	RT	14.50	14.50
88	ANTIQUE CAROUSEL HORSE, THE S3027/3	RT	14.50	14.50
89	ANTIQUE CAROUSEL CAT, THE S3027/6	RT	14.50	14.50
89	ANTIQUE CAROUSEL LION, THE S3027/5	RT	14.50	14.50
90	ANTIQUE CAROUSEL SEAHORSE, THE S3027/8	OP	14.50	14.50
90	ANTIQUE CAROUSEL ZEBRA, THE S3027/17	OP	14.50	14.50
91	ANTIQUE CAROUSEL HORSE, THE S3027/10	OP	14.50	14.50
91	ANTIQUE CAROUSEL ROOSTER, THE S3027/9	RT	14.50	14.50
92	ANTIQUE CAROUSEL ELEPHANT, THE S3027/11	OP	14.50	14.50

Elegantly attired, Madame Du Pompadour *is a majestic beauty. She was created by doll artist Eda Mann and produced by Seymour Mann Inc.*

Cherubic in every way, Merriel *was Gorham's 1992 Christmas Angel.*

Rock a bye baby! Lullaby, *by one of today's most versatile artists, is the second issue in Sandra Kuck's "Precious Memories of Motherhood" collection. Produced by Reco.*

Guinevere *is the first in the noble line of the "Legendary Heroines" series by Gorham.*

YR	NAME	LIMIT	ISSUE	QUOTE
93	ANTIQUE CAROUSEL HORSE, THE S3027/14	OP	15.00	15.00
93	ANTIQUE CAROUSEL TIGER, THE S3027/13	OP	15.00	15.00
94	ANTIQUE CAROUSEL PIG, THE S3027/15	OP	15.50	15.50
94	ANTIQUE CAROUSEL REINDEER, THE S3027/15	OP	15.50	15.50
95	ANTIQUE CAROUSEL CAMEL, THE S3027/14	OP	15.00	15.00
95	ANTIQUE FROG S32027/18	OP	15.50	15.50
95	ARMORED HORSE S3027/17	OP	15.50	15.50

K. ADLER — **MUSEUM FABRICHE**

YR	NAME	LIMIT	ISSUE	QUOTE
92	KING'S GUARD, THE ES300	OP	27.00	27.00
92	HOLIDAY DRIVE W1580	OP	38.00	38.00
92	SANTA ON A BICYCLE W1547	OP	31.00	31.00

J. MOSTROM — **ROYAL HERITAGE**

YR	NAME	LIMIT	ISSUE	QUOTE
93	ANASTASIA W2922	RT	28.00	28.00
93	CAROLINE W2924	OP	25.50	25.50
93	CHARLES W2924	OP	25.50	25.50
93	ELIZABETH W2924	OP	25.50	25.50
93	JOELLA W2979	RT	27.00	27.00
93	KELLY W2979	RT	27.00	27.00
93	NICHOLAS W2923	OP	25.50	25.50
93	PATINA W2923	OP	25.50	25.50
93	SASHA W2923	OP	25.50	25.50
94	ICE FAIRY/WINTER FAIRY W2972	OP	25.50	25.50
94	SNOW PRINCESS W2971	OP	28.00	28.00
95	BENJAMIN J5756	OP	24.50	24.50
95	BLYTHE J5756	OP	24.50	24.50

J. MOSTROM — **SMALL WONDERS**

YR	NAME	LIMIT	ISSUE	QUOTE
95	AMERICA-HOLLIE BLUE W3162	OP	30.00	30.00
95	AMERICA-TEXAS TYLER W3162	OP	30.00	30.00
95	IRELAND-CATHLEEN W3082	OP	28.00	28.00
95	IRELAND-MICHAEL W3082	OP	28.00	28.00
95	KWANZA-MUFARO W3161	OP	28.00	28.00
95	KWANZA-SHANI W3161	OP	28.00	28.00

J. MOSTROM — **WHEN I GROW UP**

YR	NAME	LIMIT	ISSUE	QUOTE
95	DR. BROWN W3079	OP	27.00	27.00
95	FREDDY THE FIREMAN W3163	OP	28.00	28.00
95	MELISSA THE TEACHER W3081	OP	28.00	28.00
95	NURSE NANCY W3079	OP	27.00	27.00
95	SCOTT THE GOLFER W3080	OP	28.00	28.00

L.L. KNICKERBOCKER CO. INC.

C. BELLSMITH — **STORY BOOK**

YR	NAME	LIMIT	ISSUE	QUOTE
94	LITTLE RED RIDING HOOD C13199	YR	48.00	48.00

B. STOEHR — **TWINS**

YR	NAME	LIMIT	ISSUE	QUOTE
94	MOPSY C13202	5000	104.00	104.00
94	RAGS C13202	5000	104.00	104.00

LAWTON'S

W. LAWTON — **CHERISHED CUSTOMS**

YR	NAME	LIMIT	ISSUE	QUOTE
90	GIRLS DAY	500	395.00	395.00
90	HIGH TEA	500	395.00	395.00
90	MIDSOMMAR	500	395.00	395.00
90	THE BLESSING	500	395.00	1200.00
91	FROLIC/AMISH	500	395.00	395.00
91	NDEKO/ZAIRE	500	395.00	750.00
92	CARNIVAL/BRAZIL	750	425.00	425.00
92	CRADLEBOARD/NAVAJO	750	425.00	425.00
92	PASCHA/UKRAINE	750	495.00	495.00
93	NALAUQATAQ--ESKIMO	500	198.00	198.00
93	TOPENG KLANA-JAVA	250	248.00	248.00
94	KWANZAA	500	213.00	213.00
95	PIPING THE HAGGIS	350	495.00	525.00

W. LAWTON — **CHILDHOOD CLASSICS**

YR	NAME	LIMIT	ISSUE	QUOTE
83	ALICE IN WONDERLAND	CL	225.00	2500.00-3000.00
84	HEIDI	CL	325.00	850.00
85	HANS BRINKER	CL	325.00	900.00-1800.00
86	ANNE OF GREEN GABLES	CL	325.00	2000.00-2400.00
86	LAURA INGALLS	CL	325.00	400.00-900.00
86	POLLYANNA	CL	325.00	1000.00-1600.00
87	JUST DAVID	CL	325.00	700.00-1100.00
87	MARY LENNOX	CL	325.00	700.00-950.00
87	POLLY PEPPER	CL	325.00	450.00-700.00
88	EVA	CL	350.00	500.00-1000.00
88	REBECCA OF SUNNYBROOK FARM	CL	350.00	850.00
88	TOPSY	CL	350.00	750.00-1200.00
89	HONEY BUNCH	CL	350.00	500.00-800.00
89	LITTLE PRINCESS	CL	395.00	650.00-950.00
90	MARY FRANCES	CL	350.00	350.00

YR	NAME	LIMIT	ISSUE	QUOTE
90	POOR LITTLE MATCH GIRL	CL	350.00	450.00
91	HIAWATHA	500	395.00	395.00
91	LITTLE BLACK SAMBO	500	395.00	395.00
91	THE BOBBSEY TWINS	350	725.00	725.00
W. LAWTON			**CHILDHOOD CLASSICS II**	
92	MARIGOLD GARDEN	750	450.00	450.00
92	OLIVER TWIST	750	450.00	450.00
92	PETER AND THE WOLF	750	495.00	495.00
93	THE VELVETEEN RABBIT	750	198.00	198.00
93	TOM SAWYER	500	198.00	198.00
95	LITTLE LORD FAUNTLEROY	350	450.00	475.00
W. LAWTON			**CHRISTMAS DOLL**	
88	CHRISTMAS JOY	CL	325.00	625.00-1200.00
89	NOEL	CL	325.00	325.00-750.00
90	CHRISTMAS ANGEL	CL	325.00	325.00
91	YULETIDE CAROLE	500	395.00	395.00
W. LAWTON			**CHRISTMAS LEGENDS**	
91	THE LEGEND OF THE POINSETTA	750	395.00	395.00
93	THE LITTLE DRUMMER BOY	500	298.00	298.00
94	SANTA LUCIA	350	213.00	213.00
95	THE NUTCRACKER	500	595.00	625.00
W. LAWTON			**CLASSIC PLAYTHINGS**	
94	KATIE AND HER KEWPIE	750	298.00	298.00
95	BESSIE AND HER BYE LO BABY	750	595.00	625.00
W. LAWTON			**EARLY AMERICAN PORTRAIT**	
94	ABIGAIL AND JANE AUGUSTA	250	498.00	498.00
95	CARRIE AND SOPHIA GRACE	350	1250.00	1300.00
W. LAWTON			**FOLKTAKES AND FAIRY STORIES**	
93	SNOW WHITE	500	198.00	198.00
W. LAWTON			**FOLKTALES AND FAIRY STORIES**	
92	LITTLE RED RIDING HOOD	750	450.00	450.00
92	SWAN PRINCESS	750	495.00	495.00
92	THE LITTLE EMPEROR'S NIGHTINGALE	750	425.00	425.00
92	WILLIAM TELL, THE YOUNGER	750	395.00	395.00
93	GOLDILOCKS AND BABY BEAR	350	298.00	298.00
94	GIRL OF THE LIMBERLOST	500	213.00	213.00
94	LITTLE GRETEL	500	198.00	198.00
95	RAPUNZEL	350	450.00	475.00
W. LAWTON			**GENTLE PURSUITS**	
94	EMILY AND HER DIARY	350	398.00	398.00
95	EUGENIA'S LITERARY SALON	350	795.00	825.00
W. LAWTON			**GRAND TOUR**	
94	SPRINGTIME IN PARIS	250	448.00	448.00
95	AFRICAN SAFARI	350	995.00	1025.00
W. LAWTON			**GUILD CENTER DISPLAY DOLL**	
95	UNIQUELY YOURS	OP	395.00	405.00
W. LAWTON			**GUILD DOLLS**	
85	BAA BAA BLACK SHEEP	CL	395.00	1000.00
90	LAVENDER BLUE	CL	395.00	450.00-600.00
91	TO MARKET, TO MARKET	YR	495.00	395.00
92	LITTLE BOY BLUE	OP	395.00	395.00
93	THE LAWTON LOGO DOLL	575	175.00	175.00
94	WEE HANDFUL	*	125.00	125.00
W. LAWTON			**MEMORIES & MELODIES**	
93	APPLE BLOSSOM TIME	500	148.00	148.00
93	IN THE GOOD OL' SUMMERTIME	500	148.00	148.00
93	LYDA ROSE	500	148.00	148.00
93	SCARLET RIBBONS	500	148.00	148.00
94	LET ME CALL YOU SWEETHEART	250	148.00	148.00
95	EASTER PARADE	250	295.00	320.00
W. LAWTON			**NEWCOMER COLLECTION**	
87	ELLIN ELIZABETH	CL	335.00	1200.00
87	ELLIN ELIZABETH, EYES CLOSED	CL	335.00	1000.00
W. LAWTON			**ONCE UPON A RHYME**	
94	AT AUNTY'S HOUSE	350	398.00	298.00
95	LUCY GRAY	350	795.00	825.00
W. LAWTON			**PLAYTHINGS PAST**	
89	EDWARD AND DOBBIN	CL	395.00	475.00-600.00
89	ELIZABETH AND BABY	CL	395.00	395.00-650.00
89	VICTORIA AND TEDDY	CL	395.00	395.00
W. LAWTON			**SEASONS**	
88	AMBER AUTUMN	CL	325.00	400.00-525.00
89	SUMMER ROSE	CL	325.00	375.00-475.00
90	CRYSTAL WINTER	CL	325.00	325.00
91	SPRING BLOSSOM	500	350.00	350.00

YR	NAME	LIMIT	ISSUE	QUOTE
W. LAWTON			**SMALL WONDERS**	
93	JAFRY	500	75.00	75.00
93	JAMILLA	500	75.00	75.00
93	MEGHAN	500	75.00	75.00
93	MICHAEL	500	75.00	75.00
W. LAWTON			**SPECIAL EDITION**	
88	MARCELLA AND RAGGEDY ANN	2500	395.00	650.00
88	MARCELLA AND RAGGEDY ANN	CL	395.00	650.00
89	AMELIA	CL	*	1400.00
90	GOLDILOCKS AND BABY BEAR	1	*	4250.00
93	FLORA MCFLIMSEY	250	448.00	448.00
94	MARY CHILTON	350	198.00	198.00
W. LAWTON			**SPECIAL OCCASION**	
88	FIRST DAY OF SCHOOL	CL	325.00	550.00
88	NANTHY	CL	325.00	525.00
90	FIRST BIRTHDAY	CL	295.00	295.00
W. LAWTON			**STORE EXCLUSIVE**	
91	GARDEN SONG MARTA	CL	335.00	335.00
91	LIBERTY SQUARE	CL	350.00	350.00
91	LITTLE COLONEL	CL	395.00	395.00
91	MAIN STREET, USA	CL	350.00	350.00
91	TISH	CL	395.00	395.00
W. LAWTON			**SUGAR 'N' SPICE**	
86	JASON	CL	250.00	600.00-925.00
86	JESSICA	CL	250.00	600.00-925.00
86	KERSTEN	CL	250.00	550.00-800.00
86	KIMBERLY	CL	250.00	550.00-800.00
87	GINGER	CL	275.00	395.00-550.00
87	MARIE	CL	275.00	395.00-550.00
W. LAWTON			**THE CHILDREN'S HOUR**	
91	EDITH WITH GOLDEN HAIR	500	395.00	395.00
91	GRAVE ALICE	500	395.00	395.00
91	LAUGHING ALLEGRA	500	395.00	395.00
W. LAWTON			**TIMELESS BALLADS**	
85	SHE WALKS IN BEAUTY	CL	550.00	600.00
87	ANNABEL LEE	CL	550.00	600.00-695.00
87	HIGHLAND MARY	CL	550.00	600.00-875.00
87	YOUNG CHARLOTTE	CL	550.00	850.00-900.00
W. LAWTON			**TREASURED TALES**	
94	THE DREAMER	500	198.00	198.00
W. LAWTON			**WEE BITS**	
88	WEE BIT O' HEAVEN	CL	295.00	450.00-600.00
88	WEE BIT O' SUNSHINE	CL	295.00	450.00-600.00
88	WEE BIT O' WOE	CL	295.00	550.00-700.00
89	WEE BIT O' BLISS	CL	295.00	350.00
89	WEE BIT O' WONDER	CL	295.00	295.00

LENOX CHINA/CRYSTAL COLLECTION

*			**BOLSHOI NUTCRACKER DOLLS**	
91	CLARA	OP	195.00	195.00
*			**BONNET BABY DOLLS**	
92	EASTER BONNET	OP	95.00	95.00
*			**CHILDREN OF THE WORLD**	
89	HANNAH, THE LITTLE DUTCH MAIDEN	OP	119.00	119.00
90	HEATHER, LITTLE HIGHLANDER	OP	119.00	119.00
90	SCOTTISH LASS	OP	119.00	119.00
91	AMMA, THE AFRICAN GIRL	OP	119.00	119.00
91	SAKURA, THE JAPANESE GIRL	OP	119.00	119.00
92	GRETCHEN, GERMAN DOLL	OP	119.00	119.00
*			**CHILDREN WITH TOYS DOLLS**	
91	TEA FOR TEDDY	OP	136.00	136.00
J. GRAMMAR			**CHINA DOLLS - CLOTH BODIES**	
85	AMY, 14 IN.	*	250.00	995.00
85	ANNABELLE, 14 IN.	*	250.00	995.00
85	ELIZABETH, 14 IN.	*	250.00	995.00
85	JENNIFER, 14 IN.	*	250.00	995.00
85	MIRANDA, 14 IN	*	250.00	995.00
85	SARAH, 14 IN.	*	250.00	995.00
*			**COUNTRY DECOR DOLLS**	
91	MOLLY	OP	150.00	150.00
P. THOMPSON			**ELLIS ISLAND DOLLS**	
91	MEGAN	TL	150.00	150.00
91	STEFAN	TL	150.00	150.00
92	ANGELINA	TL	150.00	150.00
92	ANNA	YR	152.00	152.00
92	CATHERINE	YR	152.00	152.00

YR	NAME	LIMIT	ISSUE	QUOTE
*			**FIRST COLLECTOR DOLL**	
92	LAUREN	OP	152.00	152.00
*			**INSPIRATIONAL DOLL**	
92	BLESSED ARE THE PEACEMAKERS	OP	119.00	119.00
*			**INTERNATIONAL BABY DOLL**	
92	NATALIA, RUSSIAN BABY	OP	119.00	119.00
J. GRAMMER			**LENOX CHINA DOLLS**	
84	ABIGAIL, 20 IN.	*	425.00	2000.00
84	AMANDA, 16 IN.	*	385.00	1700.00
84	JESSICA, 20 IN.	*	450.00	1900.00
84	MAGGIE, 16 IN.	*	375.00	1700.00
84	MARYANNE, 20 IN.	*	425.00	2000.00
84	MELISSA	*	450.00	3100.00
84	REBECCA, 16 IN.	*	375.00	1700.00
84	SAMANTHA	500	500.00	2800.00
*			**LENOX VICTORIAN DOLLS**	
89	THE VICTORIAN BRIDE	OP	295.00	295.00
90	CHRISTMAS DOLL, ELIZABETH	OP	195.00	195.00
91	VICTORIAN CHRISTENING DOLL	OP	295.00	295.00
92	LADY AT GALA	OP	295.00	295.00
*			**LITTLE WOMEN**	
92	AMY	OP	150.00	150.00
92	AMY, THE INSPIRING ARTIST	OP	152.00	152.00
*			**MUSICAL BABY DOLLS**	
91	PATRICK'S LULLABYE	OP	95.00	95.00
*			**NUTCRACKER DOLLS**	
92	SUGARPLUM	OP	195.00	195.00
93	NUTCRACKER	OP	195.00	195.00
*			**PRIMA BALLERINA COLLECTION**	
92	ODETTE, QUEEN OF THE SWANS	OP	195.00	195.00
93	SLEEPING BEAUTY	OP	195.00	195.00
A. LESTER			**SIBLING DOLLS**	
91	SKATING LESSON	OP	195.00	195.00

LINDA SUTTON ORIGINAL DOLLS

L. SUTTON		**L.L. SUTTON ORIGINAL PORCELAIN DOLLS**		
94	FALL BROOKE	5	1550.00	1600.00
94	SOPHIE	50	695.00	715.00
94	SPRING BROOKE	5	1550.00	1600.00
94	SUMMER BROOKE	5	1550.00	1600.00
94	WINTER BROOKE	20	1550.00	1575.00

MATTEL

*	PARISIENNE		*	110.00
90	HAPPY BIRTHDAY BARBIE		*	39.00
91	BIRTHDAY SURPRISE BARBIE		*	39.00
*	MASQUERADE	*	*	195.00
*	SILK AND FLAMES BARBIE		*	195.00
A. HIMSTEDT			**BAREFOOT CHILDREN**	
87	BASTIAN	CL	*	550.00
87	ELLEN	CL	*	650.00
87	FATOU	CL	*	800.00-900.00
87	KATHE	CL	*	550.00
87	LISA	CL	*	770.00
87	PAULA	CL	*	650.00
A. HIMSTEDT			**BLESSED ARE THE CHILDREN**	
88	FRIEDERIKE	CL	*	*
88	KASIMIR	CL	*	*
88	MAKIMURA	CL	*	495.00
88	MALIN	CL	*	500.00
88	MICHIKO	CL	*	*
A. HIMSTEDT			**FACES OF FRIENDSHIP**	
91	LILIANE (NETHERLANDS)	TL	598.00	598.00
91	NEBLINA (SWITZERLAND)	TL	598.00	598.00
91	SHIREEM (BALI)	TL	598.00	598.00
A. HIMSTEDT			**FIENE AND THE BAREFOOT BABIES**	
90	ANNCHEN-GERMAN BABY GIRL	TL	498.00	498.00
90	FIENE-BELGIAN GIRL	TL	498.00	498.00
90	MO-AMERICAN BABY BOY	TL	498.00	498.00
90	TAKI-JAPANESE BABY GIRL	TL	350.00	500.00
A. HIMSTEDT			**HEARTLAND SERIES**	
88	TIMI	CL	*	350.00-450.00
88	TONI	CL	*	350.00-450.00
*			**HOLIDAY BARBIES**	
88	HOLIDAY BARBIE	*	24.99	525.00
89	HOLIDAY BARBIE	*	34.99	105.00

YR	NAME	LIMIT	ISSUE	QUOTE
A. HIMSTEDT			**REFLECTION OF YOUTH**	
89	ADRIENNE (FRANCE)	CL	*	650.00
89	AYOKA (AFRICA)	CL	*	650.00-750.00
89	KAI (GERMAN)	CL	*	*
A. HIMSTEDT			**RELECTIONS OF YOUTH**	
89	JANKA (HUNGARY)	CL	*	350.00-500.00

MIDDLETON DOLL CO.

YR	NAME	LIMIT	ISSUE	QUOTE
L. MIDDLETON				
94	ANGEL KISSES BOY	OP	98.00	100.00
94	BLOSSOM	250	500.00	550.00
94	CHRISTMAS ANGEL 1994	500	190.00	210.00
94	HERSHEY KISSES	OP	99.50	100.00
94	TENDERNESS PETITE PIERROT	250	500.00	550.00
94	THE BRIDE	200	1390.00	1425.00
L MIDDLETON			**FIRST COLLECTIBLES**	
90	DAY DREAMER (AWAKE)	OP	42.00	42.00
90	SWEETEST LITTLE DREAMER (ASLEEP)	OP	40.00	40.00
91	DAY DREAMER SUNSHINE	OP	49.00	49.00
91	TEENIE	OP	59.00	59.00
L. MIDDLETON			**FIRST MOMENTS SERIES**	
84	FIRST MOMENTS (SLEEPING)	41,000	69.00	150.00
86	FIRST MOMENTS (BLUE EYES)	15,000	120.00	150.00
86	FIRST MOMENTS (BROWN EYES)	5490	120.00	150.00
87	FIRST MOMENTS BOY	6075	130.00	160.00
87	FIRST MOMENTS CHRISTENING (ASLEEP)	OP	160.00	180.00
87	FIRST MOMENTS CHRISTENING (AWAKE)	OP	160.00	180.00
90	FIRST MOMENTS SWEETNESS	OP	180.00	180.00
L. MIDDLETON			**LIMITED EDITION PORCELAIN**	
88	BABY GRACE	500	500.00	500.00
88	CHERISH, FIRST EDITION	750	350.00	450.00-525.00
88	DEVAN	525	500.00	500.00
88	DEVAN II	100	500.00	500.00
88	JOHANNA	500	500.00	500.00
88	MY LEE	629	500.00	500.00-525.00
88	MY LEE II	100	500.00	500.00
88	SINCERITY, FIRST EDITION	750	330.00	425.00-480.00
91	MOLLY ROSE	500	500.00	500.00
L. MIDDLETON			**LIMITED EDITION VINYL**	
81	LITTLE ANGEL-KINGDOM (HAND-PAINTED)	800	40.00	300.00
85	LITTLE ANGEL-KING II (HAND-PAINTED)	400	40.00	200.00
87	CHRISTMAS ANGEL 1987	4174	130.00	200.00
88	CHRISTMAS ANGEL 1988	6385	130.00	160.00
89	ANGEL FANCY	10,000	120.00	130.00
89	CHRISTMAS ANGEL 1989	7500	150.00	160.00
90	ANGEL LOCKS	10,000	140.00	150.00
90	BABY GRACE	5000	190.00	190.00
90	CHRISTMAS ANGEL 1990	5000	150.00	150.00
90	DEAR ONE (SUNDAY BEST)	5000	140.00	140.00
90	FIRST MOMENTS (TWIN BOY)	5000	180.00	180.00
90	FIRST MOMENTS (TWIN GIRL)	5000	180.00	180.00
90	FOREVER CHERISH	5000	170.00	170.00
90	MISSY (BUTTERCUP)	5000	160.00	170.00
90	SINCERITY (APPLES & SPICE)	5000	250.00	250.00
90	SINCERITY (PEACHES & CREAM)	5000	250.00	250.00
91	BUBBA BATBOY	5000	190.00	190.00
91	CHRISTMAS ANGEL 1991	5000	180.00	180.00
91	DEVAN DELIGHTFUL	5000	170.00	170.00
91	GRACIE MAE	5000	250.00	250.00
91	JOHANNA	5000	190.00	190.00
91	MY LEE CANDY CANE	2500	170.00	170.00
L. MIDDLETON			**LITTLEST BALLET COMPANY**	
88	APRIL (DRESSED IN PINK)	7500	100.00	110.00
88	JEANNIE (DRESSED IN WHITE)	7500	100.00	110.00
88	LISA (BLACK LEOTARDS)	7500	100.00	110.00
88	MELANIE (DRESSED IN BLUE)	7500	100.00	110.00
89	APRIL (IN LEOTARD)	7500	100.00	110.00
89	JEANNIE (IN LEOTARD)	7500	100.00	110.00
89	MELANIE (IN LEOTARD)	7500	100.00	110.00
L. MIDDLETON			**TOWN & COUNTRY**	
94	ANGEL KISSES COUNTRY BOY	OP	118.00	120.00
94	ANGEL KISSES COUNTRY GIRL	OP	118.00	120.00
94	ANGEL KISSES GIRL	OP	98.00	100.00
94	ANGEL KISSES TOWN BOY	OP	118.00	120.00
94	ANGEL KISSES TOWN GIRL	OP	118.00	120.00
94	BELOVED HAPPY BIRTHDAY BLUE	1000	220.00	230.00
94	BELOVED HAPPY BIRTHDAY PINK	1000	220.00	230.00

YR	NAME	LIMIT	ISSUE	QUOTE
94	BRIDE (RUBY SLIPPER)	1000	250.00	260.00
94	FIRST MOMENTS SWEETNESS (NEWBORN)	OP	180.00	180.00
94	JOEY (NEWBORN)	1000	180.00	190.00
94	JOHANNA (NEWBORN)	2000	180.00	190
94	LITTLE ANGEL COUNTRY BOY	OP	118.00	120.00
94	LITTLE ANGEL COUNTRY GIRL	OP	118.00	120.00
94	LITTLE ANGEL TOWN BOY	OP	118.00	120.00
94	LITTLE ANGEL TOWN GIRL	OP	118.00	120.00

L. MIDDLETON   **VINYL COLLECTORS SERIES**

YR	NAME	LIMIT	ISSUE	QUOTE
85	ANGEL FACE	OP	90.00	110.00
86	BUBBA CHUBBS	5600	100.00	200.00
86	DEAR ONE-FIRST EDITION	4935	90.00	200.00
86	LITTLE ANGEL-THIRD EDITION	OP	90.00	110.00
87	AMANDA-FIRST EDITION	4200	140.00	160.00
87	MISSY	OP	100.00	120.00
88	BUBBA CHUBBS RAILROADER	OP	140.00	160.00
88	CHERISH	OP	160.00	160.00
88	SINCERITY-LIMITED FIRST EDITION	4380	160.00	160.00
89	DEVAN	OP	170.00	170.00
89	MY LEE	OP	170.00	170.00
89	SINCERITY-SCHOOLGIRL	OP	180.00	180.00

NAHRGANG COLLECTION

J. NAHRGANG   **PORCELAIN DOLL SERIES**

YR	NAME	LIMIT	ISSUE	QUOTE
89	PALMER	250	270.00	270.00
90	ALICIA	250	330.00	330.00
90	GRANT (TAKE ME OUT TO THE BALL GAME)	500	390.00	390.00
90	KARISSA	500	350.00	395.00
90	KARMAN (GYPSY)	250	350.00	395.00
90	KASEY	250	450.00	450.00
90	KELSEY	250	350.00	350.00
90	MAGGIE	500	295.00	295.00
91	AUBRY	250	390.00	390.00
91	CARSON	250	350.00	350.00
91	ERIN	250	295.00	295.00
91	HOLLY	175	295.00	295.00
91	LAURA	250	450.00	450.00
91	MCKINSEY	250	350.00	350.00
91	RAE	250	350.00	390.00
91	SOPHIE	250	450.00	450.00
92	ALEXIS	250	390.00	390.00
92	ANNIE SULLIVAN	25	895.00	895.00
92	BROOKE	250	390.00	390.00
92	DOLLY MADISON	100	395.00	395.00
92	FLORENCE NIGHTINGALE	100	395.00	395.00
92	HARRIET TUBMAN	100	395.00	395.00
92	KATIE	250	295.00	295.00
92	MOLLY PITCHER	100	395.00	395.00
92	POCAHONTAS	100	395.00	395.00
92	TAYLOR	250	395.00	395.00

J. NAHRGANG   **PORCELIAN DOLL SERIES**

YR	NAME	LIMIT	ISSUE	QUOTE
91	ANNA MARIE	250	390.00	390.00

J. NAHRGANG   **VINYL DOLL SERIES**

YR	NAME	LIMIT	ISSUE	QUOTE
90	KARMAN (GYPSY)	2000	190.00	190.00
91	ALEXIS	500	250.00	250.00
91	ANGELA	500	190.00	190.00
91	ANN MARIE	500	225.00	225.00
91	AUBRY	2000	225.00	225.00
91	BEATRIX	500	250.00	250.00
91	BROOKE	500	250.00	250.00
91	CHELSEA	250	190.00	190.00
91	LAURA	1000	250.00	250.00
91	MOLLY	500	190.00	190.00
91	POLLY	250	225.00	225.00
91	VANESSA	250	250.00	250.00
92	DOLLY MADISON	500	199.00	199.00
92	FLORENCE NIGHTINGALE	500	199.00	199.00
92	HARRIET TUBMAN	500	199.00	199.00
92	MOLLY PITCHER	500	199.00	199.00
92	POCAHONTAS	500	199.00	199.00

ORIGINAL APPALACHIAN ARTWORKS

X. ROBERTS   **CABBAGE PATCH KIDS**

YR	NAME	LIMIT	ISSUE	QUOTE
83	ANDRE/MADEIRA	2000	250.00	1500.00-2000.00
84	DADDY'S DARLINS'-KITTEN	2000	300.00	500.00-700.00
84	DADDY'S DARLINS'-PRINCESS	2000	300.00	500.00-700.00
84	DADDY'S DARLINS'-PUN'KIN	2000	300.00	500.00-700.00

YR	NAME	LIMIT	ISSUE	QUOTE
84	DADDY'S DARLINS'-TOOTSIE	2000	300.00	500.00-700.00
88	TIGER'S EYE-VALENTINE'S DAY	5000	150.00	200.00-400.00
89	TIGER'S EYE-MOTHER'S DAY	5000	150.00	150.00-400.00
90	JOY	500	250.00	400.00-750.00
93	HAPPILY EVER AFTER BRIDE	CL	230.00	340.00
93	HAPPILY EVER AFTER GROOM	CL	230.00	340.00
93	LITTLE PEOPLE GIRLS	300	325.00	450.00
93	PREEMIE	CL	175.00	285.00
93	UNICOI BALLERINA	200	200.00	310.00
93	UNICOI KIDS	1500	195.00	325.00
94	LITTLE PEOPLE BOYS	300	325.00	425.00
94	MTN. LAUREL BABY SIDNEY & LANIER	100	390.00	490.00
94	MTN. LAUREL EASTER	200	225.00	325.00
94	MTN. LAUREL IRISH BOYS	100	210.00	310.00
94	MTN. LAUREL IRISH GIRLS	200	210.00	310.00
94	MTN. LAUREL KIDS	CL	195.00	310.00
94	MTN. LAUREL MYSTERIOUS BARRY	CL	225.00	325.00
94	MTN. LAUREL NORMAN JEAN	CL	*	*
94	NEWBORN FORM MOBILE PATCH	CL	198.00	300.00
X. ROBERTS		**CABBAGE PATCH KIDS CHRISTMAS**		
93	RUDOLPH	CL	275.00	385.00
94	NATALIE	500	275.00	375.00
X. ROBERTS		**CABBAGE PATCH KIDS CIRCUS PARADE**		
87	BIG TOP CLOWN-BABY CAKES	2000	180.00	425.00-550.00
89	HAPPY HOBO-BASHFUL BILLY	1000	180.00	225.00-400.00
91	MITZI	1000	220.00	220.00
X. ROBERTS		**CABBAGE PATCH KIDS CONV.**		
93	ELLEN	200	200.00	310.00
94	MTN. LAUREL JUSTIN	200	225.00	325.00
X. ROBERTS		**CABBAGE PATCH KIDS INTERNATIONAL**		
83	AMERICAN INDIAN	1000	150.00	800.00-1800.00
83	ORIENTAL	1000	150.00	1200.00-1500.00
X. ROBERTS		**COLLECTORS CLUB EDITIONS**		
89	ANNA RUBY	CL	250.00	250.00
90	LEE ANN	CL	250.00	250.00
91	RICHARD RUSSELL	CL	250.00	250.00
X. ROBERTS		**CONVENTION BABY**		
89	ASHLEY	CL	150.00	1000.00
90	BRADLEY	CL	175.00	600.00
91	CAROLINE	CL	200.00	200.00
X. ROBERTS		**LITTLE PEOPLE**		
78	HELEN, BLUE	1000	150.00	3000.00-7600.00
80	CELEBRITY	5000	200.00	400.00-800.00
80	NICHOLAS	2500	200.00	1500.00-2000.00
80	NOEL	2500	200.00	700.00
80	SP, PREEMIE	5000	100.00	400.00-700.00
82	AMY	2500	125.00	700.00-800.00
82	BABY RUDY	1000	200.00	800.00-900.00
82	BILLIE	2500	125.00	700.00-800.00
82	BOBBIE	2500	125.00	700.00-800.00
82	CHRISTY NICOLE	1000	200.00	800.00
82	DOROTHY	2500	125.00	700.00-900.00
82	GILDA	2500	125.00	1400.00-1600.00
82	MARILYN	2500	125.00	700.00-800.00
82	OTIS	2500	125.00	800.00-1000.00
82	PE, NEW 'EARS PREEMIE	5000	140.00	300.00-450.00
82	REBECCA	2500	125.00	700.00-900.00
82	SYBIL	2500	125.00	700.00-1000.00
82	TYLER	2500	125.00	1700.00-2500.00
X. ROBERTS		**PORCELAIN FRIENDS**		
94	ANGELICA	CL	160.00	260.00
94	KAREN LEE	CL	150.00	250.00
94	KASSIS LOU	CL	150.00	250.00
94	KATIE LYN	CL	150.00	250.00

ORIGINALS BY BEVERLY STOEHR

B. STOEHR		**BABY SERIES**		
94	AMANDA	10	1000.00	1100.00
94	KATIE BABY	10	400.00	425.00
B. STOEHR		**CHILDREN OF MEMORIES**		
94	BARBARA	50	495.00	525.00
94	JUDY	10	595.00	625.00
94	SARA	50	495.00	525.00

PEGGY MULHOLLAND INC.

B. GERARDI		**CHRISTINA DOLL COLLECTION**		
93	CHRISTINA	500	499.00	499.00

YR	NAME	LIMIT	ISSUE	QUOTE
93	EMILY	500	499.00	499.00
93	MICHAEL	500	499.00	499.00
93	ROSE	500	499.00	499.00
93	SARAH	500	499.00	499.00
B. GERARDI				**SWEETMMM'S**
93	LILI	RT	130.00	140.00
93	LIZABETH	RT	130.00	140.00
93	MARGARET	RT	130.00	140.00
93	MISSY	RT	130.00	140.00
93	PETER	RT	130.00	140.00
93	ROSEBUD	RT	130.00	140.00
93	SAMANTHA	RT	130.00	140.00
93	TIFFANY	RT	130.00	140.00
94	ANGEL	2-YR	130.00	130.00
94	PRINCESS ORIANA	500	150.00	150.00
95	BUTTONS	1000	159.00	159.00
95	GEORGETTE	1000	159.00	159.00
95	PJ	OP	159.00	159.00
95	THEODORE	1000	159.00	159.00
B. GERARDI			**SWEETMMM'S FIRST PARTY**	
94	SUZY	500	150.00	150.00
B. GERARDI			**SWEETMMM'S FIRST VIOLIN LESSON**	
95	DOROTHY	1000	179.00	179.00
B. GERARDI			**SWEETMMM'S ROCK A BYE BABY**	
94	BABY BLUE EYES	500	150.00	150.00
94	BABY BROWN EYES	500	150.00	150.00

PRINCETON GALLERY

YR	NAME	LIMIT	ISSUE	QUOTE
*			**BEST FRIENDS DOLLS**	
91	SHARING SECRETS	OP	78.00	78.00
*			**CHILD DOLLS**	
91	ABIGAIL	OP	59.00	59.00
*			**CHILDHOOD SONGS DOLLS**	
91	IT'S RAINING, IT'S POURING	OP	78.00	78.00
*			**DRESS UP DOLLS**	
91	GRANDMA'S ATTIC	OP	95.00	95.00
*			**FABRIQUE SANTA**	
91	CHRISTMAS DREAM	OP	76.00	76.00
*		**LITTLE LADIES OF VICTORIAN ENGLAND**		
90	VICTORIA ANNE	OP	59.00	59.00
91	ABIGAIL	OP	59.00	59.00
91	VALERIE	OP	58.50	58.50
92	BEVERLY	OP	58.50	58.50
92	CAROLINE	OP	58.50	58.50
92	HEATHER	OP	58.50	58.50
*			**ROCK-N-ROLL DOLLS**	
93	YELLOW DOT BIKINI	OP	95.00	95.00
91	CINDY AT THE HOP	OP	95.00	95.00
92	CHANTILLY LACE	OP	95.00	95.00
*			**SANTA DOLL**	
91	CHECKING HIS LIST	OP	119.00	119.00
M. SIRKO			**TERRIBLE TWOS DOLLS**	
91	ONE MAN BAND	OP	95.00	95.00

RECO INTERNATIONAL

YR	NAME	LIMIT	ISSUE	QUOTE
SANDRA KUCK		**CHILDHOOD DOLL COLLECTION**		
94	A KISS GOODNIGHT	OP	79.00	85.00
94	TEACHING TEDDY HIS PRAYERS	OP	79.00	85.00
95	READING WITH TEDDY	OP	79.00	79.00
J. MCCLELLAND		**CHILDREN'S CIRCUS DOLL COLLECTION**		
91	JOHNNY THE STRONGMAN	YR	83.00	83.00
91	KATIE THE TIGHTROPE WALKER	YR	78.00	78.00
91	TOMMY THE CLOWN	YR	78.00	78.00
92	MAGGIE THE ANIMAL TRAINER	YR	*	*
S. KUCK		**PRECIOUS MEMORIES OF MOTHERHOOD**		
90	LOVING STEPS	YR	125.00	195.00
90	LULLABY	YR	125.00	125.00
91	EXPECTANT MOMENTS	YR	*	*
93	BEDTIME	YR	149.00	149.00
*			**TENDER MOMENTS DOLLS**	
90	KATHY	OP	40.00	47.00
90	KELLI	OP	73.00	73.00
90	KIM	OP	40.00	43.00
90	KRISTI	OP	47.00	50.00
91	CANDI	OP	106.00	106.00
91	CARRIE	OP	30.00	30.00
91	CASEY	OP	80.00	80.00

YR	NAME	LIMIT	ISSUE	QUOTE
91	CHRISTINE	OP	85.00	85.00
91	CONNIE	OP	80.00	80.00
91	CORINNE	OP	79.00	79.00
91	KERRI	OP	64.00	64.00
91	TANYA	OP	45.00	45.00
91	TINA	OP	73.00	73.00
91	TONI	OP	47.00	47.00

RHODES STUDIO
ROCKWELL INSPIRED   **A NORMAN ROCKWELL CHRISTMAS**

YR	NAME	LIMIT	ISSUE	QUOTE
90	SCOTTY PLAYS SANTA	CL	48.00	48.00
91	SCOTTY GETS HIS TREE	CL	59.00	59.00

ROMAN INC.
E. WILLIAMS   **A CHRISTMAS DREAM**

YR	NAME	LIMIT	ISSUE	QUOTE
90	CAROLE	500	125.00	125.00
90	CHELSEA	5000	125.00	125.00

A. WILLIAMS   **ABBIE WILLIAMS COLLECTION**

91	MOLLY	5000	155.00	155.00

E. WILLIAMS   **CLASSIC BRIDES OF THE CENTURY**

90	FLORA, THE 1900'S BRIDE	CL	145.00	145.00
91	JENNIFER, THE 1980'S BRIDE	CL	149.00	149.00
92	CATHLEEN, THE 1990'S BRIDE	TL	149.95	149.95

E. WILLIAMS   **ELLEN WILLIAMS DOLLS**

89	NOELLE	5000	125.00	125.00
89	NOELLE	5000	125.00	125.00
89	REBECCA	7500	195.00	195.00
89	REBECCA	7500	195.00	195.00

*   **TYROLEAN TREASURES: SOFT BODY, HUMAN HAIR**

90	ANDREW	2000	575.00	575.00
90	EILAN	2000	575.00	575.00
90	ERIKA	2000	575.00	575.00
90	MARISA	2000	575.00	575.00
90	MATTHEW	2000	575.00	575.00
90	SARAH	2000	575.00	575.00

*   **TYROLEAN TREASURES: WOOD BODY, MOVEABLE JOINT**

90	ANN	2000	650.00	650.00
90	DAVID	2000	650.00	650.00
90	KARIN	2000	650.00	650.00
90	LISA	2000	650.00	650.00
90	MELISSA	2000	650.00	650.00
90	MONICA	2000	650.00	650.00
90	NADIA	2000	650.00	650.00
90	SUSIE	2000	650.00	650.00
90	TINA	2000	650.00	650.00
90	VERENA	2000	650.00	650.00

SALLY-LYNNE DOLLS
S. BEATTY   **FRENCH REPLICAS**

85	ANNABELLE, 30 IN.	CL	950.00	2900.00
85	CANDICE, 30 IN.	100	950.00	2200.00
85	CHARLES, 30 IN.	100	1050.00	2200.00
85	VICTORIA, 30 IN.	100	1050.00	2900.00
86	VICTORIA AT CHRISTMAS, 30 IN.	CL	2500.00	4100.00

SANDY DOLLS INC.
S. DY   **SANDRA**

94	SANDRA AUTUMN	1500	50.00	60.00
94	SANDRA WINTER	1500	60.00	65.00

S. DY   **SANDY CLOWNS**

94	JESTER	1000	75.00	80.00
94	JUJU	1000	60.00	65.00

R. TEJADA   **TRADITIONS**

94	GENTLE DOVE--WISHRAM WEDDING CEREMONY	3500	100.00	110.00
94	GREY OWL--HUNKPAPA SIOUX CHIEF	3500	250.00	275.00
94	MEADOW FLOWER--CHEROKEE PRINCESS	3500	85.00	95.00
94	SPRING WATER W/LITTLE SCOUT	3500	115.00	125.00
94	WAR CLOUD--OGLALA SIOUX CHIEF	3500	115.00	125.00

R. TEJADA   **WARRIOR AND PRICESS**

94	WHITE EAGLE--APACHE WARRIOR	5000	37.50	40.00

R. TEJADA   **WARRIOR AND PRINCESS**

94	FALLING SNOW--NEZ PERCE PRINCESS	5000	37.50	40.00
94	LAUGHING BROOK--COMANCHE PRINCESS	5000	37.50	40.00
94	ROARING RIVER--MOHAWK WARRIOR	5000	37.50	40.00
94	SHINING CLOUD--COMANCHE PRINCESS	5000	37.50	40.00
94	SOARING HAWK--COMANCHE WARRIOR	5000	37.50	40.00
94	SWIFT ELK--IROQUOIS WARRIOR	5000	37.50	40.00

He loves me, he loves me not. Daisy is *from the "Romantic Flower Maidens" series by the Ashton-Drake Galleries.*

Little Jack Horner sat in a corner. Jack *is third in the "Children of Mother Goose" collection by the Ashton-Drake Galleries.*

Remember Bye Lo Baby? Doll artist Wendy Lawton pays tribute with Bessie and Her Bye Lo Baby *from the "Classic Playthings" collection.*

Hairbrush in hand, this little lady is in for quite a job. Rapunzel *is from the "Folktales and Fairy Stories" series by Wendy Lawton. The Lawton Doll Company is the producer.*

YR	NAME	LIMIT	ISSUE	QUOTE

SARAH'S ATTIC

YR	NAME	LIMIT	ISSUE	QUOTE
*	**ANGELS IN THE ATTIC COLLECTION**			
89	GLORY ANGEL	500	50.00	50.00
89	HOLLY ANGEL	500	50.00	50.00
89	JOY ANGEL	500	50.00	50.00
89	LIBERTY ANGEL	500	50.00	50.00
*	**BEARY ADORABLES COLLECTION**			
90	AMERICANA BEAR	1000	160.00	160.00
90	BETTY BEAR SUNDAY	1000	160.00	160.00
90	TEDDY BEAR SUNDAY	1000	160.00	160.00
90	TEDDY SCHOOL BEAR	1000	160.00	160.00
91	CHRISTMAS BETTY BEAR	1000	160.00	160.00
91	CHRISTMAS TEDDY BEAR	1000	160.00	160.00
91	SPRINGTIME BETTY BEAR	1000	160.00	160.00
91	SPRINGTIME TEDDY BEAR	1000	160.00	160.00
*	**BLACK HERITAGE COLLECTION**			
90	AMERICANA HICKORY	2000	150.00	160.00
90	AMERICANA SASSAFRAS	2000	150.00	160.00
90	BEACHTIME HICKORY	2000	140.00	150.00
90	BEACHTIME SASSAFRAS	2000	140.00	150.00
90	PLAYTIME HICKORY	2000	140.00	150.00
90	PLAYTIME SASSAFRAS	2000	140.00	150.00
90	SCHOOL DAYS HICKORY	2000	140.00	150.00
90	SCHOOL DAYS SASSAFRAS	2000	140.00	150.00
90	SUNDAY'S BEST HICKORY	2000	150.00	150.00
90	SUNDAY'S BEST SASSAFRAS	2000	150.00	160.00
90	SWEET DREAMS HICKORY	2000	140.00	150.00
90	SWEET DREAMS SASSAFRAS	2000	140.00	150.00
91	CHRISTMAS HICKORY	2000	150.00	150.00
91	CHRISTMAS SASSAFRAS	2000	150.00	160.00
91	SPRINGTIME HICKORY	2000	150.00	150.00
91	SPRINGTIME SASSAFRAS	2000	150.00	150.00
*	**HAPPY COLLECTION**			
89	FREEDOM CLOWN	500	150.00	150.00
89	HARMONY CLOWN	500	150.00	150.00
89	SMILEY CLOWN	CL	118.00	118.00
89	XMAS CLOWN NOEL	500	150.00	150.00
*	**HEAVENLY WINGS**			
91	ALL CLOTH ADORA ANGEL	500	90.00	90.00
91	ALL CLOTH ENOS ANGEL	500	90.00	90.00
*	**LITTLE CHARMERS COLLECTION**			
87	MOLLY SMALL 5 PIECE DOLL	CL	36.00	36.00
87	SUNSHINE 5 PIECE DOLL	CL	79.00	79.00
88	MICHAEL 5 PIECE DOLL	CL	44.00	44.00
89	BECKY	150	120.00	120.00
89	BEVERLY JANE BLACK	500	160.00	160.00
89	BOBBY	150	120.00	120.00
89	GREEN BEVERLY JANE	500	160.00	160.00
89	RED BEVERLY JANE	500	160.00	160.00
89	SUNDAY'S BEST-BEVIE JANE	500	160.00	160.00
90	MEGAN DOLL	100	70.00	100.00
90	SCOTT DOLL	100	70.00	100.00
91	COUNTRY EDIE	500	170.00	170.00
91	COUNTRY EMILY	500	250.00	250.00
91	COUNTRY EMMA	500	160.00	160.00
91	COUNTRY HILARY	500	200.00	200.00
91	PLAYTIME EDIE	500	170.00	170.00
91	PLAYTIME EMMA	500	160.00	160.00
91	VICTORIAN EDIE	500	170.00	170.00
91	VICTORIAN EMILY	500	250.00	250.00
91	VICTORIAN EMMA	500	160.00	160.00
91	VICTORIAN HILARY	500	200.00	200.00
*	**SPIRIT OF CHRISTMAS**			
88	MRS. CLAUS 5 PIECE DOLL	OP	120.00	120.00
88	SANTA 5 PIECE DOLL	OP	120.00	120.00
89	FATHER CHRISTMAS DOLL	500	150.00	150.00
*	**TATTERED 'N TORN**			
91	ALL CLOTH MUFFIN BLACK DOLL	500	90.00	90.00
91	ALL CLOTH OPIE WHITE DOLL	500	90.00	90.00
91	ALL CLOTH POLLY WHITE DOLL	500	90.00	90.00
91	ALL CLOTH PUFFIN BLACK DOLL	500	90.00	90.00

SCHMID

J. AMOS GRAMMER

YR	NAME	LIMIT	ISSUE	QUOTE
	JUNE AMOS GRAMMER			
80	LEIGH ANN	1000	195.00	210.00
88	ROSAMUND	750	225.00	225.00

YR	NAME	LIMIT	ISSUE	QUOTE
89	KATIE	1000	180.00	180.00
89	VANESSA	1000	180.00	210.00
90	JESTER LOVE	1000	195.00	210.00
90	LAUREN	1000	279.00	280.00
90	MEGAN	750	380.00	380.00
91	HEATHER	1000	210.00	210.00
91	LAUREN	1000	280.00	280.00
91	MITSUKO	1000	210.00	210.00

SEYMOUR MANN

JAIMY *   CHRISTMAS COLLECTION

YR	NAME	LIMIT	ISSUE	QUOTE
91	FLAT SANTA CJ-115	OP	7.50	7.50
91	SANTAS, SET OF 8 CJ-12	OP	60.00	60.00
90	CUPID CPD-5	OP	13.50	13.50
90	CUPID CPD-6	OP	13.50	13.50
90	DOLL TREE TOPPER OM-124	RT	85.00	85.00
90	HAT W/STREAMERS OM-118	RT	20.00	20.00
90	HEARTFACE OM-119	RT	12.00	12.00
90	LACE BALL OM-120	RT	10.00	10.00
90	TASSEL OM-118	RT	7.50	7.50
91	ELVES W/MALL CJ-454	OP	30.00	30.00

P. APRILE   CONNOISSEUR DOLL COLLECTION

YR	NAME	LIMIT	ISSUE	QUOTE
92	BRIDE & FLOWER GRIL PAC-6	5000	800.00	800.00
92	CASSANDRA PAC-8	5000	450.00	450.00
92	CASSIE FLOWER GIRL PAC-9	5000	175.00	175.00
92	CELINE PAC-11	5000	186.00	186.00
92	CLARISSA PAC-3	5000	185.00	185.00
92	CYNTHIA PAC-10	5000	165.00	185.00
92	EUGENIE BRIDE PAC-1	5000	185.00	185.00
92	EVENING STAR PAC-5	5000	500.00	500.00
92	MELANIE PAC-14	5000	300.00	300.00
92	NADIA PAC-18	5000	175.00	175.00
92	OLIVIA PAC-12	5000	300.00	300.00
92	VANESSA PAC-15	5000	300.00	300.00
92	VIOLETTA PAC-18	5000	185.00	175.00
92	ALEXANDRIA PAC-19	5000	300.00	300.00
92	PAVLOVA PAC-17	5000	145.00	145.00
93	GRACE HKH-2	5000	250.00	250.00
93	HELENE HKH-1	5000	250.00	250.00
93	REILLY HKH-3	5000	280.00	280.00
92	BABY CAKES CRUMBS OK-CRUMBS/B	5000	17.50	17.50
92	BABY CAKES CRUMBS PK-CRUMBS	5000	17.50	17.50
92	LITTLE TURTLE INDIAN PK-110	5000	150.00	150.00
92	REVAN ESKIMO PK-106	5000	130.00	130.00
84	MISS DEBUTANTE DEBI	*	75.00	180.00
85	CHRISTMAS CHEER-124	RT	40.00	100.00
85	WENDY-C120	CL	45.00	150.00
86	CAMELOT FAIRY-C84	RT	75.00	225.00
87	AUDRINA-YK200	CL	85.00	140.00
87	CYNTHIA DOM-211	RT	85.00	85.00
87	DAWN-C185	RT	75.00	175.00
87	LINDA-C190	RT	60.00	120.00
87	MARCY-YK122	RT	55.00	100.00
87	NIRMALA YK-210	RT	50.00	60.00
87	RAPUNZEL-C158	RT	95.00	185.00
87	SABRINA-C208	RT	65.00	95.00
87	SAILORETTE-DOM217	RT	70.00	150.00
87	VIVIAN C-201P	RT	80.00	80.00
88	ASHLEY-C-278	CL	80.00	80.00
88	BRITTANY-TK-5	RT	120.00	120.00
88	CISSIE-DOM263	RT	65.00	135.00
88	CRYING COURTNEY PS75	RT	115.00	115.00
88	CYNTHIA-DOM-211	RT	85.00	85.00
88	DOLL OLIVER FH-392	RT	100.00	100.00
88	EMILY YK-243V	RT	70.00	70.00
88	FRANCES C-233	CL	80.00	125.00
88	GISELLE ON GOOSE-FH176	RT	105.00	225.00
88	JESSICA-DOM-267	RT	90.00	90.00
88	JOANNE CRY BABY PS-50	RT	100.00	100.00
88	JOLIE-C231	RT	65.00	150.00
88	JULIE-C245A	RT	65.00	160.00
88	JULIETTE BRIDE MUSICAL C246L TM	RT	150.00	150.00
88	KIRSTEN-PS-40G	RT	70.00	70.00
88	LIONEL-FH206B	RT	50.00	120.00
88	LUCINDA-DOM-293	RT	90.00	90.00
88	MICHELLE & MARCEL-YK176	RT	70.00	150.00
88	PAULINE YK-230	RT	90.00	90.00

YR	NAME	LIMIT	ISSUE	QUOTE
88	SABRINA C208	RT	65.00	95.00
88	SISTER AGNES C250	RT	75.00	75.00
88	SISTER IGNATIUS NOTRE DAME FH184	RT	75.00	75.00
88	SISTER TERESA FH187	RT	80.00	80.00
88	TRACY-C-3006	RT	95.00	150.00
88	VIVIAN-C201P	RT	80.00	80.00
89	AMBER-DOM-281A	CL	85.00	85.00
89	BETTY-PS27G	CL	65.00	125.00
89	BRETT-PS27B	RT	65.00	125.00
89	BRITTANY-TK-4	RT	150.00	150.00
89	CRYING COURTNEY PS-75	RT	115.00	115.00
89	DAPHNE ECRU/MINT GREEN C3025	RT	85.00	85.00
89	ELISABETH OM-32	RT	120.00	120.00
89	ELIZABETH-C-246P	RT	150.00	200.00
89	EMILY-PS-48	RT	110.00	110.00
89	FRANCES-C233	RT	80.00	125.00
89	HAPPY BIRTHDAY-C3012	RT	80.00	125.00
89	HEIDI-260	RT	50.00	95.00
89	JAQUELINE-DOLL-254M	RT	85.00	85.00
89	JOANNE CRY BABY PS-50	RT	100.00	100.00
89	KAYOKO-PS24	RT	75.00	175.00
89	KIRSTEN PS-40G	RT	70.00	70.00
89	LING-LING-PS-87G	RT	90.00	90.00
89	LIZ-YK-269	RT	70.00	100.00
89	LUCINDA DOM-293	RT	90.00	90.00
89	MAI-LING-PS-79	RT	100.00	100.00
89	MARCEY YK-4005	RT	90.00	90.00
89	MARGARET-245	RT	100.00	150.00
89	MAUREEN-PS-84	RT	90.00	90.00
89	MEIMEI-PS22	RT	75.00	225.00
89	MELISSA-LL-794	RT	95.00	95.00
89	MISS KIM-PS25	RT	75.00	175.00
89	PATRICIA/PATRICK-215GBB	RT	105.00	135.00
89	PAULA PS-56	RT	75.00	75.00
89	PAULINE BONAPARTE OM-68	RT	120.00	120.00
89	RAMONA PS-31B	RT	80.00	80.00
89	REBECCA PS-34V	RT	45.00	45.00
89	ROSIE-290M	RT	55.00	85.00
89	SISTER MARY-C-249	RT	75.00	125.00
89	SUNNY PS-59V	RT	71.00	71.00
89	SUZIE-PS-32	RT	80.00	80.00
89	TATIANA PINK BALLERINA OM-60	RT	120.00	120.00
89	TERRI-PS-104	RT	85.00	85.00
89	WENDY-PS-51	RT	105.00	105.00
90	ANABELLE-C-3080	2500	85.00	85.00
90	ANGEL-DOM-335	2500	105.00	105.00
90	ANGELA-C-3084	2500	105.00	105.00
90	ANGELA-C-3084M	2500	115.00	115.00
90	ANITA-FH-277G	2500	65.00	65.00
90	ASHLEY-FH-325	2500	75.00	75.00
90	AUDREY-YK-4089	3500	125.00	125.00
90	BABY BETTY-YK-4087	3500	125.00	125.00
90	BABY SUE-DOLL-402B	2500	27.50	27.50
90	BABY SUNSHINE-C-3055	CL	90.00	90.00
90	BETH-YK-4099A/B	2500	125.00	125.00
90	BETTINA-TR-4	2500	125.00	125.00
90	BEVERLY-DOLL-335	2500	110.00	110.00
90	BILLIE YK-405BV	3500	65.00	65.00
90	CAITLIN YK-4051V	CL	90.00	90.00
90	CAITLIN-DOLL-11PH	RT	60.00	60.00
90	CAROLE-YK-4085W	RT	125.00	125.00
90	CHARLENE-YK-4112	RT	90.00	90.00
90	CHIN FA-C-3061	RT	95.00	95.00
90	CHINOOK-WB-24	RT	85.00	85.00
90	CHRISTIE WB-2	RT	75.00	75.00
90	DAISY-EP-6	RT	90.00	90.00
90	DAPHNE ECRU-C-3025	RT	85.00	85.00
90	DIANE-FH-275	RT	90.00	90.00
90	DIANNA-TK-31	RT	175.00	175.00
90	DOMINO-C-3050	RT	145.00	145.00
90	DOROTHY-TR-10	RT	135.00	135.00
90	DORRI-DOLL-16PH	RT	85.00	85.00
90	EILEEN-FH-367	RT	100.00	100.00
90	FELICIA-TR-9	RT	115.00	115.00
90	FRANCESCA-C-3021	RT	100.00	175.00
90	GERRI YK-4094	RT	95.00	95.00

YR	NAME	LIMIT	ISSUE	QUOTE
90	GINNY-YK-4119	RT	100.00	100.00
90	HOPE YK-4118	RT	90.00	90.00
90	HYACINTH-DOLL-15PH	RT	85.00	85.00
90	INDIAN DOLL FH-296	RT	60.00	60.00
90	JANETTE-DOLL-385	RT	85.00	85.00
90	JILLIAN DOLL-41PH	RT	90.00	90.00
90	JOANNE-TR-12	RT	175.00	175.00
90	JULIE-WB-35	RT	70.00	70.00
90	KAREN-PS-198	RT	150.00	150.00
90	KATE-C-3060	RT	95.00	95.00
90	KATHY W/BEAR TE1	RT	70.00	70.00
90	KIKI-EP-4	RT	100.00	100.00
90	LAURA DOLL-25PH	RT	55.00	55.00
90	LAUREN-SP-300	RT	85.00	85.00
90	LAVENDER BLUE-YK-4024	RT	95.00	135.00
90	LIEN WHA-YK-4092	RT	100.00	100.00
90	LING-LING DOLL	RT	50.00	50.00
90	LISA BEIGE ACCORDION PLEAT YK-4093	RT	125.00	125.00
90	LISA-FH-379	RT	100.00	100.00
90	LIZA C-3053	RT	100.00	100.00
90	LOLA-SP-79	RT	105.00	105.00
90	LORETTA-FH-321	RT	90.00	90.00
90	LORI WB-72BM	RT	75.00	75.00
90	MADAME DU POMPADOUR-C-3088	RT	250.00	250.00
90	MAGGIE-PS-151P	RT	90.00	90.00
90	MAGGIE-WB-51	RT	105.00	105.00
90	MARIA-YK-4116	RT	85.00	85.00
90	MELANIE-YK-4115	RT	80.00	80.00
90	MELISSA-DOLL-390	RT	75.00	75.00
90	MERRY WIDOW-C-3040	RT	145.00	145.00
90	MERRY WIDOW-C-3040M	RT	140.00	140.00
90	NANOOK-WB-23	RT	75.00	75.00
90	NATASHA-PS-102	RT	100.00	100.00
90	ODESSA-FH-362	RT	65.00	65.00
90	PING-LING DOLL 363RV	RT	50.00	50.00
90	POLLY DOLL-22PH	RT	90.00	90.00
90	PRINCESS RED FEATHER PS-189	RT	90.00	90.00
90	PRINCESS-FH-268B	RT	75.00	75.00
90	PRISCILLA-WB-50	RT	105.00	105.00
90	SABRINA-C3050	RT	105.00	105.00
90	SALLY-WB-20	RT	95.00	95.00
90	SHIRLEY-WB-37	RT	65.00	65.00
90	SISTER MARY-WB-15	RT	70.00	70.00
90	SOPHIE-OM-1	RT	65.00	65.00
90	STACY-TR-5	RT	105.00	105.00
90	SUE CHUEN C-3061G	RT	95.00	95.00
90	SUNNY-FH-331	RT	70.00	70.00
90	SUSAN DOLL 364MC	RT	75.00	75.00
90	TANIA-DOL-376-P	RT	65.00	65.00
90	TINA-DOLL-371	RT	85.00	85.00
90	TINA-WB-32	RT	65.00	65.00
90	TOMMY-C-3064	RT	75.00	75.00
90	WENDY-TE-3	RT	75.00	75.00
90	WILMA-PS-174	RT	75.00	75.00
90	YEN YEN-YK-4091	RT	95.00	95.00
91	ABBY C3145	CL	100.00	100.00
91	ABIGAIL-EP-3	2500	100.00	100.00
91	ABIGAL WB-72WM	2500	75.00	75.00
91	ALEXIS EP32	2500	220.00	220.00
91	ALICIA YK-4215	3500	90.00	90.00
91	AMANDA OM-182	2500	260.00	260.00
91	AMELIA TR-47	2500	105.00	105.00
91	AMY C-3147	2600	135.00	135.00
91	ANN TR-52	2500	135.00	135.00
91	ANNETTE TR-59	2500	130.00	130.00
91	ANNIE YK-4214	3500	145.00	145.00
91	ANTOINETTE FH-452	2600	100.00	100.00
91	ARABELLA C-3183	2500	135.00	135.00
91	ARIEL EP-33	CL	175.00	175.00
91	AUDREY FH-455	2500	125.00	125.00
91	AURORA OM-181	2500	260.00	260.00
91	AZURE AM-15	2500	175.00	175.00
91	BABBY ELLIE ECRU MUSICAL 402E	2500	27.50	27.50
91	BABY BETH-DOLL-406P	2500	27.50	27.50
91	BABY BONNIE W/WALKER 409	2500	40.00	40.00
91	BABY BONNIE-SP-341	2500	55.00	55.00

YR	NAME	LIMIT	ISSUE	QUOTE
91	BABY BRENT-EP-15	RT	85.00	85.00
91	BABY CARRIE-DOLL-402P	2500	27.50	27.50
91	BABY ELLIE17	2500	65.00	65.00
91	BABY GLORIA PS-289	2500	75.00	75.00
91	BABY JOHN-PS-49B	2500	85.00	85.00
91	BABY LINDA-DOLL-406E	2500	27.50	27.50
91	BELINDA C-3164	2500	150.00	150.00
91	BERNETTA EP-40	2500	115.00	115.00
91	BETSY-AM-6	2500	105.00	105.00
91	BETTINA YK-4144	3500	105.00	105.00
91	BLAINE TR-61	CL	115.00	115.00
91	BLYTHE CH-15V	CL	135.00	135.00
91	BO-PEEP W/LAMB C-3128	CL	105.00	105.00
91	BRIDGET SP-379	2500	105.00	105.00
91	BROOKE FH-461	2500	115.00	115.00
91	BRYNA-AM-100B	2500	70.00	70.00
91	CAMELLIA FH-457	2500	100.00	100.00
91	CAROLINE LL-838	2500	110.00	110.00
91	CAROLINE LL-905	2500	110.00	110.00
91	CHERYL TR-49	2500	120.00	120.00
91	CHIN CHIN YK-4211	CL	85.00	85.00
91	CHRISTINA-PS-261	RT	115.00	115.00
91	CINDY LOU FH-264	RT	85.00	85.00
91	CISSY EP-56	RT	95.00	95.00
91	CLARE-DOLL 465	RT	100.00	100.00
91	CLAUDINE C-3146	RT	95.00	95.00
91	COLETTE-WB-7	RT	65.00	65.00
91	COLLEEN YK-4163	RT	120.00	120.00
91	COOKIE GU-6	RT	110.00	110.00
91	COURTNEY-LL-859	RT	150.00	150.00
91	CREOLE-AM-17	RT	160.00	160.00
91	CRYSTAL YK-4237	RT	125.00	125.00
91	DANIELLE-AM-5	RT	125.00	125.00
91	DARCY EP-47	RT	110.00	110.00
91	DARCY FH-451	RT	105.00	105.00
91	DARLA C-3122	RT	110.00	110.00
91	DARLENE DOLL-444	RT	75.00	75.00
91	DAWN C-3135	RT	130.00	130.00
91	DENISE-LL-852	RT	105.00	105.00
91	DEPHINE-SP-308	RT	135.00	135.00
91	DESIREE LL-898	RT	120.00	120.00
91	DUANANE-SP-366	RT	85.00	85.00
91	DULCIE-YK-4131V	RT	100.00	100.00
91	DWAYNE C-3123	RT	120.00	120.00
91	EDIE YK-4177	RT	115.00	115.00
91	ELISABETH & LISA C-3095	RT	195.00	195.00
91	ELISE-PS-259	RT	105.00	105.00
91	ELIZABETH AM-32	RT	105.00	105.00
91	EMMALINE OM-191	RT	300.00	300.00
91	EMMALINE OM-197	RT	300.00	300.00
91	EMMY-C-3099	RT	125.00	125.00
91	ERIN-DOLL-4PH	RT	60.00	60.00
91	EVALINA C-3124	RT	135.00	135.00
91	FIFI AM-100F	RT	70.00	70.00
91	FLEURETTE PS-286	RT	75.00	75.00
91	FLORA TR-46	RT	125.00	125.00
91	FRANCESCA-AM-14	RT	175.00	175.00
91	GEORGIA YK-4143	RT	150.00	150.00
91	GEORGIA-YK-4143	RT	100.00	100.00
91	GIGI-C-3107	RT	135.00	135.00
91	GINGER LL-907	RT	115.00	115.00
91	GLORIA AM-100G	RT	70.00	70.00
91	GLORIA YK-4166	RT	105.00	105.00
91	GRETCHEN DOLL-446	RT	45.00	45.00
91	GRETEL DOLL-434	RT	60.00	60.00
91	HANSEL & GRETEL DOLL-448V	RT	60.00	60.00
91	HELENE AM-29	RT	150.00	150.00
91	HOLLY CH-6	RT	100.00	100.00
91	HONEY BUNNY-WB-9	RT	70.00	70.00
91	HONEY FH-401	RT	100.00	100.00
91	HOPE FH-434	RT	90.00	90.00
91	INDIRA-AM-4	RT	125.00	125.00
91	IRIS TR-58	RT	120.00	120.00
91	IVY PS-307	RT	75.00	75.00
91	JANE-PS-243L	RT	115.00	115.00
91	JANICE OM-194	RT	300.00	300.00

YR	NAME	LIMIT	ISSUE	QUOTE
91	JESSICA-FH-423	RT	95.00	95.00
91	JOY-EP-23V	RT	130.00	130.00
91	JOYCE AM-100J	RT	35.00	35.00
91	JULIA-C-3102	RT	135.00	135.00
91	JULIETTE OM-192	RT	300.00	300.00
91	KAREN-EP-24	RT	115.00	115.00
91	KARMELA EP-57	RT	120.00	120.00
91	KELLY-AM-8	RT	125.00	125.00
91	KERRY-FH-396	RT	100.00	100.00
91	KIM AM-100K	RT	70.00	70.00
91	KINESHA SP-402	RT	110.00	110.00
91	KRISTI-FH-402	RT	100.00	100.00
91	KYLA YK-4137	RT	95.00	95.00
91	LAURA-WB-110P	RT	85.00	85.00
91	LEIGH DOLL-457	RT	95.00	95.00
91	LEILA-AM-2	RT	125.00	125.00
91	LENORE LL-911	RT	105.00	105.00
91	LENORE YK-4218	RT	135.00	135.00
91	LIBBY-EP-18	RT	85.00	85.00
91	LILA FH-404	RT	100.00	100.00
91	LILA-AM-10	RT	125.00	125.00
91	LINDSEY C-3127	RT	135.00	135.00
91	LINETTA C-3166	RT	135.00	135.00
91	LISA AM-100L	RT	70.00	70.00
91	LITTLE BOY BLUE C-3159	RT	100.00	100.00
91	LIZ C-3150	RT	100.00	100.00
91	LIZA YK-4226	RT	35.00	35.00
91	LOLA-SP-363	RT	90.00	90.00
91	LORI EP-52	RT	95.00	95.00
91	LORI FH-446	RT	100.00	100.00
91	LOUISE LL-908	RT	105.00	105.00
91	LUCY-LL-853	RT	80.00	80.00
91	MADELEINE-C-3106	RT	95.00	95.00
91	MARCY TR-55	RT	135.00	135.00
91	MARIEL C-3119	RT	125.00	125.00
91	MAUDE AM-100M	RT	70.00	70.00
91	MELISSA CH-3	RT	110.00	110.00
91	MELISSA LL-901	RT	135.00	135.00
91	MELISSA-AM-9	RT	120.00	120.00
91	MEREDITH FH-391-P	RT	95.00	95.00
91	MERYL FH-463	RT	95.00	95.00
91	MICHAEL W/SCHOOL BOOKS FH-439B	RT	95.00	95.00
91	MICHELLE EP36	RT	95.00	95.00
91	MICHELLE W/SCHOOL BOOKS FH-439G	RT	95.00	95.00
91	MIRANDA-DOLL-9PH	RT	75.00	75.00
91	MISSY DOLL-464	RT	70.00	70.00
91	MISSY PS-258	RT	90.00	90.00
91	MON YUN W/PARASOL TR-33	RT	115.00	115.00
91	NANCY W/RABBIT EP-31	RT	165.00	165.00
91	NANCY WB-73	RT	65.00	65.00
91	NELLIE-EP-1B	RT	75.00	75.00
91	NICOLE-AM-12	RT	135.00	135.00
91	NOELLE PS-239V	RT	95.00	95.00
91	PATTI DOLL-440	RT	65.00	65.00
91	PATTY YK-4221	RT	125.00	125.00
91	PEPPER PS-277	RT	130.00	130.00
91	PIA-PS-246L	RT	115.00	115.00
91	PRINCESS SUMMER WINDS FH-427	RT	120.00	120.00
91	PRISSY WHITE/BLUE-C-3140	RT	100.00	100.00
91	RAPUNZEL C-3157	RT	150.00	150.00
91	RED WING AM-30	RT	165.00	165.00
91	ROBIN AM-22	RT	120.00	120.00
91	ROSALIND-C-3090	RT	150.00	150.00
91	SAMANTHA GU-3	RT	100.00	100.00
91	SANDRA-DOLL-6PHE	RT	65.00	65.00
91	SCARLETT FH-399	RT	100.00	100.00
91	SCARLETT FH-436	RT	135.00	135.00
91	SHAKA SP-401	RT	110.00	110.00
91	SHARON BLUE-EP-34	RT	120.00	120.00
91	SHARON C-3237	2500	95.00	95.00
91	SHAU CHEN GU-2	RT	85.00	85.00
91	SHELLEY CH-1	RT	110.00	110.00
91	SOPHIE TR-53	RT	135.00	135.00
91	STACY DOLL-6PH	RT	65.00	65.00
91	STEPHANIE FH-467	RT	95.00	95.00
91	STEPHANIE PINK & WHITE-OM-196	RT	300.00	300.00

YR	NAME	LIMIT	ISSUE	QUOTE
91	STEPHANIE-AM-11	RT	105.00	105.00
91	SUMMER AM-33	RT	200.00	200.00
91	SYBIL BEIGE-C-3131	RT	135.00	135.00
91	SYBIL PINK-12PHMC	RT	75.00	75.00
91	TAMARA OM-187	RT	135.00	135.00
91	TERRI TR-62	RT	75.00	75.00
91	TESSA AM-19	RT	135.00	135.00
91	TINA-AM-16	RT	130.00	130.00
91	VANESSA AM-34	RT	90.00	90.00
91	VICKI-C-3101	RT	200.00	200.00
91	VIOLET EP-41	RT	135.00	135.00
91	VIOLET OM-186	RT	270.00	270.00
91	VIRGINIA SP-359	YR	120.00	120.00
91	WAH-CHING/ORIENTAL TODDLER-YK-4175	RT	110.00	110.00
92	ALICE JNC-4013	OP	90.00	90.00
92	AMY OM-06	2500	150.00	150.00
92	BETH OM-05	2500	135.00	135.00
92	BETTA OM-01	2500	115.00	115.00
92	CHARLOTTE FH-484	2500	115.00	115.00
92	CHELSEA IND-397	OP	85.00	85.00
92	CORDELIA OM-009	RT	250.00	250.00
92	CORDELIA OM-09	RT	250.00	250.00
92	DEBBIE JNC-4006	RT	90.00	90.00
92	DEIDRE FH-473	RT	115.00	115.00
92	DEIDRE YK-4083	RT	95.00	95.00
92	DONA FH-494	RT	100.00	100.00
92	EUGENIE OM-225	RT	300.00	300.00
92	GISELLE OM-02	RT	90.00	90.00
92	JAN OM-012	RT	135.00	135.00
92	JANET FH-496	RT	120.00	120.00
92	JET FH-478	RT	115.00	115.00
92	JODIE FH-495	RT	115.00	115.00
92	JULIETTE OM-08	2500	175.00	175.00
92	LAURA OM-010	RT	250.00	250.00
92	LAURIE JNC-4004	RT	90.00	90.00
92	LYDIA OM-226	RT	250.00	250.00
92	MAGGIE FH-505	RT	125.00	125.00
92	MELISSA OM-03	RT	135.00	135.00
92	NANCY JNC-4001	RT	90.00	90.00
92	SALLY FH-492	RT	105.00	105.00
92	SAPPHITED OM-223	RT	250.00	250.00
92	SARA ANN FH-474	RT	115.00	115.00
92	SCARLETT FH-471	RT	120.00	120.00
92	SONJA FH-486	RT	125.00	125.00
92	SUE JNC-4003	RT	90.00	90.00
92	TIFFANY OM-014	RT	150.00	150.00
92	TRINA OM-011	RT	165.00	165.00
92	VIOLETTE FH-503	RT	120.00	120.00
92	YVETTE OM-015	RT	150.00	150.00
93	ADRIENNE C-3182	2500	135.00	135.00
93	ANTONIA OM-227	2500	350.00	350.00
93	ARLENE SP-421	2500	100.00	100.00
93	BLAINE C-3167	2500	100.00	100.00
93	CAMILLE OM-230	2500	250.00	250.00
93	CINNAMON JNC-4014	RT	90.00	90.00
93	CLARE FH-497	RT	100.00	100.00
93	CLOTHILDE FH-469	RT	125.00	125.00
93	DONNA DOLL-447	RT	85.00	85.00
93	ELLEN YK-4223	RT	150.00	150.00
93	GENA OM-229	RT	250.00	250.00
93	HAPPY FH-479	RT	105.00	105.00
93	HEDY FH-449	RT	95.00	95.00
93	IRIS FH-483	RT	95.00	95.00
93	JAN DRESS UP OM-12	RT	135.00	135.00
93	JILLIAN SP-428	RT	165.00	165.00
93	JULIETTE OM-8	RT	175.00	175.00
93	KENDRA FH-481	RT	115.00	115.00
93	KIT SP-426	RT	55.00	55.00
93	LINDA SP-435	RT	95.00	95.00
93	LYNN FH-498	RT	120.00	120.00
93	MARIAH LL-909	RT	135.00	135.00
93	NINA YK-4232	RT	135.00	135.00
93	OONA TR-57	RT	135.00	135.00
93	REBECCA C-3177	RT	135.00	135.00
93	SARETTA SP-423	2500	100.00	100.00
93	SHAKA TR-45	RT	100.00	100.00

YR	NAME	LIMIT	ISSUE	QUOTE
93	SUZIE SP-422	RT	164.00	164.00
94	BLAIR YK-4532	3500	150.00	150.00
94	BOBBI NM-30	2500	135.00	135.00
94	BRANDY YK-4537	3500	165.00	165.00
94	BRONWYN IND-517	2500	140.00	140.00
94	CACTUS FLOWER INDIAN LL-944	2500	105.00	105.00
94	CALLIE TR-76	2500	140.00	140.00
94	CALYPSO LL-942	2500	150.00	150.00
94	CARMEN PS-408	2500	150.00	150.00
94	CASEY C-3197	2500	140.00	140.00
94	CATHY GU-41	2500	140.00	140.00
94	CHRIS FH-561	2500	85.00	85.00
94	CHRISSIE FH-562	2500	85.00	85.00
94	CINDY OC-58	2500	140.00	140.00
94	CLARA IND-516	2500	140.00	140.00
94	CLARA IND-524	2500	150.00	150.00
94	CLAUDETTE TR-81	2500	150.00	150.00
94	COPPER YK-4546C	3500	150.00	150.00
94	CORA FH-565	2500	140.00	140.00
94	CORY FH-564	2500	115.00	115.00
94	DALLAS PS-403	2500	150.00	150.00
94	DARYL LL-947	2500	150.00	150.00
94	DEE LL-948	2500	110.00	110.00
94	DELILAH C-3195	2500	150.00	150.00
94	FAITH IND-522	2500	135.00	135.00
94	FAITH OC-60	2500	115.00	115.00
94	FLORA FH-583	2500	115.00	115.00
94	FLORETTE IND-519	2500	140.00	140.00
94	GARDINER PS-405	2500	150.00	150.00
94	GEORGIA IND-510	2500	220.00	220.00
94	GEORGIA SP-456	2500	115.00	115.00
94	HATTY/MATTY IND-514	2500	165.00	165.00
94	HEATHER YK-4531	3500	165.00	165.00
94	HONEY LL-945	2500	150.00	150.00
94	HYACINTH LL-941	2500	90.00	90.00
94	INDIAN IND-520	2500	115.00	115.00
94	IVY C-3203	2500	85.00	85.00
94	JACQUELINE C-3202	2500	150.00	150.00
94	JAN FH-584R	2500	115.00	115.00
94	JANIS FH-584B	2500	115.00	115.00
94	JENNY OC-36M	2500	115.00	115.00
94	JILLIAN C-3196	2500	150.00	150.00
94	JO YK-4539	3500	150.00	150.00
94	JORDAN SP-455	2500	150.00	150.00
94	KATE OC-55	2500	150.00	150.00
94	KATIE IND-511	2500	110.00	110.00
94	KELLY YK-4536	3500	150.00	150.00
94	KEVIN MS-25	2500	150.00	150.00
94	KEVIN YK-4543	3500	140.00	140.00
94	KIT YK-4547	3500	115.00	115.00
94	KITTEN IND-512	2500	110.00	110.00
94	LADY CAROLINE LL-938	2500	120.00	120.00
94	LADY CAROLINE LL-939	2500	120.00	120.00
94	LAUGHING WATERS PS-410	2500	150.00	150.00
94	LAUREN SP-458	2500	125.00	125.00
94	LINDSAY SP-462	2500	150.00	150.00
94	LITTLE RED RIDING HOOD FH-557	2500	140.00	140.00
94	LORETTA SP-457	2500	140.00	140.00
94	LUCINDA PS-406	2500	150.00	150.00
94	MAGNOLIA FH-558	2500	150.00	150.00
94	MAIDEN PS-409	2500	150.00	150.00
94	MANDY YK-4548	3500	115.00	115.00
94	MARGARET C-3204	2500	150.00	150.00
94	MARIA GU-35	2500	115.00	115.00
94	MARY ANN TR-79	2500	125.00	125.00
94	MARY JO FH-552	2500	150.00	150.00
94	MARY LOU FH-565	2500	135.00	135.00
94	MARY OC-56	2500	135.00	135.00
94	MEGAN C-3192	2500	150.00	150.00
94	MISS DEBUTANTE DEBI	RT	75.00	180.00
94	MISS ELIZABETH SP-459	2500	150.00	150.00
94	MISSY FH-567	2500	140.00	140.00
94	MORNING DEW INDIAN PS-404	2500	150.00	150.00
94	MUSICAL DOLL OC-45M	2500	140.00	140.00
94	NATALIE PP-2	2500	275.00	275.00
94	NIKKI PS-401	2500	150.00	150.00

YR	NAME	LIMIT	ISSUE	QUOTE
94	NIKKI SP-461	2500	150.00	150.00
94	NOEL MS-27	2500	150.00	150.00
94	NOELLE C-3199	2500	195.00	195.00
94	NOELLE MS-28	2500	150.00	150.00
94	ODETTA IND-521	2500	140.00	140.00
94	ORIANA IND-515	2500	140.00	140.00
94	PAIGE GU-33	2500	150.00	150.00
94	PAMELA LL-949	2500	115.00	115.00
94	PANAMA OM-43	2500	195.00	195.00
94	PATTY GU-34	2500	115.00	115.00
94	PAYSON YK-4541	3500	135.00	135.00
94	PAYTON PS-407	2500	150.00	150.00
94	PEARL IND-523	2500	275.00	275.00
94	PEGEEN C-3205	2500	150.00	150.00
94	PEGGY TR-75	2500	185.00	185.00
94	PETULA C-3191	2500	140.00	140.00
94	PRINCESS FOXFIRD PS-411	2500	150.00	150.00
94	PRINCESS MOONRISE YK-4542	3500	140.00	140.00
94	PRINCESS SNOW FLOWER PS-402	2500	150.00	150.00
94	PRISCILLA YK-4538	3500	135.00	135.00
94	REBECCA C-3177	2500	135.00	135.00
94	REGINA OM-41	2500	150.00	150.00
94	RITA FH-553	2500	115.00	115.00
94	ROBBY NM-29	2500	135.00	135.00
94	SARETTA SP-423	2500	100.00	100.00
94	SHAKA TR-45	2500	100.00	100.00
94	SISTER SUZIE IND-509	2500	95.00	95.00
94	SOUTHERN BELLE FH-570	2500	140.00	140.00
94	SPARKLE OM-40	2500	150.00	150.00
94	STEPHIE OC-41M	2500	115.00	115.00
94	SUE SWEL TR-73	2500	110.00	110.00
94	SUGAR PLUM FAIRY OM-39	2500	150.00	150.00
94	SUSIE SP-422	2500	164.00	164.00
94	SUZANNE LL-943	2500	105.00	105.00
94	SUZIE GU-38	2500	135.00	135.00
94	TAFFEY TR-80	2500	150.00	150.00
94	TALLULAH OM-44	2500	275.00	150.00
94	TERESA C-3198	2500	110.00	110.00
94	TIFFANY OC-44M	2500	140.00	140.00
94	TIPPI LL-946	2500	110.00	110.00
94	TODD YK-4540	3500	45.00	45.00
94	TOPAZ TR-74	2500	195.00	195.00
94	TRIXIE TR-77	2500	110.00	110.00
94	VIRGINIA TR-78	2500	195.00	195.00
94	WENDY MS-26	2500	150.00	150.00
95	BRENDA DOLL 551	2500	60.00	60.00
95	BRIANNA GU-300B	2500	30.00	30.00
95	BRIE C-3230	2500	30.00	30.00
95	BRIE CD-1631OC	2500	30.00	30.00
95	BRIE OM-89W	2500	125.00	125.00
95	BRITT OC077	2500	40.00	40.00
95	BRITTANY DOLL 558	2500	35.00	35.00
95	BRUGUNDY ANGEL FH-291D	2500	75.00	75.00
95	BRYNA DOLL 555	2500	35.00	35.00
95	BUNNY TR-97	2500	85.00	85.00
95	CAITLIN LL-997	2500	115.00	115.00
95	CANDICE TR-94	2500	135.00	135.00
95	CARMEL TR-93	2500	125.00	125.00
95	CAROLOTTA OM-80	2500	175.00	175.00
95	CARRIE C-3231	2500	30.00	30.00
95	CATHERINE RDK-231	2500	30.00	30.00
95	CECILY DOLL 552	2500	60.00	60.00
95	CELENE FH-618	2500	120.00	120.00
95	CELESTINE LL-982	2500	100.00	100.00
95	CHELSEA DOLL 560	2500	35.00	35.00
95	CHERRY FH-616	2500	100.00	100.00
95	CHRISTMAS KITTEN IND-530	2500	100.00	100.00
95	CIANCY GU-54	2500	80.00	80.00
95	CODY FH-629	2500	120.00	120.00
95	CYNTHIA GU-300C	2500	30.00	30.00
95	DANIELLE MER-808	2500	65.00	65.00
95	DANIELLE PS-432	2500	100.00	100.00
95	DARCY FH-636	2500	80.00	80.00
95	DARCY LL-986	2500	110.00	110.00
95	DARLA LL-988	2500	100.00	100.00
95	DENISE LL-994	2500	105.00	105.00

YR	NAME	LIMIT	ISSUE	QUOTE
95	DIANA RDK-221A	2500	35.00	35.00
95	DIANE PS-444	2500	110.00	110.00
95	DINAH OC-79	2500	40.00	40.00
95	DONNA GU-300D	2500	30.00	30.00
95	DULCIE FH-622	2500	110.00	110.00
95	ELAINE CD-02210	2500	50.00	50.00
95	ELEANOR C16669	2500	35.00	35.00
95	ELIZABETH DOLL 553	2500	35.00	35.00
95	ELLIE FH-621	2500	125.00	125.00
95	EMMA DOLL-559	2500	35.00	35.00
95	EMMA GU-300E	2500	30.00	30.00
95	EMMY IND-533	2500	85.00	85.00
95	ERIN RDK-223	2500	30.00	30.00
95	FAWN C-3228	2500	55.00	55.00
95	FELICIA TR-9	2500	30.00	30.00
95	FLEUR C16415	2500	30.00	30.00
95	GEORGIA IND-528	2500	125.00	125.00
95	GINNIE FH-619	2500	110.00	110.00
95	GOLD ANGEL FH-511G	2500	85.00	85.00
95	GREEN ANGEL FH-511C	2500	85.00	85.00
95	GRETCHEN FH-620	2500	120.00	120.00
95	GUARDIAN ANGEL OM-91	2500	200.00	200.00
95	GUARDIAN ANGEL TR-98	2500	85.00	85.00
95	HAPPY RDK-238	2500	25.00	25.00
95	HEATHER LL-991	2500	115.00	115.00
95	HEATHER PS-436	2500	115.00	115.00
95	HOLLY CD-16526	2500	30.00	30.00
95	HYACINTH C-3227	2500	130.00	130.00
95	IRENE GU-56	2500	85.00	85.00
95	IRINA RDK-237	2500	35.00	35.00
95	IVANA RDK-233	2500	35.00	35.00
95	JAMAICA LL-989	2500	75.00	75.00
95	JENNIFER PS-446	2500	145.00	145.00
95	JENNY CD-16673B	2500	35.00	35.00
95	JERRI PS-434	2500	100.00	100.00
95	JESSICA RDK-225	2500	30.00	30.00
95	JEWEL TR-100	2500	110.00	110.00
95	JOELLA CD-16779	2500	35.00	35.00
95	JOY CS-1450A	2500	35.00	35.00
95	JOY TR-99	2500	85.00	85.00
95	JULIA C-3234	2500	100.00	100.00
95	JULIA RDK-222	2500	35.00	35.00
95	JUNE CD-2212	2500	50.00	50.00
95	KARYN RDK-224	2500	35.00	35.00
95	KELSEY DOLL 561	2500	35.00	35.00
95	KIMMIE CS-15816	2500	30.00	30.00
95	KITTY IND-527	2500	40.00	40.00
95	LENORE FH-617	2500	120.00	120.00
95	LENORE RDK-229	2500	50.00	50.00
95	LESLIE LL-983	2500	105.00	105.00
95	LESLIE MER-809	2500	65.00	65.00
95	LILA GU-55	2500	55.00	55.00
95	LILI CD-16888	2500	30.00	30.00
95	LILY FH-630	2500	120.00	120.00
95	LINDSAY PS-442	2500	175.00	175.00
95	LISETTE LL-993	2500	105.00	105.00
95	LITTLE BOBBY RDK-235	2500	25.00	25.00
95	LITTLE LISA OM-86	2500	125.00	125.00
95	LITTLE LORI RDK-228	2500	20.00	20.00
95	LITTLE LOU RDK-227	2500	20.00	20.00
95	LITTLE MARY RDK-234	2500	25.00	25.00
95	LITTLE PATTY PS-429	2500	50.00	50.00
95	LUCIE MER-607	2500	65.00	65.00
95	LYNN LL-995	2500	105.00	105.00
95	MAE PS-431	2500	70.00	70.00
95	MAGGIE IND-532	2500	80.00	80.00
95	MARIA PS-437	2500	125.00	125.00
95	MARIELLE PS-443	2500	175.00	175.00
95	MARTINA RDK-232	2500	35.00	35.00
95	MARY ANN FH-633	2500	110.00	110.00
95	MARY ELIZABETH OC-51	2500	50.00	50.00
95	MAXINE C-3225	2500	125.00	125.00
95	MC KENZIE LL-987	2500	100.00	100.00
95	MEGAN RDK-220	2500	30.00	30.00
95	MEREDITH MER-806	2500	65.00	65.00
95	MERRI MER-810	2500	65.00	65.00

YR	NAME	LIMIT	ISSUE	QUOTE
95	MINDI PS-441	2500	125.00	125.00
95	MINDY LL-990	2500	75.00	75.00
95	MIRANDA C16456B	2500	30.00	30.00
95	MIRANDA TR-91	2500	135.00	135.00
95	MONICA TR-95	2500	135.00	135.00
95	NANCY FH-615	2500	100.00	100.00
95	NATASHA TR-90	2500	125.00	125.00
95	NORMAN C-3226	2500	135.00	135.00
95	OUR FIRST SKATES RDK-226/BG	2500	50.00	50.00
95	PAIGE IND-529	2500	80.00	80.00
95	PAN PAN GU-52	2500	60.00	60.00
95	PATTY C-3220	2500	60.00	60.00
95	PAULETTE PS-430	2500	80.00	80.00
95	PAULINE PS-440	2500	65.00	65.00
95	PEACHES IND-531	2500	80.00	80.00
95	RAINIE LL-984	2500	125.00	125.00
95	ROBIN C-3236	2500	60.00	60.00
95	RUSTY CS-1450B	2500	35.00	35.00
95	SARAH C-3214	2500	110.00	110.00
95	SASHA GU-57	2500	75.00	75.00
95	SHIMMERING CAROLINE LL-992	2500	115.00	115.00
95	SLEEPING BEAUTY OM-88	2500	115.00	115.00
95	SOPHIA PS-445	2500	125.00	125.00
95	SOUTHERN BELLE BRIDE FH-637	2500	160.00	160.00
95	STACY FH-634	2500	110.00	110.00
95	STACY OC-75	2500	40.00	40.00
95	SUZANNE DOLL 554	2500	35.00	35.00
95	SUZIE OC-80	2500	50.00	50.00
95	SWEET PEA LL-981	2500	90.00	90.00
95	SYLVIE CD-16634B	2500	35.00	35.00
95	TABITHA C-3233	2500	50.00	50.00
95	TERRI OM-78	2500	150.00	150.00
95	TINA OM-79	2500	150.00	150.00
95	TOBEY C-3232	2500	50.00	50.00
95	WEL LIN GU-44	2500	70.00	70.00
95	WENDY FH-626	2500	200.00	200.0
95	WINNIE LL-965	2500	75.00	75.00
95	WINTER WONDERLAND RDK-301	2500	35.00	35.00
95	WOODLAND SPRITE OM-90	2500	100.00	100.00
95	YELENA RDK-236	2500	35.00	35.00
92	CREOLE BLACK HP-202	5000	250.00	250.00
92	DARLA HP-204	5000	260.00	260.00
92	DULCIE HP-200	5000	250.00	250.00
92	DUSTIN HP-201	5000	250.00	250.00
92	LITTLE MATCH GIRL HP-205	5000	150.00	150.00
92	POLLY HP-208	5000	120.00	120.00
92	SPANKY HP-25	5000	250.00	250.00
92	CODY MS-19	5000	120.00	120.00
92	KATE MS-15	5000	190.00	190.00
92	MEGAN MS-12	5000	125.00	125.00
92	REBECCA MS-17B	5000	175.00	175.00
92	RUBY MS-18	5000	135.00	135.00
92	SALLY MS-25	5000	110.00	110.00
92	STACY MS-24	5000	110.00	110.00
92	VICTORIA W/BLANKET MS-10	5000	110.00	110.00
93	BONNETT BABY MS-17W	5000	175.00	175.00
92	ABIGAIL MS-11	5000	125.00	125.00
92	ADORA MS-14	5000	185.00	185.00
P. APRILE		**SIGNATURE DOLL SERIES**		
91	PAULETTE-PAC-2	5000	250.00	250.00
91	PAULETTE-PAC-4	5000	250.00	250.00
92	BRIDE & FLOWER GIRL-PAC-6	5000	600.00	600.00
92	CASSANDRA-PAC-8	CL	450.00	450.00
92	CASSIE FLOWER GIRL-PAC-9	CL	175.00	175.00
92	CELINE-PAC-11	5000	165.00	165.00
92	CLARISSA-PAC-3	5000	165.00	165.00
92	CYNTHIA-PAC-10	RT	165.00	165.00
92	EUGENIE BRIDE-PAC-1	5000	165.00	165.00
92	EVENING STAR-PAC-5	RT	500.00	500.00
92	MELANIE PAC-14	RT	300.00	300.00
92	NADIA PAC-18	RT	175.00	175.00
92	OLIVIA PAC-12	RT	300.00	300.00
92	PAVOLVA PAC-17	RT	145.00	145.00
92	VANESSA PAC-15	RT	300.00	300.00
92	VIOLETTA PAC-16	RT	165.00	165.00
95	AMELIA PAC-28	5000	130.00	130.00

YR	NAME	LIMIT	ISSUE	QUOTE
95	BRIE PPA-26	5000	180.00	180.00
95	IMAN PPA-24	5000	110.00	110.00
91	PRECIOUS BABY-SB-100	5000	250.00	250.00
91	PRECIOUS PARTY TIME-SB-102	5000	250.00	250.00
91	PRECIOUS SPRING TIME-SB-104	CL	250.00	250.00
91	DOZY ELF WITH FEATHERBED-MAB-100	RT	110.00	110.00
91	DUBY ELF WITH FEATHERBED-MAB-103	RT	110.00	110.00
91	DUDLEY ELF WITH FEATHERBED-MAB-101	RT	110.00	110.00
91	DUFFY ELF WITH FEATHERBED-MAB-102	RT	110.00	110.00
95	CARA DALI-1	5000	400.00	400.00
95	PATRICIA DALI-3	5000	280.00	280.00
95	STACY DALI-2	5000	360.00	360.00
95	AMANDA KSFA-1	5000	175.00	175.00
95	HAPPY JFC-100	5000	120.00	120.00
94	SIS JAG-110	RT	110.00	110.00
94	TEX JAG-114	5000	110.00	110.00
94	TRACY JAG-111	5000	150.00	150.00
94	TREVOR JAG-112	5000	115.00	115.00
93	GRACE HKH-2	5000	250.00	250.00
93	HELENE HKH-1	5000	250.00	250.00
93	REILLY HKH-3	5000	260.00	260.00
95	AMY ROSE HKHF-200	5000	125.00	125.00
95	BRAD HKH-15	5000	85.00	85.00
95	LAUREL HKH-17R	5000	110.00	110.00
95	LAUREN HKH-202	5000	150.00	150.00
95	LUCY HKH-14	5000	105.00	105.00
95	NATASHA HKH-17P	5000	110.00	110.00
95	NIKKI HKHF-20	5000	125.00	125.00
95	SUZIE HKH-16	5000	100.00	100.00
91	BRIDGETTE-PK-104	RT	120.00	120.00
91	CLAIR ANN-PK-252	5000	100.00	100.00
91	ENOC-PK-100	5000	100.00	100.00
91	SHUN LEE-PK-102	CL	120.00	120.00
91	SPARKLE-PK-250	5000	100.00	100.00
91	SUSAN MARIE-PK-103	RT	120.00	120.00
91	SWEET PEA-PK-251	CL	100.00	100.00
92	BABY CAKES CRUMBS PK-CRUMBS	5000	17.50	17.50
92	BABY CAKES CRUMBS/BLACK-PK-CRUMBS/B	5000	17.50	17.50
92	RAVEN ESKIMO-PK-106	RT	130.00	130.00
95	ELEANORE GMNA-100	5000	225.00	225.00
95	HOLLY GMN-202	5000	150.00	150.00
92	CREOLE BLACK-HP-202	RT	250.00	250.00
92	DARLA-HP-204	5000	250.00	250.00
92	DULCIE-HP-200	RT	250.00	250.00
92	DUSTIN-HP-201	RT	250.00	250.00
92	LITTLE MATCH GIRL HP-205	RT	150.00	150.00
92	POLLY HP-206	5000	120.00	120.00
92	SPANKY-HP-25	RT	250.00	250.00
92	ALEXANDRIA PAC-19	5000	300.00	300.00
95	ADAK PPA-21	5000	110.00	110.00
95	ALAIN PPA-19	2500	100.00	100.00
95	CASEY PPA-23	5000	85.00	85.00
95	LATISHA PPA-25	5000	110.00	110.00
95	LENA PPA-20	5000	120.00	120.00
95	SHAO LING PPA-22	5000	110.00	110.00
95	GINNY LR-2	5000	360.00	360.00
95	LENORE LRC-100	500	140.00	140.00
95	MEREDITH LR-3	5000	375.00	375.00
95	TAMMY LR-4	5000	325.00	325.00
95	TIFFANY LR-1	5000	370.00	370.00
91	ALICE-MS-7	5000	120.00	120.00
91	AMBER-MS-1	RT	95.00	95.00
91	BECKY-MS-2	RT	95.00	95.00
91	BIANCA-PK-101	RT	120.00	120.00
91	DADDY'S LITTLE DARLING-MS-8	5000	165.00	165.00
91	MIKEY-MS-3	RT	95.00	95.00
91	MOMMY'S RAYS OF SUNSHINE-MS-9	5000	165.00	165.00
91	STEPHIE-MS-6	RT	125.00	125.00
91	SU LIN-MS-5	RT	105.00	105.00
91	YAWNING KATE-MS-4	RT	105.00	105.00
92	ABIGAIL-MS-11	RT	125.00	125.00
92	ADORA-MS-14	5000	185.00	185.00
92	CODYY MS-19	RT	120.00	120.00
92	KATE-MS-15	RT	190.00	190.00
92	MEGAN-MS-12	5000	125.00	125.00
92	REBECCA BEIGE BONNET MS-17B	5000	175.00	175.00

YR	NAME	LIMIT	ISSUE	QUOTE
92	RUBY MS-18	5000	135.00	135.00
92	SALLY-MS-25	RT	110.00	110.00
92	STACY-MS-24	RT	110.00	110.00
92	VICTORIA W/ BLANKET-MS-10	RT	110.00	110.00
93	BONNETT BABY MS-17W	5000	175.00	175.00
P. KOLESAR		**SIGNATURE DOLL SERIES SERIES**		
92	"LITTLE TURTLE" INDIAN-PK-110	RT	150.00	150.00

SPORTS IMPRESSIONS

*			**PORCELAIN DOLLS**	
90	DON MATTINGLY	1990	150.00	150.00
90	MICKEY MANTLE	1956	150.00	150.00

SUSAN WAKEEN DOLL CO. INC.

S. WAKEEN		**THE LITTLEST BALLET COMPANY**		
85	CYNTHIA	375	198.00	350.00
85	JEANNE	375	198.00	800.00
85	PATTY	375	198.00	500.00
87	ELIZABETH	250	425.00	895.00-1000.00

THE COLLECTABLES

D. EFFNER				
89	WELCOME HOME	1000	330.00	400.00
90	LIZBETH ANN	1000	420.00	420.00
86	TATIANA	1000	270.00	1200.00
87	STORYTIME BY SARAH JANE	1000	330.00	500.00
87	TASHA	1000	290.00	1400.00
89	MICHELLE	250	270.00	700.00
90	BASSINET BABY	2000	130.00	130.00
90	DANIELLE	1000	400.00	400.00
90	IN YOUR EASTER BONNET	1000	350.00	350.00
91	ADRIANNA	100	1350.00	1350.00
91	BETHANY	500	450.00	450.00
91	KELSIE	500	320.00	320.00
91	LAUREN	300	490.00	490.00
91	NATASHA	750	510.00	510.00
91	YVETTE	300	580.00	580.00
92	ANGEL ON MY SHOULDER (LILLIANNE W/CECE)	500	530.00	530.00
92	KARLIE	500	380.00	380.00
92	KARLIE	500	380.00	380.00
92	MARISSA	300	350.00	350.00
92	MARISSA	300	350.00	350.00
92	MARTY	250	190.00	190.00
92	MATIA	250	190.00	190.00
92	MISSY	OP	59.00	59.00
92	MOLLY	450	350.00	350.00
92	SHELLEY	300	450.00	450.00
92	SHELLEY	300	450.00	450.00
93	AMBER	500	330.00	390.00
93	HALEY	500	330.00	400.00
93	LITTLE DUMPLING (BLACK)	500	190.00	210.00
93	LITTLE DUMPLING (WHITE)	500	190.00	210.00
93	MAGGIE	500	330.00	390.00
93	MOLLY	450	350.00	400.00
94	AFTERNOON DELIGHT	500	410.00	425.00
94	MADISON	250	350.00	375.00
94	MADISON SAILOR	250	370.00	390.00
94	MORGAN CHRISTMAS	500	390.00	410.00
94	SUGAR PLUM FAIRY	500	250.00	270.00
P. PARKINS		**1994 COLLECTOR'S CLUB**		
93	KRYSTAL	*	380.00	590.00
P. PARKINS		**ANGELS SERIES**		
93	ANGEL ON MY SHOULDER	500	530.00	590.00
93	MY GUARDIAN ANGEL	500	590.00	700.00
94	GUARDING THE WAY	500	950.00	1050.00
P. PARKINS		**BUTTERFLY BABIES**		
89	BELINDA	1000	270.00	300.00
90	WILLOW	1000	240.00	240.00
92	LATICIA	500	320.00	320.00
D. EFFNER		**CHERISHED MEMORIES**		
88	TEA TIME	1000	380.00	400.00
86	AMY AND ANDREW	1000	220.00	325.00
88	BRITTANY	1000	240.00	1200.00
88	HEATHER	1000	280.00	300.00-350.00
88	JENNIFER	1000	380.00	500.00-600.00
88	LEIGH ANN AND LELAND	1000	250.00	250.00-300.00
89	CASSANDRA	1000	500.00	500.00
89	GENERATIONS	1000	480.00	500.00

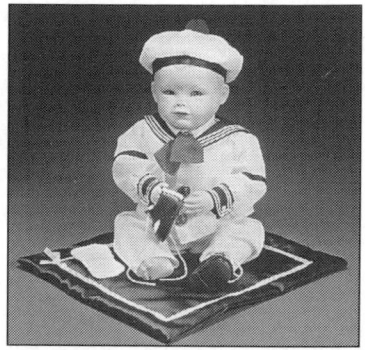

Perhaps no one knows children quite the way Yolanda Bello does. Matthew *is the fourth issue in her series of "Yolanda's Picture-Perfect Babies." Produced by Ashton-Drake Galleries.*

The popularity of ethnic dolls is on the rise. Enco *is by Seymour Mann.*

Chelsea *wears an outfit befitting little Red Riding Hood. She is produced by Roman.*

Watch your step, little one! Loving Steps *is the first issue in Sandra Kuck's "Precious Memories of Motherhood" collection. The doll is produced by Reco.*

YR NAME	LIMIT	ISSUE	QUOTE
89 TWINKLES	2000	170.00	200.00
P. PARKINS		**COLLECTOR'S CLUB DOLL**	
90 MANDY	CL	360.00	1000.00
91 KALLIE	YR	410.00	410.00
92 MOMMY AND ME	YR	*	*
P. PARKINS		**ENCHANTED CHILDREN**	
90 KARA	400	550.00	550.00
90 KATLIN	400	550.00	550.00
90 KRISTIN	400	550.00	650.00
90 TIFFY	500	370.00	700.00-1000.00
P. PARKINS		**FAIRY**	
88 TABATHA	1500	370.00	400.00-450.00
P. PARKINS		**LIMITED EDITION VINYL DOLLS**	
92 ANNIE	2500	190.00	190.00
92 BRENDA (BLUE DRESS)	2500	180.00	180.00
92 BRENDA (CHRISTMAS)	250	240.00	240.00
92 BRENDA (SPRING)	250	240.00	240.00
92 BRENT	2500	190.00	190.00
92 JENNY AND JEREMY (PUPPY LOVE)	2500	180.00	180.00
92 JESSICA	2500	190.00	190.00
D. EFFNER		**MOTHER'S LITTLE TREASURES**	
85 1ST EDITION	1000	380.00	700.00
90 2ND EDITION	1000	440.00	600.00
P. PARKINS		**SMALL ANGELS SERIES**	
94 EARTH ANGEL	500	195.00	210.00
P. PARKINS		**TINY TREASURES**	
91 HOLLY	1000	150.00	150.00
91 LITTLE GIRL	1000	140.00	140.00
91 TODDLER BOY	1000	130.00	130.00
91 TODDLER GIRL	1000	130.00	130.00
91 VICTORIAN BOY	1000	150.00	150.00
91 VICTORIAN GIRL	1000	150.00	150.00
92 NICOLAUS	500	160.00	160.00
92 NICOLE	500	180.00	180.00
92 TOMMIE	1000	160.00	160.00
92 TORI	1000	170.00	170.00
D. EFFNER		**YESTERDAY'S CHILD**	
82 CLEO	1000	180.00	250.00
82 COLUMBINE	1000	180.00	250.00
82 JASON AND JESSICA	1000	150.00	300.00
83 CHAD AND CHARITY	1000	190.00	240.00
83 NOEL	1000	190.00	240.00
84 KEVIN AND KARISSA	1000	190.00	250.00-300.00
84 REBECCA	1000	250.00	250.00-300.00
86 ASHLEY	1000	220.00	275.00
86 TODD AND TIFFANY	1000	220.00	250.00

TIMELESS CREATIONS

A. HIMSTEDT		**SUMMER DREAMS**	
91 ENZO	TL	598.00	598.00
91 JULE	TL	598.00	598.00
91 PEMBA	TL	598.00	598.00
91 SANGA	TL	598.00	598.00

TUJAYS ARTIST DOLLS

MIKO			
86 HENRY VIII	10	650.00	800.00
87 ANN BOLEYN	10	550.00	700.00
87 K. OF ARAGON	10	550.00	750.00
86 ANDREA	20	475.00	850.00
86 ANINA	20	595.00	925.00
87 AMANDA	20	595.00	950.00
87 ASHLEY	20	525.00	925.00
87 KATHERINE	20	675.00	1000.00
87 SOPHIE	20	475.00	875.00
88 ALTHEA	7	595.00	1000.00
88 ELIZABETH	25	395.00	595.00
88 MELISSA	25	325.00	350.00
88 SARAH	25	395.00	475.00
89 ALETA	20	575.00	825.00
89 CHARLOTTE	20	675.00	950.00
89 ESTELLE	20	575.00	850.00
89 HENRIETTA	20	575.00	800.00
90 GEORGETTE	100	475.00	740.00
90 LUCILLE	20	695.00	950.00
91 ABIGAIL	100	750.00	*
91 GENEVIEVE	10	975.00	*

YR	NAME	LIMIT	ISSUE	QUOTE
91	JENNIFER	100	615.00	*
91	NATALIE	100	525.00	*
91	PHYLLIS	100	595.00	*
91	REBECCA	100	615.00	*
91	STEPHANIE	20	990.00	*

VICTORIAN TRADITION

K. GLEASON — CLASSICS COLLECTION

YR	NAME	LIMIT	ISSUE	QUOTE
93	OLIVER TWIST	50	795.00	795.00

K. GLEASON — LAND OF FAERYE TALES & NURSERY RHYMES

YR	NAME	LIMIT	ISSUE	QUOTE
93	RED RIDING HOOD	50	795.00	795.00
95	MISS MUFFET	50	795.00	795.00

K. GLEASON — LIFE IS FUN!

YR	NAME	LIMIT	ISSUE	QUOTE
94	2ND CHILDHOOD	20	995.00	995.00
95	MISS AMERICA	50	795.00	795.00

K. GLEASON — NORTHERN REALM OF FAERYE

YR	NAME	LIMIT	ISSUE	QUOTE
94	BUTTONWILLOW	20	795.00	795.00
94	PTARMINI	20	795.00	795.00
94	SPRUCE	20	795.00	795.00

K. GLEASON — PEOPLE OF THE COVENANT

YR	NAME	LIMIT	ISSUE	QUOTE
94	NOAHS WIFE	50	795.00	795.00

K. GLEASON — THE ALASKANS

YR	NAME	LIMIT	ISSUE	QUOTE
94	LADY DIVINE	75	795.00	795.00

W.S. GEORGE

P. RYAN BROOKS — MY FAIR LADY

YR	NAME	LIMIT	ISSUE	QUOTE
91	ELIZA AT ASCOT	CL	125.00	150.00

M. RODERICK — ROMANTIC FLOWER MAIDENS

YR	NAME	LIMIT	ISSUE	QUOTE
88	ROSE, WHO IS LOVE	CL	87.00	125.00-150.00
89	DAISY	CL	87.00	87.00
90	LILY	TL	92.00	160.00
90	VIOLET	TL	92.00	92.00

R. AKERS/ S. GIRARDI — STEPPING OUT

YR	NAME	LIMIT	ISSUE	QUOTE
91	MILLIE	TL	99.00	99.00

P. RYAN BROOKS — THE KING & I

YR	NAME	LIMIT	ISSUE	QUOTE
91	SHALL WE DANCE?	CL	175.00	175.00

R. AKERS/ S. GIRARDI — YEAR BOOK MEMORIES

YR	NAME	LIMIT	ISSUE	QUOTE
91	PEGGY SUE	TL	87.00	87.00

Figurines

Dean Genth

"Secondary market" is often a confusing term for novice collectors. Secondary market is not an outlet for "seconds" or "rejects." It is, however, the market for collectibles after they have left the original, primary point of retail sales.

The primary market for collectibles is represented by the many authorized dealers that retail the various lines of collectibles. Secondary market transactions are represented by sales between individual collectors as well as dealers who may or may not be involved with primary retail selling.

Collectors often wonder how the prices are determined for figurines on the secondary market. In our free market society, the answer is quite simple—supply and demand. It is the buyer/collector that really determines the secondary market price.

Price guides and books that list secondary market prices generally track selling prices from a geographical cross-section of dealers, swap and sell event results, as well as auction results. Oftentimes these collectibles price guides list current market prices as well as other pertinent information regarding each figurine or item.

Selling items on the secondary market can be easily accomplished if the price requested is fair and the choice of dispersal is to the owner's liking. Once the selling price is determined, the seller must decide upon which method of selling will be employed. The seller can choose to sell directly to other collectors by advertising in the local classifieds or in one of the many collectibles publications such as *Collectors mart* magazine.

Other collectors often choose to dispose of an entire collection quickly by selling to a reputable or well-known secondary market dealer. Many secondary market dealers are experts in certain areas of collectibles and are prepared to buy large collections for their inventories.

Sometimes collectors opt to have their large collections auctioned to the highest bidders. This method assures that dispersal will be quick and almost effortless on the part of the seller. Auction prices can vary widely from time to time and locale to locale. The prices, when averaged from several auctions, usually represent what is considered to be "fair market value."

A replacement value quotation on the secondary market represents the price a buyer can expect to pay for a figurine or other collectible if that purchase must be made fairly soon. Sometimes certain items are not always readily available on the secondary market, thus driving up the price of the item.

Collectors must also determine whether they will sell to a dealer at wholesale price levels or attempt to advertise with the possibility of achieving closer to retail prices. Time availability and financial resources are considerations when undertaking the task of selling to other collectors at near-retail prices on the secondary market.

Always remember that secondary markets exist because a buyer is searching for an item no longer available though regular retail distribution channels. Many reputable secondary market dealers are in business to assist you with both selling and buying figurines.

Dealer and appraiser DEAN A. GENTH is a secondary market expert on Precious Moments, Swarovski Silver Crystal and M.I. Hummel. He serves as special consultant for The No. 1 Price Guide to M.I. Hummel *and owns Miller's Hallmark and Gift Gallery in Cincinnati, Eaton and Xenia, Ohio.*

From the tip of his arrow to the fringe on his moccasins, the detailed Resolute *makes a bold statement. The mixed media figure was created by C.A. Pardell and produced by Legends.*

Equine artist Fred Stone, typically known for his limited edition prints, aptly captures the care a young mother takes of her young foal. Arabian Mare & Foal is produced by American Artists.

The emotion and action captured by artist C.A. Pardell makes The Final Charge *a true work of art. The piece is produced by Legends.*

The legendary Chief Joseph *is captured in mixed media by artist Joe Slockbower. The piece is produced by the Lance Corp.*

Look into this wolf's eyes and you'll understand that he means no harm. Forest Spirit *was crafted by artist Kitty Cantrell and produced by Legends.*

Displaying extensive detailing, Michael Boyett's Flat Out for Red River Station *pewter sculpture, produced by the Lance Corp., is limited to 2,500.*

YR NAME	LIMIT	ISSUE	QUOTE

FIGURINES

AMERICAN ARTISTS
F. STONE · FRED STONE FIGURINES

YR	NAME	LIMIT	ISSUE	QUOTE
85	THE BLACK STALLION (BRONZE)	*	150.00	175.00
85	THE BLACK STALLION (PORCELAIN)	*	125.00	275.00
86	ARABIAN MARE & FOAL	*	150.00	225.00
86	TRANQUILITY	*	175.00	275.00
87	REARING BLACK STALLION (BRONZE)	*	175.00	195.00
87	REARING BLACK STALLION (PORCELAIN)	*	150.00	175.00

AMERICAST INC.
K. WINDRIX · THE COMMANDERS

YR	NAME	LIMIT	ISSUE	QUOTE
94	GEORGE A. CUSTER	500	195.00	200.00
94	JAMES LONGSTREET	500	195.00	200.00
94	JOSHUA L. CHAMBERLAIN	500	195.00	200.00
94	ROBERT E. LEE	5000	195.00	200.00
94	ULYSSES S. GRANT	5000	195.00	200.00
95	"STONEWALL" JACKSON	500	195.00	200.00
95	J.E.B. STUART	500	195.00	200.00
95	WILLIAM T. SHERMAN	500	195.00	200.00

ANHEUSER-BUSCH INC.
P. RADTKE · ANHEUSER-BUSCH COLL. FIGURINE

YR	NAME	LIMIT	ISSUE	QUOTE
95	HORSEPLAY F1	OP	7500.00	65.00

M. URDAHL · COLLECTIBLE FIGURINES

YR	NAME	LIMIT	ISSUE	QUOTE
94	BUDDIES N4575	7,500	65.00	65.00

ANRI
* · CLUB ANRI

YR	NAME	LIMIT	ISSUE	QUOTE
88	MAESTRO MICKEY	CL	170.00	225.00
89	DAPPER DONALD, 4 IN.	5000	199.00	199.00
89	DIVA MINNIE	5000	190.00	200.00
91	DAISY DUCK	*	250.00	250.00
83	WELCOME, 4 IN.	CL	110.00	425.00
84	MY FRIEND, 4 IN.	CL	110.00	400.00
85	HARVEST TIME, 4 IN.	CL	125.00	325.00
86	CELEBRATION MARCH, 5 IN.	CL	165.00	255.00
86	HARVEST'S HELPER, 4 IN.	CL	135.00	200.00-335.00
87	WILL YOU BE MINE	CL	135.00	250.00-325.00
88	FOREVER YOURS	CL	170.00	250.00
89	TWENTY YEARS OF LOVE	CL	190.00	190.00
89	YOU ARE MY SUNSHINE, 4 IN.	YR	220.00	220.00
91	WITH ALL MY HEART	*	250.00	250.00
84	APPLE OF MY EYE, 4 1/2 IN.	CL	135.00	150.00
85	DAD'S HELPER, 4 1/2 IN.	CL	135.00	135.00
86	MAKE A WISH	CL	165.00	350.00
86	ROMANTIC NOTIONS, 4 IN.	CL	135.00	200.00-325.00
87	A YOUNG MAN'S FANCY	CL	135.00	175.00-250.00
88	I'VE GOT A SECRET	CL	170.00	215.00
89	A LITTLE BASHFUL, 4 IN.	YR	220.00	220.00
89	I'LL NEVER TELL	CL	190.00	190.00
91	KISS ME	*	250.00	250.00

* · DISNEY WOODCARVINGS

YR	NAME	LIMIT	ISSUE	QUOTE
87	DONALD DUCK, 4 IN.	CL	150.00	195.00
87	GOOFY, 4 IN.	CL	150.00	195.00
87	MICKEY AND MINNIE, 6 IN. (MATCHING NUM.)	CL	625.00	1650.00
87	MICKEY MOUSE, 4 IN.	CL	150.00	210.00
87	MINNIE MOUSE, 4 IN.	CL	150.00	210.00
87	PINOCCHIO, 4 IN.	CL	150.00	195.00
88	DONALD DUCK, 1 3/4 IN.	CL	80.00	100.00
88	DONALD DUCK, 4 IN.	CL	180.00	180.00
88	DONALD DUCK, 6 IN.	CL	350.00	700.00
88	GOOFY, 1 3/4 IN.	CL	80.00	100.00
88	GOOFY, 4 IN.	CL	180.00	199.00
88	GOOFY, 6 IN.	500	350.00	350.00
88	GOOFY, 6 IN.	CL	350.00	700.00
88	MICKEY MOUSE, 1 3/4 IN.	CL	80.00	100.00
88	MICKEY MOUSE, 4 IN.	CL	180.00	199.00
88	MICKEY SORCERER'S APPRENTICE, 2 IN.	OP	80.00	100.00
88	MICKEY SORCERER'S APPRENTICE, 4 IN.	OP	180.00	199.00
88	MICKEY SORCERER'S APPRENTICE, 6 IN.	CL	350.00	700.00
88	PINOCCHIO, 1 3/4 IN.	CL	80.00	100.00
88	PINOCCHIO, 4 IN.	CL	180.00	180.00
88	PLUTO, 1 3/4 IN.	CL	80.00	100.00
88	PLUTO, 4 IN.	CL	180.00	180.00

YR	NAME	LIMIT	ISSUE	QUOTE
89	DAISY, 4 IN.	OP	190.00	205.00
89	DONALD, 4 IN.	OP	190.00	205.00
89	GOOFY, 4 IN.	OP	190.00	205.00
89	MICKEY & MINNIE, 6 IN. (SET)	500	700.00	700.00
89	MICKEY AND MINNIE, 20 IN. (MATCHED SET)	50	7000.00	7000.00
89	MICKEY, 10 IN.	250	700.00	750.00
89	MICKEY, 20 IN.	50	3500.00	3500.00
89	MICKEY, 4 IN.	OP	190.00	205.00
89	MINI DAISY, 2 IN.	OP	85.00	100.00
89	MINI DONALD, 2 IN.	OP	85.00	100.00
89	MINI GOOFY, 2 IN.	OP	85.00	100.00
89	MINI MICKEY, 2 IN.	OP	85.00	100.00
89	MINI MINNIE, 2 IN.	OP	85.00	100.00
89	MINI PLUTO, 2 IN.	OP	85.00	100.00
89	MINNIE, 10 IN.	250	700.00	750.00
89	MINNIE, 20 IN.	50	3500.00	3500.00
89	MINNIE, 4 IN.	OP	190.00	205.00
89	PINOCCHIO, 10 IN.	250	700.00	700.00
89	PINOCCHIO, 2 IN.	CL	85.00	100.00
89	PINOCCHIO, 20 IN.	50	3500.00	3500.00
89	PINOCCHIO, 4 IN.	CL	190.00	199.00
89	PINOCCHIO, 6 IN.	500	350.00	350.00
89	PLUTO, 4 IN.	CL	190.00	205.00
89	PLUTO, 6 IN.	500	350.00	350.00
90	CHEF GOOFY, 2 1/2 IN.	OP	125.00	125.00
90	CHEF GOOFY, 5 IN.	OP	265.00	265.00
90	DONALD AND DAISY, 6 IN. (MATCHED SET)	500	700.00	700.00
90	MICKEY MOUSE, 2 IN.	OP	100.00	100.00
90	MICKEY MOUSE, 4 IN.	OP	199.00	205.00
90	MICKEY SKATING, 4 IN.	*	250.00	250.00
90	MINNIE MOUSE, 2 IN.	OP	100.00	100.00
90	MINNIE MOUSE, 4 IN.	OP	199.00	205.00
90	MINNIE SKATING, 4 IN.	*	250.00	250.00
91	BELL BOY DONALD, 4 IN.	*	250.00	250.00
91	BELL BOY DONALD, 4 IN.	*	250.00	250.00
91	BELL BOY DONALD, 6 IN.	500	400.00	400.00
91	BELL BOY DONALD, 6 IN.	500	400.00	400.00
91	MICKEY SKATING, 2 IN.	*	120.00	120.00
91	MICKEY SKATING, 2 IN.	*	120.00	120.00
91	MICKEY SKATING, 4 IN.	*	250.00	250.00
91	MINNIE SKATING, 2 IN.	*	120.00	120.00
91	MINNIE SKATING, 2 IN.	*	120.00	120.00
91	MINNIE SKATING, 4 IN.	*	250.00	250.00
J. FERRANDIZ			**FERRANDIZ BOY & GIRL**	
76	COWBOY, 6 IN.	1500	75.00	700.00
76	HARVEST GIRL, 6 IN.	1500	75.00	800.00
77	LEADING THE WAY, 6 IN.	1500	100.00	375.00
77	TRACKER, 6 IN.	1500	100.00	375.00
78	BASKET OF JOY, 6 IN.	1500	140.00	350.00
78	PEACE PIPE, 6 IN.	1500	140.00	375.00
79	FIRST BLOSSOM, 6 IN.	2250	135.00	375.00
79	HAPPY STRUMMER, 6 IN.	2250	160.00	395.00
80	FRIENDS, 6 IN.	2250	200.00	350.00
80	MELODY FOR TWO, 6 IN.	2250	200.00	350.00
81	MERRY MELODY, 6 IN.	2250	210.00	350.00
81	TINY SOUNDS, 6 IN.	2250	210.00	350.00
82	GUIDING LIGHT, 6 IN.	2250	225.00	275.00
82	TO MARKET, 6 IN.	2250	220.00	250.00
83	ADMIRATION, 6 IN.	2250	220.00	250.00
83	BEWILDERED, 6 IN.	2250	196.00	250.00
84	FRIENDLY FACES, 3 IN.	2250	225.00	250.00
84	FRIENDLY FACES, 6 IN.	2250	210.00	225.00
84	WANDERER'S RETURN, 3 IN.	2250	93.00	125.00
84	WANDERER'S RETURN, 6 IN.	2250	195.00	250.00
85	PEACEFUL FRIENDS, 3 IN.	2250	120.00	120.00
85	PEACEFUL FRIENDS, 6 IN.	2250	250.00	250.00
85	TENDER LOVE, 3 IN.	2250	100.00	125.00
85	TENDER LOVE, 6 IN.	2250	225.00	250.00
86	GOLDEN SHEAVES, 3 IN.	2250	125.00	125.00
86	GOLDEN SHEAVES, 6 IN.	2250	245.00	245.00
86	SEASON'S BOUNTY, 3 IN.	2250	125.00	125.00
86	SEASON'S BOUNTY, 6 IN.	2250	245.00	245.00
87	DEAR SWEETHEART, 3 IN.	2250	130.00	130.00
87	DEAR SWEETHEART, 6 IN.	2250	250.00	250.00
87	FOR MY SWEETHEART, 3 IN.	2250	130.00	130.00
87	FOR MY SWEETHEART, 6 IN.	2250	250.00	250.00

YR	NAME	LIMIT	ISSUE	QUOTE
88	EXTRA, EXTRA!, 3 IN.	2250	145.00	145.00
88	EXTRA, EXTRA!, 6 IN.	2250	320.00	320.00
88	SUNNY SKIES, 3 IN.	2250	145.00	145.00
88	SUNNY SKIES, 6 IN.	2250	320.00	320.00
89	BAKER BOY, 3 IN.	1500	170.00	170.00
89	BAKER BOY, 6 IN.	1500	340.00	340.00
89	PASTRY GIRL, 3 IN.	1500	170.00	170.00
89	PASTRY GIRL, 6 IN.	1500	340.00	340.00
90	ALPINE FRIEND, 3 IN.	1500	225.00	450.00
90	ALPINE FRIEND, 6 IN.	1500	450.00	450.00
90	ALPINE MUSIC, 3 IN.	1500	225.00	225.00
90	ALPINE MUSIC, 6 IN.	1500	450.00	450.00
91	CATALONIAN BOY, 3 IN.	1500	227.50	227.50
91	CATALONIAN BOY, 6 IN.	1500	500.00	500.00
91	CATALONIAN GIRL, 3 IN.	1500	227.50	227.50
91	CATALONIAN GIRL, 6 IN.	1500	500.00	500.00

J. FERRANDIZ — FERRANDIZ MATCHING NUMBER WOODCARVINGS

YR	NAME	LIMIT	ISSUE	QUOTE
88	BON APPETIT, 3 IN. (SET)	*	*	*
88	BON APPETIT, 6 IN. (SET)	*	*	*
88	DEAR SWEETHEART, 3 IN.	100	285.00	495.00
88	EXTRA, EXTRA!, 3 IN.	100	315.00	315.00
88	EXTRA, EXTRA!, 6 IN.	100	665.00	665.00
88	FOR MY SWEETHEART, 3 IN. (SET)	*	*	*
88	PICNIC FOR TWO, 3 IN.	500	390.00	390.00
88	PICNIC FOR TWO, 6 IN.	500	845.00	845.00
88	SUNNY SKIES, 3 IN. (SET)	*	*	*
88	SUNNY SKIES, 6 IN. (SET)	*	*	*
89	BAKER/PASTRY, 3 IN.	500	340.00	340.00
89	BAKER/PASTRY, 6 IN.	500	680.00	680.00
89	DEAR SWEETHEART, 6 IN.	100	525.00	900.00
89	FOR MY SWEETHEART, 6 IN. (SET)	*	*	*
90	ALPINE MUSIC/FRIEND, 3 IN.	100	450.00	450.00
90	ALPINE MUSIC/FRIEND, 6 IN.	100	900.00	900.00
91	CATALONIAN BOY/GIRL, 3 IN.	100	455.00	455.00
91	CATALONIAN BOY/GIRL, 6 IN.	100	1000.00	1000.00

J. FERRANDIZ — FERRANDIZ MESSAGE COLLECTION

YR	NAME	LIMIT	ISSUE	QUOTE
89	GOD'S MIRACLE, 4 1/2 IN.	5000	300.00	300.00
89	GOD'S PRECIOUS GIFT, 4 1/2 IN.	5000	300.00	300.00
89	HE GUIDES US, 4 1/2 IN.	5000	300.00	300.00
89	HE IS THE LIGHT, 4 1/2 IN.	5000	300.00	300.00
89	HE IS THE LIGHT, 9 IN.	5000	600.00	600.00
89	HEAVEN SENT, 4 1/2 IN.	5000	300.00	300.00
89	LIGHT FROM WITHIN, 4 1/2 IN.	5000	300.00	300.00
89	LOVE KNOWS NO BOUNDS, 4 1/2 IN.	5000	300.00	300.00
89	LOVE SO POWERFUL, 4 1/2 IN.	5000	300.00	300.00
90	CHRISTMAS CARILLON, 4 1/2 IN.	2500	299.00	299.00
90	COUNT YOUR BLESSINGS, 4 1/2 IN.	5000	300.00	300.00
90	GOD'S CREATION, 4 1/2 IN.	5000	300.00	300.00

J. FERRANDIZ — FERRANDIZ MINI NATIVITY SET

YR	NAME	LIMIT	ISSUE	QUOTE
84	INFANT, 1 1/2 IN. (SET)	OP	*	*
84	JOSEPH, 1 1/2 IN. (SET)	OP	*	*
84	LEADING THE WAY, 1 1/2 IN. (SET)	OP	*	*
84	MARY, 1 1/2 IN.	OP	300.00	540.00
84	OX DONKEY, 1 1/2 IN. (SET)	OP	*	*
84	SHEEP KNEELING, 1 1/2 IN. (SET)	OP	*	*
84	SHEEP STANDING, 1 1/2 IN. (SET)	OP	*	*
85	BABY CAMEL, 1 1/2 IN.	OP	45.00	53.00
85	CAMEL GUIDE, 1 1/2 IN.	OP	45.00	53.00
85	CAMEL, 1 1/2 IN.	OP	45.00	53.00
85	HARMONY, 1 1/2 IN.	OP	45.00	53.00
85	REST, 1 1/2 IN.	OP	45.00	53.00
85	REVERENCE, 1 1/2 IN.	OP	45.00	53.00
85	SMALL TALK, 1 1/2 IN.	OP	45.00	53.00
85	THANKSGIVING, 1 1/2 IN.	OP	45.00	53.00
86	ANGEL, 1 1/2 IN.	OP	45.00	53.00
86	BALTHASAR, 1 1/2 IN.	OP	45.00	53.00
86	CASPAR, 1 1/2 IN.	OP	45.00	53.00
86	FREE RIDE & MINI LAMB, 1 1/2 IN.	OP	45.00	53.00
86	MELCHIOR, 1 1/2 IN.	OP	45.00	53.00
86	STAR STRUCK, 1 1/2 IN.	OP	45.00	53.00
86	THE HIKER, 1 1/2 IN.	OP	45.00	53.00
86	THE STRAY, 1 1/2 IN.	OP	45.00	53.00
86	WEARY TRAVELLER, 1 1/2 IN.	OP	45.00	53.00
88	DEVOTION, 1 1/2 IN.	OP	53.00	53.00
88	JOLLY GIFT, 1 1/2 IN.	OP	53.00	53.00
88	LONG JOURNEY, 1 1/2 IN.	OP	53.00	53.00

YR	NAME	LIMIT	ISSUE	QUOTE
88	SWEET DREAMS, 1 1/2 IN.	OP	53.00	53.00
88	SWEET INSPIRATION, 1 1/2 IN.	OP	53.00	53.00
J. FERRANDIZ		**FERRANDIZ SHEPHERDS OF THE YEAR**		
77	FRIENDSHIPS, 3 IN.	YR	53.50	330.00
77	FRIENDSHIPS, 6 IN.	YR	110.00	675.00
78	SPREADING THE WORD, 3 IN.	YR	115.00	275.00
78	SPREADING THE WORD, 6 IN.	YR	270.50	500.00
79	DRUMMER BOY, 3 IN.	YR	80.00	250.00
79	DRUMMER BOY, 6 IN.	YR	220.00	425.00
80	FREEDOM BOUND, 3 IN.	YR	90.00	225.00
80	FREEDOM BOUND, 6 IN.	YR	225.00	400.00
81	JOLLY PIPER, 6 IN.	2250	225.00	400.00
82	COMPANIONS, 6 IN.	2250	220.00	300.00
83	GOOD SAMARITAN, 6 IN.	2250	220.00	320.00
84	DEVOTION, 3 IN.	2250	82.50	125.00
84	DEVOTION, 6 IN.	2250	180.00	250.00
J. FERRANDIZ		**FERRANDIZ WOODCARVINGS**		
69	ANGEL SUGAR HEART, 6 IN.	CL	25.00	2500.00
69	HEAVENLY GARDENER, 6 IN.	CL	25.00	2000.00
69	HEAVENLY QUINTET, 6 IN.	CL	25.00	2000.00
69	LOVE LETTER, 3 IN.	CL	12.50	150.00
69	LOVE LETTER, 6 IN.	CL	25.00	250.00
69	LOVE'S MESSENGER, 6 IN.	CL	25.00	2000.00
69	SUGAR HEART, 3 IN.	CL	12.50	450.00
69	SUGAR HEART, 6 IN.	CL	25.00	525.00
69	TALKING TO THE ANIMALS, 3 IN.	CL	12.50	125.00
69	TALKING TO THE ANIMALS, 6 IN.	CL	45.00	45.00
69	THE GOOD SHEPHERD, 3 IN.	CL	12.50	120.50
69	THE GOOD SHEPHERD, 6 IN.	CL	25.00	236.50
69	THE QUINTET, 3 IN.	CL	12.50	140.00
69	THE QUINTET, 6 IN.	CL	25.00	260.00
70	ARTIST, 3 IN.	CL	30.00	175.00
70	ARTIST, 6 IN.	CL	25.00	350.00
70	DUET, 3 IN.	OP	36.00	165.00
70	DUET, 6 IN.	OP	*	355.00
71	TALKING TO THE ANIMALS, 10 IN.	CL	90.00	90.00
71	THE GOOD SHEPHERD, 10 IN.	CL	90.00	90.00
71	THE QUINTET, 10 IN.	CL	100.00	600.00
73	GIRL IN THE EGG, 3 IN.	CL	30.00	127.00
73	GIRL IN THE EGG, 6 IN.	CL	60.00	272.00
73	GIRL WITH DOVE, 3 IN.	CL	30.00	110.00
73	GIRL WITH DOVE, 6 IN.	CL	50.00	205.00
73	HAPPY WANDERER, 10 IN.	CL	120.00	500.00
73	NATURE GIRL, 3 IN.	CL	30.00	30.00
73	NATURE GIRL, 6 IN.	CL	60.00	272.00
73	SPRING ARRIVALS, 3 IN.	OP	30.00	145.00
73	SPRING ARRIVALS, 6 IN.	OP	50.00	340.00
73	SWEEPER, 3 IN.	CL	35.00	130.00
73	SWEEPER, 6 IN.	CL	75.00	425.00
73	TRUMPETER, 3 IN.	CL	69.00	115.00
73	TRUMPETER, 6 IN.	CL	120.00	240.00
74	FLIGHT INTO EGYPT, 3 IN.	CL	35.00	125.00
74	FLIGHT INTO EGYPT, 6 IN.	CL	70.00	500.00
74	GREETINGS, 3 IN.	CL	30.00	300.00
74	GREETINGS, 6 IN.	CL	55.00	475.00
74	HAPPY WANDERER, 3 IN.	CL	40.00	105.00
74	HAPPY WANDERER, 6 IN.	CL	70.00	200.00
74	HELPING HANDS, 3 IN.	CL	30.00	350.00
74	HELPING HANDS, 6 IN.	CL	55.00	700.00
74	LITTLE MOTHER, 6 IN.	CL	85.00	285.00
74	NEW FRIENDS, 3 IN.	CL	30.00	275.00
74	NEW FRIENDS, 6 IN.	CL	55.00	475.00
74	ROMEO, 3 IN.	CL	50.00	225.00
74	ROMEO, 6 IN.	CL	85.00	375.00
74	SPRING OUTING, 3 IN.	CL	30.00	625.00
74	SPRING OUTING, 6 IN.	CL	55.00	900.00
74	TENDER MOMENTS, 3 IN.	CL	30.00	375.00
74	TENDER MOMENTS, 6 IN.	CL	55.00	575.00
74	THE BOUQUET, 3 IN.	CL	35.00	175.00
74	THE BOUQUET, 6 IN.	CL	75.00	325.00
75	CHERUB, 2 IN.	OP	32.00	90.00
75	CHERUB, 4 IN.	OP	32.00	275.00
75	COURTING, 3 IN.	CL	70.00	235.00
75	COURTING, 6 IN.	CL	150.00	450.00
75	GOING HOME, 3 IN.	CL	40.00	110.00
75	GOING HOME, 6 IN.	CL	70.00	240.00

YR	NAME	LIMIT	ISSUE	QUOTE
75	HOLY FAMILY, 3 IN.	CL	75.00	250.00
75	HOLY FAMILY, 6 IN.	CL	200.00	670.00
75	INSPECTOR, 3 IN.	CL	40.00	225.00
75	INSPECTOR, 6 IN.	CL	85.00	375.00
75	LOVE GIFT, 3 IN.	CL	40.00	150.00
75	LOVE GIFT, 6 IN.	CL	70.00	250.00
75	MOTHER & CHILD, 3 IN.	CL	45.00	125.00
75	MOTHER & CHILD, 6 IN.	CL	90.00	250.00
75	SUMMERTIME, 3 IN.	CL	35.00	35.00
75	SUMMERTIME, 6 IN.	CL	70.00	70.00
75	THE GIFT, 3 IN.	CL	40.00	150.00
75	THE GIFT, 6 IN.	CL	70.00	250.00
75	WANDERLUST, 6 IN.	CL	70.00	450.00
76	CATCH A FALLING STAR, 3 IN.	CL	35.00	150.00
76	CATCH A FALLING STAR, 6 IN.	CL	75.00	250.00
76	COWBOY, 3 IN.	CL	35.00	35.00
76	FLOWER GIRL, 3 IN.	CL	40.00	40.00
76	FLOWER GIRL, 6 IN.	CL	90.00	310.00
76	GARDENER, 3 IN.	CL	32.00	105.00
76	GARDENER, 6 IN.	CL	65.00	275.00
76	GIRL W/ROOSTER, 3 IN.	CL	32.50	175.00
76	GIRL W/ROOSTER, 6 IN.	CL	60.00	275.00
76	SHARING, 3 IN.	CL	32.50	130.00
76	SHARING, 6 IN.	CL	75.00	275.00
76	THE LETTER, 3 IN.	CL	40.00	40.00
76	THE LETTER, 6 IN.	CL	90.00	600.00
76	WANDERLUST, 3 IN.	CL	32.50	125.00
77	HURDY GURDY, 3 IN.	CL	53.00	150.00
77	HURDY GURDY, 6 IN.	CL	112.00	390.00
77	JOURNEY, 3 IN.	CL	67.50	175.00
77	JOURNEY, 6 IN.	CL	120.00	400.00
77	LEADING THE WAY, 3 IN.	CL	62.50	120.00
77	NIGHT NIGHT, 3 IN.	CL	45.00	120.00
77	NIGHT NIGHT, 6 IN.	CL	67.50	315.00
77	POOR BOY, 3 IN.	CL	50.00	110.00
77	POOR BOY, 6 IN.	CL	125.00	215.00
77	PROUD MOTHER, 3 IN.	CL	52.50	150.00
77	PROUD MOTHER, 6 IN.	CL	130.00	350.00
77	RIDING THRU THE RAIN, 10 IN.	OP	400.00	1000.00
77	RIDING THRU THE RAIN, 5 IN.	OP	145.00	399.00
77	THE BLESSING, 3 IN.	CL	45.00	150.00
77	THE BLESSING, 6 IN.	CL	125.00	250.00
77	TRACKER, 3 IN.	CL	70.00	120.00
78	BASKET OF JOY, 3 IN.	CL	65.00	120.00
78	HARVEST GIRL, 3 IN.	CL	75.00	110.00
78	SPREADING THE WORD, 3 IN.	CL	115.00	193.00
78	SPREADING THE WORD, 6 IN.	CL	270.00	494.50
78	SPRING DANCE, 12 IN.	CL	950.00	1750.00
78	SPRING DANCE, 24 IN.	CL	47.50	6200.00
79	FIRST BLOSSOM, 3 IN.	CL	70.00	110.00
79	HAPPY STRUMMER, 3 IN.	CL	75.00	110.00
79	HE'S MY BROTHER, 3 IN.	CL	70.00	130.00
79	HE'S MY BROTHER, 6 IN.	CL	155.00	240.00
79	HIGH RIDING, 3 IN.	CL	145.00	200.00
79	HIGH RIDING, 6 IN.	CL	340.00	475.00
79	PEACE PIPE, 3 IN.	CL	85.00	120.00
79	STITCH IN TIME, 3 IN.	CL	75.00	125.00
79	STITCH IN TIME, 6 IN.	CL	150.00	235.00
80	DRUMMER BOY, 3 IN.	CL	130.00	200.00
80	DRUMMER BOY, 6 IN.	CL	300.00	400.00
80	SPRING ARRIVALS, 10 IN.	OP	435.00	500.00
80	SPRING ARRIVALS, 20 IN.	250	2000.00	3300.00
80	TRUMPETER, 10 IN.	CL	500.00	500.00
80	UMPAPA, 4 IN.	CL	125.00	140.00
81	JOLLY PIPER, 3 IN.	CL	100.00	120.00
81	MERRY MELODY, 3 IN.	CL	90.00	115.00
81	MUSICAL BASKET, 3 IN.	CL	90.00	115.00
81	MUSICAL BASKET, 6 IN.	CL	200.00	225.00
81	STEPPING OUT, 3 IN.	CL	95.00	110.00
81	STEPPING OUT, 6 IN.	CL	220.00	252.00
81	SWEET ARRIVAL (BLUE), 3 IN.	CL	105.00	110.00
81	SWEET ARRIVAL (BLUE), 6 IN.	CL	225.00	255.00
81	SWEET ARRIVAL (PINK), 3 IN.	CL	105.00	110.00
81	SWEET ARRIVAL (PINK), 6 IN.	CL	225.00	225.00
81	SWEET DREAMS, 3 IN.	OP	100.00	140.00
81	TINY SOUNDS, 3 IN.	CL	90.00	105.00

YR	NAME	LIMIT	ISSUE	QUOTE
82	BAGPIPE, 3 IN.	CL	80.00	95.00
82	BAGPIPE, 6 IN.	CL	175.00	190.00
82	BUNDLE OF JOY, 3 IN.	CL	100.00	300.00
82	BUNDLE OF JOY, 6 IN.	CL	225.00	322.50
82	CIRCUS SERENADE, 3 IN.	CL	100.00	160.00
82	CIRCUS SERENADE, 6 IN.	CL	220.00	220.00
82	CLARINET, 3 IN.	CL	80.00	100.00
82	CLARINET, 6 IN.	CL	175.00	200.00
82	COMPANIONS, 3 IN.	CL	95.00	115.00
82	ENCORE, 3 IN.	CL	100.00	115.00
82	ENCORE, 6 IN.	CL	225.00	235.00
82	FLUTE, 3 IN.	CL	80.00	95.00
82	FLUTE, 6 IN.	CL	175.00	190.00
82	GUIDING LIGHT, 3 IN.	CL	100.00	115.00
82	GUITAR, 3 IN.	CL	80.00	95.00
82	GUITAR, 6 IN.	CL	175.00	190.00
82	HARMONICA, 3 IN.	CL	80.00	95.00
82	HARMONICA, 6 IN.	CL	175.00	190.00
82	HITCHHIKER, 3 IN.	CL	98.00	110.00
82	HITCHHIKER, 6 IN.	CL	125.00	230.00
82	LIGHTING THE WAY, 3 IN.	CL	105.00	120.00
82	LIGHTING THE WAY, 6 IN.	CL	225.00	255.00
82	PLAY IT AGAIN, 3 IN.	CL	100.00	120.00
82	PLAY IT AGAIN, 6 IN.	CL	250.00	255.00
82	STAR BRIGHT, 3 IN.	CL	110.00	125.00
82	STAR BRIGHT, 6 IN.	CL	250.00	260.00
82	SURPRISE, 3 IN.	CL	100.00	150.00
82	SURPRISE, 6 IN.	CL	225.00	325.00
82	SWEET DREAMS, 6 IN.	TL	225.00	330.00
82	SWEET MELODY, 3 IN.	CL	80.00	90.00
82	SWEET MELODY, 6 IN.	CL	198.00	210.00
82	THE CHAMPION, 3 IN.	CL	98.00	110.00
82	THE CHAMPION, 6 IN.	CL	225.00	225.00
82	THE GOOD LIFE, 3 IN.	CL	100.00	200.00
82	THE GOOD LIFE, 6 IN.	CL	225.00	230.00
82	TO MARKET, 3 IN.	CL	95.00	115.00
82	VIOLIN, 3 IN.	CL	80.00	95.00
82	VIOLIN, 6 IN.	CL	175.00	195.00
83	COWBOY, 20 IN.	CL	2100.00	2100.00
83	EDELWEISS, 3 IN.	OP	95.00	140.00
83	EDELWEISS, 6 IN.	OP	220.00	325.00
83	GOLDEN BLOSSOM, 10 IN	OP	500.00	750.00
83	GOLDEN BLOSSOM, 20 IN	OP	3300.00	5160.00
83	GOLDEN BLOSSOM, 3 IN.	OP	95.00	140.00
83	GOLDEN BLOSSOM, 6 IN.	OP	220.00	325.00
83	LOVE MESSAGE, 3 IN.	TL	105.00	150.50
83	LOVE MESSAGE, 6 IN.	TL	240.00	365.50
83	PEACE PIPE, 10 IN.	CL	460.00	480.00
84	BIRD'S EYE VIEW, 3 IN.	CL	88.00	129.00
84	BIRD'S EYE VIEW, 6 IN.	CL	216.00	700.00
84	COWBOY, 10 IN.	CL	370.00	500.00
84	HIGH HOPES, 3 IN.	CL	81.00	81.00
84	HIGH HOPES, 6 IN.	CL	170.00	247.50
84	PEACE PIPE, 20 IN.	CL	2200.00	3500.00
84	SHIPMATES, 3 IN.	CL	81.00	118.50
84	SHIPMATES, 6 IN.	CL	170.00	247.50
84	TRUMPETER, 20 IN.	CL	2350.00	3050.00
85	BUTTERFLY BOY, 3 IN.	CL	95.00	140.00
85	BUTTERFLY BOY, 6 IN.	CL	220.00	322.00
86	A MUSICAL RIDE, 4 IN.	RT	165.00	236.50
86	A MUSICAL RIDE, 8 IN.	RT	395.00	559.00
86	EDELWEISS, 10 IN.	OP	500.00	750.00
86	EDELWEISS, 20 IN.	250	3300.00	5160.00
86	GOD'S LITTLE HELPER, 2 IN.	3500	170.00	255.00
86	GOD'S LITTLE HELPER, 4 IN.	2000	425.00	550.00
86	GOLDEN BLOSSOM, 40 IN.	OP	8300.00	12950.00
86	SWISS BOY, 3 IN.	OP	122.00	161.50
86	SWISS BOY, 6 IN.	OP	245.00	323.50
86	SWISS GIRL, 3 IN.	OP	122.00	122.00
86	SWISS GIRL, 6 IN.	OP	245.00	303.50
87	AMONG FRIENDS, 3 IN.	TL	125.00	150.50
87	AMONG FRIENDS, 6 IN.	TL	245.00	290.00
87	BLACK FOREST BOY, 3 IN.	TL	125.00	150.50
87	BLACK FOREST BOY, 6 IN.	TL	250.00	301.00
87	BLACK FOREST GIRL, 3 IN.	TL	250.00	300.00
87	BLACK FOREST GIRL, 6 IN.	TL	125.00	150.50

YR	NAME	LIMIT	ISSUE	QUOTE
87	HEAVENLY CONCERT, 2 IN.	3500	200.00	200.00
87	HEAVENLY CONCERT, 4 IN.	2000	450.00	550.00
87	NATURE'S WONDER, 3 IN.	3000	125.00	150.50
87	NATURE'S WONDER, 6 IN.	3000	245.00	290.50
87	SERENITY, 3 IN.	CL	125.00	150.50
87	SERENITY, 6 IN.	3000	245.00	290.00
88	ABRACADABRA, 3 IN.	3000	145.00	165.00
88	ABRACADABRA, 6 IN.	3000	315.00	345.00
88	BON APPETIT, 3 IN.	500	175.00	200.00
88	BON APPETIT, 6 IN.	500	395.00	440.00
88	PEACE MAKER, 3 IN.	3000	180.00	200.00
88	PEACE MAKER, 6 IN.	3000	180.00	200.00
88	PICNIC FOR TWO, 3 IN.	500	190.00	210.00
88	PICNIC FOR TWO, 6 IN.	500	425.00	465.00
88	WINTER MEMORIES, 3 IN.	1500	180.00	195.00
88	WINTER MEMORIES, 6 IN.	1500	398.00	440.00
89	MEXICAN BOY, 3 IN.	1500	170.00	175.00
89	MEXICAN BOY, 6 IN.	1500	340.00	350.00
89	MEXICAN GIRL, 3 IN.	1500	170.00	175.00
89	MEXICAN GIRL, 6 IN.	1500	340.00	350.00

J. FERRANDIZ   LIMITED EDITION COUPLES

YR	NAME	LIMIT	ISSUE	QUOTE
85	FIRST KISS, 8 IN.	750	590.00	950.00
85	SPRINGTIME STROLL, 8 IN.	750	590.00	950.00
86	A TENDER TOUCH, 8 IN.	750	590.00	850.00
86	MY HEART IS YOURS, 8 IN.	750	590.00	850.00
87	HEART TO HEART, 8 IN.	750	590.00	850.00
88	A LOVING HAND, 8 IN.	750	795.00	850.00

*   MICKEY MOUSE THROUGH THE AGES

YR	NAME	LIMIT	ISSUE	QUOTE
90	STEAM BOAT WILLIE, 4 IN.	1000	295.00	295.00
91	THE MAD DOG, 4 IN.	1000	500.00	500.00

S. KAY   SARAH KAY FIGURINES

YR	NAME	LIMIT	ISSUE	QUOTE
83	BEDTIME, 1 1/2 IN.	CL	45.00	110.00
83	BEDTIME, 4 IN.	CL	95.00	230.00
83	BEDTIME, 6 IN.	CL	195.00	435.00
83	FEEDING THE CHICKENS, 1 1/2 IN.	CL	45.00	110.00
83	FEEDING THE CHICKENS, 4 IN.	CL	95.00	230.00
83	FEEDING THE CHICKENS, 6 IN.	CL	195.00	435.00
83	FROM THE GARDEN, 1 1/2 IN.	CL	45.00	110.00
83	FROM THE GARDEN, 4 IN.	CL	95.00	235.00
83	FROM THE GARDEN, 6 IN.	CL	195.00	450.00
83	HELPING MOTHER, 1 1/2 IN.	CL	45.00	110.00
83	HELPING MOTHER, 4 IN.	CL	95.00	300.00
83	HELPING MOTHER, 6 IN.	CL	210.00	495.00
83	MORNING CHORES, 1 1/2 IN.	CL	45.00	110.00
83	MORNING CHORES, 4 IN.	CL	95.00	300.00
83	MORNING CHORES, 6 IN.	CL	210.00	495.00
83	PLAYTIME, 1 1/2 IN.	CL	45.00	110.00
83	PLAYTIME, 3 IN.	CL	95.00	230.00
83	PLAYTIME, 6 IN.	CL	195.00	445.00
83	SWEEPING, 1 1/2 IN.	CL	45.00	110.00
83	SWEEPING, 4 IN.	CL	95.00	230.00
83	SWEEPING, 6 IN.	CL	195.00	435.00
83	WAITING FOR MOTHER, 1 1/2 IN.	CL	45.00	110.00
83	WAITING FOR MOTHER, 11 IN.	CL	495.00	795.00
83	WAITING FOR MOTHER, 4 IN.	CL	95.00	230.00
83	WAITING FOR MOTHER, 6 IN.	CL	195.00	445.00
83	WAKE UP KISS, 6 IN.	CL	210.00	550.00
84	DAYDREAMING, 1 1/2 IN.	CL	45.00	125.00
84	DAYDREAMING, 4 IN.	CL	95.00	235.00
84	DAYDREAMING, 6 IN.	CL	195.00	445.00
84	FINDING R WAY, 1 1/2 IN.	CL	45.00	135.00
84	FINDING R WAY, 4 IN.	CL	95.00	245.00
84	FINDING R WAY, 6 IN.	CL	210.00	495.00
84	FLOWERS FOR YOU, 1 1/2 IN.	CL	45.00	125.00
84	FLOWERS FOR YOU, 4 IN.	CL	95.00	230.00
84	FLOWERS FOR YOU, 6 IN.	CL	195.00	430.00
84	OFF TO SCHOOL, 1 1/2 IN.	7500	45.00	125.00
84	OFF TO SCHOOL, 11 IN.	750	*	770.00
84	OFF TO SCHOOL, 20 IN.	100	*	4000.00
84	OFF TO SCHOOL, 4 IN.	4000	95.00	185.00
84	OFF TO SCHOOL, 6 IN.	4000	195.00	325.00
84	SPECIAL DELIVERY, 1 1/2 IN.	CL	45.00	125.00
84	SPECIAL DELIVERY, 4 IN.	CL	95.00	172.00
84	SPECIAL DELIVERY, 6 IN.	CL	195.00	312.00
84	TAG ALONG, 1 1/2 IN.	7500	45.00	130.00
84	TAG ALONG, 4 IN.	4000	95.00	225.00

YR	NAME	LIMIT	ISSUE	QUOTE
84	TAG ALONG, 6 IN.	4000	195.00	290.00
84	WAKE UP KISS, 1 1/2 IN.	CL	45.00	550.00
84	WAKE UP KISS, 4 IN.	CL	95.00	155.00
84	WATCHFUL EYE, 1 1/2 IN.	CL	45.00	125.00
84	WATCHFUL EYE, 4 IN.	CL	95.00	235.00
84	WATCHFUL EYE, 6 IN.	CL	195.00	445.00
85	'TIS THE SEASON, 6 IN.	CL	210.00	425.00
85	A SPECIAL DAY, 4 IN.	4000	95.00	185.00
85	A SPECIAL DAY, 6 IN.	4000	195.00	325.00
85	AFTERNOON TEA, 11 IN.	750	*	770.00
85	AFTERNOON TEA, 20 IN.	100	*	3500.00
85	AFTERNOON TEA, 4 IN.	TL	95.00	185.00
85	AFTERNOON TEA, 6 IN.	TL	195.00	325.00
85	EVERY GOOD BOY DESERVES FAVOR	4000	95.00	185.00
85	GIDDYAP!, 4 IN.	TL	95.00	185.00
85	GIDDYAP!, 6 IN.	TL	195.00	325.00
85	NIGHTIE NIGHT, 4 IN.	TL	95.00	185.00
85	NIGHTIE NIGHT, 6 IN.	TL	195.00	325.00
85	YULTIDE CHEER, 4 IN.	4000	95.00	185.00
85	YULTIDE CHEER, 6 IN.	CL	210.00	435.00
86	ALWAYS BY MY SIDE, 1 1/2 IN.	CL	45.00	95.00
86	ALWAYS BY MY SIDE, 4 IN.	CL	95.00	195.00
86	ALWAYS BY MY SIDE, 6 IN.	CL	195.00	375.00
86	BUNNY HUG, 1 1/2 IN.	7500	45.00	85.00
86	BUNNY HUG, 4 IN.	4000	95.00	172.00
86	BUNNY HUG, 6 IN.	2000	210.00	395.00
86	FINISHING TOUCH, 1 1/2 IN.	7500	45.00	85.00
86	FINISHING TOUCH, 4 IN.	4000	95.00	172.00
86	FINISHING TOUCH, 6 IN.	CL	195.00	312.00
86	GOOD AS NEW, 1 1/2 IN.	7500	45.00	90.00
86	GOOD AS NEW, 4 IN.	4000	95.00	185.00
86	GOOD AS NEW, 6 IN.	4000	195.00	325.00
86	OUR PUPPY, 1 1/2 IN.	7500	45.00	90.00
86	OUR PUPPY, 4 IN.	TL	95.00	185.00
86	OUR PUPPY, 6 IN.	TL	210.00	355.00
86	SWEET TREAT, 1 1/2 IN.	7500	45.00	85.00
86	SWEET TREAT, 4 IN.	4000	95.00	172.00
86	SWEET TREAT, 6 IN.	4000	195.00	312.00
86	TO LOVE AND CHERISH, 1 1/2 IN.	7500	45.00	85.00
86	TO LOVE AND CHERISH, 11 IN.	1000	*	667.00
86	TO LOVE AND CHERISH, 20 IN.	200	*	3600.00
86	TO LOVE AND CHERISH, 4 IN.	4000	95.00	172.00
86	TO LOVE AND CHERISH, 6 IN.	4000	195.00	312.00
86	WITH THIS RING, 1 1/2 IN.	7500	45.00	85.00
86	WITH THIS RING, 11 IN.	1000	*	667.50
86	WITH THIS RING, 20 IN.	200	*	3600.00
86	WITH THIS RING, 4 IN.	4000	95.00	172.00
86	WITH THIS RING, 6 IN.	4000	195.00	312.00
87	A LOVING SPOONFUL, 1 1/2 IN.	7500	49.50	90.00
87	A LOVING SPOONFUL, 4 IN.	4000	150.00	200.00
87	A LOVING SPOONFUL, 6 IN.	4000	295.00	400.00
87	ALL ABOARD, 1 1/2 IN.	7500	49.50	90.00
87	ALL ABOARD, 4 IN.	4000	130.00	185.00
87	ALL ABOARD, 6 IN.	2000	265.00	355.00
87	ALL MINE, 1 1/2 IN.	7500	49.50	95.00
87	ALL MINE, 4 IN.	4000	130.00	225.00
87	ALL MINE, 6 IN.	CL	245.00	465.00
87	CUDDLES, 1 1/2 IN.	7500	49.50	95.00
87	CUDDLES, 4 IN.	4000	130.00	225.00
87	CUDDLES, 6 IN.	CL	245.00	465.00
87	LET'S PLAY, 1 1/2 IN.	7500	49.50	90.00
87	LET'S PLAY, 4 IN.	TL	130.00	185.00
87	LET'S PLAY, 6 IN.	TL	265.00	355.00
87	LITTLE NANNY, 4 IN.	TL	150.00	200.00
87	LITTLE NANNY, 6 IN.	TL	295.00	400.00
87	MY LITTLE BROTHER, 1 1/2 IN.	3700	70.00	90.00
87	MY LITTLE BROTHER, 4 IN.	2000	195.00	225.00
87	MY LITTLE BROTHER, 6 IN.	2000	375.00	450.00
88	GINGER SNAP, 1 1/2 IN.	3700	70.00	90.00
88	GINGER SNAP, 4 IN.	2000	150.00	185.00
88	GINGER SNAP, 6 IN.	1000	300.00	355.00
88	HIDDEN TREASURES, 1 1/2 IN.	3700	70.00	90.00
88	HIDDEN TREASURES, 4 IN.	TL	150.00	185.00
88	HIDDEN TREASURES, 6 IN.	TL	300.00	355.00
88	NEW HOME, 1 1/2 IN.	3700	70.00	90.00
88	NEW HOME, 4 IN.	2000	185.00	240.00

YR	NAME	LIMIT	ISSUE	QUOTE
88	NEW HOME, 6 IN.	2000	365.00	500.00
88	PENNY FOR YOUR THOUGHTS, 1 1/2 IN.	3700	70.00	90.00
88	PENNY FOR YOUR THOUGHTS, 4 IN.	2000	185.00	215.00
88	PENNY FOR YOUR THOUGHTS, 6 IN.	2000	365.00	455.00
88	PURRFECT DAY, 1 1/2 IN.	3700	70.00	90.00
88	PURRFECT DAY, 4 IN.	2000	184.00	215.00
88	PURRFECT DAY, 6 IN.	2000	265.00	455.00
89	CHERISH, 1 1/2 IN.	3500	80.00	95.00
89	CHERISH, 4 IN.	2000	199.00	225.00
89	CHERISH, 6 IN.	2000	398.00	450.00
89	FIRST SCHOOL DAY, 1 1/2 IN.	3500	85.00	90.00
89	FIRST SCHOOL DAY, 4 IN.	2000	290.00	295.00
89	FIRST SCHOOL DAY, 6 IN.	2000	550.00	630.00
89	FISHERBOY, 1 1/2 IN.	3500	85.00	95.00
89	FISHERBOY, 4 IN.	2000	220.00	240.00
89	FISHERBOY, 6 IN.	1000	440.00	475.00
89	GARDEN PARTY, 1 1/2 IN.	3500	85.00	95.00
89	GARDEN PARTY, 4 IN.	2000	220.00	240.00
89	GARDEN PARTY, 6 IN.	2000	440.00	475.00
89	HOUSE CALL, 1 1/2 IN.	3500	85.00	95.00
89	HOUSE CALL, 4 IN.	2000	190.00	195.00
89	HOUSE CALL, 6 IN.	2000	390.00	390.00
89	TAKE ME ALONG, 1 1/2 IN.	3500	85.00	95.00
89	TAKE ME ALONG, 4 IN.	2000	220.00	240.00
89	TAKE ME ALONG, 6 IN.	1000	440.00	475.00
89	YEARLY CHECK-UP, 1 1/2 IN.	3500	85.00	95.00
89	YEARLY CHECK-UP, 4 IN.	2000	190.00	195.00
89	YEARLY CHECK-UP, 6 IN.	2000	390.00	390.00
90	BATTER UP, 1 1/2 IN.	3500	90.00	95.00
90	BATTER UP, 4 IN.	2000	220.00	225.00
90	BATTER UP, 6 IN.	2000	440.00	450.00
90	HOLIDAY CHEER, 1 1/2 IN.	3500	90.00	95.00
90	HOLIDAY CHEER, 4 IN.	2000	225.00	240.00
90	HOLIDAY CHEER, 6 IN.	1000	450.00	495.00
90	SEASONS GREETINGS, 1 1/2 IN.	3500	90.00	95.00
90	SEASONS GREETINGS, 4 IN.	2000	225.00	240.00
90	SEASONS GREETINGS, 6 IN.	1000	450.00	495.00
90	SHOOTIN' HOOPS, 1 1/2 IN.	3500	90.00	95.00
90	SHOOTIN' HOOPS, 4 IN.	2000	220.00	225.00
90	SHOOTIN' HOOPS, 6 IN.	2000	440.00	450.00
90	SPRING FEVER, 1 1/2 IN.	3500	90.00	95.00
90	SPRING FEVER, 4 IN.	2000	225.00	240.00
90	SPRING FEVER, 6 IN.	2000	450.00	495.00
90	TENDER LOVING CARE, 1 1/2 IN.	3500	90.00	95.00
90	TENDER LOVING CARE, 4 IN.	2000	220.00	240.00
90	TENDER LOVING CARE, 6 IN.	2000	440.00	475.00
91	DRESS UP, 1 1/2 IN.	3750	110.00	110.00
91	DRESS UP, 4 IN.	2000	270.00	270.00
91	DRESS UP, 6 IN.	2000	550.00	550.00
91	FIGURE EIGHT, 1 1/2 IN.	2000	110.00	110.00
91	FIGURE EIGHT, 4 IN.	2000	270.00	270.00
91	FIGURE EIGHT, 6 IN.	2000	550.00	550.00
91	FORE!!, 1 1/2 IN.	3750	110.00	110.00
91	FORE!!, 4 IN.	2000	270.00	270.00
91	FORE!!, 6 IN.	2000	550.00	550.00
91	SEASON'S JOY, 1 1/2 IN.	3750	110.00	110.00
91	SEASON'S JOY, 4 IN.	2000	270.00	270.00
91	SEASON'S JOY, 6 IN.	1000	550.00	550.00
91	TOUCH DOWN, 1 1/2 IN.	3750	110.00	110.00
91	TOUCH DOWN, 4 IN.	2000	270.00	270.00
91	TOUCH DOWN, 6 IN.	2000	550.00	550.00
91	WINTER SURPRISE, 1 1/2 IN.	3750	110.00	110.00
91	WINTER SURPRISE, 4 IN.	2000	270.00	270.00
91	WINTER SURPRISE, 6 IN.	1000	550.00	550.00
S. KAY			**SARAH KAY MINI SANTAS**	
91	JOLLY SANTA, 1 1/2 IN.	2500	110.00	110.00
91	JOLLY ST. NICK, 1 1/2 IN.	2500	110.00	110.00
91	KRIS KRINGLE, 1 1/2 IN.	2500	110.00	110.00
91	SARAH KAY SANTA, 1 1/2 IN.	2500	110.00	110.00
S. KAY			**SARAH KAY SANTAS**	
88	JOLLY SANTA, 12 IN.	CL	1300.00	1300.00
88	JOLLY SANTA, 4 IN.	CL	235.00	300.00
88	JOLLY SANTA, 6 IN.	CL	480.00	600.00
88	JOLLY ST. NICK, 4 IN.	CL	199.00	300.00-550.00
88	JOLLY ST. NICK, 6 IN.	CL	398.00	850.00
89	SANTA, 4 IN.	750	235.00	235.00

YR	NAME	LIMIT	ISSUE	QUOTE
89	SANTA, 6 IN.	750	480.00	480.00
89	SARAH KAY SANTA, 4 IN.	750	275.00	275.00
89	SARAH KAY SANTA, 6 IN.	750	550.00	550.00
90	KRIS KRINGLE SANTA, 4 IN.	750	275.00	275.00
90	KRIS KRINGLE SANTA, 6 IN.	750	550.00	550.00
91	A FRIEND TO ALL, 4 IN.	750	300.00	300.00
91	A FRIEND TO ALL, 6 IN.	750	590.00	590.00

ARMANI

G. ARMANI — CAN-CAN DANCERS

YR	NAME	LIMIT	ISSUE	QUOTE
89	TWO CAN-CAN DANCERS 516C	1000	820.00	975.00

G. ARMANI — DISNEYANA COLLECTION

YR	NAME	LIMIT	ISSUE	QUOTE
*	CINDERELLA 783C	RT	500.00	3000.00

G. ARMANI — FOUR SEASONS

YR	NAME	LIMIT	ISSUE	QUOTE
90	LADY ON SEASHORE (SUMMER) 540C	OP	440.00	440.00
90	LADY WITH BICYCLE (SPRING) 539C	OP	550.00	550.00
90	LADY WITH ICE SKATES (WINTER) 542C	OP	400.00	400.00
90	LADY WITH UMBRELLA (FALL) 541C	OP	475.00	475.00

G. ARMANI — G. ARMANI SOCIETY MEMBERS ONLY FIGURINES

YR	NAME	LIMIT	ISSUE	QUOTE
90	AWAKENING	CL	137.50	1000.00
90	MY FINE FEATHERED FRIENDS	CL	175.00	275.00-358.00
91	EVE 590T	RT	250.00	1320.00
91	PEACE & HARMONY 824C	7500	300.00	300.00
91	RUFFLES 745E	YR	139.00	400
92	ASCENT 866C	YR	195.00	265
92	BOY WITH DOG 409S	YR	200.00	300
92	LADY WITH BASKET OF FLOWERS 961C	YR	250.00	250.00

G. ARMANI — GARDEN SERIES

YR	NAME	LIMIT	ISSUE	QUOTE
91	LADY WITH CORNUCOPIE 870C	10,000	600.00	600.00
91	LADY WITH HARP 874C	10,000	500.00	500.00
91	LADY WITH PEACOCK 871C	10,000	585.00	585.00
91	LADY WITH VIOLIN 872C	10,000	560.00	560.00

G. ARMANI — MOONLIGHT MASQUERADE

YR	NAME	LIMIT	ISSUE	QUOTE
90	HARLEQUIN LADY 740C	7500	450.00	450.00
90	LADY CLOWN WITH CANE 742C	7500	390.00	390.00
90	LADY CLOWN WITH DOLL 743	7500	410.00	410.00
90	LADY PIERROT 741C	7500	390.00	500
90	QUEEN OF HEARTS 744	7500	450.00	450.00

G. ARMANI — MY FAIR LADIES

YR	NAME	LIMIT	ISSUE	QUOTE
87	LADY WITH PEACOCK 385C	RT	440.00	2000.00-3510.00
88	FLAMENCO DANCER 389C	RT	400.00	450.00
88	LADY WITH BOOK 384C	RT	300.00	400.00
88	LADY WITH FAN 387C	RT	300.00	370.00
88	LADY WITH GREAT DANE 429C	RT	375.00	465.00
88	LADY WITH MIRROR 386C	RT	430.00	500.00-990.00
88	LADY WITH MUFF 388C	RT	250.00	320.00
88	MOTHER AND CHILD 405C	RT	410.00	500.00
89	LADY WITH PARROT 616C	RT	460.00	460.00

G. ARMANI — PEARLS OF THE ORIENT

YR	NAME	LIMIT	ISSUE	QUOTE
89	CHU CHU SAN 612C	10,000	500.00	500.00
89	LOTUS BLOSOM 613C	10,000	450.00	450.00
89	MADAME BUTTERFFLY 610C	10,000	450.00	450.00
89	TURNADOT 611C	10,000	475.00	475.00

G. ARMANI — PREMIERE BALLERINAS

YR	NAME	LIMIT	ISSUE	QUOTE
88	BALLERINA 508C	7500	620.00	550.00-715.00
88	BALLERINA 517C	10,000	325.00	340.00
88	BALLERINA GROUP 515C	7500	620.00	775.00-1008.00
88	BALLERINA GROUP IN FLIGHT 518C	7500	810.00	900.00-1170.00
88	BALLERINA IN FLIGHT 503C	10,000	420.00	500.00-650.00
88	BALLERINA WITH DRAPE 504C	10,000	450.00	550.00-748.00

G. ARMANI — RELIGIOUS

YR	NAME	LIMIT	ISSUE	QUOTE
87	CHOIR BOYS 900	5000	350.00	660.00
88	CRUCIFIX 1158C	RT	190.00	990.00-1320.00
90	CRUCIFIX PLAQUE 711C	15,000	265.00	265.00
91	CRUCIFIX 790C	15,000	180.00	180.00

G. ARMANI — RENAISSANCE

YR	NAME	LIMIT	ISSUE	QUOTE
92	ABUNDANCE 870C	5000	600.00	600.00
92	DAWN 874C	5000	500.00	500.00
92	TWILIGHT 872C	5000	560.00	560.00
92	VANITY 871C	5000	585.00	585.00

G. ARMANI — SPECIAL TIMES

YR	NAME	LIMIT	ISSUE	QUOTE
82	CARD PLAYERS-CHEATERS 3280	OP	400.00	850.00
82	GIRL WITH CHICKS 5122	RT	95.00	495.00
82	GIRL WITH SHEEP DOG 5117	OP	100.00	180.00
82	KISSING KIDS 5138	OP	125.00	225.00
82	SLEDDING 5111	OP	115.00	200.00
82	SOCCER BOY 5199	OP	75.00	150.00

YR NAME	LIMIT	ISSUE	QUOTE
91 COUPLE IN CAR 862C	5000	1000.00	1000.00
91 LADY WITH CAR 861C	3000	900.00	900.00

G. ARMANI   WEDDING

84 WEDDING 5132	OP	175.00	225.00
89 BRIDE AND GROOM 475P	OP	280.00	295.00
89 WEDDING 407C	OP	535.00	575.00
90 JUST MARRIED 827C	5000	950.00	950.00
91 WEDDING COUPLE 813C	7500	400.00	400.00
91 WEDDING COUPLE 814C	7500	600.00	600.00
91 WEDDING COUPLE 815C	7500	500.00	500.00

G. ARMANI   WILDLIFE

82 SNOW BIRD 5548	OP	100.00	175.00
83 EAGLE 3213	OP	210.00	400.00
83 EAGLE WITH BABIES 3553	OP	215.00	375.00
88 BIRD OF PARADISE 454S	5000	475.00	475.00
88 PEACOCK 455S	5000	600.00	1100.00-2750.00
88 PEACOCK 458S	5000	630.00	675.00
90 BIRD OF PARADISE 718S	5000	550.00	550.00
90 SOARING EAGLES 97S	5000	620.00	620.00
90 THREE DOVES 996S	5000	670.00	670.00

ARMSTRONG'S

R. SKELTON   ARMSTRONG'S/RON LEE

84 CAPTAIN FREDDIE	7500	85.00	150.00
84 FREDDIE THE TORCHBEARER	7500	110.00	190.00

A. D'ESTREHAN   CERAMIC PLAQUE

85 FLAMBOROUGH HEAD	500	195.00	195.00
85 FLAMBOROUGH HEAD (ARTIST'S PROOF)	50	295.00	295.00
88 KATRINA	500	195.00	195.00
85 MOTHER'S PRIDE	400	195.00	195.00
85 MOTHER'S PRIDE (ARTIST'S PROOF)	50	295.00	295.00
85 THE STAMP COLLECTOR	400	195.00	195.00
85 THE STAMP COLLECTOR (ARTIST'S PROOF)	50	295.00	295.00

W. LANTZ   HAPPY ART

82 WOODY'S TRIPLE SELF-PORTRAIT	5000	95.00	300.00

*   PRO AUTOGRAPHED CERAMIC BASEBALL CARD PLAQUE

85 BRETT, GARVEY, JACKSON, ROSE, SEAVER,	1000	149.75	149.75

*   PRO CLASSIC CERAMIC BASEBALL CARD PLAQUES

85 GEORGE BRETT, 2 1/2 X 3 1/2 IN.	OP	9.95	9.95
85 PETE ROSE, 2 1/2 X 3 1/2 IN.	OP	9.95	9.95
85 REGGIE JACKSON, 2 1/2 X 3 1/2 IN.	OP	9.95	9.95
85 STEVE GARVEY, 2 1/2 X 3 1/2 IN.	OP	9.95	9.95
85 TOM SEAVER, 2 1/2 X 3 1/2 IN.	OP	9.95	9.95

R. SKELTON   THE RED SKELTON COLLECTION

81 CLEM KADIDDLEHOPPER	7500	75.00	75.00
81 FREDDIE IN THE BATHTUB	7500	80.00	80.00
81 FREDDIE IN THE GREEN	7500	80.00	80.00
81 FREDDIE THE FREELOADER	7500	70.00	70.00
81 JR. THE MEAN WIDDLE KID	7500	75.00	150.00
81 SAN FERNANDO RED	7500	75.00	150.00
81 SHERIFF DEADEYE	7500	75.00	75.00

ARTAFFECTS

G. PERILLO   CHILD LIFE

83 SIESTA	2500	65.00	75.00
83 SWEET DREAMS	1500	65.00	*

A. TOBEY   CHRISTIAN COLLECTION

87 BRING TO ME THE CHILDREN	OP	65.00	100.00
88 THE HEALER	OP	65.00	65.00

*   HEAVENLY BLESSINGS

85 BEDDY BYE	OP	15.00	19.00
85 BUBBLES	OP	15.00	19.00
85 DAY DREAMS	OP	15.00	19.00
85 FIRST STEP	OP	15.00	19.00
85 HAPPY BIRTHDAY	OP	15.00	19.00
85 HEAVEN SCENT	OP	15.00	19.00
85 JUST UP	OP	15.00	19.00
85 LISTEN!	OP	15.00	19.00
85 RACE YOU!	OP	15.00	19.00
85 SEE!	OP	15.00	19.00
85 SO SOFT	OP	15.00	19.00
85 YUM, YUM!	OP	15.00	19.00

G. PERILLO   MUSICAL FIGURINES

89 A BOY'S PRAYER	*	45.00	65.00
89 A GIRL'S PRAYER	*	45.00	65.00
84 THE WEDDING	OP	65.00	70.00
86 THE ANNIVERSARY	OP	65.00	70.00

YR	NAME	LIMIT	ISSUE	QUOTE
87	FATHERHOOD	OP	65.00	70.00
87	HOME SWEET HOME	OP	65.00	70.00
87	MOTHERHOOD	OP	65.00	70.00
87	NEWBORN	OP	65.00	70.00
87	SWEET SIXTEEN	OP	65.00	70.00
G. PERILLO		**PERILLO COLLECTOR CLUB PIECE**		
83	APACHE BRAVE	*	50.00	98.00
G. PERILLO		**PRIDE OF AMERICA'S INDIANS**		
88	BRAVE AND FREE	*	50.00	98.00-111.00
89	DARK EYED FRIENDS	10-DAY	45.00	75.00
89	KINDRED SPIRITS	10-DAY	45.00	50.00
89	LOYAL ALLIANCE	10-DAY	45.00	75.00
89	NOBLE COMPANIONS	10-DAY	45.00	50.00
89	PEACEFUL COMRADES	10-DAY	45.00	50.00
89	SMALL & WISE	10-DAY	45.00	50.00
89	WINTER SCOUTS	10-DAY	45.00	50.00
MAGO		**REFLECTIONS OF YOUTH**		
88	JULIA	*	29.50	70.00
89	JESSICA	14-DAY	29.50	60.00
89	SEBASTIAN	14-DAY	29.50	40.00
G. PERILLO		**SAGEBRUSH KIDS**		
85	BLUE BIRD	OP	19.50	25.00
85	BOOTS	OP	19.50	25.00
85	DRESSING UP	OP	19.50	25.00
85	FAVORITE KACHINA	OP	19.50	25.00
85	HAIL TO THE CHIEF	OP	19.50	25.00
85	MESSAGE OF JOY	OP	19.50	25.00
85	OUCH!	CL	19.50	25.00
85	ROOM FOR TWO?	OP	19.50	25.00
85	STAY AWHILE	OP	19.50	25.00
85	TAKE ONE	CL	19.50	25.00
86	COUNTRY MUSIC	OP	19.50	25.00
86	DEPUTIES	OP	19.50	25.00
86	FINISHING TOUCHES	OP	19.50	25.00
86	PRACTICE MAKES PERFECT	OP	19.50	25.00
86	PRAIRIE PLAYERS	OP	19.50	25.00
86	THE HIDING PLACE	OP	19.50	25.00
86	THE LONG WAIT	OP	19.50	25.00
86	WESTWARD HO!	OP	19.50	25.00
87	JUST PICKED	OP	19.50	25.00
87	MY PAPOOSE	OP	19.50	25.00
87	PLAYING HOUSE	OP	19.50	25.00
87	ROW, ROW	OP	19.50	25.00
87	SMALL TALK	OP	19.50	25.00
87	WAGON TRAIN	OP	19.50	25.00
89	HARMONY	OP	37.50	37.50
89	MELODY	OP	37.50	37.50
89	SANTA'S LULLABY	OP	45.00	45.00
90	EASTER OFFERING	OP	27.50	27.50
90	HOW DO I LOVE THEE?	OP	37.50	37.50
90	JUST MARRIED	OP	45.00	45.00
91	BABY BRONC	OP	27.50	27.50
91	HEAVENLY PROTECTOR	OP	75.00	75.00
91	JUST BAKED	OP	27.50	27.50
91	LITTLE WARRIORS	OP	27.50	27.50
91	LOVIN' SPOONFUL	OP	27.50	27.50
91	OUT OF THE RAIN (UMBRELLA GIRL)	OP	95.00	95.00
91	SAFE AND DRY (UMBRELLA BOY)	OP	95.00	95.00
91	TEDDY TOO?	OP	27.50	27.50
91	TOY TOTEM	OP	27.50	27.50
G. PERILLO		**SAGEBRUSH KIDS BANKS**		
90	BUCKAROO BANK	OP	39.50	39.50
90	PERILLO'S PIGGY BANK	OP	39.50	39.50
90	WAMPUM WIG-WAM BANK	OP	39.50	39.50
G. PERILLO		**SAGEBRUSH KIDS CHRISTMAS CARAVAN**		
87	COMPLETE SET	OP	165.00	255.00
87	GOLD, FRANKINCENSE & PRESENTS	OP	35.00	35.00
87	LEADING THE WAY	OP	90.00	120.00
87	SINGING PRAISES	OP	45.00	50.00
87	SLEEPY SENTINELS	OP	45.00	50.00
G. PERILLO		**SAGEBRUSH KIDS NATIVITY**		
86	4 PIECE SET	OP	50.00	65.00
86	BACKDROP DOVE	OP	17.50	21.50
86	BACKDROP POTTERY	OP	17.50	21.50
86	CHRIST CHILD	OP	12.50	13.50
86	COW	OP	12.00	13.50

Warm Wishes to Someone Special at This Joyous Time of Year *is from the Kinka Collection by Enesco Corp.*

Perhaps the beauty and grace of a ballerina can only be equaled by a porcelain figure depicting the craft. Ballet Shoes *is from Royal Doulton.*

Where's Muvver? The Long and Short of It, Got to Get Home for the Holiday *and* Just Watchin' Over You *are retired items from the Memories of Yesterday Collection from Enesco Corp.*

The elegantly attired Henley is *from the "British Sporting Heritage" series produced by Royal Doulton.*

YR	NAME	LIMIT	ISSUE	QUOTE
86	DONKEY	OP	12.00	13.50
86	GOAT	OP	8.00	9.50
86	JOSEPH	OP	17.50	19.50
86	KING WITH CORN	OP	17.50	22.50
86	KING WITH JEWELRY	OP	17.50	22.50
86	KING WITH POTTERY	OP	17.50	22.50
86	LAMB	OP	6.00	8.00
86	MARY	OP	17.50	19.50
86	SHEPHERD KNEELING	OP	17.50	22.50
86	SHEPHERD WITH LAMB	OP	17.50	22.50
86	TEE PEE	OP	17.50	22.50
89	BUFFALO	OP	17.50	17.50
89	CACTUS	OP	24.50	24.50
89	PIG	OP	15.00	15.00
89	RACCOON	OP	12.50	12.50

G. PERILLO SAGEBRUSH KIDS WEDDING PARTY

YR	NAME	LIMIT	ISSUE	QUOTE
90	BRIDE	OP	24.50	24.50
90	CHIEF	OP	24.50	24.50
90	DONKEY	OP	22.50	22.50
90	FLOWER GIRL	OP	22.50	22.50
90	GROOM	OP	24.50	24.50
90	RING BEARER	OP	22.50	22.50
90	WEDDING BACKDROP	OP	27.50	27.50
90	WEDDING PARTY OF 7	OP	165.00	165.00

G. PERILLO SAGEBRUSH KIDS-FLIGHT INTO EGYPT

YR	NAME	LIMIT	ISSUE	QUOTE
90	MARY W/BABY, JOSEPH & DONKEY (3 PC SET)	OP	65.00	65.00

G. PERILLO SAGEBRUSH KIDS-SPECIAL ISSUE

YR	NAME	LIMIT	ISSUE	QUOTE
91	ONE NATION UNDER GOD	5000	195.00	195.00

C. ROEDA SIMPLE WONDERS

YR	NAME	LIMIT	ISSUE	QUOTE
91	BABY JESUS	*	35.00	35.00
91	BABY JESUS (BLACK)	*	35.00	35.00
91	BRIDE	*	55.00	55.00
91	FOREVER FRIENDS	*	39.50	39.50
91	GROOM	*	45.00	45.00
91	I LOVE EWE	*	37.50	37.50
91	JOSEPH	*	45.00	45.00
91	JOSEPH (BLACK)	*	45.00	45.00
91	LIGHTING THE WAY	*	39.50	39.50
91	MADE WITH LOVE	*	49.50	49.50
91	MARY	*	40.00	40.00
91	MARY (BLACK)	*	40.00	40.00
91	MOMMY'S BEST	*	49.50	49.50
91	OFF TO SCHOOL	*	49.50	49.50
91	PLAYING HOOKEY	*	49.50	49.50
91	SHEEP DOG	*	15.00	15.00
91	SONG OF JOY	*	39.50	39.50
91	STAR LIGHT STAR BRIGHT	*	35.00	35.00
91	THE LITTLEST ANGEL	*	29.50	29.50
91	THE LITTLEST ANGEL (BLACK)	*	29.50	29.50
92	A PERFECT FIT	*	45.00	45.00
92	CATCH THE SPIRIT (WISECHILD)	*	35.00	35.00
92	FALLEN ANGEL	*	35.00	35.00
92	FOLLOWING THE STAR (WISECHILD)	*	45.00	45.00
92	LIL' DUMPLIN	*	25.00	25.00
92	LIL' DUMPLIN (BLACK)	*	25.00	25.00
92	LITTLE BIG SHOT	*	35.00	35.00
92	POCKETFUL OF LOVE	*	35.00	35.00
92	POCKETFUL OF LOVE (BLACK)	*	35.00	35.00
92	RAINBOW PATROL	*	39.50	39.50
92	TEN PENNY SERENADE	*	45.00	45.00
92	TEN PENNY SERENADE (BLACK)	*	45.00	45.00
92	THE THREE BEARS	*	45.00	45.00
92	THIS TOO SHALL PASS	*	35.00	35.00
92	TRICK OR TREAT	*	39.50	39.50
92	WITH OPEN ARMS (WISECHILD)	*	39.50	39.50

G. PERILLO SINGLE ISSUE

YR	NAME	LIMIT	ISSUE	QUOTE
84	BABYSITTER MUSICAL FIGURE	2500	65.00	90.00

G. PERILLO SPECIAL ISSUE

YR	NAME	LIMIT	ISSUE	QUOTE
82	THE PEACEABLE KINGDOM	950	750.00	1500.00
84	APACHE BOY BUST	*	40.00	75.00
84	NAVAJO GIRL BUST	*	40.00	75.00
84	PAPOOSE	325	500.00	975.00
85	LOVERS	*	70.00	125.00

G. PERILLO THE CHIEFTANS

YR	NAME	LIMIT	ISSUE	QUOTE
83	CRAZY HORSE	5000	65.00	200.00
83	GERONIMO	5000	65.00	135.00

YR	NAME	LIMIT	ISSUE	QUOTE
83	JOSEPH	5000	65.00	250.00
83	RED CLOUD	5000	65.00	275.00
83	SITTING BULL	5000	65.00	500.00
G. PERILLO			**THE GREAT CHIEFTAINS**	
91	CHIEF JOSEPH	5000	195.00	195.00
91	COCHISE	5000	195.00	195.00
91	CRAZY HORSE (CLUB PIECE)	*	195.00	195.00
91	GERONIMO	5000	195.00	195.00
91	RED CLOUD	5000	195.00	195.00
91	SITTING BULL	5000	195.00	195.00
G. PERILLO			**THE LITTLE INDIANS**	
82	BLUE SPRUCE	10,000	50.00	75.00
82	TENDER LOVE	10,000	65.00	39.00
82	WHITE RABBIT	10,000	50.00	39.00
G. PERILLO			**THE PRINCESSES**	
84	LILY OF THE MOHAWKS	1500	65.00	155.00
84	MINNEHAHA	1500	65.00	42.00
84	POCAHONTAS	1500	65.00	52.00-65.00
84	SACAJAWEA	1500	65.00	125.00
G. PERILLO			**THE PROFESSIONALS**	
80	BALLERINA'S DILEMMA	10,000	65.00	75.00
80	THE BIG LEAGUER	10,000	65.00	150.00
81	THE QUARTERBACK	10,000	65.00	91.00
82	MAJOR LEAGUER	10,000	65.00	98.00
82	RODEO JOE	10,000	65.00	39.00
83	HOCKEY PLAYER	10,000	65.00	125.00
G. PERILLO			**THE STORYBOOK COLLECTION**	
80	LITTLE RED RIDINGHOOD	10,000	65.00	39.00-124.00
81	CINDERELLA	10,000	65.00	39.00-46.00
82	GOLDILOCKS & THE THREE BEARS	10,000	80.00	110.00
82	HANSEL & GRETEL	10,000	80.00	46.00
G. PERILLO			**THE TRIBAL PONIES**	
84	ARAPAHO	1500	65.00	200.00
84	COMANCHE	1500	65.00	200.00
84	CROW	1500	65.00	250.00
G. PERILLO			**THE WAR PONY**	
83	APACHE WAR PONY	495	150.00	250.00
83	NEZ PERCE PONY	495	150.00	250.00
83	SIOUX WAR PONY	495	150.00	250.00
G. PERILLO			**WILDLIFE FIGURINES**	
91	BALD EAGLE	OP	65.00	65.00
91	BIGHORN SHEEP	OP	75.00	75.00
91	BUFFALO	OP	75.00	75.00
91	MOUNTAIN LION	OP	75.00	75.00
91	MUSTANG	OP	85.00	85.00
91	POLAR BEAR	OP	65.00	65.00
91	TIMBER WOLF	OP	85.00	85.00
91	WHITE-TAILED DEER	OP	95.00	95.00

ARTISTS OF THE WORLD

T. DEGRAZIA

YR	NAME	LIMIT	ISSUE	QUOTE
93	FLOWERS FOR MOTHER	*	145.00	150.00
93	LITTLE MEDICINE MAN	*	175.00	185.00
93	MOTHER SILENTLY PRAYS	3500	345.00	380.00
93	SADDLE UP	5000	195.00	215.00
94	BEARING GIFT	*	145.00	150.00
94	FIESTA FLOWERS	3500	197.50	210.00
94	LOVING MOTHER	3500	165.00	175.00
94	PEDRO	*	145.00	150.00
94	RIO GRANDE DANCER	*	97.50	100.00
94	SAGUARO DANCE	2500	495.00	510.00
94	SPRING BLOSSOMS	5000	170.00	180.00
T. DEGRAZIA			**ANNUAL CHRISTMAS**	
93	FIESTA ANGELS	YR	295.00	315.00
94	LITTLEST ANGEL	YR	165.00	175.00
T. DEGRAZIA			**DEGRAZIA FIGURINES**	
84	DISPLAY PLAQUE	CL	45.00	95.00
84	FLOWER BOY	OP	65.00	110.00
84	FLOWER GIRL	OP	65.00	110.00
84	MY FIRST HORSE	OP	65.00	110.00
84	SUNFLOWER BOY	CL	65.00	300.00
84	WHITE DOVE	OP	45.00	79.50
84	WONDERING	CL	85.00	135.00-175.00
85	JESUS	OP	25.00	55.00
85	JOSEPH	OP	55.00	90.00
85	LITTLE MADONNA	OP	80.00	125.00
85	MARY	OP	55.00	80.00

YR	NAME	LIMIT	ISSUE	QUOTE
85	NATIVITY SET (3 PIECES)	OP	135.00	195.00
85	PIMA DRUMMER BOY	CL	65.00	110.00
86	FESTIVAL LIGHTS	OP	75.00	95.00
86	MERRY LITTLE INDIAN	12,500	175.00	245.00
86	THE BLUE BOY	OP	79.00	95.00
87	LOVE ME	OP	95.00	110.00
87	WEE THREE	CL	180.00	195.00
88	BEAUTIFUL BURDEN	CL	175.00	185.00-200.00
88	CHRISTMAS PRAYER ANGEL	CL	70.00	80.00
88	FLOWER BOY PLAQUE	CL	80.00	80.00
88	LOS NINOS	5000	595.00	645.00
88	MERRILY, MERRILY, MERRILY	CL	95.00	110.00-150.00
89	LOS NINOS	48	695.00	695.00
89	MY BEAUTIFUL ROCKING HORSE	OP	225.00	245.00
89	MY FIRST ARROW	OP	95.00	110.00
89	TWO LITTLE LAMBS	OP	70.00	80.00
90	ALONE	OP	395.00	475.00
90	BIGGEST DRUM	YR	110.00	125.00
90	CRUCIFIXION	YR	295.00	295.00
90	DESERT HARVEST	5000	135.00	145.00
90	EL BURRITO	OP	60.00	75.00
90	NAVAJO BOY	YR	110.00	125.00
90	SUNFLOWER GIRL	OP	95.00	95.00

T. DEGRAZIA — **NATIVITY**

YR	NAME	LIMIT	ISSUE	QUOTE
93	BALTHASAR	*	135.00	145.00
93	EL TORO	*	95.00	98.75
93	GUSPAR	*	135.00	145.00
93	MELCHIOR	*	135.00	145.00

T. DEGRAZIA — **VILLAGE COLLECTION**

YR	NAME	LIMIT	ISSUE	QUOTE
93	LET'S COMPROMISE	*	65.00	75.00
93	PEACE PIPE	*	65.00	75.00
93	THREE FEATHERS	*	65.00	75.00
93	WATER WAGON	*	295.00	325.00

AVONLEA TRADITIONS INC.

ANNE OF GREEN GABLES

YR	NAME	LIMIT	ISSUE	QUOTE
90	ARRIVING AT THE STATION	OP	50.00	50.00
94	A SOLEMN VOW AND PROMISE	OP	120.00	120.00
94	CARROTS! CARROTS!	OP	95.00	95.00
94	PERCHED ON THE WOODPILE	OP	120.00	120.00

BAND CREATIONS

ANGELS OF THE MONTH

YR	NAME	LIMIT	ISSUE	QUOTE
95	APRIL ANGEL	OP	10.00	10.00
95	AUGUST ANGEL	OP	10.00	10.00
95	DECEMBER ANGEL	OP	10.00	10.00
95	FEBRUARY ANGEL	OP	10.00	10.00
95	JANUARY ANGEL	OP	10.00	10.00
95	JULY ANGEL	OP	10.00	10.00
95	JUNE ANGEL	OP	10.00	10.00
95	MARCH ANGEL	OP	10.00	10.00
95	MAY ANGEL	OP	10.00	10.00
95	NOVEMBER ANGEL	OP	10.00	10.00
95	OCTOBER ANGEL	OP	10.00	10.00
95	SEPTEMBER ANGEL	OP	10.00	10.00

O JOYFUL NIGHT NATIVITY

YR	NAME	LIMIT	ISSUE	QUOTE
95	ANGEL ON WALL	OP	16.00	16.00
95	CAMEL/DONKEY	OP	4.00	4.00
95	HOLY FAMILY	OP	16.00	16.00
95	SHEPHERD	OP	8.00	8.00
95	THREE KINGS	OP	8.00	8.00

BOEHM STUDIOS
*

ANIMAL SCULPTURES

YR	NAME	LIMIT	ISSUE	QUOTE
52	HUNTER	250	600.00	1300.00
57	POLO PLAYER	100	850.00	4450.00
69	ADIOS	130	1500.00	1800.00
71	BOBCATS	200	1600.00	2000.00
71	FOXES	200	1800.00	2550.00
71	RACCOONS	200	1600.00	2250.00
72	RED SQUIRRELS	100	2600.00	2800.00
73	NYALA ANTELOPE	100	4700.00	6500.00
75	GIANT PANDA	100	3800.00	6350.00
75	PUMA	50	5700.00	6800.00
76	AMERICAN MUSTANGS	75	3700.00	5700.00
76	OTTER	75	1100.00	1450.00
77	AFRICAN ELEPHANT	50	9500.00	14400.00
78	BLACK RHINOCEROS	50	9500.00	11000.00

YR	NAME	LIMIT	ISSUE	QUOTE
78	CAMEL & CALF	50	3500.00	3900.00
78	GORILLA	50	3800.00	4400.00
78	SNOW LEOPARD	75	3500.00	5500.00
78	THOROUGHBRED W/JOCKEY	25	2600.00	2800.00
79	FALLOW DEER	30	7500.00	7500.00
79	HUNTER CHASE	20	4000.00	4000.00
79	YOUNG & FREE FAWNS	160	1875.00	1875.00
80	ASIAN LION	100	1500.00	1500.00
80	CHEETAH	100	2700.00	2900.00
*			**BIRD SCULPTURES**	
51	WOOD THRUSH	2	375.00	*
52	MALLARDS, PAIR	500	650.00	1700.00
53	BOB WHITE QUAIL, PAIR	750	400.00	2600.00
54	GOLDEN PHEASANT, BISQUE	7	200.00	11250.00
54	GOLDEN PHEASANT, DECORATED	7	350.00	19000.00
54	RINGED-NECKED PHEASANTS, PAIR	500	650.00	1825.00
54	WOODCOCK	500	300.00	1950.00
55	CARDINALS, PAIR	500	550.00	3750.00
56	BLACK-TAILED BANTAMS, PAIR	57	350.00	4700.00
56	CEDAR WAXWINGS, PAIR	100	600.00	7750.00
56	GOLDEN-CROWNED KINGLETS	500	1400.00	2400.00
56	SONG SPARROWS, PAIR	50	2000.00	38000.00
57	AMERICAN EAGLE, LARGE	31	225.00	1100.00
57	AMERICAN EAGLE, SMALL	76	225.00	19200.00
57	CALIFORNIA QUAIL, PAIR	500	400.00	2900.00
57	CAROLINA WRENS	100	750.00	5500.00
57	CERULEAN WARBLERS	100	800.00	4335.00
57	DOWNY WOODPECKERS	500	450.00	1775.00
57	MEADOWLARK	750	350.00	3100.00
57	RED-WINGED BLACKBIRDS, PAIR	100	700.00	5250.00
58	AMERICAN REDSTARTS	500	350.00	2000.00
58	BLACK-THROATED BLUE WARBLER	500	400.00	1875.00
58	MOURNING DOVES	500	550.00	1250.00
58	NONPAREIL BUNTINGS	750	250.00	1075.00
59	EASTERN BLUEBIRDS, PAIR	100	1800.00	12000.00
60	RUFFED GROUSE, PAIR	250	950.00	4950.00
61	GOLDFINCHES	500	400.00	1800.00
61	MOCKINGBIRDS, PAIR	500	650.00	3800.00
61	SUGARBIRDS	100	2500.00	13250.00
62	BLUE JAYS, PAIR	250	2000.00	12750.00
62	LESSER PRAIRIE CHICKENS, PAIR	300	1200.00	2400.00
62	PTARMIGAN, PAIR	350	800.00	3575.00
63	MEARN'S QUAIL, PAIR	350	950.00	3450.00
63	MOUNTAIN BLUEBIRDS	300	1900.00	5850.00
63	TOWHEE	500	350.00	2600.00
64	BOBOLINK	500	550.00	1550.00
64	KILLDEER, PAIR	300	1750.00	4500.00
64	ROBIN (DAFFODILS)	500	600.00	5700.00
65	CATBIRD	500	900.00	2135.00
65	FLEDGLING GREAT HORNED OWL	750	350.00	1475.00
65	PARULA WARBLERS	400	1500.00	3150.00
65	TUFTED TITMICE	500	600.00	2000.00
65	VARIED BUNTINGS	300	2200.00	4500.00
66	GREEN JAYS, PAIR	400	1850.00	4200.00
66	RUFOUS HUMMINGBIRDS	500	850.00	1900.00
66	WOOD THRUSHES, PAIR	400	4200.00	8400.00
67	BLUE GROSBEAK	750	1050.00	1500.00
67	CRESTED FLYCATCHER	500	1650.00	2925.00
67	FLEDGLING CANADA WARBLER	750	550.00	2275.00
67	NORTHERN WATER THRUSH	500	800.00	1400.00
68	COMMON TERN	500	1400.00	6200.00
68	KESTRALS, PAIR	450	2300.00	3000.00
68	MERGANSERS, PAIR	440	2200.00	2825.00
68	ROADRUNNER	500	2600.00	3700.00
69	BLACK-HEADED GROSBEAK	675	1250.00	2000.00
69	VERDINS	575	1150.00	1525.00
69	WESTERN BLUEBIRDS	300	5500.00	6600.00
69	YOUNG AMERICAN EAGLE	850	700.00	1400.00
70	ORCHARD ORIOLES	550	1750.00	2200.00
70	OVEN-BIRD	450	1400.00	1800.00
70	SLATE-COLORED JUNCO	*	1600.00	2000.00
71	FLICKER	250	2400.00	2950.00
71	LITTLE OWL	350	700.00	1325.00
71	MUTE SWANS, LIFE-SIZE, PAIR	3	*	*
71	MUTE SWANS, PAIR	400	4000.00	8200.00
71	NUTHATCH	350	650.00	1100.00

YR	NAME	LIMIT	ISSUE	QUOTE
71	WESTERN MEADOWLARK	350	1425.00	1675.00
71	WINTER ROBIN	225	1150.00	1440.00
72	BARN OWL	350	3600.00	5600.00
72	BLACK GROUSE	175	2800.00	3025.00
72	BROWN PELICAN	100	10500.00	14500.00
72	CACTUS WREN	225	3000.00	3300.00
72	EUROPEAN GOLDFINCH	225	1150.00	1350.00
72	GOLDCREST	500	650.00	1200.00
72	TREE CREEPERS	200	3200.00	4200.00
72	YELLOW-BELLIED SAPSUCKER	*	2700.00	3000.00
73	BLACKBIRDS, PAIR	75	5400.00	6300.00
73	BLUE TITS	300	3000.00	3000.00
73	BROWN THRASHER	260	1850.00	1875.00
73	EVERGLADES KITES	50	5800.00	7200.00
73	GREEN WOODPECKERS	50	4200.00	4800.00
73	HORNED LARKS	200	3800.00	5000.00
73	LAPWING	100	2600.00	2975.00
73	LAZULI BUNTINGS	250	1800.00	2300.00
73	LONG TAIL TITS	200	2600.00	2900.00
73	PEREGRINE FALCON	350	4400.00	5450.00
73	SCREECH OWL	50	850.00	1425.00
73	YELLOWHAMMERS	350	3300.00	4200.00
73	YOUNG AMERICAN EAGLE, INAUGURAL	110	1500.00	2100.00
74	CHAFFINCH	125	2000.00	2200.00
74	CRESTED TIT	400	1150.00	1250.00
74	HOODED WARBLER	100	2400.00	3150.00
74	LARK SPARROW	150	100.00	2200.00
74	MYRTLE WARBLERS	210	1850.00	2075.00
74	PURPLE MARTINS	50	6700.00	8450.00
74	RUBY-THROATED HUMMINGBIRD	200	1900.00	2650.00
74	SONG THRUSHES	100	2800.00	3350.00
74	STONECHATS	150	2200.00	2400.00
74	SWALLOWS	125	3400.00	4100.00
74	VARIED THRUSH	*	2500.00	3000.00
74	YELLOW-BELLIED BLACKBIRD	75	3200.00	3600.00
74	YELLOW-BELLIED CUCKOO	*	2800.00	3000.00
75	EASTERN KINGBIRD	100	3500.00	3900.00
75	PEKIN ROBBINS	100	7000.00	8550.00
75	RED-BILLED BLUE MAGPIE	100	4600.00	5950.00
75	YOUNG AND SPIRITED, 1976	1121	950.00	1800.00
76	BLACK-THROATED BLUE WARBLER	200	900.00	1100.00
76	EAGLE OF FREEDOM I	15	35000.00	53000.00
76	KINGFISHERS	200	1900.00	2300.00
76	RIVOLI'S HUMMINGBIRD	350	950.00	1650.00
77	CAPE MAY WARBLER	400	825.00	950.00
77	CARDINALS	200	3500.00	3850.00
77	FLEDGLING BROWN THRASHERS	400	500.00	655.00
77	ROBIN (NEST)	350	1650.00	1840.00
77	SCARLET TANAGER	4	1800.00	4000.00
77	SCISSOR-TAILED FLYCATCHER	100	3200.00	3200.00
78	CANADA GEESE, PAIR	100	4200.00	4200.00
78	MOCKINGBIRDS	*	2200.00	2800.00
79	AVOCET	175	1200.00	1200.00
79	GREY WAGTAIL	150	1050.00	1260.00
79	LEAST TURN	350	1275.00	3100.00
79	SCOPS OWL	300	975.00	1500.00
80	ARCTIC TERN	350	1400.00	2850.00
80	SCREECH OWL	350	2100.00	3100.00
81	SNOW BUNTINGS	350	2400.00	2950.00
*				**BOEHM**
83	GREAT EGRET	YR	1200.00	2400.00
84	WHOOPING CRANE	YR	1800.00	2000.00
85	TRUMPETER SWAN	YR	1500.00	1800.00
*				**FIGURINES**
77	BEVERLY SILLS	100	950.00	1500.00
77	JEROME HINES	12	825.00	1000.00
*				**FLORAL SCULPTURES**
71	DAISIES	350	600.00	975.00
71	SWAN CENTERPIECE	135	1950.00	2725.00
72	CHRYSANTHEMUMS	350	1100.00	1950.00
73	DOGWOOD	250	625.00	975.00
73	STEPTOCALYX POEPPIGII	50	3400.00	4300.00
74	DEBUTANTE CAMELIA	500	625.00	800.00
74	DOUBLE PEONY	275	575.00	1050.00
74	GENTIANS	350	425.00	725.00
74	WATERLILY	350	400.00	660.00

YR	NAME	LIMIT	ISSUE	QUOTE
75	EMMETT BARNES CAMELLIA	425	550.00	780.00
75	MAGNOLIA GRANDIFLORA	750	650.00	1350.00
76	ORCHID CACTUS	100	650.00	975.00
76	QUEEN OF THE NIGHT CACTUS	125	650.00	850.00
76	ROSE, SUPREME PEACE	250	850.00	1575.00
76	ROSE, SUPREME YELLOW	250	850.00	1575.00
76	SWAN LAKE CAMELLIA	750	825.00	1725.00
76	SWEET VIBURNUM	35	650.00	1425.00
78	DOUBLE CLEMATIS CENTERPIECE	150	1500.00	1950.00
78	HELEN BOEHM CAMELLIA	500	600.00	1050.00
78	HELEN BOEHM DAYLILY	175	975.00	1160.00
78	HELEN BOEHM IRIS	175	975.00	1175.00
78	RHODODENDRON CENTERPIECE	350	1150.00	1750.00
78	ROSE, BLUE MOON	500	650.00	900.00
78	ROSE, PASCALI	500	950.00	1375.00
78	ROSE, TROPICANA	500	475.00	1085.00
78	SPANISH IRIS	500	600.00	600.00
78	WATSONII MAGNOLIA	250	575.00	690.00
79	CACTUS DAHLIA	300	800.00	960.00
79	GRAND FLORAL CENTERPIECE	15	7500.00	8700.00
79	HONEYSUCKLE	200	900.00	1080.00
80	ROSE, ALEC'S RED	500	1050.00	1300.00

BRIERCROFT

B. FARLOW   **INTERNATIONAL SANTAS**

YR	NAME	LIMIT	ISSUE	QUOTE
93	AMERICAN '40S BABY BOOMER	5000	26.50	45.00
93	ITALIAN BABBO NATALIE	5000	26.50	45.00
93	SANTA'S PUP	5000	5.00	9.00
93	SWEDISH TOMTEN & YULEBOCK	5000	26.50	45.00
94	AMERICAN '40S BABY BOOMER-BLACK	5000	26.50	45.00
94	BANJO SANTA (W/ORNAMENT)	5000	16.00	30.00
94	BELGIAN ST. NICHOLAS (W/ORNAMENT)	5000	6.00	9.50
94	DUTCH SINTER KLAAS	5000	26.50	45.00
94	DUTCH SINTER KLAAS (W/ORNAMENT)	5000	6.00	9.50
94	FRENCH PERE NOEL (W/ORNAMENT)	5000	6.00	9.50
94	MARIACHI SANTA	5000	26.50	45.00
94	POLISH GIFT GIVER	5000	26.50	45.00
94	POLISH GIFT GIVER (W/ORNAMENT)	5000	6.00	9.50
94	RUSSIAN RATHER CHRISTMAS (W/ORNAMENT)	5000	6.00	9.50
94	SPANISH GIFT GIVER	5000	26.50	45.00
94	SPANISH GIFT GIVER (W/ORNAMENT)	5000	6.00	9.50
94	SPOTTED PUP (W/ORNAMENT)	5000	6.00	9.50
94	U.S. '40S BABY BOOMER (W/ORNAMENT)	5000	6.00	9.50
94	U.S. '40S BABY BOOMER-BLACK (W/ORNAMENT)	5000	6.00	9.50

B. FARLOW   **MALE ANGELS**

YR	NAME	LIMIT	ISSUE	QUOTE
94	ANGEL AT THE TOMB	5000	25.00	39.00
94	COMMANDER ANGEL	5000	25.00	39.00
94	GABRIEL ANGEL	5000	25.00	39.00

B. FARLOW   **NATIVITY**

YR	NAME	LIMIT	ISSUE	QUOTE
93	INNKEEPER	5000	23.50	37.00
93	INNKEEPER'S WIFE	5000	23.50	37.00
94	EWE & NURSING LAMB	5000	12.50	23.50
94	EWE & SLEEPING LAMB	5000	12.50	23.50
94	GROUP OF SHEEP	5000	23.50	35.95
94	NATIVITY ANGEL	5000	26.50	45.00
94	SHEPHERD BOY WITH LAMB	5000	15.00	27.50
94	THRESHING FLOOR ANGEL	5000	25.00	39.00

BYERS' CHOICE LTD.

J. BYERS   **CAROLERS**

YR	NAME	LIMIT	ISSUE	QUOTE
82	VICTORIAN ADULT CAROLER (1ST VERSION)	CL	32.00	300.00
82	VICTORIAN CHILD CAROLER (1ST VERSION)	CL	32.00	300.00
83	VICTORIAN ADULT CAROLER (2ND VERSION)	OP	35.00	42.00
83	VICTORIAN CHILD CAROLER (2ND VERSION)	OP	33.00	41.00
86	SINGING DOGS	OP	13.00	13.00
86	TRADITIONAL GRANDPARENTS	OP	35.00	35.00
88	CHILDREN WITH SKATES	OP	40.00	46.00
88	SINGING CATS	OP	13.50	15.00
88	VICTORIAN GRANDPARENT CAROLERS	OP	40.00	45.00
91	ADULT SKATERS	OP	50.00	50.00
91	TODDLER ON SLED	OP	30.00	30.00
92	CHILDREN SKATERS	OP	50.00	50.00
92	LIL' DICKENS-SHOVEL	OP	17.00	17.00
92	LIL' DICKENS-SLED	OP	17.00	17.00
92	LIL' DICKENS-SNOWBALL (LG)	OP	17.00	17.00

J. BYERS   **COUNTRY CHRISTMAS STORE EXCLUSIVE**

YR	NAME	LIMIT	ISSUE	QUOTE
88	TOYMAKER	600	59.00	875.00

YR	NAME	LIMIT	ISSUE	QUOTE
J. BYERS				**CRIES OF LONDON**
91	LADY WITH APPLES	OP	80.00	80.00
92	CRY OF LONDON-BAKER	OP	62.00	83.00
J. BYERS				**DICKENS SERIES**
83	SCROOGE (1ST EDITION)	CL	36.00	2500.00-3000.00
84	MRS. CRATCHET (1ST EDITION)	CL	38.00	1700.00
84	SCROOGE (2ND EDITION)	OP	38.00	38.00
85	MR. FEZZIWIG (1ST EDITION)	CL	43.00	500.00
85	MRS. CRATCHIT (2ND EDITION)	OP	39.00	39.00
85	MRS. FEZZIWIG (1ST EDITION)	CL	43.00	500.00-650.00
86	MARLEY'S GHOST (1ST EDITION)	CL	40.00	500.00
86	MR. FEZZIWIG (2ND EDITION)	CL	43.00	65.00
86	MRS. FEZZIWIG (2ND EDITION)	CL	43.00	65.00
87	MARLEY'S GHOST (2ND EDITION)	OP	42.00	135
87	SPIRIT OF CHRISTMAS PAST (1ST EDITION)	CL	42.00	65.00-175.00
88	SPIRIT OF CHRISTMAS PAST (2ND EDITION)	CL	46.00	46.00
88	SPIRIT OF CHRISTMAS PRESENT (1ST ED.)	CL	44.00	165.00
89	SPIRIT OF CHRISTMAS FUTURE (1ST EDITION)	CL	46.00	165.00
89	SPIRIT OF CHRISTMAS FUTURE (1ST EDITION)	CL	46.00	100.00
89	SPIRIT OF CHRISTMAS PRESENT (2ND ED.)	CL	48.00	48.00
90	BOB CRATCHET & TINY TIM	CL	84.00	84.00
90	SPIRIT OF CHRISTMAS FUTURE (2ND ED.)	CL	48.00	48.00
91	BOB CRATCHIT & TINY TIM (2ND EDITION)	OP	86.00	86.00
91	HAPPY SCROOGE (1ST EDITION)	OP	50.00	130
92	HAPPY SCROOGE (2ND EDITION)	OP	50.00	50.00
J. BYERS				**DISPLAY FIGURES**
81	DISPLAY LADY	*	*	2000.00
81	DISPLAY MAN	*	*	2000.00
82	DISPLAY DRUMMER BOY (1ST VERSION)	CL	96.00	600.00
82	DISPLAY SANTA	CL	96.00	600.00
83	DISPLAY CAROLERS	CL	200.00	500.00
84	DISPLAY WORKING SANTA	CL	260.00	400.00
85	DISPLAY CHILDREN	CL	140.00	400.00
85	DISPLAY DRUMMER BOY (2ND VERSION)	CL	160.00	300.00
85	DISPLAY OLD WORLD SANTA	CL	260.00	500.00
86	DISPLAY ADULTS	CL	170.00	250.00-350.00
90	DISPLAY SANTA-BAYBERRY	CL	250.00	250.00
90	DISPLAY SANTA-RED	CL	250.00	250.00
J. BYERS				**MUSICIANS**
83	VIOLIN PLAYER MAN	CL	38.00	800.00
85	HORN PLAYER	CL	38.00	450.00
85	HORN PLAYER, CHUBBY FACE	CL	37.00	900.00
86	VICTORIAN GIRL WITH VIOLIN	CL	39.00	175.00
89	MUSICIAN WITH CLARINET	CL	44.00	75.00
90	MUSICIAN WITH MANDOLIN	CL	46.00	46.00
91	BOY WITH MANDOLIN	1000	48.00	150.00
91	MUSICIAN WITH ACCORDIAN	OP	48.00	110.00
92	MUSICIAN WITH FRENCH HORN	OP	52.00	52.00
J. BYERS				**NATIVITY**
87	ANGEL-GREAT STAR (BLONDE)	CL	40.00	75.00
87	ANGEL-GREAT STAR (BRUNETTE)	CL	40.00	75.00
87	ANGEL-GREAT STAR (RED HEAD)	CL	40.00	75.00
87	BLACK ANGEL	CL	36.00	200.00
88	SHEPHERDS	OP	37.00	94.00
89	KING BALTHASAR	OP	40.00	40.00
89	KING GASPER	OP	40.00	40.00
89	KING MELCHIOR	OP	40.00	40.00
90	HOLY FAMILY	OP	90.00	175
J. BYERS				**SANTAS**
78	OLD WORLD SANTA	CL	33.00	2000.00
78	VELVET SANTA	OP	*	46.00
82	SANTA IN SLEIGH (1ST VERSION)	CL	46.00	800.00
83	WORKING SANTA	OP	38.00	38.00
84	MRS. CLAUS	OP	38.00	38.00
84	SANTA IN SLEIGH (2ND VERSION)	CL	70.00	500.00
84	VIOLIN PLAYER MAN (2ND VERSION)	CL	38.00	1500.00
86	MRS. CLAUS ON ROCKER	CL	73.00	400.00
86	VICTORIAN SANTA	CL	39.00	175.00
87	VELVET MRS. CLAUS	OP	44.00	44.00
88	KNECHT RUPRECHT	CL	38.00	41.00
88	SAINT NICHOLAS	OP	44.00	94.00
89	RUSSIAN SANTA	CL	85.00	150.00
90	WEIHNACHTSMANN	OP	56.00	56.00
91	FATHER CHRISTMAS	OP	48.00	75.00
92	MRS. CLAUS (2ND EDITION)	OP	50.00	50.00
92	WORKING SANTA (2ND EDITION)	OP	52.00	90.00

YR	NAME	LIMIT	ISSUE	QUOTE
J. BYERS			**SNOW GOOSE EXCLUSIVE**	
88	MAN WITH GOOSE	600	60.00	350.00
J. BYERS			**SPECIAL CHARACTERS**	
81	THANKSGIVING LADY (CLAY HANDS)	*	*	2000.00
81	THANKSGIVING MAN (CLAY HANDS)	*	*	2000.00
82	CHOIR CHILDREN, BOY AND GIRL	CL	32.00	250.00
82	CONDUCTOR	OP	32.00	90.00
82	DRUMMER BOY	OP	34.00	150.00
82	EASTER BOY	CL	32.00	450.00
82	EASTER GIRL	CL	32.00	450.00
82	ICABOD	CL	33.00	1150.00
82	LEPRECHAUNS	CL	34.00	1200.00
82	VALENTINE BOY	CL	32.00	450.00
82	VALENTINE GIRL	CL	32.00	450.00
83	BOY ON ROCKING HORSE	300	85.00	1500.00
84	CHIMNEY SWEEP	CL	36.00	1200.00
85	PAJAMA CHILDREN	CL	35.00	60.00
87	BOY ON SLED	CL	50.00	300.00
87	CAROLER WITH LAMP	CL	40.00	130.00
87	MOTHER'S DAY	225	94.00	350.00
88	ANGEL TREE TOP	100	*	150.00
88	MOTHER HOLDING BABY	OP	40.00	40.00
88	MOTHER'S DAY (DAUGHTER)	CL	125.00	270.00
88	MOTHER'S DAY (SON)	CL	125.00	350
89	GIRL WITH HOOP	OP	44.00	100
89	MOTHER'S DAY (WITH CARRIAGE)	3000	75.00	200.00
89	NEWSBOY WITH BIKE	OP	78.00	120.00
90	GIRL ON ROCKING HORSE	CL	70.00	100
90	PARSON	OP	44.00	70.00
90	POSTMAN	OP	45.00	47.00
91	BOY WITH TREE	OP	49.00	100.00
91	CHIMNEY SWEEP (CHILD)	OP	50.00	50.00
92	SALVATION ARMY-WOMAN WITH KETTLE	OP	64.00	64.00
92	TEACHER	OP	48.00	48.00
92	VICTORIAN MOTHER WITH TODDLER	OP	60.00	60.00
J. BYERS			**STACY'S GIFTS & COLLECTIBLES EXCLUSIVES**	
87	SANTA IN ROCKING CHAIR WITH BOY	100	130.00	550.00
87	SANTA IN ROCKING CHAIR WITH GIRL	100	130.00	450.00
J. BYERS			**WAYSIDE COUNTRY STORE EXCLUSIVES**	
86	COLONIAL LAMPLIGHTER	600	46.00	500.00
87	COLONIAL WATCHMAN	600	49.00	400.00
88	COLONIAL LADY	600	49.00	350.00
J. BYERS			**WOODSTOCK INN EXCLUSIVES**	
87	SKIER BOY	200	40.00	400.00
87	SKIER GIRL	200	40.00	400.00
88	SUGARIN KIDS	*	41.00	250.00
88	SUGARIN KIDS	*	41.00	250.00
88	WOODSTOCK LADY	*	41.00	250.00
88	WOODSTOCK MAN	*	41.00	250.00

CAIRN STUDIO LTD.

*				*
*	WW II SOLDIER 328	*	*	450.00
T. CLARK			**ACORN COLLECTION**	
81	EL & EM 151	RT	5.00	30.00
81	EL KIM 152	RT	6.00	30.00
81	ELF 162	RT	7.00	30.00
81	ELK 154	RT	7.00	30.00
81	ELLA 153	RT	7.00	35.00
81	ELMER 155	RT	6.00	35.00
81	ELVA 157	RT	8.50	30.00
81	ELWOOD 156	RT	8.50	35.00
T. CLARK			**COLLECTOR SOCIETY ARTWORK SERIES**	
83	RORIE 48	RT	35.00	360.00-675.00
84	ERNEST 1030	RT	35.00	200.00-330.00
85	KILMER 1126	RT	55.00	300.00
87	HITCH 2018	RT	47.50	275.00
T. CLARK			**ESKIMOS**	
81	KANUK 165	RT	28.50	130.00-200.00
81	KEEGLOO 158	RT	32.50	300.00-475.00
81	KLONDIKE 166	RT	30.50	145.00-180.00
T. CLARK			**GNOMES & WOODSPIRITS**	
78	AMANDA 108	RT	35.00	4000.00
78	BESSIE 107	RT	35.00	4000.00
78	CALLIE 51	RT	27.50	5000.00
78	ETHAN 106	RT	35.00	2100.00
78	HAMP 105	RT	35.00	2000.00-2100.00

YR	NAME	LIMIT	ISSUE	QUOTE
78	HAP 101	RT	35.00	930.00-1050.00
78	IVY 114	RT	35.00	2000.00-4000.00
78	OBIE 104	RT	40.00	1260.00-1950.00
78	PHINEAS 103	RT	35.00	1350.00
78	REUBEN 102	RT	42.50	720.00-950.00
78	SILAS 109	RT	35.00	4000.00
78	VANYA 42	RT	35.00	5000.00
79	ABNER 10	RT	35.00	600.00-900.00
79	DAISY & ERIC 116	RT	37.50	800.00
79	HUGH ROBERT 7	RT	45.00	1200.00
79	IRVIN 9	RT	35.00	860.00-1325.00
79	LUM 18	RT	35.00	1400.00
79	MODE 8	RT	35.00	960.00-1100.00
79	MOM 4	RT	35.00	90.00-180.00
79	NAOMI 19	RT	35.00	1950.00-2200.00
79	OAKIE 3	RT	40.00	200.00-625.00
79	ROSCOE 6	RT	35.00	3000.00
79	SIMEON 2	RT	35.00	1350.00-1385.00
79	STUMPY 5	RT	35.00	2000.00-2800.00
79	WIZARD 110	RT	37.50	960.00
79	XEROX 50	RT	15.00	8000.00
80	AHAB 120	RT	32.50	354.00-625.00
80	ARNOLD 124	RT	19.00	550.00
80	CALEB 129	RT	22.00	175.00-275.00
80	CHALMERS 15	RT	27.50	102.00-265.00
80	CHASE I 14	RT	27.50	372.00-460.00
80	CHASE II 128	RT	35.00	510.00-675.00
80	DEWEY 13	RT	25.00	540.00-720.00
80	DUSTY 122	RT	35.00	3000.00-4200.00
80	FETZER 112	RT	25.00	495.00-1020.00
80	GERBER 127	RT	29.50	480.00-550.00
80	IGOR 23	RT	31.00	290.00-460.00
80	JASON 113	RT	19.50	385.00-840.00
80	JEREMIAH 119	RT	29.50	550.00
80	KATIE 125	RT	42.50	1200.00
80	LUCKY 115	RT	17.50	425.00-450.00
80	MARTIN 111	RT	27.50	390.00-550.00
80	MCMAN 21	RT	27.50	775.00
80	MCNEIL 11	RT	25.00	175.00-240.00
80	MEG 12	RT	25.00	135.00-210.00
80	NORTON 16	RT	32.50	400.00
80	O.J. 130	RT	27.50	155.00-270.00
80	OLIN 17	RT	25.00	1300.00
80	PATRICK 117	RT	19.00	720.00-850.00
80	POPS 22	RT	28.50	150.00-270.00
80	ROCKY 132	RT	32.50	210.00-310.00
80	SEAN 131	RT	27.50	275.00
80	SHAW 126	RT	22.50	450.00
80	SHELLY 123	RT	19.00	725.00
80	STARR 133	RT	32.50	500.00-600.00
80	WINK 24	RT	25.00	210.00-445.00
81	BABY JESUS 37	RT	10.00	125.00
81	BART 134	RT	27.50	285.00
81	BICK 188	RT	35.00	1020.00-1100.00
81	CAL 142	RT	45.00	1375.00-1475.00
81	CARDINAL 26	RT	19.00	*
81	DAFFY 140	RT	35.00	200.00-315.00
81	GNOME CROSSING SIGN 984	RT	39.00	90.00-200.00
81	HANS 139	RT	35.00	120.00-270.00
81	HOWDY 138	RT	35.00	235.00
81	JACKSON 149	RT	25.00	275.00-325.00
81	LENNON 135	RT	35.00	2000.00
81	LIEF 159	RT	31.00	150.00-285.00
81	PALMER 25	RT	35.00	230.00-360.00
81	PATCH 146	RT	32.50	105.00-290.00
81	RUMPKIN 160	RT	27.50	180.00
81	SANDY 93	RT	31.00	80.00-180.00
81	SECRET 190	RT	29.50	325.00
81	SOL 163	RT	35.00	150.00-240.00
81	SUNNY 150	RT	35.00	540.00-600.00
81	SWIFTY 96	RT	16.50	100.00-200.00
81	TEX 41	RT	27.50	1950.00
82	BANBURY 30	RT	25.00	215.00
82	BOOTS 31	RT	35.00	60.00-240.00
82	EGGBERT 194	RT	31.00	90.00-240.00
82	LUCKY II 198	RT	25.00	475.00

YR	NAME	LIMIT	ISSUE	QUOTE
82	MICHAEL 195	RT	27.50	190.00-300.00
82	MRS. WINK 32	RT	27.50	35.00-120.00
82	NEMO 193	RT	28.50	230.00-290.00
82	TOM CLARK CREATIONS SIGN 994	RT	*	30.00-75.00
83	ABEDNEGO 1014	RT	35.00	120.00
83	BLARNEY 1004	RT	32.50	50.00-130.00
83	BUZZY 68	RT	15.00	25.00-90.00
83	CHEESE 189	RT	25.00	180.00-290.00
83	CHEF 98	RT	13.00	27.00-75.00
83	CINDY 92	RT	35.00	200.00-225.00
83	CURTIS 94	RT	45.00	50.00-132.00
83	FRANKLIN 28	RT	65.00	80.00-300.00
83	GARLENA 97	RT	13.00	55.00-85.00
83	GUS 89	RT	26.50	140.00
83	HAZEL WITCH 1003	RT	45.00	175.00
83	HEATHER & JAN 77	RT	47.50	200.00
83	HYKE 27	RT	90.00	105.00-390.00
83	JUAN 70	RT	35.50	100.00-300.00
83	JULIE 85	RT	26.50	85.00-120.00
83	KERNEL 75	RT	50.00	90.00-175.00
83	MARTHA & JAY 73	RT	65.00	80.00-210.00
83	MESHACH 1013	RT	35.00	55.00-100.00
83	NICK O' TIME 1010	RT	31.00	325.00
83	PAPA & PRINCESS 69	RT	45.00	70.00-160.00
83	PARSLEY, SAGE, THYME 1001	RT	110.00	130.00-360.00
83	PLENTY 33	RT	32.50	45.00-180.00
83	SATURDAY 90	RT	25.00	50.00-95.00
83	SHADRACH 1012	RT	35.00	55.00-110.00
83	SKIPPER 1005	RT	37.50	60.00-170.00
83	SMOKEY 95	RT	40.00	50.00-130.00
83	SOUTH BEND 43	RT	19.00	85.00-150.00
83	SPUD 34	RT	27.50	50.00-100.00
83	STU 71	RT	40.00	60.00-70.00
83	TEDDY 81	RT	25.00	*
83	THE WIZ 87	RT	35.00	50.00-126.00
83	WILBUR 1006	RT	33.50	65.00-120.00
83	WINK TOO 88	RT	27.50	40.00-110.00
83	WOODY & CHANE 1015	RT	65.00	95.00-210.00
84	7-UP 1070	RT	500.00	1800.00
84	ACE OF SPADES 1035	RT	25.00	87.00
84	ANAHEIM 1025	RT	22.00	81.00
84	BEN 1069	RT	47.50	*
84	BONNIE 1051	RT	25.00	*
84	BUBBLES 1062	RT	15.00	30.00-55.00
84	BUTCH, WICK & BISCUIT 1056	RT	70.00	95.00-249.00
84	C.D. 1050	RT	32.50	*
84	CLAMENTINE 1064	RT	29.50	40.00-103.50
84	COLETTE 1028	RT	22.00	28.00-60.00
84	D.G. 1031	RT	33.00	210.00
84	DOUG 1045	RT	25.00	*
84	EENIE 1021	RT	27.50	45.00-97.50
84	ELIZABETH 1017	RT	25.00	35.00-50.00
84	FATHER TIME 1008	RT	33.50	45.00-110.00
84	GATOR 1032	RT	25.00	130.00-240.00
84	GEORGIA 1044	RT	31.00	95.00
84	GNOME OF ZURICH 1007	RT	33.50	70.00-175.00
84	GOODFOOT 1063	RT	29.50	125.00
84	HAL 1072	RT	40.00	*
84	HAPPY 1061	RT	35.00	*
84	HENSON 1059	RT	32.50	45.00-90.00
84	HOGAN 1033	RT	35.00	50.00-70.00
84	HOMER 1058	RT	32.50	*
84	JACK B. NIMBLE 1055	RT	29.50	55.00-120.00
84	JACK OF DIAMONDS 1038	RT	25.00	45.00-87.00
84	JACKIE B. QUICK 1065	RT	32.50	40.00-120.00
84	JOHNNY 1052	RT	25.00	*
84	KEN 1026	RT	45.00	60.00-168.00
84	KING OF CLUBS 1036	RT	25.00	50.00-85.00
84	LANCE 1042	RT	27.50	40.00-97.50
84	MABEL 1016	RT	67.50	85.00-240.00
84	MADRE 1068	RT	19.50	*
84	MCEVER 1067	RT	28.50	45.00-85.00
84	MEENIE 1022	RT	27.50	45.00-90.00
84	MELCHIOR 1060	RT	40.00	*
84	MINIE 1023	RT	25.00	35.00-70.00
84	MOE 1024	RT	25.00	35.00-90.00

YR	NAME	LIMIT	ISSUE	QUOTE
84	MOM TOO 1020	RT	40.00	55.00-85.00
84	MUGMON 1011	RT	24.50	*
84	N.O. EVELS, THE 1053	RT	70.00	*
84	NEWT 1043	RT	27.50	40.00-85.00
84	NOEL 1066	RT	55.00	75.00-175.00
84	O'NEAL 1019	RT	25.00	35.00-50.00
84	PADRE 80	RT	19.00	*
84	PAWLEY 1047	RT	31.00	*
84	PEANUT 1041	RT	27.50	35.00-85.00
84	QUEEN OF HEARTS 1037	RT	25.00	45.00-87.00
84	SANTA III 1054	RT	75.00	150.00-270.00
84	SHAKESPEARE 1039	RT	72.50	95.00-256.50
84	SHEN 1040	RT	60.00	80.00-180.00
84	SHORTY 1046	RT	32.50	*
84	SORGHUM OF GLADE VALLEY 1057	RT	35.00	70.00-110.00
84	THISTLE 1029	RT	80.00	110.00-283.50
84	TIM & RANDY 1009	RT	40.00	75.00-142.50
84	TOPSIE-TURVIE 1034	RT	37.50	90.00-190.00
84	VALENTINE (VAL) 1018	RT	30.00	*
84	WINKIN, BLINKIN & NOD 1071	RT	65.00	85.00-231.00
84	YULE 1048	RT	55.00	80.00-195.00
85	JINGLE "E" 1124	RT	15.00	27.00
85	JINGLE "G" 1122	RT	15.00	27.00
85	JINGLE "I" 1120	RT	15.00	22.00
85	JINGLE "J" 1119	RT	15.00	27.00
85	JINGLE "L" 1123	RT	15.00	27.00
85	JINGLE "N" 1121	RT	15.00	27.00
85	LILIBET 1079	RT	17.50	35.00-120.00
85	MERRILL & LYNCH 1117	RT	60.00	108.00-160.00
86	ALPHA 2014	RT	79.00	*
86	BUTTON 1092	RT	29.50	*
86	CHIP 1094	RT	37.50	*
86	HOLDER 1105	RT	37.50	*
86	JULIUS 1097	RT	40.00	*
86	MOORE OR LES 1093	RT	65.00	90.00-175.00
86	PAR 1096	RT	45.00	*
86	RACHEL 1088	RT	65.00	*
86	SAMMY 1098	RT	35.00	*
86	UNCLE WHIT 1083	RT	65.00	*
87	'TWAS THE NIGHT 1130	RT	700.00	*
87	CASPAR 1150	RT	45.00	*
87	ED 2022	RT	*	95.00-180.00
87	TELLY 1189	RT	*	205.00-375.00
88	BALTHAZAR 5012	RT	35.00	*
88	BROTHER, SIS & DAD 1181	RT	100.00	*
88	EUREKA 1115	RT	70.00	*
88	PEDRO 1158	RT	35.00	*
89	ROSEMARY 1002	RT	65.00	165.00

T. CLARK — MINIATURES

YR	NAME	LIMIT	ISSUE	QUOTE
83	BIRDIE 78	RT	*	50.00-150.00
83	EDDIE 83	RT	15.00	28.00-65.00
83	FREDDY 79	RT	17.50	95.00-115.00
83	JEFF 74	RT	17.00	40.00-75.00
83	JENNIE 84	RT	17.00	125.00
83	JOSHUA 82	RT	25.00	100.00
83	POKEY 86	RT	19.00	45.00-90.00

T. CLARK — MOUNTAINEERS

YR	NAME	LIMIT	ISSUE	QUOTE
81	APPLE ANNIE 169	RT	47.50	310.00
81	JEREMIAH SALLIE 168	RT	65.00	220.00-600.00
81	NELLIE 164	RT	55.00	540.00-840.00
82	ENOCH 186	RT	80.00	95.00-250.00
82	MATTIE 184	RT	67.50	190.00-420.00
82	NATH 185	RT	65.00	315.00-475.00

T. CLARK — NATIVITY

YR	NAME	LIMIT	ISSUE	QUOTE
81	INNKEEPER 171	RT	37.50	105.00-150.00
81	JOSEPH I 36	RT	35.00	200.00
81	MARY I 35	RT	35.00	125.00-225.00
82	ANGEL 196	RT	35.00	120.00
82	SHEPHERD 197	RT	37.50	80.00-95.00
83	HERDSMAN 72	RT	32.50	120.00

T. CLARK — SEA CAPTAINS & SAILORS

YR	NAME	LIMIT	ISSUE	QUOTE
81	ABRAHAM 173	RT	65.00	120.00-260.00
81	ABRAHAM LAMP 174	RT	80.00	180.00-420.00
81	JOCK 172	RT	40.00	155.00-200.00
82	PYRATE 181	RT	75.00	780.00
82	SVEN 180	RT	55.00	180.00-420.00

YR	NAME	LIMIT	ISSUE	QUOTE

T. CLARK — SPECIAL CHARACTERS

YR	NAME	LIMIT	ISSUE	QUOTE
80	SANTA I 121	RT	55.00	305.00-330.00
81	HATTIE 137	RT	55.00	250.00
81	LAWRENCE 136	RT	55.00	80.00-205.00
81	SLEUTH 179	RT	65.00	420.00-600.00
81	ST. FRANCIS 167	RT	50.00	120.00-180.00
81	ST. NICK 141	RT	40.00	570.00-600.00
82	BELLE KRINGLE 199	RT	55.00	96.00-300.00
82	DANIEL BOONE 182	RT	75.00	465.00-750.00
82	DANIEL BOONE LAMP 192	RT	85.00	800.00-1200.00
83	SANTA II 76	RT	55.00	90.00-300.00

T. CLARK — SPECIAL COMMISSION

YR	NAME	LIMIT	ISSUE	QUOTE
78	RUBENSTEIN 39	RT	*	5000.00
80	HARRIS 118	RT	45.00	1100.00-1200.00
81	ADAM 300	RT	*	210.00
81	FROSTY 304	RT	*	100.00-210.00
81	NEY 143	RT	35.00	95.00-150.00
81	OLLIE 303	RT	*	90.00-180.00
81	SMILEY 301	RT	*	120.00
81	STUCK 302	RT	*	95.00-155.00
82	GORDY 40	RT	*	750.00
83	BO SCHEMBECHLER 45	RT	57.50	192.00-250.00
83	COTTON 46	RT	*	205.00-230.00
83	D.C. 99	RT	*	95.00-110.00
83	HAMLET 47	RT	57.50	80.00-190.00
83	PA PAW 49	RT	*	600.00
83	WEST VIRGINIA MOUNTAINEER 91	RT	59.00	300.00-360.00

T. CLARK — SPECIAL PROMOTIONAL

YR	NAME	LIMIT	ISSUE	QUOTE
82	UNCLE SAM 83	RT	80.00	175.00-325.00

T. CLARK — THE WIND IN THE WILLOWS

YR	NAME	LIMIT	ISSUE	QUOTE
82	BADGER 177	RT	40.00	140.00
82	MOLE 176	RT	32.50	60.00-120.00
82	RATTY 175	RT	31.00	70.00-135.00
82	TOAD I 147	RT	50.00	480.00-655.00
82	TOAD II 148	RT	35.00	80.00-180.00

T. CLARK — TRUE BUILDERS OF AMERICA

YR	NAME	LIMIT	ISSUE	QUOTE
83	DR. GREY 321	RT	120.00	3700.00
83	MISS MARY 320	RT	*	840.00-1075.00
83	NEWSPAPER BOY 325	RT	120.00	510.00-750.00
84	AVIATOR 326	RT	150.00	450.00
84	PARSON PATTERSON 324	RT	150.00	190.00-485.00
84	RAILROAD CONDUCTOR 322	RT	120.00	150.00-425.00
87	BLACKSMITH 332	RT	150.00	192.00-450.00

T. CLARK — WESTERN

YR	NAME	LIMIT	ISSUE	QUOTE
83	COWBOY 306	RT	60.00	84.00-180.00
83	INDIAN 307	RT	60.00	90.00-210.00

CAST ART

KRISTIN HAYNES — DREAMSICLES

YR	NAME	LIMIT	ISSUE	QUOTE
93	BY THE SILVERY MOON	RT	100.00	175.00
93	TEETER TOTS	RT	100.00	250.00
93	THE FINISHING TOUCHES	RT	85.00	100.00
93	THE FLYING LESSON	RT	80.00	250.00
94	HOLIDAY ON ICE	OP	85.00	95.00
94	THE RECITAL	RT	135.00	150.00

KRISTIN HAYNES — DREAMSICLES COLLECTORS CLUB

YR	NAME	LIMIT	ISSUE	QUOTE
93	A STAR IS BORN	RT	30.00	30.00
93	DAYDREAM BELIEVER	RT	29.95	35.00
94	JOIN THE FUN	RT	*	0
94	MAKIN' A LIST	RT	47.95	50.00

CAVANAUGH GROUP

COCA-COLA BRAND HERITAGE COLLECTION

YR	NAME	LIMIT	ISSUE	QUOTE
94	EIGHT POLAR BEARS ON WOOD	10000	150.00	160.00
94	SANTA AT HIS DESK	OP	45.00	45.00
94	SANTA AT THE LAMPPOST	OP	50.00	50.00
94	SINGLE POLAR BEAR ON ICE	OP	40.00	40.00
94	EIGHT POLAR BEARS ON WOOD	10000	135.00	145.00
94	SANTA AT HIS DESK	5000	70.00	75.00
94	SANTA AT THE FIREPLACE	5000	70.00	75.00
94	TWO POLAR BEARS ON ICE	OP	30.00	30.00

COCA-COLA BRAND HERITAGE COLLECTION MUSICALS

YR	NAME	LIMIT	ISSUE	QUOTE
94	CALENDAR GIRL 1916	OP	60.00	60.00
94	HILDA CLARK 1901	OP	60.00	60.00
94	HILDA CLARK 1903	OP	60.00	60.00
94	SANTA'S SODA SHOP	OP	50.00	50.00
93	DEAR SANTA, PLEASE PAUSE HERE	OP	50.00	50.00

YR	NAME	LIMIT	ISSUE	QUOTE
94	SANTA AT HIS DESK	5000	95.00	100.00
94	SANTA AT THE FIREPLACE	5000	95.00	100.00
94	TWO POLAR BEARS ON ICE	OP	45.00	45.00

COCA-COLA BRAND TOWN SQUARE COLLECTION

YR	NAME	LIMIT	ISSUE	QUOTE
92	AFTER SAKTING	CL	8.00	10.00
92	BRINGING IT HOME	CL	8.00	10.00
92	COCA-COLA AD CAR	CL	9.00	10.00
92	COCA-COLA DELIVERY TRUCK	CL	15.00	18.00
92	DELIVERY MAN	CL	8.00	10.00
92	GIL THE GROCER	CL	8.00	10.00
92	HORSE-DRAWN WAGON	CL	12.00	15.00
92	THIRSTY THE SNOWMAN	CL	9.00	11.00

SANTA'S NORTH POLE BOTTLING WORKS

YR	NAME	LIMIT	ISSUE	QUOTE
95	FILLING OPERATIONS	OP	45.00	45.00
95	KITCHEN CORNER, THE	OP	55.00	55.00
95	MAKING SECRET SYRUP	OP	30.00	30.00
95	PIPE MAINTENANCE	OP	20.00	20.00
95	QUALITY CONTROL	OP	25.00	25.00
95	RESTOCKING THE VENDING MACHINE	OP	30.00	30.00
95	SANTA AT HIS DESK	OP	30.00	30.00
95	SANTA'S OFFICE	OP	50.00	50.00
95	TAKING A BREAK	OP	20.00	20.00
95	VAULT, THE	OP	25.00	25.00

COUNTRY ARTISTS

S. LANDFORD — BALD EAGLE COLLECTION

YR	NAME	LIMIT	ISSUE	QUOTE
95	BALD EAGLE SOARING	OP	62.50	74.00
95	BALD EAGLE LANDING	OP	127.50	135.00
95	HIDDEN SANCTUARY	2500	289.00	300.00
95	SPIRIT OF FREEDOM	1500	750.00	765.00

D. IVEY — BIG CAT COLLECTION

YR	NAME	LIMIT	ISSUE	QUOTE
95	CHEETAH	OP	198.00	205.00
95	COUGAR	OP	182.50	195.00
95	LEOPARD	OP	198.00	205.00
95	SNOW LEOPARD	OP	189.00	200.00
95	TIGER	OP	215.00	220.00

K. SHERWIN — GRAYWOLF COLLECTION

YR	NAME	LIMIT	ISSUE	QUOTE
92	DAWN CHORUS	OP	375.00	400.00
92	FIRST ICE OF WINTER	RT	450.00	475.00
92	HIGH GROUND	OP	225.00	250.00
92	LARGE HOWLING WOLF	OP	150.00	165
92	MEDIUM HOWLING WOLF	OP	95.00	105.00
92	MOTHER & CUB	OP	175.00	195.00
92	RUNNING FREE	OP	175.00	195.00
92	SMALL HOWLING WOLF	OP	49.00	55.00
92	WOLF CUBS	OP	135.00	145.00
92	WOLF KISS	OP	250.00	275.00
92	WOLF PAIR	OP	225.00	250.00
95	UNTAMED WILDERNESS	3500	495.00	510.00

B. PRICE — PENGUIN COLLECTION

YR	NAME	LIMIT	ISSUE	QUOTE
95	MINIATURE PENGUIN	OP	24.95	28.00
95	MOTHER & CHICKS	OP	110.00	120.00
95	PENGUIN CHICK SLIDING	OP	52.50	55.00
95	PENGUIN CHICKS KISSING	OP	57.50	62.00
95	PENGUIN CHICKS--GROUP	OP	74.50	80.00
95	PENGUIN FAMILY	OP	169.00	180.00

CREART

F. CONTRERAS — AFRICAN WILDLIFE

YR	NAME	LIMIT	ISSUE	QUOTE
93	CAPE BUFFALO	1500	418.00	418.00
94	NUMA LION'S HEAD	2500	418.00	418.00
94	GRUMBLER CAPE BUFFALO	1500	498.00	498.00
93	TRAVIESO	1500	198.00	198.00

F. CONTRERAS — AMERICAN WILDLIFE

YR	NAME	LIMIT	ISSUE	QUOTE
93	AMERICAN SYMBOL EAGLE	1500	246.00	246.00
93	THE RED FOX	1500	199.00	199.00
93	WILD AMERICAN BISON	1500	338.00	338.00
94	CATAMOUNTAIN	2500	118.00	118.00
94	OUT OF THE DEN PUMA	1500	130.00	130.00
94	PUFFINS	1500	258.00	258.00
93	BUENOS DIAS JACK RABBIT	1500	218.00	218.00
93	HOWLING COYOTE	1500	199.00	199.00
94	FREEDOM EAGLE	1500	500.00	500.00
94	AMBUSHING PUMA	1950	150.00	150.00
94	BRIEFLY REST PUMAS	1950	250.00	250.00
94	RED-TAILED HAWK	1950	130.00	130.00
93	SCENT OF HONEY BEAR	1500	398.00	398.00

YR	NAME	LIMIT	ISSUE	QUOTE
93	WHITE BLIZZARD WOLF	1500	275.00	275.00
94	OVER THE TOP PUMA	1500	398.00	398.00
94	SINGING TO THE MOON I WOLF	1500	398.00	398.00
94	SINGING TO THE MOON II WOLF	1500	358.00	358.00
J. ROBISON				**BIRDS OF PREY**
94	GYRFALCON	450	1300.00	1300.00
94	VIGILANT EAGLE	650	780.00	780.00
F. CONTRERAS				**NATURE'S CARE**
93	DOE & FAWNS	2500	99.00	99.00
93	EAGLE & EAGLET	2500	99.00	99.00
93	GORILLA & BABY	2500	99.00	99.00
93	LIONESS & CUBS	2500	99.00	99.00
93	WOLF & PUPS	2500	99.00	99.00
93	OTTERS	2500	99.00	99.00
93	JACK RABBIT & YOUNG	2500	99.00	99.00
93	GRIZZLY & CUBS	2500	99.00	99.00
93	PENGUIN AND CHICKS	2500	99.00	99.00

CRYSTAL WORLD
N. MULARGIA

YR	NAME	LIMIT	ISSUE	QUOTE
93	RIVERBOAT	350	570.00	570.00
93	VICTORIAN HOUSE	2000	190.00	190.00
93	ENCHANTED CASTLE	750	800.00	850.00
94	INDEPENDENCE HALL	750	350.00	350.00
93	COUNTRY GRISTMILL	1250	320.00	320.00
95	CLASSIC MOTORCYCLE	950	375.00	350.00

CYBIS

YR	NAME	LIMIT	ISSUE	QUOTE
*				**ANIMAL KINGDOM**
*	BULL	100	150.00	4500.00
61	HORSE	100	150.00	2000.00
65	RACCOON, RAFFLES	CL	110.00	365.00
65	SQUIRREL, MR. FLUFFY TAIL	CL	90.00	400.00
66	THOROUGHBRED	350	425.00	1650.00
67	KITTEN, BLUE RIBBON	CL	95.00	500.00
68	BEAR	CL	85.00	300.00-550.00
68	BUFFALO	CL	115.00	228.00
68	ELEPHANT	100	600.00	5000.00
68	SNAIL, SIR ESCARGOT	CL	50.00	350.00
68	STALLION	350	475.00	900.00
69	COLTS, DARBY & JOAN	CL	295.00	475.00
70	DEER MOUSE IN CLOVER	CL	65.00	160.00
71	AMERICAN BULLFROG	CL	250.00	600.00
71	APPALOOSA COLT	CL	150.00	350.00-400.00
71	NASHUA	100	2000.00	3000.00
72	PINTO COLT	CL	175.00	250.00
75	AMERICAN WHITE BUFFALO	250	1250.00	4000.00
75	KITTEN, TABITHA	CL	90.00	150.00
75	KITTEN, TOPAZ	CL	90.00	150.00
76	BUNNY, MUFFET	CL	85.00	200.00
76	CHIPMUNK WITH BLOODROOT	225	625.00	675.00
76	PRAIRIE DOG	CL	245.00	345.00
77	BUNNY PAT-A-CAKE	CL	90.00	125.00
78	DOORMOUSE MAXIMILLIAN	CL	250.00	300.00
78	DOORMOUSE MAXINE	CL	195.00	225.00
78	PINKY BUNNY/CARROT	200	200.00	265.00
80	ARCTIC WHITE FOX	100	4500.00	4700.00
80	SQUIRREL, HIGHRISE	400	475.00	525.00
81	BEAVERS, EGBERT & BREWSTER	400	285.00	335.00
82	DALL SHEEP	50	*	4250.00
84	AUSTRALIAN SULPHER CRESTED COCKATOO	25	9850.00	9850.00
84	CHANTILLY, KITTEN	OP	175.00	210.00
85	BAXTER & DOYLE	400	450.00	450.00
85	BEAGLES, BRANIGAN & CLANCY	OP	375.00	575.00
85	BUNNY, SNOWFLAKE	OP	65.00	75.00
85	ELEPHANT, WILLOUGHBY	OP	195.00	245.00
85	MONDAY, RHINOCEROS	OP	85.00	120.00
86	DAPPLE GREY FOAL	OP	195.00	225.00
86	HUEY, THE HARMONIOUS HARE	OP	175.00	275.00
86	MICK, THE MELODIOUS MUTT	OP	175.00	275.00
86	WHITE-TAILED DEER	50	9500.00	11500.00
*				**BIBLICAL**
*	HOLYWATER FONT, HOLY GHOST	CL	15.00	145.00
56	HOLY CHILD OF PRAGUE	10	1500.00	75000.00
57	MADONNA, HOUSE OF GOLD	8	125.00	4000.00
60	EXODUS	50	350.00	2600.00
60	FLIGHT INTO EGYPT	50	175.00	2500.00

YR	NAME	LIMIT	ISSUE	QUOTE
60	MADONNA LACE AND ROSE	OP	15.00	295.00
60	THE PROPHET	50	250.00	3500.00
63	MOSES THE GREAT LAWGIVER	750	250.00	5500.00
64	ALICE IN WONDERLAND	CL	50.00	850.00
64	NATIVITY, MARY	OP	*	325.00
64	ST. PETER	500	*	1250.00
76	NOAH	500	975.00	3000.00
84	CHRIST CHILD WITH LAMB	OP	*	290.00
84	NATIVITY, ANGEL, COLOR	OP	395.00	575.00
84	NATIVITY, CAMEL, COLOR	OP	625.00	825.00
84	NATIVITY, JOSEPH	OP	*	325.00
84	NATIVITY, SHEPHERD, COLOR	OP	395.00	475.00
85	NATIVITY, COW, COLOR	OP	175.00	195.00
85	NATIVITY, COW, WHITE	OP	125.00	225.00
85	NATIVITY, DONKEY, COLOR	OP	195.00	225.00
85	NATIVITY, DONKEY, WHITE	OP	130.00	150.00
85	NATIVITY, LAMB, COLOR	OP	150.00	195.00
85	NATIVITY, LAMB, WHITE	OP	115.00	125.00
*				**BIRDS & FLOWERS**
*	BIRDS & FLOWERS	250	500.00	4500.00
*	BUTTERFLY W/DOGWOOD	200	*	350.00
*	SANDPIPERS	400	700.00	2000.00-2200.00
*	SKYLARKS	350	330.00	2500.00
57	TURTLE DOVES	500	350.00	6000.00
59	HUMMINGBIRD	CL	95.00	950.00
60	BLUE-HEADED VIRIO (BUILDING NEST)	CL	60.00	1100.00
60	BLUE-HEADED VIRIO W/LILAC	275	1200.00	2200.00
60	PHEASANT	150	750.00	5000.00
61	BLUE-GREY GNATCATCHERS (PAIR)	200	400.00	2500.00
61	GOLDEN CLARION LILY	100	250.00	4500.00
62	DUCKLING (BABY BROTHER)	CL	35.00	150.00-175.00
62	SPARROW ON LOG	CL	35.00	450.00
63	IRIS	250	500.00	4500.00
63	MAGNOLIA	CL	350.00	495.00
64	DAHLIA YELLOW	350	450.00	1800.00
64	GREAT WHITE HERON	350	850.00	4000.00
65	CHRISTMAS ROSE	500	250.00	800.00
68	CALLA LILY	500	750.00	1950.00
68	NARCISSUS	500	350.00	550.00-1000.00
68	WOOD DUCK	500	325.00	900.00
69	CLEMATIS W/HOUSE WREN	350	1300.00	1400.00
70	DUTCH CROCUS	350	550.00	750.00
70	MUSHROOM W/BUTTERFLY	CL	225.00	450.00
71	LITTLE BLUE HERON	500	425.00	1500.00-2500.00
72	AMERICAN CRESTED IRIS	400	975.00	1150.00
72	AUTUMN DOGWOOD W/CHICKADEES	350	1100.00	1200.00
72	PANSIES W/CHINA MAID	1000	275.00	350.00
74	GOLDEN WINGED WARBLER	200	1075.00	1150.00
75	GREAT HORNED OWL (COLOR)	50	3250.00	7500.00
75	GREAT HORNED OWL (WHITE)	150	1950.00	6000.00
75	PANSIES W/CHINOLINA LADY	750	295.00	400.00
76	AMERICAN WHITE TURKEY	75	1450.00	1600.00
76	AMERICAN WILD TURKEY	75	1950.00	2200.00
76	COLONIAL BASKET	100	2750.00	5500.00
76	CONSTANCY FLOWER BASKET	CL	345.00	400.00
76	DEVOTION FLOWER BASKET	CL	345.00	400.00
76	FELICITY FLOWER BASKET	CL	325.00	345.00
76	MAJESTY FLOWER BASKET	CL	345.00	400.00
77	APPLE BLOSSOMS	400	350.00	550.00
77	CLEMATIS	CL	210.00	315.00
77	DUCKLING (BUTTERCUP & DAFFODIL)	CL	165.00	295.00
77	HERMIT THRUSH	150	1450.00	1450.00
77	KESTREL	175	1875.00	1925.00
78	KINGLETS ON PYRACANTHA	175	900.00	1100.00
78	NESTING BLUEBIRDS	CL	235.00	250.00
80	YELLOW CONDESA ROSE	CL	*	250.00-300.00
80	YELLOW ROSE	CL	80.00	500.00
82	SPRING BOUQUET	200	750.00	750.00
85	AMERICAN BALD EAGLE	300	2900.00	3595.00
85	SCREECH OWLS	100	3250.00	3925.00
*				**CAROUSEL-CIRCUS**
73	CAROUSEL GOAT	325	875.00	1430.00
73	CAROUSEL HORSE	325	925.00	7500.00
74	LION	325	1025.00	1400.00
74	TIGER	325	925.00	1300.00
75	BARNABY, BEAR	CL	165.00	300.00-550.00

Precious Moments figures always offer inspiration of some sort. Thank You Lord for Everything *reminds us to appreciate what we have.*

I'll Never Stop Loving You *proclaims this little porcelain bisque figure artist by Sam Butcher, creator of the Precious Moments line produced by Enesco Corp.*

Even with all these beautiful Christmas decorations, You Are My Favorite Star. *The Precious Moments figure was created by Sam Butcher for Enesco Corp.*

15 Happy Years Together, What a Tweet! *is the Enesco Precious Moments 15th anniversary commemorative figurine.*

Lord Help Us Keep Our Act Together *implore these youngsters created by Precious Moments artist Sam Butcher and produced by Enesco Corp.*

May Only Good Things Come Your Way *is from Enesco's Precious Moments collection by Sam Butcher.*

YR	NAME	LIMIT	ISSUE	QUOTE
75	BICENTENNIAL HORSE TICONDEROGA	350	925.00	4000.00
75	BOSUN, MONKEY	CL	195.00	375.00
76	FUNNY FACE, CHILD HEAD/HOLLY	CL	325.00	488.00-750.00
76	PERFORMING PONY, POPPY	1000	325.00	1200.00
76	SEBASTIAN, SEAL	CL	195.00	200.00
77	DANDY, DANCING DOG	CL	145.00	295.00
81	BEAR, BERNHARD	325	1125.00	1150.00
81	BULL, PLUTUS	325	1125.00	2050.00
81	FROLLO	1000	750.00	825.00
81	PONY	750	975.00	975.00
82	GIRAFFE	750	*	1750.00
84	PHINEAS, CIRCUS ELEPHANT	OP	325.00	425.00
85	CIRCUS RIDER EQUESTRIENNE EXTRORDINAIRE	150	2275.00	3500.00
85	JUMBLES AND FRIEND	750	675.00	725.00
85	VALENTINE	OP	335.00	375.00
86	PIERRE, THE PERFORMING POODLE	OP	225.00	275.00
*			**CHILDREN OF THE WORLD**	
72	ESKIMO CHILD HEAD	CL	165.00	400.00
75	INDIAN BOY HEAD	CL	425.00	900.00
75	INDIAN GIRL HEAD	CL	325.00	900.00
77	JEREMY	CL	315.00	475.00
78	JASON	CL	285.00	350.00
78	JENNIFER	CL	325.00	375.00
79	JESSICA	CL	325.00	475.00
*			**CHILDREN TO CHERISH**	
*	FIRST BOUQUET	250	150.00	300.00
57	THUMBELINA	CL	45.00	500.00-525.00
58	PETER PAN	CL	80.00	1000.00
59	TINKERBELL	CL	95.00	1500.00
60	BALLERINA, RED SHOES	CL	75.00	1200.00
62	HEIDI, COLOR	CL	165.00	550.00
62	HEIDI, WHITE	CL	165.00	550.00
63	BALLERINA ON CUE	CL	150.00	800.00
63	SPRINGTIME	CL	45.00	775.00
64	REBECCA	CL	110.00	400.00
66	FIRST FLIGHT	CL	50.00	475.00
68	BABY BUST	239	375.00	1000.00
68	BALLERINA, LITTLE PRINCESS	CL	125.00	700.00
71	POLLYANNA	CL	195.00	550.00
73	GOLDILOCKS	CL	145.00	400.00
73	LITTLE RED RIDING HOOD	CL	110.00	425.00-500.00
74	GRETEL	CL	260.00	455.00
74	HANSEL	CL	270.00	450.00-585.00
74	MARY, MARY	500	475.00	750.00-900.00
75	RAPUNZEL, APRICOT	1500	475.00	1200.00
75	RAPUNZEL, LILAC	1000	675.00	1000.00
75	RAPUNZEL, PINKC	1000	425.00	1100.00
75	WENDY WITH FLOWERS	*	250.00	350.00
75	YANKEE DOODLE DANDY	CL	275.00	325.00
76	ELIZABETH ANN	CL	195.00	400.00
76	MELISSA	OP	285.00	350.00-500.00
77	BOYS PLAYING MARBLES	CL	285.00	375.00
78	ALICE (SEATED)	CL	350.00	500.00
78	ALLEGRA	CL	310.00	350.00
78	EDITH	CL	310.00	325.00
78	LISA AND LYNETTE	OP	395.00	450.00
78	LITTLE BOY BLUE	CL	425.00	500.00
80	LITTLE MISS MUFFET	CL	335.00	365.00
81	FLEURETTE	1000	725.00	1075.00
82	ROBIN	1000	475.00	850.00
82	SLEEPING BEAUTY	750	695.00	1475.00
84	JACK IN THE BEANSTALK	750	575.00	575.00
84	LITTLE CHAMP	OP	325.00	375.00
84	MICHAEL	OP	235.00	350.00
84	THE CHOIRBOY	OP	325.00	345.00
85	BALLERINA, RECITAL	OP	275.00	275.00
85	BALLERINA, SWANILDA	OP	450.00	650.00
85	BETH	OP	235.00	275.00
85	CLARA	OP	395.00	395.00
85	FELECIA	OP	425.00	525.00
85	FIGURE EIGHT	750	625.00	750.00
85	JODY	OP	235.00	275.00
85	MARGUERITE	OP	425.00	525.00
85	RECITAL	OP	275.00	275.00
85	VANESSA	OP	425.00	525.00
86	CLARISSA	OP	165.00	195.00

YR	NAME	LIMIT	ISSUE	QUOTE
86	ENCORE, FIGURE SKATER	750	625.00	750.00
86	KITRI	OP	450.00	550.00
86	LULLABY, BLUE	OP	125.00	160.00
86	LULLABY, IVORY	OP	125.00	160.00
86	LULLABY, PINK	OP	125.00	160.00
87	PANDORA BLUE	CL	265.00	325.00
*			**COMMEMORATIVE**	
67	COLUMBIA	200	1000.00	2500.00
67	CONDUCTOR'S HANDS	250	250.00	1500.00
69	APOLLO II MOON MISSION	111	1500.00	2500.00
71	CREE INDIAN	100	2500.00	5500.00
72	CHESS SET	10	30000.00	60000.00
75	GEORGE WASHINGTON BUST	CL	275.00	350.00
77	OCEANIA	200	1250.00	1500.00
80	THE BRIDE	100	6500.00	10500.00
81	ARION, DOLPHIN RIDER	1000	575.00	1150.00
81	KATERI TAKAKWITHA	100	2875.00	2975.00
81	PHOENIX	100	950.00	950.00
84	1984 CYBIS HOLIDAY	OP	145.00	145.00
84	CREE INDIAN, MAGIC BOY	200	4250.00	4995.00
85	HOLIDAY ORNAMENT	OP	75.00	75.00
85	LIBERTY	100	1875.00	4000.00
86	1986 COMMEMORATIVE EGG	OP	365.00	365.00
86	LITTLE MISS LIBERTY	OP	295.00	350.00
*		**EVERYONE'S FUN TIME (LIMNETTES)**		
72	COUNTRY FAIR	500	125.00	200.00
72	THE POND	500	125.00	200.00
72	THE SEASHORE	500	125.00	200.00
72	WINDY DAY	500	125.00	200.00
*			**FANTASIA**	
69	UNICORN	500	1250.00	3750.00
74	FANTASIA	500	675.00	800.00
77	SEA KING'S STEED, OCEANIA	200	1250.00	1450.00
77	UNICORNS, GAMBOL AND FROLIC	1000	425.00	2300.00
78	SATIN HORSE HEAD	500	1100.00	2800.00
78	SHARMAINE, SEA NYMPH	250	1450.00	1650.00
80	PEGASUS	500	1450.00	3750.00
80	PEGASUS, FREE SPIRIT	1000	675.00	775.00-1000.00
81	DESIREE, WHITE DEER	400	575.00	595.00
81	PRINCE BROCADE UNICORN	500	2200.00	2600.00
82	THERON	350	675.00	850.00
84	FLIGHT AND FANCY	1000	875.00	1175.00
85	DORE'	1000	575.00	1075.00
*			**LAND OF CHEMERIC**	
77	MARIGOLD	CL	185.00	500.00
77	QUEEN TITANIA	750	725.00	2500.00
77	TIFFIN	CL	175.00	500.00
79	PIP, ELFIN PLAYER	1000	450.00	665.00
81	MELODY	1000	725.00	800.00
85	OBERON	750	825.00	825.00
*		**NORTH AMERICAN INDIAN**		
69	BLACKFEET, BEAVERHEAD MEDICINE MAN	500	2000.00	2775.00
69	DAKOTA, MINNEHAHA LAUGHING WATER	500	1500.00	2500.00
69	ONONDAGA, HIAWATHA	500	1500.00	2450.00
71	SHOSHONE, SACAJAWEA	500	2250.00	2775.00
73	ESKIMO MOTHER	200	1875.00	2650.00
73	IRIQUOIS, AT THE COUNCIL FIRE	500	4250.00	4975.00
77	CROW DANCER	200	3875.00	8500.00
79	GREAT SPIRIT, WANKAN TANKA	200	3500.00	4150.00
82	CHOCTAW, TASCULUSA	200	2475.00	4050.00
84	APACHE, CHATO	350	1950.00	3300.00
85	YAQUI, DEER DANCER	200	2095.00	2500.00
*		**PORTRAITS IN PORCELAIN**		
65	BEATRICE	700	225.00	1800.00
65	JULIET	800	175.00	4000.00
67	FOLK SINGER	283	300.00	850.00
67	GUINEVERE	800	250.00	2000.00
68	HAMLET	500	350.00	2000.00
68	SCARLETT	500	450.00	4000.00
69	OPHELIA	800	750.00	3800.00
71	ELEANOR OF AQUITAINE	750	875.00	4250.00
72	KWAN YIN	350	1250.00	2000.00
73	BALLET-PRINCE FLORIMOND	200	975.00	1100.00
73	BALLET-PRINCESS AURORA	200	1125.00	1500.00
73	PORTIA	750	825.00	3750.00
74	QUEEN ESTHER	750	925.00	1750.00

YR	NAME	LIMIT	ISSUE	QUOTE
75	LADY MACBETH	750	850.00	1400.00
76	ABIGAIL ADAMS	600	875.00	1300.00
76	PRISCILLA	500	825.00	1400.00
78	GOOD QUEEN ANNE	350	975.00	1500.00
79	BERENGARIA	500	1450.00	2340.00-4500.00
79	NEFERTITI	500	2100.00	3000.00
81	JANE EYRE	500	975.00	1500.00
82	DESDEMONA	500	1850.00	2730.00
82	LADY GODIVA	200	1875.00	3000.00
82	PERSEPHONE	200	3250.00	4850.00
84	BATHSHEBA	500	1975.00	3250.00
85	KING ARTHUR	350	2350.00	2795.00
85	KING DAVID	350	1475.00	2175.00
85	PAGLIACCI	OP	325.00	325.00
85	ROMEO AND JULIET	300	2200.00	3275.00
85	TRISTAN AND ISOLDE	200	2200.00	2200.00
86	CARMEN	500	1875.00	1975.00
*				**SPORT SCENES**
80	JOGGER, FEMALE	CL	345.00	425.00
80	JOGGER, MALE	CL	395.00	475.00
*		**THE WONDERFUL SEASONS (LIMNETTES)**		
72	AUTUMN	500	125.00	200.00
72	SPRING	500	125.00	200.00
72	SUMMER	500	125.00	200.00
72	WINTER	500	125.00	200.00
*			**THEATRE OF PORCELAIN**	
78	COURT JESTER	250	1450.00	1750.00
80	HARLEQUIN	250	1575.00	1875.00
81	COLUMBINE	250	2250.00	2250.00
81	PUCK	250	2300.00	2450.00
*		**WHEN BELLS ARE RINGING (LIMNETTES)**		
72	EASTER EGG HUNT	500	125.00	200.00
72	INDEPENDENCE CELEBRATION	500	125.00	200.00
72	MERRY CHRISTMAS	500	125.00	200.00
72	SABBATH MORNING	500	125.00	200.00

DANBURY MINT
N. ROCKWELL

				ROCKWELL FIGURINES
80	BOY ON STILTS	CL	55.00	60.00
80	CAUGHT IN THE ACT	CL	55.00	75.00
80	GRAMPS AT THE REINS	CL	55.00	75.00
80	GRANDPA SNOWMAN	CL	55.00	60.00
80	TRICK OR TREAT	CL	55.00	60.00
80	YOUNG LOVE	CL	55.00	125.00

DAVE GROSSMAN CREATIONS

93	AFTER THE PROM	7500	75.00	85.00
93	GONE FISHING	1500	65.00	75.00
93	MISSED	7500	110.00	120.00
94	ALMOST GROWN UP	7500	75.00	85.00
94	BABY'S FIRST STEP	7500	100.00	110.00
94	BED TIME	7500	100.00	110.00
94	BRIDE & GROOM	7500	100.00	110.00
94	FOR A GOOD BOY	7500	100.00	110
94	LITTLE MOTHER	7500	75.00	85.00

ROCKWELL INSPIRED

				AMERICAN ROCKWELL SERIES
81	BREAKING HOME TIES NRV-300	RT	2000.00	2300.00
82	LINCOLN NRV-301	RT	300.00	375.00
82	THANKSGIVING NRV-302	RT	2500.00	2650.00

ROCKWELL INSPIRED

				BOY SCOUT SERIES
81	CAN'T WAIT BSA-01	RT	30.00	50.00
81	GOOD FRIENDS BSA-04	RT	58.00	65.00
81	GOOD FRIENDS BSA-04	RT	58.00	65.00
81	GOOD TURN BSA-05	RT	65.00	100.00
81	PHYSICALLY STRONG BSA-03	RT	56.00	60.00
81	SCOUT IS HELPFUL BSA-02	RT	38.00	45.00
81	SCOUT MEMORIES BSA-06	RT	65.00	70.00
82	GUIDING HAND BSA-07	RT	58.00	60.00
83	TOMORROW'S LEADER BSA-08	RT	45.00	55.00

B. LEIGHTON-JONES

			EMMETT KELLY CIRCUS COLLECTION	
92	CHRISTMAS TUNES	15,000	40.00	40.00
92	EMMETT AT THE ORGAN	15,000	50.00	50.00
92	EMMETT AT WORK	15,000	45.00	45.00
92	EMMETT THE CADDY	15,000	45.00	45.00
92	LOOK AT THE BIRDIE	15,000	40.00	40.00

YR	NAME	LIMIT	ISSUE	QUOTE
	B. LEIGHTON-JONES	**EMMETT KELLY ORIGINAL CIRCUS COLLECTION**		
93	CHRISTMAS TUNES	5000	100.00	115.00
93	DEAR EMMETT	15,000	45.00	140.00
93	HARD TIMES	15,000	45.00	50.00
93	SUNDAY DRIVER	15,000	55.00	65.00
93	THE LION TAMER	15,500	55.00	65.00
93	WALL STREET	5000	120.00	135.00
94	EMMETT THE CADDY	5000	125.00	145.00
94	HOLIDAY SKATER	15,000	110.00	125.00
94	I'VE GOT IT	15,000	90.00	110.00
94	PARENTHOOD	15,000	110.00	125.00
94	STUCK ON BOWLING	15,000	90.00	100.00
*		**GONE WITH THE WIND**		
92	SCARLETT IN GREEN DRESS	TL	70.00	70.00
93	GWW-12 RHETT	*	70.00	80.00
94	ASHLEY	OP	40.00	50.00
94	GERALD O'HARA	*	70.00	80.00
94	RHETT	OP	40.00	45.00
94	SCARLETT	OP	40.00	45.00
94	SCARLETT IN BAR B QUE DRESS	*	70.00	80.00
	ROCKWELL INSPIRED	**HUCK FINN SERIES**		
79	THE SECRET HF-01	RT	110.00	130.00
80	LISTENING HF-02	RT	110.00	120.00
80	NO KINGS HF-03	RT	110.00	110.00
80	SNAKE ESCAPES HF-04	RT	110.00	110.00
	ROCKWELL INSPIRED	**LARGE LIMITED EDITIONS**		
74	DOCTOR AND DOLL NR-100	RT	300.00	1600.00
74	SEE AMERICA FIRST NR-103	RT	100.00	300.00
75	BASEBALL NR-102	RT	125.00	450.00
75	NO SWIMMING NR-101	RT	150.00	450.00
79	LEAPFROG NR-104	RT	440.00	600.00
81	DREAMS OF LONG AGO NR-105	RT	500.00	750.00
82	CIRCUS NR-106	RT	500.00	550.00
84	MARBLE PLAYERS NR-107	RT	500.00	500.00
		MINIATURE BRONZE SERIES		
93	SCENE II-TWELVE OAKS	5000	340.00	375.00
93	WIZARD OF OZ	5000	290.00	325.00
94	ATLANTA	*	340.00	365.00
	E. ROBERTS	**NATIVE AMERICAN SERIES**		
91	LONE WOLF	7500	55.00	55.00
92	TORTOISE LADY	7500	60.00	60.00
	ROCKWELL INSPIRED	**NORMAN ROCKWELL COLLECTION**		
73	BACK TO SCHOOL NR-02	RT	20.00	35.00
73	CAROLLER NR-03	RT	22.50	35.00
73	DAYDREAMER NR-04	RT	22.50	50.00
73	DOCTOR & DOLL NR-12	RT	65.00	150.00
73	LAZYBONES NR-08	RT	30.00	300.00
73	LEAPFROG NR-09	RT	50.00	550.00
73	LOVE LETTER NR-06	RT	25.00	60.00
73	LOVERS NR-07	RT	45.00	66.00
73	MARBLE PLAYERS NR-11	RT	60.00	450.00
73	NO SWIMMING NR-05	RT	25.00	50.00
73	REDHEAD NR-01	RT	20.00	200.00
73	SCHOOLMASTER NR-10	RT	55.00	225.00
74	BASEBALL NR-16	RT	45.00	120.00
74	FRIENDS IN NEED NR-13	RT	45.00	96.00
74	SEE AMERICA FIRST NR-17	RT	50.00	85.00
74	SPRINGTIME '33 NR-14	RT	30.00	45.00
74	TAKE YOUR MEDICINE NR-18	RT	50.00	95.00
75	BARBERSHOP QUARTET NR-23	RT	100.00	1400.00
75	BIG MOMENT NR-21	RT	60.00	120.00
75	CIRCUS NR-22	RT	55.00	100.00
75	DISCOVERY NR-20	RT	55.00	160.00
76	DRUM FOR TOMMY NRC-24	RT	40.00	80.00
77	PALS NR-25	RT	60.00	75.00
77	SPRINGTIME '35 NR-19	RT	50.00	55.00
78	AT THE DOCTOR NR-29	RT	108.00	160.00
78	FIRST DAY OF SCHOOL NR-27	RT	100.00	135.00
78	MAGIC POTION NR-28	RT	84.00	100.00
78	YOUNG DOCTOR NRD-26	RT	100.00	100.00
79	BACK FROM CAMP NR-33	RT	96.00	110.00
79	DREAMS OF LONG AGO NR-31	RT	100.00	160.00
79	GRANDPA'S BALLERINA NR-32	RT	100.00	110.00
79	TEACHER'S PET NRA-30	RT	35.00	80.00
80	EXASPERATED NANNY NR-35	RT	96.00	96.00
80	HANKERCHIEF NR-36	RT	110.00	110.00

YR	NAME	LIMIT	ISSUE	QUOTE
80	SANTA'S GOOD BOYS NR-37	RT	90.00	90.00
80	THE TOSS NR-34	RT	110.00	110.00
81	SPIRIT OF EDUCATION NR-38	RT	96.00	110.00
82	A VISIT WITH ROCKWELL NR-40	RT	120.00	120.00
82	AMERICAN MOTHER NRG-42	RT	100.00	110.00
82	CROQUET NR-41	RT	100.00	110.00
83	COUNTRY CRITIC NR-43	RT	75.00	75.00
83	GRADUATE NR-44	RT	30.00	35.00
83	SCOTTY'S SURPRISE NRS-20	RT	25.00	25.00
84	SCOTTY'S HOME PLATE NR-46	RT	30.00	40.00
86	RED CROSS NR-47	RT	67.00	75.00
87	YOUNG LOVE NR-48	RT	70.00	70.00
88	WEDDING MARCH NR-49	RT	110.00	110.00
92	CHOOSIN UP	7500	110.00	110.00
ROCKWELL INSPIRED		**NORMAN ROCKWELL COLLECTION MINIATURES**		
79	BACK TO SCHOOL NR-202	RT	18.00	25.00
79	CAROLLER NR-203	RT	20.00	25.00
79	DAYDREAMER NR-04	RT	20.00	30.00
79	DOCTOR AND DOLL NR-212	RT	40.00	40.00
79	LAZYBONES NR-208	RT	22.00	30.00
79	LEAPFROG NR-209	RT	32.00	32.00
79	LOVE LETTER NR-206	RT	26.00	30.00
79	LOVERS NR-207	RT	28.00	30.00
79	MARBLE PLAYERS NR-211	RT	36.00	38.00
79	NO SWIMMING NR-205	RT	22.00	30.00
79	REDHEAD NR-201	RT	18.00	48.00
79	SCHOOLMASTER NR-210	RT	34.00	40.00
80	BASEBALL NR-216	RT	40.00	50.00
80	FRIENDS IN NEED NR-213	RT	30.00	40.00
80	SEE AMERICA FIRST NR-217	RT	28.00	35.00
80	SPRINGTIME '33 NR-214	RT	24.00	80.00
80	SUMMERTIME '33 NR-215	RT	22.00	25.00
80	TAKE YOUR MEDICINE NR-218	RT	36.00	40.00
82	BARBERSHOP QUARTET NR-223	RT	40.00	50.00
82	BIG MOMENT NR-221	RT	36.00	40.00
82	CIRCUS NR-222	RT	35.00	40.00
82	DISCOVERY NR-220	RT	35.00	45.00
82	DRUM FOR TOMMY NRC-224	RT	25.00	30.00
82	SPRINGTIME '35 NR-219	RT	24.00	30.00
83	SANTA ON THE TRAIN NR-245	RT	35.00	55.00
84	AT THE DOCTOR'S NR-229	RT	35.00	35.00
84	DREAMS OF LONG AGO NR-231	RT	30.00	30.00
84	FIRST DAY OF SCHOOL NR-227	RT	35.00	35.00
84	MAGIC POTION NR-228	RT	30.00	40.00
84	PALS NR-225	RT	25.00	25.00
84	YOUNG DOCTOR NRD-226	RT	30.00	50.00
ROCKWELL INSPIRED		**ROCKWELL CLUB SERIES**		
81	YOUNG ARTISTS RCC-01	RT	96.00	105.00
82	DIARY RCC-02	RT	35.00	50.00
83	RUNAWAY PANTS RCC-03	RT	65.00	75.00
84	GONE FISHING RCC-04	RT	30.00	55.00
ROCKWELL INSPIRED		**TOM SAWYER MINIATURES**		
83	FIRST SMOKE TSM-02	RT	40.00	45.00
83	LOST IN CAVE TSM-05	RT	40.00	45.00
83	TAKE YOUR MEDICINE TSM-04	RT	40.00	45.00
83	WHITEWASHING THE FENCE TSM-01	RT	40.00	50.00
ROCKWELL INSPIRED		**TOM SAWYER SERIES**		
75	WHITEWASHING THE FENCE TS-01	RT	60.00	200.00
76	FIRST SMOKE TS-02	RT	60.00	200.00
77	TAKE YOUR MEDICINE TS-03	RT	63.00	170.00
78	LOST IN CAVE TS-04	RT	70.00	145.00

DEPARTMENT 56

*				**SNOWBABIES**
86	BEST FRIENDS 7958-8	RT	12.00	125.00-140.00
86	CLIMBING ON SNOWBALL 7965-0	RT	15.00	65.00
86	GIVE ME A PUSH 7955-3	RT	12.00	33.00-50.00
86	HANGING PAIR 7966-9	RT	15.00	135.00
86	HOLD ON TIGHT 7956-1	OP	12.00	13.50
86	I'M MAKING SNOWBALLS 7962-6	RT	12.00	19.00-35.00
86	SNOWBABY/PICTURE FRAME 7970-7 (SET OF 2)	RT	15.00	225.00
87	CLIMBING ON TREE 7971-5 (SET OF 2)	RT	25.00	475.00
87	DON'T FALL OFF 7968-5	RT	12.50	45.00-75.00
87	DOWN THE HILL WE GO 7960-0	OP	20.00	22.00
87	TUMBLING IN THE SNOW 7957-0 (SET OF 5)	RT	35.00	50.00
87	WINTER SURPRISE 7974-0	RT	15.00	23.00-38.00
88	ARE THESE MINE? 7977-4	OP	10.00	12.50

YR	NAME	LIMIT	ISSUE	QUOTE
88	FROSTY FROLIC 7981-2	4800	35.00	425.00-750.00
88	POLAR EXPRESS 7978-2	RT	22.00	49
88	TINY TRIO 7979-0 (SET OF 3)	RT	20.00	90.00-130.00
89	ALL FALL DOWN 7984-7 (SET OF 4)	RT	36.00	55.00
89	FINDING FALLEN STARS 7985-5	6000	32.50	135.00-175.00
89	FROSTY FUN 7983-9	RT	27.50	50.00-75.00
89	HELPFUL FRIENDS 7982-0	RT	30.00	34.00
89	ICY IGLOO 7987-1	OP	37.50	37.50
89	PENGUIN PARADE 7986-3	RT	25.00	55.00-75.00
89	WHO ARE YOU? 7949-9	12,500	32.50	105.00
90	A SPECIAL DELIVERY 7948-0	OP	13.50	13.50
90	I WILL PUT UP THE TREE 6800-4	OP	22.00	24.00
90	PLAYING GAMES IS FUN 7947-2	RT	30.00	30.00
90	READ ME A STORY 7945-6	OP	25.00	25.00
90	TWINKLE LITTLE STARS 7942-1 (SET OF 2)	RT	37.50	37.50
90	WE WILL MAKE IT SHINE 7946-4	RT	45.00	75.00
90	WISHING ON A STAR 7943-0	OP	20.00	20.00
91	DANCING TO A TUNE 6808-0 (SET OF 3)	OP	30.00	30.00
91	FISHING FOR DREAMS 6809-8	OP	28.00	28.00
91	I MADE THIS JUST FOR YOU 6802-0	OP	14.50	14.50
91	I WILL PUT UP THE TREE 6800-4	OP	24.00	24.00
91	IS THAT FOR ME? 6803-9 (SET OF 2)	RT	30.00	45.00
91	SNOWBABY POLAR SIGN 6804-7	OP	20.00	20.00
91	THIS IS WHERE WE LIVE 6805-5	OP	55.00	70.00
91	WAITING FOR CHRISTMAS 6807-1	RT	27.50	37.00
91	WHY DON'T YOU TALK TO ME 6801-2	OP	22.00	24.00
92	CAN I HELP TOO? 6806-3	18,500	48.00	90.00
92	I NEED A HUG 6813-6	OP	20.00	20.00
92	I NEED A HUG 6813-6	OP	20.00	20.00
92	LET'S GO SKIING 6815-2	OP	15.00	15.00
92	LET'S GO SKIING! 6815-2	OP	15.00	15.00
92	THIS WILL CHEER YOU UP 6816-0	OP	30.00	30.00
92	THIS WILL CHEER YOU UP 6816-0	OP	30.00	30.00
92	WAIT FOR ME 6812-8	OP	48.00	48.00
92	WAIT FOR ME! 6812-8	OP	48.00	48.00
92	WINKEN, BLINKEN, AND NOD 6814-4	OP	60.00	60.00
92	WINKEN, BLINKEN, AND NOD 6814-4	OP	60.00	60.00
93	BABY'S FIRST SMILE 6846-2	OP	30.00	30.00
93	CAN I OPEN IT NOW? 6838-1	YR	15.00	35.00
93	CROSSING STARRY SKIES 6834-9	OP	35.00	35.00
93	I FOUND YOUR MITTENS! 6836-5	OP	30.00	30.00
93	I'LL TEACH YOU A TRICK 6835-7	OP	24.00	24.00
93	I'M MAKING AN ICE SCULPTURE! 6842-0	OP	30.00	30.00
93	LET'S ALL CHIME IN! 6845-4 SET OF 2	OP	37.50	37.50
93	LOOK WHAT I FOUND 6833-0	OP	45.00	45.00
93	NOW I LAY ME DOWN TO SLEEP 6839-0	OP	13.50	13.50
93	SO MUCH WORK TO DO! 6837-3	OP	18.00	18.00
93	SOMEWHERE IN DREAMLAND 6840-3	OP	85.00	85.00
93	WE MAKE A GREAT PAIR 6843-8	OP	30.00	30.00
93	WHERE DID HE GO? 6841-1	OP	35.00	35.00
93	WILL IT SNOW TODAY? 6844-6	OP	45.00	45.00

THE ORIGINAL SNOW VILLAGE COLLECTION

94	SANTA COMES TO TOWN	*	30.00	33.00

THE UPSTAIRS DOWNSTAIRS BEARS

94	HENRIETTA'S TEA PARTY	5600	65.00	75.00

DUNCAN ROYALE
*

1990 & 1991 SPECIAL EVENT PIECE

*	NAST & MUSIC	5000	79.95	90.00

D. APHESSETCHE

CALENDAR SECRETS

90	APRIL	5000	350.00	370.00
90	AUGUST	5000	300.00	300.00
90	DECEMBER	5000	410.00	410.00
90	FEBRURARY	5000	370.00	370.00
90	JANUARY	5000	260.00	260.00
90	JULY	5000	280.00	280.00
90	JUNE	5000	410.00	410.00
90	MARCH	5000	280.00	350.00
90	MAY	5000	370.00	390.00
90	NOVEMBER	5000	410.00	410.00
90	OCTOBER	5000	350.00	350.00
90	SEPTEMBER	5000	300.00	300.00

CHRISTMAS IMAGES

91	THE CAROLERS	10,000	120.00	120.00
91	THE CHRISTMAS PAGEANT	10,000	175.00	175.00
92	ARE YOU REALLY SANTA?	10,000	*	*
92	SNEAKING A PEEK	10,000	*	*

YR	NAME	LIMIT	ISSUE	QUOTE
92	THE CHRISTMAS ANGEL	10,000	*	*
92	THE MIDNIGHT WATCH	10,000	*	*
*			**COLLECTORS CLUB**	
91	MUSICAL NAST	CL	80.00	95.00
94	SANTA'S GIFT	OP	100.00	100.00
94	WINTER SANTA	OP	125.00	125.00
*			**EARLY AMERICAN**	
91	ACCOUNTANT	10,000	170.00	170.00
91	BANKER	10,000	150.00	150.00
91	CHIROPRACTOR	10,000	150.00	150.00
91	DENTIST	10,000	150.00	150.00
91	DOCTOR	10,000	150.00	150.00
91	FIREMAN	10,000	150.00	150.00
91	HOMEMAKER	10,000	150.00	150.00
91	LAWYER	10,000	170.00	170.00
91	NURSE	10,000	150.00	150.00
91	PHARMACIST	10,000	150.00	150.00
91	POLICEMAN	10,000	150.00	150.00
91	SALESMAN	10,000	150.00	150.00
91	SECRETARY	10,000	150.00	150.00
91	SET OF 15	10,000	2290.00	2290.00
91	STOREKEEPER	10,000	150.00	150.00
91	TEACHER	10,000	150.00	150.00
*			**EBONY COLLECTION**	
90	BANJO MAN	5000	100.00	80.00
90	HARMONICA MAN	5000	85.00	80.00
90	THE FIDDLER	5000	100.00	90.00
91	FEMALE GOSPEL SINGER	5000	90.00	90.00
91	JUG MAN	5000	90.00	90.00
91	MALE GOSPEL SINGER	5000	90.00	90.00
91	PREACHER	5000	90.00	90.00
91	SIGNATURE PIECE	OP	50.00	50.00
91	SPOONS	5000	90.00	90.00
BUONAIUTO		**EBONY COLLECTION--FRIENDS & FAMILY**		
94	AGNES	5000	100.00	100.00
94	DADDY	5000	120.00	120.00
94	LUNCHTIME	5000	100.00	100.00
94	MILLIE	5000	100.00	100.00
94	MOMMY & ME	5000	125.00	125.00
BUONAIUTO		**EBONY COLLECTION--JUBILEE DANCERS**		
93	BUSS	5000	200.00	200.00
93	FALLANA	5000	100.00	100.00
93	KESHIA	5000	100.00	100.00
93	LAMAR	5000	100.00	100.00
93	LOTTIE	5000	125.00	125.00
93	WILFRED	5000	100.00	100.00
P. APSIT		**GREATEST GIFT...LOVE**		
88	ANNUNCIATION, MARBLE	5000	270.00	270.00
88	ANNUNCIATION, PAINTED PORCELAIN	5000	270.00	270.00
88	CRUCIFIXION MARBLE	5000	300.00	300.00
88	CRUCIFIXION, PAINTED PORCELAIN	5000	300.00	300.00
88	NATIVITY, MARBLE	5000	500.00	500.00
88	NATIVITY, PAINTED PORCELAIN	5000	500.00	500.00
P. APSIT		**HISTORY OF CLASSIC ENTERTAINERS**		
87	AMERICAN	RT	160.00	200.00
87	AUGUSTE	RT	220.00	240.00
87	GRECO-ROMAN	RT	280.00	200.00
87	GROTESQUE	RT	230.00	250.00
87	HARLEQUIN	RT	250.00	270.00
87	JESTER	RT	410.00	500.00
87	PANTALONE	RT	270.00	270.00
87	PIERROT	RT	180.00	200.00
87	PULCINELLA	RT	220.00	220.00
87	RUSSIAN	RT	190.00	875.00
87	SLAPSTICK	RT	250.00	270.00
87	UNCLE SAM	RT	160.00	160.00
90	BOB HOPE, 18 IN. (SET)	RT	1500.00	1500.00
90	MIME, 18 IN.	RT	1500.00	1500.00
P. APSIT		**HISTORY OF CLASSIC ENTERTAINERS II**		
88	BOB HOPE	20,000	250.00	250.00
88	FESTE	20,000	250.00	250.00
88	GOLIARD	20,000	200.00	200.00
88	MIME	20,000	200.00	200.00
88	MOUNTEBANK	20,000	270.00	270.00
88	PEDROLINO	20,000	200.00	200.00
88	SIGNATURE PIECE	OP	50.00	50.00

YR	NAME	LIMIT	ISSUE	QUOTE
88	TARTAGLIA	20,000	200.00	200.00
88	THOMASSI	20,000	200.00	200.00
88	TOUCHSTONE	20,000	200.00	200.00
88	TRAMP	20,000	200.00	200.00
88	WHITE FACE	20,000	250.00	250.00
88	ZANNI	20,000	200.00	200.00
P. APSIT			**HISTORY OF SANTA CLAUS**	
87	BLACK PETER, 8 IN. WOOD	500	450.00	440.00
87	CIVIL WAR, 8 IN. WOOD	500	450.00	275.00
87	DEDT MOROZ, 8 IN. WOOD	500	450.00	330.00-880.00
87	KRIS KRINGLE, 8 IN. WOOD	500	450.00	2200.00
87	MEDIEVAL, 8 IN. WOOD	500	450.00	0.00-275.00
87	NAST, 8 IN. WOOD	RT	450.00	3300.00-5200.00
87	PIONEER, 8 IN. WOOD	500	450.00	550.00
87	RUSSIAN, 8 IN. WOOD	500	450.00	875.00
87	SODA POP, 8 IN. WOOD	RT	450.00	2750.00-3200.00
87	ST. NICHOLAS, 8 IN. WOOD	500	450.00	990.00
87	VICTORIAN, 8 IN. WOOD	500	450.00	200.00-385.00
87	WASSAIL, 8 IN. WOOD	500	450.00	450.00
89	KRIS KRINGLE, 18 IN.	1000	1500.00	2200.00
89	MEDIEVAL, 18 IN.	1000	1500.00	1300.00-1430.00
89	NAST, 18 IN.	1000	1500.00	3300.00-5200.00
89	RUSSIAN, 18 IN.	1000	1500.00	1500.00
89	SODA POP, 18 IN.	1000	1500.00	2750.00-3200.00
89	ST. NICHOLAS, 18 IN.	1000	1500.00	1500.00
P. APSIT			**HISTORY OF SANTA CLAUS I**	
83	BLACK PETER	RT	145.00	440.00
83	CIVIL WAR	RT	145.00	275.00-450.00
83	DEDT MOROZ	RT	145.00	400.00
83	KRIS KRINGLE	RT	165.00	2200.00
83	MEDIEVAL	RT	220.00	2000.00
83	NAST	RT	90.00	3300.00-5500.00
83	PIONEER	RT	145.00	500.00
83	RUSSIAN	RT	145.00	875.00
83	SODA POP	RT	145.00	2500.00
83	ST. NICHOLAS	RT	165.00	990.00
83	VICTORIAN	RT	120.00	200.00
83	WASSAIL	RT	90.00	275
P. APSIT			**HISTORY OF SANTA CLAUS II**	
86	ALSACE ANGEL	10,000	250.00	300.00-325.00
86	BABOUSKA	10,000	170.00	220.00
86	BAVARIAN	10,000	250.00	325.00
86	BEFANA	10,000	200.00	270.00
86	FRAU HOLDA	10,000	160.00	200.00
86	LORD OF MISRULE	10,000	160.00	200.00
86	MONGOLIAN/ASIAN	10,000	240.00	300.00
86	ODIN	10,000	200.00	250.00
86	SIR CHRISTMAS	10,000	150.00	185.00
86	ST. LUCIA	10,000	180.00	250.00
86	THE MAGI	10,000	350.00	400.00
86	THE PIXIE	10,000	140.00	185.00
*			**HISTORY OF SANTA CLAUS III**	
90	DRUID	10,000	300.00	300.00
90	JUDAH MACCACBEE	10,000	250.00	250.00
90	JULENISSE	10,000	200.00	200.00
90	ST. BASIL	10,000	300.00	300.00
90	STAR MAN	10,000	300.00	300.00
90	UKKO	10,000	250.00	250.00
91	GRANDFATHER FROST	10,000	*	*
91	HOTEISHO	10,000	*	*
91	KNICKERBOCKER	10,000	*	*
91	SAMICHLAUS	10,000	*	*
91	SIGNATURE PIECE	OP	50.00	50.00
P. APSIT			**MINIATURE COLLECTION**	
88	ALSACE ANGEL, 6 IN. PORCELAIN	6000	80.00	90.00-120.00
88	BABOUSKA, 6 IN. PORCELAIN	6000	70.00	80.00-100.00
88	BAVARIAN, 6 IN. PORCELAIN	6000	90.00	100.00-140.00
88	BEFANA, 6 IN. PORCELAIN	6000	70.00	80.00-100.00
88	BLACK PETE, 6 IN. PORCELAIN	6000	70.00	80.00-100.00
88	CIVIL WAR, 6 IN. PORCELAIN	6000	60.00	80.00-100.00
88	DEDT MOROZ, 6 IN. PORCELAIN	6000	70.00	80.00-100.00
88	FRAU HOLDA, 6 IN. PORCELAIN	6000	50.00	80.00-100.00
88	LORD OF MISRULE, 6 IN. PORCELAIN	6000	60.00	80.00-100.00
88	MAGI, 6 IN. PORCELAIN	6000	130.00	150.00-190.00
88	MEDIEVAL, 6 IN. PORCELAIN	6000	70.00	80.00-100.00
88	MONGOLIAN/ASIAN, 6 IN. PORCELAIN	6000	80.00	120.00-140.00

YR	NAME	LIMIT	ISSUE	QUOTE
88	NAST, 6 IN. PORCELAIN	6000	60.00	80.00-100.00
88	ODIN, 6 IN. PORCELAIN	6000	80.00	90.00-120.00
88	PIONEER, 6 IN. PORCELAIN	6000	60.00	80.00-100.00
88	PIXIE, 6 IN. PORCELAIN	6000	50.00	80.00-100.00
88	RUSSIAN, 6IN. PORCELAIN	6000	70.00	80.00-100.00
88	SIR CHRISTMAS, 6 IN. PORCELAIN	6000	60.00	80.00-100.00
88	SODA POP, 6 IN. PORCELAIN	6000	60.00	80.00-100.00
88	ST. LUCIA, 6 IN. PORCELAIN	6000	70.00	80.00-100.00
88	ST. NICHOLAS, 6 IN. PORCELAIN	6000	70.00	80.00-100.00
88	VICTORIAN, 6 IN. PORCELAIN	6000	60.00	80.00-100.00
88	WASSAIL, 6 IN. PORCELAIN	6000	60.00	80.00-100.00
90	BOB HOPE, 6 IN. PORCELAIN	6000	130.00	130.00
*			**SANTA 1ST SERIES-PEWTER**	
86	BLACK PETER	500	30.00	30.00
86	CIVIL WAR	500	30.00	30.00
86	DEDT MOROZ	500	30.00	30.00
86	KRIS KRINGLE	500	30.00	30.00
86	MEDIEVAL	500	30.00	30.00
86	NAST	500	30.00	30.00
86	PIONEER	500	30.00	30.00
86	RUSSIAN	500	30.00	30.00
86	SET OF 12	500	360.00	360.00
86	SODA POP	500	30.00	30.00
86	ST. NICHOLAS	500	30.00	30.00
86	VICTORIAN	500	30.00	30.00
86	WASSAIL	500	30.00	30.00
*			**SANTA 2ND SERIES-PEWTER**	
88	ALSACE ANGEL	500	30.00	30.00
88	BABOUSKA	500	30.00	30.00
88	BAVARIAN	500	30.00	30.00
88	BEFANA	500	30.00	30.00
88	FRAU HOLDA	500	30.00	30.00
88	LORD OF MISRULE	500	30.00	30.00
88	MAGI	500	30.00	260.00
88	MONGOLIAN	500	30.00	30.00
88	ODIN	500	30.00	30.00
88	PIXIE	500	30.00	30.00
88	SET OF 12	500	360.00	360.00
88	SIR CHRISTMAS	500	30.00	30.00
88	ST. LUCIA	500	30.00	30.00
*			**WOODLAND FAIRIES**	
88	ALMOND BLOSSOM	10,000	70.00	70.00
88	APPLE	10,000	70.00	70.00
88	CALLA LILY	10,000	70.00	70.00
88	CHERRY	10,000	70.00	70.00
88	CHESTNUT	10,000	70.00	70.00
88	CHRISTMAS TREE	10,000	70.00	70.00
88	ELM	10,000	70.00	70.00
88	LIME TREE	10,000	70.00	70.00
88	MULBERRY	10,000	70.00	70.00
88	PEAR BLOSSOM	10,000	70.00	70.00
88	PINE TREE	10,000	70.00	70.00
88	POPLAR	10,000	70.00	70.00
88	SYCAMORE	10,000	70.00	70.00

EGGSPRESSIONS

* *				**EGGSHELL**
93	AMERICA'S PRIDE	OP	140.00	140.00
93	ANGELICA	OP	50.00	50.00
93	APPLE BLOSSOM BQT	OP	62.00	62.00
93	BELLS	OP	55.00	55.00
93	BILL & COO	OP	55.00	55.00
93	BIRTH DAY! DEC	OP	40.00	40.00
93	BIRTH DAY! - APR	OP	40.00	40.00
93	BIRTH DAY! - AUG	OP	40.00	40.00
93	BIRTH DAY! - FEB	OP	40.00	40.00
93	BIRTH DAY! - JAN	OP	40.00	40.00
93	BIRTH DAY! - JUL	OP	40.00	40.00
93	BIRTH DAY! - JUN	OP	40.00	40.00
93	BIRTH DAY! - MAR	OP	40.00	40.00
93	BIRTH DAY! - MAY	OP	40.00	40.00
93	BIRTH DAY! - NOV	OP	40.00	40.00
93	BIRTH DAY! - OCT	OP	40.00	40.00
93	BIRTH DAY! - SEP	OP	40.00	40.00
93	BLUE BIRDS HAPPINESS	OP	79.00	79.00
93	BLUSH	OP	105.00	105.00
93	BRR RABBIT	OP	140.00	140.00

YR	NAME	LIMIT	ISSUE	QUOTE
93	BUTTERCUP	OP	85.00	85.00
93	BUTTERFLY WINGS	OP	50.00	50.00
93	CANDYLAND	OP	100.00	100.00
93	CARDINALS	OP	70.00	70.00
93	CHOO-CHOO CHRISTMAS	OP	130.00	130.00
93	CHRISTMAS CURIOSITY	OP	110.00	110.00
93	COLOURS	OP	55.00	55.00
93	DAYTIME DEN	OP	125.00	125.00
93	DEAR ONE	OP	100.00	100.00
93	DOGWOOD	OP	50.00	50.00
93	DRUMMER BOY	OP	100.00	100.00
93	EBONY	OP	105.00	105.00
93	ELEGANT CHOICE	OP	167.00	167.00
93	FAMILY OUTING	OP	100.00	100.00
93	FANTAZIA	OP	50.00	50.00
93	GABRIELA	OP	45.00	45.00
93	GOLDEN CRYSTAL	OP	125.00	125.00
93	IN TUNE	OP	130.00	130.00
93	ISADORA	OP	130.00	130.00
93	KACHINA	OP	130.00	130.00
93	KEWPIE DOLL	OP	110.00	110.00
93	KRIS KRINGLE	OP	45.00	45.00
93	LARA	OP	115.00	115.00
93	LOBO	OP	85.00	85.00
93	LOVE DUET	OP	140.00	140.00
93	LOVE IN FLIGHT	OP	100.00	100.00
93	MARCELLA	OP	45.00	45.00
93	MARIA	OP	115.00	115.00
93	MCGREGOR'S GARDEN	OP	105.00	105.00
93	MIDAS	OP	105.00	105.00
93	MINY JULEP	OP	100.00	100.00
93	MISS ELLIE	OP	45.00	45.00
93	MISTY ROSE	OP	45.00	45.00
93	OH, NUTS	OP	100.00	100.00
93	PEARL	OP	100.00	100.00
93	PETER	OP	45.00	45.00
93	PETUNIA	OP	45.00	45.00
93	POINSETTIA	OP	60.00	60.00
93	ROMANTIQUE	OP	75.00	75.00
93	SANTA'S WORKSHOP	125	130.00	130.00
93	SECRET GARDEN	OP	158.00	158.00
93	SERENA	OP	140.00	140.00
93	SILVER JEWELS	OP	105.00	105.00
93	SKYE	OP	100.00	100.00
93	SLUMBERING STEGGY	OP	85.00	85.00
93	SNOWFLAKE	OP	50.00	50.00
93	STAR PRANCER	OP	140.00	140.00
93	STORYTELLER	OP	130.00	130.00
93	SUMMER ROSE	OP	45.00	45.00
93	TABITHA	OP	40.00	40.00
93	TANNENBAUM	OP	55.00	55.00
93	TINY TREASURES	OP	110.00	110.00
93	TOGETHERNESS	OP	100.00	100.0
93	TRYKE	OP	90.00	90.00
93	VELVET PRINCESS	OP	170.00	170.00
93	WAITING	OP	100.00	100.00
93	WARRIOR'S PRIDE	OP	85.00	85.00
93	WELCOME CANDLE	OP	63.00	63.00
93	WINTER COLT	OP	105.00	105.00
93	WINTER COLT (STAND)	OP	105.00	105.00
93	WINTER HAVEN	OP	105.00	105.00
93	WINTER SONG	OP	115.00	115.00
93	WINTER WONDERLAND	OP	105.00	105.00
93	YELLOW ROSE	OP	105.00	105.00
94	ABSOLUTELY AMETHYST	OP	100.00	100.00
94	ANGEL BUNNY	250	220.00	220.00
94	ANGEL OF HOPE	250	130.00	130.00
94	ANGEL OF LOVE	250	110.00	110.00
94	BEARY BLUE CHRISTMAS	250	100.00	100.00
94	BEARY PINK CHRISTMAS	250	100.00	100.00
94	CAROLING MICE	250	120.00	120.00
94	CHICK'S & BUNNIES	OP	88.00	88.00
94	CHRISTMAS JOY	250	105.00	105.00
94	ETERNITY	250	170.00	170.00
94	FROSTY'S CHEER	500	64.00	64.00
94	GOLDEN HARMONY	250	160.00	160.00

YR	NAME	LIMIT	ISSUE	QUOTE
94	GRANDMA'S GOODIES	OP	99.00	99.00
94	HARVEST FAIRY	OP	95.00	95.00
94	HOIDAY MEMORIES	250	190.00	190.00
94	JESSICA	125	240.00	240.00
94	LAVENDER LOVE	250	130.00	130.00
94	LOVE BIRDS	250	120.00	120.00
94	MAKING SPIRITS BRIGHT	25	300.00	300.00
94	MOTHER'S PRIDE	250	120.00	120.00
94	OH, HOLY NIGHT	250	160.00	160.00
94	OLD ST. NICKOLAS	500	64.00	64.00
94	PASSION	25	500.00	500.00
94	PASTEL & PEARLS	OP	112.00	112.00
94	PRE-SCHOOL PLAY	OP	108.00	108.00
94	PRISTINE PEARLS	OP	90.00	90.00
94	PURR-FECT HUG	RT	150.00	150.00
94	ROSE MARIE	OP	49.00	49.00
94	SANTA'S LITTLE ELVES	250	130.00	130.00
94	SANTA'S LITTLE SWEETHEART	100	100.00	100.00
94	SERENADE	250	120.00	120.00
94	SERENITY	250	115.00	115.00
94	SKIP A LONG	250	120.00	120.00
94	SPRING MELODY	250	130.00	130.00
94	SWEET DREAMS	OP	100.00	100.00
94	TEDDY BEAR SING ALONG	250	115.00	115.00
94	WEDDING IN WHITE	250	160.00	160.00
95	ANDREA	250	80.00	80.00
95	ANGEL DIVINE	250	120.00	120.00
95	CABBAGE PATCH	250	105.00	105.00
95	COO	250	115.00	115.00
95	JAMIE	250	80.00	80.00
95	TARA	250	80.00	80.00

EMI

P. APSIT — **EMMETT KELLY JR.**

YR	NAME	LIMIT	ISSUE	QUOTE
94	THINKING OF YOU	2500	640.00	670.00

R. HARRIS — **MASTERWORKS**

YR	NAME	LIMIT	ISSUE	QUOTE
94	CATTLE DRIFTING BEFORE THE STORM	500	1300.00	1400.00
94	UNKNOWN EXPLORERS	500	1100.00	1125.00
94	COW-BOY	500	930.00	950.00
94	LUMBER CAMP AT NIGHT	500	590.00	620.00

ENESCO

S. BUTCHER

YR	NAME	LIMIT	ISSUE	QUOTE
87	THE GOOD LORD HAS BLESSED US TENFOLD	LE	90.00	120.00-150.00
95	MARY LOUISE/FRANCES ANGEL W/HEARTS/STARS	2,000	60.00	60.00
95	NATHAN & SHAWNIE - BOY/GIRL INDIANS	2,000	60.00	60.00
95	THOMAS & BETH - BOY/GIRL W/SONGBOOK	2,000	60.00	60.00

* — **BALLERINA SERIES**

YR	NAME	LIMIT	ISSUE	QUOTE
91	LIFE IS ONE JOYOUS STEP 121207	YR	20.00	20.00
91	LIFE IS ONE JOYOUS STEP 121274	OP	25.00	25.00
91	YOU ARE VERY SPECIAL TO ME 121215	OP	40.00	40.00

BARBIE GLAMOUR COLLECTION

YR	NAME	LIMIT	ISSUE	QUOTE
95	MIDNIGHT BLUE '65 MUSICAL	7,500	100.00	100.00
95	SOPHISTICATED LADY '63 MUSICAL	7,500	100.00	100.00
94	SOLO IN THE SPOTLIGHT 1960	7,500	100.00	100.00
94	SOME ENCHANTED EVENING 1960	7,500	100.00	100.00
94	WEDDING ON THE CHURCH STEPS 1959	7,500	100.00	100.00
95	BRIDE 1963	7,500	100.00	100.00
95	MAGNIFICENCE 1965	7,500	100.00	100.00
95	SENIOR PROM 1963	7,500	100.00	100.00

* * — **BIRTHDAY CLUB PIECES**

YR	NAME	LIMIT	ISSUE	QUOTE
85	OUR CLUB CAN'T BE BEAT B0001	OP	10.00	60.00-95.00
88	HAVE A BEARY SPECIAL BIRTHDAY B0104	OP	11.50	25.00-45.00
88	OUR CLUB IS A TOUGH ACT TO FOLLOW B0005	OP	13.50	22.00-35.00
88	OUR CLUB IS A TOUGH ACT TO FOLLOW B0105	OP	13.50	30.00-42.00
90	LOVE PACIFIES BC911	OP	15.00	22.50-30.00
90	TRUE BLUE FRIENDS BC912	OP	15.00	25.00-35.00
91	EVERY MAN'S HOUSE IS HIS CASTLE BC921	OP	16.50	20.00-32.00
91	I'VE GOT YOU UNDER MY SKIN BC911	OP	16.50	20.00-30.00
91	OWL ALWAYS BE YOUR FRIENDS BC932	OP	16.00	16.00-20.00
91	PUT A LITTLE PUNCH...BIRTHDAY BC931	OP	16.00	16.00-18.00
92	ALL ABOARD FOR BIRTHDAY CLUB FUN B0007	OP	16.00	20.00-30.00
92	ALL ABOARD FOR BIRTHDAY CLUB FUN B0107	OP	16.00	20.00-30.00
92	HAPPINESS IS BELONGING B0008	OP	16.00	16.00-20.00
92	HAPPINESS IS BELONGING B0108	OP	16.00	16.00-20.00

P. HILLMAN — **CALICO KITTENS**

YR	NAME	LIMIT	ISSUE	QUOTE
95	ALL ABOUT ANGELS	5,000	25.00	25.00

YR	NAME	LIMIT	ISSUE	QUOTE
95	STITCH IN TIME SAVES NINE	3,000	35.00	35.00
L. RIGG				**CHAPEAU NOELLE**
94	BEAR W/HAND MIRROR - JOAN	2,000	30.00	30.00
94	BEAR W/TEA SET - LINDA	2,000	30.00	30.00
94	BRIDE BEAR - DIANE	2,000	30.00	30.00
94	MRS. SANTA - BEAR W/COOKIES	2,000	30.00	30.00
94	SANTA - BEAR W/LIST/PEN	2,000	30.00	30.00
95	ALLISON- BEAR PAINTING	2,000	30.00	30.00
95	JULIET - BEAR HOLDING DOVE	2,000	30.00	30.00
95	MARY LOUISE/FRANCES - ANGEL H/O	5,000	12.50	12.50
95	ROMEO - BEAR HOLDING ROSE	2,000	30.00	30.00
95	SANTA/MRS. SANTA H/O/	5,000	12.50	12.50
95	SUSIE- BEAR W/BASKET	2,000	30.00	30.00
95	THOMAS & BETH - CAROLERS H/O	5,000	12.50	12.50
P. HILLMAN				**CHERISHED TEDDIES**
93	ALICE	OP	17.50	17.50
93	TEDDY ROOSEVELT	OP	20.00	20.00
94	INGRID	OP	20.00	20.00
94	PRISCILLA GRETA	OP	50.00	50.00
95	AMANDA	OP	17.50	17.50
95	NICKOLAS	OP	20.00	20.00
* *				**COLLECTORS' CLUB PIECES**
86	LOVING YOU DEAR VALENTINE PM873	OP	25.00	30.00-40.00
86	LOVING YOU DEAR VALENTINE PM874	OP	25.00	35.00-45.00
92	SOWING THE SEEDS OF LOVE PM922	OP	30.00	32.00-36.00
L. RIGG				**FOUR SEASONS**
95	CAROL - WINTER ICE SKATER	2,000	30.00	30.00
95	DENISE - SPRING IN APRON	2,000	30.00	30.00
95	EMILY - SUMMER SAILOR SUIT	2,000	30.00	30.00
95	MELISSA- FALL W/CORNUCOPIA	2,000	30.00	30.00
K. WICKL				**GNOMES**
93	SIGFRIED & SOPHIA	1,000	70.00	70.00
94	HUBERT & HENRIETTA	2,000	80.00	80.00
94	LOTHAR	1,994	100.00	100.00
95	FERDINAND	15	300.00	300.00
95	JOHANN'S DANCE SCHOOL	2,000	55.00	55.00
* *				**HAPPY HOLIDAYS BARBIE**
95	HAPPY HOLIDAYS 1988 BARBIE	1,995	100.00	100.00
L. RIGG				**HISTORY OF HATS**
95	PETITE COLLECTION - 6 ASST. PREPACK	30,000	15.00	15.00
KINKA				**KINKA**
88	BABIES ARE DREAMS YOU CAN CUDDLE 117552	OP	37.50	40.00
88	BABIES ARE DREAMS YOU CAN CUDDLE 117560	OP	45.00	50.00
88	FOR YOU...JUST BECAUSE 117781	OP	37.50	40.00
88	JUST FOR YOU ON THIS SPECIAL DAY 117501	OP	22.50	25.00
88	KEEP THE WARM GLOW OF THE SEASON 117455	OP	37.50	37.50
88	LOVE TO YOU 117757	OP	37.50	40.00
88	MAY YOUR LIFE BE FILLED WITH 117498	OP	37.50	40.00
88	THINKING OF YOU 117749	OP	37.50	37.50
88	THINKING OF YOU...NOW & ALWAYS 117528	OP	22.50	25.00
88	WISHING YOU CLOUDLESS SKIES 117471	OP	37.50	40.00
88	WISHING YOU JOY, HAPPINESS 117536	OP	40.00	45.00
88	WISHING YOU JOY, HAPPINESS 117544	OP	50.00	55.00
88	YOU ARE SPECIAL TO ME 117773	OP	37.50	40.00
88	YOUR FRIENDSHIP & THOUGHTFULNESS 117463	OP	37.50	40.00
88	YOUR FRIENDSHIP WILL BE 117765	OP	37.50	40.00
89	A BOUQUET OF FLOWERS FOR YOU 119024	OP	30.00	30.00
89	BABIES ARE CHRISTMAS DREAMS 117722	YR	15.00	15.00
89	BABIES ARE CHRISTMAS DREAMS 118540	YR	15.00	15.00
89	CHRISTMAS IS A SPECIAL GIFT 117692	OP	33.50	33.50
89	CHRISTMAS IS A TIME TO GATHER 117676	OP	55.00	55.00
89	EASTER IS A TIME FILLED WITH 116629	OP	50.00	50.00
89	GATHER YOUR CHRISTMAS DREAMS 117862	OP	55.00	55.00
89	GATHER YOUR DREAMS AND WISHES 119032	OP	30.00	30.00
89	HAPPY 25TH ANNIVERSARY 119121	OP	75.00	75.00
89	HAPPY 40TH ANNIVERSARY 119148	OP	75.00	75.00
89	HAPPY 50TH ANNIVERSARY 119156	OP	75.00	75.00
89	IT'S THE TIME FOR CHRISTMAS 117889	OP	50.00	50.00
89	IT'S TIME FOR CHRISTMAS 117846	OP	37.50	37.50
89	JUST FOR YOU 119083	OP	30.00	30.00
89	KEEP ME IN YOUR DREAMS 119695	OP	50.00	50.00
89	KEEP THE SPIRIT 119113	OP	30.00	30.00
89	KEEP THE TRUE LIGHT OF CHRISTMAS 117684	OP	25.00	25.00
89	LOVE TO YOU 120391	OP	120.00	120.00
89	LOVE TO YOU AT THIS SPECIAL TIME 118877	OP	45.00	45.00
89	LOVE TO YOU AT THIS SPECIAL TIME 118885	OP	50.00	50.00

YR	NAME	LIMIT	ISSUE	QUOTE
89	MAY APRIL SHOWERS BRING 118958	OP	30.00	30.00
89	MAY GOD'S LOVE BLESS 118842	OP	45.00	45.00
89	MAY THE GLOW OF GOD'S LOVE 116661	OP	50.00	50.00
89	MAY THE GLOW OF GOD'S LOVE 116688	OP	20.00	20.00
89	MAY THE LOVE IN YOUR HEARTS 116572	OP	15.00	15.00
89	MAY THIS DAY TOUCH YOUR HEART 119105	OP	30.00	30.00
89	MAY THIS SPECIAL SEASON 118559	YR	25.00	25.00
89	MAY YOUR DAYS BE FILLED 118834	YR	45.00	45.00
89	MAY YOUR DAYS BE FILLED WITH LOVE 118915	OP	30.00	30.00
89	NATIVITY SCENE (3 WISE MEN) 118192	OP	45.00	45.00
89	NATIVITY SCENE (SET OF 9) 118214	OP	115.00	115.00
89	NATIVITY SCENE (SHEPHERD) 118206	OP	30.00	30.00
89	NATIVITY SCENE 118184	OP	40.00	40.00
89	REJOICE IN GOD'S PROMISE OF LOVE 116637	OP	37.50	37.50
89	REMEMBER THE DREAMS 118966	OP	75.00	75.00
89	THINKING OF YOU & WISHING 119016	OP	24.00	30.00
89	WILL YOU STOP & COUNT 117870	OP	50.00	50.00
89	WILL YOU STOP AND COUNT 117838	OP	37.50	37.50
89	WISH ON THE CHRISTMAS STAR 117854	OP	37.50	37.50
89	WISH ON THE CHRISTMAS STAR 117897	OP	50.00	50.00
89	WISHING YOU CLOUDLESS SKIES 408565	2500	170.00	170.00
89	WISHING YOU EVERY HAPPINESS 117730	OP	25.00	25.00
89	WISHING YOU LOVE AND HAPPINESS 116556	OP	50.00	50.00
89	WISHING YOU LOVE AND HAPPINESS 116564	OP	37.50	37.50
89	WISHING YOU PINK ROSES 119075	OP	30.00	30.00
89	WISHING YOU SPECIAL BLESSINGS 116653	OP	17.50	17.50
89	WISHING YOU SPECIAL MOMENTS 119091	OP	30.00	30.00
89	WISHING YOUR BABY 118834	OP	17.50	17.50
89	YOU BRING JOY INTO MY LIFE 119296	OP	15.00	15.00
89	YOU'RE A DOLL 118931	OP	30.00	30.00
90	CHRISTMAS FILLS YOUR HEART 119725	OP	25.00	25.00
90	CHRISTMAS IS A GIFT FROM GOD 119849	OP	20.00	20.00
90	CHRISTMAS IS A TIME OF LOVE 119822	OP	60.00	60.00
90	CHRISTMAS IS A TIME TO SHARE 119830	OP	37.50	37.50
90	CHRISTMAS IS A TIME TO SHARE 119938	OP	17.50	17.50
90	I'M WRAPPING UP ALL MY DREAMS 119717	OP	60.00	60.00
90	MAY THIS CHRISTMAS DAY 119865	OP	40.00	40.00
90	MAY YOUR HEART BE FILLED 119911	OP	65.00	65.00
90	MAY YOUR STOCKING BE FILLED 119857	OP	22.50	22.50
90	SWEET MUSIC & BEAUTIFUL MEMORIES 119873	OP	25.00	25.00
90	THE SOUND OF LOVE IS FELT 119881	OP	25.00	25.00
90	WISHING YOU GENTLE MOMENTS 119946	OP	17.50	117.50
91	BABIES ARE THE GREATEST GIFT/GOD 121266	OP	25.00	25.00
91	BABIES TOUCH YOUR HEART 118788	OP	55.00	55.00
91	KEEP THE SPECIAL MEMORIES 122777	OP	75.00	75.00
91	MAY GOD'S LOVE FILL YOUR HEART 120553	OP	50.00	50.00
91	MAY GOD'S LOVE FILL YOUR LIFE 120561	OP	45.00	45.00
91	MAY THE BLESSINGS OF EASTER BRING 120529	OP	25.00	25.00
91	MAY THIS SPECIAL SEASON REAWAKEN 122688	OP	60.00	60.00
91	MAY YOUR LIFE BE FILLED WITH 121312	OP	120.00	120.00
91	MAY YOUR LIFE TOGETHER BE FILLED 121398	OP	22.50	22.50
91	MEMORIES ARE MADE OF SIMPLE JOYS 122653	OP	60.00	60.00
91	MUSIC AND MEMORIES FILL THIS 119873	OP	27.00	27.00
91	PLEASE FEEL BETTER SOON 121258	OP	22.50	22.50
91	REJOICE IN GOD'S LOVE 120537	OP	22.50	22.50
91	SOUND OF LOVE IS FELT IN HEARTS 119881	OP	27.00	27.00
91	SPRING IS A TIME OF LOVE 120588	OP	19.00	19.00
91	WARM WISHES TO SOMEONE SPECIAL 122726	OP	60.00	60.00
91	WISHING YOU GENTLE HUGS 120510	OP	25.00	25.00
91	WISHING YOU GOD'S BLESSINGS 120545	OP	22.50	22.50
91	WITH LOVE TO MY SPECIAL ONE 120502	OP	45.00	45.00
92	CHRISTMAS FILLS YOUR HEART 119725	OP	15.00	15.00
92	CHRISTMAS IS A GIFT FROM GOD 119849	OP	12.50	12.50
92	CHRISTMAS IS A SPECIAL GIFT 117692	OP	16.75	16.75
92	CHRISTMAS IS A TIME OF LOVE 119822	OP	30.00	30.00
92	CHRISTMAS IS A TIME OF LOVE 119962	OP	13.50	13.50
92	CHRISTMAS IS A TIME TO BELIEVE 122718	OP	13.75	13.75
92	CHRISTMAS IS A TIME TO SHARE 117676	OP	27.50	27.50
92	CHRISTMAS IS A TIME TO SHARE 119830	OP	18.75	18.75
92	CHRISTMAS IS A TIME TO SHARE 119938	OP	10.00	10.00
92	CHRISTMAS IS PEACE, LOVE 118184	OP	22.50	22.50
92	CHRISTMAS IS PEACE, LOVE 118214	OP	60.00	60.00
92	GATHER YOUR CHRISTMAS DREAMS 117862	OP	27.50	27.50
92	I'M WRAPPING UP ALL MY DREAMS 119717	OP	30.00	30.00
92	IT'S THE SEASON OF SHARING 125342	OP	16.25	16.25
92	IT'S TIME FOR CHRISTMAS 117889	OP	25.00	25.00

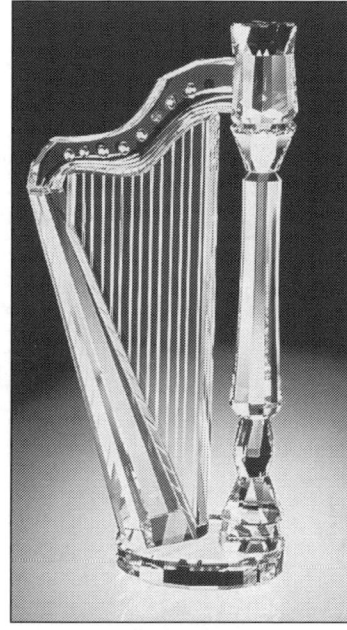

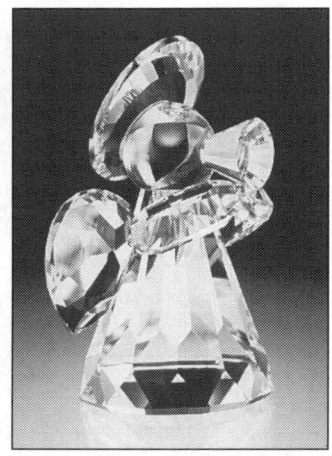

The Swarovski Silver Crystal Harp is *music to the eyes of collectors.*

This Swarovski Silver Crystal Angel *trumpets wishes for a joyous season.*

Polar Bear *is from the Swarovski Silver Crystal Collection.*

Watching over his flocks is this Swarovski Silver Crystal Shepherd.

These Swarovski Silver Crystal Wise Men *come bearing gifts for the newborn King.*

YR	NAME	LIMIT	ISSUE	QUOTE
92	JOIN IN THE CHORUS 125318	OP	10.00	10.00
92	KEEP THE SPECIAL MEMORIES 122777	OP	37.50	37.50
92	MAY CHRISTMAS BLESS YOU W/GIFTS 118192	OP	22.50	22.50
92	MAY CHRISTMAS BRING YOU ALL/JOY 120413	OP	20.00	20.00
92	MAY GOD'S SPECIAL BLESSINGS 123145	OP	33.00	33.00
92	MAY THIS CHRISTMAS DAY TOUCH 119865	OP	20.00	20.00
92	MAY THIS SPECIAL SEASON 118559	OP	15.00	15.00
92	MAY THIS SPECIAL SEASON 122688	OP	30.00	30.00
92	MAY YOU SHARE A NEW YEAR 119733	OP	11.25	11.25
92	MAY YOUR DAYS BE FILLED WITH LOVE 123188	OP	60.00	60.00
92	MAY YOUR STOCKING BE FILLED 119857	OP	12.50	12.50
92	MEMORIES ARE MADE OF SIMPLE JOYS 122653	OP	30.00	30.00
92	MY FAVORITE THINGS 125334	OP	15.00	15.00
92	REJOICE IN GOD'S LOVE 121789	OP	37.50	37.50
92	SANTA'S LITTLE HELPER 125326	OP	16.25	16.25
92	SWEET MUSIC & BEAUTIFUL MEMORIES 119873	OP	13.50	13.50
92	THE SOUND OF LOVE IS FELT 119881	OP	13.50	13.50
92	THE WONDER OF THIS SPECIAL SEASON 118206	OP	15.00	15.00
92	THREE PIECE CHRISTMAS COLLECTION 118176	OP	56.25	56.25
92	WARM WISHES TO SOMEONE SPECIAL 122726	OP	30.00	30.00
92	WILL YOU STOP AND COUNT THE STARS 117838	OP	18.75	18.75
92	WILL YOU STOP AND COUNT THE STARS 117870	OP	25.00	25.00
92	WISH ON THE CHRISTMAS STAR 117897	OP	25.00	25.00
92	WISHING YOU EVERY HAPPINESS 117730	OP	13.50	13.50
92	WISHING YOU GENTLE MOMENTS 119946	OP	10.00	10.00
92	WISHING YOU MANY MOMENTS OF LOVE 123137	OP	30.00	30.00
92	WISHING YOU SPECIAL BLESSINGS 117609	OP	12.50	12.50
L. RIGG				**LUCY & ME**
94	DIANE	2000	30.00	33.00
94	JOAN	2000	30.00	33.00
94	LINDA	2000	30.00	33.00
95	15TH ANNIVERSARY	1,993	10.00	10.00
95	ALISON	2000	30.00	30.00
95	BEAR W/COLLECTION OF LUCY & ME FIGS	2,000	30.00	30.00
95	FOUR SEASONS	2000	30.00	30.00
95	MRS. SANTA CLAUS	2000	30.00	30.00
95	ROMEO & JULIET	2000	30.00	30.00
95	SANTA CLAUS	2000	30.00	30.00
95	SUSIE	2000	30.00	30.00
M. ATTWELL			**MEMORIES OF YESTERDAY**	
88	ANYWAY, FIDO LOVES ME 114588	OP	30.00	32.50
88	CAN I KEEP HER MOMMY? 114545	OP	25.00	27.50
88	DEAR SANTA 115002	OP	50.00	75.00
88	GOOD MORNING, MR. SNOWMAN 115401	OP	75.00	85.00
88	HANG ON TO YOUR LUCK! 114510	OP	25.00	27.50
88	HE KNOWS IF YOU'VE BEEN BAD/GOOD 115355	OP	40.00	45.00
88	HOW 'BOUT A LITTLE KISS? 114987	RT	25.00	27.50
88	HOW DO YOU SPELL S-O-R-R-Y? 114529	RT	25.00	35.00-40.00
88	HUSH! 114553	RT	45.00	70.00
88	I HOPE SANTA IS HOME 115010	OP	30.00	50.00
88	I PRAY THE LORD MY SOUL TO KEEP 523259	OP	25.00	40.00-55.00
88	IF YOU CAN'T BE GOOD, BE CAREFUL 114596	OP	50.00	55.00
88	IS IT REALLY SANTA? 115347	OP	50.00	65.00
88	IT HURTS WHEN FIDO HURTS 114561	OP	30.00	32.50
88	IT'S THE THOUGHT THAT COUNTS 115029	OP	25.00	27.50
88	MOMMY, I TEARED IT 114480	OP	25.00	27.50
88	MOMMY, I TEARED IT 523488	10,000	25.00	310.00
88	MOMMY, I TEARED IT, 9 IN. 115924	CL	85.00	140.00-150.00
88	NOW HE CAN BE YOUR FRIEND, TOO! 115363	OP	45.00	50.00
88	NOW I LAY ME DOWN TO SLEEP 114499	OP	20.00	45.00
88	SPECIAL DELIVERY 114979	RT	30.00	45.00
88	WAITING FOR SANTA 114995	OP	40.00	55.00
88	WE WISH YOU A MERRY CHRISTMAS 115371	OP	70.00	75.00
88	WE'S HAPPY! HOW'S YOURSELF 114502	OP	40.00	45.00
88	WELCOME SANTA 114960	OP	45.00	60.00
88	WHAT WILL I GROW UP TO BE? 114537	OP	40.00	45.00
89	AS GOOD AS HIS MOTHER EVER MADE 522392	9600	32.50	32.50
89	AS GOOD AS HIS MOTHER EVER MADE 522392	OP	32.50	150.00
89	BLOW WIND, BLOW 520012	OP	40.00	40.00
89	DADDY, I COULD NEVER FILL/SHOES 520187	OP	30.00	30.00
89	FOR FIDO AND ME 522457	OP	70.00	70.00
89	HERE COMES THE BRIDE AND GROOM 520896	OP	50.00	50.00
89	HERE COMES THE BRIDE, 9 IN. 520527	CL	95.00	95.00
89	I'SE SPOKEN FOR 520071	RT	30.00	30.00
89	JOY TO YOU AT CHRISTMAS 522449	OP	45.00	45.00
89	KNITTING YOU A WARM & COZY WINTER 522414	OP	37.50	37.50

YR	NAME	LIMIT	ISSUE	QUOTE
89	LET'S BE NICE LIKE WE WAS BEFORE 520047	OP	50.00	50.00
89	MUST FEED THEM OVER CHRISTMAS 522406	OP	38.50	38.50
89	SHOULD I...? 520209	OP	50.00	50.00
89	THE LONG AND SHORT OF IT 522384	OP	32.50	32.50
89	THIS ONE'S FOR YOU DEAR 520195	OP	50.00	50.00
89	WE'S HAPPY! HOW'S YOURSELF? 520616	RT	70.00	70.00
90	A DASH OF SOMETHING W/SOMETHING 524727	OP	55.00	55.00
90	A LAPFUL OF LUCK 524689	OP	15.00	30.00
90	A LAPFUL OF LUCK 525014	5000	30.00	30.00
90	COLLECTION SIGN 513156	OP	7.00	7.00
90	GOT TO GET HOME FOR THE HOLIDAYS 524751	OP	100.00	100.00
90	HE HASN'T FORGOTTEN ME 523267	OP	30.00	32.00
90	HERE COMES THE BRIDE AND GROOM 520136	OP	80.00	80.00
90	HOLD IT! YOU'RE JUST SWELL 520020	OP	50.00	50.00
90	HOPING TO SEE YOU SOON 524824	OP	30.00	55.00
90	HUSH-A-BYE BABY 524778	OP	80.00	80.00
90	I'M NOT AS BACKWARD AS I LOOKS 523240	OP	32.50	32.50
90	I'SE BEEN PAINTING 524700	OP	37.50	37.50
90	KISS THE PLACE AND MAKE IT WELL 520039	OP	50.00	50.00
90	LET ME BE YOUR GUARDIAN ANGEL 524670	OP	32.50	32.50
90	LUCK AT LAST! HE LOVES ME 520217	OP	35.00	35.00
90	NOT A CREATURE WAS STIRRIN' 524697	OP	45.00	45.00
90	THE GREATEST TREASURE THE WORLD 524808	OP	50.00	50.00
90	TIME FOR BED, 9 IN. 523275	TL	95.00	95.00
90	WHERE'S MUVVER? 520101	OP	30.00	30.00
91	COULD YOU LOVE ME FOR MYSELF? 525618	OP	30.00	30.00
91	FRIENDSHIP HAS NO BOUNDARIES 525545	YR	30.00	30.00
91	GIVE IT YOUR BEST SHOT 525561	OP	35.00	35.00
91	GOOD MORNING, LITTLE BOO-BOO 525766	OP	40.00	40.00
91	HE LOVES ME, 9 IN. 525022	TL	100.00	100.00
91	I MUST BE SOMEBODY'S DARLING 522635	OP	30.00	30.00
91	I'M AS COMFY AS CAN BE 525480	OP	50.00	50.00
91	JUST THINKING 'BOUT YOU 523461	OP	70.00	70.00
91	OPENING PRESENTS IS MUCH FUN! 524735	OP	37.50	37.50
91	PULL YOURSELVES TOGETHER GIRLS 522783	OP	30.00	30.00
91	S'NO USE LOOKIN' BACK NOW! 527203	OP	75.00	75.00
91	SITTING PRETTY 522708	OP	40.00	40.00
91	THEM DISHES NEARLY DONE 524611	OP	50.00	50.00
91	TYING THE KNOT 522678	OP	60.00	60.00
91	WE ALL LOVES A CUDDLE 524832	OP	30.00	30.00
91	WE BELONG TOGETHER S-0001	OP	30.00	40.00
91	WELCOME TO YOUR NEW HOME M4911	YR	*	40.00
91	WHEREVER I AM/I'M DREAMING OF YOU 522686	OP	40.00	40.00
91	WHO EVER TOLD MOTHER/TWINS? 520063	OP	33.50	33.50
91	WHY DON'T YOU SING ALONG? 522600	OP	55.00	55.00
91	WISHFUL THINKING 522597	OP	45.00	45.00
92	A KISS FROM FIDO 523119	OP	35.00	35.00
92	A WHOLE BUNCH OF LOVE FOR YOU 522732	OP	40.00	40.00
92	HURRY UP FOR THE LAST TRAIN 525863	OP	40.00	40.00
92	I PRAY THE LORD MY SOUL TO KEEP 525596	OP	65.00	65.00
92	I'M HOPIN' YOU'RE MISSING ME TOO 525499	OP	55.00	55.00
92	I'SE SO HAPPY YOU CALLED 526401	TL	100.00	100.00
92	I'SE SUCH A GOOD LITTLE GIRL 522759	OP	30.00	30.00
92	NOW BE A GOOD DOG FIDO 524581	OP	45.00	45.00
92	SEND ALL LIFE'S LITTLE WORRIES 527505	OP	30.00	30.00
92	TIME FOR BED 527076	OP	30.00	30.00
92	YOU'LL ALWAYS BE MY HERO 524743	OP	50.00	50.00
93	HULLO! DID YOU COME BY UNDERGROUND?	500	*	
93	HULLO! DID YOU COME BY UNDERGROUND?	OP	40.00	40.00
93	I'M ALWAYS LOOKING OUT FOR YOU	OP	55.00	55.00
93	LITTLE MISS MUFFET	18,000	50.00	50.00
93	MARY HAD A LITTLE LAMB	18,000	45.00	45.00
93	MARY, MARY QUITE CONTRARY	18,000	45.00	45.00
93	MOTHER GOOSE	18,000	50.00	50.00
93	NOW I'M THE FAIREST OF THEM ALL	OP	35.00	35.00
93	SIMPLE SIMON	18,000	35.00	35.00
93	WOT'S ALL THIS TALK ABOUT LOVE?	OP	100.00	100.00
94	A LITTLE LOVE SONG-FOR YOU!	OP	35.00	35.00
94	DAYS OF THE WEEK SET	1,994	250.00	250.00
94	THANK GOD FOR FIDO	OP	30.00	30.00
94	TWEEDLE DUM & TWEEDLE DEE	10,000	25.00	25.00
94	WOT'S ALL THIS TALK ABOUT LOVE?	OP	27.50	27.50
95	A LITTLE HELP FROM FAIRYLAND	1,995	55.00	55.00
95	DEAR OLD DEAR, WHIS YOU WERE HERE	5,000	37.50	37.50
95	I COMFORT FIDO & HE COMFORTS ME	5,000	25.00	25.00
95	JOIN ME FOR A LITTLE SONG	5,000	37.50	37.50

YR	NAME	LIMIT	ISSUE	QUOTE
95	SHARING THE COMMON THREAD OF LOVE	OP	100.00	100.00
95	WON'T YOU SKATE WITH ME	5,000	35.00	35.00
95	WRAPPED IN LOVE & HAPPINESS	OP	35.00	35.00
M. ATTWELL		**MEMORIES OF YESTERDAY SYMBOL OF MEMBERSHIP**		
93	I'M THE GIRL FOR YOU	OP	*	
94	BLOWING A KISS TO A DEAR I MISS	OP	*	
95	TIME TO CELEBRATE	OP	*	
P. FAGAN			**PENNYWHISTLE LANE**	
94	TRUNK OF TEDDIES	1,000	60.00	60.00
			PRECIOUS MOMENTS	
*	DOME W/KIDS ON CLOUD FIGURINE E7350		*	750.00-850.00
76	HE CARETH FOR YOU E1377B	SU	9.00	85.00-135.00
76	LOVE ONE ANOTHER E1376	OP	10.00	37.50-130.00
76	PRAISE THE LORD ANYHOW E1374B	RT	8.00	80.00-120.00
76	PRAYER CHANGES THINGS E1375B	SU	11.00	125.00-220.00
77	BOY & GIRL ON SEESAW E1375A	RT	11.00	75.00-170.00
77	HE LEADETH ME E1377A	SU	9.00	80.00-125.00
77	HIS BURDEN IS LIGHT E1380G	RT	8.00	80.00-140.00
77	JESUS IS THE ANSWER E1381	SU	11.50	130.00-180.00
77	JESUS IS THE ANSWER E1381R	OP	55.00	55.00-65.00
77	JESUS IS THE LIGHT E1373G	RT	7.00	35.00-130.00
77	JESUS LOVES ME E1372B	CL	7.00	25.00-115.00
77	JESUS LOVES ME E1372G	CL	7.00	25.00-130.00
77	LOVE IS KIND E1379A	SU	8.00	90.00-135.00
77	O HOW I LOVE JESUS E1380B	RT	8.00	65.00-135.00
77	SMILE, GOD LOVES YOU E1373B	RT	7.00	40.00-100.00
78	COME LET US ADORE HIM E2011	RT	10.00	240.00-275.00
78	GOD UNDERSTANDS E1379B	SU	8.00	75.00-130.00
78	JESUS IS BORN E2012	SU	12.00	90.00-135.00
78	MAKE A JOYFUL NOISE E1374G	CL	8.00	30.00-125.00
78	UNTO US A CHILD IS BORN E2013	SU	12.00	90.00-135.00
78	WE HAVE SEEN HIS STAR E2010	SU	8.00	75.00-110.00
79	EGGS OVER EASY E3118	RT	12.00	80.00-130.00
79	NATIVITY SET OF 9 PCS. E2800	OP	70.00	145.00-210.00
79	TO THEE W/LOVE E3120	SU	13.00	60.00-100.00
80	MY GUARDIAN ANGEL E5207	SU	35.00	140.00-225.00
80	SILENT KNIGHT E5642	SU	55.00	175.00-240.00
81	BUT LOVES GOES ON FOREVER E6118	SU	16.00	55.00-85.00
82	BABY'S FIRST STEP E2840	SU	25.00	65.00-85.00
82	CAMEL E2363	OP	20.00	32.50-55.00
82	CHRISTMAS JOY FROM HEAD TO TOE E2361	SU	25.00	50.00-85.00
82	DROPPING IN FOR CHRISTMAS E2350	SU	18.00	72.00-80.00
82	HOLY SMOKES E2351	RT	27.00	85.00-150.00
82	I'LL PLAY MY DRUM FOR HIM E2355	SU	45.00	130.00-165.00
82	I'LL PLAY MY DRUM FOR HIM E2356	SU	30.00	85.00-130.00
82	I'LL PLAY MY DRUM FOR HIM E2360	OP	16.00	25.00-55.00
82	JOY TO THE WORLD E2343	SU	9.00	35.00-60.00
82	JOY TO THE WORLD E2344	SU	20.00	75.00-95.00
82	LET HEAVEN AND NATURE SING E2346	SU	50.00	110.00-175.00
82	LET HEAVEN AND NATURE SING E2347	15,000	40.00	40.00-45.00
82	LET LOVE REIGN E9273	RT	22.50	60.00-85.00
82	MAY YOUR CHRISTMAS BE COZY E2345	SU	23.00	70.00-85.00
82	MAY YOUR CHRISTMAS BE WARM E2348	SU	30.00	65.00-130.00
82	O COME ALL YE FAITHFUL E2352	SU	45.00	105.00-150.00
82	O COME ALL YE FAITHFUL E2353	RT	27.50	60.00-100.00
82	TELL ME THE STORY OF JESUS E2349	SU	30.00	95.00-125.00
83	BABY'S FIRST PICTURE E2841	RT	45.00	120.00-145.00
83	HIS EYE IS ON THE SPARROW E0530	RT	28.50	90.00-135.00
83	LOVE IS KIND E2847	15,000	40.00	40.00-45.00
84	AUTUMN'S PRAISE 12084	LE	30.00	65.00-75.00
84	AUTUMN'S PRAISE MUSICAL 408751	LE	200.00	130.00-200.00
84	LORD, KEEP MY LIFE IN TUNE 12165	SU	37.50	80.00-95.00
84	LOVE COVERS ALL 12009	SU	27.50	50.00-75.00
84	LOVE IS KIND E5377	RT	27.50	70.00-115.00
84	SUMMER'S JOY 12076	LE	30.00	90.00-100.00
84	SUMMER'S JOY MUSICAL 408743	LE	200.00	130.00-210.00
84	THE VOICE OF SPRING 12068	LE	30.00	250.00-300.00
84	THE VOICE OF SPRING MUSICAL 408735	LE	200.00	130.00-200.00
84	WINTER'S SONG 12092	LE	30.00	88.00-175.00
84	WINTER'S SONG MUSICAL 408778	LE	200.00	130.00-200.00
85	BABY'S FIRST TRIP 16012	SU	32.50	200.00-250.00
85	GOD SENT YOU JUST IN TIME 15504	RT	45.00	85.00-125.00
85	ISN'T EIGHT JUST GREAT 109460	OP	18.50	22.50-35.00
85	LET'S KEEP IN TOUCH 102954	OP	65.00	90.00-125.00
85	MAY YOUR BIRTHDAY BE GIGANTIC 15970	OP	12.50	18.50-45.00
85	SET OF 3-BUNNY,TURTLE & LAMB 102296	SU	5.50	20.00-30.00

YR	NAME	LIMIT	ISSUE	QUOTE
85	SILENT NIGHT 15814	SU	37.50	60.00-90.00
85	WISHING YOU GRR-EATNESS 109479	OP	18.50	22.50-35.00
86	BEAR THE GOOD NEWS OF CHRISTMAS 104515	YR	12.50	18.50-20.00
86	COME LET US ADORE HIME 104523	OP	400.00	460.00-465.00
86	CONGRATULATIONS, PRINCESS 106208	OP	20.00	30.00-42.00
86	I PICKED A VERY SPECIAL MOM 100536	LE	37.50	65.00-80.00
86	OH WHAT FUN IT IS TO RIDE 109819	OP	85.00	110.00-140.00
86	SCENT FROM ABOVE 100528	RT	19.00	55.00-80.00
86	WE BELONG TO THE LORD 103004	SP	50.00	30.00-180.00
88	PEACE ON EARTH 109749	SU	100.00	135.00-150.00
88	THE LIGHT OF THE WORLD IS JESUS 521507	OP	60.00	70.00-95.00
89	ALWAYS IN HIS CARE 225290	YR	8.00	10.00-15.00
90	A REFLECTION OF HIS LOVE 522279	OP	50.00	50.00-62.50
90	HOPPY EASTER, FRIEND 521906	OP	40.00	40.00-50.00
90	HUG ONE ANOTHER 521299	OP	45.00	50.00-60.00
90	IN THE SPOTLIGHT OF HIS GRACE 520543	OP	35.00	35.00-45.00
90	MAY YOU HAVE AN OLD.....CHRISTMAS 417777	LE	200.00	130.00-200.00
90	THERE'SA LIGHT....TUNNEL 521485	OP	55.00	55.00-65.00
90	THUMB-BODY LOVES YOU 521698	OP	55.00	60.00-70.00
90	TO A SPECIAL MUM 521965	OP	30.00	35.00-45.00
90	YOU HAVE TOUNCHED.....HEARTS 422282	LE	175.00	175.00
92	HOPE YOU'RE OVER THE HUMP 521671	OP	17.50	17.50-20.00
92	SAFE IN THE ARMS OF JESUS 521922	OP	30.00	30.00-38.00
92	THERE IS NO GREATER...A FRIEND...521000	OP	30.00	30.00-35.00
92	TO THE APPLE OF GOD'S EYE 522015	OP	32.50	32.50-35.00
94	PRECIOUS MOMENTS LAST FOEVER E6901	SU	10.00	25.00-125.00
82	PRAISE THE LORD ANYHOW E9254	LE	35.00	55.00-200.00
82	WE ARE GOD'S WORKMANSHIP 523879	2,000	500.00	625.00-675.00
82	YOU HAVE TOUCHED...HEARTS 523283	2,000	500.00	545.00-660.00
88	HAVE A BERRY MERRY CHRISTMAS 522856	SU	15.00	20.00-35.00
88	JESUS IS THE SWEETEST NAME I KNOW 523097	SU	22.50	28.00-40.00
88	OH HOLY NIGHT 522546	YR	25.00	38.00-40.00
89	CHRISTMAS FIREPLACE	SU	37.50	40.00-50.00
89	GOOD FRIENDS ARE FOREVER 525049			*
89	REJOICE O EARTH 617334	OP	125.00	100.00-125.00
90	A UNIVERSAL LOVE 527173	LE	32.50	35.00-40.00
90	HE ISMY INSPIRATION 523038	OP	60.00	60.00-70.00
90	HE LOVES ME 524263	LE	35.00	35.00-50.00
90	I CAN'T SPELL SUCCESS W/O YOU 523763	OP	40.00	45.00-55.00
90	I WILL CHERISH ..OLD RUGGED CROSS 523534	YR	27.50	35.00-40.00
90	I WOULD BE LOST W/O YOU 526142	OP	27.50	30.00-35.00
90	JOY ON ARRIVAL 523178	OP	50.00	50.00-65.00
90	MAY ONLY GOOD THINGS...YOUR WAY 524425	OP	30.00	35.00-48.00
90	MAY YOUR BIRTHDAY BE A BLESSING 524301	OP	30.00	30.00-40.00
90	THIS LAND IS OUR LAND 527777	LE	35.00	35.00-37.50
91	BLESSED ARE THE MEEK.. .EARTH 523313	LE	55.00	55.00-60.00
91	BLESSED ARE THE PEACEMAKERS..523348	LE	55.00	55.00
91	BLESSED ARE THE POOR IN SPIRIT...523437	LE	55.00	65.00-75.00
91	BLESSED ARE THE PURE IN HEART...523399	LE	55.00	55.00
91	BLESSED ARE THEY THAT MOURN..523380	LE	55.00	55.00-60.00
91	BLESSED ARE THEY...BE FILLED 523321	LE	55.00	55.00-60.00
91	BLESSED ARE....SHALL OBTAIN MERCY 523291	LE	55.00	55.00
92	A SPECIAL CHIME FOR JESUS 524468	OP	32.50	32.50
92	AMERICA, YOU'RE BEAUTIFUL 528862	OP	35.00	35.00-42.00
92	AN EVENT FOR ALL SEASONS 530158	OP	30.00	35.00-50.00
92	BABY'S FIRST BIRTHDAY 524069	OP	25.00	25.00-30.00
92	BLESS-UM YOU 527335	OP	35.00	35.00-38.00
92	BRINGING YOU A MERRY CHRISTMAS 527599	OP	45.00	45.00-48.00
92	HAPPY BIRTHDAY JESUS 530492	OP	20.00	20.00-25.00
92	I ONLY HAVE ARMS FOR YOU 527769	OP	15.00	16.00-18.00
92	I'M SO GLAD GOD...FRIEND LIKE YOU 523623	OP	50.00	50.00-55.00
92	LOVING, CARING..ALONG THE WAY C0113	OP	25.00	25.00-30.00
92	LOVING,CARING...ALONG THE WAY C0013	OP	25.00	25.00-28.00
92	MAKE A JOYFUL NOISE 528617	YR	27.50	30.00
92	MAY YOUR EVERY WISH COME TRUE 524298	OP	50.00	50.00-55.00
92	MAY YOUR FUTURE BE BLESSED	OP	35.00	35.00-37.00
92	OUR FRIENDSHIP IS SODA-LICIOUS 524336	OP	65.00	65.00-70.00
92	RING OUT THE GOOD NEWS 529966	OP	17.50	17.50-20.00
92	SEALED W/A KISS 524441	OP	50.00	50.00-58.00
92	THE MAGIC STARTS W/YOU 529648	LE	16.00	22.50-25.00
92	TIED UP FOR THE HOLIDAYS 527580	OP	40.00	40.00-45.00
92	WISHING YOU A HO HO 527629	OP	40.00	40.00-45.00
92	WISHING YOU WERE HERE 526916	OP	100.00	100.00-115.00
92	YOU'RE THE END OF MY RAINBOW C0014	OP	25.00	25.00-30.00
92	YOU'RE THE END OF MY RAINBOW C0114	OP	25.00	25.00-30.00
93	A REFLECTION OF HIS LOVE 529095	YR	27.50	27.50

YR	NAME	LIMIT	ISSUE	QUOTE
93	BRING THE LITTLE ONES TO JESUS 531359	LE	50.00	50.00
93	FRIENDS TO THE VERY END 526150	OP	40.00	40.00
93	HE IS NOT HERE FOR HE IS RISEN..527106	OP	60.00	60.00
93	I STILL DO 530999	OP	30.00	30.00
93	I STILL DO 531006	OP	30.00	30.00
93	I WILL ALWAYS BE THINKING OF YOU 523631	OP	45.00	45.00
93	I'M SO GLAD I PICKED YOU...FRIEND 524379	OP	40.00	40.00
93	LORD TEACH US TO PRAY 524158	OP	35.00	35.00
93	NOTHING CAN DAMPEN..CARING 603864	OP	35.00	35.00
93	OINKY BIRTHDAY 524506	OP	13.50	13.50-14.50
93	SERENITY PRAYER GIRL 530697	OP	35.00	35.00
93	SHARING SWEET MEMORIES TOGETHER 526487	OP	45.00	45.00
93	SURROUNDED W/JOY 531677	OP	30.00	30.00
93	SURROUNDED W/JOY 531685	OP	17.50	17.50
93	THE LORD BLESS...KEEP YOU 532134	OP	30.00	30.00
93	THE LORD BLESS..KEEP YOU 532118	OP	40.00	40.00
93	THE LORD BLESS..KEEP YOU 532126	OP	30.00	30.00
93	THE LORD IS COUNTING ON YOU 531707	OP	32.50	32.50
93	THE LORD WILL PROVIDE 523593	LE	40.00	40.00-50.00
93	TO A VERY SPECIAL SISTER 528633	OP	60.00	60.00
93	YOU SUIT ME TO A TEE 526193	OP	35.00	35.00
94	SERENITY PRAYER BOY 530700	OP	35.00	35.00
79	BUT LOVE GOES ON FOREVER E-3115	OP	16.50	35.00-105.00
79	CHRISTMAS IS A TIME TO SHARE E-2802	SU	20.00	85.00-120.00
79	CROWN HIM LORD OF ALL E-2803	SU	20.00	70.00-100.00
79	GOD UNDERSTANDS E-1379B	SU	8.00	90.00-135.00
79	HE CARETH FOR YOU E-1377B	SU	9.00	95.00-140.00
79	HE LEADETH ME E-1377A	SU	9.00	85.00-130.00
79	HE WATCHES OVER US ALL E-3105	SU	11.00	50.00-100.00
79	IT'S WHAT'S INSIDE THAT COUNTS E-3119	SU	13.00	95.00-135.00
79	JESUS IS BORN E-2012	SU	12.00	100.00-140.00
79	JESUS IS BORN E-2801	SU	37.00	285.00-350.00
79	JESUS IS THE ANSWER E-1381	SU	11.50	140.00-180.00
79	JESUS LOVES ME E-1372B	OP	7.00	25.00-105.00
79	JESUS LOVES ME E-1372G	OP	7.00	25.00-125.00
79	LOVE IS KIND E-1379A	SU	8.00	90.00-135.00
79	LOVE LIFTED ME E-1375A	OP	11.00	58.00-160.00
79	LOVE ONE ANOTHER E-1376	OP	10.00	37.50-125.00
79	LOVING IS SHARING E-3110B	RT	13.00	70.00-145.00
79	LOVING IS SHARING E-3110G	OP	13.00	30.00-100.00
79	MAKE A JOYFUL NOISE E-1374G	OP	8.00	30.00-135.00
79	MOTHER SEW DEAR E-3106	OP	13.00	30.00-100.00
79	PEACE ON EARTH E-2804	SU	20.00	130.00-165.00
79	PRAYER CHANGES THINGS E-1375B	SU	11.00	145.00-225.00
79	THE HAND THAT ROCKS THE FUTURE E-3108	SU	13.00	70.00-150.00
79	THE LORD BLESS YOU AND KEEP YOU E-3114	OP	16.00	40.00-95.00
79	THE PURR-FECT GRANDMA E-3109	OP	13.00	30.00-100.00
79	THEE I LOVE E-3116	OP	16.50	52.00-135.00
79	THOU ART MINE E-3113	OP	16.00	37.50-90.00
79	UNTO US A CHILD IS BORN E-2013	SU	12.00	90.00-125.00
79	WALKING BY FAITH E-3117	OP	35.00	75.00-125.00
79	WE HAVE SEEN HIS STAR E-2010	SU	8.00	78.00-118.00
80	BEAR YE ONE ANOTHER'S BURDENS E-5200	SU	20.00	65.00-115.00
80	BLESSED ARE THE PURE IN HEART E-3104	SU	9.00	30.00-55.00
80	COME LET US ADORE HIM 104000 (SET OF 9)	OP	70.00	125.00-130.00
80	COME LET US ADORE HIM E-5619	SU	10.00	30.00-55.00
80	COW WITH BELL FIGURINE E-5638	OP	16.00	32.50-50.00
80	DONKEY FIGURINE E-5621	OP	6.00	15.00-32.50
80	GOD IS LOVE E-5213	SU	17.00	50.00-110.00
80	ISN'T HE WONDERFUL E-5639	SU	12.00	55.00-65.00
80	ISN'T HE WONDERFUL E-5640	SU	12.00	62.00-72.00
80	LET NOT THE SUN GO DOWN...WRATH E-5203	SU	22.50	130.00-175.00
80	LOVE CANNOT BREAK/TRUE FRIENDSHIP E-4722	SU	22.50	105.00-155.00
80	LOVE LIFTED ME E-5201	SU	25.00	75.00-110.00
80	NATIVITY WALL E-5644 (SET OF 2)	OP	60.00	120.00-160.00
80	PEACE AMID THE STORM E-4723	SU	22.50	72.00-115.00
80	PRAYER CHANGES THINGS E-5214	SU	35.00	100.00-160.00
80	REJOICE O EARTH E-5636	OP	15.00	30.00-65.00
80	REJOICING WITH YOU E-4724	OP	25.00	50.00-65.00
80	THANK YOU FOR COMING TO MY AIDE E-5202	SU	22.50	105.00-150.00
80	THE HEAVENLY LIGHT E-5637	OP	15.00	30.00-95.00
80	THE LORD BLESS YOU AND KEEP YOU E-4720	SU	14.00	30.00-55.00
80	THE LORD BLESS YOU AND KEEP YOU E-4721	OP	14.00	30.00-85.00
80	THEY FOLLOWED THE STAR E-5624	OP	130.00	225.00-295.00
80	THEY FOLLOWED THE STAR E-5641	SU	75.00	180.00-210.00
80	TO A SPECIAL DAD E-5212	OP	20.00	35.00-72.00

YR	NAME	LIMIT	ISSUE	QUOTE
80	WEE THREE KINGS E-5635	OP	40.00	75.00-125.00
81	BLESS THIS HOUSE E-7164	SU	45.00	185.00-225.00
81	BUT LOVE GOES ON FOREVER E-0001	YR	*	165.00-190.00
81	FORGIVING IS FORGETTING E-9252	SU	37.50	65.00-86.00
81	GOD IS LOVE, DEAR VALENTINE E-7153	SU	16.00	35.00-60.00
81	GOD IS LOVE, DEAR VALENTINE E-7154	SU	16.00	30.00-55.00
81	GOD IS WATCHING OVER YOU E-7163	SU	27.50	85.00-100.00
81	HIS SHEEP AM I E-7161	SU	25.00	65.00-120.00
81	I BELIEVE IN MIRACLES E-7156	SU	17.00	90.00-135.00
81	LET THE WHOLE WORLD KNOW E-7165	SU	35.00	80.00-115.00
81	LORD GIVE ME PATIENCE E-7159	SU	25.00	45.00-60.00
81	LOVE BEARETH ALL THINGS E-7158	OP	25.00	40.00-75.00
81	LOVE IS SHARING E-7162	SU	25.00	155.00-175.00
81	PEACE ON EARTH E-4725	SU	25.00	65.00-100.00
81	THANKING HIM FOR YOU E-7155	SU	16.00	40.00-65.00
81	THE PERFECT GRANDPA E-7160	SU	25.00	65.00-80.00
82	3 MINI NATIVITY HOUSES/PALM TREE E-2387	OP	45.00	75.00-100.00
82	ANIMAL COLLECTION, BUNNY E-9267C	SU	6.50	20.00-30.00
82	ANIMAL COLLECTION, DOG E-9267B	SU	6.50	20.00-30.00
82	ANIMAL COLLECTION, KITTY W/BOW E-9267D	SU	6.50	20.00-30.00
82	ANIMAL COLLECTION, LAMB W/BIRD E-9267E	SU	6.50	20.00-30.00
82	ANIMAL COLLECTION, PIG W/PATCHES E-9267F	SU	6.50	20.00-30.00
82	ANIMAL COLLECTION, TEDDY BEAR E-9267A	SU	6.50	20.00-30.00
82	BLESS YOU TWO E-9255	OP	21.00	37.50-50.00
82	BUNDLES OF JOY E-2374	OP	27.50	72.00-118.00
82	BUT LOVE GOES ON FOREVER PLAQUE E-0102	YR	*	70.00-140.00
82	CAMEL FIGURINE E-2363	OP	20.00	32.50-55.00
82	CHRISTMAS JOY FROM HEAD TO TOE E-2361	SU	25.00	50.00-85.00
82	COME LET US ADORE HIM E-2395 (SET OF 11)	OP	80.00	125.00-185.00
82	DROPPING IN FOR CHRISTMAS E-2350	OP	30.00	75.00-115.00
82	DROPPING OVER FOR CHRISTMAS E-2376	RT	9.00	45.00-70.00
82	ESPECIALLY FOR EWE E-9282C	SU	8.00	25.00-40.00
82	GOAT FIGURINE E-2364	SU	10.00	40.00-60.00
82	HOW CAN 2 WALK TOGETHER...AGREE E-9263	SU	35.00	120.00-165.00
82	I'LL PLAY MY DRUM FOR HIM E-2356	SU	30.00	78.00-125.00
82	I'LL PLAY MY DRUM FOR HIM E-2360	OP	16.00	25.00-48.00
82	IF GOD BE FOR US...AGAINST US E-9285	SU	27.50	55.00-80.00
82	JESUS LOVES ME E-9278	OP	9.00	16.00-35.00
82	JESUS LOVES ME E-9279	OP	9.00	16.00-38.00
82	LET US CALL THE CLUB TO ORDER E-0103	YR	*	50.00-65.00
82	LOVE IS PATIENT E-9251	SU	35.00	82.00-90.00
82	MAY YOUR CHRISTMAS BE COZY E-2345	SU	23.00	75.00-85.00
82	MAY YOUR CHRISTMAS BE WARM E-2348	SU	30.00	95.00-130.00
82	OUR FIRST CHRISTMAS TOGETHER E-2377	SU	35.00	70.00-100.00
82	PEACE ON EARTH E-9287	SU	37.50	100.00-125.00
82	SEEK YE THE LORD E-9261	SU	21.00	42.00-55.00
82	SEEK YE THE LORD E-9262	SU	21.00	60.00-75.00
82	SENDING YOU A RAINBOW E-9288	SU	22.50	85.00-100.00
82	SHARING OUR JOY TOGETHER E-2834	SU	25.00	40.00-65.00
82	TELL ME THE STORY OF JESUS E-2349	SU	30.00	95.00-125.00
82	THE END IS IN SIGHT E-9253	SU	25.00	60.00-160.00
82	THE FIRST NOEL E-2365	SU	16.00	60.00-80.00
82	THE FIRST NOEL E-2366	SU	16.00	65.00-85.00
82	TO SOME BUNNY SPECIAL E-9282A	SU	8.00	25.00-42.00
82	TRUST IN THE LORD E-9289	SU	20.00	62.00-75.00
82	WE ARE GOD'S WORKMANSHIP E-9258	OP	19.00	30.00-55.00
82	WE'RE IN IT TOGETHER E-9259	SU	24.00	45.00-85.00
82	YOU HAVE TOUCHED SO MANY HEARTS 527661	OP	35.00	35.00-40.00
82	YOU HAVE TOUCHED SO MANY HEARTS E-2821	OP	25.00	35.00-60.00
82	YOU'RE WORTH YOUR WEIGHT IN GOLD E-9282B	SU	8.00	25.00-42.00
83	BABY FIGURINES E-2852	OP	12.00	17.50-28.00
83	BLESSINGS FROM MY HOUSE TO YOURS E-0503	SU	27.00	70.00-85.00
83	BRINGING GOD'S BLESSING TO YOU E-0509	SU	35.00	70.00-90.00
83	GOD BLESS THIS BRIDE E-2832	OP	35.00	50.00-65.00
83	GOD BLESSED OUR YEARS TOGETHER E-2853	OP	35.00	50.00-62.50
83	GOD HAS SENT HIS SON E-0507	SU	32.50	70.00-90.00
83	GOD'S PROMISES ARE SURE E-9260	SU	30.00	68.00-90.00
83	HE UPHOLDETH THOSE WHO FALL E-0526	SU	28.50	65.00-150.00
83	I GET A KICK OUT OF YOU E-2827	SU	50.00	110.00-145.00
83	IT'S A PERFECT BOY E-0512	SU	18.50	40.00-55.00
83	JESUS IS THE LIGHT THAT SHINES E-0502	SU	23.00	65.00-75.00
83	JOIN IN ON THE BLESSINGS E-0104	YR	*	50.00-65.00
83	MAY YOUR BIRTHDAY BE A BLESSING E-2826	SU	37.50	75.00-115.00
83	ONWARD CHRISTIAN SOLDIERS E-0523	OP	24.00	35.00-115.00
83	PRAISE THE LORD ANYHOW E-9254	RT	35.00	70.00-120.00
83	PRECIOUS MEMORIES E-2828	OP	45.00	65.00-85.00

YR	NAME	LIMIT	ISSUE	QUOTE
83	PREPARE YE THE WAY OF THE LORD E-0508	SU	75.00	125.00-145.00
83	PRESS ON E-9265	OP	40.00	60.00-115.00
83	SHARING OUR SEASON TOGETHER E-0501	SU	50.00	135.00-155.00
83	TO A VERY SPECIAL MOM E-2824	OP	27.50	37.50-60.00
83	TO A VERY SPECIAL SISTER E-2825	OP	37.50	50.00-75.00
83	TO GOD BE THE GLORY E-2823	SU	40.00	78.00-100.00
83	TUBBY'S FIRST CHRISTMAS E-0511	SU	12.00	28.00-45.00
84	A MONARCH IS BORN E-5380	SU	33.00	70.00-90.00
84	FOR GOD SO LOVED THE WORLD E-5382	SU	70.00	120.00-140.00
84	GET INTO THE HABIT OF PRAYER 12203	SU	19.00	40.00-55.00
84	GOD BLESS OUR HOME 12319	OP	40.00	60.00-80.00
84	GOD BLESS OUR YEARS TOGETHER 12440	CL	175.00	225.00-285.00
84	GOD BLESSED/LOVE & HAPPINESS E-2854	OP	35.00	50.00-65.00
84	GOD BLESSED/LOVE & HAPPINESS E-2855	OP	35.00	50.00-65.00
84	GOD BLESSED/LOVE & HAPPINESS E-2856	OP	35.00	50.00-65.00
84	GOD BLESSED/LOVE & HAPPINESS E-2857	OP	35.00	50.00-65.00
84	GOD BLESSED/LOVE & HAPPINESS E-2859	OP	35.00	50.00-65.00
84	GOD BLESSED/LOVE & HAPPINESS E-2860	OP	35.00	50.00-65.00
84	GOD SENDS THE GIFT OF HIS LOVE E-6613	SU	22.50	58.00-115.00
84	HIS NAME IS JESUS E-5381	SU	45.00	88.00-110.00
84	I'LL PLAY MY DRUM FOR HIM E-5384	OP	10.00	16.00-35.00
84	I'M SENDING YOU A WHITE CHRISTMAS E-2829	OP	37.50	50.00-85.00
84	ISN'T HE PRECIOUS? E-5379	OP	20.00	30.00-50.00
84	IT IS BETTER TO GIVE...TO RECEIVE 12297	SU	19.00	80.00-95.00
84	JOY TO THE WORLD E-5378	SU	18.00	36.00-48.00
84	LOVE NEVER FAILS 12300	OP	25.00	37.50-65.00
84	MAY YOUR CHRISTMAS BE BLESSED E-5376	SU	37.50	68.00-75.00
84	MINIATURE CLOWN 12238A	OP	13.50	20.00-30.00
84	MINIATURE CLOWN 12238B	OP	13.50	20.00-30.00
84	MINIATURE CLOWN 12238C	OP	13.50	20.00-30.00
84	MINIATURE CLOWN 12238D	OP	13.50	20.00-30.00
84	OH WORSHIP THE LORD E-5385	SU	10.00	35.00-50.00
84	OH WORSHIP THE LORD E-5386	SU	10.00	50.00-60.00
84	PART OF ME WANTS TO BE GOOD 12149	SU	19.00	60.00-75.00
84	SEEK AND YE SHALL FIND E-0105	YR	*	50.00-55.00
84	WISHING YOU A MERRY CHRISTMAS E-5383	YR	17.00	30.00-45.00
85	ANGEL OF MERCY 102482	OP	20.00	30.00-45.00
85	BABY'S FIRST CHRISTMAS 15539	YR	13.00	25.00-35.00
85	BABY'S FIRST CHRISTMAS 15547	YR	13.00	35.00-38.00
85	BIRDS OF A FEATHER COLLECT E-0106	YR	*	40.00-55.00
85	BROTHERLY LOVE 100544	SU	37.00	75.00-90.00
85	FRIENDS NEVER DRIFT APART 100250	OP	35.00	55.00-80.00
85	GOD BLESS AMERICA 102938	LE	30.00	75.00-80.00
85	GOD BLESS THE DAY WE FOUND YOU 100145	SU	40.00	55.00-75.00
85	GOD BLESS THE DAY WE FOUND YOU 100153	SU	40.00	55.00-75.00
85	GOD SENT HIS LOVE 15881	YR	17.00	30.00-35.00
85	HALO, AND MERRY CHRISTMAS 12351	SU	40.00	140.00-160.00
85	HE CLEASNSED MY SOUL 100277	OP	24.00	37.50-65.00
85	HONK IF YOU LOVE JESUS 15490	OP	13.00	20.00-35.00
85	I BELIEVE IN THE OLD RUGGED CROSS 103632	OP	25.00	35.00-55.00
85	I'M A POSSIBILITY 100188	RT	22.00	55.00-85.00
85	IT'S THE BIRTHDAY OF A KING 102962	SU	19.00	30.00-45.00
85	JESUS IS COMING SOON 12343	SU	22.50	38.00-42.00
85	LORD I'M COMING HOME 100110	OP	22.50	35.00-60.00
85	LOVE COVERS ALL 12009	SU	27.50	50.00-75.00
85	LOVE RESCUED ME 102393	OP	22.50	35.00-50.00
85	MAY YOUR CHRISTMAS BE DELIGHTFUL 15482	OP	25.00	35.00-55.00
85	O WORSHIP THE LORD 100064	OP	24.00	35.00-52.00
85	O WORSHIP THE LORD 102229	OP	24.00	35.00-45.00
85	SENDING MY LOVE 100056	SU	22.50	45.00-65.00
85	SERVING THE LORD 100161	SU	19.00	55.00-75.00
85	SERVING THE LORD 100293	SU	19.00	35.00-55.00
85	SHEPHERD OF LOVE 102261	OP	10.00	16.00-26.00
85	THE JOY OF THE LORD...MY STRENGTH 100137	OP	35.00	50.00-105.00
85	TO MY FAVORITE PAW 100021	SU	22.50	58.00-115.00
85	TO MY FOREVER FRIEND 100072	OP	33.00	50.00-132.00
85	WISHING YOU A COZY CHRISTMAS 102342	YR	18.00	33.00-40.00
85	YOU CAN FLY 12335	SU	25.00	60.00-70.00
86	A TUB FULL OF LOVE 104817	OP	22.50	30.00-40.00
86	CHEERS TO THE LEADER 104035	OP	22.50	30.00-47.50
86	COME LET US ADORE HIM 104000 (SET OF 9)	OP	95.00	125.00-135.00
86	GOD BLESS YOU GRADUATE 106194	OP	20.00	30.00-40.00
86	HALLELUJAH COUNTRY 105821	OP	35.00	45.00-250.00
86	HAPPY DAYS ARE HERE AGAIN 104396	SU	25.00	55.00-65.00
86	HAVE I GOT NEWS FOR YOU 105635	SU	22.50	46.00-58.00
86	HE WALKS WITH ME 107999	LE	25.00	25.00-40.00

YR	NAME	LIMIT	ISSUE	QUOTE
86	HE'S THE HEALER OF BROKEN HEARTS 100080	OP	33.00	50.00-65.00
86	HEAVEN BLESS YOUR TOGETHERNESS 106755	OP	65.00	90.00-100.00
86	I WOULD BE SUNK WITHOUT YOU 102970	OP	15.00	19.00-29.00
86	LORD. HELP US KEEP...ACT TOGETHER 101850	RT	35.00	98.00-175.00
86	LOVE IS THE BEST GIFT OF ALL 110930	YR	22.50	35.00-45.00
86	LOVE IS THE GLUE THAT MENDS 104027	SU	33.50	55.00-65.00
86	MY LOVE WILL NEVER LET YOU GO 103497	OP	25.00	35.00-50.00
86	NO TEARS PAST THE GATE 101826	OP	40.00	65.00-95.00
86	PRECIOUS MEMORIES 106763	OP	37.50	50.00-75.00
86	SHARING OUR CHRISTMAS TOGETHER 102490	SU	40.00	70.00-82.00
86	SITTING PRETTY 104825	SU	22.50	48.00-58.00
86	THE GREATEST GIFT IS A FRIEND 109231	OP	30.00	37.50-60.00
86	THE LORD GIVETH...TAKETH AWAY 100226	OP	33.50	40.00-54.00
86	THE SPIRIT IS WILLING...IS WEAK 100196	RT	19.00	50.00-100.00
86	THEY FOLLOWED THE STAR 108243	OP	75.00	110.00-125.00
86	THIS IS THE DAY THE LORD HATH MADE 12157	SU	22.50	30.00-60.00
86	TO MY DEER FRIEND 100048	OP	33.00	50.00-105.00
86	TO TELL THE TOOTH YOU'RE SPECIAL 105813	SU	38.50	95.00-115.00
86	WE ARE ALL PRECIOUS IN HIS SIGHT 102903	OP	30.00	80.00
86	WE GATHER TO ASK/LORD'S BLESSING 109762	OP	130.00	150.00-185.00
86	WE'RE PULLING FOR YOU 106151	SU	40.00	65.00-78.00
86	WISHING YOU A MERRY CHRISTMAS 109754	OP	35.00	50.00-65.00
86	WITH THIS RING... 104019	OP	40.00	60.00-75.00
87	A GROWING LOVE E-0108	YR	*	42.00-48.00
87	A TUB FULL OF LOVE 112313	OP	22.50	30.00-37.50
87	BELIEVE THE IMPOSSIBLE 109487	SU	35.00	55.00-110.00
87	BLESSED ARE THEY THAT OVERCOME 115479	YR	27.50	34.00-36.00
87	FAITH TAKES THE PLUNGE 111155	OP	27.50	35.00-60.00
87	HAPPY BIRTHDAY POPPY 106836	SU	27.50	52.00-64.00
87	LORD HELP ME MAKE THE GRADE 106216	SU	25.00	45.00-60.00
87	MOMMY, I LOVE YOU 109975	OP	22.50	27.50-42.00
87	MOMMY, I LOVE YOU 112143	OP	22.50	27.50-42.00
87	O COME LET US ADORE HIM 111333	SU	200.00	220.00-255.00
87	OH WHAT FUN IT IS TO RIDE 109819	OP	85.00	110.00-140.00
87	PUPPY LOVE IS FROM ABOVE 106798	OP	45.00	55.00-65.00
87	SCENT FROM ABOVE 100528	OP	19.00	55.00-80.00
87	SENDING YOU MY LOVE 109967	OP	35.00	45.00-65.00
87	SEW IN LOVE 106844	OP	45.00	55.00-75.00
87	SHARING IS UNIVERSAL E-0107	YR	*	35.00-50.00
87	THIS IS THE DAY...LORD HATH MADE E2838	SU	20.00	55.00-80.00
87	THIS TOO SHALL PASS 114014	OP	23.00	30.00-40.00
87	WISHING YOU A BASKET/BLESSINGS 109924	OP	23.00	30.00-50.00
88	A FRIEND IS SOMEONE WHO CARES 520632	OP	30.00	35.00-47.50
88	BELIEVE THE IMPOSSBILE 109487	OP	35.00	55.00-110.00
88	BON VOYAGE! 522201	OP	75.00	90.00-120.00
88	DON'T LET THE HOLIDAYS...DOWN 522112	RT	42.50	80.00-100.00
88	EGGSPECIALLY FOR YOU 520667	OP	45.00	50.00-70.00
88	FRIENDSHIP HITS THE SPOT 520748	OP	55.00	65.00-80.00
88	HE IS THE STAR OF THE MORNING 522252	SU	55.00	68.00-82.00
88	HIS LOVE WILL SHINE ON YOU 522376	YR	30.00	50.00-55.00
88	I BELONG TO THE LORD 520853	SU	25.00	40.00-50.00
88	ISN'T HE PRECIOUS 522988	SU	15.00	18.00-22.00
88	JESUS IS THE ONLY WAY 520756	SU	40.00	55.00-68.00
88	JESUS LOVES ME 104531	1000	500.00	1400.00-1700.00
88	JESUS THE SAVIOR IS BORN 520357	OP	25.00	42.00-55.00
88	JUST A LINE TO WISH...A HAPPY DAY 520721	OP	65.00	75.00-90.00
88	LORD, TURN MY LIFE AROUND 520551	OP	35.00	35.00-50.00
88	MAKE A JOYFUL NOISE 520322	1500	500.00	875.00-950.00
88	MAY YOUR LIFE BE...W/TOUCHDOWNS 522023	OP	45.00	50.00-70.00
88	MEOWIE CHRISTMAS 109800	OP	30.00	35.00-50.00
88	MERRY CHRISTMAS DEER 522317	OP	50.00	60.00-75.00
88	MY DAYS ARE BLUE WITHOUT YOU 520802	SU	65.00	85.00-120.00
88	MY HEART IS EXPOSED WITH LOVE 520624	OP	45.00	50.00-65.00
88	OUR FIRST CHRISTMAS TOGETHER 115290	SU	50.00	70.00-85.00
88	PUPPY LOVE 520764	OP	12.50	16.00-26.00
88	REJOICE O EARTH 520268	OP	13.00	16.00-28.00
88	SOME BUNNY'S SLEEPING 115274	OP	13.50	18.50-28.00
88	SOMETHING'S MISSING...NOT AROUND 105643	SU	32.50	65.00-75.00
88	TELL IT TO JESUS 521477	OP	35.00	37.50-55.00
88	THANK YOU LORD FOR EVERYTHING 522031	SU	55.00	70.00-85.00
88	THE GREATEST OF THESE IS LOVE 521868	SU	27.50	40.00-50.00
88	THE LORD HAS BLESSED US TENFOLD 114022	YR	90.00	165.00-175.00
88	THE LORD IS YOUR LIGHT..HAPPINESS 520837	OP	50.00	60.00-80.00
88	TIME TO WISH YOU/MERRY CHRISTMAS 115339	YR	24.00	30.00-35.00
88	TIS THE SEASON 111163	OP	27.50	35.00-47.50
88	TO BE WITH YOU IS UPLIFTING 522260	OP	20.00	30.00-42.00

YR	NAME	LIMIT	ISSUE	QUOTE
88	WE NEED A GOOD FRIEND..RUFF TIMES 520810	SU	35.00	37.50-65.00
88	WISHING YOU A COZY CHRISTMAS 521949	SU	42.50	52.00-62.00
88	WISHING YOU A HAPPY EASTER 109886	OP	23.00	30.00-40.00
88	WISHING YOU A PERFECT CHOICE 520845	OP	55.00	65.00-85.00
88	WISHING YOU A...SUCCESSFUL SEASON 522120	OP	60.00	70.00-85.00
88	WISHING YOU ROADS OF HAPPINESS 520780	OP	60.00	75.00-90.00
88	YOU ARE MY NUMBER ONE 520829	OP	25.00	30.00-37.50
88	YOUR LOVE IS SO UPLIFTING 520675	OP	60.00	75.00-85.00
89	ALWAYS IN HIS CARE 524522	YR	30.00	40.00-45.00
89	ALWAYS ROOM FOR ONE MORE C-0109	YR	*	35.00-45.00
89	BLESSINGS FROM ABOVE 523747	OP	45.00	82.00-105.00
89	EASTER'S ON ITS WAY 521892	OP	60.00	65.00-80.00
89	FAITH IS A VICTORY 521396	RT	25.00	120.00-175.00
89	GOD IS LOVE DEAR VALENTINE 523518	OP	27.50	30.00-40.00
89	GOOD FRIENDS ARE FOREVER 521817	OP	50.00	50.00-65.00
89	HAPPY BIRTHDAY DEAR JESUS 524875	SU	13.50	20.00-30.00
89	HAPPY TRIP 521280	OP	35.00	45.00-95.00
89	HEAVEN BLESS YOU 520934	OP	35.00	35.00-55.00
89	HIGH HOPES 521957	SU	30.00	40.00-55.00
89	HOPE YOU'RE UP...THE TRAIL AGAIN 521205	SU	35.00	40.00-55.00
89	I'LL NEVER STOP LOVING YOU 521418	OP	37.50	37.50-55.00
89	JESUS IS THE SWEETEST NAME I KNOW 523097	OP	22.50	32.00-45.00
89	LORD, HELP ME STICK TO MY JOB 521450	OP	30.00	35.00-52.00
89	LOVE IS FROM ABOVE 521841	OP	45.00	45.00-60.00
89	MY HAPPINESS C-0110	YR	*	35.00-42.00
89	ONCE UPON A HOLY NIGHT 523836	YR	25.00	35.00-40.00
89	SOME BUNNIES SLEEPING 522996	SU	12.00	25.00-30.00
89	SWEEP ALL YOUR WORRIES AWAY 521779	OP	40.00	40.00-135.00
89	THAT'S WHAT FRIENDS ARE FOR 521183	OP	45.00	45.00-60.00
89	THE GOOD LORD ALWAYS DELIVERS 523453	OP	27.50	30.00-40.00
89	THERE SHALL BE SHOWERS..BLESSINGS 522090	OP	60.00	70.00-90.00
89	THINKING OF YOU IS...LIKE TO DO 522287	OP	30.00	30.00-40.00
89	THIS DAY HAS BEEN MADE IN HEAVEN 523496	OP	30.00	30.00-40.00
89	TIME HEALS 523739	OP	37.50	37.50-50.00
89	WE'RE GOING TO MISS YOU 524913	OP	50.00	50.00-65.00
89	YIELD NOT TO TEMPTATION 521310	SU	27.50	42.00-50.00
90	A SPECIAL DELIVERY 521493	OP	30.00	30.00-37.50
90	ANGELS WE HAVE HEARD ON HIGH 524921	OP	60.00	65.00-75.00
90	BEING 9 IS JUST DIVINE 521833	OP	25.00	25.00-30.00
90	BLESS THOSE WHO SERVE... (A.F.) 526584	SU	32.50	45.00
90	BLESS THOSE WHO SERVE... (ARMY) 526576	SU	32.50	45.00
90	BLESS THOSE WHO SERVE... (BLACK) 527297	SU	32.50	42.00
90	BLESS THOSE WHO SERVE... (GIRL) 527289	SU	32.50	45.00
90	BLESS THOSE WHO SERVE... (MARINE) 527521	SU	32.50	42.00
90	BLESS THOSE WHO SERVE... (NAVY) 526568	SU	32.50	45.00-50.00
90	BRING THE LITTLE ONES TO JESUS 527556	OP	90.00	90.00-105.00
90	FRIENDSHIP GROWS WHEN YOU PLANT 524271	OP	40.00	75.00-110.00
90	GOD BLESS THE U.S.A. 527564	LE	32.50	35.00-45.00
90	GOOD FRIENDS ARE FOR ALWAYS 524123	OP	27.50	30.00-37.50
90	GOOD NEWS IS SO UPLIFTING 523615	OP	60.00	65.00-75.00
90	IT'S A PERFECT BOY 525286	OP	16.50	17.00-24.00
90	IT'S NO YOLK/I SAY I LOVE YOU 522104	OP	60.00	65.00-75.00
90	MAY YOUR CHRISTMAS BE MERRY 524166	YR	27.50	35.00-38.00
90	MAY YOUR WORLD BE TRIMMED W/JOY 522082	OP	55.00	55.00-65.00
90	MY WARMEST THOUGHTS ARE YOU 524085	OP	55.00	60.00-68.00
90	SHARING A GIFT OF LOVE 527114	YR	30.00	42.00-55.00
90	SHARING THE GOOD NEWS TOGETHER-C0111	YR	*	35.00-45.00
90	TAKE HEED WHEN YOU STAND 521272	OP	55.00	55.00-70.00
90	THE CLUB IS OUT OF THIS WORLD C0112	YR	*	40.00-45.00
90	TO A VERY SPECIAL MOM & DAD 521434	SU	35.00	40.00-50.00
90	WE ARE GOD'S WORKMANSHIP 525960	YR	27.50	30.00-55.00
90	WE HAVE COME FROM A FAR 526959	OP	17.50	20.00-30.00
90	WHAT THE WORLD NEEDS NOW 524352	OP	50.00	50.00-70.00
90	YOU ARE MY HAPPINESS 526185	YR	37.50	40.00-55.00
90	YOU ARE SUCH A PURR-FECT FRIEND 526010	2000	500.00	600.00-625.00
90	YOU ARE THE TYPE I LOVE 523542	OP	40.00	40.00-47.50
90	YOU DESERVE AN OVATION 520578	OP	35.00	35.00-40.00
90	YOU HAVE TOUCHED SO MANY HEARTS 523283	2000	600.00	545.00-675.00
91	GOING HOME 525979	OP	60.00	60.00-70.00
91	WE ARE GOD'S WORKMANSHIP 523879	2000	*	650.00
92	15 HAPPY YEARS TOGETHER/TWEET 530786	LE	100.00	105.00-110.00
92	A UNIVERSAL LOVE 527173	YR	32.50	45.00-50.00
92	BUT THE GREATEST OF THESE IS LOVE 527688	YR	27.50	30.00-32.00
92	GATHER YOUR DREAMS 524384	2,000	550.00	550.00-575.00
92	HAPPINESS IS AT OUR FINGERTIPS 529931	LE	35.00	50.00-70.00
92	HIS LITTLE TREASURE PM931	OP	30.00	32.00-35.00

YR	NAME	LIMIT	ISSUE	QUOTE
92	I'M LOST WITHOUT YOU 526142	YR	27.50	30.00-35.00
92	IT'S SO UPLIFTING/FRIEND LIKE YOU 524905	OP	40.00	40.00-45.00
92	JESUS IS THE ANSWER E-1381R	OP	55.00	55.00-65.00
92	LOVING PM932	OP	30.00	30.00-35.00
92	MAY YOUR BIRTHDAY BE MAMMOTH 521825	OP	25.00	25.00-30.00
92	RING THOSE CHRISTMAS BELLS 525898	OP	95.00	95.00-105.00
92	THE LORD TURNED MY LIFE AROUND 520535	OP	35.00	35.00-40.00
92	THIS LAND IS OUR LAND 527777	YR	35.00	35.00-40.00
92	TUBBY'S FIRST CHRISTMAS 525278	OP	10.00	10.00-15.00
92	WISHING YOU A COMFY CHRISTMAS 527750	OP	27.50	27.50-30.00
92	WISHING YOU/SWEETEST CHRISTMAS 530166	YR	27.50	35.00-45.00
92	YOU ARE MY FAVORITE STAR 527378	OP	60.00	60.00-65.00
92	YOU'RE MY NUMBER ONE FRIEND 530026	LE	30.00	30.00
93	IT IS NO SECRET WHAT GOD CAN DO 531111	LE	30.00	30.00
93	YOU ARE/ROSE OF HIS CREATION 531243	2,000	*	500.00
94	CARING	OP	35.00	35.00
94	SHARING	OP	35.00	35.00
94	SO GLAD I PICKED YOU AS A FRIEND	OP	40.00	40.00
94	YOU'RE AS PRETTY AS A CHRISTMAS TREE	OP	27.50	27.50
95	ALWAYS TAKE TIME TO PRAY	OP	35.00	35.00
95	HE COVERS THE EARTH W/HIS BEAUTY	OP	30.00	30.00
95	HE'S GOT THE WHOLE WORLD IN HIS HANDS	2,000	*	
95	LOVE BLOOMS ETERNAL	OP	35.00	35.00
95	SENDING MY LOVE YOUR WAY 528609	OP	40.00	40.00
95	TAKE TIME TO SMELL THE FLOWERS 524387	OP	30.00	30.00
95	YOU FILL THE PAGES OF MY LIFE	OP	67.50	67.50
95	YOU WILL ALWAYS BE OUR HERO 136271	OP	40.00	40.00
95	YOU'RE ONE IN A MILLION TO ME	OP	35.00	35.00
96	HE LOVES ME	2,000	*	
96	YOU CAN ALWAYS COUNT ON ME 526827	OP	30.00	30.00
92	THE FRUIT..SPIRIT IS LOVE 521213	OP	30.00	30.00-32.00
S. BUTCHER		**PRECIOUS MOMENTS BABY'S FIRST**		
84	BABY'S FIRST HAIRCUT 12211	SU	32.50	125.00-138.00
84	BABY'S FIRST PICTURE E-2841	RT	45.00	145.00-165.00
84	BABY'S FIRST STEP E-2840	SU	35.00	75.00-90.00
88	BABY'S FIRST PET 520705	OP	45.00	65.00-80.00
90	BABY'S FIRST MEAL 524077	OP	35.00	37.50-47.00
92	BABY'S FIRST WORD 527238	OP	25.00	25.00-30.00
S. BUTCHER		**PRECIOUS MOMENTS BIRTHDAY CLUB**		
86	FISHING FOR FRIENDS BC-861	YR	10.00	125.00-130.00
86	OUR CLUB CAN'T BE BEAT B-0001	YR	*	72.50-80.00
87	A SMILE'S THE CYMBAL OF JOY B-0002	YR	*	55.00-57.50
87	A SMILE'S THE CYMBAL OF JOY B-0102	YR	*	68.00-72.00
87	HI SUGAR BC-871	YR	11.00	80.00-100.00
88	HAVE A BEARY SPECIAL BIRTHDAY B-0004	YR	*	28.00-32.00
88	SOMEBUNNY CARES BC-881	YR	13.50	40.00-55.00
88	THE SWEETEST CLUB AROUND B-0003	YR	*	40.00-45.00
88	THE SWEETEST CLUB AROUND B-0103	YR	*	35.00-50.00
89	CAN'T BEEHIVE MYSELF WITHOUT YOU BC-891	YR	13.50	35.00-55.00
89	HAVE A BEARY SPECIAL BIRTHDAY B-0104	YR	*	32.00-48.00
90	COLLECTING MAKES GOOD SCENTS BC-901	YR	15.00	35.00-40.00
90	I'M NUTS OVER MY COLLECTION BC-902	YR	15.00	35.00-40.00
90	JEST TO LET YOU KNOW YOU'RE TOPS B-0006	YR	*	22.00-26.00
90	JEST TO LET YOU KNOW YOU'RE TOPS B-0106	YR	*	20.00-30.00
90	OUR CLUB IS A TOUGH ACT TO FOLLOW B-0005	YR	*	25.00-35.00
90	OUR CLUB IS A TOUGH ACT TO FOLLOW B-0005	YR	*	25.00-35.00
93	PUT A LITTLE PUNCH INTO YOUR BIRTHDAY	OP	15.00	15.00
94	OWL ALWAYS BE YOUR FRIEND	OP	16.00	16.00
S. BUTCHER		**PRECIOUS MOMENTS BIRTHDAY SERIES**		
86	BRIGHTEN SOMEONE'S DAY 105953	SU	12.50	28.00-45.00
86	SHOWERS OF BLESSINGS 105945	RT	16.00	40.00-60.00
88	FRIENDS TO THE END 104418	SU	15.00	30.00-52.00
88	HELLO WORLD! 521175	OP	13.50	16.00-30.00
89	NOT A CREATURE WAS STIRRING 524484	OP	17.00	27.00-35.00
89	TO MY FAVORITE FAN 521043	SU	16.00	32.00-55.00
90	CAN'T BE WITHOUT YOU 524492	OP	16.00	16.00-25.00
90	HOW CAN I EVER FORGET YOU 526924	OP	15.00	16.00-20.00
90	LET'S BE FRIENDS 527270	OP	15.00	16.00-20.00
92	HAPPY BIRDIE 527343	OP	16.00	16.00-20.00
S. BUTCHER		**PRECIOUS MOMENTS BIRTHDAY TRAIN**		
85	BLESS THE DAYS OF OUR YOUTH 16004	OP	15.00	22.50-45.00
85	GOD BLESS YOU ON YOUR BIRTHDAY 15962	OP	11.00	16.50-40.00
85	HAPPY BIRTHDAY LITTLE LAMB 15946	OP	10.00	15.00-40.00
85	HEAVEN BLESS YOUR SPECIAL DAY 15954	OP	11.00	16.50-40.00
85	KEEP LOOKING UP 15997	OP	13.50	20.00-40.00
85	MAY YOUR BIRTHDAY BE WARM 15938	OP	10.00	15.00-42.00

YR	NAME	LIMIT	ISSUE	QUOTE
85	THIS DAY IS SOMETHING...ROAR ABOUT 15989	OP	13.50	20.00-40.00
88	ISN'T EIGHT JUST GREAT 109460	OP	18.50	22.50-32.00
88	WISHING YOU GRR-EATNESS 109479	OP	18.50	22.50-32.00
90	MAY YOUR BIRTHDAY BE MAMMOTH 521825	OP	25.00	25.00-30.00
92	BEING NINE IS JUST DIVINE 521833	OP	25.00	25.00-30.00
S. BUTCHER		**PRECIOUS MOMENTS BRIDAL PARTY**		
83	BRIDE E-2846	OP	18.00	25.00-35.00
83	GROOMSMAN WITH FROG E-2836	OP	13.00	22.50-35.00
83	JUNIOR BRIDESMAID E-2845	OP	12.00	20.00-30.00
83	NO FLOWER IS AS SWEET AS YOU E-2831	OP	13.00	22.50-30.00
84	FLOWER GIRL E-2835	OP	11.00	17.00-30.00
84	RINGBEARER E-2833	OP	11.00	17.00-28.00
86	GOD BLESS..FAMILY (PARENTS/BRIDE) 100501	OP	35.00	55.00-62.00
86	GOD BLESS..FAMILY (PARENTS/GROOM) 100498	OP	35.00	50.00-62.00
86	GROOM E-2837	OP	13.50	25.00-50.00
87	WEDDING ARCH 102369	SU	22.50	40.00-52.00
S. BUTCHER		**PRECIOUS MOMENTS CALENDAR GIRL**		
87	APRIL 110027	OP	27.50	35.00-110.00
87	FEBRUARY 109991	OP	27.50	35.00-55.00
87	JANUARY 109983	OP	37.50	45.00-62.00
87	JUNE 110043	OP	40.00	50.00-120.00
87	MARCH 110019	OP	27.50	30.00-60.00
87	MAY 110035	OP	27.50	35.00-150.00
88	AUGUST 110078	OP	40.00	50.00-60.00
88	DECEMBER 110116	OP	27.50	35.00-52.00
88	JULY 110051	OP	35.00	45.00-58.00
88	NOVEMBER 110108	OP	32.50	37.50-55.00
88	OCTOBER 110094	OP	35.00	45.00-55.00
88	SEPTEMBER 110086	OP	27.50	35.00-50.00
S. BUTCHER		**PRECIOUS MOMENTS CLOWN**		
85	I GET A BANG OUT OF YOU 12262	OP	35.00	45.00-75.00
85	LORD KEEP ME ON THE BALL 12270	OP	35.00	45.00-70.00
85	THE LORD WILL CARRY YOU THROUGH 12467	RT	30.00	75.00-85.00
85	WADDLE I DO WITHOUT YOU 12459	RT	30.00	82.00-95.00
S. BUTCHER		**PRECIOUS MOMENTS COLLECTORS CLUB**		
82	BUT LOVE GOES ON FOREVER-PLAQUE E-0202	YR	*	50.00-75.00
82	LET US CALL THE CLUB TO ORDER E-0303	YR	*	55.00-60.00
83	JOIN IN ON THE BLESSINGS E-0404	YR	*	50.00-120.00
84	SEEK AND YE SHALL FIND E-0005	YR	*	45.00-50.00
86	BIRDS OF A FEATHER...TOGETHER E-0006	YR	*	45.00-50.00
87	A GROWING LOVE E-0008	YR	*	25.00-42.50
87	SHARING IS UNIVERSAL E-0007	YR	*	40.00-45.00
88	ALWAYS ROOM FOR ONE MORE C-0009	YR	*	30.00-42.50
89	MY HAPPINESS C-0010	YR	*	35.00-40.00
90	SHARING THE GOOD NEWS TOGETHER C0011	YR	*	30.00-42.00
90	THE CLUB IS OUT OF THIS WORLD C0012	YR	*	28.00-35.00
S. BUTCHER		**PRECIOUS MOMENTS EVENTS**		
87	YOU ARE MY MAIN EVENT 115231	YR	30.00	55.00-95.00
88	SHARING BEGINS IN THE HEART 520861	YR	25.00	45.00-82.00
90	I'M A PRECIOUS MOMENTS FAN 523526	YR	25.00	40.00-50.00
90	YOU CAN ALWAYS BRING A FRIEND 527122	YR	27.50	46.00-50.00
92	AN EVENT WORTH WADING FOR 527319	YR	32.50	40.00-48.00
S. BUTCHER		**PRECIOUS MOMENTS FAMILY CHRISTMAS SCENE**		
85	GOD GAVE HIS BEST 15806	SU	13.00	30.00-45.00
85	MAY YOU HAVE...SWEETEST CHRISTMAS 15776	SU	17.00	35.00-52.00
85	TELL ME A STORY 15792	SU	10.00	28.00-40.00
85	THE STORY OF GOD'S LOVE 15784	OP	22.50	46.00-60.00
86	SHARING OUR CHRISTMAS TOGETHER 102490	SU	37.00	60.00-80.00
89	HAVE A BEARY MERRY CHRISTMAS 522856	SU	15.00	16.50-25.00
90	CHRISTMAS FIREPLACE 524883	OP	37.50	50.00-62.00
		PRECIOUS MOMENTS MUSICAL		
81	LET THE WHOLE WORLD KNOW E7186	SU	60.00	115.00-160.00
90	THIS DAY HAS BEEN MADE IN HEAVEN 523682	OP	60.00	60.00-70.00
79	COME LET US ADORE HIM E-2810	SU	60.00	105.00-150.00
79	MOTHER SEW DEAR E-7182	OP	35.00	60.00-100.00
79	THE LORD BLESS YOU AND KEEP YOU E-7180	OP	55.00	85.00-140.00
79	THE PURR-FECT GRANDMA E-7184	SU	35.00	60.00-100.00
80	CHRISTMAS IS A TIME TO SHARE E-2806	RT	45.00	150.00-185.00
80	CROWN HIM LORD OF ALL E-2807	SU	45.00	90.00-130.00
80	JESUS IS BORN E-2809	SU	45.00	110.00-145.00
80	MY GUARDIAN ANGEL E-5205	SU	27.50	82.00-102.00
80	MY GUARDIAN ANGEL E-5206	SU	27.50	75.00-100.00
80	PEACE ON EARTH E-4726	SU	29.00	105.00-145.00
80	REJOICE O EARTH E-5645	RT	40.00	95.00-130.00
80	SILENT NIGHT E-5642	SU	55.00	195.00-220.00
80	UNTO US A CHILD IS BORN E-2808	SU	45.00	95.00-140.00

YR	NAME	LIMIT	ISSUE	QUOTE
81	LET THE WHOLE WORLD KNOW E-7165	SU	60.00	80.00-120.00
81	LOVE IS SHARING E-7185	RT	40.00	150.00-185.00
81	THE HAND THAT ROCKS THE FUTURE E-5204	OP	37.50	60.00-105.00
82	I'LL PLAY MY DRUM FOR HIM E-2355	SU	45.00	130.00-165.00
83	LET HEAVEN AND NATURE SING E-2345	SU	30.00	115.00-165.00
83	SHARING OUR SEASON TOGETHER E-0519	RT	70.00	135.00-165.00
83	WEE THREE KINGS E-0520	SU	60.00	115.00-135.00
84	HEAVEN BLESS YOU 100285	SU	45.00	82.00-115.00
84	WE SAW A STAR 12408	SU	50.00	90.00-105.00
84	WISHING YOU A MERRY CHRISTMAS E-5394	SU	55.00	90.00-125.00
85	OUR 1ST CHRISTMAS TOGETHER 101702	RT	50.00	100.00-128.00
87	I'M SENDING YOU A WHITE CHRISTMAS 112402	RT	55.00	120.00-145.00
88	YOU HAVE TOUCHED SO MANY HEARTS 112577	OP	40.00	60.00-75.00
90	LORD HELP KEEP ME IN BALANCE 520691	SU	60.00	68.00-85.00
91	SLEEPING BABY BOY 429570	OP	65.00	65.00-70.00
91	SLEEPING BABY GIRL 429589	OP	65.00	65.00-70.00
92	DO NOT OPEN TILL CHRISTMAS 522244	OP	75.00	85.00-95.00
92	THIS DAY HAS BEEN MADE IN HEAVEN 523682	OP	60.00	60.00-70.00
* *		**PRECIOUS MOMENTS NOAH'S ARK**		
92	BUNNIES 530123	OP	9.00	9.00-10.00
92	ELEPHANTS 530131	OP	18.00	18.00-20.00
92	GIRAFFES 530115	OP	16.00	16.00-18.00
92	NOAH'S ARK 8/PC COLL. SET 530948	OP	190.00	190.00-200.00
92	PIGS 530085	OP	12.00	12.00-14.00
92	SHEEP 530077	OP	10.00	10.00-12.00
93	LLAMAS 531375	OP	15.00	15.00
S. BUTCHER		**PRECIOUS MOMENTS REJOICE IN THE LORD**		
84	HAPPINESS IS THE LORD 12378	SU	15.00	30.00-50.00
84	HE IS MY SONG 12394	SU	17.50	40.00-50.00
84	LORD GIVE ME A SONG 12386	SU	15.00	38.00-46.00
84	THERE'S A SONG IN MY HEART 12173	SU	11.00	25.00-50.00
86	LORD KEEP MY LIFE IN TUNE 12580	SU	37.50	95.00-125.00
S. BUTCHER		**PRECIOUS MOMENTS RETIRED**		
78	WISHING YOU A SEASON FILLED W/JOY E-2805	RT	20.00	75.00-130.00
79	BE NOT WEARY IN WELL DOING E-3111	RT	14.00	82.00-190.00
79	BLESSED ARE THE PEACEMAKERS E-3107	RT	13.00	72.00-130.00
79	COME LET US ADORE HIM E-2011	RT	10.00	295.00-315.00
79	GOD LOVETH A CHEERFUL GIVER E-1378	RT	9.50	900.00
79	GOD'S SPEED E-3112	RT	14.00	70.00-105.00
79	HIS BURDEN IS LIGHT E-1380G	RT	17.00	90.00-150.00
79	JESUS IS THE LIGHT E-1373G	RT	15.00	40.00-130.00
79	O, HOW I LOVE JESUS E-1380B	RT	17.00	85.00-140.00
79	PRAISE THE LORD ANYHOW E-1374B	RT	17.00	80.00-125.00
79	SMILE, GOD LOVES YOU E-1373B	RT	15.00	60.00-135.00
81	THERE IS JOY IN SERVING JESUS E-7157	RT	17.00	48.00-70.00
82	DROPPING OVER FOR CHRISTMAS E-2375	RT	30.00	75.00-115.00
82	NOBODY'S PERFECT E-9268	RT	21.00	62.00-90.00
82	O COME ALL YE FAITHFUL E-2353	RT	27.50	60.00-100.00
82	TASTE & SEE THAT THE LORD IS GOOD E-9274	RT	22.50	68.00-250.00
83	CHRISTMASTIME IS FOR SHARING E-0504	RT	37.00	65.00-120.00
83	SURROUNDED WITH JOY E-0507	RT	35.00	70.00-85.00
83	THIS IS YOUR DAY TO SHINE E-2822	RT	37.50	80.00-155.00
83	YOU CAN'T RUN AWAY FROM GOD E-0525	RT	28.50	75.00-155.00
85	HELP, LORD, I'M IN A SPOT 100269	RT	18.50	60.00-72.00
85	LORD KEEP ME ON MY TOES 100129	RT	22.50	75.00-105.00
86	MAKE ME A BLESSING 100102	RT	35.00	65.00-135.00
86	SMILE ALONG THE WAY 101842	RT	30.00	130.00-180.00
87	HAPPINESS DIVINE 109584	RT	25.00	55.00-80.00
87	HIS EYE IS ON THE SPARROW E-0530	RT	28.50	100.00-125.00
87	HOLY SMOKES E-2351	RT	30.00	95.00-150.00
87	I BELIEVE IN MIRACLES E-7156R	RT	22.50	60.00-78.00
87	LET LOVE REIGN E-9273	RT	22.50	68.00-250.00
87	LORD/KEEP OUR ACT TOGETHER 101850	RT	35.00	115.00-155.00
87	LOVE IS KIND E-5377	RT	27.50	80.00-95.00
87	SCENT FROM ABOVE 100528	RT	19.00	55.00-80.00
87	SMILE ALONG THE WAY 101842	RT	35.00	140.00-200.00
87	THE SPIRIT IS WILLING 100196	RT	19.00	58.00-75.00
88	MANY MOONS...CANOE, BLESSUM YOU 520772	RT	50.00	200.00-250.00
88	SENDING YOU SHOWERS OF BLESSINGS 520683	RT	32.50	70.00-80.00
88	SOMEDAY MY LOVE 520799	RT	40.00	70.00-85.00
89	I'M SO GLAD YOU FLUTTERED...LIFE 520640	RT	40.00	280.00-375.00
S. BUTCHER		**PRECIOUS MOMENTS SPECIAL EDITION**		
81	HELLO, LORD, IT'S ME AGAIN PM-811	CL	25.00	425.00-450.00
81	PUT ON A HAPPY FACE PM-822	CL	25.00	190.00-215.00
82	SMILE, GOD LOVES YOU PM-821	CL	25.00	215.00-230.00
83	DAWN'S EARLY LIGHT PM-831	CL	27.50	85.00-90.00

YR	NAME	LIMIT	ISSUE	QUOTE
83	GOD'S RAY OF MERCY PM-841	CL	25.00	55.00-85.00
84	I LOVE TO TELL THE STORY PM-852	CL	27.50	50.00-60.00
84	THE LORD IS MY SHEPHERD PM-851	SU	25.00	80.00
84	TRUST IN THE LORD TO THE FINISH PM-842	CL	25.00	50.00-55.00
86	FEED MY SHEEP PM-871	CL	25.00	40.00-60.00
86	GRANDMA'S PRAYER PM-861	CL	25.00	75.00-85.00
86	I'M FOLLOWING JESUS PM-862	CL	25.00	80.00-85.00
87	IN HIS TIME PM-872	CL	25.00	38.00-55.00
88	GOD BLESS YOU/TOUCHING MY LIFE PM-881	CL	27.50	48.00-65.00
88	YOU JUST CAN'T CHUCK...FRIENDSHIP PM-882	CL	27.50	42.00-50.00
89	MOW POWER TO YOU PM-892	CL	27.50	35.00-42.00
89	YOU WILL ALWAYS BE MY CHOICE PM-891	CL	27.50	35.00-40.00
90	LORD, KEEP ME/TEE PEE TOP SHAPE PM-912	YR	27.50	35.00-42.00
90	ONE STEP AT A TIME PM-911	YR	33.00	35.00-40.00
90	TEN YEARS AND STILL GOING STRONG PM-901	CL	30.00	45.00-50.00
90	YOU ARE A BLESSING TO ME PM-902	CL	27.50	45.00-50.00
91	THIS LAND IS OUR LAND 527386	LE	350.00	350.00-385.00
92	ONLY LOVE CAN MAKE A HOME PM-921	YR	30.00	45.00-48.00
* *		**PRECIOUS MOMENTS SPECIAL EVENTS**		
93	MEMORIES ARE MADE OF THIS 529982	LE	30.00	30.00
90	AN EVENT WORTH WADING FOR 527319	YR	32.50	35.00-45.00
* *		**PRECIOUS MOMENTS SUGAR TOWN**		
92	CAR 529443	OP	22.50	22.50-24.50
92	DUSTY 529435	OP	15.00	17.00-20.00
92	FENCE 529796	OP	10.00	10.00-11.00
92	KATYLYNNE 529524	OP	20.00	20.00-22.00
92	SAM BUTCHER 529842	OP	22.50	22.50-24.50
92	SAMMY 528668	OP	17.00	17.00-220.00
92	AUNT RUTH AND AUNT DOROTHY 529486	OP	20.00	20.00-22.00
92	CHAPEL 529621	RT	85.00	85.00
92	EVERGREEN TREE 528684	OP	15.00	15.00-17.00
92	GRANDFATHER 529516	OP	15.00	15.00-17.00
92	NATIVITY 529508	OP	20.00	20.00-22.00
92	PHILIP 529494	OP	17.00	17.00-19.00
92	SAM BUTCHER 529567	LE	22.50	30.00-35.00
S. BUTCHER		**PRECIOUS MOMENTS THE FOUR SEASONS**		
85	SUMMER'S JOY 12076	YR	30.00	95.00-105.00
85	THE VOICE OF SPRING 12068	YR	30.00	275.00-300.00
86	AUTUMN'S PRAISE 12084	YR	30.00	65.00-85.00
86	WINTER'S SONG 12092	YR	30.00	115.00-135.00
* *		**SAMMY'S 1994 CIRCUS**		
93	COLLIN 529214	OP	20.00	20.00
93	DUSTY 529176	OP	22.50	22.50
93	KATIE 529184	OP	17.50	17.50
93	MARKIE 528099	OP	18.50	18.50
93	SAMMY 529222	OP	20.00	20.00
93	TIPPY 529192	OP	12.00	12.00
* *		**SHARING SEASON GIFTS**		
92	THE CLUB'S THAT'S OUT...THIS WORLD PM038	OP	*	65.00-75.00
		SMALL WORLD OF MUSIC		
94	1963 CHEVROLET CORVETTE STING RAY	7,500	300.00	300.00

FENTON ART GLASS

* *		**CHRISTMAS LIMITED EDITION**		
93	EGG 5140SV	2500	35.00	35.00
93	EGG 5140SW	2500	35.00	35.00
94	EGG 5145VG	1500	35.00	35.00
94	EGG 5145VK	1500	35.00	35.00
95	ANGEL 5542TA	900	85.00	85.00
95	ANGEL BELL 5144TW	1900	35.00	35.00
95	EGG 5145TH	900	35.00	35.00
95	EGG 5145TP	900	35.00	35.00
* *		**CHRISTMAS SERIES**		
93	CLOCK 8600HT	1500	79.00	79.00
93	FAIRY LIGHT 7300HT CHRISTMAS AT HOME	3500	39.00	39.00
93	LAMP 7204HT	1000	265.00	265.00
94	EGG CHRISTMAS STAR "SILENT NIGHT" 5145VS	1500	45.00	45.00
94	FAIRY LIGHT 7300VS	1500	45.00	45.00
94	LAMP 7204VS	500	275.00	275.00
95	EGG 5145VT	1500	45.00	45.00
95	FAIRY LIGHT 7300VT	1500	45.00	45.00
95	LAMP 2940VT	500	275.00	275.00
* *		**COLLECTIBLE EGGS**		
93	EGG 5140D1	2500	30.00	30.00
93	EGG 5140D2	2500	30.00	30.00
93	EGG 5140D3	2500	30.00	30.00
93	EGG 5140D4	2500	30.00	30.00

Simple Simon *from the "Once Upon a Fairytale" series was inspired by the artwork of Mabel Lucie Attwell. The Memories of Yesterday Collection is produced by Enesco Corp.*

With her gander standing close by, Mother Goose, *from the "Once Upon a Fairytale" series from the Memories of Yesterday line, is ready to wander.*

The price of A Dress For Cinderelly, *from the Walt Disney Classics Collection, has fluctuated on the secondary market more than the length of skirt hems.*

Jiminy Cricket *was the first gift sculpture to members of the Walt Disney Collectors Society.*

YR	NAME	LIMIT	ISSUE	QUOTE
93	EGG 5140D5	2500	30.00	30.00
93	EGG 5140D6	2500	30.00	30.00
93	EGG 5140D8	2500	35.00	35.00
94	EGG 5140A1	2500	32.50	32.50
94	EGG 5140A2	2500	32.50	32.50
94	EGG 5140A3	2500	32.50	32.50
94	EGG 5140A4	2500	32.50	32.50
94	EGG 5140A5	2500	32.50	32.50
94	EGG 5140A6	2500	32.50	32.50
94	EGG 5140A7	2500	37.50	37.50
95	EGG 5145S2	2500	32.50	32.50
95	EGG 5145S3	2500	32.50	32.50
95	EGG 5145S4	2500	32.50	32.50
95	EGG 5145S5	2500	32.50	32.50
95	EGG 5145S6	2500	32.50	32.50
95	EGG 5145S7	2500	32.50	32.50
95	EGG 5145S8	2500	35.00	35.00

* * **CONNOISSEUR COLLECTION**

YR	NAME	LIMIT	ISSUE	QUOTE
93	AMPHORA W/STAND 2748FW	850	285.00	285.00
93	BOWL 2747RX	1250	95.00	95.00
93	LAMP 2780CX	500	590.00	590.00
93	OWL 5258FN	1500	95.00	95.00
93	PERFUME/STOPPER 1710R5	1250	95.00	95.00
93	VASE 7661P4	950	175.00	175.00
93	VASE 8805X3	950	125.00	125.00
94	BOWL 7727JC	500	390.00	390.00
94	CLOCK 8691JV	850	150.00	150.00
94	LAMP 5582JB	300	590.00	590.00
94	PITCHER 2729JI	750	165.00	165.00
94	VASE 2743JP	850	185.00	185.00
94	VASE 2744JK	750	165.00	165.00
94	VASE 3161JQ	750	175.00	175.00

B. FENTON **FAMILY SIGNATURE SERIES**

YR	NAME	LIMIT	ISSUE	QUOTE
93	BASKET 6730PJ	YR	65.00	65.00
93	VASE 1640C1	YR	110.00	110.00
93	VASE 1786PV	YR	80.00	80.00
93	VASE 2752RN	YR	105.00	105.00
93	VASE 7661Z8	YR	90.00	90.00
94	BASKET 1217AO	YR	70.00	70.00
94	BASKET 2738PJ	YR	65.00	65.00
94	BASKET 2779RN	YR	65.00	65.00
94	BASKET 2787ST	YR	60.00	60.00
94	CANDY W/COVER 7380AW	YR	60.00	60.00
94	PITCHER 1568CW	YR	85.00	85.00
94	VASE 1216EH	YR	95.00	95.00
94	VASE 1559CW	YR	95.00	95.00
95	BASKET 1131DX	YR	85.00	85.00
95	BASKET 1135JE	YR	75.00	75.00
95	CANDY W/COVER 2970RN	YR	65.00	65.00
95	PITCHER 1566FS	YR	125.00	125.00
95	VASE 1649KG	YR	95.00	95.00

* * **HISTORICAL COLLECTION**

YR	NAME	LIMIT	ISSUE	QUOTE
93	BASKET 3337RV	OP	29.50	29.50
93	BASKET 3834RV	OP	25.00	25.00
93	BASKET, DRAPERY 9435XV	OP	45.00	45.00
93	BOWL 3754XV	OP	45.00	45.00
93	CANDLESTICKS, SWAN 5172XV	OP	45.00	45.00
93	CANDY W/COVER 3784RV	OP	37.50	37.50
93	CRUET W/STOPPER 3863RV	OP	47.50	47.50
93	EPERGNE 4 PC. 3701RV	OP	99.00	99.00
93	EPERGNE, MINI HOBNAIL 3801XV	OP	49.50	49.50
93	FENTON LOGO 9799RV	OP	20.00	20.00
93	LAMP 3313RV	OP	250.00	250.00
93	LAMP, POPPY GONE W/THE WING 9101XV	OP	225.00	225.00
93	PITCHER 3764RV	OP	59.00	59.00
93	PUNCH SET 14 PC. 3712RV	OP	275.00	275.00
93	ROSE BOWL, DRAPERY 8454XV	OP	25.00	25.00
93	SWAN 5127XV	OP	15.00	15.00
93	TUMBLER 3949RV	OP	12.50	12.50
93	VASE 3356RV	OP	27.50	27.50
93	VASE 3854RV	OP	17.50	17.50
93	WATER SET 5 PC. 3908RV	OP	109.00	109.00
94	BASKET 5551SS	OP	39.50	39.50
94	BASKET 5555SS	OP	29.50	29.50
94	BOW W/COVER-LION 2799SS	OP	35.00	35.00
94	BOWL 2773SS	OP	37.50	37.50

YR	NAME	LIMIT	ISSUE	QUOTE
94	BOWL 5552SS	OP	45.00	45.00
94	CANDLESTICKS 5526SS	OP	45.00	45.00
94	CANDY COVER 4381ST	OP	55.00	55.00
94	COMPORT 5554SS	OP	29.50	29.50
94	EPERGNE 2 PC. 4802SS	OP	65.00	65.00
94	EPERGNE SET 5 PC. 7601SS	OP	175.00	175.00
94	FENTON LOGO 9799SS	OP	25.00	25.00
94	GOBLET 5561SS	OP	22.50	22.50
94	JUG 5562SS	OP	60.00	60.00
94	ROSE BOWL 2759SS	OP	25.00	25.00
94	ROSE BOWL 2759ST	OP	29.50	29.50
94	SPARROW 5259ST	OP	29.50	29.50
94	URN W/COVER 4602SS	OP	65.00	65.00
94	VASE HANDERCHIEF 5559ST	OP	39.50	39.50
94	VASE HANDKERCHIEF 5559SS	OP	29.50	29.50
94	VASE, JACK IN THE PULPIT 5553SS	OP	29.50	29.50
94	WATER SET 5 PC. 5560SS	OP	150.00	150.00
95	BASKET 1142JE	OP	37.50	37.50
95	CANDLESTICKS 2911KS	OP	49.50	49.50
95	CANDY BOX W/COVER 9488KA	OP	49.50	49.50
95	CENTERPIECE 4 PC. 2990KA	OP	95.00	95.00
95	COMPORT 1134KA	OP	32.50	32.50
95	EPERGNE 5 PC. 7601KA	OP	185.00	185.00
95	FENTON LOGO 9499KA	OP	25.00	25.00
95	TOP HAT 1137JE	OP	49.50	49.50
95	TUMBLER 9049KA	OP	19.50	19.50
95	VASE 1136JE	OP	49.50	49.50
95	VASE 2767JE	OP	32.50	32.50
95	VASE W/COLBALT BASE 1141JE	OP	59.50	59.50
95	WATER SET 5 PC. 9001KA	OP	135.00	135.00
94	BASKET 2787ST	OP	60.00	60.00
95	BASKET 1135JE	OP	75.00	75.00
* *			**MARY GREGORY**	
94	BASKET 8637RY	YR	59.00	59.00
95	BASKET 8637RG	YR	65.00	65.00
95	EGG 5145RG	YR	37.50	37.50
* *			**MOUTHBLOWN EGGS**	
93	EGG 5031WE	YR	69.00	69.00
93	EGG 5031WJ	YR	69.00	69.00
94	EGG 5031FU	YR	75.00	75.00
94	EGG 5031FV	YR	75.00	75.00
95	EGG 5031YW	YR	75.00	75.00
95	EGG 5031YX	YR	75.00	75.00
* *			**VALENTINE'S DAY**	
93	BASKET 2732CR	YR	59.00	59.00
93	TRINKET BOX 2740CR	YR	79.00	79.00
93	VASE 2749CR	YR	45.00	45.00
94	BASKET 2736CR	YR	65.00	65.00
94	PERFUME W/STOPPER 2760CR	YR	75.00	75.00
94	VASE 2755CR	YR	47.50	47.50
95	BASKET 2745CR	YR	69.00	69.00
95	PITCHER 2774CR	YR	69.00	69.00

FLAMBRO
*

			ANNUAL EMMETT KELLY JR. NUTCRACKER	
90	1990 NUTCRACKER	YR	50.00	50.00
*			**CIRCUS WORLD MUSEUM CLOWNS**	
85	FELIX ADLER (GROTESQUE)	9500	80.00	80.00-110.00
85	PAUL JEROME (HOBO)	9500	80.00	80.00-150.00
85	PAUL JUNG (NEAT)	9500	80.00	110.00-120.00
87	ABE GOLDSTEIN, KEYSTONE KOP	7500	90.00	90.00
87	FELIX ADLER WITH BALLOON	7500	90.00	90.00
87	PAUL JEROME WITH DOG	7500	90.00	90.00
87	PAUL JUNG, SITTING	7500	90.00	90.00

C. PRACHT — **DADDY LOVES YOU**

YR	NAME	LIMIT	ISSUE	QUOTE
91	C'MON DADDY!	2500	100.00	100.00
91	MAKE YOU...GIGGLE!	2500	100.00	100.00
91	SOO...YOU LIKE IT?	2500	100.00	100.00
91	YOU'RE SOOO...SWEET	2500	100.00	100.00
			EKJ JAPANESE FIGURINE	
93	THE VIGILANTE	OP	75.00	75.00
*			**EKJ MEMBERS ONLY FIGURINE**	
90	MERRY-GO-ROUND	CL	125.00	125.00
91	10 YEARS OF COLLECTING	*	100.00	100.00
93	RINGMASTER	CL	125.00	125.00
94	BIRTHDAY MAIL	CL	100.00	125.00
95	SALUTE TO OUT VETS	YR	75.00	75.00

YR	NAME	LIMIT	ISSUE	QUOTE
*		**EMMETT KELLY JR. A DAY AT THE FAIR**		
90	75 CENTS PLEASE	*	65.00	65.00
90	LOOK AT YOU	RT	65.00	65.00
90	RIDE THE WILD MOUSE	*	65.00	65.00
90	STEP RIGHT UP	*	65.00	65.00
90	THANKS EMMETT	*	65.00	65.00
90	THE STILT MAN	RT	65.00	65.00
90	THREE FOR A DIME	*	65.00	65.00
90	YOU CAN DO IT, EMMETT	RT	65.00	65.00
90	YOU GO FIRST, EMMETT	RT	65.00	65.00
91	COIN TOSS	*	65.00	65.00
91	POPCORN!	*	65.00	65.00
91	THE TROUBLE WITH HOT DOGS	*	65.00	65.00
*		**EMMETT KELLY JR. FIGURINES**		
81	LOOKING OUT TO SEE	12,000	75.00	1170.00-2275.00
81	SWEEPING UP	12,000	75.00	585.00-780.00
82	THE THINKER	15,000	60.00	700.00-975.00
82	WET PAINT	15,000	80.00	455.00-806.00
82	WHY ME?	15,000	65.00	350.00-462.00
83	BALLOONS FOR SALE	10,000	75.00	480.00-570.00
83	HOLE IN THE SOLE	10,000	75.00	200.00-384.00
83	SPIRIT OF CHRISTMAS I	3500	125.00	1475.00-2080.00
83	THE BALANCING ACT	10,000	75.00	600.00-845.00
83	WISHFUL THNKING	10,000	65.00	462.00
84	BIG BUSINESS	9500	110.00	350.00-455.00
84	EATING CABBAGE	12,000	75.00	375.00-488.00
84	PIANO PLAYER	9500	160.00	455.00-553.00
84	SPIRIT OF CHRISTMAS II	3500	270.00	260.00-390.00
85	EMMETT'S FAN	12,000	80.00	585.00
85	IN THE SPOTLIGHT	12,000	103.00	125.00-325.00
85	MAN'S BEST FRIEND	9500	98.00	350.00-481.00
85	NO STRINGS ATTACHED	9500	98.00	100.00-163.00
85	SPIRIT OF CHRISTMAS III	3500	220.00	340.00-520.00
86	BEDTIME	12,000	98.00	90.00-137.00
86	COTTON CANDY	12,000	98.00	180.00-260.00
86	FAIR GAME	2500	450.00	1500.00-1900.00
86	MAKING NEW FRIENDS	9500	140.00	250.00-325.00
86	SPIRIT OF CHRISTMAS IV	3500	150.00	400.00
86	THE ENTERTAINERS	12,000	120.00	120.00-135.00
87	MY FAVORITE THINGS	9500	109.00	315.00
87	ON THE ROAD AGAIN	9500	109.00	135.00
87	OVER A BARREL	9500	130.00	150.00
87	SATURDAY NIGHT	7500	153.00	265.00-620.00
87	SPIRIT OF CHRISTMAS V	2400	170.00	585.00-700.00
87	TOOTHACHE	12000	98.00	120.00
88	AMEN	12,000	120.00	140.00
88	DINING OUT	12,000	120.00	140.00
88	SPIRIT OF CHRISTMAS VI	2400	194.00	520.00
88	WHEELER DEALER	7500	160.00	210.00
89	65TH BIRTHDAY COMMEMORATIVE	1989	275.00	2340.00
89	HURDY-GURDY MAN	9500	150.00	175.00
89	MAKING UP	7500	200.00	275.00
89	NO LOITERING	7500	200.00	260.00-300.00
90	BALLOONS FOR SALE II	7500	250.00	250.00
90	CONVENTION BOUND	7500	225.00	230.00
90	MISFORTUNE?	3500	400.00	455.00
90	SPIRIT OF CHRISTMAS VII	3500	275.00	350.00
90	WATCH THE BIRDIE	9500	200.00	210.00
91	ARTIST AT WORK	7500	295.00	295.00
91	FINISHING TOUCH	7500	245.00	245.00
91	FOLLOW THE LEADER	7500	200.00	200.00
91	SPIRIT OF CHRISTMAS VIII	3500	250.00	250.00
92	NO USE CRYING	7500	200.00	200.00
92	PEANUT BUTTER?	7500	200.00	200.00
92	READY-SET-GO	7500	200.00	200.00
95	35 YEARS OF CLOWNING	5000	240.00	240.00
95	ALL-STAR CIRCUS 20TH ANNIVERSARY	5000	240.00	240.00
95	SPIRIT OF CHRISTMAS XII	3500	200.00	200.00
M. WU		**EMMETT KELLY JR. LITTLE EMMETTS**		
94	AGE 1	OP	9.00	9.00
94	AGE 10	OP	25.00	25.00
94	AGE 2	OP	9.50	9.50
94	AGE 3	OP	12.00	12.00
94	AGE 4	OP	12.00	12.00
94	AGE 5	OP	15.00	15.00
94	AGE 6	OP	15.00	15.00

YR	NAME	LIMIT	ISSUE	QUOTE
94	AGE 7	OP	17.00	15.00
94	AGE 8	OP	21.00	21.00
94	AGE 9	OP	22.00	22.00
94	LITTLE ARTIST PICTURE FRAME	OP	22.00	22.00
94	LITTLE EMMETT COUNTING LESSON-MUSICAL	OP	30.00	30.00
94	LITTLE EMMETT COUNTRY ROAD	OP	35.00	35.00
94	LITTLE EMMETT FISHING	OP	35.00	35.00
94	LITTLE EMMETT RAINDROPS	OP	35.00	35.00
94	LITTLE EMMETT SHADOW SHOW	OP	40.00	40.00
94	LITTLE EMMETT SOMEDAY	OP	50.00	50.00
94	LITTLE EMMETT WITH BLACKBOARD	OP	30.00	30.00
94	LITTLE EMMETT YOU'VE GOT A FRIEND	OP	33.00	33.00
94	PLAYFUL BOOKENDS	OP	40.00	40.00
95	BIRTHDAY HAUL	OP	30.00	30.00
95	DANCE LESSIONS-MUSICAL	OP	50.00	50.00
95	LITTLE EMMETT NOEL, NOEL	OP	40.00	40.00
*				
	EMMETT KELLY JR. METAL SCULPTURES			
91	BALANCING ACT, TOO	5000	125.00	125.00
91	CAROUSEL RIDER	5000	125.00	125.00
91	EMMETT'S POOCHES	5000	125.00	125.00
91	THE MAGICIAN	5000	125.00	125.00
*				
	EMMETT KELLY JR. MINIATURES			
86	BALANCING ACT		25.00	40.00-50.00
86	BALLOONS FOR SALE	*	25.00	35.00-45.00
86	HOLE IN THE SOLE	RT	25.00	40.00-55.00
86	LOOKING OUT TO SEE	RT	25.00	75.00-125.00
86	SWEEPING UP	RT	25.00	75.00-125.00
86	THE THINKER	*	25.00	35.00-50.00
86	WET PAINT	*	25.00	35.00-45.00
86	WHY ME?	RT	25.00	40.00-55.00
86	WISHFUL THINKING	RT	25.00	50.00-70.00
87	EATING CABBAGE	*	30.00	35.00-50.00
87	EMMETT'S FAN	*	30.00	40.00-50.00
87	SPIRIT OF CHRISTMAS I	*	40.00	55.00-125.00
88	BIG BUSINESS	*	35.00	38.50
89	COTTON CANDY	*	30.00	30.00
89	MAN'S BEST FRIEND?	*	35.00	35.00
90	MY FAVORITE THINGS	*	45.00	45.00
90	SATURDAY NIGHT	*	50.00	50.00
90	SPIRIT OF CHRISTMAS III	*	50.00	50.00
91	IN THE SPOTLIGHT	*	35.00	35.00
91	NO STRINGS ATTACHED	*	35.00	35.00
95	BEDTIME	OP	35.00	35.00
95	DINING OUT	OP	35.00	35.00
95	HURDY GURDY MAN	OP	40.00	40.00
95	NO LOITTERING	OP	50.00	50.00
95	THE ENTERTAINERS	OP	45.00	45.00
	EMMETT KELLY JR. PROFESSIONALS			
93	AFTER THE PARADE	75000	190.00	190.00
93	KITTENS FOR SALE	75000	190.00	190.00
93	ON MANEUVERS	OP	50.00	50.00
93	PILOT	OP	50.00	50.00
93	REALTOR	OP	50.00	50.00
93	SPIRIT OF CHRISTMAS 1X	35000	200.00	200.00
93	SPIRIT OF CHRISTMAS X	35000	200.00	200.00
93	VETERINARIAN	OP	50.00	50.00
93	WORLD TRAVELER	75000	190.00	190.00
94	FOREST FRIENDS	75000	190.00	190.00
94	LET HIM EAT CAKE	RT	300.00	300-500
94	LION TAMER	75000	190.00	190.00
94	SPIRIT OF CHRISTMAS V	NUMBERED	40.00	40.00
94	SPIRIT OF CHRISTMAS X1	35000	200.00	200.00
95	COACH	OP	55.00	55.00
95	DOCTOR	OP	55.00	55.00
95	FIREMAN	OP	55.00	55.00
95	GOLFER	OP	55.00	55.00
95	LAWYER	OP	55.00	55.00
95	POLICE MAN	OP	55.00	55.00
	EMMETT KELLY JR. REAL RAGS COLLECTION			
93	BIG BUSINESS II	OP	140.00	140.00
93	CHECKING HIS LIST	OP	100.00	100.00
93	LOOKING OUT TO SEE II	OP	100.00	100.00
93	SWEEPING UP II	OP	100.00	100.00
93	THINKER	OP	120.00	120.00
94	A GOOD LIKENESS	3000	120.00	120.00
94	EATING CABBAGE TOO	3000	100.00	100.00

YR	NAME	LIMIT	ISSUE	QUOTE
94	ONE IN TWO	3000	100.00	100.00
94	RUDOLPH HAS A RED NOSE	3000	135.00	135.00
95	BALLOONS FOR SALE 2	3000	120.00	120.00
95	I'VE GOT RHYTHM	3000	140.00	140.00
95	NO STRINGS ATTACHED 2	3000	120.00	120.00
95	WATCH OUT BELOW	3000	120.00	120.00
J. BERG VICTOR			**PLEASANTVILLE 1893**	
90	1ST CHURCH OF PLEASANTVILLE	OP	35.00	35.00
90	DEPARTMENT STORE	OP	25.00	25.00
90	MASON'S HOTEL AND SALOON	OP	35.00	35.00
90	PLEASANTVILLE LIBRARY	OP	32.00	32.00
90	REVEREND LITTLEFIELD'S HOUSE	OP	34.00	34.00
90	SWEET SHOPPE & BAKERY	OP	40.00	40.00
90	THE BAND STAND	OP	12.00	12.00
90	THE GERBER HOUSE	OP	30.00	30.00
90	TOY STORE	OP	30.00	30.00
91	COURT HOUSE	OP	36.00	36.00
91	FIRE HOUSE	OP	40.00	40.00
91	METHODIST CHURCH	OP	40.00	40.00
91	SCHOOL HOUSE	OP	36.00	36.00
92	APOTHECARY/ICE CREAM SHOP	OP	*	*
92	BANK/REAL ESTATE OFFICE	OP	*	*
92	BLACKSMITH/LIVERY	OP	*	*
92	COVERED BRIDGE	OP	*	*
92	MISS FOUNTAINS	OP	*	*
92	RAILROAD STATION	OP	*	*
92	TUBBS, JR. HOUSE	OP	*	*
93	BALCOMB'S FARM	OP	40.00	40.00
93	BALCOMB'S FARMHOUSE	OP	40.00	40.00
93	BLACKSMITH SHOP	OP	40.00	40.00
93	LIVERY STABLE AND RESIDENCE	OP	40.00	40.00
94	GAZEBO/BANDSTAND	OP	25.00	25.00
94	SACRED HEART CATHOLIC CHURCH	OP	40.00	40.00
94	SACRED HEART RECTORY	OP	40.00	40.00
R. MUSGRAVE			**POCKET DRAGON**	
93	A BIG HUG	RT	35.00	30.00
93	BATH TIME	OP	90.00	90.00
93	FUZZY EARS	OP	16.50	16.50
93	I ATE THE WHOLE THING	OP	32.50	32.50
93	LET'S MAKE COOKIES	OP	90.00	90.00
93	LITTLE BIT	OP	16.50	16.50
93	LITTLE JEWEL-BROOCH	OP	19.50	19.50
93	OH GOODY!	OP	16.50	16.50
93	POCKET RIDER-BROOCH	OP	19.50	19.50
93	READING THE GOOD PARTS	OP	70.00	70.00
93	THE BOOK END	OP	90.00	90.00
93	TREASURE	OP	90.00	90.00
93	WE'RE VERY BRAVE	OP	37.50	37.50
93	YOU CAN'T MAKE ME	OP	15.00	15.00
94	A BOOK MY SIZE	OP	30.00	30.00
94	A LITTLE SECURITY	OP	20.00	20.00
94	BUTTERFLY KISSES	OP	29.50	29.50
94	CANDY CANE	OP	55.00	55.00
94	COFFEE PLEASE	OP	24.00	24.00
94	DANCE PARTNER	OP	23.00	23.00
94	GARGOYLES JUST WANT TO HAVE FUN	OP	30.00	30.00
94	IN TROUBLE AGAIN	OP	35.00	35.00
94	IT'S DARK OUT THERE	OP	45.00	45.00
94	IT'S MAGIC	OP	31.00	31.50
94	PLAYING DRESS UP	OP	30.00	30.00
94	RAIDING THE COOKIE JAR	3500	200.00	200.00
94	SNUGGLES	OP	35.00	35.00
95	BUT I'M TOO LITTLE!	OP	*	N/A
95	CLASSICAL DRAGON	OP	*	N/A
95	ELEMENTARY MY DEAR	OP	*	N/A
95	HEDGEHOG'S JOKE	OP	*	N/A
95	IT'S A PRESENT	OP	*	N/A
95	SEES ALL, KNOWS ALL	OP	*	N/A
95	TELLING SECRETS	OP	*	N/A
95	TUMBLY	OP	*	N/A
95	WATSON	OP	*	N/A
93	SANTA'S STOWAWAY	10000	30.00	30.00
94	70 TH BIRTHDAY COMMEMORATIVE	5000	30.00	30.00
R. MUSGRAVE			**POCKET DRAGON APPEARANCE FIGURINE**	
94	PACKED AND READY	OP	47.00	47.00

YR NAME	LIMIT	ISSUE	QUOTE
R. MUSGRAVE	**POCKET DRAGON CHRISTMAS EDITION**		
95 CHASING SNOWFLAKES	YR	35.00	35.00
R. MUSGRAVE	**POCKET DRAGON COLLECTORS CLUB GIFT**		
93 BITSY	RT	*	15.00
93 WANT A BITE?	RT	50.00	50.00
94 BLUE RIBBON DRAGON	CL	*	N/A
94 FRIENDSHIP PIN	RT	*	N/A
R. MUSGRAVE	**POCKET DRAGON MEMBERS ONLY**		
93 PEN PALS	RT	90.00	135.00
94 THE BEST SEAT IN THE HOUSE	5/95	75.00	75.00
R. MUSGRAVE	**POCKET DRAGONS CHRISTMAS EDITION**		
93 CHRISTMAS ANGEL	RT	45.00	65.00
94 DEAR SANTA	RT	50.00	50.00
C. BEYLON		**RAGGEDY ANN & ANDY**	
88 70 YEARS YOUNG	2500	95.00	110.00-130.00
88 GIDDY UP	3500	95.00	110.00-130.00
88 OOPS!	3500	80.00	95.00-110.00
88 WET PAINT	3500	70.00	85.00-100.00

FRANKLIN MINT

N. ROCKWELL		JOYS OF CHILDHOOD	
76 COASTING ALONG	3700	120.00	175.00
76 DRESSING UP	3700	120.00	175.00
76 HOPSCOTCH	3700	120.00	175.00
76 RIDE 'EM COWBOY	3700	120.00	175.00
76 THE FISHING HOLE	3700	120.00	175.00
76 THE MARBLE CHAMP	3700	120.00	175.00
76 THE NURSE	3700	120.00	175.00
76 THE STILT WALKER	3700	120.00	175.00
76 TIME OUT	3700	120.00	175.00
76 TRICK OR TREAT	3700	120.00	175.00

GANZ

C. THAMMAVONGSA	CHEESERVILLE PICNIC COLLECTION MINI		
91 BASKET OF APPLES	OP	2.25	2.25
91 BASKET OF PEACHES	OP	2.00	2.00
91 BLUEBERRY CAKE	RT	2.50	2.50
91 BREAD BASKET	OP	2.50	2.50
91 CANDY'	OP	2.00	2.00
91 CHERRY PIE	RT	2.00	2.00
91 CHOCOLATE CAKE	OP	2.50	2.50
91 CHOCOLATE CHEESECAKE	OP	2.00	2.00
91 DOUGHNUT BASKET	OP	2.50	2.50
91 EGG TART	OP	1.00	1.00
91 FOOD BKT. W/BLUE CLOTH	RT	6.50	6.50
91 FOOD BKT. W/GREEN CLOTH	OP	7.50	7.50
91 FOOD BKT. W/PINK CLOTH	RT	6.00	6.00
91 FOOD BKT. W/PURPLE CLOTH	OP	6.00	6.00
91 FOOD TROLLEY	RT	12.00	12.00
91 HAZELNUT ROLL	RT	2.00	2.00
91 HONEY JAR	RT	2.00	2.00
91 HOT DOG	OP	2.25	2.25
91 ICE CREAM GROUP	OP	2.00	2.00
91 LEMON CAKE	RT	2.00	2.00
91 NAPKIN IN CAN	RT	2.00	2.00
91 SET OF FOUR BOTTLES	RT	10.00	10.00
91 STRAWBERRY CAKE	OP	2.00	2.00
91 SUNDAE	OP	2.00	2.00
91 WINE GLASS	OP	1.25	1.25
94 MAYFLOWER MEADOW BASE	OP	50.00	50.00
C. THAMMAVONGSA	**CHEESERVILLE PICNIC COLLECTION MUSICALS**		
91 BLOSSOM & HICKORY JEWELRY BX	RT	65.00	65.00
91 FLORAL TRINKET BOX	OP	32.00	32.00
91 MAMA & SWEET CICELY WATERGLOBE	RT	55.00	55.00
91 MEADLEY MEADOWMOUSE WATERGLOBE	OP	47.00	47.00
91 MEDLEY MEADOWMOUSE COOKIE JAR	RT	75.00	75.00
91 PICNIC BASE	OP	60.00	60.00
91 SUNFLOWER BASE	RT	65.00	65.00
91 SWEET CICELY DOLL BASKET	OP	85.00	85.00
91 TRINKET BOX	OP	30.00	30.00
91 VIOLET WOODSWORTH COOKIE JAR	RT	75.00	75.00
92 APRIL SHOWERS BRING MAY FLWRS	OP	7.50	7.50
92 DECORATED W/LOVE	OP	7.50	7.50
92 FOR SOMEBUNNY SPECIAL	OP	7.50	7.50
93 "SECRET TREASURES" TRINKET BX	OP	35.00	35.00
93 WISHING WELL	OP	50.00	50.00
94 BANDSTAND BASE, THE	OP	48.50	48.50

YR	NAME	LIMIT	ISSUE	QUOTE
C. THAMMAVONGSA		**LITTLE CHEESERS/CHRISTMAS COLLECTION**		
91	ABNER APPLETON RINGING BELL	RT	14.00	14.00
91	AUNTIE BLOSSOM W/ORNAMENTS	OP	14.00	14.00
91	CHEESER SNOWMAN	OP	7.50	7.50
91	CHRISTMAS TREE	OP	9.00	9.00
91	COUSIN WOODY PLAYING FLUTE	OP	14.00	14.00
91	FROWZY ROQUEFORT III SKATING	RT	14.00	14.00
91	GRANDMAMA & LITTLE TRUFFLE	RT	19.00	19.00
91	GRANDPAPA & SWEET CICELY	OP	19.00	19.00
91	GRANDPAPA BLOWING HORN	OP	14.00	14.00
91	GREAT AUNT ROSE W/TRAY	OP	14.00	14.00
91	HARLEY & HARRIET DANCING	RT	19.00	19.00
91	HICKORY PLAYING CELLO	OP	14.00	14.00
91	JENNY ON SLEIGH	OP	16.00	16.00
91	JEREMY W/TEDDY BEAR	OP	12.00	12.00
91	LAMP POST	OP	8.50	8.50
91	LITTLE TRUFFLE W/STOCKING	OP	8.00	8.00
91	MAMA POURING TEA	RT	14.00	14.00
91	MARIGOLD & OSCAR STEALING A X-M KISS	OP	19.00	19.00
91	MEDLEY PLAYING DRUM	OP	8.00	8.00
91	MYRTLE MEADOWMOUSE W/BK	RT	14.00	14.00
91	OUTDOOR SCENE BASE	RT	35.00	35.00
91	PARLOR SCENE BASE	OP	37.50	37.50
91	SANTA CHEESER	OP	13.00	13.00
91	VIOLET W/SNOWBALL	OP	8.00	8.00
93	ALL I WANT FOR CHRISTMAS	OP	18.00	18.00
93	CANDLEHOLDER-SANTA CHEESER	OP	19.00	19.00
93	CANDY CANE	OP	2.00	2.00
93	CHRISTMAS GIFT	OP	3.00	3.00
93	CHRISTMAS GREETINGS	OP	16.50	16.50
93	CHRISTMAS STOCKING	OP	3.00	3.00
93	GENGERBREAD HOUSE	OP	3.00	3.00
93	ICE POND BASE	OP	5.50	5.50
93	SLEIGH RIDE	OP	11.00	11.00
93	TOY SOLDIER	OP	3.00	3.00
93	TOY TRAIN	OP	3.00	3.00
94	CHRISTMAS COLLECTION BASE	OP	50.00	50.00
94	SANTA'S SLEIGH	10,000	22.00	22.00
C. THAMMAVONGSA		**LITTLE CHEESERS/MUSICALS**		
92	J. BUTTERFIELD CHRISTMAS WATERGLOBE	RT	55.00	55.00
92	LITTLE TRUFFLE CHRISTMAS WATERGLOBE	OP	45.00	45.00
92	SANTA CHEESER ROLY-POLY	RT	55.00	55.00
93	I'LL BE HOME FOR X'MAS	OP	30.00	30.00
93	WE WISH YOU A MERRY CHRISTMAS	OP	25.00	25.00
C. THAMMAVONGSA		**SPRINGTIME/CHEESERVILLE COLLECTION**		
92	A BASKET FULL OF JOY	OP	16.00	16.00
92	A WHEELBARROW OF SUNSHINE	OP	17.00	17.00
92	HIPPITY-HOP. IT'S EASTERTIME!	OP	16.00	16.00
92	SPRINGTIME DELIGHTS	OP	12.00	12.00
93	BALLERINA SWEETHEART	OP	10.00	10.00
93	BLOSSOM HAS A LITTLE LAMB	OP	16.50	16.50
93	FIRST KISS	OP	24.00	24.00
93	FOR MY SWEETHEART	OP	22.00	22.00
93	FRIENDS FOREVER	OP	22.00	22.00
93	GENTLY DOWN THE STREAM	10,000	27.00	27.00
93	GIFT FROM HEAVEN	OP	10.00	10.00
93	HIGS & KISSES	OP	11.00	11.00
93	I LOVE YOU	OP	22.00	22.00
93	PLAYING CUPID	OP	10.00	10.00
93	SUGAR & SPICE	OP	24.00	24.00
93	SUNDAY STROLL	OP	22.00	22.00
94	BIRTHDAY PARTY	OP	22.00	22.00
94	GET WELL	OP	22.00	22.00
94	HIP HIP HOORAY	OP	22.00	22.00
C. THAMMAVONGSA		**SPRINGTIME/CHEESERVILLE MUSICAL**		
92	TULIPS & RIBBONS TRINKET BX	RT	28.00	28.00
C. THAMMAVONGSA		**THE CHRISTMAS COLLECTION**		
94	CHRISTMAS TRIMMINGS	10,000	24.00	24.00
94	JOY TO THE WORLD	OP	10.00	10.00
94	LET IT SNOW	OP	12.00	12.00
94	MISTLETOE MAGIC	OP	14.00	14.00
94	SANTA PIG	OP	11.00	11.00
94	YULETIDE CAROLS	OP	19.00	19.00
C. THAMMAVONGSA		**THE COWTOWN COLLECTION**		
93	BUFFALO BULL CODY	OP	15.00	15.00
93	BULL MASTERSON	OP	15.00	15.00

YR	NAME	LIMIT	ISSUE	QUOTE
93	BULL ROGERS	OP	17.00	17.00
93	BULL RUTH	RT	13.00	13.00
93	BUTTERMILK & BUTTERCUP	OP	16.00	16.00
93	COWLAMITY JANE	OP	15.00	15.00
93	DAISY MOO	OP	11.00	11.00
93	GLORIA BOVINE & RUDOLPH BULLENTINO	OP	20.00	20.00
93	JETHRO BOVINE	RT	15.00	15.00
93	LI'L ORPHAN ANGUS	OP	11.00	11.00
93	MOO WEST	OP	15.00	15.00
93	OLD MOODONALD	OP	13.50	13.50
94	AMOOLIA STEERHEART	OP	25.00	25.00
94	COWSEY JONES & THE CANNONBULL EXPRESS	OP	26.50	26.50
94	GERONIMOO	OP	17.00	17.00
94	HEIFERELLA	OP	16.50	16.50
94	KING COWMOOAMOOA	OP	16.50	16.50
94	MA & PA CATTLE	OP	23.50	23.50
94	POCOWHANTIS	OP	16.50	16.50
94	SET OF THREE CACTI	OP	17.00	17.00
94	TCHAICOWSKY	OP	19.00	19.00
94	TEXAS LONESTEER	10,000	50.00	50.00
C. THAMMAVONGSA		**THE LITTLE HOPPERS COLLECTION**		
94	BUBBLE BATH	OP	7.50	7.50
94	LET'S PLAY BALL	OP	7.00	7.00
94	SOMEBUNNY LOVES YOU	OP	7.50	7.50
94	SWEET NOTHINGS	OP	15.00	15.00
94	TENDER LOVING CARE	OP	10.00	10.00
94	TRICYCLE BUILT FOR TWO	OP	16.00	16.00
C. THAMMAVONGSA		**THE PIGSVILLE COLLECTION**		
93	BAKIN' AT THE BEACH	OP	11.00	11.00
93	ICE CREAM ANYONE?	RT	9.00	9.00
93	ME & MY ICE CREAM	RT	17.00	17.00
93	MOTHER LOVE	OP	13.00	13.00
93	NAP TIME	OP	11.00	11.00
93	P.O.P DISPLAY SIGN	OP	8.00	8.00
93	PIG AT THE BEACH	OP	9.00	9.00
93	PRIMA BALLERINA	RT	11.00	11.00
93	SOAP SUDS	OP	12.00	12.00
93	SQUEAKY CLEAN	OP	11.00	11.00
93	TIPSY	OP	9.00	9.00
93	TRUE LOVE	OP	12.00	12.00
93	WEE LITTLE PIGGY	OP	8.00	8.00
94	BEDTIME	OP	9.50	9.50
94	BIRTHDAY SURPRISE	OP	9.50	9.50
94	OLE FISHING HOLD	OP	16.00	16.00
94	PLAY BALL	OP	11.50	11.50
94	PRETTY PIGLET	OP	8.00	8.00
94	SANDCASTLE	OP	12.00	12.00
94	SNACKTIME	OP	11.50	11.50
94	SPECIAL TEST	OP	11.50	11.50
94	STORYTIME	OP	13.00	13.00
94	WEDDED BLISS	OP	16.00	16.00
C. THAMMAVONGSA		**THE PIGSVILLE COLLECTION ACCESSORIES**		
94	BARN	OP	35.00	35.00
94	SILO	OP	15.00	15.00
C. THAMMAVONGSA		**THE VALENTINE COLLECTION**		
94	CHAMPAGNE & ROSES	OP	14.00	14.00
94	I LOVE YOU	OP	9.50	9.50
94	I'M ALL YOURS	OP	11.50	11.50
94	LOVESTRUCK	OP	10.00	10.00
94	SWEETHEART PIG	OP	8.00	8.00
94	TOGETHER FOREVER	OP	15.00	15.00
C. THAMMAVONGSA		**THE WEDDING COLLECTION**		
92	BLOSSOM THISTLEDOWN BRIDE	OP	16.00	16.00
92	COUSIN WOODY & LI'L TRUFFLE	OP	20.00	20.00
92	FROWZY ROQUEFORT III W/GRAMOPHONE	OP	20.00	20.00
92	GRANDMAMA & GRANDPAPA THISTLEDOWN	RT	20.00	20.00
92	GREAT AUNT ROSE BESIDE TABLE	OP	20.00	20.00
92	HARLEY & HARRIET HARVESTMOUSE	OP	20.00	20.00
92	HICKORY HARVESTMOUSE GROOM	OP	16.00	16.00
92	J. BUTTERFIELD/SWEET CICELY BRIDESMAID	OP	20.00	20.00
92	LITTLE TRUFFLE RINGBEARER	OP	10.00	10.00
92	MAMA & PAPA WOODSWORTH DANCING	OP	20.00	20.00
92	MARIGOLD THISTLEDOWN & OSCAR ROBBINS	OP	20.00	20.00
92	MYRTLE MEADOWMOUSE W/MEDLEY	RT	20.00	20.00
92	PASTOR SMALLWOOD	OP	16.00	16.00
92	WEDDING PROCESSION	OP	40.00	40.00

YR	NAME	LIMIT	ISSUE	QUOTE
93	BIG DAY, THE	OP	20.00	20.00
C. THAMMAVONGSA		**THE WEDDING COLLECTION ACCESSORIES**		
93	BANQUET TABLE	OP	14.00	14.00
93	GAZEBO BASE	OP	42.00	42.00
C. THAMMAVONGSA		**THE WEDDING COLLECTION MINI**		
92	BIBLE TRINKET BOX	OP	16.50	16.50
92	BIG CHOCOLATE CAKE	RT	4.50	4.50
92	BRIDE CANDLEHOLDER	OP	20.00	20.00
92	CAKE TRINKET BOX	OP	14.00	14.00
92	CANDLES	OP	3.00	3.00
92	CHERRY JELLO	OP	3.00	3.00
92	CHOCOLATE PASTRY	RT	2.00	2.00
92	CHOCOLATE PUDDING	OP	2.50	2.50
92	FLOUR BAG	RT	2.00	2.00
92	FLOWER VASE	RT	3.00	3.00
92	FRUIT SALAD	OP	3.00	3.00
92	GRASS BASE	RT	3.50	3.50
92	GROOM CANDLEHOLDER	OP	20.00	20.00
92	HONEY POT	OP	2.00	2.00
92	RING CAKE	OP	3.00	3.00
92	SALT CAN	RT	2.00	2.00
92	SOUFFLE	RT	2.50	2.50
92	SOUP POT	OP	3.00	3.00
92	TEA POT SET	RT	3.00	3.00
92	TEDDY MOUSE	RT	2.00	2.00
93	GOOSEBERRY CHAMPAGNE	OP	3.00	3.50
93	WEDDING CAKE	OP	4.50	4.50
C. THAMMAVONGSA		**THE WEDDING COLLECTION MUSICALS**		
92	BLOSSOM & HICKORY WEDDING WATERGLOBE	OP	55.00	55.00
92	WEDDING BASE	OP	32.00	32.00
92	WOODEN BASE FOR WEDDING PROCESSIONAL	OP	25.00	25.00
93	BLOSSOM & HICKORY MUSICAL	RT	50.00	50.00
93	WHITE MUSICAL WD. BASE/GAZABO EVERGREEN	OP	25.00	25.00

GARTLAN USA

	NAME	LIMIT	ISSUE	QUOTE
*	JOE MONTAN A/P H/S	250	500.00	750.00
*	JOE MONTANA (CLUB MINI)	*	75.00	135.00
*	PETE ROSE H/S	2000	125.00	1375.00
*	YOGI BERRA H/S A/P	250	350.00	375.00
*	'JOE DIMAGGIO AP H/S	325	695.00	2400.00
*	CARL YASTREZEMSKI H/S A/P	250	150.00	495.00
*	JOHNNY BENCH H/S A/P	250	*	550.00
*	KAREEM ABDUL-JABBAR A/P	100	200.00	450.00
*	KAREEM ABDUL-JABBAR H/S	1989	175.00	495.00
*	KAREEM ABDUL-JABBAR PURPLE UNIFORM H/S	33	275.00	5500.00
*	KAREEN ABDUL-JABBAR A/P	100	200.00	600.00
*	WAYNE GRETZKY (CLUB MINI)	*	75.00	295.00
*	WAYNE GRETZKY H/S	1851	250.00	1000.00
*	MAGIC JOHNSON H/S	250	175.00	3700.00
*	MAGIC JOHNSON PURPLE UNIFORM H/S	32	275.00	6900.00
*	MIKE SCHMIDT H/S	1987	150.00	975.00
*	MIKE SCHMIDT H/S	1987	150.00	950.00
*	MIKE SCHMIDT H/S A/P	20	275.00	1500.00
ROGER		**ALL-STAR GEMS MINIATURE FIGURINES**		
90	MIKE SCHMIDT	10,000	75.00	75.00
90	GEORGE BRETT	10,000	75.00	75.00
90	PETE ROSE	10,000	75.00	75.00
90	WHITEY FORD	10,000	75.00	75.00
90	YOGI BERRA	10,000	75.00	75.00
91	JOE MONTANA	10,000	79.00	79.00
92	HANK AARON	10,000	79.00	79.00
91	MONTE IRVIN	10,000	79.00	79.00
89	CARL YASTRZEMSKI	10,000	75.00	75.00
89	JOHNNY BENCH	10,000	75.00	75.00
89	STEVE CARLTON	10,000	75.00	75.00
89	TED WILLIAMS	10,000	75.00	75.00
90	DARYL STRAWBERRY	10,000	75.00	75.00
90	JOHN WOODEN	10,000	75.00	75.00
90	WAYNE GRETZKY	10,000	75.00	75.00
91	BOBBY HULL	10,000	75.00	75.00
91	BRETT HULL	10,000	75.00	75.00
90	LUIS APARICIO	10,000	75.00	75.00
91	KEN GRIFFEY, JR.	10,000	75.00	75.00
91	ROD CAREW	10,000	75.00	75.00
91	WARREN SPAHN	10,000	75.00	75.00
92	CARLTON FISK	10,000	79.00	79.00
92	ISIAH THOMAS	10,000	79.00	79.00

YR	NAME	LIMIT	ISSUE	QUOTE
J. MARTIN		**BASEBALL/FOOTBALL/HOCKEY SERIES**		
86	GEORGE BRETT BASEBALL ROUNDER	OP	9.95	16.00
86	GEORGE BRETT BASEBALL ROUNDER, SIGNED	2000	29.95	29.95
86	GEORGE BRETT CERAMIC BASEBALL	OP	19.95	19.95
86	GEORGE BRETT CERAMIC BASEBALL, SIGNED	2000	49.50	49.50
85	PETE ROSE CERAMIC BASEBALL	OP	9.95	16.00
85	PETE ROSE CERAMIC BASEBALL, SIGNED	4192	39.00	50.00-100.00
87	ROGER STAUBACH CERAMIC FOOTBALL	OP	9.95	16.00
87	ROGER STAUBACH CERAMIC FOOTBALL, SIGNED	1979	39.00	39.00
90	WAYNE GRETZKY CERAMIC HOCKEY	OP	18.00	18.00
91	JOE MONTANA CERAMIC FOOTBALL	OP	18.00	18.00
92	CARLTON FISH CERAMIC BASEBALL	OP	18.00	18.00
L. HEYDA		**KAREEM ABDUL-JABBAR SKY HOOK COLLECTION**		
89	KAREEM ABDUL-JABBAR, THE CAPTAIN, SIGNED	1989	175.00	49.00
ROGER		**MAGIC JOHNSON GOLD RIM COLLECTION**		
88	MAGIC JOHNSON COMMEMORATIVE	32	275.00	2800.00
88	MAGIC JOHNSON-MAGIC IN MOTION	1737	125.00	650.00
88	MAGIC JOHNSON-MAGIC IN MOTION, PROOF	250	175.00	3700.00
F. BARNUM		**MASTER'S MUSEUM COLLECTION**		
91	JOE MONTANA (SET)	500	*	*
91	KAREEM ABDUL-JABBAR	500	3000.00	3000.00
91	TED WILLIAMS (SET)	500	*	*
91	WAYNE GRETZKY (SET)	500	*	*
F. BARNUM		**MEMBERS ONLY FIGURINE**		
91	JOE MONTANA-ROAD UNIFORM	*	75.00	125.00
90	WAYNE GRETZKY-HOME UNIFORM	*	75.00	150.00-250.00
91	KAREEM ABDUL-JABBAR (MINI)	*	75.00	79.00
ROGER		**MIKE SCHMIDT 500TH HOME RUN EDITION**		
87	FIGURINE, SIGNED	1987	150.00	650.00-900.00
87	PLAQUE-ONLY PERFECT, SIGNED	500	150.00	175.00-500.00
V. BOVA		**NEGRO LEAGUE SERIES**		
91	BUCK LEONARD	1972	195.00	195.00
91	JAMES (COOL PAPA) BELL	1499	195.00	195.00
91	MATCHED-NUMBER SET #1-950	950	500.00	500.00
91	RAY DANDRIDGE	1987	195.00	195.00
B. FORBES		**PETE ROSE DIAMOND COLLECTION**		
88	FAREWELL CERAMIC BASEBALL CARD	OP	9.95	16.00
88	FAREWELL CERAMIC BASEBALL CARD, SIGNED	4258	39.00	50.00-75.00
H. REED		**PETE ROSE PLATINUM EDITION**		
85	PETE ROSE-FOR THE RECORD, SIGNED	4192	125.00	1375.00
J. MARTIN		**PLAQUES**		
86	GEORGE BRETT-ROYALTY IN MOTION, SIGNED	2000	85.00	195.00
86	REGGIE JACKSON-THE ROUNDTRIPPER, PROOF	SO	200.00	250.00-350.00
86	REGGIE JACKSON-THE ROUNDTRIPPER, SIGNED	500	150.00	175.00-300.00
87	ROGER STAUBACH, SIGNED	1979	85.00	195.00
85	PETE ROSE-DESIRE TO WIN, SIGNED	4192	75.00	75.00
J. MARTIN		**REGGIE JACKSON 500TH HOME RUN EDITION**		
86	CERAMIC BASEBALL CARD	OP	9.95	16.00
86	CERAMIC BASEBALL CARD, SIGNED	500	39.00	50.00-75.00
F. BARNUM		**SIGNED FIGURINES**		
89	YOGI BERRA	2000	225.00	200.00-250.00
90	GEORGE BRETT	2500	225.00	225.00
90	WHITEY FORD	2360	225.00	225.00
91	JOE MONTANA H/S	2250	325.00	425.00
92	HANK AARON	1982	225.00	225.00
91	AL BARLICK	1989	175.00	175.00
91	MONTE IRVIN	1973	225.00	225.00
89	CARL YASTRZEMSKI-YAZ	1989	150.00	300.00-400.00
89	JOE DIMAGGIO H/S	2214	275.00	1375.00
89	JOHN WOODEN-COACHING CLASSICS	1975	175.00	175.00
89	JOHNNY BENCH H/S	1989	150.00	375.00
89	STEVE CARLTON H/S	3290	175.00	235.00
89	TED WILLIAMS H/S	2654	295.00	575.00
89	WAYNE GRETZKY	1851	225.00	500.00-800.00
89	WAYNE GRETZKY, ARTIST PROOF H/S	300	695.00	1800.00
90	DARRYL STRAWBERRY	2500	225.00	225.00
90	JOE DIMAGGIO-PINSTRIPE YANKEE CLIPPER	325	695.00	2400.00
91	BOBBY HULL-THE GOLDEN JET	1983	225.00	225.00
91	BRETT HULL-THE GOLDEN BRETT	1986	225.00	225.00
91	HULL MATCHED FIGURINES	950	500.00	500.00
90	LUIS APARICIO	1974	225.00	225.00
91	KEN GRIFFEY, JR.	1989	225.00	225.00
91	ROD CAREW-HITTING SPLENDOR	1991	225.00	225.00
91	WARREN SPAHN	1973	225.00	225.00
92	CARLTON FISK	1972	225.00	225.00
92	ISIAH THOMAS	1990	225.00	225.00

YR	NAME	LIMIT	ISSUE	QUOTE

GLASS EYE

YR	NAME	LIMIT	ISSUE	QUOTE
93	AQUARIUM	1000	17.50	20.00
93	CHERRY BLOSSOM	1000	17.50	20.00
94	CORAL REEF	1500	22.50	25.00
94	HEART AND VINES	1500	22.50	25.00
95	AURORA BOREALIS	150	165.00	175.00
95	GENESIS	500	50.00	55.00

GOEBEL INC.

YR	NAME	LIMIT	ISSUE	QUOTE
				*
*	LET'S TELL THE WORLD HUM-487	*	*	1200.00-1500.00

G. BOCHMANN

BETSEY CLARK

YR	NAME	LIMIT	ISSUE	QUOTE
72	BLESS YOU	CL	18.00	275.00
72	FRIENDS	CL	21.00	400.00
72	LITTLE MIRACLE	CL	24.50	350.00
72	SO MUCH BEAUTY	CL	24.50	350.00

LORE

BLUMENKINDER

YR	NAME	LIMIT	ISSUE	QUOTE
66	A BUTTERFLY'S KISS	CL	27.50	*
66	APRONFUL OF FLOWERS	CL	25.00	*
66	BAREFOOT LAD	CL	27.50	*
66	BEARER OF GIFTS	CL	27.50	*
66	DISPLAY PLAQUE	CL	4.00	*
66	FLUTE RECITAL	CL	25.00	*
66	GARDEN ROMANCE	CL	50.00	*
66	HER FIRST BOUQUET	CL	30.00	*
66	HER KITTEN	CL	27.50	*
66	NATURE'S TREASURES	CL	25.00	*
66	ST. VALENTINE'S MESSENGER	CL	30.00	*
66	TENDER LOVING CARE	CL	30.00	*
66	THE FLOWER FARMER	CL	30.00	*
69	FIRST JOURNEY	CL	25.00	*
69	FIRST LOVE	CL	25.00	*
69	GARDEN PRINCES	CL	50.00	*
69	SUMMER MAGIC	CL	50.00	*
71	BIRD SONG	CL	65.00	*
71	CELLO RECITAL	CL	80.00	*
71	COUNTRY LAD	CL	35.00	*
71	COUNTRY MAIDEN	CL	35.00	*
71	COURTING COUNTRY STYLE	CL	80.00	*
71	THE BOYFRIEND	CL	65.00	*
72	FIRST DATE	CL	95.00	*
72	PARTY GUEST	CL	95.00	*
73	BY A GARDEN POND	CL	75.00	*
73	EASTER TIME	CL	80.00	240.00
73	KITTENS	CL	75.00	*
73	THE ACCOMPANIST	CL	95.00	*
73	THE HITCHHIKER	CL	80.00	*
73	THE PATIENT	CL	95.00	*
75	BOTH IN HARMONY	CL	95.00	*
75	COMPANIONS	CL	85.00	*
75	FOR YOU-WITH LOVE	CL	95.00	*
75	HAPPY MINSTEL	CL	95.00	*
75	LOYAL FRIEND	CL	85.00	*
75	SPRINGTIME	CL	95.00	*
75	THE LUCKY ONE	CL	150.00	*
75	WITH LOVE	CL	150.00	*
79	BIRTHDAY MORNING	CL	201.00	*
79	FARMHOUSE COMPANIONS	CL	175.00	*
79	GARDEN FRIENDS	CL	175.00	*
79	HARVEST TREAT	CL	175.00	*
79	LOVING TOUCH	CL	201.00	*
79	SWEET TREAT	CL	149.00	*
80	DANCING SONG	CL	175.00	*
80	DRUMMER BOY	CL	180.00	*
80	FLUTIST	CL	175.00	*
80	ROMANCE	CL	175.00	*
80	SPRING SONG	CL	180.00	*
80	VIOLINIST	CL	180.00	*
82	AUTUMN DELIGHT	CL	165.00	*
82	HAPPY SAILING	CL	150.00	*
82	LITTLE MOMMY	CL	165.00	*
82	MAIL CALL	CL	165.00	*
82	PLAY BELL	CL	165.00	*
82	THE SPINNING TOP	CL	150.00	*

YR	NAME	LIMIT	ISSUE	QUOTE
M.I. HUMMEL			**CENTURY COLLECTION**	
87	PLEASANT JOURNEY HUM-406	CL	500.00	2500.00-6000.00
G. SKROBEK				**CO-BOY**
*	BERT THE SOCCER STAR	CL	*	50.00
*	CANDY THE BAKER'S DELIGHT	CL	*	50.00
*	CONNY THE NIGHT WATCHMAN	CL	*	50.00
*	ED THE WINE CELLAR STEWARD	CL	*	50.00
*	JACK THE PHARMACIST	CL	*	50.00
*	JIM THE BOWLER	CL	*	50.00
*	JOHN THE HAWKEYE HUNTER	CL	*	50.00
*	MARK-SAFETY FIRST	CL	*	50.00
*	MAX THE BOXING CHAMP	CL	*	50.00
*	PETRL THE VILLAGE ANGLER	CL	*	50.00
*	TONI THE SKIER	CL	*	50.00
71	BIT THE BACHELOR	CL	16.00	45.00
71	FIPS THE FOXY FISHERMAN	CL	16.00	*
71	FRITZ THE HAPPY BOOZER	CL	16.00	50.00
71	MIKE THE JAM MAKER	CL	16.00	*
71	PLUM THE PASTRY CHEF	CL	16.00	*
71	ROBBY THE VEGETARIAN	CL	16.00	*
71	SAM THE GOURMET	CL	16.00	*
71	TOM THE HONEY LOVER	CL	16.00	*
71	WIM THE COURT SUPPLIER	CL	16.00	*
72	BOB THE BOOKWORM	CL	20.00	50.00
72	BRUM THE LAWYER	CL	20.00	50.00
72	CO-BOY PLAQUE	CL	20.00	50.00
72	KUNI THE BIG DIPPER	CL	20.00	*
72	PORZ THE MUSHROOM MUNCHER	CL	20.00	*
72	SEPP THE BEER BUDDY	CL	20.00	*
72	UTZ THE BANKER	CL	20.00	50.00
78	GIL THE GOALIE	CL	34.00	50.00
78	PAT THE PITCHER	CL	34.00	50.00
78	TOMMY TOUCHDOWN	CL	34.00	50.00
80	CARL THE CHEF	CL	49.00	50.00
80	DOC THE DOCTOR	CL	49.00	50.00
80	GERD THE DIVER	CL	49.00	50.00
80	HERB THE HORSEMAN	CL	49.00	50.00
80	MONTY THE MOUNTAIN CLIMBER	CL	49.00	50.00
80	TED THE TENNIS PLAYER	CL	49.00	50.00
81	AL THE TRUMPET PLAYER	CL	45.00	50.00
81	BEN THE BLACKSMITH	CL	45.00	50.00
81	GEORGE THE GOURMAND	CL	45.00	50.00
81	GREG THE GOURMET	CL	45.00	50.00
81	GRETA THE HAPPY HOUSEWIFE	CL	45.00	50.00
81	NICK THE NIGHTCLUB SINGER	CL	45.00	50.00
81	NIELS THE STRUMMER	CL	45.00	50.00
81	PETER THE ACCORDIONIST	CL	45.00	50.00
81	WALTER THE JOGGER	CL	45.00	50.00
84	BRAD THE CLOCKMASTER	CL	75.00	95.00
84	CHRIS THE SHOEMAKER	CL	45.00	50.00
84	CHUCK THE CHIMNEY SWEEP	CL	45.00	50.00
84	FELIX THE BAKER	CL	45.00	50.00
84	HERMAN THE BUTCHER	CL	45.00	50.00
84	HOMER THE DRIVER	CL	45.00	50.00
84	MARTHE THE NURSE	CL	45.00	50.00
84	PAUL THE DENTIST	CL	45.00	50.00
84	RICK THE FIREMAN	CL	45.00	50.00
84	RUDY THE WORLD TRAVELER	CL	45.00	50.00
84	SID THE VINTNER	CL	45.00	50.00
87	BANK-PETE THE PIRATE	CL	80.00	80.00
87	BANK-UTZ THE MONEY BAGS	CL	80.00	80.00
87	CHUCK ON HIS PIG	CL	75.00	75.00
87	CLOCK-CONY THE WATCHMAN	CL	125.00	125.00
87	CLOCK-SEPP AND THE BEER KEG	CL	125.00	125.00
T. DEGRAZIA				**DEGRAZIA**
84	DISPLAY PLAQUE	CL	45.00	95.00
84	FLOWER BOY	OP	65.00	110.00
84	FLOWER GIRL	OP	65.00	110.00
84	MY FIRST HORSE	OP	65.00	110.00
84	SUNFLOWER BOY	CL	65.00	300.00
84	WHITE DOVE	OP	45.00	79.50
84	WONDERING	OP	85.00	135.00
85	CHILD	OP	25.00	40.00
85	JOSEPH	OP	55.00	70.00
85	LITTLE MADONNA	OP	80.00	125.00
85	MARY	OP	55.00	65.00

YR	NAME	LIMIT	ISSUE	QUOTE
85	NATIVITY SET (3 PIECES)	OP	135.00	195.00
85	PIMA DRUMMER BOY	OP	65.00	110.00
86	FESTIVAL LIGHTS	OP	75.00	95.00
86	MERRY LITTLE INDIAN	12,500	175.00	245.00
86	THE BLUE BOY	OP	70.00	95.00
87	LOVE ME	OP	95.00	110.00
87	WEE THREE	OP	180.00	195.00
88	ANGEL CHRISTMAS PRAYER	OP	70.00	79.50
88	BEAUTIFUL BURDEN	OP	175.00	185.00
88	FLOWER BOY PLAQUE	OP	80.00	79.50
88	LOS NINOS	5000	595.00	645.00
88	MERRILY, MERRILY, MERRILY	OP	95.00	110.00
89	MY BEAUTIFUL ROCKING HORSE	OP	225.00	245.00
89	MY FIRST ARROW	OP	95.00	110.00
89	TWO LITTLE LAMBS	OP	70.00	79.50
90	ALONE	OP	395.00	395.00
90	BIGGEST DRUM	YR	135.00	135.00
90	CRUCIFIXION	YR	295.00	295.00
90	DESERT HARVEST	5000	155.00	155.00
90	EL BURRITO	OP	60.00	60.00
90	LITTLE PRAYER	YR	85.00	85.00
90	NAVAJO BOY	YR	135.00	135.00
90	SUNFLOWER GIRL	OP	95.00	95.00
91	NAVAJO MOTHER	YR	*	*
91	SHEPHERD BOY	OP	95.00	95.00
91	WANDERER	YR	75.00	75.00
92	NAVAJO MADONNA	OP	135.00	135.00
92	SUN SHOWERS	5000	195.00	195.00

G. BOCHMANN · FASHIONS ON PARADE

YR	NAME	LIMIT	ISSUE	QUOTE
82	AT THE TEA DANCE	OP	30.00	50.00
82	EDWARDIAN GRACE	OP	30.00	50.00
82	STROLLING ON THE AVENUE	OP	30.00	50.00
82	THE COSMOPOLITAN	OP	30.00	50.00
82	THE GARDEN FANCIER	OP	30.00	50.00
82	THE VISITOR	OP	30.00	50.00
83	BRIDE AND GROOM	OP	65.00	100.00
83	DEMURE ELEGANCE	OP	32.50	50.00
83	GENTLE THOUGHTS	OP	32.50	50.00
83	HER TREASURED DAY (BRIDE)	OP	32.50	50.00
83	IMPATIENCE	CL	32.50	50.00
83	REFLECTIONS	OP	32.50	50.00
83	WAITING FOR HIS LOVE (GROOM)	OP	32.50	50.00
84	CENTER COURT	CL	32.50	45.00
84	ON THE FAIRWAY	CL	32.50	45.00
84	SKIMMING GENTLY	CL	32.50	45.00
85	A GENTLE MOMENT	CL	22.50	35.00
85	A LAZY DAY	CL	22.50	35.00
85	AFTERNOON TEA	OP	32.50	50.00
85	GENTLE BREEZES	OP	32.50	50.00
85	RIVER OUTING	OP	32.50	50.00
85	TO THE HUNT	OP	32.50	50.00
86	EQUESTRIAN	OP	36.00	50.00
86	FASHIONS ON PARADE PLAQUE	OP	10.00	12.50
86	SOUTHERN BELLE	OP	36.00	50.00
87	PARIS IN FALL	OP	55.00	55.00
87	PROMENADE IN NICE	OP	55.00	55.00
87	SAY PLEASE	OP	55.00	55.00
87	SILVER LACE AND RHINESTONES	OP	55.00	55.00
87	THE SHEPHERDESS	OP	55.00	55.00
87	THE VISCOUNTESS DIANA	OP	55.00	55.00
88	BRIDE AND GROOM (2ND SET)	OP	110.00	110.00
88	FOREVER AND ALWAYS (BRIDE)	OP	55.00	55.00
88	THE PROMISE (GROOM)	OP	55.00	55.00

N. ROCKWELL · GOEBEL

YR	NAME	LIMIT	ISSUE	QUOTE
63	ADVERTISING PLAQUE	CL	*	600.00
63	BOYHOOD DREAMS	CL	12.00	400.00
63	BUTTERCUP TEST (BEGUILING BUTTERCUP)	CL	10.00	400.00
63	FIRST LOVE (A SCHOLARLY PACE)	CL	30.00	400.00
63	HOME CURE	CL	16.00	400.00
63	LITTLE VETERINARIAN (MYSTERIOUS MALADY)	CL	15.00	40.00
63	MOTHER'S HELPER (PRIDE OF PARENTHOOD)	CL	15.00	400.00
63	MY FIRST SMOKE	CL	9.00	400.00
63	MY NEW PAL (A BOY MEETS HIS DOG)	CL	12.00	400.00
63	PATIENT ANGLERS (FISHERMAN'S PARADISE)	CL	18.00	400.00
63	SHE LOVES ME (DAY DREAMER)	CL	8.00	400.00
63	TIMELY ASSISTANCE (LOVE AID)	CL	16.00	400.00

The Maud Humphrey Bogart Collection features turn-of-the-century children such as the ones in Sharing Secrets. The line is produced by Hamilton Gifts.

The figurine Susanna was inspired by the art of Maud Humphrey Bogart and produced by Hamilton Gifts.

This little girl and her puppy will be Friends for Life. The figure is from the Maud Humphrey Bogart Collection produced by Hamilton Gifts.

This little gal doesn't mind always being the bridesmaid. Playing Bridesmaid is from the Maud Humphrey Bogart Collection produced by Hamilton Gifts.

YR	NAME	LIMIT	ISSUE	QUOTE
	M.I. HUMMEL		**GOEBEL COLLECTORS CLUB**	
85	SMILING THROUGH HUM-408	CL	125.00	4000.00-5000.00
88	THE SURPRISE HUM-431	CL	125.00	2000.00-3000.00
	M.I. HUMMEL			**M.I. HUMMEL**
*	A FAIR MEASURE HUM-345	OP	230.00	285.00-5000.00
*	A FARM BOY & GOOSE GIRL BOOKEND HUM60A&B	TW	*	350.00-1200.00
*	ACCORDION BOY HUM-185	RT	160.00	195.00-700.00
*	ADORATION HUM-23	CL	*	1600.00-2100.00
*	ADORATION HUM-23/I	OP	300.00	345.00-1250.00
*	ADORATION HUM-23/III	OP	470.00	535.00-2000.00
*	ADORATION WITH BIRD, HUM-105	CL	*	7000.00-8000.00
*	ADVENTURE BOUND HUM-347	OP	3300.00	3600.00-6000.00
*	ANGEL DUET HUM-261	OP	180.00	215.00-800.00
*	ANGEL DUET, CANDLEHOLDER HUM-193	OP	180.00	215.00-1700.00
*	ANGEL LIGHTS, CANDLEHOLDER HUM-241	SU	*	250.00-350.00
*	ANGEL SERENADE HUM-83	OP	180.00	215.00-700.00
*	ANGEL WITH ACCORDION HUM-238 B	OP	45.00	50.00-100.00
*	ANGEL WITH LUTE HUM-238 A	OP	45.00	50.00-100.00
*	ANGEL WITH TRUMPET HUM-238 C	OP	45.00	50.00-100.00
*	ANGEL/ACCORDION, CANDLEHLDER HUM111/39/0	SU	*	50.00-175.00
*	ANGEL/ACCORDION, CANDLEHLDER HUM111/39/1	CL	*	150.00-300.00
*	ANGEL/ACCORDION, CANDLEHOLDER HUM 1/39/0	OP	*	50.00-175.00
*	ANGEL/LUTE, CANDLEHOLDER HUM 1/38/0	OP	*	50.00-175.00
*	ANGEL/LUTE, CANDLEHOLDER HUM 111/38/0	SU	*	50.00-175.00
*	ANGEL/LUTE, CANDLEHOLDER HUM 111/38/1	CL	*	150.00-300.00
*	ANGEL/TRUMPET, CANDLEHOLDER HUM 1/40/0	SU	*	50.00-175.00
*	ANGEL/TRUMPET, CANDLEHOLDER HUM 111/40/0	SU	*	50.00-175.00
*	ANGEL/TRUMPET, CANDLEHOLDER HUM 111/40/1	CL	*	150.00-300.00
*	ANGEL/TWO CHILDREN AT FEET HUM-108	CL	*	3000.00-15000.00
*	ANGELIC SLEEP, CANDLEHOLDER HUM-25	SU	*	170.00-650.00
*	ANGELIC SONG HUM-144	OP	125.00	145.00-500.00
*	APPLE TREE BOY HUM-142	CL	*	550.00-850.00
*	APPLE TREE BOY HUM-142/3/O	OP	120.00	140.00-450.00
*	APPLE TREE BOY HUM-142/I	OP	225.00	275.00-750.00
*	APPLE TREE BOY HUM-142/V	OP	1000.00	1200.00-1600.00
*	APPLE TREE BOY HUM-142/X	CL	*	12000.00-30000.00
*	APPLE TREE BOY, CANDLEHOLDER HUM-677	OP	142.50	145.50
*	APPLE TREE BOY, TABLE LAMP HUM-230	TW	*	275.00-900.00
*	APPLE TREE BOY/GIRL-BOOKENDS HUM-252 A&B	TW	*	275.00-400.00
*	APPLE TREE GIRL HUM-141	CL	*	550.00-850.00
*	APPLE TREE GIRL HUM-141/3/O	OP	120.00	140.00-450.00
*	APPLE TREE GIRL HUM-141/I	OP	225.00	275.00-750.00
*	APPLE TREE GIRL HUM-141/V	OP	1000.00	1200.00-1600.00
*	APPLE TREE GIRL HUM-141/X	SU	*	12000.00-20000.00
*	APPLE TREE GIRL, CANDLEHOLDER HUM-676	OP	142.50	145.50
*	APPLE TREE GIRL, TABLE LAMP HUM-229	TW	*	275.00-900.00
*	ARTIST HUM-304	OP	200.00	245.00-5000.00
*	AUF WIEDERSEHEN HUM-153	CL	*	600.00-1100.00
*	AUF WIEDERSEHEN HUM-153/I	OP	250.00	295.00-1000.00
*	AUF WIEDERSEHEN HUM-153/O	OP	200.00	245.00-500.00
*	AUTHORIZED RETAILER PLAQUE HUM-460	CL	*	200.00-1500.00
*	AUTUMN HARVEST HUM-355	OP	180.00	200.00-3000.00
*	BA-BEE-RING 30/0 A&B	CL	*	6000.00-7000.00
*	BA-BEE-RING 30/I A&B	CL	*	8000.00-9000.00
*	BA-BEE-RING 30/I A&B	CL	*	2000.00-3500.00
*	BA-BEE-RING HUM-30/O A&B	OP	160.00	190.00-675.00
*	BAKER HUM-128	OP	160.00	195.00-700.00
*	BAND LEADER HUM-129	OP	170.00	200.00-700.00
*	BAND LEADER HUM-129/4/O	OP	80.00	100.00-105.00
*	BARNYARD HERO HUM-195	CL	*	600.00-1100.00
*	BARNYARD HERO HUM-195/2/O	OP	140.00	165.00-400.00
*	BARNYARD HERO HUM-195/I	OP	265.00	300.00-650.00
*	BASHFUL HUM-377	OP	170.00	195.00-1500.00
*	BE PATIENT HUM-197	CL	*	500.00-950.00
*	BE PATIENT HUM-197/2/O	OP	160.00	195.00-450.00
*	BE PATIENT HUM-197/I	OP	230.00	295.00-600.00
*	BEGGING HIS SHARE HUM-9	OP	200.00	250.00-850.00
*	BIG HOUSECLEANING HUM-363	OP	230.00	285.00-3000.00
*	BIRD DUET HUM-169	OP	120.00	140.00-500.00
*	BIRTHDAY SERENADE HUM-218	CL	*	850.00-1000.00
*	BIRTHDAY SERENADE HUM-218/2/O	OP	150.00	170.00-625.00
*	BIRTHDAY SERENADE HUM-218/O	OP	250.00	295.00-950.00
*	BIRTHDAY SERENADE, TABLE LAMP HUM-231	TW	*	400.00-3000.00
*	BIRTHDAY SERENADE, TABLE LAMP HUM-234	TW	*	325.00-2000.00
*	BLESSED CHILD (KRUMBAD) HUM-78/I	TW	*	30.00-50.00
*	BLESSED CHILD (KRUMBAD) HUM-78/II	TW	*	35.00-60.00

YR	NAME	LIMIT	ISSUE	QUOTE
*	BLESSED CHILD (KRUMBAD) HUM-78/II 1/2	OP	35.00	50.00-150.00
*	BLESSED CHILD (KRUMBAD) HUM-78/III	TW	*	45.00-400.00
*	BLESSED CHILD (KRUMBAD) HUM-78/O	CL	*	150.00-300.00
*	BLESSED CHILD (KRUMBAD) HUM-78/V	TW	*	80.00-150.00
*	BLESSED CHILD (KRUMBAD) HUM-78/VI	TW	*	150.00-850.00
*	BLESSED CHILD (KRUMBAD) HUM-78/VIII	TW	*	300.00-1000.00
*	BLESSED EVENT HUM-333	OP	280.00	320.00-5000.00
*	BOOK WORM BOOKENDS, BOY & GIRL HUM-14	CL	*	220.00-250.00
*	BOOK WORM HUM-3/I	OP	250.00	200.00-1000.00
*	BOOK WORM HUM-3/II	TW	*	1200.00-3500.00
*	BOOK WORM HUM-3/III	TW	*	1250.00-4000.00
*	BOOK WORM HUM-8	OP	180.00	215.00-750.00
*	BOOK WORM, BOOKENDS, HUM-14 A&B	SU	*	200.00-1500.00
*	BOOTS HUM-143	CL	*	600.00-1000.00
*	BOOTS HUM-143/I	OP	270.00	330.00-950.00
*	BOOTS HUM-143/O	OP	160.00	200.00-675.00
*	BOY W/HORSE, CANDLESTICK HUM-117	OP	50.00	55.00-225.00
*	BOY WITH ACCORDION HUM-390	OP	70.00	85.00-200.00
*	BOY WITH BIRD, ASHTRAY HUM-166	TW	*	130.00-600.00
*	BOY WITH HORSE HUM-239 C	OP	45.00	55.00-100.00
*	BOY WITH TOOTHACHE HUM-217	OP	185.00	210.00-500.00
*	BROTHER HUM-95	OP	165.00	200.00-700.00
*	BUILDER HUM-305	OP	200.00	245.00-5000.00
*	BUSY STUDENT HUM-367	OP	140.00	160.00-1000.00
*	CANDLELIGHT, CANDLEHOLDER HUM-192	OP	190.00	230.00-1700.00
*	CARNIVAL HUM-328	OP	190.00	215.00-5000.00
*	CELESTIAL MUSICIAN HUM-188	CL	*	310.00-1500.00
*	CELESTIAL MUSICIAN HUM-188/I	TW	230.00	275.00-310.00
*	CELESTIAL MUSICIAN HUM-188/O	OP	180.00	215.00-225.00
*	CHICK GIRL HUM-57	CL	*	450.00-1000.00
*	CHICK GIRL HUM-57/2/O	OP	125.00	145.00-150.00
*	CHICK GIRL HUM-57/I	OP	220.00	275.00-950.00
*	CHICK GIRL HUM-57/O	OP	145.00	165.00-575.00
*	CHICK GIRL, BOX (NEW STYLE) HUM III-57	TW	*	150.00-200.00
*	CHICK GIRL, BOX (OLD STYLE) HUM-III-57	CL	*	425.00-750.00
*	CHICKEN-LICKEN HUM-385	OP	240.00	280.00-1500.00
*	CHILD IN BED, LOOKING LEFT HUM-137 A	CL	*	5000.00-7000.00
*	CHILD IN BED, LOOKING RIGHT HUM-137 B	CL	*	75.00-500.00
*	CHILD IN BED, PLAQUE HUM-137	OP	55.00	65.00-75.00
*	CHIMNEY SWEEP HUM-12	CL	*	375.00-800.00
*	CHIMNEY SWEEP HUM-12/2/O	OP	110.00	120.00-300.00
*	CHIMNEY SWEEP HUM-12/I	OP	180.00	215.00-775.00
*	CHRIST CHILD HUM-18	TW	*	125.00-500.00
*	CHRISTMAS SONG HUM-343	OP	180.00	215.00-5000.00
*	CINDERELLA HUM-337	OP	240.00	285.00-5000.00
*	CLOSE HARMONY HUM-336	OP	240.00	285.00-5000.00
*	CONFIDENTIALLY HUM-314	OP	230.00	285.00-5000.00
*	CONGRATULATIONS HUM-17/2	CL	*	4500.00-8000.00
*	CONGRATULATIONS HUM-17/O	OP	160.00	200.00-700.00
*	COQUETTES HUM-179	OP	230.00	285.00-1000.00
*	CROSSROADS HUM-331	OP	350.00	400.00-5000.00
*	CULPRITS HUM-56	CL	*	750.00-950.00
*	CULPRITS HUM-56 A	OP	245.00	290.00-625.00
*	CULPRITS, TABLE LAMP HUM-44	CL	*	600.00-750.00
*	CULPRITS, TABLE LAMP HUM-44 A	TW	*	300.00-600.00
*	DOCTOR HUM-127	OP	135.00	155.00-575.00
*	DOLL BATH HUM-319	OP	230.00	285.00-5000.00
*	DOLL MOTHER HUM-67	OP	190.00	210.00-750.00
*	DOLL MOTHER/PRAYER..BKENDS HUM-76 A&B	CL	*	10000.00-15000.00
*	DUET (WITH "LIPS" BASE) HUM-130	CL	*	1000.00-1500.00
*	DUET (WITHOUT TIES), HUM-130	CL	*	2000.00-2500.00
*	DUET HUM-130	OP	225.00	280.00-950.00
*	EASTER GREETINGS! HUM-378	OP	185.00	200.00-1500.00
*	EVENTIDE (RARE) HUM-99	CL	*	3000.00-5000.00
*	EVENTIDE HUM-99	OP	290.00	325.00-1200.00
*	EVENTIDE, TABLE LAMP HUM-104	CL	*	8000.00-10000.00
*	FAREWELL HUM-65	CL	220.00	240.00-950.00
*	FAREWELL HUM-65/I	CL	*	265.00-950.00
*	FAREWELL HUM-65/O	CL	*	5000.00-8000.00
*	FAREWELL, TABLE LAMP HUM-103	CL	*	8000.00-10000.00
*	FARM BOY HUM-66	OP	190.00	225.00-800.00
*	FARM BOY/GOOSE GIRL BOOKENDS HUM-60 A&B	SU	*	350.00-1200.00
*	FAVORITE PET HUM-361	OP	230.00	285.00-1500.00
*	FEATHERED FRIENDS HUM-344	OP	220.00	275.00-5000.00
*	FEEDING TIME HUM-199	CL	*	500.00-950.00
*	FEEDING TIME HUM-199/I	OP	220.00	275.00-550.00

YR	NAME	LIMIT	ISSUE	QUOTE
*	FEEDING TIME HUM-199/O	OP	160.00	195.00-450.00
*	FESTIVAL HARMONY (FLUTE) HUM-173	CL	*	1000.00-3500.00
*	FESTIVAL HARMONY (FLUTE) HUM-173/II	TW	*	400.00-750.00
*	FESTIVAL HARMONY (FLUTE) HUM-173/O	OP	260.00	310.00-600.00
*	FESTIVAL HARMONY (MANDOLIN) HUM-172	CL	*	1000.00-3500.00
*	FESTIVAL HARMONY (MANDOLIN) HUM-172/O	OP	260.00	310.00-600.00
*	FLITTING BUTTERFLY, PLAQUE HUM-139	OP	55.00	65.00-500.00
*	FLOWER VENDOR HUM-381	OP	200.00	245.00-1500.00
*	FLYING ANGEL HUM-366	CL	105.00	125.00-250.00
*	FOLLOW THE LEADER HUM-369	OP	1000.00	1200.00-5000.00
*	FOR FATHER HUM-87	OP	180.00	210.00-750.00
*	FOR MOTHER HUM-257	CL	*	205.00-800.00
*	FOR MOTHER HUM-257/2/O	OP	105.00	120.00-125.00
*	FOR MOTHER HUM-257/O	OP	170.00	200.00-205.00
*	FOREST SHRINE HUM-183	OP	460.00	530.00-1800.00
*	FRIENDS HUM-136	CL	*	2000.00-4000.00
*	FRIENDS HUM-136/I	OP	180.00	200.00-875.00
*	FRIENDS HUM-136/V	OP	1000.00	1200.00-4000.00
*	GAY ADVENTURE HUM-356	OP	160.00	190.00-3000.00
*	GIRL W/FIR TREE, CANDLESTICK HUM-116	OP	50.00	55.00-225.00
*	GIRL W/NOSEGAY, CANDLESTICK HUM-115	OP	50.00	55.00-225.00
*	GIRL WITH DOLL HUM-239 B	OP	45.00	55.00-100.00
*	GIRL WITH NOSEGAY HUM-239 A	OP	45.00	55.00-100.00
*	GIRL WITH SHEET OF MUSIC HUM-389	OP	70.00	85.00-200.00
*	GIRL WITH TRUMPET HUM-391	OP	70.00	85.00-200.00
*	GLOBE TROTTER HUM-79	CL	170.00	190.000-725.00
*	GOING TO GRANDMA'S HUM-52	CL	*	850.00-1600.00
*	GOING TO GRANDMA'S HUM-52/I	TW	*	370.00-1500.00
*	GOING TO GRANDMA'S HUM-52/O	OP	230.00	260.00-950.00
*	GOOD FRIENDS HUM-182	OP	160.00	195.00-700.00
*	GOOD FRIENDS, BOOKENDS HUM-251 A&B	TW	*	275.00-700.00
*	GOOD FRIENDS, TABLE LAMP HUM-228	TW	*	275.00-750.00
*	GOOD HUNTING HUM-307	OP	200.00	245.00-5000.00
*	GOOD SHEPHERD HUM-42/I	CL	*	6000.00-8000.00
*	GOOD SHEPHERD HUM-42/O	OP	200.00	250.00-800.00
*	GOOSE GIRL HUM-47	CL	*	800.00-900.00
*	GOOSE GIRL HUM-47/3/O	OP	145.00	165.00-600.00
*	GOOSE GIRL HUM-47/II	OP	380.00	400.00-1300.00
*	GOOSE GIRL HUM-47/O	OP	185.00	225.00-750.00
*	GUIDING ANGEL HUM-357	OP	70.00	85.00-200.00
*	HAPPINESS HUM-86	OP	110.00	130.00-450.00
*	HAPPY BIRTHDAY HUM-176	CL	*	550.00-1000.00
*	HAPPY BIRTHDAY HUM-176/I	OP	250.00	295.00-1000.00
*	HAPPY BIRTHDAY HUM-176/O	OP	180.00	210.00-475.00
*	HAPPY DAYS HUM-150	CL	*	900.00-1600.00
*	HAPPY DAYS HUM-150/2/O	OP	150.00	170.00-375.00
*	HAPPY DAYS HUM-150/I	OP	400.00	450.00-1500.00
*	HAPPY DAYS HUM-150/O	OP	250.00	300.00-600.00
*	HAPPY DAYS, TABLE LAMP HUM-232	TW	*	400.00-1500.00
*	HAPPY DAYS, TABLE LAMP HUM-235	TW	*	350.00-1000.00
*	HAPPY PASTIME HUM-69	OP	135.00	160.00-575.00
*	HAPPY PASTIME, ASHTRAY HUM-62	TW	*	130.00-600.00
*	HAPPY PASTIME, BOX (NEW STYLE)HUM III/69	TW	*	150.00-200.00
*	HAPPY PASTIME,BOX (OLD STYLE) HUM III/69	CL	*	425.00-750.00
*	HAPPY TRAVELIER, HUM-109	CL	*	1100.00-1400.00
*	HAPPY TRAVELLER HUM-109	CL	*	145.00-225.00
*	HAPPY TRAVELLER HUM-109/II	CL	*	350.00-850.00
*	HAPPY TRAVELLER HUM-109/O	OP	120.00	140.00-300.00
*	HAPPY TRAVELLER, 7 3/4 IN. HUM-109	CL	*	1000.00-1250.00
*	HEAR YE, HEAR YE HUM-15	CL	*	1400.00-1700.00
*	HEAR YE, HEAR YE HUM-15/2/O	OP	125.00	145.00-150.00
*	HEAR YE, HEAR YE HUM-15/I	OP	200.00	250.00-850.00
*	HEAR YE, HEAR YE HUM-15/II	TW	400.00	450.00-1500.00
*	HEAR YE, HEAR YE HUM-15/O	OP	*	200.00-700.00
*	HEAVENLY ANGEL HUM-21/I	OP	210.00	250.00-900.00
*	HEAVENLY ANGEL HUM-21/II	TW	390.00	425.00-1600.00
*	HEAVENLY ANGEL HUM-21/O	OP	100.00	120.00-425.00
*	HEAVENLY ANGEL HUM-21/O 1/2	OP	170.00	215.00-750.00
*	HEAVENLY LULLABY HUM-262	OP	155.00	185.00-800.00
*	HEAVENLY PROTECTION HUM-88	CL	*	850.00-2300.00
*	HEAVENLY PROTECTION HUM-88/I	OP	370.00	425.00-650.00
*	HEAVENLY PROTECTION HUM-88/II	TW	590.00	625.00-1200.00
*	HEAVENLY SONG, CANDLEHOLDER, HUM-113	CL	*	3000.00-10000.00
*	HELLO HUM-124	CL	*	400.00-1000.00
*	HELLO HUM-124/I	TW	*	240.00-1000.00
*	HELLO HUM-124/O	OP	180.00	215.00-400.00

YR	NAME	LIMIT	ISSUE	QUOTE
*	HERALD ANGELS, CANDLEHOLDER HUM-37	TW	*	175.00-700.00
*	HOLY CHILD HUM-70	TW	*	160.00-700.00
*	HOLY WATER FONT, ANGEL CLOUD HUM-206	OP	45.00	50.00-500.00
*	HOLY WATER FONT, ANGEL DUET HUM-146	OP	45.00	50.00-200.00
*	HOLY WATER FONT, ANGEL SHRINE HUM-147	OP	45.00	50.00-250.00
*	HOLY WATER FONT, ANGEL SITTING HUM-167	OP	45.00	50.00-300.00
*	HOLY WATER FONT, ANGEL W/BIRD HUM-22	CL	*	250.00-275.00
*	HOLY WATER FONT, ANGEL W/BIRD HUM-22/I	CL	*	300.00-600.00
*	HOLY WATER FONT, ANGEL W/BIRD HUM-22/O	OP	35.00	40.00-250.00
*	HOLY WATER FONT, ANGEL/NEWS HUM-242	CL	*	1000.00-1500.00
*	HOLY WATER FONT, ANGEL/PRAYER HUM-91 A&B	OP	70.00	80.00-500.00
*	HOLY WATER FONT, ANGELS AT PRAYER HUM-91	CL	*	400.00-500.00
*	HOLY WATER FONT, CHILD JESUS HUM-26	CL	*	300.00-500.00
*	HOLY WATER FONT, CHILD JESUS HUM-26/I	CL	200.00	200.00-500.00
*	HOLY WATER FONT, CHILD JESUS HUM-26/O	OP	35.00	40.00-250.00
*	HOLY WATER FONT, CHILD W/FLOWERS HUM-36	CL	*	275.00-425.00
*	HOLY WATER FONT, CHILD/FLOWERS HUM-36/I	CL	*	150.00-400.00
*	HOLY WATER FONT, CHILD/FLOWERS HUM-36/O	OP	35.00	40.00-250.00
*	HOLY WATER FONT, CROSS WITH DOVES HUM-77	CL	*	5000.00-10000.00
*	HOLY WATER FONT, GOOD SHEPHERD HUM-35	CL	*	375.00-425.00
*	HOLY WATER FONT, GOOD SHEPHERD HUM-35/I	CL	*	150.00-400.00
*	HOLY WATER FONT, GOOD SHEPHERD HUM-35/O	OP	35.00	40.00-250.00
*	HOLY WATER FONT, GUARD. ANGEL HUM-248/I	CL	*	1300.00-1500.00
*	HOLY WATER FONT, GUARD. ANGEL HUM-248/O	OP	45.00	50.00-250.00
*	HOLY WATER FONT, GUARDIAN ANGEL HUM 29/0	CL	*	950.00-1500.00
*	HOLY WATER FONT, GUARDIAN ANGEL HUM 29/I	CL	*	1500.00-2000.00
*	HOLY WATER FONT, GUARDIAN ANGEL HUM-29	CL	*	1300.00-1500.00
*	HOLY WATER FONT, HEAVENLY ANGEL HUM-207	OP	45.00	50.00-500.00
*	HOLY WATER FONT, HOLY FAMILY HUM-246	OP	45.00	50.00-275.00
*	HOLY WATER FONT, MADONNA W/CHILD HUM-243	OP	45.00	50.00-275.00
*	HOLY WATER FONT, WHITE ANGEL HUM-75	OP	35.00	40.00-250.00
*	HOLY WATER FONT, WORSHIP HUM-164	OP	45.00	50.00-300.00
*	HOLY WATER FONT,ANGEL W/BIRD HUM-354C	CL	*	*
*	HOLY WATER FONT,ANGEL W/LANTERN HUM-354A	CL	*	*
*	HOLY WATER FONT,ANGEL W/TRUMPET	CL	*	*
*	HOME FROM MARKET HUM-198	CL	*	425.00-750.00
*	HOME FROM MARKET HUM-198/2/O	OP	120.00	145.00-325.00
*	HOME FROM MARKET HUM-198/I	OP	180.00	210.00-475.00
*	HOMEWARD BOUND HUM-334	OP	295.00	330.00-5000.00
*	HUM-253 GIRL W/BASKET	CL	*	*
*	HUM-254 GIRL PLAYING A MANDOLIN	CL	*	*
*	JOYFUL & LET'S SING WD BOOKENDS, HUM-120	CL	*	10000.00-20000.00
*	JOYFUL HUM-53	OP	100.00	120.00-425.00
*	JOYFUL, ASHTRAY HUM-33	TW	*	140.00-600.00
*	JOYFUL, BOX (OLD STYLE) HUM III/53	CL	*	425.00-500.00
*	JOYFUL, BOX(NEW STYLE)HUM III/53	CL	*	180.00-200.00
*	JOYOUS NEWS HUM-27/3	CL	*	220.00-2000.00
*	JOYOUS NEWS HUM-27/I	CL	*	250.00-500.00
*	JOYOUS NEWS HUM-27/III	OP	180.00	215.00-220.00
*	JUST RESTING HUM-112	CL	*	650.00-800.00
*	JUST RESTING HUM-112/3/O	OP	125.00	145.00-500.00
*	JUST RESTING HUM-112/I	OP	225.00	280.00-750.00
*	JUST RESTING, TABLE LAMP HUM II/112	CL	*	350.00-700.00
*	JUST RESTING, TABLE LAMP HUM-225	CL	*	475.00-800.00
*	JUST RESTING, TABLE LAMP HUM-225/I	TW	*	290.00-550.00
*	JUST RESTING, TABLE LAMP HUM-225/II	TW	*	340.00-700.00
*	KISS ME HUM-311	OP	230.00	285.00-5000.00
*	KNITTING LESSON HUM-256	OP	440.00	500.00-1100.00
*	LATEST NEWS HUM-184	OP	240.00	290.00-1000.00
*	LET'S SING HUM-110	CL	*	300.00-550.00
*	LET'S SING HUM-110/I	OP	140.00	165.00-350.00
*	LET'S SING HUM-110/O	OP	105.00	125.00-450.00
*	LET'S SING, ASHTRAY HUM-114	TW	*	130.00-1000.00
*	LET'S SING, BOX (NEW STYLE) III/110	TW	*	150.00-200.00
*	LET'S SING, BOX (OLD STYLE) III/110	CL	*	425.00-750.00
*	LETTER TO SANTA HUM-340	OP	285.00	330.00-5000.00
*	LITTLE BAND (ON BASE) HUM-392	TW	*	220.00-350.00
*	LITTLE BAND ON MUSIC BOX	TW	*	330.00-400.00
*	LITTLE BAND, CANDLEHOLDER/BOX HUM-388	TW	*	220.00-350.00
*	LITTLE BOOKKEEPER HUM-306	OP	240.00	285.00-5000.00
*	LITTLE CELLIST HUM-89	CL	*	1150.00-1500.00
*	LITTLE CELLIST HUM-89/I	OP	180.00	210.00-750.00
*	LITTLE CELLIST HUM-89/II	TW	380.00	400.00-1400.00
*	LITTLE DRUMMER HUM-240	OP	125.00	145.00-350.00
*	LITTLE FIDDLER HUM-2/4/O	OP	80.00	100.00-105.00
*	LITTLE FIDDLER HUM-2/I	TW	370.00	400.00-1500.00

YR	NAME	LIMIT	ISSUE	QUOTE
*	LITTLE FIDDLER HUM-2/II	TW	*	1200.00-3500.00
*	LITTLE FIDDLER HUM-2/III	TW	*	1300.00-4000.00
*	LITTLE FIDDLER HUM-2/O	OP	190.00	215.00-750.00
*	LITTLE FIDDLER HUM-4	OP	170.00	200.00-725.00
*	LITTLE FIDDLER, PLAQUE HUM-93	TW	*	140.00-525.00
*	LITTLE FIDDLER,PLAQUE (RARE) HUM-93	CL	*	3000.00-5000.00
*	LITTLE FIDDLER/PLAQ. WD FRAME, HUM-107	CL	*	5000.00-6000.00
*	LITTLE GABRIEL HUM-32/I	CL	*	1200.00-3500.00
*	LITTLE GABRIEL HUM-32/O	CL	*	145.00-500.00
*	LITTLE GABRIEL, 5 IN. HUM-32	OP	115.00	140.00-155.00
*	LITTLE GABRIEL, HUM-32	CL	*	1500.00-2500.00
*	LITTLE GARDENER HUM-74	OP	100.00	120.00-425.00
*	LITTLE GOAT HERDER HUM-200	CL	*	475.00-825.00
*	LITTLE GOAT HERDER HUM-200/I	OP	200.00	235.00-525.00
*	LITTLE GOAT HERDER HUM-200/O	OP	160.00	195.00-450.00
*	LITTLE GOAT HERDER, BOOKENDS HUM-250 A&B	TW	*	275.00-700.00
*	LITTLE GUARDIAN HUM-145	OP	125.00	145.00-500.00
*	LITTLE HELPER HUM-73	OP	100.00	120.00-425.00
*	LITTLE HIKER HUM-16	CL	*	450.00-750.00
*	LITTLE HIKER HUM-16/2/O	OP	100.00	120.00-425.00
*	LITTLE HIKER HUM-16/I	OP	180.00	215.00-650.00
*	LITTLE PHARMACIST HUM-322	OP	200.00	240.00-5000.00
*	LITTLE SCHOLAR HUM-80	OP	180.00	210.00-750.00
*	LITTLE SHOPPER HUM-96	OP	120.00	135.00-500.00
*	LITTLE SWEEPER HUM-171/4/O	OP	80.00	100.00-105.00
*	LITTLE SWEEPER HUM-171/O	OP	110.00	135.00-140.00
*	LITTLE TAILOR HUM-308	OP	200.00	245.00-5000.00
*	LITTLE THRIFTY, BANK HUM-118	OP	130.00	145.00-650.00
*	LOST SHEEP HUM-68	CL	*	300.00-700.00
*	LOST SHEEP HUM-68/2/O	CL	125.00	135.00-325.00
*	LOST SHEEP HUM-68/O	CL	180.00	190.00-425.00
*	LOST STOCKING HUM-374	OP	120.00	140.00-4000.00
*	LULLABY, CANDLEHOLDER HUM-24/I	TW	*	170.00-650.00
*	LULLABY, CANDLEHOLDER HUM-24/III	TW	*	450.00-1800.00
*	M.I. HUMMEL (ENGLISH), PLAQUE HUM-187 A	OP	75.00	75.00-225.00
*	MADONNA PLAQUE(WHITE OVERGLAZE)HUM 48/II	CL	*	400.00-500.00
*	MARCH WINDS HUM-43	OP	135.00	155.00-575.00
*	MAX AND MORITZ HUM-123	OP	190.00	215.00-750.00
*	MEDITATION HUM-13/2/O	OP	120.00	140.00-325.00
*	MEDITATION HUM-13/II	TW	*	350.00-5000.00
*	MEDITATION HUM-13/O	OP	190.00	215.00-800.00
*	MEDITATION HUM-13/V	TW	*	1200.00-5000.00
*	MEDITATION, HUM-13	CL	*	4000.00-5000.00
*	MERRY WANDERER HUM-11	CL	*	550.00-700.00
*	MERRY WANDERER HUM-11/2/O	OP	115.00	135.00-500.00
*	MERRY WANDERER HUM-11/O	OP	160.00	195.00-650.00
*	MERRY WANDERER HUM-7/I	TW	360.00	400.00-1600.00
*	MERRY WANDERER HUM-7/II	TW	1100.00	1200.00-3500.00
*	MERRY WANDERER HUM-7/III	TW	*	1250.00-4000.00
*	MERRY WANDERER HUM-7/O	OP	220.00	275.00-950.00
*	MERRY WANDERER HUM-7/X	TW	*	12000.00-20000.00
*	MERRY WANDERER, PLAQUE HUM-92	TW	*	140.00-525.00
*	MERRY WANDERER/PLAQ. WD FRAME, HUM-106	CL	*	5000.00-6000.00
*	MISCHIEF MAKER HUM-342	OP	220.00	275.00-5000.00
*	MOTHER'S DARLING HUM-175	OP	180.00	210.00-750.00
*	MOTHER'S HELPER HUM-133	OP	160.00	195.00-650.00
*	MOUNTAINEER HUM-315	OP	180.00	210.00-5000.00
*	NOT FOR YOU! HUM-317	OP	200.00	240.00-5000.00
*	ON SECRET PATH HUM-386	OP	210.00	245.00-1500.00
*	OUT OF DANGER HUM-56 B	OP	245.00	290.00-625.00
*	OUT OF DANGER, TABLE LAMP, HUM-44 B	TW	*	300.00-600.00
*	PHOTOGRAPHER HUM-178	OP	230.00	285.00-1000.00
*	PLAYMATES HUM-58	CL	*	450.00-1000.00
*	PLAYMATES HUM-58/2/O	OP	125.00	145.00-150.00
*	PLAYMATES HUM-58/I	OP	220.00	275.00-950.00
*	PLAYMATES HUM-58/O	OP	145.00	165.00-575.00
*	PLAYMATES, BOX (NEW STYLE) HUM III/58	TW	*	150.00-200.00
*	PLAYMATES, BOX (OLD STYLE) HUM III/58	CL	*	425.00-750.00
*	PLAYMATES/CHICK GIRL BOOKENDS HUM-61 A&B	SU	*	350.00-1200.00
*	PLAYMATES/CHICK GIRL/BOOKENDS HUM 61 A&B	TW	*	350.00-1200.00
*	POSTMAN HUM-119/2/O	OP	115.00	135.00-140.00
*	POSTMAN HUM-119/O	OP	170.00	200.00-205.00
*	PRAYER BEFORE BATTLE HUM-20	OP	145.00	165.00-600.00
*	PRAYER BEFORE BATTLE, ASHTRAY HUM-19	CL	*	5000.00-10000.00
*	PUPPY LOVE & SERENADE/DOG BKENDS HUM-122	CL	*	10000.00-20000.00
*	PUPPY LOVE HUM-1	CL	125.00	250.00-925.00

YR NAME	LIMIT	ISSUE	QUOTE
* QUARTET, PLAQUE HUM-134	TW	*	240.00-950.00
* RETEAT TO SAFETY HUM-201	CL	*	600.00-1100.00
* RETREAT TO SAFETY HUM-201/2/O	OP	140.00	160.00-400.00
* RETREAT TO SAFETY HUM-201/I	OP	250.00	300.00-650.00
* RETREAT TO SAFETY, PLAQUE HUM-126	TW	*	175.00-600.00
* RIDE INTO CHRISTMAS HUM-396	CL	*	450.00-2500.00
* RIDE INTO CHRISTMAS HUM-396/2/O	OP	200.00	235.00-245.00
* RIDE INTO CHRISTMAS HUM-396/I	OP	360.00	425.00-440.00
* RING AROUND THE ROSIE HUM-348	OP	2300.00	2600.00-5000.00
* RUN-A-WAY HUM-327	OP	210.00	250.00-5000.00
* SAINT GEORGE HUM-55	OP	280.00	320.00-3000.00
* SCHOOL BOY HUM-82	CL	*	550.00-700.00
* SCHOOL BOY HUM-82/2/O	OP	120.00	140.00-525.00
* SCHOOL BOY HUM-82/II	OP	380.00	450.00-1500.00
* SCHOOL BOY HUM-82/O	OP	160.00	195.00-675.00
* SCHOOL BOYS HUM-170	CL	*	2100.00-5000.00
* SCHOOL BOYS HUM-170/I	OP	1000.00	1200.00-1500.00
* SCHOOL BOYS HUM-170/III	CL	*	1800.00-2200.00
* SCHOOL GIRL HUM-81	CL	*	325.00-700.00
* SCHOOL GIRL HUM-81/2/O	OP	120.00	140.00-500.00
* SCHOOL GIRL HUM-81/O	OP	160.00	195.00-650.00
* SCHOOL GIRLS HUM-177	CL	*	2100.00-5000.00
* SCHOOL GIRLS HUM-177/I	OP	1000.00	1200.00-1500.00
* SCHOOL GIRLS HUM-177/III	CL	*	1800.00-2200.00
* SENSITIVE HUNTER HUM-6	CL	*	700.00-900.00
* SENSITIVE HUNTER HUM-6/2/O	OP	125.00	145.00-150.00
* SENSITIVE HUNTER HUM-6/I	OP	210.00	250.00-900.00
* SENSITIVE HUNTER HUM-6/II	TW	*	350.00-2000.00
* SENSITIVE HUNTER HUM-6/O	OP	160.00	195.00-675.00
* SERENADE HUM-85	CL	*	750.00-1500.00
* SERENADE HUM-85/4/O	OP	80.00	100.00-105.00
* SERENADE HUM-85/II	OP	380.00	450.00-1400.00
* SERENADE HUM-85/O	OP	110.00	130.00-450.00
* SHE LOVES ME, SHE LOVES ME NOT! HUM-174	OP	150.00	190.00-650.00
* SHE LOVES ME..NOT, TABLE LAMP HUM-227	TW	*	275.00-750.00
* SHEPHERD'S BOY HUM-64	OP	185.00	225.00-750.00
* SHINING LIGHT HUM-358	OP	70.00	85.00-200.00
* SHRINE, TABLE LAMP HUM-100	CL	*	8000.00-10000.00
* SIGNS OF SPRING HUM-203	CL	*	550.00-1000.00
* SIGNS OF SPRING HUM-203/2/O	CL	*	200.00-1200.00
* SIGNS OF SPRING HUM-203/I	CL	*	250.00-575.00
* SILENT NIGHT CANDLEHLDR/BLK CHILD HUM-54	CL	*	7500.00-10000.00
* SILENT NIGHT, CANDLEHOLDER HUM-54	TW	*	270.00-1000.00
* SILENT NIGHT/BLK CHILD/ADVENT GRP HUM-31	CL	*	20000.00-25000.00
* SILENT NIGHT/WHT CHILD.ADVENT GRP HUM-31	CL	*	10000.00-15000.00
* SINGING LESSON (WITHOUT BASE) HUM-41	CL	*	5000.00-10000.00
* SINGING LESSON HUM-63	OP	100.00	120.00-425.00
* SINGING LESSON, ASHTRAY HUM-34	TW	*	140.00-600.00
* SINGING LESSON, BOX(NEW STYLE)HUM III/63	TW	*	150.00-200.00
* SINGING LESSON,BOX(OLD STYLE)HUM III/63	CL	*	425.00-750.00
* SISTER HUM-98	CL	*	285.00-650.00
* SISTER HUM-98/2/O	OP	120.00	135.00-225.00
* SISTER HUM-98/O	OP	165.00	200.00-300.00
* SKIER HUM-59	OP	185.00	200.00-775.00
* SMART LITTLE SISTER HUM-346	OP	210.00	250.00-5000.00
* SOLIDIER BOY HUM-332	OP	180.00	210.00-6500.00
* SOLOIST HUM-135	CL	*	135.00-475.00
* SOLOIST HUM-135/4/O	OP	80.00	100.00-105.00
* SOLOIST HUM-135/O	OP	110.00	130.00-135.00
* SPRING CHEER HUM-72	TW	*	175.00-600.00
* SPRING DANCE HUM-353/I	TW	*	500.00-2000.00
* SPRING DANCE HUM-353/O	OP	*	310.00-4000.00
* STANDING BOY, PLAQUE HUM-168	TW	*	175.00-1000.00
* STAR GAZER HUM-132	OP	180.00	205.00-750.00
* STITCH IN TIME HUM-255	CL	*	290.00-750.00
* STITCH IN TIME HUM-255/4/O	OP	80.00	95.00-100.00
* STITCH IN TIME HUM-255/O	OP	230.00	285.00-290.00
* STORMY WEATHER HUM-71	CL	*	460.00-1250.00
* STORMY WEATHER HUM-71/2/O	OP	250.00	300.00-310.00
* STORMY WEATHER HUM-71/I	OP	380.00	450.00-460.00
* STREET SINGER HUM-131	OP	155.00	190.00-650.00
* STROLLING ALONG HUM-5	CL	120.00	225.00-900.00
* SUPREME PROTECTION HUM-364	CL	*	300.00-600.00
* SUPREME PROTECTION HUM-364 (ALTERED J)	CL	*	600.00-850.00
* SURPRISE HUM-94	CL	*	450.00-950.00
* SURPRISE HUM-94/3/O	OP	130.00	150.00-500.00

YR	NAME	LIMIT	ISSUE	QUOTE
*	SURPRISE HUM-94/I	OP	235.00	285.00-900.00
*	SWAYING LULLABY, PLAQUE HUM-165	TW	*	175.00-1000.00
*	SWEET MUSIC HUM-186	OP	160.00	200.00-700.00
*	TELLING HER SECRET HUM-196	CL	*	725.00-1350.00
*	TELLING HER SECRET HUM-196/I	TW	*	375.00-875.00
*	TELLING HER SECRET HUM-196/O	OP	250.00	295.00-675.00
*	THE MAIL IS HERE HUM-226	OP	470.00	530.00-1250.00
*	THE MAIL IS HERE, PLAQ. OVERGLAZE HUM140	CL	*	1000.00-1500.00
*	THE MAIL IS HERE, PLAQUE HUM-140	TW	*	225.00-900.00
*	TINY BABY IN CRIB, WALL PLAQ., HUM-138	CL	*	3000.00-4000.00
*	TO MARKET HUM-49	CL	*	600.00-1700.00
*	TO MARKET HUM-49/3/O	OP	140.00	160.00-600.00
*	TO MARKET HUM-49/I	TW	*	425.00-1700.00
*	TO MARKET HUM-49/O	OP	225.00	285.00-950.00
*	TO MARKET, TABLE LAMP HUM-101	CL	*	500.00-1000.00
*	TO MARKET, TABLE LAMP HUM-223	TW	*	375.00-700.00
*	TO MARKET,TABLE LAMP(PL. POST) HUM-101	CL	*	6000.00-10000.00
*	TO MARKET,TBL LAMP TREE TRK POST HUM-101	CL	*	1500.00-2000.00
*	TRUMPET BOY HUM-97	OP	110.00	130.00-475.00
*	TUNEFUL ANGEL HUM-359	OP	70.00	85.00-200.00
*	TUNEFUL GOOD NIGHT, PLAQUE HUM-180	TW	*	175.00-750.00
*	UMBRELLA BOY HUM-152	CL	*	2200.00-6000.00
*	UMBRELLA BOY HUM-152 A	CL	*	1500.00-2500.00
*	UMBRELLA BOY HUM-152/II A	OP	1200.00	1450.00-1600.00
*	UMBRELLA BOY HUM-152/O A	OP	490.00	575.00-1500.00
*	UMBRELLA GIRL HUM-152 B	CL	*	1500.00-6000.00
*	UMBRELLA GIRL HUM-152/II B	OP	1200.00	1450.00-1600.00
*	UMBRELLA GIRL HUM-152/O B	OP	490.00	575.00-1500.00
*	VACATION TIME, PLAQUE HUM-125	TW	*	175.00-700.00
*	VILLAGE BOY HUM-51	CL	*	850.00-1100.00
*	VILLAGE BOY HUM-51/2/O	OP	115.00	140.00-500.00
*	VILLAGE BOY HUM-51/3/O	OP	100.00	120.00-425.00
*	VILLAGE BOY HUM-51/I	TW	*	250.00-1000.00
*	VILLAGE BOY HUM-51/O	OP	195.00	250.00-825.00
*	VISITING AN INVALID HUM-382	OP	185.00	200.00-1500.00
*	VOLUNTEER TABLE LAMP, HUM-102	CL	*	8000.00-10000.00
*	VOLUNTEERS HUM-50	CL	*	1200.00-1500.00
*	VOLUNTEERS HUM-50/2/O	OP	190.00	215.00-450.00
*	VOLUNTEERS HUM-50/I	TW	*	425.00-1400.00
*	VOLUNTEERS HUM-50/O	OP	250.00	295.00-1000.00
*	WAITER HUM-154	CL	*	550.00-1100.00
*	WAITER HUM-154/I	OP	240.00	285.00-950.00
*	WAITER HUM-154/O	OP	180.00	210.00-725.00
*	WAITER W/WHISKY HUM 154/0	CL	*	1500.00-2000.00
*	WASH DAY HUM-321/4/O	OP	80.00	100.00-105.00
*	WASH DAY HUM-321/O	OP	230.00	285.00-290.00
*	WATCHFUL ANGEL HUM-194	OP	270.00	310.00-2000.00
*	WAYSIDE DEVOTION HUM-28	CL	*	1600.00-1850.00
*	WAYSIDE DEVOTION HUM-28/II	OP	370.00	410.00-1400.00
*	WAYSIDE DEVOTION HUM-28/III	OP	480.00	540.00-1600.00
*	WAYSIDE HARMONY HUM-111	CL	*	650.00-800.00
*	WAYSIDE HARMONY HUM-111/3/O	OP	125.00	145.00-500.00
*	WAYSIDE HARMONY HUM-111/I	OP	220.00	270.00-750.00
*	WAYSIDE HARMONY, TABLE LAMP HUM II/111	CL	*	350.00-750.00
*	WAYSIDE HARMONY, TABLE LAMP HUM-224	CL	*	475.00-800.00
*	WAYSIDE HARMONY, TABLE LAMP HUM-224/I	TW	*	290.00-550.00
*	WAYSIDE HARMONY, TABLE LAMP HUM-224/II	TW	*	340.00-700.00
*	WE CONGRATULATE (WITH BASE) HUM-220	OP	135.00	150.00-375.00
*	WEARY WANDERER HUM-204	OP	200.00	250.00-800.00
*	WHICH HAND? HUM-258	OP	165.00	195.00-800.00
*	WHITSUNTIDE HUM-163	OP	270.00	300.00-1200.00
*	WORSHIP HUM-84	CL	*	450.00-1500.00
*	WORSHIP HUM-84/O	OP	135.00	160.00-525.00
*	WORSHIP HUM-84/V	TW	*	1100.00-3000.00
41	HUM 148	CL	*	*
41	HUM 149	CL	*	*
43	HUM-155	CL	*	*
43	HUM-158 GIRL STANDING WITH DOG IN ARMS	CL	*	*
43	HUM-159 GIRL STANDING W/FLOWERS IN ARMS	CL	*	*
43	HUM-160 GIRL STANDING TIERED DRESS/FLWRS	CL	*	*
43	HUM-161 GIRL STANDING HANDS IN POCKETS	CL	*	*
46	HUM-162 GIRL STANDING WITH HANDBAG	CL	*	*
47	FESTIVAL HARMONY (FLUTE) HUM-173	CL	95.00	2500.00-3500.00
47	FESTIVAL HARMONY (FLUTE) HUM-173	CL	95.00	1000.00-1500.00
47	SWEET MUSIC W/STRIPPED SLIPPERS HUM-186	CL	*	1200.00-1600.00
48	COQUETTES HUM-179	OP	*	285.00-1000.00

YR	NAME	LIMIT	ISSUE	QUOTE
48	OLD MAN READING NEWSPAPER HUM-181	CL	*	15000.00-20000.00
48	OLD MAN READING NEWSPAPER/TBL LAMPHUM202	CL	*	15000.00-20000.00
48	OLD MAN WALKING TO MARKET HUM-191	CL	*	15000.00-20000.00
48	OLD WOMAN KNITTING HUM-189	CL	*	15000.00-20000.00
48	OLD WOMAN WALKING TO MARKET HUM-190	CL	*	15000.00-20000.00
48	SIGNS OF SPRING W/TWO SHOES HUM 203/2/O	CL	120.00	1000.00-1200.00
50	FESTIVAL HARMONY (MANDOLIN) HUM-172	CL	95.00	2500.00-3000.00
50	FESTIVAL HARMONY (MANDOLIN) HUM-172	CL	95.00	1000.00-1500.00
51	BIRTHDAY SERENADE HUM-218/1	CL	*	1000.00-1500.00
51	HUM-215 JESUS STANDING W/LAMB IN ARMS	CL	*	*
51	ORCHESTRA HUM-212	CL	*	*
52	HAPPY PASTIME/CANDY JAR HUM-221	CL	*	5000.00-10000.00
52	LITTLE VELMA HUM-219	CL	*	5000.00-7000.00
52	WE CONGRATULATE W/BASE HUM-220/2/O	CL	*	450.00-550.00
54	HUM 236A & B	CL	*	10000.00-15000.00
54	HUM-233 BOY FEEDING BIRDS	CL	*	*
55	HOLY WATER FONT, ANGEL JOYOUS NEWS H-241	CL	*	1000.00-1500.00
55	HOLY WATER FONT, ANGEL JOYOUS NEWS H-242	CL	*	1000.00-1500.00
55	HONEY LOVER HUM-312	CL	190.00	4000.00-5000.00
55	LITTLE PHARMACIST HUM-322	CL	*	2000.00-3000.00
55	MADONNA HOLDING CHILD HUM-151	CL	44.00	9000.00-12000.00
55	PROFESSOR, THE HUM-320	CL	180.00	4000.00-5000.00
55	STANDING MADONNA W/CHILD HUM-247	CL	*	10000.00-15000.00
56	BIRTHDAY PRESENT HUM-341	CL	140.00	4000.00-5000.00
56	LETTER TO SANTA CLAUS HUM-340	CL	30.00	15000.00-20000.00
57	RING AROUND THE ROSIE HUM-348	CL	70.00	10000.00-15000.00
62	GIRL W/ACCORDION HUM-259	CL	*	5000.00-10000.00
64	MORNING STROLL HUM-375	CL	170.00	3000.00-4000.00
72	CHICKEN-LICKEN HUM-385/4/O	OP	28.50	100.00-105.00
72	EASTER TIME HUM-384	OP	27.50	250.00-1500.00
72	RUN-A-WAY, THE HUM-327	OP	28.50	250.00-5000.00
74	POET, THE HUM-397	CL	220.00	2000.00-3000.00
78	LITTLE ARCHITECT, THE HUM-410	CL	290.00	2000.00-3000.00
79	BIRD WATCHER HUM-300	OP	80.00	215.00-5000.00
79	BOY AND GIRL, WALL VASE HUM-360 A	TW	*	140.00-650.00
79	BOY, WALL VASE HUM-360 B	TW	*	120.00-650.00
79	GIRL, WALL VASE HUM-360 C	TW	*	120.00-650.00
79	MERRY CHRISTMAS, PLAQUE HUM-323	OP	55.00	125.00-3000.00
79	SEARCHING ANGEL, PLAQUE HUM-310	OP	55.00	120.00-5000.00
80	VALENTINE JOY HUM-399	CL	95.00	5000.00-7500.00
81	DAISIES DON'T TELL HUM-380	CL	80.00	125.00
81	IN TUNE HUM-414	OP	115.00	280.00-3000.00
81	ON HOLIDAY "HOLIDAY SHOPPER" HUM-350	CL	85.00	4000.00-5000.00
81	ON HOLIDAY HUM-350	OP	85.00	170.00-3000.00
81	SWEET GREETINGS HUM-352	OP	85.00	200.00-3000.00
81	THOUGHTFUL HUM-415	OP	105.00	215.00-225.00
81	TIMID LITTLE SISTER HUM-394	OP	190.00	425.00-3000.00
82	BOTANIST HUM-351	OP	84.00	200.00-3000.00
82	LITTLE NURSE HUM-376	OP	95.00	245.00-4000.00
83	KNIT ONE, PURL ONE HUM-432	OP	52.00	115.00-120.00
83	WITH LOVING GREETINGS HUM-309	OP	80.00	190.00-5000.00
84	FESTIVAL HARMONY (MANDOLIN) HUM-172/II	CL	95.00	600.00-750.00
84	FLYING HIGH HUM-452	CL	75.00	150.00-250.00
84	JUST DOZING HUM-451	OP	220.00	220.00
85	BAKING DAY HUM-330	OP	95.00	275.00-5000.00
85	GOING HOME HUM-383	OP	125.00	310.00-4000.00
85	JUBILEE HUM-416	CL	200.00	350.00-500.00
85	JUST FISHING HUM-373	OP	85.00	225.00-4000.00
85	SING WITH ME HUM-405	OP	125.00	310.00-3000.00
87	GENTLE GLOW, CANDLEHOLDER HUM-439	OP	110.00	200.00-210.00
87	IN THE MEADOW HUM-459	OP	110.00	200.00-250.00
87	KINDERGARTNER HUM-467	OP	100.00	200.00-250.00
87	PEACE ON EARTH HUM-484	CL	80.00	125.00-150.00
87	SING ALONG HUM-433	OP	145.00	275.00-285.00
88	A BUDDING MAESTRO HUM-477	OP	45.00	100.00-130.00
88	LITTLE SWEEPER HUM-171	CL	*	140.00-450.00
88	SONG OF PRAISE HUM-454	OP	39.00	100.00-105.00
88	SOUND THE TRUMPET HUM-457	OP	45.00	100.00-125.00
88	SOUNDS OF THE MANDOLIN HUM-438	OP	65.00	120.00-125.00
88	THE ACCOMPANIST HUM-453	OP	39.00	100.00-105.00
88	WINTER SONG HUM-476	OP	45.00	110.00-125.00
89	AN APPLE A DAY HUM-403	OP	195.00	275.00-3000.00
89	BIRTHDAY CAKE, CANDLEHOLDER HUM-338	OP	95.00	140.00-5000.00
89	BIRTHDAY PRESENT HUM-341/3/O	OP	140.00	140.00
89	CHRISTMAS ANGEL HUM-301	OP	160.00	250.00-5000.00
89	DADDY'S GIRLS HUM-371	OP	130.00	225.00-4000.00

YR	NAME	LIMIT	ISSUE	QUOTE
89	FLYING ANGEL, HUM-366	OP	65.00	95.00-125.00
89	HOSANNA HUM-480	OP	68.00	100.00-125.00
89	I'LL PROTECT HIM HUM-483	OP	55.00	85.00-100.00
89	I'M HERE HUM-478	OP	50.00	100.00-125.00
89	IN D MAJOR HUM-430	OP	135.00	200.00-210.00
89	IS IT RAINING? HUM-420	OP	175.00	255.00-265.00
89	LOVE FROM ABOVE HUM-481	CL	75.00	125.00-150.00
89	MAKE A WISH HUM-475	OP	135.00	200.00-250.00
89	ONE FOR YOU, ONE FOR ME HUM-482	OP	50.00	100.00-125.00
89	POSTMAN HUM-119	CL	*	205.00-700.00
89	TUBA PLAYER HUM-437	OP	160.00	260.00-270.00
89	WASH DAY HUM-321	CL	*	285.00-5000.00
90	BATH TIME HUM-412	OP	300.00	375.00-3000.00
90	GOOD FRIENDS, CANDLEHOLDER HUM-679	OP	142.50	145.50
90	GRANDMAS'S GIRL HUM-561	OP	100.00	145.00-175.00
90	GRANDPA'S BOY HUM-562	OP	100.00	145.00-175.00
90	HORSE TRAINER HUM-423	OP	155.00	215.00-225.00
90	SHE LOVES ME, CANDLEHOLDER HUM-678	OP	142.50	145.50
90	SLEEP TIGHT HUM-424	OP	155.00	215.00-225.00
90	WHAT'S NEW? HUM-418	OP	200.00	275.00-285.00
91	A NAP HUM-534	OP	95.00	120.00-150.00
91	ART CRITIC HUM-318	OP	230.00	285.00-5000.00
91	EVENING PRAYER HUM-495	OP	95.00	105.00
91	FRIEND OR FOE HUM-434	OP	190.00	215.00-225.00
91	LAND IN SIGHT HUM-530	CL	1600.00	1600.00-1800.00
91	SCAMP HUM-553	OP	95.00	110.00
91	STORYBOOK TIME HUM-458	OP	330.00	380.00
91	THE GUARDIAN HUM-455	OP	140.00	165.00-190.00
91	THE PROFESSOR HUM-320/O	OP	180.00	200.00-5000.00
91	WE WISH YOU THE BEST HUM-600	CL	1300.00	1400.00-1800.00
91	WHISTLER'S DUET HUM-413	OP	235.00	280.00-3000.00
92	A SWWET OFFERING HUM-549	OP	75.00	80.00
92	LUCKY FELLOW HUM-560	CL	75.00	100.00
92	MY WISH IS SMALL HUM-463/O	CL	170.00	200.00-250.00
93	A FREE FLIGHT HUM-569	OP	185.00	195.00
93	CELESTIAL MUSICIAN (MINI) HUM-188/4/0	OP	*	310.00-1500.00
93	LITTLE ARCHITECT HUM-410/I	OP	*	300.00-3000.00
93	ONE PLUS ONE HUM-556	CL	115.00	115.00-125.00
93	PARADE OF LIGHTS HUM-616	OP	235.00	250.00
94	CALL TO GLORY HUM-739	OP	250.00	250.00
94	FESTIVAL HARMONY (MANDOLIN) HUM-172/4/O	OP	95.00	95.00
94	HEAVENLY ANGEL TREE TOPPER HUM-755	OP	450.00	450.00
94	I'M CAREFREE HUM-633	OP	365.00	375.00-750.00
94	LITTLE VISITOR HUM-563	OP	180.00	180.00
94	MORNING STROLL HUM-375/3/O	OP	170.00	175.00
94	POET, THE HUM-397/I	OP	220.00	225.00
94	WE COME IN PEACE HUM-754	OP	350.00	350.00
95	ANGLER, THE HUM-566	OP	320.00	320.00
95	COME BACK SOON HUM-545	OP	135.00	135.00
95	FESTIVAL HARMONY (FLUTE) HUM-173/4/O	OP	95.00	95.00
95	OOH, MY TOOTH HUM-533	OP	110.00	110.00
95	PIXIE HUM-768	OP	105.00	105.00
95	TO KEEP YOU WARM HUM-759	OP	195.00	195.00
MI HUMMEL		**M.I. HUMMEL ANNIVERSARY CLOCK**		
95	GOOSE GIRL ANN. CLOCK HUM-750	OP	200.00	200.00
M.I. HUMMEL		**M.I. HUMMEL CENTURY COLLECTION**		
86	CHAPEL TIME, CLOCK HUM-442	CL	500.00	1500.00-3000.00
88	CALL TO WORSHIP, CLOCK HUM-441	CL	600.00	900.00-1150.00
89	HARMONY IN FOUR PARTS HUM-471	CL	850.00	1750.00-2000.00
90	LET'S TELL THE WORLD HUM-487	CL	875.00	1250.00-1500.00
92	ON OUR WAY HUM-472	CL	950.00	950.00-1200.00
93	WELCOME SPRING HUM-635	CL	1085.00	1200.00-1500.00
94	ROCK-A-BYE HUM 574	CL	1150.00	1150.00-1200.00
95	STRIKE UP THE BAND HUM-668	OP	1200.00	1200.00
M.I. HUMMEL		**M.I. HUMMEL COLLECTORS CLUB ANNIVERSARY**		
90	FLOWER GIRL HUM-548	OP	105.00	130.00-200.00
90	THE LITTLE PAIR HUM-449	OP	170.00	200.00-350.00
91	HONEY LOVER HUM-312/I	CL	190.00	210.00-5000.00
M.I. HUMMEL		**M.I. HUMMEL COLLECTORS CLUB EXCLUSIVES**		
*	I BROUGHT YOU A GIFT HUM-479	CL	*	100.00-150.00
77	VALENTINE GIFT HUM-387	CL	45.00	600.00-3000.00
78	SMILING THROUGH, PLAQUE HUM-690	CL	50.00	200.00-250.00
80	VALENTINE JOY HUM-399	CL	95.00	250.00-7500.00
81	DAISIES DON'T TELL HUM-380	CL	80.00	300.00-4000.00
82	IT'S COLD HUM-421	CL	80.00	300.00-350.00
83	WHAT NOW? HUM-422	CL	80.00	300.00-350.00

YR	NAME	LIMIT	ISSUE	QUOTE
84	COFFEE BREAK HUM-409	CL	90.00	300.00-3000.00
85	SMILING THROUGH HUM-408	CL	125.00	300.00-350.00
86	BIRTHDAY CANDLE, CANDLEHOLDER HUM-440	CL	95.00	300.00-350.00
87	MORNING CONCERT HUM-447	CL	98.00	225.00-275.00
88	THE SURPRISE HUM-431	CL	125.00	275.00-325.00
89	HELLO WORLD HUM-429	CL	130.00	250.00-300.00
90	I WONDER HUM-486	CL	140.00	175.00-300.00
91	GIFT FROM A FRIEND HUM-485	CL	160.00	200.00-300.00
91	TWO HANDS, ONE TREAT HUM-493	CL	*	100.00-125.00
92	CHEEKY FELLOW HUM-554	CL	120.00	120.00-130.00
92	MY WISH IS SMALL HUM-463	CL	170.00	1000.00-2000.00
93	I DIDN'T DO IT HUM-626	CL	175.00	175.00-200.00
93	SWEET AS CAN BE HUM-541	OP	125.00	125.00
94	AT GRANDPA'S HUM-621	10,000	1300.00	1300.00
94	FOR KEEPS HUM-630	OP	*	80.00-100.00
94	LITTLE TROUBADOUR HUM-558	OP	130.00	130.00
95	A STORY FROM GRANDMA HUM 620	10,000	1300.00	1300.00
79	BUST OF SISTER M.I. HUMMEL HU-3	CL	75.00	300.00-350.00
M.I. HUMMEL			**M.I. HUMMEL MADONNA**	
*	FLOWER MADONNA, COLOR HUM-10/I	CL	350.00	430.00-900.00
*	FLOWER MADONNA, COLOR HUM-10/III	CL	*	475.00-1250.00
*	FLOWER MADONNA, WHITE HUM-10/I	OP	165.00	165.00-600.00
*	FLOWER MADONNA, WHITE HUM-10/III	TW	*	300.00-750.00
*	MADONNA PLAQUE HUM-48	CL	*	600.00-800.00
*	MADONNA PLAQUE HUM-48/II	TW	*	120.00-750.00
*	MADONNA PLAQUE HUM-48/O	TW	*	75.00-350.00
*	MADONNA PLAQUE HUM-48/V	CL	*	1000.00-2000.00
*	MADONNA W/HALO WHITE HUM-45/II	TW	150.00	150.00-350.00
*	MADONNA W/HALO, COLOR HUM-45/I	OP	105.00	125.00-350.00
*	MADONNA W/HALO, COLOR HUM-45/III	SU	*	150.00-600.00
*	MADONNA W/HALO, COLOR HUM-45/O	SU	*	60.00-275.00
*	MADONNA W/HALO, WHITE HUM-45	OP	*	30.00-35.00
*	MADONNA W/HALO, WHITE HUM-45/I	OP	70.00	70.00-200.00
*	MADONNA W/HALO, WHITE HUM-45/O	TW	*	40.00-175.00
*	MADONNA W/O HALO, COLOR HUM-46/I	TW	*	125.00-350.00
*	MADONNA W/O HALO, COLOR HUM-46/III	TW	*	150.00-600.00
*	MADONNA W/O HALO, COLOR HUM-46/O	TW	*	60.00-275.00
*	MADONNA W/O HALO, WHITE HUM-46/I	SU	*	70.00-200.00
*	MADONNA W/O HALO, WHITE HUM-46/III	SU	*	105.00-350.00
*	MADONNA W/O HALO, WHITE HUM-46/O	SU	*	40.00-175.00
77	MADONNA HOLDING CHILD, BLUE HUM-151	TW	*	850.00-3000.00
77	MADONNA HOLDING CHILD, WHITE HUM-151	TW	*	350.00-2500.00
M.I. HUMMEL			**M.I. HUMMEL NATIVITY**	
*	ANGEL KNEELING/SERENADE HUM-214D (COLOR)	OP	70.00	90.00-190.00
*	ANGEL KNEELING/SERENADE HUM-214D (WHITE)	CL	*	165.00-290.00
*	ANGEL SERENADE (LARGE) HUM-260E	SU	*	135.00-150.00
*	ANGEL SERENADE HUM-214/D	OP	*	90.00-290.00
*	ANGEL/GOOD NIGHT HUM-214C (COLOR)	OP	70.00	70.00-175.00
*	COW, LYING (LARGE) HUM-260M	SU	*	150.00-170.00
*	DONKEY HUM-214/J	OP	*	70.00-255.00
*	DONKEY HUM-214J (COLOR)	OP	60.00	70.00-155.00
*	DONKEY HUM-214J (WHITE)	CL	*	130.00-255.00
*	DONKEY, STANDING (LARGE) HUM-260L	SU	*	135.00-150.00
*	FLYING ANGEL HUM-366	OP	*	125.00-275.00
*	FLYING ANGEL HUM-366 (COLOR)	OP	105.00	125.00-250.00
*	FLYING ANGEL HUM-366 (WHITE)	OP	*	125.00-250.00
*	GOOD NIGHT (LARGE) HUM-260D	SU	*	140.00-160.00
*	GOOD NIGHT ANGEL HUM-214/C	OP	*	90.00-190.00
*	INFANT JESUS (LARGE) HUM-260C	SU	*	115.00-130.00
*	INFANT JESUS HUM-214A/K (COLOR)	OP	50.00	65.00-70.00
*	INFANT JESUS HUM-214A/K (WHITE)	CL	*	60.00-70.00
*	INFANT JESUS HUM-214A/K/1	OP	*	65.00
*	JOSEPH HUM-214/B	OP	*	175.00-420.00
*	JOSEPH HUM-214B (COLOR)	OP	150.00	175.00-390.00
*	JOSEPH HUM-214B (WHITE)	CL	*	145.00-420.00
*	KING ON ONE KNEE HUM 214/M	OP	*	175.00-475.00
*	KING ON ONE KNEE HUM-214 M/O	OP	*	140.00-145.00
*	KING ON ONE KNEE HUM-214M (COLOR)	OP	150.00	175.00-395.00
*	KING ON ONE KNEE HUM-214M (WHITE)	CL	*	225.00-475.00
*	KING ON TWO KNEES HUM-214 N/O	OP	*	135.00-140.00
*	KING STANDING HUM-214 L/O	OP	*	150.00-155.00
*	KING W/CASHBOX HUM 214/N	OP	*	160.00-475.00
*	KING, KNEE W/CASH BOX HUM-214N (COLOR)	OP	140.00	160.00-370.00
*	KING, KNEE W/CASH BOX HUM-214N (WHITE)	CL	*	225.00-475.00
*	KING, KNEELING (LARGE) HUM-260P	SU	*	470.00-500.00
*	KING, STANDING (LARGE) HUM-260O	SU	*	490.00-540.00

YR	NAME	LIMIT	ISSUE	QUOTE
*	LAMB HUM-214/O	OP	*	20.00-130.00
*	LAMB HUM-214O	OP	*	55.00-130.00
*	LAMB HUM-214O (COLOR)	OP	18.00	20.00-50.00
*	LITTLE TOOTER (LARGE) HUM-260K	SU	*	170.00-195.00
*	MADONNA (LARGE) HUM-260A	SU	*	520.00-550.00
*	MOORISH KING STANDING HUM 214/L	OP	*	185.00-475.00
*	MOORISH KING, STANDING (LARGE) HUM-260N	SU	*	490.00-540.00
*	MOORISH KING, STANDING HUM-214L (COLOR)	OP	155.00	185.00-400.00
*	MOORISH KING, STANDING HUM-214L (WHITE)	CL	*	225.00-475.00
*	NATIVITY SET (LARGE) 16 PIECES HUM-260	TW	*	5000.00-5500.00
*	ONE SHEEP, LYING (LARGE) HUM-260R	SU	*	50.00-70.00
*	OX (COW) HUM-214/K	OP	*	70.00-255.00
*	OX (COW) HUM-214K (COLOR)	OP	60.00	70.00-155.00
*	OX (COW) HUM-214K (WHITE)	CL	*	130.00-255.00
*	SAINT JOSEPH (LARGE) HUM-260B	SU	*	520.00-550.00
*	SHEEP, STANDING W/LAMB (LARGE) HUM-260H	SU	*	100.00-115.00
*	SHEPHERD BOY W/FLUTE HUM-214H (COLOR)	OP	100.00	125.00-270.00
*	SHEPHERD BOY W/FLUTE HUM-214H (WHITE)	CL	*	170.00-320.00
*	SHEPHERD BOY, KNEELING (LARGE) HUM-260J	SU	*	295.00-325.00
*	SHEPHERD KNEELING HUM-214/G	OP	*	130.00-320.00
*	SHEPHERD KNEELING HUM-214G (COLOR)	OP	110.00	130.00-295.00
*	SHEPHERD KNEELING HUM-214G (WHITE)	CL	*	170.00-320.00
*	SHEPHERD W/SHEEP HUM-214/F	OP	*	175.00-470.00
*	SHEPHERD W/SHEEP HUM-214F (COLOR)	OP	155.00	175.00-395.00
*	SHEPHERD W/SHEEP HUM-214F (WHITE)	CL	*	220.00-470.00
*	SHEPHERD, STANDING (LARGE) HUM-260G	SU	*	525.00-575.00
*	SHEPHERD/LI'L TOOTER HUM-214/H	OP	*	125.00-320.00
*	STABLE HUM-260S	OP	400.00	400.00
*	VIRGIN MARY HUM-214/A	OP	*	175.00
*	VIRGIN MARY HUM-214A (COLOR)	OP	150.00	175.00-2500.00
*	VIRGIN MARY HUM-214A (WHITE)	CL	*	195.00-3000.00
*	WE CONGRATULATE (LARGE) HUM-260F	SU	*	370.00-415.00
*	WE CONGRATULATE HUM-214/E	OP	*	160.00-470.00
*	WE CONGRATULATE HUM-214E (COLOR)	OP	140.00	160.00-370.00
*	WE CONGRATULATE HUM-214E (WHITE)	CL	*	270.00-470.00
51	VIRGIN MARY/INFANT JESUS H214/A	CL	*	70.00-3000.00
88	INFANT JESUS HUM-214/A/K/O	OP	*	40.00-45.00
88	INFANT JESUS HUM-214A/K/O	OP	*	40.00
88	JOSEPH HUM-214 B/O	OP	*	130.00-135.00
88	JOSEPH HUM-214B/O	OP	*	130.00
88	MARY HUM-214/A/M/O	OP	*	130.00-135.00
89	ANGEL, GOOD NIGHT HUM-214C (WHITE)	CL	*	265.00-415.00
89	DONKEY HUM-214 J/O	OP	*	50.00-55.00
89	DONKEY HUM-214J/O	OP	*	50.00
89	FLYING ANGEL HUM-366/O	CL	*	95.00-100.00
89	FLYING ANGEL HUM-366/O	OP	*	95.00
89	LAMB HUM-214 O/O	OP	*	20.00-22.00
89	LAMB HUM-214O/O	OP	*	20.00
89	MARY HUM-214A/M/O	OP	*	130.00
89	OX HUM-214 K/O	OP	*	50.00-55.00
89	OX HUM-214K/O	OP	*	50.00
90	KING ON ONE KNEE HUM-214M/O	OP	*	140.00
90	KING ON TWO KNEES HUM-214N/O	OP	*	135.00
90	KING STANDING HUM-214L/O	OP	*	130.00-135.00
91	LITTLE TOOTER HUM-214 H/O	OP	*	100.00-105.00
91	LITTLE TOOTER HUM-214H/O	OP	*	100.00
91	SHEPHERD KNEELING HUM-214 G/O	OP	*	120.00-125.00
91	SHEPHERD KNEELING HUM-214G/O	OP	*	120.00
91	SHEPHERD STANDING HUM-214 F/O	OP	*	150.00-155.00
91	SHEPHERD STANDING HUM-214F/O	OP	*	150.00

M.I. HUMMEL   **UNICEF**

YR	NAME	LIMIT	ISSUE	QUOTE
94	FRIENDS TOGETHER 662/O	OP	260.00	275.00

GOEBEL MINIATURES

R. OLSZEWSKI   **AMERICANA SERIES**

YR	NAME	LIMIT	ISSUE	QUOTE
81	THE PLAINSMAN 660-B	RT	45.00	245.00
82	AMERICAN BALD EAGLE 661-B	RT	45.00	395.00
83	SHE SOUNDS THE DEEP 662-B	RT	45.00	60.00
84	EYES ON THE HORIZON 663-B	RT	45.00	70.00
85	CENTRAL PARK SUNDAY 664-B	RT	45.00	70.00
86	AMERICANA DISPLAY 951-D	SU	80.00	105.00
86	CARROUSEL RIDE 665-B	RT	45.00	70.00
87	TO THE BANDSTAND 666-B	RT	45.00	70.00
89	BLACKSMITH 676-B	RT	55.00	165.00

R. OLSZEWSKI   **CHILDREN'S SERIES**

YR	NAME	LIMIT	ISSUE	QUOTE
80	BLUMENKINDER-COURTING 630-P	RT	55.00	475.00
81	SUMMER DAYS 631-P	RT	65.00	365.00

YR	NAME	LIMIT	ISSUE	QUOTE
82	OUT AND ABOUT 632-P	RT	85.00	385.00
83	BACKYARD FROLIC 633-P	RT	65.00	100.00
84	GRANDPA 634-P	CL	75.00	100.00
85	SNOW HOLIDAY 635-P	CL	75.00	100.00
86	CLOWNING AROUND 636-P	CL	85.00	105.00
87	CARROUSEL DAYS 637-P	CL	85.00	165.00
88	CHILDREN'S DISPLAY (SMALL)	CL	45.00	60.00
88	LITTLE BALLERINA 638-P	CL	85.00	100.00
90	BUILDING BLOCKS CASTLE (LARGE) 968-D	CL	75.00	100.00
R. OLSZEWSKI				**DEGRAZIA**
85	FLOWER BOY 502-P	SU	85.00	110.00
85	FLOWER GIRL 501-P	SU	85.00	110.00
85	MY FIRST HORSE 503-P	SU	85.00	110.00
85	SUNFLOWER BOY 551-P	7500	93.00	135.00
85	WHITE DOVE 504-P	SU	80.00	95.00-100.00
85	WONDERING 505-P	SU	93.00	95.00
86	FESTIVAL OF LIGHTS 507-P	SU	85.00	200.00
86	LITTLE MADONNA 552-P	7500	93.00	135.00
86	PIMA DRUMMER BOY 506-P	SU	85.00	250.00
87	MERRY LITTLE INDIAN 508-P	7500	95.00	295.00
88	ADOBE DISPLAY 948-D	OP	45.00	59.00
89	BEAUTIFUL BURDEN 554-P	7500	110.00	110.00
90	ADOBE HACIENDA DISPLAY (LARGE) 958-D	OP	85.00	95.00
90	CHAPEL DISPLAY 971-D	OP	95.00	100.00
91	MY BEAUTIFUL ROCKING HORSE 555-P	7500	110.00	110.00
R. OLSZEWSKI				**DISNEY-CINDERELLA**
91	ANASTASIA 172-P	SU	85.00	100.00
91	CINDERELLA 176-P	SU	85.00	125.00
91	CINDERELLA'S COACH DISPLAY 978-D	OP	95.00	120.00
91	CINDERELLA'S DREAM CASTLE 976-D	OP	95.00	115.00
91	DRIZELLA 174-P	SU	85.00	100.00
91	FAIRY GODMOTHER 180-P	SU	85.00	100.00
91	FOOTMAN 181-P	SU	85.00	100.00
91	GUS 177-P	SU	75.00	90.00
91	JAQ 173-P	SU	75.00	90.00
91	LUCIFER 175-P	SU	75.00	90.00
91	PRINCE CHARMING 179-P	SU	85.00	100.00
91	STEPMOTHER 178-P	SU	85.00	100.00
R. OLSZEWSKI				**DISNEY-PETER PAN**
92	JOHN 186-P	OP	*	110.00
92	MICHAEL 187-P	OP	*	110.00
92	NANA 189-P	OP	*	110.00
92	PETER PAN 184-P	OP	*	125.00
92	PETER PAN'S LONDON 986-D	OP	*	135.00
92	WENDY 185-P	OP	*	110.00
R. OLSZEWSKI				**DISNEY-PINOCCHIO**
90	GEPPETTO'S TOY SHOP DISPLAY 965-D	OP	95.00	120.00
90	GEPPETTO/FIGARO 682-P	OP	90.00	110.00
90	GIDEON 683-P	OP	75.00	100.00
90	J. WORTHINGTON FOULFELLOW 684-P	OP	95.00	115.00
90	JIMINY CRICKET 685-P	OP	75.00	100.00
90	PINOCCHIO 686-P	OP	75.00	110.00
91	BLUE FAIRY 693-P	OP	95.00	120.00
91	LITTLE STREET LAMP DISPLAY 964-D	OP	65.00	80.00
91	STROMBOLI 694-P	OP	95.00	120.00
91	STROMBOLI'S STREET WAGON 979-D	OP	105.00	125.00
R. OLSZEWSKI				**DISNEY-SNOW WHITE**
87	BASHFUL 165-P	19,500	60.00	85.00
87	COZY COTTAGE DISPLAY 941-D	CL	35.00	185.00
87	DOC 162-P	19,500	60.00	85.00
87	DOPEY 167-P	19,500	60.00	85.00
87	GRUMPY 166-P	19,500	60.00	85.00
87	HAPPY 164-P	19,500	60.00	85.00
87	SLEEPY 163-P	19,500	60.00	85.00
87	SNEEZY 161-P	19,500	60.00	85.00
87	SNEEZY 161-P	19,500	60.00	85.00
87	SNOW WHITE 168-P	19,500	60.00	90.00
88	HOUSE IN THE WOODS DISPLAY 944-D	OP	60.00	105.00
90	SNOW WHITE'S PRINCE 170-P	19,500	80.00	85.00
90	THE WISHING WELL DISPLAY 969-D	OP	65.00	70.00
91	CASTLE COURTYARD DISPLAY 981-D	OP	105.00	105.00
91	SNOW WHITE QUEEN 182-P	OP	*	*
R. OLSZEWSKI				**FIRST EDITION M.I. HUMMEL**
88	DOLL BATH HUM-252P	10,000	95.00	105.00
88	LITTLE FIDDLER HUM-250P	10,000	90.00	110.00-115.00
88	LITTLE SWEEPER HUM-253P	10,000	90.00	105.00

YR	NAME	LIMIT	ISSUE	QUOTE
88	MERRY WANDERER HUM-254P	10,000	95.00	170.00
88	STORMY WEATHER HUM-251P	10,000	115.00	130.00
89	APPLE TREE BOY HUM-257P	10,000	115.00	130.00
89	POSTMAN HUM-255P	10,000	95.00	105.00
89	VISITING AN INVALID HUM-256P	10,000	105.00	115.00
90	BAKER HUM-262P	10,000	100.00	105.00
90	CINDERELLA HUM-264P	10,000	115.00	115.00
90	WAITER HUM-263P	10,000	100.00	115.00
91	ACCORDION BOY HUM-266P	10,000	105.00	105.00-115.00
91	BUSY STUDENT HUM-268P	10,000	105.00	105.00-115.00
91	MERRY WANDERER DEALER PLAQUE HUM-280P	10,000	130.00	435.00
91	MORNING CONCERT HUM-269P	TL	175.00	175.00
91	RIDE INTO CHRISTMAS HUM-279P	OP	195.00	195.00
91	SERENADE HUM-265P	10,000	105.00	105.00-115.00
91	WE CONGRATULATE HUM-267P	10,000	130.00	130.00-140.00
92	GOOSE GIRL HUM-283P	OP	130.00	130.00
92	SCHOOL BOY HUM-281P	OP	120.00	120.00
92	WAYSIDE HARMONY HUM-282P	OP	140.00	180.00
R. OLSZEWSKI				**HISTORICAL SERIES**
80	CAPODIMONTE 600-P	CL	90.00	145.00
81	MASQUERADE-ST. PETERSBURG 601-P	CL	65.00	100.00
83	THE CHERRY PICKERS 602-P	OP	85.00	255.00
84	MOOR WITH SPANISH HORSE 603-P	OP	85.00	110.00
85	FLORAL BOUQUET POMPADOUR 604-P	OP	85.00	115.00
87	MEISSEN PARROT 605-P	OP	85.00	110.00
88	HISTORICAL DISPLAY 943-D	SU	45.00	60.00
88	MINTON ROOSTER 608-P	7500	85.00	110.00
89	FARMER W/DOVES 607-P	OP	85.00	110.00
90	ENGLISH COUNTRY GARDEN 970-D	OP	85.00	105.00
90	GENTLEMAN FOX HUNT 616-P	OP	145.00	145.00
R. OLSZEWSKI				**MICKEY MOUSE**
90	FANTASIA LIVING BROOMS 972-D	OP	85.00	85.00
90	THE SORCERER'S APPRENTICE 171-P	OP	80.00	90.00
R. OLSZEWSKI				**NATIVITY COLLECTION**
91	HOLY FAMILY DISPLAY 982-D	10,000	85.00	90.00
91	JOSEPH 401-P	SU	95.00	125.00
91	JOYFUL CHERUBS 403-P	SU	130.00	175.00
91	MOTHER/CHILD 400-P	SU	120.00	150.00
91	THE STABLE DONKEY 402-P	SU	95.00	125.00
92	3 KINGS DISPLAY	10,000	*	100.00
92	BALTHAZAR 405-P	SU	135.00	195.00
92	CASPAR 406-P	SU	135.00	195.00
92	MELCHIOR 404-P	SU	135.00	195.00
R. OLSZEWSKI			**NIGHT BEFORE CHRISTMAS (1ST EDITION)**	
90	EIGHT TINY REINDEER 691-P	SU	110.00	120.00
90	MAMA & PAPA 692-P	SU	110.00	125.00
90	ST. NICHOLAS 690-P	SU	95.00	115.00
90	SUGAR PLUM BOY 687-P	SU	70.00	90.00
90	SUGAR PLUM GIRL 689-P	SU	70.00	90.00
90	YULE TREE 688-P	SU	90.00	100.00
91	UP TO THE HOUSETOP 966-D	5000	95.00	95.00
R. OLSZEWSKI				**ORIENTAL SERIES**
80	KUAN YIN 640-W	CL	40.00	310.00
82	THE GEISHA 641-P	OP	65.00	195.00
85	TANG HORSE 642-P	OP	65.00	95.00
86	THE BLIND MAN AND THE ELEPHANT 643-P	OP	70.00	70.00
87	CHINESE WATER DRAGON 644-P	OP	70.00	70.00
87	ORIENTAL DISPLAY (SMALL) 945-D	SU	45.00	65.00
89	TIGER HUNT 645-P	OP	85.00	100.00
90	CHINESE TEMPLE LION 646-P	OP	90.00	90.00
90	EMPRESS GARDEN 967-D	OP	95.00	110.00
R. OLSZEWSKI				**PENDANTS**
85	FLOWER GIRL PENDANT 561-P	OP	125.00	150.00
86	CAMPER BIALOSKY	OP	95.00	145.00
87	FESTIVAL OF LIGHTS 562-P	OP	90.00	195.00
88	MICKEY MOUSE 169-P	5000	92.00	185.00
90	HUMMINGBIRD 697-P	OP	125.00	135.00
91	CHRYSANTHEMUM PENDANT	OP	135.00	135.00
91	DAFFODIL PENDANT	OP	135.00	135.00
91	POINSETTIA PENDANT	OP	135.00	135.00
91	ROSE PENDANT	OP	135.00	135.00
N. ROCKWELL				**PORTRAIT OF AMERICA**
88	BOTTOM OF THE SIXTH 365-P	OP	85.00	85.00
88	CHECK UP 363-P	OP	85.00	105.00
88	MARBLES CHAMPION 362-P	OP	85.00	85.00
88	NO SWIMMING 360-P	OP	85.00	85.00

M.I. Hummel's Pleasant Journey is the second issue in the Goebel "Century Collection."

Celestial Musician plays an angelic tune. He is just one of many children captured by artist Sister Maria Innocentia Hummel.

This delightful pair of Bavarian children are Going Home. The figure is produced by Goebel from the artwork of M.I. Hummel.

Sister Maria Innocentia Hummel's Hear Ye, Hear Ye is hand painted in the unmistakable Goebel earthtones.

YR	NAME	LIMIT	ISSUE	QUOTE
88	ROCKWELL DISPLAY 952-D	OP	80.00	93.00
88	THE DOCTOR AND THE DOLL 361-P	OP	85.00	95.00
88	TRIPLE SELF-PORTRAIT 364-P	OP	85.00	175.00
89	BOTTOM DRAWER 366-P	7500	85.00	85.00

HUGHES — SATURDAY EVENING POST

YR	NAME	LIMIT	ISSUE	QUOTE
92	BOY WITH WAGON	OP	*	*
92	CHILDREN CROSSING	OP	*	*
92	CROSSING GUARD	OP	*	*
92	MARKET VIGNETTE	OP	*	*
92	STORE OWNER	OP	*	*
92	CROSSING GUARD VIGNETTE	OP	*	*
91	CITY CLERK	OP	*	*
91	HOME COMING VIGNETTE	OP	*	*
91	MARRIAGE LICENSE VIGNETTE	OP	*	*
91	MOTHER 369-P	OP	*	*
91	SOLDIER 368-P	OP	*	*
91	WEDDING COUPLE	OP	*	*
92	TRIPLE SELF PORTRAIT	OP	*	*
92	TRIPLE SELF PORTRAIT VIGNETTE	OP	*	*

R. OLSZEWSKI — SPECIAL RELEASE-ALICE IN WONDERLAND

YR	NAME	LIMIT	ISSUE	QUOTE
82	ALICE IN THE GARDEN 670-P	5000	60.00	740.00-785.00
83	DOWN THE RABBIT HOLE 671-P	5000	75.00	450.00-480.00
84	THE CHESHIRE CAT 672-P	5000	75.00	350.00-385.00

R. OLSZEWSKI — SPECIAL RELEASE-GOOD-BYE TO OZ

YR	NAME	LIMIT	ISSUE	QUOTE
91	GOOD-BYE TO OZ DISPLAY 980-D	5000	85.00	160.00
92	DOROTHY/GLINDA 695-P	5000	120.00	120.00

R. OLSZEWSKI — SPECIAL RELEASE-WIZARD OF OZ

YR	NAME	LIMIT	ISSUE	QUOTE
84	SCARECROW 673-P	5000	75.00	350.00
85	TINMAN 674-P	5000	80.00	155.00
86	THE COWARDLY LION 675-P	5000	85.00	325.00
87	OZ DISPLAY 942-D	5000	45.00	425.00
87	THE WICKED WITCH 676-P	5000	85.00	105.00
88	THE MUNCHKINS 677-P	5000	85.00	100.00

POUNDER — THE AMERICAN FRONTIER COLLECTION

YR	NAME	LIMIT	ISSUE	QUOTE
87	EIGHT COUNT 310-B	OP	75.00	90.00
87	GRIZZLY'S LAST STAND 320-B	OP	65.00	80.00
87	INDIAN SCOUT AND BUFFALO 300-B	OP	95.00	135.00
87	THE BRONCO BUSTER 350-B	OP	80.00	80.00
87	THE END OF THE TRAIL 340-B	OP	80.00	125.00
87	THE FIRST RIDE 330-B	OP	85.00	100.00
87	AMERICAN FRONTIER DISPLAY 947-D	OP	80.00	110.00

R. OLSZEWSKI — THREE LITTLE PIGS

YR	NAME	LIMIT	ISSUE	QUOTE
89	LITTLE STICKS PIG 678-P	7500	75.00	105.00
89	THREE LITTLE PIGS HOUSE 956-D	7500	50.00	55.00
90	LITTLE STRAW PIG 679-P	7500	75.00	105.00
91	LITTLE BRICKS PIG 680-P	7500	75.00	105.00
91	THE HUNGRY WOLF 681-P	7500	80.00	105.00

R. OLSZEWSKI — WILDLIFE SERIES

YR	NAME	LIMIT	ISSUE	QUOTE
80	CHIPPING SPARROW 620-P	OP	55.00	85.00
81	OWL-DAYLIGHT ENCOUNTER 621-P	OP	65.00	365.00
82	WESTERN BLUEBIRD 622-P	OP	65.00	195.00
83	RED-WINGED BLACKBIRD 623-P	CL	65.00	190.00
84	WINTER CARDINAL 624-P	OP	65.00	225.00
85	AMERICAN GOLDFINCH 625-P	OP	65.00	90.00
86	AUTUMN BLUE JAY 626-P	OP	65.00	135.00
87	COUNTRY DISPLAY (SMALL) 940-D	OP	45.00	65.00
87	MALLARD DUCK 627-P	OP	75.00	105.00
89	HOODED ORIOLE 629-P	OP	80.00	100.00
90	HUMMINGBIRD 696-P	OP	85.00	85.00
90	WILDLIFE DISPLAY (LARGE) 957-D	OP	85.00	95.00

R. OLSZEWSKI — WOMEN'S SERIES

YR	NAME	LIMIT	ISSUE	QUOTE
80	DRESDEN DANCER 610-P	CL	55.00	75.00
81	THE HUNT WITH HOUNDS 611-P	CL	75.00	145.00
82	PRECIOUS YEARS 612-P	CL	65.00	195.00
83	ON THE AVENUE 613-P	CL	65.00	95.00
84	ROSES 614-P	CL	65.00	95.00
86	I DO 615-P	CL	85.00	195.00
89	WOMEN'S DISPLAY (SMALL) 950-D	CL	40.00	65.00

GORHAM

N. ROCKWELL — A BOY AND HIS DOG (FOUR SEASONS)

YR	NAME	LIMIT	ISSUE	QUOTE
72	A BOY MEETS HIS DOG	2500	200.00	1575.00
72	ADVENTURERS BETWEEN ADVENTURES (SET)	2500	*	*
72	PRIDE OF PARENTHOOD (SET)	2500	*	*
72	THE MYSTERIOUS MALADY (SET)	2500	*	*

N. ROCKWELL — A HELPING HAND (FOUR SEASONS)

YR	NAME	LIMIT	ISSUE	QUOTE
80	CLOSED FOR BUSINESS (SET)	2500	*	*

YR NAME	LIMIT	ISSUE	QUOTE
80 COAL SEASONS COMING (SET)	2500	*	*
80 SWATTER'S RIGHT (SET)	2500	*	*
80 YEAR END COURT	2500	650.00	700.00
N. ROCKWELL		**DAD'S BOY (FOUR SEASONS)**	
81 CAREFUL AIM (SET)	2500	*	*
81 IN HIS SPIRIT (SET)	2500	*	*
81 SKI SKILLS	2500	750.00	800.00
81 TROUT DINNER (SET)	2500	*	*
N. ROCKWELL		**FOUR AGES OF LOVE (FOUR SEASONS)**	
74 FLOWERS IN TENDER BLOOM (SET)	2500	*	*
74 FONDLY DO WE REMEMBER (SET)	2500	*	*
74 GAILY SHARING VINTAGE TIMES	2500	300.00	1250.00
74 SWEET SONG SO YOUNG (SET)	2500	*	*
N. ROCKWELL		**GOING ON SIXTEEN (FOUR SEASONS)**	
78 CHILLING CHORE	2500	400.00	675.00
78 PILGRIMAGE (SET)	2500	*	*
78 SHEAR AGONY (SET)	2500	*	*
78 SWEET SERENADE (SET)	2500	*	*
N. ROCKWELL		**GRAND PALS (FOUR SEASONS)**	
77 FISH FINDERS (SET)	2500	*	*
77 GHOSTLY GOURDS (SET)	2500	*	*
77 SNOW SCULPTURING	2500	350.00	675.00
77 SOARING SPIRITS (SET)	2500	*	*
N. ROCKWELL		**GRANDPA AND ME**	
75 DAY DREAMS (SET)	2500	*	*
75 GAY BLADES	2500	300.00	900.00
75 GOING FISHIN' (SET)	2500	*	*
75 PENSIVE PALS (SET)	2500	*	*
J.C. LEYENDECKER		**LEYENDECKER ANNUAL CHRISTMAS FIGURINES**	
88 CHRISTMAS HUG	7500	95.00	95.00
N. ROCKWELL		**LIFE WITH FATHER (FOUR SEASONS MINIATURES)**	
83 A TOUGH ONE (SET)	2500	*	*
83 BIG DECISION	2500	250.00	250.00
83 BLASTING OUT (SET)	2500	*	*
83 CHEERING CHAMPS (SET)	2500	*	*
N. ROCKWELL		**ME AND MY PAL (FOUR SEASONS)**	
76 A LICKING GOOD BATH	2500	300.00	900.00
76 DISASTROUS DARING (SET)	2500	*	*
76 FISHERMAN'S PARADISE (SET)	2500	*	*
76 YOUNG MAN'S FANCY (SET)	2500	*	*
T. NAST		**MINIATURE CHRISTMAS FIGURINES**	
85 CHRISTMAS SANTA	YR	20.00	20.00
86 CHRISTMAS SANTA	YR	25.00	25.00
87 ANNUAL THOMAS NAST SANTA	YR	25.00	25.00
79 TINY TIM	YR	15.00	15.00
80 SANTA PLANS HIS TRIP	YR	15.00	15.00
81 YULETIDE RECKONING	YR	20.00	20.00
82 CHECKING GOOD DEEDS	YR	20.00	20.00
83 SANTA'S FRIEND	YR	20.00	20.00
84 DOWNHILL DARING	YR	20.00	20.00
N. ROCKWELL			**MINIATURES**
81 AT THE VETS	OP	27.50	27.50
81 BEGUILING BUTTERCUP	OP	45.00	45.00
81 BOY MEETS HIS DOG	OP	37.50	37.50
81 DOWNHILL DARING	OP	45.00	45.00
81 FLOWERS IN TENDER BLOOM	OP	60.00	60.00
81 GAY BLADES	OP	45.00	45.00
81 SNOW SCULPTURE	OP	45.00	45.00
81 SWEET SERENADE	OP	45.00	45.00
81 SWEET SONG SO YOUNG	OP	55.00	55.00
81 YOUNG MAN'S FANCY	OP	55.00	55.00
82 MARRIAGE LICENSE	OP	60.00	60.00
82 THE ANNUAL VISIT	OP	50.00	50.00
82 THE RUNAWAY	OP	50.00	50.00
82 TRIPLE SELF PORTRAIT	OP	60.00	60.00
82 VINTAGE TIMES	OP	50.00	50.00
83 TROUT DINNER	15,000	60.00	60.00
84 CAREFUL ARMS	OP	55.00	55.00
84 GHOSTLY GOURDS	OP	60.00	60.00
84 GOIN' FISHING	OP	60.00	60.00
84 IN HIS SPIRIT	OP	60.00	60.00
84 PRIDE OF PARENTHOOD	OP	50.00	50.00
84 SHEAR AGONY	OP	60.00	60.00
84 YEARS END COURT	OP	60.00	60.00
85 BEST FRIENDS	OP	27.50	27.50
85 ENGINEER	OP	55.00	55.00

YR	NAME	LIMIT	ISSUE	QUOTE
85	LITTLE RED TRUCK	OP	25.00	25.00
85	MUSCLE BOUND	OP	30.00	30.00
85	NEW ARRIVAL	OP	32.50	32.50
85	SPRING CHECKUP	OP	60.00	60.00
85	TO LOVE AND CHERISH	OP	32.50	32.50
86	FOOTBALL SEASON	OP	60.00	60.00
86	LEMONADE STAND	OP	60.00	60.00
86	LITTLE ANGEL	OP	50.00	60.00
86	MORNING WALK	OP	60.00	60.00
86	SHOULDER RIDE	OP	50.00	50.00
86	THE GRADUATE	OP	30.00	30.00
86	THE OLD SIGN PAINTER	OP	70.00	70.00
86	WELCOME MAT	OP	70.00	70.00
87	BABYSITTER	15,000	75.00	75.00
87	BETWEEN THE ACTS	15,000	60.00	60.00
87	CINDERELLA	15,000	70.00	70.00
87	SPRINGTIME	15,000	65.00	65.00
87	STARSTRUCK	15,000	75.00	75.00
87	THE MILKMAID	15,000	80.00	80.00
87	THE PROM DRESS	15,000	75.00	75.00
N. ROCKWELL		**OLD BUDDIES (FOUR SEASONS)**		
84	ENDLESS DATES (SET)	2500	*	*
84	FINAL SPEECH (SET)	2500	*	*
84	HASTY RETREAT (SET)	2500	*	*
84	SHARED SUCCESS	2500	250.00	250.00
N. ROCKWELL		**OLD TIMERS (FOUR SEASONS MINIATURES)**		
82	CANINE SOLO	2500	250.00	250.00
82	FANCY FOOTWORK (SET)	2500	*	*
82	LAZY DAYS (SET)	2500	*	*
82	SWEET SURPRISE (SET)	2500	*	*
N. ROCKWELL				**ROCKWELL**
74	AT THE VETS	*	25.00	65.00
74	BATTER UP	*	40.00	90.00
74	CAPTAIN	*	45.00	95.00
74	FISHING	*	50.00	100.00
74	MISSING TOOTH	*	30.00	70.00
74	SKATING	*	37.50	85.00
74	TINY TIM	*	30.00	75.00
74	WEIGHING IN	*	40.00	80.00
75	BOY AND HIS DOG	*	37.50	85.00
75	NO SWIMMING	*	35.00	80.00
75	OLD MILL POND	*	45.00	95.00
76	GOD REST YE MERRY GENTLEMEN	*	50.00	800.00
76	INDEPENDENCE	*	40.00	150.00
76	MARRAIGE LICENSE	*	50.00	110.00
76	SAYING GRACE	*	75.00	120.00
76	TACKLED (AD STAND)	*	35.00	55.00
76	THE OCCULTIST	*	50.00	175.00
80	JOLLY COACHMAN	7500	75.00	125.00
81	CHRISTMAS DANCERS	7500	130.00	130.00
81	DAY IN THE LIFE BOY II	*	75.00	85.00
81	WET SPORT	*	85.00	85.00
82	A DAY IN THE LIFE BOY III	*	85.00	85.00
82	A DAY IN THE LIFE GIRL III	*	85.00	85.00
82	APRIL FOOL'S (AT THE CURIOSITY SHOP)	*	55.00	110.00
82	MARRIAGE LICENSE	5000	110.00	400.00
82	MERRIE CHRISTMAS	7500	75.00	150.00
82	SAYING GRACE	5000	110.00	450.00
82	TACKLED (ROCKWELL NAME SIGNED)	*	45.00	70.00
82	TRIPLE SELF PORTRAIT	5000	300.00	500.00
83	ANTIQUE DEALER	7500	130.00	130.00
83	CHRISTMAS GOOSE	7500	75.00	75.00
83	FACTS OF LIFE	7500	110.00	110.00
84	CARD TRICKS	7500	110.00	140.00
84	SANTA'S FRIEND	7500	75.00	75.00
84	SERENADE	7500	95.00	95.00
85	PUPPET MAKER	7500	130.00	130.00
85	THE OLD SIGN PAINTER	7500	130.00	130.00
86	DRUM FOR TOMMY	YR	90.00	90.00
87	SANTA PLANNING HIS ANNUAL VISIT	7500	95.00	95.00
88	CONFRONTATION	15,000	75.00	75.00
88	CRAMMING	15,000	80.00	80.00
88	DELORES & EDDIE	15,000	75.00	75.00
88	GARY COOPER IN HOLLYWOOD	15,000	90.00	90.00
88	HOME FOR THE HOLIDAYS	7500	100.00	100.00
88	THE DIARY	15,000	80.00	80.00

YR	NAME	LIMIT	ISSUE	QUOTE
N. ROCKWELL		**TENDER YEARS (FOUR SEASONS)**		
79	CHILLY RECEPTION (SET)	2500	*	*
79	COOL AID (SET)	2500	*	*
79	NEW YEAR LOOK	2500	500.00	550.00
79	SPRING TONIC (SET)	2500	*	*
N. ROCKWELL		**TRAVELING SALESMAN (FOUR SEASONS)**		
85	COUNTRY PEDDLER (SET)	2500	*	*
85	EXPERT SALESMAN (SET)	2500	*	*
85	HORSE TRADER	2500	275.00	275.00
85	TRAVELING SALESMAN (SET)	2500	*	*
VASARI			**VASARI FIGURINES**	
71	MERCENARY WARRIOR	250	250.00	500.00
71	MING WARRIOR	250	200.00	400.00
71	SWISS WARRIOR	250	250.00	1000.00
73	AUSTRIAN HUSSAR	250	400.00	800.00
73	CELLINI	250	400.00	800.00
73	CHRIST	250	250.00	500.00
73	CRECHE	250	500.00	1000.00
73	D'ARTAGNAN	250	250.00	800.00
73	ENGLISH CRUSADER	250	250.00	500.00
73	FRENCH CRUSADER	250	250.00	500.00
73	GERMAN HUSSAR	250	250.00	500.00
73	GERMAN MERCENARY	250	250.00	500.00
73	ITALIAN CRUSADER	250	250.00	500.00
73	LEONARDO DA VINCI	200	250.00	500.00
73	MICHELANGELO	200	250.00	500.00
73	PIRATE	250	250.00	400.00
73	PORTHOS	250	250.00	500.00
73	ROMAN CENTURION	250	250.00	400.00
73	SPANISH GRANDEE	250	250.00	400.00
73	THE COSSACK	250	250.00	500.00
73	THREE KINGS (SET OF 3)	200	750.00	1500.00
73	THREE MUSKETEERS (SET OF 3)	200	750.00	1500.00
73	VENETIAN NOBLEMAN	250	200.00	400.00
73	VIKING	250	200.00	400.00
N. ROCKWELL		**YOUNG LOVE (FOUR SEASONS)**		
73	A SCHOLARLY PACE (SET)	2500	*	*
73	BEGUILING BUTTERCUP (SET)	2500	*	*
73	DOWNHILL DARING (SET)	2500	250.00	1100.00
73	FLYING HIGH (SET)	2500	*	*

GRANGET

G. GRANGET			**GRANGET PORCELAINS**	
*	BOBWHITE QUAIL, OFF SEASON	350	*	2700.00-3300.00
*	CALIFORNIA SEA LIONS, SEA FROLIC	500	1375.00	4200.00
*	CANADIAN GEESE, HEADING SOUTH	150	4650.00	14200.00
*	CEDAR WAXWINGS, ANXIOUS MOMENTS	175	2675.00	2675.00
*	CROWNED CRANES, THE DANCE	25	20000.00	20000.00
*	DOLPHIN GROUP	350	*	5000.00
*	DOLPHINS, PLAY TIME, DECORATED	100	9000.00	*
*	DOLPHINS, PLAY TIME, UNDECORATED	500	3500.00	3000.00-3500.00
*	GREAT BLUE HERONS, THE CHALLENGE	150	5000.00	14200.00
*	HALLA	350	*	4100.00
*	MEADOWLARK, SPRING IS HERE	175	2450.00	2450.00
*	MOURNING DOVES, ENGAGES	250	*	1200.00-1750.00
*	OPEN JUMPER, THE CHAMPION	500	1350.00	1350.00
*	PEREGRINE FALCON, WOOD, 10 IN.	2500	500.00	500.00
*	PEREGRINE FALCON, WOOD, 12.5 IN.	1500	700.00	700.00
*	PEREGRINE FALCON, WOOD, 20 IN.	250	2000.00	2000.00
*	PINTAIL DUCKS, SAFE AT HOME	350	*	9700.00
*	RED DEER STAG, THE ROYAL STAG	150	4850.00	4850.00
*	RING-NECKED PHEASANTS, TAKE COVER	125	*	3800.00-6350.00
*	RUFFED GROUSE	150	2000.00	2000.00
*	SCREECH OWL WITH CHICKADEES, DISTAIN	175	2250.00	5650.00
*	SECRETARY BIRD	100	6000.00	14000.00
*	SPRINGBOK, THE SENTINEL	150	2000.00	2000.00
*	STAG	350	*	4000.00-4850.00
*	WOODCOCKS, A FAMILY AFFAIR	200	*	1500.00
74	BLUE TITMOUSE, LIVELY FELLOW	750	1295.00	1295.00
74	CATFINCH, SPRING MELODY	750	1675.00	1675.00
74	GOLDEN-CRESTED WRENS, TINY ACROBATS	700	2060.00	2060.00
74	GOLDFINCH, MORNING HOUR	750	1250.00	1250.00
74	GREAT TITMOUSE ADULTS, BUSY ACTIVITY	750	2175.00	2175.00
74	KINGFISHER, DEFECTED PREY	600	1975.00	1975.00
74	ROBIN, A DAY BEGINS	750	1795.00	1795.00
76	AMERICAN BALD EAGLE, FREEDOM IN FLIGHT	200	3400.00	9500.00
76	AMERICAN ROBIN, IT'S SPRING AGAIN	150	1950.00	1950.00

YR	NAME	LIMIT	ISSUE	QUOTE
76	BLUEBIRDS, RELUCTANT FLEDGLING	350	1750.00	4600.00
76	DOUBLE EAGLE, 24 KT GOLD VERMEIL/PEWTER	1200	250.00	250.00
76	SECRETARY BIRD, THE CONTEST	100	6000.00	11000.00
77	RELUCTANT FLEDGLING	350	1750.00	1750.00

GREENWICH WORKSHOP

J. CHRISTENSEN				**BRONZE**
*	CANDLEMAN, THE	*	*	3100.00
J. CHRISTENSEN				**FANTASY/BRONZE**
*	SIX BIRD HUNTERS	*	*	4500.00
F. MCCARTHY				**WESTERN**
*	THUNDER OF HOOVES	*	*	10500.00

HAMILTON COLLECTION

*			**A CELEBRATION OF ROSES**	
89	BRANDY	OP	55.00	55.00
89	COLOR MAGIC	OP	55.00	55.00
89	HONOR	OP	55.00	55.00
89	MISS ALL-AMERICAN BEAUTY	OP	55.00	55.00
89	TIFFANY	OP	55.00	55.00
90	OREGOLD	OP	55.00	55.00
91	PARADISE	OP	55.00	55.00
D. FRYER			**AMERICAN GARDEN FLOWERS**	
87	AZALEA	15,000	75.00	75.00
87	CAMELIA	9800	55.00	75.00
87	GARDENIA	15,000	75.00	75.00
87	ROSE	15,000	75.00	75.00
88	CALLA LILLY	15,000	75.00	75.00
88	DAY LILY	15,000	75.00	75.00
88	PETUNIA	15,000	75.00	75.00
89	PANSY	15,000	75.00	75.00
H. DEATON		**AMERICAN WILDLIFE BRONZE COLLECTION**		
79	BOBCAT	7500	60.00	75.00
79	COUGAR	7500	60.00	125.00
79	WHITE-TAILED DEER	7500	60.00	105.00
80	BEAVER	7500	60.00	65.00
80	POLAR BEAR	7500	60.00	65.00
80	SEA OTTER	7500	60.00	65.00
J. VILLENA			**CELEBRATION OF OPERA**	
86	CARMEN	7500	95.00	95.00
86	CIO-CIO-SAN	7500	95.00	95.00
87	FIGARO	7500	95.00	95.00
88	AIDA	7500	95.00	95.00
88	CANIO	7500	95.00	95.00
88	MIMI	7500	95.00	95.00
FRANCESCO			**EXOTIC BIRDS OF THE WORLD**	
84	BUDGERIGAR	7500	75.00	105.00
84	THE COCKATOO	7500	75.00	115.00
84	THE DIAMOND DOVE	7500	75.00	95.00
84	THE FISHER'S WHYDAH	7500	75.00	95.00
84	THE PEACH-FACED LOVEBIRD	7500	75.00	95.00
84	THE QUETZAL	7500	75.00	95.00
84	THE RED LOG	7500	75.00	95.00
84	THE RUBENIO PARAKEET	7500	75.00	95.00
M. WALD			**FRESHWATER CHALLENGE**	
91	RAINBOW LURE	OP	75.00	75.00
91	SUN CATCHER	OP	75.00	75.00
91	THE STRIKE	OP	75.00	75.00
H. DEATON		**GREAT ANIMALS OF THE AMERICAN WILDERNESS**		
83	BIGHORN	7500	75.00	75.00
83	ELK	7500	75.00	75.00
83	GRIZZLY BEAR	7500	75.00	75.00
83	MOUNTAIN LION	7500	75.00	75.00
83	MUSTANG	7500	75.00	75.00
83	PLAINS BISON	7500	75.00	75.00
83	PRONGHORN ANTELOPE	7500	75.00	75.00
83	TIMBER WOLF	7500	75.00	75.00
*		**HEROES OF BASEBALL-PORCELAIN BASEBALL CARDS**		
90	BROOKS ROBINSON	OP	19.50	19.50
90	CASEY STENGEL	OP	19.50	19.50
90	DUKE SNIDER	OP	19.50	19.50
90	GIL HODGES	OP	19.50	19.50
90	MICKEY MANTLE	OP	19.50	19.50
90	ROBERTO CLEMENTE	OP	19.50	19.50
90	WHITEY FORD	OP	19.50	19.50
90	WILLIE MAYS	OP	19.50	19.50
91	ERNIE BANKS	OP	19.50	19.50

YR	NAME	LIMIT	ISSUE	QUOTE
91	JACKIE ROBINSON	OP	19.50	19.50
91	SATCHEL PAGE	OP	19.50	19.50
91	YOGI BERRA	OP	19.50	19.50
ITO		**LEGENDARY FLOWERS OF THE ORIENT**		
85	CHERRY BLOSSOM	15,000	55.00	55.00
85	CHINESE PEONY	15,000	55.00	55.00
85	CHRYSANTHEMUM	15,000	55.00	55.00
85	GOLD BAND LILY	15,000	55.00	55.00
85	IRIS	15,000	55.00	55.00
85	JAPANESE ORCHID	15,000	55.00	55.00
85	LOTUS	15,000	55.00	55.00
85	WISTERIA	15,000	55.00	55.00
D.T. LYTTLETON			**LITTLE NIGHT OWLS**	
90	BARN OWL	OP	45.00	45.00
90	TAWNY OWL	OP	45.00	45.00
91	BARRED OWL	OP	45.00	45.00
91	GREAT HORNED OWL	OP	45.00	45.00
91	SNOWY OWL	OP	45.00	45.00
FRANCESCO		**MAGNIFICENT BIRDS OF PARADISE**		
85	BLACK SICKLE-BILLED BIRD OF PARADISE	12,500	75.00	95.00
85	BLUE BIRD OF PARADISE	12,500	75.00	95.00
85	EMPEROR OF GERMANY	12,500	75.00	95.00
85	GOLDIE'S BIRD OF PARADISE	12,500	75.00	95.00
85	GREATER BIRD OF PARADISE	12,500	75.00	95.00
85	MAGNIFICENT BIRD OF PARADISE	12,500	75.00	95.00
85	PRINCESS STEPHANIE BIRD OF PARADISE	12,500	75.00	95.00
85	RAGGIANA BIRD OF PARADISE	12,500	75.00	95.00
H. DEATON		**MAJESTIC WILDLIFE OF NORTH AMERICA**		
85	ALASKAN MOOSE	7500	75.00	75.00
85	BARREN GROUND CARIBOU	7500	75.00	75.00
85	BLACK BEAR	7500	75.00	75.00
85	COYOTE	7500	75.00	75.00
85	HARBOUR SEAL	7500	75.00	75.00
85	MOUNTAIN GOAT	7500	75.00	75.00
85	OCELOT	7500	75.00	75.00
85	WHITE-TAILED DEER	7500	75.00	75.00
J. LAMB		**PUPPY PLAYTIME SCULPTURE COLLECTION**		
90	DOUBLE TAKE	OP	29.50	29.50
91	CABIN FEVER	OP	29.50	29.50
91	CATCH OF THE DAY	OP	29.50	29.50
91	HANGING OUT	OP	29.50	29.50
91	WEEKEND GARDNER	OP	29.50	29.50
P. COZZOLINO		**RINGLING BROS. CIRCUS ANIMALS**		
83	ACROBATIC SEAL	9800	49.50	49.50
83	BABY ELEPHANT	9800	49.50	55.00
83	MINIATURE SHOW HORSE	9800	49.50	68.00
83	MR. CHIMPANZEE	9800	49.50	49.50
83	PERFORMING POODLES	9800	49.50	49.50
83	SKATING BEAR	9800	49.50	49.50
84	PARADE CAMEL	9800	49.50	49.50
84	ROARING LION	9800	49.50	49.60
N. ROCKWELL		**ROCKWELL HOME OF THE BRAVE**		
82	BACK TO HIS OLD JOB	7500	75.00	75.00
82	HERO'S WELCOME	7500	75.00	75.00
82	REMINISCING	7500	75.00	85.00
82	TAKING MOTHER OVER THE TOP	7500	75.00	75.00
82	UNCLE SAM TAKES WINGS	7500	75.00	75.00
82	WILLIE GILLIS IN CHURCH	7500	75.00	75.00
JACQUELINE B.			**SNUGGLE BABIES**	
88	BABY BEARS	OP	35.00	35.00
88	BABY BUNNIES	OP	35.00	35.00
88	BABY FOXES	OP	35.00	35.00
88	BABY SKUNKS	OP	35.00	35.00
89	BABY CHIPMUNKS	OP	35.00	35.00
89	BABY FAWNS	OP	35.00	35.00
89	BABY RACCOONS	OP	35.00	35.00
89	BABY SQUIRRELS	OP	35.00	35.00
*			**THE GIBSON GIRLS**	
86	THE ACTRESS	OP	75.00	75.00
87	THE BRIDE	OP	75.00	75.00
87	THE CAREER GIRL	OP	75.00	75.00
87	THE COLLEGE GIRL	OP	75.00	75.00
87	THE SPORTSWOMAN	OP	75.00	75.00
88	THE ARTIST	OP	75.00	75.00
88	THE DEBUTANTE	OP	75.00	75.00
88	THE SOCIETY GIRL	OP	75.00	75.00

YR NAME	LIMIT	ISSUE	QUOTE
G. GRANGET		**THE NOBLE SWAN**	
85 THE NOBLE SWAN	5000	295.00	295.00
*		**THE ROMANCE OF FLOWERS**	
87 SPRINGTIME BOUQUET	15,000	95.00	95.00
87 SUMMER BOUQUET	15,000	95.00	95.00
88 AUTUMN BOUQUET	15,000	95.00	95.00
88 WINTER BOUQUET	15,000	95.00	95.00
E. DAUB		**THE SPLENDOR OF BALLET**	
87 GISELLE	15,000	95.00	95.00
87 JULIET	15,000	95.00	95.00
87 KITRI	15,000	95.00	95.00
87 ODETTE	15,000	95.00	95.00
88 AURORA	15,000	95.00	95.00
89 CLARA	15,000	95.00	95.00
89 FIREBIRD	15,000	95.00	95.00
89 SWANILDA	15,000	95.00	95.00
M. WALD		**TROPICAL TREASURES**	
89 FLAG-TAIL SURGEONFISH	OP	37.50	37.50
89 PENNANT BUTTERFLY FISH	OP	37.50	37.50
89 SAIL-FINNED SURGEONFISH	OP	37.50	37.50
89 SEA HORSE	OP	37.50	37.50
90 BEAKED CORAL BUTTERFLY FISH	OP	37.50	37.50
90 BLUE GIRDLED ANGEL FISH	OP	37.50	37.50
90 SPOTTED ANGEL FISH	OP	37.50	37.50
90 ZEBRA TURKEY FISH	OP	37.50	37.50
C. BURGESS		**WILD DUCKS OF NORTH AMERICA**	
87 COMMON MALLARD	15,000	95.00	95.00
87 GREEN WINGED TAIL	15,000	95.00	95.00
87 HOODED MERGANSER	15,000	95.00	95.00
87 WOOD DUCK	15,000	95.00	95.00
88 AMERICAN WIDGEON	15,000	95.00	95.00
88 BUFFLEHEAD	15,000	95.00	95.00
88 NORTHERN PINFALL	15,000	95.00	95.00
88 RUDDY DUCK DRAKE	15,000	95.00	95.00

HAMILTON GIFTS

YR NAME	LIMIT	ISSUE	QUOTE
M. HUMPHREY	**MAUD HUMPHREY BOGART COLLECTOR'S CLUB FIGURINES**		
90 A FLOWER FOR YOU H5596	OP	65.00	65.00
91 FRIENDS FOR LIFE MH911	OP	60.00	95.00-195.00
M. HUMPHREY	**MAUD HUMPHREY BOGART FIGURINES**		
88 A PLEASURE TO MEET YOU H1310	RT	65.00	60.00-98.00
88 CLEANING HOUSE H1303	RT	60.00	50.00-91.00
88 LITTLE CHICKADEES H1306	RT	65.00	55.00-91.00
88 MY FIRST DANCE H1311	RT	60.00	125.00-260.00
88 SARAH H1312	RT	60.00	275.00
88 SEAMSTRESS H1309	RT	66.00	160.00-293.00
88 SUSANNA H1305	RT	60.00	200.00-295.00
88 TEA AND GOSSIP H1301	RT	65.00	85.00-130.00
88 THE BRIDE H1313	19,500	90.00	83.00-99.00
88 THE MAGIC KITTEN H1308	RT	66.00	70.00-104.00
89 A SUNDAY OUTING H1386	15,000	135.00	139.50
89 GIFT OF LOVE H1319	RT	65.00	45.00-98.00
89 IN THE ORCHARD H1373	24,500	33.00	36.00
89 KITTY'S LUNCH H1355	19,500	60.00	66.00
89 LITTLE BO PEEP H1382	24,000	45.00	49.00
89 LITTLE CHICKADEES-PORCELAIN H1389	15,000	*	110.00
89 LITTLE RED RIDING HOOD H1381	24,500	42.50	46.00
89 MY FIRST BIRTHDAY H1320	RT	47.00	50.00
89 NO MORE TEARS H1351	24,500	44.00	49.00
89 PLAYING BRIDESMAID H5500	19,000	125.00	90.00-120.00
89 SCHOOL DAYS H1318	RT	42.50	45.00-70.00
89 SCHOOL LESSON H1356	19,500	77.00	75.00-130.00
89 SEALED WITH A KISS H1316	RT	45.00	50.00-91.00
89 SPECIAL FRIENDS H1317	RT	66.00	90.00-130.00
89 SPECIAL FRIENDS-PORCELAIN H1390	15,000	125.00	120.00
89 SPRING BEAUTIES H1387	15,000	135.00	130.50
89 SPRINGTIME GATHERING H1385	7500	295.00	200.00
89 THE BRIDE-PORCELAIN H1388	15,000	125.00	128.00
89 THE LITTLE CAPTIVE H1374	19,500	55.00	58.00
89 THE MAGIC KITTEN-PORCELAIN H5543	19,500	125.00	125.00
89 WINTER FUN H1354	15,000	46.00	45.00-85.00
90 A CHANCE ACQUAINTANCE H5589	19,500	70.00	135.00
90 A LITTLE ROBIN H1347	19,500	55.00	58.00
90 A SPECIAL GIFT H5550	19,500	70.00	99.00
90 AUTUMN DAYS H1348	24,500	45.00	49.00
90 HOLIDAY SURPRISE H5551	24,500	50.00	55.00
90 KITTY'S BATH H1384	19,500	103.00	109.00

YR	NAME	LIMIT	ISSUE	QUOTE
90	LITTLE PLAYMATES H1349	19,500	48.00	53.00
90	MY WINTER HAT H5554	24,500	40.00	46.00
90	PLAYTIME H1383	19,500	60.00	66.00
90	SARAH (WATERBALL) H5594	19,500	75.00	79.00
90	SUSANNA (WATERBALL) H5595	19,500	75.00	79.00
90	WINTER DAYS H5553	24,500	50.00	55.00
90	WINTER FRIENDS H5552	19,500	64.00	69.00
91	ALL BUNDLED UP 910015	19,500	85.00	85.00
91	CLEANING HOUSE (WATERBALL) H5654	19,500	75.00	75.00
91	DOUBLES 910023	19,500	70.00	70.00
91	HUSH A BYE BABY H5695	19,500	62.00	62.00
91	LITTLE BOY BLUE H5612	19,500	55.00	55.00
91	LITTLE MISS MUFFET H5621	24,500	75.00	75.00
91	MELISSA (WATERBALL) 910074	19,500	40.00	40.00
91	MELISSA 910031	24,500	55.00	55.00
91	MY FIRST DANCE (WATERBALL) H5655	19,000	75.00	75.00
91	MY FIRST DANCE-PORCELAIN H5650	15,000	110.00	110.00
91	MY SNOW SHOVEL 910058	19,500	70.00	70.00
91	MY WINTER HAT 921017	15,000	80.00	80.00
91	SARAH-PORCELAIN H5651	15,000	110.00	110.00
91	SPRING BOUQUET H5598	24,500	44.00	44.00
91	SPRING FROLIC H5590	15,000	170.00	170.00
91	SUSANNA-PORCELAIN H5652	15,000	110.00	110.00
91	TEA AND GOSSIP-PORCELAIN H5653	15,000	132.00	132.00
91	THE GRADUATE H5559	19,500	75.00	75.00
91	THE PINWHEEL H5600	24,500	45.00	45.00
91	WINTER DAYS (WATERBALL) 915130	19,500	75.00	75.00
91	WINTER FRIENDS (WATERBALL) 915149	19,500	75.00	75.00
91	WINTER FUN 921025	15,000	90.00	90.00
91	WINTER RIDE 910066	19,500	60.00	60.00
M. HUMPHREY		**MAUD HUMPHREY BOGART GALLERY FIGURINES**		
91	MOTHERS TREASURES H5619	15,000	118.00	118.00
91	SHARING SECRETS 910007	15,000	120.00	120.00
M. HUMPHREY		**MAUD HUMPHREY BOGART PETITE FIGURINES**		
91	CLEANING HOUSE H5611	OP	24.00	24.00
91	GIFT OF LOVE H5620	OP	24.00	24.00
91	MY FIRST DANCE H-5623	OP	24.00	24.00
91	SARAH H5613	OP	24.00	24.00
91	SPECIAL FRIENDS H5625	OP	24.00	24.00
91	SUSANNA H5626	OP	24.00	24.00
91	THE MAGIC KITTEN H5623	OP	24.00	24.00
91	THE SEAMSTRESS H5627	OP	24.00	24.00

HAMILTON/BOEHM

*		**FAVORITE GARDEN FLOWERS**		
85	CALIFORNIA POPPY	9800	195.00	225.00
85	CARNATION	9800	195.00	225.00
85	DAFFODIL	9800	195.00	225.00
85	HIBISCUS	9800	195.00	225.00
85	MORNING GLORY	9800	195.00	225.00
85	ROSE	9800	195.00	225.00
85	SWEET PEA	9800	195.00	225.00
85	TULIP	9800	195.00	225.00
*		**ROSES OF DISTINCTION**		
83	ANGEL FACE ROSE	9800	135.00	175.00
83	ELEGANCE ROSE	9800	135.00	175.00
83	MR. LINCOLN ROSE	9800	135.00	175.00
83	PEACE ROSE	9800	135.00	195.00
83	QUEEN ELIZABETH ROSE	9800	135.00	175.00
83	ROYAL HIGHNESS ROSE	9800	135.00	175.00
83	TROPICANA ROSE	9800	135.00	175.00
83	WHITE MASTERPIECE ROSE	9800	135.00	195.00

HELEN SABATTE DESIGNS INC.

H. SABATTE		**AMER. CHRISTMAS CAROLLERS**		
93	FATHER	5000	48.00	48.00
93	GRADE SCHOOL BOY	5000	48.00	48.00
93	GRADE SCHOOL GIRL	5000	48.00	48.00
93	MOTHER	5000	48.00	48.00
93	PRE SCHOOL BOY	5000	48.00	48.00
93	PRE SCHOOL GIRL	5000	48.00	48.00
93	TEENAGE BOY	5000	48.00	48.00
93	TEENAGE GIRL	5000	48.00	48.00
93	TRADITIONAL GRANDFATHER	5000	48.00	48.00
93	TRADITIONAL GRANDMOTHER	5000	48.00	48.00
H. SABATTE		**NIGHT BEFORE CHRISTMAS**		
94	GRADE SCHOOL GIRL W/DEAR SANTA LETTER	CL	52.00	52.00

YR NAME	LIMIT	ISSUE	QUOTE
H. SABATTE		**THE COLLECTOR**	
94 BEAR COLLECTOR-MAN	5000	60.00	60.00-69.00
94 BEAR COLLECTOR-WOMAN	5000	65.00	65.00-75.00
H. SABATTE		**THE FATHER CHRISTMAS SERIES**	
94 FATHER CHRISTMAS W/CHRISTMAS GREENERY	500	75.00	75.00
94 FATHER CHRISTMAS W/TRADITIONAL TREE	500	80.00	80.00
H. SABATTE		**W/SPECIAL ACCESSORIES**	
94 TEENAGE BOY HOLDING WATER SNOWGLOBE	200	45.00	45.00-52.00
94 TEENAGER GIRL HOLDING WATER SNOWGLOBE	200	45.00	45.00-52.00

HUTSCHENREUTHER

GRANGET	AMERICAN LIMITED EDITION COLLECTION		
* A FAMILY AFFAIR	200	*	3700.00
* ANXIOUS MOMENT	175	*	5225.00
* ARABIAN STALLION	300	*	8525.00
* BLUE DOLPHINS	100	*	10000.00
* CHRISTMAS ROSE	375	*	3050.00
* DECORATED SEA LIONS	100	*	6000.00
* DISDAIN-OWL	175	*	5200.00
* DOLPHIN GROUP	500	*	4000.00
* ENGAGED	250	*	1750.00
* FIRST LESSON	175	*	3550.00
* FREEDOM IN FLIGHT	200	*	9000.00
* FRIENDLY ENEMIES-WOODPECKER	175	*	5200.00
* HEADING SOUTH	150	*	14000.00
* IT'S SPRING AGAIN	250	*	3475.00
* JOE-STAG	150	*	12000.00
* LINNET ON EAR OF RYE	250	*	1175.00
* OFF SEASON	125	*	4125.00
* OLYMPIC CHAMPION	500	*	3650.00
* PROUD PARENT	250	*	13750.00
* PYGMY OWLS	650	*	6225.00
* QUINCE	375	*	2850.00
* REDSTART ON QUINCE BRANCH	250	*	1300.00
* RELUCTANT FLEDGLING	350	*	3475.00
* SAFE AT HOME	350	*	9000.00
* SAW WHET OWL	750	*	3575.00
* SEA FROLIC-SEA LION	500	*	3500.00
* SILVER HERON	500	*	5000.00
* SPARROWHAWK W/KINGBIRD	500	*	8250.00
* SPRING IS HERE	175	*	4500.00
* TAKE COVER	125	*	14000.00
* THE CHALLENGE	150	*	14000.00
* THE CONTEST	100	*	14000.00
* THE DANCE-CROWNCRESTED CRANE	25	*	30000.00
* THE FISH HAWK	500	*	12000.00
* THE SENTINEL-SPRINGBOOK	150	*	5200.00
* TO RIDE THE WIND	500	*	8650.00
* WATER LILY	375	*	4150.00
* WHOOPING CRANES	300	*	8000.00
* WREN ON WILD ROSE	250	*	1675.00
D. VALENZA		**PORTRAIT FIGURINES**	
77 CATHERINE THE GREAT	500	500.00	1100.00
77 HELEN OF TORY	500	500.00	1050.00
77 ISOLDE	500	500.00	2650.00
77 JENNIE CHURCHHILL	500	500.00	925.00
77 JUDITH	500	500.00	1575.00
77 LILLIAN RUSSELL	500	500.00	1825.00
77 QUEEN ISABELLE	500	500.00	925.00

IRIS ARC

M. GENOA		**CRYSTAL KINGDOM**	
93 BASKET OF VIOLETS	RT	190.00	225.00
93 BIRDBATH	RT	190.00	225.00
93 COUNTRY CHURCH	OP	590.00	590.00
94 BLUEBIRD BASKET	OP	190.00	190.00
94 HUMMINGBIRDS	OP	290.00	290.00
94 MYSTIC STAR CASTLE	OP	390.00	390.00
93 NOB HILL VICTORIAN	OP	1000.00	1000.00
94 GARDEN COTTAGE	OP	390.00	390.00

ISPANKY

L. ISPANKY		**ISPANKY PORCELAINS**	
* EXODUS, BRONZE	100	1500.00	1500.00
* OWL	300	750.00	825.00
* PRINCESS OF THE NILE	500	275.00	450.00
* ROSH HASHANA, GRAY BEARD	2	275.00	10000.00
* ROSH HASHANA, WHITE BEARD	400	275.00	1300.00

YR	NAME	LIMIT	ISSUE	QUOTE
66	ORCHIDS	250	1000.00	1500.00
67	ARTIST GIRL	500	200.00	1800.00
67	BALLERINA	500	350.00	1000.00
67	BALLET DANCERS	500	350.00	1000.00
67	BIRD OF PARADISE	250	1500.00	1500.00
67	CAVALRY SCOUT, DECORATED	200	1000.00	1200.00
67	CAVALRY SCOUT, WHITE	150	675.00	900.00
67	DRUMMER BOY, DECORATED	200	250.00	285.00
67	DRUMMER BOY, WHITE	600	150.00	185.00
67	DUTCH IRIS	250	1400.00	1500.00
67	FORTY-NINER, DECORATED	200	450.00	650.00
67	FORTY-NINER, WHITE	350	250.00	250.00
67	GREAT SPIRIT, WHITE	150	750.00	750.00
67	HORSE	300	300.00	600.00
67	HUNT, DECORATED	200	2000.00	3850.00
67	HUNT, WHITE	150	1200.00	1485.00
67	KING ARTHUR	500	300.00	750.00
67	LOVE	300	375.00	950.00
67	MEDITATION	300	350.00	1000.00
67	MORNING	500	300.00	1500.00
67	MOSES	400	400.00	1800.00
67	ON THE TRAIL, WHITE	150	750.00	1125.00
67	PACK HORSE, DECORATED	200	700.00	1250.00
67	PACK HORSE, WHITE	150	500.00	350.00
67	PILGRIM FAMILY, DECORATED	200	500.00	750.00
67	PILGRIM FAMILY, WHITE	350	350.00	350.00
67	PIONEER SCOUT, DECORATED	200	1000.00	1000.00
67	PIONEER SCOUT, WHITE	200	675.00	405.00
67	PIONEER WOMAN, DECORATED	200	350.00	550.00
67	PIONEER WOMEN, WHITE	150	225.00	350.00
67	PROMISES	100	225.00	2500.00
67	TULIPS, RED	50	1800.00	4500.00
67	TULIPS, YELLOW	50	1800.00	4500.00
68	PEGASUS, DECORATED	300	375.00	800.00
68	PEGASUS, WHITE	300	300.00	800.00
68	QUEEN OF SPRING	200	750.00	1200.00
69	AUTUMN WIND	500	300.00	1500.00
69	DAFFODILS	250	950.00	950.00
69	GREAT SPIRIT, DECORATED	200	1500.00	1850.00
69	ISAIAH	300	475.00	1100.00
69	MARIA	350	750.00	1000.00
69	MERMAID GROUP, DECORATED	200	1000.00	1800.00
69	MERMAID GROUP, WHITE	200	950.00	950.00
69	STORM	500	400.00	950.00
70	CELESTE	200	475.00	500.00
70	DAWN	300	500.00	1000.00
70	EVENING	300	375.00	650.00
70	HORSEPOWER	100	1650.00	3250.00
70	ICARUS	350	350.00	650.00
70	KING AND QUEEN, PAIR	250	750.00	1200.00
70	ON THE TRAIL, DECORATED	200	1700.00	1700.00
70	PEACE, DECORATED	100	375.00	750.00
70	PEACE, WHITE	100	300.00	450.00
70	REVERIE	200	200.00	850.00
70	THRASHER	300	1000.00	1000.00
71	BEAUTY AND THE BEAST	15	4500.00	4500.00
71	BETSY ROSS	350	750.00	1325.00
71	CHRISTINE	300	350.00	800.00
71	DAVID	400	450.00	600.00
71	DEBUTANTE	500	350.00	625.00
71	ETERNAL LOVE	300	400.00	650.00
71	EXCALIBUR	15	3500.00	3500.00
71	FELICIA	15	2500.00	2500.00
71	FREEDOM	250	300.00	500.00
71	JESSAMY 1	400	450.00	600.00
71	MR. AND MRS. OTTER	500	250.00	600.00
71	PEACE RIDERS	1	35000.00	35000.00
71	QUEST	15	1500.00	1500.00
71	ROMEO AND JULIET, DECORATED	500	375.00	950.00
71	SWAN LAKE	300	1000.00	2500.00
71	TEKIEH	15	1800.00	1800.00
72	ANNABEL LEE	500	750.00	750.00
72	CINDERELLA	400	375.00	375.00
72	MADAME BUTTERFLY	300	1500.00	1500.00
72	PRINCESS AND THE FROG	500	675.00	675.00
72	SPIRIT OF THE SEA	450	500.00	500.00

YR	NAME	LIMIT	ISSUE	QUOTE
72	SPRING BALLET	400	450.00	600.00
72	SPRING BOUQUET	50	3000.00	15000.00
73	AARON	350	1200.00	2400.00
73	ABRAHAM	500	600.00	1400.00
73	EMERALD DRAGON	100	2500.00	3250.00
73	LORELEI	500	550.00	650.00
73	LOVE LETTERS	450	750.00	850.00
73	MAID OF THE MIST	350	450.00	850.00
73	MESSIAH	750	450.00	500.00
73	REBEKAH	300	400.00	775.00
73	TEXAS RANGERS	400	1650.00	1650.00
74	BANBURY CROSS	350	550.00	1025.00
74	BELLE OF THE BALL	500	550.00	950.00
74	DIANNE	500	500.00	900.00
74	HAMLET AND OPHELIA	350	1250.00	1200.00-1500.00
74	HOLY FAMILY, DECORATED	450	900.00	1595.00
74	HOLY FAMILY, WHITE	450	750.00	700.00
74	KING LEAR AND CORDELIA	250	1250.00	1250.00
74	SECOND BASE	500	650.00	1100.00
75	APOTHEOSIS OF THE SCULPTOR	250	495.00	1000.00
75	HEALING HAND, DECORATED	600	750.00	1250.00
75	HEALING HAND, WHITE	600	650.00	800.00
75	JOSHUA	350	750.00	1200.00
75	MADONNA WITH HALO, DECORATED	500	350.00	495.00
75	MADONNA WITH HALO, WHITE	500	250.00	250.00
75	MADONNA, THE BLESSED SAINT, DECORATED	500	295.00	350.00
75	MADONNA, THE BLESSED SAINT, WHITE	500	195.00	250.00
75	MEMORIES	500	600.00	900.00
75	SPRING FEVER	600	650.00	1050.00
76	LYDIA	400	450.00	835.00
76	PIANO GIRL	800	300.00	725.00
76	SOPHISTICATION	800	350.00	575.00
76	SWANILDA	1000	285.00	800.00
77	DAISY	1000	325.00	575.00
77	DAY DREAMS	1000	300.00	600.00
77	MORNING GLORY	1000	325.00	620.00
77	POPPY	1000	325.00	575.00
77	SERENE HIGHNESS	100	2500.00	4250.00
77	SNOW DROP	1000	325.00	430.00
77	THUNDER	500	500.00	795.00
78	LITTLE MERMAID	800	350.00	520.00
78	MY NAME IS IRIS	700	500.00	900.00
78	NARCISSUS	700	500.00	620.00
78	ROMANCE	500	800.00	1200.00
78	TEN COMMANDMENTS, DECORATED	500	950.00	1525.00
78	TEN COMMANDMENTS, WHITE	700	600.00	850.00
78	WATER LILY	1000	325.00	620.00

JAN HAGARA COLLECTABLES

J. HAGARA			**MINIATURES**
89	HEATHER	RT	18.00	18.00
89	MANDY	RT	18.00	25.00
89	RACHAEL	RT	18.00	18.00
89	TIPPI	RT	18.00	18.00

J. HAGARA			**SIGNATURE**
85	ALICE AND ANDREA	RT	75.00	250.00
85	BECKY	RT	55.00	350.00-400.00
85	JESSICA	RT	55.00	75.00-100.00
85	MEMORIES	RT	75.00	250.00
85	STORYTIME	RT	135.00	300.00
85	THERESA	RT	55.00	260.00
87	NIKKI & SANTA	RT	135.00	235.00-300.00

J. HAGARA			**VICTORIAN CHILDREN**
*	JAN AT AGE FOUR	*	*	75.00
*	MISSY	*	*	50.00
83	ANNE	RT	25.00	90.00
83	JENNY	RT	25.00	175.00
83	JODY	RT	25.00	60.00
83	LISA	RT	25.00	60.00
83	LYDIA	RT	25.00	75.00-100.00
83	VICTORIA	RT	25.00	60.00-75.00
84	AMANDA	RT	30.00	100.00
84	BRIAN	RT	30.00	40.00
84	CAROL	RT	30.00	200.00
84	CRISTINA	RT	30.00	75.00
85	ANGIE	RT	30.00	125.00
85	BRIAN & CINNAMON BEAR	RT	30.00	200.00

YR	NAME	LIMIT	ISSUE	QUOTE
85	DAPHNE & UNICORN	RT	45.00	85.00
85	STACY	RT	30.00	125.00
85	STEPHEN	RT	30.00	125.00
86	ASHLEY	RT	25.00	60.00
86	CHRIS	RT	30.00	100.00
86	DAISIES FROM JIMMY	RT	45.00	125.00
86	LARRY	RT	30.00	75.00
86	MEG	RT	30.00	75.00
86	MELANIE	RT	30.00	100.00

JAN'S ORIGINALS

J. BENSON		**GEORGIA & SOUTH CAROLINA SERIES**		
92	SHRIMP BOAT	500	48.00	63.00
J. BENSON		**GEORGIA OR SOUTH CAROLINA SERIES**		
92	SHRIMP BOAT	1000	48.00	60.00
J. BENSON			**GEORGIA SERIES**	
90	OLD DALLAS HIGH SCHOOL	500	48.00	48.00
90	PAULDING COURTHOUSE	500	52.00	52.00
91	LOST MOUNTAIN STORE	1000	48.00	65.00
92	1ST PRESBYTERIAN CHURCH, ST. MARY'S	500	48.00	60.00
92	BARNSLEY GARDENS RUINS	500	48.00	60.00
92	BIB CHICKEN	1000	46.00	46.00
92	CARTERSVILLE DEPOT	500	48.00	48.00
92	CLOCK TOWER	1000	46.00	55.00
92	FOX THEATRE	1000	48.00	55.00
92	GEORGIA TECH	1000	52.00	60.00
92	O'HARA HOMEPLACE	100	50.00	60.00
92	OLD ST. MARYS METHODIST CHURCH	500	48.00	60.00
92	ORANGE HALL	500	46.00	55.00
92	RIVERVIEW HOTEL	500	50.00	60.00
92	TROLLEY, THE	500	46.00	55.00
92	UNIVERSITY OF GEORGIA	1000	48.00	60.00
92	VARSITY, THE	500	50.00	50.00
92	WATERWHEEL OF BERRY COLLEGE	1000	46.00	55.00
93	1ST BAPTIST CHURCH ST. MARYS	500	48.00	48.00
93	4-WAY LUNCH	500	46.00	46.00
93	COBB CTY. COURTHOUSE	1000	50.00	50.00
93	COBB CTY. YOUTH MUSEUM	500	48.00	48.00
93	MILLER'S DOCK	500	50.00	50.00
93	ROSELAWN	500	52.00	52.00
93	SPENCER HOUSE	500	48.00	48.00
94	1902 STOCK EXCHANGE	800	48.00	48.00
94	1ST BAPTISTI CHURCH-CARTERSVILLE	500	50.00	50.00
94	1ST PRESBYTERIAN CHURCH-CARTERSVILLE	500	50.00	50.00
94	ADAITSVILLE DEPOT	500	48.00	48.00
94	BLUE GOOSE	500	48.00	48.00
94	CAMDEN CTY. HIGH SCHOOL	200	52.00	52.00
94	EPISCOPAL CHURCH OF THE ASCENIOUS	500	48.00	48.00
94	FIRST COCA COLA BOTTLING	1000	48.00	48.00
94	FLOYD CTY. COURTHOUSE	*	*	*
94	GEORGIA STATE CAPITOL	500	76.00	76.00
94	GOODBREAD HOUSE	500	48.00	48.00
94	GRAND THEATRE	500	46.00	46.00
94	JACKSON HOUSE, THE	1000	52.00	52.00
94	LOEW'S GRANT THEATRE	1000	52.00	52.00
94	MARIETTA DEPOT	1000	50.00	50.00
94	PAVILION, THE	500	48.00	48.00
94	SAM JONES MEMORIAL METHODIST	500	50.00	50.00
94	WHITE COLUMNS WSB-TV	1000	52.00	52.00
94	YOUNG BROTHERS PHARMACY	500	48.00	48.00
95	GREYFIELD PLANTATION	1000	52.00	52.00
95	OLD CAMDEN CTY. COURTHOUSE	500	52.00	52.00
95	SKYLINE OF ATLANTA, GA. 1996		54.00	54.00

JEFFREY SCOTT CO.

M. GORETTI			**THE BIRD SANCTUARY**	
93	HERITAGE EAGLE	5000	50.00	60.00
94	HARMONY IN THE WILD	2500	65.00	75.00

JOHN HINE STUDIOS LTD.

S. KUCK			**HEART STRINGS**	
92	DAY DREAMING	15,000	92.50	92.50
92	HUSH, IT'S SLEEPYTIME	15,000	97.50	97.50
92	TAKING TEA	15,000	92.50	92.50
92	WATCH ME WALTZ	15,000	97.50	97.50

YR NAME	LIMIT	ISSUE	QUOTE

JUNE MCKENNA COLLECTIBLES INC.

J. MCKENNA			**BLACK FOLK ART**
83 BLACK BOY WITH WATERMELON	CL	12.00	40.00
83 BLACK GIRL WITH WATERMELON	CL	12.00	40.00
84 BLACK MAN WITH PIG	CL	13.00	40.00
84 BLACK WOMAN WITH BROOM	CL	13.00	40.00
85 KIDS IN A TUB 3D	CL	30.00	60.00
85 KISSING COUSINS-SILL SITTER	CL	36.00	60.00
85 WATERMELON PATCH KIDS	CL	24.00	63.00
86 BLACK BUTLER	CL	13.00	40.00
87 AUNT BERTHA 3D	CL	36.00	72.00
87 LIL' WILLIE 3D	CL	36.00	72.00
87 SWEET PRISSY 3D	CL	36.00	72.00
87 UNCLE JACOB 3D	CL	36.00	72.00
88 NETTY	CL	16.00	50.00
88 RENTY	CL	16.00	40.00
89 DELIA	CL	16.00	40.00
89 JAKE	CL	16.00	40.00
90 TASHA	CL	17.00	40.00
90 TYREE	CL	17.00	40.00
J. MCKENNA			**CAROLERS**
85 BOY CAROLER	CL	36.00	75.00
85 GIRL CAROLER	CL	36.00	75.00
85 MAN CAROLER	CL	36.00	75.00
85 WOMAN CAROLER	CL	36.00	75.00
J. MCKENNA			**JUNE MCKENNA FIGURINES**
84 TREE TROPPER	CL	70.00	225.00
85 SOLDIER	CL	40.00	150.00-200.00
86 LITTLE ST. NICK	CL	50.00	75.00-125.00
86 MALE ANGEL	CL	44.00	400.00-2500.00
87 PATRIOTIC SANTA	CL	50.00	100.00-125.00
88 MRS. SANTA	CL	50.00	100.00-125.00
93 A GOOD NIGHT'S SLEEP	OP	70.00	70.00
93 ANGEL NAME PLAQUE	OP	70.00	70.00
93 BAKING COOKIES	2000	450.00	450.00
93 BELLS OF CHRISTMAS	10,000	40.00	40.00
93 CHILDREN ICE SKATERS	OP	70.00	70.00
93 CHRISTMAS CHEER	7500	120.00	120.00
93 CHRISTMAS EVE	4 YR	35.00	35.00
93 MR. SNOWMAN	OP	40.00	40.00
93 NATIVITY COW	OP	30.00	30.00
93 NATIVITY DONKEY	OP	30.00	30.00
93 NATIVITY RAM WITH EWE	OP	30.00	30.00
93 SANTA AND FRIENDS	OP	70.00	70.00
93 SANTA NAME PLAQUE	OP	70.00	70.00
93 SANTA'S LOVE	10,000	40.00	40.00
93 THE PATRIOT	4000	250.00	250.00
93 THE SNOW FAMILY	OP	40.00	40.00
93 TOMORROW'S CHRISTMAS	OP	250.00	250.00
94 ALL ABOARD NORTH POLE EXPRESS	*	500.00	500.00
94 BRINGING HOME CHRISTMAS	4 YR	35.00	35.00
94 CHILDREN CAROLERS	OP	90.00	90.00
94 CONDUCTOR	OP	70.00	70.00
94 DECORATING FOR CHRISTMAS	OP	70.00	70.00
94 MRS. CLAUS, DANCING	7500	120.00	120.00
94 NOT ONCE BUT TWICE	10,000	40.00	40.00
94 POSTMARKED NORTH POLE	10,000	40.00	40.00
94 SANTA'S ONE MAN BAND	7500	120.00	120.00
94 SAY CHEESE, PLEASE	OP	250.00	250.00
94 SNOWMAN AND CHILD	OP	70.00	70.00
94 ST. NICHOLAS	4000	250.00	250.00
94 STAR OF BETHLEHEM	OP	40.00	40.00
94 WELCOME TO THE WORLD	1500	400.00	400.00
J. MCKENNA			**LIMITED EDITION**
83 FATHER CHRISTMAS	CL	90.00	2500.00-4500.00
84 OLD SAINT NICK	CL	100.00	900.00-2000.00
85 WOODLAND	CL	140.00	1900.00
86 VICTORIAN	CL	150.00	600.00
87 CHRISTMAS EVE	CL	170.00	425.00-700.00
87 KRIS KRINGLE	CL	350.00	500.00
88 BRINGING HOME CHRISTMAS	CL	170.00	200.00-450.00
88 REMEMBERANCE OF CHRISTMAS PAST	4000	400.00	550.00
89 COMING TO TOWN	4000	220.00	220.00
89 SANTA'S WARDROBE	1500	750.00	750.00
89 SEASONS GREETINGS	CL	200.00	275.00-350.00
90 NIGHT BEFORE CHRISTMAS	1000	750.00	750.00

Lladró has a unique look all its own. Flower Song *exudes the elegance and emotion collectors of this magnificent line have come to love.*

Good Night *little darling says this Lladró mother to her young child.*

This little one is eager for the arrival of a new brother or sister. Anticipation *is produced by Lladró.*

A woman this beautiful must be a Lady of Taste. *The piece is produced by Lladró.*

YR	NAME	LIMIT	ISSUE	QUOTE
90	WILDERNESS	4000	200.00	200.00
92	BEDTIME STORIES	2000	500.00	500.00
92	CHRISTMAS GATHERING	4000	220.00	220.00
92	COMING TO TOWN	4000	220.00	220.00
92	HOT AIR BALLOON	1500	800.00	800.00
J. MCKENNA			**REGISTERED EDITION**	
86	COLONIAL	CL	150.00	200.00-650.00
87	WHITE CHRISTMAS	CL	170.00	1500.00
88	JOLLY OLE ST. NICK	CL	170.00	200.00-300.00
89	TRADITIONAL	OP	180.00	180.00
90	TOY MAKER	OP	200.00	200.00
91	CHECKING HIS LIST	OP	230.00	230.00
92	FORTY WINKS	OP	250.00	250.00
J. MCKENNA			**SPECIAL LIMITED EDITION**	
89	LAST GENTLE NUDGE	RT	280.00	280.00
89	SANTA & HIS MAGIC SLEIGH	4000	280.00	280.00
90	CHRISTMAS DREAMS	4000	280.00	280.00
90	SANTA'S REINDEER	1500	400.00	400.00
90	UP ON THE ROOFTOP	RT	280.00	280.00
J. MCKENNA			**VICTORIAN LIMITED EDITION**	
90	EDWARD 3D	CL	180.00	450.00
90	ELIZABETH 3D	CL	180.00	450.00

KAISER

W. GAWANTKA				**ANIMALS**
69	PORPOISE GROUP (3), WHITE BISQUE	CL	85.00	375.00
75	DOLPHIN GROUP (5), 520/5, WHITE BISQUE	800	850.00	3002.00
75	GERMAN SHEPHERD 528, COLOR BISQUE	CL	250.00	652.00
75	GERMAN SHEPHERD 528, WHITE BISQUE	CL	185.00	420.00
76	IRISH SETTER 535, COLOR BISQUE	1000	290.00	652.00
76	IRISH SETTER 535, WHITE/BASE	1500	*	424.00
78	DOLPHIN GROUP (4), 596/4, WHITE BISQUE	4500	75.00	956.00
78	KILLER WHALE 579, COLOR/BISQUE	2000	420.00	798.00
78	KILLER WHALE 579, WHITE/BISQUE	2000	85.00	404.00
78	KILLER WHALES (2), 594, COLOR	2000	925.00	2008.00
78	KILLER WHALES (2), 594, WHITE	2000	425.00	1024.00
79	BEAR & CUB 521, COLOR BISQUE	900	400.00	1072.00
79	BEAR & CUB 521, WHITE BISQUE	CL	125.00	378.00
85	BROOK TROUT 739, COLOR BISQUE	OP	250.00	488.00
85	PIKE 737, COLOR BISQUE	OP	350.00	682.00
85	RAINBOW TROUT 739, COLOR BISQUE	OP	250.00	488.00
85	TROUT 739, COLOR BISQUE	OP	95.00	488.00
91	LION 701201, WHITE BISQUE	1500	650.00	650.00
91	LION 701203, COLOR BISQUE	1500	1300.00	1300.00
82	TWO WILD BOARS 664, COLOR BISQUE	1000	650.00	890.00
80	BISON 630, COLOR BISQUE	2000	620.00	1044.00
80	BISON 690, WHITE BISQUE	2000	350.00	488.00
*			**BIRDS OF AMERICA COLLECTION**	
*	BALD EAGLE II 497, COLORED	CL	*	1300.00
*	ROADRUNNER 492, COLOR/BASE	CL	350.00	900.00
*	ROBIN & WORM, COLOR/BASE	CL	60.00	90.00
*	ROBIN II 537, COLOR/BASE	1000	260.00	888.00
*	SCREECH OWL 532, WHITE/BASE	CL	175.00	199.00
*	SNOWY OWL 776, COLOR/BASE	1500	*	1146.00
*	SNOWY OWL 776, WHITE/BASE	1500	*	668.00
*	SPARROW HAWK 749, COLOR/BASE	3000	575.00	906.00
70	SCARLET TANAGER, COLOR/BASE	CL	60.00	90.00
85	PINTAILS 747, COLOR/BASE	1500	*	838.00
85	PINTAILS 747, WHITE/BASE	1500	*	364.00
*	BABY TITMICE 501, COLOR/BASE	CL	400.00	500.00
*	BABY TITMICE 501, WHITE/BASE	1200	200.00	754.00
72	BLUE BIRD 496, COLOR, BASE	2500	120.00	480.00
72	GOSHAWK 491, COLOR/BASE	1500	2400.00	4326.00
72	GOSHAWK 491, WHITE/BASE	1500	850.00	1992.00
72	SEAGULL 498, COLOR/BASE	CL	850.00	1150.00
72	SEAGULL 498, WHITE/BASE	700	550.00	1586.00
73	BLUEJAY 503, COLOR/BASE	1500	475.00	1198.00
73	CARDINAL 504, COLOR/BASE	1500	60.00	600.00
73	ROBIN 502, COLOR/BASE	1500	340.00	718.00
74	FALCON 507, COLOR/BASE	1500	820.00	1928.00
76	BALD EAGLE IV 552, COLOR/BASE	1500	450.00	998.00
76	BALD EAGLE IV 552, WHITE/BASE	1500	210.00	572.00
80	BALD EAGLE VI 634, WHITE/BASE	3000	*	672.00
84	BALD EAGLE IX 714, COLOR/BASE	3500	500.00	850.00
84	BALD EAGLE IX 714, WHITE/BASE	4000	190.00	374.00
85	BALD EAGLE X 746, COLOR/BASE	1500	*	1198.00
85	BALD EAGLE X 746, WHITE/BASE	1500	375.00	672.00

YR	NAME	LIMIT	ISSUE	QUOTE
85	BALD EAGLE XI 751, COLOR/BASE	1000	880.00	1422.00
85	BALD EAGLE XI 751, WHITE/BASE	1000	*	902.00
68	PAIR OF MALLARDS 456, COLOR/BASE	CL	150.00	500.00
68	PAIR OF MALLARDS 456, WHITE/BASE	2000	75.00	518.00
68	PIDGEON GROUP 475, COLOR/BASE	1500	150.00	812.00
68	PIDGEON GROUP 475, WHITE/BASE	2000	60.00	412.00
*	BALD EAGLE VII 637, COLOR/BASE	200	*	20694.00
*	HORNED OWL II 524, COLOR/BASE	1000	650.00	2170.00
*	HORNED OWL II 524, WHITE/BASE	1000	*	918.00
*	PELICAN 534, WHITE/BASE	CL	*	625.00
75	SPARROW 516, COLOR/BASE	1500	300.00	596.00
75	WOOD DUCKS 514, COLOR/BASE	800	*	2804.00
75	WOODPECKERS 515, COLOR/BASE	800	900.00	1762.00
76	BALTIMORE ORIOLE 536, COLOR/BASE	1000	280.00	746.00
76	CANADIAN GEESE 550, WHITE/BASE	1500	1500.00	3490.00
76	PELICAN 534, COLOR/BASE	1200	925.00	1768.00
76	PHEASANT 556, COLOR/BASE	1500	3200.00	6020.00
77	OWL IV 559, COLOR/BASE	1000	*	1270.00
78	BABY TITMICE 601, COLOR/BASE	2000	*	956.00
78	BABY TITMICE 601, WHITE/BASE	2000	*	562.00
78	BALD EAGLE V 600, COLOR/BASE	1500	*	3848.00
78	PAIR OF MALLARDS II 572, COLOR/BASE	1500	*	1156.00
78	PAIR OF MALLARDS II 572, WHITE/BASE	1500	*	2366.00
79	SWAN 602, COLOR/BASE	2000	*	1370.00
81	KINGFISHER 639, COLOR/BASE	CL	45.00	60.00
81	QUAILS 640, COLOR/BASE	1500	*	2366.00
81	ROOSTER 642, COLOR/BASE	1500	860.00	1304.00
81	ROOSTER 642, WHITE/BASE	1500	380.00	688.00
82	BALD EAGLE VIII 656, COLOR/BASE	CL	800.00	880.00
82	BALD EAGLE VIII 656, WHITE/BASE	1000	400.00	904.00
82	HUMMINGBIRD GROUP 660, COLOR/BASE	3000	650.00	1232.00
84	PHEASANT 715, COLOR/BASE	1500	1000.00	1962.00
84	PEREGRINE FALCON 723, COLOR/BASE	1500	850.00	4946.00
86	SPARROW HAWK 777, COLORED BISQUE	10,000	950.00	1336.00
86	SPARROW HAWK 777, WHITE BISQUE	1000	440.00	716.00

W. GAWANTKA   **HORSE SCULPTURE**

YR	NAME	LIMIT	ISSUE	QUOTE
71	PONY GROUP 488, COLOR/BASE	CL	150.00	350.00
71	PONY GROUP 488, WHITE/BASE	2500	50.00	418.00
74	MARE & FOAL II 510, COLOR/BASE	CL	650.00	775.00
75	LIPIZZANER/MAESTOSO 517, COLOR/BASE	CL	*	1150.00
75	LIPIZZANER/MAESTOSO 517, WHITE/BASE	CL	*	750.00
76	HASSAN/ARABIAN 553, COLOR/BASE	1500	600.00	1204.00
76	HASSAN/ARABIAN 553, WHITE/BASE	CL	250.00	600.00
78	CAPITANO/LIPIZZANER 597, COLOR	1500	625.00	1496.00
78	CAPITANO/LIPIZZANER 597, WHITE	CL	275.00	574.00
80	MARE & FOAL III 636, COLOR/BASE	1500	950.00	1632.00
80	MARE & FOAL III 636, WHITE/BASE	1500	300.00	646.00
80	ORION/ARABIAN 629, COLOR/BASE	2000	600.00	1038.00
80	ORION/ARABIAN 629, WHITE/BASE	2000	250.00	442.00
87	PACER 792, COLOR/BASE	1500	1217.00	1350.00
87	PACER 792, WHITE/BASE	1500	574.00	652.00
87	TROTTER 780, COLOR/BASE	1500	1217.00	1350.00
87	TROTTER 780, WHITE/BASE	1500	574.00	652.00
90	ARGOS 633101, WHITE BISQUE/BASE	1000	578.00	672.00
90	ARGOS 633103, LIGHT COLOR/BASE	1000	1194.00	1388.00
90	ARGOS 633143, COLOR/BASE	1000	1194.00	1388.00

HUMAN FIGURES

YR	NAME	LIMIT	ISSUE	QUOTE
*	FATHER & DAUGHTER 752, COLOR	2500	390.00	710.00
*	FATHER & DAUGHTER 752, WHITE	2500	175.00	362.00
*	MOTHER & CHILD 757, COLOR	3500	600.00	864.00
*	MOTHER & CHILD 757, WHITE	4000	300.00	430.00
*	MOTHER & CHILD 775, COLOR	3500	600.00	864.00
*	MOTHER & CHILD 775, WHITE	4000	300.00	430.00
60	MOTHER & CHILD 398, WHITE BISQUE	OP	*	312.00
82	FATHER & SON 659, COLOR/BASE	2500	400.00	712.00
82	FATHER & SON 659, WHITE/BASE	2500	100.00	384.00
82	ICE PRINCESS 667, COLOR	5000	375.00	732.00
82	ICE PRINCESS 667, WHITE	5000	200.00	416.00
82	SWAN LAKE BALLET 641, COLOR	2500	650.00	1276.00
82	SWAN LAKE BALLET 641, WHITE	2500	200.00	974.00
83	MOTHER & CHILD/BUST 696, COLOR	3500	500.00	1066.00
83	MOTHER & CHILD/BUST 696, WHITE	4000	225.00	428.00

KURT S. ADLER/SANTA'S WORLD
* KSA/STEINBACH   **CAMELOT SMOKING FIGURINE**

YR	NAME	LIMIT	ISSUE	QUOTE
93	KING ARTHUR ES832	7500	175.00	175.00

YR	NAME	LIMIT	ISSUE	QUOTE
* KSA/STEINBACH		**CAMELOT SMOLING FIGURINE**		
92	MERLIN THE MAGICIAN ES830	7500	150.00	150.00
C. STEINBACH		**CAMELOT STEINBACH NUTCRACKER SERIES**		
91	MERLIN THE MAGICIAN ES610	RT	185.00	1500.00
92	KING ARTHUR ES621	10,000	195.00	195.00
J. MOSTROM		**CHRISTMAS IN CHELSEA**		
92	CHELSEA GARDEN SANTA W2721	5000	33.50	33.50
92	LARGE BLACK FOREST SANTA W2717	3000	110.00	110.00
92	LARGE FATHER CHRISTMAS W2719	3000	106.00	106.00
92	MRS. CLAUS W2714	5000	37.00	37.00
92	PATRIOTIC SANTA W2720	3000	128.00	128.00
92	PERE NOEL W2723	5000	33.50	33.50
92	SMALL BLACK FOREST SANTA W2712	5,000	40.00	40.00
92	SMALL FATHER CHRISTMAS W2712	5000	33.50	33.50
92	SMALL GRANDFATEHR FROST W2716	5000	43.00	43.00
92	SMALL GRANDFATHER FROST W2718	3000	106.00	106.00
92	ST. NICKOLAS W2713	5000	30.00	30.00
92	WORKSHOP SANTA W2715	5000	43.00	43.00
P. BOLINGER		**CHRISTMAS LEGENDS**		
94	BERWYN THE GRAND J8198	OP	175.00	175.00
94	CARADOC THE KIND J8199	OP	70.00	70.00
94	FLORIAN OF THE BERRY BUSH J8199	OP	70.00	70.00
94	GUSTAVE THE GUTSY J8199	OP	70.00	70.00
94	SILVANUS THE CHEERFUL J8197	OP	165.00	165.00
95	BOUNTIFUL J8234	OP	164.00	164.00
95	LUMINATUS J8241	OP	136.00	136.00
94	ALDWYN OF THE GREENWOOD J8196	OP	145.00	145.00
*		**CURRIER & IVES WATERGLOBE COLLECTION**		
92	OUR FIRST CHRISTMAS J1037	OP	40.00	40.00
92	WE WISH YOU A MERRY CHRISTMAS J1048	OP	40.00	40.00
*		**DISNEY CHRISTMAS NUTCRACKER COLLECTION**		
92	GOOFY H1216	OP	78.00	78.00
92	MICKEY MOUSE SORCERER H1221	OP	100.00	100.00
T. RUBEL		**FABRIC MACHE COLLECTION**		
92	HE DID IT AGAIN J7944	OP	160.00	160.00
92	I'M LATE, I'M LATE J7947	OP	100.00	100.00
92	IT'S TIME TO GO J7943	OP	150.00	150.00
*		**FABRICHE ANGEL COLLECTION**		
92	HEAVENLY MESSENGER W1584	OP	41.00	41.00
K. ADLER		**FABRICHE ANGEL SERIES**		
92	HEAVENLY MESSENGER W1584	RT	41.00	41.00
K. ADLER		**FABRICHE BEAR & FRIENDS**		
92	LAUGHING ALL THE WAY J1567	RT	83.00	83.00
92	NOT A CREATURE WAS STIRRING W1534	OP	67.00	67.00
93	TEDDY BEAR PARADE W1601	OP	73.00	73.00
P. MAUK		**FABRICHE CAMELOT FIGURE**		
93	MERLIN THE MAGICIAN J7966	7500	120.00	120.00
93	YOUNG ARTHUR J7967	7500	120.00	120.00
94	KING ARTHUR J3372	7500	110.00	110.00
*		**FABRICHE COLLECTION**		
92	BUNDLES OF JOY W1578	OP	78.00	78.00
92	CHRISTMAS IS IN THE AIR W1590	OP	110.00	110.00
92	HOMEWARD BOUND W1568	OP	61.00	61.00
92	JOLLY OLD NICK W1557	OP	56.00	56.00
92	LAUGHING ALL THE WAY W1567	OP	83.00	83.00
92	MASTER TOYMAKER W1566	OP	61.00	61.00
92	OLD FATHER FROST W1559	OP	56.00	56.00
92	SPECIAL DELIVERY W1558	OP	56.00	56.00
92	A STITCH IN TIME W1591	5000	135.00	135.00
92	APRON FULL OF LOVE W1582	OP	75.00	75.00
92	BRINGIN IN THE YULE LOG W1589	5000	200.00	200.00
92	SANTA STEALS A KISS & A COOKIE W1581	OP	150.00	150.00
92	SANTA'S ICE CAPADES W1588	OP	110.00	110.00
K. ADLER		**FABRICHE HOLIDAY FIGURINES**		
92	BUNDLES OF JOY W1578	RT	78.00	78.00
92	CHRISTMAS IS IN THE AIR W1590	OP	110.00	110.00
92	HOMEWARD BOUND W1566	OP	61.00	61.00
92	HUGS AND KISSES W1531	RT	67.00	67.00
92	ST. NICHOLAS THE BISHOP W1532	OP	78.00	78.00
93	ALL THAT JAZA W1620	RT	67.00	67.00
93	BRINGING THE GIFTS W1605	OP	60.00	60.00
93	CHECKING IT TWICE W1604	OP	56.00	56.00
93	FOREVER GREEN W1607	RT	56.00	56.00
93	PAR FOR THE CLAUS W1603	OP	60.00	60.00
93	PLAYTIME FOR SANTA W1619	RT	67.00	67.00
93	STOCKING STUFFER W1622	OP	56.00	56.00

YR	NAME	LIMIT	ISSUE	QUOTE
93	TOP BRASS W1630	OP	67.00	67.00
93	WITH ALL THE TRIMMINGS W1616	OP	76.00	76.00
94	ALL STAR SANTA W1652	OP	56.00	56.00
94	BASKET OF GOODIES W1650	OP	60.00	60.00
94	CHECKING HIS LIST W1643	OP	60.00	60.00
94	FIRELIGHTING FRIENDS W1654	OP	72.00	72.00
94	FRIENDSHIP W1642	OP	65.00	65.00
94	HO, HO, HO SANTA W1632	OP	56.00	56.00
94	HOLIDAY EXPRESS W1636	OP	100.00	100.00
94	OFFICER CLAUS W1677	OP	56.00	56.00
94	PEACE SANTA W1631	OP	60.00	60.00
94	SANTA'S FISHTALES W1640	OP	60.00	60.00
94	SCHUSSING CLAUS W1651	OP	78.00	78.00
95	ALL ABOARD FOR CHRISTMAS W1679	OP	56.00	56.00
95	ARMCHAIR QUARTERBACK W1693	OP	90.00	90.00
95	CAPTAIN CLAUS W1680	OP	56.00	56.00
95	DIET STARTS TOMORROW W1691	OP	60.00	60.00
95	FATHER CHRISTMAS W1687	OP	56.00	56.00
95	GIFT FROM HEAVEN W1694	OP	60.00	60.00
95	KRIS KINGLE W1685	OP	55.00	55.00
95	MERRY MEMORIES W1735	OP	56.00	56.00
95	PERE NOEL W1686	OP	55.00	55.00
95	STRIKE UP THE BAND W1681	OP	55.00	55.00
95	TEE TIME W1734	OP	60.00	60.00
94	MERRY ST. NICK W1641	OP	100.00	100.00
94	SANTA CALLS W1678	OP	55.00	55.00
94	MAIL MUST GO THROUGH W1667	OP	110.00	110.00
91	SANTA FIDDLER W1549	RT	100.00	100.00
92	AN APRON FULL OF LOVE W1582	OP	75.00	75.00
92	BRINGIN IN THE YULE LOG W1589	5000	200.00	200.00
92	MERRY KISSMAS W1548	RT	140.00	140.00
92	SANTA STEALS A KISS & A COOKIE W1581	RT	150.00	150.00
92	SANTA'S CAT NAP W1504	RT	98.00	98.00
92	SANTA'S ICE CAPADES W1588	OP	110.00	110.00
93	HERE KITTY W1616	RT	90.00	90.00
94	STAR GAZING SANTA W1656	OP	120.00	120.00
95	MRS. SANTA CAROLLER W1690	OP	70.00	70.00
95	SANTA CAROLER W1689	OP	70.00	70.00
92	HE DID IT AGAIN J7844	OP	160.00	160.00
92	I'M LATE, I'M LATE J7947	OP	100.00	100.00
92	IT'S TIME TO GO J7943	RT	150.00	150.00
95	WOODLAND SANTA W1731	OP	67.00	67.00
95	NIGHT BEFORE CHRISTMAS W1692	OP	60.00	60.00

M. ROTHENBERG   **FABRICHE SANTA AT HOME**

YR	NAME	LIMIT	ISSUE	QUOTE
93	GRANDPA SANTA'S PIGGYBACK RIDE W1621	7500	84.00	84.00
94	CHRISTMAS WALTZ, THE 1635	OP	135.00	135.00
94	SANTA'S NEW FRIENDS W1655	OP	110.00	110.00
95	BABY BURPING SANTA W1732	OP	80.00	80.00
95	FAMILY PORTRAIT W1727	OP	140.00	140.00
95	SANTA'S HORSEY RIDE W1728	OP	80.00	80.00

M. ROTHENBERG   **FABRICHE SANTA'S HELPERS**

YR	NAME	LIMIT	ISSUE	QUOTE
92	A STITCH IN TIME W1591	5000	135.00	135.00
93	LITTLE OLDE CLOCKMAKER W1629	5000	134.00	134.00

* KSA/SMITHSONIAN   **FABRICHE SMITHSONIAN MUSEUM**

YR	NAME	LIMIT	ISSUE	QUOTE
91	SANTA ON A BICYCLE W1527	RT	150.00	150.00
92	HOLIDAY DRIVE W1556	OP	156.00	156.00
92	PEACE ON EARTH ANGEL TREETOP W1585	OP	52.00	52.00
92	PEACE ON EARTH FLYING ANGEL W1585	OP	49.00	49.00
93	HOLIDAY FLIGHT W1617	OP	144.00	144.00
95	TOYS FOR GOOD BOYS AND GIRLS W1696	OP	75.00	75.00

K. ADLER   **GALLERY OF ANGELS**

YR	NAME	LIMIT	ISSUE	QUOTE
94	GUARDIAN ANGEL M1099	2000	150.00	150.00
94	UNSPOKEN WORD M1100	2000	150.00	150.00

C. STEINBACH   **GREAT AMERICANS STEINBACH NUTCRACKER SERIES**

YR	NAME	LIMIT	ISSUE	QUOTE
92	ABRAHAM LINCOLN ES622	12,000	195.00	195.00
92	GEORGE WASHINGTON ES623	12,000	195.00	195.00

P. BOLINGER   **HO HO HO GANG**

YR	NAME	LIMIT	ISSUE	QUOTE
94	CHRISTMAS GOOSE J8201	OP	25.00	25.00
94	HOLY MACKEREL J8202	OP	25.00	25.00
94	SANTA COB J8203	OP	28.00	28.00
94	SURPRISE J8201	OP	25.00	25.00
94	WILL HE MAKE IT? J8203	OP	28.00	28.00
95	COOKIE CLAUS J8286	OP	40.00	40.00
95	DO NOT DISTURB J8233	OP	56.00	56.00
95	NO HAIR DAY J8287	OP	50.00	50.00
95	NORTH POLE J8237	OP	60.00	60.00

YR	NAME	LIMIT	ISSUE	QUOTE
95	NORTH POLE J8238	OP	48.00	48.00
95	WILL WORK FOR COOKIES J8235	OP	40.00	40.00
95	WISHFUL THINKING J8239	OP	39.00	39.00
* KSA/JHP			**JIM HENSON'S MUPPET NUTCRACKERS**	
93	KERMIT THE FROG H1223	RT	90.00	90.00
* KSA/DISNEY			**MICKEY UNLIMITED**	
92	CHELSEA GARDEN SANTA W2721	RT	33.50	33.50
92	GOOFY H1216	OP	78.00	78.00
92	MICKEY MOUSE SOLDIER H1194	OP	72.00	72.00
92	MICKEY MOUSE SORCERER H1221	OP	100.00	100.0
93	DONALD DUCK H1235	OP	90.00	90.00
93	MICKEY MOUSE W/GIFT BOXES W1608	OP	78.00	78.00
93	PINNOCHIO H1222	OP	110.00	110.00
94	DONALD DUCK DRUMMER W1681	OP	45.00	45.00
94	MICKEY BANDLEADER W1669	OP	45.00	45.00
94	MICKEY SANTA NUTCRACKER H1237	OP	90.00	90.00
94	MINNIE MOUSE SOLDIER NUTCRACKER H1236	OP	90.00	90.00
94	MINNIE W/CYMBALS W1670	OP	45.00	45.00
* KSA/STEINBACH			**NUTCRACKER AM. PRESIDENT**	
92	ABRAHAM LINCOLN ES622	12000	195.00	195.00
92	GEORGE WASHINGTON ES623	RT	195.00	195.00
93	BEN FRANKLIN ES922	12000	225.00	225.00
93	TEDDY ROOSEVELT ES644	10000	225.00	225.00
* KSA/STEINBACH			**NUTCRACKER CAMELOT**	
91	MERLIN THE MAGICIAN ES610	RT	185.00	185.00
92	KING ARTHUR ES621	RT	195.00	195.00
93	SIR LANCELOT ES638	12000	225.00	225.00
94	SIR GALAHAD ES862	12000	225.00	225.00
94	SIR LANCELOT SMOKER ES833	7500	150.00	150.00
95	QUEEN GUENEVERE ES869	10000	245.00	245.00
* KSA/STEINBACH			**NUTCRACKER CHRISTMAS LEGENDS**	
93	FATHER CHRISTMAS ES645	7500	225.00	225.00
94	ST. NICHOLAS, THE BISHOP ES865	7500	225.00	225.00
95	1930s SANTA CLAUS ES891	7500	245.00	245.00
* KSA/STEINBACH			**NUTCRACKER COLLECTION**	
84	OIL SHELK	RT	100.00	100.00
91	COLUMBUS ES697	RT	194.00	194.00
92	HAPPY SANTA ES601	OP	190.00	190.00
* KSA/STEINBACH			**NUTCRACKER FAMOUS CHIEFTANS**	
93	CHIEF SITTING BULL ES637	8500	225.00	225.00
94	CHIEF SITTING BULL SMOKER ES834	7500	150.00	150.00
94	RED CLOUD ES864	8500	225.00	225.00
95	BLACK HAWK ES889	7500	245.00	245.00
* KSA/ZUBER			**NUTCRACKER SERIES**	
92	ANNAPOLIS MIDSHIPMAN, THE EK7	RT	125.00	125.00
92	BAVARIAN, THE EK16	RT	130.00	130.00
92	BRONCO BILLY THE COWBOY EK1	RT	125.00	125.00
92	CHIMNEY SWEEP, THE EK6	RT	125.00	125.00
92	COUNTRY SINGER, THE EK19	RT	125.00	125.00
92	FISHERMAN, THE EK17	5000	125.00	125.00
92	GEPETTO, THE TOYMAKER EK9	RT	125.00	125.00
92	GOLD PROSPECTOR, THE EK18	RT	125.00	125.00
92	GOLFER, THE EK5	RT	125.00	125.0
92	INDIAN, THE EK15	RT	135.00	135.00
92	NOR'EASTER SEA CAPTAIN, THE EK3	5000	125.00	125.00
92	PAUL BUNYAN THE LUMBERJACK EK2	RT	125.00	125.00
92	PILGRIM, THE EK14	RT	125.00	125.00
92	TYROLEAN, THE EK4	RT	125.00	125.00
92	WEST POINT CADET W/CANON, THE EK6	RT	130.00	130.00
93	HERR DROSSELMEIR NUTCRACKER EK21	RT	150.00	150.00
93	ICE CREAM VENDOR, THE EK24	5000	150.00	150.00
93	NAPOLEON BONAPARTE EK23	RT	150.00	150.00
93	PIZZAMAKER, THE EK22	5000	150.00	150.00
94	GARDNER, THE EK26	2500	150.00	150.00
94	JAZZ PLAYER EK25	2500	145.00	145.00
94	KURT THE TRAVELING SALESMAN EK28	RT	155.00	155.00
94	MOUSE KING EK31	2500	150.00	150.00
94	PETER PAN EK28	2500	145.00	145.00
94	SCUBA DIVER EK27	2500	150.00	150.00
94	SOCCER PLAYER EK30	2500	145.00	145.00
* KSA/STEINBACH			**NUTCRACKER TALES OF SHERWOOD FOREST**	
92	ROBIN HOOD ES863	7500	225.00	225.00
95	FRIAR TUCK ES890	7500	245.00	245.00
J. MOSTROM			**OLD WORLD SANTA SERIES**	
92	LARGE BLACK FOREST SANTA W2717	RT	110.00	110.00
92	LARGE FATHER CHRISTMAS W2719	RT	106.00	106.00

YR	NAME	LIMIT	ISSUE	QUOTE
92	MRS. CLAUS W2714	5000	37.00	37.00
92	PATRIOTIC SANTA W2720	3000	128.00	128.00
92	PERE NOEL W2723	RT	33.50	33.50
92	SMALL BLACK FOREST SANTA W2712	RT	40.00	40.00
92	SMALL FATHER CHRISTMAS W2712	RT	33.50	33.50
92	SMALL FATHER FROST W2716	RT	43.00	43.00
92	SMALL GRANDFATHER FROST W2718	RT	106.00	106.00
92	ST. NICHOLAS W2713	RT	30.00	30.00
92	WORKSHOP SANTA W2715	5000	43.00	43.00
93	GOOD KING WENCESLAS W2928	3000	134.00	134.00
93	MEDIEVAL KING OF CHRISTMAS W2881	3000	390.00	390.00
*		**OSCAR & BERTIE WATERGLOBE COLLECTION**		
92	BEARS ON ROCKING HORSE J1034	OP	56.00	56.00
92	SANTA BEAR WITH PACKAGES J1033	OP	41.00	41.00
*		**SATURDAY EVENING POST WATERGLOBE COLLECTION**		
92	CHRISTMAS TRIO NORMAN ROCKWELL J1035	OP	40.00	40.00
92	SANTA'S SURPRISE J.C. LEYENDECKER J1036	OP	40.00	40.00
* KSA/JHP		**SESAME STREET SERIES**		
93	BIG BIRD FIGURINE J7928	OP	60.00	60.00
93	BIG BIRD NUTCRACKER H1199	RT	60.00	60.00
*		**SMITHSONIAN MUSEUM CAROUSEL SERIES**		
92	THE BUNNY S3027/2	RT	14.50	14.50
92	THE GOAT S3027/1	RT	14.50	14.50
*		**SMITHSONIAN MUSEUM FABRICHE COLLECTION**		
92	HOLIDAY DRIVE W1556	OP	155.00	155.00
92	PEACE ON EARTH ANGEL TREETOP W1583	OP	52.00	52.00
92	PEACE ON EARTH FLYING ANGEL W1585	OP	49.00	49.00
C. STEINBACH		**STEINBACH MUSICAL COLLECTION**		
92	SKI LIFT MUSICAL ES27	2000	150.00	150.00
C. STEINBACH		**STEINBACH NUTCRACKER COLLECTION**		
92	HAPPY SANTA ES601	OP	190.00	190.00
C. STEINBACH		**STEINBACH SMOKING FIGURE SERIES**		
92	MERLIN THE MAGICIAN ES830	7500	150.00	150.00
*		**THOMAS NAST FABRICHE REPRODUCTION SERIES**		
92	CAUGHT IN THE ACT W1577	RT	133.00	133.00
92	CHRISTMAS SING-A-LONG W1576	12,000	110.00	110.00
K. ADLER		**THOMAS NAST FIGURINES**		
92	CAUGHT IN THE ACT W1577	RT	133.00	133.00
92	CHRISTMAS SING-A-LONG W1576	OP	110.00	110.00
93	DEAR SANTA W1602	RT	110.00	110.00
93	HELLO! LITTLE ONE W1552	RT	90.00	90.00
K. ADLER		**VISIONS OF SANTA SERIES**		
92	SANTA COMING OUT OF FIREPLACE J1023	RT	29.00	29.00
92	SANTA HOLDING CHILD J826	RT	24.50	24.50
92	SANTA SPILLING BAG OF TOYS J1022	RT	25.50	25.50
92	SANTA W/LITTLE GIRLS ON LAP J1024	7500	24.50	24.50
92	SANTA W/SACK HOLDING TOY J827	RT	24.50	24.50
92	WORKSHOP SANTA J825	RT	27.00	27.00
*		**WATERGLOBE COLLECTION**		
92	SANTA WITH TWO GIRLS J1038	OP	40.00	40.00
*		**ZUBER NUTCRACKER COLLECTION**		
92	THE BAVARIAN EK16	5000	130.00	130.00
92	THE COUNTRY SINGER EK19	5000	125.00	125.00
92	THE FISHERMAN EK17	5000	125.00	125.00
92	THE GOLD PROSPECTOR EK18	5000	125.00	125.00
92	THE INDIAN EK15	5000	135.00	135.00
92	THE PILGRIM EK14	5000	125.00	125.00

L.L. KNICKERBOCKER CO. INC.

M. COSTA				
92	DIANA/BLOWING DANDELIONS C11246	1500	117.00	117.00
93	ALYSSA/GIRL ON SWING C1974	2500	158.00	158.00
C. ORLANDO		**BEACH PARTY**		
94	DEDE C15004	10000	29.00	29.00
* *		**BEAN BAG**		
94	HOLLYWOOD STAR C12880	5000	29.75	29.75
93	CLEMENTINE C4735	2500	26.00	26.00
C. ORLANDO		**BEAR BUDDIES**		
94	PUPPY LUV C15006	2500	46.25	46.25
J. HAUGHEY		**BEARS ON PARADE**		
*	CLOWN #2 C9658	5000	79.50	79.50
*	LITTLE MAJORETTE C9659	YR	39.50	39.50
*	POM POM GIRL C9657	5000	59.50	59.50
92	MARINE C11513	604	47.50	47.50
92	NAVY C11512	604	47.50	47.50
93	ARMY C4756	2500	47.50	47.50
94	AIR FORCE C8146	2500	52.00	52.00

YR	NAME	LIMIT	ISSUE	QUOTE
*	APRIL C9661-765	YR	49.50	49.50
*	AUGUST C9661-769	YR	49.50	49.50
*	DECEMBER C9661-773	YR	49.50	49.50
*	FEBRUARY C9661-763	YR	49.50	49.50
*	JANUARY C9661-762	YR	49.50	49.50
*	JULY C9661-768	YR	49.50	49.50
*	JUNE C9661-767	YR	49.50	49.50
*	LITTLE LADY/LIAC C9673	YR	79.50	79.50
*	MARCH C9661-764	YR	49.50	49.50
*	MAY C9661-766	YR	49.50	49.50
*	NOVEMBER C9661-772	YR	49.50	49.50
*	OCTOBER C9661-771	YR	49.50	49.50
*	SEPTEMBER C9661-770	YR	49.50	49.50

M. NICOLE — BEST FRIENDS

YR	NAME	LIMIT	ISSUE	QUOTE
92	ERIN/GIRL W/BUNNY C9635	2500	178.50	178.50
92	GEORGIA/GIRL W/KITTEN C9637	2500	179.00	179.00
92	HILLARY/GIRL W/DUCKS C9636	2500	178.50	178.50

J. MOWRY — CHILDREN OF THE WORLD

YR	NAME	LIMIT	ISSUE	QUOTE
94	TOMIKA/ESKIMO C13710	2500	198.50	198.50
95	BONNIE JEAN C15218	2500	124.00	124.00

J. ARNETT — CHRISTMAS

YR	NAME	LIMIT	ISSUE	QUOTE
94	FATHER CHRISTMAS '94 C13427	1000	313.00	313.00
94	BRYANNA C14515	7500	149.25	149.25
92	BRYANNA/GREEN VELVET C11240	1000	183.00	183.00
94	KRIS-XMAS C8329	2500	89.00	89.00

B. MCCONNELL — CIRCUS

YR	NAME	LIMIT	ISSUE	QUOTE
93	TRIXI-ELELPHANT C4755	2500	69.50	69.50

V. DEFILIPPO — CLASSICAL BEAUTIES

YR	NAME	LIMIT	ISSUE	QUOTE
93	JULIA C11395	2500	169.00	169.00
93	PRISCILLIA/DRESSED IN PEACH C11385	2500	146.50	146.50
95	NATALIE C14829	2500	154.00	154.00

P. PARKINS — CLASSICS

YR	NAME	LIMIT	ISSUE	QUOTE
93	ALESIA/BLACK BRIDE USA C11384	250	590.00	590.00
95	LAUREN C15216	500	436.00	436.00

** — COFFEE CLUB

YR	NAME	LIMIT	ISSUE	QUOTE
94	HOLLYWOOD STAR C15002	OP	21.95	21.95

C. ROBINSON — COLLECTIBLES

YR	NAME	LIMIT	ISSUE	QUOTE
95	MORGAN C15904	1500	155.00	155.00
94	BUNNY LOVE C10941	2500	45.50	45.50
94	BUNNY LOVE CHRISTMAS C14642	2500	54.00	54.00
94	TUSH/CRAWLING BABY C10944	2500	76.50	76.50
95	BUNNY LOVE 1995 C15893	8000	41.00	41.00
95	SOME BUNNY LOVES YOU C15226	2500	45.00	45.00

G. LANGFORD — COUNTRY

YR	NAME	LIMIT	ISSUE	QUOTE
94	COWBOY GLEN C8147	2500	127.00	127.00

M. NICOLE — COUNTRY GIRL

YR	NAME	LIMIT	ISSUE	QUOTE
92	SARAH/DRESSED IN BLUE C9639	2500	159.00	159.00
92	SARITA/DRESSED IN PURPLE C9638	2500	159.00	159.00

G. LANGFORD — CUTE & CUDDY

YR	NAME	LIMIT	ISSUE	QUOTE
94	NOELLE C8188	2500	39.50	39.50
94	KASEY C8150	2500	69.00	69.00

A. FUNICELLO — CUTE CUDDY

YR	NAME	LIMIT	ISSUE	QUOTE
93	TAMMY C12199	2000	39.50	39.50

C. BELLSMITH — DEAR TO MY HEART

YR	NAME	LIMIT	ISSUE	QUOTE
92	OZEANNA/GERMAN ORIGIN C10414	2500	120.00	120.00
92	BRETA/DRESSED IN PEACH C9633	2500	115.00	115.00
92	GERRI/DRESSED IN MINT GRN. C9634	2500	115.00	115.00
92	TAMMY/DRESSED IN MAUVE C9632	2500	115.00	115.00

** — ELEGANCE

YR	NAME	LIMIT	ISSUE	QUOTE
94	JOHNNY C12882	1500	108.50	108.50
*	CYNTHIA C9686	2500	149.50	149.50

J. OPENSHAW — FAIRY TALE

YR	NAME	LIMIT	ISSUE	QUOTE
94	ALICE IN WONDERLAND C13706	5000	149.50	149.50
93	SNOW WHITE C11397	5000	177.50	177.50

B. MCCONNELL — FAMILY HELPERS

YR	NAME	LIMIT	ISSUE	QUOTE
*	JOSIE/MAMA IN KITCHEN C9687	2500	149.50	149.50

C.-L. WAUGH — FLAVORTIE

YR	NAME	LIMIT	ISSUE	QUOTE
94	CAROL C12881	1500	74.50	74.50

V. DEFILIPPO — FOUR SEASON

YR	NAME	LIMIT	ISSUE	QUOTE
93	AMBER/FALL C11380	2500	188.00	188.00

B. MCCONNELL — FOUR SEASONS

YR	NAME	LIMIT	ISSUE	QUOTE
*	DAISY C9694	2500	109.50	109.50
94	SUZANNE 13882	1500	95.00	95.00

D. STEWART — FOUR SEASONS SMALL WONDERS

YR	NAME	LIMIT	ISSUE	QUOTE
94	SMALL WONDERS C12860	4000	56.00	56.00
95	WINTER WONDER C15224	4000	61.00	61.00

YR	NAME	LIMIT	ISSUE	QUOTE
B. FINLINSON				**GREETING CARD**
95	EASTER C15753	YR	25.00	25.00
95	VALENTINE C15225	YR	25.00	25.00
93	CHRISTMAS '93 C6483	YR	25.00	25.00
93	MOTHER'S DAY '93/DRESSED IN PINK C11945	20000	25.00	25.00
95	MOTHER'S DAY '95 C15754	YR	25.00	25.00
94	LIANA C12862	2500	150.00	150.00
D. STEWART				**GREETING CARDS**
94	ALL OCCASION '94 C10943	YR	25.00	25.00
94	CHRISTMAS '94 C14645	YR	28.50	28.50
94	VALENTINE '94 C10942	YR	25.00	25.00
* *				**HARLEQUIN**
94	HARLEY C12886	1500	98.50	98.50
*	HARLEGUIN C9692	2500	99.50	99.50
*	HARLEGUIN C9691	2500	139.50	139.50
* STEWART/GRIFFITH				**HAT BOX**
93	VIRGINIA MARIE/BRIDE C11902	3000	135.00	135.00
* *				**HERMANN FACTORY**
*	FATER C9683	1000	229.50	229.50
D. CRYSTAL				**I CAN DREAM**
94	PLAYING MOMMY C13714	YR	47.00	47.00
V. DEFILIPPO				**INJURED**
92	CHELSEA/HURT LEG C11250	5000	91.50	91.50
92	DOTTIE/CHICKEN POX C11252	5000	89.00	89.00
93	MACIE/HOSPITAL GOWN C11381	5000	87.50	87.50
93	SAVANNAH/SNIFFLES C11907	5000	92.50	92.50
92	MCKENSIE/WOUNDED FINGER C9631	5000	88.00	88.00
B. STOEHR				**JESSICA'S BEST FRIEND**
94	ANGELICA/LAVENDER DRESS C13201	5000	199.50	199.50
B. STOEHR				**JESSICA'S BEST FRIENDS**
94	ANGELICA XMAS C14644	5000	228.00	228.00
C. BELLSMITH				**LARGE TRUNK**
92	TRICIA/TRAVEL THEME C10405	2500	277.00	277.00
C. BELLSMITH				**MIRACLE CHILDREN**
92	FRENDA/NEEDLEPOINT C10409	YR	91.50	91.50
92	GINA/HALLOWEEN CAT C10411	YR	88.00	88.00
93	FAITH/FLYING A KITE C1988	YR	76.50	76.50
94	BECKY/DADDY'S GIRL/BASEBALL C12857	YR	76.00	76.00
94	CAITLIN & BENTLY/GIRL W/DOG C12856	YR	79.00	79.00
92	MARILYN/PLAYING DRESS-UP C11251	YR	83.50	83.50
93	AARON/GROOM C11364	YR	75.50	75.50
93	CODY/PLAYING PIRATE C11379	YR	80.00	80.00
94	CELESTE/DRESSED LIKE AN ANGEL C14641	YR	82.00	82.00
94	TRACI/DEAF-SIGNING C13113	20000	82.00	82.00
92	BETTY/BAKING A CAKE C10413	YR	69.50	69.50
92	COURTNIE/CLOWN BABY C9627	YR	69.50	69.50
92	DANIELLE/LITTLE BALLERINA C9626	YR	69.50	69.50
92	LINDA/NO WINDOWS C10412	YR	74.00	74.00
92	PIERRE/LITTLE PICASSO C9629	YR	69.50	69.50
92	SHANNON/LITTLE NURSE C9628	YR	69.50	69.50
92	SHAWN/BORN TO SHOP C9630	YR	69.50	69.50
93	ANNIE/GIRL ON BIKE C11911	YR	74.50	74.50
93	FLORA/WEDDING THEME C11910	YR	79.50	79.50
93	MEKEL/PICNIC W/TEDDY C11909	YR	84.75	84.75
94	MOTHER'S DAY '94 C12863	YR	25.00	25.00
94	TINA/GIRL PLAYING C13711	YR	116.50	116.50
D. STEWART				**MOTHER CHILD**
94	VIRGINIA & JORDAN C13735	3000	179.00	179.00
S. & R. FOSKEY				**MUSICAL**
94	JOLLY C12883	2500	53.50	53.50
92	EMILY/MUSICAL SEWING C9640	2500	110.00	110.00
* *				**NOSTALGIC**
94	THORNEY C12887	2500	69.50	69.50
94	LITTLE JOE 13877	3000	49.00	49.00
*	BERNIE C9676	2500	59.50	59.50
*	BROWNIE C9678	2500	129.50	129.50
*	MOLLIE C9677	2500	69.50	69.50
94	DAPPER DAN C8194	1500	72.00	72.00
94	HEINZ 13878	2500	100.00	100.00
D. STEWART				**PETITE AMOUR**
93	GOLDIE/GIRL W/BEAR C11905	3000	48.50	48.50
94	ANITA C12858	3000	41.00	41.00
94	CHRISTMAS DARLINGS '94 C13428	4000	152.00	152.00
94	GRETL C13200	3000	51.00	51.00
C. BELLSMITH				**PICTURE DAY**
93	CAMILLE/DRESSED IN PINK C10406	2500	216.00	216.00

YR	NAME	LIMIT	ISSUE	QUOTE
93	CAROLINE/DRESSED IN RED VELVET C10407	2500	220.00	220.00
94	LITTLE RED RIDING HOOD C12861	5000	199.50	199.50
C.-L. WAUGH				**RUSSIAN**
*	ARTYOM/BABY C9681	5000	39.50	39.50
*	MIKHAIL/BROTHER C9679	5000	69.50	69.50
*	POLINA/SISTER C9680	5000	69.50	69.50
94	DMITRI C8281	2500	43.50	43.50
J. MITCHELL				**SCRAPBOOK**
*	BALLERINA C9695	2500	145.00	145.00
*	LET IN SNOW SNOWMAN C9698	5000	89.50	89.50
*	LET IT SNOW ANNETTE C9697	5000	145.00	145.00
*	MASQUERADE C9696	5000	145.00	145.00
*	SADDLING UP C9700	5000	79.50	79.50
*	WESTERN ROUND UP C9699	5000	145.00	145.00
D. STEWART				**SMALL TRUNK**
93	VANESSA C11386	2500	198.00	198.00
J. HOLLENBRANDS				**SOMEWHERE IN TIME**
94	ELEANOR C14755	2500	212.00	212.00
* *				**SPECIAL**
94	PEANUT BUTTER C15724	800	69.50	69.50
94	MARION C15005	1500	46.25	46.25
93	NO NO NANNETTE C4736	2500	62.00	62.00
94	TAPESTRY BEAR PURSE 13881	1500	57.00	57.00
94	GUARDIAN ANGEL BEAR C14282	10000	29.25	29.25
94	I LOVE YOU 14143	10000	40.00	40.00
*	ANETTE MOUSKEBEAR C9674	7500	79.50	79.50
*	BOBBY MOUSKEBEAR C9675	7500	79.50	79.50
*	HUGO W/JUNGLE BELLS C9690	2500	149.00	149.00
*	SKIPPER C9689	2500	149.00	149.00
94	NO NO NANETTE C4736	2500	62.00	62.00
94	MIKEY C8214	1000	71.00	71.00
94	MEL C12885	2500	66.50	66.50
C. BELLSMITH				**STORY BOOK**
93	JULIETTE/MAGIC FERRIS WHEEL C10404	2500	121.50	121.50
94	LITTLE BO PEEP C13708	YR	49.50	49.50
* *				**SWEATER**
94	JESSICA C9685	2500	39.50	39.50
94	JOSHUA 13879	2500	41.00	41.00
92	GINNY C11515	604	39.50	39.50
93	LITTLE NICK-X-MAS C4728	5000	54.50	54.50
*	JESSICA/BABY C9685	2500	39.50	39.50
*	UNCLE TEDDY C9684	2500	129.50	129.50
92	JESSICA C9685	2500	39.50	39.50
D. STEWART				**SWEET DREAMS**
93	OLIVIA/BABY ON PILLOW C11904	2500	93.00	93.00
94	SWEET DREAMS BABY/ON MOON C12859	2500	89.50	89.50
G. LANGFORD				**SWEET PRESERVES**
94	SWEET GINA C8324	2500	138.50	138.50
*	FLORA C9693	2500	119.50	119.50
* *				**T-SHIRT**
94	AF T-SHIRT A22433	*	21.75	21.75
* *			**TEDDY BEAR PICNIC/HERMANN FACTORY**	
*	MUSICAL C9682	1000	299.50	299.50
V. DEFILIPPO				**TODDLER**
92	JESSICA/1ST BIRTHDAY C10415	2500	249.00	249.00
92	RACHAEL/MARIE'S DAUGHTER C11254	2500	219.00	219.00
93	JESSICA/CHRISTMAS C6508	5000	249.00	500.00
93	DEBBIE/DONNY'S DAUGHTER C11244	2500	262.00	262.00
95	ASHLEY C15217	2500	195.50	195.50
A. JACKSON				**TWIN**
93	NATHAN/BOY IN AQUA C11382	2000	104.00	104.00
93	NICOLE/GIRL IN AQUA C11383	2000	137.00	137.00
92	ANDY & SON/COUNTRY C9641	2500	190.00	190.00
93	JENNY & JASON/CABBAGE PATCH C11430	5000	172.50	172.50
C.-L. WAUGH				**VALENTINE**
92	CANDI C11511	604	75.00	75.00
B. MCCONNELL				**VARSITY**
*	SWEATER GIRL C9688	2500	79.00	79.00
L. HENRY				**VELVETEEN**
95	BLOSSOM BUNNY C15739	5000	117.75	117.75
L. HENRY				**VELVETEEN RABBIT**
92	VELVET/WHITE PLUSH FUR C11245	5000	121.50	121.50
93	ROBBIE RABBIT C11363	5000	149.50	149.50
94	HARELOOM BUNNY C10940	5000	125.50	123.50
94	ROSEMARIE RABBIT/BRIDE W/MASK C13198	20000	149.50	149.50

YR NAME	LIMIT	ISSUE	QUOTE
D. STEWART			**XMAS**
93 HOLLY/BEAN BAG/MUSIC C2086	2500	114.00	114.00

LANCE CORP.

YR NAME	LIMIT	ISSUE	QUOTE
P.W. BASTON			**AMERICA REMEMBERS**
79 FAMILY SING	YR	29.50	90.00-125.00
80 FAMILY PICNIC	YR	29.50	45.00-60.00
81 FAMILY READS ALOUD	YR	34.50	34.50
82 FAMILY FISHING	YR	34.50	34.50
83 FAMILY FEAST	YR	37.50	100.00-150.00
P.W. BASTON			**CHILDREN AT PLAY**
78 SIDEWALK DAYS BOY	SO	19.50	35.00-50.00
78 SIDEWALK DAYS GIRL	SO	19.50	30.00-50.00
79 BUILDING DAYS BOY	SO	19.50	20.00-40.00
79 BUILDING DAYS GIRL	SO	19.50	20.00-40.00
80 SNOW DAYS BOY	SO	19.50	20.00-40.00
80 SNOW DAYS GIRL	SO	19.50	20.00-40.00
81 SAILING DAYS BOY	SO	19.50	20.00-30.00
81 SAILING DAYS GIRL	SO	19.50	20.00-30.00
82 SCHOOL DAYS BOY	SO	19.50	20.00-30.00
82 SCHOOL DAYS GIRL	SO	19.50	20.00-30.00
F. BARNUM			**CHILMARK**
87 SAVING THE COLORS	RT	350.00	350.00
87 SURPRISE ENCOUNTER	SO	250.00	730.00
89 LEE TO THE REAR	SO	300.00	580.00
90 LEE AND JACKSON	OP	375.00	620.00
91 ROBERT E. LEE	SO	350.00	1000.00
91 STONEWALL JACKSON	YR	295.00	295.00
92 KENNESAW MOUNTAIN		650.00	1000.00
92 ULYSSES S. GRANT	*	350.00	450
80 DUEL OF THE BIGHORNS	RT	725.00	1225.00
80 PRAIRIE SOVEREIGN	RT	645.00	800.00
81 APACHE SIGNALS	RT	175.00	500.00-650.00
81 BLACKFOOT SNOW HUNTER	RT	175.00	650.00
81 BUFFALO STALKER	RT	175.00	560.00
81 COMANCHE	RT	175.00	730.00
81 IROQUOIS WARFARE	RT	175.00	575.00
81 PLIGHT OF THE HUNTSMAN	SO	495.00	1000.00-1190.00
81 UNCONQUERED SEMINOLE	RT	175.00	540.00
81 VICTOR CHEYENNE	RT	175.00	500.00
82 ARAPAHO SENTINEL	RT	195.00	480.00
82 BLOOD BROTHERS	RT	250.00	610.00
82 DANCE OF THE EAGLES	RT	150.00	215.00
82 KIOWA SCOUT	RT	195.00	525.00
82 LISTENING FOR HOOVES	RT	150.00	460.00
82 MANDAN BUFFALO DANCER	RT	195.00	610.00
82 PLAINS TALK, PAWNEE	RT	195.00	525.00
82 SHOSHONE EAGLE CATCHER	SO	225.00	2040.00
82 THE TRACKER NEZ PERCE	RT	150.00	575.00
82 WINGS OF LIBERTY	SO	625.00	1250.00
83 A WARRIOR'S TRIBUTE	RT	335.00	635.00
83 ALONG THE CHEROKEE TRACE	RT	295.00	720.00
83 CIRCLING THE ENEMY	RT	295.00	395.00
83 FOREST WATCHER	RT	215.00	540.00
83 MOMENT OF TRUTH	RT	295.00	620.00
83 RITE OF THE WHITETAIL	RT	295.00	400.00
83 WINTER HUNT	RT	295.00	370.00
84 FLAT OUT FOR RED RIVER STATION	SO	3000.00	7400.00
86 EAGLE CATCHER	SO	300.00	1100.00
81 FREEDOM EAGLE	SO	195.00	950.00
80 RUBY-THROATED HUMMINGBIRD	SO	275.00	385.00
86 CAMELOT CHESS SET	RT	2250.00	2250.00
79 CAVALRY OFFICER	SO	95.00	650.00
79 COWBOY	SO	95.00	600.00-630.00
88 DRAGON SLAYER	RT	385.00	500.00
88 DRAGON SLAYER	RT	385.00	500.00
88 END OF THE TRAIL (MINI)	SO	225.00	250.00
90 SMOKE SIGNAL	SO	345.00	770.00
90 VIGIL	SO	345.00	500.00
90 WARRIOR	SO	300.00	400.00
77 FALL-MUSTANGS	3500	120.00	120.00
77 SPRING-MUSTANGS	3500	120.00	120.00
77 SUMMER-MUSTANGS	3500	120.00	120.00
77 WINTER-MUSTANGS	3500	120.00	120.00
78 BUFFALO HUNT	SO	360.00	2220.00
78 CHEYENNE	SO	285.00	2730.00
78 COLD SADDLES, MEAN HORSES	SO	250.00	1620.00

YR	NAME	LIMIT	ISSUE	QUOTE
78	COUNTING COUP	SO	275.00	1600.00
78	CROW SCOUT	SO	200.00	1700.00
78	MAVERICK CALF	SO	295.00	1300.00
78	MONDAY MORNING WASH	SO	285.00	1290.00
78	PAINTING THE TOWN	SO	400.00	1550.00
78	RESCUE	SO	315.00	2700.00
78	THE OUTLAWS	SO	325.00	725.00
79	GETTING ACQUAINTED	SO	215.00	875.00
80	AFRICAN ELEPHANT	RT	275.00	400.00
80	BORDER RUSTLERS	SO	950.00	1500.00
80	GIRAFFE	RT	125.00	145.00
80	KUDU	RT	140.00	160.00
80	MANDAN HUNTER	SO	65.00	780.00
80	RHINO	RT	115.00	135.00
81	AMBUSHED	RT	2000.00	2700.00
81	BUFFALO ROBE	RT	200.00	315.00
81	DOG SOLDIER	2500	200.00	300.00
81	ENEMY TRACKS	SO	225.00	720.00
81	U.S. MARSHAL	SO	95.00	485.00
81	WAR PARTY	RT	550.00	975.00
81	WHEN WAR CHIEFS MEET	SO	300.00	865.00
82	APACHE GAN DANCER	2500	95.00	110.00
82	APACHE HOSTILE	2500	95.00	110.00
82	ARAPAHO DRUMMER	2500	95.00	110.00
82	BUFFALO PRAYER	SO	95.00	325.00-350.00
82	COMANCHE PLAINES DRUMMER	2500	95.00	110.00
82	CROW MEDICINE DANCER	2500	95.00	110.00
82	FLATHEAD WAR DANCER	2500	95.00	110.00
82	HOPI KACHINA DANCER	2500	95.00	110.00
82	JEMEZ EAGLE DANCER	SO	95.00	145.00-325.00
82	LAST ARROW	SO	95.00	145.00-325.00
82	NAVAJO KACHINA DANCER	2500	95.00	110.00
82	SIOUX WAR CHIEF	SO	95.00	325.00-480.00
82	YAKIMA SALMON FISHERMAN	SO	200.00	1230.00
83	BOUNTY HUNTER	RT	250.00	275.00
83	LINE RIDER	SO	195.00	1410.00
83	MUSTANGER	2500	425.00	550.00
83	THE CHIEF	SO	275.00	1850.00-2050.00
83	THE WILD BUNCH	RT	215.00	225.00-260.00
83	TOO MANY ACES	2500	400.00	495.00
84	EYE TO EYE	2500	375.00	475.00
84	NOW OR NEVER	RT	275.00	800.00
84	THE GUIDON	*	*	*
84	UNIT COLORS	SO	250.00	1250.00
85	BAREBACK RIDER	2500	225.00	300.00
85	BARREL RACER	2500	275.00	325.00
85	BULL RIDER	2500	265.00	335.00
85	CALF ROPER	2500	300.00	375.00
85	OH GREAT SPIRIT	SO	300.00	1270.00
85	SADDLE BRONC RIDER	2500	250.00	300.00
85	STEER WRESTLING	2500	500.00	600.00
85	TEAM ROPING	2500	500.00	625.00
86	FIGHTING STALLIONS	2500	250.00	300.00
86	WILD STALLION	RT	145.00	160.00
88	I WILL FIGHT NO MORE FOREVER	SO	350.00	560.00
89	GERONIMO	SO	375.00	785.00
90	COCHISE	SO	400.00	745.00
90	PEQUOT WARS	SO	395.00	450.00
90	RED RIVER WARS	SO	425.00	500.00
90	TECUMSEH'S REBELLION	SO	350.00	450.00
91	CRAZY HORSE	OP	295.00	295.00
78	BUFFALO	SO	170.00	400.00
78	RISE AND SHINE	SO	135.00	200.00
78	RUNNING FREE	SO	100.00	320.00
78	STALLION	SO	100.00	260.00
78	THE CHALLENGE	SO	175.00	225.00
79	MOSES	SO	100.00	335.00
80	BORN FREE	SO	250.00	380.00
84	CHEYENNE (REMINGTON)	RT	400.00	600.00
85	BRONCO BUSTER (LARGE)	RT	400.00	400.00
84	GARDEN UNICORN	RT	160.00	200.00
92	CHIEF JOSEPH METART	*	975.00	1300
79	CAROUSEL	SO	115.00	115.00
79	UNICORN	SO	95.00	600.00

D. LIBERTY   **CRYSTALS OF ZORN**

89	BATTLE ON THE PLAINS OF XENON	950	265.00	265.00

YR	NAME	LIMIT	ISSUE	QUOTE
89	CHARGING THE STONE	950	395.00	395.00
89	GUARDING THE CRYSTAL	950	460.00	460.00
89	RESPONSE OF ORNIC FORCE	950	285.00	285.00
89	RESTORATION	950	435.00	435.00
89	U.S.S. STRIKES BACK	500	675.00	675.00
90	ASMUND'S WORKSHOP	950	275.00	275.00
90	STRUGGLING FOR SUPREMACY	950	400.00	400.00
90	VESTING THE GRAIL	950	200.00	200.00
*			**DISNEY FIGURES**	
89	GOLD EDITION HOLLYWOOD MICKEY	CL	200.00	200.00
89	HOLLYWOOD MICKEY	CL	165.00	170.00
91	MICKEY'S CAROUSEL RIDE	2500	150.00	150.00
*			**GENERATIONS OF MICKEY**	
87	ANTIQUE MICKEY	SO	130.00	350.00
89	MICKEY'S GALA PREMIERE	2500	150.00	150.00
89	SORCERER'S APPRENTICE	2500	150.00	160.00
89	STEAM BOAT WILLIE	2500	165.00	175.00
90	DISNEYLAND MICKEY	2500	150.00	150.00
90	THE BAND CONCERT	2000	185.00	185.00
90	THE BAND CONCERT (PAINTED)	500	215.00	215.00
91	PLANE CRAZY-1928	2500	175.00	175.00
91	THE MOUSE-1935	1200	185.00	185.00
P.W. BASTON, JR.			**HOLIDAY MEMORIES-MEMBER ONLY**	
90	LEPRECHAUN	YR	27.50	27.50
90	THANKSGIVING HELPER	YR	39.50	39.50
91	TRICK OR TREAT	YR	25.50	25.50
P.W. BASTON			**HUDSON PEWTER FIGURES**	
69	BETSY ROSS	CL	30.00	100.00-125.00
69	COLONIAL BLACKSMITH	CL	30.00	100.00-125.00
69	GEORGE WASHINGTON (CANNON)	CL	35.00	75.00-100.00
69	JOHN HANCOCK	CL	15.00	100.00-125.00
72	BENJAMIN FRANKLIN	CL	15.00	75.00-100.00
72	GEORGE WASHINGTON	CL	15.00	75.00-100.00
72	JAMES MADISON	CL	15.00	50.00-75.00
72	JOHN ADAMS	CL	15.00	75.00-100.00
72	THOMAS JEFFERSON	CL	15.00	75.00-100.00
75	DECLARATION WALL PLAQUE	CL	*	300.00-500.00
75	LEE'S NINTH GENERAL ORDER	CL	*	300.00-400.00
75	LINCOLN'S GETTYBURG ADDRESS	CL	*	300.00-400.00
75	NEIGHBORHOOD PEWS	CL	*	600.00-1000.00
75	SPIRIT OF '76	CL	*	750.00-1500.00
75	THE FAVORED SCHOLAR	CL	*	600.00-1000.00
75	WASHINGTON'S LETTER OF ACCEPTANCE	CL	*	300.00-400.00
75	WEIGHING THE BABY	CL	*	600.00-1000.00
76	BALD EAGLE	CL	100.00	112.50
76	GREAT HORNED OWL	CL	*	41.50
P.W. BASTON			**JIMMY FUND**	
83	SCHOOLBOY	YR	24.50	50.00-75.00
84	CATCHER	YR	24.50	50.00-75.00
85	HOCKEY PLAYER	YR	24.50	25.00-50.00
86	SOCCER PLAYER	YR	25.00	25.00
87	FOOTBALL PLAYER	YR	26.50	26.50
88	SANTA	CL	32.50	32.50
P.W. BASTON, JR.			**MEMBER ONLY**	
89	THE COLLECTORS	YR	39.50	39.50
D. LAROCCA			**MILITARY COMMEMORATIVES**	
91	DESERT LIBERATOR (PAINTED PORCELAIN)	5000	125.00	125.00
91	DESERT LIBERATOR (PEWTER)	950	295.00	295.00
POLLAND			**MINIATURE SCULP. SOC.**	
92	BLACK HAWK	*	25.00	250.00
P.W. BASTON			**SEBASTIAN EXCHANGE**	
83	NEWSPAPER BOY	YR	28.50	40.00-60.00
84	FIRST THINGS FIRST	YR	30.00	30.00
85	NEWSSTAND	YR	30.00	30.00
86	NEWS WAGON	YR	35.00	35.00
87	IT'S ABOUT TIME	YR	25.00	25.00
P.W. BASTON			**SEBASTIAN MINIATURES**	
80	S.M.C SOCIETY PLAQUE ('80 CHARTER)	YR	*	20.00-30.00
83	HARRY HOOD	SO	*	200.00-250.00
85	IT'S HOODS (WAGON)	SO	*	150.00-175.00
86	STATUE OF LIBERTY (AT&T)	SO	*	175.00-200.00
87	WHITE HOUSE (GOLD, OVAL BASE)	SO	17.00	75.00-100.00
91	AMERICA SALUTES DESERT STORM-BRONZE	1641	26.50	26.50
91	AMERICA SALUTES DESERT STORM-PAINTED	350	49.50	49.50
91	HAPPY HOOD HOLIDAYS	2000	32.50	32.50

YR	NAME	LIMIT	ISSUE	QUOTE
P.W. BASTON		**SHAKESPEAREAN-MEMBER ONLY**		
84	ANNE BOYELIN	6 MO.	17.50	17.50
84	HENRY VIII	CL	19.50	19.50
85	FALSTAFF	YR	19.50	19.50
85	MISTRESS FORD	6 MO.	17.50	17.50
86	JULIET	6 MO.	17.50	17.50
86	ROMEO	YR	19.50	19.50
87	COUNTESS OLIVIA	6 MO.	19.50	19.50
87	MALVOLIO	YR	21.50	21.50
88	AUDREY	6 MO.	22.50	22.50
88	TOUCHSTONE	YR	22.50	22.50
89	CLEOPATRA	6 MO.	27.00	27.00
89	MARK ANTHONY	YR	27.00	27.00
88	SHAKESPEARE	YR	23.50	23.50
*		**THE SORCERER'S APPRENTICE SERIES**		
90	THE DREAM	2500	225.00	225.00
90	THE INCANTATION	2500	150.00	150.00
90	THE REPENTANT APPRENTICE	2500	19598.00	195.00
90	THE SORCERER'S APPRENTICE	2500	225.00	225.00
90	THE WHIRLPOOL	2500	225.00	225.00
P.W. BASTON		**WASHINGTON IRVING-MEMBER ONLY**		
80	RIP VAN WINKLE	CL	19.50	19.50
81	DAME VAN WINKLE	CL	19.50	19.50
81	ICHABOD CRANE	CL	19.50	19.50
82	BROM BONES (HEADLESS HORSEMAN)	CL	22.50	22.50
82	KATRINA VAN TASSEL	CL	19.50	19.50
83	DIEDRICH KNICKERBOCKER	CL	22.50	22.50

LAND OF LEGEND

YR	NAME	LIMIT	ISSUE	QUOTE
T. RAINE		**CASTLE COLLECTION**		
78	DENNIS THE DRAGON/COUNTERSIGN	CL	55.00	195.00-253.00
86	CASTLE OF THE EXILED PRINCE	CL	225.00	163.00-228.00
86	CASTLE OF THE GOLDEN CHALICE	CL	60.00	60.00
86	CASTLE OF THE RANSOMED KING	CL	250.00	150.00-254.00
86	CASTLE OF THE RED KNIGHT	CL	65.00	65.00
86	CASTLE OF THE SLEEPING PRINCESS	CL	235.00	235.00
86	SORCERERS RETREAT	CL	50.00	55.00
87	WIZARD'S TOWER	CL	215.00	208.00
H. HENRIKSEN				**DRAGONS**
89	COUNTERSIGN FOR SERIES	*	75.00	90.00
90	DRAGON OF THE GOLDEN HOARD	*	270.00	350.00
90	GUARDIAN OF THE KEEP	*	295.00	375.00
90	HATCHED	*	295.00	395.00
90	LET SLEEPING DRAGONS LIE	3000	450.00	595.00
90	LEVIATHAN	*	325.00	424.00
90	WYVERN	*	295.00	375.00
T. RAINE			**DREAM CASTLES**	
88	CAMELOT	CL	32.50	32.50
88	FAIRYTALE	CL	32.50	32.50
88	GRAND VIZIERS	CL	32.50	32.50
88	VALKYRIES TOWER	CL	32.50	32.50
T. RAINE			**DREAM DRAGONS**	
88	BATHTIME	RT	31.50	31.50
88	BREAKOUT	RT	31.50	31.50
88	DOUBLE TROUBLE	RT	35.00	35.00
88	DREAM BABY	RT	31.50	31.50
88	HAZY DAZE	RT	31.50	31.50
88	HELP	RT	31.50	31.50
88	HI THERE	RT	31.50	31.50
88	LITTLE SISTER	RT	31.50	31.50
88	STRIKE ONE	RT	35.00	35.00
88	WILD WHEELS	RT	35.00	35.00
89	ESPECIALLY FOR YOU	RT	35.00	35.00
89	LIPSTICK AND LASHES	RT	35.00	35.00
89	LOVE LETTER	RT	35.00	35.00
89	OFF TO SCHOOL	RT	35.00	35.00
89	PARTY TIME	RT	45.00	45.00
89	SHE LOVES ME	RT	35.00	35.00
89	STAY COOL	RT	35.00	35.00
89	THE KISS	RT	45.00	45.00
T. RAINE			**ETHELRED FLAMETAIL**	
89	EARLY DAYS	CL	37.50	37.50
89	EUREKA	CL	49.50	49.50
89	HELLO WORLD	CL	37.50	37.50
89	JEREMY THE DANDY	CL	89.50	89.50
89	LIFT OFF	CL	105.00	105.00
89	MR. BONZER	CL	62.50	62.50

These lovely Lladró ladies chat over a cup of espresso in Cafe de Paris.

Summer Stroll *is a 1991 Lladró collectors club issue.*

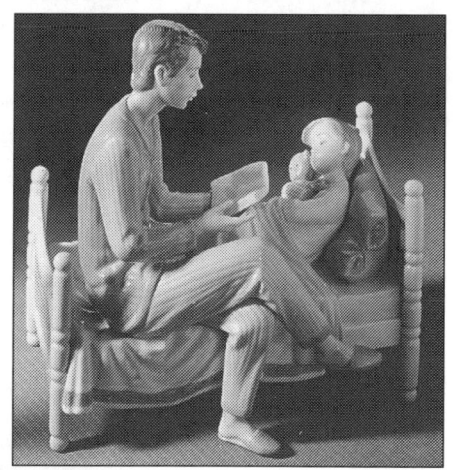

Just One More *begs this little fellow of his storytelling father. The piece is produced by Lladró.*

Jazz Horn, Jazz Sax *and* Jazz Bass *are from the "Jazz Man Collection" by Lladró.*

YR NAME	LIMIT	ISSUE	QUOTE
89 ON THE RUNWAY	CL	49.50	49.50
89 PRINCESS NYNEVE	CL	59.50	59.50
89 RANOL	CL	29.50	29.50
89 SCHOOL DAYS	CL	89.50	89.50
89 SWAMP BIRD	CL	39.50	39.50
89 TENDER LOVING CARE	CL	115.00	115.00
89 THE BLACK KNIGHT	CL	79.50	79.50
89 THE FLYING LESSON	CL	65.00	65.00
89 THE MAGIC WATER	CL	65.00	65.00
89 THE MERCHANT	CL	67.50	67.50
89 THE TROLL	CL	67.50	67.50
89 THE WILY WIZARD	CL	79.50	79.50
89 THE YOUNG INVENTOR	CL	45.00	45.00
89 THREE CHEERS	CL	115.00	115.00
89 TREE POPPER	CL	45.00	45.00

T. RAINE   **FANTASY FIGURINES**

YR NAME	LIMIT	ISSUE	QUOTE
88 BEHEMOTH ON WOODEN BASE	2500	220.00	220.00
88 ELFIN KING ON WOODEN BASE	2500	275.00	275.00
88 ETERNAL HERO ON WOODEN BASE	CL	220.00	220.00
88 UNION OF OPPOSITES ON WOODEN BASE	CL	300.00	300.00

T. RAINE   **GENIES BY TOM RAINE**

YR NAME	LIMIT	ISSUE	QUOTE
89 FLIGHT TO BAGDAD	OP	170.00	170.00
89 FREE AT LAST	OP	150.00	150.00
89 KEY OF KNOWLEDGE	OP	170.00	170.00
89 YES MASTER	OP	150.00	150.00

H. HENRIKSEN   **JESTERS**

YR NAME	LIMIT	ISSUE	QUOTE
89 COUNTERSIGN FOR SERIES	OP	75.00	90.00
89 HIS MAJESTRY BALDWICK/INCREDIBLY SIMPLE	3000	295.00	375.00
89 JOCKOMO, THE DOG	RT	59.00	59.00
89 JOLLIES PITCHBELLY	OP	175.00	200.00
89 LA DI DA TOOGOODE	RT	185.00	185.00
89 MERRY ANDREW	RT	130.00	130.00
89 PUCK, BABY BEAR	RT	59.00	59.00
89 SMACK THICKWIT	OP	185.00	230.00
89 TWIT COXCOMBE	RT	140.00	140.00
89 URSULA, MOTHER BEAR	RT	95.00	95.00

H. HENRIKSEN   **LAND OF LEGEND FELLOWSHIP**

YR NAME	LIMIT	ISSUE	QUOTE
90 SELF TAUGHT	TL	100.00	100.00
90 TAKE A CHANCE	TL	*	*
89 HUBBLE BUBBLE	RT	95.00	130.00
89 THE SWORD IN THE STONE	RT	*	75.00

T. RAINE   **LIMITED EDITION CASTLES**

YR NAME	LIMIT	ISSUE	QUOTE
88 SCHLOSS NEUSCHWANSTEIN	CL	750.00	910.00
86 SCHLOSS RHEINIUNGFRAU	1500	335.00	335.00

R. MUSGRAVE   **POCKET DRAGONS**

YR NAME	LIMIT	ISSUE	QUOTE
89 A GOOD EGG	RT	36.50	42.50
89 ATTACK	OP	45.00	55.00
89 BABY BROTHER	OP	19.50	23.50
89 DO I HAVE TO?	OP	52.50	62.50
89 DROWSY DRAGON	OP	35.00	35.00
89 FLOWERS FOR YOU	OP	42.50	47.50
89 GARGOYLE HOPING FOR RASPBERRY TEACAKE	RT	139.50	139.50
89 LOOK AT ME	RT	42.50	42.50
89 NEW BUNNY SHOES	OP	28.50	35.00
89 NO UGLY MONSTERS ALLOWED	OP	47.50	57.50
89 OPERA GARGOYLE	RT	85.00	105.00
89 PINK 'N PRETTY	OP	23.90	29.50
89 POCKET DRAGON COUNTERSIGN	RT	50.00	62.50
89 SCRIBBLES	OP	37.50	45.00
89 SEA DRAGON	RT	45.00	55.00
89 SIR NIGEL SMYTHEBE-SMOKE	OP	147.50	175.00
89 STALKING THE COOKIE JAR	OP	31.00	39.00
89 STORYTIME AT WIZARD'S HOUSE	3000	375.00	450.00
89 TEDDY MAGIC	RT	85.00	105.00
89 THE GALLANT DEFENDER	OP	36.50	42.50
89 THE POCKET MINSTREL	RT	36.50	42.50
89 TOADY GOLDTRAYLER	OP	52.50	62.50
89 WALKIES	OP	65.00	79.00
89 WHAT COOKIE?	OP	42.50	50.00
89 WIZARDRY FOR FUN AND PROFIT	3000	375.00	450.00
89 YOUR PAINT IS STIRRED	RT	42.50	52.50
90 TAG-A-LONG	OP	19.50	23.50
90 THE APPRENTICE	OP	25.00	29.50
91 A JOYFUL NOISE	OP	27.50	27.50
91 FRIENDS	OP	85.00	85.00
91 I'M A KITTY	OP	50.00	50.00

YR	NAME	LIMIT	ISSUE	QUOTE
91	PICK ME UP	OP	27.50	27.50
91	PLAYING FOOTSIE	OP	27.50	27.50
91	PRACTICE MAKES PERFECT	OP	42.50	42.50
91	SLEEPY HEAD	OP	52.50	52.50
91	TICKLE	OP	35.00	35.00
91	TWINKLE TOES	OP	27.50	27.50
T. RAINE		**THE SECRET OF THE SWAN PRINCESS**		
89	ALARCH SILVERBEARD	CL	79.50	79.50
89	ASPARD	CL	65.00	65.00
89	CASTLE OF THE SWAN PRINCESS	CL	99.50	99.50
89	DRAGON'S LAIR	CL	75.00	75.00
89	JUDGE'S RETREAT	CL	85.00	85.00
89	KIBOLD WALTER	CL	65.00	65.00
89	MASTERS OF THE FOREST	CL	75.00	75.00
89	PALACE OF THE EMPEROR CHILD	CL	75.00	75.00
89	RONTUNDO THE TUSCAN	CL	65.00	65.00
89	SALIX THE BOLD	CL	65.00	65.00
MUSGRAVE/ HENRIKSEN		**UNDER THE HEDGE**		
89	A WINTER'S FRIEND	RT	25.00	25.00
89	BASKETS OF LOVE	OP	39.50	47.50
89	CAREFULLY WRAPPED	RT	30.00	30.00
89	COUNTERSIGN	OP	39.50	47.50
89	COUSIN BERTHA'S REVENGE	OP	42.50	50.00
89	DECK THE HALLS	3000	99.50	120.00
89	FATHER CHRISTMAS	OP	45.00	55.00
89	FAVORITE UNCLE	OP	42.50	57.50
89	KEEP YOUR TAIL WARM	OP	59.50	70.00
89	OUT OF TOWN GUEST	OP	42.50	57.50
89	SNOWBALLS AND TOP HATS	RT	39.50	39.50
89	THE FASHION PLATE	RT	47.50	47.50
89	TRAPPED ON THE SUMMIT	RT	37.50	37.50
90	AUNT VIOLET & PUDGY	OP	50.00	60.00
90	COUSIN REGGIE	OP	59.50	70.00
90	JELLY SANWICHES	OP	82.50	97.50
90	JUNIUS BUG	OP	42.50	50.00
90	JUST GUARDING THE HAMPER	OP	47.50	57.50
90	MIGHTY PERCY AT THE BAT	OP	49.50	60.00
90	MISS AMELIA'S TURN	OP	45.00	55.00
90	SLOW AND STEADY	OP	59.50	70.00
90	SPARKLING CLEAN	OP	95.50	115.00
90	SPOTTING STRAYS	OP	50.00	60.00
90	STEMS AND BOWLES LTD.	OP	159.00	190.00
90	SUNDAE AFTERNOON	OP	199.00	235.00
90	THE ARTFUL BOWLER	OP	47.50	60.00
90	THE ARTIST	OP	62.50	75.00
90	THE TEA TABLE	OP	39.50	47.50
90	THE WICKET KEEPER	OP	55.00	70.00
90	WAITING FOR A LIGHT	OP	82.50	97.50
90	WATCHING THE HERD	OP	45.00	55.00
H. HENRIKSEN		**WIZARDS**		
89	COUNTERSIGN FOR WIZARDS' SERIES	OP	75.00	90.00
89	FORESHADOW THE SEER	OP	135.00	160.00
89	LACKEY	RT	95.00	95.00
89	MERLYN THE WIZARD WATCHER	RT	49.50	49.50
89	MERRYWEATHER SUNLIGHTER	3000	295.00	350.00
89	MORIAH	OP	159.00	190.00
89	MYDWYNTER	RT	135.00	135.00
89	REPOSITORY OF MAGIC	RT	130.00	130.00
89	RIMBAUGH	OP	159.00	190.00
89	THORBAULD	RT	175.00	175.00
91	BALANCE OF TRUTH	2500	270.00	270.00
91	FORESHADOW THE SEER (WITH CRYSTALS)	OP	190.00	190.00
91	HOWLAND THE WISE	2500	300.00	300.00
91	MORIAH (WITH CRYSTALS)	OP	225.00	225.00
91	PONDERING THE QUEST	2500	270.00	270.00
91	RIMBAUGH (WITH CRYSTALS)	OP	225.00	225.00
91	THE DRAGON MASTER	1500	675.00	675.00

LEGENDS

*	CHIEF JOSEPH	*	*	1650.00
*	LAKOTA LOVE SONG	*	*	965.00
*	ONE MORE COUP	*	*	1375.00
C. PARDELL		**AMERICAN WEST PREMIER EDITION**		
91	FIRST COUP	SO	1150.00	1200.00
91	UNEXPECTED RESCUER	SO	990.00	2000.00
92	AMERICAN HORSE TAKES HIS NAME	950	1300.00	1300.00

YR	NAME	LIMIT	ISSUE	QUOTE
C. PARDELL		**ANNUAL COLLECTORS EDITION**		
*	MEDICINE GIFT OF MANHOOD	*	990.00	1900.00
*	SPIRIT OF THE WOLF	*	950.00	1225.00
*	THE NIGHT BEFORE	*	990.00	1900.00
90	THE NIGHT BEFORE	SO	990.00	1900.00
91	MEDICINE GIFT OF MANHOOD	SO	990.00	1900.00
92	SPIRIT OF THE WOLF	500	950.00	1225.00
93	TOMORROW'S WARRIOR	*	590.00	1400.00
K. CANTRELL		**ENDANGERED WILDLIFE COLLECTION**		
92	SPIRIT SONG		350.00	695.00
K. CANTRELL		**ENDANGERED WILDLIFE COLLECTION-EAGLE SERIES**		
89	SENTINEL	*	280.00	585.00
C. PARDELL		**GALLERY EDITIONS**		
92	RESOLUTE	*	7950.00	13,000.00
C. PARDELL		**INDIAN ARTS COLLECTION**		
89	CHIEF'S BLANKET	SO	350.00	600.00
90	KACHINA CARVER	*	270.00	450.00
90	STORY TELLER	*	290.00	325.00
K. CANTRELL		**THE ENDANGERED WILDLIFE COLLECTION**		
90	FOREST SPIRIT	SO	290.00	1195.00
C. PARDELL		**THE LEGACIES OF THE WEST PREMIER EDITION**		
90	MYSTIC VISION	SO	990.00	2895.00
90	VICTORIOUS	SO	1275.00	3875.00
91	DEFIANT COMANCHE	SO	1300.00	2550.00
91	NO MORE, FOREVER	SO	1500.00	2900.00
C. PARDELL		**THE LEGACIES OF THE WEST PRMIER EDITION**		
92	ESTEEMED WARRIOR	SO	1750.00	2250.00
C. PARDELL		**THE LEGENDARY WEST COLLECTION**		
87	JOHNSON'S LAST FLIGHT	SO	590.00	1200.00
87	PONY EXPRESS	RT	320.00	450.00
87	WHITE FEATHER'S VISION	SO	390.00	2000.00
89	CRAZY HORSE	*	390.00	900.00
C. PARDELL		**THE LEGENDARY WEST PREMIER EDITION**		
88	RED CLOUD'S COUP	SO	480.00	5500.00
89	PURSUED	SO	750.00	4500.00
89	SONGS OF GLORY	SO	850.00	4300.00
90	CROW WARRIOR	SO	1225.00	4500.00
91	TRIUMPHANT	SO	1150.00	2000.00
92	FINAL CHARGE	*	1250.00	1600.00
92	THE FINAL CHARGE	750	1250.00	1600.00

LENOX CHINA/CRYSTAL COLLECTION

*		**AMERICAN FASHION**		
83	SPRINGTIME PROMENADE	OP	95.00	95.00
84	FIRST WALTZ	OP	95.00	95.00
84	TEA AT THE RITZ	OP	95.00	95.00
85	GOVERNOR'S GARDEN PARTY	OP	95.00	95.00
86	BELLE OF THE BALL	OP	95.00	95.00
86	GRAND TOUR	OP	95.00	95.00
87	CENTENNIAL BRIDE	OP	95.00	95.00
87	GALA AT THE WHITE HOUSE	OP	95.00	95.00
*		**BABY BEARS**		
91	POLAR BEAR	OP	45.00	45.00
*		**BABY BIRD PAIRS**		
91	ROBINS	OP	64.00	64.00
*		**BIBLICAL CHARACTERS**		
92	MOSES, THE LAWGIVER	OP	95.00	95.00
*		**CAROUSEL ANIMALS**		
87	CAROUSEL HORSE	9500	136.00	152.00
88	CAROUSEL UNICORN	9500	136.00	152.00
89	CAROUSEL CIRCUS HORSE	9500	136.00	152.00
89	CAROUSEL REINDEER	9500	136.00	152.00
90	CAROUSEL CHARGER	9500	136.00	152.00
90	CAROUSEL ELEPHANT	9500	136.00	152.00
90	CAROUSEL LION	9500	136.00	152.00
91	CAROUSEL POLAR BEAR	9500	152.00	152.00
91	PRIDE OF AMERICA	TL	152.00	152.00
91	WESTERN HORSE	OP	152.00	152.00
92	CAMELOT HORSE	OP	152.00	152.00
*		**COUNTRY KIDS**		
91	GOOSE GIRL	OP	75.00	75.00
*		**DOVES & ROSES**		
91	DOVE'S OF PEACE	OP	95.00	95.00
91	LOVE'S PROMISE	OP	95.00	95.00
92	DOVE'S OF HONOR	OP	119.00	119.00
*		**ENDANGERED BABY ANIMALS**		
90	PANDA	OP	39.00	39.00

YR	NAME	LIMIT	ISSUE	QUOTE
91	BABY FLORIDA PANTHER	OP	57.00	57.00
91	BABY GREY WOLF	OP	57.00	57.00
91	ELEPHANT	OP	57.00	57.00
*				**EXOTIC BIRDS**
91	COCKATOO	OP	49.50	49.50
*				**FLORAL SCULPTURES**
86	RUBRUM LILY	OP	119.00	136.00
87	IRIS	OP	119.00	136.00
88	MAGNOLIA	OP	119.00	136.00
88	PEACE ROSE	OP	119.00	136.00
*				**GARDEN BIRDS**
85	CHICKADEE	OP	39.00	45.00
86	BLUE JAY	OP	39.00	45.00
86	EASTERN BLUEBIRD	OP	39.00	45.00
86	TUFTED TITMOUSE	OP	39.00	45.00
87	AMERICAN GOLDFINCH	OP	39.00	45.00
87	CARDINAL	OP	39.00	45.00
87	RED-BREASTED NUTHATCH	OP	39.00	45.00
87	TURTLE DOVE	OP	39.00	45.00
88	CEDAR WAXWING	OP	39.00	45.00
88	HUMMINGBIRD	OP	39.00	45.00
89	DOWNY WOODPECKER	OP	39.00	45.00
89	ROBIN	OP	39.00	45.00
89	SAW WHET OWL	OP	45.00	45.00
90	BALTIMORE ORIOLE	OP	45.00	45.00
90	CHIPPING SPARROW	OP	45.00	45.00
90	WOOD DUCK	OP	45.00	45.00
90	WREN	OP	45.00	45.00
91	BROADBILLED HUMMINGBIRD	OP	45.00	45.00
91	DARK-EYED JUNCO	OP	45.00	45.00
91	GOLDEN CROWNED KINGLET	OP	45.00	45.00
91	PURPLE FINCH	OP	45.00	45.00
91	ROSE GROSBEAK	OP	45.00	45.00
92	SCARLET TANGER	OP	45.00	45.00
*				**GARDEN FLOWERS**
88	CATTLEYA ORCHID	OP	39.00	45.00
88	PARROT TULIP	OP	39.00	39.00
88	TEA ROSE	OP	39.00	45.00
89	IRIS	OP	45.00	45.00
90	CARNATION	OP	45.00	45.00
90	DAFFODIL	OP	45.00	45.00
90	DAY LILY	OP	45.00	45.00
91	CALLA LILY	OP	45.00	45.00
91	CAMELIA	OP	45.00	45.00
91	MAGNOLIA	OP	45.00	45.00
91	MORNING GLORY	OP	45.00	45.00
91	POINSETTIA	OP	39.00	39.00
*				**GENTLE MAJESTY**
90	BEAR HUG POLAR BEAR	OP	76.00	76.00
90	PENGUINS	OP	76.00	76.00
91	KEEPING WARM (FOXES)	OP	76.00	76.00
*				**INTERNATIONAL BRIDES**
90	RUSSIAN BRIDE	OP	136.00	136.00
*			**INTERNATIONAL HORSE SCULPTURES**	
88	ARABIAN KNIGHT	OP	136.00	136.00
89	THOROUGHBRED	OP	136.00	136.00
90	APPALOOSA	OP	136.00	136.00
90	LIPPIZAN	OP	136.00	136.00
J.W. SMITH			**JESSIE WILCOX SMITH**	
91	FEEDING KITTY	OP	60.00	60.00
91	ROSEBUDS	OP	60.00	60.00
*				**KINGS OF THE SKY**
89	AMERICAN BALD EAGLE	OP	195.00	195.00
91	DEFENDER OF FREEDOM	TL	234.00	234.00
91	GOLDEN EAGLE	OP	234.00	234.00
*				**LEGENDARY PRINCESSES**
85	RAPUNZEL	OP	119.00	136.00
86	SLEEPING BEAUTY	OP	119.00	136.00
87	SNOW QUEEN	OP	119.00	136.00
88	CINDERELLA	OP	136.00	136.00
89	SNOW WHITE	OP	136.00	136.00
89	SWAN PRINCESS	OP	136.00	136.00
90	CLEOPATRA	OP	136.00	136.00
90	GUINEVERE	OP	136.00	136.00
90	JULIET	OP	136.00	136.00
91	PEACOCK MAIDEN	OP	136.00	136.00

YR	NAME	LIMIT	ISSUE	QUOTE
91	POCOHONTAS	9500	136.00	136.00
92	FIREBIRD	OP	156.00	156.00
*	**LENOX BABY BOOK**			
90	BABY'S FIRST SHOES	OP	57.00	57.00
91	BABY'S FIRST CHRISTMAS	OP	57.00	57.00
91	BABY'S FIRST STEPS	OP	57.00	57.00
92	BABY'S FIRST PORTRAIT	OP	57.00	57.00
*	**LENOX PUPPY COLLECTION**			
90	BEAGLE	OP	76.00	76.00
91	COCKER SPANIEL	OP	76.00	76.00
92	POODLE	OP	76.00	76.00
*	**LENOX SEA ANIMALS**			
91	DANCE OF THE DOLPHINS	OP	119.00	119.00
*	**LIFE OF CHRIST**			
90	MADONNA AND CHILD	OP	95.00	95.00
90	THE CHILDREN'S BLESSING	OP	95.00	95.00
90	THE GOOD SHEPHERD	OP	95.00	95.00
91	JESUS, THE TEACHER	9500	95.00	95.00
91	THE SAVIOR	OP	95.00	95.00
92	A CHILD'S PRAYER	OP	95.00	95.00
92	CHILDREN'S DEVOTION PAINTED	OP	195.00	195.00
*	**MOTHER & CHILD**			
86	CHERISHED MOMENT	OP	119.00	119.00
86	SUNDAY IN THE PARK	OP	119.00	119.00
87	STORYTIME	OP	119.00	119.00
88	THE PRESENT	OP	119.00	119.00
89	CHRISTENING	OP	119.00	119.00
90	BEDTIME PRAYERS	OP	119.00	119.00
91	AFTERNOON STROLL	7500	136.00	136.00
91	EVENING LULLABY	7500	136.00	136.00
92	MORNING PLAYTIME	OP	136.00	136.00
*	**NATIVITY**			
86	HOLY FAMILY	OP	119.00	136.00
87	THREE ANGELS	OP	119.00	152.00
88	ANIMALS OF THE NATIVITY	OP	119.00	152.00
88	SHEPHERDS	OP	119.00	152.00
89	ANGELS OF ADORATION	OP	136.00	152.00
90	CHILDREN OF BETHLEHEM	OP	136.00	152.00
91	STANDING CAMEL & DRIVER	9500	152.00	152.00
91	TOWNSPEOPLE OF BETHLEHEM	OP	136.00	152.00
*	**NATURE'S BEAUTIFUL BUTTERFLIES**			
89	BLUE TEMORA	OP	39.00	45.00
90	MONARCH	OP	39.00	45.00
90	PURPLE EMPEROR	OP	45.00	45.00
90	YELLOW SWALLOWTAIL	OP	39.00	45.00
91	ADONIS	OP	45.00	45.00
91	MALACHITE	OP	45.00	45.00
*	**NORTH AMERICAN BIRD PAIRS**			
90	HUMMINGBIRDS	OP	119.00	119.00
91	BLUE JAY PAIRS	9500	119.00	119.00
91	CHICKADEES	9500	119.00	119.00
92	CARDINAL	OP	119.00	119.00
*	**NORTH AMERICAN WILDLIFE**			
91	WHITE-TAILED DEER	OP	195.00	195.00
*	**OWLS OF AMERICA**			
88	SNOWY OWL	OP	136.00	136.00
89	BARN OWL	OP	136.00	136.00
90	SCREECH OWL	OP	136.00	136.00
91	GREAT HORNED OWL	9500	136.00	136.00
*	**PARENT & CHILD BIRD PAIRS**			
92	BLUE JAY PAIRS	OP	119.00	119.00
*	**PORCELAIN DUCK COLLECTION**			
91	MALLARD DUCK	OP	45.00	45.00
91	WOOD DUCK	OP	45.00	45.00
92	BLUE WINGED TEAL DUCK	OP	45.00	45.00
*	**SANTA CLAUS COLLECTIONS**			
90	FATHER CHRISTMAS	OP	136.00	136.00
91	AMERICANA SANTA	OP	136.00	136.00
91	KRIS KRINGLE	OP	136.00	136.00
*	**STREET CRIER COLLECTION**			
90	FRENCH FLOWER MAIDEN	OP	136.00	136.00
91	BELGIAN LACE MAKER	OP	136.00	136.00
*	**WILDLIFE OF THE SEVEN CONTINENTS**			
84	NORTH AMERICAN BIGHORN SHEEP	OP	120.00	120.00
85	ASIAN ELEPHANT	OP	120.00	120.00
85	AUSTRAILIAN KOALA	OP	120.00	120.00

YR	NAME	LIMIT	ISSUE	QUOTE
86	SOUTH AMERICAN PUMA	OP	120.00	120.00
87	ANARCTIC SEALS	OP	136.00	136.00
87	EUROPEAN RED DEER	OP	136.00	136.00
88	AFRICAN LION	OP	136.00	136.00
*			**WOODLAND ANIMALS**	
90	RACCOON	OP	39.00	39.00
90	RED SQUIRREL	OP	39.00	39.00
91	CHIPMUNK	OP	39.00	39.00

LILLIPUT LANE LTD.

YR	NAME	LIMIT	ISSUE	QUOTE
*			**CHILDREN'S THEMES**	
*	AMY L5145	*	110.00	1500.00
*	ELLEN L5146	*	110.00	1500.00
*	IVY L5147	*	100.00	650.00
*	OLIVIA L5148	*	100.00	500.00
*	URSULA L5149	*	100.00	550.00
*			**NORMAN ROCKWELL**	
*	COURT JESTER RL405	*	*	1100.00-1200.00
*	DAY DREAMER R1411	*	*	1500.00
*	LOVE LETTER R1406	*	*	900.00
*	PRACTICE MAKES PERFECT RL408	*	*	850.00-1150.00
*	SPRINGTIME '27 R1410	*	*	1500.00
*	SUMMER STOCK RL401	*	*	1100.00
*	YOUNG LOVE R1409	*	*	900.00

R. MUSGRAVE

YR	NAME	LIMIT	ISSUE	QUOTE
*			**POCKET DRAGONS**	
*	A POCKET-SIZED TREE	*	*	65.00
*	DENNIS THE DRAGON	*	*	117.00
*	PUTTING ME ON THE TREE	*	*	78.00
*	WIZARDRY FOR FUN AND PROFIT	*	*	585.00

LLADRO
*

YR	NAME	LIMIT	ISSUE	QUOTE
*	DOG IN BASKET		*	300.00
*	LITTLE BALLET GIRL L-5104	*	*	300.00
*	RAM		*	250.00
*	SPANISH SOLDIER L-5255	*	*	700.00
93	ANGELS MELODY	RT	145.00	170.00
93	AUGUMN GLOW	1500	750.00	900.00
93	BABY'S FIRST	RT	57.00	62.00
93	DAYS OF YORE	1000	2050.00	2200.00
93	DISCOVERY MUG	1992	90.00	100.00
93	GRACEFUL MOMENT	3000	1475.00	1600.00
93	HOLIDAY GLOW	1500	750.00	900.00
93	HUMBLE GRACE	2000	2150.00	2300.00
93	INDIAN BRAVE	1500	2250.00	2500.00
93	INSPIRED VOYAGE	1000	4800.00	5000.00
93	LIMITED EDITION EGG	RT	145.00	160.00
93	OUR FIRST	RT	52.00	57.00
93	OUR LADY OF ROCIO	2000	3500.00	3800.00
93	THE BLESSING	2000	1345.00	1600.00
93	THE HAND OF JUSTICE	1000	1250.00	1400.00
93	TRAIL BOSS	1500	2450.00	2700.00
93	WHERE TO STIR	1500	5250.00	5500.00
94	1994 ETERNAL LOVE BELL	RT	95.00	110.00
94	1994 LIMITED EDITION EGG	RT	150.00	175.00
94	A MOMENT'S PAUSE	3500	1495.00	1600.00
94	ALLEGORY OF TIME	5000	1290.00	1400.00
94	AMERICAN COWBOY	3000	950.00	1050.00
94	AT PEACE	1000	1650.00	1800.00
94	AT THE HELM	3500	1495.00	1600.00
94	CIRCUS FANFARE	1500	14240.00	15000
94	CONQUERED BY LOVE	2500	2850.00	3000.00
94	ETHEREAL MUSIC	1000	2450.00	2600.00
94	FAREWELL OF THE SAMURAI	2500	3950.00	4100.00
94	FLORAL ENCHANTMENT	300	2990.00	3100.00
94	FLORAL FIGURE	300	2198.00	2300.00
94	FLOWER WAGON	3000	3290.00	3400.00
94	FLUVIAL CUP WITH BRANCH	500	1590.00	1700.00
94	FLUVIAL CUP WITH ROSES	500	1150.00	1250.00
94	FLUVIAL CUP WITH WATER LILY	500	1350.00	1450.00
94	GENTLE MOMENT	1000	1795.00	1900.00
94	HIGH SPEED	1500	3830.00	4000.00
94	INDIAN CHIEF	3000	1095.00	1200.00
94	INDIAN PRINCESS	3000	1630.00	1750.00
94	LARGE NEOCLASSIC CUP	300	2695.00	2800.00
94	NATURAL BEAUTY	500	650.00	725.00
94	NEOCLASSIC CUP (BISQUE)	500	1250.00	1350.00

YR	NAME	LIMIT	ISSUE	QUOTE
94	NEOCLASSIC CUP (COLOR)	500	1370.00	1475.00
94	PEGASUS	1500	1950.00	2100.00
94	ROMANTIC VASE (BLUE)	300	2250.00	2350.00
94	ROMANTIC VASE (WHITE)	300	2598.00	2700.00
94	SAINT JAMES THE APOSTLE	1000	950.00	1100.00
94	TRAPPER	3000	950.00	1050.00
*				*
*	1900 TREE TOPPER L-5719	*	*	250.00
*	1991 TREE TOPPER L-225	*	*	225.00
*	AEROBICS FLOOR EXERCISE L-5335	*	*	350.00
*	AEROBICS PUSH-UPS L-5334	*	*	350.00
*	AEROBICS SCISSOR FIGURE L-5336	*	*	350.00
*	AFGHAN L1069	*	*	375.00
*	AFTER THE DANCE L-5092	*	*	300.00
*	AMY SCHOOL GIRL-LETTER "A" L-5145	*	*	1050.00
*	ANGEL TREE ORNAMETNS L-1604	*	*	225.00
*	ARACELY WITH PET DUCK L-5202	*	*	300.00
*	BABY WITH DUMMY L-5102	*	*	225.00
*	BASHFUL GIRL L-5026	*	*	200.00
*	BASKET C1543	*	*	550.00
*	BASKET OF ROSES C1544	*	*	875.00
*	BEAGLE PUPPY LYING L1072	RT	*	300
*	BILLY FOOTBALL PLAYER L-5135	*	*	700.00
*	BIRD L1054	*	*	187.50
*	BOYS PLAYING WITH GOAT L1129	*	*	968.75
*	CANDID L-5039	*	*	375.00
*	CHRISTMAS BELLS 1987,88	*	*	250.00
*	CHRISTMAS BELLS 89, 90, 91 L-5525, 5616	*	*	250.00
*	CLOWN L1126	*	*	1250.00
*	DEER L1064	*	*	275.00-412.50
*	FLOWER PEDDLER L-5029	*	*	1300.00
*	FLOWER POT L-5028	*	*	650.00
*	FORD FIESTA L-7017	*	*	750.00
*	FOX AND CUB L1065	*	*	375.00-438.00
*	GARDEN CLASSIC S7617	*	*	1150.00
*	GARDEN SONG S-7618	*	*	750.00
*	GAYLE L-5109	*	*	450.00
*	GIRL MANICURING L1082	*	*	295.00-325.00
*	GIRL SOCCER PLAYER L-5134	RT	*	675
*	GIRL WITH BONNET L1147	RT	*	300
*	GIRL WITH BRUSH L1081	*	*	337.50
*	GIRL WITH MOTHER'S SHOE L1084	*	*	250.00
*	GRACEFUL SWAN L-5230	*	*	600.00
*	GREAT DANE L1068	*	*	437.50-481.25
*	GREAT HORNED OWL L-5420	*	*	175.00
*	GROUP OF EAGLE OWLS L-1223	*	*	1050.00
*	GYMNAST BALANCING BALL L-5332	*	*	400.00
*	HEN L1041	*	*	275.00
*	HOLY SHEPHERDS ORNAMENTS L-5809	*	*	175.00
*	JAPANESE VASE L-1536	*	*	1400.00
*	KARENA L-5107	*	*	425.00
*	KITTY L-5164	RT	*	500
*	LA GIOCONDA L-5337	*	*	400.00
*	LAWYER L1090	*	*	312.50
*	LITTLE BOY BULLFIGHTER L-5115	*	*	550.00
*	LITTLE FLOWER SELLER L-5082	*	*	1800.00
*	LITTLE FLOWER SELLER L-5082	*	*	1800.00
*	LITTLE LEAGUER CATCHING L-5290	*	*	350.00
*	LITTLE LEAGUER EXERCISING L-5289	*	*	425.00
*	LITTLE LEAGUER ON BENCH L-5291	*	*	375.00
*	LITTLE RED RIDING HOOD L-4965	*	*	550.00
*	MISS TERESA L-4999	*	*	350.00
*	MOTHER KISSING CHILD L-1329	*	*	1500.00
*	MOTHER, CHILD AND LAMB L-5299	*	*	400.00
*	OLD DOG L1067	*	*	450.00
*	OLD FOLKS L1033	*	*	1100.00-1870.00
*	OLYMPIC PUPPET	*	*	800.00
*	PEACOCK FLOWER VASE L-1200	*	*	2350.00
*	PENGUIN L-5247	*	*	250.00
*	PENGUIN L-5248	*	*	250.00
*	PENGUIN L-5249	*	*	250.00
*	PETITE PAIR L-5384	*	*	400.00
*	PLATES SATYR (PAN RIGHT) L1006	*	*	481.25
*	PLAYING WITH DUCKS AT POND L-5303	*	*	700.00
*	PREDICTING THE FUTURE L-5191	*	*	500.00
*	RND. BASKET-BLUE FLOWERS C1554.1	*	*	176.25

YR	NAME	LIMIT	ISSUE	QUOTE
*	RND. BRN. BASKET-PINK LACE C1553	*	*	292.50
*	RND. BRN. BASKT-BLUE LACE C1554	*	*	183.75
*	SAMSON AND DELILAH L-5051	*	*	1500.00
*	SCHOOL GIRL IVY L-5147	*	*	600.00
*	SEWING A TROUSSEAU L-5126	*	*	400.00
*	SHAKESPEARE L-1338	*	*	1050.00
*	SHEPHERDESS WITH DOG L1034	*	*	187.50
*	SHERUFF PUPPET	*	*	600.00
*	SOLDIER'S HEAD VASE L1105	*	*	375.00
*	SPRINGTIME 27 RL-406	*	*	1200.00
*	SPRINGTIME OF '27 RL-410	*	*	1100.00
*	ST. NICHOLAS L-5427	*	*	750.00
*	SUCCESSFUL HUNT WITH BASE LL-5098	*	*	4500.00
*	SWAN WITH WINGS SPREAD L-5231	*	*	750.00
*	TAILOR, THE L-5326	*	*	800.00
*	TAKING A BOW L-L5095	*	*	300.00
*	TENNIS PLAYER PUPPET L-4966	*	*	550.00
*	TINKERBELL L-7518	*	*	3200.00
*	**1990 LLADRO INTRODUCTIONS**			
90	A CHRISTMAS WISH L5711G	OP	350.00	375.00
90	A FAWN AND A FRIEND L5674G	OP	450.00	485.00
90	A QUIET MOMENT L5673G	OP	450.00	485.00
90	AFTER SCHOOL L5707G	OP	280.00	295.00
90	AFTERNOON STROLL L5687G	OP	275.00	295.00
90	ANGEL CARE L5727G	OP	190.00	195.00
90	ANGELIC VOICE L5724G	OP	125.00	135.00
90	ANTICIPATION L5650G	OP	300.00	310.00
90	BACK TO SCHOOL L5702G	OP	350.00	375.00
90	BARNYARD REFLECTIONS L5684G	OP	460.00	490.00
90	BARNYARD SCENE L5659G/M	OP	200.00	2150.00
90	BEAUTIFUL BURRO L5683G	OP	280.00	300.00
90	BEHAVE! L5703G	OP	230.00	245.00
90	BETWEEN CLASSES L5709G	OP	280.00	295.00
90	BREEZY AFTERNOON L5682G/M	OP	180.00	190.00
90	CAN I HELP? L5689G	OP	250.00	270.00
90	CAT NAP L5640G	OP	125.00	135.00
90	CATHY L5643G	OP	200.00	215.00
90	CINDY L5646G	OP	190.00	200.00
90	CIRCUS SERENADE L5694G	OP	300.00	325.00
90	CONCERTINA L5695G	OP	300.00	325.00
90	COURTNEY L5648G	OP	200.00	215.00
90	DOG'S BEST FRIEND L5688G	OP	250.00	270.00
90	DON'T LOOK DOWN L5698G	OP	330.00	355.00
90	ELIZABETH L5645G	OP	190.00	200.00
90	FANTASY FRIEND L5710G	OP	420.00	450.00
90	FIRST BALLET L5714G	OP	370.00	395.00
90	FOLLOW ME L5722G	OP	140.00	150.00
90	GIDDY UP L5664G	OP	190.00	210.00
90	HANG ON! L5665G	OP	225.00	240.00
90	HEAVENLY CHIMES L5723G	OP	100.00	110.00
90	HEAVENLY DREAMER L5728G	OP	100.00	110.00
90	HI THERE! L5672G	OP	450.00	485.00
90	I FEEL PRETTY L5678G/M	OP	190.00	210.00
90	IN NO HURRY L5679G	OP	550.00	590.00
90	JUST A LITTLE KISS L5701G	OP	320.00	340.00
90	LAND OF THE GIANTS L5716G	OP	275.00	295.00
90	LITTLE DUTCH GARDENER L5671G	OP	400.00	430.00
90	MAKING A WISH L5725G	OP	125.00	135.00
90	MANDOLIN SERENADE L5696G	OP	300.00	325.00
90	MARSHLAND MATES L5691G	OP	950.00	1100.00
90	MAY DANCE L5662G	OP	170.00	180.00
90	MOMMY, IT'S COLD L5715G	OP	360.00	385.00
90	MUSICAL MUSE L5651G	OP	375.00	400.00
90	MY FIRST CLASS L5708G	OP	280.00	295.00
90	NOTHING TO DO L5649G/M	OP	190.00	200.00
90	ON THE AVENUE L5686G	OP	275.00	295.00
90	ON THE ROAD L5681G	OP	320.00	475.00
90	ONCE UPON A TIME L5721G	OP	550.00	585.00
90	OVER THE CLOUDS L5697G	OP	275.00	295.00
90	PROMENADE L5685G	OP	275.00	295.00
90	ROCK A BYE BABY L5715G	OP	300.00	325.00
90	SARA L5647G	OP	200.00	215.00
90	SHARING SECRETS L5720G	OP	290.00	310.00
90	SITTING PRETTY L5699G	OP	300.00	320.00
90	SLEEPY KITTEN L5712G	OP	110.00	120.00
90	SOUTHERN CHARM L5700G	OP	675.00	950.00

YR	NAME	LIMIT	ISSUE	QUOTE
90	SPRING DANCE L5663G	OP	170.00	180.00
90	STREET HARMONIES L5692G	OP	3200.00	3500.00
90	SUNNING IN IPANEMA L5660G	OP	370.00	395.00
90	SUSAN L5644G	OP	190.00	200.00
90	SWAN SONG L5704G	OP	350.00	375.00
90	SWEEP AWAY THE CLOUDS L5726G	OP	125.00	135.00
90	TEE TIME L5675G	OP	280.00	295.00
90	THE KING'S GUARD L5642G	OP	950.00	1000.00
90	THE SNOW MAN L5713G	OP	300.00	325.00
90	THE SWAN AND THE PRINCESS L5705G	OP	350.00	375.00
90	TRAVELING ARTIST L5661G	OP	250.00	265.00
90	TRAVELING IN STYLE L5680G	OP	425.00	460.00
90	TRINO AT THE BEACH L5666G	OP	390.00	420.00
90	TWILIGHT YEARS L5677G	OP	370.00	395.00
90	VALENCIAN BEAUTY L5670G	OP	175.00	185.00
90	VALENCIAN FLOWERS L5669G	OP	370.00	395.00
90	VALENCIAN HARVEST L5668G	OP	175.00	185.00
90	VENECIAN CARNIVAL L5658G	OP	500.00	535.00
90	WANDERING MINSTREL L5676G	OP	270.00	290.00
90	WE CAN'T PLAY L5706G	OP	200.00	215.00
*	**1991 LLADRO INTRODUCTIONS**			
91	A CRADLE OF KITTENS L5784G	OP	360.00	360.00
91	ACADEMY DAYS L5768G	OP	280.00	280.00
91	ALICE IN WONDERLAND L5740G	OP	440.00	440.00
91	ALLEGORY OF LIBERTY L5819G	OP	1950.00	1950.00
91	ASHLEY L5756G	OP	265.00	265.00
91	BABY JESUS L5745G	OP	170.00	170.00
91	BACKSTAGE PREPARATION L5817G/M	OP	490.00	490.00
91	BEAUTIFUL TRESSES L5757G	OP	725.00	725.00
91	BEST FOOT FORWARD L5738G	OP	280.00	280.00
91	BIG SISTER L5735G	OP	650.00	650.00
91	BRIDAL PORTRAIT L5742G	OP	480.00	480.00
91	BULL & DONKEY L5744G	OP	250.00	250.00
91	CAREFREE L5790G	OP	300.00	300.00
91	CAROUSEL CANTER L57323G	OP	1700.00	1700.00
91	CAROUSEL CHARMER L5731G	OP	1700.00	1700.00
91	CHARMING DUET L5766G	OP	575.00	575.00
91	CHECKING THE TIME L5762G	OP	560.00	560.00
91	CLAUDETTE L5755G	OP	265.00	265.00
91	COME OUT AND PLAY L5797G	OP	275.00	275.00
91	CURTAIN CALL L5814G/M	OP	490.00	490.00
91	DANCE OF LOVE L5820G	OP	575.00	575.00
91	DANCING CLASS L5741G	OP	340.00	340.00
91	DON'T FORGET ME L5743G	OP	150.00	150.00
91	ELEGANT PROMENADE L5802G	OP	775.00	775.00
91	FAIRY GODMOTHER L5791G	OP	375.00	375.00
91	FAITHFUL STEED L5769G	OP	370.00	370.00
91	FIRST SAMPLER L5767G	OP	625.00	625.00
91	FLORAL GETAWAY L5795G	OP	625.00	625.00
91	GIFT OF BEAUTY L5775G	OP	850.00	850.00
91	GRACEFUL OFFERING L5773G	OP	850.00	850.00
91	HATS OFF TO FUN L5765G	OP	475.00	475.00
91	HAVING A BALL L5813G	OP	225.00	225.00
91	HOLD HER STILL L5753G	OP	650.00	650.00
91	HOLY NIGHT L5796G	OP	330.00	330.00
91	HORTICULTURIST L5733G	OP	450.00	450.00
91	I DO L5835G	OP	165.00	165.00
91	I'VE GOT IT L5827G	OP	170.00	170.00
91	IN FULL RELAVE L5815G/M	OP	490.00	490.00
91	INTERRUPTED NAP L5760G	OP	325.00	325.00
91	JAZZ BASS L5834G	OP	395.00	395.00
91	JAZZ HORN L5832G	OP	295.00	295.00
91	JAZZ SAX L5833G	OP	295.00	295.00
91	LAP FULL OF LOVE L5739G	OP	275.00	275.00
91	LITTLE DREAMERS L5772G/M	OP	230.00	230.00
91	LITTLE LAMB L5750G	OP	40.00	40.00
91	LITTLE PRINCE L5737G	OP	295.00	295.00
91	LITTLE UNICORN L5826G/M	OP	275.00	275.00
91	LITTLE VIRGIN L5752G	OP	295.00	295.00
91	LITTLEST CLOWN L5811G	OP	235.00	235.00
91	LOVER'S PARADISE L5779G	OP	2250.00	2250.00
91	MARY L5747G	OP	275.00	275.00
91	MILKMAID L5798G	OP	450.00	450.00
91	MINSTEL'S LOVE L5821G	OP	525.00	525.00
91	MUSICAL PARTNERS L5763G	OP	625.00	625.00
91	MUSICALLY INCLINED L5810G	OP	235.00	235.00

YR	NAME	LIMIT	ISSUE	QUOTE
91	MY CHORES L5782G	OP	325.00	325.00
91	MY PUPPIES L5807G	OP	325.00	325.00
91	NATURE'S GIFT L5774G	OP	900.00	900.00
91	NEXT AT BAT L5828G	OP	170.00	170.00
91	NOT TOO CLOSE L5781G	OP	365.00	365.00
91	OCEAN BEAUTY L5785G	OP	625.00	625.00
91	ON HER TOES L5818G/M	OP	490.00	490.00
91	ON THE MOVE L5838G	OP	340.00	340.00
91	OUT FOR A ROMP L5761G	OP	375.00	375.00
91	OUT FOR A SPIN L5770G	OP	390.00	390.00
91	PILGRIM COUPLE L5734G	OP	490.00	490.00
91	PLAYING TAG L5804G	OP	170.00	170.00
91	PRECIOUS BALLERINA L5793G	OP	575.00	575.00
91	PRECIOUS CARGO L5794G	OP	460.00	460.00
91	PRESTO! L5759G	OP	275.00	275.00
91	PRIMA BALLERINA L5816G/M	OP	490.00	490.00
91	PUPPET SHOW L5736G	OP	280.00	280.00
91	REVERENT MOMENT L5792G	OP	295.00	295.00
91	SEEDS OF LAUGHTER L5764G	OP	525.00	525.00
91	SHALL WE DANCE? L5799G	OP	600.00	600.00
91	SHARING SWEETS L5836G	OP	220.00	220.00
91	SHEPHERD BOY L5749G	OP	225.00	225.00
91	SHEPHERD GIRL L5748G	OP	150.00	150.00
91	SING WITH ME L5837G	OP	240.00	240.00
91	SINGAPORE DANCERS L5754G	OP	950.00	950.00
91	SOPHISTICATE L5787G	OP	185.00	185.00
91	SPECIAL DELIVERY L5783G	OP	525.00	525.00
91	ST. JOSEPH L5746G	OP	350.00	350.00
91	STORY HOUR L5786G	OP	550.00	550.00
91	SUNDAY BEST L5758G	OP	725.00	725.00
91	TALK OF THE TOWN L5788G	OP	185.00	185.00
91	THE FLIRT L5789G	OP	185.00	185.00
91	THE MAGIC OF LAUGHTER L5771G	OP	950.00	950.00
91	TICKLING L5806G/M	OP	130.00	130.00
91	TIRED FRIEND L5812G	OP	225.00	225.00
91	TUMBLING L5805G/M	OP	130.00	130.00
91	WALK WITH FATHER L5751G	OP	375.00	375.00
91	WALKING THE FIELDS L5780G	OP	725.00	725.00
*			**1992 LLADRO INTRODUCTIONS**	
92	A QUIET AFTERNOON L5843G	OP	1050.00	1050.00
92	AFTERNOON JAUNT L5855G	OP	420.00	420.00
92	AFTERNOON VERSE L2231M	OP	580.00	580.00
92	ALL DRESSED UP L5909G	OP	440.00	440.00
92	ALL TUCKERED OUT L5846G/M	OP	220.00	220.00
92	ARCTIC ALLIES L2227M	OP	585.00	585.00
92	AT THE BALL L5859G	OP	295.00	295.00
92	ATTENTIVE BUNNY L5905G	OP	75.00	75.00
92	BOUQUET OF BLOSSOMS L5895G	OP	295.00	295.00
92	BOY'S BEST FRIEND L2226M	OP	390.00	390.00
92	CHERISH L2224M	OP	1750.00	1750.00
92	CIRCUS MAGIC L5892G	OP	470.00	470.00
92	DOWN THE AISLE L5903G	OP	295.00	295.00
92	DRESSING FOR THE BALLET L5865G	OP	395.00	395.00
92	DRESSING THE BABY L5845G	OP	295.00	295.00
92	EASTER BONNETS L5852G	OP	265.00	265.00
92	EASTER BUNNIES L5902G	OP	240.00	240.00
92	FAIRY FLOWERS L5861G	OP	630.00	630.00
92	FAIRY GARLAND L5860G	OP	630.00	630.00
92	FALLAS QUEEN L5869G	OP	420.00	420.00
92	FEATHERED FANTASY L5851G	OP	1200.00	1200.00
92	FINAL TOUCHES L5866G	OP	395.00	395.00
92	FLIRTATIOUS JESTER L5844G	OP	890.00	890.00
92	FLORAL ADMIRATION L5853G	OP	690.00	690.00
92	FLORAL FANTASY L5854G	OP	690.00	690.00
92	FRAGRANT BOUQUET L5862G	OP	350.00	350.00
92	FREE SPIRIT L2220M	OP	235.00	235.00
92	FRIENDLY SPARROW L2225M	OP	295.00	295.00
92	FRIENDSHIP L5893G	OP	650.00	650.00
92	FROM THIS DAY FORWARD L5885G	OP	265.00	265.00
92	GARDEN SONG L7618G	OP	295.00	295.00
92	GRAND ENTRANCE L5857G	OP	265.00	265.00
92	GUESS WHAT I HAVE L2233M	OP	340.00	340.00
92	GUEST OF HONOR L5877G	OP	195.00	195.00
92	HIPPITY HOP L5886G	OP	95.00	95.00
92	INSPIRING MUSE L580G	OP	1200.00	1200.00
92	JAZZ CLARINET L5928G	OP	295.00	295.00

YR	NAME	LIMIT	ISSUE	QUOTE
92	JAZZ DRUMS L5929G	OP	595.00	595.00
92	JAZZ DUO L5930G	OP	795.00	795.00
92	JUST A LITTLE MORE L5908G	OP	370.00	370.00
92	JUST ONE MORE L5899G	OP	450.00	450.00
92	LOVING MOUSE L5883G	OP	285.00	285.00
92	LOVING VALENCIANA L5868G	OP	365.00	365.00
92	MAKING A WISH L5910G	OP	790.00	790.00
92	MARY'S CHILD L2230M	OP	525.00	525.00
92	MISCHIEVOUS MOUSE L5881G	OP	285.00	285.00
92	MODERN MOTHER L5873G	OP	325.00	325.00
92	NEW LAMB L2223M	OP	365.00	365.00
92	OFF WE GO L5874G	OP	365.00	365.00
92	PLAYFUL PUSH L2234M	OP	850.00	850.00
92	PLAYFUL UNICORN L5880G/M	OP	295.00	295.00
92	POOR LITTLE BEAR L2232M	OP	250.00	250.00
92	PREENING BUNNY L5906G	OP	75.00	75.00
92	RESTFUL MOUSE L5882G	OP	285.00	285.00
92	SEASONAL GIFTS L2229M	OP	450.00	450.00
92	SERENE VALENCIANA L5867G	OP	365.00	365.00
92	SHOT ON GOAL L5879G	OP	1100.00	1100.00
92	SISTER'S PRIDE L5878G	OP	595.00	595.00
92	SITTING BUNNY L5907G	OP	75.00	75.00
92	SLEEP TIGHT L5900G	OP	450.00	450.00
92	SLEEPING BUNNY L5904G	OP	75.00	75.00
92	SNACK TIME L5889G	OP	95.00	95.00
92	SNOWY SUNDAY L2228M	OP	550.00	550.00
92	SPRING SPLENDOR L5898G	OP	440.00	440.00
92	SURPRISE L5901G	OP	325.00	325.00
92	SWAN BALLET L5920G	OP	210.00	210.00
92	SWANS TAKE FLIGHT L5912G	OP	2850.00	2850.00
92	TAKE YOUR MEDICINE L5921G	OP	360.00	360.00
92	TENDER MOMENT L2222M	OP	400.00	400.00
92	THAT TICKLES L5888G	OP	95.00	95.00
92	THE AVIATOR L5891G	OP	375.00	375.00
92	THE LOAVES & FISHES L5896G	OP	695.00	695.00
92	THE LOVING FAMILY L5848G	OP	950.00	950.00
92	THE VOYAGE OF COLUMBUS LL5847	1500	1450.00	1450.00
92	TRIMMING THE TREE L5897G	OP	900.00	900.00
92	UNDERFOOT L2219M	OP	360.00	360.00
92	WAITING TO DANCE L5858G	OP	295.00	295.00
92	WASHING UP L5887G	OP	95.00	95.00
92	YOUNG MOZART LL5915	1500	500.00	500.00
*			**ASSORTED FIGURINES**	
*	CARD PLAYERS, NUMBERED L1327	RT	3800.00	5700.00
71	GIRL WITH CALLA LILLIES L4650	OP	18.00	120.00
71	VIOLINIST AND GIRL L1039	RT	120.00	950.00-1275.00
73	GIRL WITH GUITAR LL2016	RT	650.00	1800.00
73	ORIENTAL MAN LL2021	RT	500.00	1850.00
73	PEACE LL1202	RT	550.00	7500.00
73	THREE GRACES LL2028	RT	950.00	3500.00
74	PASSIONATE DANCE LL2051	RT	450.00	2750.00
74	PEASANT WOMAN LL2049	RT	400.00	1300.00
74	THE FOREST LL1243	RT	1250.00	3300.00
77	GIRL WITH CALLA LILLIES SITTING L4972	OP	65.00	150.00
77	MOUNTAIN COUNTRY LADY LL1330	RT	900.00	1950.00
81	THE RESCUE LL3506	RT	3500.00	4450.00
82	CONCERTO LL2063	RT	1000.00	1300.00
83	FEARFUL FLIGHT LL1377	750	7000.00	13500.00
84	BOY GRADUATE L5198	OP	160.00	240.00
84	CHARLIE THE TRAMP L5233	RT	150.00	675.00-1050.00
84	FLOWERS OF THE SEASON L1454	OP	1460.00	2250.00
84	GIRL GRADUATE L5199	OP	160.00	240.00
85	BUST OF LADY FROM ELCHE L5269	RT	432.00	540.00
85	CONSIDERATION L5355	RT	100.00	250.00
85	LA GIACONDA L5337	RT	350.00	450.00
86	CAN CAN L5370	RT	700.00	1100.00
86	LOVERS SERENADE L5382	RT	350.00	500.00
86	PETITE PAIR L5384	RT	225.00	565.00
86	SIDEWALK SERENADE L5388	RT	750.00	1300.00
86	THE PUPPET PAINTER L5396	OP	500.00	740.00
88	PETITE MAIDEN L5383	RT	110.00	300.00
*			**BRIDAL FIGURINES**	
75	WEDDING L4808	OP	50.00	150.00
83	MATRIMONY L1404	OP	320.00	500.00
84	HERE COMES THE BRIDE L1446	OP	517.50	850.00
85	OVER THE THRESHOLD L5282	OP	150.00	235.00

YR	NAME	LIMIT	ISSUE	QUOTE
85	WEDDING DAY L5274	OP	240.00	360.00
86	MY WEDDING DAY L1494	OP	800.00	1250.00
87	I LOVE YOU TRULY L1528	OP	375.00	500.00
87	THE BRIDE L5439	OP	250.00	335.00
89	BRIDE'S MAID L5598	OP	150.00	160.00
89	WEDDING CAKE L5587G	OP	595.00	650.00
*			**CAPRICHOS FIGURINES**	
87	IRIS BASKET C1542	RT	825.00	1400.00
87	IRIS WITH VASE C1551	RT	199.00	375.00
87	ORCHID ARRANGEMENT C1541	RT	500.00	1800.00
87	VIOLET FAN W/BASE C1546	RT	600.00	1500.00
87	WHITE FAN W/BASE C1546.3	RT	600.00	1500.00
*			**CHILDREN WITH ANIMALS**	
71	GIRL SEATED WITH FLOWERS L1088	RT	45.00	725.00
73	BOY WITH DONKEY L1181	RT	50.00	450.00
74	CARESS L1246	RT	50.00	190.00
74	FRIENDSHIP L1230	RT	68.00	250.00
74	GIRL WITH DUCKS L1267	OP	55.00	250.00
74	HONEY LICKERS L1248	RT	100.00	500.00
75	AGRESSIVE DUCK L1288	OP	170.00	450.00
75	DEVOTION L1278	RT	140.00	450.00
75	FEEDING TIME L1277	OP	120.00	360.00
76	GIRL WITH CATS L1309	OP	120.00	295.00
76	GIRL WITH PUPPIES IN BASKET L1311	OP	120.00	325.00
77	ON THE FARM L1306	RT	130.00	240.00
78	NAUGHTY DOG L4982	OP	130.00	215.00
79	AVOIDING THE DUCK L5033	OP	160.00	300.00
79	LITTLE FRISKIES L5032	OP	107.50	190.00
81	MY HUNGRY BROOD L5074	OP	295.00	370.00
83	STUBBORN MULE L5178	OP	250.00	375.00
84	A LITTER OF LOVE L1441	OP	385.00	560.00
85	PLAYING WITH DUCKS AT THE POND L5303	RT	425.00	900.00
86	LITTER OF FUN L5364	OP	275.00	400.00
86	THIS ONE'S MINE L5376	OP	300.00	440.00
87	I HOPE SHE DOES L5450	OP	190.00	260.00
87	SLEEPY TRIO L5443	OP	190.00	260.00
*			**CHILDREN'S THEMES**	
71	BEAGLE PUPPY (SITTING) L1071G/M	OP	17.50	135.00-292.50
71	PUPPY LOVE L1127	OP	50.00	270.00
71	SEESAW L4867	OP	55.00	290.00
73	GIRL WITH DOLL L1211G	OP	72.00	420.00
74	FEEDING THE DUCKS L4849	OP	60.00	220.00
74	SEESAW L1255	RT	110.00	625
80	BLOOMING ROSES L1339	RT	325.00	500.00
80	SLEIGHRIDE L5037	OP	585.00	950.00
83	A BARROW OF BLOSSOMS L1419	OP	390.00	575.00
83	AUTUMN L5218	OP	90.00	145.00
83	BALLOONS FOR SALE L5141	OP	145.00	215.00
83	FLOWER HARMONY L1418	OP	130.00	210.00
83	FROM MY GARDEN L1416	OP	140.00	235.00
83	NATURE'S BOUNTY L1417	OP	160.00	270.00
83	PONDERING L5173	OP	300.00	440.00
83	PRETTY PICKINGS L5222	OP	80.00	115.00
83	ROSES FOR MY MOM L5088	RT	645.00	810.00
83	SPRING IS HERE L5223	OP	80.00	115.00
83	SPRING L5217	OP	90.00	145.00
83	STORYTIME L5229	RT	245.00	975.00
83	SUMMER L5219	OP	90.00	145.00
83	SWEET SCENT L5221	OP	80.00	115.00
83	WINTER L5220	OP	90.00	145.00
84	BOY MEETS GIRL L1188	RT	310.00	400
84	COURTSHIP L5072	RT	327.00	525.00
84	DANCING THE POLKA L5252	OP	205.00	340.00
84	FOLK DANCING L5256	OP	205.00	550.00
84	NOSTALGIA L5071	OP	185.00	270.00
85	A VISIT WITH GRANNY L5305	OP	275.00	440.00
85	BOY ON CAROUSEL HORSE L1470	OP	470.00	750.00
85	CHILDREN AT PLAY L5304	RT	220.00	300.00-450.00
85	FALL CLEAN-UP L5286	OP	295.00	475.00
85	GIRL ON CAROUSEL HORSE L1469	OP	470.00	750.00
85	GLORIOUS SPRING L5284	OP	355.00	570.00
85	ICE CREAM L5325	OP	380.00	570.00
85	LOVE IN BLOOM L5292	OP	225.00	360.00
85	SUMMER ON THE FARM L5285	OP	235.00	375.00
85	WINTER FROST L5287	OP	270.00	475.00
85	YOUNG STREET MUSICIANS L5306	RT	300.00	950.00-1150.00

YR	NAME	LIMIT	ISSUE	QUOTE
86	A NEW FRIEND L1506	OP	110.00	165.00
86	A STITCH IN TIME L5344	OP	425.00	640.00
86	BEDTIME L5347	OP	300.00	470.00
86	BOY & HIS BUNNY L1507	OP	90.00	150.00
86	CHILDREN'S GAMES L5379	OP	325.00	480.00
86	FORGOTTEN L1502	OP	125.00	275.00
86	IN THE MEADOW L1508	OP	100.00	300.00
86	LITTLE SCULPTOR L5358	RT	160.00	390.00
86	NATURE BOY L1505	OP	100.00	300.00
86	NEGLECTED L1503	OP	125.00	195.00
86	RAG DOLL L1501	OP	*	275.00
86	RAGAMUFFIN L1500	OP	125.00	250.00
86	SPRING FLOWERS L1509	RT	100.00	350
86	STILL LIFE L5363	OP	180.00	310.00
86	SWEET HARVEST L5380	RT	450.00	610.00
86	TRY THIS ONE L5361	OP	225.00	330.00
87	AT ATTENTION L5407	RT	175.00	500
87	CADET CAPTAIN L5404	RT	175.00	500
87	CIRCUS TRAIN L1517	OP	2900.00	3750.00
87	HAPPY BIRTHDAY L5429	OP	100.00	140.00
87	IN THE GARDEN L5416	OP	200.00	310.00
87	MUSIC TIME L5430	RT	500.00	700.00
87	MY BEST FRIEND L5401	OP	150.00	200.00
87	NAPTIME L5448	OP	135.00	190.00
87	ONE, TWO, THREE L5426	OP	240.00	310.00
87	THE BUGLER L5406	RT	175.00	500
87	THE DRUMMER BOY L5403	RT	225.00	631.00
87	THE FLAG BEARER L5405	RT	200.00	500
87	THE WANDERER L5400	OP	150.00	200.00
87	TIME TO REST L5399	OP	175.00	488.00
89	BABY DOLL L5608	OP	150.00	160.00
89	HELLO FLOWERS L5543	OP	385.00	420.00
89	JOY IN A BASKET L5595	OP	215.00	235.00
89	LET'S MAKE UP L5555	OP	215.00	235.00
89	MY NEW PET L5549	OP	150.00	160.00
89	PLAYFUL ROMP L5594	OP	215.00	235.00
89	PRETTY POSIES L5548	OP	425.00	460.00
89	PUPPY DOG TAILS L5539	OP	1200.00	1300.00
*				**CLOWNS**
71	CLOWN L4618	OP	70.00	385.00
71	CLOWN L4618	OP	70.00	360.00
71	PELUSA CLOWN L1125	RT	70.00	875.00
76	SAD CLOWN L4924	RT	200.00	950.00
81	CLOWN WITH CLOCK L5056	RT	290.00	850.00-950.00
81	CLOWN WITH CONCERTINA L5058	RT	290.00	475.00
81	CLOWN WITH SAXAPHONE L5059	RT	320.00	475.00
81	CLOWN WITH VIOLIN AND TOP HAT L5057	RT	270.00	525.00
81	CLOWN WITH VIOLIN L1126	RT	71.00	1500.00
81	GIRL CLOWN WITH TRUMPET L5060	RT	290.00	550.00
82	JESTER L5129	OP	220.00	365.00
82	PENSIVE CLOWN L5130	OP	250.00	385.00
85	CLOWN WITH CONCERTINA L1027	OP	95.00	700.00
85	PIERROT WITH CONCERTINA L5279	OP	95.00	150.00
85	PIERROT WITH PUPPY & BALL L5278	OP	95.00	140.00-150.00
85	PIERROT WITH PUPPY L5277	OP	95.00	150.00
89	FINE MELODY L5585	OP	225.00	250.00
89	MELANCHOLY L5542	OP	375.00	400.00
89	REFLECTING L5612	OP	335.00	395.00
89	SAD CLOWN L5611	OP	335.00	395.00
89	SAD NOTE L5586	OP	185.00	250.00
89	STAR STRUCK L5610	OP	335.00	395.00
89	THE BLUES L5600	OP	265.00	310.00
*				**DON QUIXOTE FIGURINES**
*	RETURN TO LA MANCHA LL1580	500	*	7950.00
71	DON QUIXOTE L1030	OP	225.00	1375.00
71	SANCHO PANZA L1031	RT	65.00	525.00
74	DON QUIXOTE L4854	OP	40.00	180.00
75	MAN FROM LAMANCHA LL1269	RT	700.00	4000.00
77	IMPOSSIBLE DREAM LL1318	RT	2400.00	5000.00
77	WRATH OF DON QUIXOTE L1343	RT	250.00	850.00
78	DON QUIXOTE & SANCHO L4998	RT	875.00	2500.00
80	LETTERS TO DULCINEA L3509	OP	1275.00	2050.00
83	A TOAST BY SANCH0 L5165	RT	100.00	235.00-250.00
83	THE BRAVE KNIGHT L1385	RT	350.00	700.00
84	THE QUEST L5224	OP	125.00	230.00
85	I HAVE FOUND THEE, DUICINEA LL5341	SO	1850.00	3000.00

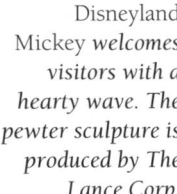

Disneyland Mickey *welcomes visitors with a hearty wave. The pewter sculpture is produced by The Lance Corp.*

This Raccoon *figure by Maruri aptly captures the nature of the animal.*

What more could she want? Sitting Pretty *is from the "Beautiful Dreamers" series produced by Rhodes Studios.*

With a handle touting the Gettysburg Address, this Abraham Lincoln Character Jug *is from a Royal Doulton collection honoring Presidents of the United States.*

This beautiful Anri wood-carved Pinocchio *figure has no strings attached. The piece is available in five sizes.*

YR	NAME	LIMIT	ISSUE	QUOTE
86	DON QUIXOTE & THE WINDMILL L1497	OP	1100.00	1750.00
86	ORATION L5357	OP	170.00	240.00
87	I AM DON QUIXOTE! L1522	OP	2600.00	3850.00
87	LISTEN TO DON QUIXOTE LL1520	750	1800.00	2750.00
				ELITE
93	ORIENTAL GARDEN	750	22500.00	24,000.00
93	PAELLA VALENCIANO	500	10000.00	11,000.00
94	CINDERELLA'S ARRIVAL	1500	25950.00	27,000.00
*				**FANTASY FIGURINES**
*	AT THE STROKE OF TWELVE L1493	1500	4250.00	7100.00
*	FANTASIA LL1487	5000	1500.00	2550.00
*	LEPRECHAUN L1721	OP	*	1325.00
*	SPRITE LL1720	OP	*	1325.00
71	CENTAUR BOY L1013	RT	45.00	350.00
71	CENTAUR GIRL L1012	RT	45.00	250.00
73	CINDERELLA L4828	OP	47.00	195.00
73	FAIRY L4595	OP	27.50	120.00
83	DAYDREAMING NYMPH L1402	RT	210.00	800.00
83	FANTASY L1414	OP	115.00	210.00
83	ILLUSION L1413	OP	115.00	210.00
83	MIRAGE L1415	OP	115.00	210.00
83	PONDERING NYMPH L1403	RT	210.00	600.00
83	SLEEPING NYMPH L1401	RT	210.00	600.00
85	CAMELOT LL1458	3000	1000.00	1550.00
85	DEMURE CENTAUR GIRL L5320	RT	157.00	225.00
85	WISTFUL CENTAUR GIRL L5319	RT	157.00	300.00
86	REY DE BASTOS LL5369	2000	325.00	575.00
86	REY DE COPAS LL5366	2000	325.00	575.00
86	REY DE ESPADAS LL5368	2000	325.00	575.00
86	REY DE OROS LL5367	2000	325.00	575.00
*				**FLOWERS**
74	FLORAL LL1184	RT	400.00	2200.00
74	FLORAL LL1185	RT	475.00	1800.00
74	FLORAL LL1185	RT	475.00	1800.00
74	FLORAL LL1186	RT	575.00	2200.00
83	BEGONIA L5186	RT	67.50	100.00
83	CALIFORNIA POPPY L5190	RT	97.50	180.00
83	CHRYSANTHEMUM L5189	RT	100.00	150.00
83	DAHLIA L5180	RT	65.00	95.00
83	JAPANESE CAMELIA L5181	RT	60.00	90.00
83	LACTIFLORA PEONY L5185	RT	65.00	100.00
83	MINIATURE BEGONIA L5188	RT	80.00	120.00
83	RHODODENDRON L5187	RT	67.50	100.00
83	THREE PINK ROSES L5181	RT	65.00	110.00
83	TWO YELLOW ROSES L5183	RT	5750.00	85.00
83	WHITE CARNATION L5184	RT	65.00	100.00
83	WHITE PEONY L5182	RT	85.00	125.00
*				**FOREIGN FIGURINES**
71	FLAMENCO DANCERS L4519	OP	495.00	800.00
71	FLAMENCO DANCERS ON HORSEBACK L4647	RT	412.00	1100.00
74	EMBROIDERER L4865	OP	115.00	550.00
74	ESKIMO L1195G	OP	30.00	125.00
75	ORIENTAL L2056	OP	35.00	85.00
75	ORIENTAL L2057	OP	30.00	85.00
75	THAILANDIA L2058	OP	650.00	1500.00
77	GRACEFUL DUO L2073	OP	775.50	1400.00
77	THAI DANCERS L2069	OP	300.00	620.00
79	GROWING ROSES L1354	RT	485.00	635.00
81	GRETEL L5064	RT	255.00	375.00
81	ILSA L5066	RT	275.00	300.00
81	INGRID L5065	RT	370.00	800.00
82	AMPARO L5125	RT	130.00	415.00
82	DRUM BEATS LL3524	1500	1875.00	2900.00
82	DUTCH WOMAN WITH TULIPS L1399	RT	*	700.00
82	PHILIPPINE FOLKLORE LL3522	1500	1450.00	2300.00
83	DESERT PEOPLE LL3555	750	1680.00	2975.00
83	ROAD TO MANDALAY LL3556	750	1390.00	1950.00
84	AZTEC DANCER L2143	RT	462.50	650.00
84	AZTEC INDIAN L2139	RT	552.50	600.00
84	BLUE GOD LL3552	1500	900.00	1500.00
84	FIRE BIRD LL3553	1500	800.00	1250.00
84	LADY FROM MAJORCA L5240	RT	120.00	375.00-425.00
85	AROMA OF THE ISLANDS L1480	OP	260.00	410.00
85	HAWAIIAN DANCER L1478	OP	230.00	375.00
85	IN A TROPICAL GARDEN L1479	OP	230.00	375.00
86	A RIDE IN THE COUNTRY L5354	OP	225.00	360.00

YR	NAME	LIMIT	ISSUE	QUOTE
86	A TIME TO REST L5391	RT	170.00	225.00-250.00
86	DEEP IN THOUGHT L5389	RT	170.00	250.00-488.00
86	ESKIMO RIDERS L5353	OP	150.00	215.00
86	HAWAIIAN FESTIVAL LL1496	4000	1850.00	3000.00
86	HINDU CHILDREN L5352	OP	250.00	350.00
86	SPANISH DANCER L5390	RT	170.00	250.00-450.00
86	TAHITIAN DANCING GIRLS L1498	OP	750.00	1100.00
87	HAWAIIAN BEAUTY L1512	RT	575.00	900.00
87	LEHUA L1532	RT	275.00	468.00-520.00
87	LEILANI L1530	RT	275.00	525.00
87	MALIA L1531	RT	275.00	468.00-520.00
87	MEXICAN DANCERS L5415	OP	800.00	1000.00
87	MOMI L1529	RT	275.00	468.00
*				**GRES FIGURINES**
75	THE WIND L1279	OP	250.00	765.00
77	GRACEFUL DUO L2073	OP	775.00	1400.00
78	RAIN IN SPAIN L2077	RT	190.00	475.00
79	A NEW HAIRDO L2070	RT	1060.00	800.00
79	PENSIVE L3514	OP	500.00	925.00
80	A WINTRY DAY L3513	RT	525.00	700.00
82	AMERICAN HERITAGE L2127	RT	525.00	750.00
82	CONTEMPLATION L3526	OP	265.00	465.00
82	LOST IN THOUGHT L2125	RT	210.00	250.00
82	MOTHER'S LOVE L3521	RT	1000.00	1150.00
82	VENUS L2128	OP	650.00	1050.00
82	WEARY L3525	OP	360.00	545.00
84	FAIRY BALLERINA L2137	RT	500.00	625.00
84	MYSTICAL JOSEPH L2135	RT	427.50	550.00
84	SEA HARVEST L2142	RT	535.00	600.00
84	THE KING L2136	RT	510.00	710.00
85	A TRIBUTE TO PEACE L2150	OP	470.00	750.00
85	YOUNG MADONNA L2149	RT	400.00	675.00
*				**HISTORICAL FIGURINES**
82	CERVANTES L5132	RT	925.00	1175.00
83	QUEEN ELIZABETH LL1275	RT	3650.00	4600.00
84	COLUMBUS LL1432	RT	575.00	1350.00
84	HENRY VIII LL1384	1200	650.00	940.00
85	NAPOLEON BONAPARTE LL5338	5000	275.00	470.00
85	NAPOLEON PLANNING BATTLE LL1459	1500	875.00	1350.00
86	EL GRECO L5359	RT	300.00	550.00
86	THE NEW WORLD LL1486	4000	700.00	1300.00
88	BEETHOVEN LL5339	3000	800.00	1250.00
*				**IN THE GARDEN FIGURINES**
71	GIRL WITH FLOWERS L1172G	OP	27.00	285.00
75	FLOWER HARVEST L1286	OP	200.00	470.00
75	LITTLE GARDENER L1283	OP	250.00	765.00
75	MY FLOWERS L1284	OP	200.00	525.00
75	MY GOODNESS L1285	OP	190.00	395.00
75	PICKING FLOWERS L1287	OP	170.00	420.00
76	VICTORIAN GIRL ON SWING L1297	RT	520.00	1800.00
78	DAUGHTERS L5013	RT	425.00	950.00
79	FLOWER CURTSY L5027	OP	230.00	400.00
79	WATERING THE FLOWER POTS L1376	RT	400.00	700.00
79	WILDFLOWER L5030	OP	360.00	600.00
86	AT THE BALL L5398	OP	375.00	560.00-700.00
86	SCARECROW & THE LADY L5385	OP	350.00	530.00
86	SUNDAY IN THE PARK L5365	OP	375.00	540.00
86	TIME FOR REFLECTION L5378	OP	425.00	640.00
87	A FLOWER FOR MY LADY L1513	RT	1150.00	1600.00
87	COURTING TIME L5409	RT	425.00	625.00
87	FEEDING THE PIGEONS L5428	OP	490.00	700.00
87	IN THE GARDEN L5416	OP	200.00	275.00
87	INSPIRATION LL5413	500	1200.00	1975.00
87	POETRY OF LOVE L5442	OP	500.00	700.00
87	STUDYING IN THE PARK L5425	OP	675.00	850.00
87	WILL YOU MARRY ME? L5447	OP	750.00	1050.00
*				**LIMITED EDITIONS**
*	A SUCCESSFUL HUNT LL5098	1000	*	7750.00
*	CHRISTOPHER COLUMBUS LL2176	1000	*	1250.00
*	CIRCUS PARADE LL1609	1000	*	6250.00
*	EIGHTEENTH CENTURY COACH LL1485	500	*	24000.00
*	GARDEN PARTY LL1578	500	*	6900.00
*	KITAKAMI CRUISE LL1605	500	*	7000.00
*	MOUNTED WARRIORS LL1608	500	*	3300.00
*	SOUTHERN TEA LL1597	1000	*	2200.00
*	TURTLE DOVE NEST LL3519	1200	*	5750.00

YR	NAME	LIMIT	ISSUE	QUOTE
90	A RIDE IN THE PARK LL5718	1000	3200.00	3675.00
90	INVINCIBLE LL2188	300	1100.00	1250.00
91	CHARM LL5801	500	650.00	680.00
91	COLUMBUS REFLECTING LL1741	1000	1850.00	1900.00
91	COLUMBUS, TWO ROUTES LL1740	1000	1500.00	1575.00
91	HEAVENLY SWING LL1739	1000	1900.00	1975.00
91	LIBERTY EAGLE LL1738	1500	1000.00	1050.00
91	NEW WORLD MEDALLION LL5808	5000	200.00	200.00
91	ONWARD! LL1742	1000	2500.00	2600.00
91	OUTING IN SEVILLE LL1756	500	23000.00	23750.00
91	THE PRINCESS AND THE UNICORN LL1755	1500	1750.00	1800.00
91	VALENCIAN CRUISE LL1731	1000	2700.00	2800.00
91	VENICE VOWS LL1732	1000	2700.00	3900.00
91	YOUTH LL5800	500	650.00	680.00
92	CIRCUS TIME LL1758	2500	9200.00	9200.00
92	HAWAIIAN CEREMONY LL1757	1000	9800.00	9800.00
92	JUSTICE EAGLE LL5863	1500	1700.00	1700.00
92	MATERNAL JOY LL5864	1500	1800.00	1800.00
92	MOTORING IN STYLE LL5884	1500	3700.00	3700.00
92	PRESENTING CREDENTIALS LL5911	1500	19500.00	19500.00
92	SORROWFUL MOTHER LL5849	1500	1750.00	1750.00
92	TEA IN THE GARDEN LL1759	2000	9500.00	9500.00
92	THE READER LL3560	200	2650.00	2650.00
92	THE VOYAGE OF COLUMBUS LL5847	7500	1450.00	1450.00
92	THE WAY OF THE CROSS LL5890	2000	975.00	975.00
92	YOUNG MOZART LL5915	2500	500.00	1200.00
*			**LITERARY FIGURINES**	
71	HAMLET LL1144	RT	250.00	2500.00
71	OTHELLO AND DESDEMONA LL1145	RT	275.00	3400.00
71	ROMEO AND JULIET L4750	OP	150.00	1050.00
74	HAMLET AND YORICK L1254	RT	325.00	1250.00-1345.00
74	LOVERS FROM VERONA L1250	RT	330.00	1300.00
84	REFLECTIONS OF HAMLET L1455	RT	1000.00	1500.00
*			**LLADRO ANGELS**	
71	ANGEL WITH CHILD L4635	OP	15.00	90.00
71	ANGEL WITH HORN L4540	OP	13.00	75.00
71	ANGEL, BLACK L4537	OP	13.00	75.00
71	ANGEL, CHINESE L4536	OP	45.00	75.00
71	ANGEL, PRAYING L4538	OP	13.00	75.00
71	ANGEL, RECLINING L4541	OP	13.00	75.00
71	ANGEL, THINKING L4539	OP	13.00	75.00
71	GROUP OF ANGELS L4542	OP	31.00	165.00
74	ANGEL WITH CLARINET L1232	RT	60.00	525.00
74	ANGEL WITH FLUTE L1233	RT	60.00	525.00
74	ANGEL WITH LUTE L1231	RT	60.00	525.00
77	CHERUB, DREAMING L4961	OP	40.00	90.00
77	CHERUB, PUZZLED L4959	OP	40.00	90.00
77	CHERUB, SMILING L4960	OP	40.00	90.00
77	CHERUB, WONDERING L4962	OP	40.00	90.00
85	CAREFREE ANGEL WITH FLUTE L1463	RT	220.00	550.00
85	CAREFREE ANGEL WITH LYRE L1464	RT	220.00	550.00
*			**LLADRO ANIMAL FIGURINES**	
71	ELEPHANTS (2) L1151	OP	45.00	375.00
71	ELEPHANTS (3) L1150	OP	100.00	775.00
71	HORSE GROUP/ALL WHITE L1022	OP	465.00	2000.00
71	HORSES L4655	OP	110.00	650.00
71	PLAYFUL HORSES L4597	RT	240.00	1200.00
71	SHEPHERDESS WITH LAMB L2005	RT	100.00	600.00
73	ORIENTAL HORSE LL2030	RT	1100.00	3500.00-500.00
74	BEAR, WHITE L1207G	OP	16.00	70.00
74	BEAR, WHITE L1208G	OP	16.00	70.00
74	BEAR, WHITE L1209G	OP	16.00	70.00
74	HUNTING SCENE LL1238	RT	800.00	3000.00
74	THE HUNT LL1308	RT	4750.00	6900.00
74	THE RACE L1249	RT	450.00	3200.00
79	HORSE HEADS L3511	RT	260.00	450.00
79	JOCKEY WITH LASS LL5036	OP	950.00	1300.00
81	SUCCESSFUL HUNT LL5098	1000	5200.00	6900.00
83	BORN FREE L1420	OP	1520.00	2450.00
83	FLIGHT OF GAZELLES LL1352	RT	2450.00	3100.00
83	WINTER WONDERLAND L1429	OP	1025.00	1675.00
84	ELK LL3501	RT	950.00	1200.00
84	HORSE GROUP L1021	RT	950.00	1950.00
84	KITTY CONFRONTATION L1442	OP	155.00	245.00
84	PURR-FECT L1444	OP	350.00	625.00
85	ANTELOPE DRINKING L5302	RT	215.00	350.00-500.00

YR	NAME	LIMIT	ISSUE	QUOTE
85	GAZELLE L5271	RT	205.00	400.00
85	PACK OF HUNTING DOGS LL5342	3000	925.00	1575.00
85	THOROUGHBRED HORSE LL5340	1000	625.00	985.00
86	FOX HUNT LL3562	RT	5200.00	8500.00
87	DESERT TOUR L5402	RT	950.00	900.00
*	**LLADRO BIRD FIGURINES**			
71	DOVE L1015G	OP	21.00	100.00
71	DOVE L1016G	OP	36.00	170.00
73	EAGLE OWL LL1223	RT	450.00	1250.00
73	EAGLES LL1189	RT	900.00	3000.00-3200.00
73	SEA BIRDS LL1174	RT	600.00	2750.00
73	SEA BIRDS WITH NEST LL1194	RT	600.00	2750.00
73	TURKEY GROUP LL1196	RT	650.00	1800.00
74	FLYING DUCK L1263G	OP	20.00	85.00
74	FLYING DUCK L1264G	OP	20.00	85.00
74	FLYING DUCK L1265G	OP	20.00	85.00
74	KISSING DOVES L1169G	OP	32.00	140.00
74	TURTLE DOVES LL1240	RT	500.00	2500.00
77	DUCKLINGS L1307	OP	47.50	145.00
77	DUCKS AT POND LL1317	RT	4250.00	6900.00
79	SPRING BIRDS L1368	RT	1600.00	2500.00
80	IBIS L1319	OP	1550.00	2500.00
83	NEST OF EAGLES LL3523	300	6900.00	9500.00-10900.00
83	TURTLE DOVES LL3520	750	6800.00	10900.00
84	CRANES L1456	OP	1000.00	1650.00
84	DOVE GROUP L1335	RT	950.00	1300.00
84	FLYING PARTRIDGES LL2064	RT	3500.00	4300.00
84	HOW DO YOU DO! L1439	OP	185.00	265.00
85	FLOCK OF BIRDS LL1462	1500	1125.00	1650.00
87	BARN OWL L5421	RT	120.00	265.00-300.00
87	GREAT GRAY OWL L5419	RT	190.00	175.00-429.00
87	HAWK OWL L5422	RT	120.00	265.00-315.00
87	HORNED OWL L5420	RT	150.00	180.00
87	SHORT EARED OWL L5418	RT	200.00	150.00-455.00
89	BOWLING CRANE L1613	OP	385.00	420.00
89	COURTING CRANES L1611	OP	565.00	600.00
89	DANCING CRANE L1614	OP	385.00	420.00
89	FLUTTERING CRANE L1598	OP	115.00	125.00
89	FREEDOM LL5602	SO	875.00	800.00-950.00
89	LANDING CRANE L1600	OP	115.00	125.00
89	NESTING CRANE L1599	OP	95.00	100.00
89	PREENING CRANES L1612	OP	985.00	420.00
*	**LLADRO COLLECTORS SOCIETY**			
85	LITTLE PALS S7600	RT	95.00	2000.00-4500.00
86	LITTLE TRAVELER S7602	RT	95.00	1250.00-2100.00
87	SPRING BOUQUETS S7603	RT	125.00	575.00-813.00
88	FLOWER SONG S7607	RT	175.00	455.00-600.00
88	SCHOOL DAYS S7604	RT	125.00	450.00
89	MY BUDDY S7609	RT	145.00	220.00
90	CAN I PLAY? S7610	YR	150.00	220.00-625.00
91	PICTURE PERFECT S7612	YR	350.00	355.00-720.00
91	SUMMER STROLL S7611	RT	195.00	390.00-400.00
*	**LLADRO HARLEQUINS AND DANCERS**			
71	IDYL L1017	OP	115.00	750.00
74	BALLERINA L4855	OP	45.00	280.00
74	CARNIVAL COUPLE L4882	OP	60.00	260.00
74	SAD HARLEQUIN L4558	OP	110.00	435.00
74	WAITING BACKSTAGE L4559	OP	110.00	380.00
74	YOUNG HARLEQUIN L1229	OP	70.00	495.00
76	CLOSING SCENE L4935	OP	180.00	475.00
79	ACT II L5035	OP	700.00	1200.00
79	DANCER L5050	OP	85.00	160.00
82	LOST LOVE L5128	RT	400.00	650.00-700.00
84	BALLERINA, WHITE L4855.3	RT	110.00	250.00
84	BALLET TRIO L5235	OP	785.00	1250.00
84	CLOSING SCENE/WHITE L4935.3	RT	202.50	265.00
*	**LLADRO MINIATURES**			
86	BALANCING ACT L5392	RT	35.00	50.00-150.00
86	CURIOSITY L5393	RT	25.00	225.00
86	ON GUARD L5350	RT	50.00	250.00
86	POOR PUPPY L5394	RT	25.00	40.00
86	WOE IS ME L5351	RT	45.00	250.00
86	WOLF HOUND L5356	RT	45.00	225
87	COUGAR L5435	RT	65.00	80.00
87	ELEPHANT L5438	RT	50.00	100.00
87	KANGAROO L5433	RT	65.00	80.00

YR	NAME	LIMIT	ISSUE	QUOTE
87	LION L5436	RT	50.00	65.00
87	MONKEY L5432	RT	60.00	150.00
87	POLAR BEAR L5434	OP	65.00	90.00
87	RHINO L5437	RT	50.00	65.00
92	CAT L5308	OP	65.00	65.00
92	COCKER SPANIEL L5310	OP	65.00	65.00
92	COCKER SPANIEL PUP L5309	OP	65.00	65.00
92	KITTEN L5307	OP	65.00	65.00
*			**LLADRO SCULPTURES**	
81	ADORATION LL3545	RT	1050.00	1600.00
81	AFRICAN WOMAN LL3546	RT	1300.00	2000.00
81	ANXIETY LL3530	125	1075.00	1775.00
81	BATHER LL3551	RT	975.00	1800.00
81	BOXER LL3550	300	850.00	1365.00
81	COMPANIONSHIP LL3529	SO	1000.00	1450.00
81	DANTINESS LL3539	RT	1000.00	1400.00
81	DEMURE LL3543	RT	1250.00	1700.00
81	DREAMING LL3537	SO	950.00	1300.00
81	IN THE DISTANCE LL3534	RT	525.00	1275.00
81	OBSERVER LL3533	115	900.00	1575.00
81	PLENTITUDE LL3532	SO	1000.00	1500.00
81	POSE LL3540	SO	1250.00	1450.00
81	RECLINING NUDE LL3547	RT	650.00	875.00
81	REFLECTIONS LL3544	75	650.00	975.00
81	RELAXATION LL3536	RT	525.00	1000.00
81	REPOSING LL3549	RT	425.00	575.00
81	SERENITY LL3548	300	925.00	1450.00
81	SLAVE LL3535	SO	950.00	1400.00
81	TOGETHERNESS LL3527	SO	750.00	1200.00
81	TRANQUILITY LL3541	SO	1000.00	1500.00
81	VICTORY LL3531	RT	1500.00	1800.00
81	WRESTLING LL3528	RT	950.00	1125.00
81	YOGA LL3542	SO	650.00	900.00
81	YOUTH LL3538	RT	525.00	1120.00
83	DAWN LL3000	300	325.00	525.00
83	INDOLENCE LL3003	SO	1465.00	1800.00
83	MONKS LL3001	300	1675.00	2400.00
83	VENUS IN THE BATH LL3005	SO	1175.00	1450.00
83	WAITING LL3002	RT	1550.00	1900.00
*			**MOTHER & CHILD SERIES**	
*	MOTHER AND SON L2131	OP	850.00	1350.00
71	MOTHER AND CHILD L4575	OP	50.00	240.00
71	MOTHER AND CHILD L4701	OP	45.00	250.00
76	BABY'S OUTING L4938	OP	250.00	685.00
77	COMFORTING BABY LL1329	RT	700.00	1500.00-2000.00
77	MY BABY LL1331	RT	550.00	1000.00
86	FAMILY ROOTS L5371	OP	575.00	875.00
87	GOODNIGHT L5449	OP	225.00	325.00
87	TENDERNESS L1527	OP	260.00	385.00
89	A GIFT OF LOVE L5596	OP	400.00	475.00
89	LATEST ADDITION L1606	OP	385.00	455.00
*			**NAUTICAL FIGURINES**	
71	SEA CAPTAIN L4621	OP	45.00	230.00
73	GOING FISHING L4809	OP	33.00	140.00
73	YOUNG SAILOR L4180	OP	33.00	140.00
76	THE HELMSMAN L1325	RT	600.00	1200.00
80	IN THE GONDOLA L1350	OP	1850.00	3100.00
83	A TALL YARN L5207	OP	260.00	440.00
83	FISHING WITH GRAMPS L5215	OP	410.00	650.00
83	ON THE LAKE L5216	RT	660.00	825.00
83	SEA FEVER L5166	OP	130.00	200.00
83	STORMY SEA L3554	OP	675.00	1100.00
83	THE WHALER L2121	RT	820.00	1400.00
83	YACHTSMAN L5206	OP	110.00	150.00
84	NAUTICAL WATCH L2134	RT	450.00	750.00
84	VENETIAN SERENADE LL1433	SO	2600.00	3750.00
85	LOVE BOAT LL5343	3000	825.00	1300.00
85	SAILOR SERENADES HIS GIRL L5276	RT	315.00	600.00
87	CARNIVAL TIME LL5423	1000	2400.00	3750.00
*			**NUDES**	
*	INNOCENCE/GREEN L3558	OP	960.00	1500.00
*	INNOCENCE/RED L3558/3	RT	960.00	1200.00
73	LYRIC MUSE LL2031	RT	750.00	2000.00
78	NATIVE L3502	OP	700.00	2100.00
79	NUDE WITH DOVE LL3503	RT	500.00	1400.00
79	NUDE WITH ROSE L3517	OP	225.00	650.00

YR	NAME	LIMIT	ISSUE	QUOTE
82	VENUS AND CUPID LL1392	RT	1100.00	2500.00
82	VENUS L2128	OP	650.00	1050.00
85	A TRIBUTE TO PEACE L2150	OP	470.00	750.00
85	CLASSIC FALL LL1466	RT	650.00	1300.00
85	CLASSIC SPRING LL1465	RT	650.00	1300.00-1400.00
85	HAWAIIAN FLOWER VENDOR L2154	OP	245.00	370.00
85	PEACE OFFERING L3559	OP	397.00	545.00
85	YOUTHFUL BEAUTY LL1461	5000	800.00	1150.00
86	NATURE GIRL L5346	RT	450.00	850.00
86	PASTORAL SCENE LL5386	OP	1100.00	2000.00
87	ARTIST'S MODEL L5417	RT	425.00	550.00

ORIENTAL FIGURINES

YR	NAME	LIMIT	ISSUE	QUOTE
73	ORIENTAL FLOWER ARRANGER L4840	OP	90.00	440.00
77	GEISHA L4807	OP	190.00	375.00
78	BUTTERFLY L4991	OP	125.00	260.00
78	CHRYSANTHEMUM L4990	OP	125.00	275.00
78	ORIENTAL SPRING L4988	OP	125.00	275.00
78	SAYONARA L4989	OP	125.00	260.00
80	A RICKSHAW RIDE L1383	OP	1500.00	1850.00
82	AUGUST MOON L5122	OP	185.00	270.00
82	MY PRECIOUS BUNDLE L5123	OP	150.00	200.00
83	FISH A'PLENTY L5172	OP	190.00	325.00
83	MARIKO L1421	OP	850.00	1350.00
84	KIYOKO L1450	OP	235.00	385.00
84	MAYUMI L1449	OP	235.00	385.00
84	MICHIKO L1447	OP	235.00	385.00
84	SPRINGTIME IN JAPAN L1445	OP	965.00	1500.00
84	TERUKO L1451	OP	235.00	385.00
84	YUKI L1448	OP	285.00	475.00
85	NIPPON LADY L5327	OP	325.00	470.00
86	LADY OF THE EAST L1488	OP	625.00	900.00
86	ORIENTAL MUSIC LL1491	5000	1350.00	2300.00

PASTORAL FIGURINES

YR	NAME	LIMIT	ISSUE	QUOTE
71	GIRL GEESE L1036G/M	OP	*	155.00
71	GIRL WITH BASKET L1034	RT	30.00	275.00
71	GIRL WITH DUCK L1052	OP	30.00	195.00
71	GIRL WITH GEESE L1035	OP	37.50	170.00
71	GIRL WITH GEESE L4568	OP	45.00	190.00
71	GIRL WITH LAMB L1010G	OP	26.00	170.00
71	GIRL WITH LAMB L4505	OP	20.00	95.00
71	GIRL WITH MILKPAIL L4682	RT	28.00	175.00
71	GIRL WITH PARASOL AND GEESE L4510	OP	40.00	210.00
71	GIRL WITH PIG L1011G/M	OP	13.00	82.00
71	GIRL WITH SHEEP L4584	OP	27.00	145.00
71	GIRL WITH SWAN AND DOG L4866	OP	26.00	180.00
71	SHEPHERDESS L4660	OP	21.00	300.00
71	SHEPHERDESS W/BASKET AND ROOSTER L4591	OP	20.00	120.00
71	SHEPHERDESS WITH GOATS L1001	RT	80.00	460.00
73	GETTING HER GOAT L4812	RT	55.00	275.00
73	GIRL WITH GEESE L4815	OP	72.00	280.00
73	GIRL WITH RABBIT L4826	OP	40.00	160.00
73	SHEPHERDESS L4835	RT	42.00	400
75	GIRL WITH PIGEONS L4915	RT	110.00	350
83	ARACELY WITH DUCKS L5202	OP	125.00	200.00
83	JOSEFA FEEDING DUCK L5201	OP	125.00	250.00
85	MOTHER AND CHILD WITH LAMB L5299	RT	180.00	325.00
86	LOVERS SERENADE L5382	RT	350.00	500.00

PERIOD FIGURINES

YR	NAME	LIMIT	ISSUE	QUOTE
71	DRESSMAKER L4700	OP	45.00	300.00
74	LADY WITH DOG L4761	OP	60.00	220.00
74	LADY WITH PARASOL L4879	OP	48.00	260.00
74	LOVERS FROM VERONA L1250	RT	330.00	900.00
75	LADY WITH SHAWL L4914	OP	220.00	575.00
76	LOVERS IN THE PARK L1274	RT	450.00	1300.00
76	MY DOG L4893	OP	85.00	195.00
76	SCHOOL GIRL L1313	RT	200.00	700
76	SPRING BREEZE L4936	OP	145.00	350.00
76	WINDBLOWN GIRL L4922	OP	150.00	250.00
79	ANNIVERSARY WALTZ L1372	OP	260.00	530.00
79	SWINGING L1366	RT	825.00	1375.00
80	READING L5000	OP	150.00	220.00
80	REMINISCING L1270	RT	975.00	1375.00
80	SUNNY DAY L5003	OP	192.50	202.00
80	UNDER THE WILLOW L1346	RT	1600.00	2400.00
80	WAITING IN THE PARK L1374	OP	235.00	425.00
83	AFTERNOON TEA L1428	OP	115.00	210.00

YR	NAME	LIMIT	ISSUE	QUOTE
83	FLAPPER L5175	OP	185.00	310.00
83	HIGH SOCIETY L1430	OP	305.00	500.00
83	ROARING 20'S L5174	OP	172.50	250.00
83	THE DEBUTANTE L1431	OP	115.00	210.00
83	THOUGHTS L1272	RT	87.50	3050.00
84	ON THE TOWN L1452	OP	220.00	365.00
84	PLEASANTRIES L1440	RT	960.00	1900.00
84	VOWS L1434	RT	600.00	675.00
85	ENGLISH LADY L5324	OP	225.00	350.00
85	MEDIEVAL COURTSHIP L5300	RT	735.00	900.00
85	MILANESE LADY L5323	OP	180.00	290.00
85	PARISIAN LADY L5321	OP	192.50	280.00
85	SOCIALITE OF THE TWENTIES L5283	OP	175.00	290.00
85	VIENNESE LADY L5322	OP	160.00	250.00
86	A LADY OF TASTE L1495	OP	575.00	900.00
86	A NEW HAT L5345	RT	200.00	270.00-400.00
86	A TOUCH OF CLASS L5377	OP	475.00	700.00
86	SERENADE L5381	RT	450.00	600.00
86	THE RECEPTION L1504	RT	625.00	965.00
86	THREE SISTERS LL1492	3000	1850.00	3100.00
87	A FLOWER FOR MY LADY L1513	RT	1150.00	1375.00
87	CAFE DE PARIS L1511	OP	1900.00	2500.00
87	INTERMEZZO L5424	R:	325.00	575.00
87	ISABEL L5412	RT	225.00	330.00-500.00
87	PILAR L5410	RT	200.00	305.00-400.00
87	STROLL IN THE PARK L1519	OP	1600.00	2200.00
87	SUNDAY STROLL L5408	RT	250.00	350.00
87	TERESA L5411	RT	225.00	475.00

PROFESSIONAL FIGURINES

YR	NAME	LIMIT	ISSUE	QUOTE
*	DENTIST L4723	RT	36.00	750.00
71	DOCTOR L4602-3	RT	33.00	160.00
71	NURSE L4603-3	RT	35.00	170.00
71	OBSTETRICIAN L4763-3	RT	40.00	290.00
73	PHARMACIST L4844	RT	70.00	1200.00
75	JUDGE LL1281	RT	325.00	1500.00
83	ARCHITECT L5214	RT	140.00	500.00
83	FEMALE PHYSICIAN L5197	OP	120.00	200.00
83	LAMPLIGHTER L5205	OP	170.00	300.00
83	LAWYER L5213	OP	250.00	450.00
83	MAESTRO, MUSIC PLEASE! L5196	RT	135.00	450.00
83	PROFESSOR L5208	RT	205.00	750.00
83	SAY CHEESE L5195	RT	170.00	375.00-435.00
83	SCHOOL MARM L5209	RT	205.00	825.00
83	SHARPENING THE CUTLERY L5204	RT	210.00	1000.00
84	ARTISTIC ENDEAVOR L5234	RT	225.00	400.00
84	WINE TASTER L5239	OP	190.00	300.00
85	CONCERT VIOLINIST L5330	RT	220.00	450.00
85	THE TAILOR L5326	RT	335.00	800.00
86	THE POET L5397	RT	425.00	750.00
87	MIDWIFE L5431	RT	175.00	400.00

RELIGIOUS FIGURINES

YR	NAME	LIMIT	ISSUE	QUOTE
*	BLESSED LADY LL1579	SO	*	1500.00
*	CHOIR LESSON L4973	RT	*	850.00
*	CHOIR LESSON L4973	RT	*	*
71	KING BALTASAR L1018M	OP	345.00	1600.00
71	KING BALTASAR L1020	OP	345.00	1795.00
71	KING GASPAR L1018	OP	345.00	1795.00
71	KING GASPAR L1020M	OP	345.00	1600.00
71	KING MELCHOR L1019	OP	345.00	1795.00
71	KING MELCHOR L1019M	OP	345.00	1600.00
71	NUNS L4611	OP	37.50	130.00
73	EVE AT TREE LL2029	RT	450.00	3000.00
73	MADONNA AND CHILD LL2043	RT	400.00	1500.00
73	MADONNA WITH CHILD LL2018	RT	450.00	1650.00
78	NUNS L2075	OP	90.00	195.00
80	HOLY MARY, NUMBERED L1394	OP	1000.00	1400.00
82	BABY JESUS L1388	OP	85.00	120.00
82	COW L1390	OP	95.00	155.00
82	DONKEY L1389	OP	95.00	155.00
82	MARY L1387	OP	240.00	325.00
82	ST. JOSEPH L1387	OP	250.00	335.00
83	JESUS IN TIBERIAS LL3557	1200	2600.00	4300.00
83	JESUS L5167	OP	130.00	225.00
83	KING BALTASAR L1425	OP	315.00	500.00
83	KING GASPAR L1424	OP	265.00	400.00
83	KING MELCHOR L1423	OP	225.00	380.00

YR	NAME	LIMIT	ISSUE	QUOTE
83	MADONNA WITH FLOWERS L5171	OP	172.50	260.00
83	MONKS AT PRAYER L5155	OP	130.00	215.00
83	MOSES L5170	OP	175.00	300.00
84	FRIAR JUNIPER L2138	OP	160.00	250.00
84	MONK L2060	OP	60.00	100.00
84	MYSTICAL JOSEPH L2135	RT	427.50	550.00
84	ST. CRISTOBAL L5246	RT	265.00	450.00
84	ST. MICHAEL LL3515	1500	2200.00	4100.00
84	ST. THERESA LL2061	RT	775.00	1800.00
85	NATIVITY SCENE, HAUTE RELIEF L5281	RT	210.00	450.00
86	BLESSED FAMILY L1499	OP	200.00	300.00
86	CONSIDERATION L5355	RT	100.00	250.00
86	SEWING CIRCLE L5360	RT	600.00	1000.00
86	ST. VINCENT L5387	RT	190.00	300.00-520.00
87	BALTASAR L1516	RT	275.00	475.00
87	GASPAR'S PAGE L1514	RT	275.00	500
87	MELCHOR L1515	RT	290.00	360.00
87	SAINT NICHOLAS L5427	OP	425.00	590.00
89	JESUS THE ROCK LL1615	1000	1175.00	1450.00
89	PIOUS LL5541	SO	1075.00	1200.00
*				**SCULPTURES**
*	CELLIST LL3018	300	*	830.00
*	CLASSIC BEAUTY LL3012	500	*	1650.00
*	DEMURENESS LL3020	300	*	525.00
*	DIGNITY LL3015	150	*	1800.00
*	MUSE LL3017	300	*	830.00
*	PASSION LL3016	750	*	1050.00
*	THE NYMPH LL3014	250	*	1350.00
*	TRUE AFFECTION LL3019	300	*	930.00
*	YOUTHFUL INNOCENCE LL3013	500	*	1650.00
90	AFTER THE BATH LL3023	SO	350.00	800.00-850.00
90	DAYDREAMING LL3022	500	550.00	730.00
90	DISCOVERIES LL3024	100	1500.00	1850.00
91	RESTING NUDE LL3025	200	650.00	650.00
91	UNADORNED BEAUTY LL3026	200	1700.00	1750.00
93	FLIGHT OF FANCY	300	1400.00	1500
93	THE AWAKENING	300	1200.00	1300.00
94	DANAE	300	2880.00	3000.00
94	EBONY	300	1295.00	1400.00
94	MODESTY	300	1295.00	1400.00
*			**SPORTS FIGURINES**	
72	FEMALE EQUESTRIAN L4516	OP	170.00	600.00
73	LADY GOLFER L4851	OP	70.00	220.00
73	MALE GOLFER L4824	OP	66.00	260.00
74	SOCCER PLAYER LL1266	RT	2000.00	7500.00
83	FEMALE TENNIS PLAYER L1427	RT	200.00	475.00
83	MALE SOCCER PLAYER L5200	RT	155.00	600.00
83	MALE TENNIS PLAYER L1426	RT	200.00	425.00
84	GOLFING COUPLE L1453	OP	248.00	425.00
84	TORCH BEARER L5251	RT	100.00	500.00
85	BIKING IN THE COUNTRY L5272	RT	295.00	430.00
85	GENTLEMAN EQUESTRIAN L5329	RT	160.00	400.00
85	HIKER L5280	RT	195.00	400.00
85	LADY EQUESTRIAN L5328	RT	160.00	500.00
85	RACING MOTORCYCLIST L5270	RT	360.00	850.00
85	WAITING TO TEE OFF L5301	OP	145.00	240.00
*			**VALENCIAN FIGURINES**	
74	GIRL FROM VALENCIA L4841	OP	35.00	170.00
76	VALENCIAN LADY WITH FLOWERS L1304	OP	200.00	595.00
83	APPRECIATION L1396	OP	420.00	660.00
83	FULL OF MISCHIEF L1395	OP	420.00	660.00
83	MS. VALENCIA L1422	OP	175.00	290.00
83	REVERIE L1398	OP	490.00	770.00
83	SECOND THOUGHTS L1397	OP	490.00	660.00
83	VALENCIAN BOY L1400	RT	297.50	450.00
84	MAKING PAELLA L5254	OP	215.00	340.00
85	FESTIVAL IN VALENCIA LL1457	3000	1475.00	2250.00
85	VALENCIAN COUPLE ON HORSE LL1472	3000	1175.00	1450.00
86	CARMENCITA L5373	OP	120.00	165.00
86	FLORAL OFFERING LL1490	3000	2500.00	4250.00
86	LOLITA L5372	OP	120.00	165.00
86	PEPITA L5374	OP	120.00	165.00
86	TERESITA L5375	OP	120.00	165.00
86	VALENCIAN BOY L5395	OP	200.00	300.00
86	VALENCIAN CHILDREN L1489	OP	700.00	1000.00
87	VALENCIAN BOUQUET L1524	OP	250.00	450.00

YR	NAME	LIMIT	ISSUE	QUOTE
87	VALENCIAN COUPLE ON HORSEBACK L4648	RT	900.00	1200.00
87	VALENCIAN DREAMS L1525	OP	240.00	450.00
87	VALENCIAN FLOWERS L1526	OP	375.00	550.00
87	VALENCIAN GARDEN L1518	OP	1100.00	1650.00
*				**VARIOUS**
*	PLAYING CARDS L1327M, NUMBERED	OP	*	6400.00
78	BETH L1358G	OP	75.00	165.00
78	HEATHER L1359G	OP	75.00	165.00
78	JULIA L1361	OP	75.00	165.00
78	LAURA L1360G	OP	75.00	165.00
78	PHYLLIS L1356G	OP	75.00	165.00
78	SHELLEY L1357G	OP	75.00	165.00
*				**VEHICULAR FIGURINES**
71	ANTIQUE AUTO LL1146	RT	1000.00	7000.00
73	HANSOM CARRIAGE LL1225	RT	1250.00	10000.00
79	CAR IN TROUBLE LL1375	RT	3000.00	5500.00-8500.00
82	FIRST DATE LL1393	1500	3800.00	5600.00
83	SCOOTING L5143	RT	575.00	735.00
85	COACH XVIII CENTURY LL1485	500	14000.00	21000.00
87	A HAPPY ENCOUNTER LL1523	1500	2900.00	4700.00
87	A SUNDAY DRIVE LL1510	1000	2600.00	4950.00
87	THE LANDAU CARRIAGE L1521	OP	2500.00	3350.00
89	HER LADYSHIP, NUMBERED L5097	OP	5900.00	6700.00

MAFEKING COLLECTION

M. GREEN			**MAN'S BEST FRIEND**	
95	MICKEY'S EYES	75	295.00	300.00

MARK HOPKINS SCULPTURE

M. HOPKINS			**KID'S PLAY GALLERY**	
93	TIRE SWING, THE	550	650.00	650.00
M. HOPKINS			**KIDS PLAY GALLERY**	
93	FASTBREAK	950	315.00	315.00
M. HOPKINS			**NAUTICAL & SEA LIFE GALLERY**	
93	FAIR WIND	RT	550.00	600.00
93	HEAVY WEATHER AHEAD	SU	500.00	500.00
93	TAKING A SIGHT	SU	450.00	450.00
M. HOPKINS			**NOBLESSENCE GALLERY**	
93	AMONG THE ASPEN	550	1125.00	1125.00
93	BREAK OUT	250	1250.00	1250.00
93	BROKEN TREATY	450	975.00	975.00
93	EAGLE DANCE	750	700.00	700.00
93	GOLDEN EAGLE	RT	975.00	1050.00
93	MOUNTAIN OVERLOOK	550	975.00	975.00
93	PHANTOMS OF THE FOREST	SU	685.00	685.00
93	SOARING	450	975.00	975.00
93	SONS & BROTHERS	250	1250.00	1250.00
94	ANCIENT OF DAYS	750	1250.00	1250.00
94	BATTLE WORN	250	975.00	975.00
94	CATCH OF THE DAY	550	1150.00	1150.00
94	CRY OF FREEDOM	450	1100.00	1100.00
94	EARTH MOTHER	750	1250.00	1250.00
94	GATHERING WISDOM	450	875.00	875.00
94	GENERATIONS OF TIME	750	1250.00	1250.00
94	GUARDIAN OF THE PLAINS	750	975.00	975.00
94	I HAVE SEEN TOMORROW	450	1000.00	1000.00
94	LICK AND A PROMISE, A	750	850.00	850.00
94	MATERNAL PRIDE	750	975.00	975.00
94	MOTHER'S NATURE	SU	685.00	685.00
94	NIGHT HUNTER	750	875.00	875.00
94	PEACE NO MORE	450	950.00	950.00
94	POUNCING LYNX	750	650.00	650.00
94	VISION QUEST	250	1500.00	1500.00
M. HOPKINS			**SPORTS & WILDLIFE GALLERY**	
93	FISHING HOLE	450	650.00	650.00
93	I CAN'T LOOK	950	325.00	325.00
93	NOT AGAIN	950	325.00	325.00
93	TEACHING THE WAY	450	750.00	750.00
94	FOREVER FREE	950	625.00	625.00
M. HOPKINS			**SPORTS AND WILDLIFE GALLERY**	
93	DOWNRIVER RUN	450	950.00	950.00
M. HOPKINS			**THE ARTS GALLERY**	
93	JAZZ BASS	750	550.00	550.00
93	JAZZ DRUMS	750	850.00	850.00
M. HOPKINS			**THE MARK HOPKINS STUDIO**	
94	BORN TO FLY	450	925.00	925.00
94	LURED AWAY	950	750.00	750.00

YR	NAME	LIMIT	ISSUE	QUOTE
93	CHASE, THE	950	695.00	695.00
93	SPOOKED	950	975.00	975.00
93	TURNING POINT	950	695.00	695.00
94	ALPHA WOLF	950	225.00	225.00
94	FACES IN THE DEEP	950	600.00	600.00
94	FIRST STRIKE	950	775.00	775.00
94	HONEY	950	225.00	225.00
94	OCEAN MONARCHS	950	575.00	575.00
94	PROTECTING THE INNOCENT	950	550.00	550.00
94	RACE TO THE FLY	950	675.00	675.00
94	RETURN TO THE SKIES	950	225.00	225.00
94	RISE TO THE CHALLENGE	950	225.00	225.00

MARURI USA

W. GAITHER — **AFRICAN SAFARI ANIMALS**

YR	NAME	LIMIT	ISSUE	QUOTE
81	MYALA	300	1450.00	1450.00
83	AFRICAN ELEPHANT	150	3500.00	3500.00
83	BLACK MANED LION	300	1450.00	1450.00
83	CAPE BUFFALO	300	2200.00	2200.00
83	GRANT'S ZEBRAS, PAIR	500	1200.00	1200.00
83	SABLE	500	1200.00	1200.00
83	SOUTHERN GREATER KUDU	300	1800.00	1800.00
83	SOUTHERN IMPALA	300	1200.00	1200.00
83	SOUTHERN LEOPARD	300	1450.00	1450.00
83	SOUTHERN WHITE RHINO	150	3200.00	3200.00

* **AMERICAN EAGLE GALLERY**

YR	NAME	LIMIT	ISSUE	QUOTE
85	E-8501	CL	45.00	45.00
85	E-8502	OP	55.00	65.00
85	E-8503	OP	60.00	60.00
85	E-8504	OP	65.00	75.00
85	E-8505	CL	65.00	65.00
85	E-8506	OP	75.00	90.00
85	E-8507	OP	75.00	90.00
85	E-8508	CL	75.00	75.00
85	E-8509	CL	85.00	85.00
85	E-8510	OP	85.00	85.00
85	E-8511	CL	85.00	85.00
85	E-8512	OP	147.50	147.50
87	E-8521	CL	40.00	50.00
87	E-8522	OP	45.00	50.00
87	E-8523	CL	55.00	55.00
87	E-8524	OP	175.00	195.00
89	E-8931	OP	55.00	60.00
89	E-8932	OP	75.00	80.00
89	E-8933	OP	95.00	95.00
89	E-8934	OP	135.00	135.00
89	E-8935	OP	175.00	185.00
89	E-8936	OP	185.00	195.00
91	E-9141 EAGLE LANDING	OP	60.00	60.00
91	E-9142 EAGLE W/TOTEM POLE	OP	75.00	75.00
91	E-9143 PAIR IN FLIGHT	OP	95.00	95.00
91	E-9144 EAGLE W/SALMON	OP	110.00	110.00
91	E-9145 EAGLE W/SNOW	OP	135.00	135.00
91	E-9146 EAGLE W/BABIES	OP	145.00	145.00

W. GAITHER — **AMERICANA**

81	GRIZZLY BEAR AND INDIAN	CL	650.00	650.00
82	SIOUX BRAVE AND BISON	300	985.00	985.00

W. GAITHER — **BABY ANIMALS**

81	AFRICAN LION CUBS	1500	195.00	195.00
81	BLACK BEAR CUBS	1500	195.00	195.00
81	MOURNING DOVES	350	780.00	780.00
81	WOLF CUBS	1500	195.00	195.00

W. GAITHER — **BIRDS OF PREY**

81	AMERICAN BALD EAGLE I	CL	165.00	1150.00
81	SCREECH OWL	300	960.00	960.00
82	AMERICAN BALD EAGLE II	CL	245.00	850.00
83	AMERICAN BALD EAGLE III	CL	445.00	445.00
84	AMERICAN BALD EAGLE IV	CL	360.00	360.00
86	AMERICAN BALD EAGLE V	CL	325.00	325.00

* **EYES OF THE NIGHT**

90	DOUBLE BARN OWL O-8807	OP	125.00	125.00
90	DOUBLE SNOWY OWL O-8809	OP	245.00	245.00
90	SINGLE GREAT HORNED OWL O-8803	OP	60.00	60.00
90	SINGLE GREAT HORNED OWL O-8808	OP	145.00	145.00
90	SINGLE SCREECH OWL O-8801	OP	50.00	50.00
90	SINGLE SCREECH OWL O-8806	OP	90.00	90.00
90	SINGLE SNOWY OWL O-8802	OP	50.00	50.00

YR	NAME	LIMIT	ISSUE	QUOTE
90	SINGLE SNOWY OWL O-8805	OP	80.00	80.00
90	SINGLE TAWNY OWL O-8804	OP	60.00	60.00
*			**GRACEFUL REFLECTIONS**	
91	MUTE SWAN WITH BABY SW-9152	OP	95.00	95.00
91	PAIR-MUTE SWAN SW-9153	OP	145.00	145.00
91	PAIR-MUTE SWAN SW-9154	OP	195.00	195.00
91	SINGLE MUTE SWAN SW-9151	OP	85.00	85.00
*			**HUMMINGBIRDS**	
91	ALLEW'S WITH HIBISCUS H-8906	OP	195.00	195.00
91	ANNA'S W/LILY H-8905	OP	160.00	160.00
91	RUBY-THROATED W/AZALEA H-8911	OP	75.00	75.00
91	RUBY-THROATED W/ORCHID H-8901	OP	150.00	150.00
91	RUFOUS WITH TRUMPET CREEPER H-8901	OP	70.00	70.00
91	VIOLET-CROWNED W/GENTIAN H-8913	OP	75.00	75.00
91	WHITE-EARED W/MORNING GLORY H-8912	OP	75.00	75.00
ITO		**LEGENDARY FLOWERS OF THE ORIENT**		
85	CHERRY BLOSSOM	15,000	45.00	55.00
85	CHINESE PEONY	15,000	45.00	55.00
85	CHRYSANTHEMUM	15,000	45.00	55.00
85	IRIS	15,000	45.00	55.00
85	LILY	15,000	45.00	55.00
85	LOTUS	15,000	45.00	45.00
85	ORCHID	15,000	45.00	55.00
85	WISTERIA	15,000	45.00	55.00
*		**MAJESTIC OWLS OF THE NIGHT**		
87	BURROWING OWL	15,000	55.00	55.00
88	BARRED OWL	15,000	55.00	55.00
88	ELF OWL	15,000	55.00	55.00
* *		**MARURI STUDIOS**		
93	WILD WINGS	3500	395.00	395.00
94	WALTZ OF THE DOLPHINS	3500	300.00	300.00
W. GAITHER		**NORTH AMERICAN GAME ANIMALS**		
84	WHITE TAIL DEER	950	285.00	285.00
W. GAITHER		**NORTH AMERICAN GAME BIRDS**		
81	CANADIAN GEESE, PAIR	CL	2000.00	2000.00
81	EASTERN WILD TURKEY	CL	300.00	300.00
82	RUFFED GROUSE	200	1745.00	1745.00
83	BOBTAIL QUAIL, FEMALE	CL	375.00	375.00
83	BOBTAIL QUAIL, MALE	CL	375.00	375.00
83	WILD TURKEY HEN WITH CHICKS	CL	300.00	300.00
W. GAITHER		**NORTH AMERICAN SONGBIRDS**		
82	BLUEBIRD	CL	95.00	95.00
82	CARDINAL, MALE	CL	95.00	95.00
82	CAROLINA WREN	CL	95.00	95.00
82	CHICKADEE	CL	95.00	95.00
82	MOCKINGBIRD	CL	95.00	95.00
83	CARDINAL, FEMALE	CL	95.00	95.00
83	ROBIN	CL	95.00	95.00
W. GAITHER		**NORTH AMERICAN WATERFOWL I**		
81	BLUE WINGED TEAL	200	980.00	980.00
81	CANVASBACK DUCKS	300	780.00	780.00
81	FLYING WOOD DUCKS	CL	880.00	880.00
81	MALLARD DUCKS	CL	2380.00	2380.00
81	WOOD DUCK, DECOY	950	480.00	480.00
W. GAITHER		**NORTH AMERICAN WATERFOWL II**		
81	MALLARD DUCKS, PAIR	1500	225.00	225.00
82	BUFFLEHEAD DUCKS, PAIR	1500	225.00	225.00
82	GOLDENEYE DUCKS, PAIR	1500	225.00	225.00
82	PINTAIL DUCKS, PAIR	1500	225.00	225.00
82	WIDGEON, FEMALE	CL	225.00	225.00
82	WIDGEON, MALE	CL	225.00	225.00
83	LOON	CL	245.00	245.00
*		**POLAR EXPEDITION**		
90	BABY ARCTIC FOX P-9002	OP	50.00	50.00
90	BABY EMPEROR PENGUIN P-9001	OP	45.00	45.00
90	BABY HARP SEALS P-9005	OP	65.00	65.00
90	MOTHER & BABY EMPEROR PENGUINS P-9006	OP	80.00	80.00
90	MOTHER & BABY HARP SEALS P-9007	OP	90.00	90.00
90	MOTHER & BABY POLAR SEALS P-9008	OP	125.00	125.00
90	POLAR BEAR CUB P-9003	OP	50.00	50.00
90	POLAR BEAR CUBS P-9004	OP	60.00	60.00
90	POLAR EXPEDITION SIGN P-9009	OP	18.00	18.00
92	ARCTIC FOX CUBS PLAYING P-9223	OP	65.00	65.00
92	BABY HARP SEAL P-221	OP	55.00	55.00
92	EMPEROR PENUINS P-9222	OP	60.00	60.00
92	POLAR BEAR FAMILY P-9224	OP	90.00	90.00

YR	NAME	LIMIT	ISSUE	QUOTE
*			**PRECIOUS PANDA**	
92	LAZY LUNCH PP-9202	OP	60.00	60.00
92	MOTHER'S CUDDLE PP-9204	OP	120.00	120.00
92	SNACK TIME PP-9201	OP	60.00	60.00
92	TUG OF WAR PP-9203	OP	70.00	70.00
W. GAITHER			**SIGNATURE COLLECTION**	
85	AMERICAN BALD EAGLE	CL	60.00	60.00
85	CANADA GOOSE	CL	60.00	60.00
85	HAWK	CL	60.00	60.00
85	PINTAIL DUCK	CL	60.00	60.00
85	SNOW GOOSE	CL	60.00	60.00
85	SWALLOW	CL	60.00	60.00
*			**SONGBIRDS OF BEAUTY**	
91	BLUEBIRD WITH APPLE BLOSSOM SB-9105	OP	85.00	85.00
91	CARDINAL WITH CHERRY BLOSSOM SB-9103	OP	85.00	85.00
91	CHICKADEE WITH ROSES SB-9101	OP	85.00	85.00
91	DOUBLE BLUEBIRD W/PEACH BLOSSOM SB-9107	OP	145.00	145.00
91	DOUBLE CARDINAL WITH DOGWOOD SB-9108	OP	145.00	145.00
91	GOLDFINCH WITH HAWTHORNE SB-9102	OP	85.00	85.00
91	ROBIN & BABY WITH AZALEA SB-9106	OP	115.00	115.00
91	ROBIN WITH LILLIES SB-9104	OP	85.00	85.00
W. GAITHER			**SPECIAL COMMISSIONS**	
81	WHITE BENGAL TIGER	240	340.00	340.00
82	CHEETAH	200	995.00	995.00
83	ORANGE BENGAL TIGER	240	340.00	340.00
*			**STUDIO COLLECTION**	
90	MAJESTIC EAGLES MS-100	CL	350.00	350.00
91	DELICATE MOTION MS-200	3500	325.00	325.00
92	IMPERIAL PANDA MS-300	3500	350.00	350.00
W. GAITHER			**STUMP ANIMALS**	
82	RED FOX	1200	175.00	175.00
83	OWL	1200	175.00	175.00
83	RACCOON	· CL	175.00	175.00
84	BOBCAT	CL	175.00	175.00
84	CHIPMUNK	1200	175.00	175.00
84	GRAY SQUIRREL	1200	175.00	175.00
84	PELICAN	CL	260.00	260.00
84	SAND PIPER	CL	260.00	260.00
*			**WINGS OF LOVE DOVES**	
87	D-8701 SINGLE DOVE	OP	45.00	55.00
87	D-8702 DOUBLE DOVE	OP	55.00	65.00
87	D-8703 SINGLE DOVE	OP	65.00	65.00
87	D-8704 DOUBLE DOVE	OP	75.00	85.00
87	D-8705 SINGLE DOVE	OP	95.00	95.00
87	D-8706 DOUBLE DOVE	OP	175.00	175.00
90	D-9021 DOUBLE DOVE	OP	50.00	55.00
90	D-9022 DOUBLE DOVE	OP	75.00	75.00
90	D-9023 DOUBLE DOVE	OP	115.00	115.00
90	D-9024 DOUBLE DOVE	OP	150.00	150.00

MIDWEST OF CANNON FALLS

L.R. SMITH				
93	DANCING SANTA	1044	170.00	170.00
93	FOLK ANGEL	2095	145.00	145.00
93	GNOME SANTA RIDING WHITE DEER	1463	270.00	270.00
93	SANTA FISHERMAN	1748	250.00	250.00
93	VOYAGEUR	788	170.00	170.00
94	GIFT GIVER SANTA	1500	180.00	180.00
94	OLD WORLD SANTA	1500	75.00	75.00
94	SANTA SKIER	1500	190.00	190.00
94	STAR OF THE ROUNDUP COWBOY	1500	100.00	100.00
94	WEATHERWISE ANGEL	1500	150.00	150.00
95	ANGEL WITH LION & LAMB FIGURE	1500	125.00	125.00
95	MAIZE MAIDEN ANGEL FIGURE	2500	45.00	45.00
95	ORCHARD SANTA	1500	125.00	125.00
95	OWL LADY FIGURE	1000	105.00	105.00
95	SANTA IN SLEIGH FIGURE	1500	125.00	125.00
95	SUNBRINGER SANTA	1500	125.00	125.00
95	WEE WILLIE SANTA	2500	50.00	50.00
C. ULBRICHT			**A CHRISTMAS CAROL**	
93	BOB CRATCHIT AND TINY TIM NUTCRACKER	6000	240.00	240.00
93	EBENEZER SCROOGE NUTCRACKER	6000	210.00	210.00
94	GHOST OF CHRISTMAS PRESENT NUTCRACKER	5000	190.00	190.00
C. ULBRICHT			**AMERICAN FOLK HERO**	
94	DAVY CROCKETT NUTCRACKER	2500	185.00	185.00
94	JOHNNY APPLESEED NUTCRACKER	2500	196.00	196.00
95	PAUL BUNYAN NUTCRACKER	2500	192.00	192.00

YR	NAME	LIMIT	ISSUE	QUOTE
			ORE MOUNTAIN -	A CHRISTMAS CAROL
93	BOB CRATCHIT WITH TINY TIM NUTCRACKER	5000	120.00	120.00
93	GHOST OF CHRISTMAS PRESENT NUTCRACKER	5000	116.00	116.00
93	SCROOGE NUTCRACKER	5000	104.00	105.00
94	GHOST OF CHRISTMAS FUTURE NUTCRACKER	4000	116.00	116.00
94	GHOST OF CHRISTMAS PAST NUTCRACKER	4000	116.00	116.00
94	MARLEY'S GHOST NUTCRACKER	4000	116.00	116.00
			ORE MOUNTAIN -	NUTCRACKER SUITE
93	THE MOUSE KING NUTCRACKER	5000	110.00	110.00
94	NUTCRACKER PRINCE NUTCRACKER	5000	104.00	104.00
			ORE MOUNTAIN -	NUTCRAKER SUITE
94	HERR DROSSELMEYER NUTCRACKER	5000	110.00	110.00
C. ULBRICHT				**SANTA SERIES**
93	MR. SANTA CLAUS NUTCRACKER	5000	180.00	180.00
93	MRS. CLAUS NUTCRACKER	5000	180.00	180.00
93	TOYMAKER NUTCRACKER	2500	220.00	200.00
94	VICTORIAN SANTA NUTCRACKER	2500	220.00	220.00
95	KING OF CHRISTMAS NUTCRACKER	2500	240.00	240.00

MILL POND PRESS
R. BATEMAN

YR	NAME	LIMIT	ISSUE	QUOTE
			BATEMAN SCULPTURES	
82	RED-TAILED HAWK STUDY	250	950.00	1750.00
83	MERGANSER DUCKLING	250	695.00	695.00
84	PEREGRINE IN FLIGHT	90	850.00	1500.00

MISS MARTHA ORIGINALS
M. HOLCOMBE

YR	NAME	LIMIT	ISSUE	QUOTE
			ALL GOD'S CHILDREN	
85	ABE 1357	RT	24.95	675.00
85	BOOKER T 1320	RT	18.95	715.00-2000.00
85	CALLIE, 2 1/4 IN. 1362	RT	12.00	150.00-175.00
85	CALLIE, 4 1/2 IN. 1361	RT	18.95	225.00-250.00
85	EMMA 1322	RT	26.95	1300.00
85	TOM 1353	RT	15.95	225.00
86	ANNIE MAE, 6 IN. 1311	RT	18.95	80.00
86	ANNIE MAE, 8 1/2 IN. 1310	RT	26.95	150.00
86	GRANDMA 1323	RT	29.95	2250.00-3000.00
86	LI'L EMMIE, 3 1/2 IN. 1345	RT	12.99	33.00
86	LI'L EMMIE, 4 1/4 IN. 1344	RT	15.99	35.00-45.00
86	SELINA JANE (6 STRANDS) 1338	RT	21.95	150.00
86	SELINA JANE (9 STRANDS) 1338	RT	21.95	100.00-250.00
86	TOBY, 3 1/2 IN. 1332	RT	12.99	40.00
86	TOBY, 4 1/2 IN. 1331	RT	15.99	50.00-70.00
86	UNCLE BUD, 6 IN. 1304	RT	18.95	80.00
86	UNCLE BUD, 8 1/2 IN. 1303	RT	26.95	160.00
87	AUNT SARAH IN BLUE 1440	RT	45.00	110.00
87	AUNT SARAH IN RED 1440	RT	45.00	200.00-400.00
87	BECKY WITH PATCH 1402	RT	18.95	115.00-150.00
87	BEN 1504	RT	21.95	150.00-175.00
87	BLOSSOM IN BLUE 1500	RT	59.95	100.00-150.00
87	BLOSSOM IN RED 1500	RT	59.95	120.00-180.00
87	CASSIE 1503	RT	21.95	45.00-80.00
87	GINNIE 1508	RT	22.00	200.00-250.00
87	JESSIE-NO BASE 1501	RT	18.95	195.00-450.00
87	PRIMAS JONES 1377	RT	39.95	455.00
87	PRIMAS JONES W/BASE	RT	39.95	455.00-650.00
87	PRISSY W/BASKET 1346	RT	16.00	40.00-80.00
87	PRISSY W/YARN HAIR (6 STRANDS) 1343	RT	18.95	90.00
87	PUD 1550	RT	10.00	800.00-1000.00
87	WILLIE-NO BASE 1406	RT	18.95	256.00
88	BETSY (CLEAR WATER) 1513	RT	36.00	100.00-175.00
88	BOONE 1510	RT	16.00	75.00
88	CALVIN 777	RT	200.00	943.00-1820.00
88	JOHN 1514	RT	30.00	55.00-100.00
88	LISA 1512	RT	30.00	75.00
88	MEG (LONG HAIR) 1505	RT	21.00	325.00
88	MEG (SHORT HAIR) 1505	RT	21.00	275.00-325.00
88	MEG IN BEIGE DRESS 1505	RT	21.00	500.00-800.00
88	PEANUT 1509	RT	16.00	46.00-100.00
88	SALLY 1507	RT	18.95	50.00-100.00
88	TANSY & TEDDY W/GREEN SOCKS 1516	RT	30.00	125.00
89	BEAN (CLEAR WATER) 1521	RT	36.00	90.00-150.00
89	BEVERLY 1525	RT	50.00	300.00
89	JESSICA & JEREMY 1522-23	RT	195.00	1150.00-1398.00
90	THALIYAH 778	RT	150.00	1000.00
91	DORI IN GREEN DRESS 1544	RT	30.00	195.00-488.00
91	FATHER CHRISTMAS BLACK 1772	RT	195.00	275.00-500.00

Cape Buffalo *by artist F. Contreras is from wildlife art producer Creart.*

Wild American Bison, *created by F. Contreras, is produced by Creart.*

Legendary Native Americans Crazy Horse, Geronimo, Red Cloud, Sitting Bull, Cochise *and* Chief Joseph *comprise "The Great Chieftains" series by western artist Gregory Perillo. The line is produced by Artaffects.*

YR	NAME	LIMIT	ISSUE	QUOTE
M. HOLCOMBE				**CHRISTMAS**
86	SAINT NICHOLAS BLACK 1316	RT	29.95	90.00-130.00
86	SAINT NICHOLAS WHITE 1315	RT	29.95	75.00-100.00
87	FATHER CHRISTMAS BLACK 1751	RT	145.00	485.00
87	FATHER CHRISTMAS WHITE 1750	RT	145.00	410.00-430.00
88	FATHER CHRISTMAS BLACK 1758	RT	195.00	350.00-390.00
88	FATHER CHRISTMAS WHITE 1757	RT	195.00	365.00-440.00
88	SANTA CLAUS BLACK 1768	RT	185.00	330.00
88	SANTA CLAUS WHITE 1767	RT	185.00	330.00
89	FATHER CHRISTMAS BLACK 1770	RT	195.00	300.00-330.00
89	FATHER CHRISTMAS WHITE 1769	RT	195.00	300.00-468.00
91	FATHER CHRISTMAS WHITE 1771	RT	195.00	450.00-500.00
M. HOLCOMBE				**COLLECTOR'S CLUB**
89	MOLLY 1524	RT	38.00	260.00
90	JOEY 1539	RT	32.00	195.00
M. HOLCOMBE				**SUGAR AND SPICE**
87	BLESSED ARE THE PEACEMAKERS (ELI) 1403	RT	21.95	420.00
87	FRIENDS SHOW LOVE (BECKY) 1402	RT	21.95	420.00
87	FRIENDSHIP WARMS...HEART (JACOB) 1407	RT	21.95	420.00
87	GOD IS LOVE (ANGEL) 1401	RT	21.95	420.00
87	JESUS LOVES ME (AMY) 1405	RT	21.95	425.00
87	OLD FRIENDS ARE BEST (RACHEL) 1404	RT	21.95	425.00
87	SHARING WITH FRIENDS (WILLIE) 1406	RT	21.95	425.00

MUSEUM COLLECTIONS INC.

YR	NAME	LIMIT	ISSUE	QUOTE
N. ROCKWELL				**AMERICAN FAMILY I**
79	BABY'S FIRST STEP	22,500	90.00	220.00
80	BIRTHDAY PARTY	22,500	110.00	150.00
80	FIRST HAIRCUT	22,500	90.00	140.00
80	HAPPY BIRTHDAY, DEAR MOTHER	22,500	90.00	150.00
80	LITTLE MOTHER	22,500	110.00	110.00
80	SWEET SIXTEEN	22,500	90.00	90.00
80	WASHING OUR DOG	22,500	110.00	110.00
81	BRIDE AND GROOM	22,500	110.00	180.00
81	MOTHER'S LITTLE HELPERS	22,500	110.00	110.00
N. ROCKWELL				**CHRISTMAS**
80	CHECKING HIS LIST	YR	65.00	85.00
81	RINGING IN GOOD CHEER	YR	95.00	95.00
82	WAITING FOR SANTA	YR	95.00	95.00
83	HIGH HOPES	YR	95.00	95.00
84	SPACE-AGE SANTA	YR	65.00	65.00
N. ROCKWELL				**CLASSIC**
80	BEDTIME	OP	65.00	95.00
80	FOR A GOOD BOY	OP	65.00	75.00
80	LIGHTHOUSE KEEPERS'S DAUGHTER	OP	65.00	65.00
80	MEMORIES	OP	65.00	65.00
80	THE COBBLER	OP	65.00	85.00
80	THE TOYMAKER	OP	65.00	85.00
81	A DOLLHOUSE FOR SIS	OP	65.00	65.00
81	MUSIC MASTER	OP	65.00	65.00
81	OFF TO SCHOOL	OP	65.00	65.00
81	PUPPY LOVE	OP	65.00	65.00
81	THE MUSIC LESSON	OP	65.00	65.00
81	WHILE THE AUDIENCE WAITS	OP	65.00	65.00
82	DREAMS IN THE ANTIQUE SHOP	OP	65.00	65.00
82	SPRING FEVER	OP	65.00	65.00
82	THE COUNTRY DOCTOR	OP	65.00	65.00
82	THE KITE MAKER	OP	65.00	65.00
82	WORDS OF WISDOM	OP	65.00	65.00
83	A FINAL TOUCH	OP	65.00	65.00
83	A SPECIAL TREAT	OP	65.00	65.00
83	BORED OF EDUCATION	OP	65.00	65.00
83	BRAVING THE STORM	OP	65.00	65.00
83	HIGH STEPPING	OP	65.00	65.00
83	WINTER FUN	OP	65.00	65.00
84	ALL WRAPPED UP	OP	65.00	65.00
84	GOIN' FISHIN'	OP	65.00	65.00
84	SATURDAY'S HERO	OP	65.00	65.00
84	THE BIG RACE	OP	65.00	65.00
N. ROCKWELL				**COMMEMORATIVE**
81	NORMAN ROCKWELL DISPLAY	5000	125.00	150.00
82	SPIRIT OF AMERICA	5000	125.00	125.00
83	NORMAN ROCKWELL, AMERICA'S ARTIST	5000	125.00	125.00
84	OUTWARD BOUND	5000	125.00	125.00
85	ANOTHER MASTERPIECE BY NORMAN ROCKWELL	5000	125.00	150.00
86	THE PAINTER AND THE PUPS	5000	125.00	150.00

YR NAME	LIMIT	ISSUE	QUOTE
OLZEWSKI STUDIOS			
R. OLSZEWSKI			**MINIATURES**
94 THE GRAND ENTRANCE	1500	225.00	300.00
94 THE LITTLE TINKER	750	235.00	400.00
94 THE TINKER'S TREASURE CHEST & TO BE...	CL	235.00	350.00
PACIFIC RIM			
			BUNNY TOES
94 MAZIE AT PLAY	OP	13.00	13.00
94 TILLIE MAKING A WREATH	OP	13.00	13.00
94 TIMOTHY WITH FLOWER CART	OP	17.00	17.00
94 TIMOTHY WITH TULIPS	OP	13.00	13.00
94 WENDELL AT THE MAILBOX	OP	17.00	17.00
94 WENDELL WITH EGGS IN HAT	OP	13.00	13.00
94 WILLIS & SKEETER	OP	17.00	17.00
94 WINIFRED WITH BLOOMS	OP	13.00	13.00
95 BUNNY GAZEBO	OP	50.00	50.00
95 GARDEN TRELLIS	OP	30.00	30.00
95 HANNAH WITH MAXIMILIAN	OP	13.00	13.00
95 TILLIE WITH HER BIKE	OP	15.00	15.00
95 TIMOTHY WITH EGGS	OP	13.00	13.00
95 WENDELL WITH FLOWERS	OP	13.00	13.00
95 WILLIS & SKEETER GARDENING	OP	15.00	15.00
95 WINIFRED PAINTS EGGS	OP	15.00	15.00
95 BUNNY TOES LOGO SIGN	OP	20.00	20.00
P. SEBERN		**BUNNY TOES BIRTHDAY BUNNIES**	
95 ANABELL GLIDING ALONG	OP	20.00	20.00
95 BETH BACK TO SCHOOL	OP	20.00	20.00
95 CALLIE BUNDLE UP	OP	20.00	20.00
95 CARLY STRIKING A POSE	OP	20.00	20.00
95 CHARLOTTE BEST OF THE BUNCH	OP	20.00	20.00
95 CHESTER SHARING WITH FRIENDS	OP	20.00	20.00
95 CHRISTOPHER & CORY THE BEST SHOT	OP	20.00	20.00
95 DINAH IRRESISTIBLE	OP	20.00	20.00
95 DOUGLAS FROSTY FRIENDS	OP	20.00	20.00
95 GOLDIE TAKING TURNS	OP	20.00	20.00
95 HARVEY GIDDY-UP AND GO	OP	20.00	20.00
95 JEREMY CLEAR SAILING	OP	20.00	20.00
95 JOEY AUTUMN CHORES	OP	20.00	20.00
95 MAGGIE JOY OF LIVING	OP	20.00	20.00
95 MOLLY SWEET WISHES	OP	20.00	20.00
95 NICHOLAS BETWEEN TIDES	OP	20.00	20.00
95 PENELOPE WISHFUL THINKING	OP	20.00	20.00
95 PHOEBE FIRST OUTING	OP	20.00	20.00
95 PIETER HIGHER EDUCATION	OP	20.00	20.00
95 RUSSEL & ROBBY SHARING THE HARVEST	OP	20.00	20.00
95 VIOLET THANK YOU NOTES	OP	20.00	20.00
95 WILBUR LAZY DAZE	OP	20.00	20.00
95 WILEY WINTER GAMES	OP	20.00	20.00
95 ZACHARY WAITIN' ON THE WIND	OP	20.00	20.00
PANTON/KRYSTONIA			
			WORLD OF KRYSTONIA
93 ALL MINE	OP	40.00	45.00
93 ESCUBLAR	7500	170.00	185.00
93 GILBRAN OF WENLOCK	15,000	65.00	75.00
93 HAGGA-BEAST	7500	125.00	150.00
93 HIS SECRET	15,000	60.00	70.00
93 HULBERT	OP	38.00	45.00
93 MUFFLER	OP	24.00	28.00
93 OOPS	OP	38.00	43.00
93 POMPON	OP	24.00	28.00
93 SHEPF	OP	23.00	28.00
93 STOOPE	OP	23.00	28.00
93 TAG THE TROLL	OP	48.00	53.00
94 CHECKIN IT OUT	15,000	36.00	40.00
94 ELDER PHYL	OP	20.00	22.00
94 IKSHAR	OP	46.00	50.00
94 LEARNING IS GWEAT	OP	48.00	52.00
94 OH SWEET DREAMS	OP	35.00	40.00
94 OKINAWATHE	7500	99.00	120.00
94 ONE UNHAAPFY RIDE	4500	125.00	140.00
94 PHYLONEOUS POOK	OP	20.00	22.00
94 POOKBALL	OP	20.00	22.00
94 SCHNOOGLES	OP	48.00	53.00
94 SPYKE	OP	20.00	25.00
94 WELCOME TO KRYSTONIA	15,000	60.00	65.00

YR	NAME	LIMIT	ISSUE	QUOTE
94	WODEMA	OP	23.00	23.00
95	A DEFINITE MAYBE	15,000	60.00	70.00
95	AH HAH!	OP	48.00	53.00
95	DELTA	OP	70.00	75.00
95	ENOUGH IS ENOUGH	2,999	250.00	280.00
95	POPOTOMPOTAN	OP	32.00	35.00
95	ROOT	15,000	85.00	95.00
95	STOOPE THE STUPENDOUS	15,000	65.00	70.00
95	TINCHACHUIK	7500	104.00	120.00
95	WHEY	OP	20.00	73.00
RT	BOLL	3000	52.00	57.00

PAPEL FREELANCE

	C. JOHNSON		LIFE'S ENDEARMENTS	
94	COACHING	OP	30.00	32.00
94	LEARNING TO SHARE	OP	25.00	27.00
94	MY FIRST FRIEND	OP	22.50	25.00
94	MY TEDDY TALKS	OP	25.00	27.00
94	PUPPY LOVE	OP	22.50	25.00
94	SISTERS	OP	30.00	32.00

PAVILION OF T'SANG YING-HSUAN

	S. FU	THE FORBIDDEN CITY MUSIC BOX COLLECTION		
91	THE EMPEROR'S WEDDING	84-DAY	39.50	45.00

PEMBERTON & OAKES

	D. ZOLAN		ZOLAN'S CHILDREN	
82	ERIK AND THE DANDELION	17,000	48.00	90.00
83	SABINA IN THE GRASS	6800	48.00	130.00
84	WINTER ANGEL	8000	28.00	150.00
85	TENDER MOMENT	10,000	29.00	60.00

POLLAND STUDIOS

	D. POLLAND		COLLECTIBLE BRONZES	
67	BULL SESSION	11	200.00	1200.00
69	BLOWIN' COLD	30	375.00	1250.00
69	BUFFALO HUNT	30	450.00	1250.00
69	COMANCHERO	30	350.00	750.00
69	DANCING INDIAN WITH LANCE	50	250.00	775.00
69	DANCING INDIAN WITH TOMAHAWK	50	250.00	775.00
69	DANCING MEDICINE MAN	50	250.00	775.00
69	DRAWN SABERS	50	2000.00	5650.00
69	LOOKOUTS	30	375.00	1300.00
69	THE BREED	30	350.00	975.00
69	TOP MONEY	30	275.00	800.00
69	TRAIL HAZZARD	30	700.00	1750.00
69	WAR CRY	30	350.00	975.00
69	WHEN ENEMIES MEET	30	700.00	2350.00
70	COFFEE TIME	50	1200.00	2900.00
70	THE LOST DISPATCH	50	1200.00	2950.00
70	WANTED	50	500.00	1150.00
71	AMBUSH AT ROCK CANYON	5	20000.00	45000.00
71	OH SUGAR!	40	700.00	1525.00
71	SHAKIN' OUT A LOOP	40	500.00	1075.00
72	BUFFALO ROBE	50	1000.00	2350.00
73	BUNCH QUITTER	60	750.00	1975.00
73	CHALLENGE	60	750.00	1800.00
73	TRACKING	60	500.00	1500.00
73	WAR PARTY	60	1500.00	5500.00
75	CHEYENNE	6	1300.00	1800.00
75	COUNTING COUP	6	1450.00	1950.00
75	CROW SCOUT	6	1300.00	1800.00
76	BUFFALO HUNT	6	2200.00	3500.00
76	MANDAN HUNTER	12	775.00	775.00
76	MONDAY MORNING WASH	6	2800.00	2800.00
76	PAINTING THE TOWN	6	3000.00	4200.00
76	RESCUE	6	2400.00	3000.00
80	BUFFALO PRAYER	25	375.00	675.00
	D. POLLAND		COLLECTOR SOCIETY	
87	I COME IN PEACE	CL	35.00	165.00-300.00
87	I COME IN PEACE, SILENT TRAIL (SET)	CL	335.00	850.00-1200.00
87	SILENT TRAIL	CL	300.00	750.00
88	DISPUTED TRAIL	CL	300.00	500.00
88	THE HUNTER	CL	35.00	250.00
88	THE HUNTER, DISPUTED TRAIL (SET)	CL	335.00	750.00-900.00
89	APACHE BIRDMAN	CL	300.00	450.00
89	CRAZY HORSE	CL	35.00	150.00
89	CRAZY HORSE, APACHE BIRDMAN (SET)	CL	335.00	700.00

YR	NAME	LIMIT	ISSUE	QUOTE
90	BUFFALO PONY	CL	300.00	350.00
90	CHIEF PONTIAC	CL	35.00	125.00
90	CHIEF PONTIAC, BUFFALO PONY (SET)	CL	335.00	625.00
91	THE SIGNAL	YR	350.00	350.00
91	WAR DANCER	YR	35.00	35.00
91	WAR DANCER & THE SIGNAL (SET)	YR	385.00	385.00
D. POLLAND			**PEWTER COLLECTION**	
84	FEDERAL STALLION	1500	145.00	185.00
85	HUNTING COUGAR	1500	145.00	180.00
85	RUNNING FREE	1500	250.00	300.00

PRECIOUS ART/PANTON

YR	NAME	LIMIT	ISSUE	QUOTE
				KRYSTONIA
*	CAUGHT AT LAST - 1107	*	*	228.00-429.00
*	DRAGONS PLAY	*	*	234.00-260.00
*	GRUMMLYE GRUNCH - 1081	*	*	163.00-221.00
*	N'BORG 6"	*	*	330.00
*	PULTZR - 501	*	*	325.00
*	SMALL TOKKEL	*	*	50.00
*	TARNHOLD - 3202	*	*	195.00-364.00
87	GRUMBLYPEG GRUNCH-1081	RT	52.00	84.00-120.00
87	LARGE GRAFFYN ON GRUMBLYPEG GRUNCH-1011	RT	52.00	86.00-120.00
87	LARGE HAAPF-1901	RT	38.00	75.00-95.00
87	LARGE KRAK N'BORG-3001	RT	240.00	600.00-700.00
87	LARGE MOPLOS-1021	RT	90.00	250.00-385.00
87	LARGE MYZER-1201	RT	50.00	110.00-250.00
87	LARGE RUEGGAN-1701	RT	55.00	90.00-130.00
87	LARGE TURFEN-1601	RT	50.00	72.00-150.00
87	LARGE WODEMA-1301	RT	50.00	75.00-120.00
87	MEDIUM STOOPE-1101	RT	52.00	70.00-100.00
87	OWHEY-1071	RT	32.00	80.00-143.00
87	SMALL GRAFFYN/GRUNCH-1012	RT	45.00	165.00-275.00
87	SMALL N'BORG-1091	RT	50.00	200.00-225.00
87	SMALL SHEPF-1152	RT	40.00	85.00-115.00
88	LARGE N'GRALL-2201	RT	108.00	180.00-260.00
88	SMALL TULAN CAPTAIN-2502	RT	44.00	66.00-125.00
88	TARNHOLD MED.-3202	RT	120.00	140.00-185.00
89	CAUGHT AT LAST!-1107	RT	150.00	175.00-240.00
*			**KRYSTONIA COLLECTOR'S CLUB**	
89	KEY	RT	*	100.00
89	PULTZR	RT	55.00	150.00
89	PULTZR W/KEY	RT	55.00	150.00
*			**WORLD OF KRYSTONIA**	
87	LARGE WODEMA-1301	RT	50.00	100.00-200.00
87	SMALL GROC-1042B	RT	34.00	3000.00-4600.00

PRINCETON GALLERY

YR	NAME	LIMIT	ISSUE	QUOTE
*				**PEGASUS**
92	WINGS OF MAGIC	OP	95.00	95.00

PRIZM

YR	NAME	LIMIT	ISSUE	QUOTE
P. ULVILDEN			**MEMORIES OF CHRISTMAS**	
94	CZECHOSLOVAKIAN SANTA	3600	85.00	90.00
94	GINGERBREAD SANTA	3600	85.00	90.00
94	MIDNIGHT VISITOR	3600	85.00	90.00
94	SANTA'S ARK	3600	85.00	90.00
94	STAR CATCHER SANTA	3600	85.00	90.00
94	STARCOAT SANTA	3600	85.00	90.00

R.J. ERNST ENTERPRISES

YR	NAME	LIMIT	ISSUE	QUOTE
A. MURRAY			**LITTLE MISSES YOUNG AND FAIR**	
82	HEART OF A CHILD	5000	65.00	65.00
83	WHERE WILD FLOWERS GROW	2000	65.00	65.00
85	FINAL TOUCH	2000	75.00	75.00
85	WHISPERED MOMENTS	2000	75.00	75.00
R. MONEY			**MY FAIR LADIES**	
82	LADY SABRINA	5000	85.00	85.00
R. MONEY			**SEEMS LIKE YESTERDAY**	
81	STOP AND SMELL THE ROSES	5000	24.50	24.50
82	HOME BY LUNCH	5000	24.50	24.50
82	IT'S GOT MY NAME ON IT	5000	24.50	24.50
82	LISA'S CREEK	5000	24.50	24.50
82	MY MAGIC HAT	5000	24.50	24.50
GLENICE			**YESTERDAYS**	
82	AMBER	5000	24.50	24.50
84	ELMER	5000	24.50	24.50
85	KATIE	600	24.50	24.50

YR NAME	LIMIT	ISSUE	QUOTE

RAWCLIFFE CORP.

J. DESTEFANO — ANGEL FAIRIES OF THE SEASONS

YR NAME	LIMIT	ISSUE	QUOTE
94 ANGEL FAIRY OF FALL	4500	95.00	95.00
94 ANGEL FAIRY OF SPRING	4500	95.00	95.00
94 ANGEL FAIRY OF SUMMER	4500	95.00	95.00
94 ANGEL FAIRY OF WINTER	4500	95.00	95.00

J. DESTEFANO — BABY BUBBLE FAIRIES

93 AMBER, OCTOBER FAIRY	6700	70.00	70.00
93 AZURE, AUGUST FAIRY	6700	70.00	70.00
93 BLUSH, MARCH FAIRY	6700	70.00	70.00
93 CHARTREUSE, APRIL FAIRY	6700	70.00	70.00
93 CORAL, JUNE FAIRY	6700	70.00	70.00
93 EMERALD, DECEMBER FAIRY	6700	70.00	70.00
93 LAVENDER, SETP, FAIRY	6700	70.00	70.00
93 MAGENTA, FEBRUARY FAIRY	6700	70.00	70.00
93 SAFFRON, JULY FAIRY	6700	70.00	70.00
93 TURQUOISE, JANUARY FAIRY	6700	70.00	70.00
93 VERMILLION, NOVEMBER FAIRY	6700	70.00	70.00
93 VIOLET, MAY FAIRY	6700	70.00	70.00

J. DESTEFANO — FOUR SEASONS FAIRIES

93 ARIA, SUMMER FAIRY	9500	95.00	95.00
93 HARVEST, FALL FAIRY	9500	95.00	95.00
93 PETAL, SPRING FAIRY	9500	95.00	95.00
93 SNOW, WINTER FAIRY	9500	95.00	95.00

J. DESTEFANO — GARDEN FAIRIES

93 DEW FAIRY, THE	4500	115.00	115.00
93 DREAM FAIRY, THE	4500	115.00	115.00
93 FAIRY SLIPPER, THE	4500	115.00	115.00
93 ILLUSIVE FAIRY, THE	4500	115.00	115.00

J. DESTEFANO — STAR TREK

93 LUKE SKYWALKER X-WING FIGHTER	15000	95.00	95.00
93 USS ENTERPRISE NCC-1701-D	4500	100.00	100.00
94 DARTH VADER TIE FIGHTER	15000	135.00	135.00
94 DEEP SPACE NINE SPACE STATION	4500	300.00	300.00
94 HAN SOLO MILLENNIUM FALCON	15000	115.00	115.00

RECO INTERNATIONAL

J. MCCLELLAND — CLOWN FIGURINES BY JOHN MCCLELLAND

87 MR. CURE-ALL	9500	35.00	35.00
87 MR. LOVABLE	9500	35.00	35.00
87 MR. ONE-NOTE	9500	35.00	35.00
87 MR. TIP	9500	35.00	35.00
88 MR. COOL	9500	35.00	35.00
88 MR. HEART-THROB	9500	35.00	35.00
88 MR. MAGIC	9500	35.00	35.00

J. MCCLELLAND — FACES OF LOVE

88 CUDDLES	OP	29.50	32.50
88 SUNSHINE	OP	29.50	32.50

G. GRANGET — GRANGET CRYSTAL SCULPTURE

* RUFFED GROUSE	350	1000.00	1000.00
73 LONG EARRED OWL, ASIO OTUS	350	2250.00	2250.00

JODY BERGSMA — LAUGHABLES

95 ANNIE, GEORGE & HARRY	OP	17.50	17.50
95 CODY & SPOT	OP	15.00	15.00
95 DAFFODIL & PRINCE	OP	13.50	13.50
95 DAISY & JEREMIAH	OP	15.00	15.00
95 JOEY & JUMPER	OP	15.00	15.00
95 MERLIN & GEMINI	OP	15.00	15.00
95 MILLIE & MITTENS	OP	15.00	15.00
95 PATCHES AND POKEY	OP	15.00	15.00
95 PATTY & PETUNIA	OP	16.50	16.50
95 SUNNY	OP	13.50	13.50
95 WHISKERS & WILLIE	OP	13.50	13.50

A. FAZIO — SOPHISTICATED LADIES FIGURINES

87 BIANKA	9500	29.50	32.50
87 CERISSA	9500	29.50	32.50
87 CHELSEA	9500	29.50	32.50
87 CLEO	9500	29.50	32.50
87 FELICIA	9500	29.50	32.50
87 NATASHA	9500	29.50	32.50
87 PHOEBE	9500	29.50	32.50
87 SAMANTHA	9500	29.50	32.50

J. MCCLELLAND — THE RECO ANGEL COLLECTION

86 ADORATION	OP	21.50	24.00
86 DEVOTION	OP	14.50	15.00
86 FAITH	OP	21.50	24.00

YR NAME	LIMIT	ISSUE	QUOTE
86 GLORIA	OP	12.00	12.00
86 HARMONY	OP	12.00	12.00
86 HOPE	OP	21.50	24.00
86 INNOCENCE	OP	12.00	12.00
86 JOY	OP	14.50	15.00
86 LOVE	OP	12.00	12.00
86 PEACE	OP	18.00	24.00
86 PRAISE	OP	18.00	20.00
86 SERENITY	OP	21.50	24.00
88 MINSTRAL	OP	12.00	12.00
88 REVERENCE	OP	12.00	12.00
J. MCCLELLAND	THE RECO CLOWN COLLECTION		
85 ARABESQUE	OP	12.00	13.00
85 BOW JANGLES	OP	12.00	13.00
85 CURLY	OP	12.00	13.00
85 HOBO	OP	12.00	13.00
85 RUFFLES	OP	12.00	13.00
85 SAD EYES	OP	12.00	13.00
85 SCAMP	OP	12.00	13.00
85 SPARKLES	OP	12.00	13.00
85 THE PROFESSOR	OP	12.00	13.00
85 TOP HAT	OP	12.00	13.00
85 WHOOPIE	OP	12.00	13.00
85 WINKIE	OP	12.00	13.00
87 DISCO DAN	OP	12.00	13.00
87 DOMINO	OP	12.00	13.00
87 HAPPY GEORGE	OP	12.00	13.00
87 JOLLY JOE	OP	12.00	13.00
87 LOVE	OP	12.00	13.00
87 MR. BIG	OP	12.00	13.00
87 SMILEY	OP	12.00	13.00
87 THE JOKER	OP	12.00	13.00
87 TRAMP	OP	12.00	13.00
87 TWINKLE	OP	12.00	13.00
87 WISTFUL	OP	12.00	13.00
87 ZANY JACK	OP	12.00	13.00
J. MCCLELLAND	THE RECO COLLECTION CLOWN BUSTS		
88 BOW JANGLES	5000	40.00	40.00
88 DOMINO	5000	40.00	40.00
88 HOBO	5000	40.00	40.00
88 LOVE	5000	40.00	40.00
88 SPARKLES	5000	40.00	40.00

RED MILL MFG.
L. JOHNSON — ANGEL II COLLECTION

94 CHRISTINA	2500	34.95	34.95
R. BENJAMIN	FLIGHTS OF FANCY		
93 LIBERTY	5000	37.95	37.95
93 INTEGRITY	3000	77.95	77.95
93 VALOR	2500	48.95	48.95
93 SENTINEL	2500	54.95	54.95
93 COURAGEOUS	2500	65.95	65.95
93 MAJESTIC	3000	74.95	74.95

RHODES STUDIO

	ROCKWELL'S AGE OF WONDER		
91 HUSH-A-BYE	CL	34.95	40.00
91 HUSH-A-BYE	TL	34.95	34.95
91 SPLISH SPLASH	TL	34.95	34.95
91 STAND BY ME	TL	36.95	36.95
ROCKWELL INSPIRED	ROCKWELL'S BEAUTIFUL DREAMERS		
91 DEAR DIARY	TL	37.95	37.95
91 SECRET SONNETS	TL	39.95	39.95
91 SITTING PRETTY	TL	37.95	37.95
ROCKWELL INSPIRED	ROCKWELL'S GEMS OF WISDOM		
91 LOVE CURES ALL	TL	39.95	39.95
91 PRACTICE MAKES PERFECT	TL	39.95	39.95
ROCKWELL INSPIRED	ROCKWELL'S HEIRLOOM SANTA COLLECTION		
90 SANTA'S WORKSHOP	150-DAY	49.95	49.95
91 CHRISTMAS DREAM	150-DAY	49.95	49.95
ROCKWELL INSPIRED	ROCKWELL'S HOMETOWN		
91 BELL TOWER	TL	36.95	36.95
91 FIREHOUSE	TL	36.95	36.95
91 GREYSTONE CHURCH	TL	34.95	34.95
91 ROCKWELL'S RESIDENCE	TL	34.95	34.95
ROCKWELL INSPIRED	ROCKWELL'S MAIN STREET		
90 ROCKWELL'S STUDIO	150-DAY	28.00	28.00

YR	NAME	LIMIT	ISSUE	QUOTE
90	THE ANTIQUE SHOP	150-DAY	28.00	28.00
90	THE COUNTRY STORE	150-DAY	32.00	32.00
90	THE TOWN OFFICES	150-DAY	32.00	32.00
91	RED LION INN	150-DAY	39.00	39.00
91	THE BANK	150-DAY	36.00	36.00
91	THE LIBRARY	150-DAY	36.00	36.00

RIVER SHORE

R. BROWN		**BABIES OF ENDANGERED SPECIES**		
84	BAXTER (BEAR)	15,000	45.00	45.00
84	CAROLINE (ANETLOPE)	15,000	45.00	45.00
84	CHESTER (PRAIRIE DOG)	15,000	45.00	45.00
84	DAISY (WOOD BISON)	15,000	45.00	45.00
84	SIDNEY (COUGAR)	15,000	45.00	45.00
84	TREVOR (FOX)	15,000	45.00	45.00
84	VIOLET (OTTER)	15,000	45.00	45.00
84	WEBSTER (TIMBERWOLF)	15,000	45.00	45.00
M. HAGUE		**LOVABLE TEDDIE MUSICAL FIGURINE COLLECTION**		
87	APRIL	OP	29.50	29.50
87	AUSTIN	OP	29.50	29.50
87	GILBERT	OP	29.50	29.50
87	WILLIAM	OP	29.50	29.50
88	ADAM	OP	29.50	29.50
88	HARVEY	OP	29.50	29.50
88	HENRY	OP	29.50	29.50
88	KATIE	OP	29.50	29.50
R. BROWN		**LOVEABLE-BABY ANIMALS**		
78	AKIKU-SEAL	15,000	37.50	150.00
78	ALFRED-RACCOON	15,000	42.50	45.00
79	MATILDA-KOALA	15,000	45.00	45.00
79	SCOOTER-CHIPMUNK	15,000	45.00	55.00
N. ROCKWELL		**ROCKWELL SINGLE ISSUES**		
81	LOOKING OUT TO SEA	9500	85.00	145.00
82	GRANDPA'S GUARDIAN	9500	125.00	125.00
R. BROWN		**WILDERNESS BABIES**		
85	ABERCROMBIE (POLAR BEAR)	15,000	45.00	45.00
85	ANNABEL (MOUNTAIN GOAT)	15,000	45.00	45.00
85	ARIANNE (RABBIT)	15,000	45.00	45.00
85	CARMEN (BURRO)	15,000	45.00	45.00
85	ELROD (FOX)	15,000	45.00	45.00
85	PENELOPE (DEER)	15,000	45.00	45.00
85	REGGIE (RACCOON)	15,000	45.00	45.00
85	ROCKY (BOBCAT)	15,000	45.00	45.00
R. BROWN		**WILDLIFE BABY ANIMALS**		
78	FANNY-FAWN	15,000	45.00	90.00
79	ROOSEVELT-BEAR	15,000	50.00	65.00
79	ROSCOE-RED FOX	15,000	50.00	50.00
80	PRISCILLA-SKUNK	15,000	50.00	50.00

RJB DESIGNS

J. DESTEFANO		**BABY BUBBLE FAIRIES**		
93	BABY BUBBLE FAIRIES	OP	*	20.00
RHONDA BRENNAN		**CINDER CLAUS**		
93	SANTA (3 FT.)	75	950.00	1000.00
93	SANTA (4 FT.)	40	1300.00	1500.00
93	SANTA-SPECIAL EDITION	850	200.00	225.00
94	AMBERT	250	200.00	225.00
94	CUTHBERT	250	200.00	225.00
94	DRUSILLA	100	20.00	23.00
94	GARRICK	250	200.00	225.00
94	MONTGOMERY	250	200.00	225.00
94	SANTA (3 FT.)	60	950.00	975.00
94	SANTA (4 FT.)	20	1300.00	1400
94	SANTA (5 FT.)	3	3500.00	3750.00

ROHN

E. ROHN		**AROUND THE WORLD**		
71	COOLIE	100	700.00	1300.00
72	GYPSY	125	1450.00	1850.00
73	MATADOR	90	2400.00	3100.00
73	SHERIFF	100	1500.00	2250.00
74	AUSSIE-HUNTER	90	1000.00	1300.00
E. ROHN		**CLOWNS-BIG TOP SERIES**		
79	WHITE FACE	100	1000.00	3500.00
80	TRAMP	100	1200.00	2500.00
81	AUGUSTE	100	1400.00	1700.00
83	SWEETHEART	200	925.00	1500.00

YR NAME	LIMIT	ISSUE	QUOTE
E. ROHN		**CLOWNS-HEY RUBE**	
79 AUGUSTE	300	190.00	350.00
79 TRAMP	300	190.00	350.00
79 WHITEFACE	300	190.00	350.00
E. ROHN		**FAMOUS PEOPLE**	
75 HARRY S. TRUMAN	75	2400.00	4000.00
79 NORMAN ROCKWELL	200	1950.00	2300.00
81 RONALD REAGAN	200	3000.00	3000.00
85 SHERLOCK HOLMES	2210	155.00	190.00
86 DR. JOHN WATSON	2210	155.00	155.00
93 SHERLOCK HOLMES & DR. WATSON	OP	185.00	200.00
E. ROHN		**FAMOUS PEOPLE-BISQUE**	
79 LINCOLN	500	100.00	500.00
79 NORMAN ROCKWELL	YR	100.00	200.00
81 REAGAN	2500	140.00	200.00
83 J.F. KENNEDY	500	140.00	400.00
E. ROHN		**KINARA SERIES**	
92 KENTE WOMAN	OP	40.00	45.00
E. ROHN		**PORTRAIT SERIES**	
92 MARTIN LUTHER KING	OP	60.00	75.00
E. ROHN		**RELIGIOUS & BIBLICAL**	
77 ZAIDE	70	1950.00	5000.00
78 SABBATH	70	1825.00	5000.00
85 THE MENTOR	15	9500.00	9500.00
E. ROHN		**REMEMBER WHEN**	
71 AMERICAN GI	100	600.00	1750.00
71 RIVERBOAT CAPTAIN	100	1000.00	2400.00
73 APPRENTICE	175	500.00	850.00
73 JAZZ MAN	150	750.00	3500.00
74 MISSY	250	250.00	500.00
74 RECRUIT (SET W/FN-5)	250	250.00	500.00
77 CASEY	300	275.00	500.00
77 FLAPPER	500	325.00	500.00
77 SOU' WESTER	450	300.00	500.00
77 WALLY	250	250.00	500.00
80 SHOWMAN (W.C. FIELDS)	300	220.00	500.00
81 CLOWN PRINCE	25	2000.00	2400.00
E. ROHN		**SMALL WORLD SERIES**	
* JOHNNIE'S	1500	90.00	90.00
74 BIG BROTHER	250	90.00	90.00
74 BURGLERS	250	120.00	120.00
74 KNEE DEEP	500	60.00	60.00
74 QUACKERS	250	75.00	75.00
75 FIELD MUSHROOMS	250	90.00	90.00
75 OYSTER MUSHROOM	250	140.00	140.00
E. ROHN		**WESTERN**	
71 APACHE INDIAN	125	800.00	2000.00
71 CHOSEN ONE (INDIAN MAID)	125	850.00	2000.00
71 CROW INDIAN	100	800.00	1500.00
71 TRAIL-HAND	100	1200.00	1600.00
E. ROHN		**WILD WEST**	
82 RODEO CLOWN	100	2600.00	3500.00

ROMAN INC.

YR NAME	LIMIT	ISSUE	QUOTE
F. HOOK		**A CHILD'S WORLD 1ST EDITION**	
80 BEACH BUDDIES, SIGNED	15,000	29.00	600.00
80 BEACH BUDDIES, UNSIGNED	15,000	29.00	450.00-520.00
80 HELPING HANDS	15,000	45.00	65.00
80 KISS ME GOOD NIGHT	15,000	29.00	40.00
80 MY BIG BROTHER	15,000	39.00	200.00
80 NIGHTTIME THOUGHTS	15,000	25.00	65.00
80 SOUNDS OF THE SEA	15,000	45.00	130.00
F. HOOK		**A CHILD'S WORLD 2ND EDITION**	
81 ALL DRESSED UP	15,000	36.00	70.00
81 CAT NAP	15,000	42.00	80.00-104.00
81 I'LL BE GOOD	15,000	36.00	70.00
81 MAKING FRIENDS	15,000	42.00	46.00
81 SUNDAY SHCOOL	15,000	39.00	75.00
81 THE SEA AND ME	15,000	39.00	50.00
F. HOOK		**A CHILD'S WORLD 3RD EDITION**	
81 BEAR HUG	15,000	42.00	55.00
81 PATHWAY TO DREAMS	15,000	47.00	80.00
81 ROAD TO ADVENTURE	15,000	47.00	50.00
81 SISTERS	15,000	64.00	110.00
81 SPRING BREEZE	15,000	37.50	40.00
81 YOUTH	15,000	37.50	40.00

YR	NAME	LIMIT	ISSUE	QUOTE
F. HOOK		**A CHILD'S WORLD 4TH EDITION**		
82	ALL BUNDLED UP	15,000	37.50	40.00
82	BEDTIME	15,000	35.00	38.00
82	BIRDIE	15,000	37.50	40.00
82	FLOWER GIRL	15,000	42.00	45.00
82	MY DOLLY!	15,000	39.00	40.00
82	RING BEARER	15,000	39.00	40.00
F. HOOK		**A CHILD'S WORLD 5TH EDITION**		
83	BROTHERS	15,000	64.00	70.00
83	FINISH LINE	15,000	39.00	42.00
83	HANDFUL OF HAPPINESS	15,000	36.00	40.00
83	HE LOVES ME...	15,000	49.00	60.00
83	PUPPY'S PAL	15,000	39.00	42.00
83	RING AROUND THE ROSIE	15,000	99.00	105.00
F. HOOK		**A CHILD'S WORLD 6TH EDITION**		
84	CAN I HELP?	15,000	37.50	40.00
84	FUTURE ARTIST	15,000	42.00	45.00
84	GOOD DOGGIE	15,000	47.00	50.00
84	LET'S PLAY CATCH	15,000	33.00	35.00
84	NATURE'S WONDERS	15,000	29.00	31.00
84	SAND CASTLES	15,000	37.50	40.00
F. HOOK		**A CHILD'S WORLD 7TH EDITION**		
85	ART CLASS	15,000	99.00	105.00
85	DON'T TELL ANYONE	15,000	49.00	50.00
85	LOOK AT ME!	15,000	42.00	45.00
85	MOTHER'S HELPER	15,000	45.00	50.00
85	PLEASE HEAR ME	15,000	29.00	30.00
85	YUMMM!	15,000	36.00	39.00
F. HOOK		**A CHILD'S WORLD 8TH EDITION**		
85	CHANCE OF SHOWERS	15,000	33.00	35.00
85	DRESS REHEARSAL	15,000	33.00	35.00
85	ENGINE	15,000	36.00	40.00
85	JUST STOPPED BY	15,000	36.00	40.00
85	PRIVATE OCEAN	15,000	29.00	31.00
85	PUZZLING	15,000	36.00	40.00
F. HOOK		**A CHILD'S WORLD 9TH EDITION**		
87	HOPSCOTCH	15,000	67.50	70.00
87	LI'L BROTHER	15,000	60.00	65.00
I. SPENCER				**CATNIPPERS**
85	A BAFFLING YARN	15,000	45.00	45.00
85	A CHRISTMAS MOURNING	15,000	45.00	45.00
85	A TAIL OF TWO KITTIES	15,000	45.00	45.00
85	CAN'T WE BE FRIENDS	15,000	45.00	45.00
85	FLORA AND FELINA	15,000	45.00	49.50
85	FLYING TIGER-RETIRED	15,000	45.00	45.00
85	SANDY CLAWS	15,000	45.00	45.00
85	THE PAW THAT REFRESHES	15,000	45.00	45.00
*			**CERAMICA EXCELSIS**	
77	CHRIST KNOCKING AT THE DOOR	5000	60.00	60.00
77	MADONNA AND CHILD WITH ANGELS	5000	60.00	60.00
77	MADONNA WITH CHILD	5000	65.00	65.00
77	ST. FRANCIS	5000	60.00	60.00
77	WHAT HAPPENED TO YOUR HAND?	5000	60.00	60.00
78	ASSUMPTION MADONNA	5000	56.00	56.00
78	CHRIST ENTERING JERUSALEM	5000	96.00	96.00
78	CHRIST IN THE GARDEN OF GETHSEMANE	5000	40.00	60.00
78	FLIGHT INTO EGYPT	5000	59.00	90.00
78	GUARDIAN ANGEL WITH BOY	5000	69.00	69.00
78	GUARDIAN ANGEL WITH GIRL	5000	69.00	69.00
78	HOLY FAMILY AT WORK	5000	96.00	96.00
78	INFANT OF PRAGUE	5000	37.50	60.00
79	JESUS SPEAKS IN PARABLES	5000	90.00	90.00
79	MOSES	5000	77.00	77.00
79	NOAH	5000	77.00	77.00
80	DANIEL IN THE LION'S DEN	5000	80.00	80.00
80	DAVID	5000	77.00	77.00
80	WAY TO EMMAUS	5000	155.00	155.00
81	INNOCENCE	5000	95.00	95.00
81	JOURNEY TO BETHLEHEM	5000	89.00	89.00
81	SERMON ON THE MOUNT	5000	56.00	56.00
81	WAY OF THE CROSS	5000	59.00	59.00
83	GOOD SHEPHERD	5000	49.00	49.00
83	HOLY FAMILY	5000	72.00	72.00
83	JESUS WITH CHILDREN	5000	74.00	74.00
83	KNEELING SANTA	5000	95.00	95.00
83	ST. ANNE	5000	49.00	49.00

YR	NAME	LIMIT	ISSUE	QUOTE
83	ST. FRANCIS	5000	59.50	59.50
E. WILLIAMS		**CLASSIC BRIDES OF THE CENTURY**		
89	1900-FLORA	5000	175.00	175.00
89	1910-ELIZABETH GRACE	5000	175.00	175.00
89	1920-MARY CLAIRE	5000	175.00	175.00
89	1930-KATHLEEN	5000	175.00	175.00
89	1940-MARGARET	5000	175.00	175.00
89	1950-BARBARA ANN	5000	175.00	175.00
89	1960-DIANNE	5000	175.00	175.00
89	1970-HEATHER	5000	175.00	175.00
89	1980-JENNIFER	5000	175.00	175.00
92	1990-STEPHANIE HELEN	5000	175.00	175.00
L. MARTIN		**DOLFI ORIGINAL-10 IN. STONEART**		
89	A SHOULDER TO LEARN ON	OP	400.00	400.00
89	BAREFOOT IN SPRING	OP	400.00	400.00
89	BIG CHIEF SITTING DOG	OP	325.00	325.00
89	BIRDLAND CAFE	OP	300.00	300.00
89	DRESS REHERSAL	OP	495.00	495.00
89	FLOWER CHILD	OP	300.00	300.00
89	FRIENDS & FLOWERS	OP	400.00	400.00
89	GARDEN SECRETS	OP	300.00	300.00
89	HAVE I BEEN THAT GOOD	OP	495.00	495.00
89	HOLIDAY HERALD	OP	300.00	300.00
89	LITTLE SANTA	OP	325.00	325.00
89	MARY & JOEY	OP	495.00	495.00
89	MERRY LITTLE LIGHT	OP	325.00	325.00
89	MOTHER HEN	OP	300.00	300.00
89	MUD PUDDLES	OP	300.00	300.00
89	MY FAVORITE THINGS	OP	400.00	400.00
89	MY FIRST CAKE	OP	300.00	300.00
89	MY FIRST KITTEN	OP	300.00	300.00
89	PAMPERED PUPPIES	OP	300.00	300.00
89	PUPPY EXPRESS	OP	300.00	300.00
89	SING A SONG OF JOY	OP	400.00	400.00
89	SLEEPYHEAD	OP	300.00	300.00
89	STUDY BREAK	OP	325.00	325.00
89	WRAPPED IN LOVE	OP	300.00	300.00
L. MARTIN		**DOLFI ORIGINAL-10 IN. WOOD**		
89	A SHOULDER TO LEAN ON	2000	1000.00	1000.00
89	BAREFOOT IN SPRINGS	2000	1000.00	1000.00
89	BIG CHIEF SITTING DOG	2000	825.00	825.00
89	BIRDLAND CAFE	2000	750.00	750.00
89	DRESS REHEARSAL	2000	1250.00	1250.00
89	FLOWER CHILD	2000	750.00	750.00
89	FRIENDS & FLOWERS	2000	1000.00	1000.00
89	GARDEN SECRETS	2000	750.00	750.00
89	HAVE I BEEN THAT GOOD	2000	1250.00	1250.00
89	HOLIDAY HERALD	2000	750.00	750.00
89	LITTLE SANTA	2000	825.00	825.00
89	MARY & JOEY	2000	1250.00	1250.00
89	MERRY LITTLE LIGHT	2000	825.00	825.00
89	MOTHER HEN	2000	750.00	750.00
89	MUD PUDDLES	2000	750.00	750.00
89	MY FAVORITE THINGS	2000	1000.00	1000.00
89	MY FIRST CAKE	2000	750.00	750.00
89	MY FIRST KITTEN	2000	750.00	750.00
89	PAMPERED PUPPIES	2000	750.00	750.00
89	PUPPY EXPRESS	2000	750.00	750.00
89	SING A SONG OF JOY	2000	1000.00	1000.00
89	SLEEPYHEAD	2000	750.00	750.00
89	STUDY BREAK	2000	825.00	825.00
89	WRAPPED IN LOVE	2000	750.00	750.00
L. MARTIN		**DOLFI ORIGINAL-5 IN. WOOD**		
89	A SHOULDER TO LEAN ON	5000	300.00	300.00
89	BAREFOOT IN SPRING	5000	300.00	300.00
89	BIG CHIEF SITTING DOG	5000	250.00	250.00
89	BIRDLAND CAFE	5000	230.00	230.00
89	DRESS REHEARSAL	5000	375.00	375.00
89	FLOWER CHILD	5000	230.00	230.00
89	FRIENDS & FLOWERS	5000	300.00	300.00
89	GARDEN SECRETS	5000	230.00	230.00
89	HAVE I BEEN THAT GOOD	5000	375.00	375.00
89	HOLIDAY HERALD	5000	230.00	230.00
89	LITTLE SANTA	5000	250.00	250.00
89	MARY & JOEY	5000	375.00	375.00
89	MERRY LITTLE LIGHT	5000	250.00	250.00

YR	NAME	LIMIT	ISSUE	QUOTE
89	MOTHER HEN	5000	230.00	230.00
89	MUD PUDDLES	5000	230.00	230.00
89	MY FAVORITE THINGS	5000	300.00	300.00
89	MY FIRST CAKE	5000	230.00	230.00
89	MY FIRST KITTEN	5000	230.00	230.00
89	PAMPERED PUPPIES	5000	230.00	230.00
89	PUPPY EXPRESS	5000	230.00	230.00
89	SING A SONG OF JOY	5000	300.00	300.00
89	SLEEPYHEAD	5000	230.00	230.00
89	STUDY BREAK	5000	250.00	250.00
89	WRAPPED IN LOVE	5000	230.00	230.00

L. MARTIN — DOLFI ORIGINAL-7 IN. STONEART

YR	NAME	LIMIT	ISSUE	QUOTE
89	A SHOULDER TO LEAN ON	OP	150.00	150.00
89	BAREFOOT IN SPRING	OP	150.00	150.00
89	BIG CHIEF SITTING DOG	OP	120.00	120.00
89	BIRDLAND CAFE	OP	110.00	110.00
89	DRESS REHEARSAL	OP	185.00	185.00
89	FLOWER CHILD	OP	110.00	110.00
89	FRIENDS & FLOWERS	OP	150.00	150.00
89	GARDEN SECRETS	OP	110.00	110.00
89	HAVE I BEEN THAT GOOD	OP	185.00	185.00
89	HOLIDAY HERALD	OP	110.00	110.00
89	LITTLE SANTA	OP	120.00	120.00
89	MARY & JOEY	OP	185.00	185.00
89	MERRY LITTLE LIGHT	OP	120.00	120.00
89	MOTHER HEN	OP	110.00	110.00
89	MUD PUDDLES	OP	110.00	110.00
89	MY FAVORITE THINGS	OP	150.00	150.00
89	MY FIRST CAKE	OP	110.00	110.00
89	MY FIRST KITTEN	OP	110.00	110.00
89	PAMPERED PUPPIES	OP	110.00	110.00
89	PUPPY EXPRESS	OP	110.00	110.00
89	SING A SONG OF JOY	OP	150.00	150.00
89	SLEEPYHEAD	OP	110.00	110.00
89	STUDY BREAK	OP	120.00	120.00
89	WRAPPED IN LOVE	OP	110.00	110.00

E. SIMONETTI — FONTANINI COLLECTOR'S CLUB MEMBERS-ONLY FIGURINES

YR	NAME	LIMIT	ISSUE	QUOTE
92	SHE RESCUED ME	YR	23.50	23.50

E. SIMONETTI — FONTANINI COLLECTORS' CLUB MEMBERS-ONLY FIGURINES

91	THE PILGRIMAGE	YR	24.95	24.95

E. SIMONETTI — FONTANINI PRESEPIO COLLECTION

92	ARIEL	TL	29.50	29.50

E. SIMONETTI — FONTANINI, THE COLLECTIBLE CRECHE

YR	NAME	LIMIT	ISSUE	QUOTE
73	10CM., (15 PIECE SET)	OP	63.60	88.50
73	12CM., (15 PIECE SET)	OP	76.50	102.00
73	19CM., (15 PIECE SET)	OP	175.50	280.00
79	16CM., (15 PIECE SET)	OP	178.50	285.00
80	30CM., (15 PIECE SET)	OP	670.00	758.50
82	17CM., (15 PIECE SET)	OP	189.00	305.00

F. HOOK — FRANCES HOOK'S FOUR SEASONS

YR	NAME	LIMIT	ISSUE	QUOTE
84	WINTER	12,500	95.00	100.00
85	FALL	12,500	95.00	100.00
85	SPRING	12,500	95.00	100.00
85	SUMMER	12,500	95.00	100.00

I. SPENCER — HEARTBEATS

86	MIRACLE	5000	145.00	145.00
87	STORYTIME	5000	145.00	145.00

F. HOOK — HOOK

YR	NAME	LIMIT	ISSUE	QUOTE
82	SAILOR MATES	2000	290.00	315.00
82	SUN SHY	2000	290.00	315.00
86	CARPENTER BUST	YR	95.00	95.00
86	CARPENTER BUST-HEIRLOOM EDITION	YR	95.00	95.00
87	LITTLE CHILDREN, COME TO ME	15,000	45.00	45.00
87	MADODNNA AND CHILD	15,000	39.50	39.50

E. ROHN — JAM SESSION

85	BANJO PLAYER	7500	145.00	145.00
85	BASS PLAYER	7500	145.00	145.00
85	CLARINET PLAYER	7500	145.00	145.00
85	CORONET PLAYER	7500	145.00	145.00
85	DRUMMER	7500	145.00	145.00
85	TROMBONE PLAYER	7500	145.00	145.00

E. ROHN — ROHN'S CLOWNS

84	AUGUSTE	7500	95.00	95.00
84	HOBO	7500	95.00	95.00
84	WHITE FACE	7500	95.00	95.00

YR	NAME	LIMIT	ISSUE	QUOTE
I. SPENCER				**SPENCER**
85	FLOWER PRINCESS	5000	195.00	195.00
85	MOON GODDESS	5000	195.00	195.00
G. DELLE NOTTI			**THE MASTERPIECE COLLECTION**	
81	THE HOLY FAMILY	5000	98.00	98.00
82	MADONNA OF THE STREETS	5000	65.00	65.00
79	ADORATION	5000	73.00	73.00
80	MADONNA WITH GRAPES	5000	85.00	85.00
A. TRIPI		**THE MUSEUM COLLECTION BY ANGELA TRIPI**		
90	THE MENTOR	1000	290.00	290.00
91	A GENTLEMAN'S GAME	1000	175.00	175.00
91	CHRISTOPHER COLUMBUS	1000	250.00	250.00
91	ST. FRANCIS OF ASSISI	1000	175.00	175.00
91	TEE TIME AT ST. ANDREW'S	1000	175.00	175.00
91	THE CADDIE	1000	135.00	135.00
91	THE FIDDLER	1000	175.00	175.00

RON LEE'S WORLD OF CLOWNS

	R. LEE	THE ORIGINAL RON LEE COLLECTION		
76	ALLIGATOR BOWLING 504	CL	15.00	35.00-78.00
76	BEAR FISHING 512	CL	15.00	35.00-78.00
76	CLOWN AND DOG ACT 101	CL	48.00	78.00-140.00
76	CLOWN AND ELEPHANT ACT 107	CL	56.00	85.00-140.00
76	CLOWN TIGHTROPE WALKER 104	CL	50.00	82.00-155.00
76	DOG FISHING 512	CL	15.00	35.00-78.00
76	FROG SURFING 502	CL	15.00	35.00-78.00
76	HIPPO ON SCOOTER 505	CL	15.00	35.00-78.00
76	HOBO JOE HITCHHIKING 116	CL	55.00	65.00
76	HOBO JOE WITH BALLOONS 120	CL	66.00	90.00
76	HOBO JOE WITH PAL 115	CL	66.00	85.00-170.00
76	HOBO JOE WITH UMBRELLA 117	CL	58.00	65.00-160.00
76	KANGAROOS BOXING 508	CL	15.00	35.00-78.00
76	OWL WITH GUITAR 500	CL	15.00	35.00-78.00
76	PENGUIN ON SNOWSKIS 503	CL	15.00	35.00-78.00
76	PIG PLAYING VIOLIN 510	CL	15.00	35.00-78.00
76	PINKY LYING DOWN 112	CL	25.00	32.00-50.00
76	PINKY SITTING 119	CL	25.00	32.00-50.00
76	PINKY STANDING 118	CL	25.00	45.00-100.00
76	PINKY UPSIDE DOWN 111	CL	25.00	32.00-50.00
76	RABBIT PLAYING TENNIS 507	CL	15.00	35.00-78.00
76	TURTLE ON SKATEBOARD 501	CL	15.00	35.00-78.00
77	BEAR ON ROCK 523	CL	18.00	30.00-80.00
77	KOALA BEAR IN TREE 514	CL	15.00	35.00-78.00
77	KOALA BEAR ON LOG 516	CL	15.00	35.00-78.00
77	KOALA BEAR WITH BABY 515	CL	15.00	35.00-78.00
77	MONKEY WITH BANANA 521	CL	18.00	30.00-80.00
77	MOUSE AND CHEESE 520	CL	18.00	30.00-80.00
77	MR. PENGUIN 518	CL	18.00	39.00-85.00
77	OWL GRADUATE 519	CL	22.00	44.00-90.00
77	PELICAN AND PYTHON 522	CL	18.00	30.00-80.00
78	BOBBI ON UNICYCLE 204	CL	45.00	65.00-98.00
78	BOW TIE 222	CL	67.50	93.00-215.00
78	BUTTERFLY AND FLOWER 529	CL	22.00	40.00-85.00
78	CLANCY, THE COP 210	CL	55.00	72.00-130.00
78	CLARA-BOW 205	CL	52.00	70.00-120.00
78	COCO-HANDS ON HIPS 218	CL	70.00	95.00-150.00
78	CORKY THE DRUMMER BOY 202	CL	53.00	85.00-130.00
78	CUDDLES 208	CL	37.00	55.00-110.00
78	DOLPHINS 525	CL	22.00	40.00-85.00
78	DRIVER THE GOLFER 211	CL	55.00	72.00-85.00
78	ELEPHANT ON BALL 214	CL	26.00	42.00-80.00
78	ELEPHANT ON STAND 213	CL	26.00	42.00-80.00
78	ELEPHANT SITTING 215	CL	26.00	42.00-80.00
78	FANCY PANTS 224	CL	55.00	90.00-120.00
78	FIREMAN WITH HOSE 216	CL	62.00	85.00-140.00
78	HEY RUBE 220	CL	35.00	53.00-92.00
78	HUMMINGBIRD 528	CL	22.00	40.00-85.00
78	JERI IN A BARREL 219	CL	75.00	110.00-180.00
78	JOCKO WITH LOLLIPOP 221	CL	67.50	93.00-215.00
78	OSCAR ON STILTS 223	CL	55.00	90.00-120.00
78	PIERROT PAINTING 207	CL	50.00	80.00-170.00
78	POLLY THE PARROT & CRACKERS 201	CL	63.00	100.00-170.00
78	POPPY WITH PUPPET 209	CL	60.00	75.00-140.00
78	PRINCE FROG 526	CL	22.00	40.00-85.00
78	SAD SACK 212	CL	48.00	62.00-210.00
78	SAILFISH 524	CL	18.00	40.00-95.00
78	SEA OTTER ON BACK 531	CL	22.00	40.00-85.00

YR	NAME	LIMIT	ISSUE	QUOTE
78	SEA OTTER ON ROCK 532	CL	22.00	40.00-85.00
78	SEAGULL 527	CL	22.00	40.00-85.00
78	SKIPPY SWINGING 239	CL	52.00	65.00-85.00
78	SPARKY SKATING 206	CL	55.00	72.00-260.00
78	TINKER BOWING 203	CL	37.00	55.00-110.00
78	TOBI-HANDS OUTSTRETCHED 217	CL	70.00	98.00-260.00
78	TURTLE ON ROCK 530	CL	22.00	40.00-85.00
79	BUTTONS BICYCLING 229	CL	75.00	110.00-150.00
79	CAROUSEL HORSE 232	CL	119.00	130.00-195.00
79	DARBY TIPPING HAT 238	CL	35.00	60.00-140.00
79	DARBY WITH FLOWER 235	CL	35.00	60.00-140.00
79	DARBY WITH UMBRELLA 236	CL	35.00	60.00-140.00
79	DARBY WITH VIOLIN 237	CL	35.00	60.00-140.00
79	DOCTOR SAWBONES 228	CL	75.00	110.00-150.00
79	FEARLESS FRED IN CANNON 234	CL	80.00	105.00-300.00
79	HARRY AND THE HARE 233	CL	69.00	102.00-180.00
79	KELLY AT THE PIANO 241	CL	185.00	280.00-510.00
79	KELLY IN KAR 230	CL	164.00	210.00-380.00
79	KELLY'S KAR 231	CL	75.00	90.00-230.00
79	LILI 227	CL	75.00	105.00-145.00
79	TIMMY TOOTING 225	CL	35.00	52.00-85.00
79	TUBBY TUBA 226	CL	35.00	55.00-90.00
80	BANJO WILLIE 258	CL	68.00	85.00-195.00
80	CAROUSEL HORSE 248	CL	88.00	115.00-285.00
80	CAROUSEL HORSE 249	CL	88.00	115.00-285.00
80	CHUCKLES JUGGLING 244	CL	98.00	105.00-150.00
80	CUBBY HOLDING BALLOON 240	CL	50.00	65.00-70.00
80	DENNIS PLAYING TENNIS 252	CL	74.00	95.00-185.00
80	DOCTOR JAWBONES 260	CL	85.00	110.00-305.00
80	DONKEY WHAT? 243	CL	60.00	92.00-250.00
80	EMILE 257	CL	43.00	82.00-190.00
80	HAPPY WAVING 255	CL	43.00	82.00-190.00
80	HOBO JOE IN TUB 259	CL	96.00	105.00-125.00
80	JAQUE DOWNHILL RACER 253	CL	74.00	90.00-210.00
80	JINGLES TELLING TIME 242	CL	75.00	90.00-190.00
80	JO-JO AT MAKE-UP MIRROR 250	CL	86.00	125.00-185.00
80	MONKEY 251	CL	60.00	85.00-210.00
80	P.T. DINGHY 245	CL	65.00	80.00-190.00
80	PEANUTS PLAYING CONCERTINA 247	CL	65.00	150.00-285.00
80	RONI RIDING HORSE 246	CL	115.00	180.00-290.00
80	RUFORD 254	CL	43.00	82.00-190.00
80	ZACH 256	CL	43.00	82.00-190.00
81	AL AT THE BASS 284	CL	48.00	52.00-112.00
81	BOSOM BUDDIES 299	CL	135.00	90.00-280.00
81	BOZO ON UNICYCLE 279	CL	28.00	49.00-185.00
81	BOZO PLAYING CYMBOLS 277	CL	28.00	49.00-185.00
81	BOZO RIDING CAR 278	CL	28.00	49.00-185.00
81	CARNEY AND SEAL ACT 300	CL	63.00	75.00-140.00
81	CAROUSEL HORSE 280	CL	88.00	125.00-240.00
81	CAROUSEL HORSE 281	CL	88.00	125.00-240.00
81	EXECUTIVE HITCHHIKING 267	CL	23.00	45.00-110.00
81	EXECUTIVE READING 264	CL	23.00	45.00-110.00
81	EXECUTIVE RESTING 266	CL	23.00	45.00-110.00
81	EXECUTIVE WITH UMBRELLA 265	CL	23.00	45.00-110.00
81	HARPO 296	CL	120.00	190.00-350.00
81	HOBO JOE PRAYING 298	CL	57.00	65.00-85.00
81	KEVIN AT THE DRUMS 283	CL	50.00	92.00-150.00
81	LARRY AND HIS HOTDOGS 274	CL	76.00	90.00-200.00
81	LOUIE HITCHING A RIDE 269	CL	47.00	58.00-135.00
81	LOUIE ON PARK BENCH 268	CL	56.00	65.00-85.00
81	LOUIE ON RAILROAD CAR 270	CL	77.00	95.00-180.00
81	MICKEY TIGHTROPE WALKER 292	CL	50.00	75.00-140.00
81	MICKEY UPSIDE DOWN 293	CL	50.00	75.00-140.00
81	MICKEY WITH UMBRELLA 291	CL	50.00	75.00-140.00
81	MY SON DARREN 295	CL	57.00	72.00-140.00
81	NICKY SITTING ON BALL 289	CL	39.00	48.00-92.00
81	NICKY STANDING ON BALL 290	CL	39.00	48.00-92.00
81	PERRY SITTING WITH BALLOON 287	CL	37.00	50.00-95.00
81	PERRY STANDING WITH BALLOON 288	CL	37.00	50.00-95.00
81	PICKLES AND POOCH 297	CL	90.00	140.00-240.00
81	PISTOL PETE 272	CL	76.00	85.00-180.00
81	ROCKETMAN 294	CL	77.00	92.00-180.00
81	RON AT THE PIANO 285	CL	46.00	55.00-110.00
81	RON LEE TRIO 282	CL	144.00	280.00-435.00
81	TIMOTHY IN BIG SHOE 286	CL	37.00	50.00-95.00
82	ALI ON HIS MAGIC CARPET 335	CL	105.00	150.00-210.00

Even the jolly old elf needs a break. For Santa *is produced by United Design.*

Artist Lowell Davis has a way of putting a humorous twist on things. Bottoms Up *was created for Schmid.*

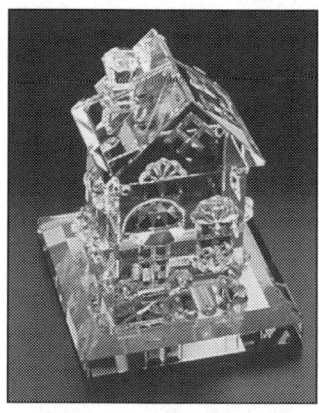

Garden Cottage *crystal figure captures all the hues of the rainbow. The piece is from Iris Arc Crystal.*

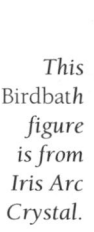

This Birdbath *figure is from Iris Arc Crystal.*

With Santa soaring high above, of course Christmas is in the Air. *The fabric mache figure is from Kurt S. Adler.*

YR	NAME	LIMIT	ISSUE	QUOTE
82	BARNUM FEEDING BACON 315	CL	120.00	160.00-270.00
82	BEAVER PLAYING ACCORDIAN 807	CL	23.00	35.00-92.00
82	BENNY PULLING CAR 310	CL	190.00	235.00-360.00
82	BURRITO BANDITO 334	CL	150.00	190.00-260.00
82	BUSTER IN BARREL 308	CL	85.00	90.00-120.00
82	CAMEL 818	CL	57.00	75.00-150.00
82	CAPTAIN CRANBERRY 320	CL	115.00	145.00-180.00
82	CAPTAIN MIS-ADVENTURE 703	CL	250.00	300.00-550.00
82	CARNEY AND DOG ACT 301	CL	63.00	75.00-150.00
82	CHARLIE CHAPLAIN 701	CL	230.00	285.00-650.00
82	CHARLIE IN THE RAIN 321	CL	80.00	90.00-160.00
82	CHICO PLAYING GUITAR 336	CL	70.00	95.00-180.00
82	CLANCY, THE COP AND DOG 333	CL	115.00	140.00-250.00
82	CLARENCE, THE LAWYER 331	CL	100.00	140.00-230.00
82	DENNY EATING ICE CREAM 305	CL	39.00	50.00-170.00
82	DENNY HOLDING GIFT BOX 306	CL	39.00	50.00-170.00
82	DENNY JUGGLING BALL 307	CL	39.00	50.00-170.00
82	DOG PLAYING GUITAR 805	CL	23.00	35.00-92.00
82	DR. PAINLESS AND PATIENT 311	CL	195.00	240.00-385.00
82	FIREMAN WATERING HOUSE 303	CL	99.00	99.00-180.00
82	FISH WITH SHOE 803	CL	23.00	35.00-92.00
82	FOX IN AN AIRPLANE 806	CL	23.00	35.00-92.00
82	GEORGIE GOING ANYWHERE 302	CL	95.00	105.00-125.00
82	GIRAFFE 816	CL	57.00	75.00-150.00
82	HERBIE BALANCING HAT 327	CL	26.00	40.00-110.00
82	HERBIE DANCING 325	CL	26.00	40.00-110.00
82	HERBIE HANDS OUTSTRETCHED 326	CL	26.00	40.00-110.00
82	HERBIE LEGS IN AIR 329	CL	26.00	40.00-110.00
82	HERBIE LYING DOWN 328	CL	26.00	40.00-110.00
82	HERBIE TOUCHING GROUND 330	CL	26.00	40.00-110.00
82	HOBO JOE ON CYCLE 322	CL	125.00	170.00-280.00
82	HORSE 819	CL	57.00	75.00-150.00
82	KUKLA AND FRIEND 316	CL	100.00	140.00-210.00
82	LAUREL & HARDY 700	CL	225.00	290.00-500.00
82	LIMOUSINE SERVICE 705	CL	330.00	375.00-750.00
82	LION 817	CL	57.00	75.00-150.00
82	LITTLE HORSE-HEAD UP 341	CL	29.00	72.00
82	MARION WITH MARRIONETTE 317	CL	105.00	135.00-225.00
82	MURPHY ON UNICYCLE 337	CL	115.00	160.00-290.00
82	NAPPY SNOOZING 346	CL	110.00	125.00-210.00
82	NORMAN PAINTING DUMBO 314	CL	126.00	150.00-210.00
82	OSTRICH 813	CL	57.00	75.00-150.00
82	PARROT ROLLERSKATING 809	CL	23.00	35.00-92.00
82	PIG BRICK LAYER 800	CL	23.00	35.00-92.00
82	PINBALL PAL 332	CL	150.00	195.00-287.00
82	QUINCY LYING DOWN 304	CL	80.00	92.00-210.00
82	RABBIT WITH EGG 801	CL	23.00	35.00-92.00
82	REINDEER 812	CL	57.00	75.00-150.00
82	ROBIN RESTING 338	CL	110.00	125.00-210.00
82	RON LEE CAROUSEL	CL	10000.00	12500.00
82	ROOSTER 815	CL	57.00	75.00-150.00
82	ROOSTER WITH BARBELL 808	CL	23.00	35.00-92.00
82	SAMMY RIDING ELEPHANT 309	CL	90.00	100.00-180.00
82	SEAL BLOWING HIS HORNS 804	CL	23.00	35.00-92.00
82	SELF PORTRAIT 702	CL	355.00	550.00-816.00
82	SELF PORTRAIT 702	CL	1000.00	1250.00-2500.00
82	SLIM CHARGING BULL 313	CL	195.00	265.00-410.00
82	SMOKEY, THE BEAR 802	CL	23.00	35.00-92.00
82	STEPPIN' OUT 704	CL	325.00	390.00-700.00
82	THREE MAN VALENTINOS 319	CL	55.00	70.00-120.00
82	TIGER 814	CL	57.00	75.00-150.00
82	TOO LOOSE-L'ARTISTE 312	CL	150.00	180.00-290.00
82	TOU TOU 323	CL	70.00	90.00-190.00
82	TOY SOLDIER 324	CL	95.00	140.00-270.00
82	TURTLE WITH GUN 811	CL	57.00	75.00-150.00
82	TWO MAN VALENTINOS 318	CL	45.00	60.00-130.00
82	WALRUS WITH UMBRELLA 810	CL	23.00	35.00-92.00
83	BEETHOVEN'S FOURTH PAWS 358	CL	59.00	60.00-110.00
83	BLACK CAROUSEL HORSE 1001	CL	450.00	525.00-750.00
83	BUMBLES SELLING BALLOONS 353	CL	80.00	95.00-170.00
83	BUSTER AND HIS BALLOONS 363	CL	47.00	55.00-90.00
83	CAPTAIN FREDDY 375	CL	85.00	200.00-425.00
83	CASEY CRUSING 351	CL	57.00	70.00-95.00
83	CATCH THE BRASS RING 708	CL	510.00	750.00-1150.00
83	CECIL AND SAUSAGE 354	CL	90.00	120.00-190.00
83	CHEF'S CUISINE 361	CL	57.00	70.00-93.00

YR	NAME	LIMIT	ISSUE	QUOTE
83	CHESTNUT CAROUSEL HORSE 1002	CL	450.00	525.00-750.00
83	CIMBA THE ELEPHANT 706	CL	225.00	290.00-450.00
83	CLYDE JUGGLING 339	CL	39.00	45.00
83	CLYDE UPSIDE DOWN 340	CL	39.00	45.00
83	COCO AND HIS COMPACT 369	CL	55.00	70.00-145.00
83	COTTON CANDY 377	CL	150.00	170.00-325.00
83	DARING DUDLEY 367	CL	65.00	75.00-172.00
83	DOOR TO DOOR DABNEY 373	CL	100.00	140.00-210.00
83	ENGINEER BILLIE 356	CL	190.00	275.00-480.00
83	FLIPPER DIVING 345	CL	115.00	140.00-205.00
83	GAZEBO 1004	CL	450.00	525.00-750.00
83	GILBERT TEE'D OFF 376	CL	60.00	85.00-100.00
83	HOBI IN HIS HAMMOCK 344	CL	85.00	90.00-175.00
83	I LOVE YOU FROM MY HEART 360	CL	35.00	50.00
83	JOSEPHINE 370	CL	55.00	70.00-145.00
83	KNICKERS BALANCING FEATHER 366	CL	47.00	55.00-116.00
83	LITTLE HORSE-HEAD DOWN 342	CL	29.00	72.00
83	LITTLE SATURDAY NIGHT 348	CL	53.00	65.00-100.00
83	LOU PROPOSING 365	CL	57.00	65.00-75.00
83	MATINEE JITTERS 378	CL	175.00	180.00-225.00
83	MATINEE JITTERS 901	CL	325.00	350.00-450.00
83	MY DAUGHTER DEBORAH 357	CL	63.00	65.00-125.00
83	NO CAMPING OR FISHING 902	CL	325.00	350.00-400.00
83	ON THE ROAD AGAIN 355	CL	220.00	290.00-500.00
83	RICHES TO RAGS 374	CL	55.00	85.00-275.00
83	RIDE 'EM RONI 347	CL	125.00	145.00-190.00
83	RUFUS AND HIS REFUSE 343	CL	65.00	160.00
83	SAY IT WITH FLOWERS 359	CL	35.00	50.00-95.00
83	SINGIN' IN THE RAIN 362	CL	105.00	129.00-225.00
83	TATTERS AND BALLOONS 352	CL	65.00	70.00-85.00
83	TEETER TOTTIE SCOTTIE 350	CL	55.00	70.00-105.00
83	THE BANDWAGON 707	CL	900.00	1200.00-2450.00
83	THE JOGGER 372	CL	75.00	80.00-115.00
83	THE LAST SCOOP 379	CL	175.00	200.00-350.00
83	THE LAST SCOOP 379	CL	175.00	200.00-350.00
83	THE LAST SCOOP 900	CL	325.00	285.00-400.00
83	TOTTIE SCOTTIE 349	CL	39.00	45.00-75.00
83	UP, UP AND AWAY 364	CL	50.00	65.00-100.00
83	WHITE CAROUSEL HORSE 1003	CL	450.00	525.00-750.00
83	WILT THE STILT 368	CL	49.00	55.00-92.00
84	A BOZO LUNCH 390	CL	148.00	160.00-300.00
84	BAGGY PANTS 387	CL	98.00	110.00-250.00
84	BLACK CIRCUS HORSE 711A	CL	305.00	350.00-520.00
84	CHESTNUT CIRCUS HORSE 710A	CL	305.00	350.00-520.00
84	GIVE A DOG A BONE 383	CL	95.00	95.00-180.00
84	JUST FOR YOU 386	CL	110.00	150.00-275.00
84	LOOK AT THE BIRDY 388	CL	138.00	160.00-255.00
84	MY FELLOW AMERICAN 391	CL	138.00	150.00-400.00
84	NO CAMPING OR FISHING 380	CL	175.00	190.00-275.00
84	NO LOITERING 392	CL	113.00	115.00-205.00
84	RUDY HOLDING BALLOONS 713	CL	230.00	230.00
84	RUDY HOLDING BALLOONS 713	CL	230.00	270.00-410.00
84	SATURDAY NIGHT 714	CL	250.00	500.00
84	T.K. AND OH!! 385	CL	85.00	95.00-210.00
84	THE PEPPERMINTS 384	CL	150.00	180.00-240.00
84	TISKET AND TASKET 393	CL	93.00	105.00-190.00
84	WHEELER SHEILA 381	CL	75.00	90.00-175.00
84	WHITE CIRCUS HORSE 709	CL	305.00	350.00-520.00
85	CLOWNS OF THE CARIBBEAN PS101	CL	1250.00	1750.00-2200.00
85	GIRAFFE GETTING A BATH 428	CL	160.00	235.00-450.00
85	WHISKERS BATHING 749	CL	305.00	305.00
85	WHISKERS HITCHHIKING 745	CL	240.00	240.00
85	WHISKERS HOLDING BALLOON 746	CL	265.00	265.00
85	WHISKERS HOLDING UMBRELLA 747	CL	265.00	265.00
85	WHISKERS ON THE BEACH 750	CL	230.00	230.00
85	WHISKERS SWEEPING 744	CL	240.00	240.00
86	BATHING BUDDIES 450	CL	145.00	150.00-245.00
86	CAPTAIN CRANBERRY 469	CL	140.00	150.00-185.00
86	GETTING EVEN 485	CL	85.00	98.00-120.00
86	HARI AND HARE 454	CL	57.00	65.00-85.00
86	RIDE 'EM PEANUTS 463	CL	55.00	68.00
86	WET PAINT 436	CL	80.00	100.00-150.00
87	FIRST & MAIN L110	CL	368.00	400.00-650.00
87	HEARTBROKEN HARRY L101	CL	63.00	100.00-150.00
87	LOVABLE LUKE L102	8500	70.00	70.00
87	PUPPY LOVE L103	8500	71.00	71.00

YR	NAME	LIMIT	ISSUE	QUOTE
87	SUGARLAND EXPRESS L109	CL	342.00	375.00
87	WOULD YOU LIKE TO RIDE? L104	CL	246.00	300.00-325.00
88	NEW RON LEE CAROUSEL	CL	7000.00	9500.00
88	THE FIFTH WHEEL L117	CL	250.00	295.00
88	TO THE RESCUE L127	CL	130.00	160.00-550.00
88	TUNNEL OF LOVE L123	CL	490.00	550.00
88	WHEN YOU'RE HOT, YOU'RE HOT! L128	CL	221.00	250.00-800.00
89	BE IT EVER SO HUMBLE L111	CL	900.00	950.00-1250.00
89	CATCH A FALLING STAR L148	CL	57.00	57.00
89	CIRCUS LITTLE L143	CL	990.00	1250.00
89	HUGHIE MUNGUS L144	CL	250.00	325.00
89	I PLEDGE ALLEGIANCE L134	3750	131.00	131.00
89	IF I WERE A RICH MAN L133	CL	315.00	375.00-500.00
89	IN OVER MY HEAD L135	CL	95.00	125.00
89	O' SOLO MIA L139	CL	85.00	150.00
89	SH-H-H-H! L146	CL	210.00	400.00-1000.00
89	SNOWDRIFTER L163	CL	230.00	275.00-450.00
89	TEE FOR TWO L141	CL	125.00	150.00
89	THE FIREMAN L169	CL	68.00	85.00
89	THE FISHERMAN L194	7500	72.00	72.00
89	THE GOLFER L188	CL	72.00	90.00
89	THE GREATEST LITTLE SHOE ON EARTH L210	CL	165.00	195.00-225.00
89	THE LAWYER L171	CL	68.00	75.00
89	THE POLICEMAN L165	CL	68.00	75.00-85.00
89	TODAY'S CATCH L147	CL	230.00	275.00-325.00
89	WISHFUL THINKING L114	CL	230.00	250.00-500.00
90	CANDY MAN L217	2750	350.00	350.00
90	FILL'ER UP L248	2250	280.00	280.00
90	HEARTBROKEN HOBO L233	CL	116.00	145.00
90	HENRY 8-3/4 L260	2750	37.00	37.00
90	HORSIN' AROUND L262	2750	37.00	37.00
90	KISS! KISS! L251	2750	37.00	37.00
90	ME TOO! L231	3500	70.00	70.00
90	NA! NA! L252	2750	33.00	33.00
90	PUSH AND PULL L249	2250	260.00	260.00
90	SCOOTER L234	2750	240.00	240.00
90	SNOWDRIFTER II L250	1250	340.00	340.00
90	TANDEM MANIA L235	2750	360.00	360.00
90	THE BIG WHEEL L236	2750	240.00	240.00
90	THE NEW SELF PORTRAIT L218	CL	800.00	950.00
90	UNI-CYCLE L237	2750	240.00	240.00
91	ANYWHERE? L269	1500	125.00	125.00
91	BUSINESS IS BUSINESS L266	1500	110.00	110.00
91	CRUISING L265	1500	170.00	170.00
91	FALL L282	1500	120.00	120.00
91	GILBERT'S DILEMMA L270	1750	90.00	90.00
91	GIVE ME LIBERTY L313	1776	155.00	155.00
91	HAPPY BIRTHDAY PUPPY LOVE L278	1750	73.00	73.00
91	I'M SINGIN' IN THE RAIN L268	1500	135.00	135.00
91	LIT'L SNOWDRIFTER L298	1750	70.00	70.00
91	OUR NATION'S PRIDE L312	1776	150.00	150.00
91	PUPPY LOVE SCOOTIN' L275	1750	73.00	73.00
91	PUPPY LOVE'S FREE RIDE L276	1750	73.00	73.00
91	PUPPY LOVE'S TREAT L277	1750	73.00	73.00
91	SPRING L280	1500	95.00	95.00
91	SUMMER L281	1500	95.00	95.00
91	TA DA! L294	1500	120.00	120.00
91	UNITED WE STAND L314	1776	150.00	150.00
91	WINTER L279	1500	115.00	115.00

R. LEE   **THE RON LEE COLLECTOR'S CLUB RENEWAL SCULPTURES**

YR	NAME	LIMIT	ISSUE	QUOTE
87	DOGGIN' ALONG CC1	YR	75.00	115.00
88	MIDSUMMER'S DREAM CC2	YR	97.00	140.00
89	PEEK-A-BOO CHARLIE CC3	YR	65.00	100.00

R. LEE   **THE RON LEE LOONEY TUNE COLLECTION**

YR	NAME	LIMIT	ISSUE	QUOTE
91	1940 BUG BUNNY LT165	2750	85.00	85.00
91	BUGS BUNNY LT150	2750	123.00	123.00
91	DAFFY DUCK LT140	2750	80.00	85.00
91	ELMER FUDD LT125	2750	87.00	90.00
91	FOGHORN LEGHORN & HENRY HAWK LT160	2750	115.00	115.00
91	MARVIN THE MARTIAN LT170	2750	75.00	75.00
91	MICHIGAN J. FROG LT110	2750	115.00	115.00
91	MT. YOSEMITE LT180	850	160.00	160.00-300.00
91	PEPE LEPEW & PENELOPE LT145	2750	115.00	115.00
91	PORKY PIG LT115	2750	97.00	100.00
91	SYLVESTER & TWEETY LT135	2750	110.00	115.00
91	TASMANIAN DEVIL LT120	2750	105.00	105.00

YR	NAME	LIMIT	ISSUE	QUOTE
91	TWEETY LT155	2750	110.00	115.00
91	WESTERN DAFFY DUCK LT105	2750	87.00	90.00
91	WILE E. COYOTE & ROADRUNNER LT175	2750	165.00	175.00
91	YOSEMITE SAM LT130	2750	110.00	110.00

ROYAL DOULTON

N. PEDLEY — **AGE OF INNOCENCE**

YR	NAME	LIMIT	ISSUE	QUOTE
91	FEEDING TIME	9500	245.00	245.00
91	MAKING FRIENDS	9500	270.00	270.00
91	PUPPY LOVE	9500	270.00	270.00

M. ABBERLEY — **ANTAGONISTS CHARACTER JUGS**

86	GEORGE III & GEORGE WASHINGTON	9500	195.00	195.00

M. ALCOCK — **BEATRIX POTTER**

93	BENJAMIN BUNNY	OP	65.00	65.00
93	JEMIMA PUDDLEDUCK	OP	65.00	65.00
93	JEREMY FISHER	OP	65.00	65.00
93	MRS. RABBIT	OP	65.00	65.00
93	PETER RABBIT	OP	65.00	65.00
93	TOM KITTEN	OP	65.00	65.00
95	PETER IN BED	OP	39.95	39.95
95	FOXY WHISKERED GENTLEMAN	OP	65.00	65.00
95	TAILOR OF GLOUCESTER	O	65.00	65.00

W. PLATT — **BRAMBLY HEDGE FIGURES**

93	MR. SALTAPPLE	OP	40.00	40.00
93	MRS. SALTAPPLE	OP	40.00	40.00

V. ANNAND — **BRITISH SPORTING HERITAGE**

93	HENLEY	5,000	475.00	475.00
94	ASCOT	5,000	450.00	450.00
95	WIMBLEDON	5,000	475.00	475.00

M. ALCOCK — **CHARACTER JUG OF THE YEAR**

94	CAPTAIN HOOK	OP	235.00	235.00
93	VICE-ADMIRAL LORD NELSON	OP	225.00	225.00
95	CAPTAIN BLIGH	OP	200.00	200.00

* — **CHARACTER JUGS**

91	FORTUNE TELLER	YR	130.00	130.00
91	SANTA CLAUS MINIATURE	5000	50.00	50.00
92	WINSTON CHURCHILL	YR	195.00	195.00
91	HENRY VIII	1991	395.00	395.00

D. BIGGS — **CHARACTER SCULPTURE**

95	GULLIVER	OP	285.00	285.00

A. MASLANKOWSKI — **CHARACTER SCULPTURES**

93	LONG JOHN SILVER	OP	250.00	250.00
93	ROBINHOOD	OP	250.00	250.00
94	PIED PIPER	OP	260.00	260.00
94	WIZARD	OP	340.00	340.00
93	CAPTAIN HOOK	OP	250.00	250.00
93	DICK TURPIN	OP	250.00	250.00
94	D'ARTAGNAN	OP	260.00	260.00

P. GEE — **CHARACTER STUDIES**

94	THE PIPER	OP	295.00	295.00
94	GRANDPA'S STORY	OP	275.00	275.00
94	WHEN I WAS YOUNG	OP	275.00	275.00
95	RICHARD THE LIONHEART	OP	500.00	500.00
93	FATHER CHRISTMAS	OP	195.00	195.00

A. MASLANKOWSKI — **CHILD FIGURES**

93	BALLET SHOES	OP	73.50	73.50
93	DADDY'S GIRL	OP	75.00	75.00
94	FLOWERS FOR MOTHER	OP	98.00	98.00
93	ALMOST GROWN	OP	65.00	65.00
93	BEST WISHES	OP	165.00	165.00
93	BIRTHDAY GIRL	OP	130.00	130.00
93	FLOWERGIRL	OP	99.00	99.00
93	MY FIRST FIGURINE	OP	110.00	110.00
94	A POSY FOR YOU	OP	98.00	98.00
94	FIRST RECITAL	OP	98.00	98.00
94	HELLO DADDY	OP	125.00	125.00
94	MOTHER'S HELPER	OP	98.00	98.00
94	SPECIAL FRIEND	OP	98.00	98.00
94	YOUNG MELODY	OP	98.00	98.00
95	HOMETIME	OP	135.00	135.00
95	SPECIAL TREAT	OP	135.00	135.00
95	WHAT'S THAT MATTER	OP	135.00	135.00

M. ALCOCK — **CHRISTMAS MINI JUGS**

94	SNOWMAN MINI	2,500	62.00	62.00
93	ELE MINI	2,500	55.00	55.00

M. DAVIES — **DANCERS OF THE WORLD**

77	DANCERS, FLAMENCO	750	400.00	1100.00-1300.00

YR	NAME	LIMIT	ISSUE	QUOTE
77	DANCERS, INDIAN TEMPLE	750	400.00	1200.00-1400.00
78	DANCERS, PHILIPPINE	750	450.00	650.00-700.00
78	DANCERS, SCOTTISH	750	450.00	900.00-1100.00
79	DANCERS, KURDISH	750	550.00	500.00-600.00
79	DANCERS, MEXICAN	750	550.00	500.00-600.00
80	DANCERS, CHINESE	750	750.00	600.00-650.00
80	DANCERS, NORTH AMERICAN INDIAN	750	950.00	500.00-650.00
80	DANCERS, POLISH	750	750.00	600.00-750.00
81	DANCERS, BRETON	750	850.00	550.00-600.00
81	DANCERS, WEST INDIAN	750	850.00	550.00-700.00
82	DANCERS, BALINESE	750	950.00	550.00-650.00
M. DAVIES				**FEMMES FATALES**
79	CLEOPATRA	750	750.00	1200.00-1400.00
81	HELEN OF TROY	750	1250.00	975.00-1200.00
82	QUEEN OF SHEBA	750	1250.00	975.00-1200.00
83	TZ'U-HSI	750	1250.00	975.00-1200.00
84	EVE	750	1250.00	975.00-1275.00
85	LUCREZIA BORGIA	750	1250.00	1150.00-1300.00
V. ANNAND				**FIGURE OF THE YEAR**
93	PATRICIA	RT	250.00	275.00
91	AMY	YR	245.00	245.00
92	MARY	YR	225.00	225.00
94	JENNIFER	OP	250.00	260.00
95	DEBORAH	OP	225.00	225.00
V. ANNAND				**FLOWERS OF LOVE**
95	CAMELLIAS	OP	325.00	325.00
95	FORGET ME NOTS	OP	325.00	325.00
V. ANNAND				**FOUR SEAONS**
95	WINTERTIME	OP	325.00	325.00
V. ANNAND				**FOUR SEASONS**
93	SPRINGTIME	OP	325.00	325.00
94	AUTUMNTIME	OP	325.00	325.00
94	SUMMERTIME	OP	325.00	325.00
P. GEE				**GAINSBOROUGH LADIES**
*	MARY, COUNTESS HOWE	5000	650.00	650.00
91	COUNTESS OF SEFTON	5000	650.00	650.00
91	HON FRANCES DUNCOMBE	5000	650.00	650.00
91	LADY SHEFFIELD	5000	650.00	650.00
*				**GENTLE ARTS**
*	ADORNMENT	750	1350.00	1350.00
*	FLOWER ARRANGING	750	1350.00	1350.00
84	SPINNING	750	1250.00	1400.00
85	TAPESTRY WEAVING	750	1250.00	1250.00
86	WRITING	750	1350.00	1350.00
87	PAINTING	750	1350.00	1350.00
R. JEFFERSON				**GREAT LOVERS**
93	ROMEO & JULIET	150	5250.00	5250.00
94	ROBINHOOD & MAID MARIAN	150	5250.00	5250.00
V. ANNAND				**HN FIGURES**
94	ANNIVERSARY	OP	575.00	575.00
P. GEE				**IMAGES**
93	GIFT OF FREEEDOM	OP	85.00	85.00
93	BROTHER & SISTER	OP	50.00	50.00
93	OUR FIRST CHRISTMAS	OP	475.00	175.00
A. HUGHES				**IMAGES OF NATURE**
93	ALWAYS AND FOREVER	OP	55.00	55.00
A. MASLANKOWSKI				**IMAGES OF NATURES**
94	NEW ARRIVAL	OP	50.00	50.00
M. DAVIES				**LADY MUSICIANS**
70	CELLO	750	250.00	1100.00
71	VIRGINALS	750	250.00	1200.00-1300.00
72	LUTE	750	250.00	675.00-900.00
72	VIOLIN	750	250.00	1000.00
73	FLUTE	750	250.00	850.00-975.00
73	HARP	750	275.00	1300.00
74	CHITARRONE	750	250.00	550.00-700.00
74	CYMBALS	750	325.00	500.00-700.00
75	DULCIMER	750	375.00	550.00-650.00
75	HURDY GURDY	750	375.00	500.00-600.00
76	FRENCH HORN	750	400.00	500.00
76	VIOLA D'AMORE	750	400.00	500.00
D. BIGGS				**LARGE SIZE JUGS**
95	ALFRED HITCHCOCK	OP	200.00	200.00
94	GLENN MILLER	OP	270.00	270.00
R. JEFFERSON				**LES SAISONS**
*	L'ETE	300	850.00	895.00

YR	NAME	LIMIT	ISSUE	QUOTE
*	L'HIVER	300	850.00	795.00
86	AUTOMNE	300	850.00	875.00-1000.00
87	PRINTEMPS	300	850.00	795.00-850.00
A. MASLANKOWSKI			**LIMITED EDITION FIGURES**	
93	WINSTON S. CHURCHILL	5,000	595.00	595.00
93	ROBERT E. LEE	5,000	1175.00	1175.00
93	ULYSSES S. GRANT	5,000	1175.00	1175.00
94	FIELD MARSHAL MONTGOMERY	1,994	1100.00	1100.00
D. BIGGS			**LIMITED EDITION JUGS**	
94	ALADDIN'S GENIE	1,500	335.00	335.00
93	WILLIAM SHAKESPHERE	2,500	625.00	625.00
94	OLIVER CROMWELL	2,500	475.00	475.00
95	CHARLES DICKENS	2,500	500.00	500.00
94	DIAMOND ANNIVERSARY TINIES	2,500	325.00	325.00
93	NAPOLEON	2,000	225.00	225.00
W. HARPER			**LIMITED EDITION TOBY JUGS**	
93	FATHER CHRISTMAS TOBY	3,500	125.00	125.00
93	CLOWN TOBY	3,000	175.00	175.00
94	KING & QUEEN OF DIAMONDS TOBY	2,500	260.00	260.00
94	LEPRECHAUN TOBY	2,500	150.00	150.00
95	JUDGE AND THIEF TOBY	OP	185.00	185.00
P. GEE			**MINIATURES**	
93	TOP O' THE HILL	OP	120.00	120.00
94	HANNAH	OP	142.00	142.00
R. JEFFERSON			**MYTHS & MAIDENS**	
82	LADY & UNICORN	300	2500.00	3000.00
83	LEDA & SWAN	300	2500.00	2950.00
84	JUNO & PEACOCK	300	2500.00	2950.00
85	EUROPA & BULL	300	2500.00	2950.00
86	DIANA THE HUNTRESS	300	2500.00	2950.00
A MASLANKOWSKI			**NATIVITY**	
93	HOLY FAMILY (JESUS, MARY & JOSEPH)	RT	250.00	275.00
S. TAYLOR			**PRESIDENTAL SERIES**	
94	THOMAS JEFFERSON	2,500	200.00	200.00
S. TAYLOR			**PRESIDENTIAL SERIES**	
93	ABRAHAM LINCOLN	2,500	190.00	190.00
95	GEORGE WASHINGTON	2,500	200.00	200.00
*			**PRESTIGE FIGURES**	
91	COLUMBINE	*	1250.00	1250.00
91	FIGHTER ELEPHANT	*	2500.00	2500.00
91	FOX	*	1550.00	1550.00
91	HARLEQUIN	*	1250.00	1250.00
91	JACK POINT	*	2900.00	2900.00
91	KING CHARLES	*	2500.00	2500.00
91	LEOPARD ON ROCK	*	3000.00	3000.00
91	LION ON ROCK	*	3000.00	3000.00
91	MATADOR AND BULL	*	21500.00	21500.00
91	PRINCESS BADOURA	*	28000.00	28000.00
91	ST. GEORGE AND DRAGON	*	13600.00	13600.00
91	THE MOOR	*	2500.00	2500.00
91	TIGER	*	1950.00	1950.00
91	TIGER ON ROCK	*	3000.00	3000.00
93	DUKE OF WELLINGTON	1,500	1750.00	1750.00
93	VICE-ADMIRAL LORD NELSON	950	1750.00	1750.00
95	CHARGE OF THE LIGHT BRIDGADE	SP	16000.00	16,000.00
P. GEE			**PRETTY LADIES**	
93	AMY'S SITER	OP	225.00	225.00
93	HELEN	OP	225.00	225.00
93	JOANNE	OP	185.00	185.00
93	NICOLE	OP	155.00	155.00
94	HOLLY	OP	195.00	195.00
95	GEMMA	OP	195.00	195.00
95	HANNAH	OP	250.00	250.00
95	HAPPY BIRTHDAY	OP	250.00	250.00
94	ALEXANDRA	OP	250.00	250.00
*			**QUEENS OF REALM**	
*	MARY, QUEEN OF SCOTS	SO	550.00	750.00
*	QUEEN ANNE	5000	525.00	550.00
*	QUEEN ELIZABETH I	SO	495.00	550.00
*	QUEEN VICTORIA	SO	495.00	950.00
P. GEE			**REYNOLDS COLLECTION**	
91	LADY WORSLEY HN3318	5000	550.00	550.00-600.00
P. GEE			**REYNOLDS LADIES**	
93	COUNTLESS SPENCER	5,000	595.00	595.00
*			**ROYAL DOULTON COLLECTORS' CLUB**	
80	JOHN DOULTON JUG (8 O'CLOCK)	YR	70.00	125.00

YR	NAME	LIMIT	ISSUE	QUOTE
81	SLEEPY DARLING FIGURE	YR	100.00	195.00
82	DOG OF FO	YR	50.00	150.00
82	PRIZED POSSESSIONS FIGURE	YR	125.00	475.00
83	LOVING CUP	YR	75.00	275.00
83	SPRINGTIME	YR	125.00	350.00
84	PRIDE & JOY FIGURE	YR	125.00	225.00
84	SIR HENRY DOULTON JUG	YR	50.00	125.00
85	TOP OF THE HILL PLATE	YR	34.95	75.00
85	WINTERTIME FIGURE	YR	125.00	195.00
86	ALBERT SAGGER TOBY JUG	YR	34.95	70.00
86	AUCTIONEER FIGURE	YR	150.00	195.00
87	COLLECTOR BUNNYKINS	YR	40.00	295.00
87	SUMMERTIME FIGURE	YR	140.00	150.00
88	BEEFEATER TINY JUG	YR	25.00	125.00
88	OLD SALT TEA POT	YR	135.00	250.00
88	TOP OF THE HILL MINIATURE FIGURINE	YR	95.00	125.00

M. DAVIES — ROYAL DOULTON FIGURINES

YR	NAME	LIMIT	ISSUE	QUOTE
67	INDIAN BRAVE	500	2500.00	6500.00-8000.00
71	THE PALIO	500	2500.00	6500.00-7000.00
33	BEETHOVEN	25	*	6000.00-6500.00

M. DAVIES — ROYALTY

YR	NAME	LIMIT	ISSUE	QUOTE
73	QUEEN ELIZABETH II	750	200.00	1900.00
80	QUEEN MOTHER	1500	650.00	1200.00-1400.00
81	DUKE OF EDINBURGH	750	395.00	400.00
82	LADY DIANA SPENCER HN2885	1500	395.00	650.00-900.00
82	PRINCE OF WALES HN2883	1500	395.00	450.00-600.00
82	PRINCE OF WALES HN2884	1500	750.00	750.00-800.00
82	PRINCESS OF WALES HN2887	1500	750.00	800.00-1250.00
86	DUCHESS OF YORK	1500	495.00	475.00-700.00

* * — SEASONAL FIGURES

YR	NAME	LIMIT	ISSUE	QUOTE
94	CHRISTMAS SURPRISE BUNNYKINS	OP	50.00	50.00
93	HALLOWEEN BUNNYKINS	OP	50.00	50.00
95	EASTER GREETINGS BUNNYKINS	OP	50.00	50.00

A. MASLANKOWSKI — SENTIMENTS

YR	NAME	LIMIT	ISSUE	QUOTE
93	CHRISTMAS DAY	OP	65.00	65.00
94	CHRISTMAS PARCELS	OP	60.00	60.00

S. KEENAN — SHIP FIGUREHEADS

YR	NAME	LIMIT	ISSUE	QUOTE
*	AJAX	950	*	550.00
*	BENMORE	950	*	550.00
*	CHIEFTAIN	950	*	650.00
*	HIBERNIA	950	*	850.00
*	LALLA ROOKH	950	*	750.00
*	LORD NELSON	950	*	750.00
*	MARY, QUEEN OF SCOTS	950	*	1200.00
*	POCAHONTAS	950	*	950.00

W. HARPER — SMALL SIZE JUGS

YR	NAME	LIMIT	ISSUE	QUOTE
93	SHAKESPHERE	OP	95.00	95.00
93	WINSTON CHURCHILL	OP	99.00	99.00

E. GRIFFITHS — SOLDIERS OF THE REVOLUTION

YR	NAME	LIMIT	ISSUE	QUOTE
75	SOLDIERS, CONNECTICUT	350	750.00	750.00-800.00
75	SOLDIERS, DELAWARE	350	750.00	750.00-800.00
75	SOLDIERS, GEORGIA	350	750.00	750.00-1000.00
75	SOLDIERS, MARYLAND	350	750.00	750.00-800.00
75	SOLDIERS, MASSACHUSETTS	350	750.00	750.00-800.00
75	SOLDIERS, NEW HAMPSHIRE	350	750.00	750.00-900.00
75	SOLDIERS, NEW JERSEY	350	750.00	1100.00-1500.00
75	SOLDIERS, NEW YORK	350	750.00	750.00-800.00
75	SOLDIERS, NORTH CAROLINA	350	750.00	750.00-800.00
75	SOLDIERS, PENNSYLVANIA	350	750.00	750.00-800.00
75	SOLDIERS, RHODE ISLAND	350	750.00	750.00-800.00
75	SOLDIERS, SOUTH CAROLINA	350	750.00	750.00-800.00
75	SOLDIERS, VIRGINIA	350	1500.00	2500.00-3200.00
77	SOLDIERS, WASHINGTON	750	*	2000.00-2500.00

M. ABBERLEY — STAR CROSSED LOVERS CHARACTER JUGS

YR	NAME	LIMIT	ISSUE	QUOTE
*	ANTHONY & CLEOPATRA	SO	195.00	195.00
86	NAPOLEON & JOSEPHINE	9500	195.00	195.00
88	SAMSON & DELILAH	9500	195.00	195.00
89	KING ARTHUR & GUINEVERE	9500	195.00	195.00

N. PEDLEY — VANITY FAIR

YR	NAME	LIMIT	ISSUE	QUOTE
93	DAWN	OP	125.00	125.00
93	GIFT OF LOVE	OP	125.00	125.00
94	GOOD COMPANION	OP	185.00	185.00
94	LINDSAY	OP	142.00	142.00
95	TAKE ME HOME	OP	195.00	195.00
93	MARIA	OP	125.00	125.00

ROYAL WORCESTER

YR	NAME	LIMIT	ISSUE	QUOTE
*			**200TH ANNIVERSARY COLLECTION**	
89	AUGUSTA VASE	200	4500.00	4500.00
89	CHAMBERLAIN CROCUS POT	200	4000.00	4000.00
89	CLARENCE VASE	200	1500.00	1500.00
89	ELIZABETH VASE	200	1500.00	1500.00
89	FLIGHT BOWL	200	1200.00	1200.00
89	GLOUCESTER ICE PAIL	200	4000.00	4000.00
89	HANCOCK VASE	200	2500.00	2500.00
89	KING GEORGE III VASE	200	4000.00	4000.00
89	QUEEN CHARLOTTE VASE	200	4000.00	4000.00
89	REGENT POT POURRI	200	3500.00	3500.00
P.W. BASTON			**BICENTENNIAL L.E. COMMEMORATIVES**	
74	BLACKSMITH	500	200.00	400.00
74	CABINETMAKER	500	200.00	400.00
74	CLOCKMAKER	500	200.00	500.00
74	POTTER	500	200.00	400.00
D. FRIAR		**BIRDS AND FLOWERS OF AMERICA SCULPTURES**		
84	THE BLUEBIRD AND FIR	9800	135.00	135.00
84	THE CARDINAL AND DOWNY HAWTHORNE	9800	135.00	135.00
84	THE CHICKADEE AND DAISY	9800	135.00	135.00
84	THE GOLDFINCH AND DOGWOOD	9800	135.00	135.00
84	THE KINGFISHER AND WATER LILY	9800	135.00	135.00
84	THE ROBIN AND NARCISSUS	9800	135.00	135.00
84	THE SWALLOW AND WILD ROSE	9800	135.00	135.00
84	THE WREN AND BLACKBERRY	9800	135.00	135.00
D. LINDER			**DORIS LINDER PORCELAINS**	
47	QUEEN ELIZABETH ON TOMMY	100	275.00	13200.00
59	HEREFORD BULL	1000	350.00	650.00-775.00
60	FOX HUNTER	500	500.00	*
61	ANGUS BULL	500	350.00	*
61	JERSEY COW	500	300.00	550.00-600.00
61	OFFICER OF ROYAL HORSE GUARDS	150	500.00	*
61	OFFICER OF THE LIFE GUARDS	150	500.00	*
61	SANTA GERTRUDIS BULL	500	350.00	675.00-700.00
62	QUARTER HORSE	500	400.00	*
63	ARAB STALLION	500	450.00	*
63	MERANO	500	500.00	1375.00
64	BRITISH FRIESIAN BULL	500	400.00	800.00-900.00
64	JERSEY BULL	500	400.00	900.00-975.00
64	SHIRE STALLION	500	700.00	1300.00-1400.00
65	HYPERION	500	525.00	850.00
66	DAIRY SHORTHORN BULL	500	475.00	875.00-900.00
66	PERCHERON STALLION	500	725.00	*
66	ROYAL CANADIAN MOUNTY	500	875.00	1400.00-1600.00
66	WELSH MOUNTAIN PONY	500	3000.00	2500.00-3000.00
67	ARKLE	500	525.00	825.00
68	BRAHMA BULL	500	400.00	*
68	BULLDOG	500	*	*
68	CHAROLAIS BULL	500	400.00	800.00-875.00
68	DUKE OF EDINBURGH	750	100.00	*
69	APPALOOSA	750	550.00	1200.00-1500.00
69	SULFOLK PUNCH	500	650.00	975.00
70	MARION COAKES-MOULD	750	750.00	1500.00
71	PALOMINO	750	975.00	*
71	PRINCESS GRACE & FOAL, COLOR	750	1500.00	1500.00-1700.00
71	PRINCESS GRACE & FOAL, WHITE	250	1400.00	1400.00-1600.00
72	NIJINSKY	500	2000.00	2000.00
73	AMERICAN SADDLE HORSE	750	1450.00	*
73	PRINCESS ANNE ON DOUBLET	750	4250.00	4250.00
75	GALLOPING PONIES, COLORED	500	3300.00	*
75	GALLOPING, CLASSIC	250	2500.00	*
76	DUKE OF MARLBOROUGH	350	5200.00	5200.00
76	GALLOPING IN WINTER	250	3500.00	*
76	HACKNEY	500	1500.00	1500.00
76	MILL REEF	500	2000.00	2000.00
76	NEW BORN, COLOR	500	1800.00	1800.00
76	NEW BORN, WHITE	150	1250.00	1250.00
76	RED RUM	250	2000.00	2000.00
76	RICHARD MEADE	500	2450.00	2450.00
77	CLYDESDALE	500	1250.00	1250.00
77	GRUNDY	500	1800.00	1800.00
77	HIGHLAND BULL	500	900.00	900.00
D. DOUGHTY			**DOROTHY DOUGHTY PORCELAINS**	
35	AMERICAN REDSTARTS AND HEMLOCK	66	*	5500.00
36	BLUEBIRDS	350	500.00	8500.00-9000.00

YR	NAME	LIMIT	ISSUE	QUOTE
36	GOLDFINCHES & THISTLE	250	350.00	2000.00-7000.00
37	CARDINALS	500	500.00	2000.00-9250.00
38	BALTIMORE ORIOLES	250	350.00	*
38	CHICKADEES & LARCH	300	350.00	8500.00-8900.00
40	BOBWHITE QUAIL	22	275.00	11000.00
40	CRABAPPLES	250	400.00	3700.00-4250.00
40	MOCKINGBIRDS	500	450.00	7200.00-7750.00
41	APPLE BLOSSOMS	250	400.00	1400.00-3750.00
42	CRABAPPLE BLOSSOM SPRAYS AND A BUTTERFLY	250	*	800.00
42	INDIGO BUNTING AND PLUM TWIG	5000	*	*
42	INDIGO BUNTINGS, BLACKBERRY SPRAYS	500	375.00	1700.00-3500.00
42	MOCKINGBIRDS AND PEACH BLOSSOM	500	*	*
47	ORANGE BLOSSOMS & BUTTERFLY	250	500.00	4200.00-4500.00
50	HUMMINGBIRDS AND FUSCHSIA	500	*	2800.00
50	MAGNOLIA WARBLER	150	1100.00	1900.00-3600.00
50	MEXICAN FEIJOA	250	600.00	2600.00-4900.00
52	KINGLETS & NOBLE PINE	500	450.00	1300.00-4800.00
52	RED-EYED VIREOS	500	450.00	2000.00
52	YELLOW-HEADED BLACKBIRDS	350	650.00	2000.00-2400.00
55	GNATCATCHERS	500	600.00	2700.00-4900.00
55	MYRTLE WARBLERS	500	550.00	1300.00-4000.00
56	BEWICK'S WRENS & YELLOW JASMINE	500	600.00	2100.00-3800.00
56	SCARLET TANAGERS	500	675.00	3000.00-4200.00
57	OVENBIRDS	250	650.00	4500.00
57	PARULA WARBLERS	500	600.00	1700.00-3600.00
58	PHOEBES ON FLAME VINE	500	750.00	2200.00-5500.00
58	YELLOWTHROATS ON WATER HYACINTH	350	750.00	1700.00-4000.00
59	CACTUS WRENS	500	1250.00	1700.00-4500.00
59	ELF OWL	500	875.00	*
60	CANYON WRENS	500	750.00	2000.00-4000.00
61	HOODED WARBLERS	500	950.00	4300.00
62	LAZULI BUNTING & CHOKECHERRIES, COLOR	500	1350.00	3000.00-4500.00
62	LAZULI BUNTING & CHOKECHERRIES, WHITE	100	1350.00	2600.00-3000.00
62	SCISSOR-TAILED FLYCATCHER, COLOR	250	950.00	*
62	SCISSOR-TAILED FLYCATCHER, WHITE	75	950.00	1300.00-1600.00
63	AUDUBON WARBLERS	500	1350.00	2100.00-4200.00
63	VERMILLION FLYCATCHERS	500	250.00	1100.00-3400.00
64	BLUE TITS & PUSSY WILLOW	500	250.00	3000.00
64	LESSER WHITETHROATS	500	350.00	1200.00-4000.00
64	MOORHEN CHICK	500	1000.00	*
64	MOUNTAIN BLUEBIRDS	500	950.00	1700.00-2300.00
64	ROBIN	500	750.00	*
64	WRENS & BURNET ROSE	500	650.00	1000.00
65	CERULEAN WARBLERS & RED MAPLE	500	1350.00	1400.00-3000.00
65	CHUFFCHAFF	500	1500.00	1300.00-2900.00
65	KINGFISHER COCK & AUTUMN BEECH	500	1250.00	1900.00-2300.00
66	LARK SPARROW	500	750.00	*
67	DOWNY WOODPECKER & PECAN, COLOR	400	1500.00	1000.00-2400.00
67	DOWNY WOODPECKER & PECAN, WHITE	75	1000.00	1900.00
68	CAROLINA PAROQUET, COLOR	350	1200.00	1900.00-2200.00
68	CAROLINA PAROQUET, WHITE	75	600.00	*
68	GRAY WAGTAIL	500	600.00	*
68	REDSTARTS & GORSE	500	1900.00	2300.00
71	NIGHTINGALE & HONEYSUCKLE	500	2500.00	100.00-2750.00
72	GOLDCRESTS, PAIR	500	4200.00	*
77	MEADOW PIPIT	500	1800.00	1800.00
N. ROESSLER		**NORBERT E.J. ROESSLER BRONZES**		
76	HUMMER, WITH FUSHSIA	500	225.00	225.00
76	MARLIN	500	250.00	250.00
R. VAN RUYCKEVELT		**RONALD VAN RUYCKEVELT PORCELAINS**		
*	ALICE	500	1875.00	1875.00
*	CECILIA	500	1875.00	1875.00
56	HOGFISH & SERGEANT MAJOR	500	375.00	650.00
58	RED HIND	500	375.00	900.00
61	PASSIONFLOWER	500	300.00	400.00
61	SQUIRRELFISH	500	400.00	9000.00
62	FLYING FISH	300	400.00	450.00
62	HIBISCUS	500	300.00	350.00
62	SAILFISH	500	400.00	550.00
64	ROCK BEAUTY	500	425.00	850.00
64	TARPON	500	500.00	975.00
65	BLUE MARLIN	500	500.00	1000.00
66	SWORDFISH	500	575.00	650.00
67	BLUEFIN TUNA	500	500.00	*
67	BUTTERFLY FISH	500	375.00	1600.00
68	BLUE ANGEL FISH	500	375.00	900.00

YR	NAME	LIMIT	ISSUE	QUOTE
68	DOLPHIN	500	500.00	900.00
68	HONFLEUR A-105	290	*	600.00
68	HONFLEUR A-106	290	*	600.00
68	MALLARDS	500	*	2000.00
68	MENNECY A-101	338	*	675.00-725.00
68	MENNECY A-102	334	*	675.00-725.00
68	RAINBOW PARROT FISH	500	1500.00	1500.00
68	RING-NECKED PHEASANTS	500	*	3200.00-3400.00
69	ARGENTEUIL A-108	338	*	*
69	BOBWHITE QUAIL, PAIR	500	*	2000.00
69	CASTELNEAU PINK	429	*	825.00-875.00
69	CASTELNEAU YELLOW	163	*	825.00-875.00
69	SAINT DENIS A-109	500	*	925.00-950.00
70	AMERICAN PINTAIL, PAIR	500	*	3000.00
71	ELAINE	750	600.00	600.00-650.00
71	GREEN-WINGED TEAL	500	1450.00	1450.00
71	LANGUEDOC	216	*	1150.00
72	WHITE DOVES	25	3600.00	27850.00
76	PICNIC	250	2850.00	2850.00
76	QUEEN ELIZABETH I	250	3850.00	3850.00
76	QUEEN MARY I	250	4850.00	4850.00
77	QUEEN ELIZABETH II	250	*	*

D. FRIAR   ROYAL WORCESTER GREAT AMERICAN BIRDS OF PREY

YR	NAME	LIMIT	ISSUE	QUOTE
85	AMERICAN KESTREL	9800	195.00	195.00
85	BALD EAGLE	9800	195.00	195.00
85	COOPERS HAWK	9800	195.00	195.00
85	GREAT HORNED OWL	9800	195.00	195.00
85	GYRFALCON	9800	195.00	195.00
85	PEREGRINE FALCON	9800	195.00	195.00
85	RED TAIL HAWK	9800	195.00	195.00
85	SCREECH OWL	9800	195.00	195.00

R. VAN RUYCKEVELT   RUTH VAN RUYCKEVELT PORCELAINS

YR	NAME	LIMIT	ISSUE	QUOTE
59	LISETTE	500	100.00	*
59	PENELOPE	500	100.00	*
60	BEATRICE	500	125.00	*
60	CAROLINE	500	125.00	*
62	LOUISA	500	400.00	975.00
63	SISTER OF LONDON HOSPITAL	500	*	475.00-500.00
63	SISTER OF ST. THOMAS HOSPITAL	500	*	475.00-500.00
64	MELANIE	500	150.00	*
64	ROSALIND	500	150.00	*
64	TEA PARTY	250	400.00	7000.00
66	SISTER OF UNIVERSITY COLLEGE HOSPITAL	500	*	475.00-500.00
67	ELIZABETH	750	300.00	750.00-800.00
68	CHARLOTTE AND JANE	500	1000.00	1500.00-1650.00
68	MADELINE	500	300.00	750.00-800.00
68	MARION	500	275.00	575.00-625.00
69	BRIDGET	500	300.00	600.00-700.00
69	EMILY	500	300.00	600.00
70	SISTER OF THE RED CROSS	750	*	525.00-500.00
71	FELICITY	750	600.00	600.00
78	ESTHER	500	*	*

K. POTTS   SPECIAL ISSUE

YR	NAME	LIMIT	ISSUE	QUOTE
88	QUEEN ELIZABETH I	100	15000.00	15000.00

SANDICAST

S. BRUE   BARKITECTURE

YR	NAME	LIMIT	ISSUE	QUOTE
93	BEACON HILL TOWNHOUSE & BOSTON TERRIER	RT	12.50	15.00
93	EIFFEL TOWER & POODLE	RT	12.50	15.00
93	ENGLISH THATCHED COTTAGE & LABRADOR	RT	12.50	15.00
93	GERMAN CASTLE & ROTTWEILER	RT	12.50	15.00
93	IGLOO & HUSKY	RT	12.50	15.00
93	IRISH COTTAGE & SETTER	RT	12.50	15.00
93	JAPANESE PAGODA & AKITA	RT	12.50	15.00
93	LOG CABIN & BLOODHOUND	RT	12.50	15.00
93	MAYAN TEMPLE & CHIHUAHUA	RT	12.50	15.00
93	SCOTTISH CASTLE & WESTIE	RT	12.50	15.00
93	SWISS CHALET & ST. BERNARD	RT	12.50	15.00
93	TIBETAN TEMPLE & LHASA	RT	12.50	15.00

S. BRUE   COLLECTOR'S GUILD

YR	NAME	LIMIT	ISSUE	QUOTE
94	COLLECTOR'S GUILD MEMBERSHIP KIT	YR	20.00	25.OO

S. BRUE   FOREVER FRIENDS

YR	NAME	LIMIT	ISSUE	QUOTE
93	BASSET & PUP	*	34.00	45.00
93	BEAGEL & PUP	*	34.00	45.00
93	BOXER PUP, BRINDLE	RT	34.00	45.00
93	BOXER PUP, FAWN	*	34.00	45.00
93	CAT & KITTEN, BLACK	*	34.00	45.00

YR	NAME	LIMIT	ISSUE	QUOTE
93	CAT & KITTEN, BLACK AND WHITE	*	34.00	45.00
93	CAT & KITTEN, CALICO	*	34.00	45.00
93	CAT & KITTEN, ORANGE AND WHITE	*	34.00	45.00
93	CAT, GRAY AND WHITE	*	34.00	45.00
93	CAT, WHITE	*	34.00	45.00
93	COCKER & PUP, BLACK	*	34.00	45.00
93	COCKER & PUP, BUFF	*	34.00	45.00
93	COCKER & PUP, PARTI BLACK	*	34.00	45.00
93	COCKER & PUP, PARTI BUFF	*	34.00	45.00
93	GOLDEN RETRIEVER & PUP	*	34.00	45.00
93	HARP SEAL & PUP	*	34.00	45.00
93	LION & CUB	*	34.00	45.00
93	PENGUIN & CHICK	*	34.00	45.00
93	SCHNAUZER & PUP	*	34.00	45.00
94	LAB & PUP, BLACK	*	34.00	40.00
94	LAB & PUP, CHOCOLATE	*	34.00	40.00
94	LAB & PUP, YELLOW	*	34.00	40.00
94	POLAR BEAR & CUB	*	31.00	37.00
S. BRUE				**LIFE SIZE**
93	CAVALIER KING CHARLES SPANIEL	*	54.00	65.00
93	PANDA CUB	*	69.00	80.00
94	COLLIE PUP, SABLE	*	54.00	60.00
94	JACK RUSSELL TERRIER	*	54.00	60.00
94	JACK RUSSELL TERRIER, BLACK AND WHITE	*	54.00	60.00
94	ST. BERNARD PUP	*	54.00	60.00
S. BRUE				**LIFESIZE**
93	CAT, BLACK AND WHITE	*	54.00	45.00
S. BRUE				**LIL' SNOOZERS**
94	KITTEN, MIDNIGHT	*	4.50	6.00
94	NODDER, MIDNIGHT	*	4.50	6.00
94	YAWNER, BLACK	*	4.50	6.00
S. BRUE				**LION KING**
94	ADULT SIMBA	*	34.00	40.00
94	MUFASA & SIMBA	*	34.00	40.00
94	PRIDE ROCK DISPLAY	*	30.00	35.00
94	SIMBA & NALA	*	34.00	40.00
94	YOUNG NALA	*	9.00	12.00
94	YOUNG SIMBA	*	9.00	12.00
S. BRUE				**NATURE'S HABITAT**
94	BISON	5000	40.00	50.00
94	GRIZZLY BEAR	5000	40.00	50.00
94	HABITAT	5000	50.00	60.00
94	MOOSE	5000	40.00	50.00
94	TIMBER WOLF	RT	20.00	25.00
S. BRUE				**ORIGINALS**
93	DOBIE, RED (II), UNCROPPED	*	20.00	25.00
94	AUSTRALIAN SHEPHERD	*	20.00	25.00
94	GREYHOUND	*	20.00	25.00
94	GREYHOUND, FAWN	*	20.00	25.00
94	GREYHOUND, WHITE & BRINDLE	*	20.00	25.00
S. BRUE				**PESKY PEEPERS**
94	CHOW, BLACK	*	5.50	7.00
94	CHOW, RED	*	5.50	7.00
94	COCKER, BLACK	*	5.50	7.00
94	JACK RUSSELL TERRIER	*	5.50	7.00
94	KITTY, BLACK	*	5.50	7.00
94	ROTTWEILER	*	5.50	7.00
94	SHIH TZU, BLACK/WHITE	*	5.50	7.00
94	SHIH TZU, GOLD/WHITE	*	5.50	7.00
94	ST. BERNARD	*	5.50	7.00
S. BRUE				**WILD CREATURES**
94	FERRET	*	24.00	30.00
94	WOLF	*	24.00	30.00

SARAH'S ATTIC

90	CRUMB RABBIT	RT	*	*
*	BEVERLY JANE AMERICAN (RED DRESS)	500	160.00	300.00
*	BEVERLY JANE SUNDAY BEST	500	160.00	300.00
*	OPIE CLOTH DOLL	500	90.00	200.00
*	POLLY COLTH DOLL	500	90.00	200.00
88	SUNSHINE DOLL	RT	118.00	700.00
88	SUNSHINE DOLL	RT	118.00	700.00
89	LONG JOURNEY	RT	19.00	35.00
90	COOKIE RABBIT	RT	29.00	40.00
90	CRUMB RABBIT	RT	29.00	40.00
90	NANA RABBIT	RT	50.00	65.00

YR	NAME	LIMIT	ISSUE	QUOTE
90	PAPA RABBIT	RT	50.00	65.00
90	SLEEPY RABBIT	RT	15.50	25.00
90	TESSY RABBIT	RT	17.00	20.00
90	TESSY RABBIT	RT	15.00	20.00
90	THELMA RABBIT	RT	33.00	40.00
90	THOMAS RABBIT	RT	33.00	40.00
90	WOODLAND SANTA	RT	100.00	125.00
91	SILENT HIGHT	RT	33.00	44.00
*	PEACE ANGEL CLOTH DOLL	500	50.00	200.00
*	VICTORIA DOLL	500	120.00	500.00
*	**AMERICANA COLLECTION**			
88	AMERICANA BEAR	CL	17.50	17.50
88	AMERICANA BEAR	CL	70.00	70.00
88	AMERICANA BUNNY	CL	70.00	70.00
88	AMERICANA CLOWN	OP	80.00	80.00
88	BETSY BEAR W/FLAG	CL	22.50	22.50
88	BETSY ROSS	OP	34.00	40.00
88	COLONIAL BEAR W/HAT	CL	22.50	22.50
88	INDIAN BRAVE	OP	10.00	10.00
88	INDIAN GIRL	OP	10.00	10.00
88	PILGRIM BOY	OP	12.50	12.50
88	PILGRIM GIRL	OP	12.50	12.50
88	TURKEY	OP	10.00	12.00
90	BRIGHT SKY	TL	70.00	70.00
90	IRON HAWK	TL	70.00	70.00
90	LITTLE DOVE	TL	40.00	40.00
90	SPOTTED EAGLE	TL	30.00	30.00
*	**ANGELS IN THE ATTIC**			
89	ANGEL ABBEE	OP	9.50	13.00
89	ANGEL ALEX	OP	10.00	14.00
89	ANGEL AMELIA	OP	10.00	14.00
89	ANGEL ASHBEE	OP	9.50	13.00
89	ANGEL ASHLEE	CL	14.00	14.00
89	ANGEL BEVIE	CL	10.00	10.00
89	ANGEL BONNIE	OP	17.00	20.00
89	ANGEL CLYDE	OP	17.00	20.00
89	ANGEL DAISY	CL	14.00	14.00
89	ANGEL DUSTY	CL	12.00	12.00
89	ANGEL EDDIE	CL	10.00	10.00
89	ANGEL EMMY LOU	CL	12.00	12.00
89	ANGEL FLOPPY	CL	10.00	10.00
89	ANGEL GRAMPS	CL	17.00	25.00
89	ANGEL GRAMS	CL	17.00	25.00
89	ANGEL JEFFREY	CL	14.00	14.00
89	ANGEL JESSICA	CL	14.00	14.00
89	ANGEL PATSY	CL	13.00	13.00
89	ANGEL RAYBURN	CL	12.00	15.00
89	ANGEL REBA	CL	12.00	12.00
89	ANGEL REGGIE	CL	12.00	15.00
89	ANGEL RUTHIE	CL	12.00	12.00
89	ANGEL SHOOTER	OP	12.50	18.00
89	ANGEL WENDALL	OP	10.00	14.00
89	ANGEL WENDY	OP	10.00	14.00
89	ANGEL WILBUR	OP	9.50	14.00
89	ANGEL WINNIE	OP	10.00	14.00
89	SAINT WILLIE BILL	OP	30.00	40.00
89	ST. ANNE	OP	29.00	32.00
89	ST. GABBE	OP	30.00	33.00
89	ST. GEORGE	OP	60.00	65.00
90	ANGEL BEAR IN BASKET	CL	23.00	23.00
90	ANGEL BILLI	OP	18.00	18.00
90	ANGEL BUSTER	OP	15.00	15.00
90	ANGEL CINDI	OP	18.00	18.00
90	ANGEL FLOSSY	OP	15.00	15.00
90	ANGEL LENA	CL	36.00	36.00
90	ANGEL LOUISE	OP	17.00	17.00
90	ANGEL RABBIT IN BASKET	CL	25.00	25.00
90	ANGEL TRAPPER	OP	17.00	17.00
90	ANGEL TRUDY	CL	36.00	36.00
91	ANGEL BERT GOLFING	1000	60.00	60.00
91	ANGEL DONALD WITH DOG	1000	50.00	50.00
91	CONTENTMENT	500	100.00	100.00
91	LOVE	500	80.00	80.00
*	**BEARY ADORABLES COLLECTION**			
87	ABBEE BEAR	CL	10.00	10.00
87	ALEX BEAR	CL	11.50	11.50

YR	NAME	LIMIT	ISSUE	QUOTE
87	AMELIA BEAR	CL	11.50	11.50
87	ASHBEE BEAR	CL	10.00	10.00
87	BEAR ON TRUNK	CL	20.00	20.00
87	COLLECTIBLE BEAR	CL	16.00	16.00
88	ARCTIC PICNIC BEAR	CL	7.00	7.00
88	BEAR IN BASKET	CL	48.00	48.00
88	BENNI BEAR	CL	7.00	7.00
88	EINSTEIN BEAR	CL	8.50	8.50
88	GHOST BEAR	CL	12.00	12.00
88	HONEY PICNIC BEAR	CL	16.50	16.50
88	JESTER CLOWN BEAR	CL	12.50	12.50
88	LEFTY BEAR	CL	80.00	80.00
88	MARTI PICNIC BEAR	CL	12.50	12.50
88	RUFUS PICNIC BEAR	CL	15.00	15.00
89	ANGEL BEAR	CL	24.50	24.50
89	DAISY BEAR	CL	48.00	55.00
89	GRISWALD BEAR	CL	48.00	55.00
89	MIKEY BEAR	CL	26.00	26.00
89	MINI TEDDY BEAR	CL	5.00	5.00
89	MISSY BEAR	CL	26.00	26.00
89	SAMMY BEAR	CL	12.00	15.00
89	SID BEAR	CL	18.00	25.00
89	SOPHIE BEAR	CL	18.00	25.00
89	SPICE BEAR	CL	12.00	15.00
89	SUGAR BEAR	CL	12.00	12.00
90	BAILEY 50'S BEAR	4000	25.00	30.00
90	BELINDA 50'S BEAR	4000	20.00	25.00
90	BEULAH 50'S BEAR	4000	25.00	30.00
90	BIRKEY 50'S BEAR	4000	20.00	25.00
90	DUDLEY BROWN BEAR	2500	32.00	32.00
90	FRANNY BROWN BEAR	2500	32.00	32.00
90	JOEY BROWN BEAR	2500	32.00	32.00
90	MARGIE BROWN BEAR	2500	32.00	32.00
90	MISS LOVE BROWN BEAR	2500	42.00	42.00
90	OLIVER BLACK BEAR	2500	32.00	32.00
*			**BLACK HERITAGE COLLECTION**	
87	GRAMPS	CL	16.00	16.00
87	GRAMS	CL	16.00	16.00
89	BROTHERLY LOVE	5000	80.00	80.00
89	CALEB	OP	21.00	23.00
89	HARPSTER W/BANJO	CL	60.00	150.00
89	HATTIE	4000	35.00	60.00
89	LIBBY W/BIBS	CL	36.00	70.00-80.00
89	LUCAS W/BIBS	CL	36.00	60.00-80.00
89	PAPPY JAKE	4000	33.00	60.00
89	PEARL, TAP DANCER	5000	40.00	47.00
89	PERCY, TAP DANCER	5000	40.00	47.00
89	PORTIA	OP	35.00	60.00
89	PREACHER I	4000	50.00	57.00
89	QUILTING LADIES	CL	80.00	90.00
89	SUSIE MAE	OP	20.00	22.00
89	WHOOPIE & WOOSTER	CL	50.00	60.00-120.00
90	BLACK BABY TANSY	10,000	40.00	40.00
90	CALEB W/VEGETABLES	4000	50.00	50.00
90	CORPORAL PERVIS	8000	60.00	60.00
90	HARPSTER W/HARMONICA	8000	60.00	60.00
90	LIBBY W/PUPPY	10,000	50.00	50.00
90	LUCAS W/DOG	10,000	50.00	50.00
90	NIGHTTIME PEARL	10,000	50.00	50.00
90	NIGHTTIME PERCY	10,000	50.00	50.00
90	PRAISE THE LORD II	5000	100.00	100.00
90	SADIE & OSIE MAE	8000	70.00	70.00
90	UNCLE REUBEN	8000	70.00	70.00
90	VICTORIAN PORTIA	7000	35.00	35.00
90	VICTORIAN WEBSTER	7000	35.00	35.00
90	WHOOPIE & WOOSTER II	8000	70.00	70.00
91	BLACK TEACHER MISS LETTIE	6000	50.00	50.00
91	BRAIDED RUG	*	35.00	35.00
91	BUFFALO SOLDIER	5000	80.00	80.00
91	CALEB WITH FOOTBALL	6000	40.00	40.00
91	CHIPS, BLACK BOY GRADUATE	6000	46.00	46.00
91	CLARENCE, PORTER	5000	80.00	80.00
91	CRICKET, BLACK GIRL GRADUATE	6000	46.00	46.00
91	ESTHER WITH BUTTER CHURN	5000	70.00	70.00
91	GENERAL OF LOVE, COOKSTOVE	*	100.00	100.00
91	GRANNY WYNNE & OLIVIA	5000	85.00	85.00

American Bald Eagle I *is from the "Birds of Prey" collection by W.D. Gaither. The porcelain sculpture is produced by Maruri.*

Artist W.D. Gaither captures the movements and majesty of the American Bald Eagle III *in his third sculpture for Maruri's "Birds of Prey" series.*

American Bald Eagle II *is crafted in porcelain by W.D. Gaither and produced by Maruri as part of the "Bird of Prey" collection.*

American Bald Eagle IV *by W.D. Gaither portrays the creature searching for food. The figure is from the "Birds of Prey" series produced by Maruri.*

YR	NAME	LIMIT	ISSUE	QUOTE
91	HATTIE QUILTING	6000	60.00	60.00
91	KETTLES	*	13.00	13.00
91	MUSIC MASTERS	CL	300.00	300.00
91	PAPPY JAKE & SUSIE MAE	6000	60.00	60.00
91	PIE	*	7.00	7.00
91	PORTIA QUILTING	6000	40.00	40.00
*			**CHERISHED MEMORIES**	
91	BLACK BABY BOY (1-2 YRS.)	*	50.00	50.00
91	BLACK BABY BOY (BIRTH-1 YR.)	*	50.00	50.00
91	BLACK BABY GIRL (1-2 YRS.)	*	50.00	50.00
91	BLACK BABY GIRL (BIRTH-1 YR.)	*	50.00	50.00
91	WHITE BABY BOY (1-2 YRS.)	*	60.00	60.00
91	WHITE BABY BOY (BIRTH-1 YR.)	*	60.00	60.00
91	WHITE BABY GIRL (1-2 YRS.)	*	60.00	60.00
91	WHITE BABY GIRL (BIRTH-1 YR.)	*	60.00	60.00
*			**CHILDREN OF LOVE**	
91	BENJAMIN WITH DRUMS	10,000	46.00	46.00
91	CHARITY SEWING FLAGS	10,000	46.00	46.00
91	SKIP BUILDING HOUSE	10,000	50.00	50.00
91	SUSIE PAINTING TRAIN	10,000	46.00	46.00
*			**CLASSROOM MEMORIES**	
88	MISS PRITCHETT	OP	28.00	35.00
91	ACHIEVING OUR GOALS	10,000	80.00	80.00
91	CLASSROOM MEMORIES	6000	80.00	80.00
*			**COTTON TALE COLLECTION**	
87	BONNIE	CL	38.00	38.00
87	CLYDE	CL	38.00	38.00
87	FLOPPY	CL	21.00	21.00
87	WENDALL BOY RABBIT	CL	13.00	25.00
87	WENDALL PA RABBIT	CL	17.00	25.00
87	WENDY GIRL RABBIT	CL	15.00	25.00
87	WINNIE MOM RABBIT	CL	17.00	17.00
88	AMOS HARE	CL	11.00	11.00
88	BILLI RABBIT	CL	27.00	35.00
88	BOY RABBIT RES. CANDLE	CL	14.00	14.00
88	CIND RABBIT	CL	27.00	35.00
88	GIRL RABBIT RES. CANDLE	CL	14.00	14.00
88	IZZY HARE	CL	10.00	10.00
88	LIZZY HARE	CL	10.00	10.00
88	MADDY HARE	CL	11.00	11.00
88	MINI BOY RABBIT	CL	7.50	7.50
88	MINI GIRL RABBIT	CL	7.50	7.50
88	MINI MAMA RABBIT	CL	8.50	8.50
88	MINI PAPA RABBIT	CL	8.50	8.50
88	RABBIT IN BASKET	CL	48.00	48.00
89	COOKIE RABBIT	CL	29.00	35.00-40.00
89	CRUMB RABBIT	CL	29.00	35.00-40.00
89	NANA RABBIT	CL	50.00	60.00-65.00
89	PAPA RABBIT	CL	50.00	60.00-65.00
89	SLEEPING BABY BUNNY	CL	15.50	15.50
89	TESSY RABBIT	CL	15.00	20.00
89	THELMA RABBIT	CL	33.00	40.00
89	THOMAS RABBIT	CL	33.00	40.00
89	TOBY RABBIT	CL	17.00	20.00
90	CHUCKLES FARM RABBIT	TL	53.00	53.00
90	COOKIE FARM RABBIT	TL	47.00	47.00
90	CRUMB FARM RABBIT	TL	53.00	53.00
90	HANNAH RABBIT QUILTING	OP	30.00	32.00
90	HEATHER RABBIT W/DOLL	OP	20.00	22.00
90	HENRY RABBIT W/PIPE	OP	30.00	32.00
90	HERBIE RABBIT W/BOOK	OP	20.00	22.00
90	MOLLY RABBIT W/VEST	4000	65.00	75.00
90	NANA FARM RABBIT	TL	100.00	100.00
90	OLLY RABBIT W/VEST	4000	65.00	75.00
90	PAPA FARM RABBIT	TL	80.00	80.00
90	SLEEPY FARM RABBIT	TL	35.00	35.00
90	VICTORIAN TABITHA	TL	30.00	30.00
90	VICTORIAN TESSY	TL	20.00	20.00
90	VICTORIAN THELMA	TL	60.00	60.00
90	VICTORIAN THOMAS	TL	60.00	60.00
90	VICTORIAN TOBY	TL	40.00	40.00
90	VICTORIAN TUCKER	TL	37.00	37.00
90	X-MAS TOBY	TL	20.00	20.00
90	ZEB SAILOR DAD	TL	26.00	28.00
90	ZEB W/CARROTS	CL	18.00	18.00
90	ZEKE SAILOR BOY	TL	24.00	26.00

YR	NAME	LIMIT	ISSUE	QUOTE
90	ZEKE W/CARROTS	CL	17.00	17.00
90	ZELDA SAILOR MOM	TL	26.00	28.00
90	ZELDA W/CARROTS	CL	18.00	18.00
90	ZOE SAILOR GIRL	TL	24.00	26.00
90	ZOE W/CARROTS	CL	17.00	17.00
*	**CUDDLY CRITTERS COLLECTION**			
87	SPARKY	OP	9.00	10.00
88	BUSTER BOY CAT	CL	14.00	14.00
88	CAROUSEL HORSE	CL	31.00	31.00
88	COW W/BELL	CL	35.00	35.00
88	FLOSSY GIRL CAT	CL	9.50	9.50
88	KITTY CAT W/BONNET	CL	12.00	12.00
88	LAZY-CAT ON BACK	CL	13.00	13.00
88	LILA MRS. MOUSE	CL	17.50	17.50
88	LOUISE MAMA CAT	CL	20.00	20.00
88	LUCKY BOY MOUSE	CL	13.00	13.00
88	LUCKY GIRL MOUSE	CL	12.00	12.00
88	MYRTLE THE PIG	CL	38.00	45.00
88	PAPA MOUSE	CL	17.50	17.50
88	ROCKING HORSE	CL	56.00	56.00
88	SLEEPING CAT	CL	6.00	6.00
88	TRAPPER PAPA CAT	CL	20.00	20.00
89	MADAM DONNA	CL	35.50	45.00
89	MESSIEUR PIERRE	CL	35.50	45.00
89	OTIS PAPA CAT	CL	13.00	13.00
89	PUDDIN GIRL CAT	CL	10.00	10.00
89	WHISKERS BOY CAT	CL	10.00	10.00
89	WIGGLY PIG	CL	17.00	25.00
90	BOY SQUIRREL SONNY	CL	18.00	18.00
90	GIRL SQUIRREL SIS	CL	18.00	18.00
90	HORACE & SISSY DOGS	OP	50.00	50.00
90	JASPER DAD CAT	OP	36.00	36.00
90	LULU GIRL CAT	OP	26.00	26.00
90	MA SQUIRREL SASHA	CL	19.00	19.00
90	PA SQUIRREL SHERMAN	CL	19.00	19.00
90	PENNY GIRL DOG	OP	35.00	35.00
90	REBECCA MOM DOG	OP	40.00	40.00
90	SCOOTER BOY DOG	OP	30.00	30.00
90	SCUFFY BOY CAT	OP	26.00	26.00
90	WINNIE MOM CAT	OP	36.00	36.00
91	JIGGS, SLEEPING CAT	*	10.00	10.00
*	**DAISY COLLECTION**			
89	SALLY BOOBA	OP	30.00	40.00
90	BOMBER	TL	50.00	52.00
90	JACK BOY BALL & GLOVE	OP	30.00	40.00
90	JEWEL	TL	60.00	62.00
90	SPARKY	TL	53.00	55.00
90	SPIKE	TL	44.00	46.00
90	STRETCH	TL	50.00	52.00
*	**GINGER BABIES COLLECTION**			
89	GINGER	CL	17.00	17.00
89	MOLASSES	CL	17.00	17.00
90	GINGER BOY NUTMEG	CL	15.50	20.00
90	GINGER GIRL CINNAMON	CL	15.50	20.00
*	**HAPPY COLLECTION**			
87	HAPPY W/BALLOONS	CL	22.00	22.00
87	LARGE HAPPY CLOWN	CL	22.00	22.00
87	SITTING HAPPY	CL	26.00	26.00
88	LADY CLOWN	CL	20.00	20.00
90	ENCORE CLOWN W/DOG	2000	100.00	100.00
*	**HEAVENLY WINGS COLLECTION**			
89	ANGELICA ANGEL	6000	21.00	25.00
89	HEAVENLY GUARDIAN	CL	40.00	40.00
89	REGINA	CL	24.00	30.00
90	ADORA W/BUNNY	10,000	50.00	50.00
90	ADORA W/PINK GOWN	CL	35.00	75.00
90	BOY ANGEL INST. ADAIR	CL	29.00	29.00
90	ENOS W/BLUE GOWN	CL	33.00	75.00
90	ENOS W/FROG	10,000	50.00	50.00
*	**LITTLE CHARMERS COLLECTION**			
87	AMBER-SMALL GIRL STANDING	CL	15.00	15.00
87	ARCHIE-SMALL BOY STANDING	CL	15.00	15.00
87	ASHLEE	CL	60.00	60.00
87	BARE BOTTOM BABY	CL	9.50	9.50
87	BASEBALL PLAYER	CL	24.00	24.00
87	BEAU-CUPIE BOY	CL	20.00	20.00

YR	NAME	LIMIT	ISSUE	QUOTE
87	BEVIE	CL	18.00	18.00
87	BLONDIE-GIRL DOLL SITTING	CL	16.00	16.00
87	BUTCH-BOY BOOK SITTING	CL	16.00	16.00
87	BUTTONS-CUPIE GIRL	CL	20.00	20.00
87	CHEERLEADER	CL	16.00	16.00
87	CLEMENTINE-GIRL SAILOR SUIT	CL	14.50	14.50
87	CORKY-BOY SAILOR SUIT	CL	14.50	14.50
87	CUPCAKE W/ROPE	CL	19.00	19.00
87	DAISY	CL	36.00	36.00
87	DUSTY	CL	19.00	19.00
87	EDDIE	CL	18.00	18.00
87	EMMY LOU	CL	14.00	14.00
87	FOOTBALL PLAYER	CL	24.00	24.00
87	MAN GOLFER	CL	24.00	24.00
87	SHOOTER	CL	19.00	19.00
87	TWINKLE W/POLE	CL	19.00	19.00
87	WILLIE BILL	CL	20.00	20.00
87	WOMAN GOLFER	CL	24.00	24.00
88	BASKETBALL PLAYER	CL	24.00	24.00
88	BOWLER	CL	24.00	24.00
88	BOY W/CLOWN DOLL	CL	40.00	40.00
88	GIRL W/DOG	CL	43.00	43.00
88	GIRL W/TEACUP	CL	37.00	37.00
88	JESSICA	CL	44.00	44.00
89	JENNIFER & DOG	CL	57.00	57.00
89	MOOSE BOY SITTING	OP	18.00	20.00
90	WHITE BABY TANSY	10,000	40.00	40.00
*			**MATT & MAGGIE**	
86	MAGGIE	*	14.00	14.00
86	MAGGIE CANDLEHOLDER	*	12.00	12.00
86	MATT	*	14.00	14.00
86	MATT CANDLEHOLDER	*	12.00	12.00
87	MAGGIE ON HEART	*	9.00	9.00
87	MATT & MAGGIE W/BEAR	100	100.00	100.00
87	MATT ON HEART	*	9.00	9.00
87	STANDING MAGGIE	*	11.00	11.00
87	STANDING MATT	*	11.00	11.00
88	LARGE MAGGIE	4000	48.00	48.00
88	LARGE MATT	4000	48.00	48.00
88	SMALL SITTING MAGGIE	*	11.50	11.50
88	SMALL SITTING MATT	*	11.50	11.50
89	MAGGIE BENCH SITTER	CL	32.00	32.00
89	MATT BENCH SITTER	CL	32.00	32.00
89	MINI MAGGIE	*	6.00	6.00
89	MINI MATT	*	6.00	6.00
*			**MEMORY LANE COLLECTION**	
87	BARBER SHOP	CL	13.00	13.00
87	BARN	CL	16.50	16.50
87	CHURCH	CL	19.00	19.00
87	COTTAGE	CL	13.00	13.00
87	DRUG STORE	CL	13.00	13.00
87	GENERAL STORE	CL	13.00	13.00
87	GRANDMA'S HOUSE	CL	13.00	13.00
87	HOUSE W/DORMERS	CL	15.00	15.00
87	MILL	CL	16.50	16.50
87	SCHOOL	CL	14.00	14.00
88	BANK	CL	13.00	13.00
88	MINI BARBER SHOP	CL	6.50	6.50
88	MINI BARN	CL	6.00	6.00
88	MINI CHURCH	CL	6.50	6.50
88	MINI DRUG STORE	CL	6.00	6.00
88	MINI GENERAL STORE	CL	6.00	6.00
88	MINI GRANDMA'S HOUSE	CL	7.00	7.00
88	MINI MILL	CL	6.50	6.50
88	MINI SALT BOX	CL	6.00	6.00
88	MINI SCHOOL	CL	6.50	6.50
88	TRAIN DEPOT	CL	13.50	13.50
89	BRITON CHURCH	CL	25.00	25.00
89	FIRE STATION	CL	20.00	20.00
89	MINI BANK	CL	6.00	6.00
89	MINI DEPOT	CL	7.00	7.00
89	POST OFFICE	CL	25.00	25.00
*			**ROSE COLLECTION**	
89	SWEET ROSE	CL	50.00	50.00
90	TIFFANY VICTORIAN GIRL	TL	40.00	40.00
90	TYLER VICTORIAN BOY	TL	40.00	40.00

YR	NAME	LIMIT	ISSUE	QUOTE
90	VICTORIAN BOY CODY	CL	46.00	46.00
*			**SANTAS OF THE MONTH**	
88	APRIL SANTA	CL	50.00	100.00-110.00
88	AUGUST SANTA	CL	50.00	100.00-110.00
88	DECEMBER SANTA	CL	50.00	100.00-110.00
88	FEBRUARY SANTA	CL	50.00	100.00-110.00
88	JANUARY SANTA	CL	50.00	100.00-110.00
88	JULY SANTA	CL	50.00	100.00-110.00
88	JUNE SANTA	CL	50.00	100.00-110.00
88	MARCH SANTA	CL	50.00	100.00-110.00
88	MAY SANTA	CL	50.00	100.00-110.00
88	MINI APRIL SANTA	CL	14.00	20.00
88	MINI AUGUST SANTA	CL	14.00	20.00
88	MINI DECEMBER SANTA	CL	14.00	20.00
88	MINI FEBRUARY SANTA	CL	14.00	20.00
88	MINI JANUARY SANTA	CL	14.00	20.00
88	MINI JULY SANTA	CL	14.00	20.00
88	MINI JUNE SANTA	CL	14.00	20.00
88	MINI MARCH SANTA	CL	14.00	20.00
88	MINI MAY SANTA	CL	14.00	20.00
88	MINI NOVEMBER SANTA	CL	14.00	20.00
88	MINI OCTOBER SANTA	CL	14.00	20.00
88	MINI SEPTEMBER SANTA	CL	14.00	20.00
88	NOVEMBER SANTA	CL	50.00	100.00-110.00
88	OCTOBER SANTA	CL	50.00	100.00-110.00
88	SEPTEMBER SANTA	CL	50.00	100.00-110.00
90	APR. SANTA SPRING/JOY	TL	150.00	150.00
90	APR. SPRING TIME	TL	90.00	90.00
90	AUG. FUN IN THE SUN	TL	90.00	90.00
90	AUGUST SANTA SUMMERS TRN.	TL	110.00	110.00
90	DEC. A GIFT OF PEACE	TL	90.00	90.00
90	DEC. SANTA PEACE	TL	120.00	120.00
90	FEB. FROM THE HEART	TL	90.00	90.00
90	FEB. SANTA CUPIDS HELP	TL	120.00	120.00
90	JAN. FRUITS OF LOVE	TL	90.00	90.00
90	JAN. SANTA WINTER FUN	TL	80.00	80.00
90	JULY CELEBRATE AMERICA	TL	90.00	90.00
90	JULY SANTA GOD BLESS	TL	100.00	100.00
90	JUNE HOMERUN	TL	90.00	90.00
90	JUNE SANTA GRADUATION	TL	70.00	70.00
90	MAR. IRISH LOVE	TL	100.00	100.00
90	MAR. SANTA IRISH DELIGHT	TL	120.00	120.00
90	MASQUERADE TILLIE	TL	45.00	45.00
90	MAY CADDY CHATTER	TL	100.00	100.00
90	MAY SANTA PAR FOR COURSE	TL	100.00	100.00
90	MRS. APRIL	TL	110.00	110.00
90	MRS. AUGUST	TL	90.00	90.00
90	MRS. DECEMBER	TL	110.00	110.00
90	MRS. FEBRUARY	TL	110.00	110.00
90	MRS. JANUARY	TL	80.00	80.00
90	MRS. JULY	TL	100.00	100.00
90	MRS. JUNE	TL	70.00	70.00
90	MRS. MARCH	TL	80.00	80.00
90	MRS. MAY	TL	80.00	80.00
90	MRS. NOVEMBER	TL	90.00	90.00
90	MRS. OCTOBER	TL	90.00	90.00
90	MRS. SEPTEMBER	TL	90.00	90.00
90	NOV. HARVEST OF LOVE	TL	120.00	120.00
90	NOV. SANTA GIVE THANKS	TL	100.00	100.00
90	OCT. MASQUERADE	TL	120.00	120.00
90	OCT. SANTA SEASONS PLENTY	TL	120.00	120.00
90	SEP. SANTA TOUCHDOWN	TL	90.00	90.00
90	SEPT. LESSONS IN LOVE	TL	90.00	90.00
*			**SARAH'S GANG COLLECTION**	
87	CUPCAKE ON HEART	CL	12.00	12.00
87	KATIE ON HEART	CL	12.00	12.00
87	ORIGINAL CUPCAKE	CL	14.00	20.00
87	ORIGINAL KATIE	CL	14.00	20.00
87	ORIGINAL TILLIE	CL	14.00	20.00
87	ORIGINAL TWINKIE	CL	14.00	20.00
87	ORIGINAL WHIMPY	CL	14.00	20.00
87	ORIGINAL WILLIE	CL	14.00	20.00
87	SITTING KATIE	CL	14.00	20.00
87	SITTING WHIMPY	CL	14.00	20.00
87	TILLIE CANDLE HOLDER	CL	15.00	20.00
87	TILLIE ON HEART	CL	12.00	12.00

YR	NAME	LIMIT	ISSUE	QUOTE
87	TWINKIE ON HEART	CL	12.00	12.00
87	WHIMPY ON HEART	CL	12.00	12.00
87	WILLIE CANDLE HOLDER	CL	15.00	20.00
87	WILLIE ON HEART	CL	12.00	12.00
88	CUPCAKE	OP	18.00	20.00
88	KATIE	OP	18.00	20.00
88	TILLIE	OP	18.00	20.00
88	TWINKIE	OP	18.00	20.00
88	WHIMPY	OP	18.00	20.00
88	WILLIE	OP	18.00	20.00
89	AMERICANA CUPCAKE	OP	19.00	21.00
89	AMERICANA KATIE	OP	19.00	21.00
89	AMERICANA TILLIE	OP	17.00	21.00
89	AMERICANA TWINKIE	OP	19.00	21.00
89	AMERICANA WHIMPY	OP	19.00	21.00
89	AMERICANA WILLIE	OP	17.00	21.00
89	BABY RACHEL	OP	17.00	20.00
89	BEACHTIME KATIE & WHIMPY	OP	53.00	60.00
89	SMALL COUNTRY TILLIE	OP	13.00	14.00
89	SMALL COUNTRY WILLIE	OP	13.00	18.00
89	SMALL SAILOR KATIE	CL	14.00	18.00
89	SMALL SAILOR WHIMPY	CL	14.00	18.00
89	SMALL SCHOOL CUPCAKE	CL	11.00	15.00
89	SMALL SCHOOL TWINKIE	CL	11.00	15.00
90	AMERICANA RACHEL	OP	30.00	30.00
90	BEACHTIME BABY RACHEL	OP	30.00	35.00
90	BEACHTIME CUPCAKE	OP	30.00	35.00
90	BEACHTIME TILLIE	OP	30.00	35.00
90	BEACHTIME TWINKIE	OP	30.00	35.00
90	BEACHTIME WILLIE	OP	30.00	35.00
90	CLOWN TILLIE	OP	40.00	40.00
90	CLOWN WILLIE	OP	40.00	40.00
90	DEVIL CUPCAKE	OP	36.00	40.00
90	DEVIL TWINKIE	OP	36.00	40.00
90	PUMPKIN RACHEL	OP	36.00	40.00
90	SCARECROW WHIMPY	OP	40.00	40.00
90	WITCH KATIE	OP	40.00	40.00
91	CRACKER, COCKER SPANIAL	TL	9.00	9.00
91	DOCTOR TWINKIE	6000	50.00	50.00
91	EXECUTIVE WHIMP	6000	46.00	46.00
91	KATIE, WHITE BRIDE	TL	47.00	47.00
91	NURSE CUPCAKE	6000	46.00	46.00
91	PEACHES, BLACK FLOWER GIRL	TL	40.00	40.00
91	PERCY, BLACK MINISTER	TL	50.00	50.00
91	PUG, BLACK RING BEARER	TL	40.00	40.00
91	RACHEL, WHITE FLOWER GIRL	TL	40.00	40.00
91	TEACHER TILLIE	6000	50.00	50.00
91	THANKSGIVING KATIE	10,000	32.00	32.00
91	THANKSGIVING RACHEL	10,000	32.00	32.00
91	THANKSGIVING TILLIE	10,000	32.00	32.00
91	THANKSGIVING WHIMPY	10,000	32.00	32.00
91	THANKSGIVING WILLIE	10,000	32.00	32.00
91	TILLIE, BLACK BRIDE	TL	47.00	47.00
91	TWINKIE, WHITE MINISTER	TL	50.00	50.00
91	TYLER, WHITE RING BEARER	TL	40.00	40.00
91	WHIMPY, WHITE GROOM	TL	47.00	47.00
91	WILLIE, BLACK GROOM	TL	47.00	47.00
*	**SARAH'S NEIGHBORHOOD FRIENDS**			
90	ANNIE W/FLOWER BASKET	TL	56.00	56.00
90	ANNIE W/VIOLIN	TL	35.00	35.00
90	BUBBA W/LANTERN	TL	35.00	35.00
90	BUBBA W/LEMONADE	TL	54.00	54.00
90	BUD W/BOOK	TL	35.00	35.00
90	BUD W/NEWSPAPER	TL	40.00	40.00
90	HEWETT W/APPLES	TL	40.00	40.00
90	HEWETT W/DRUM	TL	35.00	35.00
90	PANSY W/BUGGY	TL	50.00	50.00
90	PANSY W/SLED	TL	30.00	30.00
90	WALDO DOG	TL	10.00	10.00
90	WALDO W/FLOWERS	TL	14.00	14.00
90	WEASEL W/CAP	TL	35.00	35.00
90	WEASEL W/PAPER	TL	40.00	40.00
91	ANNIE, WHITE MARY	TL	30.00	30.00
91	BABES, BLACK BABY JESUS	TL	20.00	20.00
91	BUBBA, BLACK KING	TL	40.00	40.00
91	BUD, WHITE JOSEPH	TL	34.00	34.00

YR	NAME	LIMIT	ISSUE	QUOTE
91	CRATE OF LOVE, BLACK	TL	40.00	40.00
91	CRATE OF LOVE, WHITE	TL	40.00	40.00
91	DOLLY, WHITE BABY JESUS	TL	20.00	20.00
91	EXECUTIVE NOAH	6000	46.00	46.00
91	HEWITT, WHITE KING W/DRUM	TL	40.00	40.00
91	KITTEN IN BASKET	TL	15.00	15.00
91	NOAH, BLACK JOSEPH	TL	36.00	36.00
91	NURSE PANSY	6000	46.00	46.00
91	PANSY, BLACK ANGEL	TL	30.00	30.00
91	SHELBY, BLACK MARY	TL	30.00	30.00
91	TEACHER ANNIE	6000	55.00	55.00
91	WALDO, DOG W/SHOE	TL	15.00	15.00
91	WEASEL, WHITE KING W/KITTEN	TL	40.00	40.00
SARAH SCHULTZ				**SERIES A**
*	APRIL	TL	50.00	150.00
*	MAY SANTA	TL	50.00	150.00
90	AUGUST SANTA	TL	50.00	150.00
90	DECEMBER SANTA	TL	50.00	150.00
90	FEBRUARY SANTA	TL	50.00	150.00
90	JANUARY SANTA	TL	50.00	150.00
90	JULY SANTA	TL	50.00	150.00
90	JUNE SANTA	TL	50.00	150.00
90	JUNE SANTA	TL	50.00	150.00
90	MARCH SANTA	TL	50.00	150.00
90	MARCH SANTA	TL	50.00	150.00
90	NOVEMBER SANTA	TL	50.00	150.00
90	OCTOBER SANTA	TL	50.00	150.00
90	SEPTEMBER	TL	50.00	150.00
*			**SNOWFLAKE COLLECTION**	
89	BOO MINI SNOWMAN	OP	6.00	6.00
89	FLURRY	OP	10.00	12.00
89	WINTER FROLIC	6000	60.00	70.00
90	AMERICAN SNOW OLD GLORY	4000	24.00	26.00
*			**SPIRIT OF CHRISTMAS COLLECTION**	
87	COLONEL SANTA	CL	40.00	40.00
87	FATHER SNOW	CL	46.00	46.00
87	JINGLE BELLS	CL	28.00	28.00
87	KRIS KRINGLE	CL	120.00	120.00
87	LARGE SANTA W/CANE	CL	33.00	33.00
87	LONG JOURNEY	CL	28.00	35.00
87	MINI SANTA W/CANE	CL	11.00	11.00
87	MRS. CLAUS	CL	28.00	28.00
87	NAUGHTY OR NICE SANTA AT D	CL	100.00	100.00
87	SANTA SITTING	CL	20.50	20.50
87	SANTA W/POCKETS	CL	34.00	34.00
87	SANTA'S WORKSHOP	CL	54.00	54.00
87	SMALL SANTA W/TREE	CL	17.00	17.00
88	BLESSED CHRISTMAS	7500	100.00	100.00
88	CHRISTMAS CLOWN	CL	88.00	88.00
88	CHRISTMAS W/CHILDREN	4000	80.00	80.00
88	COW/OX	CL	16.50	16.50
88	ELF GRABBING HAT	CL	10.00	10.00
88	ELF W/GIFT	CL	8.50	8.50
88	JESUS-NATURAL	CL	7.00	7.00
88	JOSEPH-NATURAL	CL	11.00	11.00
88	LARGE MRS. CLAUS RES. CANDLE	CL	14.50	14.50
88	LARGE SANTA RES. CANDLE	CL	14.50	14.50
88	MARY-NATURAL	CL	11.00	11.00
88	MINI JESUS	CL	8.00	8.00
88	MINI JESUS-NATURAL	CL	3.50	3.50
88	MINI JOSEPH	CL	8.00	8.00
88	MINI JOSEPH-NATURAL	CL	5.00	5.00
88	MINI LONG JOURNEY	CL	11.00	11.00
88	MINI MARY	CL	8.00	8.00
88	MINI MARY-NATURAL	CL	5.00	5.00
88	MINI SANTA RES. CANDLE	CL	8.00	8.00
88	SANTA IN CHIMNEY	CL	110.00	110.00
88	SANTA KNEELING	CL	22.00	22.00
88	SANTA W/ELF	CL	90.00	90.00
88	SHEEP	CL	8.00	8.00
88	SITTING ELF	CL	7.00	7.00
88	SMALL ANGEL RES. CANDLE	CL	9.50	9.50
88	SMALL MRS. CLAUS	CL	8.50	8.50
88	SMALL MRS. CLAUS RES. CANDLE	CL	10.50	10.50
88	SMALL SANTA RES. CANDLE	CL	10.50	10.50
88	SMALL SITTING SANTA	CL	11.00	11.00

YR	NAME	LIMIT	ISSUE	QUOTE
89	BLINKEY ELF BALL	CL	16.00	20.00
89	CHRISTMAS JOY	CL	32.00	32.00
89	COLONEL SANTA 2	CL	35.00	35.00
89	FATHER SNOW 2	6000	32.00	36.00
89	JINGLE BELLS 2	CL	25.00	25.00
89	JOLLY 2	6000	15.00	17.00
89	LONG JOURNEY 2	6000	35.00	45.00
89	MAMA SANTA SITTING	CL	30.00	40.00
89	MAMA SANTA STOCKING	CL	50.00	50.00
89	MINI COLONEL SANTA	CL	14.00	20.00
89	MINI FATHER SNOW	CL	16.00	16.00
89	MINI JINGLE BELLS	CL	16.00	16.00
89	MINI JOLLY	CL	10.00	10.00
89	MINI NAUGHTY OR NICE	CL	20.00	20.00
89	MINI ST. NICK	CL	14.00	14.00
89	PAPA SANTA SITTING	CL	30.00	40.00
89	PAPA SANTA STOCKING	CL	50.00	50.00
89	SILENT NIGHT	6000	33.00	40.00
89	ST. NICK 2	CL	43.00	43.00
89	STINKY ELF SITTING	CL	16.00	16.00
89	WINKY ELF LETTER	CL	16.00	20.00
89	WOODLAND SANTA	CL	100.00	125.00
89	YULE TIDINGS 2	6000	23.00	30.00
90	BELLS OF X-MAS	5000	35.00	35.00
90	CHRISTMAS MUSIC	5000	60.00	60.00
90	CHRISTMAS WISHES	5000	50.00	50.00
90	LOVE THE CHILDREN	5000	75.00	75.00
90	SANTA CLAUS EXPRESS	4000	150.00	150.00
90	X-MAS WONDER SANTA	3000	50.00	50.00
91	SHARING LOVE SANTA	3000	120.00	120.00
91	TREASURES OF LOVE SANTA	3000	140.00	140.00
*			**TATTERED N' TORN COLLECTION**	
90	BLACK MUFFIN & PUFFIN	10,000	55.00	55.00
90	BLACK PRISSY & PEANUT	2000	120.00	120.00
90	BOY RAG DOLL OPIE	4000	50.00	50.00
90	GIRL RAG DOLL POLLY	4000	50.00	50.00
90	MUFFIN BLACK RAG DOLL	OP	30.00	30.00
90	PUFFIN BLACK RAG DOLL	OP	30.00	30.00
90	WHITE MUFFIN & PUFFIN	10,000	55.00	55.00
90	WHITE PRISSY & PEANUT	2000	120.00	120.00
*			**UNITED HEARTS COLLECTION**	
91	BARNEY THE GREAT BEAR	TL	40.00	40.00
91	BEACH ANNIE & WALDO	TL	40.00	40.00
91	BEACH BUBBA W/INNERTUBE	TL	34.00	34.00
91	BEACH PANSY WITH KITTEN	TL	34.00	34.00
91	BIBI-MISS LIBERTY BEAR	TL	30.00	30.00
91	CHILLY SNOWMAN	TL	33.00	33.00
91	CHRISTMAS ADORA	TL	36.00	36.00
91	CHRISTMAS ENOS	TL	36.00	36.00
91	CHRISTMAS TREE WITH HEARTS	TL	40.00	40.00
91	CLOWN BIBI & BIFF BEARS	TL	35.00	35.00
91	EMILY W/BUGGY	TL	53.00	53.00
91	GIDEON WITH BEAR & ROSE	TL	40.00	40.00
91	HAWITT W/LEPRECHAUN	TL	56.00	56.00
91	JACK BOY GRADUATION	TL	40.00	40.00
91	LIBERTY PAPA BARNEY & BIFF	TL	64.00	64.00
91	NOAH W/POT OF GOLD	TL	36.00	36.00
91	SALLY BOOBA GRADUATION	TL	45.00	45.00
91	SCHOOL CHUCKLES RABBIT	TL	26.00	26.00
91	SCHOOL COOKIE RABBIT W/KIT	TL	28.00	28.00
91	SCHOOL CRUMB RABBIT-DUNCE	TL	32.00	32.00
91	SCHOOL DESK WITH BOOK	TL	15.00	15.00
91	SHELBY W/SHAMROCK	TL	36.00	36.00
91	SPARKY DOG GRADUATION	TL	16.00	16.00
91	TABITHA RABBIT W/BUNNY	TL	32.00	32.00
91	THANKSGIVING CORNSTALK	TL	30.00	30.00
91	THANKSGIVING CUPCAKE	TL	36.00	36.00
91	THANKSGIVING TWINKIE	TL	32.00	32.00
91	TILLIE WITH SKATES	TL	32.00	32.00
91	TOBY & TESSIE W/WHEELBARROW	TL	44.00	44.00
91	VALENTINE PEANUT W/CANDY	TL	32.00	32.00
91	VALENTINE PRISSY WITH DOG	TL	36.00	36.00
91	WILLIE ON SLED	TL	32.00	32.00
91	WOOLY LAMB	TL	16.00	16.00

SCHMID

YR	NAME	LIMIT	ISSUE	QUOTE
L. DAVIS				**COUNTRY PRIDE**
81	BUSTIN' WITH PRIDE	RT	100.00	185.00
81	DUKE'S MIXTURE	RT	100.00	785-800
81	PLUM TUCKERED OUT	RT	100.00	650.00-700.00
81	SURPRISE IN THE CELLAR	RT	100.00	965.00
L. DAVIS				**DAVIS CAT TALES**
82	COMPANY'S COMING	RT	60.00	215.00
82	FLEW THE COOP	RT	60.00	255.00-275.00
82	ON THE MOVE	RT	70.00	550.00
82	RIGHT CHURCH, WRONG PEW	RT	70.00	370.00
L. DAVIS				**DAVIS CHRISTMAS FIGURINES**
83	HOOKER AT MAILBOX/PRESENTS	2500	80.00	750.00
84	KITTENS WITH PRESENTS	2500	80.00	450.00-475.00
85	CHRISTMAS AT FOXFIRE FARM	2500	80.00	210.00
86	CHRISTMAS AT RED OAK	2500	80.00	200.00
87	BLOSSOM'S GIFT	2500	150.00	475.00
88	CUTTING THE FAMILY CHRISTMAS TREE	2500	220.00	275.00-300.00
89	PETER AND THE WREN	2250	165.00	265.00
90	WINTERING DEER	2500	165.00	190.00
91	CHRISTMAS AT RED OAK II	2500	250.00	250.00
92	BORN ON A STARRY NIGHT	2500	225.00	225.00
L. DAVIS				**DAVIS SPECIAL EDITION FIGURINES**
83	THE CRITICS	RT	400.00	1200-1350
85	HOME FROM MARKET	RT	400.00	1200.00
89	FROM A FRIEND TO A FRIEND	RT	750.00	950.00
90	WHAT RAT RACE?	RT	800.00	950.00
92	LAST LAFF	1200	900.00	900.00
L. DAVIS				**DEALER COUNTER SIGNS**
80	RFD AMERICA	CL	40.00	175.00-275.00
81	UNCLE REMUS	CL	30.00	300.00
85	FOX FIRE FARM	CL	30.00	150.00-275.00
90	MR. LOWELL'S FARM	OP	50.00	55.00-70.00
92	LITTLE CRITTERS	OP	50.00	50.00
D. POLLAND				**DON POLLAND FIGURINES I**
83	A SECOND CHANCE	2000	350.00	650.00
83	CHALLENGE	2000	275.00	600.00
83	DANGEROUS MOMENT	2000	250.00	350.00
83	DOWNED	2500	250.00	600.00
83	ESCAPE	2500	175.00	650.00
83	FIGHTING BULLS	2500	200.00	600.00
83	HOT PURSUIT	2500	225.00	550.00
83	THE GREAT HUNT	350	3750.00	3750.00
83	THE HUNTER	2500	225.00	500.00
83	YOUNG BULL	2750	125.00	250.00
86	DOWN FROM THE HIGH COUNTRY	2250	225.00	295.00
86	EAGLE DANCER	2500	170.00	295.00
86	PLAINS WARRIOR	1250	350.00	550.00
86	RUNNING WOLF-WAR CHIEF	2500	170.00	295.00
86	SECOND CHANCE	2000	125.00	650.00
86	SHOOTING THE RAPIDS	2500	195.00	495.00
86	WAR TROPHY	2250	225.00	500.00
L. DAVIS				**FARM SET**
85	BARN	RT	47.50	250.00-300.00
85	CHICKEN HOUSE	RT	19.00	55.00
85	CORN CRIB AND SHEEP PEN	RT	25.00	55.00
85	GARDEN AND WOOD SHED	RT	25.00	55.00
85	GOAT YARD AND STUDIO	RT	32.50	80.00
85	HEN HOUSE	RT	32.50	60.00
85	HOG HOUSE	RT	27.50	65.00
85	MAIN HOUSE	RT	42.50	85.00
85	PRIVY	OP	12.50	18.00
85	REMUS' CABIN	RT	42.50	67.50
85	SMOKE HOUSE	RT	12.50	45.00
85	WINDMILL	OP	25.00	45.00
L. DAVIS				**FRIENDS OF MINE**
89	SUN WORSHIPPERS	5000	120.00	140.00
89	SUN WORSHIPPERS MINI	OP	32.50	42.50
91	WARM MILK	5000	200.00	135.00-150.00
91	WARM MILK MINI	OP	37.50	37.50
92	CAT AND JENNY WREN	5000	170.00	170.00
92	CAT AND JENNY WREN MINI	OP	35.00	35.00
92	SUNDAY AFTERNOON TREAT	5000	130.00	130.00
92	SUNDAY AFTERNOON TREAT MINI	OP	37.50	37.50
L. DAVIS				**LITTLE CRITTERS**
90	GREAT AMERICAN CHICKEN RACE	2500	225.00	250.00

YR	NAME	LIMIT	ISSUE	QUOTE
90	HOME SQUEEZINS	OP	90.00	90.00
90	MILK MOUSE	2500	175.00	228.00
90	OUTING WITH GRANDPA	2500	200.00	250.00
90	PRIVATE TIME	OP	18.00	23.50
90	PUNKIN PIG	2500	250.00	300.00
90	PUNKIN WINE	OP	100.00	120.00
91	HITTIN THE SACK	OP	70.00	70.00
91	ITISKIT, ITASKET	OP	45.00	45.00
91	TOAD STRANGLER	OP	57.00	57.00
91	WHEN COFFEE NEVER TASTED SO GOOD	1250	800.00	800.00
92	A WOLF IN SHEEP'S CLOTHING	YR	110.00	110.00
92	CHARIVARI	950	250.00	250.00
92	CHRISTOPHER CRITTER	1992	150.00	100.00-150.00
92	DOUBLE YOLKER	YR	70.00	70.00
92	MISS PRIVATE TIME	YR	35.00	35.00

L. DAVIS   **LOWELL DAVIS FARM CLUB**

YR	NAME	LIMIT	ISSUE	QUOTE
85	THE BRIDE	YR	45.00	300.00
87	THE PARTY'S OVER	YR	55.00	140.00
88	CHOW TIME	YR	65.00	120.00
89	CAN'T WAIT	YR	75.00	110.00
90	PIT STOP	YR	75.00	115.00
91	ARRIVAL OF STANLEY	YR	100.00	100.00
91	DON'T PICK THE FLOWERS	YR	100.00	100.00
92	CHECK'S IN THE MAIL	YR	100.00	100.00
92	HOG WILD	YR	100.00	100.00

L. DAVIS   **LOWELL DAVIS FARM CLUB RENEWAL FIGURINE**

YR	NAME	LIMIT	ISSUE	QUOTE
91	NEW ARRIVAL	*	*	*

L. DAVIS   **PROMOTIONAL FIGURINE**

YR	NAME	LIMIT	ISSUE	QUOTE
91	LEAVIN THE RAT RACE	*	125.00	145.00
92	HEN SCRATCH	*	90.00	100.00

L. DAVIS   **QUILTIN' BEE**

YR	NAME	LIMIT	ISSUE	QUOTE
92	BIG LIKE DADDY	OP	80.00	80.00
92	BIRDS OF A FEATHER	OP	80.00	80.00
92	CORN FLABIN	OP	80.00	80.00
92	GOLDIE AND HER PEEPS	OP	80.00	80.00
92	LUNCH BREAK	OP	80.00	80.00
92	WHAT'S FOR DESSERT	OP	80.00	80.00

L. DAVIS   **RFD AMERICA**

YR	NAME	LIMIT	ISSUE	QUOTE
79	BLOSSOM	RT	180.00	1400.00
79	BROKEN DREAMS	RT	185.00	1000.00
79	COUNTRY ROAD	RT	120.00	675.00
79	FOWL PLAY	RT	100.00	300.00
79	IGNORANCE IS BLISS	RT	165.00	1185.00
79	SLIM PICKINS	RT	185.00	785.00
80	CREEK BANK BANDIT	RT	50.00	385.00
80	FORBIDDEN FRUIT	RT	32.50	175.00-200.00
80	MILKING TIME	RT	32.50	195.00
80	SUNDAY AFTERNOON	RT	32.50	235.00
80	WILBUR	RT	110.00	585.00
81	COUNTRY BOY	RT	45.00	375.00
81	DOUBLE TROUBLE	RT	42.50	455.00
81	DRY AS A BONE	RT	45.00	250.00
81	HIGHTAILING IT	RT	50.00	345.00
81	PUNKIN SEEDS	RT	250.00	1600.00
81	SPLIT DECISION	RT	45.00	255.00
81	STUDIO MOUSE	RT	60.00	325.00
81	UP TO NO GOOD	RT	200.00	875.00-900.00
82	A SHOE TO FILL	RT	37.50	175.00
82	BABY BLOSSOM	RT	40.00	260.00
82	BABY BOBS	RT	47.50	195.00
82	BLOSSOM & CALF	RT	250.00	780.00
82	BRAND NEW DAY	RT	23.50	155.00
82	COUNTRY CROOK	RT	37.50	375.00-400.00
82	IDLE HOURS	RT	37.50	275.00
82	MOON RAIDERS	RT	180.00	495.00
82	MOVING DAY	RT	43.50	300.00
82	STRAY DOG	RT	35.00	65.00
82	THINKING BIG	RT	35.00	90.00
82	TREED	RT	155.00	280.00
82	TWO'S COMPANY	RT	43.50	245.00
82	WAITING FOR HIS MASTER	RT	50.00	150.00-300.00
82	WHEN MAMA GETS MAD	RT	37.50	250.00
83	CITY SLICKER	RT	150.00	275.00
83	FALSE ALARM	RT	65.00	140.00
83	HAPPY HUNTING GROUND	RT	160.00	235.00
83	HI GIRLS, THE NAME'S BIG JACK	RT	200.00	380.00

YR	NAME	LIMIT	ISSUE	QUOTE
83	HIS EYES ARE BIGGER THAN STOMACH	2500	235.00	330-365
83	LICKIN' GOOD	RT	35.00	250.00
83	MAMA'S PRIZE LEGHORN	RT	55.00	120.00
83	STIRRING UP TROUBLE	RT	160.00	245.00
84	ANYBODY HOME	*	35.00	125.00
84	CATNAPPING TOO	RT	70.00	115.00
84	COUNTRY KITTY	*	52.00	110.00
84	COURTIN'	RT	50.00	125.00
84	GONNA PAY FOR HIS SINS	*	27.50	50.00
84	GOSSIPS	RT	110.00	300.00
84	HEADED HOME	RT	253.00	47.50
84	HIS MASTER'S DOG	RT	45.00	100.00-270.00
84	HUH?	RT	40.00	90.00
84	MAD AS A WET HEN	RT	185.00	695.00
84	ONE FOR THE ROAD	*	37.50	60.00
84	PASTURE PALS	RT	52.00	90.00
84	PRAIRIE CHORUS	RT	135.00	1100.00-1300.00
85	BARN CATS	*	39.50	65.00
85	COUNTRY COUSINS	*	42.50	60.00
85	COUNTRY CROONER	*	25.00	42.50
85	DON'T PLAY WITH YOUR FOOD	*	28.50	80.00
85	FURS GONNA FLY	950	145.00	240.00
85	HOG HEAVEN	RT	165.00	250.00
85	LOVE AT FIRST SIGHT	*	70.00	115.00
85	OUT OF STEP	*	45.00	70.00
85	RENOIR	RT	45.00	75.00
85	TOO GOOD TO WASTE ON KIDS	*	70.00	100.00
85	WILL YOU/RESPECT ME IN THE MORNING	*	35.00	50.00
86	BIT OFF MORE THAN HE COULD CHEW	*	15.00	55.00-65.00
86	COMFY?	*	39.00	65.00
86	FEELIN' HIS OATS	1500	150.00	260.00
86	MAMA?	RT	15.00	47.50
87	BOTTOMS UP	*	80.00	90.00
87	CHICKEN THIEF	RT	200.00	360.00
87	EASY PICKINS	RT	45.00	85.00
87	GLUTTON FOR PUNISHMENT	RT	95.00	130.00-150.00
87	MAIL ORDER BRIDE	RT	150.00	175.00-300.00
87	THE ORPHANS	OP	50.00	55.00-125.00
87	TWO IN THE BUSH	RT	150.00	320.00
87	WHEN THE CAT'S AWAY	*	40.00	60.00
88	BROTHERS	RT	55.00	85.00
88	FLEAS	*	20.00	25.00
88	GOLDIE AND HER PEEPS	*	25.00	32.50
88	HAPPY HOUR	*	57.50	65.00
88	IN A PICKLE	*	40.00	43.00
88	MAKING A BEE LINE	RT	75.00	100.00
88	MISSOURI SPRING	*	115.00	125.00
88	NO PRIVATE TIME	1250	200.00	235.00
88	PERFECT TEN	RT	95.00	145.00
88	SAWIN' LOGS	*	85.00	85.00
88	WHEN THREE FOOT'S A MILE	950	230.00	270.00
88	WISHFUL THINKING	*	55.00	60.00
89	A TRIBUTE TO HOOKER	2500	180.00	215.00
89	COON CAPERS	OP	67.50	67.50
89	FAMILY OUTING	OP	45.00	45.00
89	GITTIN' A NIBBLE	OP	50.00	50.00
89	LEFTOVERS	OP	90.00	80.00-90.00
89	MEETING OF SHELDON	OP	120.00	150.00
89	MOTHER HEN	OP	37.50	40.00
89	NEW FRIEND	OP	45.00	48.00
89	SUN WORSHIPPERS	5000	120.00	140.00
89	SUN WORSHIPPERS MINI FIGURINE	OP	32.50	42.50
89	THE BOY'S NIGHT OUT	1500	190.00	225.00
89	WOODSCOLT	RT	300.00	375.00
90	CORN CRIB MOUSE	OP	35.00	40.00
90	DEALER COUNTER SIGN	OP	50.00	70.00
90	FINDERS KEEPERS	OP	39.50	39.50
90	FOREPLAY	OP	59.50	59.50
90	HANKY PANKY	OP	65.00	65.00
90	HOME SQUEEZINS	OP	90.00	90.00
90	LITTLE BLACK LAMB (BABA)	OP	30.00	30.00
90	LONG DAYS, COLD NIGHTS	OP	175.00	190.00
90	OUTING WITH GRANDPA	2500	200.00	185.00
90	PIGGIN OUT	1250	250.00	245.00
90	PRIVATE TIME	OP	18.00	18.00
90	SEEIN' RED	OP	35.00	35.00

YR	NAME	LIMIT	ISSUE	QUOTE
90	SUNDAY AFTERNOON TREAT	5000	120.00	130.00
90	SUNDAY AFTERNOON TREAT MINI	5000	32.50	30.00
90	THE LAST STRAW	OP	125.00	135.00
90	TRICKS OF THE TRADE	RT	300.00	330.00
91	COCK OF THE WALK	2500	300.00	250.00-300.00
91	FIRST OFFENSE	OP	70.00	75.00
91	GUN SHY	OP	70.00	70.00
91	HEADING FOR THE PERSIMMON GROVE	OP	80.00	80.00
91	KISSIN COUSINS	OP	80.00	80.00
91	LONG HOT SUMMER	1950	250.00	250.00
91	SOOIEEE	RT	350.00	350.00
91	WARM MILK	5000	200.00	135.00-150.00
91	WARM MILK MINI FIGURINE	OP	37.50	37.50
91	WASHED ASHORE	OP	70.00	70.00
92	DON'T PLAY WITH FIRE	OP	120.00	120.00
92	FREE LUNCH	OP	85.00	85.00
92	HEADED SOUTH	OP	45.00	45.00
92	LOWELL DAVIS PROFILE	OP	65.00	65.00
92	MY FAVORITE CHORES	1500	750.00	750.00
92	OH SHEEEEIT	OP	120.00	120.00
92	OZARK'S VITTLES	OP	50.00	50.00
92	SAFE HAVEN	OP	95.00	95.00
92	SHE LAY LOW	OP	120.00	120.00
92	SNAKE DOCTOR	OP	70.00	70.00
92	THE GRASS IS ALWAYS GREENER	OP	195.00	195.00
92	THE HONEYMOON'S OVER	1950	300.00	300.00

L. DAVIS — ROUTE 66

YR	NAME	LIMIT	ISSUE	QUOTE
91	JUST CHECK THE AIR	350	700.00	950.00-1000.00
91	JUST CHECK THE AIR	2500	550.00	550.00
91	LITTLE BIT OF SHADE	OP	100.00	100.00
91	NEL'S DINER	2500	550.00	550.00
91	NEL'S DINER	350	700.00	950.00-1000.00
92	FRESH SQUEEZED	350	700.00	700.00
92	FRESH SQUEEZED	2500	550.00	550.00
92	GOING TO GRANDMA	OP	80.00	80.00
92	QUIET DAY AT MAPLE GROVE	OP	130.00	130.00
92	RELIEF	OP	80.00	80.00
92	WELCOME MAT	1500	400.00	400.00
92	WHAT ARE PALS FOR?	OP	100.00	100.00

TOM RUBEL — SANTA'S ANIMAL KINGDOM

YR	NAME	LIMIT	ISSUE	QUOTE
94	SANTA'S ANIMAL KINGDOM-STIFFENED	2500	125.00	135.00

L. DAVIS — UNCLE REMUS

YR	NAME	LIMIT	ISSUE	QUOTE
81	BRER BEAR	RT	80.00	925.00
81	BRER COYOTE	RT	80.00	500.00
81	BRER FOX	RT	70.00	875.00
81	BRER RABBIT	RT	85.00	1600.00
81	BRER WEASEL	RT	80.00	475.00
81	BRER WOLF	RT	85.00	595.00

SCULPTURE BY SHALAH

S. PERKINS — BRONZE

YR	NAME	LIMIT	ISSUE	QUOTE
93	FARMER, THE	20	*	1800.00
93	MISS DOLLIE	20	*	1500.00
94	CALL OF THE LAND	20	*	1800.00
94	CELEBRATION OF A COWGIRL	10	*	9000.00
94	NEIGHBOR	20	*	1050.00
94	REMEMBERING	20	*	950.00

S. PERKINS — BRONZE FOUNTAIN

YR	NAME	LIMIT	ISSUE	QUOTE
94	JOY IN THE MORNING	13	*	5500.00
95	WISHFUL THINKIN	20	*	7500.00

SEBASTIAN STUDIOS

P.W. BASTON — LARGE CERAMASTONE FIGURES

YR	NAME	LIMIT	ISSUE	QUOTE
*	SANTA FE...ALL THE WAY	CL	*	600.00-1000.00
*	ST. FRANCIS PLAQUE	CL	*	600.00-1000.00
39	PAUL REVERE PLAQUE	CL	*	400.00-500.00
40	BASKET	CL	*	300.00-400.00
40	BRETON MAN	CL	*	600.00-1000.00
40	BRETON WOMAN	CL	*	600.00-1000.00
40	CANDLE HOLDER	CL	*	300.00-400.00
40	CAROLER	CL	*	300.00-400.00
40	HORN OF PLENTY	CL	*	300.00-400.00
40	JESUS	CL	*	300.00-400.00
40	LAMB	CL	*	300.00-400.00
40	MARY	CL	*	600.00-1000.00
47	LARGE VICTORIAN COUPLE	CL	*	600.00-1000.00
48	WOODY AT THREE	CL	*	600.00-1000.00

YR	NAME	LIMIT	ISSUE	QUOTE
56	JELL-O COW MILK PITCHER	CL	*	175.00-225.00
58	SWIFT INSTRUMENT GIRL	CL	*	500.00-750.00
59	WASP PLAQUE	CL	*	500.00-750.00
63	ABRAHAM LINCOLN TOBY JUG	CL	*	600.00-1000.00
63	ANNE BOLEYN	CL	*	600.00-1000.00
63	DAVID COPPERFIELD	CL	*	600.00-1000.00
63	DORA	CL	*	600.00-1000.00
63	GEORGE WASHINGTON TOBY JUG	CL	*	600.00-1000.00
63	HENRY VIII	CL	*	600.00-1000.00
63	JOHN F. KENNEDY TOBY JUG	CL	*	600.00-1000.00
63	MENDING TIME	CL	*	600.00-1000.00
63	TOM SAWYER	CL	*	600.00-1000.00
64	COLONIAL BOY	CL	*	600.00-1000.00
64	COLONIAL GIRL	CL	*	600.00-1000.00
64	COLONIAL MAN	CL	*	600.00-1000.00
64	COLONIAL WOMAN	CL	*	600.00-1000.00
64	IBM FATHER	CL	*	600.00-1000.00
64	IBM MOTHER	CL	*	600.00-1000.00
64	IBM PHOTOGRAPHER	CL	*	600.00-1000.00
64	IBM SON	CL	*	600.00-1000.00
64	IBM WOMAN	CL	*	600.00-1000.00
65	N.E. HOME FOR LITTLE WANDERERS	CL	*	600.00-1000.00
65	STANLEY MUSIC BOX	CL	*	300.00-500.00
65	THE DENTIST	CL	*	600.00-1000.00
66	GUITARIST	CL	*	600.00-1000.00
67	INFANT OF PRAGUE	CL	*	600.00-1000.00
73	BLACKSMITH	CL	*	300.00-400.00
73	CABINETMAKER	CL	*	300.00-400.00
73	CLOCKMAKER	CL	*	600.00-1000.00
73	POTTER	CL	*	300.00-400.00
75	MINUTEMAN	CL	*	600.00-1000.00
78	MT. RUSHMORE	CL	*	400.00-500.00
P.W. BASTON		**SEBASTIAN MINIATURES**		
*	BABE RUTH	CL	*	600.00-1000.00
*	BOB HOPE	CL	*	600.00-1000.00
*	CORONATION CROWN	CL	*	600.00-1000.00
*	EAGLE PLAQUE	CL	*	1000.00-1500.00
*	ORTHO GYNECIC	CL	*	600.00-1000.00
*	SYLVANIA ELECTRIC-BULB DISPLAY	CL	*	600.00-1000.00
*	THE KING	CL	*	600.00-1000.00
38	SHAKER LADY	CL	*	75.00-100.00
38	SHAKER MAN	CL	*	75.00-100.00
39	BENJAMIN FRANKLIN	CL	*	75.00-100.00
39	CORONADO	CL	*	75.00-100.00
39	CORONADO'S SENORA	CL	*	75.00-100.00
39	DEBORAH FRANKLIN	CL	*	75.00-100.00
39	EVANGELINE	CL	*	100.00-125.00
39	GABRIEL	CL	*	100.00-125.00
39	GEORGE WASHINGTON	CL	*	35.00-75.00
39	INDIAN MAIDEN	CL	*	100.00-125.00
39	INDIAN WARRIOR	CL	*	100.00-125.00
39	JOHN ALDEN	CL	*	35.00-50.00
39	MARGARET HOUSTON	CL	*	75.00-100.00
39	MARTHA WASHINGTON	CL	*	35.00-75.00
39	PRISCILLA	CL	*	35.00-50.00
39	SAM HOUSTON	CL	*	75.00-100.00
39	WILLIAMSBURG GOVERNOR	CL	*	75.00-100.00
39	WILLIAMSBURG LADY	CL	*	75.00-100.00
40	ANN STVYVESANT	CL	*	75.00-100.00
40	ANNIE OAKLEY	CL	*	75.00-100.00
40	BUFFALO BILL	CL	*	75.00-100.00
40	CATHERINE LAFITTE	CL	*	75.00-100.00
40	DAN'L BOONE	CL	*	75.00-100.00
40	ELIZABETH MONROE	CL	*	150.00-175.00
40	HANNAH PENN	CL	*	100.00-150.00
40	JAMES MONROE	CL	*	150.00-175.00
40	JEAN LAFITTE	CL	*	75.00-100.00
40	JOHN HARVARD	CL	*	125.00-150.00
40	JOHN SMITH	CL	*	125.00-150.00
40	MRS. DAN'L BOONE	CL	*	75.00-100.00
40	MRS. HARVARD	CL	*	125.00-150.00
40	PETER STVYVESANT	CL	*	75.00-100.00
40	POCOHONTAS	CL	*	125.00-150.00
40	WILLIAM PENN	CL	*	100.00-150.00
41	DOVES	CL	*	600.00-1000.00
41	DUCKLINGS	CL	*	600.00-1000.00

YR	NAME	LIMIT	ISSUE	QUOTE
41	KITTEN (SITTING)	CL	*	600.00-1000.00
41	KITTEN (SLEEPING)	CL	*	600.00-1000.00
41	PEACOCK	CL	*	600.00-1000.00
41	PHEASANT	CL	*	600.00-1000.00
41	ROOSTER	CL	*	600.00-1000.00
41	SECRETS	CL	*	600.00-1000.00
41	SWAN	CL	*	600.00-1000.00
42	ACCORDION	CL	*	325.00-375.00
42	CYMBALS	CL	*	325.00-375.00
42	DRUM	CL	*	325.00-375.00
42	HORN	CL	*	325.00-375.00
42	MAJORETTE	CL	*	325.00-375.00
42	TUBA	CL	*	325.00-375.00
46	PURITAN SPINNER	CL	*	600.00-1000.00
46	SATCHEL-EYE DYER	CL	*	125.00-150.00
47	DAHL'S FISHERMAN	CL	*	150.00-175.00
47	DILEMMA	CL	*	275.00-300.00
47	DOWN EAST	CL	*	125.00-150.00
47	FIRST COOKBOOK AUTHOR	CL	*	125.00-150.00
47	FISHER PAIR PS	CL	*	600.00-1000.00
47	HOWARD JOHNSON PIEMAN	CL	*	400.00-450.00
47	MR. BEACON HILL	CL	*	100.00-125.00
47	MRS. BEACON HILL	CL	*	100.00-125.00
47	PRINCE PHILIP	CL	*	200.00-300.00
47	PRINCESS ELIZABETH	CL	*	200.00-300.00
47	TOLLHOUSE TOWN CRIER	CL	*	125.00-175.00
48	A HARVEY GIRL	CL	*	250.00-300.00
48	DEMOCRATIC VICTORY	CL	*	350.00-500.00
48	JORDAN MARSH OBSERVER	CL	*	150.00-175.00
48	MARY LYON	CL	*	250.00-300.00
48	MR. RITTENHOUSE SQUARE	CL	*	150.00-175.00
48	MR. SHERATON	CL	*	350.00-400.00
48	MRS. RITTENHOUSE SQUARE	CL	*	150.00-175.00
48	NATHANIEL HAWTHORNE	CL	*	175.00-200.00
48	REPUBLICAN VICTORY	CL	*	600.00-1000.00
48	SITZMARK	CL	*	175.00-200.00
48	SLALOM	CL	*	175.00-200.00
48	SWEDISH BOY	CL	*	300.00-500.00
48	SWEDISH GIRL	CL	*	300.00-500.00
49	BOY SCOUT PLAQUE	CL	*	300.00-350.00
49	DUTCHMAN'S PIPE	CL	*	175.00-225.00
49	EMMETT KELLY	CL	*	250.00-300.00
49	EUSTACE TILLY	CL	*	750.00-1000.00
49	GATHERING TULIPS	CL	*	225.00-250.00
49	GIANT ROYAL BENGAL TIGER	CL	*	1000.00-1500.00
49	MENOTOMY INDIAN	CL	*	175.00-250.00
49	PATRICK HENRY	CL	*	100.00-125.00
49	PAUL BUNYAN	CL	*	250.00
49	SARAH HENRY	CL	*	100.00-125.00
49	THE MARK TWAIN HOME IN HANNIBAL, MO	CL	*	600.00-1000.00
49	THE THINKER	CL	*	175.00-250.00
49	UNCLE MISTLETOE	CL	*	200.00-300.00
50	MR. OBOCELL	CL	*	75.00-125.00
50	NATIONAL DIAPER SERVICE	CL	*	250.00-300.00
50	PHOEBE, HOUSE OF 7 GABLES	CL	*	150.00-175.00
51	CARL MOORE (WEEI)	CL	*	200.00-300.00
51	CAROLINE CABOT (WEEI)	CL	*	200.00-350.00
51	CHARLES ASHLEY (WEEI)	CL	*	200.00-350.00
51	CHIEF PONTIAC	CL	*	400.00-700.00
51	CHIQUITA BANANA	CL	*	350.00-400.00
51	CHRISTOPHER COLUMBUS	CL	*	250.00-300.00
51	E.B. RIDEOUT (WEEI)	CL	*	200.00-350.00
51	GREAT STONE FACE	CL	*	600.00-1000.00
51	JESSE BUFFMAN (WEEI)	CL	*	200.00-350.00
51	JORDON MARSH/RIDES THE A.W. HORSE	CL	*	300.00-325.00
51	JUDGE PYNCHEON	CL	*	175.00-225.00
51	MIT SEAL	CL	*	350.00-425.00
51	MOTHER PARKER (WEEI)	CL	*	200.00-350.00
51	PRISCILLA FORTESUE (WEEI)	CL	*	200.00-350.00
51	SEB. DEALER PLAQUE (MARBLEHEAD)	CL	*	300.00-350.00
51	SIR FRANCES DRAKE	CL	*	250.00-300.00
51	THE IRON MASTER'S HOUSE	CL	*	350.00-500.00
51	THE OBSERVER & DAME NEW ENGLAND	CL	*	325.00-375.00
52	AERIAL TRAMWAY	CL	*	300.00-600.00
52	BABY (JELL-O)	CL	*	525.00-600.00
52	FAVORED SCHOLAR	CL	*	200.00-300.00

YR	NAME	LIMIT	ISSUE	QUOTE
52	LOST IN THE KITCHEN (JELL-O)	CL	*	425.00-525.00
52	MARBLEHEAD HIGH SCHOOL PLAQUE	CL	*	200.00-300.00
52	NEIGHBORING PEWS	CL	*	200.00-300.00
52	OLD POWDER HOUSE	CL	*	250.00-300.00
52	OUR LADY OF GOOD VOYAGE	CL	*	200.00-250.00
52	SCOTTISH GIRL (JELL-O)	CL	*	350.00-375.00
52	ST. JOAN D'ARC	CL	*	300.00-350.00
52	ST. SEBASTIAN	CL	*	300.00-350.00
52	STORK (JELL-O)	CL	*	425.00-525.00
52	TABASCO SAUCE	CL	*	400.00-500.00
52	THE FAT MAN (JELL-O)	CL	*	525.00-600.00
52	THE FIRST HOUSE, PLYMOUTH PLANTATION	CL	*	150.00-195.00
52	WEIGHING THE BABY	CL	*	200.00-300.00
53	BLESSED JULIE BILLART	CL	*	400.00-500.00
53	BOY JESUS IN THE TEMPLE	CL	*	350.00-400.00
53	DARNED WELL HE CAN	CL	*	300.00-350.00
53	HOLGRAVE THE DAGUERROTYPIST	CL	*	200.00-250.00
53	LION (JELL-O)	CL	*	350.00-375.00
53	OLD PUT ENJOYS A LICKING	CL	*	300.00-350.00
53	R.H. STEARNS CHESTNUT HILL MALL	CL	*	225.00-275.00
53	ST. TERESA OF LISIEUX	CL	*	225.00-275.00
53	THE SCHOOLBOY OF 1850	CL	*	350.00-400.00
54	BLUEBIRD GIRL	CL	*	400.00-450.00
54	CAMPFIRE GIRL	CL	*	400.00-450.00
54	DACHSHUND (AUDIOVOX)	CL	*	300.00-350.00
54	HORIZON GIRL	CL	*	400.00-450.00
54	KERNEL-FRESH ASHTRAY	CL	*	400.00-450.00
54	MOOSE (JELL-O)	CL	*	350.00-375.00
54	OUR LADY OF LALECHE	CL	*	300.00-350.00
54	RABBIT (JELL-O)	CL	*	350.00-375.00
54	RESOLUTE INS. CO. CLIPPER PS	CL	*	300.00-325.00
54	SCUBA DIVER	CL	*	400.00-450.00
54	ST. PIUS X	CL	*	400.00-475.00
54	STIMALOSE (MEN)	CL	*	600.00-1000.00
54	STIMALOSE (WOMAN)	CL	*	175.00-200.00
54	SWAN BOAT BROOCH-EMPTY SEATS	CL	*	600.00-1000.00
54	SWAN BOAT BROOCH-FULL SEATS	CL	*	600.00-1000.00
54	WHALE (JELL-O)	CL	*	350.00-375.00
54	WILLIAM PENN	CL	*	175.00-225.00
55	CAPTAIN DOLIBER	CL	*	300.00-350.00
55	DAVY CROCKETT	CL	*	225.00-275.00
55	GIRAFFE (JELL-O)	CL	*	350.00-375.00
55	HORSE HEAD PS	CL	*	350.00-375.00
55	OLD WOMAN IN THE SHOE (JELL-O)	CL	*	500.00-600.00
55	SANTA (JELL-O)	CL	*	500.00-600.00
55	SECOND BANK-STATE ST. TRUST PS	CL	*	300.00-325.00
56	77TH BENGAL LANCER (JELL-O)	CL	*	600.00-1000.00
56	ALIKE, BUT OH SO DIFFERENT	CL	*	300.00-350.00
56	ARTHRITIC HANDS (J&J)	CL	*	600.00-1000.00
56	EASTERN PAPER PLAQUE	CL	*	350.00-400.00
56	ELSIE THE COW BILLBOARD	CL	*	600.00-1000.00
56	GIRL ON DIVING BOARD	CL	*	400.00-450.00
56	MICHIGAN MILLERS PS	CL	*	200.00-275.00
56	MRS. OBOCELL	CL	*	400.00-450.00
56	NYU GRAD SCHOOL OF BUS. ADMIN. BLDG.	CL	*	300.00-350.00
56	PERMACEL TOWER OF TAPE ASHTRAY	CL	*	600.00-1000.00
56	PRAYING HANDS	CL	*	250.00-300.00
56	RARICAL BLACKSMITH	CL	*	300.00-500.00
56	ROBIN HOOD & FRIAR TUCK	CL	*	400.00-500.00
56	ROBIN HOOD & LITTLE JOHN	CL	*	400.00-500.00
56	TEXCEL TAPE BOY	CL	*	350.00-425.00
56	THE GREEN GIANT	CL	*	400.00-500.00
56	THREE LITTLE KITTENS (JELL-O)	CL	*	375.00-400.00
57	ALONG THE ALBANY ROAD PS	CL	*	600.00-1000.00
57	BORDEN'S CENTENNIAL (ELSIE THE COW)	CL	*	600.00-1000.00
57	COLONIAL FUND DOORWAY PS	CL	*	600.00-1000.00
57	IBM 305 RAMAC	CL	*	400.00-450.00
57	JAMESTOWN CHURCH	CL	*	400.00-450.00
57	JAMESTOWN SHIPS	CL	*	350.00-475.00
57	MAYFLOWER PS	CL	*	300.00-325.00
57	NABISCO BUFFALO BEE	CL	*	600.00-1000.00
57	NABISCO SPOONMAN	CL	*	600.00-1000.00
57	OLDE JAMES FORT	CL	*	250.00-300.00
57	SPEEDY ALKA SELTZER	CL	*	600.00-1000.00
58	CBS MISS COLUMBIA PS	CL	*	600.00-1000.00
58	CLIQUOT CLUB ESKIMO PS	CL	*	1000.00-2300.00

YR	NAME	LIMIT	ISSUE	QUOTE
58	COMMODORE STEPHEN DECATUR	CL	*	125.00-175.00
58	CONNECTICUT BANK & TRUST	CL	*	225.00-275.00
58	HANNAH DUSTON PS	CL	*	250.00-325.00
58	HARVARD TRUST COLONIAL MAN	CL	*	275.00-325.00
58	JACKIE GLEASON	CL	*	600.00-1000.00
58	JORDAN MARSH OBSERVER	CL	*	175.00-275.00
58	MT. VERNON	CL	*	400.00-500.00
58	ROMEO & JULIET	CL	*	400.00-500.00
58	SALEM SAVINGS BANK	CL	*	250.00-300.00
59	ALCOA WRAP PS	CL	*	350.00-400.00
59	ALEXANDER SMITH WEAVER	CL	*	350.00-425.00
59	FIORELLO LAGUARDIA	CL	*	125.00-175.00
59	FLEISCHMAN'S MARGARINE PS	CL	*	225.00-325.00
59	GIOVANNI VERRAZZANO	CL	*	125.00-175.00
59	H.P. HOOD CO. CIGAR STORE INDIAN	CL	*	600.00-1000.00
59	HARVARD TRUST CO. TOWN CRIER	CL	*	350.00-400.00
59	HENRY HUDSON	CL	*	125.00-175.00
59	MRS. S.O.S.	CL	*	300.00-350.00
59	SIESTA COFFEE PS	CL	*	600.00-1000.00
60	MARINE MEMORIAL	CL	*	300.00-400.00
60	MASONIC BIBLE	CL	*	300.00-400.00
60	METROPOLITAN LIFE TOWER PS	CL	*	350.00-400.00
60	PETER STVYVESANT	CL	*	125.00-175.00
60	SON OF THE DESERT	CL	*	200.00-275.00
60	SUPP-HOSE LADY	CL	*	300.00-350.00
60	THE INFANTRYMAN	CL	*	600.00-1000.00
60	TONY PIET	CL	*	600.00-1000.00
61	BUNKY KNUDSEN	CL	*	600.00-1000.00
61	MERCHANT'S WARREN SEA CAPTAIN	CL	*	200.00-250.00
61	POPE JOHN 23RD	CL	*	400.00-450.00
61	ST. JUDE THADDEUS	CL	*	400.00-500.00
62	BIG BROTHER BOB EMERY	CL	*	600.00-1000.00
62	BLUE BELLE HIGHLANDER	CL	*	200.00-250.00
62	SEAMAN'S BANK FOR SAVINGS	CL	*	350.00
62	YANKEE CLIPPER SULFIDE	CL	*	600.00-1000.00
63	DIA-MEL FAT MAN	CL	*	375.00-400.00
63	JACKIE KENNEDY TOBY JUG	CL	*	600.00-1000.00
63	JOHN F. KENNEDY TOBY JUG	CL	*	600.00-1000.00
63	NAUMKEAG INDIAN	CL	*	225.00-275.00
65	HENRY WADSWORTH LONGFELLOW	CL	*	275.00-325.00
65	PANTI-LEGS GIRL PS	CL	*	250.00-300.00
65	POPE PAUL VI	CL	*	400.00-500.00
65	STATE STREET BANK GLOBE	CL	*	250.00-300.00
66	GARDENER MAN	CL	*	250.00-300.00
66	GARDENER WOMEN	CL	*	250.00-300.00
66	GARDENERS (THERMOMETER)	CL	*	300.00-400.00
66	LITTLE GEORGE	CL	*	350.00-450.00
66	MASSACHUSETTS SPCA	CL	*	250.00-350.00
66	PAUL REVERE PLAQUE (W.T. GRANT)	CL	*	300.00-350.00
66	TOWN LYNE INDIAN	CL	*	600.00-1000.00
67	DOC BERRY OF BERWICK (YELLOW SHIRT)	CL	*	300.00-350.00
67	ORTHO-NOVUM	CL	*	600.00-1000.00
68	CAPTAIN JOHN PARKER	CL	*	300.00-350.00
68	WATERMILL CANDY PLAQUE	CL	*	600.00-1000.00
70	UNCLE SAM IN ORBIT	CL	*	350.00-400.00
71	BOSTON GAS TANK	CL	*	300.00-500.00
71	TOWN MEETING PLAQUE	CL	*	350.00-400.00
72	GEORGE & HATCHET	CL	*	400.00-450.00
72	MARTHA & THE CHERRY PIE	CL	*	350.00-400.00

SEYMOUR MANN

YR	NAME	LIMIT	ISSUE	QUOTE
KENJI			**BROWN CAT IN HAT**	
91	BROWN CAT IN HAT	RT	35.00	35.00
KENJI *			**BUNNY MUSICAL**	
91	BUNNY IN TEACUP MH-781	OP	25.00	25.00
91	BUNNY IN TEAPOT MH-780	OP	25.00	25.00
KENJI			**CAT MUSICAL FIGURINES**	
85	CATS BALL SHAPE	CL	25.00	25.00
86	CATS W/RIBBON MH-481 A/C	RT	30.00	30.00
87	BROWN CAT IN BAG	CL	30.00	30.00
87	BROWN CAT IN TEACUP	RT	30.00	30.00
87	CAT IN BAG MH-614	RT	30.00	30.00
87	CAT IN TEACUP MH-600VGG	RT	30.00	30.00
87	CAT ON TIPPED GARBAGE CAN MH-498	RT	35.00	35.00
87	KITTENDS W/BALLS OF YARN MH-612	RT	30.00	30.00
87	MUSICAL BEAR MH-602	RT	27.50	27.50
87	TEAPOT CAT MH-631	RT	30.00	30.00

YR	NAME	LIMIT	ISSUE	QUOTE
87	VALENTINE CAT IN BAG MUSICAL MH-600	RT	33.50	33.50
87	VALENTINE CAT IN TEACUP MH-600VLT	RT	33.50	33.50
88	BROWN CAT IN HAT MH-634B/6	RT	35.00	35.00
88	CAT IN HAT BOX MH-634	RT	35.00	35.00
88	CAT IN HAT MH-634B	RT	35.00	35.00
89	CAT IN BASINET MH-714	RT	35.00	35.00
89	CAT IN BASKET MH-713B	RT	35.00	35.00
89	CAT IN FLOWER MH-709	RT	35.00	35.00
89	CAT IN GIFT BOX MUSICAL MH-732	RT	40.00	40.00
89	CAT IN SHOE MH-718	RT	30.00	30.00
89	CAT IN WATER CAN MUSICAL MH-712	RT	35.00	35.00
89	CAT ON BASKET MH-713	RT	35.00	35.00
89	CAT W/COFFEE CUP MUSICAL MH-706	RT	35.00	35.00
89	CAT W/SWING MUSICAL MH-710	RT	35.00	35.00
90	CAT ASLEEP MH-735	RT	17.50	37.50
90	CAT CALICO IN EASY CHAIR MH-743VG	RT	27.50	27.50
90	CAT IN BOOTIE MH-728	RT	35.00	35.00
90	CAT IN DRESS MH-751VG	RT	37.50	37.50
90	CAT ON GIFT BOX MUSIC MH-740	RT	40.00	40.00
90	CAT SAILOR IN ROCKING BOAT MH-734	RT	45.00	45.00
90	CAT W/BOW ON PINK PILLOW MH-741P	RT	33.50	35.50
90	CATS GRADUATION MH-745	RT	27.50	27.50
90	GREY CAT IN BOOTIE MH-728G/6	CL	35.00	35.00
90	KITTEN TRIO IN CARRIAGE MH-742	CL	37.50	37.50
91	BROWN CAT IN BAG	RT	30.00	30.00
91	BROWN CAT IN TEACUP	CL	30.00	30.00
91	CAT IN BAG	CL	30.00	30.00
91	CAT IN BOOTIE	CL	35.00	35.00
91	CAT IN GARBAGE CAN	RT	35.00	35.00
91	CAT IN GARBAGE CAN	CL	35.00	35.00
91	CAT IN HAT	CL	35.00	35.00
91	CAT IN HAT BOX	CL	35.00	35.00
91	CAT IN ROSE TEACUP	RT	30.00	30.00
91	CAT IN ROSE TEACUP	CL	30.00	30.00
91	CAT IN TEACUP	CL	30.00	30.00
91	CAT ON TIPPED GARBAGE CAN	CL	35.00	35.00
91	CATS BALL SHAPE	CL	25.00	25.00
91	CATS W/RIBBON	CL	30.00	30.00
91	GREY CAT IN BOOTIE	CL	35.00	35.00
91	KITTENS W/BALLS OF YARN	CL	30.00	30.00
91	MUSICAL BEAR	CL	27.50	27.50
91	TEAPOT CAT	CL	30.00	30.00
87	CAT IN BAG MH-617	RT	30.00	30.00
87	CAT IN GARBAGE CAN MH-190	RT	35.00	35.00
87	CAT IN ROSE TEACUP MH-600VG	RT	30.00	30.00
87	CAT IN TEACUP MH-600VGG	RT	30.00	30.00
90	BRIDE/GROOM CAT MH-738	RT	37.50	37.50
90	CAT ON PILLOW MH-731	RT	17.50	17.50
90	CAT W/PARROT MH-730	RT	37.50	37.50
91	CAT IN BASKET MH-768	RT	35.00	35.00
91	CAT MOMMA MH-758	RT	35.00	35.00
91	CAT W/BOW ON PINK PILLOW MH-741P	RT	33.50	33.50
91	CAT WATCHING BUTTERFLY MH-784	RT	17.50	17.50
91	CAT WATCHING CANARY MH-783	RT	25.00	25.00
91	FAMILY CAT MH-770	RT	35.00	35.00
91	LITTEN PICKING TULIPS MH-756	RT	40.00	40.00
91	REVOLVING CAT W/BUTTERFLY MH-759	RT	40.00	40.00

JAIMY   **CHRISTMAS COLLECTION**

YR	NAME	LIMIT	ISSUE	QUOTE
89	SANTA IN SLED W/REINDEER CJ-3	RT	25.00	25.00
89	SANTA MUSICALS CJ-1/4	RT	27.50	27.50
89	SANTA ON HORSE CJ-33A	RT	33.50	33.50
89	SANTA W/LIST CJ-23	RT	27.50	27.50
90	MR. & MRS. SANTA MUSICAL	CL	37.50	37.50
90	SANTA ON CHIMNEY MUSICAL	CL	33.50	33.50
90	SANTA PACKING BAG CJ-210	CL	33.50	33.50
91	REINDEER BARN LITE UP HOUSE	CL	55.00	55.00
90	ROLY POLY SANTA 3 ASST. CJ-263/4/7	RT	17.50	17.50
90	SANTA W/LIST CJ-23	RT	27.50	27.50
91	APOTHECARY LITE UP CJ-128	RT	33.50	33.50
91	BEIGE CHURCH LITE UP HOUSE MER-360A	RT	35.00	35.00
91	BOY & GIRL ON BELL CJ-132	RT	13.50	13.50
91	BOY ON HORSE CJ-457	RT	6.00	6.00
91	CAROLERS UNDER LAMPPOST CJ-114A	RT	7.50	7.50
91	CHURCH LITE UP MER-410	RT	17.50	17.50
91	COVERED BRIDGE CJ-101	RT	27.50	27.50
91	EMILY'S TOYS CJ-127	RT	35.00	35.00

YR	NAME	LIMIT	ISSUE	QUOTE
91	FATHER & MOTERH W/DAUGHTER CJ-133	RT	13.50	13.50
91	FATHER CHRISTMAS CJ-233	RT	33.50	33.50
91	FATHER CHRISTMAS W/HOLLY CJ-239	RT	35.00	35.00
91	FIRE STATION CJ-129	RT	50.00	50.00
91	FOUR MEN TALKING CJ-138	RT	27.50	27.50
91	GIFT SHOP LITE UP CJ-125	RT	33.50	33.50
91	GIRLS W/INSTRUMENTS CJ-131	RT	13.50	13.50
91	HORSE & COACH CJ-207	RT	25.00	25.00
91	KIDS BUILDING IGLOO CJ-137	RT	13.50	13.50
91	LADY W/DOGS CJ-208	RT	13.50	13.50
91	MAN W/WHEELBARROW CJ-134	RT	13.50	13.50
91	NEWSBOY UNDER LAMPPOST CJ-144B	RT	15.00	15.00
91	OLD CURIOSITY LITE UP CJ-201	RT	37.50	37.50
91	PLAYHOUSE LITE UP CJ-122	RT	50.00	50.00
91	SANTA CAT ROLY POLY CJ-252	RT	17.50	17.50
91	SANTA FIXING SLED CJ-237	RT	35.00	35.00
91	SANTA IN BARREL WATERBALL CJ-243	RT	33.50	33.50
91	SANTA IN TOY SHOP CJ-441	RT	33.50	33.50
91	SANTA ON TRAIN CJ-458	RT	6.00	6.00
91	SANTA PACKING BAG CJ-210	RT	33.50	33.50
91	SANTA PACKING BAG CJ-236	RT	35.00	35.00
91	SANTA SLEEPING MUSICAL CJ-214	RT	30.00	30.00
91	SANTA W/BAG & LIST CJ-431	RT	33.50	33.50
91	SANTA W/DEER MUSCIAL	RT	33.50	33.50
91	SANTA W/GIRL WATERBALL	RT	33.50	33.50
91	SANTA W/LANTERN MUSICAL CJ-211	RT	33.50	33.50
91	SANTA W/LIST CJ-23R	RT	27.50	27.50
91	SKATER, THE CJ-205	RT	25.00	25.00
91	SNOWBALL FIGHT CJ-124B	RT	25.00	25.00
91	SOUP SELLER WATERBALL CJ-209	RT	25.00	25.00
91	STONE COTTAGE LITE UP CJ-100	RT	37.50	37.50
91	STONE HOUSE LITE UP CJ-102	RT	45.00	45.00
91	TE OLDE TOWN TAVERN CJ-130	RT	45.00	45.00
91	THREE LADDIES W/FOOD CJ-136	RT	13.50	13.50
91	TOY SELLER, THE CJ-206	RT	13.50	13.50
91	TRADER SANTA MUSICAL CJ-442	RT	30.00	30.00
91	TWO OLD MEN TALKING CJ-107	RT	13.50	13.50
91	VILLAGE MILL LIT EUP CJ-104	RT	30.00	30.00
91	VILLAGE PEOPLE CJ-116A	RT	60.00	60.00
91	WOMAN W/COW CJ-135	RT	15.00	15.00
89	CATS IN BASKET XMAS-664	RT	7.50	7.50
90	FIRE STATION LITE UP HOUSE	CL	25.00	25.00
90	SANTA ON SEE SAW TR-14	RT	30.00	30.00
91	ELF W/DOLL HOUSE CB-14	RT	30.00	30.00
91	ELF W/HAMMER CB-11	RT	30.00	30.00
91	ELF W/ROCKING HORSE CB-10	RT	30.00	30.00
91	ELF W/TEDDY BEAR CB-12	RT	30.00	30.00
91	SANTA ON WHITE HORSE CJ-338	RT	33.50	33.50
91	TEDDY BEAR ON WHEELS CB-42	RT	25.00	25.00
85	TRUMPETING ANGEL W/JESUS XMAS-627	RT	40.00	40.00
85	VIRGIN W/CHRIST MUSICAL XMAS-528	RT	33.50	33.50
86	ANTIQUE SANTA MUSICAL XMAS-364	RT	20.00	20.00
86	JUMBO SANTA/TOYS XMAS-38	RT	45.00	45.00
89	CAT IN TEACUP MUSICAL XMAS-600	RT	30.00	30.00
90	ANTIQUE SHOP LITE UP HOUSE MER-373	RT	27.50	27.50
90	BAKERY LITE UP HOUSE MER-376	RT	27.50	27.50
90	BETHLEHEM LITE UP SET 3 CP-59893	RT	120.00	120.00
90	BRICK CHURCH LITE UP HOUSE MER-360C	RT	35.00	35.00
90	CATHEDRAL LITE UP HOUSE MER-362	RT	37.50	37.50
90	CHURCH LITE UP HOUSE MER-310	RT	27.50	27.50
90	DEEP GOLD CHURCH LITE UP HSE MER-360D	RT	35.00	35.00
90	DOUBLE STORE LITE UP HOUSE MER-311	RT	27.50	27.50
90	GRIST MILL LITE UP HOUSE MER-372	CL	27.50	27.50
90	INN LITE UP HOUSE MER-316	CL	27.50	27.50
90	LEATHERWORKS LITE UP HOUSE	CL	27.50	27.50
90	LIBRARY LITE UP HOUSES	CL	27.50	27.50
90	LIGHT HOUSE LITE UP HOUSE	CL	27.50	27.50
90	MANSION LITE UP HOUSE	CL	27.50	27.50
90	N. ENG. CHURCH LITE UP HOUSE MER-375	CL	27.50	27.50
90	N. ENG. GEN. STORE LITE UP HSE MER-377	CL	27.50	27.50
90	RAILROAD STATION LITE UP HOUSE	CL	27.50	27.50
90	SCHOOL LITE UP HOUSE	CL	27.50	27.50
90	TOWN HALL LITE UP HOUSE	CL	27.50	27.50
91	2 TONE CSTONE CHURCH MER-360B	RT	35.00	35.00
91	CHURCH W/BLU ROOF LITE UP HSE MER-360E	RT	35.00	35.00
91	FLORAL PLAQUE XMAS-911	OP	10.00	10.00

Red Fox *is from the "Stump Animal" collection by W.D. Gaither for Maruri.*

This Sand Piper *finds rest on a piece of washed up driftwood. The sculpture, produced by Maruri, is from the "Shore Birds" series by W.D. Gaither.*

This little one wants to make sure her doll isn't sick. Love Cures All *is produced by Rhodes Studios.*

The 1991 Santa Claus *motion musical plays "Have Yourself a Merry Little Christmas." The figure is by S. Nahene for WACO Products Corp.*

YR	NAME	LIMIT	ISSUE	QUOTE
91	FLOWER BASKET XMAS-912	OP	10.00	10.00
91	RESTAURANT LITE UP HOUSE	CL	27.50	27.50
91	TOY STORE LITE UP HOUSE	CL	27.50	27.50
91	TRAIN SET MER-378	RT	25.00	25.00
E. MANN			**CHRISTMAS IN AMERICA**	
88	CAPITOL, WHITE HOUSE, MT. VERNON	RT	75.00	150.00
88	DOCTOR'S OFFICE LITE UP	RT	27.50	27.50
89	SANTA IN SLEIGH	CL	25.00	45.00
90	CART WITH PEOPLE	RT	25.00	35.00
91	NEW ENGLAND CHURCH LITE UP MER-375	RT	27.50	27.50
91	NEW ENGLAND GEN'L STORE LITE UP MER-377	RT	27.50	27.50
L. SCIOLA			**CHRISTMAS VILLAGE**	
91	AWAY, AWAY	CL	30.00	30.00
91	COUNSEL HOUSE	CL	60.00	60.00
91	CURIOSITY SHOP	CL	45.00	45.00
91	EMILY'S TOYS	CL	45.00	45.00
91	ON THIN ICE	CL	30.00	30.00
91	PUBLIC LIBRARY	CL	50.00	50.00
91	SCROOGE/MARLEY'S COUNTING HOUSE	CL	45.00	45.00
91	STORY TELLER, THE CJ-204	CL	20.00	20.00
91	THE FIRE STATION	CL	60.00	60.00
91	THE PLAYHOUSE	CL	60.00	60.00
91	YE OLD GIFT SHOPPE	CL	50.00	50.00
JAIMY *			**DICKENS COLLECTION**	
91	CRATCHIT'S LITE UP HOUSE CJ-200	RT	37.50	37.50
91	CRATCHIT/TINY TIM MUSICAL CJ-117	RT	33.50	33.50
91	SCROOGE MUSICAL	RT	30.00	30.00
91	SCROOGE/MARLEY COUNTING HOUSE CJ-202	RT	37.50	37.50
89	CRATCHIT'S LITE UP XMS-7000A	RT	30.00	30.00
89	FEZZIWIG'S LITE UP XMS-7000C	RT	30.00	30.00
89	GIFT SHOPPE LITE UP XMS-7000H	RT	30.00	30.00
89	SCROOGE/MARLEY LITE UP XMS-7000B	RT	30.00	30.00
90	BLACK SWAN INN LITE UP XMS-7000E	RT	30.00	30.00
90	CRATCHIT FAMILY MER-121	RT	37.50	37.50
90	CRATCHIT/TINY TIM MUSICAL MER-105	RT	33.50	33.50
90	HEN POULTRY LITE UP	CL	30.00	30.00
90	TEA AND SPICE LITE UP	CL	30.00	30.00
90	WAITE FISH STORE LITE UP	CL	30.00	30.00
J. SAUERBREY			**GINGERBREAD CHRISTMAS COLLECTION**	
91	GINGERBREAD CHURCH LITE UP HSE CJ-403	CL	65.00	65.00
91	GINGERBREAD HOUSE LITE UP CJ-404	CL	65.00	65.00
91	GINGERBREAD MANSION LITE UP	CL	70.00	70.00
91	GINGERBREAD ROCKING HORSE MUSIC	CL	33.50	33.50
91	GINGERBREAD SWAN MUSICAL	CL	33.50	33.50
91	GINGERBREAD SWEET SHOP LITE UP HOUSE	CL	60.00	60.00
91	GINGERBREAD TEDDY BEAR MUSIC	CL	33.50	33.50
91	GINGERBREAD TOY SHOP LITE UP HOUSE	CL	60.00	60.00
91	GINGERBREAD VILLAGE LITE UP HOUSE	CL	60.00	60.00
JAIMY			**VICTORIAN CHRISTMAS COLLECTION**	
90	TWO BOYS WITH SNOWMAN	CL	12.00	12.00
91	LITTLE MATCH GIRL	CL	9.00	9.00
90	TOY/DOLL HOUSE LITE UP	CL	27.50	27.50
90	VICTORIAN HOUSE LITE UP HOUSE	CL	27.50	27.50
90	YARN SHOP LITE UP HOUSE	CL	27.50	27.50
91	ANTIQUE SHOP LITE UP HOUSE	CL	27.50	27.50
91	BEIGE CHURCH LITE UP HOUSE	CL	35.00	35.00
91	BOOK STORE LITE UP HOUSE	CL	27.50	27.50
91	CHURCH LITE UP HOUSE	CL	37.50	37.50
91	COUNTRY STORE LITE UP HOUSE	CL	27.50	27.50
91	INN LITE UP HOUSE MER-352	CL	27.50	27.50
E. MANN			**WIZARD OF OZ 40TH ANNIVERSARY**	
79	DOROTHY, SCARECROW, LION, TINMAN	RT	7.50	45.00
79	DOROTHY, SCARECROW, LION, TINMAN-MUSICAL	RT	12.50	75.00

SHADE TREE CREATIONS INC.

B. VERNON				**COWBOYS**
80	BEER DRINKER	RT	20.00	100.00
80	CARD SHARK	RT	20.00	80.00
80	EARLY RISER	RT	20.00	125.00
81	GUNFIGHTER (1ST RELEASE)	RT	20.00	100.00
81	REDNECK (1ST RELEASE)	RT	20.00	150.00
81	URBAN COWBOY (PAINTED)	RT	20.00	950.00
83	URBAN COWBOY (BROWN)	RT	15.00	550.00
87	GOLFER	RT	30.00	30.00
88	COMPUTER WIZARD	RT	25.00	45.00
89	EXECUTIVE	RT	30.00	65.00
89	HAPPY HOUR	RT	30.00	30.00

YR	NAME	LIMIT	ISSUE	QUOTE
89	HENPECKED & HOGTIED	RT	30.00	80.00
89	YEE HAW	RT	25.00	70.00
90	CAMERA CRAZY	RT	30.00	40.00
90	SMOKIN'-STURGIS RALLY	RT	35.00	400.00
90	THIS JOB	RT	30.00	30.00
90	TOURIST	RT	30.00	40.00
91	BOWLER	RT	30.00	30.00
91	GUNFIGHTER (2ND RELEASE)	RT	30.00	65.00
91	MECHANIC	RT	30.00	30.00
91	REDNECK (2ND RELEASE)	RT	30.00	125.00
91	SKIER	RT	30.00	30.00

SILVER DEER LTD.

*	CRYSTAL STARSHIP	*	*	410.00

G. TRUEX

CRYSTAL COLLECTIBLES

YR	NAME	LIMIT	ISSUE	QUOTE
84	PINOCCHIO, 120MM	CL	195.00	195.00-320.00
90	JOE COOL CRUISIN	CL	165.00	165.00

SO!

K. GRAVES

CHESS SET

YR	NAME	LIMIT	ISSUE	QUOTE
93	KATALIN'S ADV. IN ALICE'S WONDERLAND	500	1100.00	1100.00
93	TOURNAMENT OF THE TREE FROGS	500	750.00	750.00
94	A WEE MAC CHESS TOURNAMENT	500	850.00	850.00
94	IMAGES OF THE SOUTHWEST	500	2500.00	2500.00

K. GRAVES

IMAGINALS

YR	NAME	LIMIT	ISSUE	QUOTE
93	BILLY THE KITTY (KITTEN)	5000	50.00	50.00
93	BLACK BARK (STAFFORDSHIRE TERRIER)	5000	50.00	50.00
93	CHIEF SITTING BULLDOG	5000	50.00	50.00
93	CHOW MEIN	5000	50.00	50.00
93	DACHS HOLIDAY (DACHSHUND)	5000	50.00	50.00
93	DOLLY POODLE	5000	50.00	50.00
93	FLUIGATOR, THE (SKUNK)	5000	50.00	50.00
93	KAT FLOOSIE (CAT)	5000	50.00	50.00
93	MA BARKER (BEAGLE)	5000	50.00	50.00
93	MISS KITTY (CAT)	5000	50.00	50.00
93	ONE NOTE E. COYOTE	5000	50.00	50.00
93	PANCHO GATO (CAT)	5000	50.00	50.00
93	WILD NANOOK/NORTH (ALASKAN MALAMUTE)	5000	50.00	50.00
93	WYATT MOUSETRAP (CAT)	5000	50.00	50.00
94	BIG NOST KAT (WILD CAT)	5000	50.00	50.00
94	BLACK FOOTED FERRET, THE	5000	50.00	50.00
94	BOSTON BEENE (BOSTON TERRIER)	5000	50.00	50.00
94	CALAMITY CAIRN (CAIRN TERRIER)	5000	50.00	50.00
94	DANIEL SPANIEL (ENG. SPRINGER SPANIEL)	5000	50.00	50.00
94	DAVY COCKER (COCKER SPANIEL PUPPY)	5000	50.00	50.00
94	GERONIMEOW (CAT)	5000	50.00	50.00
94	GOLD N. TREEVER	5000	50.00	50.00
94	HERR MAX VON SCHAFERHUND (GERMAN SHPRD.)	5000	50.00	50.00
94	JUDGE ROY MEAN (BULL TERRIER)	5000	50.00	50.00
94	MALTESE FALCONIER, THE	5000	50.00	50.00
94	MELANIE COLLIE ROSE	5000	50.00	50.00
94	PUGLIACCI (PUG)	5000	50.00	50.00
94	RED EYED AL (ALBINO FERRET)	5000	50.00	50.00
94	REV. LUTHER ST. BERNARD	5000	50.00	50.00
94	RITA RAT	5000	50.00	50.00
94	ROUGH RIDER ROTTIE (ROTTWEILER)	5000	50.00	50.00
94	RUDOLPHO RAT	5000	50.00	50.00
94	SIAM SAM (SIAMESE CAT)	5000	50.00	50.00
94	SIAM SUE (SIAMESE CAT)	5000	50.00	50.00
94	TY-PHOON SHAR-PEI	5000	50.00	50.00
94	WILD SPOTS DOOLIN (DALMATIAN)	5000	50.00	50.00
94	WILD, WILD WESTIE (W. HIGHLAND TERRIER)	5000	50.00	50.00
94	YORKIE YORKIER PUDDIN' (YORKSHIRE TERR.)	5000	50.00	50.00

SPORTS IMPRESSIONS

*	DON MATTINGLY ERROR	500	125.00	850.00

*

500 HOME RUN CLUB

YR	NAME	LIMIT	ISSUE	QUOTE
90	EDDIE MATTHEWS	5512	100.00	125.00
90	FRANK ROBINSON	5586	150.00	150.00
90	HARMON KILLEBREW	5573	150.00	150.00
90	JIMMY FOX	5534	150.00	150.00
90	MEL OTT	5511	150.00	150.00
90	TED WILLIAMS	5251	150.00	150.00
90	WILLIE MCCOVEY	5521	150.00	150.00

*

BASEBALL SUPERSTAR FIGURINE SERIES

YR	NAME	LIMIT	ISSUE	QUOTE
88	ABBOTT & COSTELLO	5000	145.00	145.00

YR	NAME	LIMIT	ISSUE	QUOTE
88	BABE RUTH	5000	125.00	125.00
88	LOU GEHRIG	5000	125.00	125.00
88	ROBERTO CLEMENTE	5000	125.00	125.00
88	TY COBB	5000	125.00	125.00
89	CY YOUNG	5000	125.00	125.00
89	HONUS WAGNER	5000	125.00	125.00
89	THURMAN MUNSON	5000	125.00	125.00
*	**BASEBALL SUPERSTAR FIGURINES**			
87	DON MATTINGLY	CL	125.00	300.00-500.00
87	KEITH HERNANDEZ	2500	125.00	175.00-200.00
87	MICKEY MANTLE	CL	125.00	300.00
87	TED WILLIAMS F/S	CL	125.00	150.00
87	WADE BOGGS F/S	CL	125.00	150.00
88	AL KALINE G/E	2500	125.00	150.00
88	ANDRE DAWSON G/E	2500	125.00	150.00
88	BOB FELLER	2500	125.00	175.00-200.00
88	JOSE CANSECO	CL	125.00	250.00
88	PAUL MOLITOR	2500	125.00	125.00
88	REGGIE JACKSON (YANKEES)	CL	125.00	275.00
89	ALAN TRAMMELL	2500	125.00	125.00
89	DUKE SNIDER	2500	125.00	125.00
89	FRANK VIOLA	2500	125.00	125.00
89	KIRK GIBSON	CL	125.00	175.00-200.00
89	REGGIE JACKSON (ANGELS)	CL	125.00	150.00-175.00
89	WILL CLARK f/s	CL	125.00	225.00
*	**BASEBALL'S 3000 HIT CLUB**			
89	ROD CAREW	3053	150.00	150.00
*	**BASEBALL'S 3000 HIT WINNERS PITCHERS SERIES**			
89	TOM SEAVER	CL	150.00	150.00
*	**BASEBALL'S 500 HOME RUN HITTERS**			
89	ERNIE BANKS	5512	150.00	150.00
89	HANK AARON	5755	150.00	150.00
89	WILLIE MAYS	5660	150.00	150.00
*	**BASEBALL'S CY YOUNG AWARD WINNERS**			
89	OREL HERSHISER	5055	125.00	150.00-175.00
*	**COLLECTORS' CLUB FIGURINE**			
89	THE MICK-MICKEY MANTLE H/S	TL	125.00	375.00
*	**KINGS OF K**			
90	NOLAN RYAN	500	195.00	195.00
90	STEVE CARLTON	500	195.00	195.00
90	TOM SEAVER	500	195.00	195.00
*	**NEW YORK METS SUPERSTAR FIGURINES**			
89	DARRYL STRAWBERRY	5018	125.00	125.00
89	DWIGHT GOODEN	5016	125.00	125.00
89	GARY CARTER	5008	125.00	125.00
89	GREGG JEFFERIES	5009	125.00	125.00
89	HOWARD JOHNSON	5020	125.00	125.00
89	KEVIN MCREYNOLDS	5022	125.00	125.00
*	**NFL LIMITED EDITION FIGURINES**			
90	BOOMER ESIASON-AWAY	995	195.00	195.00
90	BOOMER ESIASON-HOME	995	195.00	195.00
90	DAN MARINO-AWAY	995	195.00	195.00
90	DAN MARINO-HOME	995	195.00	195.00
90	JOE MONTANA-AWAY	995	195.00	195.00
90	JOE MONTANA-HOME	995	195.00	195.00
90	JOHN ELWAY-AWAY	995	195.00	195.00
90	JOHN ELWAY-HOME	995	195.00	195.00
90	LAWRENCE TAYLOR-AWAY	995	195.00	195.00
90	LAWRENCE TAYLOR-HOME	995	195.00	195.00
90	RANDALL CUNNINGHAM-AWAY	995	195.00	195.00
90	RANDALL CUNNINGHAM-HOME	995	195.00	195.00
*	**RENAISSANCE 13 IN. SCULPTURES**			
90	DON MATTINGLY	2950	395.00	395.00
*	**SPECIAL INDIVIDUAL RELEASES**			
89	MANTLE-SWITCH HITTER	CL	295.00	295.00-375.00
90	JOE MORGAN-NEWEST HALL OF FAMER	1990	195.00	195.00
91	RICKEY HENDERSON	939	150.00	150.00
91	ROCKWELL-YER OUT	2500	195.00	195.00
*	**SUPER SIZE FIGURINES**			
89	JOSE CANSECO	CL	250.00	250.00-300.00
89	TED WILLIAMS	CL	250.00	250.00-300.00
90	MICKEY MANTLE	CL	250.00	250.00-300.00
90	REGGIE JACKSON	CL	250.00	250.00
90	THURMAN MUNSON	995	250.00	250.00
90	TOM SEAVER	CL	250.00	250.00

YR	NAME	LIMIT	ISSUE	QUOTE
*			**TEAM OF DREAMS**	
90	CAL RIPKEN, JR.	1990	150.00	150.00
90	DON MATTINGLY	1990	150.00	150.00
90	ERIC DAVIS	1990	150.00	150.00
90	KEN GRIFFEY, JR.	1990	150.00	150.00
90	KEVIN MITCHELL	1990	150.00	150.00
90	KIRBEY PUCKETT	1990	150.00	150.00
90	LENNY DYKSTRA	1990	150.00	150.00
90	MARK LANGSTON	1990	150.00	150.00
*			**TODAY'S STAR SERIES**	
90	DON MATTINGLY	2950	65.00	65.00
90	DWIGHT GOODEN	2950	65.00	65.00
90	KEN GRIFFEY, JR.	2950	65.00	65.00
90	LENNY DYKSTRA	2950	65.00	65.00
90	NOLAN RYAN	2950	65.00	65.00

SUMMERHILL CRYSTAL

YR	NAME	LIMIT	ISSUE	QUOTE
*			**SUMMERHILL CRYSTAL**	
92	BICYCLE	500	64.00	64.00
92	L'ARC DU TRIOMPHE	5000	220.00	220.00
92	LARGE DRAGON	1500	320.00	320.00
92	PRINCESS COACH	1500	700.00	700.00
92	SACRE COEUR	5000	190.00	190.00
92	VENUS	500	96.00	96.00

SWAROVSKI AMERICA
M. STAMEY

YR	NAME	LIMIT	ISSUE	QUOTE
			A PET'S CORNER	
91	KITTEN	OP	47.50	49.50
91	SITTING CAT	OP	75.00	85.00
87	MINI DACHSHUND	RT	20.00	47.50-125.00
90	BEAGLE	OP	40.00	42.50
90	TERRIER	OP	60.00	75.00
92	POODLE	OP	125.00	140.00

A. STOCKER

YR	NAME	LIMIT	ISSUE	QUOTE
			AFRICAN WILDLIFE	
88	HIPPOPOTAMUS	RT	70.00	125.00
88	LARGE ELEPHANT	RT	70.00	250.00
88	RHINOCEROS	RT	70.00	75.00
89	SMALL ELEPHANT	OP	50.00	65.00
89	SMALL HIPPOPOTAMUS	OP	70.00	75.00
90	SMALL RHINOCEROS	OP	70.00	75.00
*			**AMONG FLOWERS AND FOLIAGE**	
92	BUMBLEBEE	OP	85.00	85.00
92	HUMMINGBIRD	RT	195.00	210.00
*			**ANIMALS**	
*	BEE-GOLD 7553NR100	RT	*	1100.00
*	BEE-RHODUIM 7553NR200	RT	*	1500.00
*	BUTTERFLY-GOLD 7551NR100	*	*	1100.00
*	BUTTERFLY-RHODIUM 7551NR200	*	*	1500.00
*	GIANT BEAR 7637NR112	RT	125.00	1500.00
*	HUMMINGBIRD RHODIUM 7552NR200	*	*	1750.00
*	HUMMINGBIRD-GOLD 7552NR100	*	*	1100.00

M. SCHRECK

YR	NAME	LIMIT	ISSUE	QUOTE
			BARNYARD FRIENDS	
82	MINI PIG	OP	16.00	29.50
84	MEDIUM PIG	OP	35.00	47.50
87	MINI HEN	OP	35.00	45.00
87	MINI ROOSTER	OP	35.00	55.00
88	MINI CHICKS (SET OF 3)	RT	35.00	45.00

M. SCHRECK

YR	NAME	LIMIT	ISSUE	QUOTE
			BEAUTIES OF THE LAKE	
77	LARGE SWAN	OP	55.00	95.00
77	MEDIUM SWAN	OP	44.00	85.00
83	MINI DRAKE	OP	20.00	45.00
89	SMALL SWAN	OP	35.00	49.50
86	MALLARD	RT	80.00	135.00
89	GIANT MALLARD	OP	2000.00	4500.00
86	MINI STANDING DUCK	OP	22.00	37.50
86	MINI SWIMMING DUCK	OP	16.00	37.50
*			**COLLECTORS' SOCIETY ANNUAL EDITIONS**	
*	THE DOLPHINS DO1X901	RT	*	1500.00
*	THE ELEPHANT DO1X931	RT	325.00	1200.00
*	THE LOVEBIRDS DO1X861	RT	*	4500.00
*	THE SEALS DO1X911	RT	*	600.00
*	THE TURTLEDOVES DO1X891	RT	*	1100.00
*	THE WOODPECKERS D01X881	RT	*	1900.00
92	THE BIRTHDAY CAKE	RT	85.00	175.00
87	THE LOVE BIRDS DO1X861/TOGETHERNESS	RT	150.00	4200.00
90	THE DOLPHINS DO1X901/LEAD ME	RT	225.00	1500.00
91	THE SEALS DO1X911/SAVE ME	RT	225.00	600.00

YR	NAME	LIMIT	ISSUE	QUOTE
92	THE WHALES DO1X921/CARE FOR ME	RT	265.00	550.00
88	THE WOODPECKERS DO1X881/SHARING	RT	165.00	1900.00
89	THE TURTLEDOVES DO1X891/AMOUR	RT	195.00	1100.00
*		**COLLECTORS' SOCIETY ANNUAL EDTIONS**		
*	THE WHALES DO1X921	RT	*	550.00
*		**COMMEMORATIVE SINGLE ISSUE**		
90	ELEPHANT-COMMEMORATIVE ITEM/WALT DISNEY	CL	125.00	1200.00
	G. STAMEY			**CRYSTAL CITY**
90	SILVER CRYSTAL CITY-CATHEDRAL	RT	95.00	120.00
90	SILVER CRYSTAL CITY-HOUSES I & II	RT	75.00	75.00
90	SILVER CRYSTAL CITY-HOUSES III & IV	RT	75.00	75.00
90	SILVER CRYSTAL CITY-POPLARS	RT	40.00	49.50
91	CITY GATES	RT	95.00	95.00
91	CITY TOWER	RT	37.50	42.50
	M. ZENDRON			**CRYSTAL MELODIES**
92	HARP	OP	175.00	210.00
92	LUTE	OP	125.00	140.00
	M. SCHRECK			**ENDANGERED SPECIES**
77	LARGE TURTLE	OP	48.00	75.00
77	SMALL TURTLE	OP	35.00	49.50
81	GIANT TURTLE	OP	2500.00	4500.00
91	KIWI	OP	37.50	45.00
87	KOALA	OP	50.00	65.00
89	MINI KOALA	OP	35.00	45.00
92	LYING BABY BEAVER	OP	47.50	49.50
92	MOTHER BEAVER	OP	110.00	125.00
92	SITTING BABY BEAVER	OP	47.50	49.50
*				**EXQUISITE ACCENTS**
80	BIRDBATH	OP	150.00	210.00
87	BIRD'S NEST	OP	90.00	125.00
87	MEDIUM DINNER BELL	OP	80.00	95.00
87	SMALL DINNER BELL	OP	60.00	65.00
	M. SCHRECK			**FRUIT**
*	GIANT PINEAPPLE-RHODIUM 7507NR260002	*	*	3500.00
*	LARGE PINEAPPLE-RHODIUM 7507NR105002	*	*	450.00
*	SMALL PINEAPPLE-RHODIUM 7507NR060002	*	*	200.00
*				**IN A SUMMER MEADOW**
76	MEDIUM MOUSE	OP	48.00	85.00
82	BUTTERFLY	OP	44.00	85.00
85	LARGE HEDGEHOG	RT	120.00	300.00
85	MEDIUM HEDGEHOG	RT	70.00	250.00
86	MINI BUTTERFLY	OP	16.00	130.00
87	SMALL HEDGEHOG	OP	50.00	450.00
92	SPARROW	OP	29.50	29.50
86	SNAIL	OP	35.00	55.00
88	MINI LYING RABBIT	RT	35.00	100.00
88	MINI SITTING RABBIT	OP	35.00	45.00
88	MOTHER RABBIT	OP	60.00	75.00
91	FIELD MOUSE	OP	47.50	49.50
*				**JULIA'S WORLD**
90	JULIA	OP	29.50	29.50
90	JULIA W/MANDOLIN	OP	29.50	29.50
90	LENA & PEPI/BENCH	OP	55.00	55.00
90	LENA W/LUTE	OP	29.50	29.50
90	MARIAN	OP	29.50	29.50
90	PEPI & MOPSY	OP	55.00	55.00
90	PEPI W/DRUM	OP	29.50	29.50
90	SALI	OP	29.50	29.50
90	SALI W/ACCORDION	OP	29.50	29.50
	M. SCHRECK		**KINGDOM OF ICE AND SNOW**	
84	LARGE PENGUIN	OP	44.00	95.00
84	MINI PENGUIN	OP	16.00	37.50
85	LARGE SEAL	OP	44.00	85.00
89	WALRUS	RT	120.00	175.00
86	LARGE POLAR BEAR	OP	140.00	210.00
86	MINI BABY SEAL	OP	30.00	45.00
*				**NATIVITY**
91	HOLY FAMILY WITH ARCH	RT	250.00	300.00
92	ANGEL	RT	65.00	100.00
92	SHEPHERD	RT	65.00	100.00
92	WISE MEN (SET OF 3)	RT	175.00	225.00
*			**OUR CANDLEHOLDERS**	
87	LARGE STAR	OP	250.00	375.00
89	MEDIUM STAR	OP	200.00	260.00
83	MEDIUM WATER LILY	OP	150.00	260.00
85	LARGE WATER LILY	OP	200.00	375.00

YR	NAME	LIMIT	ISSUE	QUOTE
85	SMALL WATER LILY	OP	100.00	175.00
90	LARGE NEO-CLASSIC	RT	220.00	250.00
90	MEDIUM NEO-CLASSIC	RT	190.00	225.00
90	SMALL NEO-CLASSIC	RT	170.00	200.00
M. SCHRECK			**OUR WOODLAND FRIENDS**	
79	LARGE OWL	OP	90.00	125.00
79	MINI OWL	OP	16.00	29.50
79	SMALL OWL	OP	59.00	85.00
81	LARGE BEAR	OP	75.00	95.00
82	SMALL BEAR	OP	44.00	85.00
83	GIANT OWL	OP	1200.00	2000.00
85	MINI BEAR	RT	16.00	125.00
85	SQUIRREL	OP	35.00	65.00
87	FOX	OP	50.00	125
88	MINI RUNNING FOX	OP	35.00	45.00
88	MINI SITTING FOX	OP	35.00	45.00
89	MUSHROOMS	OP	35.00	45.00
M. SCHRECK			**PAPERWEIGHTS**	
81	EGG	RT	60.00	150.00
82	CONE	RT	80.00	225.00
87	LARGE CHATON	OP	190.00	260.00
87	LARGE PYRAMID	OP	90.00	195.00
87	SMALL CHATON	OP	50.00	65.00
87	SMALL PYRAMID	OP	100.00	125.00
90	GIANT CHATON	OP	3900.00	4500.00
*				**RETIRED**
*	DOG	RT	44.00	125.00
*	ELEPHANT	RT	90.00	1500.00
*	KING SIZE APPLE PHOTO STAND	RT	120.00	500.00
*	LARGE APPLE PHOTO STAND	RT	80.00	450.00
*	LARGE DUCK	RT	44.00	250.00
*	LARGE GRAPES	RT	250.00	995.00
*	LARGE RABBIT	RT	38.00	125.00
*	LARGE SPARROW	RT	38.00	125.00
*	MEDIUM CAT	RT	38.00	300.00
*	MEDIUM DUCK	RT	38.00	125.00
*	MINI BUTTERFLY	RT	16.00	130.00
*	MINI CHICKEN	RT	16.00	100.00
*	MINI DUCK	RT	16.00	100.00
*	MINI MOUSE	RT	16.00	125.00
*	MINI RABBIT	RT	16.00	100.00
*	SMALL APPLE PHOTO STAND	RT	40.00	275.00
84	LARGE BLOWFISH	RT	40.00	75.00-90.00
85	BEE	RT	200.00	1100.00
85	BUTTERFLY	RT	200.00	1100.00
85	HUMMINGBIRD	RT	200.00	1100.00
*	GIANT SIZE BEAR	RT	125.00	1020.00
*	KING SIZE BEAR	RT	95.00	1200.00
*	KING SIZE HEDGEHOG	RT	98.00	450.00
*	KING SIZE MOUSE	RT	95.00	650.00
*	KING SIZE TURTLE	RT	58.00	200.00
*	LARGE HEDGEHOG	RT	65.00	300.00
*	LARGE MOUSE	RT	69.00	250.00
*	LARGE PIG	RT	50.00	200.00
*	MEDIUM HEDGEHOG	RT	44.00	250.00
*	MINI SWAN	RT	16.00	125.00
*	SMALL HEDGEHOG	RT	38.00	450.00
*	SMALL MOUSE	RT	35.00	60.00
77	LARGE CAT	RT	44.00	90.00
79	MINI SPARROW	RT	16.00	60.00
81	LARGE DINNER BELL	RT	80.00	150.00
82	LARGE PINEAPPLE/RHODIUM	RT	150.00	450.00
82	MINI CAT	RT	16.00	85.00
84	DACHSHUND	RT	48.00	95.00
84	FROG	RT	30.00	125.00
84	LARGE FALCON HEAD	RT	600.00	1200.00
84	MINI BEAR	RT	16.00	125.00
85	GIANT PINEAPPLE/RHODIUM	RT	1750.00	3500.00
86	SMALL FALCON HEAD	RT	60.00	125.00
87	SMALL PINEAPPLE/RHODIUM	RT	55.00	200.00
88	WHALE	RT	70.00	125.00
*	MINI DACHSHUND	RT	20.00	125.00
87	PARTRIDGE	RT	85.00	200.00
*				**SOUTH SEA**
86	SMALL BLOWFISH	OP	35.00	55.00
87	MINI BLOWFISH	OP	22.00	29.50

YR	NAME	LIMIT	ISSUE	QUOTE
88	OPEN SHELL WITH PEARL	OP	120.00	175.00
91	BUTTERFLY FISH	OP	150.00	175.00
91	SOUTH SEA SHELL	RT	110.00	120.00
*				**SPARKLING FRUIT**
85	MEDIUM GRAPES	RT	300.00	375.00
85	SMALL GRAPES	RT	200.00	260.00
81	GIANT PINEAPPLE	OP	1750.00	3250.00
81	LARGE PINEAPPLE	RT	150.00	260.00
86	SMALL PINEAPPLE	RT	55.00	85.00
91	APPLE	OP	175.00	185.00
91	PEAR	OP	175.00	185.00
M. SCHRECK				**THE GAME OF KINGS**
84	CHESS SET	OP	950.00	1375.00
M. STAMEY				**UP IN THE TREES**
89	OWL	RT	70.00	120.00
89	PARROT	RT	70.00	120.00
89	TOUCAN	RT	70.00	120.00
90	KINGFISHER	RT	75.00	120.00
G. STAMEY				**WHEN WE WERE YOUNG**
88	LOCOMOTIVE	OP	150.00	155.00
88	TENDER	OP	55.00	55.00
88	WAGON	OP	85.00	95.00
89	OLD TIMER AUTOMOBILE	OP	130.00	155.00
90	AIRPLANE	OP	135.00	155.00
90	PETROL WAGON	OP	75.00	95.00
91	SANTA MARIA	OP	375.00	375.00

TAY PORCELAINS

YR	NAME	LIMIT	ISSUE	QUOTE
*				**TAY PORCELAINS**
*	TURTLEDOVES, GROUP OF TWO, 10 IN.	500	*	500.00-500.00
70	BLUE JAY, 13 IN.	500	375.00	675.00
70	EAGLE, 12 X 15 IN.	500	1000.00	1650.00
70	EUROPEAN WOODCOCK, 10.5 IN.	500	325.00	550.00
70	LIMPKIN, 20 IN.	500	600.00	1100.00
71	FALCON, 13 IN.	500	500.00	925.00
71	PHEASANT, 30 IN.	500	1500.00	2000.00-2700.00
71	QUAIL GROUP, 10 IN.	500	400.00	725.00
71	ROADRUNNER, 10 X 19 IN.	500	800.00	*
72	GRAY PARTRIDGE, 11.5 IN.	500	800.00	1400.00
73	AUSTRIAN OFFICER ON HORSEBACK	100	1200.00	1200.00-1500.00
74	AMERICAN WOODCOCK, 10.5 IN.	500	625.00	700.00
74	BOREAL CHICKADEE, 7 IN.	5000	275.00	360.00
74	GREAT CRESTED FLYCATCHER, 9 IN.	1000	300.00	360.00
74	GYRAFALCON, 18 IN.	300	1250.00	1500.00
74	MALLARD DUCK, 13.5 IN.	500	900.00	1050.00
74	MALLARD DUCK, FLYING, 15 IN.	500	550.00	675.00
74	OWL, 10.5 IN.	500	350.00	450.00
74	TURTLEDOVES ON ROOF TILE, 9.5 IN.	500	335.00	375.00
75	CAROLINA DUCKS, GROUP OF TWO, 13 IN.	500	1350.00	1500.00
75	ORIOLE, 9.5 IN.	1000	300.00	325.00
75	SMERGOS DUCKS, GROUP OF TWO, 10 IN.	500	1000.00	1100.00
75	WHITE-THROATED SPARROW, 5.5 IN.	500	360.00	400.00
76	BLUEBIRDS, GROUP OF TWO, 9.5 IN.	500	500.00	550.00
76	CUSTER ON HORSE, 13 X 14.5 IN.	500	1500.00	1500.00
76	INDIAN ON HORSE, 13 X 14.5 IN.	500	1500.00	1500.00
76	ROBIN, 8 IN.	500	400.00	450.00

THE BOYDS COLLECTION

G. LOWENTHAL

YR	NAME	LIMIT	ISSUE	QUOTE
			BOYDS BEARS & FRIENDS FOLKSTONE	
93	ANGEL OF FREEDOM 2820	YR	7.50	15.50-16.75
93	ANGEL OF LOVE 2821	YR	7.50	15.50-16.75
93	ANGEL OF PEACE 2822	YR	7.50	15.50-16.75
93	CHILLY & SON W/DOVE 2811	YR	8.00	16.50-18.00
93	CLASSIC ANGEL PAC 12 PCS. 2935	YR	90.00	90.00
93	HOLIDAY FOLKSTONE PAC 21 PCS. 2931-01	YR	8.00	16.50-18.00
93	JINGLES & SON W/WREATH 2812	YR	8.00	16.50-18.00
93	NICHOLAI W/TREE 2800	YR	8.00	16.50-18.00
93	NICHOLAS W/BOOK OF LIST	YR	8.00	16.50-18.00
93	NIKKI W/CANDLE 2801	YR	8.00	16.50-18.00
93	OCEANA-OCEAN ANGEL 2823	YR	7.50	15.50-16.75
93	WINDY W/BOOK 2810	YR	8.00	16.50-18.00
94	BEATRICE/BIRTHDAY ANGEL	3600	9.00	18.50-20.00
94	ELMER/COW ON HAYSTACKS	3600	8.50	17.00-19.00
94	FLORENCE/KITCHEN ANGEL	3600	9.00	18.50-20.00
94	IDA & BESSIE/THE GARDENERS	3600	8.50	17.00-19.00
94	JILL-LANGUAGE OF LOVE	3600	8.50	17.00-19.00
94	JINGLE MOOSE 2830	YR	8.00	16.50-18.00

YR	NAME	LIMIT	ISSUE	QUOTE
94	LIZZIE/SHOPPING ANGEL	3600	9.00	18.50-20.00
94	MINERVA/BASEBALL ANGEL	3600	9.00	18.50-20.00
94	MYRTLE/BELIEVE	3600	8.50	17.00-19.00
94	PETE THE WHOPPER	3600	8.50	17.00-19.00
94	RUFUS/HOE DOWN	3600	8.50	17.00-19.00

THE CAT'S MEOW

F. JONES   **19TH CENTURY MASTER BUILDERS**

YR	NAME	LIMIT	ISSUE	QUOTE
93	ALEXANDER JACKSON DAVIS	OP	*	*
93	ANDREW JACKSON DOWNING	OP	*	*
93	HENRY HOBSON RICHARDSON	OP	*	*
93	SAMUEL SLOAN	OP	*	*
93	SET	OP	41.20	41.20

F. JONES   **ACCESSORIES**

YR	NAME	LIMIT	ISSUE	QUOTE
83	FALL TREE	RT	4.00	7.00
83	PINE TREE	RT	4.00	7.00
83	SUMMER TREE	RT	4.00	7.00
83	XMAS PINE TREE	RT	4.00	7.00
83	XMAS PINE TREE W/RED BOWS	RT	3.00	100.00
84	5 IN. HEDGE	RT	3.00	7.00-30.00
84	5 IN. PICKET FENCE	RT	3.00	3.00
84	8 IN. HEDGE	RT	3.25	7.00-26.00
84	8 IN. PICKET FENCE	RT	3.25	7.00-26.00
84	BANDSTAND	RT	6.50	6.50
84	DAIRY WAGON	RT	4.00	5.00-10.00
84	GAS LIGHT	OP	3.25	3.25
84	HORSE & CARRIAGE	RT	4.00	5.00-10.00
84	HORSE & SLEIGH	RT	4.00	4.00
84	LILAC BUSHES	RT	3.00	10.00-25.00
85	CHICKENS	RT	3.25	4.00-6.50
85	COWS	RT	4.00	5.00-10.00
85	DUCKS	RT	3.25	4.00-6.50
85	F.J. REAL ESTATE SIGN	RT	3.00	4.00-6.50
85	FLOWER POTS	OP	3.00	3.00
85	MAIN ST. SIGN	OP	3.25	3.25
85	TELEPHONE BOOTH	OP	3.00	3.00
85	U.S. FLAG	OP	3.25	3.25
86	5 IN. IRON FENCE	RT	3.00	6.00-46.00
86	8 IN. IRON FENCE	RT	3.25	8.00-36.00
86	CAROLERS	RT	4.00	5.00-10.00
86	CHERRY TREE	RT	4.00	5.00-7.00
86	ICE WAGON	RT	4.00	5.00-10.00
86	IRON GATE	RT	3.00	10.00-36.00
86	MAIL WAGON	OP	4.00	4.00
86	POPLAR TREE	RT	4.00	5.00-7.00
86	SKIPJACKS	OP	6.50	6.50
86	STREET CLOCK	OP	3.25	3.25
86	WISHING WELL	RT	3.25	4.00-7.00
86	WOODEN GATE	RT	3.00	3.00
87	CABLE CAR	RT	4.00	5.00-10.00
87	F.J. EXPRESS	RT	4.00	4.00
87	LIBERTY ST. SIGN	RT	3.25	4.00-8.00
87	RAILROAD SIGN	RT	3.00	3.00
87	WINDMILL	RT	3.25	3.25
88	ADA BELLE	OP	4.00	4.00
88	BUTCH & T.J.	RT	4.00	4.00
88	CHARLIE & CO	RT	4.00	4.00
88	COLONIAL BREAD WAGON	OP	4.00	4.00
89	CLOTHESLINE	OP	4.00	4.00
89	HARRY'S HOTDOGS	OP	4.00	4.00
89	MARKET ST. SIGN	RT	3.25	5.00-7.50
89	NANNY	RT	4.00	4.00
89	PASSENGER TRAIN CAR	OP	4.00	4.00
89	PONY EXPRESS RIDER	OP	4.00	4.00
89	PUMPKIN WAGON	OP	3.25	3.25
89	QUAKER OATS TRAIN CAR	OP	4.00	4.00
89	ROSE TRELLIS	OP	3.25	3.25
89	RUDY & ALDINE	OP	4.00	4.00
89	SNOWMEN	OP	4.00	4.00
89	TAD & TONY	OP	4.00	4.00
89	TOURING CAR	RT	4.00	5.00-8.00
89	WELLS FARGO WAGON	RT	4.00	5.00-10.00
90	1909 FRANKLIN LIMOUSINE	OP	4.00	4.00
90	1913 PEERLESS TOURING CAR	OP	4.00	4.00
90	1914 FIRE PUMPER	OP	4.00	4.00
90	5 IN. WROUGHT IRON FENCE	OP	3.00	3.00
90	AMISH BUGGY	OP	4.00	4.00

YR	NAME	LIMIT	ISSUE	QUOTE
90	BLUE SPRUCE	OP	4.00	4.00
90	BUS STOP	OP	4.00	4.00
90	CHRISTMAS TREE LOT	OP	4.00	4.00
90	EUGENE	OP	4.00	4.00
90	GERSTENSLAGER BUGGY	OP	4.00	4.00
90	LITTLE RED CABOOSE	OP	4.00	4.00
90	POPCORN WAGON	OP	4.00	4.00
90	RED MAPLE TREE	OP	4.00	4.00
90	SANTA & REINDEER	OP	4.00	4.00
90	SCHOOL BUS	OP	4.00	4.00
90	TULIP TREE	OP	4.00	4.00
90	VETERINARY WAGON	OP	4.00	4.00
90	VICTORIAN OUTHOUSE	OP	4.00	4.00
90	WATKINS WAGON	OP	4.00	4.00
90	XMAS SPRUCE	OP	4.00	4.00
91	AMISH GARDEN	OP	4.00	4.00
91	BARNYARD	OP	4.00	4.00
91	CHESSIE HOPPER CAR	OP	4.00	4.00
91	CONCERT IN THE PARK	OP	4.00	4.00
91	JACK THE POSTMAN	OP	3.25	3.25
91	MARBLE GAME	OP	4.00	4.00
91	MARTIN HOUSE	OP	3.25	3.25
91	ON VACATION	OP	4.00	4.00
91	POPCORN WAGON	OP	4.00	4.00
91	SCAREY HARRY (SCARECROW)	OP	4.00	4.00
91	SKI PARTY	OP	4.00	4.00
91	USMC WAR MEMORIAL	OP	6.50	6.50
91	VILLAGE ENTRANCE SIGN	OP	6.50	6.50
92	DELIVERY TRUCK	OP	3.98	3.98
92	FORSYTHIA BUSH	OP	3.98	3.98
92	GASOLINE TRUCK	OP	3.98	3.98
92	MR. SOFTEE TRUCK	OP	3.98	3.98
92	NUTCRACKER BILLBOARD	OP	3.98	3.98
92	POLICE CAR	OP	3.98	3.98
92	SCHOOL CROSSING	OP	3.98	3.98
92	SILO	OP	3.98	3.98
92	SPRINGHOUSE	OP	3.25	3.25
93	CANNONBALL EXPRESS	OP	7.95	7.95
93	CHIPPEWA LAKE BILLBOARD	OP	7.95	7.95
93	GARDEN HOUSE	OP	6.50	6.50
93	GETTING DIRECTIONS	OP	7.95	7.95
93	GRAPE ARBOR	OP	7.95	7.95
93	JENNIE & GEORGE'S WEDDING	OP	7.95	7.95
93	JOHNNY APPLESEED STATUE	OP	7.95	7.95
93	LITTLE MARINE	OP	7.95	7.95
93	MARKET WAGON	OP	7.95	7.95
93	RUSTIC FENCE	OP	7.95	7.95

F. JONES   **AMERICAN BARNS**

YR	NAME	LIMIT	ISSUE	QUOTE
92	BANK BARN	OP	8.50	8.50
92	CRIB BARN	OP	8.50	8.50
92	OHIO BARN	OP	8.50	8.50
92	VERMONT BARN	OP	8.50	8.50

F. JONES   **CHIPPEWA LAKE AMUSEMENT PARK**

YR	NAME	LIMIT	ISSUE	QUOTE
93	BALLROOM	OP	4.50	4.50
93	BATH HOUSE	OP	4.50	4.50
93	MIDWAY	OP	4.50	4.50
93	PAVILION	OP	4.50	4.50

F. JONES   **CHRISTMAS IN NEW ENGLAND**

YR	NAME	LIMIT	ISSUE	QUOTE
89	HUNTER HOUSE	RT	8.00	32.00-55.00
89	SHELDON'S TAVERN	RT	8.00	32.00-55.00
89	THE OLD SOUTH MEETING HOUSE	RT	8.00	32.00-55.00
89	THE VERMONT COUNTRY STORE	RT	8.00	32.00-55.00

F. JONES   **COLLECTOR CLUB GIFT-HOUSES**

YR	NAME	LIMIT	ISSUE	QUOTE
89	BETSY ROSS HOUSE	CL	*	150.00
90	AMELIA EARHART	CL	*	75.00
91	LIMBERLOST CABIN	CL	*	*
92	ABIGAIL ADAMS BIRTHPLACE	YR	*	*

F. JONES   **COLLECTOR CLUB PIECES-AMERICAN SONGWRITERS**

YR	NAME	LIMIT	ISSUE	QUOTE
91	ANNA WARNER HOUSE	CL	9.25	9.25
91	BENJAMIN R. HANBY HOUSE	CL	9.25	9.25
91	OSCAR HAMMERSTEIN HOUSE	CL	9.25	9.25
91	STEPHEN FOSTER HOUSE	CL	9.25	9.25

F. JONES   **COLLECTOR CLUB PIECES-FAMOUS AUTHORS**

YR	NAME	LIMIT	ISSUE	QUOTE
89	HARRIET BEECHER STOWE	CL	8.75	85.00
89	HERMAN MELVILLE'S ARROWHEAD	CL	8.75	85.00
89	LONGFELLOW HOUSE	CL	8.75	85.00

YR NAME	LIMIT	ISSUE	QUOTE
89 ORCHARD HOUSE	CL	8.75	85.00
F. JONES	**COLLECTOR CLUB PIECES-GREAT INVENTORS**		
90 FORD MOTOR CO.	CL	9.25	30.00
90 SETH THOMAS CLOCK CO.	CL	9.25	30.00
90 THOMAS EDISON	CL	9.25	30.00
90 WRIGHT CYCLE CO.	CL	9.25	30.00
F. JONES	**COLLECTOR CLUB PIECES-SIGNERS OF THE DECLARATION**		
92 GEORGE CLYMER HOME	YR	9.75	9.75
92 JOHN WITHERSPOON HOME	YR	9.75	9.75
92 JOSIAH BARTLETT HOME	YR	9.75	9.75
92 STEPHEN HOPKINS HOME	YR	9.75	9.75
F. JONES	**COLONIAL VIRGINIA CHRISTMAS**		
90 DULANEY HOUSE	RT	8.00	10.00-25.00
90 RISING SUN TAVERN	RT	8.00	10.00-25.00
90 SHIRLEY PLANTATION	RT	8.00	10.00-25.00
90 ST. JOHN'S CHURCH	RT	8.00	10.00-25.00
F. JONES	**FALL**		
86 GOLDEN LAMB BUTTERY	RT	8.00	11.00-16.00
86 GRIMM'S FARMHOUSE	RT	8.00	11.00-16.00
86 MAIL POUCH BARN	RT	8.00	11.00-16.00
86 VOLLANT MILLS	RT	8.00	11.00-16.00
F. JONES	**HAGERSTOWN**		
88 J. HAGER HOUSE	OP	8.00	8.00
88 MILLER HOUSE	OP	8.00	8.00
88 THE YULE CUPBOARD	OP	8.00	8.00
88 WOMAN'S CLUB	OP	8.00	8.00
F. JONES	**HOMETOWN CHRISTMAS**		
92 AUGUST IMGARD HOUSE	RT	8.50	8.50
92 HOWEY HOUSE	RT	8.50	8.50
92 OVERHOLT HOUSE	RT	8.50	8.50
92 SET	RT	34.00	34.00
92 WAYNE CO. COURTHOUSE	RT	8.50	8.50
F. JONES	**LIBERTY STREET**		
88 COUNTY COURTHOUSE	OP	8.00	8.00
88 GRAF PRINTING CO	OP	8.00	8.00
88 WILTON RAILWAY DEPOT	OP	8.00	8.00
88 Z. JONES BASKETMAKER	OP	8.00	8.00
F. JONES	**LIGHTHOUSE**		
90 ADMIRALITY HEAD	OP	8.00	8.00
90 CAPE HATTERAS LIGHTHOUSE	OP	8.00	8.00
90 SANDY HOOK LIGHTHOUSE	OP	8.00	8.00
90 SPLIT ROCK LIGHTHOUSE	OP	8.00	8.00
F. JONES	**MAIN STREET**		
87 FRANKLIN LIBRARY	RT	8.00	8.00
87 GARDEN THEATRE	RT	8.00	8.00
87 HISTORICAL MUSEUM	RT	8.00	8.00
87 TELEGRAPH/POST OFFICE	RT	8.00	8.00
F. JONES	**MAINE CHRISTMAS**		
87 CAPPY'S CHOWDER HOUSE	RT	7.75	125.00
87 CAPTAIN'S HOUSE	RT	7.75	125.00
87 DAMARISCOTTA CHURCH	RT	7.75	125.00
87 PORTLAND HEAD LIGHTHOUSE	RT	7.75	125.00
F. JONES	**MARKET STREET**		
89 SCHUMACHER MILLS	OP	8.00	8.00
89 SEVILLE HARDWARE STORE	OP	8.00	8.00
89 WEST INDIA GOODS STORE	OP	8.00	8.00
89 YANKEE CANDLE COMPANY	OP	8.00	8.00
F. JONES	**MISCELLANEOUS**		
85 PENCIL HOLDER	CL	3.95	210.00
85 RECIPE HOLDER	CL	3.95	210.00
F. JONES	**NANTUCKET**		
87 JARED COFFIN HOUSE	RT	8.00	8.00
87 MARIA MITCHELL HOUSE	RT	8.00	8.00
87 NANTUCKET ATHENIUM	RT	8.00	8.00
87 UNITARIAN CHURCH	RT	8.00	8.00
F. JONES	**NANTUCKET CHRISTMAS**		
84 CHRISTMAS SHOP	RT	6.50	6.50
84 POWELL HOUSE	RT	6.50	6.50
84 SHAW HOUSE	RT	6.50	6.50
84 WINTROP HOUSE	RT	6.50	6.50
F. JONES	**NAUTICAL**		
87 H & E SHIPS CHANDLERY	RT	8.00	8.00
87 LORAIN LIGHTHOUSE	RT	8.00	8.00
87 MONHEGAN BOAT LANDING	RT	8.00	8.00
87 YACHT CLUB	RT	8.00	8.00

YR	NAME	LIMIT	ISSUE	QUOTE
F. JONES				**OHIO AMISH**
91	ADA MAE'S QUILT BARN	OP	8.00	8.00
91	BROWN SCHOOL	OP	8.00	8.00
91	ELI'S HARNESS SHOP	OP	8.00	8.00
91	JONAS TROYER HOME	OP	8.00	8.00
F. JONES		**OHIO WESTERN RESERVE CHRISTMAS**		
85	BELLEVUE HOUSE	RT	7.00	35.00-175.00
85	GATES MILLS CHURCH	RT	7.00	35.00-175.00
85	OLMSTEAD HOUSE	RT	7.00	35.00-175.00
85	WESTERN RESERVE ACCADEMY	RT	7.00	35.00-175.00
F. JONES				**PAINTED LADIES**
88	ANDREWS HOTEL	OP	8.00	8.00
88	LADY AMANDA	OP	8.00	8.00
88	LADY ELIZABETH	OP	8.00	8.00
88	LADY IRIS	OP	8.00	8.00
F. JONES			**PHILADELPHIA CHRISTMAS**	
88	ELFRETH'S ALLEY	RT	7.75	50.00-75.00
88	GRAFF HOUSE	RT	7.75	50.00-75.00
88	HILL-PHYSICK-KEITH HOUSE	RT	7.75	50.00-75.00
88	THE HEAD HOUSE	RT	7.75	50.00-75.00
F. JONES			**ROCKY MOUNTAIN CHRISTMAS**	
91	FIRST PRESBYTERIAN CHURCH	RT	8.20	14.00
91	TABOR HOUSE	RT	8.20	14.00
91	WESTERN HOTEL	RT	8.20	14.00
91	WHELLER-STALLARD HOUSE	RT	8.20	14.00
F. JONES				**ROSCOE VILLAGE**
86	CANAL COMPANY	RT	8.00	11.00-16.00
86	JACKSON TWP. HALL	RT	8.00	11.00-16.00
86	OLD WAREHOUSE REST.	RT	8.00	11.00-16.00
86	ROSCOE GENERAL STORE	RT	8.00	11.00-16.00
F. JONES			**SAVANNAH CHRISTMAS**	
86	J.J. DALE ROW HOUSE	RT	7.25	7.25
86	LAFAYETTE SQUARE HOUSE	RT	7.25	32.00
86	LIBERTY INN	RT	7.25	7.25
86	SIMON MIRAULT COTTAGE	RT	7.25	32.00
F. JONES				**SERIES I**
83	ANTIQUE SHOP	RT	8.00	35.00-56.00
83	APOTHECARY	RT	8.00	35.00-56.00
83	BARBERSHOP	RT	8.00	35.00-56.00
83	BOOK STORE	RT	8.00	35.00-56.00
83	FEDERAL HOUSE	RT	8.00	35.00-56.00
83	FLORIST SHOP	RT	8.00	35.00-56.00
83	GARRISON HOUSE	RT	8.00	35.00-56.00
83	INN	RT	8.00	35.00-56.00
83	SCHOOL	RT	8.00	35.00-56.00
83	SWEETSHOP	RT	8.00	35.00-56.00
83	TOY SHOP	RT	8.00	35.00-56.00
83	VICTORIAN HOUSE	RT	8.00	35.00-56.00
F. JONES				**SERIES II**
84	ATTORNEY/BANK	RT	8.00	25.00-36.00
84	BROCKE HOUSE	RT	8.00	25.00-36.00
84	CHURCH	RT	8.00	25.00-36.00
84	EATON HOUSE	RT	8.00	25.00-36.00
84	GRANDINERE HOUSE	RT	8.00	25.00-36.00
84	MILLINERY/QUILT	RT	8.00	25.00-36.00
84	MUSIC SHOP	RT	8.00	25.00-36.00
84	S & T CLOTHIERS	RT	8.00	25.00-36.00
84	TOBACCONIST/SHOEMAKER	RT	8.00	25.00-36.00
84	TOWN HALL	RT	8.00	25.00-36.00
F. JONES				**SERIES III**
85	ALLEN-COE HOUSE	RT	8.00	15.00-25.00
85	CONNECTICUT AVE. FIREHOUSE	RT	8.00	15.00-25.00
85	DRY GOODS STORE	RT	8.00	15.00-25.00
85	EDINBURGH TIMES	RT	8.00	15.00-25.00
85	FINE JEWELERS	RT	8.00	15.00-25.00
85	HOBART-HARLEY HOUSE	RT	8.00	15.00-25.00
85	KALORAMA GUEST HOUSE	RT	8.00	15.00-25.00
85	MAIN ST. CARRIAGE SHOP	RT	8.00	15.00-25.00
85	OPERA HOUSE	RT	8.00	15.00-25.00
85	RISTORANTE	RT	8.00	15.00-25.00
F. JONES				**SERIES IV**
86	BENNINGTON-HULL HOUSE	RT	8.00	11.00-16.00
86	CHAGRIN FALLS POPCORN SHOP	RT	8.00	11.00-16.00
86	CHEPACHET UNION CHURCH	RT	8.00	11.00-16.00
86	JOHN BELVILLE HOUSE	RT	8.00	11.00-16.00
86	JONES BROS. TEA CO.	RT	8.00	11.00-16.00

Simba, Sarabi and Mufasa *plays an excerpt from* The Lion King *theme song "Circle of Life." The musical ornament's sky also changes from dawn to dusk. It is produced by Hallmark Cards.*

We've seen many different facets of Barbie, but we never guessed that someday we'd see her as an ornament. Springtime Barbie is from the Hallmark Keepsake Ornament line.

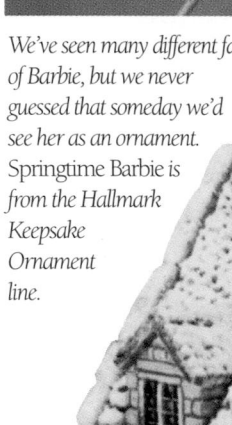

Peace on Earth *is dedicated to the military personnel involved in Operation Desert Storm. It was issued by Enesco Corp.*

One Small Step, *from Enesco's Treasury of Christmas Ornaments Collection, honors the 25th anniversary of man's walk on the moon.*

Rack 'em up! This whimsical ornament, Pool-Hall-idays, is from Enesco's Treasury of Christmas collection.

Ivy House is a 1994 ornament from Lilliput Lane.

Some things don't need to be spoken. The Eyes Say I Love You is by Armstrong artist Sue Etem.

Produced by Artists of the World, Flowers for Mother is by artist Ted Degrazia.

Ted Degrazia colorfully captures a Native American child in Little Flower Vendor produced by Artists of the World.

Morning Retreat is one of four issues in a series by nationally acclaimed wildlife artist Terry Redlin. His producer is Hadley House.

Top Left: Imperial Eagle is a regal issue from Creart. The piece was issued for $138.

Above: Sleep Tight, Horse Trainer, Bath Time and What's New? were introduced in 1990 by Goebel. They were created from the works of Sister Maria Innocentia Hummel.

Left: Even Cinderella would agree that she's never looked more beautiful than she does here. Cinderella is sculpted by Giuseppe Armani.

American Symbol Eagle is one of the fine works of wildlife art from Creart. The retail price of the sculpture was $258.

Sherman, Grant, Lee and Jackson *are from "The Adversaries" collection by P. Barnum. They are produced by Lance Corp.*

John Henry–Chris McCarron Up *celebrates the career of this popular race horse and his jockey. The piece is by equine artist Fred Stone (American Artists).*

Robert Bateman's skill as an artist is truly evident in Gray Squirrel, *which was produced in 1981 by Mill Pond Press.*

Peregrine Falcon and White-Throated Swifts *was created by Robert Bateman and produced by Mill Pond Press in the mid-1980s.*

Left: Collectors can't help but love the charm of The Old Distillery *by David Winter. The piece is produced by John Hine Studios.*

Left: The Shoemaker's Dream *is from the humorous collection of boot houses by Jon Herbert. The now-discontinued collection was produced by John Hine Studios.*

Right: Bishop's Oast is from popular collectible maker Department 56.

Long John Silver, Captain Hook, Robin Hood *and* Dick Turpin *are four famous characters from the "Classic Heroes Collection" by Royal Doulton.*

Who wouldn't want to make themselves at home at Winnie's Place? The piece is produced by Lilliput.

Castell Coch, by Patrick Gates, is produced by J.P. Editions.

The incredible amount of detail in Saxham St. Edmunds makes it all the more intriguing. The piece is by artist David Tate for Lilliput.

What collector wouldn't treasure Cherish—Lilac & Lace, *a limited edition doll by artist Lee Middleton? She is produced by Lee Middleton Original Dolls.*

Spanky *by artist Hal Payne is from the Seymour Mann Signature Series.*

Special Moments—Baby's First Christmas *holds a Gorham ornament to commemorate the occasion.*

This little gal knows where she's going. To Market, To Market is by doll artist Wendy Lawton.

Make a wish! Happy Birthday Amy is produced by Gorham.

Early American Portrait—Carrie and Sophia Grace *is a beautiful pairing from Wendy Lawton.*

YR	NAME	LIMIT	ISSUE	QUOTE
86	O'MALLEYS LIVERY STABLE	RT	8.00	11.00-16.00
86	THE LITTLE HOUSE GIFTABLES	RT	8.00	11.00-16.00
86	VANDENBERG HOUSE	RT	8.00	11.00-16.00
86	WESTBROOK HOUSE	RT	8.00	11.00-16.00
F. JONES				**SERIES IX**
91	ALL SAINTS CHAPEL	OP	8.00	8.00
91	AMERICAN RED CROSS	OP	8.00	8.00
91	CENTRAL CITY OPERA HOUSE	OP	8.00	8.00
91	CITY HALL	OP	8.00	8.00
91	CPA/LAW OFFICE	OP	8.00	8.00
91	GOV. SNYDER MANSION	OP	8.00	8.00
91	JEWELER/OPTOMETRIST	OP	8.00	8.00
91	OSBAHR'S UPHOLSTERY	OP	8.00	8.00
91	SPANKY'S HARDWARE CO	OP	8.00	8.00
91	THE TREBLE CLEF	OP	8.00	8.00
F. JONES				**SERIES V**
87	AMISH OAK/DIXIE SHOE	RT	8.00	8.00
87	ARCHITECT/TAILOR	RT	8.00	8.00
87	CONGRUITY TAVERN	RT	8.00	8.00
87	CREOLE HOUSE	RT	8.00	8.00
87	DENTIST/PHYSICIAN	RT	8.00	8.00
87	M. WASHINGTON HOUSE	RT	8.00	8.00
87	MARKETHOUSE	RT	8.00	8.00
87	MURRAY HOTEL	RT	8.00	8.00
87	POLICE DEPARTMENT	RT	8.00	8.00
87	SOUTHPORT BANK	RT	8.00	8.00
F. JONES				**SERIES VI**
88	BURTON LANCASTER HOUSE	OP	8.00	8.00
88	CITY HOSPITAL	OP	8.00	8.00
88	FIRST BAPTIST CHURCH	OP	8.00	8.00
88	FISH/MEAT MARKET	OP	8.00	8.00
88	LINCOLN SCHOOL	OP	8.00	8.00
88	NEW MASTERS GALLERY	OP	8.00	8.00
88	OHLIGER HOUSE	OP	8.00	8.00
88	PRUYN HOUSE	OP	8.00	8.00
88	STIFFENBODY FUNERAL HOME	OP	8.00	8.00
88	WILLIAMS & SONS	OP	8.00	8.00
F. JONES				**SERIES VII**
89	BLACK CAT ANTIQUES	OP	8.00	8.00
89	HAIRDRESSING PARLOR	OP	8.00	8.00
89	HANDCRAFTED TOYS	OP	8.00	8.00
89	JUSTICE OF THE PEACE	OP	8.00	8.00
89	OCTAGONAL SCHOOL	OP	8.00	8.00
89	OLD FRANKLIN BOOK SHOP	OP	8.00	8.00
89	THORPE HOUSE BED & BREAKFAST	OP	8.00	8.00
89	VILLAGE TINSMITH	OP	8.00	8.00
89	WILLIAMS APOTHECARY	OP	8.00	8.00
89	WINKLER BAKERY	OP	8.00	8.00
F. JONES				**SERIES VIII**
90	F.J. REALTY COMPANY	OP	8.00	8.00
90	GLOBE CORNER BOOKSTORE	OP	8.00	8.00
90	HABERDASHERS	OP	8.00	8.00
90	MEDINA FIRE DEPARTMENT	OP	8.00	8.00
90	NELL'S STEMS & STITCHES	OP	8.00	8.00
90	NOAH'S ARK VETERINARY	OP	8.00	8.00
90	PICCADILLI PIPE & TOBACCO	OP	8.00	8.00
90	PURITAN HOUSE	OP	8.00	8.00
90	VICTORIA'S PARLOUR	OP	8.00	8.00
90	WALLDORFF FURNITURE	OP	8.00	8.00
F. JONES				**SERIES X**
92	CITY NEWS	OP	8.50	8.50
92	FUDGE KITCHEN	OP	8.50	8.50
92	GRAND HAVEN	OP	8.50	8.50
92	HENYAN'S ATHLETIC SHOP	OP	8.50	8.50
92	LEPPERT'S 5 & 10 CENT	OP	8.50	8.50
92	MADELINE'S DRESS SHOP	OP	8.50	8.50
92	OWL AND THE PUSSYCAT	OP	8.50	8.50
92	PICKLES PUB	OP	8.50	8.50
92	PURE GAS STATION	OP	8.50	8.50
92	UNITED CHURCH OF ACWORTH	OP	8.50	8.50
F. JONES				**SERIES XI**
93	BARBERSHOP/GALLERY	OP	4.50	4.50
93	HADDONFIELD BANK	OP	4.50	4.50
93	IMMANUEL CHURCH	OP	4.50	4.50
93	JOHANN SINGER BOOTS & SHOES	OP	4.50	4.50
93	PET SHOP/GIFT SHOP	OP	4.50	4.50

YR	NAME	LIMIT	ISSUE	QUOTE
93	POLICE-TROOP C	OP	4.50	4.50
93	SHRIMPLIN & JONES PRODUCE	OP	4.50	4.50
93	STONES RESTAURANT	OP	4.50	4.50
93	U.S. ARMED FORCES	OP	4.50	4.50
93	U.S. POST OFFICE	OP	4.50	4.50
F. JONES			**ST. CHARLES CHRISTMAS**	
93	LEWIS & CLARK CENTER	OP	4.50	4.50
93	NEWBILL-MCELHINEY HOUSE	OP	4.50	4.50
93	ST. PETER'S CATHOLIC CHURCH	OP	4.50	4.50
93	STONE ROW	OP	4.50	4.50
F. JONES			**TRADESMAN**	
88	BUCKEYE CANDY & TOBACCO	OP	8.00	8.00
88	C.O. WHEEL COMPANY	OP	8.00	8.00
88	HERMANNHOF WINERY	OP	8.00	8.00
88	JENNEY GRIST MILL	OP	8.00	8.00
F. JONES			**WASHINGTON D.C.**	
91	NATIONAL ARCHIVES	OP	8.00	8.00
91	U.S. CAPITOL	OP	8.00	8.00
91	U.S. SUPREME COURT	OP	8.00	8.00
91	WHITE HOUSE	OP	8.00	8.00
F. JONES			**WILD WEST**	
89	DRINK 'EM UP SALOON	OP	8.00	8.00
89	F.C. ZIMMERMAN'S GUN SHOP	OP	8.00	8.00
89	MARSHAL'S OFFICE	OP	8.00	8.00
89	WELLS FARGO & CO.	OP	8.00	8.00
F. JONES			**WILLIAMSBURG CHRISTMAS**	
83	CHRISTMAS CHURCH	RT	6.00	6.00
83	FEDERAL HOUSE	RT	6.00	6.00
83	GARRISON HOUSE	RT	6.00	6.00
83	GEORGIAN HOUSE	RT	6.00	6.00

THE CONSTANCE COLLECTION

C. GUERRA			**ANNUAL SANTA CLAUS BY CONSTANCE**	
91	TEDDY CLAUS	YR	90.00	90.00
92	REACH FOR THE STARS SANTA	YR	90.00	90.00
C. GUERRA			**FRIENDS & FAMILY COLLECTION**	
92	A MOMENT W/MARGO	2500	55.00	55.00
92	ANNETTE & CHRISTIAN	2500	48.00	48.00
92	BUTTERCUPS	2500	35.00	35.00
92	CHELSEA'S EASTER	2500	37.00	37.00
92	CHRISTOPHER	2500	37.00	37.00
92	COVERED WITH LOVE	2500	59.90	59.90
92	ELIZABETH AND PHILLIP	2500	55.00	55.00
92	FIRST LOVE	2500	57.00	57.00
92	FOREVER FRIENDS	2500	51.00	51.00
92	GRANDPOPS ANGEL	2500	51.00	51.00
92	LITTLE SIS	2500	48.00	48.00
92	LOVES TENDER TOUCH	2500	33.00	33.00
92	MICHELLI BELLE	2500	31.00	31.00
92	MISSY	2500	31.00	31.00
92	MOTHER'S DAY BOUQUET	2500	42.00	42.00
92	ONE ON ONE FATHER/SON	2500	55.00	55.00
92	PARTY PAMMY	2500	31.00	31.00
92	PILLOW TALK	2500	42.00	42.00
92	PITZ AND SARA	2500	48.00	48.00
92	RACHEL'S BLUE BIRD	2500	42.00	42.00
92	SPECIAL SISTERS	2500	51.00	51.00
92	TIMEOUT TO LOVE	2500	37.00	37.00
92	TOGETHERNESS	2500	49.00	49.00
C. GUERRA			**HEAVEN SENT**	
92	ALLELUIA	2500	45.00	45.00
92	CHRISTENING DAY	2500	55.00	55.00
92	ENDURING FAITH	2500	55.00	55.00
92	LOVE IS PATIENT	2500	49.00	49.00
C. GUERRA			**KITTY KAT KLUB**	
90	KASSANDRA KITTY	1500	30.00	30.00
90	KATRINA	1500	30.00	30.00
90	KLARA KITTY	1500	30.00	30.00
90	KLARENCE KITTY	1500	30.00	30.00
90	KLAUDIUS KITTY	1500	30.00	30.00
90	KOCKEY KITTY	1500	30.00	30.00
90	KONRAD KITTY	1500	30.00	30.00
90	KOQUETTE KITTY	1500	30.00	30.00
C. GUERRA			**SANTA CLAUS BY CONSTANCE**	
86	JOLLY ST. NICK	4000	72.00	72.00
86	VICTORIAN SANTA	4000	90.00	90.00
86	VICTORIAN SANTA WITH BEAR	4000	80.00	80.00

YR	NAME	LIMIT	ISSUE	QUOTE
87	ANIMAL SANTA	4000	78.00	78.00
88	AMERICAN TRADITIONAL SANTA	4000	90.00	90.00
88	MIDNIGHT VISIT	4000	112.00	112.00
88	SAINT NICHOLAS OF MYRA	4000	90.00	90.00
88	SANTAS DELIVERY	4000	90.00	90.00
89	COBBLESTONE SANTA	4000	112.00	112.00
89	KITTY CHRISTMAS	4000	112.00	112.00
89	SANTA WITH BOY	1000	90.00	90.00
89	SANTA WITH DEER	4000	112.00	112.00
89	SANTA WITH GIRL	1000	90.00	90.00
89	SANTA WITH LAMB	4000	112.00	112.00
89	SANTAS SLEIGH	1000	190.00	190.00
89	SIBERIAN SANTA	1000	190.00	190.00
89	THOMAS NAST SANTA	4000	112.00	112.00
90	CANDY CANE SANTA	1000	124.00	124.00
90	ELF SANTA	1000	298.00	298.00
90	HUNT SANTA	1000	158.00	158.00
90	KITTY CLAUS	1000	78.00	78.00
90	ROCKINGHORSE SANTA	1000	124.00	124.00
91	FIRST CHRISTMAS	1000	79.00	79.00
91	FIRST FROST	1000	250.00	250.00
91	HEAVENLY BLESSING	1000	79.00	79.00
91	LITTLE BOY'S SANTA	1000	95.00	95.00
91	SANTA'S DANCE	1000	95.00	95.00
91	SANTA'S DAY OFF	1000	90.00	90.00
91	SANTA'S GIRL	1000	95.00	95.00
92	HUSH! HUSH! SANTA	2500	59.90	59.90
92	PEACE ON EARTH	2500	64.00	64.00
92	TEST RUN SANTA	2500	79.00	79.00
92	TOUCH UP SANTA	2500	64.00	64.00

C. GUERRA   **SEASONAL SANTA**

YR	NAME	LIMIT	ISSUE	QUOTE
92	BASES LOADED	2500	90.00	90.00
92	FISHING DAY FUN	2500	90.00	90.00
92	FRESH POWDER FUN	2500	72.00	72.00
92	LOST BALL SANTA	2500	90.00	90.00
92	SPRING SERENITY	2500	112.00	112.00

C. GUERRA   **TENDER TOTS**

YR	NAME	LIMIT	ISSUE	QUOTE
92	BABY BUNS	2500	31.00	31.00
92	BABY'S BLOCKS	2500	37.00	37.00
92	BABY'S FIRST ABC'S	2500	37.00	37.00
92	FIRST CRAWL	2500	37.00	37.00
92	FIRST DAY HOME (BOY)	2500	35.00	35.00
92	FIRST DAY HOME (GIRL)	2500	35.00	35.00
92	FIRST WORDS	2500	37.00	37.00
92	NIGHT-NIGHT	2500	31.00	31.00
92	PLAYMATES	2500	33.00	33.00
92	SUGARPLUM DARLINGS	2500	37.00	37.00
92	TOYLAND	2500	37.00	37.00

C. GUERRA   **THE BRIAR PATCH**

YR	NAME	LIMIT	ISSUE	QUOTE
90	BARBARA BUNNY	1500	30.00	30.00
90	BARTHOLEMUE BUNNY	1500	30.00	30.00
90	BENEDICT BUNNY	1500	30.00	30.00
90	BERNARD BUNNY	1500	30.00	30.00
90	BERNICE BUNNY	1500	30.00	30.00
90	BERTRUM BUNNY	1500	30.00	30.00
90	BETSEY BUNNY	1500	30.00	30.00
90	BIRTHA BUNNY	1500	30.00	30.00
90	BLOSSUM BUNNY	1500	30.00	30.00
90	BONNIE BUNNY	1500	30.00	30.00
90	BRAIDA BUNNY	1500	30.00	30.00
90	BROTHERLY BUNNY	1500	30.00	30.00
90	BROWNIE BUNNY	1500	30.00	30.00
90	BUSTER BUNNY	1500	30.00	30.00
92	BUNNY'S BASKET	2500	21.90	21.90
92	GRANDFATHER BUN	2500	21.90	21.90
92	GRANDMOTHER BUNNY	2500	21.90	21.90
92	LOVE BUN	2500	21.90	21.90
92	MOTHER WITH TWINS	2500	21.90	21.90
92	NEW MAMMA BUNNY	2500	21.90	21.90
92	NUMBER ONE BUN	2500	21.90	21.90
92	PAPPA BUNNY	2500	21.90	21.90
92	PONDERING BUN	2500	21.90	21.90
92	PROUD PAPPA BUNNY	2500	21.90	21.90
92	WOODLAND BUNNY	2500	31.50	31.50

C. GUERRA   **THE GOLDEN AMERICANS**

YR	NAME	LIMIT	ISSUE	QUOTE
91	ANDRES AND SAM	1500	37.00	37.00

YR	NAME	LIMIT	ISSUE	QUOTE
91	BELINDA	1500	31.00	31.00
91	BLESSED WITH LOVE	1500	55.00	55.00
91	DADDY'S DARLING	1500	48.00	48.00
91	EFFIE AND COMPANY	1500	31.00	31.00
91	EMMA AND NICKIE	1500	37.00	37.00
91	ENDLESS LOVE	1500	48.00	48.00
91	FELICIA & FLUFF	1500	37.00	37.00
91	FROZEN FRIENDS	1500	42.00	42.00
91	GILBERT	1500	31.00	31.00
91	GLORYA	1500	75.00	75.00
91	GRANDMAS LOVE	1500	65.00	65.00
91	HANNAH AND KITTY	1500	42.00	42.00
91	INTO THE LIGHT	1500	31.00	31.00
91	LEARNING TO BRAID	1500	42.00	42.00
91	LETTIE THE DOLLMAKER	1500	48.00	48.00
91	MISSING YOU	1500	37.00	37.00
91	NEW PUPS	1500	31.00	31.00
91	PARTY TIME PALS	1500	55.00	55.00
91	PENNY PINCHER	1500	48.00	48.00
91	PLAY TIME	1500	31.00	31.00
91	PRAYING PALS	1500	31.00	31.00
91	PREACHER MAN	1500	31.00	31.00
91	PUDDLES	1500	37.00	37.00
91	PUPPY LOVE	1500	37.00	37.00
91	RUBY RAE AND TOM-TOM	1500	37.00	37.00
91	SCHOOL DAZE	1500	31.00	31.00
91	SUNDAY MORNING	1500	75.00	75.00
91	SWEET ASSURANCE	1500	48.00	48.00
91	SWEET DREAMS	1500	37.00	37.00
92	ANNELLE	2500	37.00	37.00
92	BALLA RENA	2500	31.00	31.00
92	BESTEST FRIENDS	2500	31.00	31.00
92	BUNNY LOVE	2500	31.00	31.00
92	CHRIS MISS	2500	31.00	31.00
92	CHURCH LADY ELLIE	2500	37.00	37.00
92	CHURCH LADY ETHEL	2500	37.00	37.00
92	CHURCH LADY PEARLE	2500	37.00	37.00
92	DUTCHIE	2500	31.00	31.00
92	FIRST POSITION	2500	31.00	31.00
92	FREE KICK DICK	2500	31.00	31.00
92	JOY BOY	2500	31.00	31.00
92	LITTLE CHASE	2500	31.00	31.00
92	LITTLE MAGIC	2500	31.00	31.00
92	LOVING EWE	2500	31.00	31.00
92	LOVING EWE TOO!	2500	33.00	33.00
92	MANDAS NABBIT	2500	31.00	31.00
92	P.S. I LOVE YOU	2500	42.00	42.00
92	PREPIE GREGORY	2500	37.00	37.00
92	PREPIE WINTHROP	2500	31.00	31.00
92	PRIMA DONA	2500	31.00	31.00
92	PUPPY LOVING	2500	37.00	37.00
92	QUARTERBACK JACK	2500	31.00	31.00
92	SCHOOL GIRL SAL	2500	31.00	31.00
92	SCHOOL GIRL SUE	2500	31.00	31.00
92	THERE YOU ARE!	2500	48.00	48.00
92	TOO MUCH HOMEWORK	2500	48.00	48.00
92	VALENTINE OF MINE	2500	31.00	31.00
92	VICTORY	2500	31.00	31.00

C. GUERRA — VICTORIANA COLLECTION

YR	NAME	LIMIT	ISSUE	QUOTE
91	FRITZ	1500	37.00	37.00
91	JULIA	1500	37.00	37.00
91	PENELOPE	1500	37.00	37.00
91	ROSIE	1500	37.00	37.00
91	VICTORIA	1500	37.00	37.00

THE GLASS BARON

J. BECHAM — WILDLIFE SERIES

YR	NAME	LIMIT	ISSUE	QUOTE
94	LEADER OF THE PACK	250	*	

TUDOR MINT

J. WATSON

YR	NAME	LIMIT	ISSUE	QUOTE
91	THE POWER OF THE CRYSTAL	3500	478.00	525.00

S. RILEY — EXHIBITION ONLY STUDIES

YR	NAME	LIMIT	ISSUE	QUOTE
93	DACTRIUS	*	63.92	70.00
94	VEXIUS	*	66.40	70.00

S. RILEY — EXTRAVAGANZA STUDIES

YR	NAME	LIMIT	ISSUE	QUOTE
92	SAURIA	403	31.90	40.00

YR	NAME	LIMIT	ISSUE	QUOTE
94	LITHIA	*	31.90	33.00
93	DEINOS	463	31.90	35.00

S. RILEY | | | **MYTH & MAGIC CLUB** | |

YR	NAME	LIMIT	ISSUE	QUOTE
90	THE QUEST FOR THE TRUTH	1282	79.90	83.00
92	FRIENDS	*	30.30	32.00
92	PLAYMATES	3778	27.10	30.00
93	THE MYSTICAL ENCOUNTER	*	31.60	35.00
94	THE CRYSTAL SHIELD	OP	44.00	48.00
94	THE KEEPER OF THE DRAGONS	*	79.90	85.00
95	THE BATTLE FOR THE CRYSTAL	OP	108.00	108.00
91	THE GAME OF STRAX	2533	23.90	25.00
91	THE WELL OF ASPIRATIONS	2,973	79.90	85.00
92	THE ENCHANTED POOL	*	79.90	85.00

S. RILEY | | | **MYTH AND MAGIC-LARGE STUDIES** | |

YR	NAME	LIMIT	ISSUE	QUOTE
90	THE DANCE OF THE DOLPHINS	1537	280.00	300.00
90	THE DRAGON MASTER	1500	280.00	300.00
90	THE VII SEEKERS OF KNOWLEDGE	7500	280.00	300.00
92	THE GATHERING OF THE UNICORNS	5000	296.00	325.00

S. RILEY | | | **ONE YEAR ONLY STUDIES** | |

YR	NAME	LIMIT	ISSUE	QUOTE
94	THE DRAGON OF THE UNDERWORLD	YR	66.40	70.00
95	THE GUARDIAN OF THE CRYSTAL	YR	108.00	108.00
93	THE FLYING DRAGON	YR	63.90	70.00

UNITED DESIGN CORP.

S. BRADFORD | | | **ANGELS COLLECTION** | |

YR	NAME	LIMIT	ISSUE	QUOTE
91	CHRISTMAS ANGEL AA-003	10,000	125.00	125.00
91	CLASSICAL ANGEL AA-005	10,000	79.00	79.00
91	HEAVENLY SHEPHERDESS AA-008	10,000	99.00	99.00
91	MESSENGER OF PEACE AA-006	10,000	75.00	75.00
91	THE GIFT AA-009	3500	140.00	500.00
91	TRUMPETER ANGEL AA-004	10,000	99.00	99.00
91	WINTER ROSE ANGEL AA-007	10,000	65.00	65.00
93	THE GIFT '93	RT	120.00	140.00
94	EARTH ANGEL	10,000	84.00	84.00
94	HARVEST ANGEL	10,000	84.00	84.00
91	ANGEL WAIF AA-012	OP	15.00	15.00
91	PEACE DESCENDING ANGEL AA-013	OP	20.00	20.00
91	ROSETTI ANGEL AA-011	OP	20.00	20.00
91	VICTORIAN CUPID ANGEL AA-010	OP	15.00	15.00
93	ANGEL OF FLIGHT	10,000	100.00	100.00
93	MADONNA	10,000	100.00	100.00
94	ANGEL WITH CHRIST CHILD	10,000	84.00	84.00
94	DREAMING OF ANGELS	10,000	120.00	120.00
93	ANGEL WITH BIRDS	10,000	75.00	75.00
93	ANGEL WITH LEAVES	10,000	70.00	70.00
93	ANGEL WITH LEAVES, EMERALD	RT	70.00	90.00
93	ANGEL WITH LILIES	10,000	80.00	80.00
93	ANGELS WITH LILIES, CRIMSON	RT	80.00	100.00
94	ANGEL WITH BOOK	10,000	84.00	84.00
94	ANGEL, ROSES & BLUEBIRDS	10,000	65.00	65.00
94	THE GIFT '94	RT	140.00	150.00

S. BRADFORD | | | **BACKYARD BIRDS** | |

YR	NAME	LIMIT	ISSUE	QUOTE
88	BABY ROBIN, SMALL BB-006	OP	10.00	10.00
88	BABY ROBINS BB-008	OP	15.00	18.00
88	BLUEBIRD BB-009	OP	15.00	20.00
88	BLUEBIRD, SMALL BB-001	OP	10.00	10.00
88	CARDINAL, SMALL BB-002	OP	10.00	10.00
88	CHICKADEE BB-010	OP	15.00	17.00
88	CHICKADEE, SMALL BB-003	OP	10.00	10.00
88	FEMALE CARDINAL BB-011	OP	15.00	17.00
88	FEMALE HUMMINGBIRD, SMALL BB-005	OP	10.00	10.00
88	FLYING HUMMINGBIRD, SMALL BB-004	OP	10.00	10.00
88	HANGING BLUEBIRD BB-017	RT	11.00	16.50
88	HANGING CARDINAL BB-018	RT	11.00	11.00
88	HANGING HUMMINGBIRD, LARGE BB-023	RT	15.00	15.00
88	HANGING HUMMINGBIRD, SMALL BB-022	RT	11.00	11.00
88	HANGING ROBIN BB-020	RT	11.00	11.00
88	HANGING SPARROW BB-021	RT	11.00	11.00
88	HANGKING CHICKADEE BB-019	RT	11.00	11.00
88	HUMMINGBIRD BB-012	OP	15.00	17.00
88	MALE CARDIDNAL BB-013	OP	15.00	17.00
88	RED-WINGED BLACKBIRD BB-014	RT	15.00	16.50
88	ROBIN BB-015	OP	15.00	20.00
88	SPARROW BB-016	OP	15.00	17.00
88	SPARROW, SMALL BB-007	OP	10.00	10.00
89	BABY BLUE JAY BB-027	OP	15.00	15.00
89	BALTIMORE ORIOLE BB-024	OP	19.50	22.00

YR	NAME	LIMIT	ISSUE	QUOTE
89	BLUE JAY BB-026	OP	19.50	22.00
89	GOLDFINCH BB-028	OP	16.50	20.00
89	HOOT OWL BB-025	OP	15.00	20.00
89	SAW-WHET OWL BB-029	OP	15.00	18.00
89	WOODPECKER BB-030	OP	16.50	20.00
90	BABY CEDAR WAXWINGS BB-033	OP	22.00	22.00
90	BLUEBIRD (UPRIGHT) BB-031	OP	20.00	20.00
90	CEDAR WAXWING BB-032	OP	20.00	20.00
90	EVENING GROSBEAK BB-034	OP	22.00	22.00
90	FEMALE INDIGO BUNTING BB-039	OP	20.00	20.00
90	INDIGO BUNTING BB-036	OP	20.00	20.00
90	NUTHATCH, WHITE-THROATED BB-037	OP	20.00	20.00
90	PAINTED BUNTING BB-040	OP	20.00	20.00
90	PAINTED BUNTING, FEMALE BB-041	OP	20.00	20.00
90	PURPLE FINCH BB-038	OP	20.00	20.00
90	ROSE BREASTED GROSBEAK BB-042	OP	20.00	20.00

D. KENNICUTT — EASTER BUNNY FAMILY

YR	NAME	LIMIT	ISSUE	QUOTE
88	BUNNIES, BASKET OF SEC-001	RT	13.00	17.50
88	BUNNY BOY W/DUCK SEC-002	RT	13.00	17.50
88	BUNNY GIRL W/HEN SEC-004	RT	13.00	17.50
88	BUNNY, EASTER SEC-003	RT	13.00	17.50
88	RABBIT, GRANDMA SEC-005	RT	15.00	17.50
88	RABBIT, GRANPA SEC-006	RT	15.00	17.50
88	RABBIT, MOMMA W/BONNET SEC-007	RT	15.00	17.50
89	AUNTIE BUNNY SEC-008	OP	20.00	23.00
89	BUNNY W/PRIZE EGG SEC-010	OP	19.50	20.00
89	DUCKY W/BONNET, BLUE SEC-015	OP	10.00	12.00
89	DUCKY W/BONNET, PINK SEC-014	OP	10.00	12.00
89	EASTER EGG HUNT SEC-012	OP	16.50	20.00
89	LITTLE SIS W/LOLLY SEC-009	OP	14.50	17.50
89	ROCK-A-BYE BUNNY SEC-013	OP	20.00	23.00
89	SIS & BUBBA SHARING SEC-011	OP	22.50	23.00
90	BUBBA W/WAGON SEC-016	OP	16.50	17.50
90	EASTER BUNNY W/CRYSTAL SEC-017	OP	23.00	23.00
90	HEN W/CHICK SEC-018	OP	23.00	23.00
90	MOMMA MAKING BASKET SEC-019	OP	23.00	23.00
90	MOTHER GOOSE SEC-020	OP	16.50	20.00
91	BABY IN BUGGY, BOY SEC-027	OP	20.00	20.00
91	BABY IN BUGGY, GIRL SEC-029	OP	20.00	20.00
91	BUBBA IN WHEELBARROW SEC-021	OP	20.00	20.00
91	BUNNY BOY W/ BASKET SEC-025	OP	20.00	20.00
91	FANCY FIND SEC-028	OP	20.00	20.00
91	LOP-EAR W/CRYSTAL SEC-022	OP	23.00	23.00
91	NEST OF BUNNY EGGS SEC-023	OP	17.50	17.50
91	VICTORIAN AUNTIE BUNNY SEC-026	OP	20.00	20.00
91	VICTORIAN MOMMA SEC-024	OP	20.00	20.00

K. MEMOLI — FAERIE TALES

YR	NAME	LIMIT	ISSUE	QUOTE
90	FAERIE FLIGHT	7500	39.00	39.00
90	SLEEPING FAERIE	7500	39.00	39.00
90	WATER SPRITE	7500	39.00	39.00
90	WIND SPRITE	7500	39.00	39.00
90	WINTER FAERIE	7500	39.00	39.00
90	WOOD SPRITE	7500	39.00	39.00

MEMOLI/JONAS — LEGEND OF SANTA CLAUS

YR	NAME	LIMIT	ISSUE	QUOTE
90	SAFE ARRIVAL CF-027	7500	150.00	150.00
86	ROOFTOP SANTA CF-004	RT	65.00	79.00
86	SANTA WITH PUPS CF-003	RT	65.00	150.00-350.00
87	DREAMING OF SANTA CF-008	RT	65.00	150.00-350.00
87	MRS. SANTA CF-006	RT	60.00	75.00
87	ON SANTA'S KNEE CF-007	15,000	65.00	79.00
87	SANTA ON HORSEBACK CF-011	RT	75.00	150.00-350.00
88	FATHER CHRISTMAS CF-018	7500	75.00	85.00
88	LOAD 'EM UP CF-016	RT	79.00	150.00-350.00
89	A PURRR-FECT CHRISTMAS CF-019	7500	95.00	95.00
89	CHRISTMAS HARMONY CF-020	7500	85.00	85.00
90	VICTORIAN SANTA CF-028	7500	125.00	125.00
90	WAITING FOR SANTA CF-026	7500	100.00	100.00
91	VICTORIAN SANTA W/TEDDY CF-033	7500	150.00	150.00
91	BLESSED FLIGHT CF-032	7500	159.00	159.00
91	REINDEER WALK CF-031	7500	150.00	150.00
86	ELF PAIR CF-005	10,000	60.00	75.00
86	KRIS KRINGLE CF-002	RT	60.00	75.00
86	SANTA AT REST CF-001	RT	70.00	150.00-350.00
87	CHECKING HIS LIST CF-009	15,000	75.00	85.00
87	LOADING SANTA'S SLEIGH CF-010	15,000	100.00	100.00
88	ASSEMBLY REQUIRED CF-017	7500	79.00	95.00

YR	NAME	LIMIT	ISSUE	QUOTE
88	ST. NICHOLAS CF-015	7500	75.00	85.00
89	HITCHING UP CF-021	7500	90.00	90.00
90	FOREST FRIENDS CF-025	7500	90.00	90.00
90	PUPPY LOVE CF-024	7500	100.00	100.00
91	FOR SANTA CF-029	7500	99.00	99.00
91	SANTA AT WORK CF-030	7500	99.00	99.00

L. MILLER   **LEGEND OF THE LITTLE PEOPLE**

YR	NAME	LIMIT	ISSUE	QUOTE
89	A FRIENDLY TOAST LL-003	7500	35.00	45.00
89	ADVENTURE BOUND LL-002	7500	35.00	45.00
89	CADDY'S HELPER LL-007	7500	35.00	45.00
89	MAGICAL DISCOVERY LL-005	7500	45.00	45.00
89	SPRING WATER SCRUB LL-006	7500	35.00	45.00
89	TREASURE HUNT LL-004	7500	45.00	45.00
89	WOODLAND CACHE LL-001	7500	35.00	45.00
90	A LITTLE JIG LL-018	7500	45.00	45.00
90	A LOOK THROUGH THE SPYGLASS LL-015	7500	40.00	45.00
90	A PROCLAMATION LL-013	7500	45.00	50.00
90	FISHIN' HOLE LL-012	7500	35.00	45.00
90	GATHERING ACORNS LL-014	7500	100.00	100.00
90	HEDGEHOG IN HARNESS LL-010	7500	45.00	45.00
90	HUSKING ACORNS LL-008	7500	60.00	60.00
90	MINSTRAL MAGIC LL-017	7500	45.00	45.00
90	TRAVELING FAST LL-009	7500	45.00	45.00
90	WOODLAND SCOUT LL-011	7500	40.00	45.00
90	WRITING THE LEGEND LL-016	7500	65.00	65.00
91	FIRE IT UP LL-023	7500	50.00	50.00
91	GOT IT LL-021	7500	45.00	45.00
91	IT'S ABOUT TIME LL-022	7500	55.00	55.00
91	THE EASTER BUNNY'S CART LL-020	7500	45.00	45.00
91	VIKING LL-019	7500	45.00	45.00

P. JONAS   **LIL' DOLLS**

YR	NAME	LIMIT	ISSUE	QUOTE
91	ANGELA BEAR LD-010	10,000	35.00	35.00
91	ARCHIBALD BEAR LD-009	10,000	35.00	35.00
91	BETTY BUTTON'S SURPRISE LD-008	10,000	35.00	35.00
91	GEORGIE BEAR LD-001	10,000	35.00	35.00
91	JENNY BEAR LD-002	10,000	35.00	35.00
91	NUTCRACKER LD-006	10,000	35.00	35.00
91	ADDIE LD-013	10,000	35.00	35.00
91	AMY LD-003	10,000	35.00	35.00
91	BECKY BUNNY LD-005	10,000	35.00	35.00
91	KRISTA LD-014	10,000	35.00	35.00
91	MARCHING IN TIME LD-007	10,000	35.00	35.00
91	SAM LD-004	10,000	35.00	35.00
91	SARA LD-011	10,000	35.00	35.00
91	TESS LD-015	10,000	35.00	35.00
91	TOM LD-012	10,000	35.00	35.00

S. BRADFORD   **MUSICMAKERS**

YR	NAME	LIMIT	ISSUE	QUOTE
89	HERALD ANGEL MM-011	12,000	79.00	79.00
89	TEDDY BEAR BAND MM-012	12,000	99.00	99.00
89	CHRISTMAS TREE MM-008	OP	69.00	69.00
89	EVENING CAROLERS MM-005	OP	69.00	69.00
89	SNOWSHOE SLED RIDE MM-007	OP	69.00	69.00
89	TEDDIES AND FROSTY MM-010	OP	69.00	69.00
89	TEDDY DRUMMERS MM-009	OP	69.00	69.00
89	WINTER FUN MM-006	OP	69.00	69.00
91	A CHRISTMAS GIFT MM-015	OP	59.00	59.00
91	CRYSTAL ANGEL MM-017	OP	59.00	59.00
91	DASHING THROUGH THE SNOW MM-013	OP	59.00	59.00
91	TEDDY SOLDIERS MM-018	OP	69.00	69.00
91	TWO FAERIES MM-014	OP	59.00	59.00
89	COMING TO TOWN MM-001	OP	69.00	69.00
89	MERRY LITTLE CHRISTMAS MM-002	OP	69.00	69.00
89	MERRY MAKING MM-003	RT	69.00	80.00-100.00
89	SANTA'S SLEIGH MM-004	OP	69.00	69.00

D. KENNICUTT   **PARTY ANIMALS**

YR	NAME	LIMIT	ISSUE	QUOTE
84	DEMOCRATIC DONKEY ('84)	RT	14.50	16.00
90	DEMOCRATIC DONKEY ('90)	OP	16.00	16.00
90	GOP ELEPHANT ('90)	OP	16.00	16.00
84	GOP ELEPHANT ('84)	RT	14.50	16.00
86	DEMOCRATIC DONKEY ('86)	RT	14.50	14.50
86	GOP ELEPHANT ('86)	RT	14.50	14.50
88	DEMOCRATIC DONKEY ('88)	RT	14.50	16.00
88	GOP ELEPHANT ('88)	RT	14.50	16.00

P. JONAS   **PENNIBEARS**

YR	NAME	LIMIT	ISSUE	QUOTE
90	ATTIC FUN PB-019	TL	20.00	22.00
90	BABY HUGS PB-007	TL	20.00	22.00

YR	NAME	LIMIT	ISSUE	QUOTE
90	BATHTIME BUDDIES PB-023	TL	20.00	22.00
90	BEAUTIFUL BRIDE PB-004	TL	20.00	24.00
90	BIRTHDAY BEAR PB-018	TL	20.00	24.00
90	BOOOO BEAR PB-025	TL	20.00	22.00
90	BOUQUET BOY PB-003	TL	20.00	20.00
90	BOUQUET GIRL PB-001	TL	20.00	22.00
90	BUTTERFLY BEAR PB-005	TL	20.00	22.00
90	BUTTONS & BOWS PB-012	TL	20.00	22.00
90	COOKIE BANDIT PB-006	TL	20.00	22.00
90	COUNT BEARACULA PB-027	TL	22.00	24.00
90	COUNTRY QUILTER PB-030	TL	22.00	26.00
90	COUNTRY SPRING PB-013	TL	20.00	22.00
90	DOCTOR BEAR PB-008	TL	20.00	22.00
90	DRESS UP FUN PB-028	TL	22.00	24.00
90	GARDEN PATH PB-014	TL	20.00	22.00
90	GIDDIAP TEDDY PB-011	TL	20.00	24.00
90	HANDSOME GROOM PB-015	TL	20.00	22.00
90	HONEY BEAR PB-002	TL	20.00	20.00
90	LAZY DAYS PB-009	TL	20.00	22.00
90	NAP TIME PB-016	TL	20.00	22.00
90	NURSE BEAR PB-017	TL	20.00	22.00
90	PETITE MADEMOISELLE PB-010	TL	20.00	22.00
90	PUPPY BATH PB-020	TL	20.00	22.00
90	PUPPY LOVE PB-021	TL	20.00	22.00
90	SANTA BEAR-ING GIFTS PB-031	TL	24.00	26.00
90	SCARECROW TEDDY PB-029	TL	24.00	24.00
90	SNEAKY SNOWBALL PB-026	TL	20.00	22.00
90	SOUTHERN BELLE PB-024	TL	20.00	22.00
90	STOCKING SURPRISE PB-032	TL	22.00	26.00
90	TUBBY TEDDY PB-022	TL	20.00	22.00
91	A WILD RIDE PB-052	TL	26.00	26.00
91	BAKING GOODIES PB-043	TL	26.00	26.00
91	BEAR FOOTIN' IT PB-037	TL	24.00	24.00
91	BEARLY AWAKE PB-033	TL	22.00	22.00
91	BOO HOO BEAR PB-050	TL	22.00	22.00
91	BOUNTIFUL HARVEST PB-045	TL	24.00	24.00
91	BUMP-BEAR CROP PB-035	TL	26.00	26.00
91	BUNNY BUDDIES PB-042	TL	22.00	22.00
91	CHRISTMAS REINBEAR PB-046	TL	28.00	28.00
91	COUNTRY LULLABYE PB-036	TL	24.00	24.00
91	CURTAIN CALL PB-049	TL	24.00	24.00
91	GOODNIGHT LITTLE PRINCE PB-041	TL	26.00	26.00
91	GOODNIGHT SWEET PRINCESS PB-040	TL	26.00	26.00
91	HAPPY HOBO PB-051	TL	26.00	26.00
91	LIL' MER-TEDDY PB-034	TL	24.00	24.00
91	PILGRIM PROVIDER PB-047	TL	32.00	32.00
91	SUMMER SAILING PB-039	TL	26.00	26.00
91	SWEET LIL 'SIS PB-048	TL	22.00	22.00
91	SWEETHEART BEARS PB-044	TL	28.00	28.00
91	WINDY DAY PB-038	TL	24.00	24.00

P. JONAS   **PENNIBEARS COLLECTOR'S CLUB MEMBERS ONLY EDITIONS**

YR	NAME	LIMIT	ISSUE	QUOTE
90	FIRST COLLECTION PB-C90	RT	26.00	26.00
91	COLLECTING MAKES CENTS PB-C91	YR	26.00	26.00

H. HENRIKSEN   **STORYTIME RHYMES & TALES**

YR	NAME	LIMIT	ISSUE	QUOTE
91	HUMPTY DUMPTY 008	3500	64.00	64.00
91	LITTLE JACK HORNER 007	3500	50.00	50.00
91	LITTLE MISS MUFFET 006	3500	64.00	64.00
91	MISTRESS MARY 002	3500	64.00	64.00
91	MOTHER GOOSE 001	3500	64.00	64.00
91	OWL & PUSSY CAT 004	3500	100.00	100.00
91	SIMPLE SIMON 003	3500	90.00	90.00
91	THREE LITTLE PIGS 005	3500	100.00	100.00

S. BRADFORD   **SUZY'S ZOO**

YR	NAME	LIMIT	ISSUE	QUOTE
90	BABY QUACKER	OP	20.00	20.00
90	BUNNY BABY	OP	20.00	20.00
90	BUNNY BRIDE & GROOM	OP	25.00	25.00
90	CORKY PILGRIM	OP	25.00	25.00
90	CORKY TURTLE & HAT	OP	22.50	22.50
90	CORKY, HEART FELT	OP	22.50	22.50
90	JACK & FLOWERS	OP	22.50	22.50
90	MARMOT BABY, RAINY DAY	OP	20.00	20.00
90	MARMOT CAROLERS	OP	25.00	25.00
90	MARMOT SISTERS/PALS	OP	25.00	25.00
90	MARMOTS DANCING	OP	25.00	25.00
90	MARTHA MARMOT	OP	22.50	22.50
90	OLLIE MARMOT	OP	22.50	22.50

YR NAME	LIMIT	ISSUE	QUOTE
90 POLLY QUACKER	OP	22.50	22.50
90 RITZ, SIGNING-I LOVE YOU	OP	22.50	22.50
90 RITZ-HAY THERE	OP	20.00	20.00
90 SUZY & FAVORITE PILLOW	OP	22.50	22.50
90 SUZY & TEDDY	OP	22.50	22.50
90 SUZY, ARTIST	OP	22.50	22.50
90 SUZY, BEAUTY QUEEN	OP	25.00	25.00
90 TEDDY	OP	20.00	20.00
90 TILLIAMOOK & FLOWERS	OP	22.50	22.50
90 TILLIAMOOK, BALLERINA	OP	22.50	22.50

S. BRADFORD THE LEGEND OF SANTA CLAUS

YR NAME	LIMIT	ISSUE	QUOTE
93 NORTHWOODS SANTA	7500	100.00	110.00
93 VICT., LION AND LAMB SANTA	7500	100.00	110.00
94 STAR SANTA WITH POLAR BEAR	7500	130.00	130.00
93 DEAR SANTA	7500	170.00	185.00
93 JOLLY ST. NICK	7500	130.00	140.00
93 JOLLY ST. NICK, VICT.	7500	120.00	130.00
94 LONGSTOCKING DILEMMA	7500	170.00	170.00
94 LONGSTOCKING DILEMMA, VICT.	7500	170.00	170.00
94 THE STORY OF CHRISTMAS	10,000	180.00	180.00
93 NIGHT BEFORE CHRISTMAS	7500	100.00	110.00
93 SANTA'S FRIENDS	7500	100.00	110.00
94 SANTA RIDING DOVE	7500	120.00	120.00

VICKILANE
V. ANDERSON

94 BUNNY ANGEL #1610	OP	13.00	13.00
94 BUNNY ANGEL #1611	OP	13.00	13.00
94 BUNNY ANGEL #1612	OP	13.00	13.00
94 BUNNY ANGEL #1613	OP	13.00	13.00
94 BUNNY ANGEL #1614	OP	13.00	13.00
94 BUNNY ANGEL #1615	OP	13.00	13.00
94 CHILD ANGEL #6011	OP	20.00	20.00

V. ANDERSON ACCESSORIES
93 FIREPLACE	OP	20.00	20.00

V. ANDERSON AMISH/COUNTRY KIDS
94 BROTHERLY LOVE	OP	*	
94 PATIENCE	OP	20.00	20.00

V. ANDERSON BLESSINGS FROM ABOVE
94 CHILD ANGEL #6009	OP	18.00	18.00
94 CHILD ANGEL #6010	OP	25.00	25.00

V. ANDERSON CHARACTER CAPERS
94 DILIGENCE	OP	20.00	20.00
94 FAITH	OP	*	

V. ANDERSON CHRISTMAS
93 FUZZY	OP	22.50	22.50
93 GRANDMA & GRANDPA	OP	25.00	25.00
93 ROSEBERRY	OP	22.00	22.00
93 SPARKY	OP	18.00	18.00
93 SUGAR PLUM	OP	22.00	22.00

V. ANDERSON CLUB PIECE
94 MISS APRIL	OP	28.00	28.00
94 SWEET SECRETS	250	*	

V. ANDERSON COW-LLECTOR
94 COW WITH BAG OF OATS	OP	*	
94 COW WITH SUNGLASSES	OP	*	

V. ANDERSON LIL BLESSINGS
94 BUNNY ANGEL CLOUD	OP	12.00	12.00

V. ANDERSON NITE BEAR-FORE
93 PAPA BEARS	OP	22.00	22.00

V. ANDERSON PURRFECTLY PRECIOUS KITTY
94 KITTIES BEHIND FENCE	OP	*	

V. ANDERSON SCHOOL HOUSE BUNNIES
94 BOY WITH BASKETBALL	OP	18.00	18.00
94 BOYS WITH BOOKS	OP	20.00	20.00
94 GIRL READING	OP	20.00	20.00
94 SCHOOL TEACHER	OP	20.00	20.00

V. ANDERSON SKIN TONE
94 CHILD ANGEL #6013	OP	20.00	20.00
94 CHILD ANGEL #6014	OP	22.00	22.00

V. ANDERSON SWEET THUMPINS
94 BUNNY THROWING SNOW	RT	*	
94 HAPPY EARS	OP	*	
94 NEW BORN EXCITEMENT	OP	*	
94 NURSE BUNNY	OP	*	
94 SWEETHEART BUNNIES	OP	*	
94 UNJURED BUNNY	OP	*	

YR	NAME	LIMIT	ISSUE	QUOTE
V. ANDERSON			THE LORD IS MY SHEPHERD	
94	LAMB ANGEL	OP	*	
94	LAMB AT DOOR	OP	*	
94	LAMB BUILD ALTAR	OP	*	
94	LAMB READING	OP	*	
94	LAMB WORSHIPPING	OP	*	
V. ANDERSON			THIS LITTLE PIGGY	
94	PIG EATING APPLES	OP	22.00	22.00
V. ANDERSON			TIME FOR TEDDY	
93	NEWLYWED BEAR	OP	20.00	20.00
93	SNOWMEN BEARS	OP	*	
93	TEDDY BEAR	OP	10.00	10.00
V. ANDERSON			WHITE OR BLACK	
94	CHILD ANGEL #6012	OP	20.00	20.00

WACO PRODUCTS CORP.

YR	NAME	LIMIT	ISSUE	QUOTE
S. NAKANE		MELODY IN MOTION/CAROUSEL COLLECTION		
94	BLUE DANUBE CAROUSEL	OP	180.00	190.00
S. NAKANE			MELODY IN MOTION/CLOCK	
93	THE ARTIST	OP	240.00	250.00
S. NAKANE		MELODY IN MOTION/HERITAGE COLLECTION		
93	SOUTH OF THE BORDER	OP	180.00	190.00
94	CAMPFIRE COWBOY	OP	180.00	190.00
94	CHRISTMAS CAROLER BOY	10,000	172.00	180.00
94	CHRISTMAS CAROLER GIRL	10,000	172.00	180.00
94	WHEN I GROW UP	OP	200.00	210.00
S. NAKANE			MELODY IN MOTION/MADAME	
88	MADAME CELLO PLAYER	OP	130.00	130.00
88	MADAME FLUTE PLAYER	OP	130.00	130.00
88	MADAME HARP PLAYER	OP	130.00	130.00
88	MADAME HARPSICHORD PLAYER	OP	130.00	130.00
88	MADAME LYRE PLAYER	OP	130.00	130.00
88	MADAME MANDOLIN PLAYER	OP	130.00	130.00
88	MADAME VIOLIN PLAYER	OP	130.00	130.00
S. NAKANE			MELODY IN MOTION/SANTA	
86	SANTA CLAUS-1986	RT	100.00	125.00-300.00
87	SANTA CLAUS-1987	RT	104.00	125.00-225.00
88	SANTA CLAUS-1988	RT	130.00	150.00-175.00
89	WILLIE THE SANTA	RT	130.00	130.00-150.00
90	SANTA CLAUS-1990	RT	150.00	150.00
91	SANTA CLAUS-1991	12,000	150.00	150.00
93	1993 COCA-COLA SANTA	6000	180.00	190.00
94	1994 COCA-COLA SANTA	9000	190.00	
S. NAKANE		MELODY IN MOTION/SPOTLIGHT CLOWN		
89	SPOTLIGHT CLOWN BANJO	RT	120.00	120.00
89	SPOTLIGHT CLOWN CORNET	RT	120.00	120.00
89	SPOTLIGHT CLOWN TROMBONE	RT	120.00	120.00
89	SPOTLIGHT CLOWN TUBA	RT	120.00	120.00
89	SPOTLIGHT CLOWN WITH BINGO THE DOG	RT	130.00	130.00
89	SPOTLIGHT CLOWN WITH UPRIGHT BASS	RT	130.00	130.00
S. NAKANE			MELODY IN MOTION/TIMEPIECE	
89	CLOCKPOST WILLIE	OP	150.00	150.00
89	LULL'ABY WILLIE	OP	170.00	170.00
90	GRANDFATHER'S CLOCK	OP	200.00	200.00
91	HUNTER TIMEPIECE	OP	250.00	250.00
91	ROBIN HOOD TIMEPIECE	OP	300.00	300.00
C. JOHNSON			MELODY IN MOTION/VARIOUS	
91	LITTLE JOHN	7000	180.00	180.00
91	ROBIN HOOD	OP	180.00	180.00
85	SALTY N' PEPPER	RT	130.00	130.00
86	THE CELLIST	OP	130.00	130.00
86	THE FIDDLER	OP	130.00	130.00
86	THE GUITARIST	OP	130.00	130.00
87	ACCORDION CLOWN	RT	84.00	84.00
87	BALLOON CLOWN	OP	110.00	110.00
87	CLARINET CLOWN	RT	84.00	84.00
87	SAXOPHONE CLOWN	RT	84.00	84.00
87	THE CAROUSEL	OP	240.00	240.00
87	VIOLIN CLOWN	RT	84.00	84.00
89	THE GRAND CAROUSEL	OP	3000.00	3000.00
90	ACCORDION BOY	8000	120.00	120.00
90	BLACKSMITH	5000	110.00	110.00
90	HUNTER	OP	110.00	110.00
90	SHOEMAKER	5000	110.00	110.00
90	WOODCHOPPER	5000	110.00	110.00
91	VICTORIA PARK CAROUSEL	OP	300.00	300.00

YR	NAME	LIMIT	ISSUE	QUOTE
S. NAKANE			**MELODY IN MOTION/VENDOR**	
87	ORGAN GRINDER	OP	130.00	130.00
89	ICE CREAM VENDOR	OP	140.00	140.00
89	PEANUT VENDOR	OP	140.00	140.00
S. NAKANE			**MELODY IN MOTION/WILLIE**	
85	WILLIE THE HOBO	OP	96.00	130.00
85	WILLIE THE TRUMPETER	OP	96.00	130.00
85	WILLIE THE WHISTLER	OP	96.00	130.00
87	LAMPPOST WILLIE	OP	84.00	110.00
91	WILLIE THE FISHERMAN	OP	150.00	150.00
93	HEARTBREAK WILLIE	OP	180.00	190.00
93	LAMPLIGHT WILLIE	OP	240.00	250.00
93	WILLIE THE GOLFER	OP	240.00	250.00
94	CHATTANOOGA CHOO-CHOO	OP	180.00	190.00
94	DAY'S END	OP	240.00	250.00
94	JACKPOT WILLIE	OP	180.00	190.00
94	LONGEST DRIVE	OP	150.00	160.00
94	LOW PRESSURE JOB	OP	240.00	250.00
94	SMOOTH SAILING	OP	200.00	210.00
94	WILLIE THE GOLFER	OP	240.00	250.00
J. UNGER			**THE HERMAN COLLECTION**	
90	BIRTHDAY/CAKE	OP	36.00	36.00
90	BOWLING/WIFE	OP	32.00	32.00
90	DOCTOR/FAT MAN	OP	36.00	36.00
90	DOCTOR/HIGH COST	OP	32.00	32.00
90	FRY PAN	OP	40.00	40.00
90	GOLF/CAMEL	OP	44.00	44.00
90	HUSBAND/CHECK	OP	36.00	36.00
90	HUSBAND/NEWSPAPER	OP	41.00	41.00
90	LAWYER/CABINET	OP	44.00	44.00
90	STOP SMOKING	OP	40.00	40.00
90	TENNIS/WIFE	OP	32.00	32.00
90	WEDDING RING	OP	41.00	41.00

WALT DISNEY CLASSICS COLLECTIONS

				BAMBI
*	FIELD MOUSE	7,500	*	1900.00
92	BAMBI	OP	195.00	290.00
92	BAMBI & FLOWER	10,000	298.00	485.00
92	BAMBI SERIES, COMPLETE SET	*	*	2940.00
92	FIELD MOUSE-LITTLE APRIL SHOWER	7,500	198.00	1825.00
92	FLOWER	OP	78.00	175.00
92	FRIEND OWL	OP	195.00	245.00
92	SCROLL "BIG OPENING TITLE"	OP	29.00	45.00
92	THUMPER	OP	55.00	85.00
92	THUMPER'S SISTERS	OP	69.00	100.00
				CINDERELLA
*	CINDERELLA, LUCIFER, BRUNO (SET OF 3)	RT	*	550.00-780.00
92	BIRDS WITH SASH	RT	149.00	185.00
92	BRUNO-JUST LEARN TO LIKE CATS	RT	69.00	110.00
92	CHALK MOUSE	RT	65.00	95.00
92	CINDERELLA	RT	195.00	310.00
92	CINDERELLA'S DRESS	5,000	800.00	2100.00
92	CINDERELLA'S SEWING BOOK	OP	69.00	110.00
92	GUS	RT	65.00	95.00
92	JAQ	RT	65.00	90.00
92	LUCIFER	RT	69.00	110.00
92	NEEDLE MOUSE	RT	69.00	95.00
92	SCROLL "CINDERELLA OPENING TITLE"	OP	29.00	45.00
93	BRUNO	RT	69.00	100.00
93	LUCIFER	RT	69.00	100.00
				COLLECTOR'S SOCIETY
92	JIMINY CRICKET	*	52.00	180.00
				DELIVERY BOY
92	MICKEY-DELIVERY BOY	OP	125.00	245.00
92	MINNIE-DELIVERY BOY	OP	125.00	210.00
92	PLUTO (WHEEL-INCISED)	OP	125.00	325.00
92	SCROLL "THE DELIVERY BOY"	OP	29.00	29.00
				FANTASIA
92	MICKEY MOUSE "MISCHIEVOUS APPRENTICE"	OP	195.00	275.00
93	BLUE CENTAURETTE "BEAUTY IN BLOOM"	OP	195.00	335.00
93	CUPID EVENT PIECE "FLIGHT OF FANCY"		35.00	65.00
93	PINK CENTAURETTE "ROMANTIC REFLECTIONS"	OP	175.00	330.00
93	SCROLL "FANTASIA OPENING TITLE"	OP	29.00	60.00
94	CUPIDS "LOVE'S LITTLE HELPERS"	OP	290.00	290.00
94	LG. MUSHROOM "MUSHROOM DANCER"	OP	60.00	60.00
94	MED. MUSHROOM "MUSHROOM DANCER"	OP	50.00	50.00

YR	NAME	LIMIT	ISSUE	QUOTE
94	SM. MUSHROOM HOP LOW	OP	35.00	35.00

MEMBERS COMMISSION SCULPTURE

YR	NAME	LIMIT	ISSUE	QUOTE
94	PECOS BILL & WIDOWMAKER	YR	650.00	650.00

MEMBERSHIP GIFT

YR	NAME	LIMIT	ISSUE	QUOTE
93	CHESHIRE CAT "TWAS BRILLIG"		55.00	115.00
93	MICKEY MOUSE "I LET 'EM HAVE IT"	AC	160.00	285.00
94	DONALD DUCK "ADMIRAL DUCK"	AC	165.00	165.00
94	DUMBO "SIMPLY ADORABLE"		55.00	55.00
95	CRUELLA DE VIL "101 DALMATIONS"	AC		*

MR. DUCK STEPS OUT

YR	NAME	LIMIT	ISSUE	QUOTE
*	DONALD AND DAISY	7,500	*	1040.00-1300.00
92	DEWEY "I GOT SOMETHING' FOR YA"	OP	65.00	95.00
92	DONALD & DAISY "OH BOY,WHAT A JITTERBUG"	5,000	295.00	1075.00
92	NEPHEW DUCK-I'VE GOT SOMETHING FOR YA	OP	65.00	69.00-125.00
92	OH BOY, WHAT A JITTERBUG	5,000	295.00	715.00-1200.00
93	HUEY "TAG-ALONG TROUBLE"	OP	65.00	95.00
93	LOUIE "TAG-ALONG TROUBLE"	OP	65.00	95.00
93	SCROLL "MR. DUCK STEPS OUT"	OP	29.00	50.00
94	DONALD "WITH LOVE FROM DAISY"	OP	180.00	180.00

PETER PAN

YR	NAME	LIMIT	ISSUE	QUOTE
93	CAPT. HOOK "I'VE GOT YOU THIS TIME!"	OP	275.00	1100.00
93	CROCODILE "TICK-TOCK, TICK TOCK"	OP	315.00	1500.00
93	PETER PAN "NOBODY CALLS PAN A COWARD!"	OP	165.00	265.00
93	SCROLL "PETER PAN"	OP	29.00	50.00
93	TINKERBELL "A FIREFLY! A PIXIE AMAZING"	12,500	215.00	750.00
94	MR. SMEE "OH DEAR, OH DEAR" EVENT		90.00	90.00

SNOW WHITE

YR	NAME	LIMIT	ISSUE	QUOTE
94	SNOW WHITE "THE FAIREST ONE OF ALL"	OP	165.00	165.00

SYMPHONY HOUR

YR	NAME	LIMIT	ISSUE	QUOTE
92	CLARABELLE	OP	198.00	280.00
92	GOOFY (WHEEL)	OP	198.00	1200.00
92	HORACE	OP	198.00	250.00
92	MAESTRO MICHEL MOUSE	OP	185.00	230.00
92	SCROLL "SYMPHONY HOUR"	OP	29.00	55.00
94	CLARA CLUCK "BRAVO BRAVISSIMO"	OP	185.00	185.00

THE SORCERER'S APPRENTICE

YR	NAME	LIMIT	ISSUE	QUOTE
92	BROOMS--BUCKET BRIGADE	OP	75.00	175.00
92	SORCERER MICKEY--MISCHIEVOUS APPRENTICE	RT	185.00	300.00

THREE LITTLE PIGS

YR	NAME	LIMIT	ISSUE	QUOTE
93	BIG BAD WOLF "WHO'S AFRAID...?"	7,500	295.00	975.00
93	FIDDLER PIG "HEY DIDDLE,...FIDDLE"	OP	75.00	155.00
93	FIFER PIG "I TOOT MY FLUTE,..HOOT"	OP	75.00	155.00
93	PRACTICAL PIG "WORK & PLAY DON'T MIX"	OP	75.00	155.00
93	SCROLL "THREE LITTLE PIGS"	OP	29.00	29.00

WEE FOREST FOLK

A. PETERSEN

ANIMALS

YR	NAME	LIMIT	ISSUE	QUOTE
73	MISS DUCKY	CL	8.00	*
74	BABY HIPPO	CL	7.00	*
74	MISS AND BABY HIPPO	CL	15.00	*
74	MISS HIPPO	CL	8.00	*
75	"DOC" RAT	CL	12.00	200.00-300.00
75	SPEEDY RAT	CL	11.50	200.00-300.00
77	NUTSY SQUIRREL	CL	6.00	*
78	BEAVER WOOD CUTTER	CL	23.00	125.00-225.00
78	MOLE SCOUT	CL	9.00	125.00-225.00
79	TURTLE JOGGER	CL	9.00	*

A. PETERSEN

BEARS

YR	NAME	LIMIT	ISSUE	QUOTE
77	BIG LADY BEAR	CL	16.00	*
77	BLUEBERRY BEARS	CL	31.50	500.00-650.00
77	BOY BLUEBERRY BEAR	CL	17.00	200.00-400.00
77	GIRL BLUEBERRY BEAR	CL	15.00	200.00-400.00
78	TRAVELING BEAR	CL	21.50	*

A. PETERSEN

BUNNIES

YR	NAME	LIMIT	ISSUE	QUOTE
72	DOUBLE BUNNIES	CL	9.00	*
72	HOUSEKEEPING BUNNY	CL	11.00	*
73	BROOM BUNNY	CL	9.50	*
73	MARKET BUNNY	CL	9.00	*
73	MUFF BUNNY	CL	9.00	*
73	SIR RABBIT	CL	11.50	*
73	SUNDAY BUNNY	CL	9.50	*
73	THE PROFESSOR	CL	12.00	*
77	BATTER BUNNY	CL	17.00	275.00-400.00
77	TENNIS BUNNY	CL	10.50	*
78	WEDDING BUNNIES	CL	13.50	300.00-400.00
80	PROFESSOR RABBIT	CL	16.00	*
85	TINY EASTER BUNNY	CL	26.00	*

YR	NAME	LIMIT	ISSUE	QUOTE
A. PETERSEN			**FAIRY TALE SERIES**	
80	RED RIDING HOOD	CL	14.00	250.00-400.00
80	RED RIDING HOOD & WOLF	CL	34.00	700.00-1200.00
W. PETERSEN			**FOREST SCENE**	
88	WOODLAND SERENADE	RT	125.00	130.00
89	HEARTS AND FLOWERS	OP	110.00	112.00
90	MOUSIE COMES A-CALLING	OP	128.00	130.00
91	MOUNTAIN STREAM	OP	128.00	130.00
92	LOVE LETTER	OP	98.00	98.00
A. PETERSEN			**FOXES**	
77	DANDY FOX	CL	12.50	*
77	FANCY FOX	CL	10.00	*
78	BARRISTER FOX	CL	21.00	*
A. PETERSEN			**FROGS**	
74	FROG ON ROCK	CL	6.00	*
74	PRINCE CHARMING	CL	7.50	*
77	FROG FRIENDS	CL	17.50	*
77	GRAMPA FROG	CL	17.50	*
77	SPRING PEEPERS	CL	9.00	*
78	SINGING FROG	CL	12.00	*
W. PETERSEN			**LIMITED EDITION**	
81	BEAUTY AND THE BEAST	200	89.00	*
84	POSTMASTER	*	46.00	450.00-700.00
85	HELPING HAND	RT	62.00	425.00-625.00
87	STATUE IN THE PARK	2000	93.00	500.00-700.00
88	UNCLE SAMMY	2500	85.00	150.00-225.00
A. PETERSEN			**MICE**	
72	MARKET MOUSE	CL	8.00	*
72	MISS MOUSE	CL	8.00	300.00-350.00
72	MISS MOUSEY	CL	7.50	*
73	MISS NURSEY	CL	7.50	200.00-300.00
74	FARMER MOUSE	CL	7.00	*
74	GOOD KNIGHT MOUSE	CL	7.50	*
74	WOOD SPRITE	CL	7.50	300.00-550.00
75	BRIDE MOUSE	CL	7.50	375.00-500.00
75	TWO MICE WITH CANDLE	CL	8.00	300.00-400.00
75	TWO TINY MICE	CL	7.50	300.00-500.00
76	FAN MOUSE	CL	10.50	*
76	JUNE BELLE	CL	7.50	*
76	MAMA MOUSE WITH BABY	CL	12.00	325.00-450.00
76	MAY BELLE	CL	8.00	225.00-350.00
76	MOUSE WITH MUFF	CL	9.00	*
76	MRS. MOUSEY	CL	8.00	*
76	NIGHTIE MOUSE	CL	9.50	300.00-500.00
76	SHAWL MOUSE	CL	9.00	*
76	TEA MOUSE	CL	10.50	*
77	BABY SITTER	CL	9.50	200.00-300.00
77	KING "TUT" MOUSE	CL	9.50	300.00-400.00
77	QUEEN "TUT" MOUSE	CL	9.50	300.00-400.00
78	BRIDGE CLUB MOUSE	CL	12.00	*
78	BRIDGE CLUB MOUSE PARTNER	CL	12.00	*
78	CHIEF NIP-A-WAY MOUSE	CL	14.00	300.00-375.00
78	COWBOY MOUSE	CL	12.00	300.00-400.00
78	PICNIC MICE	CL	14.50	300.00-400.00
78	PIRATE MOUSE	CL	13.00	300.00-450.00
78	SECRETARY, MISS SPELL/MISS PELL	CL	9.50	300.00-425.00
78	TOWN CRIER MOUSE	CL	10.50	*
78	WEDDING MICE	CL	15.00	275.00-425.00
79	CHRIS-MISS	CL	9.00	125.00-225.00
79	CHRIS-MOUSE	CL	9.00	150.00-225.00
79	GARDENER MOUSE	CL	12.00	450.00
79	MOUSE ARTISTE	CL	12.50	300.00-450.00
79	MOUSE BABY, HEART BOOK	CL	9.50	200.00-300.00
79	MOUSE BALLERINA	CL	12.50	*
79	MOUSE DUET	CL	25.00	550.00-700.00
79	MOUSE PIANIST	CL	17.00	300.00-400.00
79	MOUSE VIOLINIST	CL	9.00	200.00-300.00
79	RAGGEDY AND MOUSE	CL	12.00	200.00-300.00
79	ROCK-A-BYE BABY MOUSE	CL	17.00	300.00-400.00
80	CARPENTER MOUSE	CL	15.00	325.00-425.00
80	COMMO-DOORMOUSE	CL	14.00	350.00-500.00
80	FISHERMOUSE	CL	16.00	350.00-450.00
80	MISS BOBBIN	*	22.00	*
80	MISS POLLY MOUSE	CL	23.00	250.00-350.00
80	MISS TEACH	CL	18.00	*
80	MRS. TIDY AND HELPER	CL	24.00	350.00-450.00

YR	NAME	LIMIT	ISSUE	QUOTE
80	PHOTOGRAPHER MOUSE	CL	23.00	400.00-600.00
80	PIRATE MOUSE	CL	16.00	325.00-425.00
80	SANTA MOUSE	CL	12.50	125.00-250.00
80	WITCH MOUSE	CL	12.00	*
81	BARRISTER MOUSE	CL	16.00	375.00-400.00
81	BLUE DEVIL	CL	12.50	*
81	DOC MOUSE & PATIENT	CL	14.00	*
81	FLOWER GIRL	CL	15.00	275.00-300.00
81	GRADUATE MOUSE	CL	15.00	75.00-125.00
81	LITTLE DEVIL	CL	*	*
81	LITTLE GHOST	CL	8.50	*
81	LONE CAROLER	CL	15.50	275.00-375.00
81	MOM AND SQUEAKY CLEAN	CL	27.00	
81	MOTHER'S HELPER	CL	11.00	150.00-225.00
81	MOUSEY EXPRESS	CL	22.00	*
81	NURSE MOUSEY	CL	*	200.00-300.00
81	PEARL KNIT MOUSE	CL	20.00	100.00-225.00
81	SCHOOL MARM MOUSE	CL	19.50	*
81	THE CAROLERS	CL	29.00	300.00-450.00
82	ARTY MOUSE	CL	19.00	60.00
82	BABY SITTER	*	23.50	*
82	BEACH MOUSEY	CL	19.00	*
82	BEDDY-BYE MOUSEY	CL	29.00	*
82	BOY SWEETHEART	CL	13.50	300.00-350.00
82	EASTER BUNNY MOUSE	CL	18.00	*
82	GIRL SWEETHEART	CL	13.50	*
82	HAPPY BIRTHDAY!	CL	17.50	*
82	HOLLY MOUSE	CL	13.50	*
82	LAMPLIGHT CAROLERS	CL	46.00	100.00-175.00
82	LITTLE FIRE CHIEF	CL	29.00	300.00-400.00
82	LITTLE SLEDDERS	CL	33.50	150.00-175.00
82	LITTLEST ANGEL	CL	15.00	100.00
82	ME AND RAGGEDY ANN	CL	18.50	*
82	MISS TEACH & PUPIL	CL	29.50	300.00-350.00
82	MOON MOUSE	CL	15.50	300.00-400.00
82	MOUSEY'S TEDDY	CL	29.00	300.00
82	POOREST ANGEL	CL	15.00	100.00
82	SAY "CHEESE"	CL	15.50	250.00-300.00
82	SNOWMOUSE & FRIEND	CL	23.50	250.00-300.00
82	SWEETHEARTS	CL	26.00	350.00-400.00
82	TEA FOR TWO	CL	26.00	300.00-460.00
82	WEDDING MICE	CL	29.50	275.00
83	BIRTHDAY GIRL	CL	18.50	275.00-325.00
83	CHIEF GERONIMOUSE	*	21.00	150.00-175.00
83	CHRISTMAS MORNING	CL	35.00	100.00-200.00
83	CLOWN MOUSE	CL	22.00	300.00-400.00
83	CUPID MOUSE	CL	22.00	*
83	FIRST CHRISTMAS	CL	16.00	100.00-150.00
83	GET WELL SOON!	CL	15.00	200.00-300.00
83	HARVEST MOUSE	CL	23.00	200.00-325.00
83	MERRY CHRIS-MISS	CL	17.50	150.00-250.00
83	MERRY CHRIS-MOUSE	CL	16.00	150.00-200.00
83	MOUSE CALL	CL	24.00	200.00-650.00
83	MOUSEY NURSE	CL	15.00	200.00-300.00
83	MOUSEY'S CONE	*	22.00	*
83	MOUSEY'S DOLLHOUSE	CL	30.00	250.00-400.00
83	MOUSEY'S TRICYCLE	*	24.00	250.00-325.00
83	PACK MOUSE	CL	19.00	200.00-280.00
83	ROCKING TOT	CL	19.50	100.00-275.00
83	ROPE 'EM MOUSEY	CL	19.00	200.00-250.00
83	WASH DAY	CL	23.00	200.00-340.00
84	CAMPFIRE MOUSE	CL	26.00	200.00-250.00
84	CHRIS-MOUSE PAGEANT	*	38.00	*
84	FIRST DAY OF SCHOOL	CL	27.00	300.00-375.00
84	MOM & GINGER BAKER	*	38.00	325.00-585.00
84	PEN PAL MOUSEY	CL	26.00	275.00-300.00
84	PETER'S PUMPKIN	*	19.00	*
84	PRUDENCE PIE MAKER	*	18.50	*
84	SANTA'S TRAINEE	CL	36.50	*
84	SPRING GARDENER	CL	26.00	200.00-300.00
84	TIDY MOUSE	CL	38.00	250.00-350.00
84	TRAVELING MOUSE	CL	28.00	150.00-300.00
84	WITCHY BOO!	RT	21.00	*
85	ATTIC TREASURE	RT	42.00	*
85	CHRIS-MOUSE TREE	*	28.00	*
85	COME PLAY!	*	18.00	*

YR	NAME	LIMIT	ISSUE	QUOTE
85	FAMILY PORTRAIT	CL	54.00	170.00-225.00
85	FIELD MOUSE	*	46.00	*
85	MOUSE TALK	*	44.00	*
85	PAGEANT SHEPHERDS	CL	35.00	50.00-100.00
85	PAGEANT WISEMAN	CL	58.00	100.00-150.00
85	PIGGY-BACK MOUSEY	CL	28.00	150.00-300.00
85	QUILTING BEE	*	30.00	*
85	SHEPHERD KNEELING	*	20.00	*
85	SHEPHERD STANDING	*	20.00	*
85	STROLLING WITH BABY	*	42.00	*
85	SUNDAY DRIVERS	*	58.00	275.00
85	UNDER THE CHRIS-MOUSE TREE	*	48.00	*
85	WISEMAN IN ROBE	*	26.00	*
85	WISEMAN KNEELING	*	29.00	*
85	WISEMAN WITH TURBAN	*	28.00	*
86	CHRIST-MOUSE STOCKING	*	34.00	*
86	COME & GET IT!	CL	34.00	50.00-100.00
86	DOWN THE CHIMNEY	CL	48.00	100.00-170.00
86	FIRST DATE	*	60.00	*
86	FIRST HAIRCUT	*	58.00	200.00
86	FUN FLOAT	*	34.00	*
86	JUST CHECKING	*	34.00	*
86	MOUSE ON CAMPUS	CL	25.00	75.00-95.00
86	SWEET DREAMS	*	58.00	*
86	WALTZING MATILDA	*	48.00	*
87	BAT MOUSE	*	25.00	*
87	CHOIR MOUSE	CL	23.00	*
87	DON'T CRY!	CL	33.00	*
87	DRUMMER MOUSE	CL	29.00	40.00-90.00
87	LITTLEST WITCH	*	24.00	*
87	LITTLEST WITCH AND SKELETON	*	49.00	*
87	MARKET MOUSE	*	49.00	*
87	MISS NOEL	*	32.00	*
87	PAGEANT ANGEL	*	19.00	*
87	PAGEANT STABLE	*	56.00	*
87	SCOOTER MOUSE	*	39.00	100.00-150.00
87	SKELETON MOUSEY	*	27.00	*
87	THE RED WAGON	CL	59.00	95.00-135.00
87	TOOTH FAIRY	*	32.00	*
87	TRUMPETER	CL	29.00	40.00-70.00
87	TUBA PLAYER	CL	29.00	40.00-70.00
88	ALOHA!	*	32.00	280.00
88	FORTY WINKS	*	36.00	*
88	MOUSEY'S EASTER BASKET	*	32.00	100.00
89	COMMENCEMENT DAY	*	28.00	*
89	ELF TALES	RT	48.00	*
89	FATHER CHRIS-MOUSE	*	34.00	*
89	HAUNTED HOUSE	*	125.00	*
89	PRIMA BALLERINA	*	35.00	*
90	CHRIS-MOUSE SLIPPER	*	35.00	35.00
90	COLLEEN O'GREEN	*	40.00	40.00
90	HANS & GRETA	*	64.00	160.00
90	POLLY'S PARASOL	*	39.00	39.00
90	STARS & STRIPES	*	34.00	65.00
90	ZELDA	*	37.00	50.00
91	APRIL SHOWERS	*	27.00	27.00
91	GRAMMY-PHONE	*	75.00	75.00
91	LITTLE SQUIRT	*	49.00	49.00
91	MOUSIE'S EGG FACTORY	*	73.00	73.00
91	NIGHT PRAYER	*	52.00	52.00
91	RED RIDING HOOD/GRANDMOTHER'S HOUSE	*	295.00	295.00
91	SEA SOUNDS	*	34.00	50.00
91	SILENT NIGHT	*	64.00	100.00
91	TEA FOR THREE	*	135.00	175.00
91	THE NUTCRACKER	*	49.00	80.00
92	ADAM'S APPLES	OP	148.00	148.00
92	HIGH ON THE HOG	OP	52.00	52.00
92	MISS DAISY	OP	42.00	42.00
92	MRS. MOUSEY'S STUDIO	OP	150.00	150.00
92	PEEKABOO!	OP	52.00	52.00
92	SNOW BUDDIES	OP	58.00	100.00
92	THE OLD BLACK STOVE	OP	130.00	130.00

A. PETERSEN

MOUSE SPORTS

YR	NAME	LIMIT	ISSUE	QUOTE
75	BOBSLED THREE	CL	12.00	*
75	SKATER MOUSE	CL	14.00	250.00-400.00
76	MOUSE SKIER	CL	12.50	250.00-400.00

YR NAME	LIMIT	ISSUE	QUOTE
76 TENNIS STAR	CL	10.50	150.00-275.00
77 GOLFER MOUSE	CL	15.50	*
77 SKATING STAR MOUSE	CL	9.00	250.00-500.00
80 SKATER MOUSE	CL	18.00	200.00-325.00
80 SKIER MOUSE	CL	13.00	*
81 GOLFER MOUSE	CL	17.00	200.00-350.00
82 TWO IN A CANOE	*	29.00	*
84 LAND HO!	CL	46.00	150.00
84 TENNIS ANYONE?	CL	18.00	125.00
85 FISHIN' CHIP	*	46.00	300.00
89 JOE DI'MOUSIO	*	39.00	*
A. PETERSEN			**OWLS**
74 MR. AND MRS. OWL	CL	19.00	300.00-375.00
74 MR. OWL	CL	10.50	100.00-200.00
74 MRS. OWL	CL	8.50	100.00-200.00
75 COLONIAL OWLS	CL	11.50	*
79 "GRAD" OWL	CL	12.50	*
80 GRADUATE OWL	CL	12.00	*
A. PETERSEN			**PIGGIES**
78 BOY PIGLET/PICNIC PIGGY	CL	12.00	100.00-125.00
78 GIRL PIGLET/PICNIC PIGGY	CL	12.00	100.00-125.00
78 JOLLY TAR PIGGY	CL	10.00	100.00-125.00
78 MISS PIGGY SCHOOL MARM	CL	12.00	100.00-225.00
78 PICNIC PIGGIES	CL	24.00	200.00-300.00
78 PIGGY BAKER	CL	14.50	100.00-225.00
78 PIGGY JOGGER	CL	13.50	100.00-125.00
80 NURSE PIGGY	CL	15.50	100.00-200.00
80 PIG O' MY HEART	CL	13.50	100.00-150.00
80 PIGGY BALLERINA	CL	15.50	100.00-175.00
80 PIGGY POLICEMAN	CL	17.50	100.00-200.00
81 HOLLY HOG	CL	25.00	100.00-225.00
A. PETERSEN			**RACCOONS**
77 HIKER RACCOON	CL	12.00	200.00-325.00
77 MOTHER RACCOON	CL	11.50	200.00-300.00
78 BIRD WATCHER RACCOON	CL	22.50	200.00-350.00
78 RACCOON SKATER	CL	12.00	200.00-400.00
79 RACCOON SKIER	CL	14.00	150.00-250.00
A. PETERSEN			**ROBIN HOOD SERIES**
90 FRIAR TUCK	*	32.00	32.00
90 MAID MARION	*	32.00	32.00
90 ROBIN HOOD	*	37.00	37.00
D. PETERSEN			**TINY TEDDIES**
83 TINY TEDDY	CL	16.00	100.00-200.00
84 BOO BEAR	SU	26.00	*
84 DRUMMER BEAR	SU	28.00	*
84 HUGGY BEAR	SU	26.00	*
84 LITTLE TEDDY	CL	26.00	100.00-150.00
84 RIDE 'EM TEDDY!	SU	38.00	*
84 SAILOR TEDDY	SU	26.00	*
84 SANTA BEAR	SU	33.00	*
84 SEASIDE TEDDY	SU	32.00	*
87 CHRISTMAS TEDDY	SU	26.00	*
87 WEDDING BEARS	SU	54.00	*
88 HANSEL & GRETEL/WITCH'S HOUSE	SU	175.00	*
89 MOMMA BEAR	SU	27.00	*
A. PETERSEN			**WIND IN THE WILLOWS**
82 BADGER	CL	18.00	200.00-300.00
82 MOLE	CL	18.00	200.00-300.00
82 RATTY	CL	18.00	200.00-300.00
82 TOAD	CL	18.00	200.00-300.00

WHITLEY BAY

L. HEYDA

			SANTA SERIES
87 GLOBE	10,000	225.00	225.00
87 SANTA	10,000	150.00	150.00
89 ELF	10,000	225.00	225.00
89 ENTRY	10,000	275.00	275.00
89 HUG	10,000	225.00	225.00
89 LETTERS	10,000	375.00	375.00
89 LISTS	10,000	275.00	275.00
89 SLEIGH	10,000	375.00	375.00

Ornaments

Clara Johnson Scroggins

Who would have guessed that one day ornament manufacturers would sponsor collector's clubs, offer special "member's only issues" and host gatherings at which "event-only" ornaments could be purchased on a limited basis?

Who could have predicted that one day collectors would be insuring their collections, carefully ascertaining reliable secondary market values for the appraisal of their ornaments? Or cataloging their collections with the aid of sourcebooks and storing their collections, carefully logged and labeled, in climate controlled quarters?

Who could have known that "first in a series" would be a phrase that sent shivers down the spines of collectors and into a buying frenzy or that one day ornaments would sell on the "secondary market" for up to 10 times their original retail value?

That's the point to which ornament collecting has evolved today. And did you notice that these once holiday-only items are rarely referred to as Christmas ornaments in today's marketplace? Ornament makers have broadened their scope to include more than just Yuletide treasures, thus making ornaments a year-round collectible. Easter, Independence Day and Thanksgiving are just some of the holidays which are often commemorated in the form of ornaments. Producers are also personalizing ornaments, making them wonderful gifts for friends and loved ones.

But more importantly, and perhaps more than any other collectible, ornaments reflect the changes in our life and times. From the early beginnings of elegant European blown glass, to the lively and often humorous artplas ornaments of today, this is a collectible that transcends all areas of passions and interests. Ornaments offer something for everyone. The themes are so varied and the media so diverse, this is a collectible with an affinity for the unique. Children thrill in owning an ornament depicting their favorite sports figure and delight in the ornaments featuring licensed characters from their favorite movies or products. Hallmark, Enesco and Carlton are just a few of the makers leading the way in this ever-changing industry rapidly aligning itself with the era of pop culture.

Timeless themes also abound in this diverse class of collecting as well. Generations-old themes, mediums and traditions are even more prevalent, and perhaps just as popular, as the "here today, gone tomorrow" themes of the '90s. Nostalgic collectors entranced by the magical look of blown glass can revel in the designs brought back by today's importers and makers such as Old World Christmas, Christopher Radko and Kurt S. Adler. Crystal, sterling silver and porcelain offered by Reed and Barton, Anna-Perenna, Swarovski and many, many more offer a variety of appealing themes in media just as alluring.

What drives the secondary market of this somewhat new arena? Perhaps its diversity is its greatest thrust. In an industry producing for the masses, it's only logical that the laws of supply and demand would dictate the growth of the secondary market. Sports collectors, car enthusiasts, train aficionados, bear lovers, angel adorers and animation zealots frequently "cross over" to the realm of ornament collecting when the subject matter lends itself to their particular area of interest—which it often does. The competition to attain an ornament aligned with that area of interest often makes buying it at the retail level somewhat difficult. That's where the secondary market begins. And so too does our chapter on the prices and trends of perhaps the world's most popular collectible.

CLARA JOHNSON SCROGGINS, who has authored six books on Hallmark ornaments, is a consultant and speaker who appears at collectible events around the country. Her ornament collection is recognized as the largest in the country.

ORNAMENTS

YR	NAME	LIMIT	ISSUE	QUOTE

AMERICAN GREETINGS

AMERICAN GREETINGS CHRISTMAS ORNAMENTS

YR	NAME	LIMIT	ISSUE	QUOTE
80	ACRYLIC DISC-HOLLY HOBBIE C-23	YR	1.75	5.00
80	ACRYLIC DISC-MOTHER C-22	YR	1.75	4.00
80	STRAWBERRY SHORTCAKE/XMAS SUGARPLUM C-27	CL	3.50	4.00
81	ACRYLIC DISC-FIRST XMAS TOGETHER WXX-240	YR	4.00	4.00
81	ACRYLIC DISC-HOLLY HOBBIE WXX-239	YR	4.00	5.00
81	ACRYLIC DISC-MOTHER WXX-237	YR	4.00	5.00
81	ACRYLIC DISC-ZIGGY & FRIENDS WXX-236	YR	4.00	5.00
81	PORCELAIN HOLLY HOBBIE WXX-56	CL	3.00	4.00
82	ACRYLIC DISC-FRIENDSHIP/DESIGN WXO-32	YR	5.00	6.00
82	HOLLY HOB. PLUM PUDD PORCLN BELL WXO-45	CL	5.25	5.25
82	HOLLY HOBBIE FIG. PORCLN BELL WXO-48	YR	12.00	14.00
83	ACRYLIC DISC-FIRST XMAS TOGETHER CO-1901	YR	5.75	7.00
83	ACRYLIC DISC-FRIENDSHIP CO-1902	YR	5.75	7.00
83	ACRYLIC DISC-LOVE CO-1903	YR	5.75	7.00
83	HIMSELF THE ELF/PORC. BELL CO-1403	CL	12.00	12.00
83	RELIGIOUS ACRYLIC DISC CO-1904	YR	5.75	7.00
83	STRAWBERRY SHORTCAKE/PORC. BELL CO-1401	CL	12.00	12.00
83	STRWBRRY SHORTCAKE..SPECIAL GIFT CO-1225	CL	9.00	12.00
83	ZIGGY PORCELAIN FIGURINE BELL CO-1402	CL	12.00	12.00
84	CAREBEARS DECORATING THE TREE AO-1102	CL	15.00	20.00
84	HIMSELF THE ELF SCULPTED ORN. AO-407	CL	7.50	7.50
84	HOLLY HOBBIE CERAMIC FIGURE BELL AO-701	CL	10.00	10.00
84	HOLLY HOBBIE SCULPTED ORNAMENT AO-403	CL	7.50	15.00
84	MUSICAL-BABY'S FIRST CHRISTMAS AO-1001	YR	17.50	22.50
84	STRAWBERRY SHORTCAKE & FRIENDS AO-1101	CL	15.00	30.00
84	STRWBRRY SHORTCAKE SCULPTED ORN. AO-402	CL	9.00	12.00
84	TENDERHEART BEAR SCULPTED ORN. AO-406	CL	6.50	10.00
85	BABY'S FIRST CHRISTMAS BX-302	YR	7.00	10.00
85	HOLLY HOBBIE PORCELAIN/BELL BX-901	YR	10.00	10.00
85	MOUSE ON WATCH BX-303	CL	7.00	7.00
85	ZIGGY & FRIENDS ADMIRING TREE BX-1102	CL	13.00	13.00
86	ACRYLIC DISC A WREATH OF LOVE DX-503	CL	3.75	5.00
86	ACRYLIC DISC BABY'S FIRST XMAS DX-504	YR	3.75	5.00
86	ACRYLIC DISC FIRST XMAS TOGETHER DX-502	YR	3.75	5.00
86	ACRYLIC DISC SPECIAL FRIEND DX-501	YR	3.75	5.00
86	BABY'S FIRST CHRISTMAS DX-1609	CL	7.50	10.00
86	CERAMIC BELL BABY'S FIRST XMAS DX-1002	YR	6.50	8.00
86	CERAMIC BELL CHRISTMAS IS LOVE DX-1003	CL	6.50	6.50
86	CERAMIC BELL FIRST XMAS TOGETHER DX-1001	YR	6.50	13.00
86	GONE FISHIN' DX-1605	CL	8.00	8.00
86	OUT W/OLD IN W/NEW - ZIGGY DX-1501	YR	6.50	6.50
87	BRASS SAILBOAT CX-702	YR	6.50	6.50
87	CERAMIC OLD-FASHIONED TEDDY CX-402	CL	5.00	5.00
87	IRIDESCENT UNICORN CX-203	CL	4.00	4.00
87	PORCELAIN BELLS 1ST XMAS TOGETHER CX-302	YR	6.50	6.50
87	PORCELAIN BELLS BABY'S FIRST XMAS CX-301	YR	6.50	6.50
87	SCULPTED DIMEN. 1ST XMAS TOGETHER CX-104	YR	7.00	9.00
87	SCULPTED DIMEN./BOY FIRST XMAS CX-403	YR	7.50	9.00
87	SCULPTED DIMEN./CAROUSEL HORSE CX-801	CL	8.50	8.50
87	SCULPTED DIMEN./GIRL FIRST XMAS CX-404	YR	7.50	9.00
87	SCULPTED DIMEN./SANTA REF CX-112	YR	7.00	7.00
87	WOODEN ORNAMENT ROCKING HORSE CX-1104	YR	3.25	5.00
87	WOODEN ORNAMENT ZIGGY & FUZZ CX-1003	CL	4.50	4.50
88	ACRYLIC DISC FIRST XMAS TOGETHER AX-1007	YR	4.00	5.00
88	ACRYLIC DISC MADONNA & CHILD AX-1039	UD	4.25	4.25
88	BABY BOY'S FIRST XMAS AX-1004	YR	7.50	7.50
88	BABY GIRL'S FIRST XMAS AX-1005	YR	7.50	7.50
88	BABY'S FIRST XMAS PHOTO FRAME AX-1001	YR	5.00	5.00
88	BOWLING MOUSE AX-1017	UD	7.00	7.00
88	BRASS OUR HOME TO YOUR HOME AX-1010	YR	5.50	5.50
88	CAROUSEL HORSE AX-1040	UD	8.50	8.50
88	CERAMIC COW BELL AX-1034	UD	6.50	6.50
88	COPPER REINDEER WEATHERVANE	YR	4.50	4.50
88	LOVEBIRDS FIRST XMAS TOGETHER AX-1006	YR	7.00	7.00
88	MUSICAL ZIGGY & FUZZ FRIENDSHIP AX-1013	YR	7.00	7.00
88	NEW YEAR ZIGGY AX-1049	YR	6.50	6.50
88	ROCKING HORSE BABY'S FIRST XMAS AX-1003	YR	3.50	3.50
89	ACRYLIC DISC REWORK DX-1012	YR	4.24	4.25
89	BEAR ON ROCKING HORSE DX-1001	YR	7.95	7.95
89	BEAR ON ROCKING HORSE DX-1002	YR	7.95	7.95
89	BEAR ON ROCKING HORSE DX-1030	YR	7.50	7.50

YR	NAME	LIMIT	ISSUE	QUOTE
89	BRASS SAILBOAT DX-1022	YR	6.50	6.50
89	BUNNIES IN SWING DX-1005	YR	8.50	8.50
89	CAMEO-LOOK DOVE DISK DX-1016	YR	5.95	5.95
89	COOKING BEAR DX-1029	YR	7.50	7.50
89	DEER LEAPING OVER LANDSCAPE DX-1004	YR	4.95	4.95
89	DINOSAUR DRIVING TRAIN DX-1010	YR	7.95	7.95
89	HEART PHOTO FRAME-CANDY CANE DX-1023	YR	5.95	5.95
89	HEART SHAPE W/HOLLY DX-1007	YR	5.95	5.95
89	KITTEN IN STOCKING DX-1011	YR	4.50	4.50
89	LACE-LOOK BEAR EMBROID HOOP DX-1003	YR	5.50	5.50
89	NAUTICAL-LIFE RING W/HOLLY DX-1028	YR	5.95	5.95
89	PAPER DOLL CHAIN ON CERAMIC BELL DX-1009	YR	6.95	6.95
89	POLAR BEARS HOLDING HANDS DX-1035	YR	6.95	6.95
89	VICTORIAN EMBROIDERY HOOP DX-1008	YR	6.50	6.50
89	VICTORIAN HOUSE DX-1013	YR	4.50	4.50
89	WOOD DISC W/TREE DX-1033	YR	4.50	4.50
89	WOOD HEART W/SILK MISTLETOE DX-1015	YR	4.50	4.50
89	ZIGGY ELF W/JINGLE BELLS DX-1014	YR	6.95	6.95
90	2 BEARS W/GIFT ON SLED DX-1010	YR	4.50	4.50
90	ANGEL HOLDING HEART DX-1012	YR	4.50	4.50
90	BEAR ON BLOCK DX-1001	YR	7.95	7.95
90	BEAR ON BLOCK DX-1002	YR	7.95	7.95
90	BEAR ON ROCKING HORSE DX-1003	YR	4.50	4.50
90	BEARS PUTTING STAR ON XMAS TREE DX-1007	YR	5.95	5.95
90	BI-PLANE WITH SANTA DX-1015	YR	7.95	7.95
90	BIRDS IN MAILBOX DX-1008	YR	6.95	6.95
90	CAROUSEL REINDEER DX-1033	YR	7.95	7.95
90	CONV. HEART SHAPED DISC W/LTG. DX-1006	YR	5.50	5.50
90	FATHER CHRISTMAS DX-1035	YR	7.50	7.50
90	NATIVITY..CHRIST CHILD DX-1019	YR	5.50	5.50
90	SLEIGH & HOUSE DX-1009	YR	5.95	5.95
90	TOY SOLDIER W/DRUM DX-1034	YR	5.95	5.95
90	VICKY BELL DX-1014	YR	7.50	7.50

ANHEUSER-BUSCH INC.

* *

				A & EAGLE COLLECTOR ORNAMENT SERIES
91	BUDWEISER GIRL N3178	OP	15.00	15.00
92	1893 COLUMBIAN EXPOSITION N3649	OP	15.00	15.00
93	GREATEST TRIUMPH N4089	OP	15.00	15.00

S. SAMPSON — **CHRISTMAS ORNAMENT SERIES**

92	CLYDESDALES MINI PLATE ORNAMENTS N3650	OP	23.00	23.00
93	BUDWEISER 6-PK MINI PLATE ORN. N4220	OP	10.00	10.00

ANNA-PERENNA

P. BUCKLEY MOSS

93	SECOND ANGEL	YR	27.50	40.00-60.00
93	THE SNOWMAN	YR	27.50	50.00-90.00
94	CHRISTMAS SKATERS	YR	27.50	27.50
94	THIRD ANGEL	YR	27.50	40.00-60.00

P. BUCKLEY MOSS — **ANNUAL CHRISTMAS ORNAMENTS**

91	NOEL	*	25.00	25.00
92	SLEIGHRIDE	*	27.50	27.50

ANNALEE MOBILITEE

A. THORNDIKE   *****

93	3" BEAR ORNAMENT W/ STAND	OP	12.95	12.95
93	5" GINGERBREAD BOY ORNAMENT	OP	16.95	16.95
93	DEER HEAR ORNAMENT	OP	34.50	34.50-750.00
93	SANTA HEAD ORNAMENT	OP	8.95	8.95
93	SNOWMAN HEAD ORNAMENT	OP	11.45	11.45
94	3" SUN W/SANTA HAT ORNAMENT	12,881	7.95	7.95
94	5" GINGERBREAD BOY ORNAMENT	4,512	17.50	17.50
94	5" OLD WORLD SANTA ORN.	7,540	23.50	23.50
94	7" SANTA HEAD ORNAMENT	12,616	9.50	9.50
94	7" SNOWMAN HEAD ORNAMENT	10,062	11.95	11.95
94	DEER HEAR ORNAMENT	8,858	10.50	10.50
94	PEPI HERRMAN CRYSTAL ORNAMENT	OP	29.95	29.95

A. THORNDIKE — **CHRISTMAS ORNAMENTS**

82	ELF HEAD	1908	2.95	25.00
83	GINGERBREAD BOY	11,835	10.95	35.00
84	SNOWMAN HEAD	13,677	7.95	25.00-30.00
84	STAR	3275	5.95	25.00
85	3 IN. ANGEL ON CLOUD	*	6.50	30.00
85	SUN	1692	6.50	25.00
86	ANGEL HEAD	*	7.95	30.00
86	BABY ANGEL	YR	11.95	35.00
86	CLOWN HEAD	5701	7.95	25.00

YR	NAME	LIMIT	ISSUE	QUOTE

ANRI
*
			DISNEY FOUR STAR COLLECTION	
89	MAESTRO MICKEY	YR	25.00	25.00
90	MINNIE MOUSE	YR	25.00	25.00

J. FERRANDIZ
			FERRANDIZ MESSAGE COLLECTION	
89	LET THE HEAVENS RING	1000	215.00	215.00
90	HEAR THE ANGELS SING	1000	225.00	225.00

J. FERRANDIZ
			FERRANDIZ WOODCARVINGS	
88	HEAVENLY DRUMMER	1000	175.00	225.00
89	HEAVENLY STRINGS	1000	190.00	190.00

ARMANI
G. AMANI
				CHRISTMAS
92	1992 CHRISTMAS ORNAMENT 788F	YR	23.50	23.50
91	1991 CHRISTMAS ORNAMENT 799A	RT	11.50	11.50

ARTAFFECTS
G. PERILLO
			ANNUAL BELL ORNAMENT	
85	HOME SWEET WIGWAM	OP	14.00	14.00
86	PEEK-A-BOO	OP	15.00	33.00
87	ANNUAL BELL ORNAMENT	YR	15.00	33.00
88	ANNUAL BELL ORNAMENT	YR	17.50	17.50
89	ANNUAL BELL ORNAMENT	YR	17.50	17.50
90	ANNUAL BELL ORNAMENT	YR	17.50	17.50
91	ANNUAL BELL ORNAMENT	YR	19.50	19.50

G. PERILLO
			ANNUAL CHRISTMAS	
85	PAPOOSE ORNAMENT	YR	14.00	33.00-46.00
86	CHRISTMAS CACTUS	YR	15.00	50.00
87	ANNUAL ORNAMENT	YR	15.00	35.00
88	ANNUAL ORNAMENT	YR	17.50	25.00
89	ANNUAL ORNAMENT	YR	17.50	25.00
90	ANNUAL ORNAMENT	YR	17.50	17.50
91	ANNUAL ORNAMENT	YR	19.50	19.50

G. PERILLO
			KACHINA ORNAMENTS	
91	DAWN KACHINA	OP	17.50	17.50
91	KACHINA MOTHER	OP	17.50	17.50
91	OLD KACHINA	OP	17.50	17.50
91	SNOW KACHINA	OP	17.50	17.50
91	SUN KACHINA	OP	17.50	17.50
91	TOTEM KACHINA	OP	17.50	17.50

G. PERILLO
			SAGEBRUSH KIDS BELL ORNAMENT	
87	CHRISTMAS CANDLE	OP	9.00	9.00
87	CHRISTMAS HORN	OP	9.00	9.00
87	THE CAROLERS	OP	9.00	9.00
87	THE FIDDLER	OP	9.00	9.00
87	THE GIFT	OP	9.00	9.00
87	THE HARPIST	OP	9.00	9.00

G. PERILLO
			SAGEBRUSH KIDS COLLECTION	
91	MOCCASIN ORNAMENT	OP	15.00	15.00
91	SHIELD ORNAMENT	OP	15.00	15.00
91	TEE-PEE ORNAMENT	OP	15.00	15.00

C. ROEDA
			SIMPLE WONDERS	
91	ASHLEY	OP	22.50	22.50
91	BRITTANY	OP	22.50	22.50
91	KIM	OP	22.50	22.50
91	LITTLE FEATHER	OP	22.50	22.50
91	MEGAN	OP	22.50	22.50
91	NICOLE	OP	22.50	22.50
92	SWEET SURPRISE	YR	15.00	15.00

ARTHUR COURT DESIGNS
A. COURT
			CHRISTMAS ORNAMENT SERIES	
94	BUNNIES ON A SLEIGH	8200	22.00	24.00

ARTISTS OF THE WORLD
T. DEGRAZIA
			ANNUAL ORNAMENT	
93	WARM WISHES	YR	65.00	75.00
94	LITTLE PRAYER	YR	49.50	52.00

T. DEGRAZIA
			DEGRAZIA ANNUAL ORNAMENTS	
86	PIMA, INDIAN DRUMMER BOY	YR	27.50	300.00-450.00
87	WHITE DOVE	YR	29.50	75.00
88	FLOWER GIRL	YR	32.50	45.00-50.00
89	FLOWER BOY	YR	35.00	45.00-50.00
90	MERRY LITTLE INDIAN	10,000	87.50	95.00-100.00
90	PINK PAPOOSE	YR	35.00	45.00-50.00
91	CHRISTMAS PRAYER	YR	49.50	49.50
92	BEARING GIFT	YR	55.00	55.00
93	LIGHTING THE WAY	YR	57.50	57.50

YR	NAME	LIMIT	ISSUE	QUOTE

BIEDERMANN & SONS

YR	NAME	LIMIT	ISSUE	QUOTE
93	BABY'S FIRST CHRISTMAS	400	12.00	13.50
93	FOUR CALLING BIRDS (BRASS)	RT	12.50	18.50
93	FOUR CALLING BIRDS (SILVER)	500	18.00	55.00
94	BABY'S FIRST CHRISTMAS	400	12.00	12.50
94	DRUMMER BOY (BRASS)	14,500	12.50	18.00
94	DRUMMER BOY (SILVER)	500	18.00	140.00

BING & GRONDAHL
J. WOODSON
CHRISTMAS IN AMERICA

YR	NAME	LIMIT	ISSUE	QUOTE
86	CHRISTMAS EVE IN WILLIAMSBURG	CL	12.50	90.00
87	CHRISTMAS EVE AT THE WHITE HOUSE	CL	15.00	15.00
88	CHRISTMAS EVE AT ROCKEFELLER CENTER	CL	18.50	18.50
89	CHRISTMAS IN NEW ENGLAND	YR	20.00	20.00
90	CHRISTMAS EVE AT THE CAPITOL	YR	20.00	20.00
91	INDEPENDENCE HALL	YR	23.50	23.50
92	CHRISTMAS IN SAN FRANCISCO	YR	25.00	25.00
93	COMING HOME FOR CHRISTMAS	YR	25.00	25.00

H. HANSEN
SANTA CLAUS

YR	NAME	LIMIT	ISSUE	QUOTE
89	SANTA'S WORKSHOP	YR	20.00	20.00
90	SANTA'S SLEIGH	YR	20.00	20.00
91	THE JOURNEY	YR	23.50	23.50
92	SANTA'S ARRIVAL	YR	25.00	25.00
93	SANTA'S GIFTS	YR	25.00	25.00

BRANDYWINE WOODCRAFTS
M. WHITING
WILLIAMSBURG ORNAMENTS

YR	NAME	LIMIT	ISSUE	QUOTE
94	GUNSMITH	350	9.50	12.00

BRIERCROFT
B. FARLOW

YR	NAME	LIMIT	ISSUE	QUOTE
94	BELL ANGEL	5000	6.00	10.00

BUCCELLATI
G. BUCCELLATI

YR	NAME	LIMIT	ISSUE	QUOTE
93	CHRISTMAS CANDLE	500	300.00	320.00
94	CHRISTMAS FIREPLACE	500	300.00	320.00

*
CHRISTMAS ORNAMENTS

YR	NAME	LIMIT	ISSUE	QUOTE
86	SNOWY VILLAGE SCENE-2464	500	195.00	400.00
87	SHOOTING STAR-2469	500	240.00	350.00
88	SANTA CLAUS-2470	500	225.00	300.00
89	CHRISTMAS TREE-2471	750	230.00	230.00
90	ZENITH-2479	750	250.00	250.00
91	WREATH-3561	750	300.00	300.00
92	CHERUBS 3562	500	300.00	300.00

CARRIAGE HOUSE STUDIO INC.
M. FURLONG
GIFTS FROM GOD

YR	NAME	LIMIT	ISSUE	QUOTE
85	THE CHARIS ANGEL	3000	45.00	100.00
86	THE ANGEL OF LIGHT	3000	45.00	100.00
86	THE HALLELUJAH ANGEL	3000	45.00	125.00
88	THE CELESTIAL ANGEL	3000	45.00	100.00
89	CORONATION ANGEL	3000	45.00	45.00-75.00

M. FURLONG
JOYEUX NOEL

YR	NAME	LIMIT	ISSUE	QUOTE
90	CELEBRATION ANGEL	10,000	45.00	45.00
91	THANKSGIVING ANGEL	10,000	45.00	45.00
92	JOYEUX NOEL ANGEL	10,000	45.00	45.00

M. FURLONG
MUSICAL SERIES

YR	NAME	LIMIT	ISSUE	QUOTE
80	THE CAROLER	3000	50.00	100.00
81	THE LYRIST	3000	45.00	50.00-75.00
82	THE LUTIST	3000	45.00	75.00
83	THE CONCERTINIST	3000	45.00	75.00
84	THE HERALD ANGEL	3000	45.00	55.00-100.00

CAVANAUGH GROUP
COCA-COLA BRAND HISTORICAL BUILDING

YR	NAME	LIMIT	ISSUE	QUOTE
91	1930's SERVICE STATION	CL	9.99	12.00
91	EARLY COCA-COLA BOTTLING COMPANY	CL	9.99	12.00
91	JACOB'S PHARMACY	CL	9.99	12.00
91	PEMBERTON HOUSE, THE	CL	9.99	12.00

COCA-COLA BRAND NORTH POLE BOTTLING WORKS

YR	NAME	LIMIT	ISSUE	QUOTE
93	BLAST OFF	OP	8.99	9.00
93	DELIVERY FOR SANTA	OP	8.99	9.00
93	FILL'ER UP	CL	8.99	10.00
93	ICE SCULPTING	OP	8.99	9.00
93	LONG WINTER'S NAP	OP	8.99	9.00
93	NORTH POLE EXPRESS	CL	8.99	10.00
93	THIRSTING FOR ADVENTURE	CL	8.99	10.00

YR	NAME	LIMIT	ISSUE	QUOTE
93	TOPS ON REFRESHMENT	OP	8.99	9.00
94	POWER DRIVE	OP	8.99	9.00
94	SANTA'S RESTAURANT	OP	8.99	9.00
94	SELTZER SURPRISE	OP	8.99	9.00
94	TOPS OFF REFRESHMENT	OP	8.99	9.00
	COCA-COLA BRAND POLAR BEAR COLLECTION			
94	DOWNHILL SLEDDER	OP	8.99	9.00
94	NORTH POLE DELIVERY	OP	8.99	9.00
94	SKATING COCA-COLA POLAR BEAR	OP	8.99	9.00
94	VNEDING MACHINE MISCHIEF	OP	8.99	9.00
SUNDBLOM		**COCA-COLA BRAND TRIM A TREE COLLECTION**		
90	HAPPY HOLIDAYS	CL	9.99	13.00
90	MERRY CHRISTMAS AND A HAPPY NEW YEAR	CL	9.99	52.50
90	SANTA ON STOOL	CL	9.99	13.00
90	SEASON'S GREETINGS	CL	9.99	13.00
91	A TIME TO SHARE	CL	9.99	12.00
91	CHRISTMAS IS LOVE	CL	9.99	12.00
92	HAPPY HOLIDAYS	CL	9.99	11.50
92	SSSHHH!	CL	9.99	11.50
93	DECORATING THE TREE	CL	9.99	11.00
93	EXTRA BRIGHT REFRESHMENT	CL	9.99	11.00
93	TRAVEL REFRESHED	CL	9.99	11.00
94	BUSY MAN'S PAUSE	OP	9.99	10.00
94	FOR SPARKLING HOLIDAYS	OP	9.99	10.00
94	THINGS GO BETTER WITH COKE	OP	9.99	10.00
	MEMBER ORNAMENT			
94	FISHING BEAR	YR	*	
95	HOSPITALITY - SANTA	YR	*	
93	HO HO HO - SANTA	YR	*	

CAZENOVIA ABROAD

*			**CHRISTMAS ORNAMENTS**	
68	BUNNY P104B	*	9.00	34.00-45.00
68	CAT P105C	*	9.00	34.00-45.00
68	DUCK P103D	*	9.00	34.00-45.00
68	ELEPHANT P102E	*	9.00	34.00-45.00
68	ROOSTER P106R	*	10.00	34.00-45.00
68	STANDING ANGEL P107SA	*	9.00	39.00-52.50
68	TEDDY BEAR P101TB	*	9.00	34.00-45.00
68	TIPTOE ANGEL P108TTA	*	10.00	34.00-45.00
69	FAWN P109F	*	12.00	45.00
70	PEACE P111P	*	12.00	45.00
70	PORKY P112PK	*	15.00	45.00
70	SNOW MAN P110SM	*	12.00	45.00
71	KNEELING ANGEL P113KA	*	15.00	48.00-65.00
72	ROCKING HORSE P114RH	*	15.00	48.00-65.00
73	TREETOP ANGEL P115TOP	*	10.00	37.00-50.00
74	OWL P116O	*	15.00	45.00
75	STAR P117ST	*	15.00	45.00
76	HATCHING CHICK P118CH	*	15.00	45.00
77	RAGGEDY ANN P119RA	*	17.50	39.00-52.50
78	SHELL P120SH	*	20.00	34.00-45.00
79	TOY SOLDIER P121TS	*	20.00	34.00-45.00
80	BURRO P122BU	*	20.00	34.00-45.00
81	CLOWN P123CL	*	25.00	34.00-45.00
82	REBECCA P124RE	*	25.00	34.00-45.00
83	MOUSE P126MO	*	27.50	39.00-52.50
83	RAGGEDY ANDY P125AND	*	27.50	39.00-52.50
84	CHERUB P127CB	*	30.00	39.00-52.50
84	REINDEER & SLEIGH H100	*	1250.00	1500.00
85	SHAGGY DOG P132SD	*	45.00	50.00
86	BIG SISTER P134BS	*	60.00	60.00
86	LITTLE BROTHER P135LB	*	55.00	55.00
86	PETER RABBIT P133PR	*	50.00	50.00
87	LAMB P136LA	*	60.00	60.00
87	SEA HORSE P137SE	*	35.00	26.00-35.00
88	PARTRIDGE P138PA	*	70.00	70.00
88	SQUIRREL P139SQ	*	70.00	70.00
89	SWAN P140SW	OP	45.00	45.00
90	MORAVIAN STAR P141PS	OP	65.00	65.00
91	ANGEL P144A	OP	63.00	63.00
91	BUNNY RABBIT P143BR	OP	65.00	65.00
91	HEDGEHOG P142HH	OP	65.00	65.00
92	HUMPTY DUMPTY P145HD	OP	70.00	70.00

YR	NAME	LIMIT	ISSUE	QUOTE

CYBIS
*
			CHRISTMAS COLLECTION	
83	1983 HOLIDAY BELL	YR	145.00	1000.00
84	1984 HOLIDAY BELL	YR	145.00	700.00
85	1985 HOLIDAY ANGEL	YR	75.00	500.00
86	1986 HOLIDAY CHERUB ORNAMENT	YR	75.00	500.00
87	1987 HEAVENLY ANGELS	YR	95.00	400.00
88	1988 HOLIDAY ORNAMENT	YR	95.00	375.00

DAVE GROSSMAN CREATIONS

94	TRIPLE SELF PORTRAIT	OP	30.00	35.00
94			*	
		ANNUAL LIMITED EDITION BALL ORNAMENT		
93	GRANPS	YR	24.00	28.00
94	COMMEMORATIVE	YR	6.00	8.00
		ANNUAL LIMITED EDITION FIGURINE ORNAMENT		
93	GRANPS	YR	6.00	8.00
94	MERRY CHRISTMAS	*	24.00	28.00

D. GROSSMAN — **ANNUAL ROCKWELL BALL ORNAMENTS**

75	SANTA WITH FEATHER QUILL	RT	3.50	25.00
76	SANTA AT GLOBE	RT	4.00	20.00
77	GRANDPA ON ROCKING HORSE	RT	4.00	15.00
78	SANTA WITH MAP	RT	4.50	15.00
79	SANTA AT DESK WITH MAIL BAG	RT	5.00	15.00
80	SANTA ASLEEP WITH TOYS	RT	5.00	12.00
81	SANTA WITH BOY ON FINGER	RT	5.00	10.00
82	SANTA FACE ON WINTER SCENE	RT	5.00	10.00
83	COACHMAN WITH WHIP	RT	5.00	10.00
84	CHRISTMAS BOUNTY MAN	RT	5.00	10.00
85	OLD ENGLISH TRIO	RT	5.00	10.00
86	TINY TIM ON SHOULDER	RT	5.00	5.00
87	SKATING LESSON	RT	5.00	5.00
88	BIG MOMENT	RT	5.50	5.50
89	DISCOVERY	RT	6.00	6.00
90	BRINGING HOME THE TREE	RT	6.00	6.00
91	DOWNHILL DARING	RT	6.00	6.00
92	ON THE ICE	YR	6.00	6.00

D. GROSSMAN — **ANNUAL ROCKWELL FIGURINE ORNAMENTS**

78	CAROLER	RT	15.00	75.00
79	DRUM FOR TOMMY	RT	20.00	50.00
80	SANTA'S GOOD BOYS	RT	20.00	40.00
81	LETTERS TO SANTA	RT	20.00	40.00
82	CORNETTIST	RT	20.00	30.00
83	FIDDLER	RT	20.00	30.00
84	CHRISTMAS BOUNTY	RT	20.00	30.00
85	JOLLY COACHMAN	RT	20.00	30.00
86	GRANDPA AND ROCKING HORSE	RT	20.00	35.00
87	SKATING LESSON	RT	20.00	30.00
88	BIG MOMENT	RT	20.00	30.00
89	DISCOVERY	RT	20.00	25.00
90	BRINGING HOME THE TREE	RT	20.00	20.00
91	DOWNHILL DARING	RT	20.00	20.00
92	ON THE ICE	YR	20.00	20.00

ROCKWELL INSPIRED — **CHARACTER DOLL ORNAMENTS**

83	DOCTOR AND DOLL	RT	20.00	30.00
83	LOVERS	RT	20.00	30.00
83	SAMPLERS	RT	20.00	30.00
*				
		EMMETT KELLY ANNUAL FIGURINE ORNAMENT		
92	CHRISTMAS TUNES	YR	15.00	15.00
86	A CHRISTMAS CAROL	CL	12.00	12.00
87	CHRISTMAS WREATH	CL	14.00	14.00
88	CHRISTMAS DINNER	CL	15.00	15.00
89	CHRISTMAS FEAST	YR	15.00	15.00
90	JUST WHAT I NEEDED	YR	15.00	15.00
91	EMMETT THE SNOWMAN	YR	15.00	15.00

B. LEIGHTON-JONES — **EMMETT KELLY ANNUAL ORNAMENT**

93	DOWNHILL ORNAMENT	YR	20.00	24.00

B. LEIGHTON-JONES — **EMMETT KELLY ORIGINAL CIRCUS COLLECTION**

94	HOLIDAY SKATER	*	20.00	24.00
*				
		GONE WITH THE WIND ORNAMENT		
92	SCARLETT-GREEN DRESS	YR	20.00	20.00
93	GWO-93 ORNAMENT	*	20.00	24.00
94	GOLD PLATED DISC ORNAMENT	OP	13.00	15.00
94	LIMITED EDITION ORNAMENT	*	20.00	24.00
94	LIMITED EDITION ORNAMENT	*	25.00	28.00

YR	NAME	LIMIT	ISSUE	QUOTE
91	PRISSY	CL	20.00	20.00
91	PRISSY	YR	20.00	20.00
87	ASHLEY	CL	15.00	45.00
87	RHETT	CL	15.00	45.00
87	SCARLETT	CL	15.00	45.00
87	TARA	CL	15.00	45.00
88	RHETT AND SCARLETT	CL	20.00	40.00
89	MAMMY	CL	20.00	20.00
90	SCARLETT-RED DRESS	CL	20.00	20.00

DEPARTMENT 56

*				**CCP ORNAMENTS**
86	APOTHECARY SHOP	CL	3.50	10.00-20.00
86	CHRISTMAS CAROL VILLAGE (SET OF 3)	CL	13.00	32.00-45.00
86	GENERAL STORE	CL	3.50	10.00-20.00
86	LIVERY STABLE & BOOT SHOP	CL	3.50	10.00-20.00
86	NATHANIEL BINGHAM FABRICS	CL	3.50	10.00-20.00
86	NEW ENGLAND VILLAGE (SET OF 7)	CL	25.00	*
86	RED SCHOOLHOUSE	CL	3.50	10.00-20.00
86	SCROOGE	CL	4.35	16.00
86	STEEPLE CHURCH	CL	3.50	10.00-20.00
*				**CHRISTMAS CAROL CHARACTER ORNAMENTS**
86	BOB CRATCHIT & TINY TIM	CL	4.35	16.00
86	CHRISTMAS CAROL CHARACTERS (SET OF 3)	CL	13.00	30.00-45.00
86	POULTERER	CL	4.35	16.00
				DICKENS' VILLAGE COLLECTION
94	DEDLOCK ARMS 9872-8	YR	12.50	12.50
*				**MISCELLANEOUS ORNAMENTS**
84	DICKENS TIN ORNAMENTS (SET OF 6)	CL	12.00	165.00
88	BALSAM BELL BRASS DICKENS' CANDLESTICK	CL	3.00	5.00-10.00
88	BOB & MRS. CRATCHIT	CL	18.00	33.00-38.00
88	SCROOGE'S HEAD	CL	12.95	20.00-28.00
88	TINY TIM'S HEAD	CL	10.00	20.00-28.00
*				**SNOWBABIES ORNAMENTS**
86	CRAWLING, LITE-UP, CLIP-ON 7953-7	OP	7.00	7.50
86	ORNAMENT ON BRASS RIBBON 7961-8	RT	8.00	50.00
86	SITTING, LITE-UP, CLIP-ON 7952-9	RT	7.00	32.00
86	WINGED, LITE-UP, CLIP-ON 7954-5	RT	7.00	35.00
87	ADRIFT, LITE-UP, CLIP-ON	RT	8.50	100.00
87	MINI, LITE-UP, CLIP-ON 7976-6	OP	9.00	12.00
87	MOON BEAMS 7951-0	OP	7.50	8.50
88	TWINKLE LITTLE STAR 7980-4	RT	7.00	25.00
89	NOEL 7988-0	OP	7.50	7.50
89	STAR BRIGHT 7990-1	OP	7.50	7.50
89	SURPRISE 7989-8	OP	12.00	12.00
90	PENGUIN, LITE-UP, CLIP ON 7940-5	OP	5.00	5.00
90	POLAR BEAR, LITE-UP, CLIP-ON 7941-3	OP	5.00	5.00
90	ROCK-A-BYE BABY 7939-1	OP	7.00	7.00
91	MY FIRST STAR 6811-0	OP	7.00	7.00
91	MY FIRST STAR 6811-0	OP	7.00	7.00
91	SWINGING ON A STAR 6810-1	OP	9.50	9.50
91	SWINGING ON A STAR 6810-1	OP	9.50	9.50
93	SPRINKLING STARS IN THE SKY 6848-9	OP	13.50	13.50
93	WEE... THIS IS FUN! 6847-9	OP	13.50	13.50
*				**VILLAGE LIGHT-UP ORNAMENTS**
85	ABEL BEASLEY BUTCHER	CL	6.00	15.00-20.00
85	BEAN AND SON SMITHY SHOP	CL	6.00	15.00-20.00
85	CANDLE SHOP	CL	6.00	16.00
85	CROWNTREE INN	CL	6.00	16.00
85	DICKENS' VILLAGE (SET OF 8)	CL	48.00	135.00-165.00
85	DICKENS' VILLAGE CHURCH	CL	6.00	16.00-35.00
85	GOLDEN SWAN BAKER	CL	6.00	15.00-20.00
85	GREEN GROCER	CL	6.00	15.00-20.00
85	JONES & CO. BRUSH & BASKET SHOP	CL	6.00	15.00-20.00
86	APOTHECARY SHOP	CL	6.00	12.00-20.00
86	BRICK TOWN HALL	CL	6.00	16.00-22.00
86	GENERAL STORE	CL	6.00	18.00-25.00
86	LIVERY STABLE & BOOT SHOP	CL	6.00	16.00-20.00
86	NATHANIEL BINGHAM FABRICS	CL	6.00	16.00-21.00
86	NEW ENGLAND VILLAGE (SET OF 7)	CL	42.00	200.00
86	RED SCHOOLHOUSE	CL	6.00	60.00-75.00
86	STEEPLE CHURCH	CL	6.00	75.00-130.00
87	BARLEY BREE FARMHOUSE	CL	6.00	15.00-20.00
87	BLYTHE POND MILL HOUSE	CL	6.00	16.00-20.00
87	BRICK ABBEY	CL	6.00	35.00-75.00
87	CHESTERTON MANOR HOUSE	CL	6.00	15.00-25.00
87	CHRISTMAS CAROL COTTAGES (SET OF 3)	CL	16.95	35.00-55.00

YR	NAME	LIMIT	ISSUE	QUOTE
87	CRAGGY COVE LIGHTHOUSE	CL	6.00	100.00
87	DICKENS' VILLAGE (SET OF 6)	CL	36.00	120.00-130.00
87	FEZZIWIG'S WAREHOUSE	CL	6.00	15.00
87	JACOB ADAMS BARN	CL	6.00	20.00-25.00
87	JACOB ADAMS FARMHOUSE	CL	6.00	25.00
87	KENILWORTH CASTLE	CL	6.00	18.00-25.00
87	NEW ENGLAND VILLAGE (SET OF 6)	CL	36.00	200.00
87	SCROOGE & MARLEY COUNTINGHOUSE	CL	6.00	15.00
87	SMYTHE WOOLEN MILL	CL	6.00	25.00
87	THE COTTAGE OF BOB CRATCHIT & TINY TIM	CL	6.00	15.00
87	THE OLD CURIOSITY SHOP	CL	6.00	15.00-18.00
87	TIMBER KNOLL LOG CABIN	CL	6.00	24.00-30.00
87	WESTON TRAIN STATION	CL	6.00	20.00-25.00

ENESCO

			ANGEL SERIES-DATED	
*				
89	WARM WISHES AND HAPPINESS-117706	YR	12.00	12.00
90	CHRISTMAS IS A TIME OF LOVE-119970	YR	17.00	17.00
90	XMAS BRING JOY OF BEAUT. SEASON-120413	YR	35.00	35.00
*			BABY'S FIRST CHRISTMAS-DATED SERIES	
89	SOMEWHERE IN THE EVENING SKY-117587	YR	12.00	15.00
90	MAY BABY'S FIRST XMAS BE FILLED-119741	YR	17.00	17.00

P. HILLMAN

			CHERISHED TEDDIES	
95	YOU'RE SKATED INTO MY HEART	OP	12.50	12.50
* *			COLLECTORS' CLUB PIECES	
84	CELEBRATING A DECADE..SHARING 227986	YR	7.00	8.50-10.00
90	7 CHAPEL WINDOWS ORNAMENT SET PM890	OP	105.00	105.00
90	BLESSED ARE THE MEEK...PM390	OP	15.00	15.00
90	BLESSED ARE THE MERCIFUL..PM590	OP	15.00	15.00
90	BLESSED ARE THE PEACEMAKERS...PM790	OP	15.00	15.00
90	BLESSED ARE THE POOR...PM190	OP	15.00	15.00
90	BLESSED ARE THE PURE... PM690	OP	15.00	15.00
90	BLESSED ARE THEY THAT HUNGER...PM490	OP	15.00	15.00
90	BLESSED ARE THEY THAT MOURN..PM290	OP	15.00	15.00
92	LOVING...SHARING ALONG THE WAY PM040	OP	12.50	27.00-30.00

KINKA

				KINKA
89	BABIES ARE CHRISTMAS DREAMS-117722	OP	15.00	15.00
89	MAY THE CHRISTMAS STAR TOUCH-117595	OP	13.50	13.50
89	MAY THIS SEASON BE FILLED WITH-117714	OP	13.50	13.50
89	MAY YOU SHARE A NEW YEAR FILLED-119733	OP	22.50	22.50
89	SOMEWHERE IN THE EVENING SKY-117587	YR	12.00	15.00
89	WARM WISHES AND EVERY HAPPINESS-117706	YR	12.00	12.00
90	LOVE TO YOU-119954	YR	13.50	*
90	MAY CHRISTMAS BRING YOU-120413	YR	35.00	*
91	CHRISTMAS IS A TIME WHEN GOD-122742	YR	22.50	22.50
91	MAY THE TRUE SPIRIT-122750 (DATED)	YR	40.00	40.00
91	MAY THIS SPECIAL SEASON-122696	OP	22.50	22.50
91	MEMORIES ARE MADE OF-122661	OP	22.50	22.50
91	WISHING YOU SPECIAL BLESSINGS-122785	YR	17.50	17.50
92	CHRISTMAS IS LOVE-125369	OP	10.00	10.00
92	HEAVEN'S BUNDLE OF JOY-122734	OP	10.00	10.00
92	LIFE IS ONE JOYOUS STEP-125350	OP	10.00	10.00
92	LOVE TO YOU/THIS WONDROUS TIME-119954	OP	7.50	7.50
92	MAY THE CHRISTMAS STAR TOUCH-117595	OP	7.50	7.50
92	MAY THIS SEASON BE FILLED W/JOY-117714	OP	7.50	7.50
92	MAY THIS SPECIAL SEASON-122688	OP	11.25	11.25
92	MEMORIES ARE MADE OF SIMPLE JOYS-122661	OP	11.25	11.25
92	SWEET MUSIC & BEAUTIFUL MEMORIES-120707	OP	10.00	10.00
92	THE SOUND OF LOVE IS FELT-120693	OP	10.00	10.00

M. ATTWELL

			MEMORIES OF YESTERDAY	
88	BABY'S FIRST CHRISTMAS 1988-520373	YR	13.50	22.00
88	BABY'S FIRST CHRISTMAS-520373	YR	13.50	25.00-30.00
88	SPECIAL DELIVERY! 1988-520381	YR	13.50	28.00
88	SPECIAL DELIVERY!-520381	YR	13.50	25.00-45.00
89	A SURPRISE FOR SANTA-522473	YR	13.50	20.00-25.00
89	A SURPRISE FOR SANTA-522473 (1989)	YR	13.50	15.00-20.00
89	BABY'S FIRST CHRISTMAS-522465	OP	15.00	22.00
89	BABY'S FIRST CHRISTMAS-522465	OP	15.00	20.00
89	CHRISTMAS TOGETHER-522562	OP	15.00	34
89	CHRISTMAS TOGETHER-522562	OP	15.00	25.00
90	MOONSTRUCK-524794	OP	15.00	15.00
90	MOONSTRUCK-524794	RT	15.00	20.00
90	NEW MOON-524646	YR	15.00	15.00
90	NEW MOON-524646	OP	15.00	25.00
90	TIME FOR BED-524638	YR	15.00	15.00
90	TIME FOR BED-524638	YR	15.00	25.00
91	JUST WATCHIN' OVER YOU-525421	OP	17.50	17.50

YR	NAME	LIMIT	ISSUE	QUOTE
91	JUST WATCHIN' OVER YOU-525421	OP	17.50	17.50
91	LUCKY ME-525448	OP	16.00	16.00
91	LUCKY ME-525448	OP	16.00	16.00
91	LUCKY YOU-525847	OP	16.00	16.00
91	LUCKY YOU-525847	OP	16.00	16.00
91	S'NO USE LOOKIN' BACK NOW!-52718	YR	17.50	17.50
91	S'NO USE LOOKIN' BACK NOW!-527181	YR	17.50	17.50
91	STAR FISHIN'-525820	OP	16.00	16.00
91	STAR FISHIN-525820	OP	16.00	16.00
92	I'LL FLY ALONG TO SEE YOU SOON-525804	YR	16.00	16.00
92	MERRY CHRISTMAS, LITTLE BOO-BOO-528803	OP	37.50	37.50
92	MOMMY, I TEARED IT-527041	YR	15.00	15.00
92	SAILIN' WITH MY FRIENDS-587575	OP	25.00	25.00
92	STAR LIGHT, STAR BRIGHT-528838	OP	16.00	16.00
92	SWINGING TOGETHER-580481	YR	17.50	17.50
93	HOW 'BOUT A LITTLE KISS?	OP	16.50	16.50
93	WISH I COULD FLY TO YOU?	OP	16.00	16.00
94	GIVE YOURSELF A HUG FROM ME	OP	17.50	17.50
95	HAPPY LANDINGS	OP	16.00	16.00

M. ATTWELL   **MEMORIES OF YESTERDAY SOCIETY MEMBERS ONLY**

YR	NAME	LIMIT	ISSUE	QUOTE
92	WITH LUCK/I'S IN HEAVEN-MY922	YR	16.00	16.00
93	I'M BRINGING GOOD LUCK-WHEREVER YOU ARE	OP	16.00	16.00

M. ATTWELL   **MEMORIES OF YESTERDAY-WINTER MEMORIES SERIES**

YR	NAME	LIMIT	ISSUE	QUOTE
89	I'SE SWINGIN'-564923 (DATED)	YR	15.00	30.00
90	MAY EVERYTHING GO WITH A SWING-569550	YR	16.00	16.00
91	SWING WITH ME-580473 (DATED	YR	16.00	16.00

PRECIOUS MOMENTS

YR	NAME	LIMIT	ISSUE	QUOTE
82	BABY'S FIRST CHRISTMAS E2362	SU	9.00	25.00-60.00
82	I'LL PLAY MY DRUM FOR HIM E2359	OP	9.00	80.00-90.00
82	OUR FIRST CHRISTMAS TOGETHER E2385	SU	9.00	22.00-50.00
82	SET OF 3-CAMEL, DONKEY & COW E2386	SU	25.00	75.00-100.00
86	BABY'S FIRST CHRISTMAS 109401	YR	12.00	40.00-45.00
86	BABY'S FIRST CHRISTMAS 109428	YR	12.00	40.00-45.00
86	I'M A POSSIBILITY 111120	SU	10.00	20.00-35.00
88	A GROWING LOVE 520349		*	80.00-90.00
88	MAY ALL YOUR CHRISTMASES..521302	OP	13.50	16.00-25.00
89	CELEBRATING...SHARING & CARING 227986	YR	7.00	8.50-10.00
90	A UNIVERSAL LOVE 238899	YR	8.00	10.00-12.00
90	SHARING A GIFT OF LOVE 233196	YR	8.00	8.00
88	ALWAYS ROOM FOR ONE MORE 522961	OP	*	95.00-110.00
88	OH NOLY NIGHT 522848	YR	13.50	30.00-35.00
89	BUNDLES OF JOY 525057	LE	17.50	30.00-35.00
90	MAY YOUR CHRISTMAS BE MERRY 526940	YR	30.00	35.00-38.00
92	IT'S SO UPLIFTING...FRIEND...YOU 528846	OP	16.00	16.00-18.00
92	SHARE IN THE WARMTH OF CHRISTMAS	OP	15.00	16.00-20.00
92	THERE'S A CHRISTIAM WELCOME HERE 528021	YR	22.50	24.00-35.00
76	LOVE ONE ANOTHER 522929	OP	17.50	17.50-25.00
80	BABY'S FIRST CHRISTMAS E-5631	SU	6.00	40.00-80.00
80	BABY'S FIRST CHRISTMAS E-5632	SU	6.00	40.00-80.00
80	WE HAVE SEEN HIS STAR E-6120	RT	9.00	48.00-75.00
80	WEE THREE KINGS (3PC SET) E-5634	SU	25.00	110.00-150.00
81	BUT LOVE GOES ON FOREVER E-5627	SU	6.00	90.00-135.00
81	BUT LOVE GOES ON FOREVER E-5628	SU	6.00	80.00-140.00
81	COME LET US ADORE HIM (4PC SET) E-5633	SU	20.00	125.00-150.00
81	LET THE HEAVENS REJOICE E-5629	YR	6.00	225.00-290.00
81	UNTO US A CHILD IS BORN E-5630	SU	6.00	50.00-75.00
82	BABY'S FIRST CHRISTMAS E-2362	SU	9.00	25.00-60.00
82	BABY'S FIRST CHRISTMAS E-2372	SU	9.00	35.00-55.00
82	CAMEL, DONKEY & COW (3 PC SET) E-2386	SU	25.00	75.00-100.00
82	DROPPING IN FOR CHRISTMAS E-2369	RT	9.00	40.00-75.00
82	DROPPING OVER FOR CHRISTMAS E-2376	RT	9.00	50.00-75.00
82	I'LL PLAY MY DRUM FOR HIM E-2359	YR	9.00	80.00-90.00
82	JOY TO THE WORLD E-2343	SU	9.00	35.00-60.00
82	MOUSE WITH CHEESE E-2381	SU	9.00	110.00-135.00
82	OUR FIRST CHRISTMAS TOGETHER E-2385	OP	9.00	20.00-50.00
82	THE FIRST NOEL E-2367	SU	9.00	50.00-65.00
82	THE FIRST NOEL E-2368	RT	9.00	35.00-75.00
82	UNICORN E-2371	RT	9.00	45.00-70.00
83	BLESSED ARE THE PURE IN HEART E-0518	YR	9.00	40.00-45.00
83	JESUS IS THE LIGHT THAT SHINES E-0537	SU	9.00	60.00-75.00
83	LET HEAVEN AND NATURE SING E-0532	RT	9.00	35.00-55.00
83	LOVE IS PATIENT E-0535	SU	9.00	45.00-60.00
83	LOVE IS PATIENT E-0536	SU	9.00	55.00-70.00
83	MOTHER SEW DEAR E-0514	OP	9.00	16.00-35.00
83	O COME ALL YE FAITHFUL E-0531	SU	10.00	45.00-60.00
83	SURROUND US WITH JOY E-0513	YR	9.00	50.00-60.00

YR	NAME	LIMIT	ISSUE	QUOTE
83	TELL ME THE STORY OF JESUS E-0533	SU	9.00	40.00-62.00
83	THE PERFECT GRANDPA E-0517	SU	9.00	25.00-65.00
83	THE PURR-FECT GRANDMA E-0516	OP	9.00	16.00-40.00
83	TO A SPECIAL DAD E-0515	SU	9.00	38.00-52.00
83	TO THEE WITH LOVE E-0534	RT	9.00	30.00-60.00
84	BLESSED ARE THE PURE IN HEART E-5392	YR	10.00	30.00-35.00
84	HAVE A HEAVENLY CHRISTMAS 12416	OP	12.00	17.50-40.00
84	JOY TO THE WORLD E-5388	RT	10.00	35.00-50.00
84	LOVE IS KIND E-5391	SU	10.00	30.00-45.00
84	MAY GOD BLESS YOU/PERFECT SEASON E-5390	SU	10.00	25.00-45.00
84	PEACE ON EARTH E-5389	SU	10.00	30.00-45.00
84	WISHING YOU A MERRY CHRISTMAS E-5387	YR	10.00	28.00-30.00
85	ANGEL OF MERCY 102407	OP	10.00	16.00-25.00
85	BABY'S FIRST CHRISTMAS 102504	YR	10.00	30.00-35.00
85	BABY'S FIRST CHRISTMAS 102512	YR	10.00	25.00-30.00
85	BABY'S FIRST CHRISTMAS 15903	YR	10.00	40.00-45.00
85	BABY'S FIRST CHRISTMAS 15911	YR	10.00	32.00-40.00
85	GOD SENT HIS LOVE 15768	YR	10.00	27.00-30.00
85	HAPPINESS IS THE LORD 15830	SU	10.00	25.00-38.00
85	HONK IF YOU LOVE JESUS 15857	SU	10.00	15.00-30.00
85	IT'S A PERFECT BOY 102415	SU	10.00	20.00-30.00
85	LORD KEEP ME ON MY TOES 102423	RT	10.00	35.00-50.00
85	LOVE RESCUE ME 102385	OP	10.00	16.00-27.50
85	MAY YOUR CHRISTMAS BE DELIGHTFUL 15849	SU	10.00	15.00-35.00
85	MAY YOUR CHRISTMAS BE HAPPY 15822	SU	10.00	30.00-40.00
85	OUR FIRST CHRISTMAS TOGETHER 102350	YR	10.00	25.00-32.50
85	ROCKING HORSE 102474	SU	10.00	18.00-30.00
85	SERVE WITH A SMILE 102431	SU	10.00	22.00-35.00
85	SERVE WITH A SMILE 102458	SU	10.00	22.00-35.00
85	SHEPHERD OF LOVE 102288	SU	10.00	18.00-35.00
85	TRUST AND OBEY 102377	OP	10.00	16.00-27.50
85	WISHING YOU A COZY CHRISTMAS 102326	YR	10.00	30.00-35.00
86	HE CLEASNSED MY SOUL 112380	OP	12.00	16.00-30.00
86	I'M SENDING YOU A WHITE CHRISTMAS 112372	SU	11.00	20.00-35.00
86	LOVE IS THE BEST GIFT OF ALL 109770	YR	11.00	25.00-35.00
86	OUR FIRST CHRISTMAS TOGETHER 112399	YR	11.00	25.00-30.00
86	REINDEER 102466	YR	11.00	165.00-190.00
86	WADDLE I DO WITHOUT YOU 112364	OP	10.00	15.00-25.50
86	YOU HAVE TOUCHED SO MANY HEARTS 112356	OP	10.00	15.00-25.00
87	BABY'S FIRST CHRISTMAS 109401	YR	12.00	40.00-45.00
87	BABY'S FIRST CHRISTMAS 109428	YR	12.00	40.00-45.00
87	BEAR THE GOOD NEWS IF CHRISTMAS 104515	YR	11.00	25.00-30.00
87	DASHING THROUGH THE SNOW 521574	OP	15.00	15.00-22.50
87	I'M A POSSIBILITY 111120	OP	10.00	18.00-35.00
88	BABY'S FIRST CHRISTMAS 115282	YR	15.00	27.50-30.00
88	BABY'S FIRST CHRISTMAS 520241	YR	13.00	25.00-30.00
88	BABY'S FIRST CHRISTMAS 523194	YR	15.00	22.00-25.00
88	BABY'S FIRST CHRISTMAS 523208	YR	15.00	23.00-27.50
88	CHEERS TO THE LEADER 113999	SU	13.50	30.00-40.00
88	CHRISTMAS IS RUFF WITHOUT YOU 520462	YR	13.00	28.00-40.00
88	DON'T LET THE HOLIDAYS..DOWN 521590	OP	15.00	15.00-22.50
88	GLIDE THROUGH THE HOLIDAYS 521566	RT	13.50	32.00-45.00
88	GOD SENT YOU JUST IN TIME 113972	SU	13.50	30.00-40.00
88	HANG ON FOR THE HOLLY DAYS 520292	YR	13.00	22.00-25.00
88	I BELIEVE IN THE OLD RUGGED CROSS 522953	OP	15.00	16.00-24.00
88	MAKE A JOYFUL NOISE 522910	OP	15.00	15.00-25.00
88	MY LOVE WILL NEVER LET YOU GO 114006	SU	13.50	25.00-40.00
88	OUR FIRST CHRISTMAS TOGETHER 520233	YR	13.00	20.00-23.00
88	OUR FIRST CHRISTMAS TOGETHER 521558	YR	17.50	35.00-38.00
88	PEACE ON EARTH 523062	YR	25.00	70.00-75.00
88	REJOICE O EARTH 113980	RT	13.50	30.00-50.00
88	SMILE ALONG THE WAY 113964	SU	15.00	20.00-35.00
88	TIME TO WISH YOU/MERRY CHRISTMAS 115320	YR	13.00	39.00-45.00
88	TO MY FOREVER FRIEND 113956	OP	16.00	17.50-35.00
88	YOU ARE MY GIFT COME TRUE 520276	YR	12.50	18.50-22.00
89	BABY'S FIRST CHRISTMAS 523771	YR	15.00	20.00-25.00
89	BABY'S FIRST CHRISTMAS 523798	YR	15.00	20.00-25.00
89	FRIENDS NEVER DRIFT APART 522937	OP	17.50	17.50-22.00
89	HAPPY TRAILS IS TRUSTING JESUS 523224	OP	15.00	15.00-22.00
89	MAY YOUR CHRISTMAS BE/HAPPY HOME 523704	YR	27.50	45.00-55.00
89	OH HOLY NIGHT 522848	YR	13.50	30.00-50.00
89	ONCE UPON A HOLY NIGHT 523852	YR	15.00	25.00-30.00
89	OUR FIRST CHRISTMAS TOGETHER 522945	YR	17.50	26.00-28.00
89	OUR FIRST CHRISTMAS TOGETHER 525324	YR	17.50	25.00-30.00
89	WISHING YOU A PURR-FECT HOLIDAY 520497	YR	15.00	28.00-33.00
90	BABY'S FIRST CHIRSTMAS (BOY) 527084	YR	15.00	20.00-25.00

Angelic Guide *lights the way as* Hear Ye, Hear Ye *proclaims his joy for the season. Each was based on artwork by M.I. Hummel and introduced in 1991 by Goebel.*

Inspired by Walt Disney's animation classic "Fantasia," Flight of Fancy *was available only at 1994 Walt Disney Classics Collection dealer events.*

Ladies and gentlemen, start your engines. This Hallmark Keepsake Ornament titled 1957 Corvette *is one fine dream machine.*

Licensed ornaments are one of the most popular collectibles around. Holiday Treats *is the second issue in the "McDonald's Dated" series from Enesco's Treasury of Christmas.*

YR	NAME	LIMIT	ISSUE	QUOTE
90	BABY'S FIRST CHIRSTMAS (GIRL) 527092	YR	15.00	22.00-25.00
90	MAY YOUR CHRISTMAS BE MERRY 524174	YR	15.00	25.00-30.00
90	SNO-BUNNY FALLS FOR YOU LIKE I DO 520438	YR	15.00	26.00-30.00
90	THE GOOD LORD ALWAYS DELIVERS 527165	SU	15.00	15.00-25.00
91	MAY YOUR CHRISTMAS BE MERRY 526940	YR	30.00	37.00-42.50
92	15 YEARS-TWEET MUSIC TOGETHER 530840	LE	15.00	18.00-22.00
92	BABY'S FIRST CHRISTMAS 527475	YR	15.00	18.00-20.00
92	BABY'S FIRST CHRISTMAS 527483	YR	15.00	18.00-20.00
92	BABY'S FIRST CHRISTMAS 530859	YR	15.00	18.00-20.00
92	BABY'S FIRST CHRISTMAS 530867	YR	15.00	18.00-20.00
92	BUT THE GREATEST OF THESE IS LOVE 527696	YR	15.00	22.50-25.00
92	BUT THE GREATEST OF THESE IS LOVE 527734	YR	30.00	30.00-32.50
92	GOOD FRIENDS ARE FOR ALWAYS 524131	OP	15.00	16.00-20.00
92	I'M NUTS ABOUT YOU 520411	YR	16.00	24.00-30.00
92	LORD KEEP ME ON MY TOES 525332	OP	15.00	16.00-18.00
92	OUR FIRST CHRISTMAS TOGETHER 528870	YR	17.50	20.00-22.00
92	OUR FIRST CHRISTMAS TOGETHER 530506	OP	17.50	18.00-20.00
92	SLOW DOWN & ENJOY THE HOLIDAYS 520489	YR	16.00	18.00-20.00
92	WISHING YOU/SWEETEST CHRISTMAS530190	YR	30.00	35.00-38.00
92	WISHING YOU/SWEETEST CHRISTMAS530212	OP	15.00	25.00-35.00
93	AN EVENT FOR ALL SEASONS 529974	LE	15.00	15.00
93	AN EVENT FOR ALL SEASONS 530158	OP	30.00	30.00
93	WISHING YOU/SWEETEST CHRISTMAS530182	OP	8.00	8.00
94	BABY'S FIRST CHRISTMAS 530255	OP	16.00	16.00
94	BABY'S FIRST CHRISTMAS 530263	OP	16.00	16.00
94	MEMORIES ARE MAD EOF THIS 529982	OP	30.00	30.00
94	OUR FIRST CHRISTMAS TOGETHER 529206	OP	18.50	18.50
94	TAKE A BOW CUZ YOU'RE MY CHRISTMAS STAR	OP	16.00	16.00
94	YER A PEL-I-CAN COUNT ON	OP	16.00	16.00
94	YOU ARE ALWAYS IN MY HEART 530972	OP	16.00	16.00
94	YOU'RE AS PRETTY AS A CHRISTMAS TREE	OP	27.50	27.50
94	YOU'RE PRETTY AS A CHRISTMAS TREE 529206	OP	16.00	16.00
94	YOU'RE PRETTY AS A CHRISTMAS TREE 530395	OP	30.00	30.00
95	BABY'S FIRST CHRISTMAS 142719	OP	17.50	17.50
95	BABY'S FIRST CHRISTMAS 142727	OP	17.50	17.50
95	FOLLOW YOUR HEART 528080	OP	30.00	30.00
95	HE COVERS THE EARTH W/HIS BEAUTY 142662	OP	17.00	17.00
95	HE COVERS THE EARTH W/HIS BEAUTY 142689	OP	30.00	30.00
95	HIPPO HOLIDAYS	OP	17.00	17.00
95	MERRY CHRISMOOSE 150134	OP	17.00	17.00
95	OUR FIRST CHRISTMAS TOGETHER 142700	OP	18.50	18.50
S. BUTCHER	**PRECIOUS MOMENTS COMMEMORATIVE EASTER SEALS ORNAMENT**			
93	YOU'RE MY NUMBER ONE FRIEND 250112	OP	8.00	8.00
94	IT IS NO SECRET WHAT GOD CAN DO	OP	6.50	6.50
95	TAKE TIME TO SMELL THE FLOWERS	OP	7.50	7.50
96	YOU CAN ALWAYS COUNT ON ME	OP	6.50	6.50
S. BUTCHER	**PRECIOUS MOMENTS SPECIAL EDITION MEMBERS ONLY**			
93	LOVING,CARING & SHARING ALONG THE WAY	OP	15.00	15.00
94	YOU ARE THE END OF MY RAINBOW	OP	15.00	15.00
* *			**SHARING SEASON GIFTS**	
86	BIRDS OF A FEATHER COLLECT... PM864	OP	*	150.00-160.00
87	BRASS FILIGREE BELL SHAPED PM009	OP	*	45.00
88	A GROWING LOVE 520349	OP	*	80.00-90.00
89	ALWAYS ROOM FOR ONE MORE 522961	OP	*	95.00-110.00
90	MY HAPPINESS PM904	OP	*	90.00-95.00
91	SHARING THE GOOD NEWS TOGETHER PM037	OP	*	75.00-80.00
* *			**SUGAR TOWN**	
92	BOY STANDING BY CHAPEL 530484	LE	17.50	17.50-20.00
*			**TREASURY OF CHRISTMAS**	
81	BABY'S FIRST CHRISTMAS 1981-E-6145	YR	6.00	22.00
81	FLYIN' SANTA CHRISTMAS SPECIAL-E6136	YR	9.00	110.00
81	LOOK OUT BELOW-E-6135	TL	6.00	60.00
81	NOT A CREATURE WAS STIRRING-E-6149	TL	4.00	45.00
81	OUR HERO-E-6146	TL	4.00	55.00
81	SAWIN' ELF HELPER-E-6138	TL	6.00	45.00
81	SNOW SHOE-IN SANTA-E-6139	TL	6.00	50.00
81	WHOOPS, IT'S 1981-E-6148	YR	7.50	75.00
81	WHOOPS-E-6147	TL	3.50	95.00
82	A SAVIOR IS BORN THIS DAY-E-6949	TL	4.00	18.00
82	BABY'S FIRST CHRISTMAS 1982-E-6952	YR	4.00	10.00
82	BABY'S FIRST CHRISTMAS 1982-E-6979	YR	10.00	35.00
82	BUNNY WINTER PLAYGROUND 1982-E-6978	YR	10.00	55.00
82	CAROUSEL HORSES-E-6958	TL	8.00	65.00
82	FLYIN' SANTA CHRISTMAS SPECIAL-E6136	YR	9.00	105.00
82	GRANDCHILD'S FIRST CHRISTMAS 1982-E-6983	YR	5.00	15.00
82	MERRY CHRISTMAS GRANDMA-E-6975	TL	5.00	5.00

YR	NAME	LIMIT	ISSUE	QUOTE
82	MERRY CHRISTMAS TEACHER-E-6984	TL	7.00	7.00
82	PENGUIN POWER-E-6977	TL	6.00	18.00
82	POLAR BEAR FUN WHOOPS IT'S 1982-E-6953	YR	10.00	85.00
82	TOY SOLDIER 1982-E-6957	YR	6.50	65.00
82	VICTORIAN SLEIGH-E-6946	TL	9.00	9.00
83	ARCTIC CHARMER-E-6945	TL	7.00	35.00
83	BABY'S FIRST CHRISTMAS-E-0271	YR	6.00	6.00
83	BABY'S FIRST CHRISTMAS-E-0273	TL	9.00	9.00
83	CAROUSEL HORSE-E-0278	TL	9.00	50.00
83	CAROUSEL HORSES-E-6980	TL	8.00	65.00
83	GRANDCHILD'S FIRST CHRISTMAS-E0272	YR	5.00	5.00
83	TO A SPECIAL TEACHER-E-0276	TL	5.00	15.00
83	TOY DRUM TEDDY-E-0274	TL	9.00	9.00
83	TOY SHOP-E-0277	TL	8.00	32
83	WATCHING AT THE WINDOW-E-0275	TL	13.00	40.00
83	WIDE OPEN THROTTLE-E-0242	TL	12.00	35.00
83	WING-A-DING ANGEL-E-6948	TL	7.00	40.00
84	BABY'S FIRST CHRISTMAS 1984-E-6215	YR	6.00	6.00
84	BUNNY'S CHRISTMAS STOCKING-E-6251	YR	2.00	28.00
84	CAROUSEL HORSE-E-6913	TL	1.50	20.00
84	CHRISTMAS NEST-E-6249	TL	3.00	3.00
84	CUCKOO CLOCK-E-6217	TL	8.00	40.00
84	FERRIS WHEEL MICE-E-6216	TL	9.00	9.00
84	GODCHILD'S FIRST CHRISTMAS-E-6287	TL	7.00	7.00
84	GRANDCHILD'S FIRST CHRISTMAS 1984-E-6286	YR	5.00	5.00
84	HAPPY HOLIDAYS-E-6248	TL	2.00	2.00
84	HOLIDAY PENGUIN-E-6240	TL	1.50	20.00
84	JOY TO THE WORLD-E-6209	TL	9.00	48.00
84	LETTER TO SANTA-E-6210	TL	5.00	35.00
84	LITTLE DRUMMER-E-6241	TL	2.00	2.00
84	LUCY & ME PHOTO FRAMES-E-6211	TL	5.00	5.00
84	MERRY CHRISTMAS MOTHER-E-6213	TL	10.00	35.00
84	OWL BE HOME FOR CHRISTMAS-E-6230	TL	10.00	10.00
84	PEEK-A-BEAR BABY'S/CHRISTMAS-E-6228	TL	10.00	10.00
84	PEEK-A-BEAR BABY'S/CHRISTMAS-E-6229	TL	9.00	9.00
84	PENGUINS ON ICE-E-6280	TL	7.50	30.00
84	SANTA IN THE BOX-E-6292	TL	6.00	35.00
84	SANTA ON ICE-E-6252	TL	2.50	25.00
84	SANTA'S TROLLEY-E-6231	TL	11.00	55.00
84	TREASURED MEMORIES THE NEW SLED-E-6256	TL	7.00	70.00
84	UP ON THE HOUSE TOP-E-6280	TL	9.00	30.00
85	A STOCKING FULL FOR 1985-56464	YR	6.00	6.00
85	ANGEL IN FLIGHT-55816	TL	8.00	25.00
85	BABY BLOCKS-55883	TL	12.00	12.00
85	BABY RATTLE PHOTO FRAME-56006	TL	5.00	5.00
85	BABY'S FIRST CHRISTMAS-55840	TL	15.00	15.00
85	CAROUSEL REINDEER-55808	TL	12.00	50.00
85	CHILD'S SECOND CHRISTMAS-55867	TL	11.00	20.00
85	CHRISTMAS LIGHTS-56200	TL	8.00	40.00
85	CHRISTMAS PENGUIN-55824	TL	7.50	40.00
85	CHRISTMAS TOY CHEST-55891	TL	10.00	25.00
85	CHRISTMAS TREE PHOTOFRAME-56871	TL	10.00	10.00
85	FISHING FOR STARS-55875	TL	9.00	15.00
85	FLYING SANTA CHRISTMAS SPECIAL-56383	TL	8.00	45.00
85	GRANDCHILD'S FIRST ORNAMENT-55921	TL	7.00	12.00
85	JOY PHOTO FRAME-55956	YR	6.00	22.00
85	LOOK OUT BELOW-56375	TL	6.00	50.00
85	MERRY CHRISTMAS GRANDMA-56197	YR	7.00	7.00
85	MERRY CHRISTMAS TEACHER-56448	YR	9.00	9.00
85	NORTH POLE EXPRESS-56073	TL	9.00	50.00
85	NOT A CREATURE WAS STIRRING-56421	YR	5.50	45.00
85	OLD FASHIONED ROCKING HORSE-55859	TL	10.00	10.00
85	OUR HERO-56413	YR	5.50	55.00
85	SANTA CLAUS BALLOON-55794	YR	8.50	40.00
85	SAWIN ELF HELPER-56391	YR	8.00	45.00
85	SCOTTIE CELEBRATING CHRISTMAS-56065	TL	10.00	15.00
85	SKATING WALRUS-56081	TL	9.00	45.00
85	SNOW SHOE-IN SANTA-56405	YR	8.00	50.00
85	ST. NICHOLAS CIRCA 1910-56359	TL	6.00	15.00
85	THE NIGHT BEFORE CHRISTMAS-55972	TL	5.00	5.00
85	TOBOGGAN RIDE-56286	TL	6.00	12.00
85	VICTORIAN DOLL HOUSE-56251	YR	13.00	30.00
85	WE THREE KINGS-55964	YR	4.50	15.00
86	1ST CHRISTMAS TOGETHER 1986-551171	YR	9.00	22.00
86	ANTIQUE TOY-551317	TL	9.00	25.00
86	BABY'S FIRST CHRISTMAS 1986-551724	YR	6.50	6.50

YR	NAME	LIMIT	ISSUE	QUOTE
86	BABY'S FIRST CHRISTMAS-551716	TL	5.50	10.00
86	BAH, HUMBUG!-553387	TL	9.00	20.00
86	CHRISTMAS CALENDAR-551333	TL	7.00	20.00
86	CHRISTMAS RATTLE-553379	TL	8.00	25.00
86	CHRISTMAS SCOTTIE-551201	TL	7.00	15.00
86	CHRISTMAS WISHES FROM PANDA-552623	TL	6.00	10.00
86	COUNTRY COUSINS MERRY XMAS, DAD-552704	TL	7.00	10.00
86	COUNTRY COUSINS MERRY XMAS, DAD-552712	TL	7.00	15.00
86	COUNTRY COUSINS MERRY XMAS, MOM-552704	TL	7.00	10.00
86	COUNTRY COUSINS MERRY XMAS, MOM-552712	TL	7.00	15.00
86	ELF STRINGING POPCORN-551198	TL	10.00	18.00
86	FIRST CHRISTMAS TOGETHER-551708	TL	6.00	23.00
86	FROM OUR HOUSE TO YOUR HOUSE-553360	TL	15.00	20.00
86	GOD BLESS US EVERYONE-553395	TL	10.00	22.00
86	GRANDMOTHER'S LITTLE ANGEL-552747	TL	8.00	15.00
86	HAVE A HEAVENLY HOLIDAY-551260	TL	9.00	1.00
86	HOLIDAY FISHERMAN-551309	TL	8.00	35.00
86	HOLIDAY TRAIN-553417	TL	10.00	24.00
86	I LOVE MY GRANDPARENTS-553263	YR	6.00	6.00
86	M.V.B. (MOST VALUABLE BEAR)-554219	TL	3.00	3.00
86	MERRY CHRISTMAS MOM & DAD-553271	YR	6.00	6.00
86	MERRY CHRISTMAS TEACHER-552666	TL	6.50	12.00
86	MERRY CHRISTMAS-553646	TL	8.00	14.00
86	MY SPECIAL FRIEND-552615	TL	2.50	18.00
86	OLD FASHIONED DOLL HOUSE-551287	TL	15.00	25.00
86	PEEK-A-BEAR GRANDCHILD'S/XMAS-552070	YR	6.00	6.00
86	PEEK-A-BEAR PRESENT-552089	TL	2.50	2.50
86	S. CLAUS HOLLYCOPTER-553344	TL	13.50	30.00
86	SANTA AND CHILD-551236	TL	13.50	25.00
86	SANTA'S HELPERS-552607	TL	2.50	2.50
86	SIAMESE KITTEN-551279	TL	9.00	20.00
86	THE BABY BEAR SLEIGH-551651	TL	9.00	25.00
86	THE CHRISTMAS ANGEL-551244	10,000	22.50	55.00
87	1ST CHRISTMAS TOGETHER 1987-556335	YR	9.00	25.00
87	BABY'S FIRST CHRISTMAS 1987-556254	YR	7.00	25.00
87	BABY'S FIRST CHRISTMAS 1987-556297	YR	2.00	5.00
87	BABY'S FIRST CHRISTMAS-555061	TL	12.00	15.00
87	BABY'S FIRST CHRISTMAS-555088	TL	7.50	12.00
87	BABY'S FIRST CHRISTMAS-555118	TL	6.00	10.00
87	BABY'S FIRST CHRISTMAS-556041	TL	10.00	10.00
87	BEARY CHRISTMAS FAMILY-556300	TL	2.00	5.00
87	BOY ON A ROCKING HORSE-555983	TL	12.00	20.00
87	BUCKET O'LOVE-556491	TL	2.50	2.50
87	CAROUSEL GOOSE-556076	TL	17.00	39.50
87	CAROUSEL MOBILE-553409	TL	15.00	60.00
87	CHRISTMAS TRAIN-557196	TL	10.00	18.00
87	COUNTRY COUSINS KATIE/ICE SKATING-556378	TL	8.00	29.50
87	COUNTRY COUSINS SCOOTER SNOWMAN-556386	TL	8.00	35.00
87	GRANDCHILD'S FIRST CHRISTMAS-556416	TL	10.00	25.00
87	I'M DREAMING OF/BRIGHT CHRISTMAS-556602	TL	2.50	2.50
87	KITTY'S 1ST CHRISTMAS-552917	TL	4.00	5.00
87	KITTY'S BED-556408	TL	12.00	50.00
87	KITTY'S JACK-IN-THE-BOX-555959	TL	11.00	15.00
87	LITTLE SAILOR ELF-556068	TL	10.00	20.00
87	MERRY CHRISTMAS KITTY-552933	TL	3.50	5.00
87	MERRY CHRISTMAS PUPPY-552925	TL	3.50	5.00
87	MERRY CHRISTMAS TEACHER-555967	TL	7.50	10.00
87	MERRY CHRISTMAS TEACHER-556319	TL	2.00	5.00
87	MOUSE IN A MITTEN-555975	TL	7.50	30.00
87	NIGHT CAPS-556084	TL	5.50	8.00
87	OUR FIRST CHRISTMAS TOGETHER-556548	TL	13.00	18.00
87	PEAK-A-BEAR MY SPECIAL FRIEND-556513	TL	6.00	20.00
87	PEEK-A-BEAR LETTER TO SANTA-555991	TL	8.00	15.00
87	PUPPY LOVE-556505	TL	6.00	15.00
87	PUPPY'S 1ST CHRISTMAS-552909	TL	4.00	5.00
87	ROCKING HORSE PAST JOYS-556157	TL	10.00	10.00
87	SANTA'S LIST-556394	TL	7.00	1815.00
87	SKATING SANTA 1987-556211	YR	13.50	9575.00
87	SLEIGH AWAY-555401	TL	12.00	20.00
87	SUGAR PLUM BEARIES-555193	TL	4.50	4.50
87	TEDDY TAKES A SPIN-556467	TL	13.00	18.00
87	TEDDY'S SUSPENDERS-556262	TL	8.50	16.00
87	THREE LITTLE BEARS-556556	TL	7.50	12.00
87	TINY TOY THIMBLE MOBILE-556475	TL	12.00	15.00
88	1ST CHRISTMAS TOGETHER 1988-554596	YR	17.50	15.00
88	BABY'S FIRST CHRISTMAS 1988-554928	YR	7.50	10.00

YR	NAME	LIMIT	ISSUE	QUOTE
88	CHRISTMAS IS COMING-554901	TL	12.00	18.00
88	CHRISTMAS PIN-UP 489409	TL	11.00	25.00
88	CHRISTMAS THIM-BELL-558389	YR	4.00	6.00
88	GRAMOPHONE KEEPSAKE-558818	TL	13.00	22.00
88	HAPPY HOWLADAYS-558605	YR	7.00	12.00
88	MERRY CHRISTMAS ENGINE-554561	TL	22.50	35.00
88	MERRY CHRISTMAS GRANDPA-560065	TL	8.00	10.00
88	NORTH POLE DEADLINE-489387	TL	13.50	18.00
88	SANTA TURTLE-558559	TL	10.00	20.00
88	SANTA'S SURVEY-554642	TL	35.00	70.00
88	THE CHRISTMAS TRAIN-554944	TL	15.00	20.00
88	THE TEDDY BEAR BALL-558567	TL	10.00	12.00
88	TURTLE GREETINGS-558583	TL	8.50	22.00
89	89 CAUGHT IN THE ACT-830046	TL	12.50	12.50
89	BABY'S FIRST CHRISTMAS 1989-562807	YR	8.00	12.00
89	BOTTOM'S UP 1989-830003	TL	11.00	20.00
89	CLARA-568406	YR	12.50	22.00
89	DOROTHY-567760	YR	12.00	25.00
89	FIRST CHRISTMAS TOGETHER 1989-562823	TL	11.00	12.00
89	GONE WITH THE WIND-567698	YR	13.50	25.00
89	HOE! HOE! HOE!-564761	YR	20.00	30.50
89	SANTA'S LITTLE REINDEAR-568430	TL	15.00	15.00
89	STATIC IN THE ATTIC-562947	TL	13.00	15.00
89	THE COWARDLY LION-567787	YR	12.00	22.00
89	THE PAUSE THAT REFRESHES-563226	TL	15.00	20.00
89	THE PURR-FECT FIT!-566462	TL	15.00	15.00
89	THE SCARECROW-567795	YR	12.00	20.00
89	THE TIN MAN-567779	YR	12.00	20.00
89	VICTORIAN SLEIGH RIDE-562890	TL	22.50	22.50
89	YE OLDE PUPPET SHOW-562939	TL	17.50	20.00
90	'TWAS THE NIGHT BEFORE CHRISTMAS-577545	TL	17.50	17.50
90	A CALLING HOME AT CHRISTMAS-568457	TL	15.00	15.00
90	BREWING WARM WISHES-564974	TL	10.00	12.00
90	CLARA'S PRINCE-568422	YR	12.50	18.00
90	FESTIVE FLIGHT-566101	TL	11.00	14.00
90	HANG IN THERE-566055	TL	13.50	13.50
90	HAPPY HOLIDAY READINGS-568104	TL	8.00	10.00
90	HAVE A COKE AND A SMILE-571512	TL	15.00	15.00
90	HEADING FOR HAPPY HOLIDAYS-577537	TL	17.50	17.50
90	MCHAPPY HOLIDAYS-577529	TL	17.50	17.50
90	MERRY CHRISTMAS TEACHER-566098	TL	11.00	11.00
90	MOUSE HOUSE-575186	TL	16.00	16.00
90	OVER ONE MILLION HOLIDAY WISHES!-577553	YR	17.50	20.00
90	PURR-FECT PALS-563218	TL	8.00	12.00
90	SANTA'S SUITCASE-566462	TL	25.00	25.00
90	SEAMAN'S GREETINGS-566047	TL	11.00	11.00
90	TEN LORDS A-LEAPING-573949	TL	15.00	15.00
90	THE NUTCRACKER-568422	YR	12.50	18.00
90	TONS OF TOYS-577510	TL	13.00	18.00
90	YOU MALT MY HEART-577596	TL	25.00	25.00
91	A REAL CLASSIC-831603	YR	10.00	10.00
91	ALL CAUGHT UP IN CHRISTMAS-583537	TL	10.00	10.00
91	ALL I WANT FOR CHRISTMAS-577596	TL	25.00	25.00
91	BABY'S FIRST CHRISTMAS 1991-586935	YR	12.50	12.50
91	CHECKING IT TWICE-583936	TL	25.00	25.00
91	CHRISTMAS CHEER-585769	TL	13.50	13.50
91	CHRISTMAS COUNTDOWN-568376	TL	20.00	20.00
91	CHRISTMAS CUTIE-576182	TL	13.50	13.50
91	CHRISTMAS IS IN THE AIR-581453	YR	15.00	15.00
91	CHRISTMAS IS MY GOAL-581550	TL	17.50	17.50
91	CHRISTMAS KAYAK-583723	TL	13.50	15.00
91	DREAM A LITTLE DREAM-575593	TL	17.50	17.50
91	FROSTY THE SNOWMAN-576425	TL	15.00	15.00
91	HAPPY MEAL ON WHEELS-583715	TL	22.50	22.50
91	HERE'S THE SCOOP-583693	TL	13.50	13.50
91	HOLIDAY AHOY-568368	TL	12.50	12.50
91	HOLIDAY TREATS-581542	YR	17.50	17.50
91	HOLIDAY WING DING-574333	TL	22.50	22.50
91	IT'S TEA-LIGHTFUL-694789	TL	13.50	15.00
91	JUGGLIN' THE HOLIDAYS-587028	TL	13.00	13.00
91	LIGHTING THE WAY-588776	TL	20.00	20.00
91	MARILYN MONROE-583774	YR	20.00	20.00
91	MEOW MATES-576220	TL	12.00	12.00
91	NORTH POLE HERE I COME-574333	TL	22.50	22.50
91	OUR MOST PRECIOUS GIFT-585726	YR	17.50	17.50
91	PEDAL PUSHIN' SANTA-566098	TL	20.00	20.00

YR	NAME	LIMIT	ISSUE	QUOTE
91	RUDOLPH-588784	TL	17.50	17.50
91	SANTA'S STEED-587044	YR	15.00	18.00
91	STARRY EYED SANTA-587176	TL	15.00	15.00
91	THE GLOW OF CHRISTMAS-581801	TL	20.00	20.00
91	THINGS GO BETTER WITH COKE-580597	TL	17.00	17.50
91	TUBA TOTIN' TEDDY-568449	TL	15.00	15.00
91	WARMEST WISHES-573825	YR	17.50	25.00
92	A CHILD'S CHRISTMAS-586358	TL	25.00	25.00
92	A CHRISTMAS TOAST-588261	TL	20.00	20.00
92	A POUND OF GOOD CHEERS-582034	TL	17.50	17.50
92	A SURE SIGN OF CHRISTMAS-588857	TL	22.50	22.50
92	A WATCHFUL EYE-595713	YR	15.00	15.00
92	A-B-C-SON'S GREETINGS-588806	TL	16.50	16.50
92	BABY'S FIRST CHRISTMAS-586943	YR	12.50	12.50
92	BEGINNING TO LOOK/CHRISTMAS-588253	TL	15.00	15.00
92	BLESS OUR HOME-595772	YR	12.00	12.00
92	CARTIN' HOME HOLIDAY TREATS-832790	TL	13.50	13.50
92	CHECKIN' HIS LIST-595756	YR	12.50	12.50
92	CHRISTMAS BIZ-593168	TL	22.50	22.50
92	CHRISTMAS CAT NAPPIN'-595764	YR	12.00	12.00
92	CHRISTMAS CURE-ALLS-588938	TL	20.00	20.00
92	CHRISTMAS EVE-MERGENCY-588849	TL	27.00	27.00
92	CHRISTMAS IS IN THE AIR-831174	TL	25.00	25.00
92	CHRISTMAS LIFTS THE SPIRITS-582018	TL	25.00	25.00
92	CHRISTMAS TRIMMIN'-590932	TL	17.00	17.00
92	DIAL 'S' FOR SANTA-589373	TL	25.00	25.00
92	FESTIVE FIDDLERS-586501	YR	20.00	20.00
92	FESTIVE NEWFLASH-588792	TL	17.50	17.50
92	FIRED UP FOR CHRISTMAS-595799	YR	12.00	12.00
92	FIRESIDE FRIENDS-588830	TL	20.00	20.00
92	GOOD CATCH-595721	YR	12.50	12.50
92	GUTEN CHEERS-587192	YR	22.50	22.50
92	HAVE A SOUP-ER CHRISTMAS-588911	TL	17.50	17.50
92	HOLIDAY TAKE-OUT-593508	YR	17.50	17.50
92	HOLIDAYS GIVE ME A LIFT-588865	TL	30.00	30.00
92	HOPPY HOLIDAYS-588814	YR	13.50	13.50
92	LIGHTS...CAMERA...CHRISTMAS!-594369	TL	20.00	20.00
92	MC HO HO HO-585181	TL	22.50	22.50
92	MERRY KISSES-831166	TL	17.50	17.50
92	MERRY MISTLE TOAD-588288	TL	15.00	15.00
92	MOON WATCH-587184	TL	20.00	20.00
92	MUSIC MICE-TRO!-575143	TL	12.00	12.00
92	ON TARGET TWO-GETHER-575623	YR	17.00	17.00
92	PUT ON A HAPPY FACE-588237	TL	15.00	15.00
92	SMALL FRY'S FIRST CHRISTMAS-586749	TL	17.00	17.00
92	SPECIAL DELIVERY-832812	TL	12.00	12.00
92	SPECIAL DELIVERY-840440	YR	22.50	22.50
92	SPIRITED STALLION-594407	YR	15.00	15.00
92	SPREADING SWEET JOY-580465	YR	13.50	13.50
92	SUNDAE RIDE-583707	TL	20.00	20.00
92	SWINGIN' CHRISTMAS-584096	TL	15.00	15.00
92	TAKE A CHANCE ON THE HOLIDAYS-594075	TL	20.00	20.00
92	TEE-RIFIC HOLIDAYS-590827	TL	25.00	25.00
92	THE COLD, CRISP TASTE OF COKE-583766	TL	17.00	17.00
92	THE HOLIDAYS ARE A HIT-581577	TL	17.50	17.50
92	THE WARMTH OF THE SEASON-586994	TL	20.00	20.00
92	TIC-TAC-MISTLE-TOE-588296	YR	23.00	23.00
92	TIP TOP TIDINGS-581828	TL	13.00	13.00
92	TO A DEAR BABY-587168	YR	18.50	18.50
92	TOYFUL' RUDOLPH-593982	TL	22.50	22.50
92	TRUNK OF TREASURES-588636	YR	20.00	20.00
92	WATCHING FOR SANTA-840432	TL	25.00	25.00
92	WEAR THE SEASON WITH A SMILE-595829	YR	10.00	10.00
92	WRAPPIN' UP WARM WISHES-593141	YR	17.50	17.50
92	YULE TIDE TOGETHER-588903	TL	20.00	20.00
93	25 POINTS FOR CHRISTMAS	OP	25.00	25.00
93	A KICK OUT OF CHRISTMAS	OP	10.00	10.00
93	A PAUSE FOR CLAUS	OP	22.50	22.50
93	ALL YOU ADD IS LOVE	OP	18.50	18.50
93	ARIEL'S UNDER-THE-SEA TREE	OP	22.50	22.50
93	BABY'S FIRST CHRISTMAS DINNER	OP	12.00	12.00
93	BEARLY BALANCED	OP	15.00	15.00
93	BORN TO SHOP	OP	26.50	26.50
93	CELEBRATING W/A SPLASH	OP	17.00	17.00
93	CHRISTMAS DANCER	OP	15.00	15.00
93	CHRISTMAS IN THE MAKING	OP	20.00	20.00

YR	NAME	LIMIT	ISSUE	QUOTE
93	CHRISTMAS IS IN THE AIR	OP	25.00	25.00
93	CHRISTMAS KICKS	OP	17.50	17.50
93	CHRISTMAS MAIL CALL	OP	20.00	20.00
93	CHRISTMAS-TO-GO	OP	25.50	25.50
93	CLOWNIN' AROUND	OP	10.00	10.00
93	COOL YULE	OP	12.00	12.00
93	COUNTIN' ON A MERRY CHRISTMAS	OP	22.50	22.50
93	DESIGNED W/YOU IN MIND	OP	16.00	16.00
93	DREAM WHEELS	OP	29.50	29.50
93	DUCKING THE SEASON'S RUSH	OP	17.50	17.50
93	DUNK THE HALLS	OP	18.50	18.50
93	FOCUSING ON CHRISTMAS	OP	27.50	27.50
93	FOR A SHARP UNCLE	OP	10.00	10.00
93	FRIENDS THROUGH THICK & THIN	OP	10.00	10.00
93	GOOFY ABOUT SKIING	OP	22.50	22.50
93	HANGINING OUT FOR THE HOLIDAYS	OP	15.00	15.00
93	HAPPILY EVER AFTER	OP	25.00	25.00
93	HAPPY HAUL-IDAYS	OP	30.00	30.00
93	HAVE A CHERRY CHRISTMAS, SISTER	OP	13.50	13.50
93	HAVE A HOLLY JELL-O CHRISTMAS	OP	19.50	19.50
93	HEART FILLED DREAMS	OP	10.00	10.00
93	HEARTS AGLOW	OP	18.50	18.50
93	HERE COMES RUDOLPH	OP	17.50	17.50
93	HERE COMES SANTA CLAWS	OP	22.50	22.50
93	HOLIDAY MEW-SIC	OP	20.00	20.00
93	HOLIDAY ORDERS	OP	20.00	20.00
93	HOLIDAY TREASURES	OP	18.50	18.50
93	HOLIDAY WISHES	OP	17.50	17.50
93	HOME TWEET HOME	OP	10.00	10.00
93	HOT OFF THE PRESS	OP	27.50	27.50
93	I'M DREAMING OF A WHITE-OUT CHRISTMAS	OP	22.50	22.50
93	IT'S BEGINNING TO LOOK A LOT LIKE...	OP	22.50	22.50
93	JOYEUX NOEL	OP	24.50	24.50
93	LIGHT UP YOUR HOLIDAYS W/COKE	OP	27.50	27.50
93	LIGHTS..CAMERA..CHRISTMAS	OP	20.00	20.00
93	LOVE'S SWEET DANCE	OP	29.50	29.50
93	MAGIC CARPET RIDE	OP	25.00	25.00
93	MERRY CHRISTMAS, BABY	OP	10.00	10.00
93	MERRY CHRISTMAS, DAUGHTER	OP	20.00	20.00
93	MERRY MC-CHOO-CHOO	OP	30.00	30.00
93	MICKEY'S HOLIDAY TREASURE	OP	12.00	12.00
93	ON YOUR MARK,GET SET,IS THAT TO GO?	OP	13.50	13.50
93	PITTER-PATTER POST OFFICE	OP	20.00	20.00
93	PLANE O' HOLIDAY FUN	OP	27.50	27.50
93	POOL HALL-IDAYS	OP	19.00	19.00
93	ROCKIN' W/SANTA	OP	13.50	13.50
93	ROUNDIN' UP CHRISTMAS TOGETHER	OP	25.00	25.00
93	SANTA'S MAGIC RIDE	OP	24.00	24.00
93	SEE-SAW SWEETHEARTS	OP	10.00	10.00
93	SLEDDIN' MR. SNOWMAN	OP	13.00	13.00
93	SLIMMIN' SANTA	OP	18.50	18.50
93	SMOOTH MOVE, MOM	OP	20.00	20.00
93	SPECIAL DELIVERY FOR SANTA	OP	10.00	10.00
93	SPOT OF LOVE	OP	20.00	20.00
93	SPREADING JOY	OP	27.50	27.50
93	SWEET SEASONS EATINGS	OP	22.50	22.50
93	SWEET WHISKERED WISHES	OP	17.00	17.00
93	T'WAY THE NIGHT BEFORE CHRISTMAS	OP	22.50	22.50
93	TANGLED UP FOR CHRISTMAS	OP	14.50	14.50
93	TERRIFIC TOYS	OP	20.00	20.00
93	THE FAIREST ONE OF ALL	OP	20.00	20.00
93	TO MY GEM	OP	27.50	27.50
93	TOASTY TIDINGS	OP	20.00	20.00
93	TOOL TIME, YULE TIME	OP	18.50	18.50
93	TOP MARKS FOR TEACHER	OP	10.00	10.00
93	TOY TO THE WORLD	OP	25.00	25.00
93	TREASURE THE HOLIDAYS, MAN'	OP	25.00	25.00
93	WARM & HEARTY WISHES	OP	17.50	17.50
93	WATCHING FOR SANTA	OP	25.00	25.00
94	'A' FOR SANTA	OP	17.50	17.50
94	A BOUGH FOR BELLE!	OP	18.50	18.50
94	A CHRISTMAS TAIL	OP	20.00	20.00
94	A HOLIDAY OPPORTUNITY	OP	20.00	20.00
94	A REAL BOY FOR CHRISTMAS	OP	15.00	15.00
94	A SIGN OF PEACE	OP	18.50	18.50
94	AHOY JOY!	OP	20.00	20.00

YR	NAME	LIMIT	ISSUE	QUOTE
94	ANSWERING CHRISTMAS WISHES	OP	17.50	17.50
94	ARIEL'S CHRISTMAS SURPRISE!	OP	20.00	20.00
94	BUBBLIN' W/JOY	OP	12.50	12.50
94	BULDING A SEW-MAN	OP	18.50	18.50
94	BUNDLE OF JOY	OP	10.00	10.00
94	CHRISTMAS CROSSROADS	OP	20.00	20.00
94	CHRISTMAS CRUSIN'	OP	22.50	22.50
94	CHRISTMAS FISHES FROM SANTA PAWS	OP	18.50	18.50
94	CHRISTMAS FLY-BY	OP	15.00	15.00
94	CHRISTMAS SWISHES	OP	17.50	17.50
94	CHRISTMAS TEE TIME	OP	25.00	25.00
94	CHRISTMAS TWO-GETHER	OP	12.50	12.50
94	COCOA 'N' KISSES FOR SANTA	OP	22.50	22.50
94	COOL CRUISE	19,640	20.00	20.00
94	EXERCISING GOOD TASTE	OP	17.50	17.50
94	FEATURED PRESENTATION	OP	20.00	20.00
94	GALIANT GREETING	OP	20.00	20.00
94	GOOD FORTUNE TO YOU	OP	25.00	25.00
94	GOOD THINGS CROP UP AT CHRISTMAS	OP	25.00	25.00
94	GOOD TIDINGS,TIDINGS,TIDINGS..	OP	20.00	20.00
94	GOOFY DELIVERY	OP	22.50	22.50
94	GRANDMAS ARE SEW SPECIAL	OP	12.50	12.50
94	HAND-TOSSED TIDINGS	OP	17.50	17.50
94	HANDLE W/CARE	OP	20.00	20.00
94	HAPPY HOWL-IDAYS	OP	22.50	22.50
94	HAVE A BALL AT CHRISTMAS	OP	15.00	15.00
94	HAVE A MERRY DAIRY CHRISTMAS	OP	22.50	22.50
94	HAVE A TOTEM-LY TERRIFIC CHRISTMAS	OP	30.00	30.00
94	HOLIDAY HONEYS	OP	20.00	20.00
94	HOLIDAY SHOW-STOPPER	OP	15.00	15.00
94	HOLIDAY STARS	OP	20.00	20.00
94	I CAN BEAR-LY WAIT FOR A COKE	OP	18.50	18.50
94	L'IL STOCKING STUFFER	OP	17.50	17.50
94	MERRY CHRISTMAS TOOL YOU, DAD	OP	22.50	22.50
94	MERRY LITTLE TWO-STEP	OP	12.50	12.50
94	MERRY MEMO-RIES	OP	22.50	22.50
94	MERRY MENAGE	OP	20.00	20.00
94	MERRY MISCHIEF	OP	15.00	15.00
94	MERRY REINDEER RIDE	OP	20.00	20.00
94	MINNIE'S HOLIDAY TREASURE	OP	12.00	12.00
94	NUTCRACKER SWEETHEART	OP	15.00	15.00
94	ON THE ROAD W/COKE	OP	25.00	25.00
94	ONCE UPON A TIME	OP	15.00	15.00
94	PEACE ON EARTH 132942	OP	12.50	12.50
94	PEACE ON EARTHWORM	OP	20.00	20.00
94	PICTURE PERFECT CHRISTMAS	OP	15.00	15.00
94	PURDY PACKAGES, PARDNER!	OP	20.00	20.00
94	PURE CHRISTMAS PLEASURE	OP	20.00	20.00
94	ROCKIN' RANGER	OP	25.00	25.00
94	SANTA CLAUS IS COMIN'	OP	20.00	20.00
94	SANTA DELIVERS	OP	12.00	12.00
94	SANTA'S L'IL HELPER	OP	12.50	12.50
94	SANTA...PHONE HOME	OP	25.00	25.00
94	SANTA..YOU'RE THE POPS!	OP	22.50	22.50
94	SEASONED W/LOVE	OP	22.50	22.50
94	SKI-SON'S GREETINGS	OP	20.00	20.00
94	SPECIAL DELIVERY	OP	20.00	20.00
94	SWEET DREAMS	OP	12.50	12.50
94	SWEET GREETINGS	OP	12.50	12.50
94	SWEETS FOR MY SWEETIE	OP	15.00	15.00
94	TEED-OFF DONALD	OP	15.00	15.00
94	THE LATEST MEWS FROM HOME	OP	16.00	16.00
94	THE WAY TO A MOUSE'S HEART	OP	15.00	15.00
94	TO COIN A PHRASE, MERRY CHRISTMAS	OP	20.00	20.00
94	TO MY FAVORITE V.I.P.	OP	20.00	20.00
94	WHAT'S SHAKIN' FOR CHRISTMAS	OP	18.50	18.50
94	WISHING UPON A STAR	OP	18.50	18.50
94	WISHING YOU WELL AT CHRISTMAS	OP	25.00	25.00
94	YULE FUEL	OP	20.00	20.00
94	YULETIDE YUMMIES	OP	20.00	20.00
95	57 HVN	OP	20.00	20.00
95	A CAROUSEL FOR ARIEL	OP	17.50	
95	A LITTLE SOMETHING EXTRA..EXTRA	10,000	25.00	
95	A SIP OF GOOD MEASURE	OP	17.50	
95	A WELL BALANCED MEAL FOR SANTA	OP	17.50	
95	ABOVE THE CROWD-R.MCDONALD HOUSE	OP	20.00	20.00

YR	NAME	LIMIT	ISSUE	QUOTE
95	ALL TUCKED IN	OP	15.00	
95	BABY'S SWEET FEAST	OP	17.50	
95	BUBBLIN' W/JOY	OP	15.00	15.00
95	CADDY	OP	20.00	20.00
95	CHOC FULL OF WISHES	OP	20.00	20.00
95	CHRISTMAS BELLE	OP	20.00	
95	CHRISTMAS FISHES, DAD	OP	17.50	
95	CHRISTMAS VACATION	OP	20.00	
95	CORVETTE	OP	20.00	20.00
95	CRACKIN' A SMILE	OP	17.50	17.50
95	DASHING THROUGH THE SNOW	OP	20.00	20.00
95	DREAMIN OF THE ONE I LOVE	OP	25.00	
95	FRIENDS FUR-EVER	OP	20.00	
95	FUN IN HAND	OP	20.00	
95	GOOFED-UP	OP	20.00	20.00
95	GOTTA HAVE A CLUE	OP	20.00	
95	HAPPY YULEGLIDE	OP	17.50	17.50
95	HAVE A COKE & A SMILE	OP	22.50	22.50
95	HO, HO, HOLE IN ONE!	OP	20.00	20.00
95	HOLIDAY BIKE HIKE	OP	20.00	20.00
95	HOLIDAY BOUND	OP	20.00	20.00
95	HOLIDAY TOY RIDE	OP	17.50	
95	HOME FOR THE HOWL-I-DAYS	OP	20.00	20.00
95	HOW..DO I LOVE THEE...	OP	22.50	22.50
95	HUSTLING UP SOME CHEER	OP	20.00	20.00
95	JUST FORE CHRISTMAS	OP	15.00	
95	LOOKING OUR HOLIDAY BEST	OP	25.00	
95	MAKE MINE A COKE	OP	25.00	25.00
95	MAKIN' TRACKS W/MICKEY	OP	20.00	20.00
95	MERRY CHRISTMAS TO ME	OP	20.00	
95	MERRY MCMEAL	OP	17.50	17.50
95	MERRY MONOPOLY	OP	22.50	22.50
95	MICKEY AT THE HELM	OP	17.50	17.50
95	MICKEY'S AIRMAIL	OP	20.00	20.00
95	MINNIE'S MERRY CHRISTMAS	OP	20.00	20.00
95	MOM'S TAXI	OP	25.00	25.00
95	NO TIME TO SPARE AT CHRISTMAS	OP	20.00	20.00
95	NUTTY ABOUT CHRISTMAS	OP	22.50	22.50
95	ON THE BALL AT CHRISTMAS	OP	15.00	15.00
95	PLANELY DELICIOUS	OP	20.00	20.00
95	PUPPY LOVE	OP	17.50	
95	RX:MAS GREETINGS	OP	17.50	17.50
95	SALUTE'	OP	22.50	
95	SANTA'S SPEEDWAY	OP	20.00	20.00
95	SCORING BIG AT CHRISTMAS	OP	20.00	20.00
95	SERVING UP THE BEST	OP	17.50	17.50
95	SNACK THAT HITS THE SPOT	OP	15.00	
95	SNEAKING A PEEK	OP	22.50	
95	STARRING ROLL AT CHRISTMAS	OP	17.50	17.50
95	SWEET ON YOU	OP	22.50	22.50
95	SWISHING YOU SWEET GREETINGS	OP	20.00	20.00
95	T-BIRD (RED)	19,550	20.00	20.00
95	T-BIRD (BLACK)	OP	20.00	
95	TAIL WAGGIN' WISHES	OP	17.50	
95	THE MAZE OF OUR LIVES	OP	17.50	
95	TIME FOR REFRESHMENTS	OP	20.00	20.00
95	TINKERTOY JOY	OP	20.00	20.00
95	TOYS TO TREASURE	OP	20.00	20.00
95	TRUCKIN'	OP	25.00	25.00
95	TRUNK FULL FO TREASURES	20,000	25.00	25.00
95	WISHING YOU A PERFECT HOLIDAY	OP	5.00	
95	YOU'RE MY CUP OF TEA	OP	20.00	20.00
95	YULE LOGON FOR CHRISTMAS CHEER	OP	20.00	20.00
95	YULE TIDE PRANCER	OP	15.00	
90	JINGLE BELL ROCK 1990-563390	YR	13.50	18.00
89	HOLLY-FAIRY-565199	YR	15.00	35.00
90	THE CHRISTMAS TREE FAIRY-565202	YR	15.00	25.00
94	'TIS THE SEASON TO GO SHOPPING	OP	22.50	22.50
94	A CHILD IS BORN	OP	25.00	25.00
94	BABY'S FIRST CHRISTMAS	OP	20.00	20.00
94	BABY'S FIRST CHRISTMAS	OP	20.00	20.00
94	DROPPING IN FOR THE HOLIDAYS	OP	20.00	20.00
94	DRUMMING UP A SEASON OF JOY	OP	18.50	18.50
94	FRIENDSHIPS WARM THE HOLIDAYS	OP	20.00	20.00
94	MAY ALL YOUR WISHES COME TRUE	OP	20.00	20.00
94	MAY YOUR HOLIDAY BE BRIGHTENED W/LOVE	OP	15.00	15.00

YR	NAME	LIMIT	ISSUE	QUOTE
94	OUR FIRST CHRISTMAS TOGETHER	OP	25.00	25.00
94	RINGING UP HOLIDAY WISHES	OP	18.50	18.50
94	SENDING YOU A SEASON'S GREETING	OP	25.00	25.00
94	SWEET HOLIDAYS	OP	11.00	11.00
95	BABY'S FIRST CHRISTMAS	OP	15.00	15.00
95	BABY'S FIRST CHRISTMAS	OP	15.00	15.00
95	BRINGING HOLIDAY WISHES TO YOU	OP	22.50	22.50
95	FRIENDS ARE THE GREATEST TREASURE	20,000	25.00	25.00
95	HAPPY BIRTHDAY JESUS	OP	15.00	15.00
95	I'M IN A SPIN OVER YOU	OP	15.00	15.00
95	LETS SNUGGLE TOGETHER FOR CHRISTMAS	OP	15.00	15.00
95	OUR FIRST CHRISTMAS TOGETHER	OP	22.50	22.50
95	PRETTY UP FOR THE HOLIDAYS	OP	20.00	20.00
95	TWINKLE, TWINKLE CHRISTMAS STAR	OP	17.50	17.50
95	YOU BRING THE LOVE TO CHRISTMAS	OP	15.00	15.00
95	YOU PULL THE STRINGS TO MY HEART	OP	20.00	20.00
88	DAIRY CHRISTMAS-557501	TL	10.00	15.00
89	CHRISTMAS COOK-OUT-561045	TL	9.00	12.00
89	DECK THE HOGS-565490	TL	12.00	16.00
89	FELIZ NAVIDAD! 1989-564842	YR	11.00	20.00
89	PINATA RIDIN'-565504	TL	11.00	18.00
89	SCRUB-A-DUB CHIPMUNK-561037	TL	8.00	10.00
89	SPREADING CHRISTMAS JOY-564850	TL	10.00	10.00
89	TOP OF THE CLASS-565237	TL	11.00	11.00
90	CHRISTMAS IS MAGIC-564826	TL	10.00	10.00
90	FLEECE NAVIDAD-571903	TL	13.50	13.50
90	HAVE A NAVAHO-HO-HO 1990-571970	YR	15.00	18.00
90	LIGHTING UP CHRISTMAS-564834	TL	10.00	14.00
90	MERRY MOUSTRONAUTS-573558	TL	20.00	20.00
90	REELING IN THE HOLIDAYS-560405	TL	8.00	10.00
91	CHRISTMAS TO GO-580600	YR	22.50	22.50
91	DOUBLE SCOOP SNOWMOUSE-564796	TL	13.50	13.50
91	HAVE A MARIACHI CHRISTMAS-580619	TL	13.50	13.50
91	WALKIN'WITH MY BABY-561029	TL	10.00	10.00
92	LA LUMINARIA-586579	TL	13.50	13.50
82	HOLIDAY SKIER-E-6954	TL	7.00	30.00
83	GARFIELD CUTS THE ICE-E-8771	TL	6.00	45.00
83	STOCKING FULL FOR 1983-E-8773	YR	8.00	45.00
84	DEER! ODIE-E6226	TL	6.00	40.00
84	FUN IN SANTA'S SLEIGH-E-6225	TL	12.00	35.00
84	GARFIELD HARK! THE HERALD ANGEL-E-6224	TL	7.50	45.00
84	GARFIELD THE SNOW CAT-E-6227	TL	12.00	12.00
84	STOCKING FULL FOR 1984-E-8773	YR	6.00	35.00
85	GARFIELD-IN-THE-BOX-56189	YR	6.50	6.50
85	HOPPY CHRISTMAS-56154	YR	8.50	30.00
85	MERRY CHRISTMAS MOTHER-56146	YR	8.50	8.50
85	MERRY CHRISTMAS TEACHER-56170	YR	6.00	6.00
85	NORTH POLE EXPRESS-56138	YR	12.00	35.00
85	SKI TIME-56111	YR	13.00	40.00
86	GIFT WRAP OLDIE-553611	YR	7.00	7.00
86	LIGHTEN UP!-553603	TL	10.00	22.00
87	GARFIELD MERRY KISSMAS-555215	TL	8.50	20.00
87	GARFIELD SUGAR PLUM FAIRY-556009	TL	8.50	25.00
87	GARFIELD THE NUTCRACKER-556017	TL	8.50	15.00
88	DEER GARFIELD-558702	TL	12.00	18.00
88	GARFIELD BAGS O'FUN-558761	YR	3.30	5.00
88	NIGHT-WATCH CAT-558362	TL	13.00	20.00
88	SPECIAL DELIVERY-558699	TL	9.00	16.00
89	A CHAINS OF PACE FOR ODIE-563269	TL	12.00	12.00
89	GOD BLESS US EVERYONE-563242	TL	13.50	13.50
89	HO-HO HOLIDAY SCROOGE-563234	TL	13.50	13.50
89	JOY RIDIN'-563463	TL	15.00	18.00
89	MINE, ALL MINE!-564079	YR	15.00	25.00
89	SCROOGE WITH THE SPIRIT-563250	TL	13.50	15.00
90	AN APPLE A DAY-572594	TL	12.00	15.00
90	DEAR SANTA-572608	TL	17.00	17.00
90	FROSTY GARFIELD 1990-572551	YR	13.50	20.00
90	GARFIELD NFL ATLANTA FALCONS-573159	TL	12.50	12.50
90	GARFIELD NFL BUFFALO BILLS-573108	TL	12.50	12.50
90	GARFIELD NFL CHICAGO BEARS-573248	TL	12.50	12.50
90	GARFIELD NFL CINCINNATI BENGALS-573000	TL	15.50	12.50
90	GARFIELD NFL CLEVELAND BROWNS-573019	TL	12.50	12.50
90	GARFIELD NFL DALLAS COWBOYS-573183	TL	12.50	12.50
90	GARFIELD NFL DENVER BRONCOS-573043	TL	12.50	12.50
90	GARFIELD NFL DETROIT LIONS-573256	TL	12.50	12.50
90	GARFIELD NFL GREEN BAY PACKERS-573264	TL	12.50	12.50

YR	NAME	LIMIT	ISSUE	QUOTE
90	GARFIELD NFL HOUSTON OILERS-573027	TL	12.50	12.50
90	GARFIELD NFL INDIANAPOLIS COLTS-573116	TL	12.50	12.50
90	GARFIELD NFL KANSAS CITY CHIEFS-573051	TL	12.50	12.50
90	GARFIELD NFL LOS ANGELES RAIDERS-573078	TL	12.50	12.50
90	GARFIELD NFL LOS ANGELES RAMS-572764	TL	12.50	12.50
90	GARFIELD NFL MIAMI DOLPHINS-573124	TL	12.50	12.50
90	GARFIELD NFL NEW ENGLAND PATRIOTS-573132	TL	12.50	12.50
90	GARFIELD NFL NEW ORLEANS SAINTS-573167	TL	12.50	12.50
90	GARFIELD NFL NEW YORK GIANTS-573191	TL	12.50	12.50
90	GARFIELD NFL NEW YORK JETS-573140	TL	12.50	12.50
90	GARFIELD NFL PHILADELPHIA EAGLES-573205	TL	12.50	12.50
90	GARFIELD NFL PHOENIX CARDINALS-573213	TL	12.50	12.50
90	GARFIELD NFL PITTSBURG STEELERS-573035	TL	12.50	12.50
90	GARFIELD NFL SAN DIEGO CHARGERS-573086	TL	12.50	12.50
90	GARFIELD NFL SAN FRANCISCO 49ERS-573175	TL	12.50	12.50
90	GARFIELD NFL SEATTLE SEAHAWKS-573094	TL	12.50	12.50
90	GARFIELD NFL TAMPA BAY BUCCANEERS-573280	TL	12.50	12.50
90	GARFIELD NFL WASHINGTON REDSKINS-573221	TL	12.50	12.50
90	LITTLE RED RIDING CAT-572632	YR	13.50	18.00
90	MINNESOTA VIKINGS-573272	TL	12.50	12.50
90	OH SHOOSH!-572624	TL	17.00	17.00
90	OVER THE ROOFTOPS-572721	TL	17.50	17.50
90	POP GOES THE ODIE-572578	TL	15.00	15.00
90	TROUBLE ON WHEELS-564052	TL	20.00	20.00
91	ALL DECKED OUT-572659	TL	13.50	13.50
91	HAVE A BALL THIS CHRISTMAS-572616	YR	15.00	20.00
91	HERE COMES SANTA PAWS-572535	TL	20.00	20.00
91	HOLIDAY HIDEOUT-585270	TL	15.00	15.00
91	HOT STUFF SANTA-573523	TL	25.00	30.00
91	MERRY CHRISTMAS GO-ROUND-585203	TL	20.00	20.00
91	PINOCCHIO-577391	TL	15.00	15.00
91	STRAIGHT TO SANTA-830534	TL	13.50	13.50
91	SWEET BEAMS-572586	TL	13.50	13.50
92	4 X 4 HOLIDAY FUN-580783	TL	20.00	20.00
92	A ROCKIN' GARFIELD CHRISTMAS-572527	TL	17.50	17.50
92	FAST TRACK CAT-585289	TL	17.50	17.50
92	HOLIDAY CAT NAPPING-585319	TL	20.00	20.00
92	HOLIDAY ON ICE-585254	TL	17.50	17.00
92	RING MY BELL-580740	YR	13.50	13.50
93	BAH HUMBUG	OP	15.00	15.00
93	GRADE A WISHES FROM GARFIELD	OP	20.00	20.00
94	MINE, MINE, MINE	OP	20.00	20.00
82	CRESCENT SANTA-E-6950	TL	10.00	65.00
82	DEAR SANTA-E-6959	TL	10.00	15.00
84	BABY'S FIRST CHRISTMAS 1984-E-6212	YR	10.00	10.00
85	BABY'S FIRST CHRISTMAS 1985-56014	YR	6.00	6.00
85	MERRY CHRISTMAS GODCHILD-55832	TL	8.00	30.00
86	BABY BEAR SLEIGH-551651	TL	9.00	30.00
86	BABY'S FIRST CHRISTMAS 1986-551678	YR	10.00	15.00
86	CAROUSEL UNICORN-551252	TL	12.00	75.00
86	MERRY CHRISTMAS-551341	TL	8.00	75.00
86	TIME FOR CHRISTMAS-551325	TL	13.00	25.00
87	BABY'S FIRST CHRISTMAS 1987-556238	YR	10.00	25.00
87	CAROUSEL LION-556025	TL	12.00	25.00
87	HOME SWEET HOME-556033	TL	15.00	55.00
87	PARTRIDGE IN A PEAR TREE-556173	TL	9.00	32.50
87	TEDDY'S STOCKING-555940	TL	10.00	20.00
87	THREE FRENCH HENS-556440	TL	9.00	25.00
87	TWINKLE BEAR-556572	TL	8.00	15.00
87	TWO TURTLEDOVES-556432	TL	9.00	32.50
88	1ST CHRISTMAS TOGETHER-554537	TL	15.00	15.00
88	A CHIPMUNK HOLIDAY-554898	TL	11.00	18.00
88	A MOUSE CHECK-554553	TL	13.50	18.00
88	AIRMAIL FOR TEACHER-489425	TL	13.50	24.50
88	AN EYE ON CHRISTMAS-554545	TL	22.50	34.50
88	BABY'S FIRST CHRISTMAS 1988-554936	YR	10.00	16.00
88	CHRISTMAS TRADITION-558400	TL	10.00	18.00
88	FIVE GOLDEN RINGS-559121	TL	11.00	29.50
88	FOREVER FRIENDS-554626	TL	12.00	27.00
88	FOUR CALLING BIRDS-556459	TL	11.00	29.50
88	LI'L DRUMMER BEAR-554952	TL	12.00	20.00
88	NORTH POLE LINEMAN-558834	TL	10.00	20.00
88	SIX GEESE A-LAYING-559148	TL	11.00	29.50
88	TWO FOR TEA-559776	TL	20.00	30.00
89	ALL SET FOR SANTA-563080	TL	17.50	17.50
89	BABY'S FIRST CHRISTMAS 1989-562815	YR	10.00	13.00

YR	NAME	LIMIT	ISSUE	QUOTE
89	BY THE LIGHT OF THE MOON-563005	TL	12.00	15.00
89	CAUGHT IN THE ACT-830046	TL	12.50	12.50
89	CHESTNUTS ROASTIN'-562912	TL	13.00	27.50
89	CHRISTMAS COOKIN'-563048	TL	22.50	25.00
89	EIGHT MAIDS A-MILKING-562750	TL	12.00	18.00
89	MERRY CHRISTMAS POPS-562971	TL	12.00	24
89	MISTLE-TOAST-1989-562963	YR	15.00	20.50
89	NINE DANCERS DANCING-562769	TL	15.00	18.00
89	OLD TOWN'S CHURCH-554871	TL	17.50	17.50
89	READIN' & RIDIN'-830054	TL	13.50	13.50
89	SARDINE EXPRESS-554588	TL	17.50	20.00
89	SEVEN SWANS A-SWIMMING-562742	TL	12.00	12.00
89	STICKIN' TO IT-563013	TL	10.00	16.00
89	TRAVELIN' TRIKE-562882	TL	15.00	15.00
90	A CAROLING WEE GO-573671	TL	12.00	12.00
90	ALL ABOARD-567671	TL	17.50	17.50
90	ALL EYE WANT FOR CHRISTMAS-573647	TL	27.50	27.50
90	BABY'S FIRST CHRISTMAS 1990-573973	YR	10.00	10.00
90	BABY'S FIRST CHRISTMAS 1990-573981	YR	12.00	14.00
90	DECK THE HALLS-573701	TL	22.50	22.50
90	ELEVEN DRUMMERS DRUMMING-573957	TL	15.00	15.00
90	FIRST CLASS CHRISTMAS-830038	TL	10.00	10.00
90	HAVE A COOL YULE-830496	TL	12.00	12.00
90	HERE'S LOOKING AT YOU-830259	TL	17.50	17.50
90	LITTLE JACK HORNER-574058	TL	17.50	17.50
90	MERRY MAILMAN-573698	TL	15.00	15.00
90	NORTH POLE OR BUST-562998	TL	25.00	25.00
90	OLD KING COLE-575682	TL	20.00	20.00
90	OLD MOTHER MOUSE-573922	TL	17.50	17.50
90	PROF. MICHAEL BEAR/ONE BEAR BAND-573663	TL	22.50	22.50
90	RAILROAD REPAIRS-573930	TL	12.50	12.50
90	SANTA'S SWEETS-563196	TL	20.00	20.00
90	STUCK ON YOU-573655	TL	12.50	12.50
90	SWEETEST GREETINGS 1990-830011	YR	10.00	15.00
90	TH-INK-IN' OF YOU-562920	TL	20.00	20.00
90	TWELVE PIPERS PIPING-573965	TL	15.00	15.00
90	WARMEST WISHES-573825	YR	17.50	24.50
90	YOU'RE WHEEL SPECIAL-573728	TL	15.00	15.00
90	YULETIDE RIDE 1990-577502	YR	13.50	22.00
91	A CHRISTMAS CAROL-583928	TL	22.50	22.50
91	A DECADE OF TREASURES-587052	YR	37.50	37.50
91	A QUARTER POUNDER WITH CHEER-581569	TL	20.00	20.00
91	A SONG FOR SANTA-573779	TL	25.00	25.00
91	AIMING FOR THE HOLIDAYS-830941	TL	12.00	12.00
91	CHRISTMAS CABBOSE-574856	TL	25.00	25.00
91	CHRISTMAS FILLS THE AIR-831921	TL	12.00	12.00
91	CHRISTMAS TRIMMINGS-575631	TL	17.00	17.00
91	COME LET US ADORE HIM-573736	TL	9.00	9.00
91	CRYSTAL BALL CHRISTMAS-575666	TL	22.50	22.50
91	DREAMIN' OF A WHITE CHRISTMAS-583669	TL	15.00	15.00
91	FIRED UP FOR CHRISTMAS-586587	TL	32.50	32.50
91	FITTIN' MITTENS-830976	TL	12.00	12.00
91	FOR A DOG-GONE GREAT UNCLE-586706	YR	12.00	12.00
91	FOR A PURR-FECT AUNT-586692	YR	12.00	12.00
91	FOR A PURR-FECT MOM-586641	YR	12.00	12.00
91	FOR A SPECIAL DAD-586668	YR	17.50	17.50
91	FROM THE SAME MOLD-581798	TL	17.00	17.00
91	GUMBALL WIZARD-575658	TL	13.00	13.00
91	KURIOUS KITTY-573868	TL	17.50	19.00
91	LETTERS TO SANTA-830925	TL	15.00	15.00
91	LIGHTS..CAMERA..KISSMAS!-583626	YR	15.00	18.00
91	MARY, MARY QUITE CONTRARY-574066	TL	22.50	22.50
91	MERRY MILLIMETERS-583677	TL	17.00	17.00
91	MOON BEAM DREAMS-573760	TL	12.00	12.00
91	MR. MAILMOUSE-587109	TL	17.00	17.00
91	ODE TO JOY-830968	TL	10.00	10.00
91	ONE FOGGY CHRISTMAS EVE-586625	TL	30.00	30.00
91	PEDDLING FUN-586714	YR	16.00	16.00
91	PETER, PETER PUMPKIN EATER-574015	TL	20.00	20.00
91	SANTA DELIVERS LOVE-562904	TL	17.50	17.50
91	SANTA'S KEY MAN-830461	TL	11.00	11.00
91	SNEAKING SANTA'S SNACK-830933	TL	13.00	13.00
91	SPECIAL KEEPSAKES-586722	YR	13.50	13.50
91	SWEET STEED-583634	TL	15.00	15.00
91	THE FINISHING TOUCH-831530	YR	10.00	12.00
91	THROUGH THE YEARS-574252	YR	17.50	17.50

YR	NAME	LIMIT	ISSUE	QUOTE
91	TIE-DINGS OF JOY-830488	YR	12.00	12.00
91	TOM, TOM THE PIPER'S SON-575690	TL	15.00	15.00
91	WITH LOVE-586676	YR	13.00	13.00
92	A BOOT-IFUL CHRISTMAS-840165	YR	20.00	20.00
92	A CHRISTMAS YARN-593516	YR	20.00	20.00
92	A GOLD STAR FOR TEACHER-831948	TL	15.00	15.00
92	A MUG FULL OF LOVE-832928	YR	13.50	13.50
92	A TALL ORDER-832758	TL	12.00	12.00
92	BEARLY SLEEPY-578029	YR	17.50	17.50
92	BUBBLE BUDDY-586978	TL	13.50	13.50
92	CANDLELIGHT SERENADE-832766	TL	12.00	12.00
92	CATCH A FALLING STAR-583944	TL	15.00	15.00
92	CATCH A FALLING STAR-583944	TL	15.00	15.00
92	CHRISTMAS NITE CAP-834424	TL	13.50	13.50
92	CHRISTOPHER COLUMOUSE-832782	YR	12.00	12.00
92	COZY CHRISTMAS CARRIAGE-586730	TL	22.50	22.50
92	FIREHOUSE FRIENDS-586951	YR	22.50	22.50
92	FUR-EVER FRIENDS-590797	TL	13.50	13.50
92	GINGER-BRED GREETING-831581	YR	12.00	12.00
92	HAVE A COOL CHRISTMAS-832944	YR	13.50	13.50
92	HOLIDAY GLOW PUPPET SHOW-832774	TL	15.00	15.00
92	HOLIDAY HAPPENINGS-588555	TL	30.00	30.00
92	HOLIDAY HONORS-833029	YR	15.00	15.00
92	HUMPTY DUMPTY-574244	TL	25.00	25.00
92	IT'S A GO FOR CHRISTMAS-587095	TL	15.00	15.00
92	KNITTEN' KITTENS-832952	YR	17.50	17.50
92	MAKING TRACKS TO SANTA-832804	TL	15.00	15.00
92	NORTH POLE PEPPERMINT PATROL-840157	TL	25.00	25.00
92	POPPIN' HOPPIN' HOLIDAYS-831263	YR	25.00	25.00
92	POST-MOUSTER GENERAL-587117	TL	20.00	20.00
92	QUEEN OF HEARTS-575712	TL	17.50	17.50
92	ROCK-A-BYE BABY-575704	TL	13.50	13.50
92	SANTA'S MIDNIGHT SNACK-588598	TL	20.00	20.00
92	SEED-SON'S GREETINGS-588571	TL	27.00	27.00
92	SEW CHRISTMASY-583820	TL	25.00	25.00
92	SWEET AS CANEBE-583642	TL	15.00	15.00
92	TANKFUL TIDINGS-831271	TL	30.00	30.00
92	THE NUTCRACKER-574023	TL	25.00	25.00
92	THROUGH THE YEARS-586862	YR	17.50	17.50
92	TO THE POINT-831182	TL	13.50	13.50
92	WINDOW WISH LIST-586854	TL	30.00	30.00
93	A BRIGHT IDEA	OP	22.50	22.50
93	A MISTLE-TOW	OP	15.00	15.00
93	BABY'S FIRST CHRISTMAS	OP	17.50	17.50
93	CARVING CHRISTMAS WISHES	OP	25.00	25.00
93	DELIVERED TO THE NICK IN TIME	OP	13.50	13.50
93	FESTIVE FIREMAN	OP	17.00	17.00
93	FOR A STAR AUNT	OP	12.00	12.00
93	GRANDMA'S LIDDLE GRIDDLE	OP	10.00	10.00
93	HAVE A COOL CHRISTMAS	OP	10.00	10.00
93	HAVE A DARN GOOD CHRISTMAS	OP	21.00	21.00
93	MY SPECIAL CHRISTMAS	OP	17.50	17.50
93	NOT A CREATURE WAS STIRRING...	OP	27.50	27.50
93	SAY CHEESE	OP	13.50	13.50
93	SEEING IS BELIEVING	OP	20.00	20.00
93	SNEAKING A PEEK	OP	10.00	10.00
93	SUGAR CHEF SHOPPE	OP	23.50	23.50
93	THE SWEETEST RIDE	OP	18.50	18.50
93	TIME FOR SANTA	OP	17.50	17.50
93	TO A GRADE A TEACHER	OP	10.00	10.00
93	TREE FOR TWO	OP	17.50	17.50
94	'TWAS THE NITE BEFORE CHRISTMAS	OP	18.50	18.50
94	ALMOST TIME FOR SANTA	OP	25.00	25.00
94	BUTTONS 'N' BOW BOUTIQUE	OP	22.50	22.50
94	CHIMINY CHEER	OP	22.50	22.50
94	CHRISTMAS CUSTOMS	10,000	17.50	17.50
94	COZY CANDLELIGHT DINNER	OP	25.00	25.00
94	ESPECIALLY FOR YOU	OP	27.50	27.50
94	FINE FEATHERED FESTIVITIES	OP	22.50	22.50
94	FINISHING FIRST	OP	20.00	20.00
94	FROM OUR HOUSE TO YOURS	OP	25.00	25.00
94	GOOD FRIENDS ARE FOREVER	OP	13.50	13.50
94	HOLIDAY CHEW-CHEW	OP	22.50	22.50
94	HOLIDAY FREEZER TEASER	OP	25.00	25.00
94	JOY FROM HEAR TO HOSE	OP	15.00	15.00
94	MELTED MY HEART	OP	15.00	15.00

YR	NAME	LIMIT	ISSUE	QUOTE
94	SANTA' S SING-A-LONG	OP	20.00	20.00
94	SANTA' SECRET TEST DRIVE	OP	20.00	20.00
94	SANTA'S GINGER-BRED DOE	OP	15.00	1500
94	SUGAR 'N SPICE FOR SOMEONE NICE	OP	30.00	30.00
94	THE LATEST SCOOP FROM SANTA	OP	18.50	18.50
94	TO THE SWEETEST BABY	OP	18.50	18.50
94	TOY TINKER TOPPER	OP	20.00	20.00
94	YOU'RE A WHEEL COOL BROTHER	OP	22.50	22.50
94	YOU'RE A WINNER SON!	OP	18.50	18.50
95	4-ALARM CHRISTMAS	OP	17.50	17.50
95	A THIMBLE OF THE SEASON	OP	22.50	
95	FILLED TO THE BRIM	OP	25.00	
95	SEA-SON'S GREETINGS, TEACHER	OP	17.50	17.50
95	SIESTA SANTA	OP	25.00	25.00
95	SWEET HARMONY	OP	17.50	
95	TO SANTA, POST HASTE	OP	15.00	15.00
95	WE'VE SHARED SEW MUCH	OP	25.00	25.00
86	THE SANTA CALUS SHOPPE CIRCA 1905-551562	TL	8.00	18.00
89	FULL HOUSE MOUSE-565016	TL	13.50	22.00
89	I FEEL PRETTY-565024	TL	20.00	25.00
90	BABY'S CHRISTMAS FEAST-565040	TL	13.50	22
90	BUBBLE TROUBLE-575038	TL	20.00	20.00
90	CATCH OF THE DAY-575070	TL	25.00	25.00
90	COFFEE BREAK-564990	TL	15.00	15.00
90	DON'T OPEN 'TIL CHRISTMAS-575089	TL	16.50	16.50
90	I CAN'T WEIGHT TIL CHRISTMAS-575119	TL	17.50	17.50
90	SLOTS O LUCK-830518	TL	13.50	22.00
90	WARMEST WISHES-565032	TL	15.00	15.00
90	YIPPIE-I-YULETIDE-564982	TL	15.00	24
90	YOU'RE SEW SPECIAL-565008	YR	20.00	25.00
91	A HOLIDAY SCENT STATION-575054	TL	15.00	15.00
91	BATHING BEAUTY-860581	TL	13.50	13.50
91	DECK THE HALLS-575127	TL	15.00	15.00
91	HATS OFF TO CHRISTMAS-586757	YR	22.50	22.50
91	MERRY MOTHER-TO-BE-575046	TL	13.50	13.50
91	TEA FOR TWO-573299	TL	30.00	30.00
92	CAMPIN' COMPANIONS-590282	TL	20.00	20.00
92	FRIENDSHIPS PRESERVED-586749	YR	22.50	22.50
92	JESUS LOVES ME-595837	YR	10.00	10.00
92	JOY TO THE WHIRLED-589551	TL	20.00	20.00
92	MERRY CHRISTMAS MOTHER EARTH-595810	YR	11.00	11.00
92	MERRY MAKE-OVER-589586	TL	20.00	20.00
92	SALUTE THE SEASON-595780	YR	12.00	12.00
92	SPINNING CHRISTMAS DREAMS-590908	TL	22.50	22.50
92	SQUIRRELIN' IT WAY-595748	YR	12.00	12.00
92	TREASURE THE EARTH-593826	TL	25.00	25.00
93	A TOAST LADLED W/LOVE	OP	15.00	15.00
93	DECEMBER 25..DEAR DIARY	OP	10.00	10.00
93	DO NOT OPEN 'TIL CHRISTMAS	OP	15.00	15.00
93	GOOD GROUNDS FOR FRIENDSHIP	OP	24.50	24.50
93	GREETINGS IN STEREO	OP	19.50	19.50
93	JEWEL BOX BALLET	OP	20.00	20.00
93	MICE CAPADES	OP	26.50	26.50
93	PAINT YOUR HOLIDAYS BRIGHT	OP	10.00	10.00
93	WHEEL MERRY WISHES	OP	15.00	15.00
93	YOU'RE A HIT W/ME, BROTHER	OP	10.00	10.00
94	BUILDING MEMORIES	OP	25.00	25.00
94	EXPECTING JOY	OP	12.50	12.50
94	FRIENDS ARE THE SPICE OF LIFE	OP	20.00	20.00
94	HAPPY HOLI-DATE	OP	22.50	22.50
94	HAVE A DINO-MITE CHRISTMAS	OP	18.50	18.50
94	HOLIDAY CATCH	OP	12.50	12.50
94	MERRY MISS MERRY	OP	12.00	12.00
94	O' COME ALL YE FAITHFUL	OP	15.00	15.00
94	ONE SMALL STEP...	19,690	30.00	30.00
94	OPEN FOR BUSINESS	OP	17.50	17.50
94	RING IN THE HOLIDAYS	OP	12.50	12.50
95	..GOOD WILL TOWARD MEN	10,000	25.00	25.00
95	FRIENDSHIPS BLOOM THROUGH ALL SEASONS	OP	22.50	22.50
95	GET IN THE SPIRIT..RECYCLE	OP	17.50	17.50
95	JACKPOT JOY!	OP	17.50	17.50
95	MISS MERRY'S SECRET	OP	20.00	20.00
95	ON THE MOVE AT CHRISTMAS	OP	17.50	
95	THE NIGHT B 4 CHRISTMAS	OP	20.00	20.00
84	MUPPET BABIES BABY'S/CHRISTMAS-E-6222	YR	10.00	60.00
84	MUPPET BABIES BABY'S/CHRISTMAS-E-6223	YR	10.00	60.00

YR	NAME	LIMIT	ISSUE	QUOTE
89	STAR OF STARS-564389	TL	9.00	10.00
89	YULETIDE TREE HOUSE-564915	TL	20.00	22.00
90	HANG ONTO YOUR HAT-564397	TL	8.00	9.00
91	SANTA WINGS IT-573612	TL	13.00	13.00
92	JOLLY OL' GENT-585645	TL	13.50	13.50
88	OLD FASHIONED ANGEL-559164	TL	12.50	15.00
88	PRETTY BABY-559156	TL	12.50	12.50
94	FORMULA FOR LOVE	OP	10.00	10.00
88	BABY'S FIRST CHRISTMAS-558397	TL	16.00	25.00
92	HEAVEN SENT-588423	TL	12.50	12.50
89	JUST WHAT I WANTED-563668	TL	13.50	13.50
90	FLEAS NAVIDAD-563978	TL	13.50	13.50
90	PUCKER UP!-563676	TL	11.00	11.00
90	TWEET GREETINGS-564044	TL	15.00	15.00
90	WHAT'S THE BRIGHT IDEA-563684	TL	13.50	13.50
91	DECK THE HALLS-860573	TL	12.00	12.00
92	SPEEDIN' MR. SNOWMAN-595802	YR	12.00	12.00
85	CHRISTMAS PLANE RIDE-56049	TL	10.00	20.00
86	LUCY & ME CHRISTMAS TREE-552542	TL	7.00	25.00
86	LUCY & ME SKI TIME-552658	TL	6.50	6.50
86	MERRY CHRISTMAS 1986-552186	YR	8.00	8.00
86	MERRY CHRISTMAS 1986-552534	YR	8.00	20.00
87	LUCY & ME ANGEL ON A CLOUD-555452	TL	12.00	20.00
87	LUCY & ME MAILBOX BEAR-556564	TL	3.00	5.00
87	LUCY & ME STORYBOOK BEAR-555444	TL	6.50	14.00
87	MERRY CHRISTMAS 1987-555428	TL	8.00	8.00
87	MERRY CHRISTMAS 1987-555436	YR	8.00	8.00
87	TIME FOR CHRISTMAS-555452	TL	12.00	20.00
88	JESTER BEAR-558222	TL	8.00	20.00
88	MERRY CHRISTMAS 1988-557595	YR	10.00	12.00
88	MERRY CHRISTMAS 1988-557609	YR	10.00	12.00
88	TEDDY BEAR GREETINGS-558214	TL	8.00	12.00
88	TOY CHEST KEEPSAKE-558206	TL	12.50	15.00
89	CHRISTMAS 1989-565210	YR	12.00	12.00
89	CHRISTMAS 1989-568325	YR	12.00	12.00
90	A SPOONFUL OF LOVE-568570	TL	10.00	10.00
90	BABY BEAR CHRISTMAS 1990-575860	YR	12.00	13.00
90	BEARING HOLIDAY WISHES-568619	TL	22.50	22.50
90	BEARY CHRISTMAS 1990-576158	YR	12.00	15.00
90	CHRISTMAS SWINGTIME 1990-568597	TL	13.00	13.00
90	CHRISTMAS SWINGTIME 1990-568600	YR	13.00	13.00
91	BEARY MERRY MAILMAN-830151	TL	13.50	13.50
91	CHRISTMAS SWINGTIME 1991-576166	YR	13.00	15.00
91	CHRISTMAS SWINGTIME 1991-5761714	YR	13.00	15.00
91	CHRISTMAS TWO-GETHER-575615	TL	22.50	22.50
91	CRANK UP THE CAROLS-575887	TL	17.50	17.50
91	LOVE IS THE SECRET INGREDIENT-568562	TL	15.00	15.00
91	TIRE-D LITTLE BEAR-575852	YR	12.50	12.50
92	MOONLIGHT SWING-568627	TL	15.00	15.00
92	TASTY TIDINGS-575836	YR	13.50	13.50
88	CHRISTMAS VACATION-558451	TL	8.00	15.00
88	CHRISTMAS WATCH-558443	TL	11.00	15.00
88	MOUSE UPON A PIPE-489220	TL	10.00	24
88	PARTY MOUSE-558435	TL	12.00	15.00
88	SANTA CLAUS BALLOON-489212	TL	10.00	16.00
88	STOCKING STORY-558419	TL	10.00	16.00
88	SWEET CHERUB-558478	TL	7.00	9.00
88	THE ICE FAIRY-558516	TL	23.00	30.00
88	TIME OUT-558486	TL	11.00	27
88	WINTER TALE-558427	TL	6.00	19
89	HO! HO! YO-YO!-565105	YR	12.00	12.00
89	SPECIAL DELIVERY-565091	YR	12.00	20.00
89	WEIGHTIN' FOR SANTA-565148	TL	7.50	8.00
90	BUMPER CAR SANTA-565083	YR	20.00	25.00
89	TEA FOR TWO-693758	TL	12.50	13.50
89	TEA TIME-694797	TL	12.50	13.50
90	FIREPLACE FROLIC-564435	TL	25.00	25.00
90	HOLIDAY TEA TOAST-694770	TL	13.50	13.50
90	A NIGHT BEFORE CHRISTMAS-572438	TL	17.50	17.50
90	CHEERS 1990-572411	YR	13.50	15.00
90	MERRY KISSMAS-572446	TL	10.00	10.00
91	RIS-SKI BUSINESS-576719	TL	10.00	10.00
92	THE FINISHING TOUCHES-585610	TL	17.50	17.50
89	HANGIN' IN THERE 1989-565598	YR	10.00	15.00
90	MEOW-Y CHRISTMAS 1990-565601	YR	10.00	12.00
89	BUNKIE-561835	TL	22.50	25.00

YR	NAME	LIMIT	ISSUE	QUOTE
89	POPPER-561878	TL	12.00	15.00
89	SPARKLES-561843	TL	17.50	20.00
90	BLINKIE-570214	TL	15.00	15.00
90	SMITCH-570184	TL	22.50	22.50
90	TUMBLES 1990-566519	YR	16.00	22.00
90	TWIDDLES-566551	TL	15.00	15.00
90	TWINKLE & SPRINKLE-570206	TL	22.50	22.50
91	SNUFFY-566578	TL	17.50	18.50
91	STAMPER-830267	YR	13.50	15.00
92	CARVER-570192	YR	17.50	17.50
92	SPARKY & BUFFER-561851	TL	25.00	25.00
93	CHIMIER	OP	25.00	25.00
93	SPEEDY	OP	25.00	25.00
94	TOODLES	OP	25.00	25.00
	TREASURY OF CHRISTMAS COLLECTORS CLUB			
93	CAN'T WEIGHT FOR THE HOLIDAYS-MOO	OP	18.50	18.50
94	SPRY FRY - MOO	OP	15.00	15.00
95	THINGS GO BETTER W/COKE - MOO	OP	15.00	15.00
93	THE TREASURE CARD - SOM	OP	20.00	20.00
95	BUTTONING UP OUR HOLIDAY BEST-MOO	OP	22.50	22.50
95	FIRST CLASS CHRISTMAS - MOO	OP	22.50	22.50
95	HOLIDAY HIGH-LIGH- MOO	OP	15.00	15.00
93	TOGETHER WE CAN SHOOT FOR THE STARS-MOO	OP	17.50	17.50
94	SEEDLINGS GREETINGS-MOO	OP	22.50	22.50
95	YOU'RE THE PERFECT FIT - SOM	OP	17.50	17.50
95	YOU'RE THE PERFECT FIT-SOM (CHARTER MEM)	OP	17.50	17.50

FLAMBRO

*			**EMMETT KELLY JR.**	
89	65TH BIRTHDAY CHRISTMAS ORNAMENT	CL	24.00	30.00-65.00
90	30 YEARS OF CLOWNING	YR	30.00	40.00-65.00
91	EKJ WITH STOCKING AND TOYS	YR	30.00	30.00
92	HOME FOR CHRISTMAS	YR	24.00	24.00
93	CHRISTMAS MAIL	YR	25.00	50.00
94	70TH BIRTHDAY COMMEMORATIVE	YR	24.00	24.00
95	ALL-STAR CIRCUS 20TH ANNIVERSARY	YR	25.00	25.00
M. WU			**LITTLE EMMETT**	
95	CHRISTMAS WRAP	OP	11.50	11.50
95	DECK THE NECK	OP	11.50	11.50
*			**RAGGEDY ANN & ANDY**	
89	RAGGEDY ANDY W/CANDY CANE	YR	13.50	18.00
89	RAGGEDY ANN W/GIFT STOCKING	YR	13.50	18.00

GANZ

C. THAMMAVONGSA			**CHEESERVILLE PICNIC COLLECTION**	
91	AUNTIE MARIGOLD EATING COOKIE	OP	13.00	13.00
91	BABY CICELY	OP	8.00	8.00
91	BABY TRUFFLE	OP	8.00	8.00
91	BLOSSOM & HICKORY IN LOVE	OP	19.00	19.00
91	COUSIN WOODY WITH BEAD & FRUIT	OP	14.00	14.00
91	FELLOW W/PICNIC HAMPER	RT	13.00	13.00
91	FELLOW W/PLATE OF COOKIES	RT	13.00	13.00
91	GRANDMAMAM THISTLEDOWN HOLDING BREAD	OP	14.00	14.00
91	GRANDPAPA THISTLEDOWN CARRYING BKT	OP	13.00	13.00
91	HARLEY HARVESTMOUSE WAVING	OP	13.00	13.00
91	HARRIET HARVESTMOUSE	RT	13.00	13.00
91	JENNY BUTTERFIELD KNEELING	OP	13.00	13.00
91	JEREMY BUTTERFIELD	OP	13.00	13.00
91	LADY W/GRAPES	RT	14.00	14.00
91	LI'L TRUFFLE EATING GRAPES	OP	8.00	8.00
91	LI'L TRUFFLE SMWLLING FLOWERS	OP	16.50	16.50
91	MAMA FIXING SWEET CICELY'S HAIR	RT	16.50	16.50
91	MAMA WITH ROLLING PIN	OP	13.00	13.00
91	MAMA WOODSWORTH W/CAFE	RT	14.00	14.00
91	MARIGOLD THISTLEDOWN PICKING UP JAR	OP	14.00	14.00
91	MEDLEY MEADOWMOUSE/BOUQUET	OP	13.00	13.00
91	PAPA WOODSWORTH	OP	13.00	13.00
91	PICNIC BUDDIES	OP	19.00	19.00
91	VIOLET WITH PEACHES	OP	13.00	13.00
92	SWEET CICELY MUSICAL DOLL IN BKT	OP	85.00	85.00
93	CHUCKLES THE CLOWN	OP	16.00	16.00
93	CLOWNIN' AROUND	OP	10.50	10.50
93	FOR SOMEONE SPECIAL	OP	13.50	13.50
93	LI'L CHEESERS DISPLAY PLAQUE	OP	25.00	25.00
93	STORYTELLER, THE	10,000	25.00	25.00
93	STRUMMIN' AWAY	OP	13.00	13.00
93	SUNDAY DRIVE	OP	40.00	40.00

"Sharing is caring" the members of the Salvation Army Band *seem to proclaim. The musical ornament, which plays "Joy to the World," is produced by Hallmark.*

Why build a snowman when a snowmouse will do? Double Scoop Snowmouse *is a three-year ornament produced by Enesco.*

Starship Enterprise *from the Hallmark Keepsake Ornament's line realized secondary market prices out of this world.*

Is somebody posing as the Jolly Old Elf? Santa *is produced by Lladró.*

YR	NAME	LIMIT	ISSUE	QUOTE
93	SWEET DREAMS	OP	27.50	27.50
93	WILLY'S TOE-TAPPIN' TUNES	OP	15.00	15.00
93	WORDS OF WISDOM	OP	14.00	14.00
94	FIDDLE-DEE-DEE	OP	13.00	13.00
94	MELODY MAKER	OP	17.00	17.00
94	OOM-PAH-PAH	OP	13.00	13.00
94	SWINGIN' SAX	OP	13.00	13.00
94	WASHBOARD BLUES	OP	13.00	13.00
94	WHAT A HOOT!	OP	13.00	13.00
C. THAMMAVONGSA		**COWTOWN/CHRISTMAS COLLECTION**		
94	BILLY THE CALF	OP	14.00	14.00
94	BRONCO BULLY	OP	13.00	13.00
94	BUFFALO BILL CODY	OP	20.00	20.00
94	CALF-IN-THE-BOX	OP	12.50	12.50
94	CHRISTMAS CACTUS	OP	13.50	13.50
94	CHRISTMOOS EVE	OP	12.00	12.00
94	DOWNHILL DAR DEBULL	OP	12.00	12.00
94	HALLEMOOAH	OP	12.00	12.00
94	JINGLE BELL	OP	15.50	15.50
94	LI'L RED GLIDING HOOF	OP	12.00	12.00
94	LITTLE DRUMMER CALF	OP	12.00	12.00
94	OLD MOODONALD	OP	20.00	20.00
94	SAINT NICOWLAS	OP	16.00	16.00
94	SANTA COWS	OP	25.00	25.00
94	SANTA COWS	OP	18.00	18.00
94	SANTA'S LITTLE HEIFER	OP	12.50	12.50
C. THAMMAVONGSA		**COWTOWN/VALENTINE COLLECTION**		
94	I LOVE MOO	OP	15.00	15.00
94	ROBIN HOOF & MAID MOOIAN	OP	23.00	23.00
94	ROMECOW & MOOLIET	OP	22.00	22.00
94	WANTED: A SWEETHEART	OP	16.00	16.00
C. THAMMAVONGSA		**LITTLE CHEESERS/CHRISTMAS COLLECTION**		
92	ABNER APPLETON ORNAMENT	OP	15.00	15.00
92	JENNY BUTTERFIELD ORNAMENT	OP	17.00	17.00
92	JEREMY/ TEDDY BEAR ORNAMENT	OP	13.00	13.00
92	LITTLE TRUFFLE ORNAMENT	OP	9.50	9.50
92	MYRTLE MEADOWMOUSE ORNAMENT	OP	15.00	15.00
92	SANTA CHEESER ORNAMENT	OP	14.00	14.00
93	BABY'S FIRST X'MAS ORNAMENT	OP	12.50	12.50
93	DASHING THROUGH THE SNOW ORN.	OP	11.00	11.00
93	LITTLE STOCKING STUFFER ORNAMENT	OP	10.50	10.50
93	MEADLEY MEADOWMOUSE X'MAS BELL	OP	17.00	17.00
93	OUR 1ST CHRISTMAS TOGETHER ORN.	OP	18.50	18.50
93	SANTA'S LITTLE HELPER ORN.	OP	11.00	11.00
93	SKATING INTO YOUR HEART ORN.	OP	10.00	10.00
94	ALL I WANT FOR CHRISTMAS	RT	13.50	13.50
94	ANGEL	OP	8.00	8.00
94	CANDY CANE CAPER	OP	9.00	9.00
94	CHEESER SHOWMAN	RT	5.00	5.00
94	CHELSEA'S STOCKING BELL	OP	15.50	15.50
94	COUSIN WOODY PLAYING FLUTE	RT	10.00	10.00
94	GRANDPA BLOWING HORN	RT	10.00	10.00
94	HICKORY PLAYING CELLO	RT	10.00	10.00
94	MEDLEY PLAYING DRUM	RT	5.50	5.50
94	MRS. CLAUS	OP	9.00	9.00
94	PEACE ON EARTH	OP	8.00	8.00
94	SANTA SILVERWOOD	OP	9.00	9.00
94	SANTA'S WORKSHOP	OP	10.00	10.00
94	SLEIGH RIDE	RT	9.00	9.00
94	SWINGING INTO THE SEASON	OP	11.00	11.00
94	VIOLET WITH SNOWBALL	RT	5.50	5.50
C. THAMMAVONGSA		**LITTLE CHEESERS/THE SILVERWOODS**		
94	CHRISTMAS SURPRISE	OP	8.50	8.50
94	COMFORT AND JOY	OP	6.00	6.00
94	DECK THE HALLS	OP	9.50	9.50
94	GIDDY UP!	OP	8.50	8.50
94	HICKORY DICKORY DOCK	OP	9.50	9.50
94	XMAS EXPRESS	OP	8.50	8.50
C. THAMMAVONGSA		**PIGSVILLE/CHRISTMAS COLLECTION**		
94	CAROLER	OP	10.00	10.00
94	CHRISTMAS TREATS	OP	9.00	9.00
94	DRUMMER PIG	OP	10.00	10.00
94	JOY TO THE WORLD	OP	10.00	10.00
94	SANTA PIG	OP	11.00	11.00
94	WHEEEEEE! PIGGY	OP	9.00	9.00

YR NAME	LIMIT	ISSUE	QUOTE
C. THAMMAVONGSA	**PIGSVILLE/THE VALENTINE COLLECTION**		
94 LOVESTRUCK	OP	10.50	10.50

GLASS EYE

93 COBALT WAVE	2000	19.00	22.00
94 CRANBERRY OPALESCENT LACE	2000	19.00	22.00

GOEBEL INC.

M.I. HUMMEL	**4TH IN ANNUAL SERIES OF ORNAMENTS**		
91 ANGELIC GUIDE HUM-571	CL	95.00	125.00-200.00
M.I. HUMMEL	**5TH IN ANNUAL SERIES OF ORNAMENTS**		
90 LIGHT UP THE NIGHT HUM-622	CL	95.00	100.00-125.00
M.I. HUMMEL	**6TH & FINAL SERIES OF ORNAMENTS**		
93 HERALD ON HIGH HUM-623	CL	155.00	155.00-160.00
*	**ANGEL BELLS ANNUAL ORNAMENT**		
76 ANGEL WITH FLUTE-BLUE	YR	9.00	100.00
76 ANGEL WITH FLUTE-PINK	YR	9.00	100.00
76 ANGEL WITH FLUTE-RED	YR	9.00	100.00
76 ANGEL WITH FLUTE-WHITE	YR	7.00	70.00
77 ANGEL WITH BANJO-GREEN	YR	9.00	35.00
77 ANGEL WITH BANJO-PURPLE	YR	9.00	35.00
77 ANGEL WITH BANJO-WHITE	YR	7.00	30.00
77 ANGEL WITH BANJO-YELLOW	YR	9.00	35.00
78 ANGEL WITH HARP-BLUE	YR	11.00	35.00
78 ANGEL WITH HARP-PINK	YR	11.00	35.00
78 ANGEL WITH HARP-RUST	YR	11.00	35.00
78 ANGEL WITH HARP-WHITE	YR	9.00	30.00
79 ANGEL WITH ACCORDION-GREEN	YR	11.00	35.00
79 ANGEL WITH ACCORDION-PURPLE	YR	11.00	35.00
79 ANGEL WITH ACCORDION-WHITE	YR	9.00	30.00
79 ANGEL WITH ACCORDION-YELLOW	YR	11.00	35.00
80 ANGEL WITH SAXAPHONE-BLUE	YR	13.50	35.00
80 ANGEL WITH SAXAPHONE-PINK	YR	13.50	35.00
80 ANGEL WITH SAXAPHONE-RUST	YR	13.50	35.00
80 ANGEL WITH SAXAPHONE-WHITE	YR	11.50	30.00
81 ANGEL WITH SONG SHEET-GREEN	YR	14.00	35.00
81 ANGEL WITH SONG SHEET-PURPLE	YR	14.00	35.00
81 ANGEL WITH SONG SHEET-WHITE	YR	12.00	30.00
81 ANGEL WITH SONG SHEET-YELLOW	YR	14.00	35.00
82 ANGEL WITH FRENCH HORN-GREEN	YR	14.00	35.00
82 ANGEL WITH FRENCH HORN-RED	YR	14.00	35.00
82 ANGEL WITH FRENCH HORN-RUST	YR	14.00	35.00
82 ANGEL WITH FRENCH HORN-WHITE	YR	12.00	30.00
83 ANGEL WITH REED PIPE-BROWN	YR	14.00	35.00
83 ANGEL WITH REED PIPE-ORANGE	YR	14.00	35.00
83 ANGEL WITH REED PIPE-PURPLE	YR	14.00	35.00
83 ANGEL WITH REED PIPE-WHITE	YR	12.00	30.00
84 ANGEL WITH DRUM-GREEN	YR	14.00	35.00
84 ANGEL WITH DRUM-RED	YR	14.00	35.00
84 ANGEL WITH DRUM-WHITE	YR	12.00	30.00
85 ANGEL WITH TRUMPET-BLUE	YR	14.00	35.00
85 ANGEL WITH TRUMPET-GREEN	YR	14.00	35.00
85 ANGEL WITH TRUMPET-RED	YR	14.00	35.00
85 ANGEL WITH TRUMPET-WHITE	YR	12.00	30.00
86 ANGEL WITH BELLS-GREEN	YR	15.00	35.00
86 ANGEL WITH BELLS-RED	YR	15.00	35.00
86 ANGEL WITH BELLS-WHITE	YR	12.50	30.00
86 ANGEL WITH BELLS-YELLOW	YR	15.00	35.00
87 ANGEL CONDUCTOR-BLUE	YR	17.25	35.00
87 ANGEL CONDUCTOR-GREEN	YR	17.25	35.00
87 ANGEL CONDUCTOR-RED	YR	17.25	35.00
87 ANGEL CONDUCTOR-WHITE	YR	15.00	30.00
88 ANGEL WITH STAR-GREEN	YR	20.00	20.00
88 ANGEL WITH STAR-RED	YR	20.00	20.00
88 ANGEL WITH STAR-WHITE	YR	17.00	17.00
88 ANGEL WITH STAR-YELLOW	YR	20.00	20.00
*	**ANNUAL CHRISTMAS BELL ORNAMENT**		
84 CHRISTMAS TREE	YR	14.00	25.00
85 SANTA	YR	14.00	15.00
86 WREATH	YR	15.00	15.00
87 TEDDY BEAR	YR	17.25	17.25
88 CRYSTAL BELL	YR	7.50	15.00
*	**ANNUAL ORNAMENT**		
78 SANTA-COLOR	YR	15.00	17.00
78 SANTA-WHITE	YR	7.50	12.00
79 ANGEL/TREE-COLOR	YR	16.00	18.00

YR	NAME	LIMIT	ISSUE	QUOTE
79	ANGEL/TREE-WHITE	YR	8.00	13.00
80	MRS. SANTA-COLOR	YR	17.00	17.00
80	MRS. SANTA-WHITE	YR	9.00	14.00
81	THE NUTCRACKER-COLOR	YR	18.00	18.00
81	THE NUTCRACKER-WHITE	YR	10.00	10.00
82	SANTA IN CHIMNEY-COLOR	YR	18.00	18.00
82	SANTA IN CHIMNEY-WHITE	YR	10.00	10.00
83	CLOWN-COLOR	YR	18.00	18.00
83	CLOWN-WHITE	YR	10.00	10.00
84	SNOWMAN-COLOR	YR	18.00	18.00
84	SNOWMAN-WHITE	YR	10.00	10.00
85	ANGEL-COLOR	YR	18.00	18.00
85	ANGEL-WHITE	YR	9.00	9.00
86	DRUMMER BOY-COLOR	YR	18.00	18.00
86	DRUMMER BOY-WHITE	YR	9.00	9.00
87	ROCKING HORSE-COLOR	YR	20.00	20.00
87	ROCKING HORSE-WHITE	YR	10.00	10.00
88	DOLL-COLOR	YR	22.50	22.50
88	DOLL-WHITE	YR	12.50	12.50
89	DOVE-COLOR	YR	20.00	20.00
89	DOVE-WHITE	YR	12.50	12.50
90	GIRL IN SLEIGH	YR	30.00	30.00
91	BABY ON MOON	YR	35.00	35.00
*		**ANNUAL ORNAMENT-GLASS**		
79	SANTA	15,000	12.00	12.00
80	ANGEL WITH TREE	15,000	12.00	12.00
81	MRS. SANTA	15,000	12.00	12.00
82	THE NUTCRACKER	15,000	4.00	4.00
C. BYJ		**CHARLOT BYJ ANNUAL ORNAMENT**		
86	SANTA LUCIA ANGEL	CL	18.00	25.00
87	CHRISTMAS PAGEANT	CL	20.00	20.00
88	ANGEL WITH SHEET MUSIC	CL	22.00	22.00
C. BYJ		**CHARLOT BYJ BABY ORNAMENT**		
86	BABY ORNAMENT	CL	18.00	18.00
87	BABY SNOW	CL	20.00	20.00
88	BABY'S 1ST STOCKING	CL	27.50	27.50
*		**CHRISTMAS ORNAMENTS**		
86	ANGEL WITH HORN-COLOR	OP	8.00	8.00
86	ANGEL WITH HORN-WHITE	OP	6.00	6.00
86	ANGEL WITH LANTERN-COLOR	OP	8.00	8.00
86	ANGEL WITH LANTERN-WHITE	OP	6.00	6.00
86	ANGEL WITH LUTE-COLOR	OP	8.00	8.00
86	ANGEL WITH LUTE-WHITE	OP	6.00	6.00
86	ANGEL-RED WITH BELL	OP	6.00	6.00
86	ANGEL-RED WITH BOOK	OP	6.00	6.00
86	ANGEL-RED WITH SONG	OP	6.00	6.00
86	TEDDY BEAR-RED BOOTS	OP	5.00	5.00
86	TEDDY BEAR-RED HAT	OP	5.00	5.00
86	TEDDY BEAR-RED SCARF	OP	5.00	5.00
87	THREE ANGELS WITH INSTRUMENTS (SET)	OP	30.00	30.00
87	THREE ANGELS WITH TOYS (SET)	OP	30.00	30.00
88	ANGEL WITH ACCORDIAN	OP	10.00	10.00
88	ANGEL WITH BANJO	OP	10.00	10.00
88	ANGEL WITH MUSIC (SET)	OP	30.00	30.00
88	ANGEL WITH TOY ROCKING HORSE	OP	10.00	10.00
88	ANGEL WITH TOY TEDDY BEAR	OP	10.00	10.00
88	ANGEL WITH TOY TRAIN	OP	10.00	10.00
88	ANGEL WITH TOYS (SET OF 3)	OP	30.00	30.00
88	ANGEL WITH VIOLIN	OP	10.00	10.00
88	NUTCRACKER	OP	15.00	15.00
88	SAINT NICK	OP	15.00	15.00
88	SANTA'S BOOT	OP	7.50	7.50
88	SNOWMAN	OP	10.00	10.00
G. SKROBEK		**CO-BOY ANNUAL ORNAMENT**		
86	COBOY WITH WREATH	CL	18.00	25.00
87	COBOY WITH CANDY CANE	CL	25.00	25.00
88	COBOY WITH TREE	CL	30.00	30.00
M.I. HUMMEL		**M.I. HUMMEL ANNUAL FIGURINE ORNAMENTS**		
88	FLYING HIGH HUM-452	CL	75.00	125.00-200.00
89	LOVE FROM ABOVE HUM-481	CL	75.00	100.00-125.00
90	PEACE ON EARTH HUM-484	CL	80.00	100.00-125.00
91	ANGELIC GUIDE HUM-571	CL	95.00	100.00-150.00
92	LIGHT UP THE NIGHT HUM-622	OP	95.00	100.00
93	HERALD ON HIGH HUM-623	YR	*	*
M.I. HUMMEL		**M.I. HUMMEL ANNUAL ORNAMENT**		
93	CELESTIAL MUSICIAN HUM-646	CL	90.00	100.00-110.00

YR	NAME	LIMIT	ISSUE	QUOTE
94	FESTIVAL HARMONY W/MANDOLIN OR. HUM-647	CL	95.00	100.00-110.00
95	FESTIVAL HARMONY W/FLUTE OR. HUM-648	OP	100.00	100.00
M.I. HUMMEL		**M.I. HUMMEL CHRISTMAS BELL ORNAMENTS**		
89	RIDE INTO CHRISTMAS HUM-775	CL	35.00	50.00-60.00
90	LETTER TO SANTA CLAUS HUM-776	CL	37.50	50.00-60.00
91	HEAR YE, HEAR YE HUM-777	CL	39.50	50.00-60.00
92	HARMONY IN FOUR PARTS HUM-778	OP	45.00	50.00
93	CELESTIAL MUSICIAN HUM-779	YR	*	*
MI HUMMEL		**M.I. HUMMEL CHRISTMAS ORNAMENT**		
*	FESTIVAL HARMONY W/FLUTE HUM-693	OP	125.00	125.00
M.I. HUMMEL				**UNICEF**
93	FRIENDS FOREVER HUM-662	25000	260.00	275.00-500.00

GORHAM

*		**ANNUAL CRYSTAL ORNAMENTS**		
85	CRYSTAL ORNAMENT	CL	22.00	22.00
86	CRYSTAL ORNAMENT	CL	25.00	25.00
87	CRYSTAL ORNAMENT	CL	25.00	25.00
88	CRYSTAL ORNAMENT	CL	28.00	28.00
89	CRYSTAL ORNAMENT	CL	28.00	28.00
90	CRYSTAL ORNAMENT	CL	30.00	30.00
91	CRYSTAL ORNAMENT	CL	35.00	35.00
92	CRYSTAL ORNAMENT	YR	32.50	32.50
*		**ANNUAL SNOWFLAKE ORNAMENTS**		
70	STERLING SNOWFLAKE	CL	10.00	250.00-325.00
71	STERLING SNOWFLAKE	CL	10.00	90.00-125.00
72	STERLING SNOWFLAKE	CL	10.00	75.00-125.00
73	STERLING SNOWFLAKE	CL	10.95	65.00-110.00
74	STERLING SNOWFLAKE	CL	17.50	45.00-75.00
75	STERLING SNOWFLAKE	CL	17.50	45.00-75.00
76	STERLING SNOWFLAKE	CL	20.00	45.00-75.00
77	STERLING SNOWFLAKE	CL	22.50	45.00-70.00
78	STERLING SNOWFLAKE	CL	22.50	45.00-70.00
79	STERLING SNOWFLAKE	CL	32.80	70.00
80	SILVERPLATED SNOWFLAKE	CL	15.00	75.00
81	STERLING SNOWFLAKE	CL	50.00	65.00
82	STERLING SNOWFLAKE	CL	37.50	75.00
83	STERLING SNOWFLAKE	CL	45.00	45.00-80.00
84	STERLING SNOWFLAKE	CL	45.00	45.00-75.00
85	STERLING SNOWFLAKE	CL	45.00	45.00-75.00
86	STERLING SNOWFLAKE	CL	45.00	45.00-60.00
87	STERLING SNOWFLAKE	CL	50.00	60.00
88	STERLING SNOWFLAKE	CL	50.00	50.00
89	STERLING SNOWFLAKE	CL	50.00	50.00
90	STERLING SNOWFLAKE	CL	50.00	50.00
91	STERLING SNOWFLAKE	CL	55.00	55.00
92	STERLING SNOWFLAKE	YR	50.00	50.00
*		**ARCHIVE COLLECTIBLE**		
88	VICTORIAN HEART	OP	50.00	50.00
89	VICTORIAN WREATH	OP	50.00	50.00
90	ELIZABETHAN CUPID	OP	60.00	60.00
91	STERLING BAROQUE ANGELS	OP	55.00	55.00
92	MADONNA AND CHILD	YR	50.00	50.00
*		**BABY'S FIRST CHRISTMAS CRYSTAL**		
91	BABY'S FIRST ROCKING HORSE	OP	35.00	35.00

HALLMARK KEEPSAKE ORNAMENTS

*				
76	BABY'S FIRST CHRISTMAS 250QX211-1	YR	2.50	100.00
76	HAPPY HOLIDAYS KISSING BALLS	YR	5.00	207.50
77	HOLLY & POINSETTIA TABLE DECOR. OHD320-2	YR	8.00	130.00
77	MR. & MRS. SNOWMAN KISSING BALL QX 225-2	YR	5.00	100.00
77	OLD FASHION CUSTOMS KISSING BALL QX225-5	YR	5.00	130.00
78	CHRISTMAS STAR TREE TOPPERS QX 702-3	YR	7.50	38.50
78	HEAVENLY MINSTREL TABLETOP QHD 921-9	YR	35.00	362.50
78	HOLIDAY MEMORIES KISSING BALL QHD 900-3	YR	5.00	110.00
78	LITTLE TRIMMER COLLECTION QX 132-3	YR	9.00	475.00
79	LITTLE TRIMMER SET QX 159-9	YR	9.00	220.00
80	BELLRINGER-2ND EDITION 1500QX157-4	YR	15.00	95.00
80	BRASS STAR TREE TOPPERS QX 705-4	YR	25.00	52.50
80	CHRISTMAS KITTEN TEST ORNAMENT QX353-4	YR	4.00	350.00
80	ROCKING HORSE, THE QX 340-7	YR	2.00	24.50
81	FROSTY FRIENDS QX 433-5	YR	8.00	395.00
81	YARN & FABRIC ORNAMENT ANGEL QX 162-1	YR	3.00	8.50
81	YARN & FABRIC ORNAMENT SANTA QX 161-4	YR	3.00	8.50
81	YARN & FABRIC ORNAMENT SNOWMAN QX 163-4	YR	3.00	8.50
81	YARN & FABRIC ORNAMENT SOLDIER QX 164-1	YR	3.00	8.50

YR	NAME	LIMIT	ISSUE	QUOTE
82	BRASS PROMOTIONAL ORNAMENT NO NUMBER	YR	3.50	32.50
83	SILVER BELL QX 110-9	YR	12.00	40.00
84	BABY'S FIRST CHRISTMAS-GIRL QX 240-1	YR	4.50	24.50
84	CHRISTMAS MEMORIES PHOTOHOLDER QX 300-4	YR	6.50	24.50
85	DISNEY CHRISTMAS QX 271-2	YR	4.75	24.00
85	HEAVENLY TRUMPETER 2750QX405-2	YR	27.50	99.00
87	ELVES-EMIL PAINTER ELF-FIGURINE QSP930-9	YR	10.00	30.00
87	ELVES-HANS CARPENTER ELF-FIGURE QSP930-7	YR	10.00	30.00
87	ELVES-KURT BLUE PRINT ELF FIGUREQSP931-7	YR	10.00	30.00
87	HALLIS STAR-TREE TOPPER EPCA	YR	*	32.50
88	THE WONDERFUL SANTACYCLE 225QX411-4	YR	22.50	47.50
89	CANDY CANE 450QXM560-2	YR	4.50	19.75
90	FESTIVE ANGEL TREE TOPPER 975QXM578-3	YR	9.75	29.50
90	PENGUIN PAL 450QXM574-6	YR	4.50	19.50
90	PORCELAIN BEAR QX 442-6	YR	8.75	14.00
93	HOLIDAY EXPRESS QXM 545-2	YR	50.00	50.00
94	BETSEY'S COUNTRY CHRISTMAS 500QX240-3	YR	5.00	14.50
94	FEELIN' GROOVY 795QX595-3	YR	7.95	22.50
94	GARFIELD 1295QX575-3	YR	12.95	28.50
94	GODPARENT 500QX242-3	YR	5.00	17.50
94	GRANDPARENTS 500QX242-6	YR	5.00	14.50
94	MARY ENGELBREIT 500QX241-6	YR	5.00	14.50
94	U.S. CHRISTMAS STAMPS 1095QX520-6	YR	10.95	24.50
93	OUR FIRST CHRISTMAS TOGETHER 975QX564-2	YR	9.75	16.50
94	CANDY CAPER 895QX577-6	YR	8.95	19.50
94	DAUGHTER 695QX562-3	YR	6.95	15.50
94	GRANDMOTHER 695QX567-3	YR	7.95	20.00
94	HEARTS OF HARMONY 1095QX440-6	YR	10.95	22.50
94	ICE SHOW 795QX594-6	YR	7.95	18.50
94	IN THE PINK 995QX576-3	YR	9.95	21.50
94	JOYOUS SONG 895QX447-3	YR	8.95	18.50
94	NEW HOME 895QX566-3	YR	8.95	19.50
94	OUR FIRST CHRISTMAS TOGETHER 1895QX570-6	YR	18.95	39.50
94	SON 695QX562-6	YR	6.95	15.50
94	TIME OF PEACE 795QX581-3	YR	7.95	16.50
94	LOU RANKIN SEAL 995QX545-6	YR	9.95	21.00
94	OUR FIRST CHRISTMAS TOGETHER 995QX564-3	YR	9.95	20.00
80	CHECKING IT TWICE 2000QX158-4	YR	20.00	195.00
94	BATMAN 1295QX585-3	YR	12.95	29.50
94	HELPFUL SHEPHERD 895QX553-6	YR	8.95	19.50
94	MERRY OLDE SANTA 1495QX525-6	YR	14.95	32.50
87	NORTH POLE POWER & LIGHT 627XPR933-3	YR	2.95	26.50
88	CHRISTMAS MORNING 2450QLX701-3	YR	24.50	49.50
88	MISTLETOAD 700QX468-7	YR	7.00	29.50
88	NIGHT BEFORE CHRISTMAS QX 451-7	YR	6.50	34.50
91	WOODLAND BABIES 600QXM566-7	YR	6.00	24.50
93	PEEK-A-BOO TREE QX524-4	YR	10.75	18.50
94	CHEERS TO YOU! 1095QX579-6	YR	10.95	24.50
94	CHEERY CYCLISTS 1295QX578-6	YR	12.95	29.50
94	DEAR SANTA MOUSE 1495QX580-6	YR	14.95	30.00
94	EXTRA-SPECIAL DELIVERY 795QX583-3	YR	7.95	17.50
94	FOLLOW THE SUN 895QX584-6	YR	8.95	19.50
94	JINGLE BELL BAND 1095QX578-3	YR	10.95	26.50
94	SANTA'S LEGO SLEIGH 1095QX545-3	YR	10.95	24.50
88	ST. LOUIE NICK QX 453-9	YR	7.75	34.50
86	CHRIS MOUSE DREAMS 1300QLX705-6	YR	13.00	74.50
87	FAVORITE SANTA 2250QX445-7	YR	22.50	65.00
94	TOBIN FRALEY CAROUSEL 2800QX522-3	YR	28.00	59.50
93	A CHILD'S CHRISTMAS QX210-5	YR	9.75	12.00
94	CHILD'S FOURTH CHRISTMAS 695QX572-6	YR	6.95	15.50
94	CHILD'S THIRD CHRISTMAS 695QX572-3	YR	6.95	15.50
94	JUMP-ALONG JACKALOPE 895QX575-6	YR	8.95	19.00
94	NEPHEW 795QX554-6	YR	7.95	16.50
94	NIECE 795QX554-3	YR	7.95	16.50
94	RELAXING MOMENT 1495QX535-6	YR	14.95	31.50
80	HEAVENLY MINSTREL 15QX156-7	YR	15.00	395.00
81	ANGEL QX 139-6	YR	5.50	77.50
83	DIANA DOLL QX 423-7	YR	9.00	22.00
84	CLASSICAL ANGEL 2750QX459-1	YR	27.50	105.00
90	GOLF'S MY BAG 775QX496-3	YR	7.75	29.50
93	FROSTY FRIENDS 975QX414-2	YR	9.75	29.50
94	FOR MY GRANDMA,PHOTOHOLDER 695QX561-3	YR	6.95	15.50
89	BROTHER 725QX445-2	YR	7.25	20.00
94	GENTLE NURSE 695QX597-3	YR	6.95	19.50
94	HAPPY BIRTHDAY JESUS 1295QX542-3	YR	12.95	29.50
94	NORMAN ROCKWELL ART 500QX241-3	YR	5.00	14.50

YR	NAME	LIMIT	ISSUE	QUOTE
86	MADONNA & CHILD QX 350-6	YR	6.75	21.00
94	MERRY FISHMAS 895QX591-3	YR	8.95	19.50
94	OUR FIRST CHRISTMAS..PHOTOHOLDER QX565-3	YR	8.95	19.50
94	PRACTICE MAKES PERFECT 895QX586-3	YR	8.95	18.50
94	SWEET GREETING 1095QX580-3	YR	10.95	22.50
85	BETSEY CLARK 13TH & FINAL 500QX263-2	YR	5.00	34.50
88	"OWLIDAY" WISH 650QX455-9	YR	6.50	24.50
90	SPENCER SPARROW, ESQ. 675QX431-2	YR	6.75	22.50
90	STOCKING KITTEN 675QX456-5	YR	6.75	19.50
94	BROTHER 695QX551-6	YR	6.95	16.50
94	DAD-TO-BE 795QX547-3	YR	7.95	17.50
94	GRANDDAUGHTER 695QX552-3	YR	6.95	16.50
94	GRANDSON 695QX552-6	YR	6.95	16.50
94	MOM-TO-BE 795QX550-6	YR	7.95	17.50
94	SISTER 695QX551-3	YR	6.95	17.50
90	FIRST CHRISTMAS TOGETHER QX 488-3	YR	9.75	17.00
94	CAT NAPS 795QX531-3	YR	7.75	22.50
94	CHILD'S FIFTH CHRISTMAS 695QX573-3	YR	6.95	16.50
94	HOLIDAY PATROL 895QX582-6	YR	8.95	19.50
94	MAKING IT BRIGHT 895QX540-3	YR	8.95	19.50
94	REINDEER PRO 795QX592-6	YR	7.95	17.50
94	SISTER TO SISTER 995QX553-3	YR	9.95	22.50
94	SPECIAL CAT, PHOTOHOLDER 795QX560-6	YR	7.95	17.50
94	SPECIAL DOG, PHOTOHOLDER 795QX560-3	YR	7.95	17.50
90	NUTSHELL HOLIDAY 575QX465-2	YR	5.75	26.50
92	THE KRINGLES 600QXM538-1	YR	6.00	22.50
93	MERRY OLDE SANTA 1475QX484-2	YR	14.75	34.50
93	PUPPY LOVE 775QX504-5	YR	7.75	26.50
94	BEATLES GIFT SET QX 537-3	YR	48.00	92.50
94	CARING DOCTOR 895QX582-3	YR	8.95	19.50
94	DAD 795QX546-3	YR	7.95	17.50
94	FELIZ NAVIDAD 895QX579-3	YR	8.95	19.50
94	GODCHILD 895QX445-3	YR	8.95	22.50
94	MOM 795QX546-6	YR	7.95	17.50
94	OUR CHRISTMAS TOGETHER 995QX481-6	YR	9.95	20.00
94	PUPPY LOVE 795QX525-3	YR	7.95	17.50
94	RED HOT HOLIDAY 795QX584-3	YR	7.95	17.50
94	THICK 'N THIN 1095QX569-3	YR	10.95	22.50
94	TOU CAN LOVE 895QX564-6	YR	8.95	19.50
87	CHRISTMAS IS GENTLE 1750QX444-9	YR	17.50	84.50
88	TREETOP DREAMS QX 459-7	YR	6.75	29.50
93	FROSTY FRIENDS 2000QX568-2	YR	20.00	50.00
93	YOU'RE ALWAYS WELCOME QXC569-2	YR	9.75	32.50
94	COLORS OF JOY 795QX589-3	YR	7.95	18.50
94	FABULOUS DECADE 795QX526-3	YR	7.95	24.50
94	FROSTY FRIENDS 995QX529-3	YR	9.95	24.50
94	HEART OF CHRISTMAS 1495QX526-6	YR	14.95	29.50
94	KITTY'S CATAMARAN 1095QX541-6	YR	10.95	22.00
94	KRINGLE'S KAYAK 795QX588-6	YR	7.95	18.50
94	MAGIC CARPET RIDE 795QX588-3	YR	7.95	24.50
94	MISTLETOE SURPRISE 1295QX599-6	YR	12.95	27.50
85	TUFTED TITMOUSE QX 479-5	YR	6.50	20.00
86	OPEN HOUSE ORNAMENT QX0440-3	YR	12.75	47.50
89	THE ORNAMENT EXPRESS 2200QX580-5	YR	22.00	49.50
90	DOVE OF PEACE 2475QXC447-6	25,400	24.75	75.00
93	SHOPPING WITH SANTA QX577-5	YR	24.00	27.50
94	FRIENDSHIP SUNDAE 1095QX476-6	YR	10.95	24.50
94	ROCKING HORSE 1095QX501-6	YR	10.95	22.50
94	STAMP OF APPROVAL 795QX570-3	YR	7.95	17.50
88	CHRIS MOUSE STAR QLX 715-4	YR	8.75	59.50
88	HAPPY HOLIDATA QX 471-4	YR	6.50	29.50
88	REINDOGGY QX 452-7	YR	5.75	34.50
93	MESSAGES OF CHRISTMAS QLX747-2	YR	35.00	27.50
94	BIG SHOT 795QX587-3	YR	7.95	18.50
94	BUSY BATTER 795QX587-6	YR	7.95	17.50
94	CHAMPION TEACHER 695QX583-6	YR	6.95	15.50
94	FRIENDLY PUSH 895QX568-6	YR	8.95	19.50
94	IT'S A STRIKE 895QX585-6	YR	8.95	19.50
94	KEEP ON MOWIN' 895QX541-3	YR	8.95	19.50
94	KICKIN' ROO 795QX591-6	YR	7.95	17.50
94	MOM AND DAD 995QX566-6	YR	9.95	22.00
94	OPEN-AND-SHUT HOLIDAY 995QX569-6	YR	9.95	22.00
94	OWLIVER 795QX522-6	YR	7.95	19.50
94	THRILL A MINUTE 895QX586-6	YR	8.95	19.50
94	WINNIE THE POOH AND TIGGER 1295QX574-6	YR	12.95	29.50
86	JOLLY ST. NICK 2250QX429-6	YR	22.50	74.50

YR	NAME	LIMIT	ISSUE	QUOTE
86	MAGICAL UNICORN 2750QX429-3	YR	27.50	175.00
87	CHRISTMAS TIME MIME 2750QX442-9	YR	27.50	64.50
88	IN A NUTSHELL 550QX469-7	YR	5.50	34.50
93	GLOWING PEWTER WREATH 1875QX530-2	YR	18.75	39.50
93	GLOWING PEWTER WREATH QX530-2	YR	18.75	27.50
94	COACH 795QX593-3	YR	7.95	17.50
94	GRANDCHILD'S FIRST CHRISTMAS 795QX567-6	YR	7.95	18.50
94	GRANDPA 795QX561-6	YR	7.95	18.50
94	LUCINDA AND TEDDY 2175QX481-3	SPEC. ED	21.75	42.50
94	OUT OF THIS WORLD TEACHER 795QX576-6	YR	7.95	19.00
94	SECRET SANTA 795QX573-6	YR	7.95	17.50
90	FIRST CHRISTMAS TOGETHER QX 213-6	YR	4.75	19.50
90	FIRST CHRISTMAS TOGETHER QX 314-6	YR	6.75	22.50
90	FIRST XMAS TOGETHER PHOTOHOLDER QX488-6	YR	7.75	19.50
93	BABY'S FIRST CHRISTMAS-GIRL 475QX209-2	YR	4.75	14.50
94	CHILD CARE GIVER 795QX590-6	YR	7.95	16.50
94	COCK-A-DOODLE CHRISTMAS QX 539-6	YR	8.95	29.50
94	OUR FIRST CHRISTMAS TOGETHER 695QX318-6	YR	6.95	15.50

D. UNRUH   **A CHRISTMAS CAROL COLLECTION**

YR	NAME	LIMIT	ISSUE	QUOTE
91	BOB CRATCHIT 1375QX499-7	YR	13.75	32.50
91	EBENEZER SCROOGE 1375QX498-9	YR	13.75	45.00
91	MERRY CAROLERS 2975QX479-9	YR	29.75	100.00
91	MRS. CRATCHIT 1375QX499-7	YR	13.75	32.50
91	TINY TIM 1075QX503-7	YR	10.75	39.50

*   **AMERICAN COUNTRY COLLECTION**

YR	NAME	LIMIT	ISSUE	QUOTE
86	MARY EMMERLING 795QX275-2	YR	7.95	29.50

ANNIVERSARY ORNAMENTS

YR	NAME	LIMIT	ISSUE	QUOTE
92	25 YEARS TOGETHER 1000AGA711-3	YR	10.00	22.50
92	25 YEARS TOGETHER ANN. BELL 800AGA713-4	YR	10.00	16.00
92	40 YEARS TOGETHER 1000AGA731-6	YR	10.00	27.50
92	50 YEARS TOGETHER 1000AGA721-4	YR	10.00	27.50
92	50 YEARS TOGETHER ANN. BELL 800AGA723-5	YR	10.00	17.50
92	OUR FIFTH ANNIVERSARY 1000AGA731-9	YR	10.00	20.00
92	OUR FIRST ANNIVERSARY 1000AGA731-8	YR	10.00	22.50
92	OUR TENTH ANNIVERSARY 1000AGA731-7	YR	10.00	20.00
93	25 YEARS TOGETHER 1000AGA768-6	YR	10.00	24.50
93	25 YEARS TOGETHER ANN. BELL 800AGA768-7	YR	10.00	24.50
93	40 YEARS TOGETHER 1000AGA786-8	YR	10.00	24.50
93	50 YEARS TOGETHER 1000AGA778-7	YR	10.00	22.50
93	50 YEARS TOGETHER ANN. BELL 800AGA778-8	YR	10.00	22.50
93	OUR FIFTH ANNIVERSARY 1000AGA786-6	YR	10.00	22.50
93	OUR FIRST ANNIVERSARY 1000AGA786-5	YR	10.00	22.50
93	OUR TENTH ANNIVERSARY 1000AGA786-7	YR	10.00	22.50

R. CHAD   **ARTISTS' FAVORITES**

YR	NAME	LIMIT	ISSUE	QUOTE
88	BABY REDBIRD 500QX410-1	YR	5.00	22.50
92	ELFIN MARIONETTE 1175QX593-1	YR	11.75	24.50
90	WELCOME, SANTA 1175QX477-3	YR	11.75	29.50
91	NOAH'S ARK 1375QX486-7	YR	13.75	39.50
92	MOTHER GOOSE 1375QX498-4	YR	13.75	34.50
88	VERY STRAWBERRY 475QX409-1	YR	4.75	24.50
89	BABY PARTRIDGE 675QX452-5	YR	6.75	17.50
90	GENTLE DREAMERS 875QX475-6	YR	8.75	29.50
91	TRAMP AND LADDIE 775QX439-7	YR	7.75	35.00
87	DECEMBER SHOWERS 550QX448-7	YR	5.50	39.50
87	THREE MEN IN A TUB 800QX454-7	YR	8.00	29.50
88	CYMBALS OF CHRISTMAS 550QX411-1	YR	5.50	29.50
89	PLAYFUL ANGEL 675QX453-5	YR	6.75	24.50
90	DONDER'S DINER 1375QX482-3	YR	13.75	27.50
90	HAPPY WOODCUTTER 975QX476-3	YR	9.75	25.00
91	HOOKED ON SANTA 775QX410-9	YR	7.75	24.50
92	TURTLE DREAMS 875QX499-1	YR	8.75	27.50
90	ANGEL KITTY 875QX474-6	YR	8.75	24.50
88	MERRY MINT UNICORN 850QX423-4	YR	8.50	24.50
89	MERRY-GO-ROUND UNICORN 1075QX447-2	YR	10.75	22.50
87	WEE CHIMNEY SWEEP 625QX451-9	YR	6.25	29.50
89	MAIL CALL 875QX452-2	YR	8.75	19.50
90	MOUSEBOAT 775QX475-3	YR	7.75	19.50
91	SANTA SAILOR 975QX438-9	YR	9.75	22.50
92	POLAR POST 875QX491-4	YR	8.75	22.50
89	CAROUSEL ZEBRA 925QX451-5	YR	9.25	19.50
89	CHERRY JUBILEE 500QX453-2	YR	5.00	24.50
91	POLAR CIRCUS WAGON 1375QX439-9	YR	13.75	29.50
92	STOCKED WITH JOY 775QX593-4	YR	7.75	19.50
87	BEARY SPECIAL 475QX455-7	YR	4.75	29.50
88	LITTLE JACK HORNER 800QX408-1	YR	8.00	29.50
88	MIDNIGHT SNACK 600QX410-4	YR	6.00	22.50

YR	NAME	LIMIT	ISSUE	QUOTE
89	BEAR-I-TONE 475QX454-2	YR	4.75	22.50
92	UNCLE ART'S ICE CREAM 875QX500-1	YR	8.75	24.50
91	FIDDLIN' AROUND 775QX438-7	YR	7.75	19.50
	BABY CELEBRATIONS			
89	BABY'S CHRISTENING KEEPSAKE 700BBY132-5	YR	7.00	35.00
89	BABY'S FIRST BIRTHDAY 5500BBY172-9	YR	5.50	35.00
89	BABY'S FIRST CHRISTMAS-BOY 475BB143-5	YR	4.75	17.50
89	BABY'S FIRST CHRISTMAS-GIRL 475BBY155-3	YR	4.75	17.50
90	BABY'S CHRISTENING 1000BBY132-6	YR	10.00	29.50
90	BABY'S FIRST CHRISTMAS-BOY PONY BBY145-4	YR	10.00	35.00
90	BABY'S FIRST CHRISTMAS-GIRL BUNNY BBY155	YR	10.00	35.00
91	BABY'S CHRISTENING LAMB 1000BBY131-7	YR	10.00	25.00
91	BABY'S FIRST CHRISTMAS-BOY PONY BBY141-6	YR	10.00	25.00
91	BABY'S FIRST CHRISTMAS-GIRL BUNNY BBY151	YR	10.00	25.00
92	BABY'S CHRISTENING-WHITE HEART BBY133-1	YR	8.50	19.50
92	BABY'S FIRST CHRISTMAS-BLUE PONYBBY145-6	YR	8.50	19.50
92	BABY'S FIRST CHRISTMAS-BUNNY 850BBY155-7	YR	8.50	19.50
93	BABY'S 1ST CHRISTMAS PHOTOHOLDERBBY147-0	YR	10.00	29.50
93	BABY'S CHRISTENING 1200BBY291-7	YR	12.00	27.50
93	BABY'S CHRISTENING PHOTOHOLDER BBY 133-5	YR	10.00	25.00
93	BABY'S FIRST CHRISTMAS MOON 1400BBY291-9	YR	14.00	29.50
93	BABY'S FIRST CHRISTMAS RABBIT BBY291-8	YR	12.00	29.50
93	GRANDDAUGHTER FIRST CHRISTMAS BBY 280-2	YR	14.00	28.00
93	GRANDSON'S FIRST CHRISTMAS BBY 280-1	YR	14.00	28.00
	BABY'S FIRST CHRISTMAS			
94	BABY'S FIRST CHRISTMAS-BOY 500QX243-6	YR	5.00	13.50
94	BABY'S FIRST CHRISTMAS-GIRL 500QX243-3	YR	5.00	13.50
94	BABY'S FIRST CHRISTMAS 795QX571-3	YR	7.95	19.50
K. CROW				
	BABY'S SECOND CHRISTMAS			
94	BABY'S SECOND CHRISTMAS 795QX571-6	YR	7.95	19.50
D. RHODUS				
	BASEBALL HEROES			
94	BABE RUTH 1295QX532-3	YR	12.95	49.50
	BEARINGERS OF VICTORIA CIRCLE			
93	ABEARNATHY/SON 495XPR974-7	YR	4.95	12.50
93	BEARNADETTE/DAUGHTER 495XPR974-8	YR	4.95	12.50
93	FIREPLACE HEARTH XPR974-9	YR	4.95	8.50
93	MAMA BEARINGER 495XPR974-5	YR	4.95	12.50
93	PAPA BEARINGER 495XPR974-6	YR	4.95	12.50
*	**BEAUTY OF AMERICA COLLECTION, THE**			
77	DESERT 250QX159-5	YR	2.50	55.00
77	MOUNTAINS 250QX158-2	YR	2.50	55.00
77	SEASHORE 250QX160-2	YR	2.50	50.00
77	WHARF 250QX161-5	YR	2.50	50.00
*	**BELLRINGER SERIES**			
81	SWINGIN' BELLRINGER QX 441-5	YR	15.00	105.00
84	ELFIN ARTIST QX 438-4	YR	15.00	28.00
82	ANGEL QX 455-6	YR	15.00	85.00
S. PIKE			**BETSEY CLARK**	
87	HOME FOR CHRISTMAS 500QX272-7	YR	5.00	24.50
	BETSEY'S COUNTRY CHRISTMAS			
93	BETSEY'S COUNTRY CHRISTMAS 500QX206-2	YR	5.00	19.50
*	**BICENTENNIAL COMMEMORATIVES**			
76	BICENTENNIAL '76 COMMEMORATIVE QX 203-1	YR	2.50	75.00
76	BICENTENNIAL CHARMERS 300QX198-1	YR	3.00	85.00
76	COLONIAL CHILDREN (2) 400QX208-1	YR	4.00	85.00
D. LEE			**BRASS ORNAMENTS**	
82	BRASS BELL 1200QX460-6	YR	12.00	25.00
82	SANTA'S SLEIGH 900QX478-6	YR	9.00	35.00
82	SANTA AND REINDEER 900QX467-6	YR	9.00	55.00
*	**CARROUSEL SERIES**			
79	CARROUSEL-2ND EDITION 650QX146-7	YR	6.50	195.00
80	MERRY CARROUSEL 750QX141-4	YR	7.50	210.00
81	CARROUSEL-4TH EDITION 900QX427-5	YR	9.00	95.00
83	SANTA & FRIENDS 1100QX401-9	YR	11.00	49.50
	CHRISTMAS CAROUSEL HORSE COLLECTION			
89	CAROUSEL DISPLAY STAND 629XPR972-3	YR	1.00	10.00
89	GINGER 629XPR972-1	YR	3.95	19.50
89	HOLLY 629XPR972-2	YR	3.95	19.50
89	SNOW 929XPR971-9	YR	3.95	29.50
89	STAR 629XPR972-0	YR	3.95	19.50
*	**CHRISTMAS CLASSICS**			
86	NUTCRACKER BALLET 1750QLX704-3	YR	17.50	85.00
87	A CHRISTMAS CAROL 1600QLX702-9	YR	16.00	74.50
90	THE LITTLEST ANGEL 1400QLX730-3	YR	14.00	40.00
89	LITTLE DRUMMER BOY 1350QLX724-2	YR	13.50	34.00

YR	NAME	LIMIT	ISSUE	QUOTE
*		**CHRISTMAS EXPRESSIONS COLLECTION**		
77	BELL 350QX154-2	YR	3.50	65.00
77	MANDOLIN 350QX157-5	YR	3.50	65.00
77	ORNAMENTS 350QX155-5	YR	3.50	65.00
77	WREATH 350QX156-2	YR	3.50	75.00
L. SICKMAN		**CHRISTMAS MEDLEY COLLECTION**		
86	FAVORITE TIN DRUM 850QX514-3	YR	8.50	29.50
86	JOYFUL CAROLERS 975QX513-6	YR	9.75	39.50
86	FESTIVE TREBLE CLEF 875QX513-3	YR	8.75	29.50
86	CHRISTMAS GUITAR 700QX512-6	YR	7.00	24.50
86	HOLIDAY HORN 800QX514-6	YR	8.00	35.00
K. CROW		**CHRISTMAS PIZZAZZ COLLECTION**		
87	JOLLY FOLLIES 850QX466-9	YR	8.50	39.50
87	MISTLETOAD 700QX468-7	YR	7.00	29.50
87	ST. LOUIE NICK 775QX453-9	YR	7.75	34.50
87	CHRISTMAS FUN PUZZLE 800QX467-9	YR	8.00	32.50
87	DOC HOLIDAY 800QX467-7	YR	8.00	44.50
87	HAPPY HOLIDATA 650QX471-7	YR	6.50	32.00
87	HOLIDAY HOURGLASS 800QX470-7	YR	8.00	27.50
L. SICKMAN		**CHRISTMAS SKY LINE COLLECTION**		
92	CABOOSE 975QX532-1	YR	9.75	25.00
92	COAL CAR 975QX540-1	YR	9.75	22.50
92	LOCOMOTIVE 975QX531-1	YR	9.75	42.50
92	STOCK CAR 975QX531-4	YR	9.75	22.50
S. PIKE			**CINNAMON BEAR**	
89	PORCELAIN BEAR-7TH EDITION 875QX461-5	YR	8.75	32.50
D. PALMITER		**CLASSIC AMERICAN CARS**		
91	1957 CORVETTE-1ST EDITION 1275QX431-9	YR	12.75	185.00
92	1966 MUSTANG 1275QX428-4	YR	12.75	49.50
93	1956 FORD THUNDERBIRD 1275QX527-5	YR	12.75	34.50
94	1957 CHEVROLET BEL AIRE 1295QX542-2	YR	12.95	29.50
D. PALMITER		**CLAUS & CO. R.R. ORNAMENTS**		
91	CABOOSE 395XPR973-3	YR	3.95	15.00
91	GIFT CAR 395XPR973-1	YR	3.95	15.00
91	PASSENGER CAR 395XPR973-2	YR	3.95	15.00
91	TRESTLE TRACK FOR TRAIN 295XPR973-4	YR	2.95	10.00
*		**CLOTH DOLL ORNAMENTS**		
77	ANGEL 175QX220-2	YR	1.75	65.00
77	SANTA 175QX221-5	YR	1.75	95.00
L. SICKMAN		**CLOTHESPIN SOLDIER**		
84	CANADIAN MOUNTIE 550QX480-7	YR	5.00	29.50
85	SCOTTISH-4TH EDITION 550QX471-5	YR	5.50	29.50
86	CLOTHESPIN SOLDIER-5TH ED. 550QX406-3	YR	5.50	32.50
87	SAILOR 550QX480-7	YR	5.50	29.50
*		**COLLECTIBLE SERIES**		
79	BELLRINGER-1ST EDITION 10QX147-9	YR	10.00	450.00
79	SNOOPY AND FRIENDS 800QX141-9	YR	8.00	145.00
80	THE BELLRINGERS-2ND EDITION 15QX157-4	YR	15.00	75.00
80	THIMBLE-3RD EDITION 400QX132-1	YR	4.00	195.00
81	NORMAN ROCKWELL-2ND EDITION 850QX511-5	YR	8.50	47.50
83	THE BELLRINGER-5TH EDITION 1500QX403-9	YR	15.00	135.00
84	BETSEY CLARK-12TH EDITION 500QX249-4	YR	5.00	34.50
84	PORCELAIN BEAR-2ND EDITION 700QX454-1	YR	7.00	27.50
84	ROCKING HORSE-4TH EDITION 1000QX435-4	YR	10.00	79.50
84	TWELVE DAYS OF CHRISTMAS 600QX348-4	YR	6.00	295.00
84	WOOD CHILDHOOD ORNAMENTS 650QX439-4	YR	6.50	49.50
86	CINNAMON BEAR-4TH EDITION 775QX405-6	YR	7.75	44.50
87	CINNAMON BEAR-5TH EDITION 775QX442-7	YR	7.75	37.50
88	FIVE GOLDEN RINGS-5TH EDITION 650QX371-4	YR	6.50	22.50
89	BETSEY CLARK: HOME FOR XMAS 500QX230-2	YR	5.00	37.50
89	WINTER SURPRISE-1ST EDITION 1075QX427-2	YR	10.75	32.50
90	BETSEY CLARK: HOME FOR XMAS 500QX203-3	YR	5.00	24.50
90	CINNAMON BEAR-8TH EDITION 875QX442-6	YR	8.75	32.50
91	BETSEY CLARK: HOME FOR XMAS 500QX210-9	YR	5.00	21.50
92	BETSEY'S COUNTRY CHRISTMAS 500QX210-4	YR	5.00	27.50
92	GIFT BRINGERS-4TH EDITION 500QX212-4	YR	5.00	19.50
89	HARK! IT'S HERALD-1ST EDITION 675QX455-5	YR	6.75	29.50
90	HARK! IT'S HERALD-2ND EDITION 675QX446-3	YR	6.75	27.50
83	CINNAMON BEAR-1ST EDITION 700QX428-9	YR	7.00	95.00
85	CINNAMON BEAR-3RD EDITION 750QX479-2	YR	7.50	59.50
85	WOOD CHILDHOOD ORNAMENTS 700QX472-2	YR	7.00	49.50
88	WOOD CHILDHOOD ORNAMENTS 750QX404-1	YR	7.50	24.50
92	TOBIN FRALEY CAROUSEL 2800QX489-1	YR	28.00	75.00
80	SNOOPY & FRIENDS 900QX154-1	YR	9.00	135.00
81	SNOOPY & FRIENDS-3RD EDITION 1200QX436-2	YR	12.00	99.00
90	WINTER SURPRISE-2ND EDITION 1075QX444-3	YR	10.75	29.50

YR	NAME	LIMIT	ISSUE	QUOTE
92	WINTER SURPRISE 1175QX427-1	YR	11.75	34.50
85	NOSTALGIC HOUSES & SHOPS 1375QX497-5	YR	13.75	115.00
91	MERRY OLDE SANTA-2ND EDITION 1475QX435-9	YR	14.75	75.00
92	FROSTY FRIENDS 975QX429-1	YR	9.75	29.50
92	HARK! IT'S HERALD 775QX446-4	YR	7.75	24.50
91	HEAVENLY ANGELS-1ST EDITION 775QX436-7	YR	7.75	37.50
91	WINTER SURPRISE-3RD EDITION 1075QX427-7	YR	10.75	34.50
92	HEAVENLY ANGELS 775QX445-4	YR	7.75	29.50
84	ART MASTERPIECE-1ST EDITION 650QX349-4	YR	6.50	19.50
85	ART MASTERPIECE-2ND EDITION 675QX377-2	YR	6.75	19.50
85	NORMAN ROCKWELL-6TH EDITION 750QX374-5	YR	7.50	32.50
87	NORMAN ROCKWELL-8TH EDITION 775QX370-7	YR	7.75	24.50
87	THE CONSTITUTION 600QZ377-7	YR	6.50	29.50
85	12 DAYS OF CHRISTMAS-2ND ED. 650QX371-2	YR	6.50	59.50
86	BETSEY CLARK: HOME FOR XMAS 500QX277-6	YR	5.00	34.50
88	BETSEY CLARK: HOME FOR XMAS 500QX271-4	YR	5.00	26.50
88	CINNAMON BEAR-PORCELAIN 800QX404-4	YR	8.00	39.50
91	FROSTY FRIENDS-12TH EDITION 975QX432-7	YR	9.75	42.50
89	CHRISTMAS KITTY-1ST EDITION 1475QX544-5	YR	14.75	32.50
89	MINIATURE CRECHE-5TH EDITION 925QX459-2	YR	9.25	26.50
90	CHRISTMAS KITTY-2ND EDITION 1475QX450-6	YR	14.75	32.50
91	CHRISTMAS KITTY-3RD EDITION 1475QX437-7	YR	14.75	32.50
91	HARK! IT'S HERALD-3RD ED. 675QX437-9	YR	6.75	29.50
91	PUPPY LOVE-1ST EDITION 775QX537-9	YR	7.75	49.50
92	PUPPY LOVE 775QX448-4	YR	7.75	39.50
82	CAROUSEL SERIES-5TH EDITION 1000QX478-3	YR	10.00	99.00
82	FROSTY FRIENDS-3RD EDITION 800QX452-3	YR	8.00	295.00
82	SNOOPY & FRIENDS-4TH EDITION 1300QX480-3	YR	13.00	95.00
83	FROSTY FRIENDS-4TH EDITION 800QX400-7	YR	8.00	275.00
84	FROSTY FRIENDS-5TH EDITION 800QX437-1	YR	8.00	79.50
85	FROSTY FRIENDS-6TH EDITION 850QX482-2	YR	8.50	69.50
85	MINIATURE CRECHE-1ST EDITION 875QX482-5	YR	8.75	45.00
86	MINIATURE CRECHE-2ND EDITION 900QX407-6	YR	9.00	59.50
87	FROSTY FRIENDS-8TH EDITION 850QX440-9	YR	8.50	59.50
87	MINIATURE CRECHE-3RD EDITION 900QX481-9	YR	9.00	37.50
88	FROSTY FRIENDS-9TH EDITION 875QX403-1	YR	8.75	65.00
89	FROSTY FRIENDS-10TH EDITION 925QX457-2	YR	9.25	44.50
90	CLAUS CONSTRUCTION 775QX488-5	YR	7.75	35.00
90	FABULOUS DECADE-1ST EDITION 775QX446-6	YR	7.75	47.50
90	FROSTY FRIENDS-11TH EDITION 975QX439-6	YR	9.75	34.50
90	HEART OF CHRISTMAS-1ST ED. 1375QX472-6	YR	13.75	80.00
90	MERRY OLDE SANTA-1ST EDITION 1475QX473-6	YR	14.75	85.00
91	FABULOUS DECADE-2ND EDITION 775QX411-9	YR	7.75	42.50
91	HEART OF CHRISTMAS-2ND ED. 1375QX435-7	YR	13.75	39.50
92	FABULOUS DECADE 775QX424-4	YR	7.75	39.50
92	HEART OF CHRISTMAS 1375QX441-1	YR	13.75	29.50
81	ROCKING HORSE-1ST EDITION 900QX422-2	YR	9.00	625.00
82	CLOTHESPIN SOLDIER-1ST ED. 500QX458-3	YR	5.00	150.00
82	ROCKING HORSE-2ND EDITION 1000QX502-3	YR	10.00	425.00
82	TIN LOCOMOTIVE-1ST EDITION 1300QX460-3	YR	13.00	600.00
83	CLOTHESPIN SOLDIER-2ND ED. 500QX402-9	YR	5.00	49.50
83	SNOOPY & FRIENDS-5TH EDITION 1300QX416-9	YR	13.00	85.00
83	TIN LOCOMOTIVE-2ND EDITION 1300QX404-9	YR	13.00	295.00
84	TIN LOCOMOTIVE-3RD EDITION 1400QX440-4	YR	14.00	90.00
85	ROCKING HORSE-5TH EDITION 1075QX493-2	YR	10.75	69.50
85	TIN LOCOMOTIVE-4TH EDITION 1475QX497-2	YR	14.75	72.50
86	ROCKING HORSE-6TH EDITION 1075QX401-6	YR	10.75	69.50
86	TIN LOCOMOTIVE-5TH EDITION 1475QX403-6	YR	14.75	75.00
87	ROCKING HORSE-7TH EDITION 1075QX482-9	YR	10.75	59.50
87	TIN LOCOMOTIVE-6TH EDITION 1475QX484-9	YR	14.75	69.50
88	ROCKING HORSE-8TH EDITION 1075QX402-4	YR	10.75	54.50
88	TIN LOCOMOTIVE-7TH EDITION 1475QX400-4	YR	14.75	59.50
89	ROCKING HORSE-9TH EDITION 1075QX462-2	YR	10.75	44.50
89	TIN LOCOMOTIVE-8TH EDITION 1475QX460-2	YR	14.75	59.50
90	ROCKING HORSE-10TH EDITION 1075QX464-6	YR	10.75	59.50
91	ROCKING HORSE-11TH EDITION 1075QX414-7	YR	10.75	37.50
92	ROCKING HORSE 1075QX426-1	YR	10.75	32.50
86	FROSTY FRIENDS-7TH EDITION 850QX405-3	YR	8.50	69.50
86	REINDEER CHAMPS-1ST EDITION 750QX422-3	YR	7.50	149.50
88	THIMBLE SNOWMAN 575QX405-4	YR	5.75	26.50
92	OWLIVER 775QX454-4	YR	7.75	23.50
87	HOLIDAY HEIRLOOM QX 485-7	34600	25.00	60.00
88	MINIATURE CRECHE-4TH EDITION 850QX403-4	YR	8.50	34.50
92	MERRY OLDE SANTA 1475QX441-4	YR	14.75	39.50
90	GIFT BRINGERS-ST. LUCIA 500QX280-3	YR	5.00	24.50
90	GREATEST STORY-1ST EDITION 1275QX465-6	YR	12.75	32.50

YR	NAME	LIMIT	ISSUE	QUOTE
91	GREATEST STORY-2ND EDITION 1275QX412-9	YR	12.75	29.50
92	GREATEST STORY 1275QX425-1	YR	12.75	24.75
*			**COLORS OF CHRISTMAS**	
77	CANDLE 350QX203-5	YR	3.50	75.00
77	JOY 350QX201-5	YR	3.50	60.00
77	WREATH 350QX202-2	YR	3.50	65.00
78	ANGEL 350QX354-3	YR	3.50	60.00
78	CANDLE 350QX357-6	YR	3.50	125.00
78	LOCOMOTIVE 350QX356-3	YR	3.50	75.00
79	HOLIDAY WREATH 350QX353-9	YR	3.50	45.00
79	PARTRIDGE IN A PEAR TREE 350QX351-9	YR	3.50	45.00
79	WORDS OF CHRISTMAS 350QX350-7	YR	3.50	95.00
80	JOY 400QX350-1	YR	4.00	35.00
82	NATIVITY 450QX308-3	YR	4.50	49.50
82	SANTA'S FLIGHT 450QX308-6	YR	4.50	45.00
78	MERRY CHRISTMAS 350QX355-6	YR	3.50	77.50
77	BELL 350QX200-2	YR	3.50	60.00
79	STAR OVER BETHLEHEM 350QX352-7	YR	3.50	75.00
*			**COMMEMORATIVES**	
77	BABY'S FIRST CHRISTMAS 350QX131-5	YR	3.50	125.00
77	FIRST CHRISTMAS TOGETHER 350QX132-2	YR	3.50	80.00
77	FOR YOUR NEW HOME 350QX263-5	YR	3.50	95.00
77	GRANDDAUGHTER 350QX208-2	YR	3.50	250.00
77	GRANDMOTHER 350QX260-2	YR	3.50	150.00
77	GRANDSON 350QX209-5	YR	3.50	225.00
77	LOVE 350QX262-2	YR	3.50	95.00
77	MOTHER 350QX261-5	YR	3.50	85.00
78	25TH CHRISTMAS TOGETHER 350QX269-3	YR	3.50	20.00
78	BABY'S FIRST CHRISTMAS 350QX200-3	YR	3.50	80.00
78	FIRST CHRISTMAS TOGETHER 350QX218-3	YR	3.50	75.00
78	FOR YOUR NEW HOME 350QX217-6	YR	3.50	75.00
78	GRANDDAUGHTER 350QX216-3	YR	3.50	60.00
78	GRANDMOTHER 350QX267-6	YR	3.50	55.00
78	GRANDSON 350QX215-6	YR	3.50	60.00
78	LOVE 350QX268-3	YR	3.50	60.00
78	MOTHER 350QX266-3	YR	3.50	45.00
79	BABY'S FIRST CHRISTMAS 350QX208-7	YR	3.50	29.50
79	BABY'S FIRST CHRISTMAS 800QX154-7	YR	8.00	195.00
79	FRIENDSHIP 350QX203-9	YR	3.50	27.50
79	GRANDDAUGHTER 350QX211-9	YR	3.50	35.00
79	GRANDMOTHER 350QX252-7	YR	3.50	24.50
79	GRANDSON 350QX210-7	YR	3.50	35.00
79	LOVE 350QX258-7	YR	3.50	39.50
79	MOTHER 350QX251-9	YR	3.50	22.50
79	NEW HOME 350QX212-7	YR	3.50	49.50
79	OUR FIRST CHRISTMAS TOGETHER 350QX209-9	YR	3.50	75.00
79	OUR TWENTY-FIFTH ANNIVERSARY 350QX250-7	YR	3.50	27.50
79	TEACHER 350QX213-9	YR	3.50	15.00
80	25TH CHRISTMAS TOGETHER 400QX206-1	YR	4.00	22.50
80	BABY'S FIRST CHRISTMAS 400QX200-1	YR	4.00	29.50
80	BEAUTY OF FRIENDSHIP 400QX303-4	YR	4.00	65.00
80	BLACK BABY'S FIRST CHRISTMAS 400QX229-4	YR	4.00	29.50
80	CHRISTMAS AT HOME 400QX210-1	YR	4.00	29.50
80	CHRISTMAS LOVE 400QX207-4	YR	4.00	39.50
80	DAD 400QX214-1	YR	4.00	25.00
80	DAUGHTER 400QX212-1	YR	4.00	39.50
80	FIRST CHRISTMAS TOGETHER 400QX205-4	YR	4.00	35.00
80	FIRST CHRISTMAS TOGETHER 400QX305-4	YR	4.00	55.00
80	FRIENDSHIP 400QX208-1	YR	4.00	29.50
80	GRANDDAUGHTER 400QX202-1	YR	4.00	35.00
80	GRANDFATHER 400QX231-4	YR	4.00	19.50
80	GRANDMOTHER 400QX204-1	YR	4.00	19.50
80	GRANDPARENTS 400QX213-4	YR	4.00	50.00
80	GRANDSON 400QX201-4	YR	4.00	35.00
80	LOVE 400QX302-1	YR	4.00	80.00
80	MOTHER 400QX203-4	YR	4.00	22.50
80	MOTHER 400QX304-1	YR	4.00	39.50
80	MOTHER AND DAD 400QX230-1	YR	4.00	24.50
80	SON 400QX211-4	YR	4.00	39.50
80	TEACHER 400QX209-4	YR	4.00	19.50
81	25TH CHRISTMAS TOGETHER 450QX707-5	YR	4.50	24.50
81	25TH CHRISTMAS TOGETHER 550QX504-2	YR	5.50	29.50
81	50TH CHRISTMAS TOGETHER QX 708-2	YR	4.50	22.50
81	BABY'S FIRST CHRISTMAS 1300QX440-2	YR	13.00	59.50
81	BABY'S FIRST CHRISTMAS 550QX516-2	YR	5.50	29.50
81	BABY'S FIRST CHRISTMAS 850QX513-5	YR	8.50	24.50

YR	NAME	LIMIT	ISSUE	QUOTE
81	BABY'S FIRST CHRISTMAS-BLACK 450QX602-2	YR	4.50	24.50
81	BABY'S FIRST CHRISTMAS-BOY 450QX601-5	YR	4.50	24.50
81	BABY'S FIRST CHRISTMAS-GIRL 450QX600-2	YR	4.50	24.50
81	DAUGHTER 450QX607-5	YR	4.50	37.50
81	FATHER 450QX609-5	YR	4.50	19.50
81	FIRST CHRISTMAS TOGETHER 450QX706-2	YR	4.50	29.50
81	FIRST CHRISTMAS TOGETHER 550QX505-5	YR	5.50	25.00
81	FRIENDSHIP 450QX704-2	YR	4.50	19.50
81	FRIENDSHIP 550QX503-5	YR	5.50	29.50
81	GODCHILD 450QX603-5	YR	4.50	19.50
81	GRANDDAUGHTER 450QX605-5	YR	4.50	29.50
81	GRANDFATHER 450QX701-5	YR	4.50	19.50
81	GRANDMOTHER 450QX702-2	YR	4.50	19.50
81	GRANDPARENTS 450QX703-5	YR	4.50	19.50
81	GRANDSON 450QX604-2	YR	4.50	29.50
81	HOME 450QX709-5	YR	4.50	19.50
81	LOVE 550QX502-2	YR	5.50	59.50
81	MOTHER 450QX608-2	YR	4.50	15.50
81	MOTHER AND DAD 450QX700-2	YR	4.50	17.50
81	SON 450QX606-2	YR	4.50	29.50
81	TEACHER 450QX800-2	YR	4.50	15.00
81	THE GIFT OF LOVE 450QX705-5	YR	4.50	25.00
82	25TH CHRISTMAS TOGETHER 450QX211-6	YR	4.50	19.50
82	50TH CHRISTMAS TOGETHER 450QX212-3	YR	4.50	19.50
82	BABY'S FIRST CHRISTMAS (BOY) 450QX216-3	YR	4.50	24.50
82	BABY'S FIRST CHRISTMAS (GIRL) 450QX207-3	YR	4.50	24.50
82	BABY'S FIRST XMAS-PHOTOHOLDER 650QX312-6	YR	6.50	32.50
82	DAUGHTER 450QX204-6	YR	4.50	35.00
82	FIRST CHRISTMAS TOGETHER 450QX211-3	YR	4.50	35.00
82	FIRST CHRISTMAS TOGETHER 550QX302-6	YR	5.50	22.50
82	FIRST CHRISTMAS TOGETHER 850QX306-6	YR	8.50	45.00
82	FIRST XMAS TOGETHER-LOCKET 1500QX456-3	YR	15.00	50.00
82	FRIENDSHIP 450QX208-6	YR	4.50	19.50
82	FRIENDSHIP 550QX304-6	YR	5.50	24.50
82	GODCHILD 450QX222-6	YR	4.50	19.50
82	GRANDDAUGHTER 450QX224-3	YR	4.50	29.50
82	GRANDFATHER 450QX207-6	YR	4.50	19.50
82	GRANDMOTHER 450QX200-3	YR	4.50	17.50
82	GRANDPARENTS 450QX214-6	YR	4.50	17.50
82	GRANDSON 450QX224-6	YR	4.50	29.50
82	LOVE 450QX209-6	YR	4.50	19.50
82	LOVE 550QX304-3	YR	5.50	29.50
82	MOMENTS OF LOVE 450QX209-3	YR	4.50	19.50
82	MOTHER 450QX205-3	YR	4.50	19.50
82	MOTHER AND DAD 450QX222-3	YR	4.50	19.50
82	NEW HOME 450QX212-6	YR	4.50	19.50
82	SISTER 450QX208-3	YR	4.50	32.50
82	SON 450QX204-3	YR	4.50	29.50
82	TEACHER 450QX214-3	YR	4.50	14.00
83	10TH CHRISTMAS TOGETHER 650QX430-7	YR	6.50	24.50
83	25TH CHRISTMAS TOGETHER 450QX224-7	YR	4.50	20.00
83	BABY'S 1ST XMAS PHOTOHOLDER QX 302-9	YR	7.00	29.50
83	BABY'S FIRST CHRISTMAS 450QX200-7	YR	4.50	22.50
83	BABY'S FIRST CHRISTMAS 450QX200-9	YR	4.50	22.50
83	BABY'S SECOND CHRISTMAS 450QX226-7	YR	4.50	35.00
83	CHILD'S THIRD CHRISTMAS 450QX226-9	YR	4.50	24.50
83	DAUGHTER 450QX203-7	YR	4.50	42.50
83	FIRST CHRISTMAS TOGETHER 600QX306-9	YR	6.00	22.50
83	FIRST CHRISTMAS TOGETHER 600QX310-7	LIMIT	6.00	42.50
83	FIRST CHRISTMAS TOGETHER 750QX301-7	YR	7.50	24.50
83	FRIENDSHIP 450QX207-7	YR	4.50	19.50
83	FRIENDSHIP 600QX305-9	YR	6.00	19.50
83	GODCHILD 450QX201-7	YR	4.50	17.50
83	GRANDCHILD'S FIRST CHRISTMAS 400Q430-9	YR	14.00	37.50
83	GRANDCHILD'S FIRST CHRISTMAS 600QX312-9	YR	6.00	22.50
83	GRANDDAUGHTER 450QX202-7	YR	4.50	29.50
83	GRANDMOTHER 450QX205-7	YR	4.50	19.00
83	GRANDPARENTS 650QX429-9	YR	6.50	19.50
83	GRANDSON 450QX201-9	YR	4.50	29.50
83	LOVE 450QX207-9	YR	4.50	29.50
83	LOVE 600QX305-7	YR	6.00	19.50
83	LOVE 600QX310-9	YR	6.00	49.50
83	LOVE IS A SONG 450QX223-9	YR	4.50	29.50
83	MOTHER 600QX306-7	YR	6.00	19.50
83	NEW HOME 450QX210-7	YR	4.50	32.50
83	SISTER 450QX206-9	YR	4.50	22.50

YR	NAME	LIMIT	ISSUE	QUOTE
83	SON 450QX202-9	YR	4.50	24.50
83	TEACHER 450QX224-9	YR	4.50	17.00
83	TEACHER 600QX304-9	YR	6.00	14.50
84	A GIFT OF FRIENDSHIP 450QX260-4	YR	4.50	19.50
84	BABY BOY FIRST CHRISTMAS 450QX240-4	YR	4.50	24.50
84	BABY GIRL FIRST CHRISTMAS 450QX340-1	YR	4.50	39.50
84	BABY'S 1ST XMAS PHOTOHOLDER QX 300-1	YR	7.00	19.50
84	BABY'S FIRST CHRISTMAS 1400QX438-1	YR	14.00	45.00
84	BABY'S FIRST CHRISTMAS 600QX340-1	YR	6.00	39.50
84	BABY'S SECOND CHRISTMAS 450QX241-1	YR	4.50	39.50
84	BABYSITTER 450QX253-1	YR	4.50	13.50
84	CHILD'S THIRD CHRISTMAS 450QX261-1	YR	4.50	19.50
84	DAUGHTER 450QX244-4	YR	4.50	29.50
84	FATHER 600QX257-1	YR	6.00	19.50
84	FIRST CHRISTMAS TOGETHER 450QX245-1	YR	4.50	24.50
84	FIRST CHRISTMAS TOGETHER 600QX342-1	YR	6.00	22.50
84	FRIENDSHIP 450QX248-1	YR	4.50	19.50
84	FROM OUR HOME TO YOURS 450QX248-4	YR	4.50	49.00
84	GODCHILD 450QX242-1	YR	4.50	19.50
84	GRANDCHILD'S FIRST CHRISTMAS 110QX460-1	YR	11.00	29.50
84	GRANDCHILD'S FIRST CHRISTMAS 450QX257-4	YR	4.50	17.00
84	GRANDDAUGHTER 450QX243-1	YR	4.50	29.50
84	GRANDMOTHER 450QX244-1	YR	4.50	17.50
84	GRANDPARENTS 450QX256-1	YR	4.50	17.50
84	GRANDSON 450QX242-4	YR	4.50	29.50
84	GRATITUDE 600QX344-4	YR	6.00	12.00
84	HEARTFUL OF LOVE 1000QX443-4	YR	10.00	45.00
84	LOVE 450QX255-4	YR	4.50	24.50
84	LOVE-THE SPIRIT OF CHRISTMAS 450QX247-4	YR	4.50	49.00
84	MOTHER 600QX343-4	YR	6.00	17.50
84	MOTHER AND DAD 650QX258-1	YR	6.50	25.00
84	NEW HOME 450QX245-4	YR	4.50	107.50
84	SISTER 650QX259-4	YR	6.50	32.00
84	SON 450QX243-4	YR	4.50	29.50
84	TEACHER 450QX249-1	YR	4.50	14.50
84	TEN YEARS TOGETHER 650QX258-4	YR	6.50	22.50
84	THE FUN OF FRIENDSHIP 600QX343-1	YR	6.00	34.50
84	THE MIRACLE OF LOVE 600QX342-4	YR	6.00	32.50
84	TWENTY-FIVE YEARS TOGETHER 650QX259-1	YR	6.50	29.50
85	BABY'S FIRST CHRISTMAS 1500QX499-2	YR	15.00	49.50
85	BABY'S FIRST CHRISTMAS 1600QX499-5	YR	16.00	50.00
85	BABY'S FIRST CHRISTMAS 500QX260-2	YR	5.00	24.50
85	BABY'S SECOND CHRISTMAS 600QX478-5	YR	6.00	35.00
85	DAUGHTER 550QX503-2	YR	5.50	17.50
85	FIRST CHRISTMAS TOGETHER 475QX261-2	YR	4.75	24.50
85	FIRST CHRISTMAS TOGETHER 675QX370-5	YR	6.75	19.50
85	FIRST CHRISTMAS TOGETHER 800QX507-2	YR	8.00	15.00
85	GOOD FRIENDS 475QX265-2	YR	4.75	29.50
85	GRANDCHILD'S FIRST CHRISTMAS 500QX260-5	YR	5.00	15.00
85	GRANDDAUGHTER 475QX263-5	YR	4.75	29.50
85	HEART FULL OF LOVE 675QX378-2	YR	6.75	19.50
85	HOLIDAY HEART 800QX498-2	YR	8.00	29.50
85	NIECE 575QX520-5	YR	5.75	12.50
85	TEACHER,OWL 600QX505-2	YR	6.00	19.50
85	TWENTY-FIVE YEARS TOGETHER 800QX500-5	YR	8.00	19.50
85	WITH APPRECIATION 675QX375-2	YR	6.75	11.50
86	BABY'S FIRST CHRISTMAS 550QX271-3	YR	5.50	24.50
86	BABY-SITTER 475QX275-6	YR	4.75	12.50
86	FIFTY YEARS TOGETHER 1000QX400-6	YR	10.00	25.00
86	FIRST CHRISTMAS TOGETHER 1600QX400-3	YR	16.00	32.00
86	FIRST CHRISTMAS TOGETHER 475QX270-3	YR	4.75	22.50
86	FIRST CHRISTMAS TOGETHER 7000QX379-3	YR	7.00	19.50
86	FRIENDSHIP GREETING 800QX427-3	YR	8.00	15.00
86	FRIENDSHIP'S GIFT 600QX381-6	YR	6.00	15.00
86	FROM OUR HOME TO YOURS 600QX383-3	YR	6.00	17.50
86	GODCHILD 475QX271-6	YR	4.75	15.50
86	GRANDCHILD'S FIRST CHRISTMAS 1000QX411-6	YR	10.00	17.50
86	GRANDPARENTS 750QX432-3	YR	7.50	22.50
86	MOTHER 700QX382-6	YR	7.00	22.50
86	NEPHEW 675QX381-3	YR	6.25	12.50
86	NIECE 600QX426-6	YR	6.00	12.00
86	SEASON OF THE HEART 475QX270-6	YR	4.75	19.50
86	TEACHER 475QX275-3	YR	4.75	14.00
86	TEN YEARS TOGETHER 750QX401-3	YR	7.50	24.50
87	BABY LOCKET 1500QX461-7	YR	15.00	29.50
87	BABY'S 1ST XMAS PHOTOHOLDER 750QX461-9	YR	7.50	39.50

Lucky You *and* Lucky Me *proclaim these adorable little ladies as they swing from their lucky horseshoes. Created from the illustrations of Mabel Lucie Attwell, these porcelain bisque ornaments were introduced in 1991 by Enesco.*

May Your Christmas Be Merry *is the 1991 Precious Moments porcelain Christmas ball ornament produced by Enesco.*

Holy Shepherds, *which sold as a set, is the final issue in the miniature series by Lladró.*

This sterling ornament speaks for itself. I Love Santa *is produced by Hand & Hammer.*

YR	NAME	LIMIT	ISSUE	QUOTE
87	BABY'S FIRST CHRISTMAS 600QX372-9	YR	6.00	22.50
87	FIRST CHRISTMAS TOGETHER 1500QX446-9	YR	15.00	32.50
87	FIRST CHRISTMAS TOGETHER 650QX371-9	YR	6.50	19.50
87	FIRST CHRISTMAS TOGETHER 800QX445-9	YR	8.00	39.50
87	GRANDMOTHER 475QX277-9	YR	4.75	17.50
87	HOLIDAY GREETINGS 600QX375-7	YR	6.00	12.75
87	NIECE 475QX275-9	YR	4.75	12.50
87	TWENTY-FIVE YEARS TOGETHER 750QX443-9	YR	7.50	29.50
87	WARMTH OF FRIENDSHIP 600QX375-9	YR	6.00	15.00
87	WORD OF LOVE 800QX447-7	YR	8.00	29.50
88	BABY BOY'S FIRST CHRISTMAS 475QX272-1	YR	4.75	24.50
88	BABY GIRL'S FIRST CHRISTMAS 475QX272-4	YR	4.75	24.50
88	BABY'S FIRST CHRISTMAS 750QX470-4	YR	7.50	29.50
88	FIFTY YEARS TOGETHER 675QX374-1	YR	6.75	19.50
88	FIRST CHRISTMAS TOGETHER 475QX274-1	YR	4.75	24.50
88	GODCHILD 475QX278-4	YR	4.75	19.50
88	GRANDMOTHER 475QX276-4	YR	4.75	19.50
88	LOVE GROWS 475QX275-4	YR	4.75	37.50
88	MOTHER 650QX375-1	YR	6.50	17.50
88	TEN YEARS TOGETHER 475QX275-1	YR	4.75	22.00
88	YEAR TO REMEMBER 700QX416-4	YR	7.00	24.50
89	FIRST CHRISTMAS TOGETHER 475QX273-2	YR	4.75	24.50
89	FIVE YEARS TOGETHER 475QX273-5	YR	4.75	22.50
89	FROM OUR HOME TO YOURS 625QX384-5	YR	6.25	17.50
89	GRANDDAUGHTER 475QX278-2	YR	4.75	22.50
89	GRANDSON 475QX278-5	YR	4.75	22.50
89	LANGUAGE OF LOVE 625QX383-5	YR	6.25	21.50
89	MOTHER 975QX440-5	YR	9.75	29.50
89	SISTER 475QX279-2	YR	4.75	19.50
89	TEACHER 575QX412-5	YR	5.75	24.50
89	WORLD OF LOVE 475QX274-5	YR	4.75	32.50
90	BABY'S FIRST CHRISTMAS:BABY BOY QX 206-3	YR	4.75	22.50
90	BABY'S FIRST CHRISTMAS:BABY GIRLQX 206-6	YR	4.75	22.50
90	BABY'S FIRST XMAS PHOTOHOLDER 775QX484-3	YR	7.75	29.50
90	CHILD CARE GIVER 675QX316-6	YR	6.75	14.50
90	FROM OUR HOME TO YOURS 475QX216-6	YR	4.75	19.50
90	GRANDPARENTS 475QX225-3	YR	4.75	17.50
90	OUR FIRST CHRISTMAS TOGETHER 475QX213-6	YR	4.75	16.50
90	OUR FIRST CHRISTMAS TOGETHER 675QX314-6	YR	6.75	17.50
90	OUR FIRST CHRISTMAS TOGETHER 975QX488-3	YR	9.75	19.50
90	OUR FIRST XMAS/PHOTOHOLDER 775QX488-6	YR	7.75	17.50
90	PEACEFUL KINGDOM 475QX210-6	YR	4.75	22.50
90	SISTER 475QX227-3	YR	4.75	19.50
91	EXTRA-SPECIAL FRIENDS 475QX227--9	YR	4.75	15.50
91	FIRST CHRISTMAS TOGETHER QX 222-9	YR	4.75	12.00
91	FIVE YEARS TOGETHER 775QX492-7	YR	7.75	20.00
91	FORTY YEARS TOGETHER 775QX493-9	YR	7.75	19.50
91	GRANDMOTHER 475QX230-7	YR	4.75	19.50
91	MOM AND DAD 975QX546-7	YR	9.75	22.50
91	MOTHER 975QX545-7	YR	9.75	35.00
91	SWEETHEART 975QX495-7	YR	9.75	27.50
91	TEN YEARS TOGETHER 775QX492-9	YR	7.75	19.50
92	FOR MY GRANDMA PHOTOHOLDER QX 518-4	YR	7.75	16.50
92	GRANDMOTHER 475QX201-1	YR	4.75	14.50
92	GRANDPARENTS 475QX200-4	YR	4.75	14.50
92	TEACHER 475QX226-4	YR	4.75	16.50
92	BABY'S FIRST CHRISTMAS 1875QX458-1	YR	18.75	39.50
91	GODCHILD 675QX548-9	YR	6.75	19.50
91	NEW HOME 675QX544-9	YR	6.75	19.50
88	CHILD'S THIRD CHRISTMAS 600QX471-4	YR	6.00	29.50
89	BABY'S FIRST CHRISTMAS 725QX449-2	YR	7.25	54.50
90	MOM AND DAD 875QX459-3	YR	8.75	24.50
91	GRANDDAUGHTER'S 1ST CHRISTMAS 675QX511-9	YR	6.75	24.50
91	GRANDSON'S FIRST CHRISTMAS 675QX511-7	YR	6.75	24.50
92	FRIENDLY GREETINGS 775QX504-1	YR	7.75	17.50
92	SPECIAL CAT PHOTOHOLDER QX 541-4	YR	7.75	19.50
92	SPECIAL DOG PHOTOHOLDER QX 542-1	YR	7.75	32.50
86	FRIENDS ARE FUN 475QX272-3	YR	4.75	39.50
86	NEW HOME 475QX274-6	YR	4.75	32.00
87	CHILD'S THIRD CHRISTMAS 575QX459-9	YR	5.75	26.50
88	BABY'S FIRST CHRISTMAS 975QX470-1	YR	9.75	49.50
91	FRIENDS ARE FUN 975QX528-9	YR	9.75	22.50
92	BROTHER 675QX468-4	YR	6.75	15.00
92	SISTER 675QX468-1	YR	6.75	17.50
89	BABY'S FIRST CHRISTMAS 675QX381-5	YR	6.75	19.50
89	BABY'S SECOND CHRISTMAS 675QX449-5	YR	6.75	29.50

YR	NAME	LIMIT	ISSUE	QUOTE
89	CHILD'S FOURTH CHRISTMAS 675QX543-2	YR	6.75	19.50
89	GODCHILD 625QX311-2	YR	6.25	14.50
89	GRANDDAUGHTER'S FIRST XMAS 675QX382-2	YR	6.75	22.50
89	GRANDSON'S FIRST CHRISTMAS 675QX382-5	YR	6.75	19.50
90	BABY'S FIRST CHRISTMAS 775QX485-6	YR	7.75	35.00
90	BABY'S FIRST CHRISTMAS 975QX485-3	YR	9.75	22.50
90	BABY'S SECOND CHRISTMAS 675QX486-3	YR	6.75	39.50
90	CHILD'S FOURTH CHRISTMAS 675QX487-3	YR	6.75	19.50
90	CHILD'S THIRD CHRISTMAS 675QX486-6	YR	6.75	22.50
90	GODCHILD 675QX317-6	YR	6.75	19.50
90	GRANDDAUGHTER'S FIRST XMAS 675QX310-6	YR	6.75	22.50
90	GRANDSON'S FIRST CHRISTMAS 675QX306-3	YR	6.75	22.50
91	A CHILD'S CHRISTMAS 975QX488-7	YR	9.75	17.50
91	BABY'S FIRST CHRISTMAS 1775QX510-7	YR	17.75	42.50
91	BABY'S FIRST CHRISTMAS 775QX488-9	YR	7.75	29.50
91	BABY'S SECOND CHRISTMAS 675QX489-7	YR	6.75	29.50
91	CHILD'S FOURTH CHRISTMAS 675QX490-7	YR	6.75	18.50
91	CHILD'S THIRD CHRISTMAS 675QX489-9	YR	6.75	29.50
92	A CHILD'S CHRISTMAS 975QX457-4	YR	9.75	17.00
92	BABY'S FIRST CHRISTMAS 775QX464-4	YR	7.75	24.50
92	BABY'S SECOND CHRISTMAS 675QX465-1	YR	6.75	17.50
92	CHILD'S FOURTH CHRISTMAS 675QX466-1	YR	6.75	24.50
92	CHILD'S THIRD CHRISTMAS 675QX465-4	YR	6.75	19.50
92	DAUGHTER 675QX503-1	YR	6.75	19.50
92	SON 675QX502-4	YR	6.75	17.50
89	CHILD'S THIRD CHRISTMAS 675QX469-5	YR	6.75	19.50
91	BABY'S FIRST CHRISTMAS-BOY 475QX221-7	YR	4.75	19.50
91	BABY'S FIRST CHRISTMAS-GIRL 475QX222-7	YR	4.75	19.50
83	BABY'S FIRST CHRISTMAS 1400QX402-7	YR	14.00	39.50
84	BABY'S FIRST CHRISTMAS 1600QX904-1	YR	16.00	49.50
85	BABY'S FIRST CHRISTMAS 575QX370-2	YR	5.75	22.50
87	BABY'S FIRST CHRISTMAS 975QX411-3	YR	9.75	29.50
87	BABY'S SECOND CHRISTMAS 575QX460-7	YR	5.75	32.50
87	FIRST CHRISTMAS TOGETHER 950QX446-7	YR	9.50	30.00
89	DAD 725QX441-2	YR	7.25	15.00
89	FRIENDSHIP TIME 975QX413-2	YR	9.75	32.50
90	DAD 675QX453-3	YR	6.75	19.50
91	DAD 775QX512-7	YR	7.75	19.50
91	DAD-TO-BE 575QX487-9	YR	5.75	16.50
91	FLAG OF LIBERTY 675QX524-9	YR	6.75	19.50
91	MOM-TO-BE 575QX487-7	YR	5.75	19.50
92	DAD-TO-BE 675QX461-1	YR	6.75	17.50
92	MOM-TO-BE 675QX461-4	YR	6.75	19.50
92	OUR FIRST CHRISTMAS TOGETHER 975QX506-1	YR	9.75	19.50
86	GRANDDAUGHTER 475QX273-6	YR	4.75	24.50
87	FIRST CHRISTMAS TOGETHER 450QX272-9	YR	4.75	22.50
87	LOVE IS EVERYWHERE 475QX278-7	YR	4.75	26.50
88	MOTHER AND DAD 800QX414-4	YR	8.00	21.50
88	SPIRIT OF CHRISTMAS 475QX276-1	YR	4.75	22.50
89	GRANDMOTHER 475QX277-5	YR	4.75	17.50
89	GRANDPARENTS 475QX277-2	YR	4.75	17.50
89	TEN YEARS TOGETHER 475QX274-2	YR	4.75	29.50
90	GRANDDAUGHTER 475QX228-6	YR	4.75	22.50
90	TEN YEARS TOGETHER 475QX215-3	YR	4.75	19.50
91	ACROSS THE MILES 675QX315-7	YR	6.75	14.50
91	SISTER 675QX548-7	YR	6.75	19.50
92	FOR THE ONE I LOVE 975QX484-4	YR	9.75	22.50
84	FIRST CHRISTMAS TOGETHER 1600QX904-4	YR	16.00	75.00
84	FIRST CHRISTMAS TOGETHER 750QX340-4	YR	7.50	24.50
85	BABY LOCKET 1600QX401-2	YR	16.00	35.00
85	GODCHILD 675QX380-2	YR	6.75	14.50
85	LOVE AT CHRISTMAS 575QX371-5	YR	5.75	42.50
86	BABY LOCKET 1600QX412-3	YR	16.00	30.00
88	FIVE YEARS TOGETHER 475QX274-4	YR	4.75	22.50
91	GIFT OF JOY 875QX531-9	YR	8.75	25.00
85	SPECIAL FRIENDS 575QX372-5	YR	5.75	15.00
86	BABY'S FIRST CHRISTMAS 600QX380-3	YR	6.00	24.50
85	FRIENDSHIP 775QX506-2	YR	7.75	15.00
85	FROM OUR HOUSE TO YOURS 775QX520-2	YR	7.75	25.00
85	GRANDMOTHER 475QX262-5	YR	4.75	15.00
85	SISTER 725QX506-5	YR	7.25	29.50
86	BABY'S FIRST XMAS PHOTOHOLDER 800QX379-2	YR	8.00	39.50
86	CHILD'S THIRD CHRISTMAS 650QX413-6	YR	6.50	26.50
86	GRANDMOTHER 475QX274-3	YR	4.75	17.50
86	JOY OF FRIENDS 675QX382-3	YR	6.75	17.50
86	SWEETHEART 1100QX408-6	YR	11.00	69.50

YR	NAME	LIMIT	ISSUE	QUOTE
87	BABY'S FIRST CHRISTMAS-BOY 475QX274-9	YR	4.75	27.50
87	BABY'S FIRST CHRISTMAS-GIRL 475QX274-7	YR	4.75	22.50
87	NEW HOME 600QX376-7	YR	6.00	32.50
88	DAUGHTER 575QX415-1	YR	5.75	52.50
88	FROM OUR HOME TO YOURS 475QX279-4	YR	4.75	19.50
88	GRANDPARENTS 475QX277-1	YR	4.75	19.50
88	GRATITUDE 600QX375-4	YR	6.00	12.00
88	SON 575QX415-4	YR	5.75	40.00
88	TWENTY-FIVE YEARS TOGETHER 675QX373-4	YR	6.75	19.00
90	FIFTY YEARS TOGETHER 975QX490-6	YR	9.75	19.50
90	FORTY YEARS TOGETHER 975QX490-3	YR	9.75	19.50
90	JESUS LOVES ME 675QX315-6	YR	6.75	19.50
90	TWENTY-FIVE YEARS TOGETHER 975QX489-6	YR	9.75	19.50
83	MOM AND DAD 650QX429-7	YR	6.50	24.50
85	GRANDPARENTS 700QX380-5	YR	7.00	12.00
85	MOTHER 675QX372-2	YR	6.75	17.50
86	GRATITUDE 600QX432-6	YR	6.00	10.50
86	HUSBAND 800QX383-6	YR	8.00	25.00
87	BABYSITTER 475QX279-7	YR	4.75	15.00
87	GRANDPARENTS 475QX277-7	YR	4.75	17.50
87	MOTHER 650QX373-7	YR	6.50	19.50
87	MOTHER AND DAD 700QX462-7	YR	7.00	22.00
88	BABY'S FIRST CHRISTMAS 600QX372-1	YR	6.00	19.50
88	BABY'S SECOND CHRISTMAS 600QX471-1	YR	6.00	32.50
88	FIRST CHRISTMAS TOGETHER 900QX489-4	YR	9.00	29.50
88	TEACHER 625QX417-1	YR	6.25	19.50
89	MOM AND DAD 975QX442-5	YR	9.75	24.00
91	FIRST CHRISTMAS TOGETHER QX 313-9	YR	6.75	16.00
91	UNDER THE MISTLETOE 875QX494-9	YR	8.75	19.50
92	NEW HOME 875QX519-1	YR	8.75	19.50
85	BABY-SITTER 475QX264-2	YR	4.75	13.00
85	FRIENDSHIP 675QX378-5	YR	6.75	19.50
85	NEW HOME 475QX269-5	YR	4.75	32.50
86	MOTHER AND DAD 750QX431-6	YR	7.50	24.50
87	FROM OUR HOME TO YOURS 475QX279-9	YR	4.75	40.00
87	GODCHILD 475QX276-7	YR	4.75	19.50
90	NEW HOME 675QX434-3	YR	6.75	29.50
91	GRANDDAUGHTER 475QX229-9	YR	4.75	22.50
91	GRANDPARENTS 475QX230-9	YR	4.75	16.50
91	GRANDSON 475QX229-7	YR	4.75	21.50
89	CHILD'S FIFTH CHRISTMAS 675QX543-5	YR	6.75	19.50
89	FIRST CHRISTMAS TOGETHER 675QX383-2	YR	6.75	24.50
90	CHILD'S FIFTH CHRISTMAS 675QX487-6	YR	6.75	19.50
90	FRIENDSHIP KITTEN 675QX414-3	YR	6.75	27.50
90	SWEETHEART 1175QX489-3	YR	11.75	29.50
91	CHILD'S FIFTH CHRISTMAS 675QX490-9	YR	6.75	20.00
91	JESUS LOVES ME 775QX314-7	YR	7.75	17.50
92	ACROSS THE MILES 675QX304-4	YR	6.75	12.00
92	CHILD'S FIFTH CHRISTMAS 675QX466-4	YR	6.75	14.50
89	25 YEARS TOGETHER PHOTOHOLDER 875QX485-5	YR	8.75	19.50
89	40 YEARS TOGETHER PHOTOHOLDER 875QX545-2	YR	8.75	22.50
89	50 YEARS TOGETHER PHOTOHOLDER 875QX486-2	YR	8.75	22.50
89	FIRST CHRISTMAS TOGETHER 675QX485-2	YR	9.75	27.50
90	BABY'S FIRST CHRISTMAS 675QX303-6	YR	6.75	22.50
91	TEACHER 475QX228-9	YR	4.75	12.50
92	HOLIDAY MEMO 775QX504-4	YR	7.75	17.50
92	LOVE TO SKATE 875QX484-1	YR	8.75	19.50
92	MOM 775QX516-4	YR	7.75	24.50
92	SECRET PAL 775QX542-4	YR	7.75	15.00
82	BABY'S FIRST CHRISTMAS 1300QX455-3	YR	13.00	49.50
82	BABY'S FIRST CHRISTMAS 550QX302-3	YR	5.50	39.50
82	TEACHER-APPLE 550QX301-6	YR	5.50	14.00
83	FIRST XMAS TOGETHER-LOCKET 1500QX432-9	YR	15.00	40.00
84	FIRST CHRISTMAS TOGETHER 1500QX436-4	YR	15.00	40.00
85	CHILD'S THIRD CHRISTMAS 600QX475-5	YR	6.00	29.50
85	FIRST CHRISTMAS TOGETHER 1675QX400-5	YR	16.75	35.00
86	DAUGHTER 575QX430-6	YR	5.75	39.50
86	LOVING MEMORIES 900QX409-3	YR	9.00	34.50
86	SON 575QX430-3	YR	5.75	39.50
87	FIFTY YEARS TOGETHER 800QX443-7	YR	8.00	24.50
87	GRANDCHILD'S FIRST CHRISTMAS 900QX460-9	YR	9.00	24.50
90	TEACHER 775QX448-3	YR	7.75	17.50
92	1ST CHRISTMAS TOGETHER PHOTO. QX 469-4	YR	8.75	27.50
92	FRIENDSHIP LINE 975QX503-4	YR	9.75	29.50
92	GRANDDAUGHTER 675QX560-4	YR	6.75	19.50
92	GRANDSON 675QX561-1	YR	6.75	19.50

YR	NAME	LIMIT	ISSUE	QUOTE
80	BABY'S FIRST CHRISTMAS 1200QX156-1	YR	12.00	49.50
82	CHRISTMAS MEMORIES 650QX311-6	YR	6.50	29.50
82	FATHER 450QX205-6	YR	4.50	19.50
82	TEACHER 650QX312-3	YR	6.50	17.50
83	BABY'S FIRST CHRISTMAS 750QX301-9	YR	7.50	17.50
83	FIRST CHRISTMAS TOGETHER 450QX208-9	YR	4.50	29.50
83	LOVE 1300QX422-7	YR	13.00	39.50
85	FIRST CHRISTMAS TOGETHER 1300QX493-5	YR	13.00	27.50
86	BABY'S FIRST CHRISTMAS 900QX412-6	YR	9.00	39.50
86	FIRST CHRISTMAS TOGETHER 1200QX409-6	YR	12.00	32.50
87	DAUGHTER 575QX463-7	YR	5.75	29.50
87	SISTER 600QX474-7	YR	6.00	15.00
87	SON 575QX463-9	YR	5.75	44.50
87	SWEETHEART 1100QX447-9	YR	11.00	32.50
88	BABYSITTER 475QX279-1	YR	4.75	12.50
89	DAUGHTER 625QX443-2	YR	6.25	19.50
89	SON 625QX444-5	YR	6.25	22.50
89	SWEETHEART 975QX486-5	YR	9.75	34.50
91	FIRST CHRISTMAS TOGETHER QX 491-9	YR	8.75	20.00
91	TERRIFIC TEACHER 675QX530-9	YR	6.75	16.50
85	SON 550QX502-5	YR	5.50	44.50
86	BABY'S SECOND CHRISTMAS 650QX413-3	YR	6.50	29.50
87	DAD 600QX462-9	YR	6.00	39.50
87	TEACHER 575QX466-7	YR	5.75	22.50
88	DAD 700QX414-1	YR	7.00	24.50
90	BROTHER 575QX449-3	YR	5.75	15.00
90	COPY OF CHEER 775QX448-6	YR	7.75	19.50
90	DAD-TO-BE 575QX491-3	YR	5.75	22.50
90	DAUGHTER 575QX449-6	YR	5.75	19.50
90	MOM-TO-BE 575QX491-6	YR	5.75	35.00
90	SON 575QX451-6	YR	5.75	19.50
91	BROTHER 675QX547-9	YR	6.75	19.50
91	DAUGHTER 575QX547-7	YR	5.75	19.50
91	SON 575QX546-9	YR	5.75	19.50
91	THE BIG CHEESE 675QX532-7	YR	6.75	19.50
92	DAD 775QX467-4	YR	7.75	19.50
92	GRANDDAUGHTER'S 1ST CHRISTMAS 675QX463-4	YR	6.75	18.50
92	GRANDSON'S 1ST CHRISTMAS 675QX462-1	YR	6.75	14.50
92	MOM AND DAD 975QX467-1	YR	9.75	37.50
92	V.P. OF IMPORTANT STUFF 675QX505-1	YR	6.75	14.50
92	WORLD-CLASS TEACHER 775QX505-4	YR	7.75	19.50
88	SWEETHEART 975QX490-1	YR	9.75	24.50
92	ANNIVERSARY YEAR, PHOTOHOLDER 975QX485-1	YR	9.75	24.50
92	GODCHILD 675QX594-1	YR	6.75	19.50
85	BABY'S FIRST CHRISTMAS 700QX478-2	YR	7.00	19.50
85	FATHER 650QX376-2	YR	6.50	12.50
85	GRANDCHILD'S FIRST CHRISTMAS 1100QX495-5	YR	11.00	24.00
85	GRANDSON 475QX262-2	YR	4.75	29.50
85	MOTHER AND DAD 775QX509-2	YR	7.75	22.50
86	FATHER 650QX431-3	YR	6.50	15.00
86	GRANDSON 475QX273-3	YR	4.75	25.00
86	SISTER 675QX380-6	YR	6.75	17.50
86	TIMELESS LOVE 600QX379-6	YR	6.00	27.50
86	TWENTY-FIVE YEARS TOGETHER 800QX410-3	YR	8.00	24.50
87	GRANDDAUGHTER 600QX374-7	YR	6.00	24.50
87	GRANDSON 475QX276-9	YR	4.75	27.50
87	HEART IN BLOSSOM 600QX372-7	YR	6.00	26.50
87	HUSBAND 700QX373-9	YR	7.00	12.00
87	TEN YEARS TOGETHER 700QX444-7	YR	7.00	24.50
88	FIRST CHRISTMAS TOGETHER 675QX373-1	YR	6.75	26.50
88	GRANDDAUGHTER 475QX277-4	YR	4.75	24.50
88	GRANDSON 475QX278-1	YR	4.75	24.50
88	LOVE FILLS THE HEART 600QX374-4	YR	6.00	24.50
88	NEW HOME 600QX376-1	YR	6.00	26.50
88	SISTER 800QX499-4	YR	8.00	32.50
89	BABY'S 1ST XMAS PHOTOHOLDER 625QX468-2	YR	6.25	49.50
89	BABY'S FIRST CHRISTMAS-BOY 475QX272-5	YR	4.75	19.50
89	BABY'S FIRST CHRISTMAS-GIRL 475QX272-2	YR	4.75	19.50
89	FESTIVE YEAR 775QX384-2	YR	7.75	19.50
89	GRATITUDE 675QX385-2	YR	6.75	13.50
89	NEW HOME 475QX275-5	YR	4.75	24.50
90	ACROSS THE MILES 675QX317-3	YR	6.75	17.50
90	FIVE YEARS TOGETHER 475QX210-3	YR	4.75	19.50
90	GRANDMOTHER 475QX223-6	YR	4.75	18.50
90	GRANDSON 475QX229-3	YR	4.75	19.50
90	MOTHER 875QX453-6	YR	8.75	19.50

YR	NAME	LIMIT	ISSUE	QUOTE
91	25 YEARS TOGETHER PHOTOHOLDER QX493-7	YR	8.75	19.50
91	BABY'S FIRST XMAS-PHOTOHOLDER 775QX486-9	YR	7.75	29.50
91	FIFTY YEARS TOGETHER-PHOTOHDR 875QX494-7	YR	8.75	19.50
91	FIRST CHRISTMAS TOGETHER QX 491-7	YR	8.75	15.00
91	FROM OUR HOME TO YOURS 475QX228-7	YR	4.75	22.50
92	BABY'S 1ST CHRISTMAS PHOTOHOLDER QX464-1	YR	7.75	22.50
92	BABY'S FIRST CHRISTMAS-GIRL 475QX220-4	YR	4.75	16.50
92	FROM OUR HOME TO YOURS 475QX213-1	YR	4.75	14.50
92	OUR FIRST CHRISTMAS TOGETHER 675QX301-1	YR	6.75	19.50
87	TIME FOR FRIENDS 475QX280-7	YR	4.75	24.50
92	BABY;S FIRST CHRISTMAS-BOY 475QX219-1	YR	4.75	16.50

COUNTRY CHRISTMAS COLLECTION

YR	NAME	LIMIT	ISSUE	QUOTE
85	OLD-FASHIONED DOLL 1450QX519-5	YR	14.50	42.50
85	WHIRLIGIG SANTA 1250QX519-2	YR	12.50	27.50
85	COUNTRY GOOSE 775QX518-5	YR	7.75	17.50
85	SHEEP AT CHRISTMAS 825QX517-5	YR	8.25	29.50
85	ROCKING HORSE MEMORIES 1000QX518-2	YR	10.00	17.50

COUNTRY TREASURES COLLECTION

YR	NAME	LIMIT	ISSUE	QUOTE
86	REMEMBERING CHRISTMAS 865QX510-6	YR	8.75	29.50
86	LITTLE DRUMMERS 1250QX511-6	YR	12.50	34.50
86	WELCOME CHRISTMAS 825QX510-3	YR	8.25	34.50
86	COUNTRY SLEIGH 1000QX511-3	YR	10.00	29.50
86	NUTCRACKER SANTA 1000QX512-3	YR	10.00	49.50

K. CROW

CRAYOLA CRAYON

YR	NAME	LIMIT	ISSUE	QUOTE
90	BRIGHT MOVING COLORS 875QX458-6	YR	8.75	42.50
91	BRIGHT VIBRANT CAROLS 975QX421-9	YR	9.75	39.50
92	BRIGHT BLAZING COLORS 975QX426-4	YR	9.75	31.50
93	BRIGHT SHINING CASTLE 1075QX442-2	YR	10.75	29.50
94	BRIGHT PLAYFUL COLORS 1095QX527-3	YR	10.95	23.50
89	BRIGHT JOURNEY 875QX-435-2	YR	8.75	44.50

CROWN CLASSICS

YR	NAME	LIMIT	ISSUE	QUOTE
81	ANGEL 450QX507-5	YR	4.50	29.50
81	TREE PHOTOHOLDER 550QX515-5	YR	5.50	29.50
81	UNICORN 850QX516-5	YR	8.50	24.50
83	ENAMELED CHRISTMAS WREATH 900QX311-9	YR	9.00	15.00
83	MEMORIES TO TREASURE 700QX303-7	YR	7.00	24.50
83	MOTHER AND CHILD 750QX302-7	YR	7.50	39.50

DECORATIVE BALL ORNAMENTS

YR	NAME	LIMIT	ISSUE	QUOTE
76	CARDINALS 225QX205-1	YR	2.25	65.00
76	CHICKADEES 225QX204-1	YR	2.25	60.00
77	CHRISTMAS MOUSE 350QX134-2	YR	3.50	85.00
77	RABBIT 250QX139-5	YR	2.50	95.00
77	SQUIRREL 250QX138-2	YR	2.50	115.00
77	STAINED GLASS 350QX152-2	YR	3.50	75.00
78	DRUMMER BOY 350QX252-3	YR	3.50	55.00
78	HALLMARK'S ANTIQUE CARD COLL. 350QX220-3	YR	3.50	44.00
78	JOY 350QX254-3	YR	3.50	50.00
78	MERRY CHRISTMAS (SANTA) 350QX202-3	YR	3.50	60.00
78	NATIVITY 350QX253-6	YR	3.50	150.00
78	THE QUAIL 350QX251-6	YR	3.50	50.00
78	YESTERDAY'S TOYS 350QX250-3	YR	3.50	75.00
79	BEHOLD THE STAR 350QX255-9	YR	3.50	45.00
79	BLACK ANGEL 350QX207-9	YR	3.50	24.50
79	CHRISTMAS CHICKADEES 350QX204-7	YR	3.50	29.50
79	CHRISTMAS COLLAGE 350QX257-9	YR	3.50	27.50
79	NIGHT BEFORE CHRISTMAS 350QX214-7	YR	3.50	39.50
79	THE LIGHT OF CHRISTMAS 350QX256-7	YR	3.50	17.00
80	CHRISTMAS CARDINALS 400QX224-1	YR	4.00	29.50
80	CHRISTMAS CHOIR 400QX228-1	YR	4.00	225.00
80	CHRISTMAS TIME 400QX226-1	YR	4.00	35.00
80	HAPPY CHRISTMAS 400QX222-1	YR	4.00	39.50
80	JOLLY SANTA 400QX227-4	YR	4.00	35.00
80	NATIVITY 400QX225-4	YR	4.00	95.00
80	SANTA'S WORKSHOP 400QX223-4	YR	4.00	29.50
81	CHRISTMAS 1981 450QX809-5	YR	4.50	22.50
81	CHRISTMAS IN THE FOREST 450QX813-5	YR	4.50	165.00
81	CHRISTMAS MAGIC 450QX810-2	YR	4.50	24.50
81	LET US ADORE HIM 450QX811-5	YR	4.50	60.00
81	MERRY CHRISTMAS 450QX814-2	YR	4.50	19.50
81	SANTA'S COMING 450QX812-2	YR	4.50	27.50
81	SANTA'S SURPRISE 450QX815-5	YR	4.50	24.50
81	TRADITIONAL (BLACK SANTA) 450QX801-5	YR	4.50	110.00
82	CHRISTMAS ANGEL 450QX220-6	YR	4.50	24.50
82	CURRIER & IVES 450QX201-3	YR	4.50	22.50
82	SEASON FOR CARING 450QX221-3	YR	4.50	24.50
83	1983 450QX220-9	YR	4.50	29.50

YR	NAME	LIMIT	ISSUE	QUOTE
83	AN OLD FASHIONED CHRISTMAS 450QX217-9	YR	4.50	32.50
83	ANGELS 500QX219-7	YR	5.00	24.00
83	CHRISTMAS JOY 450QX216-9	YR	4.50	29.50
83	CHRISTMAS WONDERLAND 450QX221-9	YR	4.50	95.00
83	CURRIER & IVES 450QX215-9	YR	4.50	22.50
83	HERE COMES SANTA 450QX217-7	YR	4.50	34.50
83	ORIENTAL BUTTERFLIES 450QX218-7	YR	4.50	22.50
83	SEASON'S GREETING 450QX219-9	YR	4.50	22.50
83	THE ANNUNCIATION 450QX216-7	YR	4.50	29.50
83	THE WISE MEN 450QX220-7	YR	4.50	39.50
82	SANTA 450QX221-6	YR	4.50	19.50
79	CHRISTMAS TRADITIONS 350QX253-9	YR	3.50	45.00
*			**DESIGNER KEEPSAKES**	
82	MERRY CHRISTMAS 450QX225-6	YR	4.50	19.50
82	OLD FASHIONED CHRISTMAS 450QX227-6	YR	4.50	39.50
82	OLD WORLD ANGELS 450QX226-3	YR	4.50	22.50
82	PATTERNS OF CHRISTMAS 450QX226-6	YR	4.50	24.50
82	STAINED GLASS 450QX228-3	YR	4.50	22.50
82	TWELVE DAYS OF CHRISTMAS 450QX203-6	YR	4.50	35.00
			EASTER ORNAMENTS COLLECTION	
91	BABY'S FIRST EASTER 875QEO518-9	YR	8.75	27.50
91	DAUGHTER 575QEO517-9	YR	5.75	29.50
91	EASTER MEMORIES PHOTOHOLDER QEO 513-7	YR	7.75	19.50
91	FULL OF LOVE 775QEO514-9	YR	7.75	39.50
91	GENTLE LAMB 675QEO515-9	YR	6.75	19.50
91	GRANDCHILD 675QEO517-7	YR	6.75	22.50
91	LI'L DIPPER 675QEO514-7	YR	6.75	22.50
91	LILY EGG 975QEO513-9	YR	9.75	24.50
91	SON 575QEO518-7	YR	5.75	24.50
91	SPIRIT OF EASTER 775QEO516-9	YR	7.75	34.50
91	SPRINGTIME STROLL 675QEO516-7	YR	6.75	24.50
94	SPRINGTIME BONNETS 775QEO809-6	YR	7.75	23.50
94	SWEET EASTER WISHES 875QEO819-6	YR	8.75	24.50
95	APRIL SHOWERS QEO 826-3	YR	6.95	6.95
95	BABY'S FIRST EASTER QEO 823-7	YR	7.95	7.95
95	BUGS BUNNY QEO 827-9	YR	8.95	8.95
95	BUNNY WITH CRAYONS QEO 824-9	YR	7.95	7.95
95	BUNNY WITH SEED PACKETS QEO 825-9	YR	8.95	8.95
95	COLLECTOR'S PLATE QEO 821-9	YR	7.95	7.95
95	DAUGHTER QEO 823-9	YR	5.95	5.95
95	EASTER BEAGLE QEO 825-7	YR	7.95	7.95
95	EASTER EGG COTTAGES QEO 820-7	YR	8.95	8.95
95	GARDEN CLUB QEO 820-9	YR	7.95	7.95
95	HAM 'N EGGS QEO 827-7	YR	7.95	7.95
95	HERE COMES EASTER QEO 821-7	YR	7.95	7.95
95	LILY QEO 826-7	YR	6.95	6.95
95	MINIATURE TRAIN QEO 826-9	YR	4.95	4.95
95	SON QEO 824-7	YR	5.95	5.95
95	SPRINGTIME BARBIE QEO 806-9	YR	12.95	25.00
95	SPRINGTIME BONNETS QEO 822-7	YR	7.95	7.95
95	THREE FLOWERPOT FRIENDS QEO 822-9	YR	14.95	14.95
93	BARRIOW OF GIGGLES 875QEO840-2	YR	8.75	24.50
93	DAUGHTER 575QEO834-2	YR	5.75	22.50
93	SON 575QEO833-5	YR	5.75	22.50
94	DAUGHTER 575QEO815-6	YR	5.75	15.00
94	SON 575QEO816-3	YR	5.75	15.00
93	TIME FOR EASTER 875QEO838-5	YR	8.75	24.50
92	EASTER PARADE 675QEO930-1	YR	6.75	36.50
92	GRANDCHILD 675QEO927-4	YR	6.75	24.50
94	COLORFUL SPRING 775QEO816-6	YR	7.75	27.50
94	HERE COMES EASTER 775QEO809-3	YR	7.75	24.50
92	BABY'S FIRST EASTER 675QEO927-1	YR	6.75	22.50
92	BLESS YOU 675QEO929-1	YR	6.75	24.50
92	SOMEBUNNY LOVES YOU 675QEO929-4	YR	6.75	27.50
93	MAYPOLE STROLL 2800QEO839-5 SET OF THREE	YR	28.00	60.00
94	BABY'S FIRST EASTER 675QEO815-3	YR	6.75	19.50
92	SPRINGTIME EGG 875QEO932-1	YR	8.75	23.50
93	BEST-DRESSED TURTLE 575QEO839-2	YR	5.75	22.50
93	EASTER PARADE 675QEO832-5	YR	6.75	29.50
93	LI'L PEPPER 775QEO831-2	YR	7.75	24.50
93	NUTTY EGGS 675QEO838-2	YR	6.75	22.50
93	SPRINGTIME BONNETS 775QEO832-2	YR	7.75	25.00
92	PROMISE OF EASTER 875QEO931-4	YR	8.75	22.50
93	CHICKS-ON-A-TWIRL 775QEO837-5	YR	7.75	22.50
92	JOY BEARER 875QEO933-4	YR	8.75	32.50
93	BABY'S FIRST EASTER 675QEO834-5	YR	6.75	19.50

YR	NAME	LIMIT	ISSUE	QUOTE
94	RIDING A BREEZE 575QEO821-3	YR	5.75	15.00
92	EVERYTHING'S DUCKY! 675QEO933-1	YR	6.75	22.50
92	SUNNY WISHER 575QEO934-4	YR	5.75	22.50
94	EASTER PARADE 675QEO813-6	YR	6.75	19.50
92	CRAYOLA BUNNY 775QEO930-4	YR	7.75	34.50
92	DAUGHTER 575QEO928-4	YR	5.75	22.50
92	SON 575QEO928-1	YR	5.75	22.50
94	SWEET AS SUGAR 875QEO808-6	YR	8.75	17.50
94	YUMMY RECIPE 775QEO814-3	YR	7.75	20.00
94	SUNNY BUNNY GARDEN 1500QEO814-6 SET OF 3	YR	15.00	30.00
93	BACKYARD BUNNY 675QEO840-5	YR	6.75	22.50
93	LOP-EARED BUNNY 575QEO831-5	YR	5.75	19.50
94	TREETOP COTTAGE 975QEO818-6	YR	9.75	20.00
92	EGGSPERT PAINTER 675QEO936-1	YR	6.75	24.50
92	COSMIC RABBIT 775QEO936-4	YR	7.75	23.50
92	CULTIVATED GARDENER 575QEO935-1	YR	5.75	19.50
92	EGGS IN SPORTS 675QEO934-1	YR	6.75	37.50
93	EGGS IN SPORTS 675QEO833-2	YR	6.75	30.00
93	GRANDCHILD 675QEO835-2	YR	6.75	22.50
94	EGGS IN SPORTS 675QEO813-3	YR	6.75	19.50
93	BEAUTIFUL MEMORIES,PHOTOHLDR 675QEO836-2	YR	6.75	18.50
93	RADIANT WINDOW 775QEO836-5	YR	7.75	24.50
94	JOYFUL LAMB 575QEO820-6	YR	5.75	15.00
94	PEANUTS 775QEO817-6	YR	7.75	27.50
94	PEEPING OUT 675QEO820-3	YR	6.75	15.00
92	BELLE BUNNY 975QEO935-4	YR	9.75	24.50
92	ROCKING BUNNY 975QEO932-4	YR	9.75	24.50
92	WARM MEMORIES 775QEO931-1	YR	7.75	19.50
93	LOVELY LAMB 975QEO837-2	YR	9.75	22.50
94	COLLECTOR'S PLATE 775QEO823-3	YR	7.75	25.00
94	DIVINE DUET 675QEO818-3	YR	6.75	16.50
94	EASTER ART SHOW 775QEO819-3	YR	7.75	17.50
*		**FABRIC ORNAMENTS**		
81	CALICO KITTY 300QX403-5	YR	3.00	24.00
81	CARDINAL CUTIE 300QX400-2	YR	3.00	22.50
81	GINGHAM DOG 300QX402-2	YR	3.00	20.00
81	PEPPERMINT MOUSE 300QX401-5	YR	3.00	37.50
D. RHODUS		**FLINTSTONES, THE**		
94	FRED & BARNEY 1495QX500-3	YR	14.95	30.00
L. SICKMAN		**FOLK ART AMERICANA**		
93	ANGEL IN FLIGHT 1575QK105-2	YR	15.75	39.50
93	POLAR BEAR ADV. 1500QK105-5	YR	15.00	55.00
93	RIDING IN THE WOODS 1575QK106-5	YR	15.75	55.00
93	RIDING THE WIND 1575QK104-5	YR	15.75	42.50
93	SANTA CLAUS 1675QK107-2	YR	16.75	225.00
94	CATCHING 40 WINKS 1675QK118-3	YR	16.75	39.50
94	GOING TO TOWN 1575QK116-6	YR	15.75	35.00
94	RACING THROUGH THE SNOW 1575QK117-3	YR	15.75	39.00
94	RARIN' TO GO 1575QK119-3	YR	15.75	35.00
94	ROUNDUP TIME 1675QK117-6	YR	16.75	35.00
*		**FROSTED IMAGES**		
80	DOVE 400QX308-1	YR	4.00	30.00
80	DRUMMER BOY 400QX309-4	YR	4.00	30.00
80	SANTA 400QX310-1	YR	4.00	30.00
81	ANGEL 400QX509-5	YR	4.00	75.00
81	MOUSE 400QX508-2	YR	4.00	25.00
81	SNOWMAN 400QX510-2	YR	4.00	25.00
R. CHAD		**GARDEN ELVES COLLECTION**		
94	DAISY DAYS 995QX598-6	YR	9.95	15.00
94	HARVEST JOY 995QX599-3	YR	9.95	15.00
94	TULIP TIME 995QX598-3	YR	9.95	15.00
94	YULETIDE CHEER 995QX597-6	YR	9.95	15.00
L. VOTRUBA		**GIFT BRINGERS**		
89	ST. NICHOLAS 550QX279-5	YR	5.00	22.50
91	CHRISTKINDL 500QX211-7	YR	5.00	24.50
93	THE MAGI 500QX206-5	YR	5.00	22.50
		GOLD CROWN ORNAMENTS		
91	SANTA'S PREMIERE 1075QX523-7	YR	10.75	49.50
86	ON THE RIGHT TRACK QSP 420-1	YR	15.00	37.50
94	EAGER FOR...TENDER TOUCHES 1500QX533-6	YR	15.00	22.00
92	"O CHRISTMAS TREE" 1075QX541-1	YR	10.75	45.00
L. SICKMAN		**HALLMARK COLLECTORS CLUB ORNAMENTS**		
87	CAROUSEL REINDEER QXC 581-7	YR	8.00	75.00
*		**HALLMARK KEEPSAKE ORNAMENTS**		
89	FESTIVE ANGEL 975QXM578-3	YR	9.75	12.00
93	MARY ENGELBREIT 500QX207-5	YR	5.00	17.50

YR	NAME	LIMIT	ISSUE	QUOTE
93	TOBIN FRALEY CAROUSEL 2800QX550-2	YR	28.00	55.00
94	BARNEY 995QX596-6	YR	9.95	17.50
93	BABY'S FIRST CHRISTMAS 1075QX551-5	YR	10.75	22.50
93	GRANDMOTHER 675QX566-5	YR	6.75	14.50
93	ON HER TOES 875QX526-5	YR	8.75	19.50
93	STAR TEACHER PHOTOHOLDER QX564-5	YR	5.75	14.50
93	SWAT TEAM, THE 1275QX539-5	YR	12.75	29.50
94	ANNIVERSARY YR. PHOTOHOLDER 1095QX568-3	YR	10.95	22.00
93	GODCHILD 875QX587-5	YR	8.75	19.50
93	GRANDDAUGHTER 675QX563-5	YR	6.75	15.00
93	GRANDSON 675QX563-2	YR	6.75	15.00
93	ONE-ELF MARCHING BAND 1275QX534-2	YR	12.75	29.50
93	POPPING GOOD TIMES 1475QX539-2	YR	14.75	29.50
93	SUPERMAN 1275QX575-2	YR	12.75	49.50
93	BABY'S FIRST CHRISTMAS 775QX552-5	YR	7.75	29.50
93	BEARY GIFTED 775QX576-2	YR	7.75	19.50
93	CURLY 'N' KINGLY 1075QX528-5	YR	10.75	23.50
93	QUICK AS A FOX 875QX579-2	YR	8.75	17.50
93	ROOM FOR ONE MORE 875QX538-2	YR	8.75	50.00
94	A FELINE OF CHRISTMAS 895QX581-6	YR	8.95	24.50
94	A SHARP FLAT 1095QX577-3	YR	8.95	22.50
93	ACROSS THE MILES 875QX591-2	YR	8.75	19.50
93	BABY'S SECOND CHRISTMAS 675QX599-2	YR	6.75	19.50
93	BOWLING FOR ZZZS 775QX556-5	YR	7.75	17.50
93	CARING NURSE 675QX578-5	YR	6.75	19.50
93	CHILD'S FOURTH CHRISTMAS 675QX521-5	YR	6.75	14.50
93	CHILD'S THIRD CHRISTMAS 675QX599-5	YR	6.75	14.50
93	GRANDCHILD'S FIRST CHRISTMAS QX 555-2	YR	6.75	15.00
93	SNOWY HIDEWAWAY 975QX531-2	YR	9.75	19.50
93	BIRD WATCHER 975QX525-2	YR	9.75	19.50
93	DAD 775QX585-5	YR	7.75	17.50
93	DAD-TO-BE 675QX553-2	YR	6.75	14.50
93	FELIZ NAVIDAD 875QX536-5	YR	8.75	19.50
93	ICICLE BICYCLE 975QX583-5	YR	9.75	18.50
93	LOOK FOR THE WONDER 1275QX568-5	YR	12.75	32.50
93	MOM 775QX585-2	YR	7.75	19.50
93	MOM-TO-BE 675QX553-5	YR	6.75	14.50
93	OUR CHRISTMAS TOGETHER 1075QX594-2	YR	10.75	22.50
93	PEEP INSIDE 1375QX532-2	YR	13.75	27.50
93	PUTT-PUTT PENGUIN 975QX579-5	YR	9.75	22.50
93	SNOW BEAR ANGEL 775QX535-5	YR	7.75	17.50
93	SNOWBIRD 775QX576-5	YR	7.75	16.50
93	TO MY GRANDMA 775QX555-5	YR	7.75	17.50
93	WATER BED SNOOZE 975QX537-5	YR	9.75	22.50
93	ANNIVERSARY YEAR PHOTOHOLDER QX597-2	YR	9.75	19.50
93	HE IS BORN 975QX536-2	YR	9.75	40.00
93	OUR FIRST CHRISTMAS TOGETHER 675QX301-5	YR	6.75	16.50
93	READY FOR FUN 775QX512-4	YR	7.75	19.50
93	SILVERY NOEL 1275QX530-5	YR	12.75	29.50
93	STAR OF WONDER 675QX598-2	YR	6.75	35.00
93	BABY'S FIRST CHRISTMAS 1875QX551-2	YR	18.75	40.00
93	COACH 675QX593-5	YR	6.75	15.50
93	LITTLE DRUMMER BOY 875QX537-2	YR	8.75	20.00
93	MAKING WAVES 975QX577-5	YR	9.75	24.50
93	MOM AND DAD 975QX584-5	YR	9.75	19.50
93	NEW HOME 775QX590-5	YR	7.75	49.50
93	PINK PANTHER, THE 1275QX575-5	YR	12.75	27.00
93	FABULOUS DECADE 775QX447-5	YR	7.75	19.50
93	CHILD'S FIFTH CHRISTMAS 675QX522-2	YR	6.75	17.50
93	LOU RANKIN POLAR BEAR 975QX574-5	YR	9.75	27.50
94	ALL PUMPED UP 895QX592-3	YR	8.95	19.50
93	BABY'S FIRST PHOTOHOLDER QX 552-2	YR	7.75	22.50
93	BROTHER 675QX554-2	YR	6.75	14.50
93	GREAT CONNECTIONS 1075QX540-2	YR	10.75	25.00
93	HOWLING GOOD TIME 975QX525-5	YR	9.75	15.50
93	NEPHEW 675QX573-5	YR	6.75	14.50
93	NIECE 675QX573-2	YR	6.75	14.50
93	SISTER 675QX554-5	YR	6.75	22.50
93	TOP BANANA 775QX592-5	YR	7.75	19.50
93	OUR FIRST CHRISTMAS TOGETHER 1875QX595-5	YR	18.75	37.50
93	APPLE FOR TEACHER 775QX590-2	YR	7.75	16.50
93	CHRISTMAS BREAK 775QX582-5	YR	7.75	21.50
93	HIGH TOP-PURR 875QX533-2	YR	8.75	24.50
93	MAKIN' MUSIC 975QX532-5	YR	9.75	19.50
93	PEOPLE FRIENDLY 875QX593-2	YR	8.75	19.50
93	SISTER TO SISTER 975QX588-5	YR	9.75	49.50

YR	NAME	LIMIT	ISSUE	QUOTE
93	SMILE! IT'S CHRISTMAS PHOTOHOLDERQX533-5	YR	9.75	20.00
94	BABY'S FIRST CHRISTMAS 1295QX574-3	YR	12.95	27.50
87	VILLAGE EXPRESS 2450QLX707-2	YR	24.50	120.00
93	CLEVER COOKIE 775QX566-2	YR	7.75	22.50
93	MAXINE 875QX538-5	YR	8.75	23.50
93	STRANGE AND WONDERFUL LOVE QX596-5	YR	8.75	17.50
93	U.S. CHRISTMAS STAMPS 1075QX529-2	YR	10.75	29.50
93	WARM AND SPECIAL FRIENDS QX589-5	YR	10.75	24.50
94	ANGEL HARE 895QX589-6	YR	8.95	20.00
93	BIG ROLLER 875QX535-2	YR	8.75	19.50
93	DUNKIN' ROO 775QX557-5	YR	7.75	17.50
93	FILLS THE BILL 875QX557-2	YR	8.75	17.50
93	HOME FOR CHRISTMAS 775QX556-2	YR	7.75	17.50
93	OWLIVER 775QX542-5	YR	7.75	17.50
93	PERFECT MATCH 875QX577-2	YR	8.75	19.50
93	THAT'S ENTERTAINMENT 875QX534-5	YR	8.75	20.00
93	JULIANNE AND TEDDY 2175QX529-5	YR	21.75	49.50
93	OUR 1ST CHRISTMAS TOGETHER PHOTO.QX595-2	YR	8.75	17.50
93	OUR FAMILY PHOTOHOLDER 775QX589-2	YR	7.75	19.50
93	WAKE-UP CALL 875QX526-2	YR	8.75	17.50
94	BABY'S FIRST CHRISTMAS 1895QX563-3	YR	18.95	39.50
93	BABY'S FIRST CHRISTMAS-BOY QX 210-5	YR	4.75	14.50
93	BIG ON GARDENING 975QX584-2	YR	9.75	19.50
93	DAUGHTER 675QX587-2	YR	6.75	19.50
93	FAITHFUL FIRE FIGHTER 775QX578-2	YR	8.00	19.50
93	GRANDPARENTS 475QX208-5	YR	4.75	14.50
93	SON 675QX586-5	YR	6.75	15.00
93	SPECIAL CAT PHOTOHOLDER QX523-5	YR	7.75	15.50
93	SPECIAL DOG PHOTOHOLDER QX596-2	YR	7.75	15.50

HALLMARK KEEPSAKE ORNAMENTS COLLECTOR'S CLUB

YR	NAME	LIMIT	ISSUE	QUOTE
91	FIVE YEARS TOGETHER QXC315-9	YR	*	75.00
94	SWEET BOUQUET QXC480-6	YR	*	15.00
90	SUGAR PLUM FAIRY 2775QXC447-3	25,400	27.75	60.00
93	GENTLE TIDINGS 2500QXC544-2	YR	25.00	50.00
92	CHRISTMAS TREASURES 2200QXC546-4	YR	22.00	150.00
89	VISIT FROM SANTA QXC580-2	YR	*	55.00
90	CLUB HOLLOW QXC445-6	YR	*	45.00
91	HIDDEN TREASURE/LI'L KEEPER 1500QXC476-9	YR	*	40.00
89	SITTING PURRTY QXC581-2	YR	*	45.00
90	ARMFUL OF JOY 975QXC445-3	YR	9.75	50.00
93	FORTY WINKS QXC 529-4	YR	*	18.50
94	HOLIDAY PURSUIT QXC 482-3	YR	*	20.00
88	ANGELIC MINSTREL 2950QX408-4	YR	29.50	49.50
92	RODNEY TAKES FLIGHT QXC508-1	YR	*	22.50
94	ON CLOUD NINE 1200QXC485-3	YR	12.00	40.00
93	SHARING CHRISTMAS 2000QXC543-5	YR	20.00	45.00
94	JOLLY HOLLY SANTA QXC 483-3	*	22.00	50.00
89	COLLECT A DREAM 900QXC428-5	YR	9.00	65.00
90	CROWN PRINCE QXC560-3	YR	*	40.00
91	SECRETS FOR SANTA 2375QXC479-7	28,700	23.75	75.00
88	CHRISTMAS IS SHARING 1750QX407-1	YR	17.50	49.50
89	CHRISTMAS IS PEACEFUL 1850QXC451-2	YR	18.50	55.00
92	CHIPMUNK PARCEL SERVICE QXC519-4	YR	*	22.50
92	SANTA'S CLUB LIST 1500QXC729-1	YR	15.00	39.50
93	IT'S IN THE MAIL QXC527-2	YR	*	22.50
88	SLEIGHFUL OF DREAMS 800QXC580-1	YR	8.00	75.00
90	CHRISTMAS LIMITED 1975QXC476-6	38,700	19.75	115.00
91	GALLOPING INTO CHRISTMAS 1975QXC477-9	28,400	19.75	125.00
93	TRIMMED W/MEMORIES 1200QXC543-2	YR	12.00	40.00
88	HOLD ON TIGHT QXC570-4	YR	*	75.00
88	OUR CLUBHOUSE QXC580-4	YR	*	55.00
91	BEARY ARTISTIC 1000QXC725-9	YR	10.00	40.00
88	HOLIDAY HEIRLOOM-2ND EDITION 2500QX406-4	34600	25.00	42.50
89	HOLIDAY HEIRLOOM-3RD ED. 2500QXC460-5	YR	25.00	40.00
89	NOELLE 1975QXC448-3	YR	19.75	60.00
92	VICTORIAN SKATER 2500QXC406-7	YR	25.00	75.00
94	MAJESTIC DEER 2500QXC483-6	*	25.00	50.00

D. UNRUH HALLMARK KEEPSAKE ORNAMENTS COLLECTORS' CLUB

YR	NAME	LIMIT	ISSUE	QUOTE
87	WREATH OF MEMORIES QXC580-9	YR	*	60.00

* HANDCRAFTED ORNAMENTS

YR	NAME	LIMIT	ISSUE	QUOTE
78	ANGELS 800QX150-3	YR	8.00	395.00
78	CALICO MOUSE 450QX137-6	YR	4.50	195.00
78	CAROUSEL SERIES-1ST EDITION 600QX146-3	YR	6.00	400.00
78	JOY 450QX138-3	YR	4.50	95.00
78	PANORAMA BALL 600QX145-6	YR	6.00	135.00
78	RED CARDINAL 450QX144-3	YR	4.50	185.00

YR	NAME	LIMIT	ISSUE	QUOTE
78	ROCKING HORSE 600QX148-3	YR	6.00	115.00
78	SCHNEEBERG BELL 800QX152-3	YR	8.00	200.00
78	SKATING RACCOON 600QX142-3	YR	6.00	110.00
79	A CHRISTMAS TREAT 500QX134-7	YR	5.00	95.00
79	CHRISTMAS EVE SURPRISE 650QX157-9	YR	6.50	65.00
79	CHRISTMAS HEART 650QX140-7	YR	6.50	125.00
79	CHRISTMAS IS FOR CHILDREN 500QX135-9	YR	5.00	95.00
79	HOLIDAY SCRIMSHAW 400QX152-7	YR	4.00	250.00
79	SANTA'S HERE 500QX138-7	YR	5.00	85.00
79	THE DRUMMER BOY 800QX143-9	YR	8.00	90.00
79	THE SKATING SNOWMAN 500QX139-9	YR	5.00	55.00
80	A CHRISTMAS TREAT 550QX134-7	YR	5.50	95.00
80	CHRISTMAS IS FOR CHILDREN 550QX135-9	YR	5.50	95.00
80	ELFIN ANTICS 900QX142-1	YR	9.00	225.00
80	HEAVENLY SOUNDS 750QX152-1	YR	7.50	110.00
80	SANTA 1980 550QX146-1	YR	5.50	125.00
80	SKATING SNOWMAN 550QX139-9	YR	5.50	90.00
80	THE SNOWFLAKE SWING 400QX133-4	YR	4.00	55.00
81	A HEAVENLY NAP 650QX139-4	YR	6.50	65.00
81	A WELL-STOCKED STOCKING 900QX154-7	YR	9.00	90.00
81	CANDYVILLE EXPRESS 750QX418-2	YR	7.50	125.00
81	CHRISTMAS FANTASY 1300QX155-4	YR	13.00	85.00
81	DOUGH ANGEL 550QX139-6	YR	5.50	90.00
81	DRUMMER BOY 250QX148-1	YR	2.50	45.00
81	LOVE AND JOY 900QX425-2	YR	9.00	95.00
81	MR. & MRS. CLAUS 1200QX448-5	YR	12.00	130.00
81	SAILING SANTA 1300QX439-5	YR	13.00	275.00
81	SPACE SANTA 650QX430-2	YR	6.50	95.00
82	CHRISTMAS FANTASY 1300QX155-4	YR	13.00	85.00
82	CLOISONNE ANGEL 1200QX145-4	YR	12.00	95.00
82	COWBOY SNOWMAN 800QX480-6	YR	8.00	60.00
82	CYCLING SANTA 2000QX435-5	YR	20.00	150.00
82	EMBROIDERED TREE 650QX494-6	YR	6.50	39.50
82	JOGGING SANTA 800QX457-6	YR	8.00	50.00
82	JOLLY CHRISTMAS TREE 650QX465-3	YR	6.50	95.00
82	PEEKING ELF 650QX419-5	YR	6.50	39.50
82	SANTA BELL 1500QX148-7	YR	15.00	65.00
82	TIN SOLDIER 650QX483-6	YR	6.50	45.00
83	CHRISTMAS KITTEN 400QX454-3	YR	4.00	37.50
83	CYCLING SANTA 2000QX435-6	YR	20.00	150.00
83	EMBROIDERED HEART 650QX421-7	YR	6.50	24.50
83	HOLIDAY PUPPY 350QX412-7	YR	3.50	29.50
83	JACK FROST 900QX407-9	YR	9.00	65.00
83	JOLLY SANTA 350QX425-9	YR	3.50	39.50
83	MADONNA AND CHILD 1200QX428-7	YR	12.00	45.00
83	MAILBOX KITTEN 650QX415-7	YR	6.50	65.00
83	MOUSE IN BELL 1000QX419-7	YR	10.00	75.00
83	PEPPERMINT PENGUIN 650QX408-9	YR	6.50	49.50
83	PORCELAIN DOLL-DIANA 900QX423-7	YR	9.00	32.50
83	SANTA'S MANY FACES 600QX311-7	YR	6.00	35.00
83	SANTA'S ON HIS WAY 1000QX426-9	YR	10.00	35.00
83	SKATING RABBIT 800QX409-7	YR	8.00	55.00
83	SKI LIFT SANTA 800QX418-7	YR	8.00	75.00
83	UNICORN 1000QX426-7	YR	10.00	69.50
88	CHRISTMAS SCENES 475QX273-1	YR	4.75	24.50
88	JINGLE BELL CLOWN 1500QX477-4	YR	15.00	37.50
88	KRINGLE PORTRAIT 750QX496-1	YR	7.50	35.00
88	KRINGLE TREE 650QX495-4	YR	6.50	39.50
88	PEANUTS 475QX280-1	YR	4.75	29.50
81	CHECKING IT TWICE 2250QX158-4	YR	22.50	195.00
82	THREE KINGS 850QX307-3	YR	8.50	24.50
88	SOFT LANDING 700QX475-1	YR	7.00	24.50
88	WINTER FUN 850QX478-1	YR	8.50	27.50
88	CHRISTMAS CUCKOO 800QX480-1	YR	8.00	32.50
88	COOL JUGGLER 650QX487-4	YR	6.50	25.00
88	PEEK-A-BOO KITTENS 750QX487-1	YR	7.50	24.50
88	SLIPPER SPANIEL 450QX472-4	YR	4.50	22.50
78	ANGEL 400QX139-6	YR	4.50	77.50
78	ANIMAL HOME 600QX149-6	YR	6.00	195.00
79	READY FOR CHRISTMAS 650QX133-9	YR	6.50	150.00
79	SKATING RACCOON 650QX142-3	YR	6.50	110.00
79	THE DOWNHILL RUN 650QX145-9	YR	6.50	135.00
80	A CHRISTMAS VIGIL 900QX144-1	YR	9.00	92.50
80	A HEAVENLY NAP 650QX139-4	YR	6.50	65.00
80	A SPOT OF CHRISTMAS CHEER 800QX153-4	YR	8.00	195.00
80	CAROLING BEAR 750QX140-1	YR	7.50	175.00

YR	NAME	LIMIT	ISSUE	QUOTE
80	DRUMMER BOY 550QX147-4	YR	5.50	95.00
80	THE ANIMAL'S CHRISTMAS 800QX150-1	YR	8.00	95.00
81	CHRISTMAS DREAMS 1200QX437-5	YR	12.00	225.00
81	ICE FAIRY 650QX431-5	YR	6.50	95.00
81	THE FRIENDLY FIDDLER 800QX434-2	YR	8.00	85.00
81	THE ICE SCULPTOR 800QX432-2	YR	8.00	99.00
81	TOPSY-TURVY TUNES 750QX429-5	YR	7.50	85.00
82	BAROQUE ANGEL 1500QX456-6	YR	15.00	175.00
82	PINECONE HOME 800QX461-3	YR	8.00	195.00
82	RACCOON SURPRISES 900QX479-3	YR	9.00	195.00
82	SANTA'S WORKSHOP 1000QX450-3	YR	10.00	85.00
82	THE ICE SCULPTOR 800QX432-2	YR	8.00	99.00
83	BAROQUE ANGELS 1300QX422-9	YR	13.00	130.00
83	RAINBOW ANGEL 550QX416-7	YR	5.50	125.00
83	SANTA'S WORKSHOP 1000QX450-3	YR	10.00	85.00
83	SKIING FOX 800QX420-7	YR	8.00	39.50
88	TRAVELS WITH SANTA 1000QX477-1	YR	10.00	39.50
88	UNCLE SAM NUTCRACKER 700QX488-4	YR	7.00	37.50
88	CHRISTMAS MEMORIES PHOTOHOLDER QX 372-4	YR	6.50	26.50
88	GLOWING WREATH 600QX492-1	YR	6.00	16.50
88	SHINY SLEIGH 575QX492-4	YR	5.75	19.50
88	SPARKLING TREE 600QX483-1	YR	6.00	22.00
88	PARTY LINE 875QX476-1	YR	8.75	29.50
88	SQUEAKY CLEAN 675QX475-4	YR	6.75	24.50
88	SANTA FLAMINGO 475QX483-4	YR	4.75	34.50
88	CHRISTMAS CARDINAL 475QX494-1	YR	4.75	19.50
88	JOLLY WALRUS 450QX473-1	YR	4.50	24.50
88	KRINGLE MOON 550QX495-1	YR	5.00	34.50
88	LOVING BEAR 475QX493-4	YR	4.75	22.50
88	PURRFECT SNUGGLE 625QX474-4	YR	6.25	29.50
88	STARRY ANGEL 475QX494-4	YR	4.75	19.50
83	ANGEL MESSENGER 650QX408-7	YR	6.50	95.00
83	BRASS SANTA 900QX423-9	YR	9.00	22.50
83	CAROLING OWL 450QX411-7	YR	4.50	39.50
83	CHRISTMAS KOALA 400QX419-9	YR	4.00	32.50
83	HITCHHIKING SANTA 800QX424-7	YR	8.00	39.50
83	MOUNTAIN CLIMBING SANTA 650QX407-7	YR	6.50	39.50
83	SCRIMSHAW REINDEER 800QX424-9	YR	8.00	35.00
83	SNEAKER MOUSE 450QX400-9	YR	4.50	39.50
88	FILLED WITH FUDGE 475QX419-1	YR	4.75	32.50
88	SWEET STAR 500QX418-4	YR	5.00	34.50
88	TEENY TASTER 475QX418-1	YR	4.75	29.50
88	THE TOWN CRIER 550QX473-4	YR	5.50	24.50
78	DOVE 450QX190-3	YR	4.50	95.00
78	HOLLY & POINSETTIA BALL 600QX147-6	YR	6.00	125.00
79	OUTDOOR FUN 800QX150-7	YR	8.00	150.00
80	SANTA'S FLIGHT 550QX138-1	YR	5.50	125.00
81	ST. NICHOLAS 550QX446-2	YR	5.50	60.00
81	STAR SWING 550QX421-5	YR	5.50	70.00
82	ELFIN ARTIST 900QX457-3	YR	9.00	49.50
82	THE SPIRIT OF CHRISTMAS 1000QX452-6	YR	10.00	125.00
83	BELL WREATH 650QX420-9	YR	6.50	35.00
83	EMBROIDERED STOCKING 650QX479-6	YR	6.50	22.50
83	MOUSE ON CHEESE 650QX413-7	YR	6.50	45.00
83	OLD-FASHIONED SANTA 1100QX409-9	YR	11.00	75.00
83	TIN ROCKING HORSE 650QX414-9	YR	6.50	47.50
88	AMERICANA DRUM 775QX488-1	YR	7.75	32.50
88	GOIN' CROSS COUNTRY 850QX476-4	YR	8.50	24.50
88	NOAH'S ARK 850QX490-4	YR	8.50	29.50
88	OLD-FASHIONED CHURCH 400QX498-1	YR	4.00	24.50
88	OLD-FASHIONED SCHOOL HOUSE 400QX497-1	YR	4.00	24.50
88	SAILING! SAILING! 850QX491-1	YR	8.50	24.50
88	ARCTIC TENOR 400QX472-1	YR	4.00	22.50
88	GO FOR THE GOLD 800QX417-4	YR	8.00	29.50
88	GONE FISHING 500QX479-4	YR	5.00	19.00
88	HOE-HOE-HOE 500QX422-1	YR	5.00	19.50
88	HOLIDAY HERO 500QX423-1	YR	5.00	19.50
88	LOVE SANTA 500QX486-4	YR	5.00	19.50
88	NICK THE KICK 500QX422-4	YR	5.00	24.50
88	PAR FOR SANTA 500QX479-1	YR	5.00	19.50
88	POLAR BOWLER 500QX478-1	YR	5.00	19.50
88	A KISS FROM SANTA 450QX482-1	YR	4.50	26.50
88	FELIZ NAVIDAD 675QX416-1	YR	6.75	34.50
88	KISS THE CLAUS 500QX486-1	YR	5.00	15.00
88	OREO 400QX481-4	YR	4.00	22.50
88	SNOOPY & WOODSTOCK 600QX474-1	YR	6.00	34.50

YR	NAME	LIMIT	ISSUE	QUOTE
D. LEE	**HANDCRAFTED ORNAMENTS: ADORABLE ADORNMENTS**			
75	BETSEY CLARK 250QX157-1	YR	2.50	350.00
75	DRUMMER BOY 250QX161-1	YR	2.50	300.00
75	MRS. SANTA 250QX156-1	YR	2.50	65.00
75	RAGGEDY ANDY 250QX160-1	YR	2.50	495.00
75	RAGGEDY ANN 250QX159-1	YR	2.50	375.00
75	SANTA 250QX155-1	YR	2.50	65.00
*	**HANDCRAFTED ORNAMENTS: NOSTALGIA**			
77	NATIVITY 500QX181-5	YR	5.00	195.00
77	ANGEL 500QX182-2	YR	5.00	125.00
75	DRUMMER BOY 350QX130-1	YR	3.50	175.00
75	JOY 350QX132-1	YR	3.50	275.00
75	LOCOMOTIVE (DATED) 350QX127-1	YR	3.50	175.00
75	PEACE ON EARTH (DATED) 350QX131-1	YR	3.50	175.00
75	ROCKING HORSE 350QX128-1	YR	3.50	175.00
75	SANTA & SLEIGH 350QX129-1	YR	3.50	295.00
76	DRUMMER BOY 400QX130-1	YR	4.00	175.00
76	LOCOMOTIVE 400QX222-1	YR	4.00	195.00
76	PEACE ON EARTH 400QX223-1	YR	4.00	185.00
76	ROCKING HORSE 400QX128-1	YR	4.00	175.00
77	ANTIQUE CAR 500QX180-2	YR	5.00	75.00
77	TOYS 500QX183-5	YR	5.00	175.00
*	**HANDCRAFTED ORNAMENTS: TREE TREATS**			
76	ANGEL 300QX176-1	YR	3.00	200.00
76	REINDEER 300QX178-1	YR	3.00	150.00
76	SANTA 300QX177-1	YR	3.00	225.00
76	SHEPHERD 300QX175-1	YR	3.00	150.00
*	**HANDCRAFTED ORNAMENTS: TWIRL-ABOUTS**			
77	BELLRINGER 600QX192-2	YR	6.00	55.00
77	WEATHER HOUSE 600QX191-5	YR	6.00	125.00
77	DELLA ROBIA WREATH 450QX193-5	YR	4.50	160.00
76	ANGEL 450QX171-1	YR	4.50	175.00
76	PARTRIDGE 450QX174-1	YR	4.50	195.00
76	SANTA 450QX172-1	YR	4.50	135.00
76	SOLDIER 450QX173-1	YR	4.50	125.00
77	SNOWMAN 450QX190-2	YR	4.50	100.00
*	**HANDCRAFTED ORNAMENTS: YESTERYEARS**			
76	DRUMMER BOY 500QX184-1	YR	5.00	160.00
76	PARTRIDGE 500QX183-1	YR	5.00	125.00
76	SANTA 500QX182-1	YR	5.00	175.00
76	TRAIN 500QX181-1	YR	5.00	175.00
E. SEALE	**HEART OF CHRISTMAS**			
93	HEART OF CHRISTMAS 1475QX448-2	YR	14.75	29.50
J. LYLE	**HEAVENLY ANGELS**			
93	HEAVENLY ANGELS 775QX494-5	YR	7.75	19.50
*	**HEIRLOOM CHRISTMAS COLLECTION**			
85	LACY HEART 875QX511-2	YR	8.75	29.50
85	VICTORIAN LADY 950QX513-2	YR	9.50	24.50
85	SNOWFLAKE 650QX510-5	YR	6.50	24.50
85	KEEPSAKE BASKET 1500QX514-5	YR	15.00	18.50
85	CHARMING ANGEL 975QX512-5	YR	9.75	24.50
*	**HERE COMES SANTA**			
79	MOTORCAR 900QX155-9	YR	9.00	500.00
80	SANTA'S EXPRESS 1200QX143-4	YR	12.00	195.00
81	ROOFTOP DELIVERIES 1300QX438-2	YR	13.00	250.00
87	SANTA'S WOODY 1400QX484-7	YR	14.00	59.50
88	KRINGLE KOACH 1400QX400-1	YR	14.00	47.50
89	CHRISTMAS CABOOSE 1475QX458-5	YR	14.75	44.50
82	JOLLY TROLLEY QX 464-3	YR	15.00	85.00
83	SANTA'S EXPRESS 1300QX403-7	YR	13.00	295.00
84	DELIVERIES 1300QX432-4	YR	13.00	89.50
85	SANTA'S FIRE ENGINE 1400QX496-5	YR	14.00	59.50
90	FESTIVE SURREY 1475QX492-3	YR	14.75	42.50
91	SANTA'S ANTIQUE CAR-13TH ED. 1475QX434-9	YR	14.75	49.50
92	KRINGLE TOURS 1475QX434-1	YR	14.75	37.50
93	HAPPY HAULI-DAYS 1475QX410-2	YR	14.75	32.50
94	MAKIN' TRACTOR TRACKS 1495QX529-6	YR	14.95	50.00
86	KRINGLES KOOL TREATS 1400QX404-3	YR	14.00	69.50
*	**HOLIDAY BARBIE COLLECTION**			
94	BARBIE 1495QX500-6	YR	14.95	35.00
94	HOLIDAY BARBIE 1495QX521-6	YR	14.95	35.00
93	HOLIDAY BARBIE 1475QX572-2	YR	14.75	125.00
*	**HOLIDAY CHIMES**			
80	SANTA MOBILE 550QX136-1	YR	5.50	60.00
81	SANTA MOBILE 550QX136-1	YR	5.50	60.00
81	SNOWMAN CHIMES 550QX445-5	YR	5.50	39.50

YR	NAME	LIMIT	ISSUE	QUOTE
82	ANGEL CHIMES 550QX502-6	YR	5.50	200.00
82	TREE CHIMES 550QX484-6	YR	5.50	55.00
78	REINDEER CHIMES 450QX320-3	YR	4.50	60.00
79	REINDEER CHIMES 450QX320-3	YR	4.50	60.00
79	STAR CHIMES 450QX137-9	YR	4.50	95.00
80	REINDEER CHIMES 550QX320-3	YR	5.50	60.00
80	SNOWFLAKE CHIMES 550QX165-4	YR	5.50	35.00
81	SNOWFLAKE CHIMES 550QX165-4	YR	5.50	35.00
82	BELL CHIMES 550QX494-3	YR	5.50	40.00
	HOLIDAY ENCHANTMENT			
93	JOURNEY TO THE FOREST 1375QK101-2	YR	13.75	32.50
93	MAGI, THE 1375QK102-5	YR	13.75	37.50
93	BRINGING HOME THE TREE 1375QK104-2	YR	13.75	35.00
93	ANGELIC MESSENGER 1375QK103-2	YR	13.75	39.50
93	VISION OF SUGARPLUMS 1375QK100-5	YR	13.75	35.00
	HOLIDAY EXPRESS			
94	REVOLVING TREE BASE QXM 545-2	YR	50.00	50.00
	L. VOTRUBA		**HOLIDAY FAVORITES**	
94	DAPPER SNOWMAN 1375QK105-3	YR	13.75	22.50
94	GRACEFUL FAWN 1175QK103-3	YR	11.75	24.50
94	JOLLY SANTA 1375QK104-6	YR	13.75	22.50
94	JOYFUL LAMB 1175QK103-6	YR	11.75	20.00
94	PEACEFUL DOVE 1175QK104-3	YR	11.75	20.00
	L. SICKMAN		**HOLIDAY FLIERS**	
93	TIN AIRPLANE 775QX562-2	YR	7.75	29.50
93	TIN BLIMP 775QX562-5	YR	7.75	18.50
93	TIN HOT AIR BALLOON 775QX561-5	YR	7.75	18.50
*			**HOLIDAY HIGHLIGHTS**	
77	DRUMMER BOY 350QX312-2	YR	3.50	75.00
77	JOY 350QX310-2	YR	3.50	45.00
77	PEACE ON EARTH 350QX311-5	YR	3.50	85.00
77	STAR 350QX313-5	YR	3.50	50.00
78	DOVE 350QX310-3	YR	3.50	125.00
78	SANTA 350QX307-6	YR	3.50	95.00
78	SNOWFLAKE 350QX308-3	YR	3.50	75.00
79	CHRISTMAS ANGEL 350QX300-7	YR	3.50	95.00
79	CHRISTMAS CHEER 350QX303-9	YR	3.50	95.00
79	CHRISTMAS TREE 350QX302-7	YR	3.50	80.00
79	LOVE 350QX304-7	YR	3.50	125.00
79	SNOWFLAKE 350QX301-9	YR	3.50	49.50
80	THREE WISE MEN 400QX300-1	YR	4.00	29.50
80	WREATH 400QX301-4	YR	4.00	95.00
81	CHRISTMAS STAR 550QX501-5	YR	5.50	25.00
81	SHEPHERD SCENE 550QX500-2	YR	5.50	29.50
82	ANGEL 550QX309-6	YR	5.50	29.50
82	CHRISTMAS MAGIC 550QX311-3	YR	5.50	29.50
82	CHRISTMAS SLEIGH 550QX309-3	YR	5.50	80.00
83	CHRISTMAS STOCKING 600QX303-9	YR	6.00	39.50
83	TIME FOR SHARING 600QX307-7	YR	6.00	39.50
78	NATIVITY 350QX309-6	YR	3.50	95.00
83	STAR OF PEACE 600QX304-7	YR	6.00	19.50
*			**HOLIDAY HUMOR**	
84	A CHRISTMAS PRAYER 450QX246-1	YR	4.50	22.50
84	FLIGHTS OF FANTASY 450QX256-4	YR	4.50	19.50
84	FRISBEE PUPPY 500QX444-4	YR	5.00	49.50
84	NAPPING MOUSE 550QX435-1	YR	5.50	49.50
84	REINDEER RACETRACK 450QX254-4	YR	4.50	22.50
84	SANTA STAR 550QX450-4	YR	5.50	39.50
84	SNOWMOBILE SANTA 650QX431-4	YR	6.50	39.50
85	DOGGY IN A STOCKING 550QX474-2	YR	5.50	42.50
85	LAMB IN LEGWARMERS 700QX480-2	YR	7.00	27.50
85	MOUSE WAGON 575QX476-2	YR	5.75	59.50
85	NATIVITY SCENE 475QX264-5	YR	4.75	29.50
86	OPEN ME FIRST 725QX422-6	YR	7.25	34.50
87	CHRISTMAS CUDDLE 575QX453-7	YR	5.75	34.50
87	DR SEUSS: GRINCH'S CHRISTMAS 475QX278-3	YR	4.75	49.50
87	JAMMIE PIES 475QX283-9	YR	4.75	17.50
87	JOY RIDE 1150QX440-7	YR	11.50	55.00
87	LET IT SNOW 650QX458-9	YR	6.50	27.50
87	PEANUTS 475QX281-9	YR	4.75	32.50
87	SANTA AT THE BAT 775QX457-9	YR	7.75	29.50
87	SPOTS 'N STRIPES 550QX452-9	YR	5.50	24.50
86	CHATTY PENGUIN 575QX417-6	YR	5.75	24.50
86	PLAYFUL POSSUM 1100QX425-3	YR	11.00	34.50
86	RAH RAH RABBIT 700QX421-6	YR	7.00	39.50
87	HAPPY SANTA 475QX456-9	YR	4.75	29.50

YR	NAME	LIMIT	ISSUE	QUOTE
87	NIGHT BEFORE CHRISTMAS 650QX451-7	YR	6.50	34.50
87	PRETTY KITTEN 1100QX448-9	YR	11.00	34.50
87	SLEEPY SANTA 625QX450-7	YR	6.25	39.50
85	KITTY MISCHIEF 500QX474-5	YR	5.00	29.50
85	MERRY MOUSE 450QX403-2	YR	4.50	29.50
85	SKATEBOARD RACCOON 650QX473-2	YR	6.50	39.50
85	SOCCER BEAVER 650QX477-5	YR	6.50	27.50
86	KITTY MISCHIEF 500QX474-5	YR	5.00	29.50
86	MERRY MOUSE 450QX403-2	YR	4.50	29.50
86	SKATEBOARD RACCOON 650QX473-2	YR	6.50	39.50
86	SNOW BUDDIES 800QX423-6	YR	8.00	39.50
86	SOCCER BEAVER 650QX477-5	YR	6.50	27.50
86	TIPPING THE SCALES 675QX418-6	YR	6.75	29.50
86	TOUCHDOWN SANTA 800QX423-3	YR	8.00	44.50
87	FUDGE FOREVER 500QX449-7	YR	5.00	39.50
87	JOGGING THROUGH THE SNOW 725QX457-7	YR	7.25	37.50
84	MUSICAL ANGEL 550QX434-4	YR	5.50	69.50
84	PEPPERMINT 1984 450QX456-1	YR	4.50	49.50
84	THREE KITTENS IN A MITTEN 800QX431-1	YR	8.00	49.50
85	SNOW-PITCHING SNOWMAN 450QX470-2	YR	4.50	27.50
85	STARDUST ANGEL 575QX475-2	YR	5.75	36.50
85	THREE KITTENS IN A MITTEN 800QX431-1	YR	8.00	49.50
86	HEAVENLY DREAMER 575QX 417-3	YR	5.75	34.50
86	SNOW-PITCHING SNOWMAN 450QX470-2	YR	4.50	27.50
86	TREETOP TRIO 975QX424-6	YR	11.00	32.50
86	WYNKEN, BLYNKEN AND NOD 975QX424-6	YR	9.75	42.50
87	TREETOP TRIO 1100QX425-6	YR	11.00	32.50
86	COOKIES FOR SANTA 450QX414-6	YR	4.50	29.50
87	OWLIDAY WISH 650QX455-9	YR	6.50	24.50
87	PADDINGTON BEAR 550QX472-7	YR	5.50	34.50
84	BELL RINGER SQUIRREL 1000QX443-1	YR	10.00	39.50
84	CHRISTMAS OWL 600QX444-1	YR	6.00	34.50
84	MARATHON SANTA 800QX456-4	YR	8.00	42.50
84	MOUNTAIN CLIMBING SANTA 650QX407-7	YR	6.50	39.50
84	POLAR BEAR DRUMMER 450QX430-1	YR	4.50	32.50
84	RACCOON'S CHRISTMAS 900QX-447-4	YR	9.00	55.00
84	ROLLER SKATING RABBIT 500QX457-1	YR	5.00	34.50
84	SNOWY SEAL 400QX450-1	YR	4.00	22.00
85	BAKER ELF 575QX491-2	YR	5.75	29.50
85	CHILDREN IN THE SHOE 950QX490-5	YR	9.50	49.50
85	DAPPER PENGUIN 500QX477-2	YR	5.00	32.50
85	DO NOT DISTURB BEAR 775QX481-2	YR	7.75	32.50
85	NIGHT BEFORE CHRISTMAS 1300QX449-4	YR	13.00	49.50
85	ROLLER SKATING RABBIT 500QX457-1	YR	5.00	34.50
85	SANTA'S SKI TRIP 1200QX496-2	YR	12.00	60.00
85	SNOWY SEAL 400QX450-1	YR	4.00	22.00
85	TRUMPET PANDA 450QX471-2	YR	4.50	26.50
86	DO NOT DISTURB BEAR 775QX481-2	YR	7.75	32.50
86	LI'L JINGLER 675QX419-3	YR	6.75	39.50
86	MOUSE IN THE MOON 550QX416-6	YR	5.50	29.50
86	SANTA'S HOT TUB 1200QX426-3	YR	12.00	60.00
86	WALNUT SHELL RIDER 600QX419-6	YR	6.00	29.50
87	CHOCOLATE CHIPMUNK 600QX456-7	YR	6.00	54.50
87	JACK FROSTING 700QX449-9	YR	7.00	59.50
87	LI'L JINGLER 675QX419-3	YR	6.75	39.50
87	MOUSE IN THE MOON 550QX416-6	YR	5.50	29.50
87	SEASONED GREETINGS 625QX454-9	YR	6.25	29.50
87	TREETOP DREAMS 675QX459-7	YR	6.75	29.50
87	WALNUT SHELL RIDER 600QX419-6	YR	6.00	29.50
84	FORTUNE COOKIE ELF 450QX452-4	YR	4.50	39.50
84	SNOWSHOE PENGUIN 650QX453-1	YR	6.50	49.50
85	BEARY SMOOTH RIDE 650QX480-5	YR	6.50	24.50
85	CANDY APPLE MOUSE 750QX470-5	YR	6.50	49.50
86	BEARY SMOOTH RIDE 650QX480-5	YR	6.50	24.50
86	MERRY KOALA 500QX415-3	YR	5.00	24.50
86	POPCORN MOUSE 675QX421-3	YR	6.75	47.50
87	MERRY KOALA 500QX415-3	YR	5.00	24.50
84	SANTA MOUSE 450QX433-4	YR	4.50	45.00
85	BOTTLECAP FUN BUNNIES 775QX481-5	YR	7.75	36.50
85	ENGINEERING MOUSE 550QX473-5	YR	5.50	32.50
85	ICE-SKATING OWL 500QX476-5	YR	5.00	27.50
85	SUN AND FUN SANTA 775QX492-2	YR	7.75	37.50
85	SWINGING ANGEL BELL 1100QX492-5	YR	11.00	36.50
86	JOLLY HIKER 500QX483-2	YR	5.00	29.50
86	SKI TRIPPER 675QX420-6	YR	6.75	24.50
86	SPECIAL DELIVERY 500QX415-6	YR	5.00	39.50

YR	NAME	LIMIT	ISSUE	QUOTE
87	BRIGHT CHRISTMAS DREAMS QX 473-7	YR	7.25	87.50
87	ICY TREAT 450QX450-9	YR	4.50	29.50
87	JOLLY HIKER 500QX483-2	YR	5.00	29.50
87	RACCOON BIKER 700QX458-7	YR	7.00	29.50
87	REINDOGGY 575QX452-7	YR	5.75	34.50
87	SNOOPY AND WOODSTOCK 725QX472-9	YR	7.25	36.50
86	ACORN INN 850QX424-3	YR	8.50	32.50
86	HAPPY CHRISTMAS TO OWL 600QX418-3	YR	6.00	24.50
86	PUPPY'S BEST FRIEND 650QX420-3	YR	6.50	29.50
87	HOT DOGGER 650QX471-9	YR	6.50	29.50
87	NATURE'S DECORATIONS 475QX273-9	YR	4.75	37.50
*				**HOLIDAY SCULPTURE**
83	SANTA 400QX308-7	YR	4.00	35.00
83	HEART 400QX307-9	YR	4.00	49.50
*				**HOLIDAY TRADITONS**
89	GENTLE FAWN 775QX548-5	YR	7.75	19.50
89	GEORGE WASHINGTON BICENTEN. 625QX386-2	YR	6.25	20.00
89	OLD-WORLD GNOME 775QX434-5	YR	7.75	29.50
89	SWEET MEMORIES PHOTOHOLDER 675QX438-5	YR	6.75	25.00
89	THE FIRST CHRISTMAS 775QX547-5	YR	7.75	15.50
89	HANG IN THERE 525QX430-5	YR	5.25	34.50
89	PEEK-A-BOO KITTIES 750QX487-1	YR	7.50	24.50
89	JOYFUL TRIO 975QX437-2	YR	9.75	17.50
89	PADDINGTON BEAR 575QX429-2	YR	5.75	19.50
89	NORMAN ROCKWELL 475QX276-2	YR	4.75	19.50
89	OWLIDAY GREETINGS 400QX436-5	YR	4.00	19.50
89	PARTY LINE 875QX476-1	YR	8.75	29.50
89	SPENCER SPARROW, ESQ. 675QX431-2	YR	6.75	22.50
89	STOCKING KITTEN 675QX456-5	YR	6.75	19.50
89	FELIZ NAVIDAD 675QX439-2	YR	6.75	29.50
89	SNOOPY & WOODSTOCK 675QX433-2	YR	6.75	24.50
89	CRANBERRY BUNNY 575QX426-2	YR	5.75	19.50
89	SPECIAL DELIVERY 525QX432-5	YR	5.75	22.50
89	TEENY TASTER 475QX418-1	YR	4.75	29.50
89	CAMERA CLAUS 575QX546-5	YR	5.75	22.50
89	DEER DISGUISE 575QX426-5	YR	5.75	26.50
89	GONE FISHING 575QX479-4	YR	5.75	19.00
89	GYM DANDY 575QX418-5	YR	5.75	17.50
89	HERE'S THE PITCH 575QX545-5	YR	5.75	19.50
89	HOPPY HOLIDAYS 775QX469-2	YR	7.75	24.50
89	KRISTY CLAUS 575QX424-5	YR	5.75	14.50
89	NORTH POLE JOGGER 575QX546-2	YR	5.75	22.50
89	ON THE LINKS 575QX419-2	YR	5.75	22.50
89	POLAR BOWLER 575QX478-4	YR	5.75	19.50
89	SEA SANTA 575QX415-2	YR	5.75	24.50
89	SNOWPLOW SANTA 575QX420-5	YR	5.75	22.50
89	A KISS FROM SANTA 450QX482-1	YR	4.50	26.50
89	OREO COOKIE 400QX481-4	YR	4.00	22.50
*				**HOLIDAY WILDLIFE**
82	CARDINALIS QX 313-3	YR	7.00	270.00
83	CHICKADEE 700QX309-9	YR	7.00	75.00
84	PHEASANTS 725QX347-4	YR	7.25	32.50
85	PARTRIDGE 750QX376-5	YR	7.50	29.50
86	CEDAR WAXWING 750QX321-6	YR	7.50	29.50
88	PURPLE FINCH 775QX371-1	YR	7.75	24.50
87	SNOW GOOSE 750QX371-7	YR	7.50	24.50
*				**ICE SCULPTURES**
82	ARCTIC PENGUIN 400QX300-3	YR	4.00	19.50
82	SNOWY SEAL 400QX300-6	YR	4.00	25.00
*				**KEEPSAKE COLLECTION**
73	BETSEY CLARK 250XHD100-2	YR	2.50	85.00
73	BETSEY CLARK-FIRST EDITION 250XHD110-2	YR	2.50	125.00
73	CHRISTMAS IS LOVE 250XHD106-2	YR	2.50	100.00
73	ELVES 250XHD103-5	YR	2.50	95.00
73	MANGER SCENE 250XHD102-2	YR	2.50	115.00
73	SANTA WITH ELVES 250XHD101-5	YR	2.50	95.00
74	ANGEL 250QX110-1	YR	2.50	75.00
74	BETSEY CLARK-SECOND EDITION 250QX108-1	YR	2.50	99.00
74	BUTTONS & BO (2) 350QX113-1	YR	3.50	55.00
74	CHARMERS 250QX109-1	YR	2.50	55.00
74	CURRIER & IVES (2) 350QX112-1	YR	3.50	55.00
74	LITTLE MIRACLES (4) 450QX115-1	YR	4.50	60.00
74	NORMAN ROCKWELL 250QX106-1	YR	2.50	95.00
74	NORMAN ROCKWELL 250QX111-1	YR	2.50	85.00
74	RAGGEDY ANN & RAGGEDY ANDY(4) 450QX114-1	YR	4.50	90.00
74	SNOWGOOSE 250QX107-1	YR	2.50	80.00

This little fellow helps Santa make dreams come true for boys and girls around the world. The Lladró Elf was introduced in 1992.

Barbie's popularity never seems to wane. Holiday Barbie, *second in a series of Hallmark Keepsake Ornaments, matches a doll offered by Mattel.*

The 1991 Christmas Ball *is the first in a series by Lladró. The 3-1/2" bas relief porcelain ornament features pink and blue trim in a matte finish.*

I'll just have the soup. Have a Soup-er Christmas *is an artplas ornament from Enesco's Treasury of Christmas collection.*

YR	NAME	LIMIT	ISSUE	QUOTE
*		**KEEPSAKE MAGIC COLLECTION**		
89	HOLIDAY BELL 1750QLX722-2	YR	17.50	35.00
89	MOONLIT NAP 875QLX713-4	YR	8.75	32.50
89	RUDOLPH RED-NOSED REINDEER 1950QLX725-2	YR	19.50	69.50
89	TINY TINKER 1950QLX717-4	YR	19.50	59.50
89	THE ANIMALS SPEAK 1350QLX723-2	YR	13.50	125.00
89	BUSY BEAVER 1750QLX724-5	YR	17.50	49.50
89	FIRST CHRISTMAS TOGETHER 1750QLX734-2	YR	17.50	47.50
89	FOREST FROLICS-1ST EDITION 2450QLX728-2	YR	24.50	87.50
89	UNICORN FANTASY 950QLX723-5	YR	9.50	35.00
89	BABY'S FIRST CHRISTMAS 3000QLX727-2	YR	30.00	67.50
89	KRINGLE'S TOY SHOP 2450QLX701-7	YR	24.50	59.50
89	SPIRIT OF ST. NICK 2450QLX728-5	YR	24.50	75.00
89	METRO EXPRESS 2800QLX727-5	YR	28.00	80.00
89	BACKSTAGE BEAR 1350QLX721-5	YR	13.50	49.50
89	LOVING SPOONFUL 1950QLX726-2	YR	19.50	39.50
89	JOYOUS CAROLERS 3000QLX729-5	YR	30.00	70.00
89	ANGEL MELODY 950QLX720-2	YR	9.50	24.50
	D. PALMITER	**KIDDIE CAR CLASSICS**		
94	MURRAY CHAMPION 1395QX542-6	YR	13.95	49.50
93	'55 MURRAY FIRE CHEIF	19,500	45.00	45.00
93	'68 MURRAY BOAT JOLLY ROGER	19,500	50.00	50.00
94	'39 LINCOLN ZEPHYR	24,500	50.00	50.00
94	'41 SPITFIRE AIRPLANE	19,500	50.00	50.00
94	'55 DUMP TRUCK	19,500	48.00	48.00
94	'55 RANCH WAGON	19,500	48.00	48.00
94	'55 RED CHAMPION	19,500	45.00	45.00
94	'56 DRAGNET POLICE CAR	24,500	50.00	50.00
94	'56 KIDILLAC PREMIUM	OP	50.00	50.00
94	'56 MARK V	24,500	45.00	45.00
94	'56 SPEEDWAY PACE CAR	24,500	45.00	45.00
94	'58 ATOMIC MISSILE	24,500	55.00	55.00
94	'61 CIRCUS CAR	24,500	48.00	48.00
	K. CROW	**KITTENS IN TOYLAND**		
88	KITTENS IN TOYALND/TRAIN 500QXM562-1	YR	5.00	29.50
89	SCOOTER 450QXM561-2	YR	4.50	19.50
90	SAILBOAT 450QXM573-6	YR	4.50	22.50
91	AIRPLANE 450QXM563-9	YR	4.50	19.50
92	POGO STICK 450QXM5391	YR	4.50	17.50
	A. ROGERS	**KRINGLES, THE**		
93	WREATH QXM 513-5	YR	5.75	12.00
*		**LIGHTED ORNAMENTS COLLECTION**		
86	MR. & MRS. SANTA 1450QLX705-2	YR	14.50	85.00
86	SANTA AND SPARKY-1ST ED. 2200QLX703-3	YR	22.00	125.00
86	SUGARPLUM COTTAGE 1100QLX701-1	YR	11.00	45.00
86	VILLAGE EXPRESS 2450QLX707-2	YR	24.50	120.00
86	BABY'S FIRST CHRISTMAS 1950QLX710-3	YR	19.50	44.50
86	KEEP ON GLOWIN' 1000QLX707-6	YR	10.00	49.50
86	SANTA'S SNACK 1000QLX706-6	YR	10.00	59.50
86	GENERAL STORE 1575QLX705-3	YR	15.75	59.50
86	CHRISTMAS SLEIGH RIDE 2450QLX701-2	YR	24.50	145.00
86	FIRST CHRISTMAS TOGETHER 2200QLX707-3	YR	14.00	42.50
86	GENTLE BLESSINGS 1500QLX708-3	YR	15.00	175.00
86	SANTA'S ON HIS WAY 1500QLX711-5	YR	15.00	69.50
86	MERRY CHRISTMAS BELL 850QLX709-3	YR	8.50	25.00
86	SHARING FRIENDSHIP 850QLX706-3	YR	8.50	24.00
		LION KING, THE		
94	MUFASA, SIMBA 1495QX540-6	YR	14.95	35.00
94	SIMBA AND NALSA 1295QX530-3	YR	12.95	30.00
94	TIMON & PUMBAA 895QX536-6	YR	8.95	29.50
94	SIMBA, SARABI AND MUFASA QLX 151-3	YR	32.00	50.00
*		**LITTLE FROSTY FRIENDS**		
80	A COOL YULE 650QX137-4	YR	6.50	695.00
90	LITTLE SEAL 620XPR972-1	YR	2.95	10.00
90	MEMORY WREATH 620XPR972-4	YR	2.95	10.00
90	LITTLE HUSKY 620XPR972-2	YR	2.95	15.00
90	LITTLE BEAR 620XPR972-3	YR	2.95	10.00
90	LITTLE FROSTY 620XPR972-0	YR	2.95	12.00
*		**LITTLE TRIMMERS**		
78	DRUMMER BOY 250QX136-3	YR	2.50	90.00
78	SANTA 250QX135-6	YR	2.50	65.00
78	THIMBLE MOUSE-1ST EDITION 250QX133-6	YR	2.50	325.00
79	A MATCHLESS CHRISTMAS 400QX132-7	YR	4.00	75.00
79	ANGEL DELIGHT 300QX130-7	YR	3.00	95.00
79	SANTA 300QX135-6	YR	3.00	65.00
79	THIMBLE SERIES-MOUSE 300QX133-6	YR	3.00	325.00

YR	NAME	LIMIT	ISSUE	QUOTE
80	CHRISTMAS OWL 400QX131-4	YR	4.00	55.00
80	CHRISTMAS TEDDY 250QX135-4	YR	2.50	150.00
80	CLOTHESPIN SOLDIER 350QX134-4	YR	3.50	50.00
80	MERRY REDBIRD 350QX160-1	YR	3.50	75.00
80	SWINGIN' ON A STAR 400QX130-1	YR	4.00	95.00
80	THIMBLE SERIES-A XMAS SALUTE 400QX131-9	YR	4.00	195.00
81	CLOTHESPIN DRUMMER BOY 450QX408-2	YR	4.50	45.00
81	JOLLY SNOWMAN 350QX407-5	YR	3.50	65.00
81	PERKY PENGUIN 350QX409-5	YR	3.50	60.00
81	PUPPY LOVE 350QX406-2	YR	3.50	45.00
81	THE STOCKING MOUSE 450QX412-2	YR	4.50	125.00
82	CHRISTMAS KITTEN 400QX454-3	YR	4.00	37.50
82	CHRISTMAS OWL 450QX131-4	YR	4.50	55.00
82	COOKIE MOUSE 450QX454-6	YR	4.50	70.00
82	JINGLING TEDDY 400QX477-6	YR	4.00	39.50
82	MERRY MOOSE 550QX415-5	YR	5.50	60.00
82	PERKY PENGUIN 400QX409-5	YR	4.00	60.00
78	PRAYING ANGEL 250QX134-3	YR	2.50	100.00
82	MUSICAL ANGEL 550QX459-6	YR	5.50	125.00
82	DOVE LOVE 450QX462-3	YR	4.50	55.00

T. ANDREWS

LOONEY TUNES COLLECTION

YR	NAME	LIMIT	ISSUE	QUOTE
93	PORKY PIG 875QX565-2	YR	8.75	19.50
94	ROAD RUNNER AND WILE E. COYOTE QX 560-2	YR	12.95	27.50
93	ELMER FUDD 875QX549-5	YR	8.75	19.50
93	SYLVESTER & TWEETY 975QX540-5	YR	9.75	39.50
94	DAFFY DUCK 895QX541-6	YR	8.95	19.50
94	SPEEDY GONZALES 895QX534-3	YR	8.95	19.50
94	TASMANIAN DEVIL 895QX560-5	YR	8.95	49.50
94	YOSEMITE SAM 895QX534-6	YR	8.95	19.50
93	BUGS BUNNY 875QX541-2	YR	9.75	29.50

*

MAGIC ORNAMENTS

YR	NAME	LIMIT	ISSUE	QUOTE
84	ALL ARE PRECIOUS 800QLX704-1	YR	8.00	24.50
84	BRASS CAROUSEL 900QLX707-1	YR	9.00	95.00
84	CHRISTMAS IN THE FOREST 800QLX703-4	YR	8.00	19.50
84	SANTA'S WORKSHOP 1300QLX700-4	YR	13.00	62.50
84	STAINED GLASS 800QLX703-1	YR	8.00	22.50
84	SUGARPLUM COTTAGE 1100QLX701-1	YR	11.00	45.00
85	ALL ARE PRECIOUS 800QLX704-4	YR	8.00	24.50
85	CHRISTMAS EVE VISIT 1200QLX710-5	YR	12.00	35.00
85	KATYBETH 1075QLX710-2	YR	10.75	44.50
85	MR. AND MRS. SANTA 1450QLX705-2	YR	14.50	85.00
85	SANTA'S WORKSHOP 1300QLX700-4	YR	13.00	62.50
85	SUGARPLUM COTTAGE 1100QLX701-1	YR	11.00	45.00
85	SWISS CHEESE LANE 1300QLX706-5	YR	13.00	59.50
87	BABY'S FIRST CHRISTMAS 1350QLX704-9	YR	13.50	37.50
87	FIRST CHRISTMAS TOGETHER 1150QLX708-7	YR	11.50	49.50
87	LACY BRASS SNOWFLAKE 1150QLX709-7	YR	11.50	32.50
87	SEASON FOR FRIENDSHIP 850QLX706-9	YR	8.50	19.50
88	FIRST CHRISTMAS TOGETHER 1200QLX702-7	YR	12.00	39.50
88	SONG OF CHRISTMAS 850QLX711-1	YR	8.50	29.50
88	TREE OF FRIENDSHIP 850QLX710-4	YR	8.50	26.50
90	BLESSINGS OF LOVE 1400QLX736-3	YR	14.00	49.50
90	OUR FIRST CHRISTMAS TOGETHER1800QLX725-5	YR	18.00	45.00
91	ANGEL OF LIGHT 3000QLT723-9	YR	30.00	60.00
92	ANGEL OF LIGHT 3000QLT723-9	YR	30.00	37.50
94	BARNEY 2400QLX750-6	YR	24.00	49.50
94	FELIZ NAVIDAD 2800QLX743-3	YR	28.00	56.00
90	ELF OF THE YEAR 1000QLX735-6	YR	10.00	27.50
91	KITTY IN A MITTY 450QXM587-9	YR	4.50	12.50
92	LIGHTING THE WAY 1800QLX723-1	YR	18.00	42.50
93	SONG OF THE CHIMES 2500QLX740-5	YR	25.00	55.00
88	MOONLIT NAP 875QLX713-4	YR	8.75	32.50
90	HOLIDAY FLASH 1800QLX733-3	YR	18.00	39.50
91	ELFIN ENGINEER 1000QLX720-9	YR	10.00	24.50
91	SPARKLING ANGEL 1800QLX715-7	YR	18.00	39.50
92	OUR FIRST CHRISTMAS TOGETHER2000QLX722-1	YR	20.00	44.50
93	OUR FIRST CHRISTMAS TOGETHER QLX735-5	YR	20.00	42.50
93	ROAD RUNNER AND WILE E COYOTE QLX741-5	YR	30.00	75.00
87	CHRISTMAS MORNING 2450QLX701-3	YR	24.50	49.50
87	KEEP ON GLOWIN! 1000QLX707-6	YR	10.00	49.50
87	KEEPING COZY 1175QLX704-7	YR	11.75	39.50
88	CHRISTMAS IS MAGIC 1200QLX717-1	YR	12.00	55.00
88	CIRCLING THE GLOBE 1050QLX712-4	YR	10.50	44.50
90	ELFIN WHITTLER 2000QLX726-5	YR	20.00	57.50
90	SANTA'S HO-HO-HOEDOWN 2500QLX725-6	YR	25.00	89.50
91	ARCTIC DOME 2500QLX711-7	YR	25.00	55.00

YR	NAME	LIMIT	ISSUE	QUOTE
91	SANTA'S HOT LINE 1800QLX715-9	YR	18.00	45.00
91	TOYLAND TOWER 2000QLX712-9	YR	20.00	44.50
92	BABY'S FIRST CHRISTMAS 2200QLX728-1	YR	22.00	95.00
92	ENCHANTED CLOCK 3000QLX727-4	YR	30.00	60.00
92	NUT SWEET NUT 1000QLX708-1	YR	10.00	22.50
92	SANTA SUB 1800QLX732-1	YR	18.00	39.50
93	BELLS ARE RINGING 2800QLX740-2	YR	28.00	59.50
93	DOLLHOUSE DREAMS 2200QLX737-2	YR	22.00	49.50
93	SANTA'S SNOW-GETTER 1800QLX735-2	YR	18.00	42.50
94	KRINGLE TROLLEY 2000QLX741-3	YR	20.00	49.50
94	SANTA'S SING-ALONG 2400QLX747-3	YR	24.00	55.00
94	WINNIE THE POOH PARADE 3200QLX749-3	YR	32.00	65.00
91	FRIENDSHIP TREE 1000QLX716-9	YR	10.00	26.50
92	WATCH OWLS 1200QLX708-4	YR	12.00	29.50
93	BABY'S FIRST CHRISTMAS 2200QLX736-5	YR	22.00	49.50
94	BABY'S FIRST CHRISTMAS 2000QLX746-6	YR	20.00	42.50
94	CANDY CANE LOOKOUT 1800QLX737-6	YR	18.00	45.00
84	SANTA'S ARRIVAL 1300QLX702-4	YR	13.00	65.00
84	VILLAGE CHURCH 1500QLX702-1	YR	15.00	50.00
85	LITTLE RED SCHOOLHOUSE 1575QLX711-2	YR	15.75	95.00
85	VILLAGE CHURCH 1500QLX702-1	YR	15.00	50.00
87	TRAIN STATION 1275QLX703-9	YR	12.75	49.50
88	CHRISTMAS CLASSICS-3RD ED. 1500QLX716-1	YR	15.00	44.50
90	FIRST CHRISTMAS TOGETHER QLX 725-5	YR	18.00	47.50
91	IT'S A WONDERFUL LIFE 2000QLX723-7	YR	20.00	75.00
91	JINGLE BEARS 2500QLX732-3	YR	25.00	57.50
91	MOLE FAMILY HOME 2000QLX714-9	YR	20.00	49.50
92	LOOK! IT'S SANTA 1400QLX709-4	YR	14.00	39.50
92	SANTA'S ANSWERING MACHINE 2200QLX724-1	YR	22.00	49.50
93	DOG'S BEST FRIEND 1200QLX717-2	YR	12.00	25.00
93	RADIO NEWS FLASH 2200QLX736-2	YR	22.00	45.00
94	WHITE CHRISTMAS 2800QLX746-3	YR	28.00	59.50
85	SEASON OF BEAUTY 800QLX712-2	YR	8.00	32.50
88	RADIANT TREE 1175QLX712-1	YR	11.75	24.50
90	PARTRIDGES IN A PEAR 1400QLX721-2	YR	14.00	35.00
94	AWAY IN A MANGER 1600QLX738-3	YR	16.00	39.50
91	FESTIVE BRASS CHURCH 1400QLX717-9	YR	14.00	32.50
91	STARSHIP ENTERPRISE 2000QLX719-9	YR	20.00	350.00
93	U.S.S ENTERPRISE 2400QLX141-2	YR	24.00	49.50
90	BABY'S FIRST CHRISTMAS 2800QLX724-6	YR	28.00	69.50
92	GOOD SLEDDING AHEAD 2800QLX724-4	YR	28.00	59.50
92	UNDER CONSTRUCTION 1800QLX732-4	YR	18.00	42.50
93	LAMPLIGHTER, THE 1800QLX719-2	YR	18.00	40.00
94	GINGERBREAD FANTASY 4400QLX738-2	YR	44.00	99.00
87	MEOWY CHRISTMAS 1000QLX708-9	YR	10.00	62.50
88	KITTY CAPERS 1300QLX716-4	YR	13.00	44.50
90	FOREST FROLICS 2500QLX723-6	YR	25.00	75.00
91	FOREST FROLICS 2500QLX721-9	YR	25.00	69.50
91	HOLIDAY GLOW 1400QLX717-7	YR	14.00	30.00
92	FOREST FROLICS 2800QLX725-4	YR	28.00	60.00
93	FOREST FROLICS 2500QLX716-5	YR	25.00	52.50
94	FOREST FROLICS 2800QLX743-6	YR	28.00	59.50
88	HEAVENLY GLOW 1175QLX711-4	YR	11.75	29.50
90	MRS. SANTA'S KITCHEN 2500QLX726-3	YR	25.00	79.50
91	PEANUTS 1800QLX722-9	YR	18.00	69.50
92	PEANUTS 1800QLX721-4	YR	18.00	54.50
92	SHUTTLE "GALILEO" 2400QLX133-1	YR	21.00	50.00
93	PEANUTS 1800QLX715-5	YR	18.00	45.00
94	PEANUTS 2000QLX740-6	YR	20.00	42.50
89	CHRIS MOUSE COOKOUT 950QLX722-5	YR	9.50	62.50
90	CHRIS MOUSE WREATH 1000QLX729-6	YR	10.00	39.50
90	LETTER TO SANTA 1400QLX722-6	YR	14.00	37.50
90	SONG AND DANCE 2000QLX725-3	YR	20.00	95.00
90	STARLIGHT ANGEL 1400QLX730-6	YR	14.00	37.50
92	CHRIS MOUSE TALES 1200QLX707-4	YR	12.00	32.50
93	CHRIS MOUSE FLIGHT 1200QLX715-2	YR	12.00	29.50
93	RAIDING THE FRIDGE 1600QLX718-5	YR	16.00	35.00
93	THE BEARYMORES 575QXM512-5	YR	5.75	18.50
94	CHRIS MOUSE JELLY 1200QLX739-3	YR	12.00	29.50
94	PEEKABOO PUP 2000QLX742-3	YR	20.00	42.50
84	NATIVITY 1200QLX700-1	YR	12.00	29.50
85	BABY'S FIRST CHRISTMAS 1650QLX700-5	YR	16.50	44.50
85	NATIVITY 1200QLX700-1	YR	12.00	29.50
87	LOVING HOLIDAY 2200QLX701-6	YR	22.00	54.50
87	MEMORIES ARE FOREVER-PHOTO 850QLX706-7	YR	8.50	34.50
88	BABY'S FIRST CHRISTMAS 2400QLX718-4	YR	24.00	59.50

YR	NAME	LIMIT	ISSUE	QUOTE
88	KRINGLE'S TOY SHOP 2450QLX701-7	YR	24.50	59.50
91	BABY'S FIRST CHRISTMAS 3000QLX724-7	YR	30.00	90.00
91	SANTA SPECIAL 4000QLX716-7	YR	40.00	80.00
91	SKI TRIP 2800QLX726-6	YR	28.00	60.00
92	SANTA SPECIAL 4000QLX716-7	YR	40.00	80.00
92	YULETIDE RIDER 2800QLX731-4	YR	28.00	59.50
93	NORTH POLE MERRYTHON QLX739-2	YR	25.00	55.00
94	CONVERSATION W/SANTA 2800QLX742-6	YR	28.00	55.00
94	THE EAGLE HAS LANDED 2400QLX748-6	YR	24.00	49.50
87	GOOD CHEER BLIMP 1600QLX704-6	YR	16.00	59.00
88	BEARLY REACHING 950QLX715-1	YR	9.50	39.50
88	COUNTRY EXPRESS 2450QLX721-1	YR	24.50	74.50
88	FESTIVE FEEDER 1150QLX720-4	YR	11.50	49.50
88	PARADE OF THE TOYS 2200QLX719-4	YR	24.50	55.00
90	CHILDREN'S EXPRESS 2800QLX724-3	YR	28.00	75.00
91	FIRST CHRISTMAS TOGETHER QX 713-7	YR	25.00	59.50
91	KRINGLES'S BUMPER CARS 2500QLX711-9	YR	25.00	55.00
92	CHRISTMAS PARADE 3000QLX727-1	YR	30.00	59.50
92	CONTINENTAL EXPRESS 3200QLX726-4	YR	32.00	69.50
92	FEATHERED FRIENDS 1400QLX709-1	YR	14.00	32.50
93	HOME ON THE RANGE 3200QLX739-5	YR	32.00	70.00
94	COUNTRY SHOWTIME 2200QLX741-6	YR	22.00	45.00
94	MAXINE 2000QLX750-3	YR	20.00	42.50
84	CITY LIGHTS 1000QLX701-4	YR	10.00	54.50
85	CHRIS MOUSE-FIRST EDITION 1250QLX703-2	YR	12.50	89.50
87	CHRIS MOUSE-3RD EDITION 100QLX705-7	YR	11.00	59.50
90	BEARY SHORT NAP 1000QLX732-6	YR	10.00	30.00
90	DEER CROSSING 1800QLX721-3	YR	18.00	49.50
90	HOP 'N POP POPPER 2000QLX735-3	YR	20.00	95.00
90	STARSHIP CHRISTMAS 1800QLX733-6	YR	18.00	55.00
91	CHRIS MOUSE MAIL 1000QLX720-7	YR	10.00	39.50
93	SANT'A WORKSHOP 2800QLX737-5	YR	28.00	60.00
93	WINNIE THE POOH 2400QLX742-2	YR	24.00	50.00
94	ROCK CANDY MINER 2000QLX740-3	YR	20.00	40.00
87	ANGELIC MESSENGERS 1875QLX711-3	YR	18.75	59.00
88	LAST-MINUTE HUG 1950QLX718-1	YR	22.00	49.00
88	SKATER'S WALTZ 2450QLX720-1	YR	24.50	65.00
90	CHRISTMAS MEMORIES 2500QLX727-6	YR	25.00	55.00
91	BRINGING HOME THE TREE 2800QLX724-9	YR	28.00	65.00
91	FATHER CHRISTMAS 1400QLX714-7	YR	14.00	37.50
91	SALVATION ARMY BAND 3000QLX727-3	YR	30.00	79.50
94	TOBIN FRALEY HOL. CAROUSEL 3200QLX749-6	YR	32.00	75.00
85	LOVE WREATH 850QLX702-5	YR	8.50	29.50
87	BRIGHT NOEL 700QLX705-9	YR	7.00	32.50
92	THE DANCING NUTCRACKER 3000QLX726-1	YR	30.00	60.00
93	LAST MINUTE SHOPPING 2800QLX738-5	YR	28.00	60.00
94	VERY MERRY MINUTES 2400QLX744-3	YR	24.00	48.00

R. CHAD

YR	NAME	LIMIT	ISSUE	QUOTE
88	BUTTERCUP 500QX407-4	YR	5.00	44.50
89	BLUEBELL/MARY'S ANGEL 2ND ED. 575QX454-5	YR	5.75	44.50
90	ROSEBUD 575QX442-3	YR	5.75	42.50
91	IRIS 675QX427-9	YR	6.75	34.50
92	LILY 675QX427-4	YR	6.75	49.50
93	IVY 675QX428-2	YR	6.75	22.50
94	JASMINE 695QX527-6	YR	6.95	17.50

E. SEALE

YR	NAME	LIMIT	ISSUE	QUOTE
91	EVERGREEN INN 875QX538-9	YR	8.75	17.50
91	HOLIDAY CAFE 875QX539-9	YR	8.75	15.50
91	SANTA'S STUDIO 875QX539-7	YR	8.75	17.50

L. SICKMAN

YR	NAME	LIMIT	ISSUE	QUOTE
77	SNOWFLAKE COLLECTION (4) 500QX210-2	YR	5.00	125.00

MARY'S ANGELS

MATCHBOX MEMORIES

METAL ORNAMENTS

MINIATURE ORNAMENTS

YR	NAME	LIMIT	ISSUE	QUOTE
*				
88	SNEAKER MOUSE 400QXM571-1	YR	4.00	19.50
88	SWEET DREAMS 700QXM560-4	YR	7.00	22.50
89	HEAVENLY GLOW TREE TOPPER QXM 566-1	YR	9.75	14.50
89	KITTENS IN TOYLAND-2ND ED. 450QXM561-2	YR	4.50	19.50
89	MOTHER 600QXM564-5	YR	6.00	14.50
89	ROLY-POLY RAM 300QXM570-5	YR	3.00	13.50
89	SPECIAL FRIEND 450QXM565-2	YR	4.50	14.00
89	THE KRINGLES-1ST EDITION 600QXM562-2	YR	6.00	33.50
90	AIR SANTA 450QXM565-6	YR	4.50	12.50
90	BRASS HORN 300QXM579-3	YR	3.00	7.50
90	BRASS PEACE 300QXM579-6	YR	3.00	7.50
90	BRASS YEAR 300QXM583-3	YR	3.00	8.00
90	LOVING HEARTS 300QXM552-3	YR	3.00	12.50
91	BRASS CHURCH 300QXM597-9	YR	3.00	9.50

YR	NAME	LIMIT	ISSUE	QUOTE
91	BRASS SOLDIER 300QXM598-7	YR	3.00	9.50
91	INN-4TH EDITION 850QXM562-7	YR	8.50	19.50
91	OUR 1ST CHRISTMAS TOGETHER 600QXM581-9	YR	6.00	17.50
92	DANCING ANGELS TREE TOPPER QXM 589-1	YR	9.75	12.00
92	HOLIDAY HOLLY 975QXM536-4	YR	9.75	21.00
93	DANCING ANGELS TREE-TOPPER QXM 589-1	YR	9.75	13.00
94	DANCING ANGELS TREE-TOPPER QXM 589-1	YR	9.75	13.00
94	GRACEFUL CAROUSEL HORSE 775QXM405-6	YR	7.75	17.50
90	FIRST CHRISTMAS TOGETHER 600QXM553-6	YR	6.00	14.50
91	BRASS BELLS 300QXM597-7	YR	3.00	9.50
92	GOING PLACES 375QXM587-1	YR	3.75	10.00
92	MOM 450QXM550-4	YR	4.50	14.50
92	SKI FOR TWO 450QXM582-1	YR	4.50	13.50
92	VISIONS OF ACORNS 450QXM585-1	YR	4.50	14.50
93	EARS TO PALS 375QXM407-5	YR	3.75	9.50
93	MOM 450QXM515-5	YR	4.50	13.50
93	NATURE'S ANGELS 450QXM512-2	YR	4.50	14.50
93	SNUGGLE BIRDS 575QXM518-2	YR	5.75	14.50
91	WEE TOYMAKER 850QXM596-7	YR	8.50	15.00
94	BEARY PERFECT TREE 475QXM407-6	YR	4.75	10.00
94	HEARTS A-SAIL 575QXM400-6	YR	5.75	12.50
94	JUST MY SIZE 375QXM408-6	YR	3.75	9.50
90	PERFECT FIT 450QXM551-6	YR	4.50	12.50
90	TYPE OF JOY 450QXM564-6	YR	4.50	9.50
91	ALL ABOARD 450QXM586-9	YR	4.50	17.50
91	RING-A-DING ELF 850QXM566-9	YR	8.50	19.50
91	TREELAND TRIO 850QXM589-9	YR	8.50	18.00
91	VISION OF SANTA 450QXM593-7	YR	4.50	15.00
92	HICKORY, DICKORY, DOCK 375QXM586-1	YR	3.75	12.50
92	SPUNKY MONKEY 300QXM592-1	YR	3.00	14.50
93	LEARNING TO SKATE 300QXM412-2	YR	3.00	9.50
93	LIGHTING A PATH 300QXM411-5	YR	3.00	9.00
93	REFRESHING FLIGHT 575QXM411-2	YR	5.75	14.50
94	POUR SOME MORE 575QXM515-6	YR	5.75	12.50
89	SANTA'S ROADSTER 600QXM566-5	YR	6.00	19.50
90	ACORN WREATH 600QXM568-6	YR	6.00	12.00
90	BUSY CARVER 450QXM567-3	YR	4.50	12.50
90	STAMP COLLECTOR 450QXM562-3	YR	4.50	10.50
91	FLY BY 450QXM585-9	YR	4.50	17.50
91	KEY TO LOVE 450QXM568-9	YR	4.50	16.50
92	BUCK-A-ROO 450QXM581-4	YR	4.50	15.00
92	FEEDING TIME 575QXM548-1	YR	5.75	15.00
92	FRIENDS ARE TOPS 450QXM552-1	YR	4.50	11.00
92	HOOP IT UP 450QXM583-1	YR	4.50	12.50
93	'ROUND THE MOUNTAIN QXM 402-5	YR	7.25	14.00
94	A MERRY FLIGHT 575QX407-3	YR	5.75	12.50
94	CUTE AS A BUTTON 375QXM410-3	YR	3.75	9.50
94	SWEET DREAMS 300QXM409-6	YR	3.00	11.00
89	SHARING A RIDE 850QXM576-5	YR	8.50	15.00
89	MERRY SEAL 600QXM575-5	YR	6.00	15.00
90	BABY'S FIRST CHRISTMAS 850QXM570-3	YR	8.50	17.00
90	HOLIDAY CARDINAL 300QXM552-6	YR	3.00	12.00
90	PANDA'S SURPRISE 450QXM561-6	YR	4.50	13.50
91	BABY'S FIRST CHRISTMAS 600QXM579-9	YR	6.00	22.50
91	UPBEAT BEAR 600QXM590-7	YR	6.00	16.50
92	BLACK-CAPPED CHICKADEE 300QXM548-4	YR	3.00	19.50
92	CHRISTMAS COPTER 575QXM584-4	YR	5.75	15.00
92	GRANDCHILD'S FIRST CHRISTMAS 575QXM550-1	YR	5.75	14.50
92	HOLIDAY SPLASH 575QXM583-4	YR	5.75	12.50
93	COUNTRY FIDDLING 375QXM406-2	YR	3.75	10.00
93	PULL OUT A PLUM 575QXM409-5	YR	5.75	12.50
93	SPECIAL FRIENDS 450QXM516-5	YR	4.50	10.00
93	WOODLAND BABIES 575QXM510-2	YR	5.75	14.50
94	SCOOTING ALONG 675QXM517-3	YR	6.75	15.00
88	BABY'S FIRST CHRISTMAS 600QXM574-4	YR	5.00	12.50
89	STOCKING PAL 450QXM567-2	YR	4.50	12.00
90	GOING SLEDDING 450QXM568-3	YR	4.50	15.00
90	SANTA'S STREETCAR 850QXM576-6	YR	8.50	19.50
90	SNOW ANGEL 600QXM577-3	YR	6.00	14.50
90	STOCKING PAL 450QXM567-2	YR	4.50	12.00
91	FRIENDLY FAWN 600QXM594-7	YR	6.00	16.50
91	HEAVENLY MINSTREL 975QXM568-7	YR	9.75	24.50
91	OLD ENGLISH VILLAGE 850QXM562-7	YR	8.50	29.50
91	SILVERY SANTA 975QXM567-9	YR	9.75	24.50
91	SPECIAL FRIENDS 850QXM579-7	YR	8.50	19.50
92	COOL UNCLE SAM 300QXM556-1	YR	3.00	15.00

YR	NAME	LIMIT	ISSUE	QUOTE
92	COZY KAYAK 375QXM555-1	YR	3.75	12.50
94	HAVE A COOKIE 575QXM516-6	YR	5.75	14.50
88	BRASS ANGEL 150QXM567-1	YR	1.50	19.50
88	BRASS STAR 150QXM566-4	YR	1.50	19.50
88	BRASS TREE 150QXM567-4	YR	1.50	19.50
89	BRASS PARTRIDGE 300QXM572-5	YR	3.00	12.00
89	BRASS SNOWFLAKE 450QXM570-2	YR	4.50	14.00
89	COZY SKATER 450QXM573-5	YR	4.50	12.50
89	LITTLE STAR BRINGER 600QXM562-2	YR	6.00	19.50
90	BRASS BOUQUET 600QMX577-6	YR	6.00	6.50
90	COZY SKATER 450QXM573-5	YR	4.50	12.50
90	MOTHER 450QXM571-6	YR	4.50	17.50
91	CARDINAL CAMEO 600QXM595-7	YR	6.00	17.50
91	CARING SHEPHERD 600QXM594-9	YR	6.00	17.50
91	FANCY WREATH 450QXM591-7	YR	4.50	14.50
92	ANGELIC HARPIST 450QXM552-4	YR	4.50	13.50
92	BABY'S FIRST CHRISTMAS 450QXM5494	YR	4.50	19.50
92	THIMBLE BELLS 600QXM546-1	YR	6.00	22.50
93	PEAR-SHAPED TONES 375QXM405-2	YR	3.75	8.50
94	BABY'S FIRST CHRISTMAS 575QXM400-3	YR	5.75	13.50
94	FRIENDS NEED HUGS 450QXM401-6	YR	4.50	12.50
94	JOURNEY TO BETHLEHEM 575QXM403-6	YR	5.75	12.50
88	FIRST CHRISTMAS TOGETHER 400QXM574-1	YR	4.00	12.50
88	JOYOUS HEART 350QXM569-1	YR	3.50	29.50
90	BEAR HUG 600QXM563-3	YR	6.00	13.50
90	PUPPY LOVE 600QXM566-6	YR	6.00	14.50
91	N. POLE BUDDY 450QXM592-7	YR	4.50	19.50
92	CHRISTMAS BONUS 300QXM581-1	YR	3.00	8.00
92	WEE THREE KINGS 575QXM553-1	YR	5.75	17.50
92	WOODLAND BABIES 600QXM544-4	YR	6.00	16.50
93	CRYSTAL ANGEL 975QXM401-5	YR	9.75	75.00
93	NORTH POLK FIRE TRUCK 475QXM410-5	YR	4.75	13.00
93	VISIONS OF SUGARPLUMS 725QXM402-2	YR	7.25	16.50
88	FOLK ART LAMB 250QXM568-1	YR	2.75	22.50
88	FOLK ART REINDEER 250QXM568-4	YR	3.00	19.50
88	FRIENDS SHARE JOY 200QXM576-4	YR	2.00	15.00
88	HAPPY SANTA 450QXM561-4	YR	4.50	20.00
88	LOVE IS FOREVER 200QXM577-4	YR	2.00	15.00
89	FOLK ART BUNNY 450QXM569-2	YR	4.50	11.00
89	KITTY CART 300QXM572-2	YR	3.00	9.50
90	BRASS SANTA 300QXM578-6	YR	3.00	7.50
90	RUBY REINDEER 600QXM581-6	YR	6.00	12.00
88	MOTHER 300QXM572-4	YR	3.00	12.50
88	THREE LITTLE KITTENS 600QXM569-4	YR	6.00	18.50
89	ACORN SQUIRREL 450QXM568-2	YR	4.50	9.00
89	BABY'S FIRST CHRISTMAS 600QXM573-2	YR	6.00	14.50
89	LOVEBIRDS 600QXM563-5	YR	6.00	14.50
89	ROLY-POLY PIG 300QXM571-2	YR	3.00	17.50
89	THREE LITTLE KITTENS 600QXM569-4	YR	6.00	18.50
90	ACORN SQUIRREL 450QXM568-2	YR	4.50	9.00
90	ROLY-POLY PIG 300QXM571-2	YR	3.00	17.50
90	SPECIAL FRIENDS 600QXM572-6	YR	6.00	13.50
90	TEACHER 450QXM565-3	YR	4.50	9.50
91	COOL 'N' SWEET 450QXM586-7	YR	4.50	19.50
91	COURIER TURTLE 450QXM585-7	YR	4.50	14.50
92	NATURE'S ANGELS 450QXM545-1	YR	4.50	19.50
92	SNUG KITTY 375QXM555-4	YR	3.75	12.50
90	THIMBLE BELLS 600QXM554-3	YR	6.00	27.50
91	THIMBLE BELLS-2ND EDITION 600QXM565-9	YR	6.00	22.50
89	LOAD OF CHEER 600QXM574-5	YR	6.00	19.50
89	PINECONE BASKET 450QXM573-4	YR	4.50	9.00
89	STARLIT MOUSE 450QXM565-5	YR	4.50	16.00
91	BRIGHT BOXERS 450QXM587-7	YR	4.50	17.50
91	BUSY BEAR 450QXM593-9	YR	4.50	12.50
91	HOLIDAY SNOWFLAKE 300QXM599-7	YR	3.00	12.50
92	FAST FINISH 375QXM530-1	YR	3.75	12.50
94	CORNY ELF 450QXM406-3	YR	4.50	10.00
88	COUNTRY WREATH 400QXM573-1	YR	4.00	12.00
89	COUNTRY WREATH 450QXM573-1	YR	4.50	12.00
89	HAPPY BLUEBIRD 450QXM566-2	YR	4.50	14.50
89	KRINGLES, THE QXM 562-5	YR	6.00	30.00
89	SANTA'S MAGIC RIDE 850QXM563-2	YR	8.50	19.50
90	BASKET BUDDY 600QXM569-6	YR	6.00	12.00
90	COUNTRY HEART 450QXM569-3	YR	4.50	9.50
90	HAPPY BLUEBIRD 450QXM566-2	YR	4.50	12.50
90	MADONNA AND CHILD 600QXM564-3	YR	6.00	12.00

YR	NAME	LIMIT	ISSUE	QUOTE
90	THE KRINGLES 600QXM575-3	YR	6.00	24.50
91	FELIZ NAVIDAD 600QXM588-7	YR	6.00	16.50
91	GRANDCHILD'S 1ST CHRISTMAS 450QXM569-7	YR	4.50	14.50
91	LULU & FAMILY 600QXM567-7	YR	6.00	18.50
91	THE KRINGLES-3RD EDITION 6000QXM564-7	YR	6.00	24.50
92	PERFECT BALANCE 300QXM557-1	YR	3.00	12.50
92	THE BEARYMORES 575QXM554-4	YR	5.75	22.50
93	SECRET PAL 375QXM517-2	YR	3.75	8.50
94	MELODIC CHERUB 375QXM406-6	YR	3.75	10.00
94	MOM 450QXM401-3	YR	4.50	10.00
94	TEA W/TEDDY 725QXM404-6	YR	7.25	16.50
94	THE BEARYMORES 575QXM513-3	YR	5.75	14.50
90	STRINGING ALONG 850QXM560-6	YR	8.50	17.00
90	WARM MEMORIES 450QXM571-3	YR	4.50	12.00
91	TINY TEA PARTY 2900QXM582-7	YR	29.00	150.00
91	TOP HATTER 600QXM588-9	YR	6.00	17.50
92	BRIGHT STRINGERS 375QXM584-1	YR	3.75	14.50
92	INSIDE STORY 725QXM588-1	YR	7.25	19.50
92	POLAR POLKA 450QXM553-4	YR	4.50	14.50
92	SEW, SEW TINY 2900QXM579-4	YR	29.00	60.00
93	CHRISTMAS CASTLE 575QXM408-5	YR	5.75	13.50
93	GRANDMA 450QXM516-2	YR	4.50	12.50
93	INTO THE WOODS 375QXM404-5	YR	3.75	8.50
93	TINY GREEN THUMBS QXM 403-2 SET OF SIX	YR	29.00	45.00
94	BAKING TINY TREATS QXM 403-3 SET OF SIX	YR	29.00	59.50
89	LITTLE SOLDIER 450QXM567-5	YR	4.50	10.00
89	PUPPY CART 300QXM571-5	YR	3.00	9.50
90	LION AND LAMB 450QXM567-6	YR	4.50	10.00
90	LITTLE SOLDIER 450QXM567-5	YR	4.50	10.00
90	SANTA'S JOURNEY 850QXM582-6	YR	8.50	19.50
91	LI'L POPPER 450QXM589-7	YR	4.50	17.50
91	NOEL 300QXM598-9	YR	3.00	12.50
92	FRIENDLY TIN SOLDIER 450QXM587-4	YR	4.50	17.50
92	LITTLE TOWN OF BETHLEHEM 300QXM586-4	YR	3.00	22.50
93	I DREAM OF SANTA 375QXM405-5	YR	3.75	12.00
93	MONKEY MELODY 575QXM409-2	YR	5.75	14.50
93	ON THE ROAD 575QXM400-2	YR	5.75	16.50
94	CENTURIES OF SANTA 600QXM515-3	YR	6.00	22.50
94	JOLLY VISITOR 575QXM405-3	YR	5.75	14.50
94	LOVE WAS BORN 450QXM404-3	YR	4.50	12.50
94	NOAH'S ARK 2450QXM410-6 SET OF THREE	YR	24.50	49.50
94	NUTCRACKER GUILD 575QXM514-6	YR	5.75	15.00
94	ON THE ROAD 575QXM510-3	YR	5.75	12.50
88	CANDY CANE ELF 300QXM570-1	YR	3.00	19.50
88	LITTLE DRUMMER BOY 450QXM578-4	YR	4.50	26.50
88	PENGUIN PAL-1ST EDITION 375QXM563-1	YR	3.75	29.50
88	SNUGGLY SKATER 450QXM571-4	YR	4.50	27.50
89	OLD-WORLD SANTA 300QXM569-5	YR	3.00	9.50
89	SLOW MOTION 600QXM575-2	YR	6.00	16.50
89	STROLLIN' SNOWMAN 450QXM574-2	YR	4.50	15.00
90	CHRISTMAS DOVE 450QXM563-6	YR	4.50	12.50
90	GRANDCHILD'S FIRST XMAS 600QXM572-3	YR	6.00	12.00
90	OLD-WORLD SANTA 300QXM569-5	YR	3.00	9.50
90	SWEET SLUMBER 450QXM566-3	YR	4.50	12.50
90	WEE NUTCRACKER 850QXM584-3	YR	8.50	17.00
91	MOM 600QXM569-9	YR	6.00	17.50
91	PENGUIN PAL-4TH EDITION 450QXM562-9	YR	4.50	17.50
91	SEASIDE OTTER 450QXM590-9	YR	4.50	12.50
92	GERBIL INC. 375QXM592-4	YR	3.75	11.00
92	PUPPET SHOW 300QXM557-4	YR	3.00	12.50
93	CHEESE PLEASE 375QXM407-2	YR	3.75	8.50
93	MERRY MASCOT 375QXM404-2	YR	3.75	10.00
88	HOLY FAMILY 850QXM561-1	YR	8.50	15.00
88	JOLLY ST. NICK 800QXM572-1	YR	8.00	36.50
88	SKATER'S WALTZ 700QXM560-1	YR	7.00	22.00
89	HOLY FAMILY 850QXM561-1	YR	8.50	15.00
90	NATIVITY 450QXM570-6	YR	4.50	14.50
91	FIRST CHRISTMAS TOGETHER QXM 581-9	YR	6.00	19.50
92	A+ TEACHER 375QXM551-1	YR	3.75	8.00
92	COCA-COLA SANTA 575QXM588-4	YR	5.75	19.50
92	GRANDMA 450QXM551-4	YR	4.50	14.50
92	MINTED FOR SANTA 375QXM585-4	YR	3.75	15.00
93	MARCH OF THE TEDDY BEARS 450QXM400-5	YR	4.50	17.50
94	MARCH OF THE TEDDY BEARS 450QXM510-6	YR	4.50	12.50
88	GENTLE ANGEL 200QXM577-1	YR	2.00	19.50
89	BUNNY HUG 300QXM577-5	YR	3.00	12.00

YR	NAME	LIMIT	ISSUE	QUOTE
89	FIRST CHRISTMAS TOGETHER 850QXM564-2	YR	8.50	12.00
89	HOLIDAY DEER 300QXM577-2	YR	3.00	12.00
89	REJOICE 300QXM578-2	YR	3.00	10.00
89	SCRIMSHAW REINDEER 450QXM568-5	YR	4.50	9.50
90	CLOISONNE POINSETTIA 1050QMX553-3	YR	10.50	24.50
91	COUNTRY SLEIGH 450QXM599-9	YR	4.50	14.50
91	LOVE IS BORN 600QXM595-9	YR	6.00	18.50
92	HARMONY TRIO 1175QXM547-1	YR	11.75	24.50
92	SNOWSHOE BUNNY 375QXM556-4	YR	3.75	12.50
93	BABY'S FIRST CHRISTMAS 575QXM514-5	YR	5.75	14.50
93	CLOISONNE SNOWFLAKE 975QXM401-2	YR	9.75	20.00
93	THIMBLE BELLS 575QXM514-2	YR	5.75	15.00
94	DAZZLING REINDEER 975QXM402-6	YR	9.75	20.00
94	JOLLY WOLLY SNOWMAN 375QXM409-3	YR	3.75	10.00
94	NATURE'S ANGELS 450QXM512-6	YR	4.50	12.50

E. SEALE — MOTHER GOOSE

| 93 | HUMPTY DUMPTY 1375QX528-2 | YR | 13.75 | 42.50 |
| 94 | HEY DIDDLE, DIDDLE 1395QX521-3 | YR | 13.95 | 39.50 |

J. FRANCIS — MR. AND MRS. CLAUS

93	A FITTING MOMENT 1475QX420-2	YR	14.75	37.50
86	MERRY MISTLETOE TIME 1300QX402-6	YR	13.00	110.00
87	HOME COOKING 1325QX483-7	YR	13.25	59.50
88	SHALL WE DANCE? 1300QX401-1	YR	13.00	49.50
89	HOLIDAY DUET 1325QX457-5	YR	13.25	44.50
90	POPCORN PARTY 1375QX439-3	YR	13.75	53.00
91	CHECKING HIS LIST 1375QX433-9	YR	13.75	40.00
92	GIFT EXCHANGE 1475QX429-4	YR	14.75	39.50
94	A HANDWARMING PRESENT 1495QX528-3	YR	14.95	29.50

MUSCIAL

| 83 | MOTHER'S DAY-A MOTHER'S LOVE MDQ 340-7 | YR | 14.00 | 85.00 |

MUSICAL

82	BABY'S FIRST CHRISTMAS 1600QMB900-7	YR	16.00	99.00
82	FIRST CHRISTMAS TOGETHER 1600QMB901-9	YR	16.00	99.00
82	LOVE 1600QMB900-9	YR	16.00	125.00
83	BABY'S FIRST CHRISTMAS 1600QMB903-9	YR	16.00	100.00
83	FRIENDSHIP 1600QMB904-7	YR	16.00	125.00
83	NATIVITY 1600QMB904-9	YR	16.00	150.00
83	TWELVE DAYS OF CHRISTMAS 1500QMB415-9	YR	15.00	100.00

S. PIKE — NATURE'S ANGELS

| 91 | PUPPY 450QXM565-7 | YR | 4.50 | 22.50 |
| 90 | BUNNY 450QXM573-3 | YR | 4.50 | 24.50 |

* — NEW ATTRACTIONS

89	FESTIVE ANGEL 675 QX463-5	YR	6.75	24.50
89	GRACEFUL SWAN 675QX464-2	YR	6.75	19.50
89	ROOSTER WEATHERVANE 575QX467-5	YR	5.75	14.50
90	COUNTRY ANGEL 675QX504-6	YR	6.75	195.00
90	FELIZ NAVIDAD 675QX517-3	YR	6.75	29.50
90	GARFIELD 475QX230-3	YR	4.75	22.50
90	GINGERBREAD ELF 575QX503-3	YR	5.75	19.50
90	GOOSE CART 775QX523-6	YR	7.75	17.50
90	HOME FOR THE OWLIDAYS 675QX518-3	YR	6.75	14.50
90	MOOY CHRISTMAS 675QX493-3	YR	6.75	23.00
90	NUTSHELL CHAT 675QX519-3	YR	6.75	26.50
90	PEANUTS 475QX223-3	YR	4.75	25.00
91	MARY ENGELBREIT 475QX223-7	YR	4.75	29.50
91	PEANUTS 500QX225-7	YR	5.00	22.50
92	DOWN-UNDER HOLIDAY 775QX514-4	YR	7.75	19.50
92	EGG NOG NEST 775QX512-1	YR	7.75	17.50
92	MEMORIES TO CHERISH 1075QX516-1	YR	10.75	24.50
92	PEANUTS 500QX224-4	YR	5.00	19.50
92	SANTA JOLLY WOLLY 775QX537-4	YR	7.75	7.75
90	SPOON RIDER 975QX549-6	YR	9.75	22.50
90	TWO PEAS IN A POD 475QX492-6	YR	4.75	34.50
92	FELIZ NAVIDAD 675QX518-1	YR	6.75	19.50
92	JESUS LOVES ME 775QX302-4	YR	7.75	16.50
92	LOVING SHEPHERD 775QX515-1	YR	7.75	19.50
92	TOBOGGAN TAIL 775QX545-9	YR	7.75	17.50
89	BALANCING ELF 675QX489-5	YR	6.75	24.50
89	NUTSHELL DREAMS 575QX465-5	YR	5.75	22.50
89	NUTSHELL WORKSHOP 575QX487-2	YR	5.75	22.50
91	DINOCLAUS 775QX527-7	YR	7.75	24.50
92	SPIRIT OF CHRISTMAS STRESS 875QX523-1	YR	8.75	19.75
89	COOL SWING 625QX487-5	YR	6.25	35.00
89	GOIN' SOUTH 425QX410-5	YR	4.25	24.50
89	LET'S PLAY 725QX488-2	YR	7.25	27.50
90	BEARBACK RIDER 975QX548-3	YR	9.75	29.50

YR	NAME	LIMIT	ISSUE	QUOTE
90	HOT DOGGER 775QX497-6	YR	7.75	22.50
90	JOY IS IN THE AIR 775QX550-3	YR	7.75	29.50
90	SANTA SCHNOZ 675QX498-3	YR	6.75	29.50
90	THREE LITTLE PIGGIES 775QX499-6	YR	7.75	19.50
91	ON A ROLL 675QX534-7	YR	6.75	21.50
91	UP 'N' DOWN JOURNEY 975QX504-7	YR	9.75	27.50
92	FUN ON A BIG SCALE 1075QX513-4	YR	10.75	23.50
92	GENIUS AT WORK 1075QX537-1	YR	10.75	22.50
92	HELLO-HO-HO 975QX514-1	YR	9.75	24.50
92	SANTA MARIA 1275QX507-4	YR	12.75	29.50
89	CACTUS COWBOY 675QX411-2	YR	6.75	45.00
89	PEPPERMINT CLOWN 2475QX450-5	YR	24.75	49.50
90	S. CLAUS TAXI 1175QX468-6	YR	11.75	32.50
90	KITTY'S BEST PAL 675QX471-6	YR	6.75	20.00
92	DECK THE HOGS 875QX520-4	YR	8.75	22.50
89	TV BREAK 625QX409-2	YR	6.25	19.50
90	BILLBOARD BUNNY 775QX519-6	YR	7.75	19.50
90	COYOTE CAROLS 875QX499-3	YR	8.75	24.50
90	POOLSIDE WALRUS 775QX498-6	YR	7.75	23.00
90	STITCHES OF JOY 775QX518-6	YR	7.75	27.50
91	CHILLY CHAP 675QX533-9	YR	6.75	19.50
91	FELIZ NAVIDAD 675QX527-9	YR	6.75	24.50
91	SKI LIFT BUNNY 675QX544-7	YR	6.75	20.00
92	A SANTA-FULL 975QX599-1	YR	9.75	42.50
92	COOL FLIERS 1075QX547-4	YR	10.75	24.50
92	GONE WISHIN' 875QX517-1	YR	8.75	22.50
92	HONEST GEORGE 775QX506-4	YR	7.75	19.50
92	PLEASE PAUSE HERE 1475QX529-1	YR	14.75	39.50
92	SANTA'S ROUNDUP 875QX508-4	YR	8.75	24.50
92	SKIING 'ROUND 875QX521-4	YR	8.75	19.50
92	TASTY CHRISTMAS 975QX599-4	YR	9.75	22.50
89	SPARKLING SNOWFLAKE 775QX547-2	YR	7.75	27.50
90	HOLIDAY CARDINALS 775QX524-3	YR	7.75	24.50
90	NORMAN ROCKWELL ART 475QX229-6	YR	4.75	24.50
91	NORMAN ROCKWELL ART 500QX225-9	YR	5.00	19.50
92	NORMAN ROCKWELL ART 500QX222-4	YR	5.00	19.50
92	GARFIELD 775QX537-4	YR	7.75	17.50
92	GREEN THUMB SANTA 775QX510-1	YR	7.75	17.50
92	RAPID DELIVERY 875QX509-4	YR	8.75	22.50
90	BORN TO DANCE 775QX504-3	YR	7.75	22.50
90	CHIMING IN 975QX436-6	YR	9.75	24.50
90	COZY GOOSE 575QX496-6	YR	5.75	17.50
90	MEOW MART 775QX444-6	YR	7.75	22.50
91	NUTTY SQUIRREL 575QX483-3	YR	5.75	14.50
92	HOLIDAY WISHES 775QX513-1	YR	7.75	19.50
89	COUNTRY CAT 625QX467-2	YR	6.25	17.50
89	NOSTALGIC LAMB 675QX466-5	YR	6.75	14.50
90	CHRISTMAS CROC 775QX437-3	YR	7.75	22.50
89	WIGGLY SNOWMAN 675QX489-2	YR	6.75	24.50
90	SNOOPY & WOODSTOCK 675QX472-3	YR	6.75	27.50
91	GARFIELD 775QX517-7	YR	7.75	24.50
91	SNOOPY AND WOODSTOCK 675QX519-7	YR	6.75	26.50
89	NUTSHELL HOLIDAY 575QX465-2	YR	5.75	26.50
90	BABY UNICORN 975QX548-6	YR	9.75	22.50
90	JOLLY DOLPHIN 675QX468-3	YR	6.75	30.00
90	LONG WINTER'S NAP 675QX470-3	YR	6.75	24.50
91	CUDDLY LAMB 675QX519-9	YR	6.75	19.50
91	NUTSHELL NATIVITY 675QX517-6	YR	6.75	29.50
92	HOLIDAY TEATIME 1475QX543-1	YR	14.75	29.50
92	SNOOPY & WOODSTOCK 875QX595-4	YR	8.75	24.50
92	GOLF'S A BALL 675QX598-4	YR	6.75	29.50
89	CLAUS CONSTRUCTION 775QX488-5	YR	7.75	35.00
90	HANG IN THERE 675QX471-3	YR	6.75	20.00
90	KING KLAUS 775QX410-6	YR	7.75	19.50
90	STOCKING PALS 1075QX549-3	YR	10.75	25.00
91	BASKET BELL PLAYERS 775QX537-7	YR	7.75	22.50
91	YULE LOGGER 875QX496-7	YR	8.75	27.50
92	BEAR BELL CHAMP 775QX507-1	YR	7.75	17.50
92	MERRY "SWISS" MOUSE 775QX511-4	YR	7.75	16.50
92	NORTH POLE FIRE FIGHTER 975QX510-4	YR	9.75	24.50
92	SANTA'S HOOK SHOT 1275QX543-4	YR	12.75	29.50
92	TREAD BEAR 875QX509-1	YR	8.75	24.50
89	HORSE WEATHERVANE 575QX463-2	YR	5.75	17.50
90	CHRISTMAS PARTRIDGE 775QX524-6	YR	7.75	24.50
91	CHRISTMAS WELCOME 975QX529-9	YR	9.75	24.50
91	JOLLY WOLLY SANTA 775QX541-9	YR	7.75	28.50

YR	NAME	LIMIT	ISSUE	QUOTE
91	JOLLY WOLLY SNOWMAN 775QX542-7	YR	7.75	22.50
91	JOLLY WOLLY SOLDIER 775QX542-9	YR	7.75	22.50
91	NIGHT BEFORE CHRISTMAS 975QX530-7	YR	9.75	24.50
91	OLD-FASHIONED SLED 875QX431-7	YR	8.75	19.50
91	PARTRIDGE IN A PEAR TREE 975QX529-7	YR	9.75	21.50
91	SNOWY OWL 775QX526-9	YR	7.75	19.50
92	SILVER STAR 2800QX532-4	YR	28.00	60.00
89	RODNEY REINDEER 675QX407-2	YR	6.75	15.00
90	BEARY GOOD DEAL 675QX473-3	YR	6.75	14.50
90	PEPPERONI MOUSE 675QX497-3	YR	6.75	20.00
90	PERFECT CATCH 775QX469-3	YR	7.75	19.50
90	POLAR JOGGER 575QX466-6	YR	5.75	17.50
90	POLAR PAIR 575QX462-6	YR	5.75	27.50
90	POLAR SPORT 775QX515-6	YR	7.75	22.50
90	POLAR TV 775QX516-6	YR	7.75	19.50
90	POLAR V.I.P. 575QX466-3	YR	5.75	17.50
90	POLAR VIDEO 575QX463-3	YR	5.75	17.50
91	ALL STAR 675QX532-9	YR	6.75	22.50
91	NOTES OF CHEER 575QX535-7	YR	5.75	14.50
91	PIGLET AND EEYORE 975QX557-7	YR	9.75	49.50
91	POLAR CLASSIC 675QX528-7	YR	6.75	19.50
92	PARTRIDGE IN PEAR TREE 875QX523-4	YR	8.75	19.50
90	LITTLE DRUMMER BOY 775QX523-3	YR	7.75	24.50
90	LOVABLE DEARS 875QX547-6	YR	8.75	20.00
91	SWEET TALK 875QX536-7	YR	8.75	23.50
92	CHEERFUL SANTA 975QX515-4	YR	9.75	39.50
90	HAPPY VOICES 675QX464-5	YR	6.75	17.50
91	FOLK ART REINDEER 875QX535-9	YR	8.75	19.50
91	JOYOUS MEMORIES-PHOTOHOLDER 675QX536-9	YR	6.75	24.50

D. UNRUH — **NIGHT BEFORE CHRISTMAS**

YR	NAME	LIMIT	ISSUE	QUOTE
94	FATHER 450QXM512-3	YR	4.50	12.50
92	HOUSE 1375QXM5541	YR	13.75	35.00
93	BED 450QXM511-5	YR	4.50	18.50

L. SICKMAN — **NOEL RAILROAD**

YR	NAME	LIMIT	ISSUE	QUOTE
89	LOCOMOTIVE 850QXM576-2	YR	8.50	44.50
90	COAL CAR 850QXM575-6	YR	8.50	29.50
91	PASSENGER CAR-3RD EDITION 850QXM564-9	YR	8.50	26.50
92	BOX CAR 700QXM5441	YR	7.00	22.50
93	FLATBED CAR 700QXM510-5	YR	7.00	19.50
94	STOCK CAR 700QXM511-3	YR	7.00	16.00

* — **NORMAN ROCKWELL**

YR	NAME	LIMIT	ISSUE	QUOTE
80	SANTA'S VISITORS 650QX306-1	YR	6.50	250.00
88	AND TO ALL A GOOD NIGHT 775QX340-4	YR	7.75	24.50
93	FILLING THE STOCKINGS 1575QK115-5	YR	15.75	36.50
93	JOLLY POSTMAN 1575QK116-2	YR	15.75	36.50
88	CHRISTMAS SCENES 475QX273-1	YR	4.75	24.50
84	CAUGHT NAPPING 750QX341-1	YR	7.50	34.50
86	CHECKING UP 775QX321-3	YR	7.75	29.50

L. SICKMAN — **NORTH POLE NUTCRACKERS**

YR	NAME	LIMIT	ISSUE	QUOTE
92	ERIC THE BAKER 875QX524-4	YR	8.75	19.50
92	FRANZ THE ARTIST 875QX526-1	YR	8.75	24.50
92	FRIEDA THE ANIMALS' FRIEND 875QX526-4	YR	8.75	24.50
92	LUDWIG THE MUSICIAN 875QX528-1	YR	8.75	19.50
92	MAX THE TAILOR 875QX525-1	YR	8.75	23.50
92	OTTO THE CARPENTER 875QX525-4	YR	8.75	23.50

D. LEE — **NOSTALGIC HOUSES & SHOPS**

YR	NAME	LIMIT	ISSUE	QUOTE
84	VICTORIAN DOLLHOUSE 1300QX448-1	YR	13.00	195.00
86	CHRISTMAS CANDY SHOPPE 1375QX403-3	YR	13.75	275.00
87	HOUSE ON MAIN ST. 1400QX483-9	YR	14.00	74.50
88	HALL BROS CARD SHOP 1450QX401-4	YR	14.50	57.50
89	U.S. POST OFFICE 1425QX458-2	YR	14.25	55.00
90	HOLIDAY HOME 1475QX469-6	YR	14.75	59.50
91	FIRE STATION-8TH EDITION 1475QX413-9	YR	14.75	49.50
92	FIVE-AND-TEN-CENT STORE 1475QX425-4	YR	14.75	39.50
93	COZY HOME 1475QX417-5	YR	14.75	39.50
93	TANNENBAUM'S DEPT. STORE 2600QX561-2	YR	26.00	60.00
94	NEIGHBORHOOD DRUGSTORE 1495QX528-6	YR	14.95	32.50

P. ANDREWS — **OLD ENGLISH VILLAGE**

YR	NAME	LIMIT	ISSUE	QUOTE
94	HAT SHOP 700QXM514-3	YR	7.00	16.50
88	FAMILY HOME-1ST EDITION 850QXM563-4	YR	8.50	44.75
89	SWEET SHOP 850QXM561-5	YR	8.50	34.50
90	SCHOOL 850QXM576-3	YR	8.50	24.50
91	COUNTRY INN QXM 562-7	YR	8.50	19.50
92	CHURCH 700QXM5384	YR	7.00	29.50
93	TOY SHOP 700QXM513-2	YR	7.00	17.50

YR	NAME	LIMIT	ISSUE	QUOTE
D. PALMITER			**OLD WORLD SILVER**	
93	SILVER DOVE OF PEACH 2475QK107-5	YR	24.75	35.00
93	SILVER SLEIGH 2475QK108-2	YR	24.75	35.00
93	SILVER STAR AND HOLLY 2475QK108-5	YR	24.75	35.00
94	SILVER BOWS 2475QK102-3	YR	24.75	49.50
93	SILVER SANTA 2475QK109-2	YR	24.75	55.00
94	SILVER BELLS 2475QK102-6	YR	24.75	49.50
94	SILVER POINSETTIA 2475QK100-6	YR	24.75	49.50
94	SILVER SNOWFLAKES 2475QK101-6	YR	24.75	49.50
P. DUTKIN		**OLD-FASHIONED CHRISTMAS COLLECTION**		
87	LITTLE WHITTLER 600QX469-9	YR	6.00	32.50
87	COUNTRY WREATH 575QX470-9	YR	5.75	29.50
87	FOLK ART SANTA 525QX474-9	YR	5.25	32.50
87	NOSTALGIC ROCKER 650QX468-9	YR	6.50	34.50
87	IN A NUTSHELL 550QX469-7	YR	5.50	34.50
			OPEN HOUSE ORNAMENTS	
86	SANTA AND HIS REINDEER 975QX0440-6	YR	9.75	44.50
86	SANTA'S PANDA PAL 550QX0441-3	YR	5.00	29.50
P. ANDREWS			**OUR FAMILY**	
94	OUR FAMILY PHOTOHOLDER 795QX557-6	YR	7.95	17.50
L. SICKMAN			**PEACE ON EARTH**	
91	ITALY 1175QX512-9	YR	11.75	35.00
92	SPAIN 1175QX517-4	YR	11.75	25.50
93	POLAND 1175QX524-2	YR	11.75	24.50
*			**PEANUTS COLLECTION**	
77	PEANUTS (2) 400QX163-5	YR	4.00	85.00
77	PEANUTS 250QX162-2	YR	2.50	75.00
77	PEANUTS 350QX135-5	YR	3.50	75.00
78	PEANUTS 250QX203-6	YR	2.50	65.00
78	PEANUTS 250QX204-3	YR	2.50	60.00
78	PEANUTS 350QX205-6	YR	3.50	85.00
78	PEANUTS 350QX206-3	YR	3.50	65.00
89	A CHARLIE BROWN CHRISTMAS 475QX276-5	YR	4.75	39.50
94	LUCY QX 520-3	YR	9.95	16.00
93	PEANUTS GANE 975QX531-5	YR	9.75	49.50
			PERSONALIZED ORNAMENTS	
93	COOL SNOWMAN 875QP605-2	YR	8.75	8.75
93	PEANUTS 900QP604-5	YR	9.00	9.00
93	REINDEER IN THE SKY 875QP605-5	YR	8.75	8.75
93	MAILBOX DELIVERY 1475QP601-5	YR	14.75	14.75
93	ON THE BILLBOARD 1275QP602-2	YR	12.75	12.75
94	ETCH-A-SKETCH 1295QP600-6	YR	12.95	12.95
94	MAILBOX DELIVERY 1495QP601-5	YR	14.95	14.95
94	ON THE BILLBOARD 1295QP602-2	YR	12.95	12.95
94	REINDEER ROOTERS 1295QP605-6	YR	12.95	12.95
93	BABY BLOCK PHOTOHOLDER QP603-5	YR	14.75	14.75
93	PLAYING BALL 1275QP603-2	YR	12.75	12.75
94	BABY BLOCK PHOTOHOLDER 1495QP603-5	YR	14.95	14.95
94	PLAYING BALL 1295QP603-2	YR	12.95	12.95
93	GOING GOLFIN' 1275QP601-2	YR	12.75	12.75
94	GOIN' FISHIN' 1495QP602-3	YR	14.95	14.95
94	GOIN' GOLFIN' 1295QP601-2	YR	12.75	12.75
94	FROM THE HEART 1495QP603-6	YR	24.95	24.95
93	FILLED W/COOKIES 1275QP604-2	YR	12.75	12.75
93	HERE'S YOUR FORTUNE 1075QP600-2	YR	10.75	10.75
93	SANTA SAYS 1475QP600-5	YR	12.75	12.75
94	COMPUTER CAT 'N' MOUSE 1295QP604-6	YR	12.95	12.95
94	SANTA SAYS 1495QP600-5	YR	14.95	14.95
94	HOLIDAY HELLO 2495QXR611-6	YR	24.95	24.95
93	FESTIVE ALBUM PHOTOHOLDER QP602-5	YR	12.75	12.75
94	COOKIE TIME 1295QP607-3	YR	12.95	12.95
94	FESTIVE ALBUM PHOTOHOLDER 1295QP602-5	YR	12.95	12.95
94	NOVEL IDEA 1295QP606-6	YR	12.95	12.95
A. ROGERS			**PLAYFUL PALS**	
93	COCA-COLA SANTA 1475QX574-2	YR	14.75	29.50
*			**PLUSH ANIMALS**	
81	CHRISTMAS TEDDY 500QX404-2	YR	5.50	29.50
81	RACCOON TUNES 550QX405-5	YR	5.50	29.50
			PORTRAITS IN BISQUE	
93	JOY OF SHARING 1575QK114-2	YR	15.75	34.50
93	CHRISTMAS FEAST 1575QK115-2	YR	15.75	34.50
93	MISTLETOE KISS 1575QK114-5	YR	15.75	32.50
*			**PROPERTY ORNAMENTS**	
75	BETSEY CLARK (2) 350QX167-1	YR	3.50	49.50
75	BETSEY CLARK (4) 450QX168-1	YR	4.50	55.00
75	BETSEY CLARK 250QX210-1	YR	2.50	50.00

YR	NAME	LIMIT	ISSUE	QUOTE
75	BETSEY CLARK-3RD EDITION 300QX133-1	YR	3.00	80.00
75	BETSEY CLARK-FOURTH EDITION 300QX195-1	YR	3.00	195.00
75	BUTTONS & BO (4) 500QX139-1	YR	5.00	50.00
75	CHARMERS 300QX135-1	YR	3.00	50.00
75	LITTLE MIRACLES (4) 500QX140-1	YR	5.00	50.00
75	MARTY LINKS 300QX136-1	YR	3.00	40.00
75	NORMAN ROCKWELL 250QX166-1	YR	2.50	65.00
75	NORMAN ROCKWELL 300QX134-1	YR	3.00	75.00
76	BETSEY CLARK (3) 450QX218-1	YR	4.50	65.00
76	CHARMERS (2) 350QX215-1	YR	3.50	65.00
76	CURRIER & IVES 250QX209-1	YR	2.50	50.00
76	CURRIER & IVES 300QX197-1	YR	3.00	50.00
76	HAPPY THE SNOWMAN (2) QX216-1	YR	3.50	55.00
76	MARTY LINKS (2) 400QX207-1	YR	4.00	65.00
76	NORMAN ROCKWELL 300QX196-1	YR	3.00	80.00
76	RAGGEDY ANN 250QX212-1	YR	2.50	65.00
76	RUDOLPH AND SANTA 250QX213-1	YR	2.50	95.00
77	BETSEY CLARK-FIFTH EDITION 350QX264-2	YR	3.50	495.00
77	CHARMERS 350QX153-5	YR	3.50	50.00
77	CURRIER & IVES 350QX130-2	YR	3.50	55.00
77	DISNEY (2) 400QX137-5	YR	4.00	85.00
77	DISNEY 350QX133-5	YR	3.50	60.00
77	GRANDMA MOSES 350QX150-2	YR	3.50	175.00
77	NORMAN ROCKWELL 350QX151-5	YR	3.50	95.00
78	BETSEY CLARK-SIXTH EDITION 350QX201-6	YR	3.50	70.00
78	DISNEY 350QX207-6	YR	3.50	95.00
78	JOAN WALSH ANGLUND 350QX221-6	YR	3.50	95.00
78	SPENCER SPARROW 350QX219-6	YR	3.50	65.00
79	BETSEY CLARK-SEVENTH EDITION 350QX201-9	YR	3.50	39.50
79	JOAN WALSH ANGLUND 350QX205-9	YR	3.50	35.00
79	MARY HAMILTON 350QX254-7	YR	3.50	30.00
79	PEANUTS-TIME TO TRIM 350QX202-7	YR	3.50	32.50
79	SPENCER SPARROW 350QX200-7	YR	3.50	39.50
79	WINNIE-THE-POOH 350QX206-7	YR	3.50	45.00
80	BETSEY CLARK 650QX307-4	YR	6.50	75.00
80	BETSEY CLARK'S CHRISTMAS 750QX149-4	YR	7.50	35.00
80	BETSEY CLARK-EIGHTH EDITION 400QX215-4	YR	4.00	40.00
80	DISNEY 400QX218-1	YR	4.00	35.00
80	JOAN WALSH ANGLUND 400QX217-4	YR	4.00	25.00
80	MARTY LINKS 400QX221-4	YR	4.00	22.50
80	MARY HAMILTON 400QX219-4	YR	4.00	24.50
80	MUPPETS 400QX220-1	YR	4.00	39.50
80	PEANUTS 400QX216-1	YR	4.00	39.50
81	BETSEY CLARK 900QX423-5	YR	9.00	75.00
81	BETSEY CLARK BLUE CAMEO QX 512-2	YR	8.50	30.00
81	BETSEY CLARK-9TH EDITION 450QX802-2	YR	4.50	32.50
81	DISNEY 450QX805-5	YR	4.50	29.50
81	JOAN WALSH ANGLUND 450QX804-2	YR	4.50	22.50
81	MARTY LINKS 450QX808-2	YR	4.50	19.50
81	MARY HAMILTON 450QX806-2	YR	4.50	19.50
81	MUPPETS 450QX807-5	YR	4.50	35.00
81	PEANUTS 450QX803-5	YR	4.50	27.50
82	BETSEY CLARK 850QX305-6	YR	8.50	24.50
82	BETSEY CLARK SERIES QX 215-6	YR	4.50	32.50
82	DISNEY 450QX217-3	YR	4.50	35.00
82	JOAN WALSH ANGLUND 450QX219-3	YR	4.50	19.50
82	MARY HAMILTON 450QX217-6	YR	4.50	19.50
82	MISS PIGGY & KERMIT 450QX218-3	YR	4.50	40.00
82	MUPPETS PARTY 450QX218-6	YR	4.50	39.50
82	NORMAN ROCKWELL 450QX202-3	YR	4.50	29.50
82	NORMAN ROCKWELL-3RD EDITION 850QX305-3	YR	8.50	29.50
82	PEANUTS 450QX200-6	YR	4.50	32.50
83	BETSEY CLARK 900QX440-1	YR	9.00	35.00
83	BETSEY CLARK-11TH EDITION 450QX211-9	YR	4.50	29.50
83	DISNEY 450QX212-9	YR	4.50	49.50
83	KERMIT THE FROG 1100QX495-6	YR	11.00	95.00
83	MARY HAMILTON 450QX213-7	YR	4.50	49.50
83	MISS PIGGY 1300QX405-7	YR	13.00	225.00
83	NORMAN ROCKWELL 450QX215-7	YR	4.50	55.00
83	NORMAN ROCKWELL-4TH EDITION 750QX300-7	YR	7.50	40.00
83	PEANUTS 450QX212-7	YR	4.50	29.50
83	SHIRT TALES 450QX214-9	YR	4.50	22.50
83	THE MUPPETS 450QX214-7	YR	4.50	49.50
84	BETSEY CLARK ANGEL 900QX462-4	YR	9.00	35.00
84	CURRIER & IVES 450QX250-1	YR	4.50	22.50
84	DISNEY 450QX250-4	YR	4.50	37.50

YR	NAME	LIMIT	ISSUE	QUOTE
84	KATYBETH 900QX463-1	YR	9.00	32.50
84	KIT 550QX453-4	YR	5.50	28.00
84	PEANUTS 450QX252-1	YR	4.50	32.50
84	SHIRT TALES 450QX252-4	YR	4.50	19.50
84	THE MUPPETS 450QX251-4	YR	4.50	34.50
85	A DISNEY CHRISTMAS 475QX271-2	YR	4.75	29.50
85	BETSEY CLARK 850QX508-5	YR	8.50	32.50
85	FRAGGLE ROCK HOLIDAY 475QX265-5	YR	4.75	22.50
85	HUGGA BUNCH 500QX271-5	YR	5.00	19.50
85	MERRY SHIRT TALES 475QX267-2	YR	4.75	19.50
85	PEANUTS 475QX266-5	YR	4.75	27.50
85	RAINBOW BRITE AND FRIENDS 475QX268-2	YR	4.75	27.50
86	KATYBETH 700QX435-3	YR	7.00	25.00
86	NORMAN ROCKWELL 475QX276-3	YR	4.75	24.50
86	PEANUTS 475QX276-6	YR	4.75	29.50
86	SHIRT TALES PARADE 475QX277-3	YR	4.75	19.50
81	KERMIT THE FROG 900QX424-2	YR	9.00	95.00
81	THE DIVINE MISS PIGGY 120QX425-5	YR	12.00	95.00
82	THE DIVINE MISS PIGGY 1200QX425-5	YR	12.00	95.00
82	KERMIT THE FROG 1100QX495-6	YR	11.00	95.00
84	MUFFIN 550QX442-1	YR	5.50	32.50
84	NORMAN ROCKWELL QX 251-1	YR	4.50	25.00
85	NORMAN ROCKWELL 475QX266-2	YR	4.75	34.50
86	THE STATUE OF LIBERTY 600QX384-3	YR	6.00	19.00
83	BETSEY CLARK 650QX404-7	YR	6.50	34.50
84	SNOOPY & WOODSTOCK 750QX439-1	YR	7.50	85.00
86	HEATHCLIFF 750QX436-3	YR	7.50	35.00
75	BETSEY CLARK 250QX163-1	YR	2.50	50.00
75	CURRIER & IVES (2) 250QX164-1	YR	2.50	50.00
75	CURRIER & IVES (2) 400QX137-1	YR	4.00	50.00
75	RAGGEDY ANN & RAGGEDY ANDY 400QX138-1	YR	4.00	95.00
75	RAGGEDY ANN 250QX165-1	YR	2.50	50.00
85	KIT THE SHEPHERD 575QX484-5	YR	5.75	29.50
85	MUFFIN THE ANGEL 575QX483-5	YR	5.75	24.00
85	SNOOPY AND WOODSTOCK 750QX491-5	YR	7.50	44.50
86	PADDINGTON BEAR 600QX435-6	YR	6.00	39.50
86	SNOOPY AND WOODSTOCK 800QX434-6	YR	8.00	42.50
B. SIEDLER			**REINDEER CHAMPS**	
87	DANCER 750QX480-9	YR	7.50	55.00
88	PRANCER 750QX405-1	YR	7.50	36.50
89	VIXEN 775QX456-2	YR	7.75	27.50
90	COMET 775QX443-3	YR	7.75	29.50
91	CUPID 775QX434-7	YR	7.75	29.50
92	DONNER 875QX528-4	YR	8.75	32.50
93	BLITZEN 875QX433-1	YR	8.75	22.50
L. SICKMAN			**ROCKING HORSE**	
88	DAPPLED 450QXM562-4	YR	4.50	42.75
89	PALOMINO 450QXM560-5	YR	4.50	27.50
90	PINTO 450QXM574-3	YR	4.50	22.50
91	GREY ARABIAN 450QXM563-7	YR	4.50	22.50
92	BROWN HORSE 450QXM5454	YR	4.50	17.50
93	APPALOOSA 450QXM511-2	YR	4.50	12.50
93	ROCKING HORSE 1075QX416-2	YR	10.75	34.50
94	WHITE 450QXM511-6	YR	4.50	11.50
K. CROW		**SANTA & HIS REINDEER COLLECTION**		
92	COMET & CUPID 495XPR973-7	YR	4.95	17.50
92	DASHER & DANCER 495XPR973-5	YR	4.95	24.50
92	DONDER & BLITZEN 495XPR973-8	YR	4.95	19.50
92	PRANCER & VIXEN 495XPR973-6	YR	4.95	17.50
92	SANTA & SLEIGH 495XPR973-9	YR	4.95	22.50
*			**SANTA & SPARKY**	
87	PERFECT PORTRAIT 1950QLX701-9	YR	19.50	75.00
88	ON WITH THE SNOW 1950QLX719-1	YR	19.50	45.00
		SANTA CLAUS-THE MOVIE		
85	SANTA CLAUS 675QX300-5	YR	6.75	12.00
85	SANTA'S VILLLAGE 675QX300-2	YR	6.75	12.00
		SARAH, PLAIN AND TALL COLLECTION, THE		
94	MRS. PARKLEY'S GENERAL STORE 795XPR945-1	YR	7.95	20.00
94	SARAH'S MAINE HOME 795XPR945-4	YR	7.95	21.50
94	SARAH'S PARIRIE HOME 795XPR945-3	YR	7.95	20.00
94	THE COUNTRY CHURCH 795XPR945-0	YR	7.95	21.50
94	THE HAYS TRAIN STATION 795XPR945-2	YR	7.95	21.50
*			**SEWN TRIMMERS**	
79	ANGEL MUSIC 200QX343-9	YR	2.00	24.50
79	MERRY SANTA 200QX342-7	YR	2.00	22.50
79	STUFFED FULL STOCKING 200QX341-9	YR	2.00	29.50

YR	NAME	LIMIT	ISSUE	QUOTE
79	THE ROCKING HORSE 200QX340-7	YR	2.00	19.00
P. ANDREWS		**SHOWCASE ORNAMENTS/CHRISTMAS LIGHTS**		
94	MOONBEAMS 1575QK111-6	YR	15.75	25.00
94	PEACEFUL VILLAGE 1575QK110-6	YR	15.75	25.00
94	HOME FOR THE HOLIDAYS 1575QK112-3	YR	15.75	25.00
94	MOTHER AND CHILD 1575QK112-6	YR	15.75	25.00
L. NORTON		**STAR TREK: THE NEXT GENERATION**		
94	KLING ON BIRD OF PREY 2400QLX738-6	YR	24.00	48.00
		TALE OF PETER RABBIT, THE		
94	BEATRIX POTTER 500QX244-3	YR	5.00	14.50
E. SEALE		**TENDER TOUCHES**		
91	FANFARE BEAR 875QX533-7	YR	8.75	19.50
91	GLEE CLUB BEARS 875QX496-9	YR	8.75	19.50
91	LOOK OUT BELOW 875QX495-9	YR	8.75	19.50
91	LOVING STITCHES 875QX498-7	YR	8.75	34.50
91	PLUM DELIGHTFUL 875QX497-7	YR	8.75	19.50
91	SNOW TWINS 875QX497-9	YR	8.75	19.50
93	DOWNHILL DASH	OP	23.00	23.00
93	GARDEN CAPERS	OP	20.00	20.00
93	HANDLING BIG THIRST	OP	21.00	21.00
93	LIBERTY MOUSE	OP	21.00	21.00
93	MR. REPAIR BEAR	OP	18.00	18.00
93	PATRIOT GEORGE	OP	25.00	25.00
93	SCULPTING SANTA	OP	20.00	20.00
93	STITCHING STARS	OP	21.00	21.00
93	TEETER FOR TWO	OP	23.00	23.00
94	"TENTS" SITUATIONS	OP	25.00	25.00
94	CHIPMUNK KETTLEDRUM	RT	18.00	21.00
94	CHRISTMAS PLAYERS	OP	25.00	25.00
94	EASTER STROLL	OP	21.00	21.00
94	LOVE AT FIRST SIGHT	OP	23.00	23.00
94	MAKING A SPLASH	OP	20.00	20.00
94	PLAYGROUND GO ROUND	OP	23.00	23.00
94	SOMETHING'S BREWING	OP	23.00	23.00
94	TEE FOR TWO	OP	23.00	23.00
94	THE OLD SWIMMING HOLE	9,500	60.00	60.00
94	WHERE'S THE FIRE	OP	25.00	25.00
*		**THIMBLE SERIES**		
79	A CHRISTMAS SALUTE 300QX131-9	YR	3.00	195.00
81	ANGEL 450QX413-5	YR	4.50	150.00
82	THIIMBLE-5TH EDITION 500QX451-3	YR	5.00	75.00
83	THIMBLE 6TH EDITION-ELF 500QX401-7	YR	5.00	39.50
86	PARTRIDGE-THIMBLE 9TH ED. 575QX406-6	YR	5.75	29.50
89	PUPPY 575QX455-2	YR	5.75	24.50
84	ANGEL 500QX430-4	YR	5.00	59.50
85	SANTA QX 472-5	YR	5.50	28.00
87	DRUMMER 575QX441-9	YR	5.75	29.50
J. LYLE		**TIME FOR LOVE**		
90	CARDINALS 475QX213-3	YR	4.75	22.50
D. PALMITER		**TINY TOON ADVENTURE**		
94	BABS BUNNY 575QXM411-6	YR	5.75	12.50
94	BUSTER BUNNY 575QXM516-3	YR	5.75	12.50
94	DIZZY DEVIL 575QXM413-3	YR	5.75	14.50
94	HAMTON 575QXM412-6	YR	5.75	12.50
94	PLUCKY DUCK 575QXM412-3	YR	5.75	12.50
*		**TRADITIONAL ORNAMENTS**		
84	A SAVIOR IS BORN 450QX254-1	YR	4.50	32.50
84	AMANDA DOLL 900QX432-1	YR	9.00	35.00
84	EMBROIDERED HEART 650QX421-7	YR	6.50	24.50
84	HOLIDAY FRIENDSHIP 1300QX445-1	YR	13.00	29.50
84	HOLIDAY STARBURST 500QX253-4	YR	5.00	22.50
84	OLD FASHIONED ROCKING HORSE 750QX346-4	YR	7.50	19.50
84	PEACE ON EARTH 750QX341-4	YR	7.50	29.50
84	SANTA 750QX458-4	YR	7.50	22.50
84	SANTA SULKY DRIVER 900QX436-1	YR	9.00	34.50
84	WHITE CHRISTMAS 1600QX905-1	YR	16.00	125.00
84	XMAS MEMORIES PHOTOHOLDER 650QX300-4	YR	6.50	24.50
85	CHRISTMAS TREATS 550QX507-5	YR	5.50	19.50
85	OLD-FASHIONED WREATH 750QX373-5	YR	7.50	19.50
86	HOLIDAY JINGLE BELL 1600QX404-6	YR	16.00	49.50
86	MEMORIES TO CHERISH PHOTO. QX 427-6	YR	7.50	45.00
87	SPECIAL MEMORIES PHOTOHOLDER 675QX464-7	YR	6.75	26.50
87	HEAVENLY HARMONY 1500QX465-9	YR	15.00	34.50
87	PROMISE OF PEACE 650QX374-9	YR	11.00	24.50
85	SANTA PIPE 950QX494-2	YR	9.50	24.50
84	CUCKOO CLOCK 1000QX455-1	YR	10.00	49.50

YR	NAME	LIMIT	ISSUE	QUOTE
85	THE SPIRIT OF SANTA CLAUS 2250QX498-5	YR	22.50	115.00
87	CURRIER & IVES: AMERICAN FARM 475QX282-9	YR	4.75	32.50
87	I REMEMBER SANTA 475QX278-9	YR	4.75	29.50
87	NORMAN ROCKWELL: XMAS SCENES 475QX282-7	YR	4.75	24.50
84	MADONNA AND CHILD 600QX344-1	YR	6.00	40.00
86	CHRISTMAS BEAUTY 600QX322-3	YR	6.00	12.00
86	GLOWING CHRISTMAS TREE 700QX428-6	YR	7.00	15.00
86	HEIRLOOM SNOWFLAKE 675QX515-3	YR	6.75	21.50
84	NEEDLEPOINT WREATH 650QX459-4	YR	6.50	14.50
85	CANDLE CAMEO 675QX374-2	YR	6.75	14.50
85	PEACEFUL KINGDOM 575QX373-2	YR	5.75	29.50
85	SEWN PHOTOHOLDER 700QX379-5	YR	7.00	35.00
86	THE MAGI 475QX272-6	YR	4.75	19.50
84	ALPINE ELF 600QX452-1	YR	6.00	39.50
84	GIFT OF MUSIC 1500QX451-1	YR	15.00	95.00
84	TWELVE DAYS OF CHRISTMAS 1500QX415-9	YR	15.00	125.00
87	JOYOUS ANGEL 775QX465-7	YR	7.75	27.50
84	CHICKADEE 600QX451-4	YR	6.00	39.50
84	EMBROIDERED STOCKING 650QX479-6	YR	6.50	22.50
84	HOLIDAY JESTER 1100QX437-4	YR	11.00	34.50
84	NOSTALGIC SLED 600QX442-4	YR	6.00	29.50
84	UNCLE SAM 600QX449-1	YR	6.00	49.50
85	NOSTALGIC SLED 600QX442-4	YR	6.00	29.50
86	BLUEBIRD 725QX428-3	YR	7.25	49.50
87	GOLDFINCH 700QX464-9	YR	7.00	95.00
87	CHRISTMAS KEYS 575QX473-9	YR	5.75	32.50
86	STAR BRIGHTENERS 600QX322-6	YR	6.00	17.50
			TREE TOPPER	
77	ANGEL TREE TOPPER 900HD230-2	YR	9.00	425.00
79	TIFFANY ANGEL TREE TOPPER 1000QX703-7	YR	10.00	39.50
84	ANGEL TREE TOPPER 2450QTT710-1	YR	24.50	49.50
86	A SHINING STAR 1750QLT709-6	YR	17.50	60.00
86	SANTA TREE TOPPER 1800QTO700-6	YR	18.00	42.50
*		**TWELVE DAYS OF CHRISTMAS**		
89	SIX GEESE A-LAYING 675QX381-2	YR	6.75	22.00
90	SEVEN SWANS-A-SWIMMING 675QX303-3	YR	6.75	29.50
91	EIGHT MAIDS-A-MILKING 675QX308-9	YR	6.75	25.00
94	ELEVEN PIPERS PIPING 695QX318-3	YR	6.95	17.50
87	FOUR COLLY BIRDS 650QX370-9	YR	6.50	39.50
88	FIVE GOLDEN RINGS 650QX371-4	YR	6.50	29.50
92	NINE LADIES DANCING 675QX303-1	YR	6.75	23.50
86	THREE FRENCH HENS 650QX378-6	YR	6.50	44.50
D. LEE		**WINDOWS OF THE WORLD**		
85	MEXICAN QX 490-2	YR	9.75	72.50
87	HAWAIIAN 1000QX482-7	YR	10.00	39.50
88	FRENCH 1000QX402-1	YR	10.00	34.50
89	GERMAN 1075QX462-5	YR	10.75	29.50
90	IRISH 1075QX463-6	YR	10.75	33.00
86	DUTCH 1000QX408-3	YR	10.00	64.50
B. SIEDLER		**WINNIE THE POOH COLLECTION**		
91	CHRISTOPHER ROBIN 975QX557-9	YR	9.75	35.00
91	KANGA AND ROO 975QX561-7	YR	9.75	52.50
91	RABBIT 975QX560-7	YR	9.75	30.00
91	TIGGER 975QX560-9	YR	9.75	125.00
91	WINNIE-THE-POOH 975QX556-9	YR	9.75	49.50
93	EEYORE 975-QX571-2	YR	9.75	19.50
93	KANGA AND ROO 975QX567-2	YR	9.75	22.50
93	OWL 975QX569-5	YR	9.75	19.50
93	RABBIT 975QX570-2	YR	9.75	19.50
93	TIGGER AND PIGLET 975QX570-5	YR	9.75	49.50
93	WINNIE THE POOH 975QX571-5	YR	9.75	29.50
B. SIEDLER		**WINNIE-THE-POOH COLLECTION**		
92	OWL 975QX561-4	YR	9.75	32.50
P. ANDREWS		**WIZARD OF OZ COLLECTION, THE**		
94	COWARDLY LION, THE 995QX544-6	YR	9.95	25.00
94	DOROTHY AND TOTO 1095QX543-3	YR	10.95	45.00
94	SCARECROW 995QX543-6	YR	9.95	27.50
94	TIN MAN 995QX544-3	YR	9.95	27.50
*		**WOOD CHILDHOOD**		
89	TRUCK 775QX459-5	YR	7.75	24.50
86	REINDEER 750QX407-3	YR	7.50	32.50
87	HORSE 750QX441-7	YR	7.50	26.50
*		**YARN ORNAMENTS**		
73	ANGEL 125XHD78-5	YR	1.25	26.50
73	BLUE GIRL 125XHD85-2	YR	1.25	24.50
73	BOY CAROLER 125XHD83-2	YR	1.25	29.50

YR	NAME	LIMIT	ISSUE	QUOTE
73	CHOIR BOY 125XHD80-5	YR	1.25	29.50
73	ELF 125XHD79-2	YR	1.25	27.50
73	GREEN GIRL 125XHD84-5	YR	1.25	24.50
73	LITTLE GIRL 125XHD82-5	YR	1.25	29.50
73	MR. SANTA 125XHD74-5	YR	1.25	27.50
73	MR. SNOWMAN 125XHD76-5	YR	1.25	29.50
73	MRS. SANTA 125XHD75-2	YR	1.25	24.50
73	MRS. SNOWMAN 125XHD77-2	YR	1.25	29.50
73	SOLDIER 100XHD81-2	YR	1.25	29.50
74	ANGEL 150QX103-1	YR	1.50	29.50
74	ELF 150QX101-1	YR	1.50	27.50
74	MRS. SANTA 150QX100-1	YR	1.50	24.50
74	SANTA 150QX105-1	YR	1.50	24.50
74	SNOWMAN 150QX104-1	YR	1.50	27.50
74	SOLDIER 150QX102-1	YR	1.50	29.50
75	DRUMMER BOY 175QX123-1	YR	1.75	27.50
75	LITTLE GIRL 175QX126-1	YR	1.75	22.50
75	MRS. SANTA 175QX125-1	YR	1.75	24.50
75	RAGGEDY ANDY 175QX122-1	YR	1.75	45.00
75	RAGGEDY ANN 175QX121-1	YR	1.75	40.00
75	SANTA 175QX124-1	YR	1.75	24.50
76	CAROLER 175QX126-1	YR	1.75	24.50
76	DRUMMER BOY 175QX123-1	YR	1.75	27.50
76	MRS. SANTA 175QX125-1	YR	1.75	24.50
76	RAGGEDY ANDY 175QX122-1	YR	1.75	45.00
76	RAGGEDY ANN 175QX121-1	YR	1.75	40.00
76	SANTA 175QX124-1	YR	1.75	24.50
78	GREEN BOY 200QX123-1	YR	2.00	25.00
78	GREEN GIRL 200QX126-1	YR	2.00	22.50
78	MR. CLAUS 200QX340-3	YR	2.00	24.50
78	MRS. CLAUS 200QX125-1	YR	2.00	24.50
80	ANGEL 300QX162-1	YR	3.00	8.50
80	SANTA 300QX161-4	YR	3.00	8.50
80	SNOWMAN 300QX163-4	YR	3.00	8.50
80	SOLDIER 300QX164-1	YR	3.00	8.50
*		**YESTERYEARS COLLECTION**		
77	ANGEL 600QX172-2	YR	6.00	150.00
77	HOUSE 600QX170-2	YR	6.00	150.00
77	JACK-IN-THE-BOX 600QX171-5	YR	6.00	135.00
77	REINDEER 600QX173-5	YR	6.00	140.00
L. SICKMAN		**YULETIDE CENTRAL**		
94	LOCOMOTIVE 1895QX531-6	YR	18.95	49.50

HAMILTON GIFTS

M. HUMPHREY

		MAUD HUMPHREY BOGART ORNAMENTS		
89	SARAH H1367	19,500	35.00	38.00
90	CATHERINE H1366	19,500	35.00	38.00
90	GRETCHEN H1369	19,500	35.00	38.00
90	MICHELLE H1370	19,500	35.00	38.00
90	REBECCA H5513	19,500	35.00	38.00
90	VICTORIA H1365	19,500	35.00	38.00
91	CLEANING HOUSE 915084	OP	24.00	24.00
91	GIFT OF LOVE 915092	OP	24.00	24.00
91	MY FIRST DANCE 915106	OP	24.00	24.00
91	SARAH 915165	OP	24.00	24.00
91	SPECIAL FRIENDS 915114	OP	24.00	24.00
91	SUSANNA 915122	OP	24.00	24.00
92	HOLLIES FOR YOU 915726	YR	24.00	24.00

HAND & HAMMER

C. DEMATTEO

		HAND & HAMMER ANNUAL ORNAMENTS		
87	SILVER BELLS-737	YR	38.00	50.00
88	SILVER BELLS-792	YR	39.50	39.50
89	SILVER BELLS-843	YR	39.50	39.50
90	SILVER BELLS REV.-964	YR	39.00	39.00
90	SILVER BELLS-1080	YR	39.50	39.50
90	SILVER BELLS-865	YR	39.00	39.00
91	SILVER BELLS-1080	OP	39.50	39.50
92	SILVER BELLS-1148	4,100	39.50	39.50

C. DEMATTEO

		HAND & HAMMER ORNAMENTS		
80	ICICLE-009	490	25.00	30.00
81	GABRIEL WITH LIBERTY CAP-301	275	25.00	50.00
81	GABRIEL-320	SU	25.00	32.00
81	ROUNDEL-109	220	25.00	45.00
82	CARVED HEART-425	SU	29.00	48.00
82	FLEUR DE LYS ANGEL-343	320	28.00	35.00
82	MADONNA & CHILD-388	175	28.00	50.00

YR	NAME	LIMIT	ISSUE	QUOTE
82	STRAW STAR-448	590	25.00	40.00
83	CALLIGRAPHIC DEER-511	SU	25.00	29.00
83	CHERUB-528	295	29.00	50.00
83	DOVE-522	*	13.00	13.00
83	EGYPTIAN CAT-521	*	13.00	13.00
83	FIRE ANGEL-473	315	25.00	28.00-36.00
83	INDIAN-494	190	29.00	50.00
83	JAPANESE SNOWFLAKE-534	350	29.00	35.00
83	POLLOCK ANGEL-502	SU	35.00	50.00
83	SARGENT ANGEL-523	690	29.00	34.00
83	SUNBURST-543	*	13.00	50.00
83	WISE MAN-549	SU	29.00	36.00
84	BEARDSLEY ANGEL-398	OP	28.00	48.00
84	BIRD & CHERUB-588	*	13.00	30.00
84	BUNNY-582	*	13.00	30.00
84	CRESCENT ANGEL-559	SU	30.00	32.00
84	FREER STAR-553	*	13.00	30.00
84	IBEX-584	400	29.00	50.00
84	MANGER-601	SU	29.00	32.00
84	MORAVIAN STAR-595	OP	38.00	50.00
84	MT. VERNON WEATHERVANE-602	SU	32.00	39.00
84	NINE HEARTS-572	275	34.00	50.00
84	PINEAPPLE-558	SU	30.00	38.00
84	PRAYING ANGEL-576	SU	29.00	30.00
84	ROCKING HORSE-581	*	13.00	13.00
84	ROSETTE-571	220	32.00	50.00
84	USHS 1984 ANGEL-574	SU	35.00	50.00
84	WILD SWAN-592	SU	35.00	50.00
84	WREATH-575	*	13.00	30.00
85	ABIGAIL-613	500	32.00	50.00
85	ANGEL-607	225	36.00	50.00
85	ANGEL-612	217	32.00	50.00
85	ART DECO DEER-620	SU	34.00	38.00
85	AUDUBON BLUEBIRD-615	SU	48.00	60.00
85	AUDUBON SWALLOW-614	SU	48.00	60.00
85	BICYCLE-669	*	13.00	30.00
85	BUTTERFLY-646	SU	39.00	39.00
85	CAMEL-655	*	13.00	30.00
85	CAROUSEL PONY-618	*	13.00	13.00
85	CHERUB-642	815	37.00	37.00
85	CRANE-606	150	39.00	50.00
85	EAGLE-652	375	30.00	50.00
85	FAMILY-659	915	32.00	40.00
85	FRENCH QUARTER HEART-647	OP	37.00	36.00
85	GEORGE WASHINGTON-629	SU	35.00	39.00
85	GRASSHOPPER-634	OP	32.00	39.00
85	GUARDIAN ANGEL-616	1340	35.00	39.00
85	HALLEY'S COMET-621	432	35.00	50.00
85	HERALD ANGEL-641	SU	36.00	40.00
85	HOSANNA-635	715	32.00	50.00
85	LAFARGE ANGEL-658	SU	32.00	50.00
85	LIBERTY BELL-611	SU	32.00	40.00
85	MADONNA-666	227	35.00	50.00
85	MERMAID-622	SU	35.00	39.00
85	MILITIAMAN-608	460	25.00	30.00
85	MODEL A FORD-604	*	13.00	30.00
85	NUTCRACKER-609	510	30.00	50.00
85	OLD NORTH CHURCH-661	OP	35.00	39.00
85	PEACOCK-603	470	34.00	37.00
85	PIAZZA-653	SU	32.00	50.00
85	REINDEER-656	*	13.00	30.00
85	SAMANTHA-648	SU	35.00	36.00
85	SHEPHERD-617	1770	35.00	39.00
85	ST. NICHOLAS-670	*	13.00	30.00
85	TEDDY-637	SU	37.00	40.00
85	UNICORN-660	SU	37.00	37.00
85	USHS BLUEBIRD-631	SU	29.00	50.00
85	USHS MADONNA-630	SU	35.00	50.00
85	USHS SWALLOW-632	SU	29.00	50.00
86	ARCHANGEL-684	SU	29.00	30.00
86	BEAR CLAUS-692	*	13.00	13.00
86	CHRISTMAS TREE-708	*	13.00	13.00
86	HALLELUJAH-686	*	38.00	38.00
86	KRINGLE BEAR-723	*	13.00	30.00
86	LAFARGE ANGEL-710	SU	31.00	50.00
86	MOTHER GOOSE-719	OP	34.00	40.00

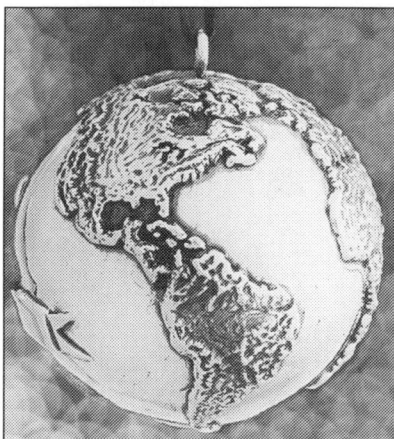

Hand & Hammer's Precious Planet *reminds us that we all have a responsibility to treat our earth as an invaluable treasure.*

Lenox ornaments are a tradition in their own right. This elegant porcelain Rocking Horse *would be perfect as a baby's first.*

With his bagful of goodies bulging at the seams, Cheerful Santa *gives a hearty wave to collectors of Hallmark Keepsake Ornaments.*

The Lladró Snowman *is certain to warm the hearts of ornament collectors.*

YR	NAME	LIMIT	ISSUE	QUOTE
86	NATIVITY-679	SU	36.00	38.00
86	NIGHTINGALE-716	SU	35.00	50.00
86	NUTCRACKER-681	1356	37.00	37.00
86	PHAETON-683	*	13.00	13.00
86	PRANCER-698	OP	38.00	38.00
86	SALEM LAMB-712	SU	32.00	40.00
86	SANTA SKATES-715	SU	36.00	36.00
86	SNOWFLAKE-713	SU	36.00	40.00
86	TEDDY BEAR-685	SU	38.00	40.00
86	TEDDY-707	*	13.00	30.00
86	USHS ANGEL-703	SU	35.00	50.00
86	VICTORIAN SANTA-724	250	32.00	35.00
86	WINGED DOVE-680	SU	35.00	36.00
86	WREATH-714	SU	36.00	38.00
87	ANGEL WITH LYRE-750	SU	32.00	40.00
87	ART DECO ANGEL-765	SU	38.00	40.00
87	BUFFALO-777	SU	36.00	36.00
87	CAT-754	OP	37.00	37.00
87	CLIPPER SHIP-756	SU	35.00	35.00
87	DOVE-747	*	13.00	13.00
87	FIRST CHRISTMAS-771	*	13.00	13.00
87	HUNTING HORN-738	OP	37.00	37.00
87	MINUTEMAN-776	SU	35.00	40.00
87	NOEL-731	OP	38.00	38.00
87	OLD IRONSIDES-767	OP	35.00	39.00
87	PEGASUS-745	*	13.00	13.00
87	REINDEER-752	OP	38.00	38.00
87	RIDE A COCK HORSE-757	SU	34.00	39.00
87	SANTA AND SLEIGH-751	SU	32.00	40.00
87	SANTA-741	*	13.00	13.00
87	SNOW QUEEN-746	SU	35.00	39.00
87	SNOWMAN-753	825	38.00	38.00
87	STOCKING-772	*	13.00	13.00
87	SWEETHEART STAR-740	SU	39.50	39.50
87	USHS GLORIA ANGEL-748	SU	39.00	50.00
88	ANGEL-797	*	13.00	13.00
88	ANGEL-818	SU	32.00	40.00
88	BANK-812	400	40.00	40.00
88	BOSTON STATE HOUSE	OP	34.00	40.00
88	BUGGY-817	*	13.00	13.00
88	CABLE CAR-848	OP	38.00	38.00
88	CAROUSEL HORSE-811	2150	34.00	34.00
88	CHRISTMAS TREE-798	*	13.00	13.00
88	CONN. STATE HOUSE-833	OP	38.00	38.00
88	CORONADO-864	OP	38.00	38.00
88	DOVE-786	112	36.00	50.00
88	DRUMMER BEAR-773	*	13.00	13.00
88	EIFFEL TOWER-861	225	38.00	40.00
88	FIRST CHRISTMAS-842	*	13.00	13.00
88	JACK IN THE BOX-789	SU	39.50	39.50
88	LOCKET BEAR-844	*	25.00	25.00
88	MADONNA-787	600	35.00	35.00
88	MADONNA-809	15	39.00	50.00
88	MADONNA-815	SU	39.00	50.00
88	MAGI-788	SU	39.50	39.50
88	NATIVITY-821	SU	32.00	39.00
88	NIGHT BEFORE CHRISTMAS COL.-841	10,000	160.00	160.00
88	OLD KING COLE-824	SU	34.00	39.00
88	RABBIT-816	*	13.00	13.00
88	SANTA WITH SCROLL-814	250	34.00	37.00
88	SKATERS-790	SU	39.50	39.50
88	SLEIGH-834	OP	34.00	38.00
88	STAR OF THE EAST-785	SU	35.00	35.00
88	STAR-806	311	13.00	150.00
88	STAR-854	275	32.00	35.00
88	STOCKING BEAR-835	*	13.00	13.00
88	STOCKING-774	*	13.00	13.00
88	STOCKING-827	*	13.00	13.00
88	THUMBELINA-803	SU	35.00	40.00
88	US CAPITOL-820	OP	38.00	40.00
89	1989 BARNESVILLE BUGGY-950	*	13.00	13.00
89	1989 NUTCRACKER-872	1790	38.00	38.00
89	1989 SANTA-856	1715	35.00	35.00
89	1989 USHS ANGEL-901	SU	38.00	38.00
89	BUGLE BEAR-935	*	12.00	12.00
89	GOOSE-857	650	37.00	37.00

YR	NAME	LIMIT	ISSUE	QUOTE
89	INDEPENDENCE HALL-908	OP	38.00	38.00
89	JACK IN THE BOX BEAR-936	*	12.00	12.00
89	L&T UGLY DUCKLING-917	SU	38.00	38.00
89	MFA ANGEL WITH TREE-906	SU	36.00	42.00
89	MFA DURER SNOWFLAKE-907	2000	36.00	42.00
89	MFA LAFARGE ANGEL SET-937	SU	98.00	98.00
89	MFA NOEL-905	SU	36.00	42.00
89	PRESIDENTIAL SEAL-858	500	39.00	39.00
89	STOCKING BEAR-95	*	12.00	12.00
89	STOCKING WITH TOYS-956	*	12.00	12.00
89	SWAN BOAT-904	OP	38.00	38.00
89	VICTORIAN HEART-954	*	13.00	13.00
90	1990 PETER RABBIT-1018	4315	39.50	39.50
90	1990 SANTA-869	2250	38.00	38.00
90	1990 SNOWFLAKE-1033	1415	36.00	38.00
90	1990 USHS ANGEL-1061	SU	39.00	39.00
90	ANGEL WITH HORN-939	*	*	*
90	ANGEL WITH STAR-871	OP	38.00	38.00
90	ANGEL WITH VIOLIN-1024	SU	39.00	39.00
90	ANGELS-1039	SU	36.00	36.00
90	BEARDSLEY ANGEL-1040	SU	34.00	34.00
90	BLAKE ANGEL-961	*	36.00	36.00
90	CARDINALS-870	OP	39.00	39.00
90	CAROUSEL HORSE-866	1915	38.00	38.00
90	CARRIAGE-960	*	13.00	13.00
90	CAT ON PILLOW-915	*	13.00	13.00
90	CHRISTMAS SEAL-931	*	25.00	25.00
90	CHURCH-921	OP	37.00	37.00
90	CLOWN WITH DOG-958	*	13.00	13.00
90	COCKATOO-969	*	13.00	13.00
90	COLONIAL CAPITOL-965	OP	39.00	39.00
90	CONESTOGA WAGON-1027	OP	38.00	38.00
90	COVERED BRIDGE-920	OP	37.00	37.00
90	CURRIER & IVES VICTORIAN VILLAGE-923	2000	140.00	140.00
90	DUCKLINGS-1114	OP	38.00	38.00
90	ELK-1023	*	13.00	13.00
90	EMBER-1124	120	*	*
90	FARMHOUSE-919	OP	37.00	37.00
90	FATHER CHRISTMAS-970	SU	36.00	36.00
90	FERREL'S ANGEL 1990-1084	*	15.00	15.00
90	FIRST BAPTIST ANGEL-997	200	35.00	35.00
90	FIRST CHRISTMAS BEAR-940	SU	35.00	35.00
90	FLOPSY BUNNIES-995	SU	39.50	39.50
90	FLORIDA STATE CAPITOL-1044	2000	39.50	39.50
90	GEORGIA STATE CAPITOL-1042	2000	39.50	39.50
90	GOOSE & WREATH-868	OP	37.00	37.00
90	GOVERNOR'S PALACE-966	OP	39.00	39.00
90	HEART ANGEL-959	SU	39.00	39.00
90	JEMIMA PUDDLEDUCK-1020	*	30.00	30.00
90	JEREMY FISHER-992	OP	39.50	39.50
90	JOY-1047	SU	39.00	39.00
90	JOY-867	1140	36.00	36.00
90	K. GREENAWAY WINDOW-924	*	*	*
90	KOALA SAN DIEGO ZOO-1095	OP	36.00	36.00
90	LANDING DUCK-1021	*	13.00	13.00
90	LIBERTY BELL-1028	OP	38.00	38.00
90	LOCOMOTIVE-1100	SU	39.00	39.00
90	MADONNA & CHILD-930	*	*	*
90	MERRY CHRISTMAS LOCKET-948	*	25.00	25.00
90	MILL-922	OP	37.00	37.00
90	MOLE & RAT WIND IN WILLOWS-944	OP	36.00	36.00
90	MONTPELIER-1113	OP	36.00	36.00
90	MOUSE WITH CANDY CANE-916	*	13.00	13.00
90	MRS. RABBIT-991	OP	39.50	39.50
90	NORTH CAROLINA STATE CAPITOL-1043	2000	39.50	39.50
90	OLD FASHIONED SANTA-971	SU	36.00	36.00
90	PATRIOTIC SANTA-972	SU	36.00	36.00
90	PEGASUS-1037	SU	35.00	35.00
90	PETER RABBIT LOCKET ORNAMENT-1019	*	30.00	30.00
90	PETER RABBIT-993	OP	39.50	39.50
90	PETER'S FIRST CHRISTMAS-994	SU	39.50	39.50
90	PRESIDENTIAL HOMES-990	OP	350.00	350.00
90	SAN FRANCISCO ROW HOUSE-1071	OP	39.50	39.50
90	SAN FRANCISCO STREET-933	*	*	*
90	SANTA & REINDEER-929	395	39.00	43.00
90	SANTA IN BALLOON-973	SU	36.00	36.00

YR	NAME	LIMIT	ISSUE	QUOTE
90	SANTA IN THE MOON-941	SU	38.00	38.00
90	SANTA ON REINDEER-974	SU	36.00	36.00
90	SANTA UP TO DATE-975	SU	36.00	36.00
90	SOUTH CAROLINA STATE CAPITOL-1045	2000	39.50	39.50
90	STEADFAST TIN SOLDIER-1050	SU	36.00	36.00
90	TEDDY BEAR LOCKET-949	*	25.00	25.00
90	TEDDY BEAR WITH HEART-957	*	13.00	13.00
90	THE BOSTON LIGHT-1032	OP	39.50	39.50
90	TOAD WIND IN WILLOWS-945	OP	38.00	38.00
90	WHITE TAIL DEER-1022	*	13.00	13.00
91	1991 SANTA-1056	OP	38.00	38.00
91	ALICE IN WONDERLAND-1159	OP	140.00	140.00
91	ALICE-1119	OP	39.00	39.00
91	ANGEL WITH HORN-1026	OP	32.00	32.00
91	APPLEY DAPPLY-1091	OP	39.50	39.50
91	CAROUSEL HORSE-1025	OP	38.00	38.00
91	COLUMBUS-1140	1500	39.00	39.00
91	COW JUMPED OVER THE MOON-1055	SU	38.00	38.00
91	FIR TREE-1145	OP	39.00	39.00
91	I LOVE SANTA-998	OP	36.00	36.00
91	LARGE JEMIMA PUDDLEDUCK-1083	OP	60.00	49.50
91	LARGE PETER RABBIT-1116	OP	49.50	49.50
91	LARGE TAILOR OF GLOUCESTER-1117	OP	49.50	49.50
91	MAD TEA PARTY-1120	OP	39.00	39.00
91	MFA SNOWFLAKE 1991-1143	OP	36.00	36.00
91	MOMMY & BABY KANGAROO-1078	OP	36.00	36.00
91	MOMMY & BABY KOALA BEAR-1077	OP	36.00	36.00
91	MOMMY & BABY PANDA BEAR-1079	OP	36.00	36.00
91	MOMMY & BABY SEAL-1075	OP	36.00	36.00
91	MOMMY & BABY WOLVES-1076	OP	36.00	36.00
91	MRS. RABBIT 1991-1086	OP	39.50	39.50
91	NATIVITY-1118	OP	38.00	38.00
91	NUTCRACKER-1151	OP	49.50	49.50
91	OLIVERS ROCKING HORSE-1085	OP	37.00	37.00
91	PAUL REVERE-1158	OP	39.00	39.00
91	PETER RABBIT WITH BOOK-1093	OP	39.50	39.50
91	PIG ROBINSON-1090	OP	39.50	39.50
91	PRECIOUS PLANET-1142	2000	120.00	120.00
91	QUEEN OF HEARTS-1122	OP	39.00	39.00
91	TAILOR OF GLOUCESTER-1087	OP	39.50	39.50
91	THE VOYAGES OF COLUMBUS-1141	1500	39.00	39.00
91	USHS ANGEL 1991-1139	OP	38.00	38.00
91	WAITING FOR SANTA-1123	OP	38.00	38.00
91	WHITE RABBIT-1121	OP	39.00	39.00
92	AMERICA AT PEACE-1245	2000	85.00	85.00
92	ANDREA-1163	OP	36.00	36.00
92	ANGEL W/DOUBLE HORN-1212	2000	49.50	49.50
92	ANGEL-1213	2000	39.00	39.00
92	BOB & TINY TIM-1242	OP	36.00	36.00
92	CHOCOLATE POT-1209	OP	49.50	49.50
92	CHRISTMAS TREE & HEART-1162	OP	36.00	36.00
92	COWARDLY LION-1287	OP	36.00	36.00
92	DELLA ROBBIA ORNAMENT-1219	OP	39.00	39.00
92	DOROTHY-1284	OP	36.00	36.00
92	FAIRY TALE ANGLE-1222	OP	36.00	36.00
92	HEART OF CHRISTMAS-1301	OP	*	*
92	JEMIMA PUDDLEDUCK 1992-1167	OP	39.50	39.50
92	JESSOPS CLOCK-1308	OP	*	*
92	JOY-1164	OP	39.50	39.50
92	MARLEY'S GHOST-1243	OP	36.00	36.00
92	MFA SNOWFLAKE-1246	OP	39.00	39.00
92	MRS. CRATCHIT-1244	OP	36.00	36.00
92	MRS. RABBIT-1181	OP	39.50	39.50
92	NOAH'S ARK-1166	OP	36.00	36.00
92	PARROT-1233	OP	37.00	37.00
92	PRINCESS & THE PEA-1247	OP	39.00	39.00
92	REVERE TEAPOT-1207	OP	49.50	49.50
92	ROUND TEAPOT-1206	OP	49.50	49.50
92	SCARECROW-1286	OP	36.00	36.00
92	SCROOGE-1241	OP	36.00	36.00
92	ST. JOHN ANGEL-1236	10,000	39.00	39.00
92	ST. JOHN LION-1235	10,000	39.00	39.00
92	TIN MAN-1285	OP	36.00	36.00
92	UNICORN-1165	OP	36.00	36.00
87	NAPTIME-732	SU	32.00	32.00
87	SANTA STAR-739	SU	32.00	32.00

YR NAME	LIMIT	ISSUE	QUOTE
HELEN SABATTE DESIGNS INC.			
E. WEIRICK		**KIDDIE CAR CLASSICS**	
95 '37 STEELCRAFT AUBURN LUXURY	24,500	65.00	65.00
95 '50 TORPEDO	OP	50.00	50.00
95 '59 DELUXE KIDILLAC	OP	55.00	55.00
95 '61 CASEY JONES LOCOMOTIVE	OP	55.00	55.00
JAN HAGARA COLLECTABLES			
J. HAGARA		**ORNAMENTS**	
84 ANNE	TL	10.00	38.00-125.00
84 JENNY	TL	10.00	60.00-85.00
84 JIMMY	TL	10.00	114.00-225.00
84 LISA	TL	10.00	40.00
J. HAGARA		**VICTORIAN CHILDREN**	
84 ANNE	RT	10.00	125.00
84 BETSY	RT	10.00	50.00
84 JENNY	RT	10.00	125.00
84 JIMMY	RT	10.00	150.00
84 JODY	RT	10.00	45.00
84 LISA	RT	10.00	50.00
84 LYDIA	RT	10.00	45.00
84 VICTORIA	RT	10.00	125.00
85 CHRIS	RT	7.00	50.00
86 JILL	RT	15.00	30.00
86 NOEL	RT	10.00	50.00
87 AMANDA	RT	14.00	45.00
87 BRIAN	RT	14.00	45.00
87 CRISTINA	RT	14.00	30.00
87 HOLLY	RT	15.00	18.00
87 LAURIE	RT	14.00	30.00
87 MARC	RT	14.00	35.00
87 NIKKI	RT	10.00	50.00
87 STACY	RT	14.00	45.00
87 STEPHEN	RT	14.00	45.00
JOHN HINE STUDIOS LTD.			
D. WINTER		**CHRISTMAS ORNAMENTS**	
92 FAIRYTALE CASTLE	OP	15.00	15.00
92 FRED'S HOME	OP	15.00	15.00
92 SUFFOLK HOUSE	OP	15.00	15.00
92 TUDOR MANOR HOUSE	OP	15.00	15.00
D. WINTER		**DAVID WINTER ORNAMENTS**	
92 A CHRISTMAS CAROL	CL	15.00	25.00
92 FAIRYTALE CASTLE	YR	15.00	15.00
92 FRED'S HOME	YR	15.00	15.00
92 HOGMANY	CL	15.00	25.00
92 MISTER FEZZIWIG'S EMPORIUM	CL	15.00	25.00
92 SCROOGE'S COUNTING HOUSE	CL	15.00	140.00-240.00
92 SET	YR	60.00	100.00
92 SUFFOLK HOUSE	YR	15.00	15.00
92 TUDOR MANOR	YR	15.00	15.00
JUNE MCKENNA COLLECTIBLES INC.			
JUNE MCKENNA			
93 ANGEL OF PEACE-PINK	OP	30.00	30.00
93 ANGEL OF PEACE-WHITE	OP	30.00	30.00
93 CHRISTMAS TREAT	OP	30.00	30.00
93 ELF BERNIE	OP	30.00	30.00
93 FINAL NOTES	OP	30.00	30.00
93 OLD LAMPLIGHTER	OP	30.00	30.00
94 ELF RICKEY	OP	30.00	30.00
94 ELF TAMMY	OP	30.00	30.00
94 GUIDING LIGHT ANGEL-GREEN	OP	30.00	30.00
94 GUIDING LIGHT ANGEL-PINK	OP	30.00	30.00
94 GUIDING LIGHT ANGEL-WHITE	OP	30.00	30.00
94 NUTCRACKER	OP	30.00	30.00
94 PRIMITIVE	OP	16.00	17.00
94 QUICK AS A WINK	OP	16.00	17.00
94 RINGING IN CHRISTMAS	OP	30.00	30.00
94 SANTA WITH PIPE	OP	30.00	30.00
94 SANTA WITH SKIS	OP	30.00	30.00
94 SNOW SHOWERS	OP	30.00	30.00
94 WHISPERING	OP	16.00	17.00
J. MCKENNA		**FLATBACK ORNAMENTS**	
82 ANGEL WITH TOYS	CL	14.00	85.00
82 BABY BEAR, TEESHIRT	CL	11.00	60.00
82 CANDY CANE	CL	10.00	45.00

YR	NAME	LIMIT	ISSUE	QUOTE
82	COLONIAL MAN	CL	12.00	150.00
82	COLONIAL WOMAN	CL	12.00	150.00
82	KATE GREENAWAY BOY	CL	12.00	250.00-300.00
82	KATE GREENAWAY GIRL	CL	12.00	250.00-350.00
82	MAMA BEAR, BLUE CAP	CL	12.00	85.00
82	PAPA BEAR, RED CAPE	CL	12.00	85.00
82	SANTA WITH TOYS	CL	14.00	80.00
83	BABY	CL	11.00	60.00
83	BABY BEAR IN VEST	CL	11.00	50.00
83	FATHER BEAR IN SUIT	CL	12.00	75.00
83	GLORIA ANGEL	CL	14.00	450.00-500.00
83	GRANDMA	CL	12.00	65.00
83	GRANDPA	CL	12.00	65.00
83	MOTHER BEAR IN DRESS	CL	12.00	75.00
83	RAGGEDY ANDY	CL	12.00	75.00
83	RAGGEDY ANN	CL	12.00	75.00
83	ST. NICK WITH LANTERN	CL	14.00	75.00
84	ANGEL WITH HORN	CL	14.00	75.00
84	COUNTRY BOY	CL	12.00	70.00
84	COUNTRY GIRL	CL	12.00	70.00
84	MR. CLAUS	CL	14.00	52.00-80.00
84	MRS. CLAUS	CL	14.00	60.00
84	OLD WORLD SANTA	CL	14.00	65.00
85	AMISH MAN	CL	13.00	50.00
85	AMISH WOMAN	CL	13.00	50.00
85	BABY PIG	CL	11.00	60.00
85	BRIDE	CL	25.00	125.00
85	FATHER PIG	CL	12.00	75.00
85	GROOM	CL	25.00	125.00
85	MOTHER PIG	CL	12.00	75.00
85	PRIMITIVE SANTA	CL	17.00	85.00
86	AMISH BOY	CL	13.00	65.00
86	SANTA WITH BAG	CL	16.00	65.00
86	SANTA WITH BEAR	CL	14.00	*
86	SANTA WITH BELLS (BLUE)	CL	14.00	65.00
86	SANTA WITH BELLS (GREEN)	CL	14.00	60.00
88	1776 SANTA	CL	17.00	40.00
88	ELIZABETH, SILL SITTER	CL	*	60.00
88	GUARDIAN ANGEL	CL	16.00	40.00
88	SANTA WITH BOOK (BLUE & RED)	CL	17.00	40.00-110.00
88	SANTA WITH TOYS	CL	17.00	40.00
88	SANTA WITH WREATH	CL	17.00	40.00
89	GLORIOUS ANGEL	OP	17.00	17.00
89	SANTA WITH TREE	CL	17.00	40.00
89	WINKING SANTA	CL	17.00	40.00
90	ELF JEFFREY	CL	17.00	40.00
90	HARVEST SANTA	CL	17.00	40.00
90	HO HO HO	CL	17.00	40.00
91	BOY ANGEL	CL	20.00	20.00
91	ELF JOEY	OP	20.00	20.00
91	GIRL ANGEL	OP	20.00	20.00
91	SANTA WITH BANNER	OP	20.00	20.00
91	SANTA WITH LIGHTS, BLACK	OP	20.00	20.00
92	ELF SCOTTY	OP	25.00	25.00
92	NORTH POLE NEWS	OP	25.00	25.00
92	PRAYING ANGEL	OP	25.00	25.00
92	SANTA WITH BASKET	OP	25.00	25.00
92	SANTA WITH SACK	OP	25.00	25.00

KIRK STIEFF

	D. BACORN		COLONIAL WILLIAMSBURG	
83	SILVERPLATE TREETOP STAR	YR	29.50	29.50
87	SILVERPLATE ROCKING HORSE	OP	19.95	30.00
87	SILVERPLATE TIN DRUM	OP	19.95	30.00
88	SILVERPLATE LAMB	OP	19.95	22.00
88	SILVERPLATE UNICORN	YR	22.00	22.00
89	SILVERPLATE DOLL ORNAMENT	YR	22.00	22.00
	D. BACORN		KIRK STIEFF ORNAMENTS	
83	CHARLESTON LOCOMOTIVE	CL	17.50	19.95
84	UNICORN	CL	17.50	19.95
86	STERLING SILVER ICICLE	OP	35.00	50.00
89	SMITHSONIAN CAROUSEL HORSE	YR	50.00	50.00
89	SMITHSONIAN CAROUSEL SEAHORSE	YR	50.00	50.00
90	TOY SHIP	YR	23.00	23.00
	K. STIEFF	THE NUTCRACKER STAINED GLASS ORNAMENT		
86	CLARA'S GIFT	CL	17.50	17.50
86	SET OF FOUR	CL	69.95	39.95

YR	NAME	LIMIT	ISSUE	QUOTE
86	THE BATTLE	CL	17.50	17.50
86	THE NUTCRACKER PRINCE	CL	17.50	17.50
86	THE SUGAR PLUM FAIRY	CL	17.50	17.50

J. BARATA   **TWELVE DAYS OF CHRISTMAS**

YR	NAME	LIMIT	ISSUE	QUOTE
85	PARTRIDGE IN A PEAR TREE	YR	9.95	10.95
85	TWO TURTLE DOVES	YR	9.95	10.95
86	FOUR CALLING BIRDS	YR	9.95	10.95
86	THREE FRENCH HENS	YR	9.95	10.95
87	FIVE GOLDEN RINGS	YR	9.95	10.95
87	SIX GEESE A-LAYING	YR	9.95	10.95
88	EIGHT MAIDS A-MILKING	YR	9.95	10.95
88	SEVEN SWANS A-SWIMMING	YR	9.95	10.95
89	NINE LADIES DANCING	YR	10.95	10.95
89	TEN LORDS A-LEAPING	YR	10.95	10.95

KURT S. ADLER/SANTA'S WORLD

J. MOSTROM   **CHILDREN'S HOUR**

YR	NAME	LIMIT	ISSUE	QUOTE
95	ALICE IN WONDERLAND J5751	OP	22.50	22.50
95	BOW PEEP J5753	OP	27.00	27.00
95	CINDERELLA J5762	OP	28.00	28.00
95	LITTLE BOY BLUE J5755	OP	18.00	18.00
95	MISS MUFFET J5753	OP	27.00	27.00
95	MOTHER GOOSE J5754	OP	27.00	27.00
95	RED RIDING HOOD J5751	OP	22.50	22.50

J. MOSTROM   **CHRISTMAS IN CHELSEA**

YR	NAME	LIMIT	ISSUE	QUOTE
92	ALLISON SITTING IN CHAIR W2812	RT	25.50	25.50
92	ALLISON W2729	RT	21.00	21.00
92	AMANDA W2709	RT	21.00	21.00
92	AMY W2729	RT	21.00	21.00
92	CHRISTINA W2812	RT	25.50	25.50
92	CHRISTOPHER W2709	RT	21.00	21.00
92	DELPHINIUM W2728	OP	20.00	20.00
92	HOLLY HOCK W2728	OP	20.00	20.00
92	HOLLY W2709	RT	21.00	21.00
92	PEONY W2728	OP	20.00	20.00
92	ROSE W2728	OP	20.00	20.00
94	ALICE,MARGUERITE W2973	OP	28.00	28.00
94	GUARDIAN ANGEL W/BABY W2974	OP	31.00	31.00
95	EDMOND W/VIOLIN W3078	OP	32.00	32.00
95	JOSE W/VIOLIN W3078	OP	32.00	32.00
95	PAULINE W/VIOLIN W3078	OP	32.00	32.00

M. ROTHENBERG   **CORNHUSK MICE**

YR	NAME	LIMIT	ISSUE	QUOTE
93	BALLERINA CORNHUSK MICE W2700	RT	13.50	13.50
93	NUTCRACKER STE. FANTASY CORNHUSK MOUSE	RT	15.50	15.50
94	CLARA, PRINCE W2948	OP	16.00	16.00
94	COWBOY W2951	OP	18.00	18.00
94	DROSSELMEIR FAIRY, MOUSE KING W2949	OP	16.00	16.00
94	FATHER CHRISTMAS W2979	OP	18.00	18.00
94	FATHER CHRISTMAS W2982	OP	25.00	25.00
94	LITTLE POCAHONTAS, INDIAN BRAVE W2950	OP	18.00	18.00
95	ANGEL MICE W3088	OP	10.00	10.00
95	BABY'S FIRST MOUSE W3087	OP	10.00	10.00
95	MISS TAMMIE MOUSE W3086	OP	17.00	17.00
95	MR. JAMIE MOUSE W3086	OP	17.00	17.00
95	MRS. MOLLY MOUSE W3086	OP	17.00	17.00

*   **FABRICHE COLLECTION**

YR	NAME	LIMIT	ISSUE	QUOTE
92	HELLO LITTLE ONE! W1561	OP	22.00	22.00
92	HUGS AND KISSES W1560	OP	22.00	22.00
92	MERRY CHRISMOUSE W1565	RT	10.00	10.00
92	NOT A CREATURE WAS STIRRING W1563	OP	22.00	22.00
94	HOIDAY FLIGHT W1637	OP	40.00	40.00
92	CHRISTMAS IN THE AIR W1593	OP	35.50	35.50
93	HOMEWARD BOUND W1596	OP	27.00	27.00
93	MASTER TOYMAKER W1595	OP	27.00	27.00
93	PAR FOR THE CLAUS W1625	OP	27.00	27.00
93	SANTA W/LIST W1510	OP	20.00	20.00
94	ALL STAR SANTA W1665	OP	27.00	27.00
94	CHECKING HIS LIST W1634	OP	23.50	23.50
94	COOKIES FOR SANTA W1639	OP	28.00	28.00
94	FIREFIGHTING FRIENDS W1668	OP	28.00	28.00
94	SANTA'S FISHTALES W1666	OP	29.00	29.00
95	CAPTAIN CLAUS W1711	OP	25.00	25.00
95	STRIKE UP THE BAND W1710	OP	25.00	25.00
92	AN APRON FULL OF LOVE W1594	OP	27.00	27.00

J. MOSTROM   **INTERNATIONAL CHRISTMAS**

YR	NAME	LIMIT	ISSUE	QUOTE
94	CATHY, JOHNNY	OP	24.00	24.00
94	ESKIMO-ATOM UKPIK W2967	OP	28.00	28.000

YR	NAME	LIMIT	ISSUE	QUOTE
94	GERMANY-KATERINA,HANS W2969	OP	27.00	27.00
94	NATIVE AMERICAN-WHITE DOVE,LITTLE WOLF	RT	28.00	28.00
94	POLAND-MARISSA,HEDWIG W2965	OP	27.00	27.00
94	SCOTLAND-BONNIE, DOUGLAS W2966	OP	27.00	27.00
94	SPAIN-MARTA. MIGUEL W2968	OP	27.00	27.00
J. MOSTROM				**LITTLE DICKENS**
94	LITTLE BOB CRACHIT W2961	OP	30.00	30.00
94	LITTLE MARLEY'S GHOST W2964	OP	33.50	33.50
94	LITTLE MRS. CRACHIT W2962	OP	27.00	27.00
94	LITTLE SCROOGE IN BATHROBE W2959	OP	30.00	30.00
94	LITTLE SCROOGE IN OVERCOAT W2960	OP	30.00	30.00
94	LITTLE TINY TIM W2963	OP	22.50	22.50
* KSA/KORNOZJA				**POLONAISE**
94	ANGEL HEAD GP372	OP	18.00	18.00
94	ANGEL W/BELL GP396	OP	20.20	20.20
94	BEER GLASS GP366	OP	18.00	18.00
94	CARDINAL GP420	OP	18.00	18.00
94	CAT W/BALL GP390	OP	23.00	23.00
94	DINOSAURS GP397	OP	22.50	22.50
94	EGYPTIANS 12 PC. GP500	OP	200.00	200.00
94	GLASS ACORN GP342	OP	11.00	11.00
94	GLASS ANGEL GP309	OP	18.00	18.00
94	GLASS APPLE GP339	OP	11.00	11.00
94	GLASS CHURCH GP369	OP	18.00	18.00
94	GLASS CLOWN GP301	OP	13.50	13.50
94	GLASS CLOWN GP302	OP	22.50	22.50
94	GLASS CLOWN GP303	OP	22.50	22.50
94	GLASS DICE GP363	OP	18.00	18.00
94	GLASS DOLL GP377	OP	13.50	13.50
94	GLASS GNOME GP347	OP	18.00	18.00
94	GLASS KNIGHT GP304	OP	18.00	18.00
94	GLASS OWL GP328	OP	20.00	20.00
94	GLASS TOP GP359	OP	9.00	9.00
94	GLASS TURKEY GP326	OP	20.00	20.00
94	GUARDMAN GP407	OP	15.50	15.50
94	HOLY FAMILY GP371	OP	28.00	28.00
94	LOCOMOTIVE GP353	OP	22.50	22.50
94	MADONNA W/CHILD GP370	OP	22.50	22.50
94	MERLIN GP373	OP	20.00	20.00
94	MOOSE KING GP406	OP	20.00	20.00
94	NEFERTITI GP349	OP	25.00	25.00
94	NIGHT & DAY GP307	OP	22.50	22.50
94	NUTCRACKER GP404	OP	20.00	20.00
94	OLD FASHIONED CAR GP380	OP	13.50	13.50
94	PARROTT GP332	OP	15.50	15.50
94	PEACOCK GP323	OP	28.00	28.00
94	PEACOCK GP324	OP	18.00	18.00
94	PIERROT CLOWN GP405	OP	18.00	18.00
94	PUPPY GP333	OP	15.50	15.50
94	PYRAMID GP352	OP	22.50	22.50
94	ROCKING HORSE GP355	OP	22.50	22.50
94	ROCKING HORSE GP356	OP	22.50	22.50
94	SAINT NICK GP316	OP	28.00	28.00
94	SANTA BOOT GP375	OP	20.00	20.00
94	SANTA GP317	OP	22.50	22.50
94	SANTA HEAD GP315	OP	13.50	13.50
94	SANTA HEAD GP374	OP	18.00	18.00
94	SNOWMAN W/PARCEL GP313	OP	22.50	22.50
94	SNOWMAN W/SPECS GP312	OP	20.00	20.00
94	SPARROW GP329	OP	15.50	15.50
94	SPHINX GP350	OP	22.50	22.50
94	SWAN GP325	OP	20.00	20.00
94	TEDDY BEAR GP338	OP	15.50	15.50
94	TRAIN COACHES GP354	OP	15.50	15.50
94	TRAIN SET GP501	OP	90.00	90.00
94	TROPICAL FISH GP409	OP	22.50	22.50
94	TUTENKHAMEN GP348	OP	25.00	25.00
94	ZODIAC SUN GP381	OP	22.50	22.50
95	ALARM CLOCK GP452	OP	25.00	25.00
95	BLESSED MOTHER GP413	OP	22.50	22.50
95	CAT IN BOOT GP478	OP	28.00	28.00
95	CAT W/BOW GP446	OP	22.50	22.50
95	CEASAR GP422	OP	25.00	25.00
95	CHRIST CHILD GP414	OP	20.00	20.00
95	CHRISTMAS TREE GP461	OP	22.50	22.50
95	CLARA GP408	OP	20.00	20.00

YR	NAME	LIMIT	ISSUE	QUOTE
95	CLOWN HEAD GP460	OP	25.00	25.00
95	COWBOY HEAD GP462	OP	30.00	30.00
95	CROCODILE GP468	OP	28.00	28.00
95	EAGLE GP453	OP	28.00	28.00
95	EGYPTIAN SET 4 PC. GP500/4	OP	110.00	110.00
95	ELEPHANT GP	OP	28.00	28.00
95	FISH 4 PC. GP506	OP	110.00	110.00
95	HERR DROSSELMEIR GP465	OP	30.00	30.00
95	HOLY FAMILY 3 PC. GP504	OP	84.00	84.00
95	INDIAN GP463	OP	30.00	30.00
95	LOCOMOTIVE GP447	OP	28.00	28.00
95	NOAH'S ARK GP469	OP	25.00	25.00
95	NUTCRACKER SUITE 4 PC. GP507	OP	110.00	110.00
95	PETER PAN GP419	OP	22.50	22.50
95	PETER PAN SET 4 PC. GP503	OP	124.00	124.00
95	POLONAISE AFRO-AM. SANTA GP389/1	OP	25.00	25.00
95	POLONAISE CARDINAL GP473	OP	25.00	25.00
95	POLONAISE HOUSE GP455	OP	25.00	25.00
95	POLONAISE SANTA GP389	OP	25.00	25.00
95	ROMAN CENTURIAN GP427	OP	22.50	22.50
95	ROMAN SET 7 PC. GP402	OP	164.00	164.00
95	SAILING SHIP GP415	OP	30.00	30.00
95	SANTA GP442	OP	25.00	25.00
95	SANTA ON GOOSE ON SLED GP479	OP	30.00	30.00
95	SHARK GP417	OP	18.00	18.00
95	ST. JOSEPH GP412	OP	22.50	22.50
95	TELEPHONE GP448	OP	25.00	25.00
95	TREASURE CHEST GP416	OP	20.00	20.00
95	WIZARD OF OZ 6 PC. GP508	5000	170.00	170.00
95	WIZARD OF OZ DOROTHY GP434	OP	25.00	25.00
95	WIZARD OF OZ LION GP433	OP	22.50	22.50
95	WIZARD OF OZ SCARECROW GP435	OP	25.00	25.00
95	WIZARD OF OZ TINMAN GP436	OP	25.00	25.00
95	CRECHE GP358	OP	28.00	28.00
95	DOVE ON BALL GP472	OP	25.00	25.00
95	GOOSE W/WREATH GP475	OP	25.00	25.00
95	HUMPTY DUMPTY GP477	OP	25.00	25.00
95	ICICLE SANTA GP474	OP	25.00	25.00
95	PARTIDGE GP467	OP	33.50	33.50
95	SANTA MOON GP454	OP	28.00	28.00
95	STAR SANTA GP470	OP	25.00	25.00
95	TURTLE DOVES GP471	OP	25.00	25.00
*		**SMITHSONIAN FABRICHE COLLECTION**		
92	FABRICHE SANTA BEAR W1563	OP	22.00	22.00
92	HOLIDAY DRIVE W1580	OP	30.00	30.00
92	HOLIDAY DRIVE W1580	OP	38.00	38.00
92	SANTA ON A BICYCLE W1547	OP	31.00	31.00
*		**STEINBACH ORNAMENT COLLECTION**		
92	THE KING'S GUARDS ES300	OP	27.00	27.00

LANCE CORP.
P.W. BASTON

			SEBASTIAN CHRISTMAS ORNAMENTS	
43	MADONNA OF THE CHAIR	CL	2.00	150.00-200.00
81	SANTA CLAUS	CL	28.50	30.00
82	MADONNA OF THE CHAIR (REISSUE)	CL	15.00	30.00-45.00
92	FINAL CHECK	OP	14.50	14.50
85	HOME FOR THE HOLIDAYS	CL	10.00	13.00-17.00
86	HOLIDAY SLEIGH RIDE	CL	10.00	14.00
87	SANTA	CL	10.00	12.50
88	DECORATING THE TREE	CL	12.50	14.00
89	FINAL PREPARATIONS FOR CHRISTMAS	CL	13.90	13.90
90	STUFFING THE STOCKINGS	CL	14.00	14.00
91	MERRY CHRISTMAS	OP	14.50	14.50

LAND OF LEGEND
R. MUSGRAVE

			POCKET DRAGONS	
90	ONE SIZE FITS ALL	OP	19.50	19.50
90	PUTTING ME ON THE TREE	5000	47.50	47.50

LENOX CHINA/CRYSTAL COLLECTION

*			ANNUAL BELL SERIES	
87	PARTRIDGE BELL	YR	45.00	45.00
88	ANGEL BELL	OP	45.00	45.00
89	ST. NICHOLAS BELL	OP	45.00	45.00
90	CHRISTMAS TREE BELL	OP	49.00	49.00
91	TEDDY BEAR BELL	YR	49.00	49.00
92	SNOWMAN BELL	YR	49.00	49.00

YR	NAME	LIMIT	ISSUE	QUOTE
*			**ANNUAL ORNAMENT**	
82	1982 ORNAMENT	YR	30.00	50.00-90.00
83	1983 ORNAMENT	YR	35.00	75.00
84	1984 ORNAMENT	YR	38.00	65.00
85	1985 ORNAMENT	YR	37.50	60.00
86	1986 ORNAMENT	YR	38.50	50.00
87	1987 ORNAMENT	YR	39.00	45.00
88	1988 ORNAMENT	YR	39.00	45.00
89	1989 ORNAMENT	YR	39.00	39.00
90	1990 ORNAMENT	YR	42.00	42.00
91	1991 ORNAMENT	YR	39.00	39.00
92	1992 ORNAMENT	YR	39.00	39.00
	BOTTICELLI		**CATHEDRAL PORTRAITS**	
91	15TH CENTURY MADONNA & CHILD	OP	29.00	29.00
91	16TH CENTURY MADONNA & CHILD	OP	29.00	29.00
*			**COMMEMORATIVES**	
89	BABY'S FIRST CHRISTMAS (DATED)	YR	22.50	25.00
89	FIRST CHRISTMAS TOGETHER (DATED)	YR	22.50	25.00
*			**CRYSTAL BALL ORNAMENTS**	
91	CRYSTAL ABBEY BALL	OP	45.00	45.00
91	CRYSTAL STARLIGHT BALL-BLUE	OP	45.00	45.00
91	CRYSTAL STARLIGHT BALL-GREEN	OP	45.00	45.00
91	CRYSTAL STARLIGHT BALL-RED	OP	45.00	45.00
92	CRYSTAL OPTIKA	OP	37.00	37.00
*			**DAYS OF CHRISTMAS**	
87	PARTRIDGE	OP	22.50	22.50
88	TWO TURTLE DOVES	OP	22.50	22.50
89	THREE FRENCH HENS	OP	22.50	22.50
90	FOUR CALLING BIRDS	OP	25.00	25.00
91	FIVE GOLDEN RINGS	OP	25.00	25.00
92	SIX GEESE A-LAYING	OP	25.00	25.00
*			**GOLDEN RENAISSANCE ANGELS**	
91	ANGEL WITH MANDOLIN	OP	25.00	25.00
91	ANGEL WITH TRUMPET	OP	25.00	25.00
91	ANGEL WITH VIOLIN	OP	25.00	25.00
*			**HOLIDAY HOMECOMING**	
88	HEARTH	CL	22.50	22.50
89	DOOR-DATED	OP	22.50	22.50
90	HUTCH-DATED	YR	25.00	25.00
91	WINDOW (DATED)	YR	25.00	25.00
92	STOVE (DATED)	YR	25.00	25.00
*			**LENOX CARVED ORNAMENTS**	
87	PORTRAIT WREATH	CL	21.00	21.00
89	GEORGIAN FRAME	OP	21.00	25.00
*			**LENOX CHINA ANNUAL ORNAMENTS**	
82	1982 ORNAMENT	YR	30.00	90.00
83	1983 ORNAMENT	YR	35.00	75.00
84	1984 ORNAMENT	YR	38.00	65.00
85	1985 ORNAMENT	YR	37.50	60.00
86	1986 ORNAMENT	YR	38.50	50.00
87	1987 ORNAMENT	YR	39.00	45.00
88	1988 ORNAMENT	YR	39.00	45.00
89	1989 ORNAMENT	YR	39.00	39.00
90	1990 ORNAMENT	YR	42.00	42.00
*			**LENOX CHRISTMAS KEEPSAKES**	
90	ROCKING HORSE	OP	42.00	42.00
90	SWAN	OP	42.00	42.00
91	SLEIGH	OP	42.00	42.00
92	FIRE ENGINE	OP	42.00	42.00
*			**LENOX CHRISTMAS VILLAGE**	
89	VILLAGE CHURCH-DATED	OP	39.00	39.00
90	VILLAGE INN-DATED	YR	39.00	39.00
91	VILLAGE TOWN HALL (DATED)	YR	39.00	39.00
92	SWEET SHOP (DATED)	YR	39.00	39.00
*			**LENOX CRYSTAL BALL ORNAMENTS**	
84	DEEP CUT BALL	YR	35.00	50.00
85	CUT BALL	YR	35.00	50.00
86	CUT BALL	YR	35.00	45.00
87	CUT BALL	YR	29.00	29.00
88	CHRISTMAS LIGHTS BALL	YR	30.00	30.00
89	CRYSTAL LIGHTS ORNAMENT	OP	30.00	30.00
89	STARLIGHT ORNAMENT	OP	34.00	34.00
*			**LENOX CRYSTAL ORNAMENTS**	
89	ANNUAL CHRISTMAS TREE	YR	26.00	26.00
89	BABY'S FIRST CHRISTMAS	YR	26.00	26.00
89	CANDLELIGHT BELL	OP	38.00	38.00

YR	NAME	LIMIT	ISSUE	QUOTE
89	CHRISTMAS LIGHTS TREE TOP ORNAMENT	OP	55.00	55.00
89	CRYSTAL ICICLE	OP	30.00	30.00
89	NATIVITY	OP	26.00	26.00
89	OUR FIRST CHRISTMAS	YR	26.00	26.00
89	SNOWFLAKE	OP	26.00	32.00
90	1990 CHRISTMAS TREE	YR	30.00	30.00
90	BABY'S FIRST CHRISTMAS-1990	YR	30.00	30.00
90	CANDY CANE	OP	30.00	30.00
90	CHRISTMAS GOOSE	OP	30.00	29.00
90	OUR FIRST CHRISTMAS-1990	YR	32.00	32.00
91	ABBEY TREETOPPER	OP	54.00	54.00
91	ANGEL PENDENT	OP	29.00	29.00
91	BABY'S FIRST CHRISTMAS-1991	YR	29.00	29.00
91	BIRD-BLUE	OP	29.00	29.00
91	BIRD-CLEAR	OP	29.00	29.00
91	BIRD-GREEN	OP	29.00	29.00
91	BIRD-RED	OP	29.00	29.00
91	CHRISTMAS STOCKING	OP	29.00	29.00
91	CHRISTMAS TREE-1991	YR	29.00	29.00
91	DOVE	OP	32.00	32.00
91	HERALD ANGEL-BLUE	OP	29.00	29.00
91	HERALD ANGEL-CLEAR	OP	29.00	29.00
91	HERALD ANGEL-GREEN	OP	29.00	29.00
91	HERALD ANGEL-RED	OP	29.00	29.00
91	OUR FIRST CHRISTMAS-1991	YR	29.00	29.00
91	SNOWMAN	OP	32.00	32.00
*				**NATIVITY**
89	JOSEPH	OP	21.00	21.00
89	MARY & CHILD	OP	21.00	21.00
90	BALTHAZAR	OP	22.00	22.00
90	GASPAR	OP	22.00	22.00
90	MELCHIOR	OP	22.00	22.00
*			**RENAISSANCE ANGEL TREETOPPER**	
89	ANGEL TREETOPPER	OP	100.00	100.00
*			**RENAISSANCE ANGELS**	
87	ANGEL WITH MANDOLIN	CL	21.00	21.00
87	ANGEL WITH TRUMPET	OP	21.00	21.00
87	ANGEL WITH VIOLIN	CL	21.00	21.00
*			**SANTA'S PORTRAITS**	
89	SANTA'S VISIT	OP	27.00	27.00
90	SANTA WITH GARLAND	OP	29.00	29.00
90	SANTA'S RIDE	OP	29.00	29.00
91	SANTA AND CHILD	OP	29.00	29.00
92	SANTA IN CHIMNEY	OP	29.00	29.00
*			**THE CHRISTMAS CAROUSEL**	
89	BLACK HORSE	OP	19.50	19.50
89	CAT	OP	19.50	19.50
89	CHRISTMAS CAROUSEL SET	OP	312.00	315.00
89	ELEPHANT	OP	19.50	19.50
89	GOAT	OP	19.50	19.50
89	HARE	OP	19.50	19.50
89	LION	OP	19.50	19.50
89	PALOMINO	OP	19.50	19.50
89	PINTO	OP	19.50	19.50
89	POLAR BEAR	OP	19.50	19.50
89	REINDEER	OP	19.50	19.50
89	SEA HORSE	OP	19.50	19.50
89	SWAN	OP	19.50	19.50
89	TIGER	OP	19.50	19.50
89	UNICORN	OP	19.50	19.50
89	WHITE HORSE	OP	19.50	19.50
89	ZEBRA	OP	19.50	19.50
90	CAMEL	OP	19.50	19.50
90	FROG	OP	19.50	19.50
90	GIRAFFE	OP	19.50	19.50
90	MEDIEVAL HORSE	OP	19.50	19.50
90	PANDA	OP	19.50	19.50
90	PIG	OP	19.50	19.50
90	ROOSTER	OP	19.50	19.50
90	SET OF 24	OP	468.00	468.00
90	ST. BERNARD	OP	19.50	19.50
*			**VICTORIAN HOMES**	
90	SHEFFIELD MANOR	OP	25.00	25.00
91	CAMBRIDGE MANOR	OP	25.00	25.00
*			**VICTORIAN LACE**	
91	CHRISTMAS TREE	OP	25.00	25.00

YR	NAME	LIMIT	ISSUE	QUOTE
91	FAN	OP	25.00	25.00
*				**YULETIDE**
85	CHRISTMAS TREE	OP	18.00	18.00
85	TEDDY BEAR	CL	18.00	18.00
89	ANGEL WITH HORN	OP	18.00	18.00
89	SANTA WITH TREE	OP	18.00	18.00
90	DOVE	OP	19.50	19.50
91	SNOWMAN	OP	19.50	19.50
92	GOOSE	OP	20.00	20.00
*				**YULETIDE EXPRESS**
88	LOCOMOTIVE	OP	39.00	39.00
89	CABOOSE-DATED	OP	39.00	90.00
90	PASSENGER-DATED	OP	39.00	39.00
91	DINING CAR (DATED)	YR	39.00	39.00
92	TENDER CAR (DATED)	YR	39.00	39.00

LILLIPUT LANE LTD.

YR	NAME	LIMIT	ISSUE	QUOTE
*				**CHRISTMAS ORNAMENT SERIES**
92	MISTLETOE COTTAGE	YR	27.50	27.50
93	ROBIN COTTAGE	RT	35.00	100.00
94	IVY HOUSE	*	37.50	50.00
95	PLUM COTTAGE	*	40.00	40.00

LLADRO

YR	NAME	LIMIT	ISSUE	QUOTE
*				
92	BABY'S FIRST L5922G	YR	55.00	55.00
92	CHRISTMAS MORNING L5940G	YR	97.50	97.50
92	ELF L5938G	YR	50.00	50.00
92	MRS. CLAUS L5939G	YR	55.00	55.00
92	OUR FIRST L5923G	YR	50.00	50.00
92	SANTA L5842G	YR	55.00	55.00
92	SNOWMAN L5841G	YR	50.00	50.00
93	1993 CHRISTMAS BALL	RT	54.00	60.00
93	1993 CHRISTMAS BELL	RT	39.50	45.00
94	1994 CHRISTMAS BALL	RT	55.00	65.00
94	1994 CHRISTMAS BELL	RT	39.50	45.00
94	ANGELIS VIOLINIST	RT	150.00	175.00
94	JOYFUL OFFERING	RT	245.00	275.00
*				*
*	HOLY FAMILY ORNAMENTS LL-5657	*	*	175.00
*	THREE KINGS ORNAMETNS LL-5729	*	*	150.00
*				**ANGEL ORCHESTRA**
91	HEAVENLY HARPIST	YR	135.00	135.00
92	ANGELIC CYMBALIST	YR	140.00	140.00
*				**ANNUAL ORNAMENT**
88	CHRISTMAS BALL L1603M	YR	60.00	100.00
88	CHRISTMAS BALL L5656M	YR	65.00	75.00-125.00
90	CHRISTMAS BALL L5730M	YR	70.00	70.00
91	CHRISTMAS BALL L5829M	YR	*	59.00-85.00
92	CHRISTMAS BALL L5914M	YR	52.00	52.00
*				**MINIATURE ORNAMENTS**
88	MINIATURE ANGELS L1604 (SET OF 3)	YR	75.00	150.00-250.00
89	HOLY FAMILY L5657G (SET OF 3)	YR	79.50	90.00-150.00
90	THREE KINGS L5729G (SET OF 3)	YR	87.50	87.50
91	HOLY SHEPHERDS L5809G	YR	*	100.00
*				**TREE TOPPER ORNAMENTS**
90	ANGEL TREE TOPPER (BLUE)	YR	115.00	115.00
91	ANGEL TREE TOPPER L5831G (PINK)	YR	115.00	160.00
92	ANGEL TREE TOPPER L5875G (GREEN)	YR	120.00	120.00

MIDWEST OF CANNON FALLS
L.R. SMITH

YR	NAME	LIMIT	ISSUE	QUOTE
94	FLYING WOODSMAN SANTA	2500	35.00	35.00
95	PARTRIDGE ANGEL ORNAMENT	3500	30.00	30.00
95	SANTA ON REINDEER ORNAMENT	3500	35.00	35.00
				MOUSEKINS
94	HEATHCLIFF GREY "TIME TO CELEBRATE"	YR	10.00	10.00

MISS MARTHA ORIGINALS
M. HOLCOMBE

YR	NAME	LIMIT	ISSUE	QUOTE
				ALL GOD'S CHILDREN
87	CAMEO D-1912	ST	24.00	100.00
87	DOLL D-1924 (SET OF 24)	ST	28.00	2080.00

ORREFORS
O. ALBERIUS

YR	NAME	LIMIT	ISSUE	QUOTE
				CHRISTMAS ORNAMENTS
84	DOVE	YR	30.00	45.00
85	ANGEL	YR	30.00	40.00
86	REINDEER	YR	30.00	35.00
87	SNOWMAN	YR	30.00	35.00

YR	NAME	LIMIT	ISSUE	QUOTE
88	SLEIGH	YR	30.00	35.00
89	CHRISTMAS TREE 1989	YR	35.00	35.00
90	HOLLY LEAVES AND BERRIES	YR	35.00	35.00
91	STOCKING	YR	40.00	40.00
92	STAR	YR	35.00	35.00
93	BELL	OP	35.00	35.00

PANTON/KRYSTONIA

			WORLD OF KRYSTONIA	
94	GRAFYNSSORPRISE	RT	19.00	23.00
94	WHAT KRYSTAL	RT	19.00	23.00

PFALTZGRAFF
B.B. RICHARDS

93	LITTLEST ANGEL	5000	12.50	15.00

RECO INTERNATIONAL
J. MCCLELLAND

			THE RECO ANGEL COLLECTION HANG-UPS	
87	ADORATION	OP	10.00	10.00
87	DEVOTION	OP	7.50	7.50
87	GLORIA	OP	7.50	7.50
87	HARMONY	OP	7.50	7.50
87	HOPE	OP	10.00	10.00
87	INNOCENCE	OP	7.50	7.50
87	JOY	OP	7.50	7.50
87	LOVE	OP	7.50	7.50
87	PEACE	OP	10.00	10.00
87	SERENITY	OP	10.00	10.00

J. MCCLELLAND

			THE RECO CLOWN COLLECTION HANG-UPS	
87	ARABESQUE	OP	8.00	8.00
87	BOW JANGLES	OP	8.00	8.00
87	CURLY	OP	8.00	8.00
87	HOBO	OP	8.00	8.00
87	RUFFLES	OP	8.00	8.00
87	SAD EYES	OP	8.00	8.00
87	SCAMP	OP	8.00	8.00
87	SPARKLES	OP	8.00	8.00
87	THE PROFESSOR	OP	8.00	8.00
87	TOP HAT	OP	8.00	8.00
87	WHOOPIE	OP	8.00	8.00
87	WINKIE	OP	8.00	8.00

S. KUCK

			THE RECO ORNAMENT COLLECTION	
88	BILLY	YR	15.00	15.00
88	LISA	YR	15.00	15.00
89	HEATHER	YR	15.00	15.00
89	TIMOTHY	YR	15.00	15.00
90	AMY	YR	15.00	15.00
90	JOHNNY	YR	15.00	15.00
90	PEACE ON EARTH	17,500	17.50	17.50

REED & BARTON

	*		12 DAYS OF CHRISTMAS	
83	PARTRIDGE IN A PEAR TREE	YR	16.50	20.00
83	TURTLE DOVES	YR	16.50	20.00
84	CALLING BIRDS	YR	18.50	20.00
84	FRENCH HENS	YR	18.50	20.00
85	GEESE A'LAYING	YR	20.00	20.00
85	GOLD RINGS	YR	20.00	20.00
86	MAIDS A'MILKING	YR	20.00	20.00
86	SWANS A'SWIMMING	YR	20.00	20.00
87	LADIES DANCING	YR	20.00	20.00
87	LORDS A'LEAPING	YR	20.00	20.00
88	DRUMMERS DRUMMING	YR	20.00	20.00
88	PIPERS PIPING	YR	20.00	20.00
	*	12 DAYS OF CHRISTMAS STERLING & LEAD CRYSTAL		
88	PARTRIDGE IN A PEAR TREE	YR	25.00	27.50
89	TWO TURTLE DOVES	YR	25.00	27.50
90	FRENCH HENS	YR	27.50	27.50
91	CALLING BIRDS	YR	27.50	27.50
92	FIVE GOLDEN RINGS	YR	27.50	27.50
	*		CAROUSEL HORSE	
88	GOLD COVERED-1988	YR	15.00	15.00
88	SILVERPLATE-1988	YR	13.50	13.50
89	GOLD COVERED-1989	YR	15.00	15.00
89	SILVERPLATE-1989	YR	13.50	13.50
90	GOLD COVERED-1990	YR	14.50	15.00
90	SILVERPLATE-1990	YR	13.50	13.50
91	GOLD COVERED-1991	YR	15.00	15.00

YR	NAME	LIMIT	ISSUE	QUOTE
91	SILVERPLATE-1991	YR	13.50	13.50
92	GOLD COVERED-1992	YR	15.00	15.00
92	SILVERPLATE-1992	YR	13.50	13.50
*				**CATHEDRALS**
90	GOTHIC	YR	12.50	12.50
90	MOORISH	YR	12.50	12.50
*				**CHRISTMAS CROSS**
71	24KT. GOLD OVER STERLING-V1971	YR	17.50	225.00
71	STERLING SILVER-1971	YR	10.00	300.00
72	24KT. GOLD OVER STERLING-V1972	YR	17.50	65.00-105.00
72	STERLING SILVER-1972	YR	10.00	125.00
73	24KT. GOLD OVER STERLING-V1973	YR	17.50	55.00-65.00
73	STERLING SILVER-1973	YR	10.00	60.00-75.00
74	24KT. GOLD OVER STERLING-V1974	YR	20.00	50.00-60.00
74	STERLING SILVER-1974	YR	12.95	35.00-60.00
75	24KT. GOLD OVER STERLING-V1975	YR	20.00	45.00-50.00
75	STERLING SILVER-1975	YR	12.95	35.00-55.00
76	24KT. GOLD OVER STERLING-V1976	YR	19.95	45.00-50.00
76	STERLING SILVER-1976	YR	13.95	55.00
77	24KT. GOLD OVER STERLING-V1977	YR	18.50	45.00-50.00
77	STERLING SILVER-1977	YR	15.00	35.00-55.00
78	24KT. GOLD OVER STERLING-V1978	YR	20.00	45.00-55.00
78	STERLING SILVER-1978	YR	16.00	60.00
79	24KT. GOLD OVER STERLING-V1979	YR	24.00	32.00-57.00
79	STERLING SILVER-1979	YR	20.00	60.00
80	24KT. GOLD OVER STERLING-V1980	YR	40.00	45.00-50.00
80	STERLING SILVER-1980	YR	35.00	60.00
81	24KT. GOLD OVER STERLING-V1981	YR	40.00	45.00
81	STERLING SILVER-1981	YR	35.00	45.00
82	24KT. GOLD OVER STERLING-V1982	YR	40.00	45.00
82	STERLING SILVER-1982	YR	35.00	53.00
83	24KT. GOLD OVER STERLING-V1983	YR	40.00	40.00-45.00
83	STERLING SILVER-1983	YR	35.00	50.00
84	24KT. GOLD OVER STERLING-V1984	YR	45.00	45.00
84	STERLING SILVER-1984	YR	35.00	45.00
85	24KT. GOLD OVER STERLING-V1985	YR	40.00	40.00
85	STERLING SILVER-1985	YR	35.00	40.00
86	24KT. GOLD OVER STERLING-V1986	YR	40.00	40.00
86	STERLING SILVER-1986	YR	38.50	38.50
87	24KT. GOLD OVER STERLING-V1987	YR	40.00	40.00
87	STERLING SILVER-1987	YR	35.00	35.00
88	24KT. GOLD OVER STERLING-V1988	YR	40.00	40.00
88	STERLING SILVER-1988	YR	35.00	35.00
89	24KT. GOLD OVER STERLING-V1989	YR	40.00	40.00
89	STERLING SILVER-1989	YR	35.00	35.00
90	24KT. GOLD OVER STERLING-V1990	YR	45.00	45.00
90	STERLING SILVER-1990	YR	40.00	40.00
91	24KT. GOLD OVER STERLING-V1991	YR	45.00	45.00
91	STERLING SILVER-1991	YR	40.00	40.00
92	24KT GOLD OVER STERLING-1992	YR	45.00	45.00
92	STERLING SILVER-1992	YR	40.00	40.00
*				**COLORS OF CHRISTMAS**
90	VICTORIAN HOUSE	YR	12.50	12.50
90	WREATH	YR	12.50	12.50
*				**DISNEY CHRISTMAS ORNAMENTS**
87	MICKEY	YR	25.00	40.00
88	MINNIE	YR	25.00	25.00
*				**FLORA OF CHRISTMAS**
90	POINSETTIA/SNOWDROP (PAIR)	YR	25.00	25.00
91	MISTLETOE & CHRISTMAS IVY	YR	25.00	25.00
*				**HOLLY BALL**
76	1976 SILVER PLATED	YR	13.95	50.00
77	1977 SILVER PLATED	YR	15.00	35.00
78	1978 SILVER PLATED	YR	15.00	35.00
79	1979 SILVER PLATED	YR	15.00	35.00
*				**HOLLY BELL**
80	1980 BELL	YR	22.50	40.00
80	GOLD PLATE BELL-V1980	YR	25.00	45.00
81	1981 BELL	YR	22.50	35.00
81	GOLD PLATE BELL-V1981	YR	27.50	35.00
82	1982 BELL	YR	22.50	35.00
82	GOLD PLATE BELL-V1982	YR	27.50	35.00
83	1983 BELL	YR	23.50	40.00
83	GOLD PLATE BELL-V1983	YR	30.00	35.00
84	1984 BELL	YR	25.00	30.00
84	GOLD PLATE BELL-V1984	YR	28.50	35.00

YR	NAME	LIMIT	ISSUE	QUOTE
85	1985 BELL	YR	25.00	35.00
85	GOLD PLATE BELL-V1985	YR	28.50	28.50
86	1986 BELL	YR	25.00	35.00
86	GOLD PLATE BELL-V1986	YR	28.50	32.50
87	1987 BELL	YR	27.50	30.00
87	GOLD PLATE BELL-V1987	YR	30.00	30.00
88	1988 BELL	YR	27.50	30.00
88	GOLD PLATE BELL-V1988	YR	30.00	30.00
89	1989 BELL	YR	27.50	27.50
89	GOLD PLATE BELL-V1989	YR	30.00	30.00
90	1990 BELL	YR	27.50	27.50
90	GOLD PLATE BELL-V1990	YR	30.00	30.00
91	1991 BELL	YR	27.50	27.50
91	GOLD PLATE BELL-V1991	YR	30.00	30.00
92	GOLD PLATE BELL-V1992	YR	30.00	30.00
92	SILVER PLATE BELL-1992	YR	27.50	27.50

RJB DESIGNS
RHONDA BRENNAN
CINDER CLAUS

YR	NAME	LIMIT	ISSUE	QUOTE
93	'93 CINDER CLAUS	1000	42.00	45.00
94	'94 CINDER CLAUS	1000	42.00	45.00

ROMAN INC.
I. SPENCER
CATNIPPERS

YR	NAME	LIMIT	ISSUE	QUOTE
88	CHRISTMAS MOURNING	OP	15.00	15.00
88	PUSS IN BERRIES	OP	15.00	15.00
88	RING A DING-DING	OP	15.00	15.00
89	BOW BRUMMEL	OP	15.00	15.00
89	HAPPY HOLIDAZE	OP	15.00	15.00
89	SANDY CLAWS	OP	15.00	15.00
90	FELIX NAVIDAD	OP	15.00	15.00
90	SOCK IT TO ME SANTA	OP	15.00	15.00
90	STUCK ON CHRISTMAS	OP	15.00	15.00
91	CHRISTMAS KNIGHT	OP	15.00	15.00
91	FAUX PAW	OP	15.00	15.00
91	MEOWY CHRISTMAS	OP	15.00	15.00
92	HOLLY DAYS ARE HAPPY DAYS	OP	15.00	15.00
92	PAWTRIDGE IN A PURR TREE	OP	15.00	15.00
92	SNOW BIZ	OP	15.00	15.00

E. SIMONETTI
FONTANINI ANNUAL CHRISTMAS ORNAMENT

YR	NAME	LIMIT	ISSUE	QUOTE
91	1991 ANNUAL (BOY)	YR	8.50	8.50
91	1991 ANNUAL (GIRL)	YR	8.50	8.50
92	1992 ANNUAL (BOY)	YR	8.50	8.50
92	1992 ANNUAL (GIRL)	YR	8.50	8.50

I. SPENCER
THE DISCOVERY OF AMERICA

YR	NAME	LIMIT	ISSUE	QUOTE
91	KITSTOPHER KOLUMBUS	1992	15.00	15.00
91	QUEEN KITSABELLA	1992	15.00	15.00

SARAH'S ATTIC
*
SANTAS OF THE MONTH ORNAMENTS

YR	NAME	LIMIT	ISSUE	QUOTE
88	APRIL MINI SANTA	CL	14.00	14.00-20.00
88	AUG. MINI SANTA	CL	14.00	14.00-20.00
88	DEC. MINI SANTA	CL	14.00	14.00-20.00
88	FEB. MINI SANTA	CL	14.00	14.00-20.00
88	JAN. MINI SANTA	CL	14.00	14.00-20.00
88	JULY MINI SANTA	CL	14.00	14.00-20.00
88	JUNE MINI SANTA	CL	14.00	14.00-20.00
88	MARCH MINI SANTA	CL	14.00	14.00-20.00
88	MAY MINI SANTA	CL	14.00	14.00-20.00
88	NOV. MINI SANTA	CL	14.00	14.00-20.00
88	OCT. MINI SANTA	CL	14.00	14.00-20.00
88	SEPT. MINI SANTA	CL	14.00	14.00-20.00

SCHMID
*
DISNEY ANNUAL

YR	NAME	LIMIT	ISSUE	QUOTE
85	SNOW BIZ	YR	8.50	20.00
86	TREE FOR TWO	YR	8.50	15.00
87	MERRY MOUSE MEDLEY	YR	8.50	10.00
88	WARM WINTER RIDE	YR	11.00	45.00
89	MERRY MICKEY CLAUS	YR	11.00	11.00
90	HOLLY JOLLY CHRISTMAS	YR	13.50	30.00
91	MICKEY & MINNIE'S ROCKIN' CHRISTMAS	YR	13.50	13.50

L. DAVIS
FRIENDS OF MINE

YR	NAME	LIMIT	ISSUE	QUOTE
89	SUN WORSHIPPERS	YR	32.50	35.00
90	SUNDAY AFTERNOON TREAT	YR	37.50	35.00
91	WARM MILK	YR	37.50	37.50
92	CAT AND JENNY WREN	YR	35.00	35.00

YR	NAME	LIMIT	ISSUE	QUOTE
	M. LILLEMOE		**KITTY CUCUMBER ANNUAL**	
89	RING AROUND THE ROSIE	YR	25.00	25.00
90	SWAN LAKE	YR	12.00	12.00
91	TEA PARTY	YR	12.00	24.00
	L. DAVIS		**LOWELL DAVIS COUNTRY CHRISTMAS**	
83	MAILBOX & GIFTS	YR	17.50	55.00-60.00
84	CAT IN BOOT	YR	17.50	28.00-44.00
85	WILBUR IN TROUGH	YR	17.50	60.00
86	CHURCH	YR	17.50	33.00-44.00
87	BLOSSOM IN WREATH	YR	19.50	46.00-59.00
88	WISTERIA IN WREATH	YR	19.50	33.00
89	WREN	YR	19.50	44.00
90	BARN	YR	19.50	20.00
91	CHURCH AT RED OAK II	YR	25.00	3025.00
92	BORN ON A STARRY NIGHT	YR	25.00	25.00
	L. DAVIS		**LOWELL DAVIS GLASS ORNAMENTS**	
86	CHRISTMAS AT RED OAK	YR	5.00	20.00
87	BLOSSOM'S GIFT	YR	5.50	10.00
88	HOPE MOM LIKES IT	YR	6.00	18.00
89	PETER AND THE WREN	YR	6.50	10.00
90	WINTERING DEER	YR	6.50	10.00
91	CHURCH AT RED OAK II	YR	7.50	28.00
92	BORN ON A STARRY NIGHT BALL	YR	7.50	7.50

SCUPLTURE WORKSHOP DESIGNS

YR	NAME	LIMIT	ISSUE	QUOTE
	F. KREITCHET			**ANNUAL**
85	THE RETURN OF THE CHRISTMAS COMET	7500	39.00	100.00
86	LIBERTY/PEACE	7500	49.00	150.00
87	CHRISTMAS AT HOME	2500	57.00	90.00
88	CHRISTMAS DOVES	2500	57.00	80.00
89	SANTA'S REINDEER	2500	60.00	75.00
90	JOYFUL ANGELS	2500	75.00	75.00
91	ANGEL & SHEPHERDS	2500	75.00	75.00
	F. KREITCHET		**ANNUAL-SPECIAL COMMEMORATIVE**	
87	THE BICENTENNIAL OF/U.S. CONSTITUTION	200	95.00	250.00
89	THE PRESIDENTIAL SIGNATURES	200	95.00	125.00
91	THE U.S. BILL OF RIGHTS	200	150.00	150.00
	F. KREITCHET			**SANTA SERIES**
92	FOREVER SANTA	2500	68.00	68.00

SEYMOUR MANN

YR	NAME	LIMIT	ISSUE	QUOTE
	JAIMY		**CHRISTMAS COLLECTION**	
89	FLAT RED SANTA ORNAMENT CJ-115R	OP	2.88	2.88
89	FLAT SANTA ORNAMENT CJ-115	OP	7.50	7.50
91	ELF WITH REINDEER CJ-422	CL	9.00	9.00
85	ANGEL WALL ORNAMENT CHRISTMAS-523	CL	12.00	12.00
86	CUPID HEAD ORNAMENT CHRISTMAS-53	OP	25.00	25.00
86	SANTA ORNAMENT CHRISTMAS-384	CL	7.50	7.50
89	CHRISTMAS CAT IN TEACUP CHRISTMAS-660	OP	13.50	13.50
	J. SAUERBREY		**GINGERBREAD CHRISTMAS COLLECTION**	
91	GINGERBREAD ANGEL CJ-411	CL	7.50	7.50
91	GINGERBREAD HOUSE CJ-416	CL	7.50	7.50
91	GINGERBREAD MAN CJ-415	CL	7.50	7.50
91	GINGERBREAD MOUSE/BOOT CJ-409	CL	7.50	7.50
91	GINGERBREAD MRS. CLAUS CJ-414	CL	7.50	7.50
91	GINGERBREAD REINDEER CJ-410	CL	7.50	7.50
91	GINGERBREAD SANTA CJ-408	CL	7.50	7.50
91	GINGERBREAD SLEIGH CJ-406	CL	7.50	7.50
91	GINGERBREAD SNOWMAN CJ-412	CL	7.50	7.50
91	GINGERBREAD TREE CJ-407	CL	7.50	7.50
	JAIMY		**VICTORIAN CHRISTMAS COLLECTION**	
93	COUPLE AGAINST WIND CJ-420	CL	15.00	15.00

SWAROVSKI AMERICA

YR	NAME	LIMIT	ISSUE	QUOTE
	*		**HOLIDAY ORNAMENTS**	
86	LARGE ANGEL/NOEL	YR	35.00	35.00
86	LARGE PARTRIDGE/MERRY CHRISTMAS	YR	35.00	35.00
86	MEDIUM ANGEL/JOYEUX NOEL	YR	22.50	22.50
86	MEDIUM BELL/MERRY CHRISTMAS	YR	22.50	22.50
86	MEDIUM SNOWFLAKE	YR	22.50	22.50
86	SMALL ANGEL/NOEL	YR	18.00	18.00
86	SMALL BELL/MERRY CHRISTMAS	YR	18.00	18.00
86	SMALL DOVE/PEACE	YR	18.00	18.00
86	SMALL HOLLY/MERRY CHRISTMAS	YR	18.00	18.00
86	SMALL SNOWFLAKE	YR	18.00	18.00
87	1987 HOLIDAY ETCHING-CANDLE	YR	20.00	35.00
88	1988 HOLIDAY ETCHING-WREATH	YR	25.00	25.00
89	1989 HOLIDAY ETCHING-DOVE	YR	35.00	35.00

Angelic Symbolist *is an elegant tree topper produced by Lladró.*

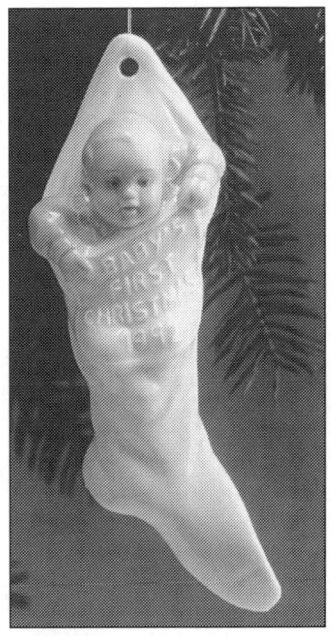

What child wouldn't grow up to treasure this Baby's First Christmas *dated ornament? Lladró is the maker.*

Is Mrs. Claus *ringing the dinner bell to call Santa or is it her turn to feed the reindeer? The porcelain ornament is produced by Lladró.*

Hallmark was the first to introduce a voice-recordable ornament. Messages of Christmas *enables a collector to record a special message in his own voice.*

YR	NAME	LIMIT	ISSUE	QUOTE
90	1990 HOLIDAY ETCHING	YR	25.00	25.00
91	1991 HOLIDAY ORNAMENT	YR	35.00	35.00

TOWLE SILVERSMITHS
*

			CHRISTMAS ANGEL	
91	1991 ANGEL	*	45.00	45.00
*			**REMEMBRANCE COLLECTION**	
90	OLD MASTER SNOWFLAKE-1990	*	45.00	45.00
91	OLD MASTER SNOWFLAKE-1991	*	45.00	45.00
92	OLD MASTER SNOWFLAKE-1992	*	45.00	45.00
*		**SONGS OF CHRISTMAS MEDALLIONS**		
78	SILENT NIGHT MEDALLION	25,000	35.00	60.00
79	DECK THE HALLS	5000	*	50.00
80	JINGLE BELLS	5000	52.50	60.00
81	HARK THE HEARLD ANGELS SING	5000	52.50	60.00
82	O CHRISTMAS TREE	2000	35.00	50.00
83	SILVER BELLS	2500	40.00	60.00
84	LET IT SNOW	6500	30.00	50.00
85	CHESTNUTS ROASTING ON OPEN FIRE	3000	35.00	50.00
86	IT CAME UPON A MIDNIGHT CLEAR	3500	35.00	45.00
87	WHITE CHRISTMAS	3500	35.00	45.00
*		**STERLING CHRISTMAS ORNAMENTS**		
89	FACETED BALL	OP	38.00	38.00
89	FLUTED BALL	OP	38.00	38.00
89	PLAIN BALL	OP	38.00	38.00
89	POMANDER BALL	OP	33.00	33.00
*		**STERLING FLORAL MEDALLIONS**		
83	CHRISTMAS ROSE	20,000	40.00	50.00
84	HAWTHORNE/GLASTONBURY THORN	20,000	40.00	50.00
85	POINSETTIA	14,000	35.00	40.00
86	LAUREL BAY	12,000	35.00	40.00
87	MISTLETOE	10,000	35.00	40.00
88	HOLLY	10,000	40.00	40.00
89	IVY	10,000	35.00	35.00
90	CHRISTMAS CACTUS	10,000	40.00	40.00
91	CHRYSANTHEMUM	*	40.00	40.00
92	STAR OF BETHLEHEM	*	40.00	40.00
*		**STERLING NATIVITY MEDALLION**		
88	ANGEL GABRIEL	7500	40.00	60.00
89	THE JOURNEY	7500	40.00	50.00
90	NO ROOM AT THE INN	7500	40.00	40.00
91	TIDINGS OF JOY	*	40.00	40.00
92	STAR OF BETHLEHEM	*	40.00	40.00
*		**STERLING TWELVE DAYS OF CHRISTMAS MEDALLIONS**		
71	PARTRIDGE IN PEAR TREE	15,000	20.00	700.00
72	TWO TURTLE DOVES	45,000	20.00	250.00
73	THREE FRENCH HENS	75,000	20.00	150.00
74	FOUR MOCKINGBIRDS	60,000	30.00	100.00
75	FIVE GOLDEN RINGS	60,000	30.00	65.00
76	SIX GEESE-A-LAYING	60,000	30.00	90.00
77	SEVEN SWANS-A-SWIMMING	60,000	35.00	50.00
78	EIGHT MAIDS-A-MILKING	60,000	37.00	50.00
79	NINE LADIES DANCING	40,000	*	50.00
80	TEN LORDS-A-LEAPING	25,000	76.00	50.00
81	ELEVEN PIPERS PIPING	25,000	50.00	50.00
82	TWELVE DRUMMERS DRUMMING	20,000	35.00	40.00
*		**TWELVE DAYS OF CHRISTMAS**		
79	SILVERPLATE ETCHED	1000	3.60	10.00
79	SILVERPLATE ETCHED	1000	3.60	10.00
79	SILVERPLATE ETCHED	1000	3.60	10.00
79	SILVERPLATE ETCHED	1000	3.60	10.00
79	SILVERPLATE ETCHED	1000	3.60	10.00
79	SILVERPLATE ETCHED	1000	3.60	10.00
79	SILVERPLATE ETCHED	1000	3.60	10.00
79	SILVERPLATE ETCHED	1000	3.60	10.00
79	SILVERPLATE ETCHED	1000	3.60	10.00
79	SILVERPLATE ETCHED	1000	3.60	10.00
79	SILVERPLATE ETCHED	1000	3.60	10.00
79	SILVERPLATE ETCHED	1000	3.60	10.00
88	GOLDPLATE ETCHED	2500	7.00	7.00
88	GOLDPLATE ETCHED	2500	7.00	7.00
88	GOLDPLATE ETCHED	2500	7.00	7.00
88	GOLDPLATE ETCHED	2500	7.00	7.00
88	GOLDPLATE ETCHED	2500	7.00	7.00
88	GOLDPLATE ETCHED	2500	7.00	7.00
88	GOLDPLATE ETCHED	2500	7.00	7.00
88	GOLDPLATE ETCHED	2500	7.00	7.00
88	GOLDPLATE ETCHED	2500	7.00	7.00

YR	NAME	LIMIT	ISSUE	QUOTE
88	GOLDPLATE ETCHED	2500	7.00	7.00
88	GOLDPLATE ETCHED	2500	7.00	7.00
88	GOLDPLATE ETCHED	2500	7.00	7.00
88	GOLDPLATE ETCHED	2500	7.00	7.00
91	PARTRIDGE IN WREATH	*	45.00	45.00
92	TWO TURTLEDOVES IN WREATH	*	45.00	45.00

UNITED DESIGN CORP.

	S. BRADFORD	ANGELS COLLECTION-TREE ORNAMENTS		
91	FRA ANGELICO DRUMMER, BLUE IBO-414	OP	20.00	20.00
91	FRA ANGELICO DRUMMER, IVORY IBO-420	OP	20.00	20.00
91	FRA ANGELICO DRUMMER, IVORY IBO-420	OP	20.00	20.00
91	GIRL CUPID W/ROSE, IVORY IBO-413	OP	15.00	15.00
91	VICTORIAN CUPID IBO-415	OP	15.00	15.00
92	ANGEL AND TAMBOURINE IBO-422	OP	20.00	20.00
92	ANGEL AND TAMBOURINE, IVORY IBO-425	OP	20.00	20.00
92	MARY AND DOVE IBO-424	OP	20.00	20.00
92	ST. FRANCIS AND CRITTERS IBO-423	OP	20.00	20.00
90	CRYSTAL ANGEL IBO-401	OP	20.00	20.00
90	CRYSTAL ANGEL, IVORY IBO-405	OP	20.00	20.00
90	ROSE OF SHARON IBO-402	OP	20.00	20.00
90	ROSE OF SHARON, IVORY IBO-406	OP	20.00	20.00
90	STAR GLORY IBO-403	OP	15.00	15.00
90	STAR GLORY, IVORY IBO-407	OP	15.00	15.00
90	VICTORIAN ANGEL IBO-404	OP	15.00	15.00
90	VICTORIAN ANGEL, IVORY IBO-408	OP	15.00	15.00
91	ANGEL WAIF, IVORY IBO-411	OP	15.00	15.00
91	PEACE DESCENDING IBO-418	OP	20.00	20.00
91	PEACE DESCENDING, IVORY IBO-412	OP	20.00	20.00
91	ROSETTI ANGEL IBO-416	OP	20.00	20.00
91	ROSETTI ANGEL, IVORY IBO-410	OP	20.00	20.00
91	VICTORIAN CUPID, IVORY IBO-409	OP	15.00	15.00

VICKILANE

	V. ANDERSON	LIL BLESSINGS		
94	BUNNY ANGEL #1610	OP	13.00	13.00
	V. ANDERSON	ORNAMENTS		
94	BUNNY ANGEL #1611	OP	13.00	13.00
94	BUNNY ANGEL #1612	OP	13.00	13.00
94	BUNNY ANGEL #1613	OP	13.00	13.00
94	BUNNY ANGEL #1614	OP	13.00	13.00
94	BUNNY ANGEL #1615	OP	13.00	13.00

WALLACE SILVERSMITHS

	*	24K GOLDPLATE SCULPTURES		
88	ANGEL	OP	15.99	15.99
88	CANDY CANE	OP	15.99	15.99
88	CHRISTMAS TREE	OP	15.99	15.99
88	DOVE	OP	15.99	15.99
88	NATIVITY SCENE	OP	15.99	15.99
88	SNOWFLAKE	OP	15.99	15.99
	*	ANNUAL SILVERPLATED BELLS		
71	1ST EDITION SLEIGH BELL	CL	12.95	1000.00
72	2ND EDITION SLEIGH BELL	CL	12.95	400.00
73	3RD EDITION SLEIGH BELL	CL	12.95	400.00
74	4TH EDITION SLEIGH BELL	CL	13.95	300.00
75	5TH EDITION SLEIGH BELL	CL	13.95	250.00
76	6TH EDITION SLEIGH BELL	CL	13.95	300.00
77	7TH EDITION SLEIGH BELL	CL	14.95	150.00
78	8TH EDITION SLEIGH BELL	CL	14.95	85.00
79	9TH EDITION SLEIGH BELL	CL	15.95	100.00
80	10TH EDITION SLEIGH BELL	CL	18.95	50.00
81	11TH EDITION SLEIGH BELL	CL	18.95	60.00
82	12TH EDITION SLEIGH BELL	CL	19.95	80.00
83	13TH EDITION SLEIGH BELL	CL	19.95	80.00
84	14TH EDITION SLEIGH BELL	CL	21.95	75.00
85	15TH EDITION SLEIGH BELL	CL	21.95	40.00
86	16TH EDITION SLEIGH BELL	CL	21.95	35.00
87	17TH EDITION SLEIGH BELL	CL	21.99	25.00
88	18TH EDITION SLEIGH BELL	CL	21.99	25.00
89	19TH EDITION SLEIGH BELL	CL	24.99	25.00
90	20TH EDITION SLEIGH BELL	YR	25.00	25.00
90	SPECIAL EDITION SLEIGH BELL, GOLD	YR	35.00	35.00
92	22ND EDITION SLEIGH BELL	YR	25.00	25.00
	*	ANTIQUE PEWTER BELLS		
89	REINDEER	OP	15.99	15.99
89	TEDDY BEAR	OP	15.99	15.99
89	TOY SOLDIER	OP	15.99	15.99

YR	NAME	LIMIT	ISSUE	QUOTE
90	CAROUSEL HORSE	OP	16.00	16.00
90	SANTA CLAUS	OP	16.00	16.00
*				

ANTIQUE PEWTER ORNAMENTS

YR	NAME	LIMIT	ISSUE	QUOTE
*	CANDY CANE	OP	9.99	9.99
*	DOVE	OP	9.99	9.99
*	GINGERBREAD HOUSE	OP	9.99	9.99
*	ROCKING HORSE	OP	9.99	9.99
*	TEDDY BEAR	OP	9.99	9.99
*	TOY SOLDIER	OP	9.99	9.99
89	ANGEL WITH CANDLES	OP	9.99	9.99
89	CHERUB WITH HORN	OP	9.99	9.99
89	SANTA	OP	9.99	9.99
89	TEDDY BEAR	OP	9.99	9.99
89	WREATH	OP	9.99	9.99
*				

CAMEO FRAME ORNAMENTS

YR	NAME	LIMIT	ISSUE	QUOTE
89	ANGEL	OP	14.99	14.99
89	CHRISTMAS BALL	OP	14.99	14.99
89	DINO	OP	14.99	14.99
89	ELEPHANT	OP	14.99	14.99
89	KITTEN	OP	14.99	14.99
89	SANTA	OP	14.99	14.99
89	SNOWMAN	OP	14.99	14.99
89	SOLDIER	OP	14.99	14.99
89	WREATH	OP	14.99	14.99
*				

CANDY CANES

YR	NAME	LIMIT	ISSUE	QUOTE
81	PEPPERMINT	CL	8.95	225.00
82	WINTERGREEN	CL	9.95	60.00
83	CINNAMON	CL	10.95	50.00
84	CLOVE	CL	10.95	50.00
85	DOVE MOTIF	CL	11.95	50.00
86	BELL MOTIF	CL	11.95	80.00
87	TEDDY BEAR	CL	12.95	50.00
88	CHRISTMAS ROSE	CL	13.99	40.00
89	CHRISTMAS CANDLE	CL	14.99	35.00
90	REINDEER	CL	16.00	20.00
*				

CATHEDRAL ORNAMENT

YR	NAME	LIMIT	ISSUE	QUOTE
88	1988-1ST EDITION	CL	24.99	24.99
89	1989-2ND EDITION	YR	24.99	24.99
90	1990-3RD EDITION	YR	25.00	25.00
*				

CHRISTMAS COOKIE ORNAMENT

YR	NAME	LIMIT	ISSUE	QUOTE
80	ANGEL	CL	5.95	20.00
80	SANTA	CL	5.95	10.00
80	SNOWMAN	CL	5.95	15.00
80	TREE	CL	5.95	15.00
81	BELL	CL	5.95	15.00
81	DRUM	CL	5.95	15.00
81	REINDEER	CL	5.95	15.00
82	DOVE	CL	5.95	20.00
82	MOUSE	CL	5.95	15.00
82	TRAIN	CL	5.95	15.00
83	BOY CAROLER	CL	5.95	15.00
83	GINGERBREAD HOUSE	CL	5.95	10.00
83	HUSKY	CL	5.95	20.00
83	JACK-IN-THE-BOX	CL	5.95	10.00
83	MRS. CLAUS	CL	5.95	10.00
83	ROCKING HORSE	CL	5.95	10.00
83	TOY SOLDIER	CL	5.95	10.00
84	CAROL SINGER	CL	6.95	15.00
84	HORN	CL	6.95	10.00
84	MOTHER AND CHILD	CL	6.95	15.00
84	PUPPY IN BOOT	CL	6.95	10.00
85	BOY SKATER	CL	10.95	10.00
85	CLOWN	CL	6.95	10.00
85	HOT-AIR BALLOON	CL	10.95	10.00
85	TEDDY BEAR	OP	6.95	10.00
85	UNICORN	CL	6.95	10.00
86	CARROUSEL HORSE	CL	6.95	20.00
86	DOG ON SLED	CL	6.95	20.00
86	DRESSED KITTEN	CL	6.95	15.00
86	GIRL HONEY BEAR	CL	6.95	10.00
86	GOOSE	CL	6.95	15.00
86	NEW DESIGN SNOWMAN	CL	6.95	20.00
86	PANDA	CL	5.95	10.00
86	PENGUIN	CL	6.95	10.00
86	SANTA HEAD	CL	6.95	10.00
86	TUGBOAT	CL	6.95	10.00

YR	NAME	LIMIT	ISSUE	QUOTE
87	ANGEL WITH HEART	OP	7.95	10.00
87	GIRAFFE	CL	7.95	10.00
87	POLAR BEAR	OP	7.95	10.00
87	SKI CABIN	CL	7.95	10.00
87	SNOWBIRD	CL	7.95	10.00
88	ANGEL	OP	8.99	10.00
88	BABY BEAR	OP	8.99	10.00
88	CHRISTMAS VILLAGE	OP	8.99	10.00
88	DRAGON	OP	8.99	10.00
88	ELEPHANT	OP	8.99	10.00
88	GOOSE	OP	8.99	10.00
88	POLAR BEAR	OP	8.99	10.00
88	TEDDY BEAR	OP	8.99	10.00
88	THE NIGHT BEFORE	OP	8.99	10.00
89	ROCKING HORSE	OP	9.99	10.00
89	SANTA	OP	9.99	10.00
89	SNOWBIRD	OP	9.99	10.00
*	GRANDE BAROQUE 12 DAY SERIES			
88	PARTRIDGE	CL	39.99	55.00
89	TWO TURTLE DOVES	YR	39.99	50.00
90	THREE FRENCH HENS	YR	40.00	40.00
*	STERLING MEMORIES			
89	BEAR WITH BLOCKS	OP	34.99	34.99
89	CAROLERS	OP	34.99	34.99
89	CHURCH	OP	34.99	34.99
89	DOVE	OP	34.99	34.99
89	DRUMMER BOY	OP	34.99	34.99
89	MOTHER & CHILD	OP	34.99	34.99
89	NATIVITY ANGEL	OP	34.99	34.99
89	REINDEER	OP	34.99	34.99
89	ROCKING HORSE	OP	34.99	34.99
89	SLEIGH	OP	34.99	34.99
89	SNOWFLAKE	OP	34.99	34.99
89	SNOWMAN	OP	34.99	34.99
*	STERLING MEMORIES-HAND ENAMELED WITH COLOR			
89	CANDY CANE	OP	34.99	34.99
89	CHURCH	OP	34.99	34.99
89	ELF WITH GIFT	OP	34.99	34.99
89	FIREPLACE	OP	34.99	34.99
89	KNEELING ANGEL	OP	34.99	34.99
89	SANTA	OP	34.99	34.99
89	SINGLE CANDLE	OP	34.99	34.99
89	TOY SOLDIER	OP	34.99	34.99
89	TRAIN	OP	34.99	34.99

WALT DISNEY CLASSICS COLLECTION

		COLLECTOR'S SOCIETY		
93	FLIGHT OF FANCY	*	35.00	50.00

WATERFORD WEDGWOOD USA

*	WATERFORD CRYSTAL CHRISTMAS ORNAMENTS			
78	1978 ORNAMENT	YR	25.00	60.00
79	1979 ORNAMENT	YR	28.00	50.00
80	1980 ORNAMENT	YR	28.00	44.50
81	1981 ORNAMENT	YR	28.00	44.50
82	1982 ORNAMENT	YR	28.00	44.50
83	1983 ORNAMENT	YR	28.00	39.00
84	1984 ORNAMENT	YR	28.00	39.00
85	1985 ORNAMENT	YR	28.00	39.00 .
86	1986 ORNAMENT	YR	28.00	31.00
87	1987 ORNAMENT	YR	29.00	29.00
88	1988 ORNAMENT	YR	30.00	30.00
89	1989 ORNAMENT	YR	32.00	32.00
*	WEDGWOOD CHRISTMAS ORNAMENTS			
88	JASPER CHRISTMAS TREE ORNAMENT	OP	20.00	28.00
89	JASPER ANGEL ORNAMENT	OP	25.00	28.00
90	JASPER SANTA CLAUS ORNAMENT	OP	28.00	28.00
91	JASPER WREATH ORNAMENT	OP	28.00	28.00
92	JASPER STOCKING ORNAMENT	OP	25.00	25.00

WILLITTS DESIGNS
C. SCHULTZ

		CERAMIC PEANUTS ORNAMENTS		
88	CHARLIE BROWN	SO	7.50	7.50
88	FLYING ACE	SO	7.50	7.50
88	JOE COOL	SO	7.50	7.50
88	LUCY	SO	7.50	7.50
88	SKATING SNOOPY	SO	7.50	7.50
88	SLEDDING SNOOPY	SO	7.50	7.50

YR	NAME	LIMIT	ISSUE	QUOTE
88	WOODSTOCK (BELL)	SO	7.50	7.50
*			**COCA-COLA SANTA**	
90	COCA-COLA SIX PACK ORNAMENT	OP	20.00	20.00
90	HAPPY HOLIDAYS COKE BOTTLE	OP	10.00	10.00
C. SCHULZ			**PEANUTS**	
90	CHARLIE BROWN SHEPERD ORNAMENT	SO	10.00	10.00
90	SNOOPY SHEPERD ORNAMENT	SO	10.00	10.00
C. SCHULTZ		**PEANUTS BASEBALL ORNAMENTS**		
88	CHARLIE BROWN	SO	10.00	10.00
88	LINUS	SO	10.00	10.00
88	LUCY	SO	10.00	10.00
88	PEPPERMINT PATTY	SO	10.00	10.00
88	SCHROEDER	SO	10.00	10.00
88	SNOOPY	SO	10.00	10.00
C. SCHULTZ		**WOODEN SNOOPY ORNAMENTS**		
88	SNOOPY-8438	SO	5.50	5.50
88	SNOOPY-8439	OP	5.50	5.50
88	SNOOPY-8440	SO	5.50	5.50

Plates

Susan K. Elliott

If the circle can be considered a form of perfection, then plate collectors enjoy a perfect form of art.

Since the first dated annual Christmas plates appeared in 1895 in Denmark, collectors have been happily anticipating the "next" edition to be released. Bing & Grondahl issued that first blue and white collector's plate, *Behind the Frozen Window*, at approximately 50 cents. Today, as the series celebrates its 100th anniversary of continuous production, that rare first edition sells for about $5,000.

Of course, these days not all plates are round, made of porcelain, or colored blue and white. New shapes include ovals, rounded squares, and even hearts. Today's plates may be sculpted in bas relief, incised, lighted or able to play a tune. They're made of wood, molded resin, pewter, crystal or porcelain. Subjects range from cute to elegant, with every possibility in between, and in a full range of colors and accent borders.

Until the 1960s, collector's plates continued to be made in Europe and produced only for Christmas. Royal Copenhagen introduced a second Danish Christmas series in 1908, and Rosenthal began a dated Christmas series in Germany in 1907.

Other key events in plate collecting history include:

- 1965: Lalique introduces a crystal plate, *Deux Oiseeaux (Two Birds)*
- 1969: Bing & Grondahl releases the first Mother's Day plate, *Dog and Puppies*, in blue and white
- 1969: Wedgwood issues *Windsor Castle* as first in a new Christmas series, produced in its famous blue and white jasperware
- 1970: Franklin Mint introduces original art by Norman Rockwell on a sterling silver plate, *Bringing Home the Tree*
- 1971: two Christmas series featuring art by Sister Maria Innocentia Hummel begin, with the Goebel Hummel issue, *Heavenly Angel*, later becoming one of the most valuable plates in the market.

The 1970s saw a boom in collecting of all types, spurred by the celebration of the U.S. Bicentennial in 1976. Historical subject plates abounded, and more and more makers, both American and European, focused on plates as a collectible. New artists entered the field, elevating the art and generating more attention to the artists themselves.

The development of the First International Plate Collectors Convention in 1975 provided a platform for the limited edition hobby to grow, and grow it has, expanding into many related types of art forms such as figurines, cottages, ornaments, dolls and graphics. The number of platemakers peaked in the 1980s, with production shifting to fewer, major producers such as The Bradford Exchange by the 1990s.

Plate collectors of the '90s are likely to collect other media besides plates, searching for graphics by favorite artists such as Thomas Kinkade, Sandra Kuck, Terry Redlin and Lena Liu to round out their collections.

As plate collecting enters its second hundred years, the art form remains an ever-changing and always growing collectible.

SUSAN K. ELLIOTT began enjoying plates just before attending the first international plate convention in 1975. She writes extensively about collectibles and is the executive director of the National Association of Limited Edition Dealers (NALED).

PLATES

YR	NAME	LIMIT	ISSUE	QUOTE

AMERICAN ARTISTS

D. ZOLAN — FAMILY TREASURES

YR	NAME	LIMIT	ISSUE	QUOTE
81	CORA'S RECITAL	18,500	39.50	39.50
82	CORA'S TEA PARTY	18,500	39.50	39.50
83	CORA'S GARDEN PARTY	18,500	39.50	39.50

F. STONE — FAMOUS FILLIES

YR	NAME	LIMIT	ISSUE	QUOTE
87	LADY'S SECRET	9500	65.00	65.00
88	GENUINE RISK	9500	65.00	65.00
88	RUFFIAN	9500	65.00	75.00
89	GO FOR THE WAND	9500	65.00	65.00
92	GO FOR THE WAND	9500	65.00	85.00

F. STONE — FRED STONE CLASSIC SERIES

YR	NAME	LIMIT	ISSUE	QUOTE
86	THE ETERNAL LEGACY	950	75.00	863.00
86	THE SHOE-8,000 WINS	9500	75.00	85.00
88	FOREVER FRIENDS	9500	75.00	75.00
89	ALYSHEBA	9500	75.00	75.00

F. STONE — MARE AND FOAL SERIES

YR	NAME	LIMIT	ISSUE	QUOTE
86	PASTURE PEST	12,500	49.50	125.00
86	TRANQUILITY	12,500	49.50	75.00
86	WATER TROUGH	12,500	49.50	150.00
87	THE ARABIANS	12,500	49.50	49.00

M. SEELEY — OLD FRENCH DOLL COLLECTION

YR	NAME	LIMIT	ISSUE	QUOTE
79	THE A.T.	5000	39.00	55.00
79	THE BRU	5000	39.00	200.00
79	THE E.J.	5000	39.00	75.00
80	ALEZANDRE	5000	39.00	45.00
81	THE MARQUE	5000	39.00	43.00
81	THE SCHMITT	5000	39.00	43.00

F. STONE — SPORT OF KINGS SERIES

YR	NAME	LIMIT	ISSUE	QUOTE
84	MAN O'WAR	9500	65.00	185.00
84	SECRETARIAT	9500	65.00	225.00-295.00
85	JOHN HENRY-MCCARRON	9500	65.00	105.00
86	SEATTLE SLEW	9500	65.00	65.00

F. STONE — THE HORSES OF FRED STONE

YR	NAME	LIMIT	ISSUE	QUOTE
82	ARABIAN MARE AND FOAL	9500	55.00	150.00
82	PATIENCE	9500	55.00	250.00
82	SAFE AND SOUND	9500	55.00	195.00
83	CONTENTMENT	9500	55.00	175.00

F. STONE — THE STALLION SERIES

YR	NAME	LIMIT	ISSUE	QUOTE
83	ANDALUSIAN	12,500	49.50	125.00
83	BLACK STALLION	12,500	49.50	125.00

AMERICAN ROSE SOCIETY

* — ALL-AMERICAN ROSE

YR	NAME	LIMIT	ISSUE	QUOTE
75	ARIZONA	9800	39.00	142.00
75	OREGOLD	9800	39.00	142.00
75	ROSE PARADE	9800	39.00	137.00
76	AMERICA	9800	39.00	135.50
76	CATHEDRAL	9800	39.00	135.50
76	SEASHELL	9800	39.00	135.50
76	YANKEE DOODLE	9800	39.00	135.50
77	DOUBLE DELIGHT	9800	39.00	115.00
77	FIRST EDITION	9800	39.00	115.00
77	PROMINENT	9800	39.00	115.00
78	CHARISMA	9800	39.00	89.00
78	COLOR MAGIC	9800	39.00	107.00
79	FRIENDSHIP	9800	39.00	79.00
79	PARADISE	9800	39.00	39.00
79	SUNDOWNER	9800	39.00	75.00
80	CHERISH	9800	49.00	80.00
80	HONOR	9800	49.00	55.00
80	LOVE	9800	49.00	80.00
81	BING CROSBY	9800	49.00	49.00
81	MARINA	9800	49.00	69.00
81	WHITE LIGHTNIN'	9800	49.00	69.00
82	BRANDY	9800	49.00	69.00
82	FRENCH LACE	9800	49.00	54.00
82	MON CHERI	9800	49.00	49.00
82	SHREVEPORT	9800	49.00	54.00
83	SUN FLARE	9800	49.00	69.00
83	SWEET SURRENDER	9800	49.00	55.00
84	IMPATIENT	9800	49.00	55.00
84	INTRIGUE	9800	49.00	58.00
84	OLYMPIAD	9800	49.00	55.00

YR	NAME	LIMIT	ISSUE	QUOTE
85	PEACE	9800	49.50	49.50
85	QUEEN ELIZABETH	9800	49.50	49.50
85	SHOWBIZ	9800	49.50	49.50

ANHEUSER-BUSCH INC.
M. URDAHL

YR	NAME	LIMIT	ISSUE	QUOTE
95	THIS BUD'S FOR YOU N4945	25-DAY	27.50	27.50

D. LANGENECKERT   **ARCHIVES PLATE SERIES**

YR	NAME	LIMIT	ISSUE	QUOTE
92	1893 COLUMBIAN EXPOSITION N3477	25-DAY	27.50	27.50
92	GANYMEDE N4004	25-DAY	45.00	45.00

D. LANGENECKERT   **CIVIL WAR SERIES**

YR	NAME	LIMIT	ISSUE	QUOTE
92	GENERAL GRANT N3478	25-DAY	45.00	45.00
93	GENERAL ROBERT E. LEE N3590	25-DAY	45.00	45.00
93	PRESIDENT ABRAHAM LINCOLN N3591	25-DAY	45.00	45.00

B. KEMPER   **HOLIDAY PLATE SERIES**

YR	NAME	LIMIT	ISSUE	QUOTE
89	WINTERS DAY N2295	RT	30.00	50.00-150.00
89	WINTERS EVENING N2295	RT	30.00	75.00
94	HOMETOWN HOLIDAY N4572	25-DAY	27.50	27.50
93	SPECIAL DELIVERY N4002	RT	27.50	27.50
90	AN AMERICAN TRADITION N2767	RT	30.00	35.00
90	AN AMERICAN TRADITION N2767	RT	30.00	75.00
91	THE SEASON'S BEST N3034	25,000	30.00	30.00
91	THE SEASON'S BEST N3034	25-DAY	30.00	30.00
92	A PERFECT CHRISTMAS N3440	25,000	27.50	27.50
92	A PERFECT CHRISTMAS N3440	25-DAY	27.50	27.50

M. URDAHL   **MAN'S BEST FRIEND SERIES**

YR	NAME	LIMIT	ISSUE	QUOTE
*	BUDDIES N2615	RT	30.00	40.00-45.00
90	BUDDIES N2615	RT	30.00	75.00
90	SIX PACK N3005	RT	30.00	30.00-105.00
90	SIX PACK N3005	RT	30.00	40.00
92	SOMETHING'S BREWING N3147	25,000	30.00	30.00
92	SOMETHING'S BREWING N3147	25-DAY	30.00	30.00
93	OUTSTANDING IN THEIR FIELD N4003	25-DAY	27.50	27.50

* *   **OLYMPIC TEAM SERIES**

YR	NAME	LIMIT	ISSUE	QUOTE
91	'92 OLYMPIC TEAM WINTER PLATE N3180	25-DAY	35.00	35.00
92	'92 OLYMPIC TEAM SUMMER PLATE N3122	25-DAY	35.00	35.00

ANNA-PERENNA
P. BUCKLEY MOSS

YR	NAME	LIMIT	ISSUE	QUOTE
93	FRIENDS FOREVER	5000	85.00	85.00
93	THE STORYTELLER	5000	100.00	100.00
94	SCHOOL DAYS	5000	85.00	85.00
94	VISITNG NURSE	5000	85.00	85.00

P. BUCKLEY MOSS   **AMERICAN SILHOUETTES FAMILY SERIES**

YR	NAME	LIMIT	ISSUE	QUOTE
81	FAMILY OUTING	5000	85.00	85.00
82	HOMEMAKERS QUILTING	SO	75.00	225.00-250.00
82	JOHN AND MARY	5000	75.00	125.00-200.00
84	LEISURE TIME	5000	75.00	150.00-225.00

P. BUCKLEY MOSS   **AMERICAN SILHOUETTES VALLEY SERIES**

YR	NAME	LIMIT	ISSUE	QUOTE
81	FROSTY FROLIC	SO	85.00	250.00-350.00
82	HAY RIDE	5000	85.00	85.00
83	SUNDAY RIDE	5000	75.00	200.00-250.00
84	MARKET DAY	5000	75.00	175.00-250.00

P. BUCKLEY MOSS   **AMERICAN SILHOUETTES-CHILDREN'S SERIES**

YR	NAME	LIMIT	ISSUE	QUOTE
81	FIDDLERS TWO	5000	75.00	200.00-225.00
83	MARY WITH THE LAMBS	5000	75.00	175.00-250.00
84	RING-AROUND-THE-ROSIE	5000	75.00	500.00-600.00
84	WAITING FOR TOM	5000	75.00	450.00-550.00

P. BUCKLEY MOSS   **AMERICAN WILDLIFE**

YR	NAME	LIMIT	ISSUE	QUOTE
93	SUMMER WEDDING	5000	100.00	100.00

P. BUCKELY MOSS   **ANNUAL CHRISTMAS PLATE**

YR	NAME	LIMIT	ISSUE	QUOTE
91	THE SNOWMAN	7500	80.00	80.00
84	NOEL, NOEL	SO	75.00	500.00-600.00
85	HELPING HANDS	SO	75.00	150.00-275.00
86	NIGHT BEFORE CHRISTMAS	SO	75.00	150.00-250.00
87	CHRISTMAS SLEIGH	5000	75.00	175.00-250.00
88	CHRISTMAS JOY	7500	75.00	75.00
89	CHRISTMAS CAROL	7500	80.00	95.00
90	CHRISTMAS EVE	7500	80.00	80.00
92	CHRISTMAS WARMTH	7500	85.00	85.00

P. BUCKLEY MOSS   **CHRISTMAS PLATE SERIES**

YR	NAME	LIMIT	ISSUE	QUOTE
93	JOY TO THE WORLD	7500	85.00	85.00
94	CHRISTMAS NIGHT	7500	85.00	85.00

P. BUCKLEY MOSS   **JOYFUL CHILDREN COLLECTION**

YR	NAME	LIMIT	ISSUE	QUOTE
93	DANCE OF THE BUTTERFLIES	5000	70.00	70.00
93	PURPLE UMBRELLA	5000	70.00	70.00
94	THE DOLL'S HOUSE	5000	70.00	70.00

YR	NAME	LIMIT	ISSUE	QUOTE
94	THE MEDICS	5000	70.00	70.00
P. BUCKLEY MOSS			**MOTHER'S LOVE SERIES**	
93	MOTHER'S WORLD	5000	80.00	80.00
94	MOTHER'S JOY	5000	80.00	80.00
P. BUCKLEY MOSS			**THE CELEBRATION SERIES**	
86	WEDDING JOY	SO	100.00	400.00
87	THE CHRISTENING	SO	100.00	125.00-250.00
88	THE ANNIVERSARY	5000	100.00	250.00-300.00
89	FAMILY REUNION	5000	100.00	100.00
P. BUCKLEY MOSS			**THE HEARTLAND SERIES**	
93	THE SCHOOLHOUSE	5000	90.00	90.00
T. KRUMEICH			**UNCLE TAD'S CATS**	
79	OLIVER'S BIRTHDAY	5000	75.00	260.00
80	PEACHES & CREAM	5000	75.00	90.00
81	PRINCESS AURORA	5000	80.00	100.00
81	WALTER'S WINDOW	5000	80.00	100.00

ANRI

YR	NAME	LIMIT	ISSUE	QUOTE
*			**ANRI FATHER'S DAY**	
72	ALPINE FATHER & CHILDREN	5000	35.00	100.00
73	ALPINE FATHER & CHILDREN	5000	40.00	95.00
74	CLIFF GAZING	5000	50.00	100.00
76	SAILING	5000	60.00	90.00
*			**ANRI MOTHER'S DAY**	
72	ALPINE MOTHER & CHILDREN	5000	35.00	50.00
73	ALPINE MOTHER & CHILDREN	5000	40.00	50.00
74	ALPINE MOTHER & CHILDREN	5000	50.00	55.00
75	ALPINE STROLL	5000	60.00	65.00
76	KNITTING	5000	60.00	65.00
*			**CHRISTMAS**	
79	MOSS GATHERERS	6000	135.00	135.00
80	WINTRY CHURCHGOING	6000	165.00	135.00
81	SANTA CLAUS IN TYROL	6000	165.00	200.00
82	THE STAR SINGERS	6000	165.00	170.00
83	UNTO US A CHILD IS BORN	6000	165.00	325.00
84	YULETIDE IN THE VALLEY	6000	165.00	185.00
71	ST. JAKOB IN GARDEN	10,000	37.50	75.00
72	PIPERS AT ALBEROBELLO	10,000	45.00	90.00
73	ALPINE HORN	10,000	45.00	400.00
74	YOUNG MAN AND GIRL	10,000	50.00	110.00
75	CHRISTMAS IN IRELAND	10,000	60.00	76.00
76	ALPINE CHRISTMAS	6000	65.00	160.00
77	LEGEND OF HELIGENBLUT	6000	65.00	120.00
78	KLOCKLER SINGERS	6000	80.00	105.00
85	GOOD MORNING, GOOD CHEER	6000	165.00	165.00
86	A GRODEN CHRISTMAS	6000	165.00	200.00
87	DOWN FROM THE ALPS	6000	195.00	250.00
88	CHRISTKINDL MARKT	6000	220.00	230.00
88	FLIGHT INTO EGYPT	6000	275.00	275.00
90	HOLY NIGHT	6000	300.00	310.00
*			**DISNEY FOUR STAR COLLECTION**	
89	MICKEY MINI PLATE	5000	40.00	45.00
90	MINNIE MINI PLATE	5000	40.00	45.00
91	DONALD MINI PLATE	5000	50.00	50.00
J. FERRANDIZ			**FERRANDIZ CHRISTMAS**	
72	CHRIST IN THE MANGER	2500	35.00	230.00
73	CHRISTMAS	*	40.00	225.00
74	HOLY NIGHT	*	50.00	100.00
75	FLIGHT INTO EGYPT	*	60.00	95.00
76	GIRL WITH FLOWERS	4000	65.00	185.00
76	TREE OF LIFE	*	60.00	60.00
78	LEADING THE WAY	4000	77.50	180.00
79	THE DRUMMER	4000	120.00	175.00
80	REJOICE	4000	150.00	160.00
81	SPREADING THE WORD	4000	150.00	150.00
82	THE SHEPHERD FAMILY	4000	150.00	150.00
83	PEACE ATTEND THEE	4000	150.00	150.00
J. FERRANDIZ			**FERRANDIZ MOTHER'S DAY SERIES**	
72	MOTHER SEWING	2500	35.00	200.00
73	ALPINE MOTHER & CHILD	1500	40.00	150.00
74	MOTHER HOLDING CHILD	1500	50.00	150.00
75	DOVE GIRL	1500	60.00	150.00
76	MOTHER KNITTING	1500	60.00	200.00
77	ALPINE STROLL	3000	65.00	125.00
78	THE BEGINNING	3000	75.00	150.00
79	ALL HEARTS	3000	120.00	170.00
80	SPRING ARRIVALS	3000	150.00	165.00

YR	NAME	LIMIT	ISSUE	QUOTE
81	HARMONY	3000	150.00	150.00
82	WITH LOVE	3000	150.00	150.00

J. FERRANDIZ   **FERRANDIZ WOODEN WEDDING PLATES**

YR	NAME	LIMIT	ISSUE	QUOTE
72	BOY AND GIRL EMBRACING	*	40.00	150.00
73	WEDDING SCENE	*	40.00	150.00
74	WEDDING	*	48.00	150.00
75	WEDDING	*	60.00	150.00
76	WEDDING	*	60.00	90.00-150.00

ARABIA ANNUAL
R. UOSIKKINEN   **KALEVALA**

YR	NAME	LIMIT	ISSUE	QUOTE
76	VAINAMOINEN'S SOWING	*	30.00	250.00
77	AINO'S FATE	*	30.00	35.00
78	LEMMINKAINEN'S CHASE	2500	39.00	44.00
79	KULLERVO'S REVENGE	YR	39.50	47.00
80	VAINAMOINEN'S RESCUE	YR	45.00	65.00
81	VAINAMOINEN'S MAGIC	YR	49.50	49.50
82	JOUKAHAINEN SHOOTS THE HORSE	YR	55.50	67.50
83	LEMMINKAINEN'S ESCAPE	YR	60.00	90.00
84	LEMMINKAINEN'S MAGIC FEATHERS	YR	49.50	93.00
85	LEMMINKAINEN'S GRIEF	YR	60.00	80.00
86	OSMATAR CREATING ALE	YR	60.00	80.00
87	VAINAMOINEN TRICKS ILMARINEN	YR	65.00	85.00
88	HEAR VAINAMOINEN WEEP	YR	69.00	115.00
89	FOUR MAIDENS	YR	75.00	87.00
90	ANNIKKA	YR	85.00	105.00
91	LEMMINKAIN'S MOTHER SAYS DON'T/WAR	YR	85.00	89.00

ARMSTRONG'S
R. SKELTON   **COMMEMORATIVE ISSUES**

YR	NAME	LIMIT	ISSUE	QUOTE
83	70 YEARS YOUNG	15,000	85.00	85.00
84	FREDDIE THE TORCHBEARER	15,000	62.50	62.50

L. DEWINNE   **FACES OF THE WORLD**

YR	NAME	LIMIT	ISSUE	QUOTE
88	CLARA (BELGIUM)	14-DAY	24.50	24.50
88	COLLETTE (FRANCE)	14-DAY	24.50	24.50
88	ERIN (IRELAND)	14-DAY	24.50	24.50
88	GRETA (AUSTRIA)	14-DAY	24.50	24.50
88	HEATHER (ENGLAND)	14-DAY	24.50	24.50
88	LUISA (SPAIN)	14-DAY	24.50	24.50
88	MARIA (ITALY)	14-DAY	24.50	24.50
88	TAMIKO (JAPAN)	14-DAY	24.50	24.50

R. SKELTON   **FREDDIE THE FREELOADER**

YR	NAME	LIMIT	ISSUE	QUOTE
79	FREDDIE IN THE BATHTUB	10,000	55.00	450.00
80	FREDDIE'S SHACK	10,000	55.00	300.00
81	FREDDIE ON THE GREEN	10,000	60.00	200.00
82	LOVE THAT FREDDIE	10,000	60.00	100.00

R. SKELTON   **FREDDIE'S ADVENTURES**

YR	NAME	LIMIT	ISSUE	QUOTE
82	BRONCO FREDDIE	15,000	60.00	62.50
82	CAPTAIN FREDDIE	15,000	60.00	150.00
83	SIR FREDDIE	15,000	62.50	62.50
84	GERTRUDE AND HEATHCLIFFE	15,000	62.50	70.00

W. LANTZ   **HAPPY ART SERIES**

YR	NAME	LIMIT	ISSUE	QUOTE
81	WOODY'S TRIPLE SELF-PORTRAIT	9000	39.50	39.50
81	WOODY'S TRIPLE SELF-PORTRAIT-SIGNED	1000	100.00	100.00
83	GOTHIC WOODY	9000	39.50	39.50
83	GOTHIC WOODY-SIGNED	1000	100.00	100.00
84	BLUE BOY WOODY	9000	39.50	39.50
84	BLUE BOY WOODY-SIGNED	1000	100.00	100.00

S. ETEM   **INFINITE LOVE**

YR	NAME	LIMIT	ISSUE	QUOTE
87	A PAIR OF DREAMS	14-DAY	24.50	24.50
87	KISS A LITTLE GIGGLE	14-DAY	24.50	24.50
87	ONCE UPON A SMILE	14-DAY	24.50	24.50
87	THE EYES SAY I LOVE YOU	14-DAY	24.50	24.50
88	BUNDLE OF JOY	14-DAY	24.50	24.50
88	GRINS FOR GRANDMA	14-DAY	24.50	24.50
88	LOVE GOES FORTH IN LITTLE FEET	14-DAY	24.50	24.50
89	A MOMENT TO CHERISH	14-DAY	24.50	24.50

A. D'ESTREHAN   **STATUE OF LIBERTY**

YR	NAME	LIMIT	ISSUE	QUOTE
86	DEDICATION	10,000	39.50	49.50
86	INDEPENDENCE	10,000	39.50	49.50
86	RE-DEDICATION	10,000	39.50	49.50
86	THE IMMIGRANTS	10,000	39.50	49.50

A. D'ESTREHAN   **THE CONSTITUTION SERIES**

YR	NAME	LIMIT	ISSUE	QUOTE
87	THE GREAT CHASE	10,000	39.50	39.50
87	U.S. CONSTITUTION VS. GUERRIERE	10,000	39.50	39.50
87	U.S. CONSTITUTION VS. JAVA	10,000	39.50	39.50
87	U.S. CONSTITUTION VS. TRIPOLI	10,000	39.50	39.50

YR	NAME	LIMIT	ISSUE	QUOTE
S. ETEM			THE MISCHIEF MAKERS	
86	BUCKLES	10,000	39.95	39.95
86	PUDDLES	10,000	39.95	39.95
87	TRIX	10,000	39.95	39.95
88	NAP	10,000	39.95	39.95
R. SKELTON			THE SIGNATURE COLLECTION	
86	ANYONE FOR TENNIS?	9000	62.50	62.50
86	ANYONE FOR TENNIS?-SIGNED	1000	125.00	650.00
87	IRONING THE WAVES	9000	62.50	62.50
87	IRONING THE WAVES-SIGNED	1000	125.00	175.00
88	THE CLIFFHANGER	9000	62.50	62.50
88	THE CLIFFHANGER-SIGNED	1000	150.00	150.00

ART WORLD OF BOURGEAULT

YR	NAME	LIMIT	ISSUE	QUOTE
R. BOURGEAULT			THE ENGLISH COUNTRYSIDE	
80	THE COUNTRY SQUIRE	1500	70.00	370.00
81	THE WILLOWS	1500	85.00	370.00
82	ROSE COTTAGE	1500	90.00	370.00
83	THATCHED BEAUTY	1500	95.00	370.00
R. BOURGEAULT		THE ENGLISH COUNTRYSIDE SINGLE ISSUES		
84	THE ANNE HATHAWAY COTTAGE	500	150.00	640.00
85	LILAC COTTAGE	500	125.00	350.00
87	SUFFOLK PINK	50	220.00	427.00
88	STUART HOUSE	50	325.00	571.00
89	LARK RISE	50	450.00	603.00
R. BOURGEAULT			THE ROYAL GAINSBOROUGH SERIES	
90	THE LISA-CAROLINE	*	65.00	65.00
91	A GAINSBOROUGH LADY	*	*	*
R. BOURGEAULT			THE ROYAL LITERARY SERIES	
85	THE JOHN BUNYAN COTTAGE	4500	60.00	90.00
87	THE THOMAS HARTY COTTAGE	4500	65.00	90.00
88	THE JOHN MILTON COTTAGE	4500	65.00	90.00
89	THE ANNE HATHAWAY COTTAGE	4500	65.00	90.00
R. BOURGEAULT			WHERE IS ENGLAND	
90	FORGET-ME-NOT	50	525.00	705.00
91	THE FLEECE INN	50	525.00	705.00
92	MILLBROOK HOUSE	50	525.00	525.00
93	COTSWOLD BEAUTY	50	525.00	525.00

ARTAFFECTS

YR	NAME	LIMIT	ISSUE	QUOTE
G. PERILLO			AMERICA'S INDIAN HERITAGE	
87	CHEYENNE NATION	10-DAY	24.50	80.00
88	ARAPAHO NATION	10-DAY	24.50	26.00-104.00
88	BLACKFOOT NATION	10-DAY	24.50	28.00
88	CHIPPEWA NATION	10-DAY	24.50	28.00
88	CROW NATION	10-DAY	24.50	28.00
88	KIOWA NATION	10-DAY	24.50	28.00
88	NEZ PERCE NATION	10-DAY	24.50	28.00
88	SIOUX NATION	10-DAY	24.50	30.00
K. SOLDWEDEL			AMERICAN MARITIME HERITAGE	
87	U.S.S. CONSTITUTION	14-DAY	35.00	35.00
J. EGGERT			ANGLER'S DREAM	
83	BROOK TROUT	9800	55.00	75.00
83	CHINOOK SALMON	9800	55.00	75.00
83	LARGEMOUTH BASS	9800	55.00	75.00
83	STRIPED BASS	9800	55.00	75.00
G. PERILLO			ARCTIC FRIENDS	
82	SIBERIAN LOVE	7500	100.00	650.00
82	SNOW PALS	7500	*	*
R. SAUBER			BABY'S FIRSTS	
89	BABY'S FIRST STEP	14-DAY	21.50	22.50
89	CHRISTMAS MORN	14-DAY	21.50	22.50
89	FIRST BIRTHDAY	14-DAY	21.50	22.50
89	PICTURE PERFECT	14-DAY	21.50	22.50
89	VISITING THE DOCTOR	14-DAY	21.50	22.50
B. LEIGHTON-JONES			BACKSTAGE	
90	BUBBLING OVER	14-DAY	29.50	29.50
90	THE LETTER	14-DAY	29.50	29.50
90	THE RUNAWAY	14-DAY	29.50	29.50
M. HOOKS			BAKER STREET	
83	SHERLOCK HOLMES	9800	55.00	150.00
83	WATSON	9800	55.00	125.00
C. BECKER			BECKER BABIES	
83	SNOW PUFF	OP	29.95	60.00
84	PALS	OP	29.95	60.00
84	SMILING THROUGH	OP	29.95	60.00

YR NAME	LIMIT	ISSUE	QUOTE
B.P. GUTMANN			**BESSIE'S BEST**
84 LOOKING FOR TROUBLE	OP	29.95	65.00
84 MY BABY	OP	29.95	65.00
84 OH! OH! A BUNNY	OP	29.95	65.00
84 TAPS	OP	29.95	65.00
84 THE NEW LOVE	OP	29.95	65.00
G. PERILLO			**CHIEFTANS 2**
83 CHIEF PONTIAC	7500	70.00	110.00-150.00
83 CHIEF VICTORIO	7500	70.00	52.00
84 CHIEF BLACK KETTLE	7500	70.00	110.00-125.00
84 CHIEF COCHISE	7500	70.00	110.00-125.00
84 CHIEF TECUMSEH	7500	70.00	52.00
G. PERILLO			**CHILD LIFE**
83 SIESTA	10,000	45.00	60.00-100.00
84 SWEET DREAMS	10,000	45.00	46.00
R. SAUBER			**CHILDHOOD DELIGHTS**
83 AMANDA	7500	45.00	75.00
A. TOBEY			**CHRISTIAN COLLECTION**
87 BRING TO ME THE CHILDREN	*	35.00	35.00
87 THE HEALER	*	35.00	35.00
87 WEDDING FEAST AT CANA	*	35.00	35.00
J. DENEEN			**CLASSIC AMERICAN CARS**
89 CADILLAC	14-DAY	35.00	35.00
89 CORD	14-DAY	35.00	35.00
89 DUESENBERG	14-DAY	35.00	40.00
89 RUXTON	14-DAY	35.00	35.00
90 HUDSON	14-DAY	35.00	35.00
90 LINCOLN	14-DAY	35.00	35.00
90 PACKARD	14-DAY	35.00	35.00
90 PIERCE-ARROW	14-DAY	35.00	35.00
J. DENEEN			**CLASSIC AMERICAN TRAINS**
88 A RACE AGAINST TIME	14-DAY	35.00	35.00
88 COMPETITION	14-DAY	35.00	40.00
88 HOMEWARD BOUND	14-DAY	35.00	52.00
88 MIDDAY STOP	14-DAY	35.00	35.00
88 ROUND THE BEND	14-DAY	35.00	35.00
88 TAKING THE HIGH ROAD	14-DAY	35.00	45.00
88 THE SILVER BULLET	14-DAY	35.00	54.00
88 TRAVELING IN STYLE	14-DAY	35.00	50.00
G. PERILLO			**COUNCIL OF NATIONS**
92 BOLDNESS OF THE SENECA	14-DAY	29.50	29.50
92 COURAGE OF THE ARAPATTO	14-DAY	29.50	29.50
92 DIGNITY OF THE NEZPERCE	14-DAY	29.50	29.50
92 NOBILITY OF THE ALGONQUIN	14-DAY	29.50	29.50
92 POWER OF THE BLACKFOOT	14-DAY	29.50	29.50
92 PRIDE OF THE CHEYENNE	14-DAY	29.50	29.50
92 STRENGTH OF THE SIOUX	14-DAY	29.50	29.50
92 WISDOM OF THE CHEROKEE	14-DAY	29.50	29.50
S. MILLER-MAXWELL			**GOOD SPORTS**
89 ALLEY CATS	14-DAY	22.50	25.00
89 PURRFECT GAME	14-DAY	22.50	25.00
89 QUARTERBACK SNEAK	14-DAY	22.50	25.00
89 TEE TIME	14-DAY	22.50	25.00
89 TWO/LOVE	14-DAY	22.50	25.00
89 WHAT'S THE CATCH?	14-DAY	22.50	25.00
J. DENEEN			**GREAT AMERICAN TRAINS**
92 THE ALTON LIMITED	75-DAY	27.00	27.00
92 THE BLACKHAWK LIMITED	75-DAY	27.00	27.00
92 THE BROADWAY LIMITED	75-DAY	27.00	27.00
92 THE CAPITOL LIMITED	75-DAY	27.00	27.00
92 THE MERCHANTS LIMITED	75-DAY	27.00	27.00
92 THE PANAMA SPECIAL LIMITED	75-DAY	27.00	27.00
92 THE SOUTHWESTERN LIMITED	75-DAY	27.00	27.00
92 THE SUNSHINE SPECIAL LIMITED	75-DAY	27.00	27.00
MAGO			**HEAVENLY ANGELS**
92 ANGEL CAKE	75-DAY	27.00	27.00
92 CAUGHT IN THE ACT	75-DAY	27.00	27.00
92 HEAVENLY HELPER	75-DAY	27.00	27.00
92 HEAVENLY LIGHT	75-DAY	27.00	27.00
92 HUSH-A-BYE	75-DAY	27.00	27.00
92 MY ANGEL	75-DAY	27.00	27.00
92 SLEEPY SENTINEL	75-DAY	27.00	27.00
92 THE ANGEL'S KISS	75-DAY	27.00	27.00
R. SAUBER			**HOW DO I LOVE THEE?**
82 ALAINA	19,500	39.95	60.00
82 TAYLOR	19,500	39.95	60.00

YR	NAME	LIMIT	ISSUE	QUOTE
83	EMBRACE	19,500	39.95	60.00
83	RENDEZVOUS	19,500	39.95	60.00
G. PERILLO				**INDIAN BRIDAL**
90	AUTUMN BLOSSOM	14-DAY	25.00	25.00
90	MISTY WATERS	14-DAY	25.00	25.00
90	SUNNY SKIES	14-DAY	25.00	25.00
90	YELLOW BIRD	14-DAY	25.00	25.00
G. PERILLO				**INDIAN NATIONS**
83	APACHE (SET)	7500	*	*
83	BLACKFOOT	7500	140.00	1000.00
83	CHEYENNE (SET)	7500	*	*
83	SIOUX (SET)	7500	*	*
G. PERILLO				**LEGENDS OF THE WEST**
82	DANIEL BOONE	10,000	65.00	39.00
83	BUFFALO BILL	10,000	65.00	80.00
83	DAVY CROCKETT	10,000	65.00	80.00
83	KIT CARSON	10,000	65.00	80.00
B.P. GUTMANN				**MAGICAL MOMENT**
81	HAPPY DREAMS	OP	29.95	100.00
81	HARMONY	OP	29.95	90.00
82	HIS MAJESTY	OP	29.95	60.00
82	THANK YOU GOD	OP	29.95	50.00
82	WAITING FOR DADDY	OP	29.95	50.00
83	THE LULLABY	OP	29.95	50.00
MAGO				**MAGO'S MOTHERHOOD**
90	SERENITY	14-DAY	50.00	50.00
G. PERILLO		**MARCH OF DIMES: OUR CHILDREN, OUR FUTURE**		
89	A TIME TO BE BORN	150-DAY	29.00	29.00
MONET/ CASSAT			**MASTERPIECES OF IMPRESSIONISM**	
80	WOMAN WITH PARASOL	17,500	35.00	75.00
81	YOUNG MOTHER SEWING	17,500	35.00	60.00
82	SARA IN GREEN BONNET	17,500	35.00	60.00
83	MARGOT IN BLUE	17,500	35.00	50.00
N. ROCKWELL				**MASTERPIECES OF ROCKWELL**
80	AFTER THE PROM	17,500	42.50	150.00
80	THE CHALLENGER	17,500	50.00	75.00
82	GIRL IN THE MIRROR	17,500	50.00	100.00
82	MISSING TOOTH	17,500	50.00	75.00
REMINGTON				**MASTERPIECES OF THE WEST**
80	INDIAN TRAPPER	17,500	35.00	100.00
82	COWBOY STYLE	17,500	35.00	75.00
82	INDIAN STYLE	17,500	35.00	150.00
80	TEXAS NIGHT HERDER	17,500	35.00	75.00
H. GARRIDO				**MELODIES OF CHILDHOOD**
83	MARY HAD A LITTLE LAMB	19,500	35.00	50.00
83	ROW, ROW, ROW YOUR BOAT	19,500	35.00	50.00
83	TWINKLE, TWINKLE, LITTLE STAR	19,500	35.00	50.00
B.P. GUTMANN				**MOTHER'S LOVE**
84	DADDY'S HERE	OP	29.95	60.00
88	FEELINGS	YR	35.00	175.00
89	MOONLIGHT	YR	35.00	100.00
90	PRIDE & JOY	YR	35.00	50.00
91	LITTLE SHADOW	YR	39.50	45.00
G. PERILLO				**MOTHERHOOD SERIES**
83	MADRE	10,000	50.00	52.00-65.00
84	MADONNA OF THE PLAINS	3500	50.00	65.00-104.00
85	ABUELA	3500	50.00	100.00
86	NAP TIME	3500	50.00	100.00
G. PERILLO				**NATURE'S HARMONY**
82	BENGAL TIGER	12,500	50.00	65.00
82	THE PEACEABLE KINGDOM	12,500	100.00	195.00
82	ZEBRA	12,500	50.00	52.00-98.00
83	BLACK PANTHER	12,500	50.00	150.00
83	ELEPHANT	12,500	50.00	78.00
C. BECKER				**NURSERY PAIR**
83	IN SLUMBERLAND	OP	25.00	60.00
83	THE AWAKENING	OP	25.00	60.00
N. ROCKWELL				**ON THE ROAD SERIES**
84	CITY PRIDE	OP	35.00	75.00
84	COUNTRY PRIDE	OP	35.00	75.00
84	PRIDE OF STOCKBRIDGE	OP	35.00	75.00
G. PERILLO				**PERILLO CHRISTMAS**
87	SHINING STAR	YR	29.50	130.00-163.00
88	SILENT LIGHT	YR	35.00	200.00
89	SNOW FLAKE	YR	35.00	95.00
90	BUNDLE UP	YR	35.00	50.00

YR	NAME	LIMIT	ISSUE	QUOTE
91	CHRISTMAS JOURNEY	YR	39.50	39.50
G. PERILLO				**PERILLO SANTAS**
80	SANTA'S JOY	*	29.95	75.00-100.00
81	SANTA'S BUNDLE	*	29.95	75.00-100.00
G. PERILLO			**PERILLO'S FOUR SEASONS**	
91	AUTUMN	14-DAY	25.00	25.00
91	SPRING	14-DAY	25.00	25.00
91	SUMMER	14-DAY	25.00	25.00
91	WINTER	14-DAY	25.00	25.00
G. PERILLO				**PERILLO'S WILDLIFE**
89	MOUNTAIN LION	14-DAY	29.50	29.50
89	MUSTANG	14-DAY	29.50	29.50
89	WHITE-TAILED DEER	14-DAY	29.50	29.50
90	AMERICAN BALD EAGLE	14-DAY	29.50	29.50
90	BIGHORN SHEEP	14-DAY	29.50	29.50
90	BUFFALO	14-DAY	29.50	29.50
90	POLAR BEAR	14-DAY	29.50	29.50
90	TIMBER WOLF	14-DAY	29.50	29.50
J.H. DOLPH				**PLAYFUL PETS**
82	CURIOSITY	7500	45.00	75.00
82	MASTER'S HAT	7500	45.00	75.00
J. EGGERT				**PORTRAIT SERIES**
86	CHANTILLY	14-DAY	24.50	40.00
86	DYNASTY	14-DAY	24.50	40.00
86	JAMBALAYA	14-DAY	24.50	40.00
86	VELVET	14-DAY	24.50	40.00
G. PERILLO		**PORTRAITS BY PERILLO-MINI PLATES**		
89	BRIGHT SKY	9500	19.50	19.50
89	LITTLE FEATHER	9500	19.50	19.50
89	RUNNING BEAR	9500	19.50	19.50
89	SMILING EYES	9500	19.50	19.50
90	BLUE BIRD	9500	19.50	19.50
90	PROUD EAGLE	9500	19.50	19.50
90	SPRING BREEZE	9500	19.50	19.50
90	WILDFLOWER	9500	19.50	19.50
R. SAUBER		**PORTRAITS OF AMERICAN BRIDES**		
86	CAROLINE	10-DAY	29.50	100.00
86	JACQUELINE	10-DAY	29.50	35.00
87	ELIZABETH	10-DAY	29.50	35.00
87	EMILY	10-DAY	29.50	35.00
87	LAURA	10-DAY	29.50	35.00
87	MEREDITH	10-DAY	29.50	35.00
87	REBECCA	10-DAY	29.50	35.00
87	SARAH	10-DAY	29.50	35.00
G. PERILLO		**PRIDE OF AMERICA'S INDIANS**		
86	BRAVE AND FREE	10-DAY	24.50	78.00-91.00
86	DARK-EYED FRIENDS	10-DAY	24.50	39.00-52.00
86	NOBLE COMPANIONS	10-DAY	24.50	36.00
87	KINDRED SPIRITS	10-DAY	24.50	48.00
87	LOYAL ALLIANCE	10-DAY	24.50	80.00
87	PEACEFUL COMRADES	10-DAY	24.50	34.00-39.00
87	SMALL AND WISE	10-DAY	24.50	45.00
87	WINTER SCOUTS	10-DAY	24.50	35.00-58.00
G. PERILLO			**PROUD YOUNG SPIRITS**	
90	BIRDS OF A FEATHER	14-DAY	29.50	29.50
90	FAST FRIENDS	14-DAY	29.50	29.50
90	FREEDOMS WATCH	14-DAY	29.50	29.50
90	LOYAL GUARDIAN	14-DAY	29.50	29.50
90	PRAIRIE PALS	14-DAY	29.50	29.50
90	PROTECTOR OF THE PLAINS	14-DAY	29.50	29.50
90	WATCHFUL EYES	14-DAY	29.50	29.50
90	WOODLAND SCOUTS	14-DAY	29.50	29.50
MAGO			**REFLECTIONS OF YOUTH**	
88	AMY	14-DAY	29.50	29.50
88	ANDREW	14-DAY	29.50	29.50
88	BETH	14-DAY	29.50	29.50
88	JESSICA	14-DAY	29.50	29.50
88	JULIA	14-DAY	29.50	29.50
88	LAUREN	14-DAY	29.50	29.50
88	MICHELLE	14-DAY	29.50	29.50
88	SEBASTIAN	14-DAY	29.50	29.50
N. ROCKWELL			**ROCKWELL AMERICANA**	
81	SHUFFLETON'S BARBERSHOP	17,500	75.00	150.00
82	BREAKING HOME TIES	17,500	75.00	125.00
83	WALKING TO CHURCH	17,500	75.00	125.00

YR	NAME	LIMIT	ISSUE	QUOTE
N. ROCKWELL			**ROCKWELL TRILOGY**	
81	STOCKBRIDGE IN WINTER 1	OP	35.00	50.00
82	STOCKBRIDGE IN WINTER 2	OP	35.00	50.00
82	STOCKBRIDGE IN WINTER 3	OP	35.00	50.00
L. MARCHETTI			**ROMANTIC CITIES OF EUROPE**	
89	PARIS	14-DAY	35.00	35.00
89	VENICE	14-DAY	35.00	35.00
90	LONDON	14-DAY	35.00	35.00
90	MOSCOW	14-DAY	35.00	35.00
K. SOLDWEDEL			**SAILING THROUGH HISTORY**	
86	FLYING CLOUD	14-DAY	29.50	60.00
86	MAYFLOWER	14-DAY	29.50	60.00
86	SANTA MARIA	14-DAY	29.50	60.00
N. ROCKWELL			**SIMPLER TIMES SERIES**	
84	LAZY DAZE	7500	35.00	75.00
84	ONE FOR THE ROAD	7500	35.00	75.00
R. SAUBER			**SONGS OF STEPHEN FOSTER**	
84	BEAUTIFUL DREAMER	3500	60.00	80.00
84	JEANIE WITH THE LIGHT BROWN HAIR	3500	60.00	80.00
84	OH! SUSANNAH	3500	60.00	80.00
H.C. CHRISTY			**SPECIAL ISSUE**	
87	WE THE PEOPLE	OP	35.00	35.00
81	APACHE BOY	5000	95.00	117.00-156.00
83	PAPOOSE	3000	100.00	250.00
84	NAVAJO GIRL	3500	95.00	350.00
84	THE LOVERS	*	50.00	100.00
86	NAVAJO BOY	3500	95.00	250.00
F. TIPTON HUNTER			**SPECIAL OCCASIONS**	
82	BUBBLES	OP	29.95	50.00
82	BUTTERFLIES	OP	29.95	50.00
MAGO			**STUDIES OF EARLY CHILDHOOD**	
90	ANYBODY HOME?	150-DAY	34.90	37.00
90	CHRISTOPHER & KATE	150-DAY	34.90	48.00
90	PEEK-A-BOO	150-DAY	34.90	37.00
89	CHRISTOPHER & KATE	OP	34.90	37.00
90	THREE-PART HARMONY	OP	34.90	58.00
G. PERILLO			**TENDER MOMENTS**	
85	SUNSET	2000	150.00	250.00
85	WINTER ROMANCE	2000	*	*
T. NEWSOM			**THE ADVENTURES OF PETER PAN**	
90	FLYING OVER LONDON	14-DAY	29.50	29.50
90	LOOK AT ME	14-DAY	29.50	29.50
90	NEVER LAND	14-DAY	29.50	30.00
90	THE ENCOUNTER	14-DAY	29.50	30.00
G. PERILLO			**THE ARABIANS**	
86	SILVER STREAK	3500	95.00	98.00
T. NEWSOM			**THE CARNIVAL SERIES**	
82	CAROUSEL	19,500	35.00	50.00
82	KNOCK EM' DOWN	19,500	35.00	50.00
G. PERILLO			**THE CHIEFTAINS**	
79	CHIEF JOSEPH	7500	65.00	241.00
79	CHIEF SITTING BULL	7500	65.00	293.00-488.00
80	CHIEF GERONIMO	7500	65.00	98.00-130.00
80	CHIEF RED CLOUD	7500	65.00	165.00
81	CHIEF CRAZY HORSE	7500	65.00	182.00
G. PERILLO			**THE COLTS**	
85	APPALOOSA	5000	40.00	100.00
85	ARABIAN	5000	40.00	39.00
85	PINTO	5000	40.00	100.00
85	THE THOROUGHBRED	5000	40.00	39.00-52.00
J. DENEEN			**THE GREAT TRAINS**	
85	SANTA FE	7500	35.00	100.00
85	TWENTIETH CENTURY LTD.	7500	35.00	100.00
86	EMPIRE BUILDER	7500	35.00	100.00
L. MARCHETTI			**THE LIFE OF JESUS**	
92	THE AGONY IN THE GARDEN	25-DAY	27.00	27.00
92	THE BLESSING OF THE CHILDREN	25-DAY	27.00	27.00
92	THE DESCENT FROM THE CROSS	25-DAY	27.00	27.00
92	THE ENTRY INTO JERUSALEM	25-DAY	27.00	27.00
92	THE HEALING OF THE SICK	25-DAY	27.00	27.00
92	THE LAST SUPPER	25-DAY	27.00	27.00
92	THE RESURRECTION	25-DAY	27.00	27.00
92	THE SERMON ON THE MOUNT	25-DAY	27.00	27.00
G. PERILLO			**THE MAIDENS**	
85	SHIMMERING WATERS	5000	60.00	150.00
85	SNOW BLANKET	5000	60.00	150.00

YR	NAME	LIMIT	ISSUE	QUOTE
85	SONG BIRD	5000	60.00	150.00
G. PERILLO				**THE PLAINSMEN**
78	BUFFALO HUNT (BRONZE)	2500	300.00	500.00
79	THE PROUD ONE (BRONZE)	2500	300.00	800.00
G. PERILLO				**THE PRINCESSES**
82	LILY OF THE MOHAWKS	7500	50.00	65.00-377.00
82	MINNEHAHA	7500	50.00	26.00-221.00
82	POCAHONTAS	7500	50.00	65.00-234.00
82	SACAJAWEA	7500	50.00	46.00-221.00
G. PERILLO				**THE PROFESSIONALS**
79	THE BIG LEAGUER	15,000	29.95	30.00-150.00
80	BALLERINA'S DILEMMA	15,000	32.50	33.00-100.00
81	QUARTERBACK	15,000	32.50	33.00-100.00
81	RODEO JOE	15,000	35.00	35.00-100.00
82	MAJOR LEAGUER	15,000	35.00	35.00-100.00
83	THE HOCKEY PLAYER	15,000	35.00	35.00-100.00
G. PERILLO				**THE STORYBOOK COLLECTION**
80	LITTLE RED RIDING HOOD	18-DAY	45.00	45.00
81	CINDERELLA	18-DAY	45.00	45.00
81	HANSEL & GRETEL	18-DAY	45.00	45.00
82	GOLDILOCKS & THE 3 BEARS	18-DAY	45.00	45.00
G. PERILLO				**THE THOROUGHBREDS**
84	MAN O' WAR	9500	50.00	78.00
84	SEABISCUIT	9500	50.00	65.00
84	SECRETARIAT	9500	50.00	350.00
84	WHIRLAWAY	9500	50.00	65.00
G. PERILLO				**THE TRIBAL PONIES**
84	ARAPAHO TRIBAL PONY	3500	65.00	150.00
84	COMANCHE TRIBAL PONY	3500	65.00	150.00
84	CROW TRIBAL PONY	3500	65.00	200.00
H.C. CHRISTY				**THE TRIBUTE SERIES**
82	GEE, I WISH	OP	29.95	50.00
82	I WANT YOU	OP	29.95	50.00
83	SOLDIER'S FAREWELL	OP	29.95	50.00
G. PERILLO				**THE WAR PONIES**
83	APACHE WAR PONY	7500	60.00	350.00
83	NEZ PERCE WAR PONY	7500	60.00	250.00
83	SIOUX WAR PONY	7500	60.00	400.00
G. PERILLO				**THE YOUNG CHIEFTAINS**
85	YOUNG JOSEPH	5000	50.00	100.00
85	YOUNG SITTING BULL	5000	50.00	59.00
86	YOUNG CRAZY HORSE	5000	50.00	100.00
86	YOUNG GERONIMO	5000	50.00	100.00
86	YOUNG RED CLOUD	5000	50.00	100.00
R. SAUBER				**TIMELESS LOVE**
89	SWEET EMBRACE	14-DAY	35.00	35.00
89	THE PROPOSAL	14-DAY	35.00	38.00
90	AFTERNOON LIGHT	14-DAY	35.00	35.00
90	QUIET MOMENTS	14-DAY	35.00	35.00
R. SAUBER			**TIMES OF OUR LIVES COLLECTION**	
82	THE WEDDING	OP	37.50	39.50
84	HAPPY BIRTHDAY	OP	37.50	39.50
85	ALL ADORE HIM	OP	37.50	39.50
85	HOME SWEET HOME	OP	37.50	39.50
86	SWEETHEARTS	OP	37.50	39.50
86	THE ANNIVERSARY	OP	37.50	39.50
86	THE CHRISTENING	OP	37.50	39.50
87	FATHERHOOD	OP	37.50	39.50
87	MOTHERHOOD	OP	37.50	39.50
87	SWEET SIXTEEN	OP	37.50	39.50
88	ALL ADORE HIM	OP	19.50	22.50
88	FATHERHOOD	OP	19.50	22.50
88	HAPPY BIRTHDAY	OP	19.50	22.50
88	HOME SWEET HOME	OP	19.50	22.50
88	MOTHERHOOD	OP	19.50	22.50
88	SWEETHEARTS	OP	19.50	22.50
88	THE ANNIVERSARY	OP	19.50	22.50
88	THE CHRISTENING	OP	19.50	22.50
88	THE WEDDING	OP	19.50	22.50
89	GOD BLESS AMERICA	14-DAY	39.50	39.50
89	GOD BLESS AMERICA	14-DAY	21.50	22.50
89	VISITING THE DOCTOR	14-DAY	39.50	39.50
90	MOTHER'S JOY	OP	39.50	39.50
90	MOTHER'S JOY	OP	22.50	22.50
J. TERRESON				**UNICORN MAGIC**
83	AFTERNOON OFFERING	7500	50.00	60.00

Valentine sweethearts make the best kind. Be Mine *was created by Sandra Kuck as part of "A Childhood Almanac" series for Reco.*

John McClelland adds elements of humor and charm to Breakfast, *produced by Reco.*

Artist Sandra Kuck paints sentiment into each and every work. Loving Touch, *featuring a young mother with her two favorite helpers, is a fine example of her sensitive style. Produced by Reco.*

Corinne Layton captures the pastime of playing dress-up in Olivia, *fourth issue in the "Heirlooms and Lace" series produced by Edwin M. Knowles.*

YR	NAME	LIMIT	ISSUE	QUOTE
83	MORNING ENCOUNTER	7500	50.00	60.00

G. PERILLO — WAR PONIES OF THE PLAINS

YR	NAME	LIMIT	ISSUE	QUOTE
92	FREE SPIRIT	75-DAY	27.00	27.00
92	GENTLE WARRIOR	75-DAY	27.00	27.00
92	NIGHTSHADOW	75-DAY	27.00	27.00
92	PRAIRIE PRANCER	75-DAY	27.00	27.00
92	PROUND COMPANION	75-DAY	27.00	27.00
92	SUN DANCER	75-DAY	27.00	27.00
92	THUNDERFOOT	75-DAY	27.00	27.00
92	WINDCATCHER	75-DAY	27.00	27.00

R. SAUBER — WINTER MINDSCAPE

YR	NAME	LIMIT	ISSUE	QUOTE
89	PEACEFUL VILLAGE	14-DAY	29.50	65.00
89	SNOWBOUND	14-DAY	29.50	40.00
90	COUNTRY MORNING	14-DAY	29.50	40.00
90	FIRST FREEZE	14-DAY	29.50	40.00
90	JANUARY THAW	14-DAY	29.50	40.00
90	PAPA'S SURPRISE	14-DAY	29.50	40.00
90	SLEIGH RIDE	14-DAY	29.50	40.00
90	WELL TRAVELED ROAD	14-DAY	29.50	40.00

G. PERILLO — YOUNG EMOTIONS

YR	NAME	LIMIT	ISSUE	QUOTE
86	SMILES	5000	*	
86	TEARS	5000	75.00	98.00

ARTISTS OF THE WORLD

T. DEGRAZIA — CELEBRATION

YR	NAME	LIMIT	ISSUE	QUOTE
93	CAROLING	5000	39.50	42.00
93	HOLIDAY LULLABY	5000	39.50	42.00

T. DEGRAZIA — CHILDREN

YR	NAME	LIMIT	ISSUE	QUOTE
76	LOS NINOS	5000	35.00	1000.00
77	WHITE DOVE	5000	40.00	100.00
78	FLOWER GIRL	9500	45.00	105.00
78	FLOWER GIRL-SIGNED	500	100.00	450.00
78	LOS NINOS-SIGNED	500	100.00	3000.00
78	WHITE DOVE-SIGNED	500	100.00	450.00
79	FLOWER BOY	9500	45.00	65.00
79	FLOWER BOY-SIGNED	500	100.00	450.00
80	LITTLE COCOPAH	9500	50.00	80.00
80	LITTLE COCOPAH GIRL-SIGNED	500	100.00	320.00
81	BEAUTIFUL BURDEN	9500	50.00	65.00
81	BEAUTIFUL BURDEN-SIGNED	500	100.00	320.00
81	MERRY LITTLE INDIAN-SIGNED	500	100.00	450.00
82	MERRY LITTLE INDIAN	9500	55.00	85
83	WONDERING	10,000	60.00	60.00
84	PINK PAPOOSE	10,000	65.00	65.00
85	SUNFLOWER BOY	10,000	65.00	65.00

K. FUNG NG — CHILDREN OF ABERDEEN

YR	NAME	LIMIT	ISSUE	QUOTE
79	GIRL WITH LITTLE BROTHER	*	50.00	50.00
80	SAMPAN GIRL	*	50.00	50.00
81	GIRL WITH LITTLE SISTER	*	55.00	55.00
82	GIRL WITH SEASHELLS	*	60.00	60.00
83	GIRL WITH SEABIRDS	*	60.00	60.00
84	BROTHER AND SISTER	*	60.00	60.00

T. DEGRAZIA — CHILDREN-MINI PLATES

YR	NAME	LIMIT	ISSUE	QUOTE
80	LOS NINOS	5000	15.00	300.00
81	WHITE DOVE	5000	15.00	35.00
82	FLOWER BOY	5000	15.00	35.00
82	FLOWER GIRL	5000	15.00	35.00
83	BEAUTIFUL BURDEN	5000	17.50	20.00
83	LITTLE COCOPAH INDIAN GIRL	5000	15.00	25.00
84	MERRY LITTLE INDIAN	5000	17.50	20.00
84	WONDERING	5000	17.50	20.00
85	PINK PAPOOSE	5000	17.50	20.00
85	SUNFLOWER BOY	5000	17.50	20.00

T. DEGRAZIA — FIESTA OF THE CHILDREN

YR	NAME	LIMIT	ISSUE	QUOTE
90	CASTANETS IN BLOOM	CL	34.50	44.00
90	WELCOME TO THE FIESTA	150-DAY	34.50	36.00
91	FIESTA FLOWERS	150-DAY	34.50	45.00
92	FIESTA ANGELS	150-DAY	34.50	40.00

T. DEGRAZIA — FLORAL FIESTA

YR	NAME	LIMIT	ISSUE	QUOTE
94	FLOWERS FOR MOTHER	5000	39.50	42.00
94	LITTLE FLOWER VENDOR	5000	39.50	42.00

T. DEGRAZIA — HOLIDAY

YR	NAME	LIMIT	ISSUE	QUOTE
76	FESTIVAL OF LIGHTS	9500	45.00	110.00
76	FESTIVAL OF LIGHTS-SIGNED	500	100.00	250.00
77	BELL OF HOPE	9500	45.00	65.00
77	BELL OF HOPE-SIGNED	500	100.00	200.00
78	LITTLE MADONNA	9500	45.00	70.00

YR	NAME	LIMIT	ISSUE	QUOTE
78	LITTLE MADONNA-SIGNED	500	100.00	350.00
79	THE NATIVITY	9500	50.00	130.00
79	THE NATIVITY-SIGNED	500	100.00	200.00
80	LITTLE PIMA DRUMMER	9500	50.00	60.00
80	LITTLE PIMA DRUMMER-SIGNED	500	100.00	200.00
81	A LITTLE PRAYER	9500	55.00	65.00
81	A LITTLE PRAYER-SIGNED	500	100.00	200.00
82	BLUE BOY	10,000	60.00	65.00
82	BLUE BOY-SIGNED	96	100.00	200.00
83	HEAVENLY BLESSINGS	10,000	65.00	65.00
84	NAVAJO MADONNA	10,000	65.00	65.00
85	SAGUARO DANCE	10,000	65.00	65.00

T. DEGRAZIA — HOLIDAY-MINI PLATES

YR	NAME	LIMIT	ISSUE	QUOTE
80	FESTIVAL OF LIGHTS	5000	15.00	250.00
81	BELL OF HOPE	5000	15.00	200.00
82	LITTLE MADONNA	5000	15.00	350.00
82	THE NATIVITY	5000	15.00	200.00
83	LITTLE PIMA DRUMMER	5000	15.00	200.00
83	LITTLE PRAYER	5000	17.50	20.00
84	BLUE BOY	5000	17.50	20.00
84	HEAVENLY BLESSINGS	5000	17.50	20.00
85	NAVAJO MADONNA	5000	17.50	20.00
85	SAGUARO DANCE	5000	17.50	20.00

BAREUTHER
H. MUELLER — CHRISTMAS

YR	NAME	LIMIT	ISSUE	QUOTE
67	STIFTSKIRCHE	10,000	12.00	85.00
68	KAPPLKIRCHE	10,000	12.00	25.00
69	CHRISTKINDLESMARKT	10,000	12.00	18.00
70	CHAPEL IN OBERNDORF	10,000	12.50	22.00
72	CHRISTMAS IN MUNICH	10,000	14.50	25.00
73	SLEIGH RIDE	10,000	15.00	35.00
74	BLACK FOREST CHURCH	10,000	19.00	19.00
75	SNOWMAN	10,000	21.50	30.00
76	CHAPEL IN THE HILLS	10,000	23.50	26.00
77	STORY TIME	10,000	24.50	40.00
78	MITTENWALD	10,000	27.50	31.00
79	WINTER DAY	10,000	35.00	35.00
80	MITTENBERG	10,000	37.50	39.00
81	WALK IN THE FOREST	10,000	39.50	39.50
82	BAD WIMPFEN	10,000	39.50	43.00
83	THE NIGHT BEFORE CHRISTMAS	10,000	39.50	39.50
84	ZEIL ON THE RIVER MAIN	10,000	42.50	45.00
85	WINTER WONDERLAND	10,000	42.50	57.00
86	CHRISTMAS IN FORCHHEIM	10,000	42.50	70.00
87	DECORATING THE TREE	10,000	42.50	85.00
88	ST. COLOMAN CHURCH	10,000	52.50	65.00
89	SLEIGH RIDE	10,000	52.50	80.00-90.00
90	THE OLD FORGE IN ROTHENBURG	10,000	52.50	52.50
91	CHRISTMAS JOY	10,000	56.50	56.50
92	MARKET PLACE IN HEPPENHEIM	10,000	56.50	56.50
71	TOYS FOR SALE	10,000	12.75	27.00

BELLEEK
*
CHRISTMAS

YR	NAME	LIMIT	ISSUE	QUOTE
70	CASTLE CALDWELL	7500	25.00	85.00
71	CELTIC CROSS	7500	25.00	75.00
72	FLIGHT OF THE EARLS	7500	30.00	35.00
73	TRIBUTE TO YEATS	7500	38.50	47.00
74	DEVENISH ISLAND	7500	45.00	200.00
75	THE CELTIC CROSS	7500	48.00	80.00
76	DOVE OF PEACE	7500	55.00	55.00
77	WREN	7500	55.00	57.00

BERLIN DESIGN
*
CHRISTMAS

YR	NAME	LIMIT	ISSUE	QUOTE
70	CHRISTMAS IN BERNKASTEL	4000	14.50	125.00
71	CHRISTMAS IN ROTHENBURG	20,000	14.50	45.00
72	CHRISTMAS IN MICHELSTADT	20,000	15.00	55.00
73	CHRISTMAS IN WENDLESTEIN	20,000	20.00	55.00
74	CHRISTMAS IN BREMEN	20,000	25.00	53.00
75	CHRISTMAS IN DORTLAND	20,000	30.00	35.00
76	CHRISTMAS IN AUGSBURG	20,000	32.00	75.00
77	CHRISTMAS IN HAMBURG	20,000	32.00	32.00
78	CHRISTMAS IN BERLIN	20,000	36.00	85.00
79	CHRISTMAS IN GREETSIEL	20,000	47.50	60.00
80	CHRISTMAS IN MITTENBERG	20,000	50.00	55.00
81	CHRISTMAS EVE IN HAHNENKLEE	20,000	55.00	55.00

YR	NAME	LIMIT	ISSUE	QUOTE
82	CHRISTMAS EVE IN WASSERBERG	20,000	55.00	50.00
83	CHRISTMAS IN OBERNDORF	20,000	55.00	65.00
84	CHRISTMAS IN RAMSAU	20,000	55.00	55.00
85	CHRISTMAS IN BAD WIMPFEN	20,000	55.00	59.00
86	CHRISTMAS EVE IN GELNHAUS	20,000	65.00	65.00
87	CHRISTMAS EVE IN GOSLAR	20,000	65.00	65.00
88	CHRISTMAS EVE IN RUHPOLDING	20,000	65.00	90.00
89	CHRISTMAS EVE IN FRIEDECHSDADT	20,000	80.00	80.00
90	CHRISTMAS EVE IN PARTENKIRCHEN	20,000	80.00	80.00
91	CHRISTMAS EE IN ALLENDORF	20,000	80.00	80.00
*				HISTORICAL
75	WASHINGTON CROSSING THE DELAWARE	YR	30.00	40.00
76	TOM THUMB	YR	32.00	35.00
77	ZEPPELIN	YR	32.00	35.00
78	BENZ MOTOR CAR MUNICH	10,000	36.00	36.00
79	JOHANNES GUTENBERG	10,000	47.50	48.00
*		HOLIDAY WEEK OF THE FAMILY KAPPELMANN		
84	MONDAY	*	33.00	33.00
84	TUESDAY	*	33.00	37.00
85	FRIDAY	*	35.00	40.00
85	THURSDAY	*	35.00	38.00
85	WEDNESDAY	*	33.00	37.00
86	SATURDAY	*	35.00	40.00
86	SUNDAY	*	35.00	40.00

BIEDERMANN & SONS

YR	NAME	LIMIT	ISSUE	QUOTE
93	FOUR CALLING BIRDS	250	17.50	20.00
94	DRUMMER BOY	250	20.00	50.00

BING & GRONDAHL
E. JENSEN

YR	NAME	LIMIT	ISSUE	QUOTE
85	CHRISTMAS EVE AT THE FARMHOUSE	YR	54.50	72.00

D. JENSEN — CENTENNIAL COLLECTION

92	CROWS ENJOYING CHRISTMAS	YR	59.50	63.00

C. ROLLER — CHILDREN'S DAY PLATE SERIES

85	THE MAGICAL TEA PARTY	YR	24.50	25.00-30.00
86	A JOYFUL FLIGHT	YR	26.50	30.00
86	THE LITTLE GARDENERS	YR	29.50	42.00
88	WASH DAY	YR	34.50	50.00
89	BEDTIME	YR	37.00	58.00-80.00
90	MY FAVORITE DRESS	YR	37.00	40.00
91	FUN ON THE BEACH	YR	45.00	48.00
92	A SUMMER DAY IN THE MEADOW	YR	45.00	50.00
93	THE CAROUSEL	YR	45.00	47.00

AARESTRUP — CHRISTMAS

09	YULE TREE	YR	1.50	135.00
54	ROYAL BOAT	YR	7.00	115.00
55	KAULUNDORG CHURCH	YR	8.00	150.00
56	CHRISTMAS IN COPENHAGEN	YR	8.50	180.00
57	CHRISTMAS CANDLES	YR	9.00	175.00
58	SANTA CLAUS	YR	9.50	108.00
59	CHRISTMAS EVE	YR	10.00	150.00
60	VILLAGE CHURCH	YR	10.00	175.00
61	WINTER HARMONY	YR	10.50	83.00
62	WINTER NIGHT	YR	11.00	65.00
10	THE OLD ORGANIST	YR	1.50	100.00
31	TOWN HALL SQUARE	YR	2.50	100.00
32	LIFE BOAT	YR	2.50	90.00
33	KORSOR-NYBORG FERRY	YR	3.00	100.00
34	CHURCH BELL IN TOWER	YR	3.00	90.00
17	CHRISTMAS BOAT	YR	1.50	100.00
18	FISHING BOAT	YR	1.50	105.00
19	OUTSIDE LIGHTED WINDOW	YR	2.00	85.00
20	HARE IN THE SNOW	YR	2.00	150.00
21	PIGEONS	YR	2.00	100.00
22	STAR OF BETHLEHEM	YR	2.00	90.00
23	THE ERMITAGE	YR	2.00	80.00
24	LIGHTHOUSE	YR	2.50	105.00
25	CHILD'S CHRISTMAS	YR	2.50	125.00
26	CHURCHGOERS	YR	2.50	100.00
27	SKATING COUPLE	YR	2.50	145.00
28	ESKIMOS	YR	2.50	90.00
29	FOX OUTSIDE FARM	YR	2.50	95.00
30	CHRISTMAS TRAIN	YR	2.50	120.00
00	CHURCH BELLS	YR	0.75	1100.00
98	ROSES AND STAR	YR	0.75	890.00

YR	NAME	LIMIT	ISSUE	QUOTE
99	CROWS	YR	0.75	925.00
95	BEHIND THE FROZEN WINDOW	YR	0.50	5000.00
96	NEW MOON	YR	0.50	1950.00
97	SPARROWS	YR	0.75	1135.00
12	GOING TO CHURCH	YR	1.50	130.00
03	EXPECTANT CHILDREN	YR	1.00	325.00
46	COMMEMORATION CROSS	YR	5.00	105.00
47	DYBBOL MILL	YR	5.00	150.00
48	WATCHMAN	YR	5.50	160.00
49	LANDSOLDATEN	YR	5.50	115.00
50	KRONBORG CASTLE	YR	5.50	150.00
51	JENS BANG	YR	6.00	120.00
02	GOTHIC CHURCH INTERIOR	YR	1.00	215.00
05	CHRISTMAS NIGHT	YR	1.00	180.00
06	SLEIGHING TO CHURCH	YR	1.00	110.00
15	DOG OUTSIDE WINDOW	YR	1.50	195.00
84	THE CHRISTMAS LETTER	YR	54.50	70.00
86	SILENT NIGHT, HOLY NIGHT	YR	54.50	70
87	THE SNOWMAN'S CHRISTMAS EVE	YR	59.50	62.00
88	IN THE KINGS GARDEN	YR	64.50	75.00
89	CHRISTMAS ANCHORAGE	YR	59.50	70.00
90	CHANGING OF THE GUARDS	YR	64.50	68.00
91	COPENHAGEN STOCK EXCHANGE	YR	69.50	74.00
08	ST. PETRI CHURCH	YR	1.00	85.00
16	SPARROWS AT CHRISTMAS	YR	1.50	100.00
13	BRINGING HOME THE TREE	YR	1.50	105.00
14	AMALIENBORG CASTLE	YR	1.50	95.00
35	LILLEBELT BRIDGE	YR	3.00	85.00
36	ROYAL GUARD	YR	3.00	100.00
37	ARRIVAL OF CHRISTMAS GUESTS	YR	3.00	100.00
40	CHRISTMAS LETTERS	YR	4.00	235.00
41	HORSES ENJOYING MEAL	YR	4.00	270.00
42	DANISH FARM	YR	4.00	235.00
43	RIBE CATHEDRAL	YR	5.00	210.00
44	SORGENFRI CASTLE	YR	5.00	155.00
45	THE OLD WATER MILL	YR	5.00	160.00
11	ANGELS AND SHEPHERDS	YR	1.50	110.00
04	FREDERICKSBERG HILL	YR	1.00	129.00
07	LITTLE MATCH GIRL	YR	1.00	125.00
52	THORSVALDSEN MUSEUM	YR	6.00	135.00
53	SNOWMAN	YR	7.50	115.00
01	THREE WISE MEN	YR	1.00	400.00
92	CHRISTMAS AT THE RECTORY	YR	69.50	72.00
93	FATHER CHRISTMAS IN COPENHAGEN	YR	69.50	72.00
64	THE FIR TREE AND HARE	YR	11.50	40.00
65	BRINGING HOME THE TREE	YR	12.00	47.00
65	THE CHRISTMAS ELF	YR	11.00	96.00
66	HOME FOR CHRISTMAS	YR	12.00	29.00
67	SHARING THE JOY	YR	13.00	25.00
68	CHRISTMAS IN CHURCH	YR	14.00	26.00
69	ARRIVAL OF GUESTS	YR	14.00	15.00
70	PHEASANTS IN SNOW	YR	14.50	15.00
71	CHRISTMAS AT HOME	YR	15.00	15.00
72	CHRISTMAS IN GREENLAND	YR	16.50	16.50
73	COUNTRY CHRISTMAS	YR	19.50	19.50
74	CHRISTMAS IN THE VILLAGE	YR	22.00	22.00
75	OLD WATER MILL	YR	27.50	27.50
76	CHRISTMAS WELCOME	YR	27.50	27.50
77	COPENHAGEN CHRISTMAS	YR	29.50	29.50
78	CHRISTMAS TALE	YR	32.00	32.00
79	WHITE CHRISTMAS	YR	36.50	50.00
80	CHRISTMAS IN WOODS	YR	42.50	42.50
81	CHRISTMAS PEACE	YR	49.50	70.00
82	CHRISTMAS TREE	YR	54.50	70.00
83	CHRISTMAS IN OLD TOWN	YR	54.50	70.00
38	LIGHTING THE CANDLES	YR	3.00	135.00
39	OLD LOCK-EYE, THE SANDMAN	YR	3.00	250.00

J. WOODSON — **CHRISTMAS IN AMERICA**

YR	NAME	LIMIT	ISSUE	QUOTE
86	CHRISTMAS EVE IN WILLIAMSBURG	YR	29.50	110.00-250.00
87	CHRISTMAS EVE AT THE WHITE HOUSE	YR	34.50	34.50-85.00
88	CHRISTMAS EVE AT ROCKEFELLER CENTER	YR	34.50	55.00-60.00
89	CHRISTMAS IN NEW ENGLAND	YR	37.00	37.00-65.00
90	CHRISTMAS EVE AT THE CAPITOL	YR	39.50	50.00
91	CHRISTMAS EVE AT INDEPENDENCE HALL	YR	45.00	50.00
92	CHRISTMAS IN SAN FRANCISCO	YR	47.50	49.00
93	COMING HOME FOR CHRISTMAS	YR	47.50	50.00

YR	NAME	LIMIT	ISSUE	QUOTE
J. WOODSON		**CHRISTMAS IN AMERICA ANNIVERSARY PLATE**		
91	CHRISTMAS EVE IN WILLIAMSBURG	YR	69.50	74.00
AARESTRUP		**JUBILEE-5 YEAR CYCLE**		
80	YULE TREE	YR	60.00	75.00
90	THE ROYAL YACHT DANNEBROG	YR	95.00	100.00
30	THE OLD ORGANIST	YR	*	225.00
85	LIFEBOAT AT WORK	YR	65.00	93.00
50	ESKIMOS	YR	*	180.00
65	CHURCHGOERS	YR	25.00	90.00
20	CHURCH BELLS	YR	*	60.00
15	FROZEN WINDOW	YR	*	225.00
55	DYBBOL MILL	YR	*	210.00
60	KRONBORG CASTLE	YR	25.00	90.00
25	DOG OUTSIDE WINDOW	YR	*	300.00
45	AMALIENBORG CASTLE	YR	*	150.00
70	AMALIENBORG CASTLE	YR	30.00	30.00
75	HORSES ENJOYING MEAL	YR	40.00	50.00
35	LITTLE MATCH GIRL	YR	*	1000.00
40	THREE WISE MEN	YR	*	2000.00
L. JENSEN		**MOTHER'S DAY**		
90	HEN WITH CHICKS	YR	52.50	63.00
91	THE NANNY GOAT AND HER TWO FRISKY KIDS	YR	54.50	70.00
92	PANDA WITH CUBS	YR	59.50	63.00
69	DOGS AND PUPPIES	YR	9.75	350.00-390.00
70	BIRD AND CHICKS	YR	10.00	20.00
71	CAT AND KITTEN	YR	11.00	11.00
72	MARE AND FOAL	YR	12.00	14.00
73	DUCK AND DUCKLINGS	YR	13.00	13.00
74	BEAR AND CUBS	YR	16.50	16.50
75	DOE AND FAWNS	YR	19.50	19.50
76	SWAN FAMILY	YR	22.50	25.00
77	SQUIRREL AND YOUNG	YR	23.50	25.00
78	HERON	YR	24.50	25.00
79	FOX AND CUBS	YR	27.50	27.50
80	WOODPECKER AND YOUNG	YR	29.50	39.00
81	HARE AND YOUNG	YR	36.50	45.00
82	LIONESS AND CUBS	YR	39.50	50.00
83	RACCOON AND YOUNG	YR	39.50	50.00
84	STORK AND NESTLINGS	YR	39.50	50.00
85	BEAR AND CUBS	YR	39.50	50.00
86	ELEPHANT WITH CALF	YR	39.50	43.00
87	SHEEP WITH LAMBS	YR	42.50	65.00
88	CRESTED PLOYER & YOUNG	YR	47.50	57.00
88	LAPWING MOTHER WITH CHICKS	YR	49.50	60.00
89	COW WITH CALF	YR	49.50	60.00
93	ST. BERNARD DOG AND PUPPIES	YR	59.50	62.00
H. HANSEN		**SANTA CLAUS COLLECTION**		
89	SANTA'S WORKSHOP	YR	59.50	70.00
90	SANTA'S SLEIGH	YR	59.50	65.00
91	SANTA'S JOURNEY	YR	69.50	75.00
92	SANTA'S ARRIVAL	YR	74.50	78.00
93	SANTA'S GIFTS	YR	74.50	78.00
*		**STATUE OF LIBERTY**		
85	STATUE OF LIBERTY	10,000	60.00	75.00
S. VESTERGAARD		**YOUNG ADVENTURER PLATE**		
90	THE LITTLE VIKING	YR	52.50	54.00-65.00

BOEHM STUDIOS

*		**EGYPTIAN COMMEMORATIVE**		
78	TUTANKHAMUN	5000	125.00	170.00
78	TUTANKHAMUN, HANDPAINTED	225	975.00	975.00
*		**PANDA**		
82	PANDA, HARMONY	5000	65.00	65.00
82	PANDA, PEACE	5000	65.00	65.00

BRADFORD EXCHANGE

A. WHITE		**101 DALMATIONS**		
94	HALFWAY HOME	95-DAY	32.90	37.00
* *		**ALICE IN WONDERLAND**		
93	ADVICE FROM A CATERPILLAR	OP	29.90	29.90
93	CROQUET WITH THE QUEEN	OP	29.90	29.90
93	THE CHESHIRE CAT	OP	29.90	29.90
93	THE MAD TEA PARTY	OP	29.90	29.90
* *		**AMERICA'S TRIUMPH IN SPACE**		
93	BEYOND THE BOUNDS OF EARTH	OP	32.90	32.90
93	CONQUERING THE NEW FRONTIER	OP	32.90	32.90
93	FLIGHT OF GLORY	OP	32.90	32.90

YR	NAME	LIMIT	ISSUE	QUOTE
93	THE EAGLE HAS LANDED	OP	29.90	29.90
93	THE MARCH TOWARDS DESTINY	OP	29.90	29.90
94	RENDEVOUS W/VICTORY	OP	34.90	34.90
94	THE NEW EXPLORERS	OP	34.90	34.90
94	THE TRIUMPHANT FINALE	OP	34.90	34.90
94	CONQUERING THE NEW FRONTIER	95-DAY	32.90	32.90

T. KINKADE   AN OLD-FASHIONED CHRISTMAS WITH THOMAS KINKADE

YR	NAME	LIMIT	ISSUE	QUOTE
93	ALL FRIENDS ARE WELCOME	95-DAY	29.90	29.90

L. LIU   BEAUTIFUL GARDENS

YR	NAME	LIMIT	ISSUE	QUOTE
94	PEONY GARDEN	*	34.00	39.00

BEAUTY & THE BEAST

YR	NAME	LIMIT	ISSUE	QUOTE
94	A SPOT OF TEA	150-DAY	34.90	40.00

C. WYSOCKI   CHARLES WYSOCKI'S PEPPERCRICKET GROVE

YR	NAME	LIMIT	ISSUE	QUOTE
93	PEPPERCRICKET FARMS	95-DAY	24.90	30.00

W. BOUGUEREAU   CHERUBS OF INNOCENCE

YR	NAME	LIMIT	ISSUE	QUOTE
94	THE FIRST KISS	95-DAY	29.90	35.00

G. RUNNING WOLF   CHOSEN MESSENGERS

YR	NAME	LIMIT	ISSUE	QUOTE
94	THE SURVEYORS	95-DAY	32.90	37.00

R. AKERS   CHRISTMAS CAMEOS

YR	NAME	LIMIT	ISSUE	QUOTE
94	PROPOSAL UNDER THE STARS	*	65.00	70.00

M. STUTZMAN   COMMEMORATING THE KING

YR	NAME	LIMIT	ISSUE	QUOTE
93	ROCK AND ROLL LEGEND	95-DAY	29.75	35.00
94	THE TIGER: FAITH, SPIRIT, DISCIPLINE	95-DAY	29.75	35.00

J. THORNBRUGH   DEER FRIENDS AT CHRISTMAS

YR	NAME	LIMIT	ISSUE	QUOTE
94	A GLISTENING SEASON	95-DAY	29.90	35.00
94	ALL A GLOW	95-DAY	29.90	35.00
94	ALL AGLOW	95-DAY	29.90	35.00

DISNEY TREASURED MOMENTS PLATE COLLECTION

YR	NAME	LIMIT	ISSUE	QUOTE
94	CINDERELLA	150-DAY	29.90	35.00

D.R. PIERCE   EYES OF THE WILD

YR	NAME	LIMIT	ISSUE	QUOTE
93	EYES IN THE MIST	95-DAY	29.50	35.00

G. ANGELINI   FABULOUS CARS OF THE FIFTIES

YR	NAME	LIMIT	ISSUE	QUOTE
94	'59 RED FORD FAIRLANE	95-DAY	27.75	32.00

L. KAATZ   FIELD PUP FOLLIES

YR	NAME	LIMIT	ISSUE	QUOTE
94	FOWL PLAY	*	29.90	35.00
94	HAT CHECK	*	29.90	35.00

G. KURZ   FLORAL FROLICS

YR	NAME	LIMIT	ISSUE	QUOTE
94	SPRING SURPRISES	95-DAY	29.90	35.00

D. SIVAVEC   FOOTSTEPS OF KING

YR	NAME	LIMIT	ISSUE	QUOTE
94	FLYING CIRCLE G RANCH: WALLS, MS	95-DAY	32.75	35.00

* *   FOOTSTEPS OF THE BRAVE

YR	NAME	LIMIT	ISSUE	QUOTE
93	AT JOURNEY'S END	OP	29.90	29.90
93	AT STORM'S PASSAGE	OP	24.90	24.90
93	HORIZONS OF DESTINY	OP	27.90	27.90
93	NOBLE QUEST	OP	24.90	24.90
93	PATH OF HIS FOREFATHERS	OP	27.90	27.90
93	SOULFUL REFLECTION	OP	29.90	29.90
93	THE REVERENT TRAIL	OP	29.90	29.90
93	WITH BOUNDLESS VISION	OP	27.90	27.90

L. CHANG   FRIENDSHIP IN BLOOM

YR	NAME	LIMIT	ISSUE	QUOTE
94	PAWS IN THE POSIES	95-DAY	29.90	35.00

D. RICHARDSON   GARDENS OF INNOCENCE

YR	NAME	LIMIT	ISSUE	QUOTE
94	HOPE	95-DAY	29.90	35.00

L. CHANG   GARDENS OF PARADISE

YR	NAME	LIMIT	ISSUE	QUOTE
93	TRANQUILITY	150-DAY	29.50	35.00

S. GARDNER   GREAT MOMENTS IN BASEBALL

YR	NAME	LIMIT	ISSUE	QUOTE
93	JOE DIMAGGIO: THE STREAK	95-DAY	29.90	35.00
94	SATCHEL PAIGE	95-DAY	34.90	40.00

* *   HIDEAWAY LAKE

YR	NAME	LIMIT	ISSUE	QUOTE
93	ECHOES OF MORNING	OP	34.90	34.90
93	FISHING FOR DREAMS	OP	34.90	34.90
93	RUSTY'S RETREAT	OP	34.90	34.90
93	SUNSET CABIN	OP	34.90	34.90

T. KINKADE   KINKADE'S ILLUMINATED COTTAGES

YR	NAME	LIMIT	ISSUE	QUOTE
94	THE FLAGSTONE PATH	95-DAY	*	

J. BARSON   LEGENDS OF BASEBALL

YR	NAME	LIMIT	ISSUE	QUOTE
94	LEFTY GROVE	150-DAY	31.75	36.00

L. LIU   LENA LIU'S FLOWER FAIRIES

YR	NAME	LIMIT	ISSUE	QUOTE
93	MAGIC MAKERS	95-DAY	29.50	35.00

LITTLE MERMAID

YR	NAME	LIMIT	ISSUE	QUOTE
94	FIREWORKS AT FIRST SIGHT	95-DAY	34.90	40.00

B. LANGTON   MOMENTS OF SERENITY

YR	NAME	LIMIT	ISSUE	QUOTE
94	MORNING REFLECTIONS	95-DAY	*	

B. EMMETT   MUSICAL TRIBUTE TO ELVIS THE KING

YR	NAME	LIMIT	ISSUE	QUOTE
94	ROCKIN' BLUE SUEDE SHOES	95-DAY	29.90	35.00

YR	NAME	LIMIT	ISSUE	QUOTE
	R. AKERS	**MUSICAL CAROUSEL TREASURES**		
93	SWEET STANDER	150-DAY	49.00	55.00
	K. MILNAZIK	**MUSICAL MOMENTS FROM THE WIZARD OF OZ**		
93	OVER THE RAINBOW	95-DAY	29.90	35.00
* *			**MYSTIC GARDENS**	
93	COMPANION SPIRITS	OP	32.90	32.90
93	FAITHFUL FELLOWSHIP	OP	32.90	32.90
93	MAJESTIC MESSENGER	OP	29.90	29.90
93	ROYAL UNITY	OP	34.90	34.90
93	SOUL MATES	OP	29.90	29.90
93	SPIRITUAL HARMONY	OP	32.90	32.90
	C. JACKSON	**NATIVE AMERICAN LEGENDS**		
94	SITTING BULL	*	*	
	L. BOGLE		**NATIVE BEAUTY**	
94	THE PROMISE	95-DAY	29.90	35.00
	L. MARTIN	**NATURE'S LITTLE TREASURES**		
93	GARDEN WHISPERS	95-DAY	29.90	35.00
94	MINUTE ENCHANTMENT	95-DAY	34.90	40.00
* *			**NEW HORIZONS**	
93	BLDG. FOR A NEW GENERATION	OP	29.90	29.90
93	THE POWER OF GOD	OP	29.90	29.90
93	WINGS OF SNOWY GRANDEUR	OP	32.90	32.90
94	MASTER OF THE CHASE	OP	32.90	32.90
94	MASTER OF THE CHASE	95-DAY	32.90	32.90
			NORTHWOODS SPIRIT	
94	TIMELESS WATCH	95-DAY	29.90	35.00
* *		**NOTORIOUS DISNEY VILLAINS**		
93	THE WICKED QUEEN	OP	29.90	29.90
94	CRUELLA DE VIL	OP	29.90	29.90
94	MALEFICENT	OP	29.90	29.90
94	URSELLA	OP	29.90	29.90
* *		**OLD FASHIONED CHRISTMAS W/T. KINKADE**		
93	A HOLIDAY GATHERING	OP	32.90	32.90
93	ALL FRIENDS ARE WELCOME	OP	29.90	29.90
93	CHRISTMAS TREE COTTAGE	OP	32.90	32.90
93	WINTER'S MEMORIES	OP	29.90	29.90
	D. GEISNESS		**PEACE ON EARTH**	
94	SNOWY SILENCE	95-DAY	32.90	37.00
	M. HARVEY		**PEACEABLE KINGDOM**	
94	NOAH'S ARK	95-DAY	29.90	35.00
* *			**PORTRAITS OF VALOR**	
93	EMANCIPATION PROCLAMATION	OP	29.90	29.90
93	THE GETTYSBURG ADDRESS	OP	29.90	29.90
93	THE LINCOLN-DOUGLAS DEBATE	OP	29.90	29.90
* *			**PROMISE OF A SAVIOR**	
93	A CHILD IS BORN	OP	29.90	29.90
93	AN ANGEL'S MESSAGE	OP	29.90	29.90
93	ANGELS WERE WATCHING	OP	29.90	29.90
93	GIFTS TO JESUS	OP	29.90	29.90
93	HOLY MOTHER AND CHILD	OP	29.90	29.90
93	THE HEAVENLY KING	OP	29.90	29.90
	L. MARTIN		**RADIANT MESSENGERS**	
94	BEAUTY	95-DAY	29.90	35.00
	C. NOTARILE		**REFLECTIONS OF MARILYN**	
94	SHIMMERING HEAT	95-DAY	29.90	35.00
	N. ROCKWELL	**ROCKWELL COMMEMORATIVE STAMPS**		
94	FREEDOM FROM FEAR	95-DAY	29.90	35.00
94	FREEDOM FROM WANT	95-DAY	29.90	35.00
	N. ROCKWELL	**ROCKWELL SOCIETY CHRISTMAS**		
94	CHRISTMAS MARVEL	*	32.90	37.00
	N. ROCKWELL	**ROCKWELL SOCIETY HERITAGE**		
94	THE APPRENTICE	*	29.90	35.00
	H. BOND		**SANTA'S LITTLE HELPERS**	
94	STOCKING STUFFERS	95-DAY	29.90	35.00
94	WRAPPING UP THE HOLIDAYS	95-DAY	24.90	30.00
	S. GUSTAFSON		**SANTA'S ON HIS WAY**	
94	CHECKING IT TWICE	95-DAY	29.90	35.00
	L. GARRISON	**SCENES OF CHRISTMAS PAST**		
94	A GATHERING OF FAITH	150-DAY	32.50	37.00
	J. THORNBRUGH		**SIGNS OF SPRING**	
94	A FAMILY FEAST	95-DAY	*	
	J. TANTON	**SOME BEARY NICE PLACES**		
94	WELCOME TO THE LIBEARY	95-DAY	29.90	35.00
	S. KUCK		**SUGAR AND SPICE**	
93	BEST FRIENDS	95-DAY	29.90	35.00
94	MORNING PRAYERS	95-DAY	32.90	37.00

YR NAME	LIMIT	ISSUE	QUOTE
* *		**SUPERSTAR OF CTY MUSIC**	
93 BARBARA MANDRELL	OP	32.90	32.90
93 DOLLY PARTON: I WILL ALWAYS LOVE YOU	OP	29.90	29.90
93 GLEN CAMPBELL: RHINESTONE COWBOY	OP	32.90	32.90
93 KENNY ROGERS: SWEET MUSIC MAN	OP	29.90	29.90
T. SIZEMORE		**SUPERSTARS OF BASEBALL**	
94 WILLIE 'SAY HEY' MAYS	95-DAY	29.90	35.00
D. HENDERSON		**TAKE ME OUT TO THE BALLGAME**	
94 COUNTY STADIUM	95-DAY	34.75	40.00
A. ISAKOV		**THAT'S WHAT FRIENDS ARE FOR**	
94 FRIENDS ARE FOREVER	95-DAY	29.90	35.00
D. KLAUBA	**THE COSTUMING OF A LEGEND: DRESSING GONE WITH THE WIND**		
93 THE RED DRESS	95-DAY	29.90	35.00
B. BENGER		**THE LEGENDS OF BASEBALL**	
92 BABE RUTH: THE CALLED SHOT	150-DAY	24.75	28.00
		THE LITTLE MERMAID	
94 FOREVER LOVE	95-DAY	34.90	40.00
C. NOTARILE		**THE MAGIC OF MARILYN**	
93 FOR OUR BOYS IN KOREA, 1954	95-DAY	24.75	30.00
	THE TALE OF PETER RABBIT AND BENJAMIN BUNNY		
94 A POCKET FULL OF ONIONS	*	39.00	44.00
T. KINKADE	**THOMAS KINKADE'S HOME IS WHERE THE HEART IS**		
92 HOME SWEET HOME	150-DAY	29.90	35.00
K. NOLES		**THROUGH A CHILD'S EYES**	
94 LITTLE BUTTERFLY	95-DAY	29.90	35.00
J.K. COLE		**TOUCHING THE SPIRIT**	
93 RUNNING WITH THE WIND	95-DAY	29.50	35.00
H. GARRIDO		**VISIONS OF OUR LADY**	
94 OUR LADY OF GRACE	95-DAY	29.90	35.00
* *		**WHEN ALL HEARTS COME HOME**	
93 CHRISTMAS WISH	OP	29.90	29.90
93 COMFORT AND JOY	OP	29.90	29.90
93 GRANDPA'S FARM	OP	29.90	29.90
93 NIGHT BEFORE CHRISTMAS	OP	29.90	29.90
93 NIGHT DEPARTURE	OP	29.90	29.90
93 OH CHRISTMAS TREE	OP	29.90	29.90
93 PEACE ON EARTH	OP	29.90	29.90
93 SUPPER AND SMALL TALK	OP	29.90	29.90
93 OH CHRISTMAS TREE	95-DAY	29.90	29.90
T. HIRATA		**WILD SPIRITS**	
93 SOLITARY WATCH	150-DAY	29.50	35.00
J. WELTY		**WINDOWS OF GLORY**	
93 KING OF KINGS	95-DAY	29.90	35.00
D.L. RUST		**WINGS OF WINTER**	
93 MOONLIGHT RETREAT	150-DAY	29.50	35.00
C. JACKSON		**WINNIE THE POOH AND FRIENDS**	
94 TIME FOR A LITTLE SOMETHING	*	39.90	45.00
		WOODLAND TRANQUILITY	
94 WINTER'S CALM	95-DAY	29.90	35.00

BYLINY'S PORCELAIN
U.L. DUBOVIKOV

	JEWELS OF THE GOLDEN RING		
91 ST. BASIL'S, MOSCOW	195-DAY	29.87	35.00

CAVANAUGH GROUP
SUNDBLOM

	COCA-COLA BRAND HERITAGE COLLECTION		
94 SANTA AT THIS DESK	5000	60.00	65.00

CLARISSA'S CREATIONS
C. JOHNSON

90 LITTLE BALLERINA	14-DAY	48.00	55.00
94 MEMORIES	25,000	48.00	50.00

CRESTLEY COLLECTION

		A TRIBUTE TO ROY ROGERS	
94 HAPPY TRAILS TO YOU	*	19.95	22.00
S. WOODS		**BACKYARD BUDDIES**	
94 OCTOBER HARVEST	*	19.95	22.00
S. WHEELER		**CHRISTMAS/PRIMROSE HILL**	
94 BE IT EVER SO HUMBLE	*	19.95	22.00
T. CATHEY		**HEAVENLY HEARTS**	
94 PRUDENCE	*	19.95	22.00
T. DUBOIS		**MONDAY'S TROLL FAIR OF FACE**	
94 SUNDAY'S TROLL	*	19.95	22.00
		PICTURE PURRFECT	
94 EVERYONE NEEDS A TEDDY	*	19.95	22.00
S. EVANS		**PROFILES OF BRAVERY**	
94 THE FIERCE & THE MIGHTY	*	19.95	22.00

YR	NAME	LIMIT	ISSUE	QUOTE
	T. DUBOIS		**TEDDY BEAR FAIR**	
94	THE POWER OF LOVE	*	19.95	22.00
	L. KENDRICK		**VISION QUEST**	
94	VALLEY OF THE SPIRIT	*	19.95	22.00

CROWN PARIAN

YR	NAME	LIMIT	ISSUE	QUOTE
	*** PARIAN**		**FREDDIE THE FREELOADER**	
79	FREDDIE IN THE BATHTUB	OP	55.00	174.00
80	FREDDIE'S SHACK	OP	55.00	78.00
81	FREDDIE ON THE GREEN	OP	60.00	51.00
82	LOVE THAT FREDDIE	OP	60.00	34.00
	*** PARIAN**		**FREDDIE'S ADVENTURE**	
82	BRONCO FREDDIE	OP	60.00	27.00
82	CAPTAIN FREDDIE	OP	60.00	29.00
83	SIR FREDDIE	OP	62.50	25.00
84	GERTRUDE AND HEATHCLIFFE	OP	62.50	75.00

D'ARCEAU LIMOGES

YR	NAME	LIMIT	ISSUE	QUOTE
	A. RESTIEAU		**CHRISTMAS**	
75	LA FRUITE EN EGYPTE	*	24.32	30.00
76	DANS LA CRECHE	*	24.32	29.00
77	REFUS D'HEBERGEMENT	*	24.32	29.00
78	LA PURIFICATION	YR	26.81	29.00
79	L'ADORATION DES ROIS	YR	26.81	31.00
80	JOYEUSE NOUVELLE	YR	28.74	32.00
81	GUIDES PAR L'ETOILE	YR	28.74	30.00
82	L'ANNUCIATION	YR	30.74	35.00
	A. RESTIEAU		**LAFAYETTE**	
73	NORTH ISLAND LANDING	*	19.82	20.00-25.00
73	THE SECRET CONTRACT	*	14.82	20.00-25.00
74	BATTLE OF BRANDYWINE	*	19.82	20.00-25.00
74	CITY TAVERN MEETING	*	19.82	20.00-25.00
75	MESSAGES TO FRANKLIN	*	19.82	20.00-25.00
75	SIEGE AT YORKTOWN	*	19.82	20.00-25.00

DAVE GROSSMAN CREATIONS

YR	NAME	LIMIT	ISSUE	QUOTE
	ROCKWELL INSPIRED		**BOY SCOUT**	
81	CAN'T WAIT	RT	30.00	45.00
82	GUIDING HAND	RT	30.00	45.00
83	TOMORROW'S LEADER	RT	30.00	45.00
	B. LEIGHTON-JONES		**EMMETT KELLY CHRISTMAS PLATE**	
93	DOWNHILL PLATE	YR	30.00	35.00
	B. LEIGHTON-JONES		**EMMETT KELLY ORIGINAL CIRCUS COLLECTION**	
94	HOLIDAY SKATER	*	30.00	35.00
	B. LEIGHTON-JONES		**EMMETT KELLY PLATES**	
86	CHRISTMAS CAROL	CL	20.00	25.00
87	CHRISTMAS WREATH	YR	20.00	25.00
88	CHRISTMAS DINNER	YR	20.00	25.00
89	CHRISTMAS FEAST	YR	20.00	25.00
90	JUST WHAT I NEEDED	YR	24.00	29.00
91	EMMETT THE SNOWMAN	YR	25.00	27.00
92	CHRISTMAS TUNES	YR	25.00	27.00
	ROCKWELL INSPIRED		**HUCK FINN**	
79	SECRET	RT	40.00	50.00
80	LISTENING	RT	40.00	50.00
80	NO KINGS	RT	40.00	50.00
81	SNAKE ESCAPES	RT	40.00	45.00
	E. ROBERTS		**NATIVE AMERICAN SERIES**	
91	LONE WOLF	10,000	45.00	48.00
92	TORTOISE LADY	10,000	45.00	48.00
	ROCKWELL INSPIRED		**NORMAN ROCKWELL COLLECTION**	
78	YOUNG DOCTOR	RT	50.00	65.00
79	BUTTERBOY	RT	40.00	45.00
79	LEAPFROG	RT	50.00	75.00
80	BACK TO SCHOOL	RT	24.00	30.00
80	CHRISTMAS TRIO	RT	75.00	90.00
80	LOVERS	RT	60.00	70.00
81	DREAMS OF LONG AGO	RT	60.00	75.00
81	NO SWIMMING	RT	25.00	35.00
81	SANTA'S GOOD BOYS	RT	75.00	90.00
82	AMERICAN MOTHER	RT	45.00	50.00
82	DOCTOR AND DOLL	RT	65.00	95.00
82	FACES OF CHRISTMAS	RT	75.00	90.00
82	LOVE LETTER	RT	27.00	40.00
83	CHRISTMAS CHORES	RT	75.00	85.00
83	CIRCUS	RT	65.00	70.00
83	DOCTOR AND DOLL	RT	27.00	30.00
83	DREAMBOAT	RT	24.00	30.00

YR NAME	LIMIT	ISSUE	QUOTE
84 BIG MOMENT	RT	27.00	30.00
84 TINY TIM	RT	75.00	85.00
84 VISIT WITH ROCKWELL	RT	65.00	75.00
ROCKWELL INSPIRED		**SATURDAY EVENING POST**	
91 DOWNHILL DARING	YR	25.00	30.00
91 MISSED	YR	25.00	27.00
92 CHOOSIN UP	YR	25.00	27.00
ROCKWELL INSPIRED		**TOM SAWYER**	
75 WHITEWASHING THE FENCE	RT	26.00	35.00
76 FIRST SMOKE	RT	26.00	35.00
77 TAKE YOUR MEDICINE	RT	26.00	40.00
78 LOST IN CAVE	RT	26.00	40.00

DELPHI

YR NAME	LIMIT	ISSUE	QUOTE
* *		**COMMEMORATING THE KING**	
93 BLUES AND BLACK LEATHER	OP	29.75	29.75
93 GOLDEN BOY	OP	29.75	29.75
93 LAS VEGAS, LIVE	OP	29.75	60.00
93 OUTSTANDING YOUNG MAN	OP	29.75	29.75
93 PRIVATE PRESLEY	OP	29.75	29.75
93 SCREEN IDOL	OP	29.75	29.75
93 THE ROCK AND ROLL LEGEND	OP	29.75	59.00
93 THE TIGER'S FAITH, SPIRT & DISCIPLINE	OP	29.75	29.75
P. PALMA		**DREAM MACHINES**	
88 '56 T-BIRD	150-DAY	24.75	30/00
88 '57 'VETTE	150-DAY	24.75	25.00
89 '56 CONTINENTAL	150-DAY	27.75	28.00
89 '57 BEL AIR	150-DAY	27.75	29.00
89 '57 CHRYSLER 300C	150-DAY	27.75	35.00
89 '58 BIARRITZ	150-DAY	27.75	28.00
* *		**ELVIS ON THE BIG SCREEN**	
92 G.I. BLUES	OP	29.75	50.00
92 LOVING YOU	OP	29.75	45.00
92 VIVA LAS VEGAS	OP	32.75	70.00
93 BLUE HAWAII	OP	32.75	32.75
93 JAILHOUSE ROCK	OP	32.75	32.75
93 SPEEDWAY	OP	34.75	34.75
93 SPINOUT	OP	34.75	34.75
* *		**ELVIS PRESLEY HIT PARADE**	
92 BLUE CHRISTMAS	OP	32.75	32.75
92 BLUE SUEDE SHOES	OP	29.75	29.75
92 HEARTBREAK	OP	29.75	29.75
92 HOUND DOG	OP	32.75	32.75
92 RETURN TO SENDER	OP	32.75	32.75
93 ALWAYS ON MY MIND	OP	34.75	34.75
93 BLUE MOONN OF KENTUCKY	OP	34.75	34.75
93 MYSTERY TRAIN	OP	34.75	34.75
93 PEACE IN THE VALLEY	OP	36.75	36.75
93 SUSPICIOUS MINDS	OP	36.75	36.75
93 TEDDY BEAR	OP	34.75	34.75
93 WEAR MY RING ROUND YOUR NECK	OP	36.75	36.75
92 HEARTBRAK HOTEL	150-DAY	29.75	29.75
* *		**ELVIS PRESLEY: IN PERFORMANCE**	
92 IN THE SPOTLIGHT:HAWAII '72	OP	31.75	31.75
92 TOUR FINALE: INDIANAPOLIS '77	OP	31.75	31.75
90 '68 COMEBACK SPECIAL	150-DAY	24.75	61.00
91 ALOHA FROM HAWAII	150-DAY	27.75	55.00
91 BACK IN TUPELO, 1956	150-DAY	27.75	69.00
91 BENEFIT FOR THE USS ARIZONA	150-DAY	29.75	59.00
91 CONCERT IN BATON ROUGE, 1974	150-DAY	29.75	40.00
91 IF I CAN DREAM	150-DAY	27.75	54.00
91 KING OF LAS VEGAS	150-DAY	24.75	62.00
91 MADISON SQUARE GARDEN, 1972	150-DAY	29.75	75.00
91 TAMPA, 1955	150-DAY	29.75	30.00
92 ON STAGE IN WICHITA, 1974	150-DAY	31.75	50.00
B. EMMETT		**ELVIS PRESLEY: LOOKING AT A LEGEND**	
88 ELVIS AT/GATES OF GRACELAND	150-DAY	24.75	90.00
89 HOMECOMING	150-DAY	27.75	64.00
89 JAILHOUSE ROCK	150-DAY	24.75	95.00
89 THE MEMPHIS FLASH	150-DAY	27.75	60.00
90 A STUDIO SESSION	150-DAY	27.75	50.00
90 ELVIS AND GLADYS	150-DAY	27.75	60.00
90 ELVIS IN HOLLYWOOD	150-DAY	29.75	65.00
90 ELVIS ON HIS HARLEY	150-DAY	29.75	80.00
90 STAGE DOOR AUTOGRAPHS	150-DAY	29.75	62.00
91 CHRISTMAS AT GRACELAND	150-DAY	32.75	70.00
91 CLOSING THE DEAL	150-DAY	34.75	35.00

YR	NAME	LIMIT	ISSUE	QUOTE
91	ENTERING SUN STUDIO	150-DAY	32.75	69.00
91	GOING FOR THE BLACK BELT	150-DAY	32.75	52.00
91	HIS HAND IN MINE	150-DAY	32.75	35.00
91	LETTERS FROM FANS	150-DAY	32.75	40.00
92	ELVIS RETURNS TO THE STAGE	150-DAY	34.75	40.00
* *		**ELVIS PRESLEY:LOOKING AT A LEGEND**		
89	THE MEMPHIS FLASH	OP	27.75	60.00
* *		**FABULOUS CARS OF THE FIFTIES**		
93	'57 BLUE BELAIR	OP	27.75	29.00
93	'57 RED CORVETTE	OP	24.75	59.00
93	'57 WHITE T-BIRD	OP	24.75	26.00
93	'59 PINK CADILLAC	OP	27.75	29.00
94	'56 LINCOLN PREMIER	OP	27.75	29.00
94	'59 RED FORD FAIRLANE	OP	27.75	29.00

V. GADINO

YR	NAME	LIMIT	ISSUE	QUOTE
		INDIANA JONES		
89	INDIANA JONES	150-DAY	24.75	25.00
89	INDIANA JONES AND HIS DAD	150-DAY	24.75	45.00
90	A FAMILY DISCUSSION	150-DAY	27.75	40.00
90	INDIANA JONES/DR. SCHNEIDER	150-DAY	27.75	30.00
90	YOUNG INDIANA JONES	150-DAY	27.75	50.00
91	INDIANA JONES/THE HOLY GRAIL	150-DAY	27.75	60.00
* *		**MARILYN MONROE**		
92	ALL ABOUT EVE	OP	29.75	59.00
92	DON'T BOTHER TO KNOCK	OP	31.75	42.00
92	MONKEY BUSINESS	OP	31.75	65.00
92	WE'RE NOT MARRIED	OP	31.75	45.00
89	MARILYN MONROE/7 YEAR ITCH	150-DAY	24.75	73.00
90	DIAMONDS/GIRL'S BEST FRIEND	150-DAY	24.75	82.00
91	MARILYN MONROE/RIVER OF NO RETURN	150-DAY	27.75	49.00
92	HOW TO MARRY A MILLIONAIRE	150-DAY	27.75	50.00
92	MARILYN MONROE AS CHERIE IN BUS STOP	150-DAY	29.75	60.00
92	MARILYN MONROE IN NIAGARA	150-DAY	29.75	80.00
92	MY HEART BELONGS TO DADDY	150-DAY	29.75	57.00
92	THERE'S NO BUSINESS/SHOW BUSINESS	150-DAY	27.75	80.00
* *		**PORTRAITS OF THE KING**		
92	FOLLOW THAT DREAM	OP	32.75	32.75
92	JUST BECAUSE	OP	32.75	32.75
92	YOU'RE A HEARTBREAKER	OP	32.75	32.75
91	ARE YOU LONESOME TONIGHT?	150-DAY	27.75	33.00
91	I'M YOURS	150-DAY	30.75	31.00
91	LOVE ME TENDER	150-DAY	27.75	45.00
91	TREAT ME NICE	150-DAY	30.75	35.00
92	THE WONDER OF YOU	150-DAY	30.75	30.75
* *		**TAKE ME OUT TO THE BALLGAME**		
93	BRIGGS STADIUM:HOME OF THE TIGERS	OP	32.75	32.75
93	CLEVELAND STADIUM:HOME OF THE INDIANS	OP	34.75	34.75
93	COMISKEY PARK:HOME OF THE WHITE SOX	OP	32.75	32.75
93	COUNTY STADIUM:HOME OF THE CHAMPS	OP	34.75	34.75
93	FENWAY PARK:HOME OF THE GREEN MONSTER	OP	32.75	32.75
93	MEMORIAL STADIUM:HOME OF THE ORIOLES	OP	34.75	34.75
93	WRIGLEY FIELD:THE FRIENDLY CONFINES	OP	29.75	29.75
93	YANKEE STADIUM:HOUSE THAT RUTH BUILT	OP	29.75	29.75
94	EBBETS FIELD:HOME OF THE DODGERS	OP	34.75	34.75
* *		**THE BEATLES COLLECTION**		
92	BEATLES '65	OP	27.75	27.75
92	HELP	OP	27.75	27.75
92	RUBBER SOUL	OP	29.75	29.75
92	THE BEATLES AT SHEA STADIUM	OP	29.75	29.75
92	YESTERDAY AND TODAY	OP	29.75	29.75
91	A HARD DAY'S NIGHT	150-DAY	27.75	58.00
91	HELLO AMERICA	150-DAY	24.75	60.00
91	THE BEATLES, LIVE IN CONCERT	150-DAY	24.75	45.00
* *		**THE MAGIC OF MARILYN**		
92	FOR OUR BOYS IN KOREA, 1954	OP	24.75	24.75
92	OPENING NIGHT	OP	24.75	24.75
93	CURTAIN CALL	OP	29.75	29.75
93	PHOTO OPPORTUNITY	OP	29.75	29.75
93	RISING STAR	OP	27.75	27.75
93	SHINING STAR	OP	29.75	29.75
93	STOPPING TRAFFIC	OP	27.75	27.75

DEPARTMENT 56

YR	NAME	LIMIT	ISSUE	QUOTE
*		**A CHRISTMAS CAROL**		
91	THE CRATCHIT'S CHRISTMAS PUDDING	18,000	60.00	75.00
92	MARLEY'S GHOST APPEARS TO SCROOGE	18,000	60.00	60.00
*		**DICKENS' VILLAGE COLLECTION**		
87	DICKENS' VILLAGE 5917-0 (SET OF 4)	CL	140.00	140.00

Shuffleton's Barbershop, *the first issue in the "Rockwell Annual" series, recaptures the days when a trip to the barber resulted in more than a haircut. Produced by Artaffects.*

What collector could resist sweet Julia *created by artist Mago for Artaffects?*

Guess who's been sleeping in their bed? Goldilocks *is the first issue in the "Classic Fairy Tales" series produced by Edwin M. Knowles.*

Iris Quartet *strikes a note of sentiment in the hearts of flower lovers. It is the first issue in Lena Liu's series "Symphony of Shimmering Beauty" by W.S. George.*

YR	NAME	LIMIT	ISSUE	QUOTE

DUNCAN ROYALE

S. MORTON — HISTORY OF SANTA CLAUS I

YR	NAME	LIMIT	ISSUE	QUOTE
*	COLLECTION OF 12 PLATES	RT	480.00	480.00
85	KRIS KRINGLE	RT	40.00	65.00
85	MEDIEVAL	RT	40.00	75.00
85	PIONEER	10,000	40.00	40.00
86	CIVIL WAR	10,000	40.00	40.00
86	NAST	10,000	40.00	75.00
86	RUSSIAN	10,000	40.00	40.00
86	SODA POP	RT	40.00	65.00
87	BLACK PETER	10,000	40.00	40.00
87	DEDT MOROZ	10,000	40.00	40.00
87	ST. NICHOLAS	RT	40.00	75.00
87	VICTORIAN	10,000	40.00	40.00
87	WASSAIL	RT	40.00	40.00

EDNA HIBEL STUDIOS

E. HIBEL — ARTE OVALE

YR	NAME	LIMIT	ISSUE	QUOTE
80	TAKARA, BLANCO	700	450.00	1100.00
80	TAKARA, COBALT BLUE	1000	595.00	2220.00
80	TAKARA, GOLD	300	1000.00	4000.00
84	TARO-KUN, BLANCO	700	450.00	750.00
84	TARO-KUN, COBALT BLUE	1000	595.00	975.00
84	TARO-KUN, GOLD	300	1000.00	2500.00

E. HIBEL — MARCH OF DIMES: OUR CHILDREN, OUR FUTURE

YR	NAME	LIMIT	ISSUE	QUOTE
90	A TIME TO EMBRACE	150-DAY	29.00	29.00

E. HIBEL — THE WORLD I LOVE

YR	NAME	LIMIT	ISSUE	QUOTE
81	LEAH'S FAMILY	17,500	85.00	26.00-65.00
82	KAYLIN	17,500	85.00	325.00
83	EDNA'S MUSIC	17,500	85.00	195.00
83	O, HANA	17,500	85.00	195.00

EDWIN M. KNOWLES

* CASTARI — GRANDPARENTS

YR	NAME	LIMIT	ISSUE	QUOTE
80	BEDTIME STORY	OP	18.00	18.00
81	THE SKATING LESSON	OP	20.00	20.00
82	THE COOKIE TASTING	OP	20.00	20.00
83	THE SWINGER	OP	20.00	20.00
84	THE SKATING QUEEN	OP	22.00	22.00
85	THE PATRIOT'S PARADE	OP	22.00	22.00
86	THE HOME RUN	OP	22.00	22.00
87	THE SNEAK PREVIEW	OP	22.00	22.00

B. LANGTON — A LOVING LOOK: DUCK FAMILIES

YR	NAME	LIMIT	ISSUE	QUOTE
91	FAMILY OUTING	150-DAY	34.50	40.00

E. HIBEL — A SWAN IS BORN

YR	NAME	LIMIT	ISSUE	QUOTE
87	AT THE BARRE	OP	24.50	25.00
87	HOPES AND DREAMS	OP	24.50	25.00
87	IN POSITION	OP	24.50	17.00
88	JUST FOR SIZE	OP	24.50	45.00
87	AT THE BARRE	150-DAY	24.50	38.00
87	HOPES AND DREAMS	150-DAY	24.50	28.00-45.00
87	IN POSITION	150-DAY	24.50	42.00-50.00
88	JUST FOR SIZE	150-DAY	24.50	45.00

* * — AESOP'S FABLES

YR	NAME	LIMIT	ISSUE	QUOTE
88	THE GOOSE THAT LAID THE GOLDEN EGG	OP	27.90	28.00
88	THE HARE & THE TORTOISE	OP	27.90	28.00
89	THE FOX & THE GRAPES	OP	30.90	31.00
89	THE JAY & THE PEACOCK	OP	30.90	28.00
89	THE LION & THE MOUSE	OP	30.90	35.00
89	THE MILK MAID & HER PAIL	OP	30.90	32.00
88	THE FOX AND THE GRAPES	150-DAY	30.90	40.00
88	THE GOOSE THAT LAID THE GOLDEN EGG	150-DAY	27.90	30.00
88	THE HARE AND THE TORTOISE	150-DAY	27.90	33.00
89	THE JAY AND THE PEACOCK	150-DAY	30.90	54.00
89	THE LION AND THE MOUSE	150-DAY	30.90	31.00-40.00
89	THE MILK MAID AND HER PAIL	150-DAY	30.90	31.00-60.00

E. HIBEL — AMERICAN INNOCENTS

YR	NAME	LIMIT	ISSUE	QUOTE
86	ABIGAIL IN THE ROSE GARDEN	OP	19.50	20.00
86	ANN BY THE TERRACE	OP	19.50	20.00
86	ELLEN & JOHN IN THE PARLOR	OP	19.50	20.00
87	WILLIAM ON THE ROCKING HORSE	OP	19.50	46.00
86	ABIGAIL IN THE ROSE GARDEN	100-DAY	19.50	25.00
86	ANN BY THE TERRACE	100-DAY	19.50	29.00
86	ELLEN AND JOHN IN THE PARLOR	100-DAY	19.50	35.00
86	WILLIAM ON THE ROCKING HORSE	100-DAY	19.50	60.00

* * — AMERICANA HOLIDAYS

YR	NAME	LIMIT	ISSUE	QUOTE
78	FOURTH OF JULY	OP	26.00	26.00

YR	NAME	LIMIT	ISSUE	QUOTE
79	THANKSGIVING	OP	26.00	26.00
80	EASTER	OP	26.00	26.00
81	VALENTINE'S DAY	OP	26.00	26.00
82	FATHER'S DAY	OP	26.00	26.00
83	CHRISTMAS	OP	26.00	26.00
84	MOTHER'S DAY	OP	26.00	26.00
78	FOURTH OF JULY	YR	26.00	29.00
79	THANKSGIVING	YR	26.00	30.00
80	EASTER	YR	26.00	26.00
81	VALENTINE'S DAY	YR	26.00	27.00
82	FATHER'S DAY	YR	26.00	27.00
83	CHRISTMAS	YR	26.00	26.00
84	MOTHER'S DAY	YR	26.00	27.00
A. BRACKENBURY		**AMY BRACKENBURY'S CAT TALES**		
87	A CHANCE MEETING: WHITE AM. SHORTHAIRS	150-DAY	21.50	45.00
87	GONE FISHING: MAINE COONS	150-DAY	21.50	65.00
88	ALL WRAPPED UP: HIMALAYANS	150-DAY	24.90	65.00
88	FLOWER BED: BRITISH SHORTHAIRS	150-DAY	24.90	40.00
88	KITTENS AND MITTENS: SILVER TABBIES	150-DAY	24.90	45.00
88	STRAWBERRIES AND CREAM: CREAM PERSIANS	150-DAY	24.90	50.00
* *				**ANNIE**
83	ANNIE AND GRACE	OP	19.00	19.00
83	ANNIE AND SANDY	OP	19.00	19.00
83	DADDY WARBUCKS	OP	19.00	19.00
84	ANNIE AND THE ORPHANS	OP	21.00	21.00
85	ANNIE AND MISS HANNIGAN	OP	21.00	21.00
85	TOMORROW	OP	21.00	21.00
86	ANNIE, LILY AND ROOSTER	OP	24.00	44.00
86	GRAND FINALE	OP	24.00	25.00
83	ANNIE AND GRACE	100-DAY	19.00	22.00-35.00
83	ANNIE AND SANDY	100-DAY	19.00	22.00-50.00
83	DADDY WARBUCKS	100-DAY	19.00	19.00-35.00
84	ANNIE AND THE ORPHANS	100-DAY	21.00	24.00-32.00
85	TOMORROW	100-DAY	21.00	22.00-32.50
86	ANNIE AND MISS HANNIGAN	100-DAY	21.00	29.50
86	ANNIE, LILLY AND ROOSTER	100-DAY	24.00	27.50
86	GRAND FINALE	100-DAY	24.00	24.00
* *		**BABY OWLS OF NORTH AMERICA**		
91	3 OF A KIND: GREAT HORNED OWLS	OP	30.90	35.00
91	BEGINNING TO EXPLORE:BOREAL OWLS	OP	32.90	50.00
91	FORTY WINKS:SAW-WHET OWLS	OP	27.90	38.00
91	OUT ON A LIMB:GREAT GRAY OWL	OP	30.90	45.00
91	PEEK-A-WHOO:SCREECH OWLS	OP	27.90	39.00
91	THE TREE HOUSE:NORTHERNPYGMY OWLS	OP	30.90	48.00
92	THREE COMPANY:LONG EARED OWLS	OP	32.90	45.00
92	WHOO'S THERE: BARRED OWLS	OP	32.90	32.90
91	BEGINNING TO EXPLORE: BOREAL OWLS	150-DAY	32.90	32.90
91	FORTY WINKS: SAW-WHET OWLS	150-DAY	29.90	29.90
91	OUT ON A LIMB: GREAT GRAY OWLS	150-DAY	30.90	30.90
91	PEEK-A-WHOO: SCREECH OWLS	150-DAY	27.90	27.90
91	THE TREE HOUSE: NORTHERN PYGMY OWLS	150-DAY	30.90	30.90
91	THREE OF A KIND: GREAT HORNED OWLS	150-DAY	30.90	30.90
92	THREE'S COMPANY: LONG EARED OWLS	150-DAY	32.90	32.90
* *			**BACKYARD HARMONY**	
91	ANNOUNCING SPRING	OP	30.90	58.00
91	THE SINGING LESSON	OP	27.90	39.00
91	WELCOMING A NEW DAY	OP	27.90	30.00
92	AT THE PEEP OF DAY	OP	32.90	40.00
92	SPRING TIME PRIDE	OP	30.90	50.00
92	THE MORNING HARVEST	OP	30.90	48.00
92	TODAY'S DISCOVERIES	OP	32.90	32.90
92	TREETOP SERENADE	OP	32.90	59.00
* *				**BAMBI**
91	BASHFUL BAMBI	OP	34.90	35.00
92	BAMBI'S MORNING GREETINGS	OP	37.90	37.90
92	BAMBI'S NEW FRIENDS	OP	34.90	34.90
92	BAMBI'S SKATING LESSON	OP	37.90	37.90
92	HELLO LITTLE PRINCE	OP	37.90	37.90
93	WHAT'S UP POSSUMS?	OP	37.90	37.90
		BEAUTY AND THE BEAST		
93	A BLOSSOMING ROMANCE	OP	29.90	29.90
93	A MISMATCH	OP	34.90	34.90
93	BE OUR GUEST	OP	34.90	34.90
93	BELLE'S FAVORITE STORY	OP	34.90	34.90
93	LEARNING TO LOVE	OP	32.90	32.90
93	LOVE'S FIRST DANCE	OP	29.90	29.90

YR	NAME	LIMIT	ISSUE	QUOTE
93	PAPA'S WORKSHOP	OP	32.90	32.90
93	WARMING UP	OP	32.90	32.90
94	A GIFT FOR BELLE	OP	36.90	36.90
94	A SPOT OF TEA	OP	34.90	34.90
94	ENCHANTE'S CHERIE	OP	36.90	36.90
**			**BIBLICAL MOTHERS**	
83	BATHSHEBA AND SOLOMON	OP	39.50	40.00
84	JUDGMENT OF SOLOMON	OP	39.50	40.00
84	PHAROH'S DAUGHTER & MOSES	OP	39.50	40.00
85	MARY AND JESUS	OP	39.50	40.00
85	REBECCA, JACOB & ESAU	OP	44.50	44.00
85	SARAH AND ISAAC	OP	44.50	45.00
83	BETHSHEBA AND SOLOMON	YR	39.50	39.00-67.50
84	JUDGMENT OF SOLOMON	YR	39.50	40.00-65.00
84	PHARAOH'S DAUGHTER AND MOSES	YR	39.50	39.50-55.00
85	MARY AND JESUS	YR	39.50	39.50-42.00
85	SARAH AND ISAAC	YR	44.50	51.00
86	REBEKAH, JACOB AND ESAU	YR	44.50	45.00
**			**BIRDS OF THE SEASONS**	
90	BLUEBIRDS IN SPRING	OP	24.90	31.00
90	CARDINAL IN WINTER	OP	24.90	44.00
91	BALTIMORE ORIOLES IN SUMMER	OP	27.90	30.00
91	BLUE JAYS IN EARLY FALL	OP	27.90	43.00
91	CEDAR WAXWINGS IN FALL	OP	29.90	64.00
91	CHICKADEES IN WINTER	OP	29.90	55.00
91	NUTATCHES IN FALL	OP	27.90	28.00
91	ROBINS IN EARLY SPRING	OP	27.90	30.00
90	BLUEBIRDS IN SPRING	150-DAY	24.90	24.90
90	CARDINALS IN WINTER	150-DAY	24.90	24.90
91	BALTIMORE ORIOLES IN SUMMER	150-DAY	27.90	27.90
91	BLUE JAYS IN EARLY FALL	150-DAY	27.90	27.90
91	CEDAR WAXWINGS IN FALL	150-DAY	29.90	29.90
91	CHICKADEES IN WINTER	150-DAY	29.90	29.90
91	NUTHATCHES IN FALL	150-DAY	27.90	27.90
91	ROBINS IN EARLY SPRING	150-DAY	27.90	27.90
**			**BRITANNICA'S BIRDS OF YOUR GARDEN**	
85	THE BALTIMORE ORIOLE	OP	22.50	30.00
85	THE BLUE JAY	OP	19.50	28.00
85	THE CARDINAL	OP	19.50	32.00
86	THE BLUEBIRD	OP	22.50	28.00
86	THE CHICKADEES	OP	22.50	20.00
86	THE HUMMINGBIRD	OP	24.50	32.00
86	THE ROBIN	OP	22.50	33.00
87	THE CEDAR WAXWING	OP	24.90	40.00
87	THE DOWNY WOODPECKER	OP	24.50	40.00
87	THE GOLDFINCH	OP	24.50	30.00
85	BLUE JAY	100-DAY	19.50	34.00
85	CARDINAL	100-DAY	19.50	36.00
85	ORIOLE	100-DAY	22.50	32.00
86	BLUEBIRD	100-DAY	22.50	34.00
86	CHICKADEES	100-DAY	22.50	37.00
86	HUMMINGBIRD	100-DAY	24.50	27.00
86	ROBIN	100-DAY	22.50	23.00
87	CEDAR WAXWING	100-DAY	24.90	25.00
87	DOWNY WOODPECKER	100-DAY	24.50	25.00
87	GOLDFINCH	100-DAY	24.50	34.00
**			**CALL OF THE WILDERNESS**	
91	FIRST OUTING	OP	29.90	53.00
91	HOWLING LESSON	OP	29.90	60.00
91	SILENT WATCH	OP	32.90	50.00
91	WINTER TRAVELERS	OP	32.90	33.00
92	A NEW FUTURE	OP	34.90	34.90
92	AHEAD OF THE PACK	OP	32.90	32.90
92	MORNING MIST	OP	36.90	36.90
92	NORTHERN SPIRITS	OP	34.90	34.90
92	THE SILENT ONE	OP	36.90	36.90
92	TWILIGHT FRIENDS	OP	34.90	34.90
**			**CAROUSEL**	
87	IF I LOVED YOU	OP	24.90	25.00
88	MR. SNOW	OP	24.90	25.00
88	THE CAROUSEL WALTZ	OP	24.90	30.00
88	YOU'LL NEVER WALK ALONG	OP	24.90	25.00
87	IF I LOVED YOU	150-DAY	24.90	30.00
88	MR. SNOW	150-DAY	24.90	27.00
88	THE CAROUSEL WALTZ	150-DAY	24.90	48.00-67.00
88	YOU'LL NEVER WALK ALONE	150-DAY	24.90	54.00

YR	NAME	LIMIT	ISSUE	QUOTE
* *				**CASABLANCA**
90	HERE'S LOOKING AT YOU, KID	OP	34.90	36.00
90	WE'LL ALWAYS HAVE PARIS	OP	34.90	41.00
91	A FRANC FOR YOUR THOUGHTS	OP	37.90	58.00
91	PLAY IT SAM	OP	37.90	59.00
91	RICK'S CAFE AMERICCAIN	OP	37.90	38.00
91	WE LOVED EACH OTHER ONCE	OP	37.90	35.00
90	HERE'S LOOKING AT YOU, KID	150-DAY	34.90	34.90
90	WE'LL ALWAYS HAVE PARIS	150-DAY	34.90	34.90
91	A FRANC FOR YOUR THOUGHTS	150-DAY	37.90	37.90
91	PLAY IT AGAIN SAM	150-DAY	37.90	37.90
91	RICK'S CAFE AMERICAN	150-DAY	37.90	37.90
91	WE LOVED EACH OTHER ONCE	150-DAY	37.90	37.90
A. BRACKENBURY				**CAT TALES**
87	A CHANCE MEETING:SHORTHAIRS	OP	21.50	26.00
87	GONE FISHING:MAINE COONS	OP	21.50	78.00
88	ALL WRAPPE DUP: HIMALAYANS	OP	24.90	45.00
88	FLOWER BED:BRITISH SHORTHAIRS	OP	24.90	25.00
88	KITTENS/MITTENS:SILVER TABBIE	OP	24.90	25.00
88	STRAWBERRIES/CREAM: PERSIANS	OP	24.90	65.00
J.W. SMITH				**CHILDHOOD HOLIDAYS**
86	CHRISTMAS	CL	19.50	20.00
86	EASTER	CL	19.50	20.00
86	THANKSGIVING	CL	19.50	20.00
86	VALENTINE'S DAY	CL	22.50	23.00
87	FOURTH OF JULY	CL	22.50	23.00
87	MOTHER'S DAY	CL	22.50	23.00
* *				**CHINA'S NATURAL TREASURES**
91	THE GIANT PANDA	OP	32.90	35.00
91	THE SIBERIAN TIGER	OP	29.90	44.00
91	THE SNOW LEOPARD	OP	29.90	30.00
92	THE ASIAN ELEPHANT	OP	32.90	45.00
92	THE GOLDEN MONKEY	OP	34.90	50.00
92	THE TIBETAN BROWN BEAR	OP	32.90	40.00
E. HIBEL				**CHRISTMAS**
85	THE ANGEL'S MESSAGE	OP	45.00	45.00
86	THE GIFTS OF THE MAGI	OP	45.00	45.00
87	THE FIGHT INTO EGYPT	OP	49.00	50.00
88	ADORATION OF THE SHEPHERD	OP	49.00	77.00
89	PEACEFUL KINGDOM	OP	49.00	49.00
90	THE NATIVITY	OP	49.00	55.00
88	THE ANNUNCIATION	OP	44.90	45.00
88	THE NATIVITY	OP	44.90	45.00
89	ADORATION OF THE SHEPHERDS	OP	49.90	50.00
90	JOURNEY OF THE MAGI	OP	49.90	56.00
91	GIFTS OF THE MAGI	OP	49.90	52.00
92	REST ON THE FLIGHT INTO EGYPT	OP	49.90	51.00
				CHRISTMAS IN THE CITY
92	A CHRISTMAS SNOWFALL	OP	34.90	44.00
92	YULETIDE CELEBRATION	OP	34.90	54.00
93	HOLIDAY CHEER	OP	34.90	34.90
93	THE MAGIC OF CHRISTMAS	OP	34.90	35.00
*				**CINDERELLA**
88	A DREAM IS A WISH YOUR HEART MAKES	150-DAY	29.90	95.00
88	BIBBIDI, BOBBIDI, BOO	150-DAY	29.90	50.00-60.00
89	A DRESS FOR CINDERELLY	150-DAY	32.90	105.00
89	OH SING SWEET NIGHTENGALE	150-DAY	32.90	32.90
89	SO THIS IS LOVE	150-DAY	32.90	32.90
90	AT THE STROKE OF MIDNIGHT	150-DAY	32.90	32.90
90	HAPPILY EVER AFTER	150-DAY	34.90	34.90
90	IF THE SHOE FITS	150-DAY	34.90	34.90
88	BIBBIDI-BOBBIDI-BOO	OP	29.90	61.00
89	A DREAM/WISH/HEART MAKES	OP	29.90	60.00
89	A DRESS OF CINDERELLY	OP	32.90	80.00
89	OH SING SWEET NIGHTINGALE	OP	32.90	50.00
89	SO THIS IS LOVE	OP	32.90	70.00
90	AT THE STROKE OF MIDNIGHT	OP	32.90	58.00
90	HAPPILY EVER AFTER	OP	35.00	35.00
90	IF THE SHOE FITS	OP	34.90	58.00
* *				**CLASSIC FAIRY TALES**
91	GOLDILOCKS AND THE 3 BEARS	OP	29.90	53.00
91	LITTLE RED RIDING HOOD	OP	29.90	54.00
91	THE FROG PRINCE	OP	32.90	60.00
91	THE THREE LITTLE PIGS	OP	32.90	55.00
92	HANSEL AND GRETEL	OP	34.90	66.00
92	JACK AND THE BEANSTALK	OP	32.90	56.00

YR	NAME	LIMIT	ISSUE	QUOTE
92	PUSS IN BOOTS	OP	34.90	34.90
92	TOM THUMB	OP	34.90	34.90
**			**CLASSIC MOTHER GOOSE**	
92	LITTLE MISS MUFFET	OP	29.90	45.00
92	MARY HAD A LITTLE LAMB	OP	29.90	49.00
92	MARY,MARY, QUITE CONTRARY	OP	29.90	55.00
**			**COZY COUNTRY CORNERS**	
90	LAZY MORNING	OP	24.90	51.00
90	WARM RETREAT	OP	24.90	50.00
91	A SUNNY SPOT	OP	27.90	38.00
91	APPLE ANTICS	OP	29.90	74.00
91	ATTIC AFTERNOON	OP	27.90	50.00
91	HIDE AND SEEK	OP	29.90	45.00
91	MIRROR MISCHIEF	OP	27.90	58.00
91	TABLE TROUBLE	OP	29.90	65.00
90	LAZY MORNING	150-DAY	24.90	24.90
90	WARM RETREAT	150-DAY	24.90	24.90
91	A SUNNY SPOT	150-DAY	27.90	27.90
91	APPLE ANTICS	150-DAY	29.90	29.90
91	ATTIC AFTERNOON	150-DAY	27.90	27.90
91	HIDE AND SEEK	150-DAY	29.90	29.90
91	MIRROR MISCHIEF	150-DAY	27.90	27.90
91	TABLE TROUBLE	150-DAY	29.90	29.90
J. CSATARI			**CSATARI GRANDPARENT**	
80	BEDTIME STORY	100-DAY	18.00	18.00
81	THE SKATING LESSON	100-DAY	20.00	23.00
82	THE COOKIE TASTING	100-DAY	20.00	20.00
83	THE SWINGER	100-DAY	20.00	20.00
84	THE SKATING QUEEN	100-DAY	22.00	25.00
85	THE PATRIOT'S PARADE	100-DAY	22.00	22.00
86	THE HOME RUN	100-DAY	22.00	29.00
87	THE SNEAK PREVIEW	100-DAY	22.00	34.00
*		**FANTASIA: (THE SORCERER'S APPRENTICE) GOLDEN ANNIVERSARY**		
90	MISCHIEVOUS APPRENTICE	150-DAY	29.90	45.00
90	THE APPRENTICE'S DREAM	150-DAY	29.90	58.00
91	DREAMS OF POWER	150-DAY	32.90	68.00
91	MICKEY MAKES MAGIC	150-DAY	34.90	39.90
91	MICKEY'S MAGICAL WHIRLPOOL	150-DAY	32.90	33.00
91	THE PENITENT APPRENTICE	150-DAY	34.90	34.90
91	WIZARDRY GONE WILD	150-DAY	32.90	32.90
**			**FANTASIA:SORCERER'S APPRENTICE**	
90	MISCHIEVOUS APPRENTICE	OP	29.90	71.00
90	THE APPRENTICE'S DREAM	OP	29.90	60.00
91	DREAMS OF POWER	OP	32.90	60.00
91	MICKEY MAKES MAGIC	OP	34.90	59.00
91	MICKEY'S MAGICAL WHIRLPOOL	OP	32.90	40.00
91	THE PENITENT APPRENTICE	OP	34.90	34.90
91	WIZARDRY GONE WILD	OP	32.90	45.00
92	AN APPRENTICE AGAIN	OP	34.90	34.90
**			**FATHER'S LOVE**	
84	BATTER UP	OP	19.50	20.00
84	OPEN WIDE	OP	19.50	20.00
85	LITTLE SHAVER	OP	19.50	20.00
85	SWING TIME	OP	22.50	23.00
84	BATTER UP	100-DAY	19.50	20.00
84	OPEN WIDE	100-DAY	19.50	20.00
85	LITTLE SHAVER	100-DAY	19.50	23.00
85	SWING TIME	100-DAY	22.50	26.00
**			**FIELD PUPPIES**	
87	CAUGHT/ACT-GOLDEN RETRIEVER	OP	24.90	40.00
87	DOG TIRED-SPRINGER SPANIEL	OP	24.90	45.00
88	A PERFECT SET-LABRADOR	OP	27.90	42.00
88	FRITZ'S FOLLY-GERMAN/POINTER	OP	27.90	40.00
88	MISSING/POINT-IRISH SETTER	OP	27.90	28.00
88	SHIRT TALES-COCKER SPANIEL	OP	27.90	45.00
89	COMMAND PERFORMANCE/WELMARANER	OP	29.90	34.00
89	FINE/FRIENDS-ENGLISH SETTER	OP	29.90	30.00
87	CAUGHT IN THE ACT-THE GOLDEN RETRIEVER	150-DAY	24.90	60.00
87	DOG TIRED-THE SPRINGER SPANIEL	150-DAY	24.90	62.00-65.00
88	A PERFECT SET-LABRADOR	150-DAY	27.90	52.00
88	FRITZ'S FOLLY-GERMAN SHORTHAIRED POINTER	150-DAY	27.90	29.90
88	MISSING/POINT/IRISH SETTER	150-DAY	27.90	40.00
88	SHIRT TALES-COCKER SPANIEL	150-DAY	27.90	29.90
89	FINE FEATHERED FRIENDS-ENGLISH SETTER	150-DAY	29.90	29.90
89	PERFORMANCE-WIEMARANER	150-DAY	29.90	29.90

YR	NAME	LIMIT	ISSUE	QUOTE
* *				**FIELD TRIPS**
90	GONE FISHING	OP	24.90	24.00
91	BOXED IN	OP	27.90	25.00
91	DUCKING DUTY	OP	24.90	24.00
91	PAIL PALS	OP	29.90	34.00
91	PUPPY TALES	OP	27.90	28.00
91	PUPS 'N BOOTS	OP	27.90	30.00
92	CHESAPEAKE BAY RETRIEVERS	OP	29.90	32.00
92	HAT TRICK	OP	29.90	30.00
90	GONE FISHING	150-DAY	24.90	24.90
91	BOXED IN	150-DAY	27.90	27.90
91	CHESAPEAKE BAY RETRIEVERS	150-DAY	29.90	29.90
91	DUCKING DUTY	150-DAY	24.90	24.90
91	HAT TRICK	150-DAY	29.90	29.90
91	PAIL PALS	150-DAY	29.90	29.90
91	PUPPY TALES	150-DAY	27.90	27.90
91	PUPS 'N BOOTS	150-DAY	27.90	27.90
* *				**FIRST IMPRESSIONS**
91	ALL EARS	OP	32.90	65.00
91	FINE FEATHERED FRIEND	OP	32.90	44.00
91	TAKING A GANDER	OP	29.90	40.00
91	TWOS' COMPANY	OP	29.90	35.00
91	WHAT'S UP?	OP	32.90	35.00
92	BETWEEM FRIENDS	OP	32.90	35.00
* *				**FOUR ANCIENT ELEMENTS**
84	AIR	OP	29.50	30.00
84	EARTH	OP	27.50	28.00
84	FIRE	OP	29.50	44.00
84	WATER	OP	27.50	28.00
* *				**FRANCES HOOK LEGACY**
85	DAYDREAMING	OP	19.50	20.00
85	FACSINATION	OP	19.50	20.00
86	DISAPPOINTMENT	OP	22.50	23.00
86	DISCOVERY	OP	22.50	23.00
86	WONDERMENT	OP	22.50	23.00
87	EXPECTATION	OP	22.50	23.00
85	DAYDREAMING	100-DAY	19.50	22.50
85	FASCINATION	100-DAY	19.50	22.50
86	DISAPPOINTMENT	100-DAY	22.50	22.50
86	DISCOVERY	100-DAY	22.50	22.50
86	WONDERMENT	100-DAY	22.50	22.50
87	EXPECTATION	100-DAY	22.50	33.00
				FREE AS THE WIND
92	AIRBORNE	OP	32.90	32.90
92	ALOFT	OP	29.90	50.00
92	SKYWARD	OP	29.90	52.00
93	ASCENT	OP	32.90	32.90
93	FLIGHT	OP	32.90	32.90
93	HEAVENWARD	OP	32.90	32.90
J. DOWN				**FRIENDS I REMEMBER**
83	FISH STORY	97-DAY	17.50	20.00-40.00
83	FISH STORY	CL	17.50	18.00
84	OFFICE HOURS	97-DAY	17.50	20.00-39.00
84	OFFICE HOURS	CL	17.50	18.00
85	A COAT OF PAINT	97-DAY	17.50	21.00-38.00
85	A COAT OF PAINT	CL	17.50	18.00
85	FRINGE BENEFITS	97-DAY	19.50	20.00-36.00
85	FRINGE BENEFITS	CL	19.50	20.00
85	HERE COMES THE BRIDE	97-DAY	19.50	20.00-37.00
85	HERE COMES THE BRIDE	CL	19.50	20.00
86	FLOWER ARRANGEMENT	97-DAY	21.50	25.00-35.00
86	FLOWER ARRANGEMENT	CL	21.50	22.00
86	HIGH SOCIETY	97-DAY	19.50	20.00-35.00
86	HIGH SOCIETY	CL	19.50	20.00
86	TASTE TEST	97-DAY	21.50	25.00
86	TASTE TEST	CL	21.50	22.00
* *				**FRIENDS OF THE FOREST**
87	THE RABBIT	OP	24.50	25.00
87	THE RACCOON	OP	24.50	32.00
87	THE SQUIRREL	OP	27.90	28.00
88	THE CHIPMUNK	OP	27.90	28.00
88	THE FOX	OP	27.90	28.00
88	THE OTTER	OP	27.90	28.00
87	THE RABBIT	150-DAY	24.50	45.00
87	THE RACCOON	150-DAY	24.50	62.00
87	THE SQUIRREL	150-DAY	27.90	36.00-46.00

YR	NAME	LIMIT	ISSUE	QUOTE
88	THE CHIPMUNK	150-DAY	27.90	36.00-47.00
88	THE FOX	150-DAY	27.90	55.00
88	THE OTTER	150-DAY	27.90	40.00-50.00

** **

GARDEN COTTAGES OF ENGLAND

YR	NAME	LIMIT	ISSUE	QUOTE
91	CANDLELIT COTTAGE	OP	30.90	45.00
91	CEDAR NOOK COTTAGE	OP	27.90	34.00
91	CHANDLER'S COTTAGE	OP	27.90	59.00
91	MCKENNA'S COTTAGE	OP	32.90	57.00
91	OPEN GATE COTTAGE	OP	30.09	50.00
91	WOODSMAN'S THATCH	OP	32.90	58.00
92	MERRITT'S COTTAGE	OP	32.90	55.00
92	STONEGATE COTTAGE	OP	32.90	60.00
91	CANDLELIT COTTAGE	150	30.90	30.90
91	CEDAR NOOK COTTAGE	150-DAY	27.90	27.90
91	CHANDLER'S COTTAGE	150-DAY	27.90	27.90
91	MCKENNA'S COTTAGE	150-DAY	30.90	30.90
91	OPEN GATE COTTAGE	150-DAY	30.90	30.90
91	WOODSMAN'S THATCH COTTAGE	150-DAY	32.90	32.90

GARDEN SECRETS

YR	NAME	LIMIT	ISSUE	QUOTE
93	BLOOMIN' KITTIES	OP	24.90	24.90
93	FLORAL PURR-FRAME	OP	24.90	24.90
93	FLOWER FANCIERS	OP	24.90	24.90
93	FRISKY BUSINESS	OP	24.90	24.90
93	KITTY CORNER	OP	24.90	24.90
93	MEADOWN MISCHIEF	OP	24.90	24.90
93	NINE LIVES	OP	24.90	25.00
93	PUSSYCAT POTPOURRI	OP	24.90	24.90

** **

GONE WITH THE WIND

YR	NAME	LIMIT	ISSUE	QUOTE
78	SCARLETT	OP	21.50	16.00
79	ASHLEY	OP	21.50	80.00
80	MELANIE	OP	21.50	50.00
81	RHETT	OP	23.50	40.00
82	MAMMY LACING SCARLETT	OP	23.50	55.00
83	MELANIE GIVES BIRTH	OP	23.50	55.00
84	SCARLETT'S GREEN DRESS	OP	25.50	55.00
85	RHETT AND BONNIE	OP	25.50	59.00
85	SCARLETT & RHETT: THE FINALE	OP	29.50	54.00
78	SCARLETT	100-DAY	21.50	210.00
79	ASHLEY	100-DAY	21.50	120.00
80	MELANIE	100-DAY	21.50	60.00
81	RHETT	100-DAY	23.50	45.00
82	MAMMY LACING SCARLETT	100-DAY	23.50	80.00
83	MELANIE GIVES BIRTH	100-DAY	23.50	86.00
84	SCARLET'S GREEN DRESS	100-DAY	25.50	65.00
85	RHETT AND BONNIE	100-DAY	25.50	95.00
85	SCARLETT AND RHETT: THE FINALE	100-DAY	29.50	80.00

** **

GREAT CATS OF THE AMERICAS

YR	NAME	LIMIT	ISSUE	QUOTE
89	THE COUGAR	OP	29.90	43.00
89	THE JAGUAR	OP	29.90	50.00
89	THE LYNX	OP	32.90	33.00
90	THE BOBCAT	OP	32.90	33.00
90	THE JAGUARUNDI	OP	32.90	33.00
90	THE MARGAY	OP	34.90	35.00
90	THE OCELOT	OP	32.90	33.00
91	THE PAMPAS CAT	OP	34.90	35.00
89	THE COUGAR	150-DAY	29.90	60.00
89	THE JAGUAR	150-DAY	29.90	105.00
89	THE LYNX	150-DAY	32.90	32.90
90	THE BOBCAT	150-DAY	32.90	32.90
90	THE JAGUARUNDI	150-DAY	32.90	32.90
90	THE MARGAY	150-DAY	34.90	34.90
90	THE OCELOT	150-DAY	32.90	32.90
91	THE PAMPAS CAT	150-DAY	34.90	34.90

** **

HEIRLOOMS AND LACE

YR	NAME	LIMIT	ISSUE	QUOTE
89	ANNA	OP	34.90	53.00
89	VICTORIA	OP	34.90	63.00
90	OLIVIA	OP	37.90	100.00
90	TESS	OP	37.90	82.00
91	BRIDGET	OP	37.90	108.00
91	REBECCA	OP	37.90	85.00
89	ANNA	150-DAY	34.90	34.90
89	VICTORIA	150-DAY	34.90	34.90
90	OLIVIA	150-DAY	37.90	37.90
90	TESS	150-DAY	37.90	37.90
91	BRIDGET	150-DAY	37.90	37.90
91	REBECCA	150-DAY	37.90	37.90

YR	NAME	LIMIT	ISSUE	QUOTE
E. HIBEL			**HIBEL CHRISTMAS**	
85	THE ANGEL'S MESSAGE	YR	45.00	44.00
86	THE GIFTS OF THE MAGI	YR	45.00	60.00
87	THE FLIGHT INTO EGYPT	YR	49.00	58.00
88	ADORATION OF THE SHEPHERD	YR	49.00	50.00
89	PEACEFUL KINGDOM	YR	49.00	49.00-65.00
90	NATIVITY	YR	49.00	65.00
E. HIBEL			**HIBEL MOTHER'S DAY**	
84	ABBY AND LISA	YR	29.50	50.00-150.00
85	ERICA AND JAMIE	YR	29.50	30.00-45.00
86	EMILY AND JENNIFER	YR	29.50	79.00-150.00
87	CATHERINE AND HEATHER	YR	34.50	65.00
88	SARAH AND TESS	YR	34.90	58.00
89	JESSICA AND KATE	YR	34.90	45.00-54.00
90	ELIZABETH, JORDAN & JANIE	YR	36.90	40.00
91	MICHELE AND ANNA	YR	36.90	36.90
* *			**HOME FOR THE HOLIDAYS**	
91	HOME BEFORE CHRISTMAS	OP	32.90	50.00
91	HOME TO GRANDMA'S	OP	29.90	40.00
91	SLEIGH RIDE HOME	OP	29.90	49.00
92	HOME AWAY FROM HOME	OP	34.90	52.00
92	HOMESPUN HOLIDAY	OP	32.90	45.00
92	HOMETIME YULETIDE	OP	34.90	65.00
92	THE JOURNEY HOME	OP	34.90	35.00
92	THE WARMTH OF HOME	OP	32.90	59.00
91	SLEIGHRIDE HOME	150-DAY	29.90	35.00
			HOME IS WHERE THE HEART IS	
92	A CARRIAGE RIDE HOME	OP	32.90	32.90
92	A WARM WELCOME HOME	OP	29.90	29.90
92	HOME SWEET HOME	OP	29.90	65.00
93	AMBER AFTERNOON	OP	32.90	32.90
93	COUNTRY MEMORIES	OP	32.90	32.90
93	HOMETOWN HOSPITALITY	OP	34.90	34.90
93	OUR SUMMER HOME	OP	34.90	34.90
93	THE TWILIGHT CAFE	OP	34.90	34.90
* *			**HOME SWEET HOME**	
88	THE VICTORIAN	OP	39.90	40.00
89	THE GEORGIAN	OP	39.90	40.00
89	THE GREEK REVIVAL	OP	39.90	40.00
90	THE MISSION	OP	39.90	40.00
89	THE GEORGIAN	150-DAY	39.90	60.00
89	THE GREEK REVIVAL	150-DAY	39.90	42.50
89	THE VICTORIAN	150-DAY	39.90	45.00
90	THE MISSION	150-DAY	39.90	42.00
* *			**IT'S A DOG'S LIFE**	
92	LITERARY LABS	OP	29.90	29.90
92	WE'VE BEEN SPOTTED	OP	29.90	29.90
93	BARRELING ALONG	OP	32.90	32.90
93	DOGS AND SUDS	OP	34.90	34.90
93	LODGING A COMPLAINT	OP	32.90	32.90
93	PAWS FOR A PICNIC	OP	34.90	34.90
93	PLAY BALL	OP	34.90	34.90
93	RETRIEVING OUR DIGNITY	OP	32.90	32.90
J.W. SMITH			**J.W. SMITH CHILDHOOD HOLIDAYS**	
86	CHRISTMAS	97-DAY	19.50	24.00
86	EASTER	97-DAY	19.50	23.00
86	THANKSGIVING	97-DAY	19.50	20.00
86	VALENTINE'S DAY	97-DAY	22.50	22.50
87	FOURTH OF JULY	97-DAY	22.50	22.50
87	MOTHER'S DAY	97-DAY	22.50	32.00
* *			**JERNER'S LESS TRAVELED ROAD**	
88	THE COVERED BRIDGE	OP	32.90	33.00
88	THE MURMURING STREAM	OP	29.90	30.00
88	THE WEATHERED BAM	OP	29.90	30.00
89	THE FLOWERING MEADOW	OP	32.90	33.00
89	THE HIDDEN WATERFALL	OP	32.90	60.00
89	WINTER'S PEACE	OP	32.90	33.00
88	THE COVERED BRIDGE	150-DAY	32.90	44.00
88	THE MURMURING STREAM	150-DAY	29.90	40.00
88	THE WEATHERED BARN	150-DAY	29.90	40.00-45.00
89	THE FLOWERING MEADOW	150-DAY	32.90	36.00
89	THE HIDDEN WATERFALL	150-DAY	32.90	40.00
89	WINTER'S PEACE	150-DAY	32.90	55.00
* *			**JEWELS OF THE FLOWERS**	
91	AMETHYST FLIGHT	OP	32.90	35.00
91	EMERALD PAIR	OP	32.90	45.00

YR	NAME	LIMIT	ISSUE	QUOTE
91	FISH TALES	OP	24.90	22.00
91	OPAL SPLENDOR	OP	34.90	49.00
91	RUBY ELEGANCE	OP	32.90	50.00
91	SAPPHIRE WINGS	OP	29.90	33.00
91	TEATIME TABBIES	OP	24.90	25.00
91	TOPAZ BEAUTIES	OP	29.90	37.00
91	TWO MAESTROS	OP	24.90	27.00
91	YAM SPINNERS	OP	24.90	30.00
92	AQUAMARINE GLIMMER	OP	34.90	35.00
92	PEARL LUSTER	OP	34.90	60.00
91	AMETHYST FLIGHT	150-DAY	32.90	32.90
91	EMERALD PAIR	150-DAY	32.90	32.90
91	OPAL SPLENDOR	150-DAY	34.90	34.90
91	RUBY ELEGANCE	150-DAY	32.90	32.90
91	SAPPHIRE WINGS	150-DAY	29.90	29.90
91	TOPAZ BEAUTIES	150-DAY	29.90	29.90
92	AQUAMARINE GLIMMER	150-DAY	34.90	34.90
92	PEARL LUSTER	150-DAY	34.90	34.90
* *	**KEEPSAKE RHYMES**			
92	HUMPTY DUMPTY	OP	29.90	43.00
93	OLD KING COLE	OP	29.90	30.00
93	PAT-A-CAKE	OP	29.90	90.00
93	PETER PUMPKIN EATER	OP	29.90	60.00
* *	**LADY AND THE TRAMP**			
92	DOG POUND BLUES	OP	37.90	37.90
92	FIRST DATE	OP	34.90	34.90
92	MERRY CHRISTMAS TO ALL	OP	37.90	37.90
92	PUPPY LOVE	OP	34.90	34.90
93	DOUBLE SIAMESE TROUBLE	OP	37.90	37.90
93	MOONLIGHT ROMANCE	OP	39.90	39.90
93	RUFF HOUSE	OP	39.90	39.90
93	TELLING TAILS	OP	39.90	39.90
* *	**LINCOLN, MAN OF AMERICA**			
86	THE GETTYSBURG ADDRESS	OP	24.50	25.00
87	BEGINNINGS IN NEW SALEM	OP	27.90	28.00
87	THE INAUGURATION	OP	24.50	25.00
87	THE LINCOLN-DOUGLAS DEBATES	OP	27.50	28.00
88	EMANCIPATION PROCLAMATION	OP	27.90	28.00
88	THE FAMILY MAN	OP	27.90	28.00
86	THE GETTYSBURG ADDRESS	150-DAY	29.90	29.90
87	BEGINNINGS IN NEW SALEM	150-DAY	27.90	35.00
87	THE INAUGURATION	150-DAY	24.50	26.00
87	THE LINCOLN-DOUGLAS DEBATES	150-DAY	27.50	27.50
88	EMANCIPATION PROCLAMATION	150-DAY	27.90	27.90-45.00
88	THE FAMILY MAN	150-DAY	27.90	27.90
* *	**LIVING WITH NATURE-JERNER'S DUCKS**			
86	THE MALLARD	OP	19.50	33.00
86	THE PINTAIL	OP	19.50	28.00
87	THE AMERICAN WIGEON	OP	22.90	40.00
87	THE GADWALL	OP	24.90	39.00
87	THE GREEN WINGED TEAL	OP	22.50	39.00
87	THE NORTHERN SHOVELER	OP	22.90	36.00
87	THE WOOD DUCK	OP	22.50	36.00
88	THE BLUE WINGED TEAL	OP	24.90	33.00
86	THE MALLARD	150-DAY	19.50	60.00
86	THE PINTAIL	150-DAY	19.50	74.00
87	THE AMERICAN WIDGEON	150-DAY	22.90	45.00
87	THE GADWALL	150-DAY	24.90	46.00
87	THE GREEN-WINGED TEAL	150-DAY	22.50	39.50-66.00
87	THE NORTHERN SHOVELER	150-DAY	22.90	42.00
87	THE WOOD DUCK	150-DAY	22.50	45.00
88	THE BLUE-WINGED TEAL	150-DAY	24.90	43.00
* *	**MAJESTIC BIRDS OF NORTH AMERICA**			
88	THE BALD EAGLE	OP	29.90	30.00
88	THE GREAT HOMED OWL	OP	32.90	33.00
88	THE PEREGRINE FLACON	OP	29.90	30.00
89	THE AMERICAN KESTRAL	OP	32.90	33.00
89	THE RED-TAILED HAWK	OP	32.90	33.00
89	THE WHITE GYRFALCON	OP	32.90	33.00
90	THE GOLDEN EAGLE	OP	34.90	35.00
90	THE OSPREY	OP	34.90	35.00
88	PEREGRINE FALCON	150-DAY	29.90	44.00
88	THE BALD EAGLE	150-DAY	29.90	52.00
88	THE GREAT HORNED OWL	150-DAY	32.90	36.00
89	THE AMERICAN KESTRAL	150-DAY	32.90	32.90
89	THE RED-TAILED HAWK	150-DAY	32.90	34.00-50.00

YR	NAME	LIMIT	ISSUE	QUOTE
89	THE WHITE GYRFALCON	150-DAY	32.90	32.90
90	THE GOLDEN EAGLE	150-DAY	34.90	34.90
90	THE OSPREY	150-DAY	34.90	34.90

MARY POPPINS

YR	NAME	LIMIT	ISSUE	QUOTE
89	A SPOONFUL OF SUGAR	OP	29.90	30.00
89	MARY POPPINS	OP	29.90	25.00
90	A JOLLY HOLIDAY W/MARY	OP	32.90	37.00
90	WE LOVE TO LAUGH	OP	32.90	45.00
91	CHIM CHIM CHER-EE	OP	32.90	35.00
91	TUPPENCE A BAG	OP	32.90	50.00
89	A SPOONFUL OF SUGAR	150-DAY	29.90	38.00
89	MARY POPPINS	150-DAY	29.90	39.00-44.00
90	A JOLLY HOLIDAY WITH MARY	150-DAY	32.90	55.00
90	WE LOVE TO LAUGH	150-DAY	32.90	66.00
91	CHIM CHIM CHER-EE	150-DAY	32.90	32.90
91	TUPPENCE A BAG	150-DAY	32.90	66.00

MICKEY'S CHRISTMAS CAROL

YR	NAME	LIMIT	ISSUE	QUOTE
92	BAH HUMBUG!	OP	29.90	30.00
92	WHAT'S SO MERRY ABOUT CHRISTMAS?	OP	29.90	29.90
93	A CHRISTMAS FEAST	OP	34.90	34.90
93	A CHRISTMAS SURPRISE	OP	32.90	32.90
93	A COZY CHRISTMAS	OP	34.90	34.90
93	GOD BLESS US EVERY ONE	OP	32.90	32.90
93	MARLEY'S WARNING	OP	34.90	34.90
93	YULETIDE GREETINGS	OP	32.90	32.90

E. HIBEL

MOTHER'S DAY

YR	NAME	LIMIT	ISSUE	QUOTE
84	ABBYA ND LISA	OP	29.50	30.00
85	ERICA AND JAMIE	OP	29.50	30.00
86	EMILY AND JENNIFER	OP	29.50	44.00
87	CATHERINE AND HEATHER	OP	34.50	49.00
88	SARAH AND TESS	OP	34.90	35.00
89	JESSICA AND KATE	OP	34.90	35.00
90	ELIZABATH, JORDAN & JANIE	OP	36.90	46.00
91	MICHELE AND ANNA	OP	36.90	37.00

MY FAIR LADY

YR	NAME	LIMIT	ISSUE	QUOTE
89	I COULD HAVE DANCED ALL NIGHT	OP	24.90	25.00
89	OPENING DAY AT ASCOT	OP	24.90	25.00
89	SHOW ME	OP	27.90	28.00
89	THE RAIN IN SPAIN	OP	27.90	28.00
90	GET ME TO/CHURCH ON TIME	OP	27.90	27.00
90	I'VE GROWN ACCUSTOMED TO HER FACE	OP	27.90	50.00
89	I COULD HAVE DANCED ALL NIGHT	150-DAY	24.90	24.90
89	OPENING DAY AT ASCOT	150-DAY	24.90	24.90
89	SHOW ME	150-DAY	27.90	27.90
89	THE RAIN IN SPAIN	150-DAY	27.90	27.90
90	GET ME TO THE CHURCH ON TIME	150-DAY	27.90	27.90
90	I'VE GROWN ACCUSTOMED TO YOUR FACE	150-DAY	27.90	27.90

NATURE'S CHILD

YR	NAME	LIMIT	ISSUE	QUOTE
90	FAITHFUL FRIENDS	OP	32.90	33.00
90	SEEMS LIKD YESTERDAY	OP	32.90	32.00
90	SHARING	OP	29.90	30.00
90	THE LOST LAMB	OP	29.90	30.00
90	TRUSTED COMPANION	OP	32.90	47.00
91	HAND IN HAND	OP	32.90	44.00
90	FAITHFUL FRIENDS	150-DAY	32.90	32.90
90	SEEMS LIKE YESTERDAY	150-DAY	32.90	32.90
90	SHARING	150-DAY	29.90	29.90
90	THE LOST LAMB	150-DAY	29.90	29.90
90	TRUSTED COMPANION	150-DAY	32.90	49.00
91	HAND IN HAND	150-DAY	32.90	32.90

NATURE'S NURSERY

YR	NAME	LIMIT	ISSUE	QUOTE
92	TESTING THE WATERS	OP	29.90	30.00
93	HIDE AND SEEK	OP	29.90	29.90
93	PIGGYBACK RIDE	OP	29.90	29.90
93	RACE YA MOM	OP	29.90	29.90
93	TAKING THE PLUNGE	OP	29.90	30.00
93	TIME TO WAKE UP	OP	29.90	29.90

J.W. SMITH

NOT SO LONG AGO

YR	NAME	LIMIT	ISSUE	QUOTE
88	MOTHER'S LITTLE HELPER	150-DAY	24.90	40.00
88	MOTHER'S LITTLE HELPER	OP	24.90	28.00
88	STORY TIME	150-DAY	24.90	24.90
88	STORY TIME	OP	24.90	25.00
88	SUPPERTIME FOR KITTY	150-DAY	24.90	45.00
88	SUPPERTIME FOR KITTY	OP	24.90	27.00
88	WASH DAY FOR DOLLY	150-DAY	24.90	28.00
88	WASH DAY FOR DOLLY	OP	24.90	25.00

YR	NAME	LIMIT	ISSUE	QUOTE
E. HIBEL				**OKLAHOMA!**
85	OH, WHAT A BEAUTIFUL MORNIN'	OP	19.50	20.00
86	I CAIN'T SAY NO	OP	19.50	20.00
86	OKLAHOMA!	OP	19.50	20.00
86	SURREY W/THE FRINGE ON TOP	OP	19.50	20.00
85	OH, WHAT A BEAUTIFUL MORNIN'	150-DAY	19.50	20.00-35.00
86	I CAIN'T SAY NO	150-DAY	19.50	20.00-35.00
86	OKLAHOMA	150-DAY	19.50	20.00-35.00
86	SURREY WITH THE FRINGE ON TOP'	150-DAY	19.50	20.00-35.00
* *				**OLD FASHIONED FAVORITES**
91	APPLE CRISP	OP	29.90	73.00
91	BLUEBERRY MUFFINS	OP	29.90	60.00
91	CHOCOLATE CHIP OATMEAL COOKIES	OP	29.90	110.00
91	PEACH COBBLER	OP	29.90	75.00
C. TENNANT				**OLD MILL STREAM**
91	NEW LONDON GRIST MILL	150-DAY	39.90	45.00
* *				**ONCE UPON A TIME**
88	LITTLE RED RIDING HOOD	OP	24.90	25.00
88	RAPUNZEL	OP	24.90	25.00
88	THREE LITTLE PIGS	OP	27.90	30.00
89	BEAUTY AND THE BEAST	OP	27.90	49.00
89	GOLDILOCKS/THREE BEARS	OP	27.90	34.00
89	THE PRINCESS AND THE PEA	OP	27.90	30.00
88	LITTLE RED RIDING HOOD	150-DAY	24.90	24.90-33.00
88	RAPUNZEL	150-DAY	24.90	29.00
88	THREE LITTLE PIGS	150-DAY	27.90	40.00
89	BEAUTY AND THE BEAST	150-DAY	27.90	27.90
89	GOLDILOCKS AND THE THREE BEARS	150-DAY	27.90	27.90
89	THE PRINCESS AND THE PEA	150-DAY	27.90	27.90
*				**PINOCCHIO**
89	GEPETTO CREATES PINOCCHIO	150-DAY	29.90	29.90
90	I'VE GOT NO STRINGS ON ME	150-DAY	32.90	32.90
90	IT'S AN ACTOR'S LIFE FOR ME	150-DAY	32.90	32.90
90	PINOCCHIO AND THE BLUE FAIRY	150-DAY	29.90	29.90
91	A REAL BOY	150-DAY	32.90	32.90
91	PLEASURE ISLAND	150-DAY	32.90	32.90
89	GEPETTO CREATES PINOCCHIO	OP	29.90	40.00
90	I'VE GOT NO STRINGS ON ME	OP	32.90	44.00
90	IT'A AN ACTOR' S LIFE FOR ME	OP	32.90	39.00
90	PINOCCHIO & THE BLYE FAIRY	OP	29.90	67.00
91	A REAL BOY	OP	32.90	50.00
91	PLEASURE ISLAND	OP	32.90	40.00
* *				**PORTRAITS OF MOTHERHOOD**
87	MOTHER'S HERE	OP	29.50	30.00
88	FIRST TOUCH	OP	29.90	30.00
87	MOTHER'S HERE	150-DAY	29.50	35.00
88	FIRST TOUCH	150-DAY	29.50	32.00
M.T. FANGEL				**PRECIOUS LITTLE ONES**
88	LITTLE FLEDGLINGS	150-DAY	29.90	29.90-34.00
88	LITTLE RED ROBINS	150-DAY	29.90	29.90-33.00
88	PEEK-A-BOO	150-DAY	29.90	29.90-44.00
88	SATURDAY NIGHT BATH	150-DAY	29.90	29.90-33.00
88	LITTLE FLEDGLINGS	OP	29.90	30.00
88	LITTLE RED ROBINS	OP	29.90	30.00
88	SATURDAY NIGHT BATH	OP	29.90	31.00
89	PEEK-A-BOO	OP	29.90	34.00
		PROUD SENTIANALS OF THE AMERICAN WEST		
93	CAT NAP	OP	29.90	29.90
93	CROWN PRINCE	OP	32.90	32.90
93	DESERT BIGHORN-MORMON RIDGE	OP	32.90	32.90
93	YOUNGBLOOD	OP	29.90	45.00
* *				**PURRFECT POINT OF VIEW**
91	UNEXPECTED VISITORS	OP	29.90	30.00
92	AFTERNOON CATNAP	OP	29.90	30.00
92	COZY COMPANY	OP	29.90	29.90
92	WISTFUL MORNING	OP	29.90	40.00
C. WILSON				**PUSSYFOOTING AROUND**
91	FISH TALES	150-DAY	24.90	24.90
91	TEATIME TABBIES	150-DAY	24.90	24.90
91	TWO MAESTROS	150-DAY	24.90	24.90
91	YARN SPINNERS	150-DAY	24.90	24.90
N. ROCKWELL				**ROCKWELL HERITAGE**
91	THE YOUNG SCHOLAR	YR	24.90	30.00
* *				**ROMANTIC AGE OF STEAM**
92	LITTLE BO PEEP	OP	29.90	55.00
92	THE BROADWAY LIMITED	OP	29.90	29.90

This nostalgic image takes collectors on a walk down Memory Lane. Walking to Church *by Norman Rockwell is produced by Artaffects.*

Like a soft lullaby, Bessie Pease Gutmann captures the sweet sight and sound of Harmony. *The plate is second in the "Magical Moments" series produced by Artaffects.*

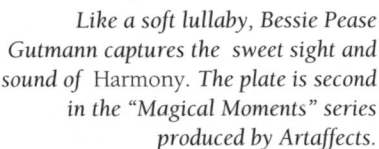

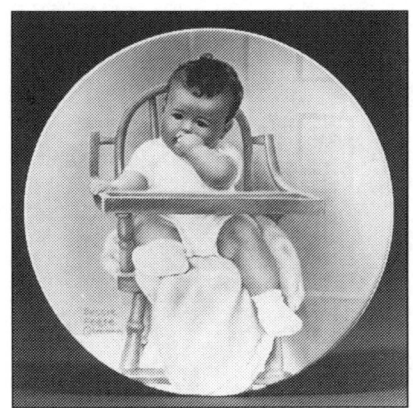

Capturing the simple delights of children in a way only she could do, Bessie Pease Gutmann portrays this little king atop his mighty throne in His Majesty. *Produced by Artaffects.*

Bubbles, *the first issue in the "Special Occasions" series by Francis Tipton Hunter, captures the daydreams of little girls around the world. Produced by Artaffects.*

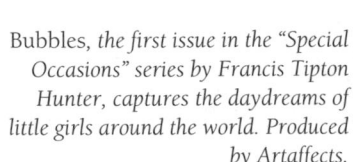

YR	NAME	LIMIT	ISSUE	QUOTE
92	THE CHIEF	OP	32.90	32.90
92	THE EMPIRE BUILDER	OP	29.90	29.90
92	THEC RESCENT LIMITED	OP	32.90	32.90
92	TWENTIETH CENTURY LIMITED	OP	32.90	32.90
93	THE DAYLIGHT	OP	34.90	34.90
93	THE JUPITER	OP	34.90	34.90
93	THE OVERLAND LIMITED	OP	34.90	34.90
* *				
			SANTA'S CHRISTMAS	
91	SANTA'S CHEER	OP	29.90	44.00
91	SANTA'S GIFT	OP	32.90	50.00
91	SANTA'S LOVE	OP	29.90	40.00
91	SANTA'S PROMISE	OP	32.90	65.00
92	SANTA'S MAGIC	OP	32.90	69.00
92	SANTA'S SURPRISE	OP	32.90	60.00
91	SANTA'S LOVE	150-DAY	29.90	35.00
* *				
			SEASON FOR SONG	
91	FROSTY CHORUS	OP	34.90	40.00
91	SILVER SERENADE	OP	34.90	40.00
91	SNOWY SYMPHONY	OP	34.90	58.00
91	WINTER CONCERT	OP	34.90	40.00
91	FROSTY CHORUS	150-DAY	34.90	34.90
91	SILVER SERENADE	150-DAY	34.90	34.90
91	SNOWY SYMPHONY	150-DAY	34.90	34.90
91	WINTER CONCERT	150-DAY	34.90	34.90
			SEASON OF SPLENDOR	
92	A COUNTRY WEEKEND	OP	32.90	45.00
92	AUTUMN GRANDEUR	OP	29.90	43.00
92	HARVEST MEMORIES	OP	32.90	54.00
92	SCHOOL DAYS	OP	29.90	38.00
92	WOODLAND MILL STREAM	OP	32.90	64.00
93	INDIAN SUMMER	OP	32.90	59.00
			SHADOWS & LIGHT:WINTER'S WILDLIFE	
92	WINTER'S CHILDREN	OP	29.90	50.00
93	CUB SCOUTS	OP	29.90	59.00
93	LITTLE SNOWMAN	OP	29.90	47.00
93	THE SNOW CAVE	OP	29.90	40.00
* *				
			SINGIN' IN THE RAIN	
90	GOOD MORNING	OP	32.90	33.00
90	SINGIN' IN THE RAIN	OP	32.90	33.00
91	BROADWAY MELODY	OP	32.90	45.00
91	WE'RE HAPPY AGAIN	OP	32.90	40.00
90	GOOD MORNING	150-DAY	32.90	37.00
90	SINGIN' IN THE RAIN	150-DAY	32.90	32.90-47.00
91	BROADWAY MELODY	150-DAY	32.90	32.90
91	WE'RE HAPPY AGAIN	150-DAY	32.90	62.00
*				
			SLEEPING BEAUTY	
91	AWAKENED BY A KISS	150-DAY	39.90	39.90
91	HAPPY BIRTHDAY BRIAR ROSE	150-DAY	42.90	42.90
91	ONCE UPON A DREAM	150-DAY	39.90	39.90
91	AWAKENED BY A KISS	OP	39.90	83.00
91	HAPPY BIRTHDAY BRIAR ROSE	OP	42.90	58.00
91	ONCE UPON A DREAM	OP	39.90	43.00
92	TPGETHER AT LAST	OP	42.90	60.00
			SMALL BLESSINGS	
92	BLESS US O LORD FOR THESE, THY GIFTS	OP	29.90	62.00
92	BLESSED ARE THE PURE IN HEART	OP	32.90	32.90
92	JESUS LOVES ME, THIS I KNOW	OP	32.90	32.90
92	NOW I LAY ME DOWN TO SLEEP	OP	29.90	59.00
92	THIS LITTLE LIGHT OF MINE	OP	32.90	32.90
93	BLESS OUR HOME	OP	32.90	32.90
* *				
			SNOW WHITE AND THE 7 DWARFS	
91	A SPECIAL TREAT	OP	32.90	49.00
91	THE DANCE OF SNOW WHITE/SEVEN DWARFS	OP	29.90	55.00
91	WITH A SMLE AND A SONG	OP	29.90	30.00
92	A KISS FOR DOPEY	OP	32.90	35.00
92	A WISH COME TRUE	OP	34.90	34.90
92	FIRESIDE LOVE STORY	OP	34.90	68.00
92	STUBBORN GRUMPY	OP	34.90	34.90
92	THE POISON APPLE	OP	32.90	66.00
92	TIME TO TIDY UP	OP	34.90	34.90
93	A SURPRISE IN THE CLEARING	OP	36.90	36.90
93	HAPPY ENDING	OP	36.90	36.90
93	MAY I HAVE THIS DANCE?	OP	36.90	36.90
* *				
			SONGS OF THE AMERICAN SPIRIT	
91	AMERICA THE BEAUTIFUL	OP	29.90	45.00
91	BATTLE HYMN OF THE REPLUBLIC	OP	29.90	49.00

YR	NAME	LIMIT	ISSUE	QUOTE
91	MY COUNTRY 'TIS OF THEE	OP	29.90	44.00
91	THE STAR SPANGLED BANNER	OP	29.90	30.00
T. CRNKOVICH			**SOUND OF MUSIC**	
86	DO-RE-MI	150-DAY	19.50	26.00-35.00
86	LAENDLER WALTZ	150-DAY	22.50	28.00
86	MY FAVORITE THINGS	150-DAY	22.50	35.00
86	SOUND OF MUSIC	150-DAY	19.50	23.00-35.00
87	CLIMB EV'RY MOUNTAIN	150-DAY	24.90	43.00
87	EDELWEISS	150-DAY	22.50	31.00-35.00
87	I HAVE CONFIDENCE	150-DAY	22.50	30.00-34.00
87	MARIA	150-DAY	24.90	40.00
86	DO-RE-MI	OP	19.50	20.00
86	MY FAVORITE THINGS	OP	22.50	23.00
86	SOUND OF MUSIC	OP	19.50	20.00
87	CLIMB EV'RE MOUNTAIN	OP	24.90	36.00
87	EDELWEISS	OP	22.50	24.00
87	I HAVE CONFIDENCE	OP	22.50	23.00
87	LAENDLER	OP	22.50	23.00
87	MARIA-WEDDING SCENE	OP	24.90	33.00
* *			**SOUTH PACIFIC**	
87	DITES MOI	OP	24.90	25.00
87	HAPPY TALK	OP	24.50	25.00
87	SOME ENCHANTED EVENING	OP	24.50	25.00
88	HONEY BUN	OP	24.90	25.00
87	DITES MOI	150-DAY	24.90	24.50
87	HAPPY TALK	150-DAY	24.50	24.50
87	SOME ENCHANTED EVENING	150-DAY	24.50	24.50
88	HONEY BUN	150-DAY	24.90	24.90-34.00
* *			**STATELY OWLS**	
89	THE GREAT HORNED OWL	OP	29.90	30.00
89	THE SNOWY OWL	OP	29.90	35.00
90	THE BARN OWL	OP	32.90	33.00
90	THE BARRED OWL	OP	32.90	40.00
90	THE GREAT GRAY OWL	OP	34.90	36.00
90	THE SCREECH OWL	OP	32.90	33.00
90	THE SHORT-EARED OWL	OP	32.90	33.00
91	THE SAW-WHET OWL	OP	34.90	40.00
89	THE GREAT HORNED OWL	150-DAY	29.90	29.90
89	THE SNOWY OWL	150-DAY	29.90	29.90
90	THE BARN OWL	150-DAY	32.90	32.90
90	THE BARRED OWL	150-DAY	32.90	32.90
90	THE GREAT GREY OWL	150-DAY	34.90	34.90
90	THE SCREECH OWL	150-DAY	32.90	32.90
90	THE SHORT-EARED OWL	150-DAY	32.90	32.90
91	THE SAW-WHET OWL	150-DAY	34.90	34.90
* *			**SUNDBLOM SANTAS**	
89	SANTA BY THE FIRE	OP	27.90	30.00
90	CHRISTMAS VIGIL	OP	27.90	45.00
91	TO ALL A GOOD NIGHT	OP	32.90	47.00
92	SANTA'S ON HIS WAY	OP	32.90	68.00
89	SANTA BY THE FIRE	TL	27.90	44.00
90	CHRISTMAS VIGIL	TL	27.90	27.90
91	TO ALL A GOOD NIGHT	CL	32.90	45.00
* *			**SWEETNESS AND GRACE**	
92	FAVORITE BUDDY	OP	34.90	35.00
92	GOD BLESS TEDDY	OP	34.90	40.00
92	SUNSHINE AND SMILES	OP	34.90	59.00
92	SWEET DREAMS	OP	34.90	34.90
* *			**THE AMERICAN JOURNEY**	
87	WESTWARD HO	OP	29.90	30.00
88	CHRISTMAS AT THE NEW CABIN	OP	29.90	30.00
88	CROSSING THE RIVER	OP	29.90	30.00
88	KITCHEN W/A VIEW	OP	29.90	30.00
87	WESTWARD HO	150-DAY	29.90	35.00
88	CHRISTMAS AT THE NEW CABIN	150-DAY	29.90	45.00
88	CROSSING THE RIVER	150-DAY	29.90	60.00
88	KITCHEN WITH A VIEW	150-DAY	29.90	40.00
			THE COMFORTS OF HOME	
92	CURIOUS PAIR	OP	24.90	24.90
92	SLEEPYHEADS	OP	24.90	24.90
93	A COZY FIRESIDE	OP	29.90	29.90
93	FELINE FROLIC	OP	29.90	29.90
93	MOTHER'S RETREAT	OP	27.90	27.90
93	PLAYTIME	OP	27.90	27.90
93	WASHDAY HELPERS	OP	29.90	29.90
93	WELCOME FRIENDS	OP	27.90	27.90

YR	NAME	LIMIT	ISSUE	QUOTE

THE DISNEY TREASURED MOMENTS COLLECTION

YR	NAME	LIMIT	ISSUE	QUOTE
92	CINDERELLA	OP	29.90	29.90
92	SNOW WHITE & THE SEVEN DWARFS	OP	29.90	29.90
93	ALICE IN WONDERLAND	OP	32.90	32.90
93	BEAUTY AND THE BEAST	OP	34.90	34.90
93	PETER PAN	OP	32.90	32.90
93	PINOCCHIO	OP	34.90	34.90
93	SLEEPING BEAUTY	OP	32.90	32.90
93	THE JUNGLE BOOK	OP	34.90	34.90

G. LAMBERT — **THE FOUR ANCIENT ELEMENTS**

YR	NAME	LIMIT	ISSUE	QUOTE
84	EARTH	75-DAY	27.50	30.00-43.00
84	WATER	75-DAY	27.50	30.00-40.00
85	AIR	75-DAY	29.50	31.00-45.00
85	FIRE	75-DAY	29.50	29.50-38.00

* *   **THE KING AND I**

YR	NAME	LIMIT	ISSUE	QUOTE
84	A PUZZLEMENT	OP	19.50	20.00
85	GETTING TO KNOW YOU	OP	19.50	20.00
85	SHALL WE DANCE?	OP	19.50	20.00
85	WE KISS IN A SHADOW	OP	19.50	20.00
84	A PUZZLEMENT	150-DAY	19.50	30.00
85	GETTING TO KNOW YOU	150-DAY	19.50	24.00-48.00
85	SHALL WE DANCE?	150-DAY	19.50	42.00-53.00
85	WE KISS IN A SHADOW	150-DAY	19.50	25.00-34.00

* *   **THE OLD MILL STREAM**

YR	NAME	LIMIT	ISSUE	QUOTE
90	NE WLONDON GRIST MILL	OP	39.90	40.00
91	GLADE CREEK GRIST MILL	OP	39.90	41.00
91	THE OLD RED MILL	OP	39.90	41.00
91	WAYSIDE INN GRIST MILL	OP	39.90	39.00
90	NEW LONDON GRIST MILL	150-DAY	39.90	39.90
91	GLADE CREEK GRIST MILL	150-DAY	39.90	39.90
91	OLD RED MILL	150-DAY	39.90	39.90
91	WAYSIDE INN GRIST MILL	150-DAY	39.90	39.90

E. LICEA — **THE STORY OF CHRISTMAS BY EVE LICEA**

YR	NAME	LIMIT	ISSUE	QUOTE
87	THE ANNUNCIATION	YR	44.90	46.00
88	THE NATIVITY	YR	44.90	45.00
89	ADORATION OF THE SHEPHERDS	YR	49.90	50.00
90	JOURNEY OF THE MAGI	TL	49.90	59.00
91	GIFTS OF THE MAGI	YR	49.90	65.00

T. KINKADE — **THOMASHIRE**

YR	NAME	LIMIT	ISSUE	QUOTE
92	OLD THOMASHIRE MILL	OP	29.90	29.90
92	OLDE PORTERFIELD TEA ROOM	OP	29.90	29.90
92	PYR CORNER COTTAGE	OP	32.90	32.90
92	SWANBROOK COTTAGE	OP	32.90	32.90
93	BLOSSOM HILL CHURCH	OP	32.90	32.90
93	OLDE GARDEN COTTAGE	OP	32.90	32.90

* *   **TOM SAWYER**

YR	NAME	LIMIT	ISSUE	QUOTE
87	TOM & BECKY	OP	27.90	28.00
87	TOM SAWYER THE PIRATE	OP	27.90	28.00
87	WHITEWASHING THE FENCE	OP	27.50	28.00
88	FIRST PIPES	OP	27.90	30.00
87	TOM AND BECKY	150-DAY	27.90	27.90
87	TOM SAWYER THE PIRATE	150-DAY	27.90	27.90
87	WHITEWASHING THE FENCE	150-DAY	27.50	27.50
88	FIRST PIPES	150-DAY	27.90	27.90

* *   **UNDER MOTHER'S WING**

YR	NAME	LIMIT	ISSUE	QUOTE
92	ARCTIC SPRING:SNOWY OWLS	OP	29.90	44.00
92	FOREST EDGE:GREAT GRAY OWLS	OP	29.90	35.00
92	LOFTY-LIMB:GREAT HORNED OWLS	OP	34.90	40.00
92	TREETOP TRIO:LONG EARED OWLS	OP	32.90	40.00
92	VAST VIEW:SAW WHET OWLS	OP	32.90	50.00
92	WOODLAND WATCH:SPOTTED OWLS	OP	32.90	60.00
93	HAPPY HOME:SHORT EARED OWL	OP	34.90	34.90
93	PERFECT PERCH:BARRED OWL	OP	34.90	35.00

W. ANDERSON — **UPLAND BIRDS OF NORTH AMERICA**

YR	NAME	LIMIT	ISSUE	QUOTE
86	THE GROUSE	150-DAY	24.50	25.00-37.50
86	THE PHEASANT	150-DAY	24.50	25.00-37.50
87	THE GRAY PARTRIDGE	150-DAY	27.50	28.00
87	THE QUAIL	150-DAY	27.50	28.00-37.50
87	THE WILD TURKEY	150-DAY	27.50	28.00
87	THE WOODCOCK	150-DAY	27.50	28.00
86	THE GROUSE	OP	24.50	15.00
86	THE PHEASANT	OP	24.50	25.00
87	THE GRAY PARTRIDGE	OP	27.50	28.00
87	THE QUAIL	OP	27.50	28.00
87	THE WILD TURKEY	OP	27.50	28.00
87	THE WOODCOCK	OP	27.90	28.00

YR	NAME	LIMIT	ISSUE	QUOTE
			WINDOWS OF GLORY	
93	KING OF KINGS	OP	29.90	29.90
93	PRINCE OF PEACE	OP	29.90	29.90
93	THE GOOD SHEPHERD	OP	32.90	32.90
93	THE LIGHT OF THE WORLD	OP	32.90	32.90
93	THE MESSIAH	OP	32.90	32.90
* *			**WIZARD OF OZ**	
77	OVER THE RAINBOW	OP	19.00	43.00
78	IF I ONLY HAD A BRAIN	OP	19.00	30.00
78	IF I ONLY HAD A HEART	OP	19.00	51.00
78	IF I WERE KING OF THE FOREST	OP	19.00	48.00
79	FOLLOW THE YELLOW BRICK RD.	OP	19.00	50.00
79	WICKED WITCH OF THE WEST	OP	19.00	60.00
79	WONDERFUL WIZARD OF OZ	OP	19.00	63.00
80	THE GRAND FINALE	OP	24.00	58.00
77	OVER THE RAINBOW	100-DAY	19.00	64.00-140.00
78	IF I ONLY HAD A BRAIN	100-DAY	19.00	40.00
78	IF I ONLY HAD A HEART	100-DAY	19.00	45.00
78	IF I WERE KING OF THE FOREST	100-DAY	19.00	46.00
79	FOLLOW THE YELLOW BRICK ROAD	100-DAY	19.00	53.00
79	WICKED WITCH OF THE WEST	100-DAY	19.00	55.00
79	WONDERFUL WIZARD OF OZ	100-DAY	19.00	56.OO
80	THE GRAND FINALE	100-DAY	24.00	58.00
* *		**WIZARD OF OZ: A NATIONAL TREASURE**		
91	FOLLOW THE YELLOW BRICK RD.	OP	29.90	57.00
91	I HAVEN'T GOT A BRAIN	OP	29.90	29.90
91	I'M A LITTLE RUSTY YET	OP	32.90	32.90
92	I EVEN SCARE MYSELF	OP	32.90	32.90
92	I'LL NEVER GET HOME	OP	34.90	34.90
92	I'M MELTING	OP	34.90	34.90
92	THERE'S NO PLACE LIKE HOME	OP	34.90	34.90
92	WE'RE OFF TO SEE THE WIZARD	OP	32.90	32.90
			YESTERDAY'S INNOCENTS	
92	MY FIRST BOOK	OP	29.90	30.00
92	TIME TO SMELL THE ROSES	OP	29.90	53.00
93	HUSH, BABY'S SLEEPING	OP	32.90	45.00
93	READY AND WAITING	OP	32.90	49.00
T. KINKADE			**YULETIDE MEMORIES**	
92	A BEACON OF FAITH	OP	29.90	29.90
92	THE MAGIC OF CHRISTMAS	OP	29.90	84.00
93	A WINTER'S TALK	OP	29.90	29.90
93	MOONLIT SLEIGHRIDE	OP	29.90	29.90
93	OLDE PORTERFIELD GIFT SHOPPE	OP	29.90	29.90
93	SILENT NIGHT	OP	29.90	29.90
93	SKATER'S DELIGHT	OP	29.90	29.90
93	THE WONDER OF THE SEASON	OP	29.90	29.90

ENESCO

YR	NAME	LIMIT	ISSUE	QUOTE
* *			**BARBIE**	
94	35TH ANNIVERSARY	5,000	30.00	30.00
94	HOLIDAY 1994	5,000	30.00	30.00
95	SOLO IN THE SPOTLIGHT 1960	5,000	30.00	30.00
P. HILLMAN			**CHERISHED TEDDIES**	
95	THE SEASON OF JOY	OP	35.00	35.00
* *		**HAPPY HOLIDAYS BARBIE**		
95	HAPPY HOLIDAYS BARBIE 1988	1,995	30.00	30.00
95	HAPPY HOLIDAYS BARBIE 1995	1,995	30.00	30.00
KINKA		**KINKA COLLECTOR PLAQUE**		
89	KINKA 119601	OP	10.00	10.00
M. ATTWELL			**MEMORIES OF YESTERDAY**	
93	LOOK OUT-SOMETHING GOOD..YOUR WAY!	OP	50.00	50.00
M. ATTWELL		**MEMORIES OF YESTERDAY PLATE SERIES**		
94	PLEASANT DREAMS & SWEET REPOSE	OP	25.00	25.00
96	JOIN ME FOR A LITTLE SONG	OP	50.00	50.00
			PRECIOUS MOMENTS	
80	LOVE ONE ANOTHER E5215	15,000	20.00	40.00-55.00
82	I'LL PLAY MY DRUM FOR HIM E2357	OP	40.00	60.00-70.00
83	LOVING THEY NEIGHBOR E2848	15,000	40.00	35.00-40.00
93	THINKING OU YOU...REALLY..TO DO 531766	OP	50.00	50.00
S. BUTCHER		**PRECIOUS MOMENTS CHRISTMAS BLESSINGS**		
89	WISHING YOU A YUMMY CHRISTMAS 523801	YR	50.00	50.00-55.00
90	BLESSING FROM ME TO THEE 523860	YR	50.00	55.00-65.00
92	BUT THE GREATEST/LOVE 527742	YR	50.00	50.00
S. BUTCHER		**PRECIOUS MOMENTS CHRISTMAS COLLECTION**		
80	COME LET US ADORE HIM E-5646	15,000	40.00	45.00-55.00
82	LET HEAVEN AND NATURE SING E-2347	15,000	40.00	45.00
83	WEE THREE KINGS E-0538	15,000	40.00	40.00-55.00

YR NAME	LIMIT	ISSUE	QUOTE
84 UNTO US A CHILD IS BORN E-5395	15,000	40.00	35.00-55.00

S. BUTCHER — PRECIOUS MOMENTS CHRISTMAS LOVE

YR NAME	LIMIT	ISSUE	QUOTE
86 I'M SENDING YOU A WHITE CHRISTMAS 101834	YR	45.00	50.00-60.00
86 MY PEACE I GIVE TO THEE 102954	YR	45.00	45.00-55.00
88 MAY YOUR CHRISTMAS BE/HAPPY HOME 523003	YR	50.00	55.00-60.00
88 MERRY CHRISTMAS DEER 520284	YR	50.00	50.00-60.00

S. BUTCHER — PRECIOUS MOMENTS COLLECTION

YR NAME	LIMIT	ISSUE	QUOTE
92 WISHING YOU/SWEETEST CHRISTMAS 530204	YR	50.00	55.00-60.00
94 YOU'RE AS PRETTY AS A CHRISTMAS TREE	OP	50.00	50.00
95 HE COVERS THE EARTH W/HIS BEAUTY 142670	OP	50.00	50.00

S. BUTCHER — PRECIOUS MOMENTS INSPIRED THOUGHTS

YR NAME	LIMIT	ISSUE	QUOTE
81 MAKE A JOYFUL NOISE E-7174	15,000	40.00	40.00-42.00
82 I BELIEVE IN MIRACLES E-9257	15,000	40.00	35.00-40.00
84 LOVE IS KIND E-2847	15,000	40.00	45.00
85 LOVE ONE ANOTHER E-5215	15,000	27.50	30.00-50.00

S. BUTCHER — PRECIOUS MOMENTS JOY OF CHRISTMAS

YR NAME	LIMIT	ISSUE	QUOTE
82 I'LL PLAY MY DRUM FOR HIM E-2357	YR	40.00	60.00-70.00
83 CHRISTMASTIME IS FOR SHARING E-0505	YR	40.00	50.00-75.00
84 TELL ME THE STORY OF JESUS 15237	YR	40.00	75.00-80.00
84 THE WONDER OF CHRISTMAS E-5396	YR	40.00	35.00-50.00

S. BUTCHER — PRECIOUS MOMENTS MOTHER'S LOVE PLATE

YR NAME	LIMIT	ISSUE	QUOTE
80 MOTHER SEW DEAR E-5217	15,000	40.00	40.00-50.00
82 THE PURR-FECT GRANDMA E-7173	15,000	40.00	35.00-45.00
83 THE HAND THAT ROCKS THE FUTURE E-9256	15,000	40.00	38.00-40.00
84 LOVING THY NEIGHBOR E-2848	15,000	40.00	35.00-40.00

S. BUTCHER — PRECIOUS MOMENTS OPEN EDITIONS

YR NAME	LIMIT	ISSUE	QUOTE
81 REJOICING WITH YOU E-7172	SU	30.00	30.00-40.00
81 THE LORD BLESS YOU AND KEEP YOU E-5216	SU	30.00	35.00-45.00
82 JESUS LOVES ME E-9275	SU	30.00	30.00-40.00
82 JESUS LOVES ME E-9276	SU	30.00	30.00-40.00
82 OUR FIRST CHRISTMAS TOGETHER E-2378	SU	30.00	30.00-40.00

S. BUTCHER — PRECIOUS MOMENTS THE FOUR SEASONS SERIES

YR NAME	LIMIT	ISSUE	QUOTE
84 AUTUMN'S PRAISE 12122	YR	40.00	45.00-55.00
84 SUMMER'S JOY 12114	YR	40.00	55.00-80.00
84 THE VOICE OF SPRING 12106	YR	40.00	65.00-90.00
84 WINTER'S SONG 12130	YR	40.00	55.00-65.00

FAIRMONT

* DEGRAZIA — ARTISTS OF THE WORLD

YR NAME	LIMIT	ISSUE	QUOTE
76 FESTIVAL OF LIGHTS	OP	45.00	120.00
77 BELL OF HOPE	OP	45.00	43.00
78 LITTLE MADONNA	OP	45.00	50.00
79 THE NAVTITY	OP	50.00	63.00
80 PRIME INDIAN DRUMMER	OP	50.00	61.00
81 LITTLE PRAYER ANGEL	OP	55.00	33.00
82 BLUE BOY	OP	60.00	34.00
83 HEAVENLY BLESSINGS	OP	65.00	24.00
84 NAVAJO MADONNA	OP	65.00	27.00
85 SAGUARO DANCE	OP	65.00	40.00

* DEGRAZIA — ARTISTS OF THE WORLD/CHILDREN

YR NAME	LIMIT	ISSUE	QUOTE
78 FLOWER GIRL	OP	45.00	50.00
79 FLOWER BOY	OP	45.00	59.00
80 LITTLE COCOPAH INDIAN GIRL	OP	50.00	65.00
81 BEAUTIFUL BURDEN	OP	50.00	59.00
82 MERRY LITTLE INDIAN	OP	55.00	85.00
83 WONDERING	OP	60.00	27.00
84 PINK PAPOOSE	OP	65.00	24.00
84 SUNFLOWER BOY	OP	65.00	32.00
85 MY FIRST HORSE	OP	65.00	65.00
86 GIRL AT SEWING MACHINE	OP	65.00	65.00
87 LOVE ME	OP	65.00	60.00
88 MERRILY, MERRILY, MERRILY	OP	65.00	65.00
89 MY FIRST ARROWN	OP	65.00	83.00
90 AWAY WITH MY KITE	OP	65.00	80.00

* * — FAMOUS CLOWNS

YR NAME	LIMIT	ISSUE	QUOTE
76 FREDDIE THE FREELOADER	OP	55.00	450.00
77 W.C. FIELDS	OP	55.00	39.00
78 HAPPY	OP	55.00	70.00
79 THE PLEDGE	OP	55.00	62.00
76 FREDDIE THE FREELOADER	10,000	55.00	472.00-550.00
77 W.C. FIELDS	10,000	55.00	73.00
78 HAPPY	10,000	55.00	92.00
79 THE PLEDGE	10,000	55.00	85.00

I. SPENCER — SPENCER SPECIAL

YR NAME	LIMIT	ISSUE	QUOTE
78 HUG ME	10,000	55.00	150.00
78 SLEEP LITTLE BABY	10,000	65.00	125.00

YR	NAME	LIMIT	ISSUE	QUOTE

FENTON ART GLASS
*

		AMERICAN CRAFTSMAN CARNIVAL		
70	GLASSMAKER	600	10.00	140.00
70	GLASSMAKER	200	10.00	220.00
70	GLASSMAKER	YR	10.00	68.00
71	PRINTER	YR	10.00	80.00
72	BLACKSMITH	YR	10.00	150.00
73	SHOEMAKER	YR	12.50	70.00
74	COOPER	YR	12.50	55.00
75	SILVERSMITH REVERE	YR	12.50	60.00
76	GUNSMITH	YR	15.00	45.00
77	POTTER	YR	15.00	35.00
78	WHEELWRIGHT	YR	15.00	25.00
79	CABINETMAKER	YR	15.00	23.00
80	TANNER	YR	16.50	20.00
81	HOUSEWRIGHT	YR	17.50	18.00

* *

		CHRISTMAS SERIES		
93	PLATE 7418HT	3500	49.00	49.00
94	PLATE 7418VS	1500	65.00	65.00
95	PLATE 7418VT	1500	65.00	65.00

* *

		MARY GREGORY		
94	PLATE 8319RY	YR	65.00	65.00
95	PLATE 8319RG	YR	65.00	65.00

FLAMBRO

		EMMETT KELLY JR. CHRISTMAS PLATE		
95	ALL WRAPPED UP IN CHRISTMAS	5000	30.00	30.00

C. KELLY

		EMMETT KELLY JR. PLATES		
83	WHY ME?-PLATE I	10,000	40.00	300.00-390.00
84	BALLOONS FOR SALE-PLATE II	10,000	40.00	300.00-350.00
85	BIG BUSINESS-PLATE III	10,000	40.00	250.00-300.00
86	AND GOD BLESS AMERICA-PLATE IV	10,000	40.00	125.00-200.00
88	TIS THE SEASON	10,000	40.00	40.00
89	LOOKING BACK-65TH BIRTHDAY	6500	50.00	75.00-125.00
91	WINTER	10,000	30.00	30.00
92	AUTUMN	10,000	30.00	30.00
92	SPRING	10,000	30.00	30.00
92	SUMMER	10,000	30.00	30.00

C. BEYLON

		RAGGEDY ANN & ANDY		
88	70 YEARS YOUNG	10,000	35.00	35.00

FOUNTAINHEAD
M. FERNANDEZ

		AS FREE AS THE WIND		
89	AS FREE AS THE WIND	*	295.00	220.00-600.00

M. FERNANDEZ

		THE SEASONS		
86	FALL CARDINALS	5000	85.00	85.00
87	SPRING ROBINS	5000	85.00	85.00
87	SUMMER GOLDFINCHES	5000	85.00	85.00
87	WINTER CHICKADEES	5000	85.00	85.00

M. FERNANDEZ

		THE TWELVE DAYS OF CHRISTMAS		
88	A PARTRIDGE IN A PEAR TREE	7500	155.00	155.00
88	TWO TURTLE DOVES	7500	*	*
89	FOUR CALLING BIRDS	7500	*	*
89	THREE FRENCH HENS	7500	155.00	155.00

M. FERNANDEZ

		THE WINGS OF FREEDOM		
85	COURTSHIP FLIGHT	2500	250.00	1600.00-2080.00
86	WINGS OF FREEDOM	2500	250.00	440.00

GARTLAN USA

*	PETE ROSE H/S	4192	*	*
*	MIKE SCHMIDT H/S DATED	50	*	795.00
*	KAREEM ABDUL-JABBAR H/S	1989	100.00	295.00

M. TAYLOR

		AL BARLICK		
91	PLATE	*	19.00	19.00

M. TAYLOR

		BRETT & BOBBY HULL		
91	HOCKEY'S GOLDEN BOYS	*	18.00	18.00
91	HOCKEY'S GOLDEN BOYS	10,000	45.00	45.00
91	HOCKEY'S GOLDEN BOYS	950	250.00	250.00

M. TAYLOR

		CARLTON FISK		
92	PLATE	10,000	45.00	45.00
92	PLATE	*	19.00	19.00
92	SIGNED PLATE	950	150.00	150.00
92	SIGNED PLATE, A/P	300	175.00	175.00

M. TAYLOR

		COACHING CLASSICS-JOHN WOODEN		
89	COLLECTOR PLATE	1975	100.00	100.00
89	COLLECTOR PLATE	*	16.00	18.00

YR	NAME	LIMIT	ISSUE	QUOTE
89	COLLECTOR PLATE	*	45.00	45.00
M. TAYLOR			**DARRYL STRAWBERRY**	
90	PLATE	*	16.00	18.00
90	PLATE	10,000	45.00	45.00
90	SIGNED PLATE	2500	125.00	125.00
J. MARTIN		**GEORGE BRETT GOLD CROWN COLLECTION**		
86	GEORGE BRETT	*	12.95	18.00
86	GEORGE BRETT	2000	100.00	395.00
M. TAYLOR			**JOE MONTANA**	
91	PLATE	10,000	45.00	45.00
91	SIGNED PLATE	2250	125.00	125.00
91	SIGNED PLATE, A/P	250	195.00	195.00
M. TAYLOR			**JOHNNY BENCH**	
89	COLLECTOR PLATE	1989	100.00	195.00
89	COLLECTOR PLATE	*	16.00	18.00
M. TAYLOR		**KAREEM ABDUL-JABBAR SKY-HOOK COLLECTION**		
89	COLLECTOR PLATE	*	16.00	18.00
89	KAREEM ABDUL-JABBAR	1851	100.00	195.00
M. TAYLOR			**LUIS APARICIO**	
90	PLATE	10,000	45.00	45.00
90	PLATE	*	16.00	18.00
90	SIGNED PLATE	1974	125.00	125.00
R. WINSLOW		**MAGIC JOHNSON GOLD RIM COLLECTION**		
87	MAGIC JOHNSON-THE MAGIC SHOW	1987	100.00	795.00
87	MAGIC JOHNSON-THE MAGIC SHOW	*	14.50	18.00
C. PALUSO		**MIKE SCHMIDT 500TH HOME RUN EDITION**		
87	MIKE SCHMIDT (A/P)	56	150.00	150.00
87	MIKE SCHMIDT-POWER AT THE PLATE	*	14.50	18.00
87	MIKE SCHMIDT-POWER AT THE PLATE H/S	1987	100.00	495.00
T. SIZEMORE			**PETE ROSE**	
*	PETE ROSE H/S DATED	50	100.00	695.00
B. FORBES		**PETE ROSE DIAMOND COLLECTION**		
88	PETE ROSE-THE REIGNING LEGEND	950	195.00	295.00
88	PETE ROSE-THE REIGNING LEGEND	*	14.50	18.00
T. SIZEMORE		**PETE ROSE PLATINUM EDITION**		
85	PETE ROSE-THE BEST OF BASEBALL	*	12.95	18.00
85	PETE ROSE-THE BEST OF BASEBALL	4192	100.00	395.00
M. TAYLOR			**PLATE**	
91	PLATE	*	19.00	19.00
M. TAYLOR			**ROD CAREW**	
91	HITTING FOR THE HALL	950	150.00	150.00
91	HITTING FOR THE HALL	10,000	45.00	45.00
91	HITTING FOR THE HALL	*	18.00	18.00
C. SOILEAU		**ROGER STAUBACH STERLING COLLECTION**		
87	ROGER STAUBACH	*	12.95	18.00
87	ROGER STAUBACH	1979	100.00	195.00
J. MARTIN			**THE ROUND TRIPPER**	
86	REGGIE JACKSON	*	12.95	18.00
M. TAYLOR			**WAYNE GRETZKY**	
89	COLLECTOR PLATE	300	300.00	500.00
89	COLLECTOR PLATE	*	16.00	18.00
89	COLLECTOR PLATE	10,000	45.00	45.00
89	COLLECTOR PLATE, H/S BY GRETZKY & HOWE	1851	225.00	395.00
M. TAYLOR			**WHITEY FORD**	
90	PLATE	10,000	45.00	45.00
90	PLATE	*	16.00	18.00
90	SIGNED PLATE	2360	125.00	125.00
M. TAYLOR			**YOGI BERRA**	
*	COLLECTOR PLATE	10,000	45.00	45.00
89	COLLECTOR PLATE	*	16.00	18.00
89	COLLECTOR PLATE	2000	125.00	125.00

GHENT COLLECTION

E. BIERLY		**AMERICAN BICENTENNIAL WILDLIFE**		
76	AMERICAN WHITETAIL DEER	2500	95.00	95.00
76	AMERICAN BISON	2500	95.00	95.00
76	AMERICAN WILD TURKEY	2500	95.00	95.00
76	AMERICAN BALD EAGLE	2500	95.00	95.00
N. ROCKWELL			**APRIL FOOL ANNUAL**	
78	APRIL FOOL	10,000	35.00	60.00
79	APRIL FOOL	10,000	35.00	35.00
80	APRIL FOOL	10,000	37.50	45.00

GOEBEL INC.

				*
*	GUIDING ANGEL	*	47.50	50.00
*	TENDER WATCH	*	47.50	50.00

YR	NAME	LIMIT	ISSUE	QUOTE
75	ANNIVERSARY PLATE 1975	*	100.00	175.00
80	ANNIVERSARY PLATE 1980	*	225.00	300.00
85	ANNIVERSARY PLATE 1985	*	225.00	250.00
M.I. HUMMEL		**M.I. HUMMEL ANNIVERSARY PLATES**		
75	STORMY WEATHER HUM-280	CL	100.00	200.00-250.00
80	RING AROUND THE ROSIE HUM-281	CL	225.00	175.00-225.00
85	AUF WIEDERSEHEN HUM-282	CL	225.00	250.00-300.00
M.I. HUMMEL		**M.I. HUMMEL ANNUAL PLATES**		
71	HEAVENLY ANGEL HUM-264	CL	25.00	750.00-1500.00
72	HEAR YE, HEAR YE HUM-265	CL	30.00	80.00-125.00
73	GLOBE TROTTER HUM-266	CL	32.50	200.00-250.00
74	GOOSE GIRL HUM-267	CL	40.00	80.00-125.00
75	RIDE INTO CHRISTMAS HUM-268	CL	50.00	80.00-125.00
76	APPLE TREE GIRL HUM-269	CL	50.00	80.00-125.00
77	APPLE TREE BOY HUM-270	CL	52.50	80.00-5000.00
78	HAPPY PASTIME HUM-271	CL	65.00	80.00-125.00
79	SINGING LESSON HUM-272	CL	90.00	75.00-100.00
80	SCHOOL GIRL HUM-273	CL	100.00	75.00-100.00
81	UMBRELLA BOY HUM-274	CL	100.00	80.00-125.00
82	UMBRELLA GIRL HUM-275	CL	100.00	175.00-200.00
83	POSTMAN HUM-276	CL	108.00	250.00-275.00
84	LITTLE HELPER HUM-277	CL	108.00	100.00-150.00
85	CHICK GIRL HUM-278	CL	110.00	100.00-150.00
86	PLAYMATES HUM-279	CL	125.00	175.00-225.00
87	FEEDING TIME HUM-283	CL	135.00	350.00-400.00
88	LITTLE GOAT HERDER HUM-284	CL	145.00	175.00-200.00
89	FARM BOY HUM-285	CL	160.00	200.00-225.00
90	SHEPHERD'S BOY HUM-286	CL	170.00	225.00-250.00
91	JUST RESTING HUM-287	CL	196.00	225.00-250.00
92	WAYSIDE HARMONY HUM-288	CL	210.00	225.00-250.00
93	DOLL BATH HUM-289	CL	210.00	225.00-250.00
M.I. HUMMEL		**M.I. HUMMEL CHRISTMAS PLATES**		
87	CELESTIAL MUSICIAN	20,000	35.00	60.00
88	ANGEL DUET	20,000	40.00	50.00
89	GUIDING LIGHT	20,000	*	50.00-60.00
90	TENDER WATCH	20,000	*	50.00-60.00
M.I. HUMMEL		**M.I. HUMMEL CLUB EXCLUSIVE-CELEBRATION**		
86	VALENTINE GIFT HUM-738	CL	90.00	125.00
87	VALENTINE JOY HUM-737	CL	98.00	125.00
88	DAISIES DON'T TELL HUM-736	CL	115.00	125.00
89	IT'S COLD HUM-735	CL	120.00	125.00
M.I. HUMMEL		**M.I. HUMMEL PLATE**		
83	ANNUAL PLATE, 1994 DOCTOR HUM-290	CL	210.00	225.00-250.00
83	ANNUAL PLATE, 1995 COME BK SOON HUM-291	OP	250.00	250.00
M.I. HUMMEL		**M.I. HUMMEL-FRIENDS FOREVER**		
92	MEDITATION HUM-292	CL	180.00	195.00-210.00
93	FOR FATHER HUM-293	CL	195.00	195.00-210.00
94	SWEET GREETINGS PLATE HUM-294	CL	205.00	205.00-210.00
95	SURPRISE PLATE HUM-295	OP	210.00	210.00
M.I. HUMMEL		**M.I. HUMMEL-LITTLE MUSIC MAKER**		
84	LITTLE FIDDLER HUM-744	CL	30.00	75.00-100.00
85	SERENADE HUM-741	CL	30.00	75.00-100.00
86	SOLOIST HUM-743	CL	35.00	75.00-100.00
87	BAND LEADER HUM-742	CL	40.00	75.00-100.00
M.I. HUMMEL		**M.I. HUMMEL-THE LITTLE HOMEMAKERS**		
88	LITTLE SWEEPER HUM-745	CL	45.00	75.00-100.00
89	WASH DAY HUM-746	CL	50.00	75.00-100.00
90	A STITCH IN TIME HUM-747	CL	50.00	75.00-100.00
91	CHICKEN LICKEN HUM-748	CL	70.00	75.00-100.00
M.I. HUMME		**MAIL ORDER/M.I. HUMMEL PLATE**		
91	KITCHEN MOULD COLLECTON HUM-670	CL	99.00	125.00-150.00
91	KITCHEN MOULD COLLECTION HUM-669	CL	99.00	125.00-150.00
91	KITCHEN MOULD COLLECTION HUM-672	CL	99.00	125.00-150.00
91	KITHCEN MOULD COLLECTION HUM-671	CL	99.00	125.00-150.00

GORHAM

N. ROCKWELL		**A BOY AND HIS DOG FOUR SEASONS PLATES-SET OF FOUR**		
71	ADVENTURES BETWEEN ADVENTURES (SET)	YR	*	*
71	BOY MEETS HIS DOG	YR	50.00	250.00-650.00
71	PRIDE OF PARENTHOOD (SET)	YR	*	*
71	THE MYSTERIOUS MALADY (SET)	YR	*	*
N. ROCKWELL		**A HELPING HAND FOUR SEASONS PLATES**		
79	CLOSED FOR BUSINESS (SET)	YR	*	*
79	COAL SEASON'S COMING (SET)	YR	*	*
79	SWATTER'S RIGHTS (SET)	YR	*	*
79	YEAR END COURT	YR	100.00	55.00-140.00

YR NAME	LIMIT	ISSUE	QUOTE
R. DONNELLY		**AMERICAN ARTIST**	
76 APACHE MOTHER & CHILD	9800	25.00	56.00
BARRYMORE		**BARRYMORE**	
71 QUIET WATERS	15,000	25.00	25.00
72 LITTLE BOATYARD, STERLING	1000	100.00	145.00
72 NANTUCKET, STERLING	1000	100.00	100.00
72 SAN PEDRO HARBOR	15,000	25.00	25.00
N. ROCKWELL		**BAS RELIEF**	
81 BEGUILING BUTTERCUP	UD	62.50	70.00
81 SWEET SONG SO YOUNG	UD	100.00	100.00
82 FLOWERS IN TENDER BLOOM	UD	100.00	100.00
82 FLYING HIGH	UD	62.50	65.00
N. ROCKWELL		**BOY SCOUT PLATES**	
75 OUR HERITAGE	18,500	19.50	40.00
76 A SCOUT IS LOYAL	18,500	19.50	55.00
77 A GOOD SIGN	18,500	19.50	50.00
77 THE SCOUTMASTER	18,500	19.50	60.00
78 CAMPFIRE STORY	18,500	19.50	25.00
78 POINTING THE WAY	18,500	19.50	50.00
80 BEYOND THE EASEL	18,500	45.00	45.00
C. RUSSELL		**CHARLES RUSSELL**	
80 IN WITHOUT KNOCKING	9800	38.00	75.00
81 BRONC TO BREAKFAST	9800	38.00	75.00-115.00
82 WHEN IGNORANCE IS BLISS	9800	45.00	75.00-115.00
83 COWBOY LIFE	9800	45.00	45.00
*		**CHINA BICENTENNIAL**	
72 1776 PLATE	18,500	17.50	35.00
76 1776 BICENTENNIAL	8000	17.50	35.00
N. ROCKWELL		**CHRISTMAS**	
74 TINY TIM	YR	12.50	45.00
75 GOOD DEEDS	YR	17.50	49.00
76 CHRISTMAS TRIO	YR	19.50	21.00
77 YULETIDE RECKONING	YR	19.50	45.00
78 PLANNING CHRISTMAS VISIT	YR	24.50	24.50
79 SANTA'S HELPERS	YR	24.50	27.00
80 LETTER TO SANTA	YR	27.50	35.00
81 SANTA PLANS HIS VISIT	YR	29.50	60.00
82 JOLLY COACHMAN	YR	29.50	29.50
83 CHRISTMAS DANCERS	YR	29.50	35.00
84 CHRISTMAS MEDLEY	17,500	29.95	29.95
85 HOME FOR THE HOLIDAYS	17,500	29.95	35.00
86 MERRY CHRISTMAS GRANDMA	17,500	29.95	65.00
87 THE HOMECOMING	17,500	35.00	50.00
88 DISCOVERY	17,500	37.50	40.00
*	**CHRISTMAS/CHILDREN'S TELEVISION WORKSHOP**		
81 SESAME STREET CHRISTMAS	YR	17.50	17.50
82 SESAME STREET CHRISTMAS	YR	17.50	17.50
83 SESAME STREET CHRISTMAS	YR	19.50	19.50
N. ROCKWELL	**DAD'S BOYS FOUR SEASONS PLATES**		
80 CAREFUL AIM (SET)	YR	*	*
80 IN HIS SPIRITS (SET)	YR	*	*
80 SKI SKILLS	YR	135.00	138.00-155.00
80 TROUT DINNER (SET)	YR	*	*
T. DEGRAZIA		**DEGARZIA CHILDREN**	
76 LOS NINOS	OP	35.00	35.00-675.00
77 THE WHITE DOVE	OP	40.00	40.00-75.00
J. CLYMER	**ENCOUNTERS, SURVIVAL AND CELEBRATIONS**		
82 A FINE WELCOME	7500	50.00	62.50
83 ALOUETTE	7500	62.50	62.50
83 THE TRADER	7500	62.50	62.50
83 THE TRAPPER TAKES A WIFE	7500	62.50	62.50
83 WINTER CAMP	7500	62.50	62.50
83 WINTER TRAIL	7500	50.00	62.50
N. ROCKWELL	**FOUR AGES OF LOVE-SET OF FOUR**		
73 FLOWERS IN TENDER BLOOM (SET)	YR	*	*
73 FONDLY WE DO REMEMBER (SET)	YR	*	*
73 GAILY SHARING VINTAGE TIME	YR	60.00	229.00
73 SWEET SONG SO YOUNG (SET)	YR	*	*
N. ROCKWELL		**FOUR SEASONS LANDSCAPES**	
80 SUMMER RESPITE	YR	45.00	67.50
81 AUTUMN REFLECTION	YR	45.00	65.00
82 WINTER DELIGHT	YR	50.00	62.50
83 SPRING RECESS	YR	60.00	60.00
* *		**FOUR SEASONS- 4 PC. SET**	
71 BOY AND HIS DOG	OP	50.00	50.00-224.00
72 YOUNG LOVE	OP	60.00	60.00-100.00

Listen closely for the mysterious sound of Garden Whispers by Larry K. Martinez from the "Nature's Little Treasures" series produced by The Bradford Exchange.

Issued in 1986, Lesley was the third release in the "Country Series" by Jan Hagara, an artist known for her elegantly dressed Victorian-era children.

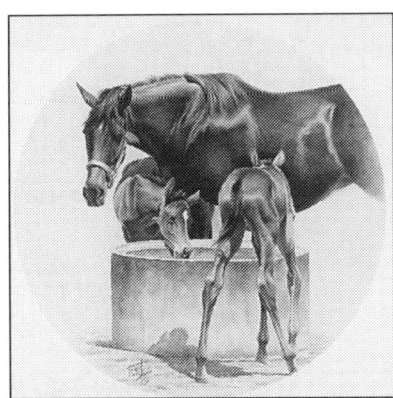

Equine artist Fred Stone is capable of capturing perfectly the sinewy stance of a horse from any angle. In The Water Trough, first in the "Mare & Foal" series, Stone also captures the special bond between a mother and her young foal. Produced by Artaffects.

Christmas Homecoming, from the "Holiday Traditions" series, harkens back to a time when the holidays meant visiting grandma's house for a festive reunion with loved ones. The Bradford Exchange.

Early Riser by P.D. Jackson is produced by Reco.

YR	NAME	LIMIT	ISSUE	QUOTE
73	AGES OF LOVE	OP	60.00	60.00-165.00
74	GRANDPA AND ME	OP	60.00	60.00-89.00
75	ME AND MY PAL	OP	70.00	70.00-115.00
76	GRAND PALS	OP	70.00	70.00-118.00
77	GOING ON SIXTEEN	OP	75.00	75.00-95.00
78	TENDER YEARS	OP	100.00	100.00
79	A HELPING HAND	OP	100.00	100.00
80	DAD'S BOY	OP	135.00	89.00
REMBRANDT			**GALLERY OF MASTERS**	
71	MAN WITH A GILT HELMET	10,000	50.00	50.00
72	SELF PORTRAIT WITH SASKIA	10,000	50.00	50.00
73	THE HONORABLE MRS. GRAHAM	7500	50.00	50.00
N. ROCKWELL		**GOING ON SIXTEEN FOUR SEASONS PLATES**		
77	CHILLING CHORE	YR	75.00	110.00
77	PILGRIMAGE (SET)	YR	*	*
77	SHEAR AGONY (SET)	YR	*	*
77	SWEET SERENADE (SET)	YR	*	*
*			**GORHAM MUSEUM DOLL PLATES**	
84	BELTON BEBE	5000	29.00	55.00
84	CHRISTMAS LADY	7500	32.50	32.50
84	LYDIA	5000	29.00	125.00
85	JUMEAU	5000	29.00	29.00
85	LUCILLE	5000	29.00	35.00
N. ROCKWELL		**GRAND PALS FOUR SEASONS PLATES-SET OF FOUR**		
76	FISH FINDERS (SET)	YR	*	*
76	GHOSTLY GOURDS (SET)	YR	*	*
76	SNOW SCULPTURING	YR	70.00	160.00
76	SOARING SPIRITS (SET)	YR	*	*
N. ROCKWELL		**GRANDPA AND ME FOUR SEASONS PLATES-SET OF FOUR**		
74	DAY DREAMERS (SET)	YR	*	*
74	GAY BLADES	YR	60.00	100.00-200.00
74	GOIN' FISHING (SET)	YR	*	*
74	PENSIVE PALS (SET)	YR	*	*
J. RITTER				**JULIAN RITTER**
77	A CHRISTMAS VISIT	9800	24.50	29.00
78	VALENTINE, FLUTTERING HEART	7500	45.00	45.00
J. RITTER			**JULIAN RITTER, FALL IN LOVE**	
77	ENCHANTMENT	5000	100.00	100.00
77	FROLIC (SET)	5000	*	*
77	GUTSY GAL (SET)	5000	*	*
77	LONELY CHILL (SET)	5000	*	*
J. RITTER			**JULIAN RITTER, TO LOVE A CLOWN**	
78	AWAITED REUNION	5000	120.00	120.00
78	SHOWTIME BECKONS	5000	120.00	120.00
78	TOGETHER IN MEMORIES	5000	120.00	120.00
78	TWOSOME TIME	5000	120.00	120.00
J.C. LEYENDECKER		**LEYENDECKER ANNUAL CHRISTMAS PLATES**		
88	CHRISTMAS HUG	10,000	37.50	37.50
N. ROCKWELL		**LIFE WITH FATHER FOUR SEASONS PLATES**		
82	A TOUGH ONE (SET)	YR	*	*
82	BIG DECISION	YR	100.00	200.00
82	BLASTING OUT (SET)	YR	*	*
82	CHEERING THE CHAMPS (SET)	YR	*	*
N. ROCKWELL		**ME AND MY PALS FOUR SEASONS PLATES**		
75	A LICKIN' GOOD BATH	YR	70.00	150.00
75	DISASTROUS DARING (SET)	YR	*	*
75	FISHERMAN'S PARADISE (SET)	YR	*	*
75	YOUNG MAN'S FANCY (SET)	YR	*	*
*			**MOPPET PLATES-ANNIVERSARY**	
76	M. PLATE ANNIVERSARY	20,000	13.00	13.00
*			**MOPPET PLATES-CHRISTMAS**	
73	M. PLATE CHRISTMAS	YR	10.00	35.00
74	M. PLATE CHRISTMAS	YR	12.00	12.00
75	M. PLATE CHRISTMAS	YR	13.00	13.00
76	M. PLATE CHRISTMAS	YR	13.00	15.00
77	M. PLATE CHRISTMAS	YR	13.00	14.00
78	M. PLATE CHRISTMAS	YR	10.00	10.00
79	M. PLATE CHRISTMAS	YR	12.00	12.00
80	M. PLATE CHRISTMAS	YR	12.00	12.00
81	M. PLATE CHRISTMAS	YR	12.00	12.00
82	M. PLATE CHRISTMAS	YR	12.00	12.00
83	M. PLATE CHRISTMAS	YR	12.00	12.00
*			**MOPPET PLATES-MOTHER'S DAY**	
73	M. PLATE MOTHER'S DAY	YR	10.00	30.00
74	M. PLATE MOTHER'S DAY	YR	12.00	20.00
75	M. PLATE MOTHER'S DAY	YR	13.00	15.00

YR	NAME	LIMIT	ISSUE	QUOTE
76	M. PLATE MOTHER'S DAY	YR	13.00	15.00
77	M. PLATE MOTHER'S DAY	YR	13.00	15.00
78	M. PLATE MOTHER'S DAY	YR	10.00	10.00
N. ROCKWELL		**OLD BUDDIES FOUR SEASONS PLATES**		
83	ENDLESS DEBATE (SET)	YR	*	*
83	FINAL SPEECH (SET)	YR	*	*
83	HASTY RETREAT (SET)	YR	*	*
83	SHARED SUCCESS	YR	115.00	115.00
N. ROCKWELL		**OLD TIMERS FOUR SEASONS PLATES**		
81	CANINE SOLO	YR	100.00	100.00
81	FANCY FOOTWORK (SET)	YR	*	*
81	LAZY DAYS (SET)	YR	*	*
81	SWEET SURPRISE (SET)	YR	*	*
B. FELDER		**PASTORAL SYMPHONY**		
*	HE LOVES ME	7500	42.50	50.00
82	GATHER THE CHILDREN	7500	42.50	50.00
82	WHEN I WAS A CHILD	7500	42.50	50.00
84	SUGAR AND SPICE	7500	42.50	50.00
R. PAILTHORPE		**PEWTER BICENTENNIAL**		
71	BURNING OF THE GASPEE	5000	35.00	35.00
72	BOSTON TEA PARTY	5000	35.00	35.00
N. ROCKWELL		**PRESIDENTIAL**		
76	DWIGHT D. EISENHOWER	9800	30.00	35.00
76	JOHN F. KENNEDY	9800	30.00	65.00
F. REMINGTON		**REMINGTON WESTERN**		
73	A NEW YEAR ON THE CIMARRON	YR	25.00	35.00
73	AIDING A COMRADE	YR	25.00	30.00
73	THE FIGHT FOR THE WATER HOLE	YR	25.00	30.00
73	THE FLIGHT	YR	25.00	30.00
75	A BREED	YR	20.00	35.00
75	OLD RAMOND	YR	20.00	35.00
76	A TRAPPER	5000	37.50	75.00
76	CAVALRY OFFICER	5000	37.50	75.00
*		**SILVER BICENTENNIAL**		
72	1776 PLATE	500	500.00	500.00
72	BURNING OF THE GASPEE	750	500.00	500.00
73	BOSTON TEA PARTY	750	550.00	575.00
F. QUAGON		**SINGLE RELEASE**		
76	THE BLACK REGIMENT 1778	7500	25.00	58.00
74	THE GOLDEN RULE	YR	12.50	30.00
74	WEIGHING IN	YR	12.50	99.00
75	BEN FRANKLIN	YR	19.50	35.00
76	THE MARRIAGE LICENSE	*	37.50	52.00
78	TRIPLE SELF PORTRAIT MEMORIAL PLATE	YR	37.50	47.50
80	THE ANNUAL VISIT	YR	32.50	35.00
81	DAY IN LIFE OF BOY	YR	50.00	80.00
81	DAY IN LIFE OF GIRL	YR	50.00	80.00
N. ROCKWELL		**TENDER YEARS FOUR SEASONS PLATES**		
78	CHILLY RECEPTION (SET)	YR	*	*
78	COOL AID (SET)	YR	*	*
78	NEW YEAR LOOK	YR	100.00	80.00-275.00
78	SPRING TONIC (SET)	YR	*	*
B. PORT		**TIME MACHINE TEDDIES PLATES**		
86	MISS EMILY, BEARING UP	5000	32.50	32.50
87	BIG BEAR, THE TOY COLLECTOR	5000	32.50	32.50
88	HUNNY MUNNY	5000	37.50	37.50
*		**VERMEIL BICENTENNIAL**		
72	1776 PLATE	250	750.00	800.00
N. ROCKWELL		**YOUNG LOVE FOUR SEASONS PLATES**		
72	A SCHOLARLY PACE (SET)	YR	*	*
72	BEGUILING BUTTERCUP (SET)	YR	*	*
72	DOWNHILL DARING	YR	60.00	140.00
72	FLYING HIGH (SET)	YR	*	*

GRANDE COPENHAGEN

YR	NAME	LIMIT	ISSUE	QUOTE
*				**CHRISTMAS**
75	ALONE TOGETHER	UD	24.50	24.50
76	CHRISTMAS WREATH	UD	24.50	29.50
77	FISHWIVES AT GAMMELSTRAND	UD	26.50	30.00
78	HANS CHRISTIAN ANDERSON	UD	32.50	38.00
79	PHEASANTS	UD	34.50	53.00
80	SNOW QUEEN IN THE TIVOLI	UD	39.50	40.00
81	LITTLE MATCH GIRL IN NYHAVN	UD	42.50	43.00
82	SHEPHERDESS/CHIMNEY SWEEP	UD	45.00	55.00
83	LITTLE MERMAID NEAR KRONBORG	UD	45.00	115.00
84	SANDMAN AT AMALIENBORG	UD	45.00	60.00

YR NAME	LIMIT	ISSUE	QUOTE

HACKETT AMERICAN
PALUSO

		LIMIT	ISSUE	QUOTE
*	BABE RUTH	10,000	35.00	110.00
*	E. MATHEWS D/S	540	125.00	295.00
*	H. KILLEBREW D/S	573	125.00	325.00
*	H. KILLEBREW U/S	5000	45.00	60.00
*	HANK AARON H/S	755	125.00	445.00
*	HANK AARON U/S	5000	45.00	60.00
*	NOLAN RYAN H/S	1598	100.00	850.00
*	REGGIE JACKSON H/S	464	100.00	975.00
*	SANDY KOUFAX H/S	1000	125.00	595.00
*	STEVE CARLTON H/S	600	100.00	350.00
*	STEVE CARLTON U/S	5000	45.00	60.00
*	STEVE GARVEY H/S	1207	100.00	245.00
*	TOM SEAVER H/S	3272	100.00	350.00
*	TOM SEAVER U/S	5000	45.00	60.00
*	WHITEY FORD H/S	472	125.00	295.00
*	WHITEY FORD U/S	5000	45.00	60.00
*	WHITEY FORD U/S	5000	45.00	60.00
*	WILLIE MAYS H/S	660	125.00	495.00
*	WILLIE MAYS U/S	5000	45.00	60.00

PALUSO *

		LIMIT	ISSUE	QUOTE
*	NOLAN RYAN U/S	5000	45.00	125.00

HADLEY COMPANIES
T. REDLIN GLOW SERIES

85	EVENING GLOW	5000	55.00	350.00-450.00
85	MORNING GLOW	5000	55.00	295.00
85	TWILIGHT GLOW	5000	55.00	95.00-125.00
87	COMING HOME	9500	85.00	85.00
87	EVENING RETREAT	9500	65.00	75.00
87	MORNING RETREAT	9500	65.00	65.00-125.00
88	AFTERNOON GLOW	5000	55.00	55.00
88	GOLDEN RETREAT	9500	65.00	95.00
88	LIGHTS OF HOME	9500	85.00	85.00
89	HOMEWARD BOUND	9500	85.00	85.00
89	MOONLIGHT RETREAT	9500	65.00	65.00

HALLMARK KEEPSAKE ORNAMENTS
L. VOTRUBA

87	LIGHT SHINES AT CHRISTMAS 800QX481-7	YR	8.00	75.00
88	WAITING FOR SANTA 800QX406-1	YR	8.00	49.50
89	MORNING OF WONDER 825QX461-2	YR	8.25	35.00
90	COOKIES FOR SANTA 875QX443-6	YR	8.75	34.50
91	LET IT SNOW!-5TH EDITION 875QX436-9	YR	8.75	29.50
92	SWEET HOLIDAY HARMONY 875QX446-1	YR	8.75	29.50

HAMILTON COLLECTION
T. UTZ

83	PRINCESS GRACE	21-DAY	39.50	52.00

B.P. GUTMANN A CHILD'S BEST FRIEND

85	GOING TO TOWN	14-DAY	24.50	60.00
85	GOOD MORNING	14-DAY	24.50	45.00
85	IN DISGRACE	14-DAY	24.50	180.00
85	MINE	14-DAY	24.50	90.00
85	ON THE UP AND UP	14-DAY	24.50	54.00
85	SYMPATHY	14-DAY	24.50	24.00-65.00
85	THE REWARD	14-DAY	24.50	60.00
85	WHO'S SLEEPY	14-DAY	24.50	45.00

J.M. VASS A COUNTRY SEASON OF HORSES

90	A WINTER'S WALK	14-DAY	29.50	29.50
90	AUTUMN GRANDEUR	14-DAY	29.50	29.50
90	CLIFFSIDE BEAUTY	14-DAY	29.50	29.50
90	CRISP COUNTRY MORNING	14-DAY	29.50	29.50
90	FIRST DAY OF SPRING	14-DAY	29.50	36.00
90	FROSTY MORNING	14-DAY	29.50	29.50
90	RIVER RETREAT	14-DAY	29.50	29.50
90	SUMMER SPLENDOR	14-DAY	29.50	29.50

N. NOEL A COUNTRY SUMMER

85	BUTTERFLY BEAUTY	10-DAY	29.50	36.00
85	THE GOLDEN PUPPY	10-DAY	29.50	35.00
86	MY BUNNY	10-DAY	29.50	33.00
86	THE ROCKING CHAIR	10-DAY	29.50	36.00
88	TEAMMATES	10-DAY	29.50	35.00
88	THE PIGLET	10-DAY	29.50	35.00

T. FREEMAN AMERICA'S GREATEST SAILING SHIPS

88	AMERICA	14-DAY	29.50	45.00

YR	NAME	LIMIT	ISSUE	QUOTE
88	BONHOMME RICHARD	14-DAY	29.50	45.00
88	CHARLES W. MORGAN	14-DAY	29.50	36.00
88	EAGLE	14-DAY	29.50	48.00
88	ENTERPRISE	14-DAY	29.50	37.50
88	GERTRUDE L. THEBAUD	14-DAY	29.50	35.00
88	GREAT REPUBLIC	14-DAY	29.50	36.00
88	U.S.S. CONSTITUTION	14-DAY	29.50	36.00
D. MANNING		**BIG CATS OF THE WORLD**		
89	AFRICAN SHADE	14-DAY	29.50	35.00
89	VIEW FROM ABOVE	14-DAY	29.50	29.50
90	ABOVE THE TREETOPS	14-DAY	29.50	29.50
90	DEEP IN THE JUNGLE	14-DAY	29.50	29.50
90	MOUNTAIN DWELLER	14-DAY	29.50	29.50
90	ON THE PROWL	14-DAY	29.50	29.50
90	SPIRIT OF THE MOUNTAIN	14-DAY	29.50	29.50
90	SPOTTED SENTINEL	14-DAY	29.50	29.50
J. CHENG		**BIRDS OF THE TEMPLE GARDENS**		
89	CRANES OF ETERNAL LIFE	14-DAY	29.50	35.00
89	DOVES OF FIDELITY	14-DAY	29.50	35.00
89	GOLDFINCHES OF VIRTUE	14-DAY	29.50	35.00
89	HONORABLE SWALLOWS	14-DAY	29.50	35.00
89	IMPERIAL GOLDCREST	14-DAY	29.50	29.50
89	MAGPIES: BIRDS OF GOOD OMEN	14-DAY	29.50	29.50
89	ORIENTAL WHITE EYES OF BEAUTY	14-DAY	29.50	29.50
89	PHEASANTS OF GOOD FORTUNE	14-DAY	29.50	29.50
B.P. GUTMANN		**BUNDLES OF JOY**		
88	A LITTLE BIT OF HEAVEN	14-DAY	24.50	45.00
88	AWAKENING	14-DAY	24.50	75.00
88	BILLY	14-DAY	24.50	30.00
88	HAPPY DREAMS	14-DAY	24.50	39.00
88	SUN KISSED	14-DAY	24.50	30.00
88	SWEET INNOCENCE	14-DAY	24.50	30.00
88	TASTING	14-DAY	24.50	30.00
88	TOMMY	14-DAY	24.50	30.00
P. SWEANY		**BUTTERFLY GARDEN**		
87	COMMON BLUE	14-DAY	29.50	37.50
87	CRIMSON PATCHED LONGWING	14-DAY	29.50	37.50
87	MONARCH	14-DAY	29.50	37.50
87	ORANGE SULPHUR	14-DAY	29.50	30.00
87	SPICEBUSH SWALLOWTAIL	14-DAY	29.50	45.00
87	TIGER SWALLOWTAIL	14-DAY	29.50	30.00
88	MORNING CLOAK	14-DAY	29.50	35.00
88	RED ADMIRAL	14-DAY	29.50	37.50
T. UTZ		**CAREFREE DAYS**		
82	AUTUMN WANDERER	10-DAY	24.50	30.00
82	BATHTIME VISITOR	10-DAY	24.50	30.00
82	BEST FRIENDS	10-DAY	24.50	30.00
82	FEEDING TIME	10-DAY	24.50	30.00
82	FIRST CATCH	10-DAY	24.50	30.00
82	MONKEY BUSINESS	10-DAY	24.50	30.00
82	NATURE HUNT	10-DAY	24.50	30.00
82	TOUCHDOWN	10-DAY	24.50	30.00
B.P. GUTMANN		**CHILDHOOD REFLECTIONS**		
91	FRIENDLY ENEMIES	14-DAY	29.50	29.50
91	HARMONY	14-DAY	29.50	29.50
91	KITTY'S BREAKFAST	14-DAY	29.50	29.50
91	LITTLE MOTHER	14-DAY	29.50	29.50
91	LULLABY	14-DAY	29.50	29.50
91	OH! OH! A BUNNY	14-DAY	29.50	29.50
91	SMILE, SMILE, SMILE	14-DAY	29.50	29.50
91	THANK YOU, GOD	14-DAY	29.50	29.50
D. CROOK		**CHILDREN OF THE AMERICAN FRONTIER**		
86	A LADY NEEDS A LITTLE PRIVACY	10-DAY	24.50	30.00
86	IN TROUBLE AGAIN	10-DAY	24.50	30.00
86	RIDERS WANTED	10-DAY	24.50	27.00
86	THE DESPERADOES	10-DAY	24.50	30.00
86	TUBS AND SUDS	10-DAY	24.50	27.00
87	A COWBOY'S DOWNFALL	10-DAY	24.50	34.00
87	A SPECIAL PATIENT	10-DAY	24.50	30.00
87	RUNAWAY BLUES	10-DAY	24.50	30.00
B. CHRISTIE		**CLASSIC SPORTING DOGS**		
89	BEAGLES	14-DAY	24.50	30.00
89	GOLDEN RETRIEVERS	14-DAY	24.50	36.00
89	LABRADOR RETRIEVERS	14-DAY	24.50	36.00
89	POINTERS	14-DAY	24.50	27.00
89	SPRINGER SPANIELS	14-DAY	24.50	30.00

YR	NAME	LIMIT	ISSUE	QUOTE
90	BRITTANY SPANIELS	14-DAY	24.50	30.00
90	GERMAN SHORT-HAIRED POINTERS	14-DAY	24.50	45.00
90	IRISH SETTERS	14-DAY	24.50	24.50

K. MILNAZIK — CLASSIC TV WESTERNS

YR	NAME	LIMIT	ISSUE	QUOTE
90	BONANZA	14-DAY	29.50	29.50
90	ROY ROGERS AND DALE EVANS	14-DAY	29.50	29.50
90	THE LONE RANGER AND TONTO	14-DAY	29.50	29.50
91	HAVE GUN, WILL TRAVEL	14-DAY	29.50	29.50
91	HOPALONG CASSIDY	14-DAY	29.50	29.50
91	RAWHIDE	14-DAY	29.50	29.50
91	THE VIRGINIAN	14-DAY	29.50	29.50
91	WILD WILD WEST	14-DAY	29.50	29.50

H. BOND — CORAL PARADISE

YR	NAME	LIMIT	ISSUE	QUOTE
89	THE LIVING OASIS	14-DAY	29.50	29.50
90	CARIBBEAN SPECTACLE	14-DAY	29.50	29.50
90	FOREST BENEATH THE SEA	14-DAY	29.50	29.50
90	MYSTERIES OF THE GALAPAGOS	14-DAY	29.50	29.50
90	RICHES OF THE CORAL SEA	14-DAY	29.50	29.50
90	SHIMMERING REEF DWELLERS	14-DAY	29.50	29.50
90	TROPICAL PAGEANTRY	14-DAY	29.50	29.50
90	UNDERSEA VILLAGE	14-DAY	29.50	29.50

G. GERARDI — COUNTRY KITTIES

YR	NAME	LIMIT	ISSUE	QUOTE
89	ALL WASHED UP	14-DAY	24.50	39.00
89	ATTIC ATTACK	14-DAY	24.50	45.00
89	CAPTIVE AUDIENCE	14-DAY	24.50	39.00
89	JUST FOR THE FERN OF IT	14-DAY	24.50	27.00
89	MISCHIEF MAKERS	14-DAY	24.50	30.00
89	ROCK AND ROLLERS	14-DAY	24.50	30.00
89	STROLLER DERBY	14-DAY	24.50	36.00
89	TABLE MANNERS	14-DAY	24.50	27.00

B. HARRISON — CURIOUS KITTENS

YR	NAME	LIMIT	ISSUE	QUOTE
90	KEEPING IN STEP	14-DAY	29.50	29.50
90	RAINY DAY FRIENDS	14-DAY	29.50	29.50
91	A PAW'S IN THE ACTION	14-DAY	29.50	29.50
91	ALL WOUND UP	14-DAY	29.50	29.50
91	CHANCE MEETING	14-DAY	29.50	29.50
91	DELIGHTFUL DISCOVERY	14-DAY	29.50	29.50
91	MAKING TRACKS	14-DAY	29.50	29.50
91	PLAYING CAT AND MOUSE	14-DAY	29.50	29.50

J. HAGARA — DEAR TO MY HEART

YR	NAME	LIMIT	ISSUE	QUOTE
90	ADDIE	14-DAY	29.50	29.50
90	CATHY	14-DAY	29.50	29.50
90	DACY	14-DAY	29.50	29.50
90	JIMMY	14-DAY	29.50	29.50
90	PAUL	14-DAY	29.50	29.50
91	JENNY	14-DAY	29.50	29.50
91	JOY	14-DAY	29.50	29.50
91	SHELLY	14-DAY	29.50	29.50

J. LAMB — DELIGHTS OF CHILDHOOD

YR	NAME	LIMIT	ISSUE	QUOTE
89	CRAYON CREATIONS	14-DAY	29.50	35.00
89	LITTLE MOTHER	14-DAY	29.50	29.50
90	BATHING BEAUTY	14-DAY	29.50	29.50
90	IS THAT YOU, GRANNY?	14-DAY	29.50	29.50
90	NATURE'S LITTLE HELPER	14-DAY	29.50	29.50
90	SHOWER TIME	14-DAY	29.50	29.50
90	SO SORRY	14-DAY	29.50	29.50
90	STORYTIME FRIENDS	14-DAY	29.50	29.50

S. MORTON — ELVIS REMEMBERED

YR	NAME	LIMIT	ISSUE	QUOTE
89	EARLY YEARS	90-DAY	37.50	37.50
89	ELVIS PRESLEY	90-DAY	37.50	37.50
89	FOREVER YOURS	90-DAY	37.50	37.50
89	LOVING YOU	90-DAY	37.50	55.00
89	MOODY BLUES	90-DAY	37.50	45.00
89	ROCKIN' IN THE MOONLIGHT	90-DAY	37.50	37.50
89	TENDERLY	90-DAY	37.50	37.50-55.00
89	THE KING	90-DAY	37.50	37.50

M. BELL — ENGLISH COUNTRY COTTAGES

YR	NAME	LIMIT	ISSUE	QUOTE
90	PERIWINKLE TEA ROOM	14-DAY	29.50	29.50
91	GAMEKEEPER'S COTTAGE	14-DAY	29.50	29.50
91	GINGER COTTAGE	14-DAY	29.50	29.50
91	LORNA DOONE COTTAGE	14-DAY	29.50	29.50
91	LULLABYE COTTAGE	14-DAY	29.50	29.50
91	MURRLE COTTAGE	14-DAY	29.50	29.50
91	THE CHAPLAIN'S GARDEN	14-DAY	29.50	29.50

D. O'DRISCOLL — FAVORITE AMERICAN SONGBIRDS

YR	NAME	LIMIT	ISSUE	QUOTE
89	BLUE JAYS OF SPRING	14-DAY	29.50	35.00

YR	NAME	LIMIT	ISSUE	QUOTE
89	GOLDFINCHES OF SUMMER	14-DAY	29.50	35.00
89	RED CARDINALS OF WINTER	14-DAY	29.50	29.50
89	ROBINS & APPLE BLOSSOMS	14-DAY	29.50	35.00
90	AUTUMN CHICKADEES	14-DAY	29.50	29.50
90	BLUEBIRDS AND MORNING GLORIES	14-DAY	29.50	35.00
90	TUFTED TITMOUSE AND HOLLY	14-DAY	29.50	29.50
91	CAROLINA WRENS OF SPRING	14-DAY	29.50	29.50

T. BLACKSHEAR — **FIFTY YEARS OF OZ**

YR	NAME	LIMIT	ISSUE	QUOTE
89	FIFTY YEARS OF OZ	14-DAY	37.50	90.00

J. LAMB — **GOOD SPORTS**

YR	NAME	LIMIT	ISSUE	QUOTE
90	DOUBLE PLAY	14-DAY	29.50	29.50
90	HOLE IN ONE	14-DAY	29.50	29.50
90	SLAP SHOT	14-DAY	29.50	29.50
90	SPOTTED ON THE SIDELINE	14-DAY	29.50	29.50
90	THE BASS MASTERS	14-DAY	29.50	29.50
90	WIDE RETRIEVER	14-DAY	29.50	29.50
91	BASSETBALL	14-DAY	29.50	29.50
91	NET PLAY	14-DAY	29.50	29.50

WYLAND — **GREAT MAMMALS OF THE SEA**

YR	NAME	LIMIT	ISSUE	QUOTE
91	CHILDREN OF THE SEA	14DAY	35.00	35.00
91	DOLPHIN PARADISE	14-DAY	35.00	35.00
91	HAWAII DOLPHINS	14-DAY	35.00	35.00
91	ISLANDS	14DAY	35.00	35.00
91	KISSING DOLPHINS	14DAY	35.00	35.00
91	ORCA JOURNEY	14-DAY	35.00	35.00
91	ORCA TRIO	14-DAY	35.00	35.00
91	ORCAS	14-DAY	35.00	35.00

P. BROOKS — **GROWING UP TOGETHER**

YR	NAME	LIMIT	ISSUE	QUOTE
90	MY VERY BEST FRIENDS	14-DAY	29.50	29.50
90	PICNIC PALS	14-DAY	29.50	29.50
90	TEA FOR TWO	14-DAY	29.50	29.50
90	TENDER LOVING CARE	14-DAY	29.50	29.50
91	BEDTIME BLESSINGS	14-DAY	29.50	29.50
91	FISHING BUDDIES	14-DAY	29.50	29.50
91	KITTEN CABOODLE	14-DAY	29.50	29.50
91	NEWFOUND FRIENDS	14-DAY	29.50	29.50

S. KUCK — **HEARTS AND FLOWERS**

YR	NAME	LIMIT	ISSUE	QUOTE
92	CAROUSEL OF DREAMS	120-DAY	32.50	32.50

SHUHO/KAGE — **JAPANESE FLORAL CALENDAR**

YR	NAME	LIMIT	ISSUE	QUOTE
81	NEW YEAR'S DAY	10-DAY	32.50	60.00
82	AUTUMN	10-DAY	32.50	35.00
82	BOY'S DOLL DAY FESTIVAL	10-DAY	32.50	35.00
82	BUDDHA'S BIRTHDAY	10-DAY	32.50	35.00
82	EARLY SPRING	10-DAY	32.50	40.00
82	EARLY SUMMER	10-DAY	32.50	35.00
82	GIRL'S DOLL DAY FESTIVAL	10-DAY	32.50	35.00
82	SPRING	10-DAY	32.50	35.00
82	SUMMER	10-DAY	32.50	35.00
83	FESTIVAL OF THE FULL MOON	10-DAY	32.50	37.00
83	LATE AUTUMN	10-DAY	32.50	38.00
83	WINTER	10-DAY	32.50	38.00

M. HUMPHREY — **LITTLE LADIES**

YR	NAME	LIMIT	ISSUE	QUOTE
89	PLAYING BRIDESMAID	14-DAY	29.50	60.00
90	A DAY IN THE COUNTRY	14-DAY	29.50	29.50
90	KITTY'S BATH	14-DAY	29.50	29.50
90	LITTLE CAPTIVE	14-DAY	29.50	29.50
90	PLAYING MAMA	14-DAY	29.50	29.50
90	SUSANNA	14-DAY	29.50	29.50
90	THE SEAMSTRESS	14-DAY	29.50	29.50
91	SARAH	14-DAY	29.50	29.50

G. GERARDI — **LITTLE SHOPKEEPERS**

YR	NAME	LIMIT	ISSUE	QUOTE
90	SEW TIRED	14-DAY	29.50	29.50
91	BREAK TIME	14-DAY	29.50	29.50
91	CANDY CAPERS	14-DAY	29.50	33.00
91	CHAIN REACTION	14-DAY	29.50	29.50
91	INFERIOR DECORATORS	14-DAY	29.50	29.50
91	PURRFECT FIT	14-DAY	29.50	29.50
91	TOYING AROUND	14-DAY	29.50	29.50
91	TULIP TAG	14-DAY	29.50	29.50

T. HIRATA — **MAJESTY OF FLIGHT**

YR	NAME	LIMIT	ISSUE	QUOTE
89	COASTAL JOURNEY	14-DAY	37.50	37.50
89	COMMANDING THE MARSH	14-DAY	37.50	37.50
89	REALM OF THE RED-TAIL	14-DAY	37.50	39.00
89	SENTRY OF THE NORTH	14-DAY	37.50	37.50
89	THE EAGLE SOARS	14-DAY	37.50	37.50
90	FIERCE AND FREE	14-DAY	29.50	45.00

YR	NAME	LIMIT	ISSUE	QUOTE
90	SILENT WATCH	14-DAY	29.50	37.50
90	THE VANTAGE POINT	14-DAY	29.50	37.50
P. COOPER			**MIXED COMPANY**	
90	A STICKY SITUATION	14-DAY	29.50	29.50
90	ALL WRAPPED UP	14-DAY	29.50	29.50
90	PICTURE PERFECT	14-DAY	29.50	29.50
90	TWO AGAINST ONE	14-DAY	29.50	29.50
90	WHAT'S UP	14-DAY	29.50	29.50
91	A MOMENT TO UNWIND	14-DAY	29.50	29.50
91	OLE	14-DAY	29.50	29.50
91	PICNIC PROWLERS	14-DAY	29.50	29.50
R. PARKER			**NATURE'S QUIET MOMENTS**	
88	A CURIOUS PAIR	14-DAY	37.50	37.50
88	JUST RESTING	14-DAY	37.50	37.50
88	NORTHERN MORNINGS	14-DAY	37.50	37.50
89	AUTUMN FORAGING	14-DAY	37.50	37.50
89	CREEKSIDE	14-DAY	37.50	37.50
89	MOUNTAIN BLOOMS	14-DAY	37.50	37.50
89	OLD MAN OF THE MOUNTAIN	14-DAY	37.50	37.50
89	WAITING OUT THE STORM	14-DAY	37.50	37.50
D. WRIGHT			**NOBLE AMERICAN INDIAN WOMEN**	
89	SACAJAWEA	14-DAY	29.50	29.50
90	LILY OF THE MOHAWK	14-DAY	29.50	29.50
90	MINNEHAHA	14-DAY	29.50	29.50
90	PINE LEAF	14-DAY	29.50	29.50
90	POCAHONTAS	14-DAY	29.50	29.50
90	WHITE ROSE	14-DAY	29.50	29.50
91	FALLING STAR	14-DAY	29.50	29.50
91	LOZEN	14-DAY	29.50	29.50
J. SEEREY-LESTER			**NOBLE OWLS OF AMERICA**	
86	MORNING MIST	15,000	55.00	60.00
87	AUTUMN MIST	15,000	55.00	60.00
87	DAWN IN THE WILLOWS	15,000	55.00	60.00
87	PRAIRIE SUNDOWN	15,000	55.00	60.00
87	SNOWY WATCH	15,000	55.00	60.00
87	WINTER VIGIL	15,000	55.00	60.00
88	HIDING PLACE	15,000	55.00	60.00
88	WAITING FOR DUSK	15,000	55.00	60.00
R. LAWRENCE			**NORTH AMERICAN DUCKS**	
91	AUTUMN FLIGHT	14-DAY	29.50	29.59
91	THE RESTING PLACE	14-DAY	29.50	29.59
91	TWIN FLIGHT	14-DAY	29.50	29.50
92	MISTY MORNING	14-DAY	29.50	29.50
92	OVERCAST	14-DAY	29.50	29.50
92	PERFECT PINTAILS	14-DAY	29.50	29.50
92	SPRINGTIME THAW	14-DAY	29.50	29.50
92	SUMMER RETREAT	14-DAY	29.50	29.50
J. KILLEN			**NORTH AMERICAN GAMEBIRDS**	
90	BOBWHITE QUAIL	14-DAY	37.50	45.00
90	GAMBEL QUAIL	14-DAY	37.50	37.50
90	MOURNING DOVE	14-DAY	37.50	37.50
90	RING-NECKED PHEASANT	14-DAY	37.50	44.00
90	RUFFED GROUSE	14-DAY	37.50	37.50
90	WOODCOCK	14-DAY	37.50	37.50
91	CHUKAR PARTRIDGE	14-DAY	37.50	37.50
91	WILD TURKEY	14-DAY	37.50	37.50
R. LAWRENCE			**NORTH AMERICAN WATERBIRDS**	
88	CANADA GEESE	14-DAY	37.50	45.00
88	HOODED MERGANSERS	14-DAY	37.50	54.00
88	PINTAILS	14-DAY	37.50	45.00
88	WOOD DUCKS	14-DAY	37.50	55.00
89	AMERICAN WIDGEONS	14-DAY	37.50	54.00
89	CANVASBACKS	14-DAY	37.50	55.00
89	MALLARD PAIR	14-DAY	37.50	55.00
89	SNOW GEESE	14-DAY	37.50	55.00
R. MASSEY			**PASSAGE TO CHINA**	
83	ALLIANCE	15,000	55.00	65.00
83	EMPRESS OF CHINA	15,000	55.00	65.00
85	CHALLENGE	15,000	55.00	55.00
85	FLYING CLOUD	15,000	55.00	55.00
85	GRAND TURK	15,000	55.00	60.00
85	ROMANCE OF THE SEAS	15,000	55.00	60.00
85	SEA SERPENT	15,000	55.00	60.00
85	SEA WITCH	15,000	55.00	60.00
B. HARRISON			**PETALS AND PURRS**	
88	BLUSHING BEAUTIES	14-DAY	24.50	30.00

YR	NAME	LIMIT	ISSUE	QUOTE
88	FORGET-ME-NOT	14-DAY	24.50	30.00
88	MORNING GLORIES	14-DAY	24.50	30.00
88	SPRING FEVER	14-DAY	24.50	37.50
89	GOLDEN FANCY	14-DAY	24.50	30.00
89	PINK LILLIES	14-DAY	24.50	30.00
89	SIEMESE SUMMER	14-DAY	24.50	24.50
89	SUMMER SUNSHINE	14-DAY	24.50	24.50
T. BLACKSHEAR			**PORTRAITS FROM OZ**	
89	DOROTHY	14-DAY	29.50	35.00-38.00
89	SCARECROW	14-DAY	29.50	41.00-45.00
89	TIN MAN	14-DAY	29.50	29.50-37.00
90	COWARDLY LION	14-DAY	29.50	41.00
90	GLINDA	14-DAY	29.50	45.00-50.00
90	TOTO	14-DAY	29.50	140.00
90	WICKED WITCH	14-DAY	29.50	35.00-39.00
90	WIZARD	14-DAY	29.50	36.00-42.00
T. UTZ			**PORTRAITS OF CHILDHOOD**	
81	BUTTERFLY MAGIC	28-DAY	24.95	45.00
82	SWEET DREAMS	28-DAY	24.95	30.00
83	TURTLE TALK	28-DAY	24.95	36.00
84	FRIENDS FOREVER	28-DAY	24.95	30.00
T. UTZ			**PRECIOUS MOMENTS PLATES**	
79	FRIEND IN THE SKY	28-DAY	21.50	50.00
80	SAND IN HER SHOE	28-DAY	21.50	40.00
80	SEASHELLS	28-DAY	21.50	37.50
80	SNOW BUNNY	28-DAY	21.50	40.00
81	DAWN	28-DAY	21.50	27.00
82	MY KITTY	28-DAY	21.50	36.00
B.P. GUTMANN			**PRECIOUS PORTRAITS**	
87	BUNNY	14-DAY	24.50	30.00
87	FAIRY GOLD	14-DAY	24.50	30.00
87	GOLDILOCKS	14-DAY	24.50	27.00
87	MISCHIEF	14-DAY	24.50	27.00
87	PEACH BLOSSOM	14-DAY	24.50	30.00
87	SUNBEAM	14-DAY	24.50	30.00
K. FREEMAN			**PROUD INDIAN FAMILIES**	
91	PLAYING WITH TRADITION	14DAY	29.50	29.50
91	THE NAMING CEREMONY	14-DAY	29.50	29.50
91	THE POWER OF THE BASKET	14-DAY	29.50	29.50
91	THE STORYTELLER	14-DAY	29.50	29.59
92	CEREMONIAL DRESS	14-DAY	29.50	29.50
92	PREPARING THE BERRY HARVEST	14-DAY	29.50	29.50
92	SOUNDS OF THE FOREST	14-DAY	29.50	29.50
92	THE MARRIAGE CEREMONY	14-DAY	29.50	29.50
N. ROCKWELL			**ROCKWELL HOME OF THE BRAVE**	
81	BACK TO HIS OLD JOB	18,000	35.00	40.00
81	HERO'S WELCOME	18,000	35.00	50.00
81	REMINISCING	18,000	35.00	75.00
81	WAR HERO	18,000	35.00	45.00
82	TAKING MOTHER OVER THE TOP	18,000	35.00	40.00
82	UNCLE SAM TAKES WINGS	18,000	35.00	40.00
82	WAR BOND	18,000	35.00	40.00
82	WILLIE GILLIS IN CHURCH	18,000	35.00	40.00
D. SWEET			**ROMANTIC CASTLES OF EUROPE**	
90	LUDWIG'S CASTLE	19,500	55.00	55.00
91	DAVINCI'S CHAMBORD	19,500	55.00	55.00
91	EILEAN DONAN	19,500	55.00	55.00
91	PALACE OF THE MOORS	19,500	55.00	55.00
91	SWISS ISLE FORTRESS	19,500	55.00	55.00
91	THE LEGENDARY CASTLE OF LEEDS	19,500	55.00	55.00
92	ELTZ CASTLE	19,500	55.00	55.00
92	KYLEMORE ABBEY	19,500	55.00	55.00
J. PITCHER			**SEASONS OF THE BALD EAGLE**	
91	AUTUMN IN THE MOUNTAINS	14-DAY	37.50	37.50
91	SPRING ON THE RIVER	14-DAY	37.50	37.50
91	WINTER IN THE VALLEY	14-DAY	37.50	37.50
C. FRACE			**SMALL WONDERS OF THE WILD**	
89	HIDEAWAY	14-DAY	29.50	35.00
90	EXPLORING A NEW WORLD	14-DAY	29.50	29.50
90	EYES OF WONDER	14-DAY	29.50	29.50
90	QUIET MORNING	14-DAY	29.50	29.50
90	READY FOR ADVENTURE	14-DAY	29.50	29.50
90	THREE OF A KIND	14-DAY	29.50	45.00
90	UNO	14-DAY	29.50	29.50
90	YOUNG EXPLORERS	14-DAY	29.50	29.50

YR NAME	LIMIT	ISSUE	QUOTE
J. LAMB		**SPORTING GENERATION**	
91 GOLDEN MOMENTS	14-DAY	29.50	29.50
91 LIKE FATHER, LIKE SON	14-DAY	29.50	29.50
91 THE LOOKOUT	14-DAY	29.50	29.50
T. UTZ		**SPRINGTIME OF LIFE**	
85 AMONG THE DAFFODILS	14-DAY	29.50	35.00
85 AUNT TILLIE'S HATS	14-DAY	29.50	35.00
85 GRANNY'S BOOTS	14-DAY	29.50	35.00
85 JUST LIKE MOMMY	14-DAY	29.50	35.00
85 LITTLE EMILY	14-DAY	29.50	35.00
85 MY FAVORITE DOLLS	14-DAY	29.50	35.00
85 MY MASTERPIECE	14-DAY	29.50	35.00
85 TEDDY'S BATHTIME	14-DAY	29.50	35.00
*		**STAINED GLASS GARDENS**	
89 GARDEN SUNSET	15,000	55.00	60.00
89 PEACOCK AND WISTERIA	15,000	55.00	60.00
89 THE COCKATOO'S GARDEN	15,000	55.00	60.00
89 WATERFALL AND IRIS	15,000	55.00	55.00
90 A HOLLYHOCK SUNRISE	15,000	55.00	55.00
90 PEACEFUL WATERS	15,000	55.00	55.00
90 ROSES AND MAGNOLIAS	15,000	55.00	55.00
90 SPRINGTIME IN THE VALLEY	15,000	55.00	55.00
T. UTZ		**SUMMER DAYS OF CHILDHOOD**	
83 A JUMPING CONTEST	10-DAY	29.50	35.00
83 A STOLEN KISS	10-DAY	29.50	35.00
83 BALLOON CARNIVAL	10-DAY	29.50	35.00
83 BLOWING BUBBLES	10-DAY	29.50	35.00
83 COOLING OFF	10-DAY	29.50	35.00
83 FIRST CUSTOMER	10-DAY	29.50	35.00
83 GARDEN MAGIC	10-DAY	29.50	35.00
83 KITTY'S BATHTIME	10-DAY	29.50	35.00
83 LITTLE BEACHCOMBER	10-DAY	29.50	35.00
83 MOUNTAIN FRIENDS	10-DAY	29.50	35.00
83 PLAYING DOCTOR	10-DAY	29.50	35.00
83 THE BIRTHDAY PARTY	10-DAY	29.50	35.00
D. PRECHTEL		**THE AMERICAN CIVIL WAR**	
90 ABRAHAM LINCOLN	14-DAY	37.50	37.50
90 GENERAL ROBERT E. LEE	14-DAY	37.50	37.50
90 GENERAL THOMAS STONEWALL JACKSON	14-DAY	37.50	37.50
90 GENERALS GRANT AND LEE AT APPOMATTOX	14-DAY	37.50	37.50
91 A LETTER FORM HOME	14-DAY	37.50	37.50
91 GENERAL JEB STUART	14-DAY	37.50	37.50
91 GENERAL PHILIP SHERIDAN	14-DAY	37.50	37.50
P.J. SWEANY		**THE AMERICAN ROSE GARDEN**	
88 AMERICAN SPIRIT	14-DAY	29.50	35.00
88 PEACE ROSE	14-DAY	29.50	35.00
89 AMERICAN HERITAGE	14-DAY	29.50	36.00
89 BLUE MOON	14-DAY	29.50	36.00
89 CORAL CLUSTER	14-DAY	29.50	33.00
89 ECLIPSE	14-DAY	29.50	33.00
89 PRESIDENT HERBERT HOOVER	14-DAY	29.50	29.50
89 WHITE KNIGHT	14-DAY	29.50	36.00
M. SUSINNO		**THE ANGLER'S PRIZE**	
91 AUTUMN BEAUTY	14-DAY	29.50	36.00
91 BLUE RIBBON TROUT	14-DAY	29.50	29.50
91 BRONZEBACK FIGHTER	14-DAY	29.50	36.00
91 FRESHWATER BARRACUDA	14-DAY	29.50	36.00
91 SUN DANCERS	14-DAY	29.50	29.50
91 TROPHY BASS	14-DAY	29.50	29.50
92 OLD MOONEYES	14-DAY	29.50	29.50
92 SILVER KING	14-DAY	29.50	29.50
C. LAWSON		**THE GOLDEN CLASSICS**	
87 HANSEL AND GRETEL	10-DAY	37.50	37.50
87 JACK AND THE BEANSTALK	10-DAY	37.50	37.50
87 RUMPELSTILTSKIN	10-DAY	37.50	37.50
87 SLEEPING BEAUTY	10-DAY	37.50	37.50
87 SNOW WHITE AND ROSE RED	10-DAY	37.50	37.50
88 CINDERELLA	10-DAY	37.50	37.50
88 THE GOLDEN GOOSE	10-DAY	37.50	37.50
88 THE SNOW QUEEN	10-DAY	37.50	37.50
F. MOODY		**THE GREATEST SHOW ON EARTH**	
81 AERIALISTS	10-DAY	30.00	35.00
81 CLOWNS	10-DAY	30.00	75.00
81 ELEPHANTS	10-DAY	30.00	40.00
81 EQUESTRIANS	10-DAY	30.00	40.00
81 GREAT PARADE	10-DAY	30.00	40.00

YR	NAME	LIMIT	ISSUE	QUOTE
81	MIDWAY	10-DAY	30.00	40.00
82	GRANDE FINALE	10-DAY	30.00	35.00
82	LION TAMER	10-DAY	30.00	35.00
J. KRITZ		**THE I LOVE LUCY PLATE COLLECTION**		
89	CALIFORNIA HERE WE COME	14-DAY	29.50	35.00
89	ITS JUST LIKE CANDY	14-DAY	29.50	29.50
90	EATING THE EVIDENCE	14-DAY	29.50	29.50
90	THE BIG SQUEEZE	14-DAY	29.50	29.50-49.00
90	TWO OF A KIND	14-DAY	29.50	29.50
91	QUEEN OF THE GYPSIES	14-DAY	29.50	29.50
92	A RISING PROBLEM	14-DAY	29.50	29.50
92	NIGHT AT THE COPA	14-DAY	29.50	29.50
KOSEKI/ EBIHARA		**THE JAPANESE BLOSSOMS OF AUTUMN**		
85	ARROWROOT	10-DAY	45.00	50.00
85	BELLFLOWER	10-DAY	45.00	50.00
85	BUSH CLOVER	10-DAY	45.00	50.00
85	MAIDEN FLOWER	10-DAY	45.00	50.00
85	PAMPAS GRASS	10-DAY	45.00	50.00
85	PURPLE TROUSERS	10-DAY	45.00	50.00
85	WILD CARNATION	10-DAY	45.00	50.00
J. LANDENBERGER		**THE JEWELED HUMMINGBIRDS PLATE COLLECTION**		
89	AMETHYST-THROATED HUMMINGBIRDS	14-DAY	37.50	37.50
89	ANDEAN EMERALD HUMMINGBIRDS	14-DAY	37.50	37.50
89	BLUE-HEADED SAPPHIRE HUMMINGBIRDS	14-DAY	37.50	37.50
89	GARNET-THROATED HUMMINGBIRDS	14-DAY	37.50	37.50
89	GREAT SAPPHIRE WING HUMMINGBIRDS	14-DAY	37.50	37.50
89	PEARL CORONET HUMMINGBIRDS	14-DAY	37.50	37.50
89	RUBY-THROATED HUMMINGBIRDS	14-DAY	37.50	37.50
89	RUBY-TOPAZ HUMMINGBIRDS	14-DAY	37.50	37.50
*		**THE LITTLE RASCALS**		
85	BUTCH'S CHALLENGE	10-DAY	24.50	30.00
85	DARLA'S DEBUT	10-DAY	24.50	30.00
85	MY GAL	10-DAY	24.50	30.00
85	PETE'S PAL	10-DAY	24.50	30.00
85	ROUGHIN' IT	10-DAY	24.50	30.00
85	SKELETON CREW	10-DAY	24.50	30.00
85	SPANKY'S PRANKS	10-DAY	24.50	30.00
85	THREE FOR THE SHOW	10-DAY	24.50	30.00
S. FISHER		**THE NUTCRACKER BALLET**		
78	CLARA	28-DAY	19.50	125.00
79	GODFATHER	28-DAY	19.50	65.00
79	SNOW QUEEN AND KING	28-DAY	19.50	47.00
79	SUGAR PLUM FAIRY	28-DAY	19.50	55.00
80	CLARA AND THE PRINCE	28-DAY	19.50	47.00
80	WALTZ OF THE FLOWERS	28-DAY	19.50	47.00
D. KILMER		**THE OFFICIAL HONEYMOONERS PLATE COLLECTION**		
87	BABY, YOU'RE THE GREATEST	14-DAY	24.50	75.00
87	THE HONEYMOONERS	14-DAY	24.50	60.00
87	THE HUCKLEBUCK	14-DAY	24.50	67.50
88	BANG! ZOOM!	14-DAY	24.50	75.00
88	THE GOLFER	14-DAY	24.50	90.00
88	THE HONEYMOON EXPRESS	14-DAY	24.50	150.00
88	THE ONLY WAY TO TRAVEL	14-DAY	24.50	90.00
88	THE TV CHEFS	14-DAY	24.50	90.00
R. SWANSON		**THE PROUD NATION**		
89	AUTUMN TREAT	14-DAY	24.50	45.00
89	DRESSED UP FOR THE POW WOW	14-DAY	24.50	35.00
89	IN A BIG LAND	14-DAY	24.50	31.00
89	JUST A FEW DAYS OLD	14-DAY	24.50	30.00-49.00
89	NAVAJO LITTLE ONE	14-DAY	24.50	35.00-45.00
89	NEWEST LITTLE SHEEPHERDER	14-DAY	24.50	35.00
89	OUT WITH MAMA'S FLOCK	14-DAY	24.50	33.00
89	UP THE RED ROCKS	14-DAY	24.50	30.00
M. STEELE		**THE QUILTED COUNTRYSIDE**		
91	SPRING CLEANING	14-DAY	29.50	29.50
91	SUMMER HARVEST	14-DAY	29.50	29.50
91	THE COUNTRY MERCHANT	14-DAY	29.50	29.50
91	THE OLD COUNTRY STORE	14-DAY	29.50	29.50
91	THE QUILTER'S CABIN	14-DAY	29.50	29.50
91	WINTER'S END	14-DAY	29.50	29.50
92	THE ANTIQUES STORE	14-DAY	29.50	29.50
92	WASH DAY	14-DAY	29.50	29.50
N. ROCKWELL		**THE SATURDAY EVENING POST PLATE COLLECTION**		
89	EASTER MORNING	14-DAY	35.00	50.00
89	THE FACTS OF LIFE	14-DAY	35.00	54.00
89	THE WONDERS OF RADIO	14-DAY	35.00	39.00

YR	NAME	LIMIT	ISSUE	QUOTE
90	FIRST FLIGHT	14-DAY	35.00	50.00
90	FURLOUGH	14-DAY	35.00	53.00
90	JURY ROOM	14-DAY	35.00	53.00
90	THE WINDOW WASHER	14-DAY	35.00	38.00
90	TRAVELING COMPANION	14-DAY	35.00	53.00

T. BLACKSHEAR   THE STAR TREK 25TH ANNIVERSARY COMMEMORATIVE COLLECTION

YR	NAME	LIMIT	ISSUE	QUOTE
91	KIRK	14-DAY	35.00	35.00
91	SPOCK	14-DAY	35.00	35.00
91	STAR TREK 25TH ANNIVERSARY PLATE	14-DAY	37.50	37.50
92	MCCOY	14-DAY	35.00	35.00
92	SCOTTY	14-DAY	35.00	35.00
92	UHURA	14-DAY	35.00	35.00

T. BLACKSHEAR   THE STAR WARS 10TH ANNIVERSARY COMMEMORATIVE PLATE

YR	NAME	LIMIT	ISSUE	QUOTE
90	STAR WARS 10TH ANNIVERSARY PLATE	14-DAY	39.50	60.00-90.00

T. BLACKSHEAR   THE STAR WARS PLATE COLLECTION

YR	NAME	LIMIT	ISSUE	QUOTE
87	HANS SOLO	14-DAY	29.50	36.00
87	LUKE AND YODA	14-DAY	29.50	54.00
87	LUKE SKYWALKER AND DARTH VADER	14-DAY	29.50	60.00
87	PRINCESS LEIA	14-DAY	29.50	60.00
87	R2-D2 AND WICKET	14-DAY	29.50	45.00
87	THE IMPERIAL WALKERS	14-DAY	29.50	45.00
88	CREW IN THE COCKPIT	14-DAY	29.50	75.00
88	SPACE BATTLE	14-DAY	29.50	35.00-170.00

F. MCCARTHY   THE WEST OF FRANK MCCARTHY

YR	NAME	LIMIT	ISSUE	QUOTE
91	ATTACKING THE IRON HORSE	14-DAY	37.50	37.50
91	ATTEMPT ON THE STAGE	14-DAY	37.50	37.50
91	BRINGING OUT THE FURS	14-DAY	37.50	37.50
91	HEADED NORTH	14-DAY	37.50	37.50
91	KIOWA RAIDER	14-DAY	37.50	37.50
91	ON THE OLD NORTH TRAIL	14-DAY	37.50	37.50
91	THE HOSTILE THREAT	14-DAY	37.50	37.50
91	THE PRAYER	14-DAY	37.50	37.50

T. UTZ   THORNTON UTZ 10TH ANNIVERSARY PLATE COLLECTION

YR	NAME	LIMIT	ISSUE	QUOTE
89	AMONG THE DAFFODILS	14-DAY	29.50	35.00
89	BEST FRIENDS	14-DAY	29.50	35.00
89	DAWN	14-DAY	29.50	35.00
89	FRIENDS IN THE SKY	14-DAY	29.50	35.00
89	JUST LIKE MOMMY	14-DAY	29.50	29.50
89	LITTLE EMILY	14-DAY	29.50	29.50
89	MY KITTY	14-DAY	29.50	29.50
89	PLAYING DOCTOR	14-DAY	29.50	29.50
89	TEDDY'S BATHTIME	14-DAY	29.50	29.50
89	TURTLE TALK	14-DAY	29.50	29.50

M. TSANG   TIMELESS EXPRESSIONS OF THE ORIENT

YR	NAME	LIMIT	ISSUE	QUOTE
90	FIDELITY	15,000	75.00	75.00
91	BEAUTY	15,000	55.00	55.00
91	FEMININITY	15,000	75.00	75.00
91	LONGEVITY	15,000	75.00	75.00
92	COURAGE	15,000	55.00	55.00

H. BOND   TREASURED DAYS

YR	NAME	LIMIT	ISSUE	QUOTE
87	AMANDA	14-DAY	24.50	45.00
87	ASHLEY	14-DAY	29.50	50.00-60.00
87	CHRISTOPHER	14-DAY	24.50	45.00
87	JEREMY	14-DAY	24.50	45.00
87	SARA	14-DAY	24.50	30.00
88	JUSTIN	14-DAY	24.50	45.00
88	LINDSAY	14-DAY	24.50	45.00
88	NICHOLAS	14-DAY	24.50	45.00

T. UTZ   UTZ MOTHER'S DAY

YR	NAME	LIMIT	ISSUE	QUOTE
83	A GIFT OF LOVE	TL	27.50	45.00
83	MOTHER'S ANGEL	TL	27.50	32.00
83	MOTHER'S HELPING HAND	TL	27.50	32.00

J. HARRISON   VANISHING RURAL AMERICA

YR	NAME	LIMIT	ISSUE	QUOTE
91	AMERICA'S HEARTLAND	14-DAY	29.50	29.50
91	AUTUMN'S PASSAGE	14-DAY	29.50	29.50
91	COUNTRY PATH	14-DAY	29.50	29.50
91	COVERED IN FALL	14DAY	29.50	29.50
91	QUIET REFLECTIONS	14-DAY	29.50	29.50
91	RURAL DELIVERY	14-DAY	29.50	29.50
91	STOREFRONT MEMORIES	14-DAY	29.50	29.50
91	WHEN THE CIRCUS CAME TO TOWN	14DAY	29.50	29.50

R. PARKER   WINGED REFLECTIONS

YR	NAME	LIMIT	ISSUE	QUOTE
89	ABOVE THE BREAKERS	14-DAY	37.50	37.50
89	AMONG THE REEDS	14-DAY	37.50	37.50
89	FOLLOWING MAMA	14-DAY	37.50	37.50
89	FREEZE UP	14-DAY	37.50	37.50

1991 Marry Me, Scarlett *is the first issue in the "Critic's Choice: Gone With the Wind" series produced by W.S. George.*

This playful pair is twice as nice. Produced as both a plate and an ornament, Irene Spencer's Happy Holidaze *captures the capriciousness of kittens celebrating Christmas in their own special way. Produced by Roman Inc.*

This little lass looks high above her head in search of the treetops in Trees So Tall. *The legendary children's artist, Francis Hook, best known for the children on the Charmin tissue illustrations, is the artist. Roman is the producer.*

Thy Kingdom Come *by Abbie Williams is the second issue in "The Lord's Prayer" series produced by Roman. The piece was limited to just a 10-day firing period.*

YR	NAME	LIMIT	ISSUE	QUOTE
89	WINGS ABOVE THE WATER	14-DAY	37.50	37.50
90	AT THE WATER'S EDGE	14-DAY	29.50	29.50
90	EARLY SPRING	14-DAY	29.50	29.50
90	SUMMER LOON	14-DAY	29.50	29.50

J. SEEREY-LESTER WINTER WILDLIFE

YR	NAME	LIMIT	ISSUE	QUOTE
89	AMONG THE CATTAILS	15,000	55.00	60.00
89	CLOSE ENCOUNTERS	15,000	55.00	60.00
89	EARLY SNOW	15,000	55.00	60.00
89	FIRST SNOW	15,000	55.00	60.00
89	LYING IN WAIT	15,000	55.00	60.00
89	OUT OF THE BLIZZARD	15,000	55.00	60.00
89	THE REFUGE	15,000	55.00	55.00
89	WINTER HIDING	15,000	55.00	55.00

T. BLACKSHEAR WIZARD OF OZ COMMEMORATIVE

YR	NAME	LIMIT	ISSUE	QUOTE
88	DOROTHY MEETS THE SCARECROW	14-DAY	24.50	30.00
88	WE'RE OFF TO SEE THE WIZARD	14-DAY	24.50	125.00
89	A GLIMPSE OF THE MUNCHKINS	14-DAY	24.50	30.00
89	IF I WERE KING OF THE FOREST	14-DAY	24.50	30.00
89	THE GREAT AND POWERFUL OZ	14-DAY	24.50	30.00
89	THE TIN MAN SPEAKS	14-DAY	24.50	45.00
89	THE WITCH CASTS A SPELL	14-DAY	24.50	45.00
89	THERE'S NO PLACE LIKE HOME	14-DAY	24.50	120.00

G. GIORDANO WOODLAND ENCOUNTERS

YR	NAME	LIMIT	ISSUE	QUOTE
91	ANYONE FOR A SWIM?	14-DAY	29.50	29.50
91	HI NEIGHBOR	14-DAY	29.50	29.50
91	LUNCHTIME VISITOR	14-DAY	29.50	29.50
91	MEADOW MEETING	14-DAY	29.50	29.50
91	NATURE SCOUTS	14-DAY	29.50	29.50
91	PEEK-A-BOO!	14-DAY	29.50	29.50
91	WANT TO PLAY?	14-DAY	29.50	29.50
92	FIELD DAY	14-DAY	29.50	29.50

HAMILTON/BOEHM

*

AWARD WINNING ROSES

YR	NAME	LIMIT	ISSUE	QUOTE
79	ANGEL FACE ROSE	15,000	45.00	55.00
79	ELEGANCE ROSE	15,000	45.00	55.00
79	MR. LINCOLN ROSE	15,000	45.00	55.00
79	PEACE ROSE	15,000	45.00	100.00
79	QUEEN ELIZABETH ROSE	15,000	45.00	55.00
79	ROYAL HIGHNESS ROSE	15,000	45.00	55.00
79	TROPICANA ROSE	15,000	45.00	65.00
79	WHITE MASTERPIECE ROSE	15,000	45.00	75.00

*

GAMEBIRDS OF NORTH AMERICA

YR	NAME	LIMIT	ISSUE	QUOTE
84	AMERICAN WOODCOCK	15,000	62.50	62.50
84	BOB WHITE QUAIL	15,000	62.50	62.50
84	CALIFORNIA QUAIL	15,000	62.50	62.50
84	PRAIRIE GROUSE	15,000	62.50	62.50
84	RING-NECKED PHEASANT	15,000	62.50	62.50
84	RUFFED GROUSE	15,000	62.50	62.50
84	WILD TURKEY	15,000	62.50	62.50
84	WILLOW PARTRIDGE	15,000	62.50	62.50

*

HUMMINGBIRD COLLECTION

YR	NAME	LIMIT	ISSUE	QUOTE
80	BLUE THROATED	15,000	62.50	80.00
80	BRAZILIAN RUBY	15,000	62.50	80.00
80	BROADBILLED	15,000	62.50	62.50
80	BROADTAIL	15,000	62.50	62.50
80	CALLIOPE	15,000	62.50	80.00
80	CRIMSON TOPAZ	15,000	62.50	62.50
80	RUFOUS FLAME BEARER	15,000	62.50	80.00
80	STREAMERTAIL	15,000	62.50	80.00

*

OWL COLLECTION

YR	NAME	LIMIT	ISSUE	QUOTE
80	BARN OWL	15,000	45.00	62.50
80	BARRED OWL	15,000	45.00	62.50
80	BOREAL OWL	15,000	45.00	75.00
80	GREAT HORNED OWL	15,000	45.00	62.50
80	SAW WHET OWL	15,000	45.00	62.50
80	SCREECH OWL	15,000	45.00	62.50
80	SHORT EARED OWL	15,000	45.00	62.50
80	SNOWY OWL	15,000	45.00	62.50

*

WATER BIRDS

YR	NAME	LIMIT	ISSUE	QUOTE
81	AMERICAN PINTAIL	15,000	62.50	62.50
81	CANADA GEESE	15,000	62.50	75.00
81	CANVAS BACK	15,000	62.50	62.50
81	COMMON MALLARD	15,000	62.50	62.50
81	GREEN WINGED TEAL	15,000	62.50	62.50
81	HOODED MERGANSER	15,000	62.50	62.50
81	ROSS'S GEESE	15,000	62.50	62.50
81	WOOD DUCKS	15,000	62.50	62.50

YR NAME	LIMIT	ISSUE	QUOTE

HAVILAND
R. HETREAU — **TWELVE DAYS OF CHRISTMAS**

YR NAME	LIMIT	ISSUE	QUOTE
70 PARTRIDGE	30,000	25.00	54.00
71 TWO TURTLE DOVES	30,000	25.00	25.00
72 THREE FRENCH HENS	30,000	27.50	27.50
73 FOUR CALLING BIRDS	30,000	28.50	30.00
74 FIVE GOLDEN RINGS	30,000	30.00	30.00
75 SIX GEESE A'LAYING	30,000	32.50	32.50
76 SEVEN SWANS	30,000	38.00	38.00
77 EIGHT MAIDS	30,000	40.00	40.00
78 NINE LADIES DANCING	30,000	45.00	67.00
79 TEN LORDS A'LEAPING	30,000	50.00	50.00
80 ELEVEN PIPERS PIPING	30,000	55.00	65.00
81 TWELVE DRUMMERS	30,000	60.00	60.00

HAVILAND & PARLON
RAPHAEL — **CHRISTMAS MADONNAS**

YR NAME	LIMIT	ISSUE	QUOTE
72 BY RAPHAEL	5000	35.00	55.00
73 BY FERUZZI	5000	40.00	78.00-86.00
74 BY RAPHAEL	5000	42.50	40.00
75 BY MURILLO	7500	42.50	42.50
76 BY BOTTICELLI	7500	45.00	53.00
77 BY BELLINI	7500	48.00	48.00
78 BY LIPPI	7500	48.00	53.00
79 BY BOTTICELLI	7500	49.50	110.00
79 MADONNA OF THE EUCHARIST	7500	49.50	110.00
*			**TAPESTRY I**
71 UNICORN IN CAPTIVITY	10,000	35.00	70.00
72 START OF THE HUNT	10,000	35.00	35.00
73 CHASE OF THE UNICORN	10,000	35.00	76.00
74 END OF THE HUNT	10,000	37.50	74.00
75 UNICORN SURROUNDED	10,000	40.00	40.00
76 BROUGHT TO THE CASTLE	10,000	42.50	42.50
*		**THE LADY AND THE UNICORN**	
77 TO MY ONLY DESIRE	20,000	45.00	45.00
78 SIGHT	20,000	45.00	45.00
79 SOUND	20,000	47.50	48.00
80 TOUCH	15,000	52.50	110.00
81 SCENT	10,000	59.00	59.00
82 TASTE	10,000	59.00	65.00

HUTSCHENREUTHER
G. GRANGET — **GUNTHER GRANGET**

YR NAME	LIMIT	ISSUE	QUOTE
72 AMERICAN SPARROWS	5000	50.00	150.00
72 EUROPEAN SPARROWS	5000	30.00	65.00
73 AMERICAN KILDEER	2250	75.00	90.00
73 AMERICAN SQUIRREL	2500	75.00	75.00
73 EUROPEAN SQUIRREL	2500	35.00	50.00
74 AMERICAN PARTRIDGE	2500	75.00	90.00
75 AMERICAN RABBITS	2500	90.00	90.00
76 FREEDOM IN FLIGHT	5000	100.00	100.00
76 FREEDOM IN FLIGHT, GOLD	200	200.00	200.00
76 WRENS	2500	100.00	110.00
77 BEARS	2500	100.00	100.00
78 FOXES' SPRING JOURNEY	1000	125.00	200.00

W.C. HALLETT — **THE GLORY OF CHRISTMAS**

YR NAME	LIMIT	ISSUE	QUOTE
82 THE NATIVITY	25,000	80.00	125.00
83 THE ANNUNCIATION	25,000	80.00	115.00
84 THE SHEPHERDS	25,000	80.00	100.00
85 THE WISEMAN	25,000	80.00	100.00

IMPERIAL CHING-TE CHEN
Z. HUIMIN — **BEAUTIES OF THE RED MANSION**

YR NAME	LIMIT	ISSUE	QUOTE
86 PAO-CHAI	115-DAY	27.92	39.00
86 YUAN-CHUN	115-DAY	27.92	41.00
87 HSI-CHUN	115-DAY	30.92	45.00
87 HSI-FENG	115-DAY	30.92	44.00
88 HSIANG-YUN	115-DAY	34.92	38.00
88 KO-CHING	115-DAY	32.92	35.00
88 LI-WAN	115-DAY	32.92	44.00
88 MIAO-YU	115-DAY	30.92	51.00
88 TAI-YU	115-DAY	32.92	40.00
88 YING-CHUN	115-DAY	30.92	50.00
89 CHIAO-CHIEH	115-DAY	34.92	38.00
89 TAN-CHUN	115-DAY	34.92	38.00

Z. SONG MAO — **BLESSINGS FROM A CHINESE GARDEN**

YR NAME	LIMIT	ISSUE	QUOTE
88 THE GIFT OF PURITY	175-DAY	39.92	44.00

YR	NAME	LIMIT	ISSUE	QUOTE
89	THE GIFT OF BEAUTY	175-DAY	42.92	49.00
89	THE GIFT OF GRACE	175-DAY	39.92	43.00
89	THE GIFT OF HAPPINESS	175-DAY	42.92	45.00
90	THE GIFT OF JOY	175-DAY	42.92	42.92
90	THE GIFT OF TRUTH	175-DAY	42.92	42.92
Z. HUIMIN		**FLOWER GODDESSES OF CHINA**		
91	THE CAMELLIA GODDESS	175-DAY	37.92	42.00
91	THE CHRYSANTHEMUM GODDESS	175-DAY	34.92	39.00
91	THE LOTUS GODDESS	175-DAY	34.92	39.00
91	THE NARCISSUS GODDESS	175-DAY	37.92	42.00
91	THE PEONY GODDESS	175-DAY	37.92	42.00
91	THE PLUM BLOSSOM GODDESS	175-DAY	34.92	38.00
91	THE PLUM BLOSSOM GODDESS	175-DAY	37.92	41.00
J. XUE-BING		**LEGENDS OF WEST LAKE**		
89	LADY WHITE	175-DAY	32.00	32.00
90	BRIGHT PEARL	175-DAY	32.92	35.00
90	LADY SILKWORM	175-DAY	29.92	33.00
90	LAUREL PEAK	175-DAY	29.92	33.00
90	RISING SUN TERRACE	175-DAY	32.92	35.00
90	THE APRICOT FAIRY	175-DAY	32.92	35.00
90	THREAD OF SKY	175-DAY	34.92	38.00
91	ANCESTORS OF TEA	175-DAY	34.92	38.00
91	FLY-IN PEAK	175-DAY	36.92	36.92
91	PHOENIX MOUNTAIN	175-DAY	34.92	38.00
91	THE CASE OF THE FOLDING FANS	175-DAY	36.92	41.00
91	THREE POOLS MIRRORING/MOON	175-DAY	36.92	40.00
Z. SONG MAO		**SCENES FROM THE SUMMER PALACE**		
88	JADE BELT BRIDGE	175-DAY	29.92	38.00
88	THE MARBLE BOAT	175-DAY	29.92	45.00
89	BOATERS ON KUMMING LAKE	175-DAY	34.92	38.00
89	GARDEN/HARMONIOUS PLEASURE	175-DAY	32.92	35.00
89	HALL THAT DISPELS THE CLOUDS	175-DAY	32.92	35.00
89	SEVENTEEN ARCH BRIDGE	175-DAY	34.92	38.00
89	THE GREAT STAGE	175-DAY	32.92	35.00
89	THE LONG PROMENADE	175-DAY	32.92	35.00
Z. HUIMIN		**THE FLOWER GODDESSES OF CHINA**		
91	THE LOTUS GODDESS	175-DAY	34.92	45.00
S. FU		**THE FORBIDDEN CITY**		
90	FLYING KITES/SPRING DAY	150-DAY	39.92	44.00
90	PAVILION OF 10,000 SPRINGS	150-DAY	39.92	44.00
90	PAVILION/FLOATING JADE GREEN	150-DAY	42.92	42.92
91	DRESSING THE EMPRESS	150-DAY	45.92	48.00
91	NINE DRAGON SCREEN	150-DAY	42.92	42.92
91	PAVILION OF FLOATING CUPS	150-DAY	45.92	48.00
91	THE HALL OF THE CULTIVATING MIND	150-DAY	42.92	42.92
91	THE LATERN FESTIVAL	150-DAY	42.92	42.92

INCOLAY

**		**'TWAS THE NIGHT BEFORE CHRISTMAS**		
92	HAPPY CHRISTMAS TO ALL	OP	69.00	90.00
92	IT MUST BE ST. NICK	OP	74.00	150.00
92	UP ON THE ROOFTOP	OP	69.00	130.00
92	WITH VISIONS OF SUGAR PLUMS	OP	74.00	125.00
93	I SPRANG FROM MY BED	OP	74.00	148.00
93	UP THE CHIMNEY HE ROSE	OP	74.00	145.00
**		**CHRISTMAS CAMEO COLLECTION**		
92	EVENING CAROLERS	OP	65.00	84.00
90	HOME WITH THE TREE	*	60.00	73.00
91	SKATERS AT TWILIGHT	YR	60.00	76.00
93	SLEDING BY STARLIGHT	YR	65.00	99.00
94	PROPOSAL UNDER THE STARS	YR	65.00	65.00
**		**LOVE SONNETS OF SHAKESPEARE**		
87	LOVE ALTERS NOT	OP	60.00	65.00
87	SHALL I COMPARE THEE	OP	55.00	55.00
87	SINCE I FIRST SAW YOU	OP	60.00	65.00
87	THOU ART TOO DEAR	OP	55.00	55.00
88	YOU SHALL SHINE MORE BRIGHT	OP	60.00	65.00
88	YOUR FAIR EYES	OP	60.00	65.00
**		**LOVE THEMES FROM GRAND OPERA**		
90	MADAME BUTTERFLY	OP	65.00	65.00
90	THE MARRIAGE OF FIGARO	OP	70.00	89.00
91	AIDA	OP	70.00	100.00
91	LA TRAVIATA	OP	70.00	80.00
91	TRISTAN AND ISOIDE	OP	70.00	77.00
90	CARMEN	*	65.00	65.00
**		**MAJESTIC SAILING SHIPS**		
92	FLYING CLOUD	OP	65.00	80.00

YR	NAME	LIMIT	ISSUE	QUOTE
92	THE BREDNOUGHT	OP	65.00	80.00
92	THE CHARLES W. MORGAN	OP	65.00	75.00
92	THE SEA WITCH	OP	65.00	70.00
93	CHARLES W. MORGAN	YR	65.00	65.00
93	FLYING CLOUD, THE	YR	65.00	65.00
94	DREADNOUGHT, THE	YR	65.00	65.00
94	SEA WITCH, THE	YR	65.00	65.00
R. AKERS		**NIGHT BEFORE CHRISTMAS**		
93	HAPPY CHRISTMAS	YR	69.00	69.00
94	I SPRANG FROM MY BED	YR	74.00	74.00
94	IT MUST BE ST. NICK	YR	74.00	74.00
94	UP ON THE ROOFTOP	YR	69.00	69.00
94	UP THE CHIMNEY	YR	74.00	74.00
94	VISIONS OF SUGAR PLUMS	YR	74.00	74.00
* *		**NORTH AMERICA'S WILDLIFE HERITAGE**		
91	AT STREAM'S EDGE	OP	65.00	68.00
91	IN THE POND'S SHALLOWS	OP	65.00	65.00
92	BENEATH THE OPEN SKY	OP	70.00	70.00
92	BESIDE THE SHELTERING KNOLL	OP	75.00	75.00
92	ON THE RIVERBANK	OP	70.00	100.00
92	THROUGH THE GRASSY CLEARING	OP	75.00	75.00
92	UPON THE ROCKY LEDGE	OP	70.00	100.00
93	NEAR THE RUNNING BROOK	OP	75.00	75.00
D. CLIFF		**NORTH AMERICAN WILDLIFE HERITAGE**		
93	AT STREAMS EDGE (DEER)	YR	65.00	65.00
93	IN PONDS SHALLOW (MOOSE)	YR	65.00	65.00
94	BENEATH THE OPEN SKY (RAM)	YR	70.00	70.00
94	BESIDE THE SHELTERING KNOLL (WOLF)	YR	70.00	70.00
94	GRASSY CLEARING, THE (ELK)	YR	75.00	75.00
94	NEAR THE RUNNIN BROOK (BISON)	YR	75.00	75.00
94	ON THE RIVERBANK	YR	70.00	70.00
94	UPON THE ROCKY LEDGE (MTN. LION)	YR	70.00	70.00
R. AKERS		**ROMANTIC POET SERIES**		
81	THE KISS	YR	65.00	70.00
82	MY HEART LEAPS UP	YR	70.00	75.00
83	I STOOD TIPTOE	YR	70.00	75.00
84	THE DREAM	YR	70.00	75.00
85	THE RECOLLECTION	YR	70.00	75.00
77	SHE WALKS IN BEAUTY	YR	60.00	60.00
78	A THING OF BEAUTY	YR	60.00	65.00
79	ODE TO A SKYLARK	YR	65.00	70.00
80	PHANTOM OF DELIGHT	YR	65.00	70.00
* *		**SHAKESPEARE LOVERS**		
88	ROMEO AND JULIET	OP	65.00	65.00-81.00
89	HAMLET AND OPHELIA	OP	65.00	65.00-110.00
89	MACBETH AND LADY MACBETH	OP	70.00	70.00-109.00
89	PETRUCHIO AND KATHARINA	OP	70.00	70.00-81.00
90	BENEDICK AND BEATRICE	OP	70.00	70.00-114.00
90	FERDINAND AND MIRANDA	OP	75.00	75.00-106.00
90	LYSANDER AND HERMIA	OP	70.00	70.00-109.00
90	OTHELLO AND DESDEMONA	OP	75.00	75.00-115.00
90	ROMEO & JULIET	*	65.00	105.00
* *		**THE FALL OF TROY**		
87	THE JUDGMENT OF PARIS	OP	55.00	55.00
88	HECTOR AND ANDROMACHE	OP	55.00	55.00
88	HELEN AND PARIS	OP	55.00	55.00
88	THE TROJAN HORSE	OP	55.00	55.00
* *		**VICTORIAN DREAM HOMES**		
92	125 MAIN STREET	OP	55.00	90.00
92	212 THIRD AVENUE	OP	55.00	79.00
92	367 RIVERSIDE DRIVE	OP	60.00	85.00
92	432 FAIRVIEW LANE	OP	60.00	78.00
93	125 MAIN STREET	YR	55.00	55.00
94	212 THIRD AVENUE	YR	55.00	55.00
94	367 RIVERSIDE DRIVE	YR	60.00	60.00
94	432 FAIRVIEW LANE	YR	60.00	60.00

INTERNATIONAL SILVER

M. DEOLIVEIRA				**BICENTENNIAL**
72	SIGNING DECLARATION	7500	40.00	310.00
73	PAUL REVERE	7500	40.00	160.00
74	CONCORD BRIDGE	7500	40.00	115.00
75	CROSSING DELAWARE	7500	50.00	80.00
76	VALLEY FORGE	7500	50.00	65.00
77	SURRENDER AT YORKTOWN	7500	50.00	60.00

YR	NAME	LIMIT	ISSUE	QUOTE

JAN HAGARA COLLECTABLES
J. HAGARA
VICTORIAN CHILDREN

YR	NAME	LIMIT	ISSUE	QUOTE
79	DAISIES FROM MARYBETH	*	37.50	150.00
79	LISA	5000	60.00	90.00
80	ADRIANNE	5000	60.00	250.00
80	CARA	*	24.50	250.00
80	DAISIES FROM JIMMY	*	37.50	300.00
81	HEARTS & FLOWERS	*	24.50	250.00
81	LYDIA	5000	60.00	175.00
82	DAISIES FOR MOMMY	*	37.50	120.00
82	MELANEE	5000	60.00	125.00
83	CAROL	15,000	45.00	210.00
84	CHRIS	15,000	45.00	150.00
85	NOEL	15,000	45.00	100.00
86	LESLEY	RT	42.50	120.00
86	NIKKI	15,000	45.00	100.00
88	HANNAH	15,000	50.00	125.00

JOHN HINE STUDIOS LTD.
D. WINTER
DAVID WINTER CAMEOS

YR	NAME	LIMIT	ISSUE	QUOTE
92	OXFORDSHIRE GOAT YARD	RT	*	

*
DAVID WINTER PLATE COLLECTION

YR	NAME	LIMIT	ISSUE	QUOTE
92	OLD CURIOSTY SHOP	10,000	30.00	30.00
92	CHINCHESTER CROSS PLATE	10,000	30.00	30.00
92	LITTLE MILL PLATE	10,000	30.00	55.00
91	A CHRISTMAS CAROL	10,000	30.00	105.00-110.00
91	COTSWOLD VILLAGE PLATE	10,000	30.00	30.00
92	EBENEZER SCROOGE'S COUNTING HOUSE	10,000	30.00	30.00
92	SCROOGE'S COUNTING HOUSE	10,000	30.00	55.00
92	THE OLD CURIOSITY SHOP	10,000	30.00	55.00

KAISER
G. NEUBACHER
AMERICA, THE BEAUTIFUL

YR	NAME	LIMIT	ISSUE	QUOTE
88	CALIFORNIA QUAIL	9500	49.50	59.00
88	SNOWY EGRET	9500	49.50	49.50
90	BROWSING FOR DELICACIES	9500	49.50	59.00
90	SCANNING THE TERRITORY	9500	49.50	59.00

G. WILLIAMS
AMERICAN CATS

YR	NAME	LIMIT	ISSUE	QUOTE
91	KITS IN A CRADLE, SIAMESE	7500	49.50	49.50
91	LAZY RIVER DAYS, SHORTHAIRS	7500	49.50	49.50
91	TAKING IT EASY, PERSIANS	7500	49.50	49.50
91	TREE VIEW, SHORTHAIRS	7500	49.50	49.50

K. BAUER
ANNIVERSARY

YR	NAME	LIMIT	ISSUE	QUOTE
75	TENDER MOMENT	CL	25.00	27.50
82	BETROTHAL	CL	40.00	40.00
79	ROMANTIC INTERLUDE	CL	32.00	32.00
80	LOVE AT PLAY	CL	40.00	40.00
81	RENDEZVOUS	CL	40.00	40.00
72	LOVE BIRDS	CL	16.50	30.00
73	IN THE PARK	CL	16.50	24.50
74	CANOEING	CL	20.00	30.00
76	SERENADE	CL	25.00	25.00
77	SIMPLE GIFT	CL	25.00	25.00
78	VIKING TOAST	CL	30.00	30.00
83	SUNDAY AFTERNOON	CL	40.00	40.00

R. HERSEY
ARABIAN NIGHTS

YR	NAME	LIMIT	ISSUE	QUOTE
89	SCHEHERAZADE	9500	75.00	75.00

J. TRUMBALL
BICENTENNIAL PLATE

YR	NAME	LIMIT	ISSUE	QUOTE
76	SIGNING DECLARATION	CL	75.00	150.00

J. FRANCIS
BIRD DOG SERIES

YR	NAME	LIMIT	ISSUE	QUOTE
*	BEAGLE	19,500	39.50	49.50
*	BLACK LABRADOR	19,500	39.50	49.50
*	COCKER SPANIEL	19,500	39.50	49.50
*	ENGLISH POINTER	19,500	39.50	49.50
*	ENGLISH SETTER	19,500	39.50	49.50
*	GERMAN SHORT HAIR POINTER	19,500	39.50	49.50
*	GOLDEN LABRADOR	19,500	39.50	49.50
*	IRISH SETTER	19,500	39.50	49.50

A. SCHLESINGER
CHILDHOOD MEMORIES

YR	NAME	LIMIT	ISSUE	QUOTE
85	WAIT A LITTLE	CL	29.00	29.00

W. ZEUNER
CHILDREN'S PRAYER

YR	NAME	LIMIT	ISSUE	QUOTE
82	NOW I LAY ME DOWN TO SLEEP	CL	29.50	29.50
82	SAYING GRACE	CL	29.50	29.50

K. BAUER
CHRISTMAS PLATES

YR	NAME	LIMIT	ISSUE	QUOTE
71	SILENT NIGHT	CL	13.50	23.00
72	WELCOME HOME	CL	16.50	43.00
74	CHRISTMAS CAROLERS	CL	25.00	30.00

YR	NAME	LIMIT	ISSUE	QUOTE
81	ADORATION BY THREE KINGS	CL	40.00	41.00
82	BRINGING HOME THE TREE	CL	40.00	45.00
79	CHRISTMAS EVE	CL	32.00	45.00
80	JOYS OF WINTER	CL	40.00	43.00
76	CHRIST/SAVIOUR BORN	CL	25.00	35.00
75	BRINGING HOME THE TREE	CL	25.00	30.00
70	WAITING FOR SANTA CLAUS	CL	12.50	25.00
73	HOLY NIGHT	CL	18.00	44.00
77	THE THREE KINGS	CL	25.00	25.00
78	SHEPHERDS IN THE FIELD	CL	30.00	30.00
G. NEUBACHER		**CLASSIC FAIRY TALES COLLECTION**		
82	FROG KING	*	39.50	39.50
83	LITTLE RED RIDING HOOD	*	39.50	39.50
83	PUSS IN BOOTS	*	39.50	39.50
84	CINDERELLA	*	39.50	39.50
84	HANSEL AND GRETEL	*	39.50	39.50
84	SLEEPING BEAUTY	*	39.50	39.50
R. CLARKE		**DANCE, BALLERINA, DANCE**		
*	OPENING NIGHT	CL	47.50	47.50
*	PIROUETTE	CL	47.50	47.50
*	SWAN LAKE	CL	47.50	47.50
*	THE RECITAL	CL	47.50	47.50
82	FIRST SLIPPERS	CL	47.50	47.50
83	AT THE BARRE	CL	47.50	47.50
*				**EGYPTIAN**
80	NEFERTITI	10,000	275.00	458.00
80	TUTANKHAMEN	10,000	275.00	458.00
R.J. MAY		**FAITHFUL COMPANIONS**		
90	BEAGLE	9500	49.50	49.50
90	COCKER SPANIEL	9500	49.50	49.50
90	DASHCHUND	9500	49.50	49.50
90	DOBERMAN	9500	49.50	49.50
90	ENGLISH SPRINGER SPANIEL	9500	49.50	49.50
90	GERMAN SHEPHERD	9500	49.50	49.50
90	GOLDEN RETRIEVER	9500	49.50	49.50
90	ROTTWEILER	9500	49.50	49.50
A. LOHMANN		**FAMOUS HORSES**		
83	SNOW KNIGHT	CL	95.00	95.00
84	NORTHERN DANCER	CL	95.00	95.00
G. NEUBACHER		**FAMOUS LULLABIES**		
85	SLEEP BABY SLEEP	*	39.50	40.00
86	A MOCKINGBIRD	*	39.50	46.00
86	AU CLAIR DE LUNE	*	39.50	44.00
86	ROCKABYE BABY	*	39.50	41.00
87	WELSH LULLABYE	*	39.50	57.00
88	BRAHMS' LULLABYE	*	39.50	45.00
G. LOATES		**FEATHERED FRIENDS**		
78	BLUE JAYS	CL	70.00	100.00
79	CARDINALS	CL	80.00	90.00
80	WAXWINGS	CL	80.00	85.00
81	GOLDFINCH	CL	80.00	85.00
I. CENKOVCAN		**FOUR SEASONS**		
81	AUTUMN	*	50.00	64.00
81	SPRING	*	50.00	64.00
81	SUMMER	*	50.00	64.00
81	WINTER	*	50.00	64.00
W. GAWANTKA		**GARDEN AND SONG BIRDS**		
73	CARDINALS	CL	200.00	250.00
73	TITMOUSE	CL	200.00	250.00
K. BAUER		**GREAT YACHTS**		
72	CETONIA	CL	50.00	50.00
72	WESTWARD	CL	50.00	50.00
G. NEUBACHER		**HAPPY DAYS**		
79	THE AEROPLANE	CL	75.00	75.00
80	JULIE	CL	75.00	75.00
81	WINTER FUN	CL	75.00	75.00
82	THE LOOKOUT	CL	75.00	75.00
J. LITTLEJOHN		**HARMONY AND NATURE**		
85	SPRING ENCORE	CL	39.50	39.50
*				**KING TUT**
78	KING TUT	CL	65.00	100.00
G. NEUBACHER		**MEMORIES OF CHRISTMAS**		
83	THE WONDER OF CHRISTMAS	CL	42.50	42.50
84	A CHRISTMAS DREAM	CL	39.50	42.50
85	CHRISTMAS EVE	CL	39.50	39.50
86	A VISIT WITH SANTA	CL	39.50	39.50

YR NAME	LIMIT	ISSUE	QUOTE
K. BAUER			**MOTHER'S DAY**
82 PHEASANT FAMILY	CL	40.00	44.00
83 TENDER CARE	CL	40.00	65.00
81 SAFE NEAR MOTHER	CL	40.00	40.00
80 RACCOON FAMILY	CL	40.00	45.00
79 A MOTHER'S DEVOTION	CL	32.00	40.00
71 MARE AND FOAL	CL	13.00	25.00
72 FLOWERS FOR MOTHER	CL	16.50	20.00
73 CATS	CL	17.00	40.00
74 FOX	CL	20.00	40.00
75 GERMAN SHEPHERD	CL	25.00	100.00
76 SWAN AND CYGNETS	CL	25.00	27.50
77 MOTHER RABBIT AND YOUNG	CL	25.00	30.00
78 HEN AND CHICKS	CL	30.00	50.00
*			**OBERAMMERGAU PASSION PLAY**
91 OBERAMMERGAU, COBALT	400	64.00	64.00
91 OBERAMMERGAU, SEPIA	700	38.00	38.00
70 OBERAMMERGAU	CL	40.00	40.00
70 OBERAMMERGAU	CL	25.00	30.00
A. LOHMANN			**ON THE FARM**
* DUCKS ON THE POND	*	50.00	108.00
* GIRL FEEDING ANIMALS	*	50.00	108.00
* GIRL WITH GOATS	*	50.00	108.00
* WHITE HORSE	*	50.00	108.00
81 THE DUCK	*	50.00	108.00
82 THE ROOSTER	*	50.00	108.00
83 THE HORSES	*	50.00	108.00
83 THE POND	*	50.00	108.00
R. HORTON			**RACING FOR PRIDE AND PROFIT**
* PROFIT OR PRISON	9500	*	60.00
84 THE AGING VICTOR	9500	50.00	50.00
85 SECOND GOES HUNGRY	9500	50.00	50.00
86 NO TIME TO BOAST	9500	50.00	50.00
87 FIRST FISH TO MARKET	9500	50.00	60.00
88 GYPSY TRADERS	9500	60.00	60.00
G. NEUBACHER			**ROMANTIC PORTRAITS**
81 LILIE	CL	200.00	210.00
82 CAMELIA	CL	175.00	180.00
83 ROSE	CL	175.00	185.00
84 DAISY	CL	175.00	180.00
J. MCKERNAN			**THE GRADUATE**
86 BOY	7500	39.50	39.50
86 GIRL	7500	39.50	39.50
D. KING			**TRADITIONAL FAIRY TALES**
83 CINDERELLA	*	39.50	39.50
83 JACK AND THE BEANSTALK	*	39.50	39.50
84 THREE LITTLE PIGS	*	39.50	39.50
84 TOM THUMB	*	39.50	39.50
85 DICK WITTINGTON	*	39.50	39.50
85 GOLDILOCKS	*	39.50	39.50
T. BOYER		**WALLPLATES: #837 WATER FOWL COLLECTION**	
89 PAIR OF CANVASBACKS	15,000	49.50	49.50
89 PAIR OF CAROLINA WOOD DUCKS	15,000	49.50	49.50
89 PAIR OF GREENWINGED TEALS	15,000	49.50	49.50
89 PAIR OF MALLARD	15,000	49.50	49.50
89 PAIR OF PINTAILS	15,000	49.50	49.50
89 PAIR OF REDHEADS	15,000	49.50	49.50
G. NEUBACHER		**WALLPLATES: FOREST SURPRISES**	
89 DEERHEAD ORCHID	9500	49.50	59.00
89 MARSH MARIGOLD	9500	49.50	59.00
90 VIOLETS	9500	49.50	59.00
90 WILD IRIS	9500	49.50	59.00
L. TURNER		**WALLPLATES: NOBLE HORSE COLLECTION**	
88 ARABIAN	OP	49.50	49.50
88 GELDERLANDER	OP	49.50	49.50
88 HOLSTEIN	OP	49.50	49.50
88 QUARTER HORSE	OP	49.50	49.50
88 THOROUGHBRED	OP	49.50	49.50
88 TRAKEHNER	OP	49.50	49.50
D. TWINNEY		**WALLPLATES: STABLE DOOR COLLECTION**	
88 FIRST STEPS	OP	29.50	29.50
88 IMPUDENCE	OP	29.50	29.50
88 PRIDE	OP	29.50	29.50
88 THE VISITOR	OP	29.50	29.50
E. BIERLY			**WATER FOWL**
85 CANVASBACK DUCKS	19,500	55.00	89.00

YR	NAME	LIMIT	ISSUE	QUOTE
85	MALLARD DUCKS	19,500	55.00	89.00
85	PINTAIL DUCKS	19,500	55.00	89.00
85	WOOD DUCKS	19,500	55.00	89.00
G. NEUBACHER				**WILDFLOWERS**
86	TRILLIUM	9500	39.50	65.00
87	SPRING BEAUTY	9500	45.00	64.00
87	WILD ASTERS	9500	49.50	59.00
87	WILD ROSES	9500	49.50	59.00
R. ORR			**WOODLAND**	**CREATURES**
85	FIRST ADVENTURE	10-DAY	37.50	37.50
85	FISHING TRIP	10-DAY	37.50	37.50
85	MEADOWLAND VIGIL	10-DAY	37.50	37.50
85	MORNING LESSON	10-DAY	37.50	37.50
85	RESTING IN THE GLEN	10-DAY	37.50	37.50
85	SPRINGTIME FROLIC	10-DAY	37.50	37.50
85	STARTLED SENTRY	10-DAY	37.50	37.50
85	THE HIDING PLACE	10-DAY	37.50	37.50

KONIGSZELT BAYERN

H. KELLER			**HEDI KELLER**	**CHRISTMAS**
79	THE ADORATION	*	29.50	33.00
80	FLIGHT INTO EGYPT	*	29.50	33.00
81	RETURN INTO GALILEE	*	29.50	31.00
82	FOLLOWING THE STAR	*	29.50	32.00
83	REST ON THE FLIGHT	*	29.50	35.00
84	THE NATIVITY	*	29.50	35.00
85	GIFT OF THE MAGI	*	34.50	40.00
86	ANNUNCIATION	*	34.50	34.50-45.00

KPM-ROYAL CORPORATION

*				**CHRISTMAS**
69	CHRISTMAS STAR	5000	28.00	380.00
70	THREE KINGS	5000	28.00	300.00
71	CHRISTMAS TREE	5000	28.00	290.00
72	CHRISTMAS ANGEL	5000	31.00	300.00
73	CHRIST CHILD ON SLED	5000	33.00	280.00
74	ANGEL AND HORN	5000	35.00	180.00
75	SHEPHERDS	5000	40.00	165.00
76	STAR OF BETHLEHEM	5000	43.00	140.00
77	MARY AT CRIB	5000	46.00	100.00
78	THREE WISE MEN	5000	49.00	54.00
79	THE MANGER	5000	55.00	55.00
80	SHEPHERDS IN FIELDS	5000	55.00	55.00

L.L. KNICKERBOCKER CO. INC.

R.T. GORDON				
94	VARSITY BEAR PHOTO C15001	2500	31.25	31.25

LALIQUE

M. LALIQUE				**ANNUAL**
65	DEUX OISEAUX (TWO BIRDS)	2000	25.00	1200.00
66	ROSE DE SONGERIE (DREAM ROSE)	5000	25.00	185.00
67	BALLET DE POISSON (FISH BALLET)	5000	25.00	125.00
68	GAZELLE FANTAISIE (GAZELLE FANTASY)	5000	25.00	120.00
69	PAPILLON (BUTTERFLY)	5000	30.00	98.00
70	PAON (PEACOCK)	5000	30.00	80.00
71	HIBOU (OWL)	5000	35.00	75.00
72	COQUILLAGE (SHELL)	5000	40.00	70.00
73	PETIT GEAI (JAYLING)	5000	42.50	130.00
74	SOUS D'ARGENT (SILVER PENNIES)	5000	47.50	120.00
75	DUO DE POISSON (FISH DUET)	5000	50.00	140.00
76	AIGLE (EAGLE)	5000	60.00	100.00

LANCE CORP.

A. PETITTO		**A CHILD'S CHRISTMAS (HUDSON PEWTER)**		
78	BEDTIME STORY	10,000	35.00	60.00
79	LITTLEST ANGELS	10,000	35.00	60.00
80	HEAVEN'S CHRISTMAS TREE	10,000	42.50	60.00
81	FILLING THE SKY	10,000	47.50	60.00
P.W. BASTON			**SEBASTIAN**	**PLATES**
78	MOTIF NO. 1	4878	75.00	50.00-75.00
79	GRAND CANYON	2492	75.00	50.00-75.00
80	IN THE CANDY STORE	9098	39.50	39.50
80	LONE CYPRESS	718	75.00	150.00-175.00
81	THE DOCTOR	7547	39.50	39.50
83	LITTLE MOTHER	2710	39.50	39.50
84	SWITCHING THE FREIGHT	706	42.50	80.00-100.00

YR	NAME	LIMIT	ISSUE	QUOTE
P.W. BASTON		**THE AMERICAN EXPANSION (HUDSON PEWTER)**		
75	AMERICAN EXPANSION	2250	*	50.00-75.00
75	AMERICAN INDEPENDENCE	18,462	*	100.00-125.00
75	SPIRIT OF '76 (6 IN. PLATE)	4812	*	100.00-120.00
75	THE AMERICAN WAR BETWEEN THE STATES	825	*	150.00-200.00
A. MCGRORY		**THE SONGS OF CHRISTMAS (HUDSON PEWTER)**		
88	SILENT NIGHT	2500	55.00	60.00
89	HARK! THE HERALD ANGELS SING	2000	60.00	60.00
90	THE FIRST NOEL	2500	60.00	60.00
91	WE THREE KINGS	2500	60.00	60.00
A. HOLLIS		**TWAS THE NIGHT BEFORE CHRISTMAS (HUDSON PEWTER)**		
82	NOT A CREATURE WAS STIRRING	10,000	47.50	60.00
83	VISIONS OF SUGAR PLUMS	10,000	47.50	60.00
84	HIS EYES HOW THEY TWINKLED	10,000	47.50	60.00
85	HAPPY CHRISTMAS TO ALL	10,000	47.50	60.00
86	BRINGING HOME THE TREE	10,000	47.50	60.00
D. EVERHART		**WALT DISNEY (HUDSON PEWTER)**		
86	GOD BLESS US, EVERY ONE	10,000	47.50	60.00
87	JOLLY OLD SAINT NICK	10,000	55.00	60.00
88	HE'S CHECKING IT TWICE	10,000	50.00	60.00
87	THE CAROLING ANGELS	10,000	47.50	60.00

LENOX CHINA/CRYSTAL COLLECTION

YR	NAME	LIMIT	ISSUE	QUOTE
N. ADAMS			**AMERICAN WILDLIFE**	
82	BLACK BEARS	9500	65.00	70.00
82	BUFFALO	9500	65.00	70.00
82	DALL SHEEP	9500	65.00	70.00
82	JACK RABBITS	9500	65.00	70.00
82	MOUNTAIN LIONS	9500	65.00	70.00
82	OCELOTS	9500	65.00	70.00
82	OTTERS	9500	65.00	70.00
82	POLAR BEARS	9500	65.00	70.00
82	RACCOONS	9500	65.00	70.00
82	RED FOXES	9500	65.00	70.00
82	SEA LIONS	9500	65.00	70.00
82	WHITE TAILED DEER	9500	65.00	70.00
*			**ANNUAL HOLIDAY**	
91	SLEIGH	YR	75.00	78.00
E. BOEHM			**BOEHM BIRDS**	
70	WOOD THRUSH	YR	35.00	98.00
71	GOLDFINCH	YR	35.00	49.00
72	MOUNTAIN BLUEBIRD	YR	37.50	48.00
73	MEADOWLARK	YR	41.00	30.00
74	RUFOUS HUMMINGBIRD	YR	45.00	50.00
75	AMERICAN REDSTART	YR	50.00	60.00
76	CARDINALS	YR	53.00	80.00
77	ROBINS	YR	55.00	44.00
78	MOCKINGBIRDS	YR	58.00	60.00
79	GOLDEN-CROWNED KINGLETS	YR	65.00	94.00
80	BLACK-THROATED BLUE WARBLERS	YR	80.00	112.00
81	EASTERN PHOEBES	YR	90.00	100.00
E. BOEHM			**BOEHM WOODLAND WILDLIFE**	
73	RACCOONS	YR	50.00	55.00
74	RED FOXES	YR	52.50	57.00
75	COTTONTAIL RABBITS	YR	58.50	63.00
76	EASTERN CHIPMUNKS	YR	62.50	65.00
77	BEAVER	YR	67.50	72.00
78	WHITETAIL DEER	YR	70.00	75.00
79	SQUIRRELS	YR	76.00	76.00
80	BOBCATS	YR	82.50	87.00
81	MARTENS	YR	100.00	150.00
82	RIVER OTTERS	YR	100.00	180.00
*			**CHRISTMAS TREES AROUND THE WORLD**	
91	GERMANY	YR	75.00	78.00
92	FRANCE	YR	75.00	80.00
*			**COLONIAL CHRISTMAS WREATH**	
81	COLONIAL VIRGINIA	YR	65.00	76.00
82	MASSACHUSETTS	YR	70.00	93.00
83	MARYLAND	YR	70.00	79.00
84	RHODE ISLAND	YR	70.00	82.00
85	CONNECTICUT	YR	70.00	79.00
86	NEW HAMPSHIRE	YR	70.00	70.00
87	PENNSYLVANIA	YR	70.00	78.00
88	DELAWARE	YR	70.00	70.00
89	NEW YORK	YR	75.00	82.00
90	NEW JERSEY	YR	75.00	78.00
91	SOUTH CAROLINA	YR	75.00	78.00
92	NORTH CAROLINA	YR	75.00	80.00

YR	NAME	LIMIT	ISSUE	QUOTE
*		GARDEN BIRD PLATE COLLECTION		
88	BLUEJAY	OP	48.00	53.00
88	CHICKADEE	OP	48.00	53.00
89	HUMMINGBIRD	OP	48.00	53.00
91	CARDINAL	OP	48.00	53.00
91	DOVE	OP	48.00	53.00
92	GOLDFINCH	OP	48.00	53.00
C. MCCLUNG			NATURE'S COLLAGE	
92	CEDAR WAXWING, AMONG THE BERRIES	OP	34.50	34.50
92	GOLD FINCHES, GOLDEN SPLENDOR	OP	34.50	34.50

LILLIPUT LANE LTD.

R. DAY

YR	NAME	LIMIT	ISSUE	QUOTE
		AMERICAN LANDMARKS COLLECTION		
90	COUNTRY CHURCH	5000	35.00	35.00
90	RIVERSIDE CHAPEL	5000	35.00	35.00

LLADRO
*
YR	NAME	LIMIT	ISSUE	QUOTE
*				*
*	1972 MOTHERS DAY PLATE L-7007	*	*	150.00

MAFEKING COLLECTION

M. GREEN

YR	NAME	LIMIT	ISSUE	QUOTE
			FOREVER FRIENDS	
93	THE HIDE AWAY	500	85.00	100.00
94	RUFOUS (THE HUMMINGBIRD)	500	34.75	85.00
M. GREEN			MAN'S BEST FRIEND	
93	DEREK (THE LABRADOR RETRIEVER)	500	65.00	85.00
93	DIVOT (THE GERMAN SHEPHERD)	500	85.00	100.00
94	MICKEY (SPANIEL CROSS)	500	39.95	45.00
94	PEPPER (THE AIREDALE)	500	39.95	85.00
M. GREEN			MY LITTLE BEAR	
93	BEAR WITH ME	500	85.00	100.00
93	SHIZAM (THE MAGICIAN)	500	85.00	100.00
M. GREEN			THE LORD'S CHILDREN	
93	A FRAGRANCE IN TIME	500	85.00	100.00
93	HEAR MY PRAYERS	500	75.00	85.00
94	TRADITIONS	500	39.95	85.00

MARCH OF DIMES

YR	NAME	LIMIT	ISSUE	QUOTE
			OUR CHILDREN, OUR FUTURE	
89	A TIME FOR PEACE	OP	29.00	29.00
89	A TIME TO BE BORN	OP	29.00	30.00
89	A TIME TO LOVE	OP	29.00	46.00
89	A TIME TO PLANT	OP	29.00	29.00
90	A TIME TO EMBRACE	OP	29.00	29.00
90	A TIME TO LAUGH	OP	29.00	29.00

MARURI USA

W. GAITHER

YR	NAME	LIMIT	ISSUE	QUOTE
			EAGLE PLATE SERIES	
84	FREE FLIGHT	995	150.00	150.00-198.00

MORGANTOWN

C. YATES

YR	NAME	LIMIT	ISSUE	QUOTE
			YATE'S COUNTRY LADIES	
81	ANGELICA	OP	75.00	75.00
82	VIOLET	OP	75.00	75.00
83	HEATHER	OP	75.00	75.00
84	LAUREL	OP	75.00	90.00
C. YATES			HEAVENS ABOVE	
89	CASSIOPEIA	OP	64.50	65.00
90	ORION	OP	64.50	120.00
90	PEGASUS	OP	64.50	200.00
91	CYGNUS	OP	64.50	150.00
C. YATES			THE STAR OF BETHLEHEM	
88	THE HOLY FAMILY	OP	34.50	35.00
89	SHEPHERDS IN THE FIELD	OP	34.50	54.00
90	LED BY THE STAR	OP	37.50	50.00
91	TIDINGS OF GREAT JOY	OP	37.50	200.00

MUSEUM COLLECTIONS INC.

N. ROCKWELL

YR	NAME	LIMIT	ISSUE	QUOTE
			AMERICAN FAMILY I	
79	BABY'S FIRST STEP	9900	28.50	61.00
79	BIRTHDAY PARTY	9900	28.50	35.00
79	BRIDE AND GROOM	9900	28.50	35.00
79	FIRST HAIRCUT	9900	28.50	35.00
79	FIRST PROM	9900	28.50	35.00
79	HAPPY BIRTHDAY DEAR MOTHER	9900	28.50	45.00
79	LITTLE MOTHER	9900	28.50	35.00
79	MOTHER'S LITTLE HELPERS	9900	28.50	35.00
79	SWEET SIXTEEN	9900	28.50	35.00
79	THE STUDENT	9900	28.50	35.00

YR	NAME	LIMIT	ISSUE	QUOTE
79	WASHING OUR DOG	9900	28.50	35.00
79	WRAPPING CHRISTMAS PRESENTS	9900	28.50	35.00
N. ROCKWELL			**AMERICAN FAMILY II**	
80	ALMOST GROWN UP	22,500	35.00	40.00
80	COURAGEOUS HERO	22,500	35.00	40.00
80	GIVING THANKS	22,500	35.00	40.00
80	HOME RUN SLUGGER	22,500	35.00	40.00
80	LITTLE SALESMAN	22,500	35.00	40.00
80	LITTLE SHAVER	22,500	35.00	40.00
80	NEW ARRIVAL	22,500	35.00	55.00
80	SPACE PIONEERS	22,500	35.00	40.00
80	SWEET DREAMS	22,500	35.00	40.00
80	WE MISSED YOU DADDY	22,500	35.00	40.00
81	AT THE CIRCUS	22,500	35.00	40.00
81	GOOD FOOD, GOOD FRIENDS	22,500	35.00	40.00
N. ROCKWELL			**CHRISTMAS**	
79	DAY AFTER CHRISTMAS	YR	75.00	85.00
80	CHECKING HIS LIST	YR	75.00	85.00
81	RINGING IN GOOD CHEER	YR	75.00	85.00
82	WAITING FOR SANTA	YR	75.00	85.00
83	HIGH HOPES	YR	75.00	85.00
84	SPACE AGE SANTA	YR	55.00	65.00

NEWELL
S. STILWELL   **WEBER'S CALENDAR**

YR	NAME	LIMIT	ISSUE	QUOTE
84	JULY	OP	19.00	19.00
84	JUNE	OP	19.00	19.00
85	AUGUST	OP	19.00	19.00
85	NOVEMBER	OP	19.00	19.00
85	OCTOBER	OP	19.00	19.00
85	SEPTEMBER	OP	19.00	19.00
86	APRIL	OP	19.00	25.00
86	DECEMBER	OP	19.00	20.00
86	FEBRUARY	OP	19.00	19.00
86	JANUARY	OP	19.00	19.00
86	MARCH	OP	19.00	22.00
86	MAY	OP	19.00	55.00

OSIRIS PORCELAIN
N.N. BICHAY   **LEGEND OF TUTANKHAMUN**

YR	NAME	LIMIT	ISSUE	QUOTE
91	TUTANKHUMUN AND HIS PRINCESS	195-DAY	39.84	45.00

PEMBERTON & OAKES
D. ZOLAN   **ADVENTURES OF CHILDHOOD**

YR	NAME	LIMIT	ISSUE	QUOTE
89	ALMOST HOME	44-DAY	19.60	60.00
89	CRYSTAL'S CREEK	44-DAY	19.60	36.00
89	SUMMER SUDS	44-DAY	22.00	27.00
90	SNOWY ADVENTURE	44-DAY	22.00	22.00
91	FORESTS & FAIRY TALES	44-DAY	24.40	25.00
D. ZOLAN			**ANNIVERSARY (10TH)**	
88	RIBBONS AND ROSES	19-DAY	24.40	45.00
D. ZOLAN			**CHILDHOOD FRIENDSHIP**	
86	BEACH BREAK	17-DAY	19.00	69.00
87	LITTLE ENGINEERS	17-DAY	19.00	75.00
88	DOZENS OF DAISIES	17-DAY	19.00	39.00
88	SHARING SECRETS	17-DAY	19.00	60.00
89	TINY TREASURES	17-DAY	19.00	44.00
90	COUNTRY WALK	17-DAY	19.00	24.00
D. ZOLAN			**CHILDREN AND PETS**	
84	GOLDEN MOMENT	UD	19.00	23.00
84	TENDER MOMENT	UD	19.00	37.00
85	MAKING FRIENDS	UD	19.00	22.00
85	TENDER BEGINNING	UD	19.00	32.00
86	BACKYARD DISCOVERY	UD	19.00	23.00
86	WAITING TO PLAY	UD	19.00	27.00
			CHILDREN AT CHRISTMAS	
81	GIFT FOR LAURIE	OP	48.00	48.00
81	A GIFT FOR LAURIE	15,000	48.00	109.00
82	CHRISTMAS PRAYER	15,000	48.00	70.00
83	ERIK'S DELIGHT	15,000	48.00	65.00
84	CHRISTMAS SECRET	15,000	48.00	50.00
85	CHRISTMAS KITTEN	15,000	48.00	59.00
86	LAURIE AND THE CRECHE	15,000	48.00	64.00
D. ZOLAN			**FATHERS DAY**	
86	DADDY'S HOME	UD	19.00	90.00
			LOCKHART WILDLIFE	
70	WOODCOCK-GROUSE	OP	150.00	209.00
71	TEAL-MALLARD	OP	150.00	170.00

YR NAME	LIMIT	ISSUE	QUOTE
72 MOCKINGBIRD-CARDINAL	OP	162.50	140.00
73 TURKEY-PHEASANT	OP	162.50	225.00
74 AMERICAN BOLD EAGLE	OP	150.00	675.00
75 WHITE-TAILED DEER	OP	100.00	109.00
76 AMERICAN BUFFALO	OP	165.00	124.00
77 GREAT HORNED OWL	OP	100.00	100.00
78 AMERICAN PANTHER	OP	175.00	75.00
79 RED FOXES	OP	120.00	65.00
80 TRUMPETER SWAN	OP	200.00	220.00
D. ZOLAN	**MARCH OF DIMES: OUR CHILDREN, OUR FUTURE**		
87 A TIME FOR PEACE (1ST IN SERIES)	150-DAY	29.00	35.00
D. ZOLAN		**MOTHER'S DAY**	
88 MOTHER'S ANGELS	UD	19.00	40.00
R. ANDERSON		**NUTCRACKER II**	
88 THE ROYAL WELCOME	UD	24.40	30.00
81 GRAND FINALE	UD	24.40	36.00
82 ARABIAN DANCERS	UD	24.40	67.50
83 DEW DROP FAIRY	UD	24.40	36.00
84 CLARA'S DELIGHT	UD	24.40	42.00
85 BEDTIME FOR NUTCRACKER	UD	24.40	48.00
86 THE CROWNING OF CLARA	UD	24.40	36.00
89 THE SPANISH DANCER	UD	24.40	26.00
87 DANCE OF THE SNOWFLAKES	UD	24.40	48.00
D. ZOLAN	**SPECIAL ISSUE (MINIATURE)**		
90 FIRST KISS (VALENTINE'S DAY)	19-DAY	14.50	55.00
90 FLOWERS FOR MOTHER (MOTHER'S DAY)	19-DAY	14.40	49.00
91 EASTER MORNING (EASTER)	19-DAY	16.60	35.00
92 TWILIGHT PRAYER (MOTHER'S DAY)	19-DAY	16.60	18.00
89 MEADOW MAGIC	OP	22.00	24.00
D. ZOLAN	**SPECIAL MOMENTS OF CHILDHOOD**		
88 BROTHERLY LOVE	19-DAY	19.00	45.00
88 SUNNY SURPRISE	19-DAY	19.00	27.00
89 SUMMER'S CHILD	19-DAY	22.00	26.00
90 CONE FOR TWO	19-DAY	24.60	25.00
90 MEADOW MAGIC	19-DAY	22.00	45.00
90 RODEO GIRL	19-DAY	24.60	25.00
D. ZOLAN		**THANKSGIVING**	
81 I'M THANKFUL TOO	UD	19.00	30.00
D. ZOLAN	**THE BEST OF ZOLAN IN MINIATURE**		
85 SABINA	SO	12.50	110.00
86 ERIK AND DANDELION	UD	12.50	96.00
86 TENDER MOMENT	UD	12.50	65.00
86 TOUCHING THE SKY	UD	12.50	52.00
87 A GIFT FOR LAURIE	UD	12.50	44.00-82.00
87 SMALL WONDER	UD	12.50	38.00-70.00
		WONDER OF CHILDHOOD	
85 GRANDMA'S GARDEN	OP	22.00	30.00
86 DAYDREAMER	CL	22.00	25.00
82 TOUCHING THE SKY	UD	19.00	25.00
83 SPRING INNOCENCE	UD	19.00	24.00
84 WINTER ANGEL	UD	22.00	30.00
85 SMALL WONDER	UD	22.00	30.00
86 GRANDMA'S GARDEN	UD	22.00	39.00
87 DAY DREAMER	UD	22.00	29.00
D. ZOLAN		**ZOLAN'S CHILDREN**	
78 ERIK AND DANDELION	UD	19.00	270.00
79 SABINA IN THE GRASS	UD	22.00	210.00
80 BY MYSELF	UD	24.00	60.00
81 FOR YOU	UD	24.00	44.00

PFALTZGRAFF
B.B. RICHARDS

93 LITTLEST ANGEL	5000	18.50	23.00
94 CHRISTMAS TRADITION	10,000	15.00	18.00
94 HARVEST MEMORIES	10,000	15.00	18.00

PICKARD
RAPHAEL

		ANNUAL CHRISTMAS	
76 ALBA MADONNA	7500	60.00	100.00
79 ADORATION OF THE MAGI	10,000	70.00	75.00
80 MADONNA AND CHILD	10,000	80.00	85.00
81 MADONNA AND CHILD WITH ANGELS	10,000	90.00	100.00
78 REST ON FLIGHT INTO EGYPT	10,000	65.00	85.00
77 THE NATIVITY	7500	65.00	90.00
J. SANCHEZ		**CHILDREN OF MEXICO**	
81 MARIA	5000	85.00	95.00

YR	NAME	LIMIT	ISSUE	QUOTE
81	MIGUEL	5000	85.00	95.00
82	REGINA	5000	90.00	100.00
83	RAPHAEL	5000	90.00	100.00

GEMS OF NATURE: HUMMINGBIRDS

YR	NAME	LIMIT	ISSUE	QUOTE
89	RUDY-THROATED HUMMINGBIRD	CL	29.00	29.00
90	BLACK-CHINNED HUMMINGBIRD	CL	32.00	35.00
90	BROAD-BILLED HUMMINGBIRD	CL	32.00	32.00
90	CALLIOPE HUMMINGBIRD	CL	32.00	45.00
90	RUFOUS HUMMINGBIRD	CL	29.00	38.00
91	ANNA'S HUMMINGBIRD/PETUNIAS	CL	34.00	38.00
91	COSTA'S HUMMINGBIRD & HOLLYHOCKS	CL	34.00	44.00
91	WHITE-EARED HUMMINGBIRD	CL	32.00	44.00

HAWAIIAN SPLENDOR

YR	NAME	LIMIT	ISSUE	QUOTE
92	AN EVENING IN THE ISLANDS	CL	34.00	50.00
92	COASTAL HARMONY	CL	34.00	52.00
92	TROPICAL ENCHANTMENT	CL	34.00	37.00
92	TWILIGHT PARADISE	CL	34.00	55.00

HOLIDAY TRADITIONS

YR	NAME	LIMIT	ISSUE	QUOTE
92	CHRISTMAS HOMECOMING	CL	29.00	45.00
92	QUIET UNDER THE EAVES	CL	29.00	65.00
93	SNOWS OF YESTERYEAR	CL	29.00	30.00
93	THE HEART OF CHRISTMAS	CL	29.00	29.00

INNOCENT ENCOUNTERS

YR	NAME	LIMIT	ISSUE	QUOTE
88	JUST PASSING BY	CL	34.00	29.00
88	MAKING FRIENDS	CL	34.00	37.00
89	EYE TO EYE	CL	34.00	25.00
89	LET'S PLAY	CL	34.00	30.00

J. LOCKHART — **LOCKHART WILDLIFE**

YR	NAME	LIMIT	ISSUE	QUOTE
70	WOODCOCK/RUFFED GROUSE, PAIR	2000	150.00	264.00
71	TEAL/MALLARD, PAIR	2000	150.00	170.00
72	MOCKINGBIRD/CARDINAL, PAIR	2000	162.50	180.00
73	TURKEY/PHEASANT, PAIR	2000	162.50	264.00
74	AMERICAN BALD EAGLE	2000	150.00	700.00
75	WHITE TAILED DEER	2500	100.00	140.00
76	AMERICAN BUFFALO	2500	165.00	180.00
77	GREAT HORN OWL	2500	100.00	115.00
78	AMERICAN PANTHER	2000	175.00	200.00
79	RED FOXES	2500	120.00	130.00
80	TRUMPETER SWAN	2000	200.00	220.00

I. SPENCER — **MOTHER'S LOVE**

YR	NAME	LIMIT	ISSUE	QUOTE
80	MIRACLE	7500	95.00	105.00
81	STORY TIME	7500	110.00	120.00
82	FIRST EDITION	7500	115.00	125.00
83	PRECIOUS MOMENT	7500	120.00	145.00

I. SPENCER — **SYMPHONY OF ROSES**

YR	NAME	LIMIT	ISSUE	QUOTE
82	WILD IRISH ROSE	10,000	85.00	95.00
83	YELLOW ROSE OF TEXAS	10,000	90.00	100.00
84	HONEYSUCKLE ROSE	10,000	95.00	134.00
85	ROSE OF WASHINGTON SQUARE	10,000	100.00	218.00

PORSGRUND

G. BRATILE — **CHRISTMAS (ANNUAL)**

YR	NAME	LIMIT	ISSUE	QUOTE
68	CHURCH SCENE	UD	12.00	125.00
69	THREE KINGS	UD	12.00	12.00
70	ROAD TO BETHLEHEM	UD	12.00	12.00
71	A CHILD IS BORN	UD	12.00	12.00
72	HARK THE HERALD ANGELS	UD	12.00	12.00
73	PROMISE OF THE SAVIOR	UD	12.00	12.00
74	THE SHEPHERDS	UD	15.00	36.00
75	ROAD TO TEMPLE	UD	19.50	19.50
76	JESUS AND THE ELDERS	UD	22.00	26.00
77	DRAUGHT OF THE FISH	UD	24.00	28.00

PRINCETON GALLERY

J. VAN ZYLE — **ARCTIC WOLVES**

YR	NAME	LIMIT	ISSUE	QUOTE
91	SONG OF THE WILDERNESS	90-DAY	29.50	29.50

R. SANDERSON — **CIRCUS FRIENDS COLLECTION**

YR	NAME	LIMIT	ISSUE	QUOTE
89	DON'T BE SHY	*	29.50	29.50
90	CHEER UP MR. CLOWN	*	29.50	29.50
90	LOOKS LIKE RAIN	*	29.50	29.50
90	MAKE ME A CLOWN	*	29.50	29.50

Q. LEMOND — **CUBS OF THE BIG CATS**

YR	NAME	LIMIT	ISSUE	QUOTE
90	COUGAR CUB	*	29.50	29.50
91	CHEETAH	90-DAY	29.50	29.50
91	LION CUB	90-DAY	29.50	29.50
91	SNOW LEOPARD	90-DAY	29.50	29.50
91	TIGER	90-DAY	29.50	29.50

Curiosity: Asian Elephants *from the "Tomorrow's Promise" series, is one of many wildlife plates produced by The Bradford Exchange.*

These newborn cardinals offer a Morning Serenade *to their proud parents. This is the first issue in the "Nature's Poetry" series created by Lena Liu for W.S. George.*

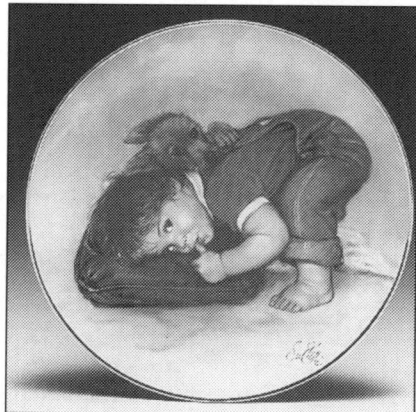

This little guy isn't sleepy. Nap *is the fourth issue in the "Mischief Makers" series by Sue Etem. Armstrong's is the producer.*

Portraying a bond that will last forever is Sue Etem's A Pair of Dreams *from the "Infinite Love" series produced by Armstrong's.*

YR	NAME	LIMIT	ISSUE	QUOTE
L. PICKEN			**DARLING DALMATIONS**	
91	DALMATION	90-DAY	29.50	29.50
92	FIREHOUSE FROLIC	90-DAY	29.50	29.50

R.J. ERNST ENTERPRISES

YR	NAME	LIMIT	ISSUE	QUOTE
S. MORTON			**A BEAUTIFUL WORLD**	
81	TAHITIAN DREAMER	27,500	27.50	30.00
82	FLIRTATION	27,500	27.50	27.50
84	ELKE OF OSLO	27,500	27.50	27.50
S. KUHNLY			**CLASSY CARS**	
82	THE 26T	20-DAY	24.50	32.00
82	THE 31A	20-DAY	24.50	30.00
83	THE PICKUP	20-DAY	24.50	27.50
84	PANEL VAN	20-DAY	24.50	35.00
S. MORTON			**COMMEMORATIVES**	
81	JOHN LENNON	30-DAY	39.50	75.90
82	ELVIS PRESLEY	30-DAY	39.50	39.50
82	MARILYN MONROE	30-DAY	39.50	39.50
83	JUDY GARLAND	30-DAY	39.50	39.50
84	JOHN WAYNE	2500	39.50	39.50
S. MORTON			**ELVIRA**	
86	NIGHT ROSE	90-DAY	29.50	29.50
S. MORTON			**HOLLYWOOD GREATS**	
81	GARY COOPER	27,500	29.95	32.50
81	JOHN WAYNE	27,500	29.95	50.00
82	CLARK GABLE	27,500	29.95	65.00
84	ALAN LADD	27,500	29.95	60.00
R. MONEY			**SEEMS LIKE YESTERDAY**	
81	STOP & SMELL THE ROSES	10-DAY	24.50	24.50
82	HOME BY LUNCH	10-DAY	24.50	24.50
82	LISA'S CREEK	10-DAY	24.50	24.50
83	IT'S GOT MY NAME ON IT	10-DAY	24.50	24.50
83	MY MAGIC HAT	10-DAY	24.50	24.50
84	LITTLE PRINCE	10-DAY	24.50	24.50
S. MORTON			**STAR TREK**	
84	MR. SPOCK	90-DAY	29.50	35.00-75.00
85	BEAM US DOWN SCOTTY	90-DAY	29.50	75.00
85	CAPTAIN KIRK	90-DAY	29.50	60.00-95.00
85	CHEKOV	90-DAY	29.50	35.00-75.00
85	DR. MCCOY	90-DAY	29.50	35.00-75.00
85	SCOTTY	90-DAY	29.50	35.00-75.00
85	SULU	90-DAY	29.50	35.00-75.00
85	THE ENTERPRISE	90-DAY	39.50	50.00-125.00
85	UHURA	90-DAY	29.50	35.00-75.00
R. MONEY			**TURN OF THE CENTURY**	
81	RIVERBOAT HONEYMOON	10-DAY	35.00	35.00
82	CHILDREN'S CAROUSEL	10-DAY	35.00	37.50
84	FLOWER MARKET	10-DAY	35.00	35.00
85	BALLOON RACE	10-DAY	35.00	35.00
D. PUTNAM			**WOMEN OF THE WEST**	
79	EXPECTATIONS	10,000	39.50	39.50
81	SILVER DOLLAR SAL	10,000	39.50	45.00
82	SCHOOL MARM	10,000	39.50	39.50
83	DOLLY	10,000	39.50	39.50

RECO INTERNATIONAL

YR	NAME	LIMIT	ISSUE	QUOTE
S. KUCK			**A CHILDHOOD ALMANAC**	
85	BE MINE-FEBRUARY	14-DAY	29.50	36.00
85	CHRISTMAS MAGIC-DECEMBER	14-DAY	29.50	45.00
85	EASTER MORNING-APRIL	14-DAY	29.50	35.00
85	FIRESIDE DREAMS-JANUARY	14-DAY	29.50	31.00
85	FOR MOM-MAY	14-DAY	29.50	33.00-35.00
85	GIVING THANKS-NOVEMBER	14-DAY	29.50	33.00
85	INDIAN SUMMER-OCTOBER	14-DAY	29.50	35.00
85	JUST DREAMING-JUNE	14-DAY	29.50	29.50
85	SCHOOL DAYS-SEPTEMBER	14-DAY	29.50	38.00
85	STAR SPANGLED SKY-JULY	14-DAY	29.50	33.00
85	SUMMER SECRETS-AUGUST	14-DAY	29.50	33.00
85	WINDS OF MARCH-MARCH	14-DAY	29.50	35.00
S. KUCK			**A CHILDREN'S CHRISTMAS PAGEANT**	
86	SILENT NIGHT	YR	32.50	55.00
87	HARK THE HERALD ANGELS SING	YR	32.50	36.00
88	WHILE SHEPHERDS WATCHED...	YR	32.50	51.00
89	WE THREE KINGS	TL	32.50	37.00
S. DEVLIN			**AMERICANA**	
72	GASPEE INCIDENT	1500	200.00	325.00

YR	NAME	LIMIT	ISSUE	QUOTE
B. FARNSWORTH		**AMISH TRADITIONS**		
94	FAMILY OUTING	95-DAY	29.50	32.00
94	GOLDEN HARVEST	95-DAY	29.50	32.00
94	THE QUILTING BEE	95-DAY	29.50	32.00
95	LAST DAY OF SCHOOL	95-DAY	29.50	29.50
S. KUCK		**BAREFOOT CHILDREN**		
87	GOLDEN AFTERNOON	14-DAY	29.50	32.00
87	NIGHT-TIME STORY	14-DAY	29.50	29.50-35.00
88	CAROUSEL MAGIC	14-DAY	29.50	35.00-42.00
88	GRANDMA'S TRUNK	14-DAY	29.50	32.00
88	LITTLE SWEETHEARTS	14-DAY	29.50	29.50-36.00
88	PRETTY AS A PICTURE	14-DAY	29.50	35.00
88	THE REHEARSAL	14-DAY	29.50	35.00
88	UNDER THE APPLE TREE	14-DAY	29.50	29.50-35.00
J. MCCLELLAND		**BECKY'S DAY**		
85	AWAKENING	90-DAY	24.50	29.00
85	GETTING DRESSED	90-DAY	24.50	28.00
86	BREAKFAST	90-DAY	27.50	32.00
86	EVENING PRAYER	90-DAY	27.50	32.00
86	LEARNING IS FUN	90-DAY	27.50	32.00
86	MUFFIN MAKING	90-DAY	27.50	32.00
86	TUB TIME	90-DAY	27.50	32.00
G. RATNAVIRA		**BIRDS OF THE HIDDEN FOREST**		
94	MACAW WATERFALL	96-DAY	29.50	32.00
94	PARADISE VALLEY	96-DAY	29.50	32.00
95	TOUCAN TREASURE	96-DAY	29.50	29.50
*		**BOHEMIAN ANNUALS**		
74	1974	500	130.00	155.00
75	1975	500	140.00	160.00
76	1976	500	150.00	160.00
S. KUCK		**CHRISTENING GIFT**		
95	GOD'S GIFT	OP	29.90	29.90
J. BERGSMA		**CHRISTMAS WISHES**		
94	I WISH YOU LOVE	75-DAY	29.50	32.00
* *		**DAYS GONE BY**		
85	SURREY RIDE	OP	29.50	28.00
83	AMY'S MAGIC HORSE	14-DAY	29.50	29.00
83	SUNDAY BEST	14-DAY	29.50	38.00
84	AFTERNOON RECITAL	14-DAY	29.50	50.00
84	EASTER AT GRANDMA'S	14-DAY	29.50	23.00
84	LITTLE ANGLERS	14-DAY	29.50	27.00
84	LITTLE TUTOR	14-DAY	29.50	20.00
85	MORNING SONG	14-DAY	29.50	13.00
85	THE SURREY RIDE	14-DAY	29.50	40.00
*		**DRESDEN CHRISTMAS**		
71	SHEPHERD SCENE	3500	15.00	50.00
72	NIKLAS CHURCH	6000	15.00	25.00
73	SCHWANSTEIN CHURCH	6000	18.00	35.00
74	VILLAGE SCENE	5000	20.00	30.00
75	ROTHENBURG SCENE	5000	24.00	30.00
76	VILLAGE CHURCH	5000	26.00	35.00
77	OLD MILL (ISSUE CLOSED)	5000	28.00	30.00
*		**DRESDEN MOTHER'S DAY**		
72	DOE AND FAWN	8000	15.00	20.00
73	MARE AND COLT	6000	16.00	25.00
74	TIGER AND CUB	5000	20.00	23.00
75	DACHSHUNDS	5000	24.00	28.00
76	OWL AND OFFSPRING	5000	26.00	30.00
77	CHAMOIS (ISSUE CLOSED)	5000	28.00	30.00
C. HOPKINS		**ENCHANTED NORFIN TROLLS**		
94	CHEF LE TROLL	75-DAY	19.50	21.00
94	IF TROLLS COULD FLY	75-DAY	19.50	21.00
94	QUEEN OF THE TROLLS	75-DAY	19.50	21.00
J. POLUSZYNSKI		**FOUR SEASONS**		
73	FALL	2500	50.00	75.00
73	SPRING	2500	50.00	75.00
73	SUMMER	2500	50.00	75.00
73	WINTER	2500	50.00	75.00
*		**FURSTENBERG CHRISTMAS**		
71	RABBITS	7500	15.00	30.00
72	SNOWY VILLAGE	6000	15.00	20.00
73	CHRISTMAS EVE	4000	18.00	35.00
74	SPARROWS	4000	20.00	30.00
75	DEER FAMILY	4000	22.00	30.00
76	WINTER BIRDS	4000	25.00	30.00

YR NAME	LIMIT	ISSUE	QUOTE
E. GROSSBERG	**FURSTENBERG DELUXE CHRISTMAS**		
71 WISE MEN	1500	45.00	65.00
72 HOLY FAMILY	2000	45.00	60.00
73 CHRISTMAS EVE	2000	60.00	65.00
*	**FURSTENBERG EASTER**		
71 SHEEP	3500	15.00	150.00
72 CHICKS	6500	15.00	60.00
73 BUNNIES	4000	16.00	80.00
74 PUSSYWILLOW	4000	20.00	35.00
75 EASTER WINDOW	4000	22.00	30.00
76 FLOWER COLLECTING	4000	25.00	30.00
*	**FURSTENBERG MOTHER'S DAY**		
72 HUMMINGBIRDS, FE	6000	15.00	45.00
73 HEDGEHOGS	5000	16.00	40.00
74 DOE AND FAWN	4000	20.00	30.00
75 SWANS	4000	22.00	30.00
76 KOALA BEARS	4000	25.00	30.00
J. POLUSZYNSKI	**FURSTENBERG OLYMPIC**		
72 MUNICH	5000	20.00	75.00
76 MONTREAL	5000	37.50	42.00
S. KUCK	**GAMES CHILDREN PLAY**		
79 ME FIRST	10,000	45.00	50.00
80 FOREVER BUBBLES	10,000	45.00	48.00
81 SKATING PALS	10,000	45.00	47.50
82 JOIN ME	10,000	45.00	50.00
D. BARLOWE	**GARDENS OF AMERICA**		
92 COLONIAL SPLENDOR	48-DAY	29.50	29.50
92 COLONIAL SPLENDOR	48-DAY	29.50	29.50
D. BARLOWE	**GARDENS OF BEAUTY**		
88 DUTCH COUNTRY GARDEN	14-DAY	29.50	32.00
88 ENGLISH COUNTRY GARDEN	14-DAY	29.50	32.00
88 JAPANESE GARDEN	14-DAY	29.50	32.00
88 NEW ENGLAND GARDEN	14-DAY	29.50	32.00
89 GERMAN COUNTRY GARDEN	14-DAY	29.50	32.00
89 HAWAIIAN GARDEN	14-DAY	29.50	32.00
89 ITALIAN GARDEN	14-DAY	29.50	32.00
89 MEXICAN GARDEN	14-DAY	29.50	29.50
I. DRECHSLER	**GOD'S OWN COUNTRY**		
90 COMING HOME	14-DAY	30.00	32.00
90 DAYBREAK	14-DAY	30.00	34.00
90 PEACEFUL GATHERING	14-DAY	30.00	32.00
90 QUIET WATERS	14-DAY	30.00	32.00
*	**GRAFBURG CHRISTMAS**		
75 BLACK-CAPPED CHICKADEE	5000	20.00	60.00
76 SQUIRRELS	5000	22.00	30.00
G. KATZ	**GREAT STORIES FROM THE BIBLE**		
87 JOSEPH'S COAT OF MANY COLORS	14-DAY	29.50	35.00
87 KING SAUL & DAVID	14-DAY	29.50	35.00
87 MOSES AND THE TEN COMMANDMENTS	14-DAY	29.50	38.00
87 MOSES IN THE BULRUSHES	14-DAY	29.50	35.00
88 DANIEL READS THE WRITING ON THE WALL	14-DAY	29.50	35.00
88 KING SOLOMON	14-DAY	29.50	35.00
88 REBEKAH AT THE WELL	14-DAY	29.50	35.00
88 THE STORY OF RUTH	14-DAY	29.50	35.00
J. BERGSMA	**GUARDIANS OF THE KINGDOM**		
90 GUARDIANS OF THE INNOCENT CHILDREN	17,500	35.00	38.00
90 RAINBOW TO RIDE ON	17,500	35.00	37.00
90 SPECIAL FRIENDS ARE FEW	17,500	35.00	37.00
90 THE MIRACLE OF LOVE	17,500	35.00	37.00
91 IN FAITH I AM FREE	17,500	35.00	35.00
91 ONLY WITH THE HEART	17,500	35.00	35.00
91 THE MAGIC OF LOVE	17,500	35.00	35.00
91 TO FLY WITHOUT WINGS	17,500	35.00	35.00
H. ROE	**HAVEN OF THE HUNTERS**		
94 EAGLE'S CASTLE	96-DAY	29.50	32.00
94 SANCTUARY OF THE HAWK	96-DAY	29.50	32.00
S. KUCK	**HEARTS & FLOWERS**		
91 CATS IN THE CRADLE	OP	32.50	40.00
92 CAROUSEL OF DREAMS	OP	32.50	32.50
92 DELIGHTFUL BUNDLE	OP	34.50	34.50
92 STORYBOOK MEMORIES	OP	32.50	32.50
93 EASTER MORNING VISITOR	OP	34.50	34.50
93 ME AND MY PONY	OP	34.50	34.50
S. KUCK	**HEARTS AND FLOWERS**		
91 PATIENCE	120-DAY	29.50	44.00
91 TEA PARTY	120-DAY	29.50	55.00

YR	NAME	LIMIT	ISSUE	QUOTE
92	CAT'S IN THE CRADLE	120-DAY	32.50	32.50
W. LOWE		**IN THE EYE OF THE STORM**		
91	FIRST STRIKE	120-DAY	29.50	29.50
92	NIGHT FORCE	120-DAY	29.50	29.50
92	TRACKS ACROSS THE SAND	120-DAY	29.50	29.50
J. BERGSMA		**J. BERGSMA MOTHER'S DAY SERIES**		
90	THE BEAUTY OF LIFE	14-DAY	35.00	40.00
92	MOTHER'S LOVE	14-DAY	35.00	35.00
MERLI		**KING'S CHRISTMAS**		
73	ADORATION	1500	100.00	265.00
74	MADONNA	1500	150.00	250.00
75	HEAVENLY CHOIR	1500	160.00	235.00
76	SIBLINGS	1500	200.00	225.00
A. FALCHI		**KING'S FLOWERS**		
73	CARNATION	1000	85.00	130.00
74	RED ROSE	1000	100.00	145.00
75	YELLOW DAHLIA	1000	110.00	162.00
76	BLUEBELLS	1000	130.00	165.00
77	ANEMONES	1000	130.00	175.00
MERLI		**KING'S MOTHER'S DAY**		
73	DANCING GIRL	1500	100.00	225.00
74	DANCING BOY	1500	115.00	250.00
75	MOTHERLY LOVE	1500	140.00	225.00
76	MAIDEN	1500	180.00	200.00
P. JEPSON		**KINGDOM OF THE GREAT CATS**		
94	SUMMIT SANCTUARY	36-DAY	29.50	32.00
95	OUT OF THE MIST	36-DAY	29.50	29.50
S. SOMERVILLE		**KITTENS 'N HATS**		
94	OPENING NIGHT	48-DAY	29.50	32.00
94	SITTING PRETTY	48-DAY	29.50	32.00
95	LITTLE LEAGUE	48-DAY	29.50	29.5
J. BERGSMA		**LAND OF OUR DREAMS**		
89	LAND OF NOD	19,000	35.00	40.00
89	THE SECRET DOOR	19,000	35.00	40.00
89	THE STARS	19,500	35.00	40.00
89	THE SWING	19,000	35.00	40.00
S. KUCK		**LITTLE PROFESSIONALS**		
82	ALL IS WELL	10,000	39.50	47.50-95.00
83	TENDER LOVING CARE	10,000	39.50	46.00-110.00
84	LOST AND FOUND	10,000	39.50	42.50-85.00
85	READING, WRITING AND...	10,000	39.50	47.50-85.00
J. BERGSMA		**MAGIC COMPANIONS**		
94	BELIEVE IN LOVE	48-DAY	29.50	32.00
94	IMAGINE PEACE	48-DAY	29.50	32.00
S. KUCK		**MARCH OF DIMES: OUR CHILDREN, OUR FUTURE**		
89	A TIME TO LOVE (2ND IN SERIES)	150-DAY	29.00	45.00
89	A TIME TO PLANT (3RD IN SERIES)	150-DAY	29.00	32.00
*		**MARMOT CHRISTMAS**		
70	POLAR BEAR, FE	5000	13.00	60.00
71	AMERICAN BUFFALO	6000	14.50	35.00
71	BUFFALO BILL	6000	16.00	55.00
72	BOY AND GRANDFATHER	5000	20.00	50.00
73	SNOWMAN	3000	22.00	45.00
74	DANCING	2000	24.00	30.00
75	QUAIL	2000	30.00	40.00
76	WINDMILL	2000	40.00	45.00
*		**MARMOT FATHER'S DAY**		
70	STAG	3500	12.00	100.00
71	HORSE	3500	12.50	40.00
*		**MARMOT MOTHER'S DAY**		
72	SEAL	6000	16.00	60.00
73	BEAR WITH CUB	3000	20.00	140.00
74	PENGUINS	2000	24.00	50.00
75	RACCOONS	2000	30.00	45.00
76	DUCKS	2000	40.00	45.00
*		**MOSER CHRISTMAS**		
70	HARDCANY CASTLE	400	75.00	170.00
71	KARLSTEIN CASTLE	1365	75.00	80.00
72	OLD TOWN HALL	1000	85.00	90.00
73	KARLOVY VARY CASTLE	500	90.00	100.00
*		**MOSER MOTHER'S DAY**		
71	PEACOCKS	350	75.00	100.00
72	BUTTERFLIES	750	85.00	90.00
73	SQUIRRELS	500	90.00	95.00
J. MCCLELLAND		**MOTHER GOOSE**		
79	MARY, MARY	YR	22.50	75.00

YR	NAME	LIMIT	ISSUE	QUOTE
80	LITTLE BOY BLUE	YR	22.50	24.00
81	LITTLE MISS MUFFET	YR	24.50	30.00
82	LITTLE JACK HORNER	YR	24.50	28.00
83	LITTLE BO PEEP	YR	24.50	25.00
84	DIDDLE, DIDDLE DUMPLING	YR	24.50	25.00
85	MARY HAD A LITTLE LAMB	YR	27.50	28.00
86	JACK AND JILL	YR	27.50	28.00
S. KUCK		**MOTHER'S DAY COLLECTION**		
85	ONCE UPON A TIME	YR	29.50	135.00
86	TIMES REMEMBERED	YR	29.50	40.00-75.00
87	A CHERISHED TIME	YR	29.50	30.00-40.00
88	A TIME TOGETHER	YR	29.50	50.00
* KELLY		**NOBLE & FREE**		
94	MOONLIGHT RUN	95-DAY	29.50	32.00
94	PROTECTED JOURNEY	95-DAY	29.50	32.00
P.D. JACKSON		**OSCAR & BERTIE'S EDWARDIAN HOLIDAY**		
92	EARLY RISE	48-DAY	29.50	29.50
P.D. JACKSON		**OSCAR & BERTIE'S VICTORIAN HOLIDAY**		
91	SNAPSHOT	48-DAY	29.50	29.50
S. BARLOWE		**OUR CHERISHED SEAS**		
91	FLIGHT OF THE DOLPHINS	48-DAY	37.50	37.50
91	LIONS OF THE SEA	48-DAY	37.50	37.50
91	WHALE SONG	48-DAY	37.50	37.50
92	PALACE OF THE SEALS	48-DAY	37.50	37.50
S. KUCK		**PLATE OF THE MONTH COLLECTION**		
90	APRIL	28-DAY	25.00	30.00
90	AUGUST	28-DAY	25.00	25.00
90	DECEMBER	28-DAY	25.00	30.00
90	FEBRUARY	28-DAY	25.00	30.00
90	JANUARY	28-DAY	25.00	30.00
90	JULY	28-DAY	25.00	30.00
90	JUNE	28-DAY	25.00	30.00
90	MARCH	28-DAY	25.00	30.00
90	MAY	28-DAY	25.00	30.00
90	NOVEMBER	28-DAY	25.00	30.00
90	OCTOBER	28-DAY	25.00	30.00
90	SEPTEMBER	28-DAY	25.00	30.00
S. KUCK		**PRECIOUS ANGELS**		
94	ANGEL OF SHARING	95-DAY	29.90	32.00
95	ANGEL OF GRACE	95-DAY	29.90	29.90
95	ANGEL OF HOPE	95-DAY	29.90	29.90
95	ANGEL OF LAUGHTER	95-DAY	29.90	29.90
95	ANGEL OF SUNSHINE	95-DAY	29.90	32.00
S. KUCK		**PREMIER COLLECTION**		
91	KITTEN	7500	95.00	97.00
91	PUPPY	7500	95.00	97.00
*		**ROYALE**		
69	APOLLO MOON LANDING	2000	30.00	80.00
*		**ROYALE CHRISTMAS**		
69	CHRISTMAS FAIR	6000	12.00	125.00
70	VIGIL MASS	10,000	13.00	110.00
71	CHRISTMAS NIGHT	8000	16.00	50.00
72	ELKS	8000	16.00	45.00
73	CHRISTMAS DOWN	6000	20.00	37.50
74	VILLAGE CHRISTMAS	5000	22.00	60.00
75	FEEDING TIME	5000	26.00	35.00
76	SEAPORT CHRISTMAS	5000	27.50	30.00
77	SLEDDING	5000	30.00	35.00
*		**ROYALE FATHER'S DAY**		
70	FRIGATE CONSTITUTION	5000	13.00	80.00
71	MAN FISHING	5000	13.00	35.00
72	MOUNTAINEER	5000	16.00	55.00
73	CAMPING	4000	18.00	45.00
74	EAGLE	2500	22.00	35.00
75	REGATTA	2500	26.00	35.00
76	HUNTING	2500	27.50	33.00
77	FISHING	2500	30.00	35.00
J. POLUSZYNSKI		**ROYALE GAME PLATES**		
72	SETTERS	500	180.00	200.00
73	FOX	500	200.00	250.00
74	OSPREY	250	250.00	270.00
75	CALIFORNIA QUAIL	250	265.00	280.00
*		**ROYALE GERMANIA CHRISTMAS ANNUAL**		
70	ORCHID	600	200.00	650.00
71	CYCLAMEN	1000	200.00	325.00
72	SILVER THISTLE	1000	250.00	290.00

YR	NAME	LIMIT	ISSUE	QUOTE
73	TULIPS	600	275.00	310.00
74	SUNFLOWERS	500	300.00	320.00
75	SNOWDROPS	350	450.00	500.00
76	FLAMING HEART	350	450.00	490.00
*		**ROYALE GERMANIA CRYSTAL MOTHER'S DAY**		
71	ROSES	250	135.00	650.00
72	ELEPHANT AND YOUNGSTER	750	180.00	250.00
73	KOALA BEAR AND CUB	600	200.00	225.00
74	SQUIRRELS	500	240.00	250.00
75	SWAN AND YOUNG	350	350.00	375.00
*		**ROYALE MOTHER'S DAY**		
70	SWAN AND YOUNG	6000	12.00	80.00
71	DOE AND FAWN	9000	13.00	55.00
72	RABBITS	9000	16.00	40.00
73	OWL FAMILY	6000	18.00	40.00
74	DUCK AND YOUNG	5000	22.00	40.00
75	LYNX AND CUBS	5000	26.00	40.00
76	WOODCOCK AND YOUNG	5000	27.50	35.00
77	KOALA BEAR	5000	30.00	35.00
S. KUCK		**SANDRA KUCK MOTHER'S DAY**		
95	HOME IS WHERE THE HEART IS	48-DAY	35.00	35.00
S. KUCK		**SPECIAL OCCASIONS BY RECO**		
88	THE WEDDING	CL	35.00	40.00
89	WEDDING DAY (6 1/2 IN.)	OP	20.00	25.00
90	THE SPECIAL DAY	CL	25.00	30.00
C. MICARELLI		**SPECIAL OCCASIONS-WEDDING**		
91	FROM THIS DAY FORWARD	OP	25.00	25.00
91	FROM THIS DAY FORWARD	OP	35.00	35.00
91	TO HAVE AND TO HOLD	OP	35.00	35.00
91	TO HAVE AND TO HOLD	OP	25.00	25.00
S. KUCK		**SUGAR & SPICE**		
94	GARDEN OF SUNSHINE	95-DAY	34.90	38.00
94	MORNING PRAYERS	95-DAY	32.90	35.00
94	TEDDY BEAR TALES	95-DAY	32.90	35.00
95	A SPECIAL DAY	95-DAY	34.90	34.90
95	FIRST SNOW	95-DAY	34.90	34.90
J. BERGSMA		**THE CHRISTMAS SERIES**		
90	DOWN THE GLISTENING LANE	14-DAY	35.00	39.00
91	A CHILD IS BORN	14-DAY	35.00	35.00
C.M. BARKER		**THE FLOWER FAIRIES YEAR COLLECTION**		
90	THE PINE TREE FAIRY	14-DAY	29.50	32.00
90	THE RED CLOVER FAIRY	14-DAY	29.50	32.00
90	THE ROSE HIP FAIRY	14-DAY	29.50	32.00
90	THE WILD CHERRY BLOSSOM FAIRY	14-DAY	29.50	32.00
S. KUCK		**THE GRANDPARENT COLLECTOR'S PLATES**		
81	GRANDMA'S COOKIE JAR	YR	37.50	40.00
81	GRANDPA AND THE DOLLHOUSE	YR	37.50	40.00
J. MCCLELLAND		**THE MCCLELLAND CHILDREN'S CIRCUS COLLECTION**		
82	KATIE THE TIGHTROPE WALKER	100-DAY	29.50	35.00
82	TOMMY THE CLOWN	100-DAY	29.50	30.00-37.50
83	JOHNNY THE STRONGMAN	100-DAY	29.50	30.00
84	MAGGIE THE ANIMAL TRAINER	100-DAY	29.50	30.00
C. MICARELLI		**THE NUTCRACKER BALLET**		
89	CHRISTMAS EVE PARTY	28-DAY	35.00	40.00
90	CLARA AND HER PRINCE	28-DAY	35.00	37.00
90	THE DREAM BEGINS	28-DAY	35.00	40.00
91	DANCE OF THE SNOW FAIRIES	28-DAY	35.00	35.00
92	THE LAND OF SWEETS	14-DAY	35.00	35.00
92	THE SUGAR PLUM FAIRY	14-DAY	35.00	35.00
J. MCCLELLAND		**THE PREMIER COLLECTION**		
91	LOVE	7500	75.00	75.00
A. FAZIO		**THE SOPHISTICATED LADIES COLLECTION**		
85	CLEO	21-DAY	29.50	32.50
85	FELICIA	21-DAY	29.50	32.50
85	PHOEBE	21-DAY	29.50	33.00
85	SAMANTHA	21-DAY	29.50	32.50
86	BIANKA	21-DAY	29.50	32.00
86	CERISSA	21-DAY	29.50	32.00
86	CHELSEA	21-DAY	29.50	32.00
86	NATASHA	21-DAY	29.50	32.50
T. UTZ		**THE SPRINGTIME OF LIFE**		
85	TEDDY'S BATHTIME	14-DAY	29.50	32.50
86	AMONG THE DAFFODILS	14-DAY	29.50	32.00
86	AUNT TILLIE'S HATS	14-DAY	29.50	32.00
86	GRANNY'S BOOTS	14-DAY	29.50	32.00
86	JUST LIKE MOMMY	14-DAY	29.50	32.00

YR	NAME	LIMIT	ISSUE	QUOTE
86	LITTLE EMILY	14-DAY	29.50	32.00
86	MY FAVORITE DOLLS	14-DAY	29.50	35.00
86	MY MASTERPIECE	14-DAY	29.50	35.00
J. MCCLELLAND			THE WONDER OF CHRISTMAS	
91	SANTA'S SECRET	48-DAY	29.50	29.50
92	MY FAVORITE ORNAMENT	48-DAY	24.50	24.50
J. MCCLELLAND			THE WORLD OF CHILDREN	
77	RAINY DAY FUN	10,000	50.00	55.00
78	WHEN I GROW UP	15,000	50.00	55.00
79	YOU'RE INVITED	15,000	50.00	55.00
80	KITTENS FOR SALE	15,000	50.00	55.00
* *			TIDINGS OF JOY	
92	PEACE ON EARTH	OP	35.00	50.00
93	REJOICE	OP	35.00	49.00
94	NOEL	OP	38.00	38.00
94	NOEL	75-DAY	35.00	38.00
J. BERGSMA			TOTEMS OF THE WEST	
94	PEACE AT LAST	96-DAY	29.50	32.00
94	THE WATCHMEN	96-DAY	29.50	32.00
S. BARLOWE			TOWN AND COUNTRY DOGS	
90	FOX HUNT	36-DAY	35.00	35.00
91	GOLDEN FIELDS (GOLDEN RETRIEVER)	36-DAY	35.00	35.00
91	THE RETRIEVAL	36-DAY	35.00	35.00
* *			TREASURED SONGS OF CHILDHOOD	
88	ROUND THE MULBERRY BUSH	CL	32.90	33.00
88	A TISKET, A TASKET	150-DAY	29.50	32.00
88	BAA, BAA, BLACK SHEEP	150-DAY	32.90	33.00
88	TWINKLE, TWINKLE, LITTLE STAR	150-DAY	29.50	30.00
89	I'M A LITTLE TEAPOT	150-DAY	32.90	33.00
89	PAT-A-CAKE	150-DAY	34.90	34.90-48.00
89	RAIN, RAIN GO AWAY	150-DAY	32.90	33.00
89	ROUND THE MULBERRY BUSH	150-DAY	32.90	36.00
90	HUSH LITTLE BABY	150-DAY	34.90	34.90-47.00
S. BARLOWE			VANISHING ANIMAL KINGDOMS	
86	OLEPI THE BUFFALO	21,500	35.00	40.00
86	RAMA THE TIGER	21,500	35.00	40.00
87	COOLIBAH THE KOALA	21,500	35.00	42.00
87	ORTWIN THE DEER	21,500	35.00	39.00
87	YEN-POH THE PANDA	21,500	35.00	40.00
88	MAMAKUU THE ELEPHANT	21,500	35.00	59.00
S. KUCK			VICTORIAN CHRISTMAS	
95	DEAR SANTA	72-DAY	35.00	35.00
S. KUCK			VICTORIAN MOTHER'S DAY	
89	MOTHER'S SUNSHINE	YR	35.00	65.00
90	REFLECTION OF LOVE	YR	35.00	37.00
91	A PRECIOUS TIME	YR	35.00	37.00
91	BOUQUETS OF LOVE	YR	35.00	37.00
92	LOVING TOUCH	YR	35.00	35.00
92	TO BE ANNOUNCED	YR	35.00	35.00
E. BERKE				WESTERN
74	MOUNTAIN MAN	1000	165.00	180.00
C. CORCILIUS			WOMEN OF THE PLAINS	
94	NO BOURDENES	36-DAY	29.50	32.00
94	PRIDE OF A MAIDEN	36-DAY	29.50	32.00

REECE

	*			WATERFOWL
73	MALLARDS & WOOD DUCKS (PAIR)	900	250.00	375.00
74	CANVASBACK & CANADIAN GEESE (PAIR)	900	250.00	375.00
75	PINTAILS & TEAL (PAIR)	900	250.00	425.00

REED & BARTON

	*	'TWAS THE NIGHT BEFORE CHRISTMAS		
89	'TWAS THE NIGHT BEFORE CHRISTMAS	4000	75.00	85.00
90	VISIONS OF SUGARPLUMS	3500	75.00	85.00
91	AWAY TO THE WINDOW	3500	74.00	79.00
	*			AUDUBON
70	PINE SISKIN	5000	60.00	175.00
71	RED-SHOULDERED HAWK	5000	60.00	75.00
72	STILT SANDPIPER	5000	60.00	70.00
73	RED CARDINAL	5000	60.00	65.00
74	BOREAL CHICKADEE	5000	65.00	75.00
75	YELLOW-BREASTED CHAT	5000	65.00	75.00
76	BAY-BREASTED WARBLER	5000	65.00	75.00
77	PURPLE FINCH	5000	65.00	75.00

YR NAME	LIMIT	ISSUE	QUOTE

RHODES STUDIO

BOUNTIFUL HARVEST

YR NAME	LIMIT	ISSUE	QUOTE
92 BASKET FULL OF APPLES	OP	39.00	120.00
92 BUSHEL OF PEACHES	OP	39.00	65.00
93 FRESH OFF THE PLUM TREE	OP	39.00	50.00
93 PEARS FROM THE GROVE	OP	39.00	65.00

LEGENDARY STEAM TRAINS

89 AMERICAN STANDARD 4-4-0	OP	65.00	89.00
90 BEST FRIEND/CHARLESTON 0-4-OT	OP	70.00	110.00
90 HUDSON J3 STREAMLINER 4-6-4	OP	65.00	92.00
90 THE CHALLENGER CLASS 4-6-6-4	OP	70.00	110.00
91 THE K-28 2-8-2	OP	70.00	100.00
91 THE K4 CLASS 4-6-2	OP	70.00	125.00

MIRACLES OF LIGHT

92 NATIVITY OF HOPE	OP	90.00	90.00
92 NATIVITY OF JOY	OP	90.00	90.00
92 NATIVITY OF LOVE	OP	85.00	90.00
92 NATIVITY OF PEACE	OP	85.00	90.00
93 NATIVITY OF FAITH	OP	90.00	90.00
93 NATIVITY OF PRAISE	OP	90.00	90.00

TREASURES OF THE DORE BIBLE

86 MOSES/TEN COMMANDMENTS	OP	59.00	59.00
87 JACOB AND THE ANGEL	OP	59.00	59.00
87 REBEKAH AT THE WELL	OP	64.00	70.00
88 DANIEL IN THE LION'S DEN	OP	64.00	65.00
88 ELIJAH AND/CHARIOT OF FIRE	OP	64.00	75.00
88 JUDGMENT OF SOLOMON	OP	64.00	64.00

VILLAGE LIGHTS

93 CHURCH AT THE BEND	OP	54.00	54.00
93 EVERGREEN BOOKS	OP	54.00	54.00
93 HOLLY STREET BAKERY	OP	49.00	49.00
93 KRINGLE'S GENERAL STORE	OP	54.00	54.00
93 MISTLETOE TOY SHOP	OP	49.00	49.00
93 MRS. SUGARPLUM'S CHOCOLATES	OP	54.00	54.00

WATERFOWL LEGACY

91 MALLARD'S DESCENT	OP	69.00	120.00
92 IN FLIGHT	OP	69.00	100.00
92 TAKING OFF	OP	74.00	135.00
92 WIND RIDERS	OP	74.00	150.00
93 FLYING IN	OP	74.00	125.00
93 RISING UP	OP	74.00	74.00

RICHARD DI SILVIO STUDIO

R. DISILVIO

92 COLUMBUS DISCOVERY OF AMERICA	2000	29.95	29.95

R. DISILVIO   **PANTHEON OF COMPOSERS**

92 GIACOMO PUCCINI	YR	29.95	29.95
92 GIOACCHINO ROSSINI	YR	29.95	29.95
92 LUDWIG VAN BEETHOVEN	YR	29.95	29.95
92 WOLFGANG A. MOZART	YR	29.95	29.95
93 FRANZ LISZT	YR	29.95	29.95
93 GIUSEPPE VERDI	YR	29.95	29.95
93 PETER TEHACKOVSKY	YR	29.95	29.95
93 RICHARD WAGNER	YR	29.95	29.95

R. DISILVIO   **WEDDING COLLECTION**

93 KISS OF ETERNAL LOVE	10000	29.95	29.95

RIVER SHORE

R. BROWN   **BABY ANIMALS**

79 AKIKU	20,000	50.00	80.00
80 ROOSEVELT	20,000	50.00	90.00
81 CLOVER	20,000	50.00	65.00
82 ZUELA	20,000	50.00	65.00

ROCKWELL/ BROWN   **FAMOUS AMERICANS**

76 BROWN'S LINCOLN	9500	40.00	40.00
77 ROCKWELL'S TRIPLE SELF-PORTRAIT	9500	45.00	45.00
78 PEACE CORPS	9500	45.00	45.00
79 SPIRIT OF LINDBERGH	9500	50.00	50.00

E. CHRISTOPHERSON   **LITTLE HOUSE ON THE PRAIRIE**

85 A BELL FOR WALNUT GROVE	10-DAY	29.50	45.00
85 CAROLINE'S EGGS	10-DAY	29.50	45.00
85 FOUNDER'S DAY PICNIC	10-DAY	29.50	50.00
85 INGALL'S FAMILY	10-DAY	29.50	45.00
85 MARY'S GIFT	10-DAY	29.50	45.00
85 MEDICINE SHOW	10-DAY	29.50	45.00
85 THE SWEETHEART TREE	10-DAY	29.50	45.00
85 WOMEN'S HARVEST	10-DAY	29.50	45.00

YR NAME	LIMIT	ISSUE	QUOTE
M. HAGUE		**LOVABLE TEDDIES**	
85 BEARLY FRIGHTFUL	10-DAY	21.50	21.50
85 BEDTIME BLUES	10-DAY	21.50	21.50
85 CAUGHT IN THE ACT	10-DAY	21.50	21.50
85 FIRESIDE FRIENDS	10-DAY	21.50	21.50
85 HARVEST TIME	10-DAY	21.50	21.50
85 MISSED A BUTTON	10-DAY	21.50	21.50
85 SUNDAY STROLL	10-DAY	21.50	21.50
85 TENDER LOVING BEAR	10-DAY	21.50	21.50
N. ROCKWELL		**NORMAN ROCKWELL SINGLE ISSUE**	
79 SPRING FLOWERS	17,000	75.00	145.00
80 LOOKING OUT TO SEA	17,000	75.00	130.00
82 GRANDPA'S GUARDIAN	17,000	80.00	80.00
82 GRANDPA'S TREASURES	17,000	80.00	80.00
J. LAMB		**PUPPY PLAYTIME**	
87 DOUBLE TAKE	14-DAY	24.50	32.00-35.00
87 FUN AND GAMES	14-DAY	24.50	29.50
88 A NEW LEASH ON LIFE	14-DAY	24.50	29.50
88 CABIN FEVER	14-DAY	24.50	24.50
88 CATCH OF THE DAY	14-DAY	24.50	24.50
88 GETTING ACQUAINTED	14-DAY	24.50	24.50
88 HANGING OUT	14-DAY	24.50	24.50
88 WEEKEND GARDENER	14-DAY	24.50	24.50
N. ROCKWELL		**ROCKWELL FOUR FREEDOMS**	
81 FREEDOM OF SPEECH	17,000	65.00	65.00
82 FREEDOM FROM FEAR	17,000	65.00	65.00
82 FREEDOM FROM WANT	17,000	65.00	65.00
82 FREEDOM OF WORSHIP	17,000	65.00	65.00
* *		**SIGNS OF LOVE**	
81 A KISS FOR MOTHER	OP	18.50	8.00
81 A WATCHFUL EYE	OP	21.50	6.00
82 A GENTLE PERSUASION	OP	23.50	5.00
83 A PROTECTIVE EMBRACE	OP	23.50	8.00
83 A TENDER COAXING	OP	23.50	8.00
84 A REASSURING TOUCH	OP	23.50	8.00
85 A LOVING GUIDANCE	OP	26.50	14.00
85 A TRUSTING HUG	OP	26.50	34.00
D. CROOK		**WE THE CHILDREN**	
87 THE FREEDOM OF SPEECH	14-DAY	24.50	24.50
88 CRUEL AND UNUSUAL PUNISHMENT	14-DAY	24.50	24.50
88 QUARTERING OF SOLDIERS	14-DAY	24.50	24.50
88 RIGHT TO BEAR ARMS	14-DAY	24.50	24.50
88 RIGHT TO VOTE	14-DAY	24.50	24.50
88 SELF INCRIMINATION	14-DAY	24.50	24.50
88 TRIAL BY JURY	14-DAY	24.50	24.50
88 UNREASONABLE SEARCH AND SEIZURE	14-DAY	24.50	24.50

ROCKWELL SOCIETY

YR NAME	LIMIT	ISSUE	QUOTE
N. ROCKWELL		**A MIND OF HER OWN**	
86 SITTING PRETTY	150-DAY	24.90	25.00
87 BREAKING THE RULES	150-DAY	27.90	30.00
87 GOOD INTENTIONS	150-DAY	27.90	25.00
87 SERIOUS BUSINESS	150-DAY	24.90	25.00
88 KISS AND TELL	150-DAY	29.90	30.00
88 ON MY HONOR	150-DAY	29.90	30.00
88 SECOND THOUGHTS	150-DAY	27.90	28.00
88 WORLD'S AWAY	150-DAY	27.90	28.00
* *		**AMERICAN DREAM**	
86 YOUNG MAN'S DREAM	OP	22.90	20.00
* *		**CHRISTMAS**	
92 THE CHRISTMAS SURPRISE	OP	32.90	44.00
93 THE TREE BRIGADE	OP	32.90	39.00
94 CHRISTMAS MARVEL	OP	32.90	32.90
74 SCOTTY GETS HIS TREE	YR	24.50	90.00
75 ANGEL WITH BLACK EYE	YR	24.50	34.00
76 GOLDEN CHRISTMAS	YR	24.50	35.00
77 TOY SHOP WINDOW	YR	24.50	25.00
78 CHRISTMAS DREAM	YR	24.50	24.00
79 SOMEBODY'S UP THERE	YR	24.50	24.00
80 SCOTTY PLAYS SANTA	YR	24.50	28.00
81 WRAPPED UP IN CHRISTMAS	YR	25.50	25.00
82 CHRISTMAS COURTSHIP	YR	25.50	26.00
83 SANTA IN THE SUBWAY	YR	25.50	26.00
84 SANTA IN THE WORKSHOP	YR	27.50	28.00
85 GRANDPA PLAYS SANTA	YR	27.50	28.00
86 DEAR SANTY CLAUS	YR	27.90	27.00
87 SANTA'S GOLDEN GIFT	YR	29.90	30.00

"Bah Humbug" *says old Mr. Scrooge to Tiny Tim. The Disney plate is from the "Mickey's Christmas Carol" series distributed by The Bradford Exchange.*

Blue Boy Woody *is a dapper dandy from cartoonist Walter Lantz. The piece was produced by Armstrong's.*

This bas-relief plate, Santa's Workshop, *was inspired by the art of Norman Rockwell. It is one issue in the "Rockwell's Christmas Legacy" series produced by The Bradford Exchange.*

Is the Santa Fe *picking up speed or rolling into the train station? The work was created by Jim Deneen for Artaffects.*

YR	NAME	LIMIT	ISSUE	QUOTE
88	SANTA CLAUS	YR	29.90	30.00
89	JOLLY OLD ST. NICK	YR	29.90	30.00
90	A CHRISTMAS PRAYER	YR	29.90	30.00
91	SANTA'S HELPERS	YR	32.90	33.00
★ ★			**CHRISTMAS LEGACY**	
92	SANTA'S WORKSHOP	OP	49.90	49.90
93	FILLING EVERY STOCKING	OP	54.90	54.90
93	MAKING A LIST	OP	49.90	49.90
93	SANTA'S MAGICAL VIEW	OP	54.90	54.90
93	VISIONS OF SANTA	OP	54.90	54.90
93	WHILE SANTA SLUMBERS	OP	54.90	54.90
★ ★			**COLONIALS-THE RAREST ROCKWELLS**	
86	UNEXPECTED PROPOSAL	OP	27.90	27.00
85	UNEXPECTED PROPOSAL	150-DAY	27.90	31.00
86	LIGHT FOR THE WINTER	150-DAY	30.90	38.00
86	WORDS OF COMFORT	150-DAY	27.90	28.00
87	CLINCHING THE DEAL	150-DAY	30.90	31.00
87	PORTRAIT FOR A BRIDEGROOM	150-DAY	30.90	31.00
87	THE JOURNEY HOME	150-DAY	30.90	31.00
88	SIGN OF THE TIMES	150-DAY	32.90	33.00
88	YE GLUTTON	150-DAY	32.90	33.00
★ ★			**COLONIALS:THE RAREST ROCKWELLS**	
87	LIGHT FOR THE WINTER	OP	30.90	31.00
N. ROCKWELL			**COMING OF AGE**	
90	A NEW LOOK	150-DAY	32.90	35.00
90	BACK TO SCHOOL	150-DAY	29.90	30.00
90	HER FIRST FORMAL	150-DAY	32.90	40.00
90	HOME FROM CAMP	150-DAY	29.90	30.00
90	THE MUSCLEMAN	150-DAY	32.90	33.00
91	A BALCONY SEAT	150-DAY	32.90	33.00
91	DOORWAY TO THE PAST	150-DAY	34.90	49.00
91	MEN ABOUT TOWN	150-DAY	34.90	35.00
91	PATHS OF GLORY	150-DAY	34.90	35.00
91	SCHOOL'S OUT!	150-DAY	34.90	60.00
★ ★			**GOLDEN MOMENTS**	
88	GRANDMA'S LOVE	OP	19.90	30.00
N. ROCKWELL			**HERITAGE**	
77	TOY MAKER	YR	14.50	100.00
78	COBBLER	YR	19.50	70.00
79	LIGHTHOUSE KEEPER'S DAUGHTER	YR	19.50	26.00
80	SHIP BUILDER	YR	19.50	42.00
81	MUSIC MAKER	YR	19.50	42.00
82	TYCOON	YR	19.50	35.00
83	PAINTER	YR	19.50	30.00
84	STORYTELLER	YR	19.50	31.00
85	GOURMET	YR	19.50	30.00-36.00
86	PROFESSOR	YR	22.90	32.00
87	SHADOW ARTIST	YR	22.90	60.00
88	THE BANJO PLAYER	YR	22.90	50.00-55.00
88	THE VETERAN	YR	22.90	53.00-60.00
90	THE OLD SCOUT	YR	24.90	32.00-55.00
91	THE FAMILY DOCTOR	YR	27.90	49
91	THE YOUNG SCHOLAR	YR	24.90	33.00
★ ★			**INNOCENCE & EXPERIENCE**	
91	THE AMERICAN HEROES	OP	32.90	35.00
91	THE MAGICIAN	OP	32.90	36.00
91	THE RADIO OPERATOR	OP	29.90	28.00
91	THE SEA CAPTAIN	OP	29.90	30.00
★ ★			**LIGHT CAMPAIGN**	
83	THE ROOM THAT LIGHT MADE	OP	19.50	20.00
★ ★			**MOTHER'S DAY**	
92	A SPECIAL DELIVERY	OP	32.90	34.00
76	A MOTHER'S LOVE	YR	24.50	75.00
77	FAITH	YR	24.50	35.00
78	BEDTIME	YR	24.50	28.00
79	REFLECTIONS	YR	24.50	25.00
80	A MOTHER'S PRIDE	YR	24.50	25.00
81	AFTER THE PARTY	YR	24.50	25.00
82	THE COOKING LESSON	YR	25.50	26.00
83	ADD TWO CUPS AND LOVE	YR	25.50	26.00
84	GRANDMA'S COURTING DRESS	YR	25.50	26.00
85	MENDING TIME	YR	27.50	28.00
86	PANTRY RAID	YR	27.90	28.00
87	GRANDMA'S SURPRISE	YR	29.90	29.00
88	MY MOTHER	YR	29.90	30.00
89	SUNDAY DINNER	YR	29.90	30.00

YR	NAME	LIMIT	ISSUE	QUOTE
90	EVENING PRAYERS	YR	29.90	30.00
91	BUILDING OUR FUTURE	YR	32.90	33.00
91	GENTLE REASSURANCE	YR	32.90	33.00
* *			**REDISCOVERED WOMEN**	
81	DREAMING IN THE ATTIC	OP	19.50	20.00
82	WAITING ON THE SHORE	OP	22.50	23.00
83	FLIRTING IN THE PARLOR	OP	22.50	23.00
83	GOSSIPING IN THE ALCOVE	OP	22.50	23.00
83	MAKING BELIEVE AT THE MIRROR	OP	22.50	23.00
83	PONDERING ON THE PORCH	OP	22.50	23.00
83	STANDING IN THE DOORWAY	OP	22.50	23.00
83	WALKING AT THE DANCE	OP	22.50	23.00
* *			**ROCKWELL HERITAGE**	
92	THE FAMILY DOCTOR	OP	27.90	43.00
93	THE JEWELER	OP	27.90	46.00
94	HALLOWEEN FROLIC	OP	27.90	27.90
95	THE APPRENTICE	OP	29.90	29.90
N. ROCKWELL			**ROCKWELL ON TOUR**	
83	PROMENADE A PARIS	150-DAY	16.00	16.00
83	WALKING THROUGH MERRIE ENGLANDE	150-DAY	16.00	16.00
83	WHEN IN ROME	150-DAY	16.00	16.00
84	DIE WALK AM RHEIN	150-DAY	16.00	16.00
N. ROCKWELL			**ROCKWELL'S AMERICAN DREAM**	
85	A COUPLE'S COMMITMENT	150-DAY	19.90	27.00
85	A FAMILY'S FULL MEASURE	150-DAY	22.90	34.00
85	A YOUNG GIRL'S DREAM	150-DAY	19.90	19.00
86	A MOTHER'S WELCOME	150-DAY	22.90	23.00
86	A YOUNG MAN'S DREAM	150-DAY	22.90	39.00
86	THE MUSICIAN'S MAGIC	150-DAY	22.90	23.00
87	AN ORPHAN'S HOPE	150-DAY	24.90	26.00
87	LOVE'S REWARD	150-DAY	24.90	35.00
N. ROCKWELL			**ROCKWELL'S GOLDEN MOMENTS**	
87	GRANDMA'S LOVE	150-DAY	19.90	44.00
87	GRANDPA'S GIFT	150-DAY	19.90	30.00
88	BEST FRIENDS	150-DAY	22.90	23.00
88	END OF DAY	150-DAY	22.90	25.00
89	EVENING'S REPOSE	150-DAY	24.90	25.00
89	KEEPING COMPANY	150-DAY	24.90	25.00
89	LOVE LETTERS	150-DAY	22.90	23.00
89	NEWFOUND WORLDS	150-DAY	22.90	23.00
N. ROCKWELL			**ROCKWELL'S LIGHT CAMPAIGN**	
83	THIS IS THE ROOM THAT LIGHT MADE	150-DAY	19.50	51.00
84	CLOSE HARMONY	150-DAY	21.50	22.00
84	EVENING'S EASE	150-DAY	19.50	20.00
84	FATHER'S HELP	150-DAY	19.50	20.00
84	GRANDPA'S TREASURE CHEST	150-DAY	19.50	20.00
84	THE BIRTHDAY WISH	150-DAY	21.50	22.00
N. ROCKWELL			**ROCKWELL'S REDISCOVERED WOMEN**	
*	COMPLETE COLLECTION	100-DAY	267.00	370.00
84	CONFIDING IN THE DEN	100-DAY	22.50	23.00
84	DREAMING IN THE ATTIC	100-DAY	19.50	30.00
84	FLIRTING IN THE PARLOR	100-DAY	22.50	35.00
84	GOSSIPING IN THE ALCOVE	100-DAY	22.50	26.00
84	MAKING BELIEVE AT THE MIRROR	100-DAY	22.50	27.00
84	MEETING ON THE PATH	100-DAY	22.50	23.00
84	PONDERING ON THE PORCH	100-DAY	22.50	26.00
84	REMINISCING IN THE QUIET	100-DAY	22.50	23.00
84	STANDING IN THE DOORWAY	100-DAY	22.50	35.00-48.00
84	WAITING AT THE DANCE	100-DAY	22.50	45.00
84	WAITING ON THE SHORE	100-DAY	22.50	24.00
84	WORKING IN THE KITCHEN	100-DAY	22.50	23.00
N. ROCKWELL			**ROCKWELL'S THE ONES WE LOVE**	
88	TENDER LOVING CARE	150-DAY	19.90	35.00
89	A TIME TO KEEP	150-DAY	19.90	27.00
89	GROWING STRONG	150-DAY	22.90	23.00
89	READY FOR THE WORLD	150-DAY	22.90	23.00
89	THE INVENTOR AND THE JUDGE	150-DAY	22.90	30.00
90	OUR LOVE OF COUNTRY	150-DAY	24.90	25.00
90	THE COUNTRY DOCTOR	150-DAY	24.90	25.00
90	THE HOMECOMING	150-DAY	24.90	22.00
90	THE STORY HOUR	150-DAY	22.90	24.00
91	A HELPING HAND	150-DAY	24.90	25.00
N. ROCKWELL			**ROCKWELL'S TREASURED MEMORIES**	
91	QUIET REFLECTIONS	150-DAY	29.90	15.00
91	ROMANTIC REVERIE	150-DAY	29.90	30.00
91	TENDER ROMANCE	150-DAY	32.90	33.00

YR NAME	LIMIT	ISSUE	QUOTE
* *		**TREASURED MEMORIES**	
91 EVENING PASSAGE	OP	32.90	33.00
91 HEAVENLY DREAMS	OP	32.90	33.00
91 SENTIMENTAL SHORES	OP	32.90	35.00

ROMAN INC.

YR NAME	LIMIT	ISSUE	QUOTE
F. HOOK		**A CHILD'S PLAY**	
82 BREEZY DAY	30-DAY	29.95	35.00
82 KITE FLYING	30-DAY	29.95	35.00
84 BATHTUB SAILOR	30-DAY	29.95	35.00
84 THE FIRST SNOW	30-DAY	29.95	35.00
F. HOOK		**A CHILD'S WORLD**	
80 LITTLE CHILDREN, COME TO ME	15,000	45.00	65.00
A. WILLIAMS		**ABBIE WILLIAMS COLLECTION**	
91 BLESS THE CHILD	OP	29.50	35.00
91 LEGACY OF LOVE	OP	29.50	35.00
I. SPENCER		**CATNIPPERS**	
86 CHRISTMAS MOURNING	9500	34.50	40.00
92 HAPPY HOLIDAZE	9500	34.50	34.50
E. SIMONETTI		**FONTANINI ANNUAL CHRISTMAS PLATE**	
86 A KING IS BORN	1986	60.00	60.00
87 O COME, LET US ADORE HIM	1987	60.00	65.00
88 ADORATION OF THE MAGI	1988	70.00	75.00
89 FLIGHT INTO EGYPT	1989	75.00	85.00
F. HOOK		**FRANCES HOOK COLLECTION-SET I**	
82 BABY BLOSSOMS	15,000	24.95	75.00
82 DAISY DREAMER	15,000	24.95	75.00
82 I WISH, I WISH	15,000	24.95	75.00
82 TREES SO TALL	15,000	24.95	75.00
F. HOOK		**FRANCES HOOK COLLECTION-SET II**	
83 CAN I KEEP HIM	15,000	24.95	50.00
83 CAUGHT IT MYSELF	15,000	24.95	50.00
83 SO CUDDLY	15,000	24.95	50.00
83 WINTER WRAPPINGS	15,000	24.95	50.00
F. HOOK		**FRANCES HOOK LEGACY**	
85 DAYDREAMING	100-DAY	19.50	23.00
85 DISAPPOINTMENT	100-DAY	22.50	26.00
85 DISCOVERY	100-DAY	22.50	26.00
85 EXPECTATION	100-DAY	22.50	26.00
85 FASCINATION	100-DAY	19.50	23.00
85 WONDERMENT	100-DAY	22.50	26.00
A. WILLIAMS		**GOD BLESS YOU, LITTLE ONE**	
91 BABY'S FIRST BIRTHDAY (BOY)	OP	29.50	35.00
91 BABY'S FIRST BIRTHDAY (GIRL)	OP	29.50	35.00
91 BABY'S FIRST SMILE	OP	19.50	25.00
91 BABY'S FIRST STEP	OP	19.50	25.00
91 BABY'S FIRST TOOTH	OP	19.50	25.00
91 BABY'S FIRST WORD	OP	19.50	25.00
A. WILLIAMS		**MARCH OF DIMES: OUR CHILDREN, OUR FUTURE**	
90 A TIME TO LAUGH	150-DAY	29.00	29.00
G. PETTY		**PRETTY GIRLS OF THE ICE CAPADES**	
83 ICE PRINCESS	30-DAY	24.50	35.00
*		**ROMAN CATS**	
84 GRIZABELLA	30-DAY	29.50	35.00
84 MR. MISTOFFELEES	30-DAY	29.50	35.00
84 RUM RUM TUGGER	30-DAY	29.50	35.00
F. HOOK		**ROMAN MEMORIAL**	
84 THE CARPENTER	YR	100.00	300.00
G. PETTY		**THE ICE CAPADES CLOWN**	
83 PRESENTING FREDDIE TRENKLER	30-DAY	24.50	35.00
A. WILLIAMS		**THE LORD'S PRAYER**	
86 AS WE FORGIVE	10-DAY	24.50	30.00
86 DELIVER US FROM EVIL	10-DAY	24.50	30.00
86 FORGIVE OUR TRESPASSES	10-DAY	24.50	30.00
86 GIVE US THIS DAY	10-DAY	24.50	30.00
86 LEAD US NOT	10-DAY	24.50	30.00
86 OUR FATHER	10-DAY	24.50	30.00
86 THINE IS THE KINGDOM	10-DAY	24.50	30.00
86 THY KINGDOM COME	10-DAY	24.50	30.00
A. WILLIAMS		**THE LOVE'S PRAYER**	
88 LOVE BELIEVES ALL THINGS	14-DAY	29.50	35.00
88 LOVE DOES NOT INSIST ON ITS OWN WAY	14-DAY	29.50	35.00
88 LOVE IS NEVER ARROGANT OR RUDE	14-DAY	29.50	35.00
88 LOVE IS NEVER IRRITABLE OR RESENTFUL	14-DAY	29.50	35.00
88 LOVE IS NEVER JEALOUS OR BOASTFUL	14-DAY	29.50	35.00
88 LOVE IS PATIENT AND KIND	14-DAY	29.50	35.00
88 LOVE NEVER ENDS	14-DAY	29.50	35.00
88 LOVE REJOICES IN THE RIGHT	14-DAY	29.50	35.00

YR	NAME	LIMIT	ISSUE	QUOTE
	A. WILLIAMS		**THE MAGIC OF CHILDHOOD**	
85	BEST BUDDIES	10-DAY	24.50	35.00
85	FEEDING TIME	10-DAY	24.50	30.00
85	GETTING ACQUAINTED	10-DAY	24.50	30.00
85	SPECIAL FRIENDS	10-DAY	24.50	30.00
86	A HANDFUL OF LOVE	10-DAY	24.50	30.00
86	LAST ONE IN	10-DAY	24.50	30.00
86	LOOK ALIKES	10-DAY	24.50	30.00
86	NO FAIR PEEKING	10-DAY	24.50	30.00
	G. DELLE NOTTI		**THE MASTERPIECE COLLECTION**	
81	THE HOLY FAMILY	5000	95.00	115.00
82	MADONNA OF THE STREETS	5000	85.00	100.00
79	ADORATION	5000	65.00	75.00
80	MADONNA WITH GRAPES	5000	87.50	100.00
	I. SPENCER		**THE SWEETEST SONGS**	
86	A BABY'S PRAYER	30-DAY	39.50	45.00
86	THIS LITTLE PIGGIE	30-DAY	39.50	45.00
88	LONG, LONG AGO	30-DAY	39.50	45.00
89	ROCKABYE	30-DAY	39.50	45.00

RORSTRAND

YR	NAME	LIMIT	ISSUE	QUOTE
	G. NYLUND		**CHRISTMAS**	
68	BRINGING HOME THE TREE	YR	12.00	520.00
69	FISHERMAN SAILING HOME	YR	13.50	20.00
70	NILS WITH HIS GEESE	YR	13.50	17.00
71	NILS IN LAPLAND	YR	15.00	20.00
72	DALECARLIAN FIDDLER	YR	15.00	21.00
73	FARM IN SMALAND	YR	16.00	60.00
74	VADSLENA	YR	19.00	41.00
75	NILS IN VASTMANLAND	YR	20.00	35.00
76	NILS IN UAPLAND	YR	20.00	55.00
77	NILS IN VARMLAND	YR	29.50	29.50
78	NILS IN FJALLBACKA	YR	32.50	50.00
79	NILS IN VAESTERGOETLAND	YR	38.50	38.50
80	NILS IN HALLAND	YR	55.00	70.00
81	NILS IN GOTLAND	YR	55.00	45.00
82	NILS AT SKANSEN	YR	47.50	40.00
83	NILS IN OLAND	YR	42.50	55.00
84	ANGERMAN LAND	YR	42.50	35.00
85	NILS IN JAMTLAND	YR	42.50	65.00
86	NILS IN KARLSKR	YR	42.50	50.00
87	CHRISTMAS	YR	47.50	160.00
88	CHRISTMAS	YR	55.00	60.00
89	NILS VISITS GOTHENBORG	YR	60.00	65.00

ROSENTHAL

*

YR	NAME	LIMIT	ISSUE	QUOTE
				CHRISTMAS
10	WINTER PEACE	YR	*	550.00
11	THREE WISE MEN	YR	*	325.00
12	STARDUST	YR	*	255.00
13	CHRISTMAS LIGHTS	YR	*	235.00
14	CHRISTMAS SONG	YR	*	350.00
15	WALKING TO CHURCH	YR	*	180.00
16	CHRISTMAS DURING WAR	YR	*	240.00
17	ANGEL OF PEACE	YR	*	200.00
18	PEACE ON EARTH	YR	*	200.00
19	ST. CHRISTOPHER WITH CHRIST CHILD	YR	*	225.00
20	MANGER IN BETHLEHEM	YR	*	325.00
21	CHRISTMAS IN MOUNTAINS	YR	*	200.00
22	ADVENT BRANCH	YR	*	200.00
23	CHILDREN IN WINTER WOODS	YR	*	200.00
24	DEER IN THE WOODS	YR	*	200.00
25	THREE WISE MEN	YR	*	200.00
26	CHRISTMAS IN MOUNTAINS	YR	*	195.00
27	STATION ON THE WAY	YR	*	200.00
28	CHALET CHRISTMAS	YR	*	185.00
29	CHRISTMAS IN ALPS	YR	*	225.00
30	GROUP OF DEER UNDER PINES	YR	*	225.00
31	PATH OF THE MAGI	YR	*	225.00
32	CHRIST CHILD	YR	*	185.00
33	THRU THE NIGHT TO LIGHT	YR	*	190.00
34	CHRISTMAS PEACE	YR	*	190.00
35	CHRISTMAS BY THE SEA	YR	*	190.00
36	NURNBERG ANGELS	YR	*	195.00
37	BERCHTESGADEN	YR	*	195.00
38	CHRISTMAS IN THE ALPS	YR	*	195.00
39	SCHNEEKOPPE MOUNTAIN	YR	*	195.00
40	MARIEN CHURCH IN DANZIG	YR	*	250.00

YR	NAME	LIMIT	ISSUE	QUOTE
41	STRASSBURG CATHEDRAL	YR	*	250.00
42	MARIANBURG CASTLE	YR	*	300.00
43	WINTER IDYL	YR	*	300.00
44	WOOD SCAPE	YR	*	300.00
45	CHRISTMAS PEACE	YR	*	400.00
46	CHRISTMAS IN AN ALPINE VALLEY	YR	*	240.00
47	DILLINGEN MADONNA	YR	*	985.00
48	MESSAGE TO THE SHEPHERDS	YR	*	875.00
49	THE HOLY FAMILY	YR	*	185.00
50	CHRISTMAS IN THE FOREST	YR	*	185.00
51	STAR OF BETHLEHEM	YR	*	450.00
52	CHRISTMAS IN THE ALPS	YR	*	195.00
53	THE HOLY LIGHT	YR	*	195.00
54	CHRISTMAS EVE	YR	*	195.00
55	CHRISTMAS IN A VILLAGE	YR	*	195.00
56	CHRISTMAS IN THE ALPS	YR	*	195.00
57	CHRISTMAS BY THE SEA	YR	*	195.00
58	CHRISTMAS EVE	YR	*	195.00
59	MIDNIGHT MASS	YR	*	195.00
60	CHRISTMAS IN A SMALL VILLAGE	YR	*	195.00
61	SOLITARY CHRISTMAS	YR	*	225.00
62	CHRISTMAS EVE	YR	*	195.00
63	SILENT NIGHT	YR	*	195.00
64	CHRISTMAS MARKET IN NUREMBERG	YR	*	225.00
65	CHRISTMAS MUNICH	YR	*	185.00
66	CHRISTMAS IN ULM	YR	*	275.00
67	CHRISTMAS IN REGINBURG	YR	*	185.00
68	CHRISTMAS IN BREMEN	YR	*	195.00
69	CHRISTMAS IN ROTHENBURG	YR	*	220.00
70	CHRISTMAS IN COLOGNE	YR	*	175.00
71	CHRISTMAS IN GARMISCH	YR	42.00	100.00
72	CHRISTMAS IN FRANCONIA	YR	50.00	95.00
73	LUBECK-HOLSTEIN	YR	77.00	105.00
74	CHRISTMAS IN WURZBURG	YR	85.00	100.00

H. DREXEL   **CLASSIC ROSE CHRISTMAS**

YR	NAME	LIMIT	ISSUE	QUOTE
71	CHRISTMAS IN GARMISCH	YR	66.00	79.00
72	CHRISTMAS IN FRANCONIA	YR	66.00	85.00
73	LUBECK-HOLSTEIN	YR	84.00	75.00
74	CHRISTMAS IN WURZBURG	YR	85.00	110.00
74	MEMORIAL CHURCH IN BERLIN	YR	84.00	200.00
75	FREIBURG CATHEDRAL	YR	75.00	105.00
76	CASTLE OF COCHEM	YR	95.00	85.00
77	HANOVER TOWN HALL	YR	125.00	125.00
78	CATHEDRAL AT AACHEN	YR	150.00	150.00
79	CATHEDRAL IN LUXENBOURG	YR	165.00	165.00
80	CHRISTMAS IN BRUSSELS	YR	190.00	190.00
81	CHRISTMAS IN TRIER	YR	190.00	190.00
82	MILAN CATHEDRAL	YR	190.00	190.00
83	CHURCH AT CASTLE WITTENBERG	YR	195.00	195.00
84	CITY HALL OF STOCKHOLM	YR	195.00	195.00
85	CHRISTMAS IN AUGSBURG	YR	195.00	195.00
86	CHRISTMAS IN AMSTERDAM	YR	210.00	210.00
87	TRADITIONAL CHRISTMAS	YR	210.00	210.00

E. HIBEL   **NOBILITY OF CHILDREN**

YR	NAME	LIMIT	ISSUE	QUOTE
76	LA CONTESSA ISABELLA	12,750	120.00	120.00
77	LA MARQUIS MAURICE-PIERRE	12,750	120.00	120.00
78	BARONESSE JOHANNA	12,750	130.00	140.00
79	CHIEF RED FEATHER	12,750	140.00	180.00

E. HIBEL   **ORIENTAL GOLD**

YR	NAME	LIMIT	ISSUE	QUOTE
76	YASUKO	2000	275.00	630.00
77	MR. OBATA	2000	275.00	425.00
78	SAKURA	2000	295.00	390.00
79	MICHIO	2000	325.00	375.00

B. WIINBLAD   **WIINBLAD CHRISTMAS**

YR	NAME	LIMIT	ISSUE	QUOTE
71	MARIA & CHILD	UD	100.00	700.00
72	CASPAR	UD	100.00	425.00
73	MELCHIOR	UD	125.00	400.00
74	BALTHAZAR	UD	125.00	200.00
75	THE ANNUNCIATION	UD	195.00	195.00
76	ANGEL WITH TRUMPET	UD	195.00	150.00
77	ADORATION OF SHEPHERDS	UD	225.00	250.00
78	ANGEL WITH HARP	UD	275.00	295.00
79	EXODUS FROM EGYPT	UD	310.00	310.00
80	ANGEL WITH GLOCKENSPIEL	UD	360.00	360.00
81	CHRIST CHILD VISITS TEMPLE	UD	375.00	375.00
82	CHRISTENING OF CHRIST	UD	375.00	435.00

YR	NAME	LIMIT	ISSUE	QUOTE

ROYAL BAYREUTH
*

				CHRISTMAS
72	CARRIAGE IN THE VILLAGE	4000	15.00	80.00
73	SCOW SCENE	4000	16.50	20.00
74	THE OLD MILL	4000	24.00	24.00
75	FOREST CHALET 'SERENITY'	4000	27.50	27.50
76	CHRISTMAS IN THE COUNTRY	5000	40.00	40.00
77	PEACE ON EARTH	5000	40.00	40.00
78	PEACEFUL INTERLUDE	5000	45.00	45.00
79	HOMEWARD BOUND	5000	50.00	50.00

ROYAL COPENHAGEN
*

				CHRISTMAS
62	THE LITTLE MERMAID	YR	11.00	160.00
16	SHEPHERD AT CHRISTMAS	YR	1.50	100.00
26	CHRISTIANSHAVN CANAL	YR	2.00	75.00
36	ROSKILDE CATHEDRAL	YR	2.50	190.00
45	A PEACEFUL MOTIF	YR	4.00	330.00
51	CHRISTMAS ANGEL	YR	5.00	280.00
13	FREDERIK CHURCH SPIRE	YR	1.50	135.00
14	HOLY SPIRIT CHURCH	YR	1.50	215.00
49	OUR LADY'S CATHEDRAL	YR	5.00	225.00
57	THE GOOD SHEPHERD	YR	8.00	85.00
58	SUNSHINE OVER GREENLAND	YR	9.00	125.00
59	CHRISTMAS NIGHT	YR	9.00	140.00
60	THE STAG	YR	10.00	90.00
11	DANISH LANDSCAPE	YR	1.00	185.00
17	OUR SAVIOR CHURCH	YR	2.00	130.00
18	SHEEP AND SHEPHERDS	YR	2.00	160.00
19	IN THE PARK	YR	2.00	110.00
21	AABENRAA MARKETPLACE	YR	2.00	65.00
23	DANISH LANDSCAPE	YR	2.00	120.00
25	CHRISTIANSHAVN	YR	2.00	100.00
29	GRUNDTVIG CHURCH	YR	2.00	140.00
32	FREDERIKSBERG GARDENS	YR	2.50	135.00
34	THE HERMITAGE CASTLE	YR	2.50	120.00
41	DANISH VILLAGE CHURCH	YR	3.00	315.00
48	NODEBO CHURCH	YR	4.50	190.00
53	FREDERIKSBERG CASTLE	YR	6.00	110.00
15	DANISH LANDSCAPE	YR	1.50	105.00
40	THE GOOD SHEPHERD	YR	3.00	285.00
47	THE GOOD SHEPHERD	YR	4.50	255.00
52	CHRISTMAS IN THE FOREST	YR	5.00	90.00
54	AMALIENBORG PALACE	YR	6.00	120.00
55	FANO GIRL	YR	7.00	155.00
56	ROSENBORG CASTLE	YR	7.00	120.00
61	TRAINING SHIP	YR	10.00	115.00
63	HOJSAGER MILL	YR	11.00	63.00
64	FETCHING THE TREE	YR	11.00	55.00
65	LITTLE SKATERS	YR	12.00	40.00
66	BLACKBIRD	YR	12.00	30.00
67	THE ROYAL OAK	YR	13.00	24.00
68	THE LAST UMIAK	YR	13.00	20.00
69	THE OLD FARMYARD	YR	14.00	22.00
70	CHRISTMAS ROSE AND CAT	YR	14.00	40.00
71	HARE IN WINTER	YR	15.00	16.00
72	IN THE DESERT	YR	16.00	20.00
73	TRAIN HOMEWARD BOUND	YR	22.00	25.00
74	WINTER TWILIGHT	YR	22.00	25.00
75	QUEEN'S PALACE	YR	27.50	25.00
77	IMMERVAD BRIDGE	YR	32.00	32.00
78	GREENLAND SCENERY	YR	35.00	35.00
79	CHOOSING CHRISTMAS TREE	YR	42.50	50.00
80	BRINGING HOME THE TREE	YR	49.50	49.50
81	ADMIRING CHRISTMAS TREE	YR	52.50	52.50
82	WAITING FOR CHRISTMAS	YR	54.50	67.00
83	MERRY CHRISTMAS	YR	54.50	54.50
84	JINGLE BELLS	YR	54.50	54.50
85	SNOWMAN	YR	54.50	59.00
86	CHRISTMAS VACATION	YR	54.50	54.50
38	ROUND CHURCH IN OSTERLARS	YR	3.00	315.00
39	GREENLAND PACK-ICE	YR	3.00	385.00
24	SAILING SHIP	YR	2.00	135.00
27	SHIP'S BOY AT TILLER	YR	2.00	140.00
30	FISHING BOATS	YR	2.50	160.00
33	FERRY AND THE GREAT BELT	YR	2.50	185.00

YR	NAME	LIMIT	ISSUE	QUOTE
35	KRONBORG CASTLE	YR	2.50	185.00
44	DANISH VILLAGE SCENE	YR	4.00	210.00
50	BOESLUNDE CHURCH	YR	5.00	225.00
20	MARY AND CHILD JESUS	YR	2.00	135.00
28	VICAR'S FAMILY	YR	2.00	75.00
31	MOTHER AND CHILD	YR	2.50	125.00
22	THREE SINGING ANGELS	YR	2.00	90.00
08	MADONNA AND CHILD	YR	1.00	2100.00
10	THE MAGI	YR	1.00	165.00
12	CHRISTMAS TREE	YR	1.00	180.00
37	MAIN STREET COPENHAGEN	YR	2.50	310.00
42	BELL TOWER	YR	4.00	270.00
43	FLIGHT INTO EGYPT	YR	4.00	550.00
46	ZEALAND VILLAGE CHURCH	YR	4.00	220.00
09	DANISH LANDSCAPE	YR	1.00	199.00
76	DANISH WATERMILL	YR	27.50	32.00
87	WINTER BIRDS	YR	59.50	59.50
88	CHRISTMAS EVE IN COPENHAGEN	YR	59.50	59.50
89	THE OLD SKATING POND	YR	59.50	69.00
90	CHRISTMAS AT TIVOLI	YR	69.50	76.00
91	THE FESTIVAL OF SANTA LUCIA	YR	69.50	69.50
93	CHRISTMAS GUESTS	YR	69.50	69.50

ROYAL CORNWALL
Y. KOUTSIS

				CREATION
77	IN HIS IMAGE	10,000	45.00	130.00
77	IN THE BEGINNING	10,000	37.50	90.00
78	ADAM'S RIB	10,000	45.00	125.00
78	BANISHED FROM EDEN	10,000	45.00	125.00
78	NOAH AND THE ARK	10,000	45.00	120.00
80	JACOB'S LADDER	10,000	45.00	75.00
80	JACOB'S WEDDING	10,000	45.00	75.00
80	JOSEPH INTERPRETS PHARAOH'S DREAM	10,000	45.00	75.00
80	JOSEPH'S COAT OF MANY COLORS	10,000	45.00	75.00
80	REBEKAH AT THE WELL	10,000	45.00	75.00
80	SODOM AND GOMORRAH	10,000	45.00	75.00
80	TOWER OF BABEL	10,000	45.00	75.00

Y. KOUTSIS

		CREATION CALHOUN CHARTER RELEASE		
77	ADAM'S RIB	19,500	29.50	100.00
77	IN HIS IMAGE	19,500	29.50	120.00
77	IN THE BEGINNING	19,500	29.50	152.00
77	NOAH AND THE ARK	19,500	29.50	90.00
78	JACOB'S LADDER	19,500	29.50	80.00
78	JACOB'S WEDDING	19,500	29.50	80.00
78	JOSEPH INTERPRETS PHARAOH'S DREAM	19,500	29.50	80.00
78	JOSEPH'S COAT OF MANY COLORS	19,500	29.50	80.00
78	REBEKAH AT THE WELL	19,500	29.50	80.00
78	SODOM AND GOMORRAH	19,500	29.50	80.00
78	TOWER OF BABEL	19,500	29.50	80.00

ROYAL DEVON
N. ROCKWELL

			ROCKWELL CHRISTMAS	
75	DOWNHILL DARING	YR	24.50	30.00
76	THE CHRISTMAS GIFT	YR	24.50	35.00
77	THE BIG MOMENT	YR	27.50	50.00
78	PUPPETS FOR CHRISTMAS	YR	27.50	27.50
79	ONE PRESENT TOO MANY	YR	31.50	31.50
80	GRAMPS MEETS GRAMPS	YR	33.00	33.00

N. ROCKWELL

			ROCKWELL MOTHER'S DAY	
75	DOCTOR AND DOLL	YR	23.50	65.00
76	PUPPY LOVE	YR	24.50	115.00
77	THE FAMILY	YR	24.50	165.00
78	MOTHER'S DAY OFF	YR	27.00	35.00
79	MOTHER'S EVENING OUT	YR	30.00	32.00
80	MOTHER'S TREAT	YR	32.50	35.00

ROYAL DOULTON
*

			FAMILY CHRISTMAS PLATES	
91	DAD PLAYS SANTA	*	60.00	60.00

ROYAL GRAFTON/THE COLLECTOR'S
M. JACKSON

			THE BEAUTY OF POLAR WILDLIFE	
91	BABY SEALS	150-DAY	27.50	35.00

ROYAL WICKFORD PORCELAIN
G. TERP

			ALICE IN WONDERLAND	
87	THE CATERPILLAR	45-DAY	29.50	48.00
87	THE DUCHESS AND COOK	45-DAY	29.50	48.00

Sports Impressions says Farewell *to 27-year baseball veteran Nolan Ryan.*

Animation artist Walter Lantz put a new spin on an old classic. Gothic Woody *is produced by Armstrong's.*

Famous for capturing the graceful beauty of his subjects, artist Fred Stone sets the pace in the area of equine art. Patience *is the first issue in his series "The Horses of Fred Stone" issued by Artaffects.*

Gone With the Wind *fans fell head over heels for Scarlett and Rhett locked in the heat of a* Fiery Embrace. *The plate is from "The Passions of Scarlett O'Hara" series produced by The Bradford Exchange.*

In creating a royal wonderland for these gentle giants of the sea, nature artist Sy Barlowe designed Palace of the Seals, *produced by Reco.*

YR	NAME	LIMIT	ISSUE	QUOTE
87	THE TEA PARTY	45-DAY	29.50	43.00
87	THE WHITE KNIGHT	45-DAY	29.50	48.00
87	TWEEDLEDEE-TWEEDLEDUM	45-DAY	29.50	29.50
88	HUMPTY DUMPTY	45-DAY	29.50	29.50
88	OFF WITH THEIR HEADS	45-DAY	29.50	29.50
88	RED AND WHITE QUEENS	45-DAY	29.50	29.50
88	TALKING FLOWERS	45-DAY	29.50	29.50
88	THE LION AND THE UNICORN	45-DAY	29.50	29.50
88	THE WHITE RABBIT	45-DAY	29.50	29.50
88	WALRUS AND CARPENTER	45-DAY	29.50	29.50

L. DUBIN | | | | **THE LIL' PEDDLERS**

YR	NAME	LIMIT	ISSUE	QUOTE
87	APPLE A DAY	YR	29.50	48.00
87	BALLOONS N' THINGS	YR	29.50	29.50
87	CHIMNEY SWEEP	YR	29.50	29.50
87	COBBLESTONE DELI	YR	29.50	29.50
87	COOLIN' OFF	YR	29.50	50.00
87	EXTRA, EXTRA	YR	29.50	50.00
87	FORGET ME NOTS	YR	29.50	50.00
87	JUST PICKED	YR	29.50	29.50
87	OVEN FRESH	YR	29.50	29.50
87	PENNY CANDY	YR	29.50	29.50
87	POPPIN' CORN	YR	29.50	29.50
87	TODAY'S CATCH	YR	29.50	29.50

ROYAL WORCESTER

P.W. BASTON | | | | **BIRTH OF A NATION**

YR	NAME	LIMIT	ISSUE	QUOTE
72	BOSTON TEA PARTY	10,000	45.00	325.00
73	PAUL REVERE	10,000	45.00	300.00
74	CONCORD BRIDGE	10,000	50.00	200.00
75	SIGNING DECLARATION	10,000	65.00	200.00
76	CROSSING DELAWARE	10,000	65.00	175.00
77	WASHINGTON'S INAUGURATION	1250	65.00	300.00

P.W. BASTON | | | | **CURRIER AND IVES PLATES**

YR	NAME	LIMIT	ISSUE	QUOTE
74	ROAD IN WINTER	5570	59.50	125.00
75	OLD GRIST MILL	3200	59.50	125.00
76	WINTER PASTIME	1500	59.50	150.00
77	HOME TO THANKSGIVING	546	59.50	200.00

P. COOPER | | | | **KITTEN CLASSICS**

YR	NAME	LIMIT	ISSUE	QUOTE
85	BIRDWATCHER	14-DAY	29.50	29.50
85	CAT NAP	14-DAY	29.50	36.00
85	COUNTRY KITTY	14-DAY	29.50	33.00
85	FIRST PRIZE	14-DAY	29.50	29.50
85	LITTLE RASCAL	14-DAY	29.50	29.50
85	PURRFECT TREASURE	14-DAY	29.50	29.50
85	TIGER'S FANCY	14-DAY	29.50	33.00
85	WILD FLOWER	14-DAY	29.50	29.50

P. COOPER | | | | **KITTEN ENCOUNTERS**

YR	NAME	LIMIT	ISSUE	QUOTE
87	BEDTIME BUDDIES	14-DAY	29.50	30.00
87	BUNNY CHASE	14-DAY	29.50	30.00
87	FISHFUL THINKING	14-DAY	29.50	54.00
87	FLUTTER BY	14-DAY	29.50	30.00
87	JUST DUCKY	14-DAY	29.50	36.00
87	PUPPY PAL	14-DAY	29.50	36.00
88	CAT AND MOUSE	14-DAY	29.50	33.00
88	STABLEMATES	14-DAY	29.50	48.00

* | | | | **SPODE MARITIME PLATES**

YR	NAME	LIMIT	ISSUE	QUOTE
80	CONSTITUTION & GUERRIRE	2000	150.00	150.00
80	CONSTITUTION & JAVA	2000	150.00	150.00
80	PELICAN & ARGUS	2000	150.00	150.00
80	PRESIDENT & LITTLE BELT	2000	150.00	150.00
80	SHANNON & CHESAPEAKE	2000	150.00	150.00
80	UNITED STATES/MACEDONIAN	2000	150.00	150.00

J. COOKE | | | | **WATER BIRDS OF NORTH AMERICA**

YR	NAME	LIMIT	ISSUE	QUOTE
85	AMERICAN PINTAILS	15,000	55.00	55.00
85	CANADA GEESE	15,000	55.00	55.00
85	CANVASBACKS	15,000	55.00	55.00
85	GREEN WINGED TEALS	15,000	55.00	55.00
85	HOODED MERGANSERS	15,000	55.00	55.00
85	MALLARDS	15,000	55.00	55.00
85	SNOW GEESE	15,000	55.00	55.00
85	WOOD DUCKS	15,000	55.00	55.00

SARAH'S ATTIC

* | | | | **CLASSROOM MEMORIES**

YR	NAME	LIMIT	ISSUE	QUOTE
91	CLASSROOM MEMORIES	6000	80.00	80.00

YR	NAME	LIMIT	ISSUE	QUOTE

SCHMID
*

A YEAR WITH PADDINGTON BEAR PLATES

YR	NAME	LIMIT	ISSUE	QUOTE
79	PYRAMID OF PRESENTS	25,000	12.50	27.50
80	SPRINGTIME	25,000	12.50	25.00
81	SANDCASTLES	25,000	12.50	22.50
82	SCHOOL DAYS	25,000	12.50	12.50

M.I. HUMMEL
CHRISTMAS

YR	NAME	LIMIT	ISSUE	QUOTE
71	ANGEL	YR	15.00	30.00
72	ANGEL WITH FLUTE	YR	15.00	25.00
73	THE NATIVITY	YR	15.00	110.00
74	THE GUARDIAN ANGEL	YR	18.50	22.50
75	CHRISTMAS CHILD	YR	25.00	25.00
76	SACRED JOURNEY	YR	27.50	45.00
77	HERALD ANGEL	YR	27.50	27.50
78	HEAVENLY TRIO	YR	32.50	32.50
79	STARLIGHT ANGEL	YR	38.00	38.00
80	PARADE INTO TOYLAND	YR	45.00	45.00
81	A TIME TO REMEMBER	YR	45.00	45.00
82	ANGELIC PROCESSION	YR	45.00	45.00
83	ANGELIC MESSENGER	YR	45.00	45.00
84	A GIFT FROM HEAVEN	YR	45.00	47.50
85	HEAVENLY LIGHT	YR	45.00	46.50
86	TELL THE HEAVENS	YR	45.00	55.00-86.00
87	ANGELIC GIFTS	YR	47.50	50.00
88	CHEERFUL CHERUBS	YR	53.00	70.00-91.00
89	ANGELIC MUSICIAN	YR	53.00	70.00
90	ANGEL'S LIGHT	YR	53.00	53.00
91	MESSAGE FROM ABOVE	YR	60.00	60.00
92	SWEET BLESSINGS	YR	65.00	65.00

L. DAVIS
DAVIS CAT TALES PLATES

YR	NAME	LIMIT	ISSUE	QUOTE
83	COMPANY'S COMING	12,500	37.50	45.00-104.00
83	FLEW THE COOP	12,500	37.50	39.00-104.00
83	ON THE MOVE	12,500	37.50	325.00-480.00
83	RIGHT CHURCH, WRONG PEW	12,500	37.50	67.50

L. DAVIS
DAVIS CHRISTMAS PLATES

YR	NAME	LIMIT	ISSUE	QUOTE
83	COUNTRY CHRISTMAS	7500	45.00	65.00
84	COUNTRY CHRISTMAS	7500	45.00	85.00
85	CHRISTMAS AT FOXFIRE FARM	7500	45.00	115.00
86	CHRISTMAS AT RED OAK	7500	45.00	160.00-220.00
87	BLOSSOM'S GIFT	7500	47.50	25.00-33.00
88	COUNTRY CHRISTMAS	7500	47.50	60.00
89	PETER AND THE WREN	7500	47.50	295.00-355.00
90	WINTERING DEER	7500	47.50	52.50
91	CHRISTMAS AT RED OAK II	7500	55.00	285.00
92	BORN ON A STARRY NIGHT	7500	55.00	55.00

L. DAVIS
DAVIS COUNTRY PRIDE PLATES

YR	NAME	LIMIT	ISSUE	QUOTE
81	PLUM TUCKERED OUT	7500	35.00	26.00-33.00
81	SURPRISE IN THE CELLAR	7500	35.00	60.00-85.00
82	BUSTIN' WITH PRIDE	7500	35.00	40.00-100.00
82	DUKE'S MIXTURE	7500	35.00	140.00-180.00

L. DAVIS
DAVIS RED OAK SAMPLER

YR	NAME	LIMIT	ISSUE	QUOTE
85	GENERAL STORE	5000	45.00	40.00-111.00
87	COUNTRY WEDDING	5000	45.00	65.00-104.00
89	COUNTRY SCHOOL	5000	45.00	30.00-65.00
90	BLACKSMITH SHOP	5000	47.50	60.00

L. DAVIS
DAVIS SPECIAL EDITION PLATES

YR	NAME	LIMIT	ISSUE	QUOTE
84	GOOD OLE DAYS PRIVY SET 2	5000	60.00	100.00
84	THE CRITICS	12,500	45.00	59.00-195.00
85	HOME FROM MARKET	7500	55.00	80.00-100.00

*
DISNEY ANNUAL

YR	NAME	LIMIT	ISSUE	QUOTE
83	SNEAK PREVIEW	20,000	22.50	22.50
84	COMMAND PERFORMANCE	20,000	22.50	22.50
85	SHOW BIZ	20,000	22.50	22.50
86	TREE FOR TWO	20,000	22.50	22.50
87	MERRY MOUSE MEDLEY	20,000	25.00	25.00
88	WARM WINTER RIDE	20,000	25.00	25.00
89	MERRY MICKEY CLAUS	20,000	32.50	32.50
90	HOLLY JOLLY CHRISTMAS	20,000	32.50	32.50
91	MICKEY AND MINNIE'S ROCKIN' CHRISTMAS	20,000	37.00	37.00

*
DISNEY CHRISTMAS

YR	NAME	LIMIT	ISSUE	QUOTE
73	SLEIGH RIDE	YR	10.00	360.00
74	DECORATING THE TREE	YR	10.00	105.00
75	CAROLING	YR	12.50	120.00
76	BUILDING A SNOWMAN	YR	13.00	23.00
77	DOWN THE CHIMNEY	YR	13.00	20.00
78	NIGHT BEFORE CHRISTMAS	YR	15.00	35.00

YR	NAME	LIMIT	ISSUE	QUOTE
79	SANTA'S SURPRISE	15,000	17.50	35.00
80	SLEIGH RIDE	15,000	17.50	35.00
81	HAPPY HOLIDAYS	15,000	17.50	22.00
82	WINTER GAMES	15,000	18.50	29.00
*			DISNEY MOTHER'S DAY	
74	FLOWERS FOR MOTHER	YR	10.00	45.00
75	SNOW WHITE & DWARFS	YR	12.50	50.00
76	MINNIE MOUSE	YR	13.00	25.00
77	PLUTO'S PALS	YR	13.00	18.00
78	FLOWERS FOR BAMBI	YR	15.00	25.00
79	HAPPY FEET	10,000	17.50	20.00
80	MINNIE'S SURPRISE	10,000	17.50	35.00
81	PLAYMATES	10,000	17.50	35.00
82	A DREAM COME TRUE	10,000	18.50	40.00
J. FERRANDIZ		FERRANDIZ BEAUTIFUL BOUNTY PORCELAIN PLATES		
82	A MID-WINTER'S DREAM	10,000	40.00	78.00
82	AUTUMN'S BLESSING	10,000	40.00	45.00
82	SPRING BLOSSOMS	10,000	40.00	40.00
82	SUMMER'S GOLDEN HARVEST	10,000	40.00	47.50
J. FERRANDIZ		FERRANDIZ MUSIC MAKERS PORCELAIN PLATES		
81	THE ENTERTAINER	10,000	25.00	25.00
81	THE FLUTIST	10,000	25.00	25.00
82	MAGICAL MEDLEY	10,000	25.00	27.50
82	SWEET SERENADE	10,000	25.00	25.00
J. FERRANDIZ		FERRANDIZ PORCELAIN CHRISTMAS PLATES		
72	CHRIST IN THE MANAGER	*	30.00	179.00
73	CHRISTMAS	*	30.00	229.00
J. FERRANDIZ		FERRANDIZ WOODEN BIRTHDAY PLATES		
72	BOY	*	15.00	150.00
72	GIRL	*	15.00	160.00
73	BOY	*	20.00	200.00
73	GIRL	*	20.00	150.00
74	BOY	*	22.00	160.00
74	GIRL	*	22.00	160.00
L. DAVIS			FRIENDS OF MINE	
89	SUNDAY WORSHIPPERS	7500	53.00	45.00-65.00
90	SUNDAY AFTERNOON TREAT	7500	53.00	50.00-75.00
91	WARM MILK	7500	55.00	55.00
92	CAT AND JENNY WREN	7500	55.00	55.00
M. LILLEMOE		KITTY CUCUMBER ANNUAL		
89	RING AROUND THE ROSIE	20,000	25.00	25.00
90	SWAN LAKE	20,000	25.00	25.00
91	TEA PARTY	2500	25.00	25.00
92	DANCE ROUND THE MAYPOLE	2500	25.00	45.00
M.I. HUMMEL			MOTHER'S DAY	
72	PLAYING HOOKY	YR	15.00	15.00
73	LITTLE FISHERMAN	YR	15.00	33.00
74	BUMBLEBEE	YR	18.50	20.00
75	MESSAGE OF LOVE	YR	25.00	29.00
76	DEVOTION FOR MOTHER	YR	27.50	30.00
77	MOONLIGHT RETURN	YR	27.50	29.00
78	AFTERNOON STROLL	YR	32.50	32.50
79	CHERUB'S GIFT	YR	38.00	38.00
80	MOTHER'S LITTLE HELPERS	YR	45.00	52.00
81	PLAYTIME	YR	45.00	52.00
82	THE FLOWER BASKET	YR	45.00	47.50
83	SPRING BOUQUET	YR	45.00	54.00
84	A JOY TO SHARE	YR	45.00	45.00
85	A MOTHER'S JOURNEY	YR	45.00	45.00
86	HOME FROM SCHOOL	YR	45.00	55.00
88	YOUNG READER	YR	52.50	81.00
89	PRETTY AS A PICTURE	YR	53.00	75.00
90	MOTHER'S LITTLE ATHLETE	YR	53.00	53.00
91	SOFT & GENTLE	YR	55.00	55.00
*		PADDINGTON BEAR/MUSICIAN'S DREAM PLATES		
83	KNOWING THE SCORE	10,000	17.50	20.00
83	PERFECT HARMONY	10,000	17.50	17.50
83	THE BEAT GOES ON	10,000	17.50	22.50
83	TICKLING THE IVORY	10,000	17.50	17.50
C. SCHULZ			PEANUTS CHRISTMAS	
72	SNOOPY GUIDES THE SLEIGH	YR	10.00	30.00
73	CHRISTMAS EVE AT DOGHOUSE	YR	10.00	100.00
74	CHRISTMAS AT FIREPLACE	YR	10.00	31.00
75	WOODSTOCK AND SANTA CLAUS	YR	12.50	14.00
76	WOODSTOCK'S CHRISTMAS	YR	13.00	19.00
77	DECK THE DOGHOUSE	YR	13.00	15.00

YR	NAME	LIMIT	ISSUE	QUOTE
78	FILLING THE STOCKING	YR	15.00	17.00
79	CHRISTMAS AT HAND	15,000	17.50	20.00
80	WAITING FOR SANTA	15,000	17.50	32.00
81	A CHRISTMAS WISH	15,000	17.50	20.00
82	PERFECT PERFORMANCE	15,000	18.50	25.00

C. SCHULZ — PEANUTS MOTHER'S DAY PLATES

YR	NAME	LIMIT	ISSUE	QUOTE
72	LINUS	*	10.00	55.00
73	MOM?	*	10.00	50.00
74	SNOOPY/WOODSTOCK/PARADE	*	10.00	45.00
75	A KISS FOR LUCY	*	12.50	40.00
76	LINUS AND SNOOPY	*	13.00	35.00
77	DEAR MOM	*	13.00	30.00
78	THOUGHTS THAT COUNT	*	15.00	25.00
79	A SPECIAL LETTER	*	17.50	22.50
80	A TRIBUTE TO MOM	*	17.50	22.50
81	MISSION FOR MOM	*	17.50	20.00
82	WHICH WAY TO MOTHER	*	18.50	18.50

C. SCHULZ — PEANUTS SPECIAL EDITION PLATE

YR	NAME	LIMIT	ISSUE	QUOTE
76	BICENTENNIAL	*	13.00	30.00

C. SCHULZ — PEANUTS VALENTINE'S DAY PLATES

YR	NAME	LIMIT	ISSUE	QUOTE
77	HOME IS WHERE THE HEART IS	*	13.00	32.50
78	HEAVENLY BLISS	*	13.00	30.00
79	LOVE MATCH	*	17.50	27.50
80	FROM SNOOPY, WITH LOVE	*	17.50	25.00
81	HEARTS-A-FLUTTER	*	17.50	20.00
82	LOVE PATCH	*	17.50	17.50

C. SCHULZ — PEANUTS WORLD'S GREATEST ATHLETE

YR	NAME	LIMIT	ISSUE	QUOTE
82	GO DEEP	10,000	17.50	25.00
82	THE CROWD WENT WILD	10,000	17.50	17.50
82	THE PUCK STOPS HERE	10,000	17.50	22.50
82	THE WAY YOU PLAY THE GAME	10,000	17.50	20.00

* RAGGEDY ANN ANNUAL PLATES

YR	NAME	LIMIT	ISSUE	QUOTE
80	THE SUNSHINE WAGON	10,000	17.50	80.00
81	THE RAGGEDY SHUFFLE	10,000	17.50	27.50
82	FLYING HIGH	10,000	18.50	18.50
83	WINNING STREAK	10,000	22.50	22.50
84	ROCKING RODEO	10,000	22.50	22.50

* RAGGEDY ANN BICENTENNIAL PLATE

YR	NAME	LIMIT	ISSUE	QUOTE
76	BICENTENNIAL PLATE	*	13.00	30.00

* RAGGEDY ANN CHRISTMAS PLATES

YR	NAME	LIMIT	ISSUE	QUOTE
75	GIFTS OF LOVE	*	12.50	45.00
76	MERRY BLADES	*	13.00	37.50
77	CHRISTMAS MORNING	*	13.00	22.50
78	CHECKING THE LIST	*	15.00	20.00
79	LITTLE HELPER	*	17.50	19.50

* RAGGEDY ANN VALENTINE'S DAY PLATES

YR	NAME	LIMIT	ISSUE	QUOTE
78	AS TIME GOES BY	*	13.00	25.00
79	DAISIES DO TELL	*	17.50	20.00

* WALT DISNEY SPECIAL EDITION PLATES

YR	NAME	LIMIT	ISSUE	QUOTE
78	MICKEY MOUSE AT FIFTY	15,000	25.00	65.00
80	HAPPY BIRTHDAY PINOCCHIO	7500	17.50	25.00
81	ALICE IN WONDERLAND	7500	17.50	17.50
82	GOOFY'S GOLDEN JUBILEE	7500	18.50	18.50
82	HAPPY BIRTHDAY PLUTO	7500	17.50	17.50
87	SNOW WHITE GOLDEN ANNIVERSARY	5000	47.50	47.50
88	MICKEY MOUSE & MINNIE MOUSE-60TH ANNIV.	10,000	50.00	95.00
89	SLEEPING BEAUTY-30TH ANNIVERSARY	5000	80.00	80.00
90	FANTASIA RELIEF PLATE	20,000	25.00	25.00
90	FANTASIA-SORCERER'S APPRENTICE	5000	59.00	59.00
90	PINOCCHIO'S FRIEND	YR	25.00	25.00

SILVER DEER LTD.
E. ERIKSEN
CHRISTMAS

YR	NAME	LIMIT	ISSUE	QUOTE
72	MAID OF COPENHAGEN	YR	16.50	37.00
73	THE FIR TREE	YR	22.00	25.00
74	THE CHIMNEY SWEEP	YR	25.00	25.00
75	THE UGLY DUCKLING	YR	27.50	27.50
77	SNOWMAN	YR	29.50	29.50
78	LAST DREAM OF THE OLD OAK TREE	YR	32.00	32.00
79	THE OLD STREET LAMP	YR	36.50	36.50
80	WILLIE WINKIE	YR	42.50	42.50
81	UTTERMOST PARTS OF THE SEA	YR	49.50	49.50
82	TWELVE BY THE MAILCOACH	YR	54.50	54.50
83	THE STORY OF THE YEAR	YR	54.50	54.50
84	THE NIGHTINGALE	YR	54.50	54.50
85	KRONBERG CASTLE	YR	60.00	60.00
86	THE BELL	YR	60.00	75.00

YR	NAME	LIMIT	ISSUE	QUOTE
87	THUMBELINA	YR	60.00	60.00
88	THE BELL DEEP	YR	60.00	60.00
89	THE OLD HOUSE	YR	60.00	60.00
90	GRANDFATHER'S PICTURE BOOK	YR	64.50	72.00
91	THE WINDMILL	YR	64.50	75.00
70	H.C. ANDERSON HOUSE	YR	14.50	39.00
71	LITTLE MATCH GIRL	YR	15.00	38.00
76	THE SNOW QUEEN	YR	27.50	27.50
*				**MOTHER'S DAY**
70	BOUQUET FOR MOTHER	*	14.50	75.00
71	MOTHER'S LOVE	*	15.00	40.00
72	GOOD NIGHT	*	16.50	35.00
73	FLOWERS FOR MOTHER	*	20.00	35.00
74	DAISIES FOR MOTHER	*	25.00	35.00
75	SURPRISE FOR MOTHER	*	27.50	27.50
76	THE COMPLETE GARDENER	*	27.50	27.50
77	LITTLE FRIENDS	*	29.50	29.50
78	DREAMS	*	32.00	32.00
79	PROMENADE	*	36.50	36.50
80	NURSERY SCENE	*	42.50	42.50
81	DAILY DUTIES	*	49.50	49.50
82	MY BEST FRIEND	*	54.50	54.50
83	AN UNEXPECTED MEETING	*	54.50	54.50
87	THE COMPLETE ANGLER	YR	60.00	60.00
88	THE LITTLE BAKERY	YR	60.00	60.00
89	SPRINGTIME	YR	60.00	60.00
90	THE SPRING EXCURSION	YR	64.50	64.50
91	WALKING AT THE BEACH	YR	64.50	64.50
84	WHO ARE YOU?	YR	54.50	54.50
86	MEETING ON THE MEADOW	YR	60.00	60.00

SPODE
R. HARM
				AMERICAN SONG BIRDS
72	SET OF TWELVE	UD	350.00	765.00

G. WEST
				CHRISTMAS
70	PARTRIDGE	UD	35.00	35.00
71	ANGEL'S SINGING	UD	35.00	35.00
72	THREE SHIPS A'SAILING	UD	35.00	38.00
73	WE THREE KINGS OF ORIENT	UD	35.00	55.00
74	DECK THE HALLS	UD	35.00	55.00
75	CHRISTBAUM	UD	45.00	45.00
76	GOOD KING WENCESLAS	UD	45.00	55.00
77	HOLLY & IVY	UD	45.00	45.00
78	WHILE SHEPHERDS WATCHED	UD	45.00	45.00
79	AWAY IN A MANGER	UD	50.00	50.00
80	BRINGING IN THE BOAR'S HEAD	UD	60.00	60.00
81	MAKE WE MERRY	UD	65.00	65.00

SPORTS IMPRESSIONS
*				*
*	JACKIE ROBINSON G/E	1956	150.00	150.00
*	MICHAEL JORDAN G/E	1991	150.00	275.00
*	MAGIC JOHNSON G/E	1991	150.00	200.00
*	TEAM USA BASKETBALL G/E	1992*	150.00	250.00

GLENICE
				CELEBRITY IMPRESSIONS
*	HULK HOGAN	5000	39.50	39.50
*	MIKE TYSON	5000	39.50	39.50

J. CATALANO
				COLLECTOVAL PLATES
90	KINGS OF K	1990	195.00	195.00
90	LIFE OF A LEGEND	1968	195.00	195.00
90	FENWAY TRADITION	1000	195.00	195.00
90	GOLDEN YEARS	1000	195.00	195.00
*				**GOLD EDITION PLATES**
89	KIRK GIBSON	2500	125.00	125.00
88	JOSE CANSECO	2500	125.00	125.00
88	YANKEE TRADITION	2500	150.00	225.00
89	MANTLE SWITCH HITTER	2401	150.00	250.00
89	OREL HERSHISER	2500	125.00	125.00
89	WILL CLARK	2500	125.00	125.00-175.00
88	PAUL MOLITOR	1000	125.00	125.00
89	DARRYL STRAWBERRY #2 G/E	3500	125.00	195.00
89	DWIGHT GOODEN	5000	125.00	125.00
89	FRANK VIOLA	2500	125.00	125.00
86	DON MATTINGLY	2500	125.00	195.00
86	WADE BOGGS	1000	125.00	150.00
88	DUKE SNIDER	1500	125.00	125.00
87	AL KALINE	1000	125.00	125.00

YR	NAME	LIMIT	ISSUE	QUOTE
88	BOB FELLER	2500	125.00	125.00
89	ALAN TRAMMELL	1000	125.00	125.00
87	LIVING TRIPLE CROWN WINNERS	1000	150.00	150.00
88	ANDRE DAWSON	1000	125.00	125.00
89	GREATEST CENTERFIELDERS	5000	150.00	150.00
89	TOM SEAVER	3311	125.00	255.00
86	KEITH HERNANDEZ	1000	125.00	175.00
86	LARRY BIRD F/S	1000	125.00	180.00
86	MICKEY MANTLE AT NIGHT U/S	CL	95.00	395.00
87	CARL YASTRZEMSKI	1500	125.00	125.00
87	DARRYL STRAWBERRY #1	CL	125.00	195.00
87	GARY CARTER	CL	125.00	150.00
87	LENNY DYKSTRA	1000	125.00	125.00
87	MICKEY, WILLIE, & DUKE H/S	1500	150.00	395.00
87	TED WILLIAMS U/S	CL	95.00	335.00
88	BROOKS ROBINSON	CL	125.00	295.00

J. CATALANO — **NFL GOLD EDITION PLATES**

YR	NAME	LIMIT	ISSUE	QUOTE
90	BOOMER ESIASON	1990	150.00	150.00
90	DAN MARINO	1990	150.00	150.00
90	JOE MONTANA	1990	150.00	150.00
90	JOHN ELWAY	1990	150.00	150.00
90	LAWRENCE TAYLOR	1990	150.00	150.00
90	RANDALL CUNNINGHAM	1990	150.00	150.00

M. PETRONELLA — **NFL PLATINUM EDITION PLATES**

YR	NAME	LIMIT	ISSUE	QUOTE
90	BOOMER ESIASON	5000	49.95	49.95
90	DAN MARINO	5000	49.95	49.95
90	JOE MONTANA	5000	49.95	49.95
90	JOHN ELWAY	5000	49.95	49.95
90	LAWRENCE TAYLOR	5000	49.95	49.95
90	RANDALL CUNNINGHAM	5000	49.95	49.95

J. CATALANO — **REGULAR EDITION PLATES**

YR	NAME	LIMIT	ISSUE	QUOTE
*	JOSE CANSECO	10,000	49.50	65.00
*	WHO'S ON FIRST	10,000	49.50	75.00
*	WILL CLARK	10,000	49.50	65.00
*	YANKEE TRADITION	10,000	49.50	65.00
*	FRANK VIOLA	10,000	49.50	65.00
*	KIRK GIBSON	10,000	49.50	65.00
*	PAUL MOLITOR	10,000	49.50	65.00
*	BABE RUTH	10,000	49.50	75.00
*	DON MATTINGLY R/E	5000	49.50	75.00
*	DUKE SNIDER	5000	49.50	75.00
*	LOU GEHRIG	10,000	49.50	75.00
*	WADE BOGGS	2000	49.50	65.00
*	AL KALINE	10,000	49.50	65.00
*	ALAN TRAMMEL	10,000	49.50	65.00
*	BOB FELLER	10,000	49.50	65.00
*	ANDRE DAWSON	10,000	49.50	65.00
*	CY YOUNG	10,000	49.50	75.00
*	HONUS WAGNER	10,000	49.50	75.00
*	LIVING TRIPLE CROWN	10,000	49.50	75.00
*	NOLAN RYAN	5000	150.00	150.00
*	R. CLEMENTE	10,000	49.50	75.00
*	TY COBB	10,000	49.50	75.00
*	B. ROBINSON	2000	49.50	75.00
*	CARL YASTRZEMSKI	3000	49.50	65.00
*	CARY CARTER	2000	49.50	65.00
*	DARRYL STRAWBERRY R/E	2000	49.50	75.00
*	DEM BUMS	10,000	49.50	75.00
*	K. HERNANDEZ	2000	49.50	65.00
*	LARRY BIRD	2000	49.50	65.00
*	LENNY DYKSTRA	2000	49.50	65.00
*	MICKEY MANTLE R/E	3500	49.50	75.00
*	MICKEY, WILLIE, DUKE F/S	3500	49.50	175.00
*	TED WILLIAMS	3000	49.50	65.00
*	THURMAN MUNSON	10,000	49.50	75.00

M. PETRONELLA — **THE GOLDEN YEARS**

YR	NAME	LIMIT	ISSUE	QUOTE
90	DUKE SNIDER	5000	60.00	60.00
90	MICKEY MANTLE	5000	60.00	60.00
90	WILLIE MAYS	5000	60.00	60.00

STUDIO COLLECTION
TOM RUBEL — **SANTA'S ANIMAL KINGDOM**

YR	NAME	LIMIT	ISSUE	QUOTE
94	SANTA'S ANIMAL KINGDOM COLLECTORS PLATE	5000	30.00	32.00

U.S. HISTORICAL SOCIETY
W. HOMER — **YOUNG AMERICA**

YR	NAME	LIMIT	ISSUE	QUOTE
73	YOUNG AMERICA OF WINSLOW HOMER-6 PLATES	2500	425.00	1100.00

YR	NAME	LIMIT	ISSUE	QUOTE

VAGUE SHADOWS

* *
PRIDE OF AMERICA'S INDIAN

YR	NAME	LIMIT	ISSUE	QUOTE
86	DARK-EYED FRIENDS	OP	24.50	20.00
86	NOBLE COMPANIONS	OP	24.50	19.00
87	KINDRED SPIRITS	OP	24.50	26.00
87	LOYAL ALLIANCE	OP	24.50	50.00
87	PEACEFUL COMMRADES	OP	24.50	36.00
87	SMALL AND WISE	OP	24.50	35.00
87	WINTER SCOUTS	OP	24.50	28.00

* *
THE CHIEFTAINS

YR	NAME	LIMIT	ISSUE	QUOTE
79	CHIEF JOSEPH	OP	65.00	105.00
79	CHIEF SITTING BULL	OP	65.00	400.00
80	CHIEF RED CLOUD	OP	65.00	119.00
80	GERONIMO	OP	65.00	82.00
81	CHIEF CRAZY HORSE	OP	65.00	140.00

VALEKH ART STUDIOS
A. KOVALEV
RUSSIAN LEGENDS

YR	NAME	LIMIT	ISSUE	QUOTE
88	THE PRINCESS/SEVEN BOGATYRS	195	29.87	60.00
88	RUSSIAN AND LUDMILLA	195	29.87	55.00
88	LUKOMORYA	195	32.87	32.87
88	THE GOLDEN COCKEREL	195	32.87	32.87
89	FISHERMAN AND THE MAGIC FISH	195	32.87	32.87
89	THE PRIEST AND HIS SERVANT	195	34.87	34.87
89	TSAR SALTAN	195	32.87	32.87
90	MOROZKO	195	36.87	36.87
90	SADKO	195	34.87	34.87
90	SILVER HOOF	195	36.87	36.87
90	STONE FLOWER	195	34.87	34.87
90	THE TWELVE MONTHS	195	36.87	36.87

VENETO FLAIR
V. TIZIANO
BELLINI

YR	NAME	LIMIT	ISSUE	QUOTE
71	MADONNA	500	45.00	400.00

*
BIRDS

YR	NAME	LIMIT	ISSUE	QUOTE
72	FALCON	2000	37.50	37.50
72	OWL	2000	37.50	100.00
73	MALLARD	2000	45.00	45.00

V. TIZIANO
CHRISTMAS

YR	NAME	LIMIT	ISSUE	QUOTE
71	THREE KINGS	1500	55.00	160.00
72	SHEPHERDS	2000	55.00	90.00
73	CHRIST CHILD	2000	55.00	55.00
74	ANGEL	*	55.00	55.00

V. TIZIANO
DOGS

YR	NAME	LIMIT	ISSUE	QUOTE
72	GERMAN SHEPHERD	2000	37.50	75.00
73	COLLIE	2000	40.00	45.00
73	DACHSHUND	2000	45.00	43.00
73	DOBERMAN	2000	37.50	35.00
73	POODLE	2000	37.50	45.00

*
EASTER

YR	NAME	LIMIT	ISSUE	QUOTE
73	RABBITS	2000	50.00	90.00
74	CHICKS	2000	50.00	55.00
75	LAMB	2000	50.00	55.00
76	COMPOSITE	2000	55.00	55.00

*
ST. MARK'S OF VENICE

YR	NAME	LIMIT	ISSUE	QUOTE
84	NOAH AND THE DOVE	UD	60.00	65.00
85	MOSES AND THE BURNING BUSH	UD	60.00	65.00
86	ABRAHAM AND THE JOURNEY	UD	60.00	66.00
86	JOSEPH AND THE COAT	UD	63.00	65.00

V. TIZIANO
WILDLIFE

YR	NAME	LIMIT	ISSUE	QUOTE
71	DEER	500	37.50	450.00
72	ELEPHANT	1000	37.50	275.00
73	PUMA	2000	37.50	65.00
74	TIGER	2000	40.00	50.00

VILETTA
*
DISNEYLAND

YR	NAME	LIMIT	ISSUE	QUOTE
76	BETSY ROSS	3000	15.00	100.00
76	CROSSING THE DELAWARE	3000	15.00	100.00
76	SIGNING THE DECLARATION	3000	15.00	100.00
76	SPIRIT OF '76	3000	15.00	100.00
79	MICKEY'S 50TH ANNIVERSARY	5000	37.00	50.00

* *
NUTCRACKER BALLET

YR	NAME	LIMIT	ISSUE	QUOTE
78	CLARA AND NUTCRACKER	OP	19.50	10.00
79	GIFT FROM GODFATHER	OP	19.50	9.00
79	SNOW KING AND QUEEN	OP	19.50	24.00
79	THE SUGARPLUM FAIRY	OP	19.50	10.00

YR	NAME	LIMIT	ISSUE	QUOTE
80	CARLA AND THE PRINCE	OP	19.50	15.00
80	WALTZ OF THE FLOWERS	OP	19.50	11.00
* ZOLAN			ZOLAN'S CHILDREN	
78	ERIK AND DANDELION	OP	19.00	240.00
79	SABRINA IN THE GRASS	OP	22.00	150.00
80	BY MYSELF	OP	24.00	24.00
81	FOR YOU	OP	24.00	24.00

VILLEROY & BOCH

C. BARKER			**FLOWER FAIRY**	
79	LAVENDER	21-DAY	35.00	125.00
80	CANDYTUFT	21-DAY	35.00	125.00
80	SWEET PEA	21-DAY	35.00	125.00
81	APPLEBLOSSOM	21-DAY	35.00	95.00
81	BLACKTHORN	21-DAY	35.00	75.00
81	HELIOTROPE	21-DAY	35.00	75.00
B. ZVORYKIN		**RUSSIAN FAIRYTALES MARIA MOREVNA**		
82	KOSHCHEY CARRIES OFF MARIA MOREVNA	27,500	70.00	81.00
82	MARIA MOREVNA AND TSAREVICH IVAN	27,500	70.00	78.00
82	TSAREVICH IVAN AND THE BEAUTIFUL CASTLE	27,500	70.00	76.00
B. ZVORYKIN		**RUSSIAN FAIRYTALES SNOW MAIDEN**		
80	THE SNOW MAIDEN	27,500	70.00	260.00
81	SNEGUROCHKA AND LEI, THE SHEPHERD BOY	27,500	70.00	100.00
81	SNEGUROCHKA AT THE COURT/TSAR BERENDEI	27,500	70.00	90.00
B. ZVORYKIN		**RUSSIAN FAIRYTALES THE FIREBIRD**		
81	IN SEARCH OF THE FIREBIRD	27,500	70.00	125.00
81	IVAN AND TSAREVNA ON THE GREY WOLF	27,500	70.00	93.00
81	THE WEDDING OF TSAREVNA ELENA THE FAIR	27,500	70.00	170.00
B. ZVORYKIN		**RUSSIAN FAIRYTALES THE RED KNIGHT**		
81	THE RED KNIGHT	27,500	70.00	90.00-135.00
81	VASSILISSA AND HER STEPSISTERS	27,500	70.00	77.00
81	VASSILISSA IS PRESENTED TO THE TSAR	27,500	70.00	100.00

W.S. GEORGE

B. LANGTON			**A LOVING LOOK: DUCK FAMILIES**	
90	FAMILY OUTING	150-DAY	34.50	35.00
91	QUIET MOMENT	150-DAY	37.50	40.00
91	SAFE AND SOUND	150-DAY	37.50	38.00
91	SLEEPY START	150-DAY	34.50	35.00
91	SPRING ARRIVALS	150-DAY	37.50	68.00
91	THE FAMILY TREE	150-DAY	37.50	50.00
* *			**ALASKA: THE LAST FRONTIER**	
92	ARCTIC JOURNEY	OP	39.50	39.50
92	DOWN THE TRAIL	OP	37.50	39.00
92	GRACEFUL PASSAGE	OP	39.50	39.50
92	MOONLIGHT LOOKOUT	OP	37.50	60.00
92	SUMMIT DOMAIN	OP	39.50	39.50
91	AUTUMN GRANDEUR	150-DAY	34.50	39.00
91	ICY MAJESTY	150-DAY	34.50	35.00
92	MOUNTAIN MONARCH	150-DAY	37.50	44.00
H. JOHNSON			**AMERICA THE BEAUTIFUL**	
88	THE GRAND CANYON	150-DAY	34.50	35.00
88	YOSEMITE FALLS	150-DAY	34.50	35.00
89	THE GREAT SMOKEY MOUNTAINS	150-DAY	37.50	38.00
89	YELLOWSTONE RIVER	150-DAY	37.50	38.00
90	ACADIA	150-DAY	37.50	39.00
90	CRATER LAKE	150-DAY	39.50	40.00
90	THE EVERGLADES	150-DAY	37.50	38.00
90	THE GRAND TETONS	150-DAY	39.50	45.00
* *			**AMERICA'S PRIDE**	
92	RUGGED SHORES	OP	29.50	45.00
93	CANYON CLIMB	OP	34.50	34.50
93	GOLDEN VISTA	OP	34.50	34.50
93	LOFTY REFLECTIONS	OP	32.50	49.00
93	MIGHTY SUMMIT	OP	32.50	35.00
93	MOUNTAIN MAJESTY	OP	34.50	35.00
93	TRANQUIL QATERS	OP	32.50	65.00
M. MCDONALD			**ART DECO**	
89	A FLAPPER WITH GREYHOUNDS	150-DAY	39.50	47.00
90	ARRIVING IN STYLE	150-DAY	39.50	50.00
90	ON THE TOWN	150-DAY	39.50	75.00
90	TANGO DANCERS	150-DAY	39.50	83.00
L. LIU			**BASKET BOUQUETS**	
92	IRISES	OP	32.50	32.50
92	LILLIES	OP	32.50	32.50
92	PANSIES	OP	29.50	29.50
92	PARROT TULIPS	OP	32.50	32.50

YR	NAME	LIMIT	ISSUE	QUOTE
92	PEONIES	OP	32.50	32.50
92	TULIPS AND LILACS	OP	32.50	32.50
93	BEGONIAS	OP	32.50	32.50
93	CALLA LILLIES	OP	32.50	32.50
93	HYDRANGEAS	OP	32.50	32.50
93	MAGNOLIAS	OP	32.50	32.50
93	ORCHIDS	OP	32.50	32.50
**			**BELOVED HYMNS OF CHILDHOOD**	
90	LOVING SHEPHERS OF THY SHEEP	OP	34.50	35.00
88	AWAY IN A MANGER	150-DAY	29.50	40.00
88	THE LORD'S MY SHEPHERD	150-DAY	29.50	50.00
89	ALL GLORY, LAUD AND HONOUR	150-DAY	32.50	33.00
89	I LOVE TO HEAR THE STORY	150-DAY	32.50	35.00
89	LOVE DIVINE	150-DAY	32.50	32.00
89	NOW THANK WE ALL OUR GOD	150-DAY	32.50	32.00
90	ALL PEOPLE ON EARTH DO DWELL	150-DAY	34.50	35.00
W. RANE			**BLESSED ARE THE CHILDREN**	
90	I AM THE GOOD SHEPHERD	150-DAY	29.50	49.00
90	LET THE/CHILDREN COME TO ME	150-DAY	29.50	39.00
91	BLESSED ARE THE PEACEMAKERS	150-DAY	34.50	55.00
91	HOSANNA IN THE HIGHEST	150-DAY	32.50	40.00
91	I AM THE VINE, YOU ARE THE BRANCHES	150-DAY	34.50	60.00
91	JESUS HAD COMPASSION ON THEM	150-DAY	32.50	45.00
91	LET THE LITTLE CHILDREN COME TO ME	150-DAY	29.50	35.00
91	SEEK AND YOU WILL FIND	150-DAY	34.50	42.00
91	WHOEVER WELCOMES THIS LITTLE CHILD	150-DAY	32.50	44.00
**			**BONDS OF LOVE**	
92	TREASURED KISSES	OP	32.50	40.00
94	ENDEARING WHISPERS	OP	32.50	40.00
89	PRECIOUS EMBRACE	150-DAY	29.50	30.00
90	CHERISHED MOMENT	150-DAY	29.50	30.00
91	TENDER CARESS	150-DAY	32.50	35.00
92	LOVING TOUCH	150-DAY	32.50	36.00
L. KAATZ		**CLASSIC WATERFOWL: THE DUCKS UNLIMITED**		
88	GEESE IN THE AUTUMN FIELDS	150-DAY	36.50	36.50-69.00
88	MALLARDS AT SUNRISE	150-DAY	36.50	38.00
89	CANVASBACKS, BREAKING AWAY	150-DAY	39.50	40.00
89	GREEN WINGS/MORNING MARSH	150-DAY	39.50	40.00
89	PINTAILS IN INDIAN SUMMER	150-DAY	39.50	39.50
90	WOOD DUCKS TAKING FLIGHT	150-DAY	39.50	40.00
**		**COLUMBUS DISCOVERS AMERICA: THE 500TH ANNIVERSARY**		
92	BRINGING TOGETHER TWO CULTURES	OP	32.50	32.00
92	THE QUEEN'S APPROVAL	OP	32.50	51.00
92	TREASURES FROM THE NEW WORLD	OP	32.50	92.00
92	ASHORE AT DAWN	150-DAY	29.50	42.00
92	COLUMBUS RAISES THE FLAG	150-DAY	32.50	32.00
92	UNDER FULL SAIL	150-DAY	29.50	29.50
G. KURZ			**COUNTRY BOUQUETS**	
91	GARDEN'S BOUNTY	150-DAY	32.50	35.00
91	MORNING SUNSHINE	150-DAY	29.50	49.00
91	SUMMER PERFUME	150-DAY	29.50	49.00
91	WARM WELCOME	150-DAY	32.50	49.00
M. HARVEY			**COUNTRY NOSTALGIA**	
89	THE APPLE CIDER PRESS	150-DAY	32.50	40.00
89	THE OLD HAND PUMP	150-DAY	32.50	54.00
89	THE SPRING BUGGY	150-DAY	29.50	30.00
89	THE VINTAGE SEED PLANTER	150-DAY	29.50	40.00
90	THE ANTIQUE SPINNING WHEEL	150-DAY	34.50	39.00
90	THE DAIRY CANS	150-DAY	32.50	33.00
90	THE FORGOTTEN PLOW	150-DAY	34.50	39.00
90	THE WOODEN BUTTER CHURN	150-DAY	32.50	44.00
**		**CRITIC'S CHOICE: GONE WITH THE WIND**		
92	SCARLETT GETS HER WAY	OP	32.50	50.00
92	SCARLETT'S GETS DOWN TO BUSINESS	OP	34.50	34.50
92	SCARLETT'S SHOPPING SPREE	OP	32.50	32.50
92	THE BUGGY RIDE	OP	32.50	32.50
92	THE SMITTEN SUITOR	OP	32.50	45.00
93	AT CROSS PURPOSES	OP	34.50	34.50
93	SCARLETT'S HEART IS W/TARA	OP	34.50	34.50
91	"MARRY ME, SCARLETT!"	150-DAY	27.50	33.00
91	A DECLARATION OF LOVE	150-DAY	30.50	36.00
91	MARRY ME, SCARLETT	150-DAY	27.50	49.00
91	SCARLETT ASKS A FAVOR	150-DAY	30.50	47.00
91	THE PARIS HAT	150-DAY	30.50	49.00
91	WAITING FOR RHETT	150-DAY	27.50	52.00

YR	NAME	LIMIT	ISSUE	QUOTE
G. BUSH			**DR. ZHIVAGO**	
90	ZHIVAGO AND LARA	150-DAY	39.50	40.00
91	LARA'S LOVE	150-DAY	39.50	60.00
91	LOVE POEMS FOR LARA	150-DAY	39.50	40.00
91	ZHIVAGO AND LARA	150-DAY	39.50	45.00
91	ZHIVAGO SAYS FAREWELL	150-DAY	39.50	45.00
* *			**FIELD BIRDS OF NORTH AMERICA**	
92	SEASON'S END:WILLOW PTARMIGAN	OP	42.50	60.00
* *			**FIELD BIRDS OF NORTH AMERICA**	
92	AUTUMN MOMENT:AM. WOODCOCK	OP	42.50	55.00
91	AUTUMN MOMENT: AMERICAN WOOD	150-DAY	42.50	42.50
91	IN DISPLAY: RUFFED GOOSE	150-DAY	39.50	41.00
91	MISTY CLEARING: WILD TURKEY	150-DAY	42.50	85.00
91	WINTER COLORS: RING-NECKED PHEASANT	150-DAY	39.50	47.00
D. BUSH			**FIELD BRIDS OF NORTH AMERICA**	
91	MORNING LIGHT: BOBWHITE QUAIL	150-DAY	42.50	50.00
G. KURZ			**FLOWERS FROM GRANDMA'S GARDEN**	
90	COUNTRY CUTTINGS	150-DAY	24.50	45.00
90	THE MORNING BOUQUET	150-DAY	24.50	40.00
91	A COUNTRY WELCOME	150-DAY	29.50	55.00
91	GARDENER'S DELIGHT	150-DAY	27.50	50.00
91	HARVEST IN THE MEADOW	150-DAY	27.50	40.00
91	HOMESPUN BEAUTY	150-DAY	27.50	35.00
91	NATURE'S BOUNTY	150-DAY	27.50	45.00
91	THE SPRINGTIME ARRANGEMENT	150-DAY	29.50	54.00
V. MORLEY			**FLOWERS OF YOUR GARDEN**	
88	CHRYSANTHEMUMS	150-DAY	27.50	28.00
88	DAISIES	150-DAY	27.50	37.00
88	LILACS	150-DAY	24.50	45.00
88	PEONIES	150-DAY	27.50	27.00
88	ROSES	150-DAY	24.50	33.00
89	DAFFODILS	150-DAY	27.50	28.00
89	IRISES	150-DAY	29.50	34.00
89	TULIPS	150-DAY	29.50	29.00
C. GILLIES			**GARDEN OF THE LORD**	
92	LOVE ONE ANOTHER	150-DAY	29.50	29.50
* *			**GENTLE BEGINNINGS**	
92	FIRST STEPS	OP	37.50	50.00
92	HAPPY TOGETHER	OP	37.50	55.00
91	A TOUCH OF LOVE	150-DAY	34.50	40.00
91	LAP OF LOVE	150-DAY	37.50	42.00
91	TENDER LOVING CARE	150-DAY	34.50	43.00
91	UNDER WATCHFUL EYES	150-DAY	37.50	40.00
R. COBANE			**GLORIOUS SONGBIRDS**	
91	BALTIMORE ORIOLES/AUTUMN LEAVES	150-DAY	34.50	50.00
91	BLUEBIRDS IN A BLUEBERRY BUSH	150-DAY	34.50	35.00
91	CARDINALS ON A SNOW BRANCH	150-DAY	29.50	30.00
91	CARDINALS ON A SNOWY BRANCH	150-DAY	29.50	35.00
91	CEDAR WAXWING/WINTER BERRIES	150-DAY	32.50	34.00
91	CHICKADEES AMONG THE LILACS	150-DAY	32.50	33.00
91	GOLDFINCHES IN/THISTLE	150-DAY	32.50	33.00
91	INDIGO BUNTINGS AND/BLOSSOMS	150-DAY	29.50	30.00
91	ROBINS WITH DOGWOOD IN BLOOM	150-DAY	34.50	45.00
* *			**GOLDEN AGE OF THE CLIPPER SHIP**	
89	TWILIGHT UNDER FULL SAIL	OP	29.50	30.00
* *		**GONE WITH THE WIND: GOLDEN ANNIVERSARY**		
90	SCARLETT & RHETT'S HONEYMOON	OP	32.50	47.00
88	SCARLETT AND ASHLEY AFTER THE WAR	150-DAY	27.50	60.00
88	SCARLETT AND HER SUITORS	150-DAY	24.50	55.00
88	THE BURNING OF ATLANTA	150-DAY	24.50	55.00
88	THE PROPOSAL	150-DAY	27.50	75.00
89	A QUESTION OF HONOR	150-DAY	29.50	47.00
89	FRANKLY MY DEAR	150-DAY	29.50	63.00
89	HOME TO TARA	150-DAY	27.50	45.00
89	MELANIE AND ASHLEY	150-DAY	32.50	35.00
89	SCARLETT'S RESOLVE	150-DAY	29.50	47.00
89	STROLLING IN ATLANTA	150-DAY	27.50	44.00
90	A TOAST TO BONNIE BLUE	150-DAY	32.50	50.00
P. JENNIS		**GONE WITH THE WIND: THE PASSIONS OF SCARLETT O'HARA**		
92	FIERY EMBRACE	150-DAY	29.50	65.00
92	PRIDE AND PASSION	150-DAY	29.50	62.00
C. FRACE			**GRAND SAFARI**	
92	IMAGES OF AFRICA	150-DAY	29.50	29.50
* *			**HEART OF THE WILD**	
91	A GENTLE TOUCH	OP	29.50	50.00
92	AN AFTERNOON TOGETHER	OP	32.50	50.00
92	QUIET TIME?	OP	32.50	59.00

YR	NAME	LIMIT	ISSUE	QUOTE
E. DZENIS		**HOLLYWOOD'S GLAMOUR GIRLS**		
89	JEAN HARLOW-DINNER AT EIGHT	150-DAY	29.50	34.00
90	CAROLE LOMBAR/THE GAY BRIDE	150-DAY	29.50	30.00
90	GRETA GARBO-IN GRAND HOTEL	150-DAY	29.50	30.00
90	LANA TURNER-POSTMAN RINGS TWICE	150-DAY	29.50	30.00
L. LIU		**HUMMINGBIRD TREASURY**		
92	ANNA'S HUMMINGBIRD	OP	29.50	29.50
92	THE RUBY-THROATED HUMMINGBIRD	OP	29.50	29.50
92	THE RUFOUS HUMMINGBIRD	OP	32.50	32.50
92	VIOLET-CROWNED HUMMINGBIRD	OP	32.50	32.50
93	BROAD-BILLED HUMMINGBIRD	OP	34.50	34.50
93	CALLIOPE HUMMINGBIRD	OP	34.50	34.50
93	THE ALLEN'S HUMMINGBIRD	OP	34.50	34.50
93	WHITE-EARED HJUMMINGBIRD	OP	32.50	32.50
W. NELSON		**LAST OF THEIR KIND: THE ENDANGERED SPECIES**		
88	THE PANDA	150-DAY	27.50	40.00
88	THE SNOW LEOPARD	150-DAY	27.50	36.00
89	THE ASIAN ELEPHANT	150-DAY	30.50	31.00
89	THE RED WOLF	150-DAY	30.50	31.00
90	THE BLACK-FOOTED FERRET	150-DAY	33.50	34.00
90	THE BRIDLED WALLABY	150-DAY	30.50	31.00
90	THE SIBERIAN TIGER	150-DAY	33.50	34.00
90	THE SLENDER-HORNED GAZELLE	150-DAY	30.50	31.00
91	PRZEWALSKI'S HORSE	150-DAY	33.50	34.00
91	THE VICUNA	150-DAY	33.50	34.00
L. LIU		**LENA LIU'S BASKET BOUQUETS**		
92	ROSES	150-DAY	29.50	29.50
**		**NATURE'S LEGACY**		
91	MT. RANIER/TWILIGHT REFLECTIONS	OP	27.50	22.00
90	BLUE SNOW AT HALF DOME	150-DAY	24.50	28.00
91	AUTUMN SPLENDOR IN THE SMOKEY MTNS.	150-DAY	27.50	28.00
91	GOLDEN MAJESTY/ROCKY MOUNTAINS	150-DAY	29.50	35.00
91	HAVASU CANYON	150-DAY	27.50	28.00
91	MISTY MORNING/MT. MCKINLEY	150-DAY	24.50	25.00
91	MOUNT RANIER	150-DAY	27.50	27.50
91	RADIANT SUNSET OVER THE EVERGLADES	150-DAY	29.50	32.00
91	WINTER PEACE IN YELLOWSTONE PARK	150-DAY	29.50	28.00
C. FRACE		**NATURE'S LOVABLES**		
90	THE KOALA	150-DAY	27.50	41.00
91	BABY HARP SEAL	150-DAY	30.50	41.00
91	BANDIT	150-DAY	32.50	44.00
91	BOBCAT: NATURE'S DAWN	150-DAY	30.50	40.00
91	CHINESE TREASURE	150-DAY	27.50	28.00
91	CLOUDED LEOPARD	150-DAY	32.50	33.00
91	NEW ARRIVAL	150-DAY	27.50	39.00
91	ZEBRA FOAL	150-DAY	32.50	40.00
**		**NATURE'S PLAYMATES**		
92	AMBASSADORS	OP	36.50	70.00
92	PEACE ON ICE	OP	36.50	65.00
92	PLAYMATES	OP	34.50	64.00
92	SURPRISE	OP	34.50	123.00
91	DOUBLE TROUBLE	150-DAY	32.50	44.00
91	PALS	150-DAY	32.50	45.00
91	PARTNERS	150-DAY	29.50	43.00
91	RECESS	150-DAY	32.50	33.00
91	SECRET HEIGHTS	150-DAY	29.50	45.00
92	CURIOUS TRIO	150-DAY	34.50	50.00
L. LIU		**NATURE'S POETRY**		
89	MORNING SERENADE	150-DAY	24.50	45.00
89	SONG OF PROMISE	150-DAY	24.50	44.00
90	GENTLE REFRAIN	150-DAY	27.50	29.00
90	MELODY AT DAYBREAK	150-DAY	29.50	30.00
90	MORNING CHORUS	150-DAY	27.50	34.00
90	NATURE'S HARMONY	150-DAY	27.50	45.00
90	TENDER LULLABY	150-DAY	27.50	28.00
91	CHERUB CHORALE	150-DAY	32.50	55.00
91	DELICATE ACCORD	150-DAY	29.50	32.00
91	LYRICAL BEGINNINGS	150-DAY	29.50	32.00
91	MOTHER'S MELODY	150-DAY	32.50	40.00
91	SONG OF SPRING	150-DAY	32.50	35.00
L. LIU		**ON GOSSAMER WINGS**		
88	MALACHITES	150-DAY	27.50	28.00
88	MONARCH BUTTERFLIES	150-DAY	24.50	34.00
88	RED-SPOTTED PURPLE	150-DAY	27.50	29.00
88	WESTERN TIGER SWALLOWTAILS	150-DAY	24.50	35.00
88	WHITE PEACOCKS	150-DAY	27.50	35.00

Artist P. Buckley Moss captures the simplistic pleasures of Amish life in Family Outing, *the first issue in "The Family Collection" produced by Anna Perenna.*

This merry duo strikes a chord with collectors. Fiddlers Two, *by artist P. Buckley Moss, is the first issue in "The Children Collection" series.*

Valentine Joy was produced as a M.I. Hummel Club exclusive available to members only.

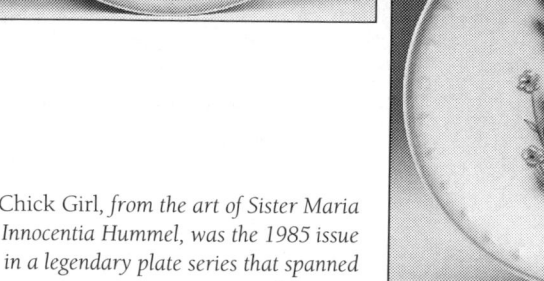

Chick Girl, from the art of Sister Maria Innocentia Hummel, was the 1985 issue in a legendary plate series that spanned 25 years.

YR	NAME	LIMIT	ISSUE	QUOTE
89	EASTERN TAILED BLUES	150-DAY	27.50	28.00
89	RED ADMIRALS	150-DAY	29.50	30.00
89	ZEBRA SWALLOWTAILS	150-DAY	29.50	30.00
* *				**ON THE WING**
92	GLORIOUS ASCENT	OP	32.50	60.00
92	TAKING WING	OP	32.50	45.00
92	UPWARD BOUND	OP	32.50	32.50
93	WONDROUS MOTION	OP	34.50	34.50
92	RISING MALLARD	150-DAY	29.50	45.00
92	WINGED SPLENDOR	150-DAY	29.50	30.00
* *				**ON WINGS OF SNOW**
91	THE COCKATOOS	OP	37.50	37.50
92	THE HERONS	OP	37.50	37.50
91	THE DOVES	150-DAY	34.50	79.00
91	THE EGRETS	150-DAY	37.50	58.00
91	THE PEACOCKS	150-DAY	37.50	53.00
91	THE SWANS	150-DAY	34.50	40.00
91	THE SWANS	150-DAY	34.50	40.00
C. BRENDERS				**OUR WOODLAND FRIENDS**
89	FASCINATION	150-DAY	29.50	30.00
90	BENEATH THE PINES	150-DAY	29.50	30.00
90	HIGH ADVENTURE	150-DAY	32.50	33.00
90	SHY EXPLORERS	150-DAY	32.50	39.00
91	A JUMP INTO LIFE: SPRING FAWN	150-DAY	34.50	32.00
91	FOREST SENTINEL: BOBCAT	150-DAY	34.50	40.00
91	FULL HOUSE FOX FAMILY	150-DAY	32.50	54.00
91	GOLDEN SEASON: GRAY SQUIRREL	150-DAY	32.50	35.00
* *				**PORTRAITS OF CHRIST**
92	FOLLOW ME	OP	34.50	57.00
92	FOR GOD SO LOVED THE WORLD	OP	34.50	72.00
92	I AM THE WAY, THE TRUTH & THE LIFE	OP	34.50	73.00
92	WEEP NOT FOR ME	OP	34.50	63.00
91	BECOME AS LITTLE CHILDREN	150-DAY	32.50	60.00
91	FATHER, FORGIVE THEM	150-DAY	29.50	75.00
91	LO, I AM WITH YOU	150-DAY	32.50	54.00
91	PEACE I LEAVE WITH YOU	150-DAY	34.50	35.00
91	THIS IS MY BELOVED SON	150-DAY	32.50	58.00
91	THY WILL BE DONE	150-DAY	29.50	51.00
C. BRENDERS				**PORTRAITS OF EXQUISITE BIRDS**
90	BACKYARD TREASURE-CHICKADEE	150-DAY	29.50	30.00
90	THE BEAUTIFUL BLUEBIRD	150-DAY	29.50	30.00
91	IVORY-BILLED WOODPECKER	150-DAY	32.50	33.00
91	RED-WINGED BLACKBIRD	150-DAY	32.50	33.00
91	SUMMER GOLD: THE ROBIN	150-DAY	32.50	33.00
91	THE MEADOWLARK'S SONG	150-DAY	32.50	33.00
D. SCHWARTZ				**PUREBRED HORSES OF THE AMERICAS**
89	THE APPALOOSA	150-DAY	34.50	36.00
89	THE TENNESSEE WALKER	150-DAY	34.50	35.00
90	THE MORGAN	150-DAY	37.50	65.00
90	THE MUSTANG	150-DAY	37.50	39.00
90	THE QUARTERHORSE	150-DAY	37.50	38.00
90	THE SADDLEBRED	150-DAY	37.50	45.00
C. SMITH				**ROMANTIC GARDENS**
89	THE PLANTATION GARDEN	150-DAY	29.50	30.00
89	THE WOODLAND GARDEN	150-DAY	29.50	30.00
90	THE COLONIAL GARDEN	150-DAY	32.50	33.00
90	THE COTTAGE GARDEN	150-DAY	32.50	40.00
V. MORLEY				**ROMANTIC ROSES**
93	COUNTRY CHARM	OP	32.50	32.50
93	OLD-FASHIONED GRACE	OP	29.50	29.50
93	PASTORAL DELIGHT	OP	32.50	32.50
93	SPRINGTIME ELEGANCE	OP	34.50	34.50
93	SUMMER ROMANCE	OP	32.50	32.50
93	VICTORIAN BEAUTY	OP	29.50	29.50
93	VINTAGE SPLENDOR	OP	34.50	34.50
* *				**SCENES OF CHRISTMAS PAST**
92	FAMILY TRADITIONS	OP	32.50	33.00
93	HOLIDAY PAST	OP	32.50	45.00
94	A GATHERING OF FAITH	OP	32.50	32.50
87	HOLIDAY SKATERS	150-DAY	27.50	34.00
88	CHRISTMAS EVE	150-DAY	27.50	30.00
89	THE HOMECOMING	150-DAY	30.50	31.00
90	THE TOY STORE	150-DAY	30.50	31.00
91	THE CAROLLERS	150-DAY	30.50	31.00
C. FRACE				**SOARING MAJESTY**
91	FREEDOM	150-DAY	29.50	30.00

YR	NAME	LIMIT	ISSUE	QUOTE
91	PEREGRINE FALCON	150-DAY	32.50	33.00
91	RED-TAILED HAWK	150-DAY	32.50	33.00
91	THE GOLDEN EAGLE	150-DAY	34.50	45.00
91	THE GYRFALCON	150-DAY	34.50	50.00
91	THE NORTHERN GOSHHAWK	150-DAY	29.50	40.00
91	THE OSPRAY	150-DAY	32.50	34.00
92	RED-SHOULDERED HAWK	150-DAY	34.50	35.00
* *			**SONNETS IN FLOWERS**	
92	SONNET OF HAPPINESS	OP	34.50	44.00
92	SONNET OF LOVE	OP	34.50	35.00
92	SONNET OF PEACE	OP	34.50	55.00
92	SONNET OF BEAUTY	150-DAY	34.50	35.00
J. SIAS			**SPIRIT OF CHIRSTMAS**	
90	SILENT NIGHT	150-DAY	29.50	33.00
91	DECK THE HALLS	150-DAY	32.50	44.00
91	I'LL BE HOME FOR CHRISTMAS	150-DAY	32.50	45.00
91	JINGLE BELLS	150-DAY	29.50	30.00
J. SIAS			**SPIRIT OF CHRISTMAS**	
91	O CHRISTMAS TREE	150-DAY	32.50	35.00
91	WINTER WONDERLAND	150-DAY	32.50	37.00
L. LIU		**SYMPHONY OF SHIMMERING BEAUTIES**		
91	IRIS QUARTET	150-DAY	29.50	50.00
91	LILY CONCERTO	150-DAY	32.50	55.00
91	PEONY PRELUDE	150-DAY	32.50	49.00
91	POPPY PASTORALE	150-DAY	32.50	32.00
91	ROSE FANTASY	150-DAY	34.50	35.00
91	TULIP ENSEMBLE	150-DAY	29.50	35.00
* *		**SYMPHONY OF SHIMMERING BEAUTY**		
91	HIBISCUS MEDLEY	OP	34.50	34.50
92	CARNATION SERENADE	OP	36.50	36.50
92	DAHLIA MELODY	OP	34.50	34.50
92	GLADIOLUS ROMANCE	OP	36.50	36.50
92	HOLLYHOCK MARCH	OP	34.50	34.50
92	ZINNIA FINALE	OP	36.50	36.50
* *			**THE CHRISTMAS STORY**	
92	GIFTS OF THE MAGI	OP	29.50	29.50
93	ADORATION OF THE SHEPHERDS	OP	29.50	29.50
93	JOURNEY OF THE MAGI	OP	29.50	29.50
93	REST ON THE FLIGHT INTO EGYPT	OP	29.50	29.50
93	THE ANNUNCIATION	OP	29.50	29.50
93	THE NATIVITY	OP	29.50	29.50
* *			**THE DUCKS UNLIMITED**	
88	CANADA GEESE/AUTUMN FIELDS	OP	36.50	37.00
90	BLUEBILLS COMING IN	OP	41.50	42.00
90	PINTAILS IN INDIAN SUMMER	OP	39.50	40.00
90	SNOW GEESE AGAINST NOV. SKIES	OP	41.50	40.00
* *			**THE ELEGANT BIRDS**	
88	SNOWY EGRET	OP	35.50	36.00
88	GREAT BLUE HERON	150-DAY	32.50	33.00
88	THE SWAN	150-DAY	32.50	33.00
89	SNOWY EGRET	150-DAY	32.50	35.00-45.00
89	THE ANHINGA	150-DAY	35.50	36.00
89	THE FLAMINGO	150-DAY	35.50	36.00
90	SANDHILL AND WHOOPING CRANE	150-DAY	35.50	36.00
* *			**THE ENDANGERED SPECIES**	
89	THE RED WOLF	OP	30.50	31.00
91	THE VICUNA	OP	33.50	34.00
N. ANDERSON		**THE FEDERAL DUCK STAMP PLATE COLLECTION**		
90	CANVASBACKS	150-DAY	30.50	38.00
90	MALLARD	150-DAY	27.50	55.00
90	THE LESSER SCAUP	150-DAY	27.50	42.00
90	THE RUDDY DUCKS	150-DAY	30.50	31.00
91	CINNAMON TEAL	150-DAY	32.50	33.00
91	FULVOUS WISTLING DUCK	150-DAY	32.50	59.00
91	PINTAILS	150-DAY	30.50	35.00
91	SNOW GOOSE	150-DAY	32.50	35.00
91	THE REDHEADS	150-DAY	32.50	55.00
91	WIGEONS	150-DAY	30.50	31.00
C. VICKERY		**THE GOLDEN AGE OF THE CLIPPER SHIPS**		
89	THE BLUE JACKET AT SUNSET	150-DAY	29.50	30.00
89	THE TWILIGHT UNDER FULL SAIL	150-DAY	29.50	29.50-51.00
89	YOUNG AMERICA, HOMEWARD	150-DAY	32.50	33.00
90	DAVY CROCKET AT DAYBREAK	150-DAY	32.50	37.00
90	FLYING CLOUD	150-DAY	32.50	33.00
90	GOLDEN EAGLE CONQUERS WIND	150-DAY	32.50	35.00
90	SEA WITCH, MISTRESS/OCEANS	150-DAY	34.50	38.00

YR	NAME	LIMIT	ISSUE	QUOTE
90	THE LIGHTNING IN LIFTING FOG	150-DAY	34.50	35.00

THE MAJESTIC HORSE

YR	NAME	LIMIT	ISSUE	QUOTE
92	REGAL SPIRIT:THE ARABIAN	OP	34.50	48.00
92	WESTERN: AM. PAINT HORSE	OP	34.50	74.00
92	AMERICAN GOLD: THE QUARTERHORSE	150-DAY	34.50	36.00
92	CLASSIC BEAUTY: THOROUGHBRED	150-DAY	34.50	35.00

J. BRIDGETT — THE SECRET WORLD OF THE PANDA

YR	NAME	LIMIT	ISSUE	QUOTE
90	A MOTHER'S CARE	150-DAY	27.50	28.00
91	A BAMBOO FEAST	150-DAY	32.50	70.00
91	A DAY OF EXPLORING	150-DAY	30.50	31.00
91	A FROLIC IN THE SNOW	150-DAY	27.50	28.00
91	A GENTLE HUG	150-DAY	32.50	33.00
91	LAZY AFTERNOON	150-DAY	30.50	31.00

THE SOUND OF MUSIC: SILVER ANNIVERSARY

YR	NAME	LIMIT	ISSUE	QUOTE
92	MARIA'S WEDDING DAY	OP	32.50	50.00
91	THE HILLS ARE ALIVE	150-DAY	29.50	34.00
92	LET'S START AT THE VERY BEGINNING	150-DAY	29.50	39.00
92	SOMETHING GOOD	150-DAY	32.50	45.00

A. CASAY — THE VANISHING GENTLE GIANTS

YR	NAME	LIMIT	ISSUE	QUOTE
91	JUMPING FOR JOY	150-DAY	32.50	35.00
91	MONARCH OF THE DEEP	150-DAY	35.50	44.00
91	SONG OF THE HUMPBACK	150-DAY	32.50	34.00
91	TRAVELERS OF THE SEA	150-DAY	35.50	66.00
91	UNICORN OF THE SEA	150-DAY	35.50	55.00
91	WHITE WHALE OF THE NORTH	150-DAY	35.50	54.00

THE WORLD'S MOST MAGNIFICENT CATS

YR	NAME	LIMIT	ISSUE	QUOTE
92	SIBERIAN TIGER	OP	31.50	70.00
92	THE CHEETAH	OP	31.50	55.00
91	COUGAR	150-DAY	24.50	68.00
91	FLEETING ENCOUNTER	150-DAY	24.50	49.00
91	JAGUAR	150-DAY	27.50	42.00
91	MIGHTY WARRIOR	150-DAY	29.50	50.00
91	POWERFUL PRESENCE	150-DAY	27.50	59.00
91	ROYAL BENGAL	150-DAY	27.50	39.00
91	THE AFRICAN LEOPARD	150-DAY	29.50	49.00
91	THE CLOUDED LEOPARD	150-DAY	29.50	60.00

TOMORROW'S PROMISE

YR	NAME	LIMIT	ISSUE	QUOTE
92	FRISKINESS: KIT FOXES	OP	32.50	45.00
92	INNOCENCE: RHINOS	OP	32.50	35.00
92	PLAYTIME PANDAS	OP	29.50	40.00
92	CURIOSITY: ASIAN ELEPHANTS	150-DAY	29.50	55.00

R. STINE — TREASURY OF SONGBIRDS

YR	NAME	LIMIT	ISSUE	QUOTE
92	MORNING'S GLORY	150-DAY	29.50	30.00
92	SPRINGTIME SPLENDOR	150-DAY	29.50	50.00

H. BONNER — VICTORIAN CAT

YR	NAME	LIMIT	ISSUE	QUOTE
90	MISCHIEF WITH THE HATBOX	150-DAY	24.50	50.00
91	DAYDREAMS	150-DAY	27.50	35.00
91	FRISKY FELINES	150-DAY	27.50	40.00
91	KITTENS AT PLAY	150-DAY	27.50	46.00
91	PERFECTLY POISED	150-DAY	29.50	60.00
91	PLAYING IN THE PARLOR	150-DAY	29.50	51.00
91	STRING QUARTET	150-DAY	24.50	50.00
92	MIDDAY REPOSE	150-DAY	29.50	45.00

WINTER'S MAJESTY

YR	NAME	LIMIT	ISSUE	QUOTE
92	THE CHASE	OP	34.50	34.50
92	THE QUEST	OP	34.50	34.50
93	ALASKAN FRIEND	OP	34.50	34.50
93	AMERICAN COUGAR	OP	34.50	34.50
93	ON WATCH	OP	34.50	34.50
93	SOLITUDE	OP	34.50	34.50

R. HARM — WONDERS OF THE SEA

YR	NAME	LIMIT	ISSUE	QUOTE
91	A FAMILY AFFAIR	150-DAY	34.50	35.00
91	HEART TO HEART	150-DAY	34.50	35.00
91	STAND BY ME	150-DAY	34.50	35.00
91	STAND BY ME	150-DAY	34.50	40.00
91	WARM EMBRACE	150-DAY	34.50	45.00

WALLACE SILVERSMITHS

'TIS THE SEASON

YR	NAME	LIMIT	ISSUE	QUOTE
93	A TIME FOR TRADITION	OP	29.50	29.50
93	A WORLD DRESSED IN SNOW	OP	29.50	29.50
93	WE SHALL COME REJOICING	OP	29.50	29.50

A BLACK TIE AFFAIR: THE PENGUIN

YR	NAME	LIMIT	ISSUE	QUOTE
92	BABY-SITTERS	OP	29.50	29.50
92	LITTLE EXPLORER	OP	29.50	30.00
92	PENGUIN PARADE	OP	29.50	29.50
93	BELLY FLOPPING	OP	29.50	29.50

YR	NAME	LIMIT	ISSUE	QUOTE
**		A DELICATE BALANCE:VANISHING WILDLIFE		
92	TOMORROW'S HOPE	OP	29.50	29.50
93	EYES ON THE NEW DAY	OP	32.50	32.50
93	PRESENT DREAMS	OP	32.50	32.50
93	TODAY'S FUTURE	OP	29.50	29.50
**		A TREASURY OF SONGBIRDS		
92	AFTERNOON CALM	OP	32.50	32.50
92	DAWN'S RADIANCE	OP	32.50	32.50
92	GOLDEN DAYBREAK	OP	32.50	33.00
93	ALLURING DAYLIGHT	OP	34.50	34.50
93	SAPPHIRE DAWN	OP	34.50	34.50
93	SCARLET SUNRISE	OP	34.50	34.50
**		ALONG AN ENGLISH LANE		
93	COTTAGE AROUND THE BEND	OP	29.50	29.50
93	FRIENDS AND FLOWERS	OP	29.50	29.50
93	GREETING THE DAY	OP	29.50	29.50
93	SUMMER'S BRIGHT WELCOME	OP	29.50	29.50
**		AMERIC'A PRIDE		
92	MISTY FJORDS	OP	29.50	62.00
**		BABY CATS OF THE WILD		
92	MORNING MISCHIEF	OP	29.50	29.50
93	NAP TIME	OP	32.50	32.50
93	THE BUDDY SYSTEM	OP	32.90	32.90
93	TOGETHERNESS	OP	29.50	29.50
**		BEAR TRACKS		
92	DENAIL FAMILY	OP	29.50	29.50
93	ALONG THE ICE FLOW	OP	29.50	29.50
93	BREAKING COVER	OP	29.50	29.50
93	HEAVY GOING	OP	29.50	29.50
93	HIGH COUNTRY CHAMPION	OP	29.50	29.50
93	THEIR FIRST SEASON	OP	29.50	29.50
**		ENCHANTED GARDENS		
93	A PEACEFUL RETREAT	OP	24.50	24.50
93	A PLACE TO DREAM	OP	24.50	24.50
93	PLEASANT PATHWAYS	OP	24.50	24.50
93	TRANQUIL HIDEAWAY	OP	24.50	24.50
**		EYES OF THE WILD		
93	EYES IN THE MIST	OP	29.50	29.50
93	EYES IN THE PINES	OP	29.50	29.50
93	EYES IN THE SNOW	OP	29.50	29.50
93	EYES OF GOLD	OP	29.50	29.50
93	EYES OF SILENCE	OP	29.50	29.50
93	EYES OF STRENGTH	OP	29.50	29.50
93	EYES OF WONDER	OP	29.50	29.50
93	EYES ON THE SLY	OP	29.50	29.50
**		FELINE FANCY		
93	GLOBETROTTERS	OP	34.50	39.00
93	LITTLE ATHLETES	OP	34.50	34.50
93	THE GEOGRAPHERS	OP	34.50	34.50
93	YOUNG ADVENTURERS	OP	34.50	34.50
**		FLORAL FANCIES		
93	SITTING PINK	OP	34.50	34.50
93	SITTING PRETTY	OP	34.50	34.50
93	SITTING SOFTLY	OP	34.50	34.50
93	SITTING SUNNY	OP	34.50	34.50
L. LIU		FLOWER FAIRIES		
93	ARMOROUS ANGELS	OP	32.50	32.50
93	DELICATE DANCERS	OP	32.50	32.50
93	FANCIFUL FAIRIES	OP	34.50	34.50
93	MAGIC MAKERS	OP	29.50	29.50
93	MINIATURE MERMAIDS	OP	34.50	34.50
93	MISCHIEF MASTERS	OP	32.50	32.50
93	PETAL PLAYMATES	OP	29.50	29.50
93	WINGED WONDERS	OP	34.50	34.50
**		GARDENS OF PARADISE		
92	SERENITY	OP	29.50	29.50
92	TRANQUILITY	OP	29.50	29.50
93	BEAUTY	OP	32.50	32.50
93	ELEGANCE	OP	32.50	32.50
93	GRANDEUR	OP	32.50	32.50
93	HARMONY	OP	32.50	32.50
93	MAJESTY	OP	32.50	32.50
93	SPLENDOR	OP	32.50	32.50
**		GRAND SAFARI:IMAGES OF AFRICA		
92	A MOMENT'S REST	OP	34.50	34.50
92	ELEPHANT'S OF KILIMANJARO	OP	34.50	34.50

YR	NAME	LIMIT	ISSUE	QUOTE
92	UNDIVIDED ATTENTION	OP	37.50	37.50
93	LONE HUNTER	OP	37.50	37.50
93	QUIET TIME IN SAMBURU	OP	37.50	37.50
93	THE GREATER KUDO	OP	37.50	37.50
**			**HOMETOWN MEMORIES**	
93	A WINTER RIDE	OP	29.50	29.50
93	HEADING HOME	OP	29.50	29.50
93	MOONLIGHT SKATERS	OP	29.50	29.50
93	MOUNTAIN SLEIGH RIDE	OP	29.50	29.50
**			**LITTLE ANGELS**	
92	ANGELS WE HAVE HEARD ON HIGH	OP	29.50	48.00
92	O TANNENBAUM	OP	29.50	60.00
93	HARK THE HERALD ANGELS SING	OP	32.50	32.50
93	IT CAME UPON A MIDNIGHT CLEAR	OP	32.50	32.50
93	JOY TO THE WORLD	OP	32.50	33.00
93	THE FIRST NOEL	OP	32.50	32.50
**			**MELODIES IN THE MIST**	
93	AMONG THE DEWDROPS	OP	34.50	34.50
93	EARLY MORNING RAIN	OP	34.50	34.50
93	FEEDING TIME	OP	37.50	37.50
93	SPRING RAIN	OP	37.50	37.50
93	THE GARDEN PARTY	OP	37.50	37.50
93	UNPLEASANT SURPRISE	OP	37.50	37.50
**			**MEMORIES OF A VICTORIAN CHILDHOOD**	
92	AN ARMFUL OF TREASURES	OP	32.50	60.00
92	SWEET SLUMBER	OP	29.50	55.00
92	THROUGH THICK AND THIN	OP	32.50	50.00
92	YOU'D BETTER NOT POUT	OP	29.50	29.00
93	A TRIO OF BOOKWORMS	OP	32.50	57.00
93	PUGNACIOUS PLAYMATE	OP	32.50	57.00
**			**ON GOLDEN WINGS**	
93	AS DAY BREAKS	OP	32.50	32.50
93	DAYLIGHT FLIGHT	OP	32.50	32.50
93	EARLY RISERS	OP	29.50	29.50
93	FIRST LIGHT	OP	32.90	32.90
93	MORNING LIGHT	OP	29.50	29.50
93	WINTER DAWN	OP	32.50	32.50
**			**ON THE WING**	
93	ON THE WING	OP	34.50	34.50
93	SPRINGING FORTH	OP	34.50	34.50
**			**PETER PALS**	
92	FLOWERING FASCINATION	OP	24.50	24.50
92	GARDEN DISCOVERY	OP	24.50	24.50
93	ALLURING LILLIES	OP	24.50	24.50
93	BLOSSOMING ADVENTURE	OP	24.50	24.50
93	DANCING DAFFODILS	OP	24.50	24.50
93	MORNING MELODY	OP	24.50	24.50
93	OUR FAMILY TREE	OP	29.50	29.50
93	SPRINGTIME OASIS	OP	24.50	24.50
93	SUMMER SURPRISE	OP	24.50	24.50
**			**POETIC COTTAGES**	
92	BEDFORDSHIRE EVENING SKY	OP	32.50	32.50
92	GARDEN PATHS OF OXFORDSHIRE	OP	29.50	50.00
92	STONWALL BROOK BLOSSOMS	OP	32.50	32.50
92	TWILIGHT AT WOODGREEN POND	OP	29.50	65.00
93	ALDERBURY GARDENS	OP	32.50	32.50
93	HAMPSHIRE SPRING SPLENDOR	OP	32.50	32.50
93	WISTERIA SUMMER	OP	32.50	32.50
93	WITTSHIRE ROSE ARBOR	OP	32.50	32.50
**			**RARE ENCOUNTERS**	
93	BLACK MAGIC	OP	29.50	29.50
93	FUTURE SONG	OP	32.50	32.50
93	HIGH AND MIGHTY	OP	32.50	32.50
93	LAST SANCTUARY	OP	32.50	32.50
93	SOFTLY, SOFTLY	OP	29.50	29.50
93	SOMETHING STIRRED	OP	34.50	34.50
C. VICKERY			**ROMANTIC HARBORS**	
93	ADVENT OF THE GOLDEN BOUGH	OP	34.50	34.50
93	CHRISTMAS TREE SCHOONER	OP	34.50	34.50
93	PRELUDE TO THE JOURNEY	OP	34.50	34.50
93	SHIMMERING LIGHT OF DUSK	OP	34.50	34.50
**			**SPIRITS OF THE SKY**	
92	EVENING GLIMMER	OP	32.50	32.50
92	FIRST LIGHT	OP	29.50	29.50
92	GOLDEN DUSK	OP	32.50	32.50
92	TWILIGHT GLOW	OP	29.50	40.00

YR	NAME	LIMIT	ISSUE	QUOTE
93	AMBER FIGHT	OP	34.50	34.50
93	DAY'S END	OP	34.50	34.50
93	SUNSET SPLENDOR	OP	32.50	32.50
93	WINGED RADIANCE	OP	34.50	34.50
* *			THE FACES OF NATURE	
92	CANYON OF THE CAT	RT	29.50	50.00
92	WOLFE RIDGE	OP	29.50	29.50
93	TRAIL OF THE TALISMAN	OP	29.50	29.50
93	TWO BEARS CAMP	OP	29.50	29.50
93	WAMBLI OKIYE	OP	29.50	29.50
93	WINTERING WITH THE WAPITI	OP	29.50	29.50
93	WITHIN SUNRISE	OP	29.50	29.50
93	WOLFPACK OF THE ANCIENTS	OP	29.50	29.50
* *			THE PASSIONS OF SCARLETT O'HARA	
92	AS GOD IS MY WITNESS	OP	34.50	55.00
92	DREAMS OF ASHLEY	OP	32.50	64.00
92	THE FOND FAREWELL	OP	32.50	44.00
92	THE WALTZ	OP	32.50	60.00
93	BRAVE SCARLETT	OP	34.50	34.50
93	DANGEROUS ATTRACTION	OP	36.50	36.50
93	EVENING PRAYERS	OP	34.50	34.50
93	NAPTIME	OP	36.50	36.50
93	NIGHTMARE	OP	34.50	34.50
93	THE END OF AN ERA	OP	36.50	36.50
* *			TOUCHING THE SPIRIT	
93	CAMP OF THE SACRED DOGS	OP	29.50	29.50
93	HE WHO WATCHES	OP	29.50	29.50
93	KEEPER OF THE SECRET	OP	29.50	29.50
93	KINDRED SPIRITS	OP	29.50	29.50
93	RUNNING WITH THE WIND	OP	29.50	29.50
93	THE MARKING TREE	OP	29.50	29.50
93	TWICE TRAVELED TRAIL	OP	29.50	29.50
93	WAKAN TANKA	OP	29.50	29.50
* *			VICTORIAN CAT CAPERS	
92	A CURIOUS KITTY	OP	27.50	55.00
92	FORBIDDEN FRUIT	OP	29.50	29.50
92	MY BOWL IS EMPTY	OP	27.50	36.00
92	PUSS IN BOOT	OP	24.50	62.00
92	VANITY FAIR	OP	27.50	27.50
92	WHO'S THE FAIREST OF THEM ALL?	OP	24.50	68.00
93	THE KITTEN EXPRESS	OP	29.50	29.50
93	THE PURR-FECT PEN PAL	OP	29.50	29.50
* *			WILD INNOCENTS	
93	LION CLUB	OP	29.50	29.50
93	REFLECTIONS	OP	29.50	29.50
93	SPIRITUAL HEIR	OP	29.50	29.50
93	SUNNY SPOT	OP	29.50	29.50
* *			WILD SPIRITS	
92	MOUNTAIN MAGIC	OP	32.50	32.50
92	SOLITARY WATCH	OP	29.50	29.50
92	TIMBER GHOST	OP	29.50	29.50
93	LONE VANGUARD	OP	34.50	34.50
93	MIGHTY PRESENCE	OP	34.50	34.50
93	QUIET VIGIL	OP	34.50	34.50
93	SILENT GUARD	OP	32.50	32.50
93	SLY EYES	OP	32.50	32.50
* *			WINGS OF WINTER	
92	MOONLIGHT RETREAT	OP	29.50	29.50
93	FULL MOON COMPANIONS	OP	29.50	29.50
93	NIGHT LIGHTS	OP	29.50	29.50
93	SILENT SUNSET	OP	29.50	29.50
93	TWILIGHT SERENADE	OP	29.50	29.50
93	WHITE NIGHT	OP	29.50	29.50
93	WINTER HAVEN	OP	29.50	29.50
93	WINTER REFLECTIONS	OP	29.50	29.50

WATERFORD WEDGWOOD USA

			BICENTENNIAL	
*				
72	BOSTON TEA PARTY	YR	40.00	40.00
73	PAUL REVERE'S RIDE	YR	40.00	115.00
74	BATTLE OF CONCORD	YR	40.00	55.00
75	ACROSS THE DELAWARE	YR	40.00	105.00
75	VICTORY AT YORKTOWN	YR	45.00	53.00
76	DECLARATION SIGNED	YR	45.00	45.00
*			MOTHER'S DAY	
71	SPORTIVE LOVE	*	20.00	20.00
72	THE SEWING LESSON	*	20.00	20.00

YR	NAME	LIMIT	ISSUE	QUOTE
73	THE BAPTISM OF ACHILLES	*	20.00	25.00
74	DOMESTIC EMPLOYMENT	*	30.00	33.00
75	MOTHER AND CHILD	*	35.00	37.00
76	THE SPINNER	*	35.00	35.00
77	LEISURE TIME	*	35.00	35.00
78	SWAN AND CYGNETS	*	40.00	40.00
79	DEER AND FAWN	*	45.00	45.00
80	BIRDS	*	47.50	47.50
81	MARE AND FOAL	*	50.00	60.00
82	CHERUBS WITH SWING	*	55.00	60.00
83	CUPID AND BUTTERFLY	*	55.00	55.00
84	MUSICAL CUPIDS	*	55.00	59.00
85	CUPIDS AND DOVES	YR	55.00	80.00
86	CUPIDS FISHING	YR	55.00	55.00
87	SPRING FLOWERS	YR	55.00	80.00
88	TIGER LILY	YR	55.00	59.00
89	IRISES	YR	65.00	65.00
91	PEONIES	YR	65.00	65.00
*			**WEDGWOOD CHRISTMAS**	
79	BUCKINGHAM PALACE	YR	65.00	65.00
80	ST. JAMES PALACE	YR	70.00	70.00
81	MARBLE ARCH	YR	75.00	75.00
82	LAMBETH PALACE	YR	80.00	90.00
83	ALL SOULS, LANGHAM PALACE	YR	80.00	80.00
84	CONSTITUTION HILL	YR	80.00	80.00
85	THE TATE GALLERY	YR	80.00	80.00
86	THE ALBERT MEMORIAL	YR	80.00	150.00
87	GUILDHALL	YR	80.00	110.00
88	THE OBSERVATORY/GREENWICH	YR	80.00	95.00
89	WINCHESTER CATHEDRAL	YR	88.00	88.00
69	WINDSOR CASTLE	YR	25.00	155.00
70	TRAFALGAR SQUARE	YR	30.00	30.00
71	PICADILLY CIRCUS	YR	30.00	40.00
72	ST. PAUL'S CATHEDRAL	YR	35.00	40.00
73	TOWER OF LONDON	YR	40.00	90.00
74	HOUSES OF PARLIAMENT	YR	40.00	40.00
75	TOWER BRIDGE	YR	45.00	45.00
76	HAMPTON COURT	YR	50.00	50.00
77	WESTMINISTER ABBEY	YR	55.00	60.00
78	HORSE GUARDS	YR	60.00	60.00

WILDLIFE INTERNATIONALE
J. RUTHVEN

			SPORTING DOGS	
85	DECOY (LABORADOR RETRIEVER)	5000	55.00	150.00
85	DUSTY (GOLDEN RETRIEVER)	5000	55.00	80.00
85	RUMMY (ENGLISH SETTER)	5000	55.00	55.00
85	SCARLETT (IRISH SETTER)	5000	55.00	150.00

Prints

Jay Brown

Selling a print can be as emotional as losing a favorite pet. But often with art, the financial reward can be the perfect compensation. Perhaps you need a few quick bucks or want to clear a little wall space for a new masterpiece. What do you do?

The first thing is to determine the value of the work you wish to sell. There are magazines such as *Collector's mart* on the market which can give you some idea of the current trend. The gallery where the print was purchased or the publisher of the print should also be able to give you an idea of the current market price.

Remember that a framed or unframed print in mint condition is easier to sell and will bring you more dollars than the same print in average condition. Hopefully, you will find that the current market price is in line with what is personally acceptable to you. If you are lucky, the gallery or publisher with which you're dealing may make a good offer or direct you to a collector or gallery who is looking for the work you wish to sell.

If not, you have two main options: sell at retail to a private collector, perhaps someone you know, or sell (usually on consignment) at wholesale through a dealer. In either case, it often helps to show a would-be buyer evidence that the print was purchased from (and was framed, if applicable) by a gallery with a good reputation.

One way to locate a retail buyer is to place a classified advertisement in a local newspaper and/or check to see if your friends are interested in buying the print. If the artist is in high demand, your chances for making a sale will be increased tremendously.

If your ad doesn't result in a buyer, don't fret. Selling your print through a reputable gallery is often the preferred way to go. Look for a gallery with experience in dealing with the artist whose work you wish to sell. That gallery should have a marketing plan and a clientele interested in the print. The sales commission that the gallery receives will vary from 10-50 percent of the selling price. The most common commission is 33-40 percent.

Occasionally, a print will be difficult to sell due to the timing of the attempted resale. Perhaps the economy is in a decline or the artist is not in demand due to a change in collecting trends. Remember, as with any investment, there are peak times to sell. For example, you'll have better luck with an artist who is in his prime as opposed to one whose art is not as popular.

There are special companies that specialize in matching buyers with sellers on the secondary market. These companies provide dealers and collectors with listings of clients interested in selling works of art. Such listings are based on information provided by the sellers. Using such a list, galleries are able to see what it costs to obtain a work of art.

Even though these listing companies make locating works on the secondary market easy for art dealers, many reputable galleries prefer to use their own client base whenever possible. By using their own collector base, galleries can normally avoid shipping costs and be assured that the condition of the work of art is as represented. But most important, by using their own client base, galleries are able to reward clients who exhibit loyalty to them.

Art is a fabulous investment, not because of the amount of potential profit that can be made upon its sale, but because of the amount of enjoyment it can give. Even though many prints turn out to be great monetary investments, it is highly recommended that buyers follow the golden rule of collecting: "Buy what you like, and all your purchases are guaranteed to be good investments."

JAY BROWN owns and operates Gallery One with locations in Mentor and Akron, Ohio, where he specializes in the retail sales of limited edition prints and original paintings and sculptures by the industry's most popular artists. He also deals extensively in the secondary market sale of these collectibles.

PRINTS

YR	NAME	LIMIT	ISSUE	QUOTE

AMERICAN ARTISTS
F. STONE

YR	NAME	LIMIT	ISSUE	QUOTE
79	AFFIRMED, STEVE CAUTHEN UP	750	100.00	600.00
79	MARE AND FOAL	500	90.00	1000.00
79	MOMENT AFTER, THE	500	90.00	350.00
79	ONE, TWO, THREE	500	100.00	1000.00
79	PATIENCE	1000	90.00	1000.00
79	RIVALS, THE: AFFIRMED & ALYDAR	500	90.00	500.00
80	BELMONT, THE: BOLD FORBES	500	100.00	800.00
80	EXCELLER: BILL SHOEMAKER	500	90.00	800.00
80	GENUINE RISK	500	100.00	600.00
80	KENTUCKY DERBY, THE	750	100.00	1400.00
80	KIDNAPPED MARE: FRANFRELUCHE	750	115.00	575.00
80	PASTURE PEST, THE	500	100.00	1400.00
80	SPECTACULAR BID	500	65.00	350.00
81	ARABIANS, THE	750	115.00	450.00
81	CONTENTMENT	750	115.00	600.00
81	JOHN HENRY: BILL SHOEMAKER UP	595	160.00	900.00
81	SHOE, THE: 8,000 WINS	395	200.00	7500.00
81	THOROUGHBREDS, THE	750	115.00	650.00
82	MAN O' WAR: FINAL THUNDER	750	175.00	3000.00
82	OFF AND RUNNING	750	125.00	600.00
82	POWER HORSES, THE	750	125.00	250.00
82	WATER TROUGH, THE	750	125.00	575.00
83	ANDALUSIAN, THE	750	150.00	350.00
83	DUEL, THE	750	150.00	450.00
83	FOR ONLY A MOMENT: RUFFIAN	750	175.00	1600.00
83	SECRETARIAT	950	175.00	1100.00
83	TRANQUILITY	750	150.00	650.00
84	NORTHERN DANCER	950	175.00	1000.00
84	TURNING FOR HOME	750	150.00	650.00
85	FRED STONE PAINTS THE SPORT OF KINGS	750	265.00	750.00
85	JOHN HENRY: MCCARRON UP	750	175.00	900.00
85	KELSO	950	175.00	600.00
85	LEGACY, THE	950	175.00	950.00
86	FOREVER FRIENDS	950	175.00	1000.00
86	NIJINSKI II	950	175.00	225.00
86	RUFFIAN & FOOLISH PLEASURE	950	175.00	375.00
87	FIRST DAY, THE	950	175.00	500.00
87	LADY'S SECRET	950	175.00	275.00
87	RIVALRY, THE: ALYSHEBA AND BET TWICE	950	195.00	500.00
88	ALYSHEBA	950	195.00	540.00
88	CAM-FELLA	950	175.00	175.00
89	BATTLE FOR THE TRIPLE CROWN	950	225.00	550.00
89	PHAR LAP	950	195.00	275.00
89	SHOE BALD EAGLE	950	195.00	495.00
90	FINA TRIBUTE: SECRETARIAT	1150	265.00	800.00
90	OLD WARRIORS SHOEMAKER: JOHN HENRY	1950	265.00	400.00
91	BLACK STALLION	1500	225.00	175.00
91	FOREGO	1150	225.00	160.00
91	GO FOR WAND: A CANDLE IN THE WIND	1150	225.00	150.00
92	DANCE SMARTLY	950	225.00	225.00

AMERICAN LEGACY
S. ETEM

YR	NAME	LIMIT	ISSUE	QUOTE
*	INDIANA SUMMER	CL	150.00	150.00
*	LITTLE BANDIT	CL	150.00	150.00
*	THE FOUNTAIN	CL	150.00	150.00

AMERICAN MASTERS
P. CROWE

YR	NAME	LIMIT	ISSUE	QUOTE
85	FOGGY MORNING MALLARDS	950	90.00	170.00
86	OUTLAWS II, THE	1950	60.00	340.00
87	MASTERS OF DISASTER, THE	950	90.00	100.00
87	WILD BUNCH, THE	950	90.00	170.00
87	WINTER RETREAT	950	90.00	150.00
78	ISAIAH 40:3 S/N	1000	40.00	450.00
78	ISAIAH 40:3 S/O	1500	30.00	115.00
78	ISAIAH 58:8 S/N	1000	35.00	120.00
78	JOHN 3:8 S/N	1000	30.00	320.00
78	PSALM 27:4 S/N	1000	40.00	350.00
79	COLLECTOR'S SUITE S/N	1000	48.00	125.00
79	JOHN 9:4 S/N	1000	45.00	130.00
79	JOHN 9:4 S/O	2000	30.00	120.00

YR	NAME	LIMIT	ISSUE	QUOTE
79	PROVERBS 8:25 S/N	1000	45.00	120.00
79	PROVERBS 8:25 S/O	1800	30.00	120.00
79	PSALM 113:3 S/N	1000	40.00	120.00
79	PSALM 113:3 S/O	1500	30.00	120.00
79	PSALM 147:16 S/N	1000	45.00	125.00
79	PSALM 147:16 S/O	1200	30.00	125.00
79	SONG OF SOLOMON 2:17 S/N	1000	45.00	120.00
79	SONG OF SOLOMON 2:17 S/O	1800	30.00	95.00
80	COLLECTOR'S SUITE S/O	1800	35.00	120.00
80	DEUTERONOMY 28:8 S/N	1000	55.00	125.00
80	DEUTERONOMY 28:8 S/O	1800	37.50	115.00
80	EZEKIEL 34:15 S/N	1000	55.00	130.00
80	EZEKIEL 34:15 S/O	1800	37.50	120.00
80	PSALM 42:1 S/N	1000	55.00	140.00
80	PSALM 42:1 S/O	1200	37.50	120.00
80	PSALM 91:1 S/N	1000	45.00	120.00
80	PSALM 91:1 S/O	2200	30.00	120.00
80	REVELATIONS 21:6 S/N	1000	55.00	1000.00
80	REVELATIONS 21:6 S/O	1800	35.00	900.00
80	ROMANS 15:32 S/N	1000	57.50	120.00
80	ROMANS 15:32 S/O	2200	37.50	115.00
81	EZEKIEL 32:14 S/N	1500	65.00	130.00
81	EZEKIEL 32:14 S/O	2500	40.00	120.00
81	JOHN 10:27 S/N	1000	60.00	120.00
81	JOHN 10:27 S/O	2700	37.50	100.00
81	LAMENTATIONS 3:28 S/N	1500	68.00	240.00
81	LAMENTATIONS 3:28 S/O	2500	45.00	200.00
81	MATTHEW 6:30 S/N	1000	40.00	120.00
81	MATTHEW 9:37 S/N	1000	65.00	120.00
81	MATTHEW 9:37 S/O	2200	38.00	50.00
81	PROVERBS 23:10 S/N	1000	60.00	130.00
81	PROVERBS 23:10 S/O	2200	37.50	130.00
81	PSALM 90:2 S/N	1500	67.50	120.00
81	PSALM 90:2 S/O	2500	45.00	115.00
82	DANIEL 2:21 S/N	1500	70.00	130.00
82	DANIEL 2:21 S/O	2500	45.00	60.00
82	ECCLESIASTES 3:1 S/N	1500	70.00	130.00
82	ISAIAH 45:3 S/N	1950	80.00	135.00
82	JOB 39:8 S/N	1500	70.00	175.00
82	JOB 39:8 S/O	2500	45.00	45.00
82	JOHN 8:32 S/N	1500	85.00	135.00
82	JOSHUA 2:22 S/N	1500	70.00	120.00
82	JOSHUA 2:22 S/O	2500	45.00	60.00
83	EARLY ARRIVAL (EPHESIANS 5:8) S/N	1600	75.00	250.00
83	ISAIAH 58:11 S/N	1600	85.00	350.00
83	MATTHEW 18:12 S/N	1500	75.00	140.00
83	ZACHARIAH 14:7 S/N	1600	85.00	100.00
84	MAJESTIC MORNING (AMOS 4:13) S/N	1600	85.00	175.00
84	MORGAN'S CLEARING S/N	1600	80.00	140.00
84	SHARING THE FAITH (PSALM 23) S/N	5000	85.00	140.00
84	TRANQUIL REFUGE (JEREMIAH 48:40) S/N	1600	80.00	120.00
85	A NEW PROMISE (GENESIS 9:16) S/N	1600	85.00	200.00
85	OFFERING, THE (MARK 12:41-44) S/N	3000	125.00	165.00
85	SHADY CREEK MILL (JOB 40:22) S/N	1600	85.00	220.00
87	MISSION, THE (ISAIAH 40:8) S/N	1503	85.00	310.00
87	QUIET ENCOUNTER (PSALM 104:13) S/N	1600	85.00	220.00
88	AFTER THE STORM (LAMENTATIONS 3:26) S/N	1000	110.00	300.00
73	AFRICAN LION	3000	35.00	200.00
73	GIANT PANDA	5000	45.00	200.00
73	GOLDEN EAGLE	1000	75.00	200.00
73	PRONGHORN	5000	50.00	150.00
73	TIGER	3000	35.00	500.00
74	CHEETAH KITTEN	5000	40.00	550.00
74	HERRING GULL	5000	45.00	175.00
74	LIONS, THE	5000	40.00	175.00
74	RACCOON	5000	50.00	400.00
74	ZEBRA	4000	60.00	160.00
75	BISON	2000	50.00	250.00
75	LION CUB	3500	35.00	175.00
75	NORTHERN GOSHAWK	4000	50.00	1700.00
75	SCREECH OWLS	3500	20.00	130.00
75	SNOW LEOPARD	1500	75.00	1800.00
75	SNOW LEOPARD (REMARQUE)	1000	125.00	2200.00
75	TIGER CUB	3500	35.00	200.00
75	ZEBRA FOAL	4000	35.00	250.00
76	CAVALIER SPANIELS	1500	35.00	275.00

YR	NAME	LIMIT	ISSUE	QUOTE
76	ELEPHANTS AT KILIMANJARO	1000	75.00	450.00
76	FLORIDA BOBCAT	3000	40.00	320.00
76	GYRFALCON	3000	40.00	145.00
76	MASAI GIRAFFES	3000	40.00	400.00
76	MORRIS THE CAT	5000	30.00	550.00
76	OCELOTS	5000	35.00	250.00
76	WHITE TIGER	1500	75.00	350.00
76	WHITE TIGER (REMARQUE)	1000	125.00	350.00
77	AFRICAN LEOPARD	1500	75.00	500.00
77	AFRICAN LEOPARD (REMARQUE)	1000	125.00	600.00
77	CANADA LYNX	3000	50.00	175.00
77	CHEETAH	3000	50.00	125.00
77	COUGAR CUB	3000	50.00	200.00
77	GREATER KUDU	3000	50.00	150.00
77	HARLAN'S HAWK	1500	60.00	150.00
78	AFRICAN LEOPARD CUB	2000	65.00	450.00
78	BLACK LEOPARD	3000	50.00	700.00
78	COUGAR	1000	90.00	1800.00
78	IMPALA	2000	60.00	110.00
78	RACCOONS (3)	5000	50.00	100.00
78	RED SHOULDERED HAWK	2000	60.00	175.00
79	CLOUDED LEOPARD	2000	65.00	160.00
79	CLOUDED LEOPARD CUB	2000	75.00	180.00
79	KOALA	2000	65.00	850.00
79	SIBERIAN TIGER	2000	100.00	180.00
79	SNOW LEOPARD HEAD	15,000	20.00	290.00
79	SNOWY OWLS	2000	65.00	175.00
80	AMERICAN EAGLE	2000	75.00	175.00
80	HARP SEAL	2000	75.00	1200.00
80	JAGUAR	2000	75.00	950.00
80	POLAR BEAR	2000	100.00	125.00
80	SIBERIAN LYNX CUB	2000	75.00	150.00
80	WHITE TIGER HEAD	20,000	25.00	125.00
81	AFRICAN LEOPARD HEAD	12,500	25.00	115.00
81	BIGHORN COUNTRY	2500	75.00	300.00
81	HIMALAYAN PRINCE	2000	75.00	650.00
81	LOFTY VIEW	2500	75.00	250.00
81	ROYAL PRIDE	2500	100.00	150.00
82	JAGUAR HEAD	12,500	25.00	115.00
82	LONE HUNTER	2500	100.00	220.00
82	MAJESTY	2500	80.00	125.00
82	ON WATCH	2500	80.00	1100.00
82	RACCOON (TENNESSEE CONSERVATION STAMP)	2000	50.00	150.00
82	UNO	2500	75.00	150.00
83	A MOMENT'S REST	2500	100.00	240.00
83	ALASKAN AUTUMN	2500	80.00	560.00
83	BOBCAT (MS WILDLIFE FED. STAMP)	5000	90.00	175.00
83	LABRADOR RETRIEVER (NTL. RETR. CLUB)	2192	125.00	175.00
83	LABRADOR RETRIEVER (NTL. RETR. CLUB/REM)	190	250.00	400.00
83	MY FRIEND	7500	35.00	120.00
83	RED RASCAL	2500	80.00	800.00
83	YOUNG EXPLORER	2500	80.00	150.00
84	AMERICAN MONARCH	3750	120.00	400.00
84	BANDIT	2500	90.00	150.00
84	DOUBLE TROUBLE	2500	90.00	360.00
84	NEW ARRIVAL	7500	35.00	150.00
84	SOLITUDE	2500	100.00	300.00
85	A SUNNY SPOT	2500	100.00	125.00
85	KING'S FAVORITE	2500	110.00	130.00
85	PALS	2500	70.00	150.00
85	QUIET TIME IN SAMBURU	2500	100.00	125.00
85	ROYAL BENGAL	3950	125.00	160.00
86	FIRST LIGHT	3950	125.00	135.00
86	FREEDOM	2500	120.00	750.00
86	HIDEAWAY	3950	85.00	225.00
86	THREE OF A KIND	3950	110.00	200.00
86	TREASURES OF THE SEA (FRIEND/SEA OTTER)	500	150.00	175.00
87	CHALLENGER, THE	3000	140.00	150.00
87	MIGHTY WARRIOR	3000	140.00	130.00
87	PLAYMATES	2500	120.00	220.00
87	READY FOR ADVENTURE	3950	115.00	125.00
87	TAKING A BREAK	3950	100.00	125.00
88	FLEETING ENCOUNTER	3000	150.00	1000.00
88	HIGH MOUNTAIN PATH	3000	140.00	145.00
88	OUT ON A LIMB	3000	140.00	150.00
88	RECESS	2500	140.00	150.00

YR	NAME	LIMIT	ISSUE	QUOTE
88	WANDERER, THE	3000	140.00	480.00
89	CHINESE TREASURE	3000	140.00	240.00
89	NATURE'S DAWN	3000	140.00	140.00
89	POWERFUL PRESENCE	5619	155.00	150.00
89	SAFE RETURN	3000	140.00	125.00
89	SURPRISE	3000	140.00	165.00
90	A RADIANT MOMENT	3000	155.00	150.00
90	AMBASSADORS	3000	155.00	130.00
90	PARTNERS	3000	155.00	700.00
87	BURST OF SPRING	950	65.00	90.00
87	PARADISAL SETTING	950	65.00	90.00
87	PASSING THROUGH	950	65.00	200.00
87	ROSE GARDENS	950	65.00	200.00
88	EVENING RIDE	950	75.00	250.00
88	FLOWER MARKET, THE	950	70.00	200.00
88	PLEASANT PROMENADE	950	70.00	170.00
88	SUMMER CAROUSEL	950	70.00	225.00
78	BOSQUE TERRITORY	1500	35.00	200.00
78	FORBIDDING WILDERNESS	1500	35.00	175.00
78	WHITE BUFFALO	1500	35.00	380.00
79	COLTER'S QUEST	1500	50.00	160.00
79	COMANCHE MOON	1500	36.00	120.00
79	FOOTPRINTS IN THE SNOW	1500	40.00	1100.00
79	MIGHTY OAK ENDURETH, THE	1500	25.00	130.00
80	ANOTHER DAY	1500	52.00	300.00
80	NATURE'S CLASSROOM	1500	52.00	130.00
80	RECEDING STORM	1500	50.00	175.00
80	SLICKER TIME	1500	52.00	1500.00
81	CAMP COFFEE	1500	75.00	140.00
81	COMMUNE WITH GOD	1500	75.00	250.00
81	FIRST VISIT	1500	62.00	180.00
81	HEADIN' HOME	1500	57.00	140.00
81	LEADIN' LOOSE	1500	60.00	120.00
81	RENDEZVOUS	1500	55.00	120.00
82	BOOM TOWN	1950	75.00	300.00
82	COOLING OFF	1500	80.00	130.00
82	FAMILY TREE	1500	85.00	145.00
82	I'D LIKE TO BE THERE	1500	80.00	135.00
82	PEACEFUL VALLEY	1500	80.00	140.00
82	TEXAS GOLD	1950	90.00	150.00
83	AGAINST THE WIND	1500	90.00	135.00
83	ALL IS CALM	1500	90.00	120.00
83	PERFECT DAY, THE	1500	90.00	140.00
83	RANGE FARE	1500	95.00	150.00
84	CHANGING TIMES	1500	85.00	225.00
84	COWTOWN	1500	90.00	160.00
86	LEGEND OF THE WEST	1500	85.00	145.00
87	BARON'S DAUGHTER	750	100.00	500.00
87	COUNTRY SLICKERS	750	100.00	325.00

ANNA-PERENNA
T. KRUMEICH

			KRUMEICH HECTOR'S WINDOW	
*	13-COLOR LITHO, FRAMED	995	95.00	95.00
*	GENUINE STONE LITHO	325	175.00	225.00

ARMSTRONG'S
A. D'ESTREHAN

87	SAN PEDRO	500	95.00	95.00
87	SAN PEDRO A/P	CL	95.00	95.00
87	U.S.S. CONSTITUTION	500	95.00	95.00
87	U.S.S. CONSTITUTION A/P	CL	95.00	95.00
87	WINDSWEPT	500	95.00	95.00
87	WINDSWEPT A/P	CL	95.00	95.00
87	BOYS, THE	500	70.00	70.00
87	BOYS, THE A/P	CL	70.00	70.00
87	SISSY AND MISSY	500	70.00	70.00
87	SISSY AND MISSY A/P	CL	70.00	70.00
87	LADY CUNNINGHAM	500	95.00	95.00
87	LADY CUNNINGHAM A/P	CL	95.00	95.00

ART WORLD OF BOURGEAULT
R. BOURGEAULT

			ROYAL LITERARY SERIES	
89	ANNE HATHAWAY COTTAGE	OP	75.00	90.00
89	JOHN BUNYAN COTTAGE	OP	75.00	90.00
89	JOHN MILTON COTTAGE	OP	75.00	90.00
89	THOMAS HARDY COTTAGE	OP	75.00	90.00

R. BOURGEAULT

			THE ENGLISH COUNTRYSIDE	
89	COUNTRY SQUIRE, THE	550	130.00	295.00

YR	NAME	LIMIT	ISSUE	QUOTE

ARTAFFECTS
MAGO

YR	NAME	LIMIT	ISSUE	QUOTE
88	BETH	950	95.00	200.00
88	JESSICA AND SEBASTIAN (PR.)	550	225.00	325.00
88	SERENITY	950	95.00	200.00
88	EMPIRE BUILDER	950	75.00	75.00
88	SANTA FE	950	75.00	75.00
88	TWENTIETH CENTURY LIMITED	950	75.00	75.00
*	BRAVE AND FREE	*	*	83.00
*	CHEIF RED CLOUD	*	*	83.00
77	MADRE	500	125.00	410.00
78	MADONNA OF THE PLAINS	500	125.00	500.00
78	SNOW PALS	500	125.00	260.00
79	SIOUX SCOUT/BUFFALO HUNT (PR.)	500	150.00	750.00
80	BABYSITTER	3000	60.00	98.00-130.00
80	PUPPIES	3000	45.00	260.00
81	PEACEABLE KINGDOM	950	100.00	104.00
82	CHIEF PONTIAC	950	75.00	100.00
82	HOOFBEATS	950	100.00	150.00
82	INDIAN STYLE	950	75.00	325.00
82	LONESOME COWBOY	950	75.00	390.00
82	MARIA	550	150.00	350.00
82	TENDER LOVE	950	75.00	104.00
82	TINKER	3000	45.00	100.00
83	MOMENT, THE (POSTER)	OP	20.00	60.00
84	NAVAJO LOVE	300	125.00	550.00
84	OUT OF THE FOREST	*	*	450.00
85	CHIEF CRAZY HORSE	950	125.00	450.00
85	CHIEF SITTING BULL	500	125.00	350.00
85	MARIGOLD	500	125.00	350.00
85	SECRETARIAT	950	125.00	125.00
85	WHIRLAWAY	950	125.00	125.00
86	LEARNING HIS WAYS	325	150.00	150.00
86	POUT	325	150.00	350.00
86	RESCUE, THE	325	150.00	450.00
86	WAR PONY	325	150.00	250.00
88	BY THE STREAM	950	100.00	100.00
88	MAGNIFICENT SEVEN	950	125.00	125.00
90	PACK, THE	950	150.00	150.00
82	BUTTERFLY	3000	45.00	100.00

MAGO
GRAND GALLERY COLLECTION

YR	NAME	LIMIT	ISSUE	QUOTE
88	AMY	2500	75.00	90.00
88	LAUREN	2500	75.00	90.00
88	MISCHIEF	2500	75.00	90.00
88	TOMORROWS	2500	75.00	90.00
88	PARIS	2500	75.00	90.00
88	VENICE	2500	75.00	90.00
88	BLACKFOOT HUNTER	2500	75.00	90.00
88	BRAVE & FREE	2500	75.00	98.00
88	CHEYENNE NATION, THE	2500	75.00	90.00
88	CHIEF CRAZY HORSE	2500	75.00	90.00
88	CHIEF RED CLOUD	2500	75.00	98.00
88	LAST FRONTIER, THE	2500	75.00	90.00
88	LATE MAIL	2500	75.00	98.00
88	LILY OF THE MOHAWKS	2500	75.00	90.00
88	NATIVE AMERICAN	2500	75.00	90.00
88	NOBLE HERITAGE	2500	75.00	90.00
88	PEACEABLE KINGDOM, THE	2500	75.00	90.00
88	TENDER LOVE	2500	75.00	130.00
88	GOD BLESS AMERICA	2500	75.00	90.00
88	HOME SWEET HOME	2500	75.00	90.00
88	MOTHERHOOD	2500	75.00	90.00
88	VISITING THE DOCTOR	2500	75.00	90.00
88	WEDDING, THE	2500	75.00	90.00

ARTISTS OF THE WORLD
T. DEGRAZIA

YR	NAME	LIMIT	ISSUE	QUOTE
94	ADORATION	950	79.50	83.00
94	BEAUTIFUL HARVEST	950	79.50	83.00
94	SPRING BLOSSOMS	950	79.50	83.00
94	YOUNG MADONNA	950	79.50	83.00

B. BOURGEAU RICHARDS COLLECTION
B.B. RICHARDS

YR	NAME	LIMIT	ISSUE	QUOTE
93	ALWAYS	1000	25.00	30.00
93	BARNEY	1000	20.00	23.00
93	DAPHNEY DUBUNNY	1000	20.00	23.00

YR	NAME	LIMIT	ISSUE	QUOTE
93	FOR THE CHILDREN	1000	45.00	55.00
93	GRANDMA'S TEAPOT	1000	20.00	23.00
93	MARY & PETE NEWEST ARRIVAL	1000	20.00	23.00
93	MEDORE'S PRIZE PIG	1000	40.00	45.00
93	RED ROSES FOR CONSTANCE	1000	30.00	35.00
93	SUNFLOWER FOR FLORENCE	1000	20.00	23.00
94	BIRD WATCHING	1000	15.00	18.00
94	CYNTHIA'S TEAPOT	1000	15.00	18.00
94	FROM THE HEART	1000	15.00	18.00
94	INDIAN SUMMER	1000	37.00	42.00
94	INNOCENCE	1000	40.00	45.00
94	JOSEPHINE WEDS CHARLES	1000	15.00	18.00
94	JUST THREE ANGELS	1000	15.00	18.00
94	MA	1000	35.00	40.00
94	PEARL LOVES HELEN	1000	15.00	18.00
94	SARAH ON WASH DAY	1000	15.00	18.00
94	THE FISHERMAN	1000	15.00	18.00
94	THE FRIENDSHIP GARDEN	1000	37.00	42.00
94	WAITING FOR PAPA	1000	25.00	30.00
B.B. RICHARDS		**AMAMDA MOORE SERIES**		
93	APPLE FOR MISS AMANDA	1000	40.00	45.00
B.B. RICHARDS		**AMANDA MOORE SERIES**		
93	HOUSE ON HOLLISTER	1000	30.00	35.00
B.B. RICHARDS		**CHRISTMAS SERIES**		
93	PEACE, LOVE AND JOY	1050	32.00	40.00
94	WHERE MY HEART FINDS CHRISTMAS	1452	32.00	40.00
B.B. RICHARDS		**FLORAL SERIES**		
93	WILD ROSES	1000	40.00	45.00
94	PURPLE IRIS	1000	40.00	45.00
B.B. RICHARDS		**FOUR SEASONS WEDDING COLLECTION**		
94	WEDDING IN SPRING	1000	35.00	40.00
B.B. RICHARDS		**FOUR SEASONS WEDDING SERIES**		
93	WINTER WEDDING BELLS	1000	34.00	40.00

CAVANAUGH GROUP

SUNDBLOM		**COCA-COLA BRAND SANTA ANIMATION**		
91	SSSHH!	CL	99.99	125.00
92	SANTA'S PAUSE FOR REFRESHMENT	CL	99.99	125.00
93	TRIMMING THE TREE	CL	99.99	120.00
95	SANTA AT THE LAMPPOST	OP	110.00	115.00

CHRISTOPHER PALUSO ART WORKS

C. PALUSO				
*	AL KALINE	750	5.00	30.00
*	ALAN TRAMMELL	750	5.00	30.00
*	ANDY HAWKINS	750	5.00	30.00
*	BABE RUTH	500	85.00	125.00
*	BASEBALL'S IRON MAN	10,000	15.00	35.00
*	CHUCK CONNORS	750	5.00	50.00
*	DARRYL STRAWBERRY	1000	10.00	30.00
*	DAVE DRAVECKY	750	5.00	30.00
*	DON MATTINGLY	1000	10.00	30.00
*	DUKE SNIDER	500	5.00	30.00
*	DWIGHT GOODEN	1000	10.00	30.00
*	K. MCREYNOLDS	500	5.00	30.00
*	NOLAN RYAN	1000	50.00	300.00
*	OREL HERSHISER	750	5.00	30.00
*	RICKY HENDERSON	1000	10.00	30.00
*	RON CEY	250	5.00	30.00
*	RUPPERT JONES	750	5.00	30.00
*	RYNE SANDBERG	500	5.00	30.00
*	SPARKY ANDERSON	250	5.00	30.00
*	STEVE GARVEY	1000	10.00	30.00
*	TED WILLIAMS	500	5.00	35.00
*	TERRY KENNEDY	750	5.00	30.00
*	TONY GWYNN	351	85.00	150.00
*	WILLIE MAYS	500	5.00	35.00
*	WILLIE McCOVEY	500	5.00	30.00

CIRCLE FINE ART

L. NEIMAN				**NEIMAN**
*	12 METER YACHT RACE	250	*	1800.00
*	AL CAPONE	300	*	2400.00
*	BACKHAND	300	*	1450.00
*	CASINO	300	*	5500.00
*	CHIPPING ON	275	*	1500.00
*	DEUCE	275	*	3000.00
*	DOUBLES	300	*	3150.00

YR	NAME	LIMIT	ISSUE	QUOTE
*	DOWNHILL	600	*	1800.00
*	END AROUND	300	*	1700.00
*	FOUR ACES	300	*	1500.00
*	FOX HUNT	300	*	1500.00
*	GOAL	300	*	1500.00
*	HARLEQUIN	200	*	2600.00
*	HARLEQUIN W/SWORD	250	*	1150.00
*	HARLEQUIN W/TEXT	200	*	1150.00
*	HOCKEY PLAYER	300	*	2800.00
*	HOMMAGE TO BOUCHER	250	*	1700.00
*	IN THE STRETCH	250	*	1400.00
*	INNSBRUCK	300	*	3500.00
*	JOCKEY	300	*	1600.00
*	LEOPARD	300	*	7500.00
*	LION PRIDE	300	*	5000.00
*	MARATHON	300	*	1800.00
*	OCELOT	250	*	2000.00
*	PADDOCK	300	*	3900.00
*	PIERROT	250	*	1150.00
*	PIERROT THE JUGGLER	200	*	1150.00
*	POOL ROOM	350	*	6500.00
*	PUNCHINELLO	250	*	2600.00
*	PUNCHINELLO W/TEXT	200	*	1600.00
*	RACE, THE	300	*	1300.00
*	ROULETTE	40	*	10000.00
*	SAILING	275	*	1700.00
*	SCRAMBLE	300	*	1800.00
*	SKIER	300	*	1500.00
*	SLALOM	300	*	1500.00
*	SLAPSHOT	300	*	1600.00
*	SLIDING HOME	300	*	4200.00
*	SMASH	300	*	1850.00
*	STOCK MARKET	300	*	9000.00
*	SUDDEN DEATH	250	*	5000.00
*	TEE SHOT	300	*	1850.00
*	TENNIS PLAYER	300	*	1500.00
*	TIGER	300	*	5100.00
*	TROTTERS	300	*	1850.00

N. ROCKWELL · ROCKWELL

YR	NAME	LIMIT	ISSUE	QUOTE
*	A DAY IN THE LIFE OF A BOY	200	*	6200.00
*	AMERICAN FAMILY FOLIO	200	*	17500.00
*	ARTIST AT WORK, THE	130	*	3500.00
*	AT THE BARBER	200	*	4900.00
*	AUTUMN	200	*	3500.00
*	AUTUMN/JAPON	25	*	3600.00
*	AVIARY	200	*	4200.00
*	BARBERSHOP QUARTET	200	*	6000.00
*	BASEBALL	200	*	3600.00
*	BEN FRANKLIN'S PHILADELPHIA	200	*	3600.00
*	BEN'S BELLES	200	*	3600.00
*	BIG DAY, THE	200	*	3400.00
*	BIG TOP, THE	148	*	3400.00
*	BLACKSMITH SHOP	200	*	6500.00
*	BOOKSELLER	200	*	2700.00
*	BOOKSELLER/JAPON	25	*	2750.00
*	BRIDGE, THE	200	*	3100.00
*	CAT	200	*	5400.00
*	CAT/COLLOTYPE	200	*	4000.00
*	CHEERING	200	*	3600.00
*	CHILDREN AT WINDOW	200	*	3600.00
*	CHURCH	200	*	3400.00
*	CHURCH/COLLOTYPE	200	*	4000.00
*	CIRCUS	200	*	2650.00
*	COUNTY AGRICULTURAL	200	*	3900.00
*	CRITIC, THE	200	*	4650.00
*	DAY IN THE LIFE OF A BOY	25	*	6500.00
*	DEBUT	200	*	3600.00
*	DISCOVERY	200	*	5900.00
*	DOCTOR AND BOY	200	*	9400.00
*	DOCTOR AND DOLL	200	*	11900.00
*	DRESSING UP/INK	60	*	4400.00
*	DRESSING UP/PENCIL	200	*	3700.00
*	DRUNKARD, THE	200	*	3600.00
*	EXPECTED AND UNEXPECTED, THE	200	*	3700.00
*	FAMILY TREE	200	*	5900.00
*	FIDO'S HOUSE	200	*	3600.00

YR	NAME	LIMIT	ISSUE	QUOTE
*	FOOTBALL MASCOT	200	*	3700.00
*	FOUR SEASONS FOLIO	200	*	8000.00
*	FOUR SEASONS FOLIO	25	*	14000.00
*	FREEDOM FROM FEAR	200	*	6400.00
*	FREEDOM FROM WANT	200	*	6400.00
*	FREEDOM OF RELIGION	200	*	6400.00
*	FREEDOM OF SPEECH	200	*	6400.00
*	GAIETY DANCE TEAM	200	*	4500.00
*	GIRL AT MIRROR	200	*	8400.00
*	GOLDEN AGE, THE	200	*	3500.00
*	GOLDEN RULE	200	*	4400.00
*	GOLF	200	*	3600.00
*	GOSSIPS	200	*	5000.00
*	GOSSIPS/JAPON	25	*	5100.00
*	GROTTO	200	*	3400.00
*	GROTTO/COLLOTYPE	200	*	4000.00
*	HIGH DIVE	200	*	3000.00
*	HOMECOMING, THE	200	*	3700.00
*	HOUSE, THE	200	*	3700.00
*	HUCK FINN FOLIO	200	*	19500.00
*	ICHABOD CRANE	200	*	6700.00
*	INVENTOR, THE	200	*	3600.00
*	JERRY	200	*	4700.00
*	JIM GOT DOWN ON HIS KNEES	200	*	4500.00
*	LINCOLN	200	*	11400.00
*	LOBSTERMAN	200	*	5500.00
*	LOBSTERMAN/JAPON	25	*	5500.00
*	MARRIAGE LICENSE	200	*	6900.00
*	MEDICINE	200	*	3400.00
*	MEDICINE/COLOR LITHO	200	*	6000.00
*	MISS MARY JANE	200	*	4500.00
*	MOVING DAY	200	*	3900.00
*	MUSIC HATH CHARMS	200	*	4200.00
*	MY HAND SHOOK	200	*	4500.00
*	OUT THE WINDON	200	*	3400.00
*	OUT THE WINDOW/COLLOTYPE	200	*	4000.00
*	OUTWARD BOUND	200	*	7900.00
*	POOR RICHARD'S ALMANAC	200	*	11500.00
*	PRESCRIPTION	200	*	4900.00
*	PRESCRIPTION/JAPON	25	*	4900.00
*	PROBLEM WE ALL LIVE WITH, THE	200	*	6000.00
*	PUPPIES	200	*	3700.00
*	RALEIGH THE DOG	200	*	3900.00
*	ROCKET SHIP	200	*	6000.00
*	ROYAL CROWN, THE	200	*	3500.00
*	RUNAWAY	200	*	4600.00
*	SAFE AND SOUND	200	*	3800.00
*	SATURDAY PEOPLE	200	*	3300.00
*	SAVE ME	200	*	3600.00
*	SAVING GRACE	200	*	7400.00
*	SCHOOL DAYS FOLIO	200	*	14000.00
*	SCHOOLHOUSE, THE	200	*	4500.00
*	SCHOOLHOUSE/JAPON	25	*	4650.00
*	SEE AMERICA FIRST	200	*	5650.00
*	SEE AMERICA FIRST/JAPON	25	*	5650.00
*	SETTING IN	200	*	3600.00
*	SHUFFELTON'S BARBERS	200	*	7400.00
*	SMOKING	200	*	3400.00
*	SMOKING/COLLOTYPE	200	*	4000.00
*	SPANKING	200	*	3400.00
*	SPANKING/COLLOTYPE	200	*	3300.00
*	SPELLING BEE	200	*	5000.00
*	SPRING	200	*	3500.00
*	SPRING FLOWERS	200	*	5200.00
*	SPRING/JAPON	25	*	3600.00
*	STUDY FOR THE DOCTOR	200	*	6000.00
*	STUDYING	200	*	3600.00
*	SUMMER	200	*	3500.00
*	SUMMER STOCK	200	*	4900.00
*	SUMMER/JAPON	25	*	3600.00
*	SUMMERSTOCK/JAPON	25	*	5000.00
*	TEACHER'S PET	200	*	3600.00
*	TEACHER, THE	200	*	3400.00
*	TEACHER, THE/JAPON	25	*	3500.00
*	TEXAN THE	200	*	3700.00
*	THEN FOR THREE MINUTES	200	*	4500.00

YR	NAME	LIMIT	ISSUE	QUOTE
*	THEN MISS WATSON	200	*	4500.00
*	THERE WARN'T NO HARM	200	*	4500.00
*	THREE FARMERS	200	*	3600.00
*	TICKETSELLER	200	*	4400.00
*	TOM SAWYER COLOR SUITE	200	*	30000.00
*	TOM SAWYER FOLIO	200	*	14000.00
*	TOP OF THE WORLD	200	*	4200.00
*	TRUMPETER	200	*	3900.00
*	TRUMPETER/JAPON	25	*	4100.00
*	TWO O'CLOCK FEEDING	200	*	3600.00
*	VILLAGE SMITHY, THE	200	*	3500.00
*	WELCOME	200	*	3500.00
*	WET PAINT	200	*	3800.00
*	WHEN I LIT MY CANDLE	200	*	4500.00
*	WHITEWASHING	200	*	3400.00
*	WHITEWASHING THE FENCE	200	*	4000.00
*	WINDOW WASHER	200	*	4800.00
*	WINTER	200	*	3500.00
*	WINTER/JAPON	25	*	3600.00
*	YE OLD PRINT SHOPPE	200	*	3500.00
*	YOUR EYES IS LOOKIN'	200	*	4500.00

COMPETITIVE IMAGES
RUSH

YR	NAME	LIMIT	ISSUE	QUOTE
76	GUARANTEED WINNER (SUPER BOWL III)	900	100.00	1150.00
78	SUGAR BOWL 1987: ALABAMA VS OHIO STATE	275	200.00	3000.00
79	TURN, THE (THOROUGHBRED)	275	300.00	900.00
79	YOU BETTER PASS (SUGAR BOWL)	130	300.00	4500.00
80	SPINNAKER RUN (12 M. YACHTS)	325	400.00	1000.00
80	SPIRIT OF VICTORY (USA OLYM. HOCKEY)	325	400.00	3500.00
81	CHAMPIONSHIP SEASON (U. OF GEORGIA)	325	400.00	500.00
81	HAPPY BIRTHDAY AMERICA (MCENROE)	325	400.00	1500.00
81	JACK NICKLAUS: THE GOLDEN BEAR	325	400.00	800.00
81	SLALOM	325	400.00	2500.00
81	SUPER BOWL GIANTS	410	500.00	550.00
82	COACH PAUL BEAR BRYANT	200	425.00	2500.00
82	HILTON HEAD: THE HERITAGE CLASSIC	325	425.00	2500.00
82	LAST CHUKKER, THE (POLO)	500	400.00	500.00
82	NATIONAL CHAMPION CLEMSON UNIV.	500	450.00	450.00
82	NORTH CAROLINA NATIONAL CHAMPION	500	450.00	500.00
82	PEBBLE BEACH	500	500.00	1200.00
83	DINNER WHITE NIGHT (PENN STATE)	350	450.00	500.00
83	GREENTRACK (GREYHOUND RACING)	225	425.00	500.00
83	UCLA	500	450.00	500.00
84	A DREAM OF GOLD (XXIII OLYMPIAD)	500	500.00	600.00
84	FAIRBANKS, THE (XXXIII OLYM. EQUES.)	200	500.00	550.00
84	ONE AND ONLY, THE (NEBRASKA)	225	450.00	500.00
84	WIMBLEDON WOMEN (100TH ANNIVERSARY)	500	450.00	800.00
85	A CENTURY OF EXCELLENCE (GA TECH)	225	500.00	550.00
85	CHRIS EVERT LLOYD	275	500.00	500.00
85	MIAMI ON THE MOVE (DOLPHINS)	225	500.00	600.00
85	TWENTY SIX & GLORY (OK STATE)	100	450.00	450.00
86	GLORY YEARS, THE (ICE BOWL)	135	500.00	2000.00
86	INDY 500, THE	175	500.00	600.00
86	KENTUCKY DERBY, THE	500	450.00	550.00
86	MARTINA NAVRATILOVA	275	500.00	550.00
86	OKLAHOMA NATIONAL CHAMPION (B. SWITZER)	100	500.00	800.00
86	ROYAL FINISH (KANSAS CITY)	300	522.00	600.00
86	SHOW ME SERIES, THE (K.C. WORLD SERIES)	375	450.00	550.00
86	WON FOR PAPA (SUPER BOWL)	200	500.00	4000.00
87	AMAZIN AGAIN: N.Y. METS	320	525.00	550.00
87	AMERICA'S COWBOYS (DALLAS)	310	500.00	550.00
87	BURGANDY IN GOLD (REDSKINS)	165	500.00	550.00
87	MILE HIGH DENVER BRONCOS	425	500.00	500.00
88	CUMMINGS AGAIN: BUCKS	175	500.00	550.00
88	LED BY THE SPIRIT (COTTON BOWL 88)	150	525.00	1500.00
88	NATIONAL CHAMPION HOOSIERS	250	525.00	525.00
88	NATIONAL CHAMPION JAYHAWKS	275	450.00	450.00
88	ON WISCONSIN	185	500.00	500.00
88	REACHING THE MARK (AMERICA'S CUP)	*	525.00	700.00
89	A TRADITION OF GOLD (NOTRE DAME)	275	550.00	550.00
89	HIGH FLYING CARDINALS (BASEBALL)	190	525.00	525.00
89	HIT & RUN BREWERS 1987	190	525.00	550.00
89	SECOND AND GOLD: 1987 ROSE BOWL	150	525.00	525.00
90	ABOVE THE CROWD (M. JORDAN)	200	525.00	600.00

YR	NAME	LIMIT	ISSUE	QUOTE

CROSS GALLERY

P. CROSS — **HALF BREED SERIES**

YR	NAME	LIMIT	ISSUE	QUOTE
89	ACH-HUA DLUBH: HALF BREED	475	190.00	1400.00
89	ACH-HUA DLUBH: HALF BREED II	475	225.00	675.00
90	ACH-HUA DLUBH: HALF BREED III	475	225.00	800.00

P. CROSS — **LIMITED EDITION ORIGINAL GRAPHICS**

YR	NAME	LIMIT	ISSUE	QUOTE
87	CAROLINE (STONE LITHO)	47	300.00	150.00
88	MAIDENHOOD HOPI (STONE LITHO)	74	950.00	600.00
89	RED CAPOTE, THE (SERIGRAPH)	275	750.00	400.00
89	ROSAPINA (ETCHING)	74	1200.00	800.00
90	NIGHTEYES I (SERIGRAPH)	275	225.00	175.00

P. CROSS — **LIMITED EDITION PRINTS**

YR	NAME	LIMIT	ISSUE	QUOTE
83	AYLA-SA-XUH-XAH (PRETTY COLOURS)	475	150.00	150.00
83	ISBAALOO EETSCHIILEEHCHEE (SORTING BEAD)	475	150.00	1750.00
84	BLUE BEADED HAIR TIES	475	85.00	400.00
84	DII-TAH-SHTEH EE-WIHZA-AHOOK (COAT)	475	90.00	2000.00
84	PROFILE OF CAROLINE	475	85.00	165.00
84	THICK LODGE CLAN BOY: CROW	475	85.00	180.00
84	WHISTLING WATER CLAN GIRL: CROW	475	85.00	125.00
84	WINTER MORNING	475	185.00	1400.00
85	WATER VISION, THE	475	150.00	200.00
86	GRAND ENTRY	475	85.00	175.00
86	RED CAPOTE, THE	475	150.00	200.00
86	WINTER SHAWL, THE	475	150.00	2600.00
87	CAROLINE	475	45.00	150.00
87	ELKSKIN ROBE, THE	475	190.00	400.00
87	RED NECKLACE, THE	475	90.00	150.00
87	TINA	475	45.00	175.00
88	DANCE APACHE	475	190.00	200.00
88	MA-A-LUPPIS-SHE-LA-DUS (SHE IS ABOVE)	475	190.00	775.00
89	B'ACHUA DLUBH-BIA BII NOSKIIYAHI, II	475	225.00	415.00
89	BIAACHEE-ITAH BAH-ACHBEH	475	225.00	250.00
89	CHEY-AYJEH: PREY	475	190.00	600.00
89	DREAMER, THE	475	190.00	150.00
89	TEESA WAITS TO DANCE	475	135.00	135.00
90	BAAPE OCHIA (NIGHT WIND, TURQUOISE)	475	185.00	175.00
90	ESHTE	475	185.00	175.00
90	ISHIA-KAHDA #1 (QUIET ONE)	475	185.00	150.00

P.A. CROSS — **MINIATURE LINE**

YR	NAME	LIMIT	ISSUE	QUOTE
91	BJ	447	80.00	150.00
91	KENDRA	447	80.00	150.00
91	THE FLORAL SHAWL	447	80.00	175.00
91	WATERCOLOR STUDY #32 FOR HALF BREED	447	80.00	80.00

P. CROSS — **STAR QUILT**

YR	NAME	LIMIT	ISSUE	QUOTE
85	WINTER WARMTH	475	150.00	1600.00
86	REFLECTIONS	475	185.00	850.00
88	QUILT MAKERS, THE	475	190.00	450.00

P. CROSS — **THE PAINTED LADIES' SUITE**

YR	NAME	LIMIT	ISSUE	QUOTE
92	ACORIA (CROW: SEAT OF HONOR)	447	80.00	175.00
92	AVISOLA	475	185.00	185.00
92	DAH-SAY (CROW: HEART)	475	185.00	185.00
92	ITZA-CHU (APACHE: THE EAGLE)	475	185.00	185.00
92	KEL'HOYA (HOPI: LITTLE SPARROW HAWK)	475	185.00	185.00
92	SUS(H)GAH-DAYDUS(H) (CROW: QUICK)	447	80.00	80.00
92	THE PAINTED LADIES	475	225.00	1200.00
92	TZE-GO-JUNI (CHIRICAHUA APACHE)	447	80.00	80.00

P. CROSS — **WOLF SERIES**

YR	NAME	LIMIT	ISSUE	QUOTE
85	DII-TAH-SHTEH BII-WIK; CHEDAH-BAH LIIDAH	475	185.00	2200.00
87	MORNING STAR GIVES LONG OTTER HIS HOOP	475	190.00	1850.00
89	BIAGOHT EECUEBEH HEHSHEESH-CHEDAH	475	225.00	175.00
90	AGNJNAUG AMAGUUT; INUPIAG (WOMEN/WOLVES)	1050	325.00	175.00

DELGADO STUDIO

YR	NAME	LIMIT	ISSUE	QUOTE
*	MICKEY AT NIGHT H/S	750	125.00	450.00
*	CAMACHO VS MACINI S/N	500	25.00	100.00
*	JOHN HENRY	750	75.00	275.00
*	THE CATCH A/P	49	149.00	275.00
*	THE CATCH S/N H/S	750	100.00	200.00
*	THE SHOES ROSES A/P	25	150.00	300.00
*	THE SHOES ROSES S/N	500	50.00	200.00

DELGADO — *

YR	NAME	LIMIT	ISSUE	QUOTE
*	HEAD TO HEAD EASY GOER & SUNDAY SILENCE	500	100.00	250.00
*	MONTANA TO RICE A/P	49	300.00	400.00
*	MONTANTA TO RICE H/S S/N	500	250.00	300.00
*	PAEZ VS LOPEZ S/N	500	25.00	100.00

YR	NAME	LIMIT	ISSUE	QUOTE
*	RONNIE LOTT H/S S/N	1049	149.00	225.00
*	WITAKER, TAYLER, CAMACHO AT CAESARS S/N	500	25.00	125.00

DIMENSIONAL AESTHETICS
B. HAILS

YR	NAME	LIMIT	ISSUE	QUOTE
*	CITY BREEZES	*	80.00	160.00
*	RIVER VISTA (THE GAP)	*	40.00	60.00
85	GAZEBO, THE	*	40.00	65.00
86	BRIGHT NEW DAY	*	40.00	60.00
86	SOLITUDE	*	40.00	60.00
86	TAVERN, THE	*	40.00	65.00
87	INDIAN SUMMER	*	40.00	60.00
87	LOCK, THE	*	75.00	95.00
87	QUIET LIGHT	*	40.00	60.00
88	AZALEA BANK A/P	*	90.00	180.00
89	AZALEA GLOW	*	40.00	40.00
89	TRACERY	*	40.00	50.00

EAGLE EDITIONS LTD.
J. CRANDALL

YR	NAME	LIMIT	ISSUE	QUOTE
77	SMOKE UP AHEAD	450	60.00	500.00
79	I FOUND THE PASS	500	60.00	550.00
79	PURSUED	525	60.00	650.00
80	ON TO TAOS	560	65.00	300.00
80	SHRINE TO THE BUFFALO	525	65.00	650.00
81	CAUTION	650	40.00	250.00
81	NOT ALONE	650	55.00	350.00
82	COUREURS DES BOIS	1000	75.00	250.00
83	AN EARLY SNOW	750	85.00	100.00

J. CRANDALL — WINGS OF VALOR

YR	NAME	LIMIT	ISSUE	QUOTE
85	MOUSE AND THE FLEA, THE: B-17	950	85.00	250.00
87	TOMCATS 2-FITTERS 0: F-14	950	85.00	750.00-1000.00
89	BLOND KNIGHT, THE: ME 109	950	145.00	850.00-1200.00

EDNA HIBEL STUDIOS
E. HIBEL — HIBEL LITHOGRAPHY ON PORCELAIN

YR	NAME	LIMIT	ISSUE	QUOTE
78	LENORE AND CHILD (ON PORCELAIN)	395	600.00	2100.00
80	CHERYLL AND WENDY (ON PORCELAIN)	100	3900.00	11500.00

E. HIBEL — HIBEL STONE LITHOGRAPHY

YR	NAME	LIMIT	ISSUE	QUOTE
*	BEGGAR	70	250.00	4700.00
74	MOTHER AND FOUR CHILDREN	60	150.00	1550.00
75	SANDY (STONE LITHO)	140	75.00	1550.00
76	ELSA & BABY	300	150.00	4200.00
76	JAPANESE DOLL	28	160.00	2600.00
76	KIKUE (SILK)	145	195.00	2700.00
76	MOTHER & FOUR CHILDREN (HORIZONTAL)	300	250.00	2000.00
76	SOPHIA & CHILDREN	296	325.00	4300.00
76	SWITZERLAND	270	350.00	2300.00
77	COLETTE & CHILD	275	195.00	1750.00
77	MAYAN MAN	295	350.00	4300.00
77	MUSEUM SUITE	375	1900.00	9700.00
78	FELICIA	148	900.00	3850.00
79	AKIKO & CHILDREN	335	450.00	2800.00
79	INTERNATIONAL YEAR OF THE CHILD SUITE	420	900.00	4200.00
79	JOSEPH	335	495.00	1325.00
79	NORA	394	175.00	850.00
79	PETRA MIT KINDER	320	345.00	4000.00
79	THAI PRINCESS	335	495.00	1450.00
80	CHERYLL & WENDY	100	3900.00	11500.00
80	CHO CHO SAN	396	500.00	1050.00
80	HOPE	396	400.00	1100.00
80	SPIRIT OF MAINAU SUITE, THE	385	1200.00	3150.00
80	TINA	200	750.00	1625.00
81	JACKLIN & CHILD	197	110.00	400.00
81	LITTLE EMPEROR, THE	275	1000.00	2250.00
81	LITTLE EMPRESS	319	1000.00	2100.00
82	BETTINA AND CHILDREN	300	310.00	1400.00
82	FAMILY OF THE MOUNTAIN LAKE	305	395.00	2900.00
82	JOELLE	348	295.00	1800.00
82	KELLY	347	320.00	1700.00
82	LYDIA	298	295.00	650.00
82	NARO-SAN	322	310.00	675.00
82	RENA & RACHEL	329	345.00	1025.00
83	VALERIE & CHILDREN	400	295.00	625.00
84	ARIELLE & AMY	275	295.00	675.00
84	BEVERLY & CHILD	216	160.00	425.00
84	CARESS, THE	430	325.00	700.00
84	CELESTE	256	175.00	400.00

YR	NAME	LIMIT	ISSUE	QUOTE
84	CLAIRE	206	335.00	975.00
84	DES FLEURS ROUGES	298	245.00	750.00
84	DORENE & CHILD	331	250.00	525.00
84	DREAM SKETCHBOOK	298	175.00	475.00
84	GERARD	200	250.00	725.00
84	JENNIFER & CHILDREN	318	445.00	775.00
84	NATASHA & CHILDREN	308	195.00	500.00
84	NAVA & CHILDREN	385	385.00	750.00
84	SANDY & CHILDREN	419	365.00	750.00
84	SARAH & JOSHUA	343	475.00	850.00
84	WENDY WITH HAT	308	395.00	725.00
85	LA TOSCA	355	595.00	725.00
86	BELINDA & NINA	320	295.00	625.00
86	DUCHESS	320	325.00	525.00
86	NANCY WITH MEGAN	367	450.00	900.00
87	FINNISH MOTHER & CHILD	343	185.00	325.00
87	FLOWERS OF KASHMIR	297	275.00	525.00
87	MONICA MATTEAO & VANESSA	300	350.00	650.00
87	ONCE UPON A TIME	287	365.00	550.00
88	AMELIA & CHILDREN	268	675.00	825.00
88	FLOWERS OF THE ADRIATIC	286	300.00	500.00
88	JOHN M	308	185.00	325.00
88	LINDA T	302	185.00	325.00
88	NEW HAT, THE	298	310.00	550.00
88	XIN-XIN OF THE HIGH MOUNTAINS	325	1300.00	2000.00
89	HELENE & CHILDREN	280	365.00	495.00
90	TAMARA	254	360.00	500.00

FOUNTAINHEAD
M. FERNANDEZ

	NAME	LIMIT	ISSUE	QUOTE
*	HEART OF SEVEN COLORS	*	*	950.00
*	MOST PRECIOUS GIFT	*	*	950.00
*	OH, SMALL CHILD	*	*	245.00
*	SPREADING THE WORD	*	*	100.00

FRAME HOUSE
C. HARPER

	NAME	LIMIT	ISSUE	QUOTE
*	ARCTIC CIRCLE-MUSKOX	*	*	175.00
*	BARK EYES-OWL	*	90.00	90.00
*	BIG RAC' ATTACK-RACCOON	*	*	125.00
*	BLACKBERRY JAM	*	90.00	90.00
*	BRRRRRDBATH	*	150.00	150.00
*	CARDINAL COURTSHIP	*	175.00	175.00
*	CARDINAL CRADLE	*	*	175.00
*	CHRISTMAS CAPER	*	25.00	25.00
*	CLAIR DE LOON	*	175.00	175.00
*	CONFISKATION-ROBIN	*	90.00	90.00
*	CONVIVIAL PURSUIT	*	125.00	125.00
*	COTTONTAIL IN A COTTONFIELD-RABBIT	*	*	125.00
*	CRABITAT	*	*	125.00
*	DREAM TEAM	*	*	20.00
*	EVERGLADE KITE	*	*	250.00
*	FEARLESS FEATHERS	*	125.00	125.00
*	FEARLESS FEATHERS	*	125.00	125.00
*	FLAMINGO A GO	*	150.00	150.00
*	FROG IN GRASS	*	*	250.00
*	GIFT RAPT-RACCOON	*	175.00	175.00
*	KOALA, KOALA-KOALA BEAR	*	*	20.00
*	LOVE ON A LIMB-MONKEY	*	125.00	125.00
*	LUCKY LADYBUG	*	*	55.00
*	MANATEE IN THE MANGROVE	*	195.00	195.00
*	MYSTERY OF THE MISSING MIGRANT-BIRD	*	*	30.00
*	OWLTERCATION	*	175.00	175.00
*	PACK PACT-MILL	*	175.00	175.00
*	PELICAN PANTRY	*	*	100.00
*	PFWHOOOO	*	*	145.00
*	PISCINE QUEUES	*	125.00	125.00
*	QUAILSAFE	*	*	90.00
*	RACCROBAT	*	*	10.00
*	RACCSNACK-RACCOON	*	*	120.00
*	SQUIRREL IN A SQUALL	*	135.00	135.00
*	SUGAR FREE	*	185.00	185.00
*	TAILGATOR	*	*	125.00
*	UPSIDE DOWNY	*	125.00	125.00
*	WINGDING	*	*	90.00
68	HOUSE WRENS	500	20.00	175.00
68	LADYBUG	500	20.00	300.00

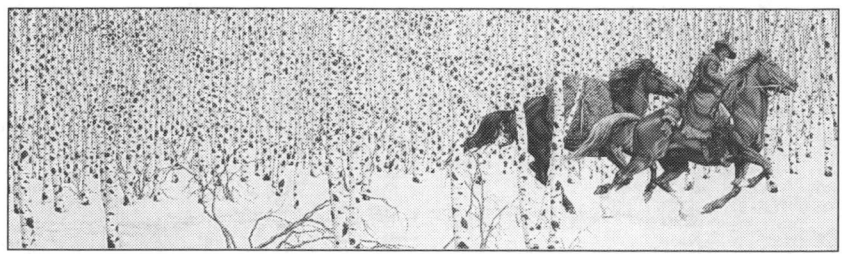

An Indian spirit and his eagles watch over Sacred Ground *in Bev Doolittle's limited edition print of the same name. Published by The Greenwich Workshop.*

How many hidden images can you find in Bev Doolittle's Eagle Heart? *Produced by The Greenwich Workshop.*

YR	NAME	LIMIT	ISSUE	QUOTE
68	LADYBUG (LITHO)	10,000	6.00	50.00
68	PORTFOLIO OF FOUR PRINTS	500	60.00	375.00
69	ANHINGA (LITHO ON CANVAS)	500	50.00	225.00
69	HUNGRY EYES	500	20.00	600.00
69	WATER STRIDER	500	40.00	475.00
70	BOBWHITE FAMILY	750	30.00	150.00
70	BURROWING OWL	500	30.00	200.00
70	CARDINAL (ON CORN)	500	30.00	400.00
70	CRAYFISH MOLTING	750	30.00	150.00
70	PILEATED WOODPECKER	750	30.00	150.00
71	BEETLE BATTLE	750	30.00	100.00
71	BLUE JAY BATHING	1500	30.00	90.00
71	LADYBUG LOVERS	1500	30.00	145.00
71	PUFFIN	750	30.00	140.00
71	RED-BELLIED WOODPECKER	1500	30.00	100.00
72	BEAR IN THE BIRCHES	1500	35.00	525.00
72	BOX TURTLE	1500	30.00	95.00
72	CHIPMUNK	1500	30.00	120.00
72	FAMILY OWLBUM	1500	30.00	110.00
72	PELICAN IN A DOWNPOUR	1500	30.00	400.00
72	YELLOW BELLIED SAPSUCKER	1500	30.00	110.00
73	LAST SUNFLOWER SEED, THE	1500	30.00	300.00
73	ROUND ROBIN	1500	30.00	90.00
73	WATERMELON MOON	1500	30.00	450.00
73	WEDDING FEAST	1500	30.00	100.00
73	WOOD DUCK	1500	30.00	325.00
74	BIRDS OF A FEATHER	2000	50.00	100.00
74	COOL CARDINAL	2000	30.00	435.00
74	CROW IN THE SNOW	1500	35.00	300.00
74	FINE FEATHER	1500	30.00	120.00
74	PAINTED BUNTING	1500	30.00	90.00
74	TALL TAIL	2000	30.00	100.00
75	BIRDWATCHER	2000	40.00	325.00
75	BLUEBIRDS IN THE BLUEGRASS	2000	45.00	90.00
75	RACCPACK	2000	35.00	150.00
75	WHITECOAT	2000	30.00	200.00
76	CLAWS	2000	40.00	120.00
76	CORNPONE	2500	40.00	150.00
76	DEVOTION IN THE OCEAN	2000	40.00	120.00
76	LOVE FROM ABOVE	2000	40.00	375.00
76	SKIMMERSCAPE	2000	40.00	110.00
77	BRRRTHDAY	2500	40.00	90.00
77	CATNIP	2500	50.00	125.00
77	DOLFUN	2500	50.00	90.00
77	DOWN UNDER, DOWN UNDER	2500	40.00	80.00
77	PHANCY PHEATHERS	2500	50.00	125.00
77	SEEING RED	2500	40.00	125.00
77	SKIPPING SCHOOL	2500	50.00	80.00
78	BITTERN SUITE	2500	50.00	75.00
78	CRAWLING TALL	3500	50.00	90.00
78	FROG EAT FROG	2500	50.00	100.00
78	HARE'S BREADTH	2500	50.00	70.00
78	LOVEY DOVEY	2500	50.00	100.00
79	BUZZ OFF YOU TURKEY	2500	55.00	75.00
79	COOL CARNIVORE	2500	50.00	60.00
79	FURRED FEEDER	2500	50.00	100.00
79	SERENGETI SPAGHETTI	2500	40.00	110.00
80	HEXIT	1500	60.00	90.00
80	JUMBRELLA	1500	60.00	100.00
80	POTLUCK	1500	60.00	110.00
80	REDBIRDS AND REDBUDS	1500	60.00	120.00
81	FOXSIMILES	1500	60.00	60.00
81	LAST APHID	1500	60.00	135.00
81	RACC & RUIN	1500	60.00	150.00
81	ROMANCE ON THE RICHTER SCALE-WHALE	1500	60.00	140.00
82	ARMADITTO	1500	60.00	90.00
82	PRICKLEY PAIR	1500	60.00	90.00
82	TERN, STONES, AND TURNSTONES	1500	60.00	85.00
84	GREEN CUISINE	1000	90.00	110.00
84	PIER GROUP	1000	90.00	250.00
84	RACCOONNAISSANCE	1000	90.00	120.00
85	HERONDIPITY-HERON	500	175.00	225.00
85	VOWLENTINE	1000	45.00	75.00
86	B-R-R-R-R-R-DBATH	1000	125.00	150.00
86	LOONRISE-LOON DUCK	500	175.00	175.00
74	RURAL AMERICANA	1500	40.00	310.00

YR	NAME	LIMIT	ISSUE	QUOTE
75	AMERICAN BYWAYS	1500	40.00	385.00
75	COUNTRY SEASONIN'	1500	40.00	245.00
75	DISAPPEARING AMERICA	1500	40.00	1200.00
76	RURAL DELIVERY	1500	40.00	315.00
76	YESTERYEAR	1500	50.00	145.00
77	BURMA SHAVE	1500	50.00	260.00
77	COMMUNITY CHURCH	1500	50.00	175.00
77	DR. PEPPER	1500	50.00	170.00
77	FALLOW AND FORGOTTON	1500	50.00	165.00
78	666 COLD TABLETS	1500	50.00	150.00
78	PHILIP MORRIS	1500	50.00	180.00
78	RC COLA	975	135.00	135.00
78	RED COVERED BRIDGE	1500	50.00	300.00
78	TOOLS	300	275.00	350.00
78	WOODPILE	1500	75.00	150.00
79	CLABBER GIRL	1500	75.00	350.00
79	GOLD DUST TWINS	1500	55.00	135.00
79	GOODY'S	1500	50.00	150.00
79	LUCKY STRIKE	1500	50.00	200.00
80	PEANUTS AND PEPSI	1500	60.00	270.00
80	TONIC AND LINIMENT	1500	85.00	195.00
80	TUBE ROSE SNUFF	1500	60.00	120.00
80	UNPAINTED COVERED BRIDGE	1500	60.00	150.00
81	7-UP AND BLACK EYED SUSANS	1500	75.00	90.00
81	BRUSH AND BUCKET	300	300.00	300.00
81	HOUSE AND BARN	1500	50.00	120.00
81	OLD DUTCH CLEANSER	1500	75.00	135.00
82	BULL OF THE WOODS	1500	75.00	115.00
82	RAILROAD CROSSING	1500	75.00	400.00
82	WINDMILL	1500	75.00	115.00
83	FILLIN' STATION	1500	80.00	200.00
83	FRESH GRITS	1500	80.00	808.00
83	LEE OVERALLS	OP	7.50	20.00
83	LIGHTHOUSE	975	135.00	315.00
83	MOUNTAIN BRIDGE	1500	80.00	200.00
83	SHRINE CIRCUS	1500	80.00	80.00
84	MEMORIES	408	90.00	250.00
84	MORTON SALT AND ROCK CITY	1500	135.00	190.00
84	RED GOOSE SHOES	1500	90.00	90.00
85	MEMORIES II	431	90.00	150.00
85	OLD STONE BARN	1500	90.00	90.00
85	SPRING CLOUDS	1500	90.00	150.00
86	FISHING VILLAGE	975	135.00	175.00
87	COCA-COLA BRIDGE	975	135.00	468.00
87	JEFFERSON ISLAND SALT	975	135.00	160.00
87	UNCLE JOHN'S SYRUP	975	135.00	150.00
88	HERSHEY BAR	975	135.00	200.00
88	RED BOAT	975	135.00	175.00
84	LAZY AFTERNOON	1500	75.00	130.00
85	FOX IN REEDS	1500	75.00	135.00
86	SNOW LEOPARD	1000	150.00	380.00
88	DAWN ALERT	TL	160.00	195.00

GARTLAN USA
TAYLOR *

*	JOE MONTANA, SIGNED, H/S	500	495.00	545.00
*	KAREEM ABDUL-JABBAR, PRINT	1989	175.00	350.00

J. MARTIN LITHOGRAPH

86	GEORGE BRETT: THE SWING	2000	85.00	85.00
87	ROGER STAUBACK	1979	85.00	85.00
89	KAREEM ABDUL-JABBAR: THE RECORD SETTER	1989	125.00	175.00
90	DARRYL STRAWBERRY	500	295.00	295.00

GREENWICH WORKSHOP
J. CHRISTENSEN CHRISTENSEN

*	ANGEL WITH FISH	*	*	275.00
*	BIRDS HUNTERS FULL CAMO.	*	*	165.00
*	COLLEGE MAGIC	*	*	650.00
*	FISH WATER	*	*	3200.00
*	RHYMES & REASONS	OP	*	150.00
85	THE GIFT FOR MRS. CLAUS	3,500	80.00	675.00
86	JONAH	850	95.00	225.00
86	OLDE WORLD SANTA	3,500	80.00	375.00
86	YOUR PLACE, OR MINE?	850	125.00	175.00
87	OLD MAN WITH ALOT ON HIS MIND	850	85.00	675.00
87	VOYAGE OF THE BASSET	850	225.00	1350.00
88	MAN WHO MINDS THE MOON, THE	850	145.00	750.00

YR	NAME	LIMIT	ISSUE	QUOTE
88	WIDOW'S MITE, THE	850	145.00	2500.00
89	ANNUNCIATION, THE	850	175.00	175.00
90	BURDEN OF THE RESPONSIBLE MAN, THE	850	145.00	1300.00
90	RHYMES & REASONS	OP	150.00	675.00
90	TWO SISTERS	650	325.00	325.00
91	CANDLEMAN, THE	850	160.00	185.00
91	LAWRENCE AND A BEAR	850	145.00	250.00
91	ONCE UPON A TIME	1,500	175.00	1450.00
91	ONCE UPON A TIME (REMARQUE)	500	375.00	1650.00
91	PELICAN KING	850	115.00	450.00
92	OLDEST ANGEL, THE	850	125.00	715.00
92	RESPONSIBLE WOMAN, THE	2,500	175.00	175.00
92	ROYAL PROCESSIONAL, THE	1,500	185.00	550.00
92	ROYAL PROCESSIONAL, THE- REMARQUE	1,500	185.00	850.00
93	COLLEGE OF MAGICAL KNOWLEDGE	4,500	185.00	185.00
93	GETTING IT RIGHT	4,000	185.00	185.00
93	ROYAL MUSIC BARQUE, THE	2,750	375.00	375.00
93	SCHOLAR, THE	3,250	125.00	125.00
93	WAITING FOR THE TIDE	2,250	150.00	150.00
B. DOOLITTLE				**DOOLITTLE**
*	EAGLE HEART, NOT FRAMED	*	*	715.00
*	GHOST OF THE GRIZZLY	*	*	3500.00
*	GRIZZLY TREE	*	*	3500.00
*	HIDE AND SEEK-7 PC. COMP SET	*	*	1200.00
*	HIDE AND SEEK-LG	*	*	300.00
*	HIDE AND SEEK-MINI	*	*	250.00
*	PRAYER FOR THE WILD THINGS	*	*	375.00
*	SACRED CIRCLE	*	*	450.00
*	TWO MORE INDIAN HORSES	*	*	345.00
*	WHEN THE WIND HAD WINGS	*	*	325.00
*	WILDERNESS...WILDERNESS!!!	*	*	65.00
79	PINTOS	1000	65.00	11500.00
80	BUGGED BEAR	1000	85.00	3500.00
80	GOOD OMEN, THE	1000	85.00	4250.00
80	WHOO!?	1000	75.00	1800.00
81	SPIRIT OF THE GRIZZLY	1500	150.00	4600.00
81	UNKNOWN PRESENCE	1500	150.00	3400.00
81	WOODLAND ENCOUNTER	1500	145.00	9500.00
82	EAGLE'S FLIGHT	1500	185.00	3900.00
83	CHRISTMAS DAY, GIVE OR TAKE A WEEK	4800	80.00	2300.00
83	ESCAPE BY A HARE	1500	80.00	950.00
83	RUNS WITH THUNDER	1500	150.00	2100.00
83	RUSHING WAR EAGLE	1500	150.00	1850.00
84	LET MY SPIRIT SOAR	1500	195.00	7650.00
85	TWO INDIAN HORSES	12,253	225.00	3650.00
85	WOLVES OF THE CROW	2650	225.00	2450.00
86	TWO BEARS OF THE BLACKFEET	2650	225.00	1600.00
86	WHERE SILENCE SPEAKS, ART OF DOOLITTLE	3500	650.00	3500.00
87	CALLING THE BUFFALO	8500	245.00	1550.00
87	GUARDIAN SPIRITS	13,238	295.00	1400.00
87	SEASON OF THE EAGLE	36,548	245.00	800.00
88	DOUBLED BACK-BEAR	15,000	245.00	1850.00
89	SACRED GROUND	70,000	265.00	925.00
90	HIDE AND SEEK SUITE	25,000	1200.00	1980.00
91	SACRED CIRCLE (PC)	40,192	325.00	1540.00
91	SENTINEL, THE	35,000	275.00	825.00
92	EAGLE HEART	48,000	285.00	345.00
J. CHRISTENSEN				**ETCHING**
*	ARTIST, THE	*	*	450.00
*	GIFT, THE	*	*	350.00
*	OLD ANGEL	*	*	350.00
*	WIZARD	*	*	50.00
J. CHRISTENSEN				**FANTASY**
*	EVENING ANGELS	*	*	195.00
*	PISCATORIAL PERCUSSIONIST	*	*	125.00
*	SERENADE FOR AN ORANGE CAT	*	*	125.00
*	SISTERS OF THE SEA	*	*	195.00
*	SOMETIMES THE SPIRIT..W/BOOK	*	*	195.00
*	TWO ANGEL DISCUSS BOTTICELI	*	*	145.00
J. CHRISTENSEN				**FANTASY/ETCHING**
*	FISH WATER	*	*	300.00
*	FISHE	*	*	325.00
*	MECHANICAL FISH	*	*	300.00
*	MIDNIGHT SCHOLAR	*	*	350.00
*	MUSICIAN	*	*	300.00

YR	NAME	LIMIT	ISSUE	QUOTE
J. CHRISTENSEN				**FANTASY/LITHO**
*	ANGEL IN PURSUIT FISH KNOW.	*	*	300.00
*	CONVERSATION AROUND FISH	*	*	600.00
*	FISH ANGEL	*	*	400.00
B. DOOLITTLE				**HORSE**
*	HIDE AND SEEK-NUM MINI-1C	*	*	150.00
*	HIDE AND SEEK-NUM MINI-2A	*	*	150.00
*	HIDE AND SEEK-NUM MINI-2C	*	*	150.00
*	HIDE AND SEEK-NUM MINI-3B	*	*	150.00
*	HIDE AND SEEK-NUM MINI-3D	*	*	150.00
B. DOOLITTLE				**INDIAN**
*	FOREST HAS EYES, THE	*	*	5250.00
*	IN THE LAND OF ANCIENT ONES	*	*	245.00
*	NAVAJO PONIES FOR COMANCHE	*	*	225.00
*	SHOW OF DEFIANCE	*	*	195.00
*	SIGHTING THE INTRUDERS	*	*	225.00
*	WAY OF ANCIENT MIGRATION	*	*	245.00
*	WHEN THE LAND WAS THEIRS	*	*	225.00
*	WHERE OTHERS HAD PASSED	*	*	245.00
S. LYMAN				**LANDSCAPE**
*	CATHEDRAL SNOW-LANDSCAPE	*	*	245.00
*	LAKE OF THE SHINING ROCKS-LANDSCAPE	*	*	300.00
*	NORTH COUNTRY SHORES-LANDSCAPE	*	*	225.00
J. CHRISTENSEN				**LITHO**
*	COPADEORA	*	350.00	350.00
S. LYMAN				**LYMAN**
*	BIG COUNTRY, THE-GRIZZLY	*	*	20.00
*	FIRE DANCE-CAMPFIRE	*	*	300.00
*	MIDNIGHT FIRE	*	*	245.00
*	MOONFIRE	*	*	475.00
*	MOONLIT FLIGHT,CHRISTMAS	*	*	165.00
*	NEW KID ON THE ROCK-OTTER	*	*	185.00
*	NEW TERRITORY-GRIZZLY BEAR	*	*	225.00
*	RIPARIAN RICHES-G/B HERON	*	*	235.00
*	RIVER OF LIGHT	*	*	225.00
*	SPIRIT OF CHRISTMAS-SANTA	*	*	300.00
*	THUNDERBOLT	*	*	235.00
*	WILDERNESS WELCOME	*	*	595.00
*	WILDFLOWER SUITE	*	*	175.00
*	WOODLAND HAVEN-ELK	*	*	195.00
83	EARLY WINTER IN THE MOUNTAINS	850	95.00	150.00
83	END OF THE RIDGE	850	95.00	200.00
83	PASS, THE	850	95.00	450.00
84	FREE FLIGHT	850	70.00	70.00
84	NOISY NEIGHBORS (R)	25	215.00	95.00
85	AUTUMN GATHERING-LANDSCAPE	850	115.00	250.00
85	BEAR & BLOSSOMS-BLACK BEAR	850	75.00	75.00
86	COLORS OF TWILIGHT	850	*	*
86	HIGH TRAIL AT SUNSET-MOUNTAIN GOAT	1000	125.00	650.00
86	MORNING SOLITUDE-GREY BLUE HERON	850	115.00	150.00
86	SNOWY THRONE (C)	850	85.00	85.00
87	AN ELEGANT COUPLE	1000	125.00	150.00
87	CANADIAN AUTUMN-MOOSE	1500	165.00	200.00
87	ELEGANT COUPLE-WOOD DUCK	*	*	150.00
87	HIGH CREEK CROSSING-BISON	1000	165.00	825.00
87	MOON SHADOWS-CANADA GOOSE	1500	135.00	135.00
87	TWILIGHT SNOW-BLUE JAY	950	85.00	195.00
88	INTRUDER, THE	1500	150.00	150.00
88	RAPTOR'S WATCH, THE-EAGLE	1500	150.00	300.00
88	RETURN OF THE FALCON	1500	150.00	150.00
88	SNOW HUNTER-BOBCAT	1500	135.00	135.00
88	UZUMATI: GREAT BEAR OF YOSEMITE	1750	150.00	150.00
89	COLOR IN THE SNOW-PHEASANT	1500	165.00	165.00
89	HIGH LIGHT	1250	165.00	480.00
89	LAST LIGHT OF WINTER-CANADA GOOSE	1500	175.00	1500.00
89	QUIET RAIN-CANADA GOOSE	1500	165.00	350.00
90	A MOUNTAIN CAMPFIRE	1500	195.00	2850.00
90	AMONG THE WILD BRAMBLES-KESTREL	1750	185.00	185.00
90	EVENING LIGHT	2500	225.00	1450.00
90	SILENT SNOWS-WOLF	1750	210.00	210.00
91	DANCE OF CLOUD AND CLIFF-LANDSCAPE	1500	225.00	325.00
91	DANCE OF WATER AND LIGHT	*	225.00	275.00
91	EMBERS AT DAWN	3500	225.00	1600.00
91	SECRET WATCH-LYNX	2250	150.00	150.00
92	WARMED BY THE VIEW-CAMPFIRE	8500	235.00	325.00

YR	NAME	LIMIT	ISSUE	QUOTE
	F. MCCARTHY			**MCCARTHY**
*	ON THE OLD NORTH TRAIL	*	*	900.00
*	SHADOWS OF THE WARRIORS	*	*	225.00
74	HUNT, THE	1000	75.00	800.00
74	LONE SENTINEL	1000	55.00	1175.00
74	LONG COLUMN	1000	75.00	600.00
74	NIGHT THEY NEEDED A GOOD RIBBON MAN, THE	1000	65.00	300.00
75	RETURNING RAIDERS	1000	75.00	460.00
75	SMOKE WAS THEIR ALLY	1000	75.00	310.00
75	SURVIVOR, THE	1000	65.00	380.00
75	WAITING FOR THE ESCORT	1000	75.00	170.00
76	HOSTILES, THE	1000	75.00	690.00
76	PACKING IN	1000	65.00	700.00
76	SIOUX WARRIORS	650	55.00	440.00
76	WARRIOR, THE	650	50.00	170.00
77	AN OLD TIME MOUNTAIN MAN	1000	65.00	225.00
77	BEAVER MEN, THE	1000	75.00	590.00
77	COMANCHE MOON	1000	75.00	340.00
77	DISTANT THUNDER	1500	75.00	1000.00
77	DUST STAINED POSSE	1000	75.00	400.00
77	ROBE SIGNAL	850	60.00	550.00
78	AMBUSH, THE	1000	125.00	375.00
78	BEFORE THE NORTHER	1000	90.00	550.00
78	FORDING, THE	1000	75.00	350.00
78	IN THE PASS	1500	90.00	190.00
78	NIGHT CROSSING	1000	75.00	280.00
78	SINGLE FILE	1000	75.00	600.00
78	TO BATTLE	1000	75.00	500.00
79	LONER, THE	1000	75.00	380.00
79	ON THE WARPATH	1000	75.00	185.00
79	PRAYER, THE	1500	90.00	550.00
79	RETREAT TO HIGHER GROUND	2000	90.00	830.00
80	A TIME OF DECISION	1150	125.00	310.00
80	BEFORE THE CHARGE	1000	115.00	195.00
80	FORBIDDEN LAND	1000	125.00	165.00
80	ROAR OF THE NORTHER	1000	90.00	260.00
80	SNOW MOON	1000	115.00	300.00
80	TROOPER, THE	1000	90.00	220.00
81	COUP, THE	1000	125.00	440.00
81	CROSSING THE DIVIDE/THE OLD WEST	1500	850.00	1900.00
81	HEADED NORTH	1000	150.00	370.00
81	RACE WITH THE HOSTILES	1000	135.00	150.00
81	SURROUNDED	1000	150.00	275.00
81	UNDER HOSTILE FIRE	1000	150.00	195.00
82	ALERT	1000	135.00	150.00
82	APACHE SCOUT	1000	165.00	165.00
82	ATTACK ON THE WAGON TRAIN	1400	150.00	200.00
82	CHALLENGE, THE	1000	175.00	500.00
82	WARRIORS, THE	1000	150.00	160.00
83	BLACKFOOT RAIDERS	1000	90.00	340.00
83	BURNING THE WAY STATION	1000	175.00	400.00
83	IN THE LAND OF THE SPARROW HAWK PEOPLE	1000	165.00	165.00
83	MOONLIT TRAIL	1000	90.00	195.00
83	OUT OF THE MIST THEY CAME	1000	165.00	300.00
83	UNDER ATTACK	5676	125.00	920.00
84	AFTER THE DUST STORM	1000	145.00	140.00
84	ALONG THE WEST FORK	1000	175.00	320.00
84	DECOYS, THE	450	325.00	690.00
84	SAVAGE TAUNT, THE	1000	225.00	690.00
84	WATCHING THE WAGONS	1400	175.00	750.00
84	WHIRLING HE RACED TO MEET THE CHALLENGE	1000	175.00	790.00
85	CHARGING THE CHALLENGER	1000	150.00	875.00
85	FIREBOAT, THE	1000	175.00	175.00
85	LAST CROSSING, THE	550	*	450.00
85	LONG KNIVES, THE	1000	175.00	1290.00
85	SCOUTING THE LONG KNIVES	1400	195.00	390.00
85	TRADERS, THE	1000	195.00	150.00
86	CHILDREN OF THE RAVEN	1000	185.00	980.00
86	COMANCHE WAR TRAIL	1000	165.00	165.00
86	DRIVE, THE	1000	95.00	190.00
86	RED BULL'S WAR PARTY	1000	165.00	160.00
86	SPOOKED	1400	195.00	195.00
86	WHERE TRACKS WILL BE LOST	550	350.00	500.00
87	CHIRICAHUA RAIDERS	1000	165.00	300.00
87	FOLLOWING THE HERDS	1000	195.00	670.00
87	FROM THE RIM	1000	225.00	250.00

YR	NAME	LIMIT	ISSUE	QUOTE
87	IN THE LAND OF THE WINTER HAWK	1000	225.00	550.00
87	WHEN OMENS TURN BAD	1000	165.00	770.00
88	APACHE TRACKERS	1000	95.00	150.00
88	BUFFALO RUNNERS, THE	1000	195.00	300.00
88	HOSTILE LAND, THE	1000	225.00	225.00
88	IN PURSUIT OF THE WHITE BUFFALO	1500	225.00	950.00
88	LAST STAND, THE: LITTLE BIG HORN	2250	225.00	190.00
88	SABER CHARGE	2250	225.00	225.00
88	TURNING THE LEADERS	1500	225.00	150.00
89	BIG MEDICINE	1000	225.00	580.00
89	CANYON LANDS	1250	225.00	225.00
89	COMING OF THE IRON HORSE, THE	1500	225.00	225.00
89	COMING OF/IRON HORSE, THE (PRINT/PEWTER)	100	1500.00	3600.00
89	DOWN FROM THE MOUNTAINS	1500	245.00	240.00
89	LOS DIABLOS	1250	225.00	225.00
90	BELOW THE BREAKING DAWN	1250	225.00	225.00
90	HOKA HEY: SIOUX WAR CRY	1250	225.00	225.00
90	OUT OF THE WINDSWEPT RAMPARTS	1250	225.00	225.00
90	WINTER TRAIL	1500	235.00	235.00
91	PONY EXPRESS	1000	225.00	225.00
91	PURSUIT, THE	650	550.00	550.00
91	WILD ONES, THE	1000	225.00	225.00
F. MCCARTHY				**WESTERN**
*	BENEATH THE CLIFF OF SPIRIT	*	*	295.00
*	BREAK'G THE MOONLIT SILENCE	*	*	375.00
*	BY ANICENT TRAILS THEY PASS	*	*	245.00
*	CHARGE OF BUFFALO SOLDIERS	*	*	195.00
*	CHASE, THE	*	*	225.00
*	FLASHES OF LIGHTNING	*	*	435.00
*	HEADING BACK	*	*	225.00
*	SPLITTING THE HERD	*	*	465.00
*	WHERE ANCIENT ONES HUNTED	*	*	300.00
*	WITH PISTOLS DRAWN	*	*	195.00
C. WYSOCKI				**WYSOCKI**
*	CARNIVAL CAPERS	*	*	200.00
*	CHUMBUDDIES (SIGNED FAP)	*	*	55.00
*	CHUMBUDDIES (UNSIGNED FAP)	*	*	40.00
*	COMMEMORATIVE PRINT-1984	*	*	55.00
*	COMMEMORATIVE PRINT-1985	*	*	55.00
*	COMMEMORATIVE PRINT-1986	*	*	55.00
*	ETHEL THE GOURMET-CAT	*	*	385.00
*	GANG'S ALL HERE, THE W/REM	*	*	90.00
*	GANG'S ALL HERE, THE/TEDDY BEAR	*	*	65.00
*	GAY HEAD LIGHT/LIGHTHOUSE	*	*	165.00
*	HOME SWEET HOME	*	*	25.00
*	I LOVE AMERICA	*	*	20.00
*	LOST IN THE WOODIES	*	*	195.00
*	LOVE LETTER FROM LARAMIE	*	*	150.00
*	MABEL THE STOWAWAY	*	*	175.00
*	MABEL THE STOWAWAY/CANVAS	*	*	495.00
*	MABEL THE STOWAWAY/FRAMED	*	*	
*	OLD BUCKS COUNTY	*	*	275.00
*	PLUM ISLAND SOUND POSTER	*	*	40.00
*	PROUD LITTLE ANGLER	*	*	190.00
*	REMINGTON, HORT/W BOOK, CAT	*	*	300.00
*	ROOT BEAR BREAK/BUTTERFIELD	*	*	160.00
*	SMALL TOWN CHRISTMAS	*	*	145.00
*	THREE SISTERS OF NAUSET/LIGHTHOUSE	*	*	165.00
*	WARM CHRISTMAS LOVE	*	*	450.00
79	BUTTERNUT FARMS	1000	75.00	1150.00
79	FAIRHAVEN BY THE SEA	1000	75.00	800.00
79	FOX RUN	1000	75.00	1600.00
79	SHALL WE?	1000	75.00	425.00
80	CALEB'S BUGGY BARN	1000	80.00	275.00
80	DERBY SQUARE	1000	90.00	825.00
80	JOLLY HILL FARMS	1000	75.00	700.00
81	CARVER COGGINS	1000	145.00	800.00
81	OLDE AMERICA	1500	125.00	475.00
81	PAGE'S BAKE SHOPPE	1000	115.00	550.00
81	PRAIRIE WIND FLOWERS	1000	125.00	2475.00
82	CHRISTMAS PRINT, 1982	2000	80.00	800.00
82	NANTUCKET, THE	1000	145.00	145.00
82	SLEEPY TOWN WEST	1500	150.00	400.00
82	SUNSET HILLS, TEXAS WILDCATTERS	1000	125.00	150.00
83	AMISH NEIGHBORS	1000	150.00	500.00
83	APPLEBUTTER MAKERS	1000	135.00	675.00

YR	NAME	LIMIT	ISSUE	QUOTE
83	COMMEMORATIVE PRINT, 1983	2000	55.00	55.00
83	COUNTRY RACE	1000	150.00	300.00
83	TEA BY THE SEA	1000	145.00	1200.00
84	A WARM CHRISTMAS LOVE	3951	80.00	425.00
84	BIRD HOUSE	1000	85.00	200.00
84	CAPE COD COLD FISH PARTY	1000	150.00	225.00
84	COTTON COUNTRY	1000	150.00	250.00
84	FOXY FOX OUTFOXES THE FOX HUNTERS, THE	1500	150.00	500.00
84	STORIN' UP	450	325.00	750.00
84	SWEETHEART CHESSMATE	1000	95.00	350.00
84	YANKEE WINK HOLLOW	1000	95.00	900.00
85	BIRDS OF A FEATHER	1250	145.00	300.00
85	CLAMMERS AT HODGE'S HORN	1000	150.00	900.00
85	DEVILSTONE HARBOR/AN AMERICAN CELEB.	3500	195.00	350.00
85	MERRYMAKERS SERENADE	1250	135.00	135.00
85	SALTY WITCH BAY	475	350.00	2500.00
86	DADDY'S COMING HOME	1250	150.00	1200.00
86	DANCING PHEASANT FARMS	1750	165.00	325.00
86	DEVILBELLY BAY	1000	145.00	275.00
86	HICKORY HAVEN CANAL	1500	165.00	725.00
86	LADY LIBERTY INDEPENDENCE DAY	1500	140.00	300.00
86	MR. SWALLOBARK	2000	145.00	450.00
87	BACH'S MAGNIFICAT IN D MINOR	2250	150.00	500.00
87	DAHALIA DINALHAVEN MAKES A DORY DEAL	2250	150.00	250.00
87	TWAS THE TWILIGHT BEFORE CHRISTMAS	7500	95.00	165.00
87	YEARNING FOR MY CAPTAIN	2000	150.00	300.00
87	YOU'VE BEEN SO LONG AT SEA, HORATIO	2500	150.00	225.00
88	AMERICANA BOWL, THE	3500	295.00	295.00
88	FEATHERED CRITICS	2500	150.00	150.00
88	HOME IS MY SAILOR	2500	150.00	150.00
89	ANOTHER YEAR AT SEA	2500	175.00	800.00
89	BOSTONIANS AND BEANS	6711	225.00	600.00
89	CHRISTMAS GREETING	11,000	125.00	150.00
89	DREAMERS	3000	175.00	325.00
89	FUN LOVIN' SILLY FOLKS	3000	185.00	185.00
89	MEMORY MAKER, THE	2500	165.00	165.00
90	BELLY WARMERS	2500	150.00	150.00
90	JINGLE BELL TEDDY AND FRIENDS	5000	125.00	125.00
90	ROBIN HOOD	2000	165.00	165.00
90	WEDNESDAY NIGHT CHECKERS	2500	175.00	175.00
90	WHERE THE BOUYS ARE	2750	175.00	175.00
91	BEAUTY AND THE BEAST	2000	125.00	125.00
91	ROCKLAND BREAKWATER LIGHT	2500	165.00	300.00
91	SEA CAPTAIN'S WIFE ABIDING	1500	150.00	150.00
91	WEST QUODDY HEAD LIGHT	*	165.00	165.00
91	WHISTLE STOP CHRISTMAS	5000	125.00	125.00
92	FREDERICK THE LITERATE-CAT	6500	150.00	2550.00

GUILDHALL INC.
W. BAIZE

88	BEST OF FRIENDS	575	85.00	175.00
88	WINTER ARRIVAL	575	85.00	95.00
75	THREE OF A KIND	1000	30.00	140.00
79	FOGGY MORNIN' WAIT	650	75.00	2000.00
80	CIRCLE, THE	1000	30.00	140.00
80	TEXAS PANHANDLE	650	75.00	1250.00
81	FORGIN' THE KEECHI	85	650.00	380.00
81	MAC TAVISH	650	65.00	1480.00
81	SURPRISE ENCOUNTER	750	85.00	199.00
82	O' THAT STRAWBERRY ROAN	750	85.00	384.00
83	CROSSIN' HORSE CREEK	650	100.00	320.00
83	KEEP A MOVIN' DAN	750	85.00	200.00
83	RIDIN' OL' PAINT	750	85.00	1000.00
83	TWO OLD RENEGADES	150	150.00	3600.00
84	JAKE	650	100.00	450.00
84	SPOOKED	650	95.00	1400.00
85	HORSEMEN OF THE WEST (SUITE OF 3)	650	145.00	750.00
85	KEECHI COUNTRY	750	100.00	180.00
85	OKLAHOMA PAINTS	750	100.00	420.00
85	UP THE CHISHOLM	750	85.00	200.00
86	LONER, THE (W/BELT BUCKLE)	750	145.00	640.00
86	MOON DANCERS	750	100.00	220.00
86	MUSTANGERS, THE	750	100.00	440.00
86	SEARCHERS, THE	650	100.00	270.00
87	CROW CEREMONIAL DRESS	750	100.00	220.00
87	MURPHY'S LAW	750	100.00	350.00
87	SNOW BIRDS	750	100.00	280.00

YR	NAME	LIMIT	ISSUE	QUOTE
87	SUPREMECY	750	100.00	300.00
87	WINTER SONGSINGER	750	95.00	190.00
88	MORNIN' GATHER	750	100.00	700.00
88	STAGE TO DEADWOOD	750	100.00	300.00
88	WATER BREAKIN'	750	125.00	700.00
89	CROWS	800	135.00	850.00
89	KENTUCKY BLUE	750	125.00	700.00
89	QUARTER HORSE, THE	800	125.00	160.00
89	VILLAGE MARKERS	750	125.00	300.00
90	CROW AUTUMN	925	135.00	190.00
90	ESCAPE	925	135.00	155.00
90	HIGH PLAINS DRIFTERS	925	140.00	135.00
90	WAR CRY	750	125.00	140.00
91	ENCOUNTER, THE	925	140.00	160.00
91	PIPE CARRIER, THE	925	140.00	150.00
91	SUNDANCE	925	140.00	150.00
91	THE PRIDEFUL ONES	925	150.00	160.00
92	73 DEGREES IN AMARILLO...YESTERDAY	925	140.00	195.00
92	CROSSING AT THE BIG TREES	925	140.00	154.00
92	SILENT TRAIL TALK	925	140.00	150.00
88	COMPANIONS	575	85.00	185.00
88	PROTRAYING HIS HERITAGE	575	85.00	185.00

HADLEY COMPANIES
O. FRANCA

*	THE LOVERS	*	*	1250.00
*	WIND SONG	*	*	300.00
*	EVENING SOLITUDE	*	*	300.00
*	BEEF HERD	*	*	550.00
*	HIS SPOTTED PONY	*	*	450.00
*	LONESOME TRAIL W/ COMPANION PRINT	*	*	800.00
*	NOMADS OF THE PLAINS	*	*	620.00
73	CORRALLING THE CAVVY	1000	100.00	600.00
74	BUFFALO SCOUT	1000	100.00	950.00
74	CALIFORNIA WRANGLER	1000	100.00	470.00
74	MISSING IN THE ROUNDUP	1000	100.00	440.00
74	NAVAJO PORTRAIT	1000	75.00	360.00
74	PACKING IN	1000	100.00	316.00
77	BOYS IN THE BUNKHOUSE	1000	150.00	400.00

T. REDLIN

YR	NAME	LIMIT	ISSUE	REDLIN
77	APPLE RIVER MALLARDS	OP	10.00	200.00
77	OVER THE BLOWDOWN	OP	20.00	900.00
77	WINTER SNOWS	OP	20.00	500.00
78	BACK FROM THE FIELDS	720	40.00	400.00
78	BACKWATER MALLARDS	720	40.00	1200.00
78	OLD LOGGERS TRAIL	720	40.00	1500.00
78	OVER THE RUSHES	720	40.00	300.00
78	QUIET AFTERNOON	720	40.00	750.00
78	STARTLED	720	30.00	1500.00
79	AGEING SHORELINE	960	40.00	400.00
79	COLORFUL TRIO	960	40.00	580.00
79	FIGHTING A HEADWIND	960	30.00	440.00
79	LONER, THE	960	40.00	350.00
79	MORNING CHORES	960	40.00	1700.00
79	WHITECAPS	960	40.00	590.00
80	AUTUMN RUN	960	60.00	400.00
80	BREAKING AWAY	960	60.00	400.00
80	CLEARING THE RAIL	960	60.00	900.00
80	COUNTRY ROAD	960	60.00	900.00
80	DRIFTING	960	60.00	390.00
80	HOMESTEAD, THE	960	60.00	790.00
80	INTRUDERS	960	60.00	330.00
80	NIGHT WATCH	2400	60.00	800.00
80	RUSTY REFUGE	960	60.00	530.00
80	SECLUDED POND	960	60.00	300.00
80	SILENT SUNSET	960	60.00	1000.00
80	SPRING THAW	960	60.00	500.00
80	SQUALL LINE	960	60.00	360.00
81	1981 MINNESOTA DUCK STAMP	7800	125.00	185.00
81	ALL CLEAR	960	150.00	300.00
81	APRIL SNOW	960	100.00	790.00
81	BROKEN COVEY	960	100.00	770.00
81	HIGH COUNTRY	960	100.00	750.00
81	HIGHTAILING	960	75.00	340.00
81	LANDMARK, THE	960	100.00	400.00
81	MORNING RETREAT	240	400.00	3800.00
81	PASSING THROUGH	960	100.00	220.00

YR	NAME	LIMIT	ISSUE	QUOTE
81	RUSTY REFUGE II	960	100.00	780.00
81	SHARING THE BOUNTY	960	100.00	2800.00
81	SOFT SHADOWS	960	100.00	400.00
81	SPRING RUN-OFF	1700	125.00	690.00
82	1982 MINNESOTA TROUT STAMP	960	125.00	650.00
82	BIRCH LINE, THE	960	100.00	1350.00
82	EVENING RETREAT A/P	300	400.00	1600.00
82	LANDING, THE	OP	30.00	80.00
82	OCTOBER EVENING	960	100.00	1000.00
82	REFLECTIONS	960	100.00	600.00
82	SEED HUNTERS	960	100.00	800.00
82	SPRING MAPLING	960	100.00	1300.00
82	WHITEWATER	960	100.00	400.00
82	WINTER HAVEN	500	85.00	1400.00
83	1983 NORTH DAKOTA DUCK STAMP	3438	135.00	190.00
83	AUTUMN SHORELINE	OP	50.00	850.00
83	BACKWOODS CABIN	960	150.00	1500.00
83	EVENING GLOW	960	150.00	2600.00
83	EVENING SURPRISE	960	150.00	3000.00
83	HIDDEN POINT	960	150.00	725.00
83	ON THE ALERT	960	125.00	400.00
83	PEACEFUL EVENING	960	100.00	1500.00
83	PRAIRIE SPRINGS	960	150.00	600.00
83	RUSHING RAPIDS	960	125.00	1200.00
84	1984 QUAIL CONSERVATION	1500	135.00	135.00
84	BLUEBILL POINT A/P	240	300.00	900.00
84	CHANGING SEASONS-SUMMER	960	150.00	2300.00
84	CLOSED FOR THE SEASON	960	150.00	600.00
84	LEAVING THE SANCTUARY	960	150.00	2000.00
84	MORNING GLOW	960	150.00	2600.00
84	NIGHT HARVEST	960	150.00	2800.00
84	NIGHTFLIGHT	360	600.00	2800.00
84	PRAIRIE SKYLINE	960	150.00	2400.00
84	RURAL ROUTE	960	150.00	540.00
84	RUSTY REFUGE III	960	150.00	790.00
84	SILENT WINGS SUITE (SET OF 4)	960	200.00	1150.00
84	SUNDOWN	960	300.00	575.00
84	SUNNY AFTERNOON	960	150.00	980.00
84	WINTER WINDBREAK	960	150.00	1050.00
85	1985 MINNESOTA DUCK STAMP	4385	135.00	175.00
85	AFTERNOON GLOW	960	150.00	2250.00
85	BREAKING COVER	960	150.00	725.00
85	BROWSING	960	150.00	1200.00
85	CLEAR VIEW	1500	300.00	450.00
85	DELAYED DEPARTURE	1500	150.00	1700.00
85	EVENING COMPANY	960	150.00	950.00
85	NIGHT LIGHT	1500	300.00	2400.00
85	RIVERSIDE POND	960	150.00	1000.00
85	RUSTY REFUGE IV	960	150.00	375.00
85	SHARING SEASON, THE	OP	60.00	250.00
85	WHISTLE STOP	960	150.00	900.00
86	BACK TO THE SANTUARY	960	150.00	600.00
86	CHANGING SEASONS-AUTUMN	960	150.00	600.00
86	CHANGING SEASONS-WINTER	960	200.00	925.00
86	COMING HOME	2400	100.00	1350.00
86	HAZY AFTERNOON	2560	200.00	1100.00
86	NIGHT MAPLING	2560	200.00	550.00
86	PRAIRIE MONUMENTS	2560	200.00	1000.00
86	SHARING SEASON II, THE	OP	60.00	190.00
86	SILENT FLIGHT	960	150.00	420.00
86	STORMY WEATHER	1500	200.00	990.00
86	SUNLIT TRAIL	960	150.00	440.00
86	TWILIGHT GLOW	960	200.00	2000.00
87	AUTUMN AFTERNOON	4800	100.00	900.00
87	CHANGING SEASONS-SPRING	960	200.00	850.00
87	DEER CROSSING	2400	200.00	1850.00
87	EVENING CHORES (PRINT/BOOK)	2400	400.00	1000.00
87	EVENING HARVEST	960	200.00	2000.00
87	GOLDEN RETREAT A/P	500	800.00	2350.00
87	PREPARED FOR THE SEASON	OP	70.00	250.00
87	SHARING THE SOLITUDE	2400	125.00	700.00
87	THAT SPECIAL TIME	2400	125.00	1600.00
87	TOGETHER FOR THE SEASON	OP	70.00	170.00
88	BOULDER RIDGE	4800	150.00	200.00
88	CATCHING THE SCENT	2400	200.00	200.00
88	COUNTRY NEIGHBORS	4800	150.00	575.00

YR	NAME	LIMIT	ISSUE	QUOTE
88	HOMEWARD BOUND	OP	70.00	385.00
88	HOUSE CALL	6800	175.00	1350.00
88	LIGHTS OF HOME	9500	125.00	1000.00
88	MASTER'S DOMAIN, THE	2400	225.00	1000.00
88	MOONLIGHT RETREAT	530	1000.00	1390.00
88	PRAIRIE MORNING	4800	150.00	620.00
88	QUIET OF THE EVENING	4800	150.00	760.00
88	WEDNESDAY AFTERNOON	6800	175.00	1200.00
89	AROMA OF FALL	6800	200.00	2000.00
89	HOMEWARD BOUND	OP	80.00	385.00
89	INDIAN SUMMER	4800	200.00	1000.00
89	MORNING ROUNDS	6800	175.00	600.00
89	OFFICE HOURS	6800	175.00	1350.00
89	SPECIAL MEMORIES	570	1000.00	1690.00
90	BEST FRIENDS	570	1000.00	2200.00
90	EVENING SOLITUDE	9500	200.00	1100.00
90	EVENING WITH FRIENDS	19,500	225.00	1800.00
90	FAMILY TRADITIONS	OP	80.00	200.00
90	HEADING HOME	OP	80.00	400.00
90	MASTER OF THE VALLEY	6800	200.00	200.00
90	PURE CONTENTMENT	9500	150.00	740.00
90	WELCOME TO PARADISE	14,500	150.00	900.00
91	COMFORTS OF HOME, THE	22,900	175.00	570.00
91	FLYING FREE	14,500	200.00	325.00
91	HUNTER'S HAVEN	*	1000.00	1200.00
91	MORNING SOLITUDE	12,107	250.00	745.00
91	PLEASURES OF WINTER, THE	24,500	150.00	300.00
92	SUMMERTIME	24,900	225.00	200.00

HAROLD RIGSBY
H. RIGSBY

				RIGSBY
78	AFRICAN LION	500	20.00	200.00
78	CHEETAH	500	20.00	250.00
78	SIBERIAN TIGER	500	20.00	400.00
79	BOBCAT	500	15.00	75.00
79	RACCOON	500	15.00	75.00
79	SNOW LEOPARD	500	25.00	100.00
79	SNOW TIGER	500	25.00	250.00
80	AFRICAN LION II	200	50.00	250.00
80	BENGAL TIGER II	200	50.00	400.00
80	GIRAFFE	500	25.00	250.00
80	KOALA	500	25.00	75.00
80	RED FOX I	950	30.00	150.00
80	RED FOX II	950	30.00	150.00
80	TIGER CUB	500	20.00	400.00
80	WHITE TIGER CUB	500	20.00	400.00
81	AFRICAN LION CUB	950	30.00	100.00
81	COTTONTAIL RABBIT	950	15.00	75.00
81	ZEBRA FOAL	500	50.00	375.00
82	COUGAR	500	50.00	425.00
82	GREY SQUIRREL	950	15.00	50.00
82	TIGER IV	950	20.00	75.00
83	BABY HARP SEAL	950	25.00	250.00
83	BALD EAGLE	950	15.00	50.00
83	BENGAL TIGER CUB	500	50.00	375.00
83	PANDA	950	35.00	450.00
83	WHITE BENGAL TIGER	950	20.00	75.00
84	BENGAL TIGER V	975	40.00	275.00
85	BLACK LEOPARD	975	50.00	250.00
85	GRAY WOLF	975	35.00	225.00

HISTORICAL ART PRINTS LTD.
D. TROIANI

82	CONFEDERATE STANDARD BEARER	600	75.00	2300.00
82	CPL. WHEAT'S FIRST SPEC. BAT.	600	40.00	260.00
83	BEFORE THE STORM (T.J. JACKSON)	600	75.00	2300.00
83	FORWARD THE COLORS	750	85.00	1050.00
83	UNION STANDARD BEARER	600	75.00	1600.00
84	CONFEDERATE DRUMMER	625	75.00	1000.00
84	J.E.B. STUART	850	95.00	1700.00
84	LEE'S TEXANS	950	95.00	1200.00
84	UNION DRUMMER	625	75.00	675.00
85	FIGHT FOR THE COLORS, THE	950	95.00	2100.00
85	GRAY WALL, THE	950	95.00	1800.00
85	REBEL YELL	950	95.00	1250.00
85	SOUTHERN STEEL (N.B. FOREST)	950	95.00	2300.00
86	BRONZE GUNS & IRON MEN	950	95.00	1700.00

YR	NAME	LIMIT	ISSUE	QUOTE
86	LAST ROUNDS, THE	950	95.00	1600.00
86	MEN MUST SEE US TODAY, THE	950	95.00	850.00
86	OLD JACK	950	95.00	800.00
87	114TH PA/COLLIS ZOUAVES	750	65.00	400.00
87	2ND MD INFANTRY	750	65.00	150.00
87	8TH TEXAS CAVALRY	750	65.00	475.00
87	CLEAR THE WAY	950	125.00	2100.00
87	CO.D 2ND U.S. SHARP SHOOTER	750	65.00	450.00
87	GIVE THEM COLD STEEL...	950	95.00	2250.00
87	STARS & BARS	950	125.00	540.00
88	BAYONET	1000	100.00	700.00
88	BOY COLONEL, THE	1000	125.00	500.00
88	EAGLE OF THE 8TH	1000	125.00	760.00
88	GENERAL ROBERT E. LEE	950	125.00	480.00
88	LAST SALUTE, THE	1000	125.00	2000.00
88	SAVING THE FLAG	1000	125.00	785.00
89	12TH VIRGINIA CAVALRY, 1864	750	75.00	195.00
89	2ND U.S. CAVALRY, 1861	750	75.00	200.00
89	EMBLEMS OF VALOR	1000	125.00	600.00
89	FORLORN HOPE, THE	1000	150.00	340.00
89	THUNDER ON LITTLE KENNESAW	1000	150.00	1200.00
89	UNITED STATES MARINES 1861-1865	750	65.00	225.00
90	BONNIE BLUE FLAG, THE	1000	150.00	400.00
90	CHARGE	1000	200.00	540.00
90	GRAY COMANCHES, THE	1000	175.00	750.00
90	OPDYCKE'S TIGERS	1000	200.00	400.00
91	1ST S.C. RIFLES, 1861	950	75.00	95.00
91	DIEHARDS, THE	1000	200.00	900.00
91	MEN OF ARKANSAS	1000	200.00	440.00
91	RED DEVILS, THE	1000	200.00	740.00
91	WASHINGTON ARTILLERY OF NEW ORLEANS	950	75.00	300.00
92	RANGER MOSBY	1000	250.00	335.00
92	RETREAT BY RECOIL	1000	250.00	470.00
92	UNTIL SUNDOWN	1000	200.00	800.00

IMPERIAL GRAPHICS LTD.

L. LIU

LENA Y. LIU LIMITED EDITION IMAGES

	NAME	LIMIT	ISSUE	QUOTE
*	BASKET OF PANSIES	2500	40.00	85.00
*	CHICKADEES	950	35.00	160.00
*	FLORAL SYMPHONY	1950	95.00	180.00
*	HUMMINGBIRDS & IRIS	1950	40.00	140.00
*	IRIS GARDEN	1950	45.00	100.00
*	MIXED IRISES I	2500	50.00	65.00
*	MIXED IRISES II	2500	50.00	130.00
*	MOONLIGHT SPLENDOR	1950	60.00	175.00
*	MORNING GLORIES & HUMMER	1950	45.00	56.00-70.00
*	MORNING ROOM, THE	2500	95.00	260.00
*	ORIENTAL SCREEN	2500	95.00	190.00
*	PARENTHOOD	1950	45.00	100.00
*	PEONIES & AZALEAS	1950	35.00	70.00
*	PEONIES & FORSYTHIA	1950	35.00	70.00
*	PEONIES & WATERFALL	1950	65.00	130.00
*	ROMANTIC ABUNDANCE	1950	95.00	200.00
*	SOLITUDE	1950	60.00	225.00
*	SPRING DUET	1950	60.00	150.00
*	SWANS & CALLAS	1950	65.00	120.00
*	TWO WHITE IRISES	2500	40.00	60.00
*	WATERFALL W/BLOSSOMS	1950	65.00	100.00

J.S. PERRY ORIGINALS

J.S. PERRY

YR	NAME	LIMIT	ISSUE	QUOTE
84	MEW'S MIX	SO	38.00	500.00
84	PUSSYWILLOWS	800	38.00	72.00
84	STILL LIFE WITH CUPCATS	800	38.00	96.00
85	CALL OF THE WILD	800	95.00	220.00
85	CATTAILS	SO	38.00	500.00
85	FRIENDS IN HIGH PLACES	800	95.00	165.00
85	PAPA WAS A ROLLING STONE	800	38.00	96.00
85	THREE SCOOPS	800	38.00	48.00
86	HOME SWEET HOME	800	48.00	96.00
86	SUMMER TALES	800	48.00	72.00
87	BACKYARD JUNGLE GYM, THE	800	48.00	96.00
87	BOXING MATCH, THE	800	65.00	97.50
87	PEEKABOO	800	65.00	97.50
87	YOGA YOU CAN DO AT HOME	800	35.00	70.00
88	HOT PINK BIKINI, THE	800	35.00	52.50
90	GIRL'S NIGHT OUT	800	48.00	72.00

YR	NAME	LIMIT	ISSUE	QUOTE

JAN HAGARA COLLECTABLES
J. HAGARA — VICTORIAN CHILDREN

YR	NAME	LIMIT	ISSUE	QUOTE
*	BONNIE	*	*	50.00-85.00
*	HANNAH	*	*	150.00
75	TRINA	600	7.00	500.00
76	CHRIS	2000	5.00	75.00
77	SPRING & LANCE	2000	12.00	175.00
78	JUMEAU DOLL	1200	20.00	50.00
78	OLIVIA	600	55.00	800.00
79	DAISIES FROM MARYBETH	900	20.00	100.00
80	BETSY	750	45.00	400.00
80	JIMMY	750	45.00	300.00
80	LYDIA	650	65.00	350.00
81	JENNY	2000	45.00	300.00
81	STORYTIME	450	125.00	600.00
82	CAROL	2000	25.00	175.00
82	IN LINE	1000	65.00	1200.00
82	MANDY	500	60.00	400.00
83	JENNIFER	700	60.00	250.00
83	PAIGE	2000	47.50	200.00
85	CYNTHIA	600	50.00	175.00
85	GOLDIE	1200	47.50	125.00
85	NOEL	2000	30.00	95.00
86	PHILLIP'S COUSINS	1000	60.00	800.00-1300.00
86	SOPHIE	1200	50.00	125.00
87	CATHY	2000	30.00	150.00
87	NIKKI	2000	30.00	95.00
87	RENNY & BLUEBEARY	950	125.00	550.00
88	ADDIE	2000	65.00	150.00-250.00
88	MATTIE-FIRST COLLECTOR'S CLUB PRINT	YR	55.00	165.00-350.00

JOHN M. BARBER ART LTD.
J. BARBER

YR	NAME	LIMIT	ISSUE	QUOTE
*	BAY COUNTRY MILL	950	135.00	200.00
*	BOAT SHED	750	40.00	350.00
*	BREEZING UP	950	140.00	300.00
*	BUTLER'S BOAT YARD	500	40.00	350.00
*	BUYBOATS JACKSON CREEK	950	65.00	400.00
*	BUYBOATS WM. B. TENNISON	950	55.00	300.00
*	BUYING OYSTERS AT DRUM POINT	950	100.00	195.00
*	CHESAPEAKE MORNING	1450	130.00	500.00
*	COMING SQUALL	950	50.00	225.00
*	DAWN ON THE CHOPTANK	950	95.00	245.00
*	DAWN'S EARLY LIGHT	950	85.00	300.00
*	DISTANT THUNDER	950	75.00	300.00
*	FOG OVER BLOODY POINT BAR	950	165.00	225.00
*	GLOUCESTER PT. WATERMEN	950	75.00	200.00
*	GUARDIAN OF DIAMOND SHOALS	950	65.00	150.00
*	HAMPTON CREEK DERELICT	500	40.00	500.00
*	MOONLIGHT HARBOR	950	175.00	1100.00
*	MORNING AT COVE POINT	950	75.00	500.00
*	NELLIE CROCKETT OYSTER BOAT	750	40.00	750.00
*	NIGHT PASSAGE	950	225.00	350.00
*	ON THE RAILWAY	950	75.00	175.00
*	RACING FOR THE OYSTERS	950	175.00	400.00
*	RETURNING HOME	950	145.00	400.00
*	SIGSBEE (B/W)	500	25.00	50.00
*	SKIPJACK MAGGIE LEE, THE	950	55.00	330.00
*	SPINNAKER REACH	950	85.00	350.00
*	SPRING PAINTING	500	40.00	160.00
*	SUNRISE OVER MOBJACK BAY	950	185.00	350.00
*	TOWN DOCK	950	95.00	150.00
*	TRADEWINDS	950	65.00	165.00
*	TWILIGHT HARBOR	950	125.00	1250.00
*	UNCERTAIN WEATHER	950	125.00	250.00
*	UP FOR REPAIR	950	95.00	150.00
*	VANISHING FLEET, THE	1650	145.00	320.00
*	WINDWARD START	950	85.00	300.00

KRAPF IMAGES
P. KRAPF — KRAPF IMAGES PRINTS

YR	NAME	LIMIT	ISSUE	QUOTE
89	ANOTHER SEASON	*	90.00	90.00
89	CLOSE TO COVER	*	60.00	60.00
89	GRIZZLY COUNTRY	*	85.00	85.00
89	HUNTER'S REST	*	95.00	95.00
89	SURPRISED	*	55.00	55.00
90	AMERICAN ORIGINAL	*	80.00	80.00

YR	NAME	LIMIT	ISSUE	QUOTE
90	CHIPPY ON THE ROCKS	*	50.00	50.00
90	DISTANT BUGLE	*	95.00	95.00
90	EDGE OF THE BURN	*	80.00	80.00
90	OCTOBER MORNING, CANYON DE CHELLY	*	85.00	85.00
90	ON HIS WAY	*	75.00	75.00
90	ON THE EDGE	*	90.00	90.00
90	READY	*	95.00	95.00
90	YELLOWSTONE CANYON	*	80.00	80.00
91	ABOVE AND BEYOND	*	95.00	95.00
91	CAUGHT NAPPING	*	65.00	65.00

LIGHTPOST PUBLISHING
T. KINKADE

YR	NAME	LIMIT	ISSUE	QUOTE
*	HOMETOWN CHAPEL	*	95.00	95.00
*	LAMPLIGHT BROOKE	*	385.00	385.00
*	LAMPLIGHT INN	*	235.00	235.00
*	LAMPLIGHT LANE	*	975.00	975.00
*	NATIONAL PARK STAMP PRINT-1	*	200.00	200.00
*	NEW YORK-SNOW ON 7TH AVE-CITY SCENE	*	1350.00	1350.00
*	PARIS, ST. MICHEL	*	125.00	125.00
*	POWER & THE MAJESTY, THE	*	39.95	39.95
*	PUERTA VALLARTA BEACH	*	125.00	125.00
*	ROSE ARBOR COTTAGE, THE	*	500.00	500.00
*	SAN FRANCISCO, ALCATRAZ	*	145.00	145.00
*	SAN FRANCISCO, CALIFORNIA ST.	*	1800.00	1800.00
*	SAN FRANCISCO, MARKET ST.	*	375.00	375.00
*	SPRING IN THE ALPS	*	225.00	225.00
*	SWEETHEART COTTAGE III-LANDSCAPE	*	235.00	235.00
*	VENICE CANAL	*	95.00	95.00
*	VICTORIA'S GARDEN	*	*	1475.00
*	VICTORIAN CHRISTMAS III	*	250.00	250.00
*	WISTERIA ARBOR	*	125.00	125.00

T. KINKADE

YR	NAME	LIMIT	ISSUE	ARCHIVAL PAPER QUOTE
84	DAWSON	CL	150.00	200.00-750.00
84	PLACERVILLE, 1916	CL	90.00	1500.00-2000.00
85	BIRTH OF A CITY	CL	150.00	200.00-950.00
85	EVENING SERVICE	CL	90.00	200.00-475.00
85	MOONLIGHT ON THE WATERFRONT	CL	150.00	200.00-475.00
86	NEW YORK, 6TH AVENUE	CL	150.00	200.00-1000.00
86	ROOM WITH A VIEW	CL	150.00	300.00-550.00
86	SAN FRANCISCO, 1909	CL	150.00	2650.00
89	CARMEL, OCEAN AVENUE	CL	225.00	450.00-750.00
89	ENTRANCE TO THE MANOR HOUSE	CL	125.00	300.00-675.00
89	EVENING AT MERRITT'S COTTAGE	CL	125.00	675.00
89	SAN FRANCISCO, UNION SQUARE-CITYSCAPE	CL	225.00	450.00-750.00
90	CHANDLER'S COTTAGE	CL	125.00	350.00
90	CHRISTMAS COTTAGE	CL	95.00	150.00
90	HIDDEN COTTAGE	CL	125.00	350.00
90	ROSE ARBOR	CL	125.00	300.00
90	SPRING AT STONEGATE-COTTAGE	550	95.00	175.00
91	AUTUMN GATE, THE	980	225.00	1100.00
91	BOSTON	550	175.00	765.00
91	CARMEL, TUCK BOX TEA ROOM	980	275.00	275.00
91	CHRISTMAS EVE-COTTAGE	980	125.00	175.00
91	FLAGS OVER THE CAPITOL-CITYSCAPE	1991	195.00	235.00
91	HOME FOR THE EVENING-COTTAGE	980	100.00	225.00
91	HOME FOR THE HOLIDAYS	980	225.00	375.00
91	MCKENNA'S COTTAGE	980	150.00	195.00
91	OLDE PORTERFIELD TEA ROOM-COTTAGE	980	150.00	195.00
91	OPEN GATE, SUSSEX	980	100.00	110.00
91	VICTORIAN EVENING	980	150.00	475.00
92	AFTERNOON LIGHT, DOGWOODS	980	185.00	680.00
92	BLOSSOM HILL CHURCH-COTTAGE	980	225.00	235.00
92	BROADWATER BRIDGE-LANDSCAPE	980	225.00	500.00
92	CHRISTMAS AT THE AHWAHNEE-COTTAGE	980	175.00	195.00
92	COTTAGE-BY-THE-SEA-COTTAGE	980	250.00	425.00
92	COUNTRY MEMORIES-LANDSCAPE	980	185.00	175.00
92	FALL COLORS VICTORIAN	980	175.00	175.00
92	GARDEN PARTY, THE-COTTAGE	980	175.00	195.00
92	HOME IS WHERE THE HEART IS	980	225.00	235.00
92	JULIANNE'S COTTAGE	980	185.00	975.00
92	MILLER' COTTAGE	980	175.00	195.00
92	OLDE PORTERFIELD GIFT SHOPPE-COTTAGE	980	175.00	195.00
92	PARIS, CITY OF LIGHTS	980	225.00	285.00
92	SAN FRANCISCO	980	275.00	275.00
92	SILENT NIGHT-COTTAGE	980	185.00	500.00
92	SUNDAY AT APPLE HILL	980	175.00	595.00

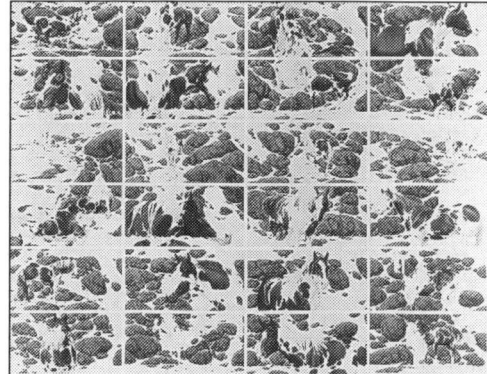

Bev Doolittle has charmed collectors with her images of Native American symbolism and her intriguing ability to play Hide and Seek *evident in this example of her famous camouflage technique. Her publisher is The Greenwich Workshop.*

Anyone studying this breathtaking work by artist and naturalist Stephen Lyman is sure to be Warmed by the View, *third in a series produced by The Greenwich Workshop.*

Ozz França masterfully paints the beauty of a Native American couple locked in a warm embrace. The Lovers *is part of a series produced by Hadley House.*

YR	NAME	LIMIT	ISSUE	QUOTE
92	SWANBROOKE COTTAGE	980	225.00	800.00
92	SWEETHEART COTTAGE	980	150.00	325.00
92	VICTORIAN CHRISTMAS	980	225.00	850.00
92	VICTORIAN GARDEN-COTTAGE	980	275.00	2500.00
92	YOSEMITE	980	225.00	235.00
T. KINKADE			**ARCHIVAL PAPER/CANVAS**	
90	BLUE COTTAGE	750	125.00	255.00
90	MOONLIT VILLAGE	935	225.00	1200.00
90	NEW YORK, 1932-CITYSCAPE	935	225.00	495.00
90	SKATING IN THE PARK	750	275.00	1875.00
T. KINKADE			**CANVAS EDITION**	
*	AUTUMN AT ASHLEY'S-LANDSCAPE	*	390.00	390.00
*	BROOKSIDE HIDEAWAY-COTTAGE	*	485.00	485.00
*	CHRISTMAS MEMORIES-COTTAGE	*	485.00	485.00
*	COUNTRY MEMORIES	980	265.00	595.00-773.50
*	CREEKSIDE TRAIL	*	590.00	590.00
*	DAYS OF PEACE	*	590.00	590.00
*	DUSK IN THE VALLEY	*	590.00	590.00
*	EMERALD ISLE COTTAGE-LANDSCAPE	*	455.00	455.00
*	END OF PERFECT DAY III	*	845.00	845.00
*	GARDENS BEYOND A. GATE	*	875.00	875.00
*	GLORY OF WINTER-COTTAGE	*	515.00	515.00
*	GUARDIAN CASTLE	*	765.00	765.00
*	HIDDEN ARBOR	*	455.00	455.00
*	HOMESTEAD HOUSE	*	515.00	515.00
*	HOMETOWN CHAPEL	*	795.00	795.00
*	HOMETOWN MEMORIES I	*	765.00	765.00
*	LAMPLIGHT VILLAGE	*	550.00	550.00
*	MOONLIGHT LANE I	*	455.00	455.00
*	MORNING DOGWOOD	*	445.00	445.00
*	POWER & THE MAJESTY, THE	*	235.00	515.00
*	SAN FRANCISCO, MARKET ST.	*	695.00	695.00
*	SAN FRANCISCO, VIEW FROM CAL.-CITYSCAPE	*	4200.00	4200.00
*	SILENT NIGHT-COTTAGE	980	265.00	395.00-513.50
*	SPRING IN THA ALPS	*	515.00	515.00
*	ST. NICHOLAS CIRCLE	*	615.00	615.00
*	STUDIO IN THE GARDEN	*	365.00	365.00
*	VICTORIAN CHRISTMAS III	*	550.00	550.00
*	VILLAGE INN, THE	*	555.00	555.00
*	WARMTH OF HOME, THE	*	390.00	390.00
*	WINTER'S END-LANDSCAPE	*	515.00	515.00
89	CARMEL, OCEAN AVENUE	CL	595.00	950.00-3500
89	ENTRANCE TO THE MANOR HOUSE	CL	495.00	1000.00-1500.00
89	EVENING AT MERRITT'S COTTAGE	CL	495.00	850.00
89	SAN FRANCISCO, UNION SQUARE-CITYSCAPE	CL	595.00	2000.00
90	CHANDLER'S COTTAGE	CL	495.00	1000.00-1500.00
90	CHRISTMAS COTTAGE	CL	295.00	1450.00
90	CHRISTMAS EVE-COTTAGE	CL	395.00	175.00
90	HIDDEN COTTAGE	CL	495.00	1000.00-1500.00
90	MORNING LIGHT A/P	CL	695.00	800.00
90	ROSE ARBOR	CL	495.00	500.00
90	SPRING AT STONEGATE-COTTAGE	550	295.00	365.00
91	AFTERNOON LIGHT, DOGWOODS	980	435.00	680.00
91	BOSTON	550	435.00	765.00
91	CARMEL, TUCK BOX TEA ROOM	980	545.00	765.00
91	CEDAR NOOK COTTAGE	1960	165.00	165.00
91	FLAGS OVER THE CAPITOL-CITYSCAPE	980	495.00	515.00
91	HOME FOR THE EVENING-COTTAGE	980	165.00	225.00
91	HOME FOR THE HOLIDAYS	CL	595.00	375.00
91	LIT PATH, THE-COTTAGE	1960	165.00	165.00
91	MCKENNA'S COTTAGE	980	435.00	195.00
91	OLDE PORTERFIELD TEA ROOM-COTTAGE	980	435.00	195.00
91	OPEN GATE, SUSSEX	980	165.00	110.00
91	PYE CORNER COTTAGE	1960	165.00	185.00
91	VICTORIAN EVENING	980	435.00	435.00
91	WOODMAN'S THATCH	1960	165.00	165.00
92	BLOSSOM HILL CHURCH-COTTAGE	980	495.00	235.00
92	BROADWATER BRIDGE-LANDSCAPE	980	435.00	500.00
92	CHRISTMAS AT THE AHWAHNEE-COTTAGE	980	435.00	455.00
92	COTTAGE-BY-THE-SEA-COTTAGE	980	495.00	495.00
92	COUNTRY MEMORIES-LANDSCAPE	980	295.00	875.00
92	EVENING CAROLERS-COTTAGE	980	245.00	255.00
92	FALL COLORS VICTORIAN	980	435.00	435.00
92	GARDEN PARTY, THE-COTTAGE	980	435.00	455.00
92	HOME IS WHERE THE HEART IS	980	495.00	495.00
92	JULIANNE'S COTTAGE	980	345.00	940.00

YR	NAME	LIMIT	ISSUE	QUOTE
92	MILLER'S COTTAGE	980	435.00	435.00
92	MOONLIT SLEIGH RIDE-LANDSCAPE	980	245.00	245.00
92	OLDE PORTERFIELD GIFT SHOPPE-COTTAGE	980	435.00	555.00
92	PARIS, CITY OF LIGHTS	980	495.00	495.00
92	SAN FRANCISCO, NOB HILL	980	545.00	545.00
92	SILENT NIGHT-COTTAGE	980	345.00	345.00
92	SUNDAY AT APPLE HILL	980	435.00	435.00
92	SWANBROOKE COTTAGE	980	495.00	800.00
92	SWEETHEART COTTAGE	980	435.00	435.00
92	VICTORIAN CHRISTMAS	980	495.00	495.00
92	VICTORIAN GARDEN	980	695.00	1100.00
92	WEATHERVANE HUTCH-COTTAGE	1960	245.00	355.00
92	YOSEMITE	980	495.00	515.00

T. KINKADE

	NAME	LIMIT	ISSUE	PAPER EDITION
*	AMBER AFTERNOON-COTTAGE	*	235.00	235.00
*	AUTUMN AT ASHLEY'S-LANDSCAPE	*	185.00	185.00
*	BEACON OF HOPE	*	235.00	235.00
*	BESIDE STILL WATERS-LANDSCAPE	*	680.00	680.00
*	BEYOND AUTUMN GATE-COTTAGE	*	825.00	825.00
*	BIARRITZ	*	95.00	95.00
*	BLESSINGS OF AUTUMN-LANDSCAPE	*	235.00	235.00
*	BLESSINGS OF SPRING	*	195.00	195.00
*	BLOOMSBURY CAFE	*	145.00	145.00
*	BROOKSIDE HIDEAWAY-COTTAGE	*	205.00	205.00
*	CARMEL, DOLORES ST.-COTTAGE	*	765.00	765.00
*	CHRISTMAS MEMORIES-COTTAGE	*	205.00	205.00
*	CHRISTMAS TREE COTTAGE	*	185.00	185.00
*	CREEKSIDE TRAIL	*	275.00	275.00
*	DAYS OF PEACE	*	275.00	275.00
*	DUSK IN THE VALLEY	*	275.00	275.00
*	EMERALD ISLE COTTAGE-LANDSCAPE	*	195.00	195.00
*	END/PERFECT DAY	*	800.00	800.00
*	END/PERFECT DAY II	*	285.00	285.00
*	END/PERFECT DAY III	*	325.00	325.00
*	FISHERMAN'S WHARF	*	305.00	305.00
*	GARDEN OF PROMISE-GATE	*	425.00	425.00
*	GARDENS BEYOND A. GATE	*	325.00	325.00
*	GLORY OF WINTER-COTTAGE	*	235.00	235.00
*	GUARDIAN CASTLE	*	300.00	300.00
*	HEATHER'S HUTCH-COTTAGE	*	175.00	175.00
*	HIDDEN ARBOR	*	340.00	340.00
*	HIDDEN COTTAGE II	*	195.00	195.00
*	HIDDEN GAZEBO	*	195.00	195.00
*	HOMESTEAD HOUSE	*	235.00	235.00
*	HOMETOWN MEMORIES I	*	300.00	300.00
*	LAMPLIGHT VILLAGE	*	250.00	250.00
*	LUXEMBOURG GARDENS	*	95.00	95.00
*	MOONLIGHT LANE I	*	195.00	195.00
*	MORNING DOGWOOD	*	195.00	195.00
*	MORNING LIGHT-LANDSCAPE	*	800.00	800.00
*	PACIFIC GROVE	*	125.00	125.00
*	PARIS, EIFFEL TOWER	*	295.00	295.00
*	ST. NICHOLAS CIRCLE	*	235.00	235.00
*	STONEHEARTH HUTCH	*	175.00	175.00
*	STUDIO IN THE GARDEN	*	175.00	175.00
*	SUNDAY OUTING	*	195.00	195.00
*	SWEETHEART COTTAGE II	*	315.00	315.00
*	VICTORIAN CHRISTMAS II	*	235.00	235.00
*	VILLAGE INN, THE	*	195.00	195.00
*	WARMTH OF HOME, THE-LANDSCAPE	*	185.00	185.00
*	WINTER'S END-LANDSCAPE	*	235.00	235.00

LYNN'S PRINTS

L. GRAEBNER

YR	NAME	LIMIT	ISSUE	THE AMISH
87	BACKFIRE	750	40.00	125.00
87	BREAD AND MILK	*	40.00	40.00
87	FIRST LOVE	*	40.00	40.00
87	HORSEY'S TREAT	750	40.00	100.00
87	LITTLE APPLE PICKER	*	40.00	40.00
87	SUNDAY MEETING	750	25.00	65.00
88	AUCTION, THE	*	25.00	25.00
88	BACK PORCH QUILT FIXIN	750	25.00	65.00
88	BARN RAISING LUNCH	*	25.00	25.00
88	BARNYARD FRIENDS	*	25.00	25.00
88	CART FULL OF APPLES	750	25.00	75.00
88	MOTHERS SPECIAL DAY '88	750	20.00	60.00
88	ROADSIDE BERRY PICKIN	750	25.00	75.00

YR	NAME	LIMIT	ISSUE	QUOTE
88	SHARING	*	15.00	45.00
88	SHARING THE LOAD	750	25.00	85.00
88	SWEET SMELLS	750	25.00	65.00
88	TALKING WITH DOLLY	750	15.00	45.00
89	AUTUMN PLAYTIME	*	85.00	85.00
89	CART FOR DOLLIES	*	30.00	30.00
89	COME A COURTIN	*	20.00	20.00
89	FALL AFTERNOON	*	30.00	30.00
89	FEEDING TIME BEFORE SCHOOL	*	30.00	30.00
89	FISHERMAN'S HELPER	*	30.00	30.00
89	IN TOWN CHRISTMAS	*	100.00	200.00
89	WILD GOOSE CHASE	*	30.00	30.00
89	YOU CAN'T HAVE MY DOLLY	*	20.00	20.00
90	AFTERNOON AT THE POND	*	65.00	65.00
90	AIRING THE QUILTS	*	30.00	30.00
90	BE GOOD TO EACH OTHER	50	100.00	250.00
90	CHRISTMASTIME IN THE COUNTRY	*	65.00	65.00
90	DOLLY'S QUILT	*	20.00	20.00
90	FETCH	*	20.00	20.00
90	FIRST QUILT	*	20.00	20.00
90	FIRST ROSE OF SUMMER	*	30.00	30.00
90	FOREVER YOURS DAD	*	20.00	20.00
90	FRIENDS	*	30.00	30.00
90	FRONT PORCH TEA PARTY	*	30.00	30.00
90	GRAPE PICKIN	*	30.00	30.00
90	LET'S BE FRIENDS	*	30.00	30.00
90	MMM GOOD	*	20.00	20.00
90	SUMMER SCENTS	*	20.00	20.00
90	SUNDAY MEETING HOOKY	*	65.00	65.00
91	CLOAK ROOM	*	150.00	150.00
91	COME DOWN AND HAVE A TREAT	*	25.00	25.00
91	HITCHIN A RIDE	*	25.00	25.00
91	KNIT PICKIN	*	25.00	25.00
91	MOTHER'S DAY SPECIAL 1991	*	25.00	25.00
91	ROUNDING UP THE PIGS	*	25.00	25.00
91	SEEDS FOR YOU MR. CARDINAL	*	25.00	25.00

MAFEKING COLLECTION
M. GREEN

MAN'S BEST FRIEND

94	DEREK (THE LABRADOR RETRIEVER)	1500	17.39	25.00
94	MICKEY (SPANIEL CROSS)	1500	17.39	25.00
94	PEPPER (THE AIREDALE)	1500	17.39	25.00

MARTY BELL FINE ART
M. BELL

LIMITED EDITION LITHOGRAPHS

82	BIBURY COTTAGE	550	280.00	800.00-1000.00
82	BIG DADDY'S SHOE	950	64.00	150.00-300.00
82	CASTLE COMBE COTTAGE	550	230.00	400.00-1000.00
82	CROSSROADS COTTAGE	950	38.00	200.00
83	NESTLEWOOD	550	300.00	2500.00
84	PENHURST TEA ROOMS (ARCHIVAL)	1000	335.00	795.00-1800.00
84	PENHURST TEA ROOMS (CANVAS)	550	335.00	1500.00-3600.00
84	WEST KINGTON DELL	550	480.00	999.00
85	FIDDLEFORD COTTAGE	550	78.00	500.00-1950.00
85	LITTLE BOXFORD	550	156.00	300.00-900.00
85	MEADOWLARK COTTAGE	550	156.00	450.00-699.00
85	SUMMER'S GLOW	550	196.00	1000.00
85	SURREY GARDEN HOUSE	550	98.00	850.00-1499.00
85	SWEET PINE COTTAGE	550	78.00	350.00-1499.00
85	WINDSONG COTTAGE	550	156.00	350.00-799.00
86	BURFORD VILLAGE STORE	550	106.00	500.00-1500.00
86	COTSWOLD PARISH CHURCH	1850	98.00	500.00-1500.00
86	HOUSEWIVES CHOICE	550	98.00	400.00-1000.00
86	LORNA DOONE COTTAGE	550	380.00	8000.00-9000.00
86	YORK GARDEN SHOP	550	98.00	250.00-999.00
87	ALDERTON VILLAGE	550	235.00	500.00-899.00
87	BROUGHTON VILLAGE	950	128.00	500.00
87	CHAPLAIN'S GARDEN, THE	550	235.00	2200.00
87	CHIPPENHAM FARM	550	120.00	900.00
87	DOVE COTTAGE GARDEN	950	272.00	495.00
87	DRIFTSONE MANOR	550	400.00	3950.00
87	DUCKSBRIDGE COTTAGE	550	400.00	2500.00
87	EASHING COTTAGE	950	120.00	350.00
87	HALFWAY COTTAGE	950	260.00	800.00
87	LITTLE TULIP THATCH	550	120.00	600.00
87	MAY COTTAGE	950	120.00	700.00
87	MILLPOND STOCKBRIDGE, THE	550	120.00	1800.00

YR	NAME	LIMIT	ISSUE	QUOTE
87	MORNING GLORY COTTAGE	550	120.00	600.00
87	SUNRISE THATCH	950	120.00	350.00
87	VICAR'S GATE, THE	550	110.00	900.00
87	WAKEHURST PLACE	950	480.00	2700.00
87	WELL COTTAGE, SANDY LANE	550	440.00	1600.00
87	WHITE LILAC THATCH	950	260.00	700.00
88	BISHOP'S ROSES, THE	2450	220.00	500.00
88	CLOVE COTTAGE	950	128.00	800.00
88	CLOVER LANE COTTAGE	1850	272.00	1400.00
88	COTSWOLD TWILIGHT	950	128.00	495.00
88	GINGER COTTAGE	1850	320.00	800.00
88	ICOMB VILLAGE GARDEN	2450	620.00	1800.00
88	JASMINE THATCH	950	272.00	695.00
88	LULLABYE COTTAGE	2450	220.00	525.00
88	MORNING'S GLOW	1850	280.00	650.00
88	MURRLE COTTAGE	1850	320.00	1000.00
88	RODWAY COTTAGE	2450	694.00	2000.00
88	SHERE VILLAGE ANTIQUES	950	272.00	825.00
88	SWEET TWILIGHT	2450	220.00	600.00
89	BLUSH OF SPRING	1250	96.00	225.00
89	FIRESIDE CHRISTMAS	550	136.00	800.00
89	GAMEKEEPER'S COTTAGE, THE	950	396.00	2000.00
89	LARKSPUR COTTAGE	2450	220.00	450.00
89	OLD BEAMS COTTAGE	950	368.00	700.00
89	PRIDE OF SPRING	1250	96.00	225.00
89	PRIMROSE COTTAGE	2450	88.00	88.00
90	ARBOR COTTAGE	950	130.00	250.00
90	BRYANTS PUDDLE THATCH	950	130.00	250.00
90	GOMSHALL FLOWER SHOP	950	396.00	2050.00
90	LITTLE WELL THATCH	950	130.00	250.00
90	LONGSTOCK LANE	950	130.00	250.00
90	LOWER BROCKHAMPTON MANOR	950	640.00	2300.00
90	OLD HERTFORDSHIRE COTTAGE	950	396.00	1500.00
90	READY FOR CHRISTMAS	550	130.00	1050.00
91	DEVON ROSES	*	96.00	196.00
91	DORSET ROSES	*	96.00	196.00
91	TEA TIME	*	130.00	200.00
91	WINDWARD COTTAGE, RYE	*	228.00	620.00

M. BELL — MEMBERS ONLY COLLECTORS CLUB

YR	NAME	LIMIT	ISSUE	QUOTE
91	LITTLE THATCH TWILIGHT	YR	288.00	320.00-380.00
92	BLOSSOM LANE	YR	288.00	288.00
92	CANDLE AT EVENTIDE	YR	*	*

MILL POND PRESS
R. BATEMAN

	NAME	LIMIT	ISSUE	QUOTE
*	1987 NFWF W/BOTH STAMPS PRIDE/AUTUMN	*	200.00	200.00
*	1990 NFWF W/BOTH STAMPS WIDE HORIZON	*	152.50	152.50
*	AFRICAN FISH EAGLE	*	265.00	265.00
*	AIR FOREST & WATCH 2 PC. ETCHING	*	1200.00	1200.00
*	ARCTIC LANDSCAPE-POLAR BEAR	*	345.00	345.00
*	ARKANSAS DUCK STAMP 1987-WOOD DUCK	*	200.00	200.00
*	ARTCIC LANDSCAPE-POLAR BEAR	*	800.00	800.00
*	AT THE FEEDER-CARDINAL	*	125.00	125.00
*	BEACH GRASS & TREE FROG	*	345.00	345.00
*	BUFFALO AT AMBOSELI-CAPE BUFFALO	*	400.00	400.00
*	CANADA DUCK PRINT W/S 1988-PINTAILS	*	175.00	175.00
*	CANADA DUCK STAMP-1985 W/2 MALLARD DUCKS	*	200.00	200.00
*	CANADA GEESE IN WINTER	*	2500.00	2500.00
*	CARDINAL & SUMAC	*	650.00	650.00
*	CARDINAL & SUMAC	*	275.00	275.00
*	CARDINAL & SUMAC	*	175.00	175.00
*	CARDINAL & SUMAC	*	1500.00	1500.00
*	CARDINAL & SUMAC	*	400.00	400.00
*	CARDINAL & SUMAC	*	235.00	235.00
*	CHEETAH SIESTA	*	2500.00	2500.00
*	CHICKADEE ON PINECONE-ETCHING	*	2000.00	2000.00
*	CLAN OF THE RAVEN	*	850.00	850.00
*	COUGAR IN THE SNOW	*	450.00	450.00
*	CRIES OF COURTSHIP-CRANE	*	675.00	675.00
*	DAY LILIES AND DRAGONFLIES	*	345.00	345.00
*	DECENDING SHADOWS-WOLVES	*	295.00	295.00
*	DIK-DIKS	*	600.00	600.00
*	DISTANT DANGER-RACCOON	*	225.00	225.00
*	ENDANGERED SPACES-GRIZZLY	*	625.00	625.00
*	ENDANGERED SPACES-ROYAL-BEAR	*	925.00	925.00
*	FIRST ARRIVAL-KILLDEER BIRD	*	265.00	265.00
*	FOX-ETCHING	*	2200.00	2200.00

YR	NAME	LIMIT	ISSUE	QUOTE
*	GIANT PANDA	*	750.00	750.00
*	GIANT PANDA IN THE WILD	*	295.00	295.00
*	GOLDFINCH WITH MULLEIN	*	225.00	225.00
*	GRIZZLY AND CUBS	*	335.00	335.00
*	GRIZZLY BEAR-ETCHING	*	2200.00	2200.00
*	HOODED MERGANSER-DUCK	*	700.00	700.00
*	IN HIS PRIME-MALLARD DUCK	*	295.00	295.00
*	INTRUSION-MOUNTAIN GORILLA	*	325.00	325.00
*	JUNCO IN WINTER	*	210.00	210.00
*	KESTREL AND GRASSHOPPER	*	335.00	335.00
*	LION CUBS B/W	*	1000.00	1000.00
*	LION-ETCHING	*	2200.00	2200.00
*	LIONESS-ETCHING	*	2200.00	2200.00
*	LOON PAIR AND YOUNG	*	425.00	425.00
*	MANGROVE SHADOW-COMMON EGRET	*	285.00	285.00
*	MARBLED MURRELET-DUCK	*	1200.00	1200.00
*	MERGANSER DUCK-BRONZE	*	695.00	695.00
*	MERU DUCK - LESSER KUDUS	*	135.00	135.00
*	MEXICAN WOLF	*	285.00	285.00
*	MIDNIGHT-BLACK WOLF	*	2250.00	2250.00
*	MOOSE	*	1200.00	1200.00
*	MOSSY BRANCHES-SPOTTED OWL	*	995.00	995.00
*	NEW YORK DUCK STAMP W/2 S	*	175.00	175.00
*	NO. AMERICAN WILD SHEEP STAMP	*	300.00	300.00
*	OLD WILLOW AND MALLARDS	*	390.00	390.00
*	ON THE BRINK-RIVER OTTERS	*	345.00	345.00
*	PATH OF THE PANTHER	*	295.00	295.00
*	PEACEFUL FLOCK-AMERICAN WIGEON	*	225.00	225.00
*	PEREGRINE IN FLIGHT-BRONZE	*	1500.00	1500.00
*	PICNIC TABLE	*	250.00	250.00
*	PREDATOR PORTFOLIO-BLACK BEAR	*	475.00	475.00
*	PREDATOR PORTFOLIO-COUGAR	*	465.00	465.00
*	PREDATOR PORTFOLIO-GRIZZLY	*	475.00	475.00
*	PREDATOR PORTFOLIO-POLAR BEAR	*	485.00	485.00
*	PREDATOR PORTFOLIO-WOLF	*	475.00	475.00
*	PREDATOR PORTFOLIO-WOLVERINE	*	275.00	275.00
*	RECLINING SNOW LEOPARD	*	335.00	335.00
*	RED FOX ON THE PROWL	*	1500.00	1500.00
*	RED-TAILED HAWK STUDY-BRONZE	*	1750.00	1750.00
*	RIVER OTTER	*	1500.00	1500.00
*	ROSE-BREASTED GROSBEAK	*	450.00	450.00
*	SALT SPRING SHEEP	*	235.00	235.00
*	SAP BUCKET-MYRTLE WARBLER	*	195.00	195.00
*	SAW WHET OWL & WILD GRAPES	*	185.00	185.00
*	SHADOW OF RAINFOREST-JAGUAR	*	1200.00	1200.00
*	SHADOWS OF THE RAINFOREST	*	510.00	510.00
*	SIBERIAN TIGER	*	325.00	325.00
*	SIBERIAN TIGER - PRESTIGE	*	625.00	625.00
*	SIERRA EVENING-MEXICAN WOLF	*	285.00	285.00
*	SNOWY NAP-TIGER	*	525.00	525.00
*	SNOWY OWL	*	1275.00	1275.00
*	SPARRING ELEPHANTS	*	325.00	325.00
*	SPIRITS OF THE FOREST-WOODTHRUSH	*	1750.00	1750.00
*	SUMMER GARDEN - YOUNG ROBIN	*	235.00	235.00
*	SYMBOL OF RAINFOREST - JAGUAR	*	235.00	235.00
*	TEMOB-ELEPHANT	*	350.00	350.00
*	TEXAS DUCK STAMP 1990-AMERICAN WIGEON	*	135.00	135.00
*	VERMILION FLYCATCHER	*	95.00	95.00
*	VIGILANCE	*	330.00	330.00
*	VIGILANCE - PREMIER	*	650.00	650.00
*	WHITE FOOTED MOUSE DRAWING	*	95.00	95.00
*	WHITE TAILED DEER THROUGH BIRCH	*	335.00	335.00
*	WILDEBEEST AT SUNSET	*	400.00	400.00
*	WINGED SPIRIT - 2 PC. SNOWY OWL	*	1100.00	1100.00
*	WINTER COAT-LANDSCAPE	*	245.00	245.00
*	WINTER PINE- G/H OWL	*	265.00	265.00
*	WINTER TRACKS-COYOTE	*	335.00	335.00
*	WOLF PAIR IN WINTER	*	795.00	795.00
*	WOLF SKETCH	*	250.00	250.00
*	YOUNG GIRAFFE	*	850.00	850.00
90	AIR, FOREST AND WATCH-EAGLE	42,558	325.00	325.00
90	SNOW LEOPARD	290	2500.00	3500.00
*	COTTONTAIL FAMILY-RABBIT	*	120.00	120.00
*	CRAB APPLE CRAVING-SQUIRREL	*	60.00	60.00
*	BLACK SPHINX	*	235.00	235.00
*	BROKEN SILENCE-FAWNS	*	195.00	195.00

YR	NAME	LIMIT	ISSUE	QUOTE
*	BUTTERFLY COLLECTION - 2ND	*	375.00	375.00
*	BUTTERFLY COLLECTION - 3RD	*	375.00	375.00
*	BUTTERFLY COLLECTION, THE	*	375.00	375.00
*	CLOSE-UP, JAGUAR	*	110.00	110.00
*	DALL SHEEP PORTRAIT	*	115.00	115.00
*	DEN MOTHER - MOTHER WOLF	*	135.00	135.00
*	DEN MOTHER - WOLF FAMILY	*	250.00	250.00
*	DEN MOTHER-PREMIER-WOLF	*	700.00	700.00
*	FAMILY TREE, THE-OWLS	*	225.00	225.00
*	FOREST CARPENTER-PILEATED-WOODPECKER	*	195.00	195.00
*	FULL HOUSE-PREMIER ED.- FOXES	*	900.00	900.00
*	GOSLING STUDY	*	35.00	35.00
*	IN THE NORTHERN HUNTING GROUNDS-LYNX	*	375.00	375.00
*	ISLAND SHORES - SNOWY EGRET	*	250.00	250.00
*	IVORY BILLED WOODPECKER	*	600.00	600.00
*	MONARCH IS ALIVE-PREMIER-EAGLE	*	900.00	900.00
*	MOTHER OF PEARLS-POLAR BEAR	*	275.00	275.00
*	NARROW ESCAPE - CHIPMUNK	*	150.00	150.00
*	ONE TO ONE - GRAY WOLF STUDY	*	220.00	220.00
*	PATHFINDER - RED FOX	*	245.00	245.00
*	POLAR BEAR CUB STUDY	*	35.00	35.00
*	POWER AND GRACE-DEER	*	525.00	525.00
*	RED FOX STUDY	*	125.00	125.00
*	RIVERBANK KESTREL	*	325.00	325.00
*	ROCKY CAMP - COUGAR (GICLEE)	*	500.00	500.00
*	ROCKY CAMP - COUGAR FAMILY	*	275.00	275.00
*	ROCKY CAMP CUBS	*	225.00	225.00
*	ROCKY KINGDOM - BIGHORN SHEEP	*	255.00	255.00
*	SILENT PASSAGE-LION	*	400.00	400.00
*	SNOW LEOPARD PORTRAIT	*	150.00	150.00
*	SUMMER ROSES - WINTER WREN	*	425.00	425.00
*	TAKE FIVE - CANADA LYNX	*	340.00	340.00
*	TUNDRA SUMMIT-ARCTIC WOLVES	*	340.00	340.00
*	WOLF SCOUT #1-WOLF CUB	*	105.00	105.00
*	WOLF SCOUT #2-WOLF CUB	*	105.00	105.00
*	WREN STUDY	*	35.00	35.00
91	SHADOWS IN THE GRASS (PRESTIGE ED.)	*	450.00	450.00
*	LONELY WATCH	*	100.00	100.00
*	NEW DAY, A	*	150.00	150.00
*	PAUSE FOR A DRINK	*	100.00	100.00
*	TRAIL BOSS	*	100.00	100.00
*	WHEN TRAPPERS MEET (PENCIL)	*	165.00	165.00
*	A GIFT OF TIME	*	395.00	395.00
*	A GIFT OF TIME-SCHOOL TEACHER	*	145.00	145.00
*	FIRST DAY IN HARNESS	*	225.00	225.00
*	FISHING RIGHTS-BROWN BEAR	*	195.00	195.00
*	RARIN' TO GO DOG SLED	*	225.00	225.00
*	BLUE SHADOWS-ARCTIC FOX	*	175.00	175.00
*	COASTAL MORNING-GRIZZLY	*	195.00	195.00
*	EVENING SILHOUETTE-COYOTES	*	225.00	225.00
*	EVENING SOLITUDE-WOLF	*	195.00	195.00
*	FALLEN TOTEM-EAGLE	*	300.00	300.00
*	FOREST FLIGHT-EAGLE	*	195.00	195.00
*	FROSTY ALDER-EVENING GROSBEAK	*	125.00	125.00
*	GRIZZLES AT THE FALLS	*	225.00	225.00
*	ICY CREEK-MINK	*	105.00	105.00
*	LAST LIGHT-COUGAR	*	235.00	235.00
*	MOUNTAIN BLOOMS-GROUND SQUIRREL	*	50.00	50.00
*	OLD MAN OF THE MOUNTAIN-BLACK BEAR	*	185.00	185.00
*	RAIDING THE CACHE	*	95.00	95.00
*	RAMPARTS-MOUNTAIN GOATS	*	200.00	200.00
*	RED-BREASTED NUTHATCH ON PI	*	95.00	95.00
*	RED-COCKADED WOODPECKER	*	120.00	120.00
*	REFLECTIONS-MALLARD DUCK	*	175.00	175.00
*	SEA OTTER WITH URCHIN	*	150.00	150.00
*	STILL WATER - MALLARD DUCK	*	105.00	105.00
*	THROUGH THE FIRS-EAGLE	*	500.00	500.00
*	WAPITI PORTRAIT-AMERICAN ELK	*	105.00	105.00
*	WARY GLANCE - CHIPMUNK	*	70.00	70.00
*	WHITE-TAILED TROPICBIRDS	*	130.00	130.00
*	WINTER'S FURY-MOUNTAIN GOATS	*	195.00	195.00
*	VOLUNTEERS	*	255.00	255.00
*	ALERT-WHITETAILED DEER	*	175.00	175.00
*	BERRY FOOD-CEDAR WAXWINGS	*	85.00	85.00
*	COASTING DOWN-CANADA GEESE	*	40.00	40.00
*	COLD MORNING-MALLARDS	*	175.00	175.00

YR	NAME	LIMIT	ISSUE	QUOTE
*	DARK SKY-PINTAILS	*	125.00	125.00
*	DARK SKY-SNOW GEESE	*	175.00	350.00
*	FAMILY, THE - CANADA GEESE	*	95.00	95.00
*	FLARING-MALLARDS	*	175.00	175.00
*	FLIGHT- CANADA GEESE - BRONZE	*	4000.00	4000.00
*	HEAVY SNOW-RUFFED GROUSE	*	150.00	150.00
*	HIGH COUNTRY SKIER	*	125.00	125.00
*	MADISON COUNTY BRIDGE-PHEASANTS	*	135.00	135.00
*	MISTY FLIGHT-CANADA GEESE	*	150.00	150.00
*	PREENING-BLUE WINGED TEAL	*	115.00	115.00
*	QUAIL RIDGE-BOBWHITES	*	175.00	175.00
*	QUIET LANDING-MALLARD-BRONZE	*	3000.00	3000.00
*	ROSEMAN BRIDGE-MADISON CITY	*	135.00	135.00
*	SHALLOW RIVER-AMERICAN WIGEON	*	.195.00	195.00
*	SUNSET-CANADA GEESE	*	195.00	195.00
*	TWIN FAWNS-WHITE-TAILED DEER	*	235.00	235.00
*	WASHINGTON DUCK 1989 - AMERICAN WIGEON	*	135.00	135.00
*	WATERFOWL ART OF MAYNARD	*	650.00	650.00
*	WHITE PINE- BLUE JAY	*	85.00	85.00
*	ABANDONED-WOLF PUPS	*	175.00	175.00
*	AMBOSELI CHILD-AF/ELEPHANT	*	160.00	160.00
*	BANYAN AMBUSH-BLACK PANTHER	*	235.00	235.00
*	BLACK JADE-WOLVES	*	550.00	550.00
*	BLACK MAGIC-PANTHER	*	475.00	475.00
*	CANADA D.U. DUCK STAMP PRIN	*	135.00	135.00
*	CANADA D.U. DUCK STAMP-EXEC.	*	375.00	375.00
*	CHASE-SNOW LEOPARD, THE	*	200.00	200.00
*	CHILD OF THE OUTBACK-KOALA	*	175.00	175.00
*	COUGAR HEAD STUDY	*	60.00	60.00
*	COURTSHIP, THE-EGERTS	*	175.00	175.00
*	DARK ENCOUNTER-BLACK WOLF	*	200.00	200.00
*	EARLY SNOW-RED FOX	*	200.00	200.00
*	FOREST GLOW-JAGUAR	*	225.00	225.00
*	FREEDOM I -HARPY EAGLE	*	500.00	500.00
*	FROZEN MOONLIGHT-ARCTIC WOLVES	*	225.00	225.00
*	GRIZZLY IMPACT	*	225.00	225.00
*	HIGH REFUGE-RED SQUIRREL	*	120.00	120.00
*	ICE COMPANIONS-HARP SEAL-SEAL PUPS	*	175.00	175.00
*	ICE FISHING-POLAR BEAR	*	225.00	225.00
*	IMPRESS, OF INDIA/NEPAL-W/C WILDLIFE	*	550.00	550.00
*	KEEPING PACE-GRIZZLY W/CUBS	*	200.00	200.00
*	LEAVING THE NEST-WOOD DUCK	*	150.00	150.00
*	LOONLIGHT-LOON	*	225.00	225.00
*	MONSOON-WHITE TIGER	*	195.00	195.00
*	MOONLIGHT FISHERMAN-RACCOON	*	175.00	175.00
*	MORNING FORAGE-GROUND SQUIRREL	*	75.00	75.00
*	MORNING GLORY-BALD EAGLE	*	225.00	225.00
*	N.Y. DUCK STAMP - 1990 W/	*	300.00	300.00
*	N.Y. DUCK STAMP -1990 W/MEDAL	*	550.00	550.00
*	NIGHT PROWLER-WOLF	*	225.00	225.00
*	NIGHT SPECTER- BLACK JAGUAR	*	195.00	195.00
*	OUT OF THE DARKNESS-BLACK PANTHER	*	200.00	200.00
*	PHANTOMS OF THE TUNDRA-WOLVES	*	235.00	235.00
*	QINLING PANDA	*	225.00	225.00
*	RAINS-TIGER, THE	*	225.00	225.00
*	RANTHAMBHORE RUSH-TIGER	*	225.00	225.00
*	RED FOX KIT STUDY	*	60.00	60.00
*	REGAL MAJESTY-BLACK PANTHER	*	200.00	200.00
*	RETURN TO WINTER-PINTAILS	*	135.00	135.00
*	RETURN TO YELLOWSTONE-WOLVES	*	235.00	235.00
*	SEEKING ATTENTION-GRIZZLY	*	200.00	200.00
*	SILENT WATERS-MOOSE	*	175.00	175.00
*	SNOWBOUNDING-GRIZZLY	*	225.00	225.00
*	SQUIRREL MONKEY STUDY	*	145.00	145.00
*	SUNDOWN REFLECTIONS-WOOD DUCK	*	85.00	85.00
*	WOLONG WHITEOUT-PANDA	*	225.00	225.00
*	YOUNG PREDATOR-LEOPARD CUB	*	200.00	200.00
89	GORILLA	290	400.00	600.00
90	SUMMER RAIN-COMMON LOONS (SPECIAL)	450	425.00	425.00
*	ACCEPT MY FATHERS SPIRIT	*	175.00	175.00
*	ACROSS THE TUNDRA	*	135.00	135.00
*	AFTERNOON SHADOWS-MULE DEER	*	145.00	145.00
*	ANTELOPE RIDGE	*	150.00	150.00
*	BANDITS, THE	*	125.00	125.00
*	BENGAL TIGER	*	175.00	175.00
*	BUFFALO BROTHERS	*	175.00	175.00

YR	NAME	LIMIT	ISSUE	QUOTE
*	CHALLENGE OF THE WILD	*	225.00	225.00
*	DARK WATERS-HERON	*	70.00	70.00
*	FEMALE TIMBER WOLF	*	100.00	100.00
*	GARDEN VISITOR-RED FOX	*	210.00	210.00
*	ICE BEAR	*	210.00	210.00
*	MALE TIMBER WOLF	*	100.00	100.00
*	MCNEIL RIVER FISHERMAN-BROWN BEAR	*	175.00	175.00
*	TIMBER WOLF STUDY	*	75.00	75.00
*	TIMBER WOLF STUDY COMPANION	*	185.00	185.00
*	TOMORROW MAY BE COOLER-LION	*	135.00	135.00
*	WHITE WOLF STUDY	*	75.00	75.00
F. MACHETANZ				**ALASKAN**
*	HARPOONER'S MOMENT-ALASKAN	*	225.00	225.00
*	TRAIL OF GREAT WHITE BEAR-ALASKA	*	225.00	225.00
R. BATEMAN				**BATEMAN**
*	WASHINGTON DUCK STAMP	*	150.00	150.00
*	WINTER RUN-BULL MOOSE	*	295.00	295.00
78	BY THE TRACKS-KILLDEER	950	75.00	1200.00
78	CHEETAH WITH CUBS	950	95.00	450.00
78	DOWNY WOODPECKER ON GOLDENROD	950	50.00	1425.00
78	LION CUBS	950	125.00	750.00
78	MAJESTY ON THE WING-BALD EAGLE	950	150.00	4000.00
78	YOUNG BARN SWALLOW	950	75.00	700.00
79	AFTERNOON GLOW-SNOWY OWL	950	125.00	625.00
79	AMONG THE LEAVES-COTTONTAIL RABBIT	950	75.00	1400.00
79	BULL MOOSE	950	125.00	1275.00
79	COUNTRY LANE-PHEASANTS	950	85.00	300.00
79	EVENING SNOWFALL-AMERICAN ELK	950	150.00	1900.00
79	GOLDEN EAGLE	950	150.00	250.00
79	GREAT BLUE HERON	950	125.00	1300.00
79	HIGH COUNTRY-STONE SHEEP	950	125.00	325.00
79	KING OF THE REALM-LION	950	125.00	675.00
79	MASTER OF THE HERD-AMERICAN BUFFALO	950	150.00	2250.00
79	SURF AND SANDERLINGS	950	65.00	600.00
79	UP IN THE PINE-GREAT HORNED OWL	950	150.00	730.00
79	WILY AND WARY-RED FOX	950	125.00	1500.00
79	WINTER CARDINAL	950	75.00	3550.00
79	WINTER-SNOWSHOE HARE	950	95.00	1200.00
79	WOLF PACK IN MOONLIGHT	950	95.00	3000.00
79	YELLOW-RUMPED WARBLER	950	50.00	575.00
80	AFRICAN AMBER-LIONESS PAIR	950	175.00	525.00
80	ANTARCTIC ELEMENTS-SEA GULL	950	125.00	150.00
80	ARCTIC FAMILY-POLAR BEARS	950	150.00	2250.00
80	ASLEEP ON THE HEMLOCK-SCREECH OWL	950	125.00	1150.00
80	AUTUMN OVERTURE-MOOSE	950	245.00	1450.00
80	AWESOME LAND-AMERICAN ELK	950	245.00	1785.00
80	BARN OWL IN THE CHURCHYARD	950	125.00	775.00
80	BLUFFING BULL-AFRICAN ELEPHANT	950	135.00	1125.00
80	BROWN PELICAN AND PILINGS	950	165.00	950.00
80	CHAPEL DOORS	950	135.00	375.00
80	COYOTE IN WINTER SAGE	950	245.00	3600.00
80	CURIOUS GLANCE-RED FOX	950	135.00	1200.00
80	EVENING GROSBEAK	950	125.00	1175.00
80	FALLEN WILLOW-SNOWY OWL	950	200.00	950.00
80	FLYING HIGH-GOLDEN EAGLE	950	150.00	1500.00
80	HERON ON THE ROCKS	950	75.00	300.00
80	KINGFISHER IN WINTER	950	175.00	825.00
80	KITTIWAKES GREETING	950	75.00	550.00
80	LEOPARD IN A SAUSAGE TREE	950	150.00	1250.00
80	LION AT TSAVO	950	150.00	275.00
80	MISCHIEF ON THE PROWL-RACCOON	950	85.00	350.00
80	MISTY COAST-GULLS	950	135.00	600.00
80	ON THE ALERT-CHIPMUNK	950	60.00	500.00
80	PRAIRIE EVENING-SHORT-EARED OWL	950	150.00	200.00
80	ROCKY WILDERNESS-COUGAR	950	175.00	1425.00
80	SPRING CARDINAL	950	125.00	600.00
80	SPRING THAW-KILLDEER	950	85.00	150.00
80	VANTAGE POINT-BALD EAGLE	950	245.00	2100.00
80	WHITE ENCOUNTER-POLAR BEAR	950	245.00	4250.00
80	WHITE-FOOTED MOUSE IN WINTERGREEN	950	60.00	650.00
80	WINTER ELM-AMERICAN KESTREL	950	135.00	600.00
80	WINTER SONG-CHICKADEES	950	95.00	900.00
81	ARTIST AND HIS DOG	950	150.00	550.00
81	BRIGHT DAY-ATLANTIC PUFFINS	950	175.00	875.00
81	CANADA GEESE-NESTING	950	295.00	3500.00
81	CLEAR NIGHT-WOLVES	950	245.00	6500.00

YR	NAME	LIMIT	ISSUE	QUOTE
81	COURTING PAIR-WHISTLING SWAN	950	245.00	550.00
81	COURTSHIP DISPLAY-WILD TURKEY	950	175.00	175.00
81	EDGE OF THE ICE-ERMINE	950	175.00	475.00
81	EVENING LIGHT-WHITE GYRFALCON	950	245.00	1100.00
81	GALLOPING HERD-GIRAFFES	950	175.00	1200.00
81	GRAY SQUIRREL	950	180.00	1250.00
81	HIGH CAMP AT DUSK-HORSE	950	245.00	300.00
81	IN FOR THE EVENING-SHEEP	950	150.00	1500.00
81	KINGFISHER AND ASPENS	950	225.00	720.00
81	LAST LOOK-BIGHORN SHEEP	950	195.00	225.00
81	LAUGHING GULL AND HORSESHOE CRAB	950	125.00	125.00
81	LITTLE BLUE HERON	950	95.00	275.00
81	MISTY MORNING-LOONS	950	150.00	3600.00
81	OSPREY FAMILY	950	245.00	325.00
81	PAIR OF SKIMMERS	950	150.00	200.00
81	RED-TAILED HAWK BY THE CLIFF	950	245.00	550.00
81	RED-WINGED BLACKBIRD AND RAIL FENCE	950	195.00	225.00
81	ROUGH-LEGGED HAWK IN THE ELM	950	175.00	175.00
81	ROYAL FAMILY-MUTE SWANS	950	245.00	1100.00
81	SARAH E. WITH GULLS	950	245.00	3650.00
81	SHEER DROP-MOUNTAIN GOATS	950	245.00	2800.00
81	SWIFT FOX	950	175.00	350.00
81	WATCHFUL REPOSE-BLACK BEAR	950	245.00	700.00
81	WINTER MIST-GREAT HORNED OWL	950	245.00	900.00
81	WINTER WREN	950	135.00	250.00
81	WRANGLER'S CAMPSITE-GRAY JAY	950	195.00	550.00
82	ABOVE THE RIVER-TRUMPETER SWANS	950	200.00	1050.00
82	ARCTIC EVENING-WHITE WOLF	950	185.00	1750.00
82	ARCTIC PORTRAIT-WHITE GYRFALCON	950	175.00	250.00
82	AT THE ROADSIDE-RED TAILED HAWK	950	185.00	550.00
82	BAOBAB TREE AND IMPALA	950	245.00	350.00
82	BARN SWALLOWS IN AUGUST	950	245.00	425.00
82	CHEETAH PROFILE	950	245.00	500.00
82	DIPPER BY THE WATERFALL	950	165.00	200.00
82	EDGE OF THE WOODS-WHITETAIL DEER/BOOK	950	745.00	1400.00
82	FOX AT THE GRANARY	950	165.00	225.00
82	FROSTY MORNING-BLUE JAY	950	185.00	1000.00
82	GALLINULE FAMILY	950	135.00	135.00
82	GENTOO PENGUINS AND WHALE BONES	950	205.00	525.00
82	GOLDEN CROWNED KINGLET W/RHODODENDRON	950	150.00	2575.00
82	LEOPARD AMBUSH	950	150.00	600.00
82	LIVELY PAIR-CHICKADEES	950	160.00	450.00
82	MEADOW'S EDGE-MALLARD	950	175.00	1000.00
82	MERGANSER FAMILY IN HIDING	950	200.00	525.00
82	PILEATED WOODPECKER ON BEECH TREE	950	175.00	850.00
82	PIONEER MEMORIES-MAGPIE PAIR	950	175.00	250.00
82	POLAR BEAR PROFILE	950	210.00	2350.00
82	POLAR BEARS AT BAFFIN ISLAND	950	245.00	875.00
82	QUEEN ANNE'S LACE/AMERICAN GOLDFINCH	950	150.00	1000.00
82	READY FOR THE HUNT-SNOWY OWL	950	245.00	775.00
82	RED SQUIRREL	950	245.00	700.00
82	RED WOLF	950	175.00	525.00
82	SPRING MARSH-PINTAIL PAIR	950	200.00	275.00
82	STILL MORNING-HERRING GULLS	950	200.00	250.00
82	WHITE WORLD-DALL SHEEP	950	200.00	450.00
82	WHITE-FOOTED MOUSE ON ASPEN	950	90.00	225.00
82	WILLET ON THE SHORE	950	125.00	225.00
83	BALD EAGLE PORTRAIT	950	185.00	350.00
83	CALL OF THE WILD-BALD EAGLE	950	200.00	250.00
83	EARLY SNOWFALL-RUFFED GROUSE	950	195.00	225.00
83	EARLY SPRING-BLUEBIRD	950	185.00	975.00
83	EVENING IDYLL-MUTE SWANS	950	245.00	525.00
83	GHOST OF THE NORTH-GREAT GREY OWL	950	200.00	2675.00
83	GOSHAWK AND RUFFED GROUSE	950	185.00	700.00
83	GREAT HORNED OWL IN THE WHITE PINE	950	225.00	575.00
83	LOON FAMILY	950	200.00	750.00
83	MORNING ON THE FLATS-BISON	950	200.00	350.00
83	MULE DEER IN WINTER	950	200.00	350.00
83	NEW SEASON-AMERICAN ROBIN	950	200.00	450.00
83	OSPREY IN THE RAIN	950	110.00	650.00
83	PHEASANT IN CORNFIELD	950	200.00	375.00
83	RUBY-THROAT AND COLUMBINE-HUMMINGBIRD	950	150.00	3400.00
83	SNOWY OWL ON DRIFTWOOD	950	170.00	1450.00
83	TIGER PORTRAIT	950	130.00	400.00
83	WINTER BARN-SHEEP	950	170.00	400.00
83	WINTER LADY-CARDINAL	950	200.00	1500.00

YR	NAME	LIMIT	ISSUE	QUOTE
83	WOLVES ON THE TRAIL	950	225.00	700.00
83	WOODLAND DRUMMER-RUFFED GROUSE	950	185.00	250.00
83	YOUNG ELF OWL-OLD SAGUARO	950	95.00	250.00
84	ACROSS THE SKY-SNOW GOOSE	950	220.00	675.00
84	ALONG THE RIDGE-GRIZZLY BEARS	950	200.00	950.00
84	AMERICAN GOLDFINCH-WINTER DRESS	950	75.00	225.00
84	BIG COUNTRY-PRONGHORN ANTELOPE	950	185.00	200.00
84	COUGAR PORTRAIT	950	95.00	200.00
84	DOWN FOR A DRINK-MOURNING DOVE	950	135.00	230.00
84	HOODED MERGANSERS IN WINTER	950	210.00	650.00
84	HOUSE FINCH AND YUCCA	950	95.00	175.00
84	IN THE BRIER PATCH-COTTONTAIL	950	165.00	350.00
84	LILY PADS AND LOON	950	200.00	1875.00
84	MAY MAPLE-SCARLET TANAGER	950	175.00	750.00
84	MISTY LAKE-OSPREY	950	95.00	300.00
84	MORNING ON THE RIVER-TRUMPETER SWANS	950	185.00	300.00
84	PEREGRINE AND RUDDY TURNSTONES	950	200.00	350.00
84	READY FOR FLIGHT-PEREGRINE FALCON	950	185.00	500.00
84	REEDS- STILLIFE	950	185.00	575.00
84	SMALLWOOD-LABRADOR DOG	950	200.00	500.00
84	STRETCHING-CANADA GOOSE	950	225.00	3600.00
84	SUMMER MORNING-LOON	950	185.00	1250.00
84	TADPOLE TIME	950	135.00	475.00
84	TIGER AT DAWN	950	225.00	2500.00
84	WHITE-THROATED SPARROW AND PUSSY WILLOW	950	150.00	580.00
84	WINDOW INTO ONTARIO	950	265.00	1500.00
84	WINTER SUNSET-MOOSE	950	245.00	2700.00
85	ARCTIC TERN PAIR	950	175.00	200.00
85	BEAVER POND REFLECTIONS	950	185.00	225.00
85	CANADA GEESE FAMILY (STONE LITHO)	260	350.00	1000.00
85	CANADA GEESE OVER THE ESCARPMENT	950	135.00	275.00
85	ENTERING THE WATER-COMMON GULLS	950	195.00	200.00
85	GAMBEL'S QUAIL PAIR	950	95.00	350.00
85	GOLDEN EAGLE PORTRAIT	950	115.00	175.00
85	IN THE HIGHLANDS-GOLDEN EAGLE	950	235.00	425.00
85	IN THE MOUNTAINS-OSPREY	950	95.00	200.00
85	IRISH COTTAGE AND WAGTAIL	950	175.00	325.00
85	LEOPARD AT SERONERA	950	175.00	300.00
85	LIONS IN THE GRASS	950	265.00	1250.00
85	MORNING DEW-ROE DEER	950	175.00	175.00
85	OLD WHALING BASE AND FUR SEALS	950	195.00	550.00
85	ON THE GARDEN WALL-CHAFFINCH	950	115.00	300.00
85	ORCA PROCESSION	950	245.00	2525.00
85	PEREGRINE FALCON & WHITE-THROATED SWIFTS	950	245.00	725.00
85	SNOWY HEMLOCK-BARRED OWL	950	245.00	400.00
85	STREAM BANK-JUNE-BIRD	950	160.00	175.00
85	STRUTTING-RING-NECKED PHEASANT	950	225.00	325.00
85	SUDDEN BLIZZARD-RED-TAILED HAWK	950	245.00	600.00
85	TRUMPETER SWANS AND ASPEN	950	245.00	550.00
85	WEATHERED BRANCH-BALD EAGLE	950	115.00	300.00
85	WHITE-BREASTED NUTHATCH ON A BEECH TREE	950	175.00	300.00
85	WINTER COMPANION-YELLOW LAB. DOG	950	175.00	500.00
85	WOOD BISON PORTRAIT	950	165.00	200.00
86	A RESTING PLACE-CAPE BUFFALO	950	265.00	265.00
86	BLACK EAGLE	950	200.00	200.00
86	BLACK-TAILED DEER IN THE OLYMPICS	950	245.00	300.00
86	BLACKSMITH PLOVER	950	185.00	185.00
86	CANADA GEESE WITH YOUNG	950	195.00	325.00
86	CHARGING RHINO	950	325.00	500.00
86	DARK GYRFALCON	950	225.00	325.00
86	DRIFTWOOD PERCH-STRIPED SWALLOWS	950	195.00	250.00
86	ELEPHANT HERD AND SANDGROUSE	950	235.00	235.00
86	EUROPEAN ROBIN AND HYDRANGEAS	950	130.00	245.00
86	FENCE POST AND BURDOCK	950	130.00	160.00
86	HOUSE SPARROW	950	125.00	150.00
86	HUMMINGBIRD PAIR (DIPTYCH)	950	330.00	475.00
86	IN THE GRASS-LIONESS	950	245.00	245.00
86	MALLARD FAMILY-MISTY MARSH	950	130.00	175.00
86	MALLARD PAIR-EARLY WINTER	41,740	135.00	200.00
86	MALLARD PAIR-EARLY WINTER (24K GOLD)	950	1650.00	2000.00
86	MALLARD PAIR-EARLY WINTER (GOLD)	7691	250.00	375.00
86	MARGINAL MEADOW-LANDSCAPE	950	220.00	350.00
86	MOOSE AT WATER'S EDGE	950	130.00	225.00
86	MULE DEER IN ASPEN	950	175.00	175.00
86	NORTHERN REFLECTIONS-LOON FAMILY	8631	255.00	2100.00
86	PROUD SWIMMER-SNOW GOOSE	950	185.00	185.00

YR	NAME	LIMIT	ISSUE	QUOTE
86	RESTING PLACE-CAPE BUFFALO	950	265.00	265.00
86	ROBINS AT THE NEST	950	185.00	225.00
86	SPLIT RAILS-SNOW BUNTINGS	950	220.00	220.00
86	SUMMERTIME-POLAR BEARS	950	225.00	475.00
86	SWIFT FOX STUDY	950	115.00	150.00
86	WILDEBEEST	950	185.00	185.00
86	WINTER IN THE MOUNTAINS-RAVEN	950	200.00	200.00
87	AT THE NEST-SECRETARY BIRDS	950	290.00	290.00
87	CONTINUING GENERATIONS-SPOTTED OWLS	950	525.00	1150.00
87	END OF SEASON-GRIZZLY	950	325.00	500.00
87	EVERGLADES-EGRET	950	360.00	360.00
87	FARM LANE AND BLUE JAYS	950	225.00	500.00
87	GREAT BLUE HERON IN FLIGHT	950	295.00	550.00
87	GREAT EGRET PREENING	950	315.00	500.00
87	GREATER KUDU BULL	950	145.00	145.00
87	HIGH KINGDOM-SNOW LEOPARD	950	325.00	875.00
87	HOUSE SPARROWS AND BITTERSWEET	950	220.00	400.00
87	HURRICAN LAKE-WOOD DUCKS	950	135.00	200.00
87	KING PENGUINS	950	130.00	135.00
87	LATE WINTER-BLACK SQUIRREL	950	165.00	175.00
87	LION AND WILDEBEEST	950	265.00	265.00
87	LIONESS AT SERENGETI	950	325.00	325.00
87	OTTER STUDY	950	235.00	375.00
87	PEREGRINE FALCON/CLIFF (STONE LITHO)	525	350.00	625.00
87	PLOWED FIELD-SNOWY OWL	290	145.00	400.00
87	PRIDE OF AUTUMN-CANADA GOOSE	950	135.00	200.00
87	RHINO AT NGORO NGORO	950	325.00	325.00
87	ROCKY POINT-OCTOBER-BOAT	950	195.00	275.00
87	RUDDY TURNSTONES	950	175.00	175.00
87	SNOWY OWL AND MILKWEED	950	235.00	950.00
87	STONE SHEEP RAM	950	175.00	175.00
87	SYLVAN STREAM-MUTE SWANS	950	125.00	125.00
87	WISE ONE, THE-ELEPHANT	950	325.00	800.00
88	CARDINAL AND WILD APPLES	950	235.00	255.00
88	CATTAILS, FIREWEED,YELLOWTHROAT WARBLER	950	235.00	275.00
88	CHALLENGE, THE-BULL MOOSE	10,671	325.00	325.00
88	CHERRYWOOD WITH JUNCOS	950	245.00	245.00
88	COLONIAL GARDEN-LANDSCAPE	950	245.00	300.00
88	DOZING LYNX	950	335.00	1750.00
88	GRASSY BANK-GREAT BLUE HERON	950	285.00	285.00
88	GREAT CRESTED GREBE	950	135.00	135.00
88	HARDWOOD FOREST-WHITE TAILED BUCK	950	345.00	2100.00
88	HARLEQUIN DUCK-BULL KELP (EXEC.)	950	550.00	550.00
88	HARLEQUIN DUCK-BULL KELP (GOLD)	950	300.00	300.00
88	LEOPARD AND THOMSON GAZELLE KILL	950	275.00	275.00
88	MALLARD FAMILY AT SUNSET	950	235.00	235.00
88	MUSKOKA LAKE-COMMON LOONS	950	265.00	450.00
88	PANDAS AT PLAY (STONE LITHO)	160	400.00	2500.00
88	PHEASANTS AT DUSK	950	325.00	675.00
88	PREENING PAIR-CANADA GEESE	950	235.00	300.00
88	RED CROSSBILLS	950	125.00	150.00
88	SHELTER-RURAL LANDSCAPE	950	325.00	1150.00
88	TAWNY OWL IN BEECH	950	325.00	600.00
88	TREE SWALLOW OVER POND	950	290.00	290.00
88	YOUNG SANDHILL CRANES	950	325.00	325.00
89	BACKLIGHT-MUTE SWAN	950	275.00	600.00
89	BARN SWALLOW AND HORSE COLLAR	950	225.00	225.00
89	BROAD-TAILED HUMMINGBIRD PAIR	950	225.00	225.00
89	CATCHING THE LIGHT-BARN OWL	2000	295.00	295.00
89	CENTENNIAL FARM	950	295.00	450.00
89	DISPUTE OVER PREY	950	325.00	325.00
89	EVENING CALL-COMMON LOON	950	235.00	525.00
89	GOLDFINCH IN THE MEADOW	1600	150.00	200.00
89	MANGROVE MORNING-ROSEATE SPOONBILLS	2000	325.00	325.00
89	MIDNIGHT-BLACK WOLF	25,352	325.00	1850.00
89	NEAR GLENBURNIE-ROCK	950	265.00	265.00
89	PUMPKIN TIME	950	195.00	195.00
89	VULTURE AND WILDEBEEST	550	295.00	295.00
89	YOUNG KITTIWAKE-BIRD	950	195.00	195.00
89	YOUNG SNOWY OWL	950	195.00	195.00
90	CHINSTRAP PENGUIN	810	150.00	150.00
90	HOMAGE TO AHMED-ELEPHANT	290	3300.00	3300.00
90	IRELAND HOUSE-LANDSCAPE	950	265.00	265.00
90	KEEPER OF THE LAND-GRIZZLY	290	3300.00	3300.00
90	LUNGING HERON	1250	225.00	225.00
90	MORNING COVE-COMMON LOON	950	165.00	165.00

YR	NAME	LIMIT	ISSUE	QUOTE
90	MOSSY BRANCHES-SPOTTED OWL	4500	300.00	525.00
90	MOWED MEADOW	950	190.00	190.00
90	PINTAILS IN SPRING	9651	135.00	360.00
90	POLAR BEAR	290	3300.00	3300.00
90	POWERPLAY-RHINOCEROS	950	320.00	320.00
90	ROLLING WAVES-LESSER SCAUP	3330	125.00	125.00
90	SUMMER MORNING PASTURE-COWS	290	175.00	175.00
90	WHITE ON WHITE-SNOWSHOE HARE	290	195.00	590.00
91	ARCTIC CLIFF-WHITE WOLVES	13,000	325.00	525.00
91	ARCTIC CLIFF-WHITE WOLVES (CONSERV.)	*	325.00	525.00
91	ARCTIC CLIFF-WHITE WOLVES (PREMIER ED.)	*	625.00	950.00
91	AT THE CLIFF-BOBCAT	*	325.00	325.00
91	AT THE CLIFF-BOBCAT (SIGNATURE ED.)	*	400.00	400.00
91	BLUEBIRD AND BLOSSOMS	4500	235.00	235.00
91	BLUEBIRD AND BLOSSOMS (PRESTIGE ED.)	450	625.00	625.00
91	CEREMONIAL POSE-JAPANESE CRANE	*	3300.00	3300.00
91	COTTAGE LANE-RED FOX	950	285.00	285.00
91	ELEPHANT COW AND CALF	950	300.00	300.00
91	ENCOUNTER IN THE BUSH-AFRICAN LIONS	950	295.00	295.00
91	ENDANGERED SPACES-GRIZZLY	4008	325.00	325.00
91	FLUID POWER-ORCA	290	2500.00	2500.00
91	GULLS ON PILINGS	1950	265.00	265.00
91	SCOLDING, THE-CHICKADEES AND SCREECH OWL	*	235.00	425.00
91	SEA OTTER STUDY	*	150.00	250.00
91	TRUMPETER SWAN FAMILY	290	2500.00	2500.00
91	WHISTLING SWAN-LAKE ERIE	1950	325.00	325.00
91	WIDE HORIZON-TUNDRA SWANS	2862	325.00	385.00

J. DALY **BOY**

	NAME	LIMIT	ISSUE	QUOTE
*	FAVORITE READER	*	425.00	425.00

A. BRACKENBURY **BRACKENBURY**

YR	NAME	LIMIT	ISSUE	QUOTE
83	GREAT EXPECTATIONS	950	40.00	80.00
83	UNDER THE RED TWIGS-COTTONTAIL	950	40.00	80.00
84	CATTAILS	950	60.00	225.00
84	FIRST EXCURSION-CHICKEN	*	40.00	40.00
84	GRIZZLY IN CHOKEBERRIES	*	60.00	60.00
85	PROWLING BANDITS-RACCOONS	*	50.00	50.00
85	SLED DOGS	950	50.00	50.00
85	TOADALLY CAPTIVATED-DOG	950	60.00	72.00
86	CHILLY DOG-YELLOW LAB	*	75.00	75.00
87	STONE LYIN'-CAT	*	85.00	85.00
88	CAT IN THE MAIZE	*	80.00	80.00
88	CHOCOLATE CLUSTER-CHOCOLATE LAB	*	80.00	80.00
88	CORN DOGS-LAB. DOG	*	85.00	85.00
88	FEATHERBRAIN-LAB. DOG	*	80.00	150.00
88	POLE CAT	*	85.00	85.00
89	BASKET CASE-PUPPIES	950	95.00	95.00
89	BUREAUCATS-KITTENS	*	95.00	95.00
89	RED TAPE-LAB. DOG	950	95.00	95.00
89	WINTER COAT-GOLDEN RETRIEVER	*	85.00	85.00
90	PUPULATION EXPLOSION-BLK VARI.-COCKER	950	95.00	95.00
90	PUPULATION EXPLOSION-GLD VARI.-COCKER	950	95.00	95.00
90	WAGGIN' TAILS-PUPPIES	950	95.00	95.00
91	DAWN ON THE BEACH-SNOWY EGRET	*	95.00	95.00

C. BRENDERS **BRENDERS**

YR	NAME	LIMIT	ISSUE	QUOTE
*	HUNTER'S DREAM-ELK	*	950.00	950.00
84	ON THE ALERT-RED FOX	950	95.00	475.00
84	PLAYFUL PAIR-CHIPMUNKS	950	40.00	400.00
84	SILENT HUNTER-GREAT HORNED OWL	950	95.00	600.00
84	SILENT PASSAGE-COUGAR	950	150.00	455.00
84	WATERSIDE ENCOUNTER-RACCOON	950	95.00	1000.00
85	MIGHTY INTRUDER-BLACK BEAR	950	95.00	275.00
86	ACROBATS MEAL, THE-RED SQUIRREL	950	65.00	275.00
86	BLACK-CAPPED CHICKADEES	950	40.00	525.00
86	BLUEBIRDS	950	40.00	200.00
86	COLORFUL PLAYGROUND-COTTONTAILS	950	75.00	500.00
86	DISTRIBUTED DAYDREAMS	950	95.00	370.00
86	GOLDEN SEASON-GRAY SQUIRREL	950	85.00	525.00
86	HARVEST TIME-CHIPMUNK	950	65.00	250.00
86	LATE SNOW-GREAT BLUE HERON	*	90.00	175.00
86	MEADOWLARK	1250	165.00	275.00
86	ROBINS	950	40.00	125.00
87	AUTUMN LADY-DEER	950	150.00	375.00
87	CLOSE TO MOM-BEAR	950	150.00	1500.00
87	DOUBLE TROUBLE-RACCOONS	950	120.00	650.00
87	IVORY-BILLED WOODPECKER	950	95.00	515.00
87	MIGRATION FEVER-BARN SWALLOWS	950	150.00	350.00

YR	NAME	LIMIT	ISSUE	QUOTE
87	MYSTERIOUS VISITOR-BARN OWL	950	150.00	375.00
87	UNDER THE PINE TREES-CHIPMUNKS	*	65.00	225.00
87	WHITE ELEGANCE-TRUMPETER SWANS	950	115.00	390.00
87	YELLOW-BELLIED MARMOT	950	95.00	425.00
88	A HUNTER'S DREAM	950	165.00	950.00
88	APPLE HARVEST	950	115.00	290.00
88	CALIFORNIA QUAIL	*	95.00	375.00
88	FOREST SENTINEL-BOBCAT	950	135.00	500.00
88	HIDDEN IN THE PINES-GREAT HORNED OWL	950	175.00	1500.00
88	HIGH ADVENTURE-BLACK BEAR CUBS	950	105.00	425.00
88	LONG DISTANCE HUNTERS-WOLF	1250	175.00	2250.00
88	ROAMING THE PLAINS-PRONGHORNS	*	150.00	250.00
88	TALK ON THE OLD FENCE	950	165.00	775.00
88	WITNESS OF A PAST-BISON	*	110.00	175.00
89	A YOUNG GENERATION-RABBIT	1250	165.00	375.00
89	APPLE LOVER, THE-ROBIN	1500	125.00	275.00
89	COMPANIONS, THE-WOLF	18036	200.00	675.00
89	FORAGER'S REWARD-RED SQUIRREL	*	135.00	250.00
89	LORD OF THE MARSHES-BLUE HERON	950	40.00	175.00
89	MERLINS AT THE NEST	1250	165.00	375.00
89	NORTHERN COUSINS-BLACK SQUIRREL	950	95.00	250.00
89	PREDATORS WALK, THE-COUGAR	*	150.00	375.00
89	RED-WINGED BLACKBIRDS	*	40.00	100.00
89	STELLER'S JAY	1250	135.00	175.00
89	SURVIVORS, THE-CANADA GEESE	*	225.00	850.00
90	A THREATENED SYMBOL-BALD EAGLE	1950	145.00	300.00
90	BLOND BEAUTY-HORSE	1950	185.00	185.00
90	FULL HOUSE-FOX FAMILY	20,106	235.00	275.00
90	GHOSTLY QUIET-SPANISH LYNX	1950	200.00	200.00
90	MONARCH IS ALIVE,THE-EAGLE	*	265.00	325.00
90	MOUNTAIN BABY-BIGHORN SHEEP	1950	165.00	165.00
90	ON THE OLD FARM DOOR-BLUEBIRD	1500	225.00	450.00
90	SHORELINE QUARTET-WHITE IBIS	1950	265.00	265.00
90	SMALL TALK	1500	125.00	250.00
90	SPRING FAWN	1500	125.00	300.00
90	SQUIRREL'S DISH	*	110.00	110.00
91	BALANCE OF NATURE, THE-HAWK & RABBIT	*	225.00	225.00
91	CALM BEFORE THE CHALLENGE-MOOSE	1950	225.00	225.00
91	NESTING SEASON, THE-HOUSE SPARROW	1950	195.00	250.00
91	ONE TO ONE-GRAY WOLF	10,000	245.00	510.00
91	SHADOWS IN THE GRASS-YOUNG COUGARS	*	235.00	235.00
91	STUDY FOR ONE TO ONE	1950	120.00	285.00
91	WOLF STUDY	*	125.00	125.00
J. CHRISTENSEN				**BRONZE**
*	SIX BIRD HUNTERS	*	4500.00	4500.00
*	COYOTE	*	950.00	950.00
*	RIMROCK - BRONZE	*	1450.00	1450.00
P. CALLE				**CALLE**
*	EARLY ARRIVALS	*	245.00	245.00
*	THEY CALL ME WILLIAM	*	265.00	265.00
*	WINTER FEAST	*	265.00	430.00
80	CARING FOR THE HERD	950	110.00	110.00
80	CHIEF HIGH PIPE (PENCIL)	950	75.00	165.00
80	CHIEF JOSEPH-MAN OF PEACE	950	135.00	150.00
80	LANDMARK TREE	950	125.00	225.00
80	PRAYER TO THE GREAT MYSTERY	950	245.00	450.00
80	SIOUX CHIEF	950	85.00	85.00
80	SOMETHING FOR THE POT	950	175.00	1700.00
80	VIEW FROM THE HEIGHTS	950	245.00	350.00
80	WHEN SNOW CAME EARLY	950	85.00	250.00
80	WINTER HUNTER, THE (PENCIL)	950	65.00	450.00
81	ALMOST HOME	950	150.00	150.00
81	AND STILL MILES TO GO	950	245.00	300.00
81	ANDREW AT THE FALLS	950	150.00	175.00
81	CHIEF HIGH PIPE (COLOR)	950	265.00	275.00
81	END OF A LONG DAY	950	150.00	150.00
81	FRESH TRACKS	*	150.00	165.00
81	FRIENDS	950	150.00	150.00
81	JUST OVER THE RIDGE	950	245.00	320.00
81	ONE WITH THE LAND	950	245.00	320.00
81	PAUSE AT THE LOWER FALLS	950	110.00	350.00
81	TETON FRIENDS	950	150.00	200.00
81	WINTER HUNTER, THE (COLOR)	950	245.00	725.00
82	BREATH OF FRIENDSHIP, THE	950	225.00	295.00
82	EMERGING FROM THE WOODS	950	110.00	110.00
82	GENERATIONS IN THE VALLEY	950	245.00	245.00

YR	NAME	LIMIT	ISSUE	QUOTE
82	RETURN TO CAMP	950	245.00	400.00
82	TWO FROM THE FLOCK	950	245.00	425.00
83	A WINTER'S SURPRISE	950	195.00	800.00
83	COMPANIONS	*	150.00	150.00
83	FREE SPIRITS	950	195.00	325.00
83	IN SEARCH OF BEAVER	950	225.00	950.00
83	STRAYS FROM THE FLYWAY	950	195.00	250.00
84	A BRACE FOR THE SPIT	950	110.00	275.00
84	CHANCE ENCOUNTER	950	225.00	300.00
84	FATE OF THE LATE MIGRANT	950	110.00	300.00
84	HEAR ME O' GREAT SPIRIT	*	175.00	275.00
84	MOUNTAIN MAN, THE	950	95.00	135.00
84	TRAPPER, THE	*	95.00	95.00
84	WHEN TRAILS CROSS	950	245.00	750.00
85	CARRYING PLACE, THE	*	195.00	195.00
85	GRANDMOTHER, THE	950	150.00	150.00
85	STORYTELLER OF THE MOUNTAINS	950	225.00	575.00
86	FREE TRAPPER, THE	*	200.00	200.00
86	SNOW HUNTER, THE	950	150.00	250.00
87	IN THE LAND OF THE GIANTS	950	245.00	780.00
87	INTO THE GREAT ALONE	950	245.00	600.00
88	VOYAGEURS & WATERFOWL	*	265.00	300.00
89	AND A GOOD BOOK FOR COMPANY	950	135.00	190.00
89	BEAVER MEN, THE	950	125.00	125.00
89	FUR TRAPPER, THE	550	75.00	75.00
89	GREAT MOMENT, THE	*	350.00	350.00
89	MOUNTAIN MEN, THE (LITHO)	*	400.00	400.00
89	NAVAJO MADONNA	650	95.00	95.00
89	WHERE EAGLES FLY	*	265.00	350.00
90	CHILDREN OF WALPI	350	160.00	160.00
90	DOLL MAKER, THE	950	95.00	95.00
90	INTERRUPTED JOURNEY	1750	265.00	300.00
90	INTERRUPTED JOURNEY (PRESTIGE ED.)	290	465.00	465.00
90	SON OF SITTING BULL	950	95.00	95.00
91	ALMOST THERE	*	165.00	240.00
91	IN THE BEGINNING...FRIENDS	1250	250.00	250.00
91	MAN OF THE FUR TRADE	550	110.00	110.00
91	SILENCED HONKERS, THE	*	250.00	250.00
91	THEY CALL ME MATTHEW	*	125.00	125.00
91	WHEN TRAILS GROW COLD	2500	265.00	265.00
91	WHEN TRAILS GROW COLD (PRESTIGE ED.)	290	465.00	465.00
J. DALY				**DALY**
*	ANNIE'S RAGGEDY	*	175.00	175.00
*	CATCH OF MY DREAMS	*	45.00	45.00
*	MARSHALL, THE	*	150.00	150.00
*	MUD MATES	*	150.00	150.00
*	MY BEST FRIENDS	*	140.00	140.00
*	SATURDAY MORNING	*	150.00	150.00
*	SLUGGER	*	75.00	75.00
*	SUNDAY MORNING	*	350.00	350.00
*	TO ALL A GOOD NIGHT	*	160.00	160.00
*	WALKING THE RAILS	*	175.00	175.00
*	WIND-UP, THE	*	75.00	75.00
82	SPRING FEVER	950	85.00	1450.00
83	SATURDAY NIGHT	950	85.00	1500.00
86	FLYING HIGH-CHILDREN	950	50.00	750.00
87	FAVORITE READER-BOY	*	85.00	425.00
87	ODD MAN OUT-BOY	*	85.00	675.00
88	ON THIN ICE-BOY ICE SKATING	*	95.00	150.00
88	TERRITORIAL RIGHTS-BOY	*	85.00	350.00
88	TIE BREAKER-CHECKERS	*	95.00	275.00
88	WIPED OUT-MARBLES	*	125.00	500.00
89	IN THE DOGHOUSE-BOY/DOG	1500	75.00	300.00
89	LET'S PLAY BALL-BOY/DOG	1500	75.00	200.00
89	THIEF, THE-BOY/DOG	1500	95.00	450.00
89	THORN, THE	*	125.00	675.00
90	BIG MOMENT, THE-CLOWN W/CHILD	1500	125.00	125.00
90	CONFRONTATION	1500	85.00	145.00
90	CONTENTMENT	1500	95.00	550.00
90	HONOR AND ALLEGIANCE	1500	110.00	160.00
90	ICE MAN, THE-BOY	1500	125.00	200.00
90	IT'S THAT TIME AGAIN	1500	120.00	120.00
90	MAKE BELIEVE-LITTLE GIRLS	1500	75.00	425.00
90	RADIO DAZE	1500	150.00	150.00
90	SCHOLAR, THE	1500	110.00	110.00
91	A NEW BEGINNING	*	125.00	125.00

YR	NAME	LIMIT	ISSUE	QUOTE
91	CAT'S CRADLE	*	450.00	450.00
91	HOME TEAM: ZERO-BASEBALL	1500	150.00	150.00
91	HOMEMADE	1500	125.00	175.00
91	PILLARS OF A NATION-ELLIS ISLAND	20,000	175.00	175.00
91	TIME-OUT-CHILDREN	*	125.00	125.00
N. ENGLE				**ENGLE**
81	HOUSE BY THE SEA	950	75.00	1005.00
81	WILDERNESS MARSH	950	75.00	815.00
83	MORNING ON THE YELLOWDOG RIVER	950	75.00	170.00
83	QUIET WATERS	950	75.00	275.00
83	SUMMER RIVER	950	75.00	240.00
83	WILD OCTOBER	*	75.00	125.00
83	WINTER BROOK	*	75.00	75.00
84	APRIL LIGHT	*	95.00	95.00
84	AUTUMN BLUEBERRIES	950	75.00	125.00
84	EVENING HARBOR	950	75.00	135.00
84	ISLAND HOME	*	75.00	135.00
84	ISLAND LAKE	950	95.00	160.00
84	LOST CREEK	*	15.00	135.00
84	MARCH THAW	*	95.00	175.00
84	MELTING INTO SPRING	*	95.00	175.00
84	MIDDLE ISLAND POINT	*	115.00	165.00
84	PEACEFUL MORNING-CANADAS	*	50.00	50.00
85	AUTUMN GOLD	*	85.00	160.00
85	AUTUMN RIVER	*	50.00	120.00
85	GREAT PASSAGE	*	175.00	215.00
85	GROUSE COUNTRY	950	85.00	300.00
85	HEMLOCK MARSH	*	115.00	160.00
85	MISTY ISLE	*	150.00	180.00
85	MOUNTAIN COVE	*	125.00	180.00
85	SALTY DOG	*	95.00	170.00
85	WILD ROSE MARSH	950	95.00	760.00
86	SUNSET SWAMP	*	75.00	75.00
87	FISHERMAN AT DAWN	*	95.00	245.00
87	MOUNTAIN MEADOW	*	95.00	290.00
87	SAFE HARBOR	*	95.00	130.00
88	DEEP WOODS WINTER	*	95.00	160.00
88	EDGE OF WINTER-LAKE SUPERIOR	*	150.00	255.00
88	FOREST POOL	*	110.00	180.00
88	LIGHT IN THE WILLOWS-GREAT WHITE HERON	*	145.00	145.00
88	VICTORIAN SPRING-GRAND HOTEL	*	150.00	170.00
89	BRIGHT RIVER	950	150.00	165.00
89	CARRIAGE WAITING	950	75.00	110.00
89	DAISY BAY	*	150.00	205.00
89	FIRST COLOR	*	135.00	180.00
89	GOLDEN BEACH	*	110.00	180.00
90	AFTERNOON VISITOR	950	75.00	75.00
90	FEEDER STREAM	950	150.00	195.00
90	WILD ROSES BY THE SEA	*	150.00	265.00
P. CALLE				**INDIAN**
*	BUFFALO SKULL BUCKEL - BRONZE	*	95.00	95.00
*	BUFFALO SKULL BUCKEL - SILVER	*	750.00	750.00
*	ONE STAR	*	125.00	125.00
R. BATEMAN				**LITHO**
*	BULL MOOSE	*	1250.00	1250.00
*	CANADA GOOSE	*	450.00	450.00
*	COUGAR AND KIT	*	495.00	495.00
*	GOLDEN-HEADED LION TAMARIN	*	350.00	350.00
*	GREAT BLUE HERON	*	950.00	950.00
*	PEREGRINE AND YOUN	*	395.00	395.00
F. MACHETANZ				**MACHETANZ**
*	CHANGE OF DIRECTION W/MEDAL-ESKIMO	*	320.00	320.00
*	SEARCH ON THE PRESSURE ICE	*	245.00	245.00
78	FACE TO FACE	950	150.00	1890.00
78	HUNTER'S DAWN	950	125.00	525.00
78	INTO THE HOME STRETCH	950	175.00	700.00
79	BEGINNINGS	950	175.00	575.00
79	DECISIONS ON THE ICE FIELD	950	150.00	465.00
79	PICK OF THE LITTER	950	165.00	250.00
79	REACHING THE CAMPSITE	950	200.00	400.00
80	KING OF THE MOUNTAIN	950	200.00	250.00
80	NELCHINA TRAIL	950	245.00	1015.00
80	SOURDOUGH	950	245.00	1085.00
80	WHEN THREE'S A CROWD	950	225.00	850.00
81	GOLDEN YEARS	950	245.00	615.00
81	MIDDAY MOONLIGHT	950	265.00	425.00

After brushing up on his reading, Frederick the Literate *is too pooped to ponder the true meaning of book titles such as "A Tale of Two Kitties," one of the imaginary novels dreamed up by Americana artist Charles Wysocki. His limited edition print is published by The Greenwich Workshop.*

Charles Wysocki paints a nostalgic picture in Memory Maker. *Produced by The Greenwich Workshop.*

A picture is worth a thousand words. Artist Jim Daly captures the curiosity of youngsters, the optimism of adolescents, and the serenity of the older generation in his limited edition print Pillars of a Nation. *Published by Mill Pond Press.*

In Harmony, *by the late artist Alan Maley, captures the quiet feeling of comfort felt by this family. Published by Past Impressions.*

YR	NAME	LIMIT	ISSUE	QUOTE
81	WHAT EVERY HUNTER FEARS	950	245.00	850.00
81	WHERE MEN AND DOGS SEEM SMALL	950	245.00	1500.00
81	WINTER HARVEST	950	265.00	280.00
82	MIGHTY HUNTER	950	265.00	775.00
82	MOONLIGHT STAKEOUT	950	265.00	540.00
82	MOOSE TRACKS	950	265.00	465.00
82	TENDER ARCTIC, THE	950	295.00	775.00
83	NANOOK	950	295.00	295.00
83	THEY OPENED THE NORTH COUNTRY	950	245.00	275.00
84	END OF A LONG DAY-POLAR BEAR	950	200.00	200.00
84	MANY MILES TOGETHER-ESKIMO	950	245.00	245.00
84	MIDNIGHT WATCH	950	250.00	250.00
84	SMOKE DREAMS	950	250.00	400.00
84	STORY OF THE BEADS	950	245.00	300.00
85	END OF THE HUNT-ESKIMO	950	245.00	245.00
85	LAND OF THE MIDNIGHT SUN-POLAR BEAR	950	245.00	245.00
85	LANGUAGE OF THE SNOW-ESKIMO	950	195.00	195.00
85	REACHING THE PASS-DOG SLED	950	265.00	1050.00
86	KYROK-ESKIMO SEAMSTRESS	950	225.00	225.00
86	LEAVING THE NEST-POLAR BEAR	950	245.00	245.00
86	LONE MUSHER-ALASKA	950	245.00	245.00
86	MT. BLACKBURN-SOVEREIGN OF THE WRANGELLS	950	245.00	245.00
86	SON OF THE NORTH-ESKIMO	*	175.00	175.00
87	SPRING FEVER-POLAR BEAR	950	225.00	225.00
87	START OF THE DAY-ALASKA	*	200.00	200.00
87	TRAIL THROUGH THE PRESSURE ICE-ALASKA	*	225.00	225.00
88	CHANGE OF DIRECTION W/MEDAL	950	320.00	320.00
88	TENSE MOMENT-POLAR BEAR	*	200.00	200.00
88	VETERAN OF THE TRAIL-DOG SLED	*	175.00	175.00
88	WHALING LOOKOUT-ESKIMO WHALING	*	195.00	195.00
89	CHIEF DANCES, THE-ESKIMO	950	235.00	235.00
89	INVADERS, THE-POLAR BEAR	*	235.00	235.00
89	TWO OF MY FAVORITE SUBJECTS	*	225.00	225.00
90	GLORY OF THE TRAIL-DOG MUSHING	950	225.00	225.00
90	GRASS IS ALWAYS GREENER, THE-DOG	950	200.00	200.00
90	QUALITY TIME-POLAR BEAR	950	200.00	200.00
91	KAYAK MAN	950	215.00	215.00
91	SEARCH FOR GOLD, THE	*	225.00	225.00
91	TUNDRA FLOWER	950	235.00	235.00

B. MOORE, JR. — MOORE, JR.

YR	NAME	LIMIT	ISSUE	QUOTE
79	HARRY SHOURDES REDHEAD	950	65.00	135.00
79	LEE DUDLEY-CANVASBACK	950	65.00	250.00
79	WARD BROTHERS-CANADAS	950	85.00	135.00
80	WARD BROTHERS-CANVASBACKS	*	85.00	135.00
81	JOSEPH LINCOLN PINTAIL ON THE SANTEE	*	85.00	135.00
81	WAITING, THE	950	85.00	330.00
81	WIND CALLED HIS NAME, THE	950	85.00	500.00
82	GOLDEN DAWN	950	85.00	110.00
82	POINT AND HONOR	*	115.00	195.00
83	BECKY	*	75.00	225.00
86	THIS PLACE NOT FOR SALE	*	85.00	160.00

P. CALLE — MOUNTAIN MAN

YR	NAME	LIMIT	ISSUE	QUOTE
*	AND A GRIZZLY CLAW NECKLACE	*	150.00	150.00
*	FIRESIDE COMPANIONS	*	150.00	150.00
*	FREE TRAPPER STUDY	*	125.00	125.00
*	FREE TRAPPER, THE - BRONZE	*	*	0.00
*	FRIEND OR FOE	*	125.00	125.00
*	FRONTIER BLACKSMITH	*	245.00	245.00
*	HUNTER OF GEESE	*	125.00	125.00
*	I CALL HIM FRIEND	*	235.00	235.00
*	I CALL HIM FRIEND - PRESTIGE	*	375.00	375.00
*	MOUNTAIN MAN, THE (COLOR)	*	150.00	150.00
*	MOUNTAIN MAN, THE (PENCIL)	*	250.00	250.00
*	NEAR JOURNEY'S END	*	245.00	245.00
*	OUT OF THE SILENCE	*	265.00	265.00
*	OUT OF THE SILENCE - PRESTIGE	*	465.00	465.00
*	THROUGH THE TALL GRASS	*	175.00	175.00
*	TRAPPER AT REST	*	95.00	95.00
*	WINTER FEAST, A PREMIER ED.	*	465.00	465.00

R. PARKER — PARKER

YR	NAME	LIMIT	ISSUE	QUOTE
*	BREAK IN THE ICE-CANADA GOOSE	*	*	175.00
*	CROSSING THE RIDGE-WOLVES	*	*	265.00
82	RACCOON PAIR	950	95.00	400.00
82	SNOW ON THE PINE-CHICKADEES	950	95.00	100.00
82	SPRING MIST-GRAY WOLF	950	155.00	375.00
82	WEATHERED WOOD-BLUEBIRDS	950	75.00	175.00

YR	NAME	LIMIT	ISSUE	QUOTE
83	MALLARD FAMILY	950	95.00	175.00
83	RED SQUIRREL	*	65.00	65.00
83	RIVERSIDE PAUSE-RIVER OTTER	950	95.00	150.00
83	YELLOW DAWN-AMERICAN ELK	950	130.00	200.00
84	CHICKADEES IN AUTUMN	950	75.00	75.00
84	FACE OF THE NORTH-WOLF	950	95.00	250.00
84	FAT AND SASSY-ROBIN	*	95.00	95.00
84	GRAY WOLF PORTRAIT	950	115.00	175.00
84	SILENT STEPS-LYNX	950	145.00	325.00
84	WHEN PATHS CROSS	950	185.00	400.00
84	WINTER JAY-BLUE JAY	950	95.00	150.00
85	AFTERNOON SHADOWS-MULE DEER	*	105.00	105.00
85	MISTY DAWN-LOON	950	120.00	525.00
85	SPRING ARRIVALS-CANADA GEESE	950	120.00	200.00
85	WAITING OUT THE STORM-WOLF	950	105.00	400.00
85	WINGS OVER WINTER-BALD EAGLE	950	135.00	350.00
85	WINTER CLOAK-ERMINE	*	105.00	105.00
86	ABOVE THE BREAKERS-OSPREY	950	150.00	175.00
86	AT END OF DAY-WOLVES	950	235.00	325.00
86	AUTUMN FIELDS-RED FOX	*	220.00	220.00
86	AUTUMN FORAGING-MOOSE	950	175.00	425.00
86	AUTUMN LEAVES-RED FOX	950	95.00	100.00
86	AUTUMN MEADOW-ELK	950	195.00	200.00
86	BEHIND THE HEMLOCK-LYNX	*	105.00	105.00
86	CARDINAL IN BLUE SPRUCE	950	125.00	150.00
86	CARDINAL IN BRAMBLES	950	125.00	150.00
86	CREEKSIDE-COUGAR	950	225.00	350.00
86	FOLLOWING MAMA-MUTE SWANS	950	165.00	475.00
86	JUST RESTING-SEA OTTER	950	85.00	250.00
86	MORNING ON THE LAGOON-MUTE SWAN	950	95.00	100.00
86	NORTHERN MORNING-ARCTIC FOX	950	125.00	175.00
86	RIMROCK-COUGAR	950	200.00	900.00
86	WHITETAIL AND WOLVES	950	180.00	300.00
86	WINTER CREEK-COYOTE	950	130.00	275.00
87	A BREAK IN THE ICE-CANADA GEESE	*	150.00	175.00
87	ABOVE THE WAVES-COMMON TERNS	*	95.00	95.00
87	ARCTIC SPRING-WHITE GYRFALCON	*	185.00	185.00
87	ARCTIC WOLF PORTRAIT	*	105.00	105.00
87	AUTUMN MORNING-GRIZZLY	*	200.00	200.00
87	BARN SWALLOWS ON FENCE POST	*	105.00	105.00
87	DESERT RESPITE-KIT FOX	*	125.00	125.00
87	EVENING GLOW-WOLF PACK	950	245.00	275.00
87	EVENING REFLECTIONS-TRUMPETER SWAN	*	115.00	115.00
87	FREEZE UP-CANADA GEESE	950	85.00	100.00
87	GOLDEN GRASSES-CALIFORNIA QUAIL	*	95.00	95.00
87	LOW WATER-RACCOON	*	125.00	125.00
87	ON THE RUN-WOLF PACK	950	245.00	245.00
87	RAIL FENCE-BLUEBIRDS	950	105.00	125.00
87	SHELTERED SPOT-LYNX	*	150.00	150.00
87	WALKING THE RIDGE-PRONGHORN	*	185.00	185.00
87	WHITE-CROWNED SPARROW ON DRIFTWOOD	*	125.00	125.00
87	WINTER CREEK AND WHITETAILS	950	185.00	185.00
87	WINTER ENCOUNTER-WOLF	950	235.00	350.00
87	WINTER PINE-DOWNY WOODPECKER	*	110.00	110.00
87	WINTER SAGE-COYOTE	950	225.00	350.00
87	WINTER STORM-COYOTES	950	245.00	325.00
88	EAGLES IN THE PINES	*	200.00	200.00
88	FIRST SNOW-ARCTIC WOLVES	*	175.00	175.00
88	FOX PUP AT THE DEN ENTRANCE	*	115.00	115.00
88	SEARCHING THE STREAM-RACCOON	*	125.00	125.00
88	SILENT PASSAGE-ORCAS WHALE	950	175.00	175.00
88	SNOW PALACE-MULE DEER	*	225.00	225.00
88	SUMMER-LOON	*	125.00	125.00
88	WINTER VALLEY-ELK	*	150.00	150.00
88	WINTER WREN ON IVY	*	95.00	95.00
89	AUTUMN ASPEN-WHITE-TAILED DEER	*	175.00	175.00
89	AUTUMN CORNFIELD-CARDINAL	*	115.00	115.00
89	AUTUMN MAPLES-WOLVES	950	195.00	195.00
89	DEEP WATER-ORCAS WHALE	1250	195.00	195.00
89	EARLY SNOWFALL-ELK	950	185.00	185.00
89	EARLY SPRING-GREAT BLUE HERON	*	135.00	135.00
89	EUCALYPTUS CLIMBER-KOALA BEAR	*	110.00	110.00
89	EVENING AMBER-TRUMPETER SWAN	*	125.00	125.00
89	FLYING REDTAIL HAWK-ORIGINAL	290	295.00	295.00
90	BREAKING THE SILENCE-WOLVES	1250	195.00	300.00
90	ICE MORNING-RED FOX	950	150.00	150.00

YR	NAME	LIMIT	ISSUE	QUOTE
90	INSIDE PASSAGE-ORCAS WHALE	1500	195.00	195.00
90	LIONESS AND CUBS	150	295.00	295.00
90	MOOSE IN THE BRUSH	950	195.00	195.00
90	WINTER LOOKOUT-COUGAR	950	175.00	175.00
91	DEEP SNOW-WHITETAIL DEER	950	175.00	175.00
91	FOREST TREK-GRAY WOLF	950	185.00	185.00
91	GILA WOODPECKER	950	135.00	135.00
91	MOONLIT TRACKS-WOLF	1500	200.00	225.00
91	MOTHER AND SON-ORCAS	950	185.00	185.00
R. PETERSON				**PETERSON**
73	BALTIMORE ORIOLE	450	150.00	300.00
73	CARDINAL	450	150.00	580.00
73	FLICKER	450	150.00	275.00
73	WOOD THRUSH	450	150.00	370.00
74	BALD EAGLE	950	150.00	500.00
74	BARN SWALLOW	750	150.00	350.00
74	BLUE JAYS	950	150.00	350.00
74	BOBOLINK	750	150.00	275.00
74	GREAT HORNED OWL	950	150.00	525.00
75	BOBWHITES	950	150.00	320.00
75	FUR SEALS	*	25.00	25.00
75	JAYS-COLOR PLATE #30-BLUE JAY	*	150.00	150.00
75	OWLS-COLOR PLATE #16	*	150.00	150.00
75	RUFFED GROUSE	950	150.00	350.00
75	SEA OTTERS	*	25.00	150.00
76	ADELIE PENQUINS	950	35.00	35.00
76	BARN OWL	950	225.00	300.00
76	GOLDEN EAGLE	950	200.00	200.00
76	QUAILS-COLOR PLATE #9	*	150.00	150.00
76	ROADRUNNER	*	25.00	175.00
76	SNOWY OWL	950	175.00	525.00
77	BLUEBIRD	950	75.00	225.00
77	PEREGRINE FALCON	950	175.00	300.00
77	SCARLET TANAGER	950	125.00	200.00
77	SOOTY TERNS	450	50.00	85.00
77	WILD ORCHIDS AND TRILLIUMS	*	75.00	75.00
77	WILLETS	450	50.00	75.00
78	MOCKINGBIRD	950	125.00	250.00
78	RING-NECKED PHEASANT	950	200.00	250.00
78	ROBIN	950	125.00	420.00
78	ROSE-BREASTED GROSBEAK	950	125.00	125.00
78	SHOWY WAYSIDE FLOWERS	*	75.00	75.00
79	GYRFALCON	950	225.00	360.00
79	PUFFIN	*	175.00	175.00
81	WILD TURKEYS	*	195.00	195.00
83	ARCTIC GLOW-SNOWY OWL	*	200.00	200.00
86	LORD OF THE AIR-PEREGRINE FALCON	*	120.00	120.00
P. CALLE				**PORTRAIT**
*	JIMMY DOOLITTLE PORTRAIT	*	425.00	425.00
*	ALL ABOARD	*	145.00	145.00
*	CHILDHOOD FRIENDS	*	110.00	110.00
*	DOMINOES	*	155.00	155.00
*	EYE TO EYE	*	95.00	95.00
*	FAVORITE GIFT	*	175.00	175.00
*	FLYING HORSES, THE	*	325.00	325.00
*	GOOD COMPANY	*	155.00	155.00
*	HER SECRET PLACE	*	275.00	275.00
*	IMMIGRANT SPIRIT, THE	*	125.00	125.00
*	LEFT OUT	*	110.00	110.00
*	NEW CITIZEN, THE	*	125.00	125.00
*	PLAYMATES	*	355.00	355.00
*	SECRET ADMIRER	*	150.00	150.00
*	SLIDING HOME	*	75.00	75.00
*	SUNDAY AFTERNOON	*	185.00	185.00
*	WHEN I GROW UP	*	175.00	175.00
*	WINNING COACH	*	75.00	75.00
M. REECE				**REECE**
*	BURST OF COLOR-RING NECKED PHEASANT	*	*	200.00
*	PAIR-TRUMPETER SWAN, THE	*	*	95.00
*	QUAIL COVEY-BOBWHITES	*	*	245.00
48	FEDERAL DUCK STAMP-BUFFLEHEADS	200	15.00	1200.00
51	FEDERAL DUCK STAMP-GADWALLS	250	15.00	1200.00
59	FEDERAL DUCK STAMP-RETRIEVER	400	15.00	4000.00
64	BOBWHITES (STONE LITHO)	950	20.00	650.00
64	MALLARDS (STONE LITHO)	950	20.00	650.00
69	FEDERAL DUCK STAMP-WHITE-WINGED SCOTERS	750	50.00	1000.00

YR NAME	LIMIT	ISSUE	QUOTE
69 MALLARDS-PITCHING IN	500	40.00	600.00
70 EDGE OF THE HEDGEROW-BOBWHITES	950	60.00	700.00
71 FEDERAL DUCK STAMP-CINNAMON TEAL	950	75.00	5000.00
72 AGAINST THE WIND-CANVASBACKS	950	60.00	400.00
73 FEEDING TIME-CANADA GEESE	550	75.00	350.00
73 LATE AFTERNOON-MALLARD	450	150.00	245.00
73 MARSHLANDER MALLARDS	600	60.00	275.00
73 PHEASANT COUNTRY	550	60.00	275.00
73 WOOD DUCKS	550	125.00	200.00
74 A BURST OF COLOR-RING-NECKED PHESANTS	950	75.00	200.00
74 COURTSHIP FLIGHT-PINTAILS	950	75.00	190.00
74 EARLY ARRIVALS-MALLARDS	950	50.00	125.00
74 FLOODED OAKS-MALLARDS	850	150.00	300.00
74 MALLARDS-DROPPING IN	950	75.00	225.00
74 PASSING STORM, THE-CANVASBACKS	950	50.00	145.00
74 QUAIL COVER	750	150.00	300.00
74 SANDBAR, THE-CANADA GEESE	950	50.00	75.00
74 SNOW GEESE-BLUE GEESE	750	150.00	150.00
74 SNOWY CREEK-MALLARDS	950	75.00	200.00
74 SOLITUDE-WHITETAIL DEER	950	85.00	125.00
74 WINGING SOUTH-CANADA GEESE	750	150.00	245.00
74 WOODED SECLUSION-TURKEY	950	75.00	110.00
75 AFTERNOON SHADOWS-BOBWHITES	950	100.00	350.00
76 AUTUMN TRIO-RING-NECKED PHEASANTS	950	85.00	250.00
76 CANADA GEESE-COMING IN	950	85.00	200.00
76 DARK SKY-MALLARDS	950	85.00	600.00
76 FLIGHT-CANADA GEESE	950	50.00	125.00
76 GENTOO-PENGUINS	260	125.00	150.00
76 GOOD FETCH-LABRADOR RETRIEVER	950	150.00	200.00
76 RAIL FENCE, THE-BOBWHITES	950	85.00	200.00
76 SHALLOW POND-MALLARDS	950	125.00	225.00
76 THUNDERHEAD-CANADA GEESE	260	125.00	1160.00
76 WEATHERED WOOD-BOBWHITES	950	50.00	150.00
77 COVEY RISE-BOBWHITES	950	150.00	850.00
77 DARK SHADOWS-WHITETAIL DEER	950	85.00	102.00
77 EASY LANDING-PINTAILS	950	95.00	175.00
77 GRACEFUL PAIR-RING-NECKED PHEASANTS	950	50.00	100.00
77 JUMPING GREENWINGS-GREEN-WINGED TEAL	950	85.00	150.00
77 NINE TRAVELERS-CANADA GEESE	950	95.00	150.00
77 QUIET POND-MALLARDS	950	95.00	150.00
77 RESTING-WOOD DUCKS	950	50.00	100.00
77 SENTINEL, THE-WHITETAIL DEER	950	150.00	180.00
77 STICK POND-MALLARDS	950	125.00	200.00
77 THROUGH THE TREES-WOOD DUCKS	950	95.00	375.00
78 CHINSTRAP PENQUINS	*	50.00	60.00
78 CRESCENT LAKE-MALLARDS	950	125.00	225.00
78 DARK SKY-CANADA GEESE	950	175.00	350.00
78 NEW SNOW-WHITE TAIL DEER	950	95.00	114.00
78 OAK FOREST-TURKEY	950	124.00	200.00
78 OUT OF THE PINES-BOBWHITES	950	245.00	300.00
78 OVER THE POINT-LESSER SCAUPS	950	125.00	150.00
78 ROUGH WATER-CANVASBACKS	950	150.00	235.00
78 WINTER COVEY-BOBWHITES	950	225.00	575.00
79 DARK SKY-BOBWHITES	950	225.00	375.00
79 MARSH, THE	950	75.00	90.00
79 PHEASANT COVER	950	175.00	250.00
79 REGAL FLIGHT-WHISTLING SWANS	950	125.00	150.00
79 RENDEZVOUS-WHITE-FRONTED GEESE	950	85.00	85.00
79 SUNRISE-GREEN WINGED TEAL	950	150.00	300.00
79 VALLEY, THE-PINTAILS	950	150.00	180.00
79 WINDY DAY-MALLARDS	950	150.00	180.00
79 WINTER-RING-NECKED PHEASANTS	950	125.00	150.00
80 ALONG THE SHORE-REDHEADS	950	160.00	160.00
80 DARK SKY-CANVASBACKS	950	195.00	235.00
80 DIAMOND ISLAND-MALLARDS	950	195.00	350.00
80 LANDING-CANADA GEESE	950	125.00	150.00
80 MOUNTAIN SNOW	950	95.00	225.00
80 POINTERS AND BOBWHITES	950	245.00	300.00
80 QUAIL COUNTRY	950	250.00	300.00
80 QUIET PLACE, THE-CANADA GEESE	950	175.00	380.00
80 TIMBER-WOOD DUCKS	950	160.00	300.00
80 TUNDRA-BLACK BRANT	950	85.00	102.00
80 TWILIGHT-AMERICAN WIDGEON	950	75.00	190.00
80 WILLOW, THE-GREEN-WINGED TEAL	950	160.00	160.00
81 DARK SKY-RUFFED GROUSE	950	245.00	350.00
81 EARLY SPRING-WILD TURKEYS	950	220.00	220.00

YR	NAME	LIMIT	ISSUE	QUOTE
81	ESCAPE-RING-NECKED PHEASANTS	950	195.00	195.00
81	FROSTY MORNING-CANADA GEESE	950	175.00	350.00
82	BREAKING AWAY-PINTAILS	*	150.00	150.00
82	FLOODED TIMBER-MALLARDS	950	150.00	250.00
82	MINIATURE SERIES I-MALLARDS	950	75.00	75.00
82	MINIATURE SERIES II-WOOD DUCKS	950	75.00	75.00
82	QUAIL CONVEY-BOBWHITES	950	245.00	245.00
82	SPLASH, THE-SMALLMOUTH BASS	950	95.00	150.00
82	STONY LAKE-MALLARDS	*	100.00	100.00
83	ALONG THE RIVER-TRUMPETER SWANS	*	50.00	50.00
83	DARK SKY-PHEASANTS	950	125.00	125.00
83	PASSING THROUGH-LESSER SCAUP	*	100.00	100.00
83	RUNNING BLUES-SCALED QUAILS	*	100.00	100.00
83	TRANQUIL MARSH MALLARDS	*	60.00	60.00
84	MINIATURE SERIES III-BOBWHITES	950	75.00	75.00
84	MINIATURE SERIES IV-PHEASANTS	*	75.00	75.00
84	SECLUSION-WOOD DUCKS	*	150.00	150.00
85	HAZY DAY-BOBWHITES	950	150.00	350.00
85	MUSKRAT HOUSE, THE-CANVASBACKS	*	95.00	95.00
85	SNOWSTORM, THE-MALLARDS	950	95.00	95.00
85	STORM CLOUDS-CANADA GOOSE	950	125.00	250.00
85	WATER'S EDGE-CANADA GEESE	950	95.00	200.00
86	AUTUMN MARSH-MALLARDS	950	120.00	250.00
86	NORTHERN LAKE-COMMON LOONS		125.00	125.00
86	SNOW COVER-CARDINAL	*	95.00	95.00
87	BIRCH, THE-RUFFED GROUSE	*	85.00	85.00
87	CAREFUL LANDING-CANADA GEESE	*	175.00	175.00
87	OLD TREE-BOBWHITE QUAIL	*	195.00	195.00
87	RED PINE-BLACK-CAPPED CHICKADEES	*	95.00	95.00
87	WINTER SOLITUDE-MALLARDS	*	125.00	125.00
88	AUTUMN WINGS-MALLARDS	950	135.00	230.00
88	LEAPING-RAINBOW TROUT	*	110.00	110.00
88	OAK TIMBER-MALLARDS		165.00	165.00
88	SONORAN DESERT-GAMBEL'S QUAIL	*	150.00	150.00
89	FLYING LOW-CANADA GEESE	*	225.00	225.00
89	ICY WATER-MALLARDS	*	175.00	175.00
89	OVER THE MARSH-CANADA GEESE	*	165.00	165.00
89	UPLAND SERIES I-BOBWHITES	950	125.00	125.00
89	WEEDY DRAW-RING-NECKED PHEASANTS	*	150.00	150.00
90	AMERICAN WIGEON-WASHINGTON CENNTENIAL	1058	135.00	135.00
90	GREENHEAD-MALLARD	150	245.00	245.00
90	UPLAND SERIES II-WILD TURKEYS & REDBUD	950	125.00	125.00
90	UPLAND SERIES III-RING-NECKED PHEASANT	*	125.00	125.00
91	CHASE, THE-WOLF PACK	550	150.00	150.00
91	OFFSHORE LUNCH-COMMON LOONS	550	195.00	195.00
91	UPLAND SERIES IV-RUFFED GOOSE	950	125.00	125.00

J. SEEREY-LESTER **SEEREY-LESTER**

YR	NAME	LIMIT	ISSUE	QUOTE
*	NEW YORK DUCK STAMP 1990 RE	*	*	135.00
*	PLUNGE-NORTHERN SEA LIONS	*	*	200.00
83	COOL RETREAT-LYNX	950	85.00	100.00
83	EARLY WINDFALL-GRAY SQUIRRELS	*	85.00	85.00
83	FIRST SNOW-GRIZZLY BEARS	950	95.00	250.00
83	LONE FISHERMAN-GREAT BLUE HERON	950	85.00	300.00
83	REFUGE, THE-RACCOONS	950	85.00	300.00
83	RIVER WATCH-PEREGRINE FALCON	*	85.00	85.00
83	WINTER LOOKOUT-COUGAR	950	85.00	500.00
84	AMONG THE CATTAILS-CANADA GEESE	950	130.00	425.00
84	ARCTIC PROCESSION-WILLOW PTARMIGAN	950	220.00	600.00
84	BASKING-BROWN PELICANS	950	115.00	125.00
84	BREAKING COVER-BLACK BEAR	*	130.00	130.00
84	CLOSE ENCOUNTER-BOBCAT	950	130.00	190.00
84	HIGH GROUND-WOLVES	950	130.00	325.00
84	ICY OUTCROP-WHITE GYRFALCON	950	115.00	200.00
84	LYING LOW-COUGAR	950	85.00	450.00
84	MORNING MIST-SNOWY OWL	950	95.00	95.00
84	PLAINS HUNTER-PRAIRIE FALCON	*	95.00	95.00
84	SPIRIT OF THE NORTH-WHITE WOLF	950	130.00	185.00
85	AWAKENING MEADOW-COTTONTAIL	*	50.00	50.00
85	CHILDREN OF THE FOREST-RED FOX KITS	950	110.00	150.00
85	CHILDREN OF THE TUNDRA-ARCTIC WOLF PUP	950	110.00	225.00
85	DAYBREAK-MOOSE	*	135.00	135.00
85	FALLEN BIRCH-CHIPMUNK	950	60.00	250.00
85	FIRST LIGHT-GRAY JAYS	950	130.00	200.00
85	GATHERING, THE-GRAY WOLVES	950	165.00	350.00
85	ISLAND SANCTUARY-MALLARDS	950	95.00	175.00
85	UNDER THE PINES-BOBCAT	950	95.00	275.00

YR	NAME	LIMIT	ISSUE	QUOTE
85	WINTER RENDEZVOUS-COYOTES	950	140.00	225.00
86	ABOVE THE TREELINE-COUGAR	950	139.00	130.00
86	AFTER THE FIRE-GRIZZLY BEAR	*	95.00	95.00
86	ALONG THE ICE FLOW-POLAR BEARS	*	200.00	200.00
86	CONFLICT AT DAWN-HERON AND OSPREY	*	130.00	175.00
86	COTTONWOOD GOLD-BALTIMORE ORIOLE	*	85.00	85.00
86	EARLY ARRIVALS-SNOW BUNTINGS	*	75.00	75.00
86	HIDDEN ADMIRER-MOOSE	950	165.00	275.00
86	HIGH COUNTRY CHAMPION-GRIZZLY	950	175.00	250.00
86	KENYAN FAMILY-CHEETAHS	*	130.00	130.00
86	LAKESIDE FAMILY-CANADA GEESE	*	75.00	75.00
86	LOW TIDE-BALD EAGLES	*	130.00	130.00
86	RACING THE STORM-ARCTIC WOLVES	950	200.00	350.00
86	SNOWY EXCURSION-RED SQUIRREL	*	75.00	75.00
86	SPRING MIST-CHICKADEES	950	105.00	150.00
86	TREADING THIN ICE-CHIPMUNK	*	75.00	75.00
86	WINTER HIDING-COTTONTAIL	*	75.00	75.00
86	WINTER PERCH-CARDINAL	950	85.00	175.00
86	YOUNG EXPLORER, THE-RED FOX KIT	*	75.00	75.00
87	ALPENGLOW-ARCTIC WOLF	950	200.00	275.00
87	AUTUMN MIST-BARRED OWL	950	160.00	225.00
87	AUTUMN THUNDER-MUSK OXEN	*	150.00	150.00
87	BATHING-MUTE SWAN	175	*	175.00
87	CANYON CREEK-COUGAR	950	195.00	450.00
87	DAWN ON THE MARSH-COYOTE	*	200.00	200.00
87	FIRST TRACKS-COUGAR	*	150.00	150.00
87	IN DEEP-BLACK BEAR CUB	*	135.00	135.00
87	LYING IN WAIT-ARCTIC FOX	*	175.00	175.00
87	OUT OF THE BLIZZARD-TIMBER WOLVES	950	215.00	500.00
87	OUT OF THE MIST-GRIZZLY	*	200.00	325.00
87	RAIN WATCH-BELTED KINGFISHER	*	125.00	200.00
87	SUNDOWN ALERT-BOBCAT	*	150.00	150.00
87	WINTER VIGIL-GREAT HORNED OWL	*	175.00	175.00
88	BATHING-BLUE JAY	*	95.00	95.00
88	CLIFF HANGER-BOBCAT	*	200.00	200.00
88	COASTAL CLIQUE-HARBOR SEALS	*	160.00	160.00
88	EDGE OF THE FOREST-TIMBER WOLVES	950	500.00	700.00
88	EVENING MEADOW-AMERICAN GOLDFINCH	*	150.00	150.00
88	HIDING PLACE-SAW-WHET OWL	*	95.00	95.00
88	LAST SANCTUARY-FLORIDA PANTHER	*	175.00	175.00
88	MOOSE HAIR	*	165.00	230.00
88	MORNING DISPLAY-COMMON LOONS	950	135.00	330.00
88	NIGHT MOVES-AFRICAN ELEPHANTS	*	150.00	150.00
88	NORTHWOODS FAMILY-MOOSE	*	75.00	75.00
88	SAVANNA SIESTA-AFRICAN LIONS	*	165.00	165.00
88	SNOWY WATCH-GREAT GRAY OWL	*	175.00	175.00
88	SPANISH MIST-YOUNG BARRED OWL	*	165.00	165.00
88	TUNDRA FAMILY-ARCTIC WOLVES	*	200.00	200.00
88	WINTER GRAZING-BISON	*	185.00	185.00
88	WINTER SPIRIT-GRAY WOLF	*	200.00	200.00
89	BEFORE THE FREEZE-BEAVER	*	165.00	195.00
89	COUGAR RUN	950	185.00	450.00
89	EVENING DUET-SNOWY EGRETS	1250	185.00	185.00
89	FLUKE SIGHTING-HUMPBACK WHALES	*	185.00	185.00
89	HEAVY GOING-GRIZZLY	950	175.00	175.00
89	HIGH AND MIGHTY-GORILLA	950	185.00	225.00
89	SNEAK PEAK-CHICKEN	950	950.00	185.00
89	SOFTLY, SOFTLY-WHITE TIGER	950	220.00	500.00
89	SPRING FLURRY-ADELIE PENGUINS	950	185.00	185.00
89	WATER SPORT-BOBCAT	950	185.00	185.00
90	ARCTIC WOLF PUPS	290	500.00	500.00
90	BITTERSWEET WINTER-CARDINAL	1250	150.00	275.00
90	DAWN MAJESTY-WHITE TIGER	1250	185.00	185.00
90	GRIZZLY-ORIGINAL	290	400.00	400.00
90	IN THEIR PRESENCE-ORCAS	250	200.00	200.00
90	MARKER 221-CANVASBACKS NEW YORK	*	135.00	135.00
90	MOUNTAIN CRADLE-GORILLA	1250	200.00	200.00
90	NIGHT RUN-ARCTIC WOLVES	1250	200.00	250.00
90	NORTHERN PLUNGE, THE-SEA LIONS	1250	200.00	200.00
90	SEASONAL GREETING-CARDINAL	1250	150.00	200.00
90	SPOUT-WHALES	290	500.00	500.00
90	SUITORS, THE-WOOD DUCKS	3313	135.00	185.00
90	SUMMER RAIN-COMMON LOONS	4500	200.00	200.00
90	THEIR FIRST SEASON-GRIZZLY BEAR	1250	200.00	200.00
90	TOGETHERNESS-LION	1250	125.00	125.00
90	WHITETAIL SPRING-WHITETAIL DEER	1250	185.00	185.00

YR	NAME	LIMIT	ISSUE	QUOTE
91	DENALI FAMILY-GRIZZLY BEAR	*	195.00	225.00
91	EVENING ENCOUNTER-GRIZZLY & WOLF	1250	185.00	185.00
91	FACE TO FACE	*	200.00	200.00
91	MOONLIGHT CHASE-COUGAR	250	195.00	195.00
91	OUT ON A LIMB-YOUNG BARRED OWL	950	185.00	185.00
91	PANDA TRILOGY	*	375.00	375.00
91	SISTERS-ARCTIC WOLVES	1250	185.00	185.00
91	SOMETHING STIRRED-BENGAL TIGER	950	195.00	195.00
M. SOLBERG				**SOLBERG**
86	CHECKING FOR STRAYS	*	85.00	85.00
86	EARLY MORNING CHALLENGE-ELK	*	150.00	150.00
86	EDGE OF NIGHT-BARN OWL	*	150.00	245.00
86	LONG CAST, THE-FISHERMAN	*	95.00	95.00
86	MORNING MIST-CANADA GEESE	*	95.00	125.00
86	MOUNTAIN VISTA-LANDSCAPE	950	95.00	1175.00
86	ON SCENT-GERMAN SHORTHAIRS	*	95.00	95.00
86	SUNLIT MIST-ELK	*	85.00	85.00
86	VIRGIN WATERS-LANDSCAPE	*	150.00	150.00
86	WHERE THE TRAIL ENDS-SNOW LEOPARD	*	150.00	150.00
86	WINGS OF WONDER-BALD EAGLE	950	150.00	400.00
86	WINTER REFLECTION-BEAR	*	150.00	150.00
87	ALERT-DOE AND FAWN	*	125.00	125.00
87	BAD WATER BEAR	*	150.00	150.00
87	FROM NORTH THEY CAME-WOLF	*	85.00	85.00
87	GRAND DUCK, THE-OWL	*	150.00	150.00
87	HANDSOME HUNTER-AMERICAN KESTREL	950	115.00	375.00
87	HIGH COUNTRY MORNING-BIGHORN SHEEP	*	125.00	125.00
87	MONARCH OF THE SKY-GOLDEN EAGLE	950	200.00	275.00
87	MOUNTAIN SENTINEL-LION	*	125.00	125.00
87	ON THE HIGH SIDE-MOUNTAIN GOAT	*	95.00	95.00
87	SOMETHING MOVED-BOBCAT	*	125.00	125.00
87	YELLOWSTONE OSPREY	*	75.00	75.00
88	ARCTIC NOMADS	950	150.00	150.00
88	BLACK-CAPPED CHICKADEE	*	95.00	95.00
88	GATEFUL MOMENT-EAGLE	*	150.00	150.00
88	INTO THE STORM-CARIBOU	*	140.00	140.00
88	MORNING MEMORIES	*	135.00	135.00
88	ON SILENT WINGS-BALD EAGLE	*	150.00	275.00
88	RIVER OF DREAMS-FISHING	*	150.00	150.00
89	DECEPTIVE CALM-GOSHAWK	950	95.00	195.00
89	REFLECTION-WOLF	950	150.00	150.00
89	WHEN WINTER WARMS-POLAR BEAR	950	115.00	115.00
89	WHISPERING WINGS-TRUMPETER SWAN	*	135.00	135.00
89	WINTER WHITE-SNOWY OWL	*	95.00	95.00
90	BY FIRELIGHT-MOUNTAIN LION	*	160.00	150.00
90	NOMAD OF THE ICE-POLAR BEAR	1250	165.00	225.00
90	ON WATCH	950	150.00	150.00
90	OUT OF THE FOG-GRIZZLY BEAR	*	150.00	150.00
90	SERENE SETTING-AMERICAN KESTRELS	1250	150.00	250.00
90	SIGNS OF SPRING-HORSE	*	150.00	150.00
90	SMALL WONDER-CHIPMUNK	*	110.00	110.00
90	THISTLEDOWN-KESTREL	*	150.00	150.00
91	AUTUMN CHALLENGE-ELK	*	150.00	150.00
91	KORBEL GARDENS-FLORAL	*	150.00	150.00
91	MOUSE TRACKS-COYOTE	*	150.00	150.00
T. UTZ				**UTZ**
81	GREENHOUSE NUDE, THE	550	95.00	135.00
81	LAVENDER LACE	950	75.00	145.00
81	MELANIE	450	85.00	150.00
81	PICNIC	550	110.00	115.00
81	PINK LADY	450	85.00	175.00
81	SOFT WIND, THE	950	75.00	75.00
83	INTERLUDE	*	40.00	40.00
86	MORNING MELODY	*	90.00	90.00
86	STRAND OF PEARLS	*	90.00	90.00
87	ANGELICA	*	85.00	85.00
87	GABRIELLA	*	85.00	85.00
88	GRANNY'S BOOTS	*	95.00	95.00
88	SOLITUDE	*	95.00	95.00
90	CONTEMPLATION	*	150.00	150.00
90	DRAGON SLAYER, THE	*	95.00	95.00
90	EARLY LIGHT	*	110.00	110.00
90	END OF THE RAINBOW	*	95.00	95.00
90	GOSSAMER	*	150.00	250.00
M. WARREN				**WARREN**
74	TOP HAND OF THE CONCHO	950	150.00	260.00

YR	NAME	LIMIT	ISSUE	QUOTE
81	A COLD DAY	950	245.00	775.00
81	APPROACHING STORM	*	195.00	195.00
81	WHEN COWBOYS GET EDGY	*	245.00	245.00
82	NIGHT IN CHIMAYO	*	125.00	225.00
J. ZEMSKY				**ZEMSKY**
79	COME AND SEE THE NEW COLT	950	65.00	70.00
79	JORDAN AT THE WEDDING	950	65.00	160.00
79	JORDAN'S DOLLY	950	65.00	400.00
79	LOVE AT FIRST SIGHT	950	75.00	175.00
79	WHEN THE THEN AND THE NOW HOLD HANDS	950	65.00	200.00
80	JORDAN'S SPRING	*	65.00	350.00
84	JENNY IN THE ATTIC	*	75.00	175.00
84	THEY'LL BE SORRY WHEN WE'RE GONE	*	75.00	85.00

MOSS PORTFOLIO
P. BUCKLEY MOSS

	NAME	LIMIT	ISSUE	QUOTE
				MOSS
*	APPLE PICKER	1000	30.00	70.00
*	BARELIMBED REFLECTIONS	1000	25.00	70.00
*	BECKY AND TOM	1000	10.00	55.00
*	BLUE BOUQUET	1000	16.00	32.00
*	CANADA GEESE	1000	60.00	140.00
*	CANADA GEESE (ETCHING)	99	600.00	1200.00
*	CENTRAL PARK	1000	80.00	200.00
*	DAILY CHORES	1000	16.00	40.00
*	EMILY	1000	30.00	100.00
*	EVENING RUN	1000	55.00	110.00
*	FAMILY OUTING	1000	75.00	300.00
*	FLAG BOY	1000	16.00	40.00
*	FOUR LITTLE GIRLS	1000	30.00	80.00
*	FRESH BOUQUET	1000	16.00	40.00
*	FRIENDLY STEED	1000	50.00	110.00
*	FRIENDS	1000	35.00	80.00
*	FROSTY FROLIC	1000	75.00	400.00
*	GINNY	1000	16.00	45.00
*	GINNY AND CHRIS WITH LAMBS	1000	35.00	100.00
*	GOLDEN WINTER	1000	150.00	430.00
*	GOSSIP	1000	45.00	95.00
*	GRANDMOTHER	1000	60.00	120.00
*	HELPERS	1000	35.00	70.00
*	HOMESTEADERS	99	1200.00	2300.00
*	HUNGRY BABY BIRD	1000	15.00	50.00
*	JOHN	1000	16.00	45.00
*	LANDSCAPE W/GEESE (GOLD)	1000	500.00	1000.00
*	LESSON IN PATIENCE	1000	150.00	300.00
*	LITTLE APPLES IN A ROW	1000	100.00	200.00
*	LITTLE FELLOW	1000	57.00	115.00
*	LITTLE GIRL IN BLUE	1000	16.00	40.00
*	LORDS OF THE REALM	1000	80.00	210.00
*	MARY AND MAGNOLIA	1000	15.00	42.00
*	MARY'S LAMB (LARGE)	1000	75.00	215.00
*	MILK LAD	1000	15.00	45.00
*	MILK MAID	1000	15.00	45.00
*	MOMMA APPLE (BLUE)	1000	10.00	50.00
*	MOMMA APPLE (GOLD)	1000	16.00	50.00
*	MOONLIT SKATERS I (LARGE)	1000	75.00	200.00
*	MOONLIT SKATERS II (SMALL)	1000	40.00	80.00
*	MUFFET BOY I	1000	10.00	40.00
*	MUFFET GIRL I	1000	10.00	40.00
*	NINE MENNONITES GIRLS	1000	40.00	90.00
*	ORCHARD HELPERS	1000	75.00	250.00
*	PERFECT PET	1000	15.00	30.00
*	POPPA APPLE (BLUE)	1000	10.00	50.00
*	POPPA APPLE (GOLD)	1000	15.00	50.00
*	QUILTING BEE	1000	55.00	110.00
*	QUILTING LADIES	1000	40.00	100.00
*	RACHEL & JACOB	1000	150.00	400.00
*	RELUCTANT BALLERINA	1000	15.00	48.00
*	SEASON'S OVER	1000	35.00	90.00
*	SERENITY IN BLACK AND WHITE	1000	120.00	300.00
*	SHENANDOAH SILHOUETTE	1000	25.00	60.00
*	SHOWALTER'S FARM	1000	100.00	200.00
*	SKATING AWAY I	1000	70.00	200.00
*	SKATING LESSON	1000	50.00	400.00
*	SNOW GOOSE	1000	50.00	170.00
*	SNOWY BIRCHES	1000	60.00	160.00
*	SOLITARY SKATER	1000	35.00	100.00
*	SPIRIT OF EQUUS	1000	100.00	150.00

YR	NAME	LIMIT	ISSUE	QUOTE
*	STACK OF GIRLS	1000	25.00	75.00
*	STONE HOUSE	99	600.00	1250.00
*	TENDER SHEPHERD	1000	50.00	100.00
*	TENDING HER FLOCK	1000	80.00	170.00
*	WAYSIDE INN (ETCHING)	99	1800.00	3250.00
*	WINTER CAMEO	1000	30.00	95.00
*	WINTER GEESE (ETCHING)	99	400.00	1100.00
*	WINTER VISITOR	1000	80.00	180.00
*	WOMAN TALK	1000	35.00	70.00
*	WORKDAY'S O'ER	1000	110.00	350.00
79	A WELCOME	1000	45.00	110.00
79	APPLE HARVEST	1000	75.00	150.00
79	AWAKE, O EARTH	1000	50.00	90.00
79	BEHOLD	1000	35.00	70.00
79	EVERY BLESSING	1000	50.00	100.00
79	FANEUIL HALL	1000	40.00	80.00
79	GRANNY'S FAVORITE	1000	40.00	110.00
79	HAIL THE DAY, SOLACE	1000	75.00	200.00
79	HARK	1000	40.00	100.00
79	HE LIVES	1000	25.00	60.00
79	HOW CALM THE MORNING	1000	75.00	200.00
79	JOY	1000	10.00	40.00
79	LOVE	1000	10.00	40.00
79	MARY'S LAMBS (SMALL)	1000	40.00	100.00
79	MY HANDS TO THEE	1000	75.00	200.00
79	NEVER ALONE	1000	35.00	75.00
79	O GENTLE FRIEND	1000	40.00	90.00
79	OH LIFE	1000	40.00	80.00
79	PAVILION AT WOLFEBORO	1000	40.00	80.00
79	PROMISED	1000	40.00	80.00
79	PUBLIC GARDENS AND BEACON STREET	1000	50.00	210.00
79	TARRY NOT	1000	35.00	100.00
79	TIS GRACE	1000	20.00	50.00
79	TWO LITTLE HANDS	1000	35.00	80.00
80	CAPITOL SKATERS	1000	80.00	160.00
80	ON THE CANAL	1000	60.00	125.00
80	PEACH HARVEST	1000	150.00	500.00
80	RING AROUND A ROSIE	1000	40.00	115.00
80	STREET BY THE PARK	1000	200.00	600.00
80	WAYSIDE INN	1000	65.00	500.00
80	WINTER'S HOUSE	1000	350.00	750.00
81	BLACK CAT	1000	50.00	100.00
81	BLACK CAT ON PINK CUSHION	1000	40.00	80.00
81	QUILTING DREAMS	1000	40.00	70.00
81	SAM	1000	16.00	55.00
81	SARAH	1000	16.00	80.00
81	SKATING JOY	1000	200.00	400.00
81	SOLITARY SKATER II	1000	35.00	100.00
81	SOLO	1000	15.00	75.00
81	SPRING LOVE	1000	25.00	60.00
81	STREET BY THE PARK II	1000	125.00	275.00
81	SUNDAY MORNING	1000	60.00	200.00
81	SUNDAY'S RIDE	1000	60.00	123.00
81	TOGETHER	99	450.00	2000.00
81	WAITING FOR TOM	1000	40.00	100.00
81	WINTER AT THE MILL	1000	80.00	250.00
82	APPLE DAY	1000	80.00	165.00
82	APPLE GIRL	1000	30.00	75.00
82	AUTUMN RIDE	1000	80.00	160.00
82	BALLOON RIDE	1000	100.00	200.00
82	BLUE WINTER	1000	100.00	200.00
82	CAMEO GEESE	1000	40.00	115.00
82	CHRIS	1000	25.00	70.00
82	DANIEL	1000	20.00	80.00
82	DASHING AWAY	1000	100.00	210.00
82	DONKEY BOY	1000	40.00	80.00
82	EBONY'S JET	1000	150.00	300.00
82	FLAG GIRL	1000	10.00	50.00
82	FLOWER GIRL	1000	20.00	50.00
82	FRUIT OF THE VALLEY	1000	80.00	300.00
82	GAGGLE OF GEESE	1000	125.00	275.00
82	GRANDPA'S HOUSE	1000	40.00	110.00
82	HAND IN HAND	1000	40.00	105.00
82	HAYRIDE	1000	75.00	110.00
82	HURRAH!	1000	20.00	40.00
82	LISA AND TIGER	1000	30.00	70.00

YR	NAME	LIMIT	ISSUE	QUOTE
82	LITTLE GIRL'S PRAYER	1000	35.00	95.00
82	MY PLACE	1000	30.00	60.00
82	MY SISTERS	1000	40.00	90.00
82	ON THE SWING	1000	40.00	80.00
82	OUR LITTLE BROTHER	1000	50.00	115.00
82	OUR LITTLE SISTER	1000	50.00	115.00
82	PALS	1000	25.00	50.00
82	PINK BALLERINA	1000	25.00	50.00
82	PLEASE GOD	1000	50.00	150.00
82	PLEASE!	1000	35.00	70.00
82	ROCKING	1000	40.00	98.00
82	SHENANDOAH HARVEST	1000	60.00	125.00
82	SKATING DUET	1000	40.00	80.00
82	SLEIGH RIDE	1000	50.00	110.00
82	STACK OF BOYS	1000	30.00	70.00
82	TAKING TURNS	1000	50.00	120.00
82	TOGETHER IN THE PARK	1000	80.00	120.00
82	TWO ON A BARREL	1000	25.00	65.00
82	TWO ON A SWING	1000	50.00	110.00
82	WEDDING	1000	80.00	300.00
82	WEDDING DAY	1000	160.00	320.00
82	WEDDING II	1000	90.00	220.00
82	WINTER DUET	1000	90.00	200.00
82	WINTER'S GLIMPSE	1000	40.00	90.00
83	ADAM	1000	20.00	85.00
83	AMY	1000	20.00	90.00
83	BECKY	1000	20.00	75.00
83	BROTHERS	1000	35.00	80.00
83	CARRIE	1000	30.00	70.00
83	CHERISHED	1000	35.00	110.00
83	CHICKEN FARMERS	1000	40.00	80.00
83	CHRISTMAS CAROL	1000	60.00	520.00
83	COLONIAL SLEIGH RIDE	1000	125.00	250.00
83	COUNTRY CHURCH	1000	80.00	170.00
83	EVENING GUESTS	1000	60.00	125.00
83	EVENING WELCOME	1000	60.00	125.00
83	FAMILY, THE	1000	125.00	300.00
83	FINISHING TOUCHES	1000	60.00	130.00
83	FIRST LOVE	1000	60.00	120.00
83	GAGGLE OF GEESE (SILKSCREEN)	99	600.00	2000.00
83	GINGER	1000	40.00	80.00
83	GIRLS IN GREEN	1000	40.00	80.00
83	GOLDEN AUTUMN	1000	110.00	250.00
83	GOVERNOR'S PALACE	1000	50.00	210.00
83	GRANNY'S GIRL	1000	50.00	100.00
83	JOSHUA	1000	25.00	60.00
83	KATIE	1000	30.00	90.00
83	LONG GROVE CHURCH	1000	100.00	225.00
83	LORDS OF THE VALLEY	1000	175.00	350.00
83	MARY ANN	1000	20.00	55.00
83	MONARCH	1000	35.00	55.00
83	MY GIRLS	1000	60.00	130.00
83	NOTRE DAME	1000	90.00	180.00
83	OLD MILL HOUSE	1000	125.00	260.00
83	ORCHARD GIRL	1000	40.00	85.00
83	OUR BIG BROTHER	1000	35.00	80.00
83	QUILT, THE	1000	90.00	200.00
83	RED BIKE	1000	35.00	80.00
83	RED HOUSE	1000	100.00	220.00
83	ROTHENBURG	1000	40.00	80.00
83	SISTERS FOUR	1000	60.00	150.00
83	SPRING BOUQUET	1000	40.00	85.00
83	SPRING SHEPHERDS	1000	40.00	80.00
83	SUMMER LOVE	1000	50.00	100.00
83	SUNDAY'S APPLES	1000	50.00	120.00
83	TERRACE HILL	1000	110.00	210.00
83	TIMOTHY	1000	30.00	70.00
83	TOGETHER ON SUNDAY (SILKSCREEN)	99	600.00	2050.00
83	WEDDING III	1000	90.00	180.00
83	WHITE CHURCH, THE	1000	80.00	167.00
83	WINTER RIDE	1000	60.00	130.00
83	WINTER SKATER	1000	40.00	100.00
83	WINTER'S DAY	1000	50.00	110.00
83	WINTER'S JOY (SILKSCREEN)	99	500.00	1050.00
84	AUTUMN TRIPTYCH	1000	150.00	300.00
84	BALLOON GIRL	1000	20.00	45.00

YR	NAME	LIMIT	ISSUE	QUOTE
84	BLESSING, THE	1000	60.00	260.00
84	BROWER HOMESTEAD	1000	100.00	200.00
84	CRAZY QUILT	1000	50.00	105.00
84	ENGAGEMENT, THE	1000	40.00	80.00
84	EVENING HOUR, THE	1000	70.00	130.00
84	FIRST BORN	1000	50.00	100.00
84	FROSTY RIDE	1000	70.00	150.00
84	GRANDMA'S BED	1000	60.00	225.00
84	HITCHING A RIDE	1000	60.00	120.00
84	HOMEWARD BOUND	1000	90.00	200.00
84	LOUDMOUTHS	1000	125.00	250.00
84	MAGGIE	1000	30.00	60.00
84	MARY JEN	1000	20.00	50.00
84	MIKE AND JESSIE	1000	60.00	120.00
84	MOLLY	1000	30.00	70.00
84	NEWBORN, THE	1000	55.00	160.00
84	OHIO STAR	1000	60.00	130.00
84	PRINCELY PAIR	1000	60.00	130.00
84	RED WAGON	1000	50.00	120.00
84	SCHOOL YARD, THE	1000	60.00	120.00
84	SECRET, THE	1000	50.00	100.00
84	SUNDAY'S PRAYER	1000	50.00	105.00
84	SWAN HOUSE	1000	80.00	160.00
84	TO GRANDMOTHER'S HOUSE WE GO	1000	80.00	160.00
84	VICTORIAN LEGACY	1000	150.00	315.00
84	WEDDING RIDE, THE	1000	130.00	260.00
84	WEDDING RING	1000	75.00	165.00
84	WINTER'S GLORY	1000	200.00	350.00
85	A VISIT TO THE CAPITOL	1000	30.00	65.00
85	BILLY	1000	25.00	55.00
85	CATHY	1000	20.00	70.00
85	CHILDREN'S MUSEUM CAROUSEL, THE	1000	80.00	165.00
85	CINDY	1000	40.00	80.00
85	COUNTRY ROAD	1000	160.00	320.00
85	DANIEL HARRISON HOUSE, THE	1000	100.00	200.00
85	DAREDEVIL SKATERS	1000	100.00	185.00
85	ERIN	1000	25.00	60.00
85	EVENING HOUR IN LONG GROVE	1000	70.00	165.00
85	EVERYTHING NICE	1000	65.00	130.00
85	FAMILY HEIRLOOM	1000	80.00	160.00
85	HEARTLAND, THE	1000	80.00	170.00
85	HEATHER	1000	25.00	60.00
85	IMPERIAL MAJESTY	99	600.00	1200.00
85	JAKE	1000	25.00	50.00
85	KENTUCKY	1000	70.00	140.00
85	LANCASTER MORN	1000	275.00	565.00
85	LITTLE SISTER	1000	35.00	70.00
85	MARY'S WEDDING	1000	65.00	125.00
85	MIKE	1000	25.00	75.00
85	MINNESOTA	1000	70.00	165.00
85	MY LITTLE BROTHERS	1000	50.00	115.00
85	NANCY	1000	40.00	95.00
85	NIGHT BEFORE CHRISTMAS, THE	1000	65.00	200.00
85	NURSES, THE	1000	70.00	150.00
85	NURSING TEAM	1000	70.00	140.00
85	OUR GIRLS	1000	60.00	135.00
85	PAT	1000	25.00	60.00
85	PICKET FENCE	1000	60.00	120.00
85	PIE MAKERS, THE	1000	80.00	165.00
85	PLAYMATES	1000	70.00	140.00
85	PLEASE MA'AM	1000	50.00	100.00
85	RED CARRIAGE	1000	65.00	130.00
85	ROBBIE	1000	20.00	55.00
85	SCREECH OWL TWINS	1000	75.00	150.00
85	SENATORS, THE	1000	275.00	500.00
85	SENTINELS, THE	1000	65.00	120.00
85	SUMMER'S BLESSING	1000	65.00	130.00
85	THREE SISTERS	1000	70.00	160.00
85	TO EACH OTHER	1000	40.00	85.00
85	TWILIGHT RIDE	1000	80.00	160.00
85	WATCH, THE	1000	70.00	50.00
85	WEDDING BOUQUET	1000	75.00	150.00
85	WEDDING JOY	5000	100.00	400.00
85	WEDDING MORN	1000	70.00	150.00
85	WINTER'S TRAVELERS	1000	60.00	120.00
86	ALLELUIA!	1000	70.00	160.00

YR	NAME	LIMIT	ISSUE	QUOTE
86	ALLISON	1000	20.00	60.00
86	AMY'S FLOWERS	1000	50.00	115.00
86	ANDREW	1000	20.00	65.00
86	ANNIE & TEDDY	1000	20.00	60.00
86	BRANDON	1000	20.00	50.00
86	BRIAN	1000	20.00	50.00
86	CAROLINE	1000	30.00	60.00
86	DEAR LORD (LONG)	1000	30.00	75.00
86	DEAR LORD (SHORT)	1000	30.00	75.00
86	DIANA	1000	25.00	55.00
86	EVELYN	1000	40.00	80.00
86	FIRST PROMISE	1000	70.00	150.00
86	GENTLE SWING	1000	50.00	95.00
86	JACK	1000	25.00	70.00
86	KIM	1000	20.00	55.00
86	MAID MARION	1000	50.00	100.00
86	PROFESSOR, THE	1000	40.00	80.00
86	SCHOOL DAYS	1000	70.00	160.00
86	SKATING WALTZ	1000	60.00	125.00
86	SPRING WEDDING	1000	70.00	155.00
86	STEPHANIE	1000	35.00	85.00
86	SUNDAY STROLL	1000	50.00	100.00
86	WINTER WEDDING	1000	80.00	170.00
86	WINTER'S EVE	1000	100.00	200.00
86	WINTER'S MATES	1000	50.00	110.00
87	BETTY	1000	20.00	40.00
87	BILL	1000	20.00	40.00
87	CHAMPIONS	1000	80.00	138.00
87	CHRISTMAS DANCE	1000	70.00	125.00
87	CONTEMPLATION	1000	75.00	130.00
87	SITTING PRETTY	1000	60.00	120.00
87	THREE LITTLE SISTERS	1000	70.00	140.00
87	YOUNG MAESTRO	1000	60.00	85.00
88	ANGEL'S PRAYER	1000	70.00	125.00
88	ANGEL'S TWO	1000	40.00	80.00
88	CAROL	1000	25.00	45.00
88	CHELSEA	1000	30.00	55.00
88	GEORGETOWN (ETCHING)	1000	1000.00	2000.00
88	GRANDAD'S BUDDY	1000	45.00	90.00
88	LITTLE BROWN CHURCH	1000	100.00	175.00
89	A MOTHER'S LOVE	1000	45.00	90.00
89	FOREVER YOURS	1000	125.00	250.00
89	KATIE'S FLOWERS	1000	30.00	100.00
89	MY BIG SISTER	1000	50.00	95.00
89	OUR BEDROOM	1000	70.00	130.00
89	PARTNERS	1000	40.00	70.00
90	BABY BOY	1000	25.00	60.00
90	BABY GIRL	1000	25.00	60.00
90	CALLING ON FRIENDS	1000	110.00	160.00
90	SHADOWS OF ETERNITY	1000	50.00	90.00
90	SISTER LOVE	1000	40.00	90.00
90	SISTERS	1000	20.00	70.00
90	SPRING MORN	1000	125.00	200.00
90	TAMMY	1000	30.00	50.00

NEW MASTERS PUBLISHING
P. BANNISTER
BANNISTER

YR	NAME	LIMIT	ISSUE	QUOTE
78	BANDSTAND	250	75.00	375.00
80	DUST OF AUTUMN	200	200.00	1225.00
80	FADED GLORY	200	200.00	1225.00
80	GIFT OF HAPPINESS	200	200.00	2000.00
80	GIRL ON THE BEACH	200	200.00	1200.00
80	SILVER BELL, THE	200	200.00	2000.00
81	APRIL	SO	200.00	1050.00
81	CRYSTAL	300	260.00	500.00
81	EASTER	SO	260.00	950.00
81	JULIET	SO	260.00	4800.00
81	MY SPECIAL PLACE	SO	260.00	2500.00
81	PORCELAIN ROSE	SO	260.00	2000.00
81	REHEARSAL	SO	260.00	1000.00
81	SEA HAVEN	SO	260.00	1140.00
81	TITANIA	SO	260.00	900.00
82	AMARYLLIS	SO	285.00	1900.00
82	CINDERELLA	500	285.00	500.00
82	EMILY	SO	285.00	1300.00
82	IVY	SO	285.00	700.00
82	JASMINE	SO	235.00	1000.00

YR	NAME	LIMIT	ISSUE	QUOTE
82	LILY	500	285.00	470.00
82	MAIL ORDER BRIDES	SO	325.00	2300.00
82	MEMORIES	SO	235.00	500.00
82	NUANCE	SO	235.00	490.00
82	PARASOLS	500	235.00	300.00
82	PRESENT, THE	SO	260.00	1000.00
83	DUCHESS, THE	SO	250.00	2500.00
83	MEMENTOS	SO	150.00	1200.00
83	OPHELIA	SO	150.00	1000.00
84	APRIL LIGHT	SO	150.00	300.00
84	FAN WINDOW, THE	SO	195.00	390.00
84	MAKE BELIEVE	SO	150.00	590.00
84	SCARLET RIBBONS	SO	150.00	350.00
84	WINDOW SEAT	SO	150.00	600.00
86	PRIDE & JOY	SO	150.00	200.00
86	SOIREE	950	150.00	200.00
87	AUTUMN FIELDS	950	150.00	380.00
87	FIRST PRIZE	950	115.00	115.00
87	QUIET CORNER	SO	115.00	250.00
87	SEPTEMBER HARVEST	SO	150.00	300.00
88	APPLES AND ORANGES	SO	265.00	900.00
88	FLORIBUNDA	SO	265.00	550.00
88	GUINEVERE	485	265.00	1600.00
88	LOVE SEAT	SO	230.00	450.00
88	SUMMER CHOICES	300	250.00	900.00
89	CHAPTER ONE	SO	265.00	2050.00
89	DAYDREAMS	SO	265.00	530.00
89	LOW TIDE	SO	265.00	550.00
89	MARCH WINDS	SO	265.00	300.00
89	PEACE	SO	265.00	1100.00
89	QUILT, THE	SO	265.00	1600.00
90	GOOD FRIENDS	SO	265.00	760.00
90	LAVENDER HILL	SO	265.00	600.00
90	RENDEZVOUS	SO	265.00	700.00
90	SEASCAPES	SO	265.00	390.00
90	SISTERS	SO	265.00	1300.00
90	SONGBIRD	SO	265.00	450.00
90	STRING OF PEARLS	SO	265.00	790.00
91	CELEBRATION	SO	350.00	995.00
91	CROSSROADS	SO	295.00	500.00
91	PUDDING & PIES	SO	265.00	440.00
91	TEATIME	SO	295.00	600.00
91	WILDFLOWERS	SO	295.00	420.00

ON THE WILD SIDE
J. MEGER

YR	NAME	LIMIT	ISSUE	MEGER
79	WILDSIDE I-CANVASBACKS	*	75.00	800.00
80	MANITOBA MEMORIES-CANVASBACKS	*	100.00	140.00
80	SPLIT DECISION-CANVASBACKS	*	100.00	350.00
81	STACK OF BILLS-LESSER SCAUP	*	100.00	220.00
81	WINGS IN THE WILLOWS	*	100.00	150.00
82	PRAIRIE POTHOLES-CANVASBACKS	*	60.00	150.00
82	STOP ON RED-REDHEADS	100	100.00	190.00
83	RISKY BUSINESS	75	85.00	100.00
84	BLUE BANDITS	60	60.00	120.00
84	GOOD MORNING	45	45.00	70.00
84	LEADING LADY	*	60.00	70.00
84	LEGACY-LOON	60	85.00	750.00
85	BURNING THROUGH	*	100.00	250.00
85	FIELDSTONES-PHEASANTS	125	125.00	300.00
85	LEGACY-EAGLE	85	85.00	550.00
85	WINDSONG-CANADA GEESE	225	225.00	470.00
86	FIRST LIGHT-LOONS	95	95.00	150.00
86	SUNDANCE-SNOWY OWL	125	125.00	650.00
86	UNINVITED GUESTS	60	75.00	80.00
87	COMING HOME	125	125.00	185.00
87	HEARTLAND-PHEASANTS	100	100.00	470.00
87	INTERLUDE	75	75.00	160.00
87	LEGACY-MOOSE	85	85.00	165.00
87	ONE MORE PASS	60	75.00	160.00
87	OUTBACK-PHEASANTS	*	75.00	225.00
87	UP AT THE LAKE	95	95.00	160.00
88	FAST MOVING GAME	60	75.00	80.00
88	HERITAGE CARDINAL	*	85.00	145.00
88	LEGACY-TIMBERWOLVES (AP)	125	85.00	600.00
88	SEPTEMBER PASSAGE	*	125.00	190.00
88	SNOWY COURTSHIP-SNOWY OWLS	125	125.00	250.00

Artist Terry Redlin knows how to capture the best of any season. The Pleasures of Winter *is produced by Hadley House.*

Terry Redlin never fails to leave out even the smallest of detail. In Welcome to Paradise, *limited to 14,500, the artist captures the anticipation of a long and prosperous fishing trip. Hadley House is the publisher.*

The title says it all. Yellowstone Magic *exudes the mysterious beauty enjoyed by visitors this breathtaking national park. Created by Adriano Manocchia and co-signed by Silvio Calabi.*

There's no room at this inn. Full House—Fox Family, *by wildlife artist Carl Brenders, reveals a mother tending to the needs of her young pups. Published by Mill Pond Press.*

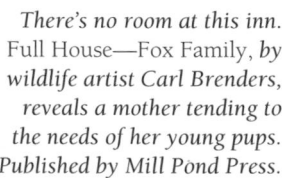

YR	NAME	LIMIT	ISSUE	QUOTE
89	EDGE OF TOWN	95	95.00	145.00
89	HOMESTEAD-PHEASANTS (AP)	125	125.00	300.00
89	MOONRIDE-LOONS	95	95.00	990.00
89	PRAIRIE DANCEHALL-PHEASANTS	95	75.00	135.00
89	THREE'S A CROWD	60	60.00	175.00
90	ALPHA-TIMBER WOLF	*	150.00	340.00
90	ALPHA-TIMBER WOLF (AP)	225	225.00	400.00
90	ALPHA-TIMBER WOLF (COLLECTOR'S EDITION)	225	275.00	600.00
90	BREEZING UP-WOOD DUCKS (AP)	*	145.00	195.00
90	FANFARE-TRUMPETER SWANS	150	150.00	195.00
90	FIRST OUTING	60	60.00	130.00
90	HIDDEN GAME-TIMBER WOLF (AP)	75	75.00	140.00
90	MOON SHADOWS-WHITE-TAILED DEER	95	95.00	300.00
90	STORM WARNING-PHEASANTS	95	125.00	550.00
91	PROMISE, THE	*	150.00	135.00
91	PROMISE, THE (COLLECTOR'S EDITION)	295	295.00	150.00
91	SNOWY PURSUIT	*	125.00	200.00
SI	SILHOUETTE-TIMBER WOLF	*	95.00	300.00

PAST IMPRESSIONS
A. MALEY
				MALEY
84	GLORIOUS SUMMER	CL	150.00	970.00
84	SECLUDED GARDEN	CL	150.00	970.00
85	PASSING ELEGANCE	CL	150.00	600.00
85	SECRET THOUGHTS	CL	150.00	970.00
86	TELL ME	CL	150.00	600.00
86	WINTER ROMANCE	CL	150.00	750.00
87	DAY DREAMS	500	*	450.00
87	LOVE LETTER	450	200.00	650.00
87	LOVE LETTER A/P	450	300.00	350.00
87	PROMISE, THE	450	200.00	400.00
88	BOARDWALK, THE	500	250.00	450.00
88	JOYS OF CHILDHOOD	500	250.00	400.00
88	OPENING NIGHT	CL	250.00	1500.00
88	TRANQUIL MOMENT	500	250.00	400.00
88	VICTORIAN TRIO	500	250.00	440.00
89	ENGLISH ROSE	750	250.00	480.00
89	IN HARMONY	750	250.00	500.00
89	WINTER IMPRESSIONS	750	250.00	550.00
90	CAFE ROYALE	750	275.00	440.00
90	FESTIVE OCCASION	750	250.00	250.00
90	GRACIOUS ERA	750	275.00	275.00
90	ROMANTIC ENGAGEMENT	750	275.00	400.00
90	SUMMER PASTIME	750	250.00	250.00
91	BETWEEN FRIENDS	750	275.00	250.00
91	SUMMER CAROUSEL	750	200.00	200.00
91	SUNDAY AFTERNOON	750	275.00	600.00
91	WINTER CAROUSEL	750	200.00	200.00
92	A WALK IN THE PARK	500	260.00	260.00
92	AN ELEGANT AFFAIR	500	260.00	420.00
92	EVENING PERFORMANCE	750	150.00	300.00
92	INTIMATE MOMENT	750	250.00	500.00

A. MALEY
			WOMEN OF ELEGANCE	
89	ALEXANDRA	750	125.00	200.00
89	BETH	750	125.00	200.00
89	CATHERINE	750	125.00	125.00
89	VICTORIA	750	125.00	125.00

PEMBERTON & OAKES
D. ZOLAN
82	ERIK AND DANDELION	880	98.00	400.00
83	BY MYSELF	880	98.00	290.00
84	SABINA IN THE GRASS	880	98.00	625.00
86	TENDER MOMENT	880	98.00	330.00
87	TOUCHING THE SKY	880	98.00	290.00
88	DAY DREAMER	1000	35.00	150.00
88	SMALL WONDER	880	98.00	312.00
88	TINY TREASURES	450	150.00	250.00
88	WAITING TO PLAY	1000	35.00	125.00
88	WINTER ANGEL	880	98.00	270.00
89	ALMOST HOME	880	98.00	310.00
89	BROTHERLY LOVE	880	98.00	360.00
89	DADDY'S HOME	880	98.00	294.00
89	GRANDMA'S MIRROR	*	98.00	320.00
89	MOTHER'S ANGELS	880	98.00	283.00
89	RODEO GIRL	*	98.00	210.00
89	SNOWY ADVENTURE	880	98.00	175.00-270.00

YR	NAME	LIMIT	ISSUE	QUOTE
89	SUMMER'S CHILD	*	98.00	200.00
90	CHRISTMAS PRAYER	880	98.00	195.00-245.00
90	COLORS OF SPRING	880	98.00	200.00-300.00
90	CRYSTAL'S CREEK	880	98.00	320.00
90	LAURIE AND THE CRECHE	*	98.00	185.00
91	FLOWERS FOR MOTHER	*	98.00	205.00

RECO INTERNATIONAL
J. MCCLELLAND

			FINE ART CANVAS REPRODUCTION	
90	BEACH PLAY	350	80.00	80.00
91	FLOWER SWING	350	100.00	100.00
91	SUMMER CONVERSATION	350	80.00	80.00

S. KUCK

			LIMITED EDITION PRINT	
84	JESSICA	500	60.00	400.00
85	HEATHER	500	75.00	150.00
86	ASHLEY	500	85.00	155.00

J. MCCLELLAND

				MCCLELLAND
*	I LOVE TAMMY	500	75.00	100.00
*	JUST FOR YOU	300	155.00	155.00
*	OLIVIA	300	175.00	175.00
*	REVERIE	300	110.00	110.00
*	SWEET DREAMS	300	145.00	145.00

RIE MUNOZ LTD.
R. MUNOZ

YR	NAME	LIMIT	ISSUE	QUOTE
71	DANCE IN KASHIM	100	8.00	450.00
73	ESKIMO STORY TELLER	300	30.00	825.00
74	KING ISLAND	300	30.00	1600.00
74	SCARY SEA	500	30.00	1500.00
75	CREATION OF MAN	500	30.00	2000.00
75	CROW IN A MOUNTAIN ASH	950	30.00	845.00
77	CANNERY WORKERS, NAKNEK	500	30.00	820.00
77	CRABBING	100	30.00	350.00
77	CRANE LEGEND	500	40.00	1900.00
77	GATHERING EGGS	500	30.00	1250.00
77	GOSSIPING WOMEN	500	27.00	200.00
77	KOTZEBU BREAKUP	500	36.00	990.00
77	WINTER SUN, GAMBELL	500	30.00	540.00
78	BERRY PICKERS	500	36.00	415.00
78	RAFT OF DUCKS	950	30.00	715.00
78	RIBBON SEALS	950	20.00	480.00
79	BUTCHERING CRABS, TENAKEE	500	36.00	775.00
79	FISHING FOR KING CRAB, UKIVOK	500	36.00	875.00
79	LADIES IN THE BATH	500	36.00	495.00
80	BLUEBERRIES, BLUEBIRDS	500	30.00	295.00
80	CATS CRADLE	500	27.00	760.00
80	DOUGLAS CRAB BOAT	500	60.00	895.00
80	HAPPY HOUR, NOME	500	40.00	795.00
80	KETCHIKAN ALASKA	500	12.00	365.00
80	LAST CARIBOU	500	35.00	860.00
80	LOOSE DOGS	500	32.00	490.00
80	MIDDLETON	500	36.00	645.00
80	OFF TO SUMMER CAMP	500	40.00	590.00
80	RECESS AUKE BAY SCHOOL	500	42.00	870.00
80	STRING GAME	250	75.00	895.00
80	TUNDRA	500	32.00	440.00
81	BERRY PICKERS	550	40.00	450.00
81	BOOM BOAT	750	45.00	980.00
81	CRAB BUTCHERING PARTY	500	40.00	645.00
81	DANCER IN MOTION	500	36.00	365.00
81	FISHERMAN, KETCHIKAN	500	40.00	645.00
81	FRIENDS, GAMBELL	500	30.00	390.00
81	GATHERING GRASS	500	30.00	265.00
81	GOING BERRY PICKING, HOONAH	500	40.00	750.00
81	HOPKINS ALLEY	750	45.00	595.00
81	INTERVIEWING THE WINNER	500	40.00	650.00
81	MONKEY TREE	500	40.00	665.00
81	REINDEER ROUNDUP	200	200.00	995.00
81	SEALIONS AT UNALASKA	750	50.00	685.00
81	STARRING	500	36.00	595.00
82	DRYING LAUNDRY & FISH	750	40.00	415.00
82	EVERGREEN BOWL	750	45.00	750.00
82	HAULING IN CRABS	750	40.00	540.00
82	ICE FISHING	750	32.00	720.00
82	IDITAROD RACE HEADQUARTERS	750	40.00	580.00
82	NOAH	750	36.00	685.00
82	RIE MUNOZ IN TAPESTRY	OP	20.00	40.00

YR	NAME	LIMIT	ISSUE	QUOTE
82	SIGNS OF SPRING	750	30.00	465.00
82	SOME ALASKA BIRDS	175	45.00	565.00
82	SUMMER CAMP	750	45.00	490.00
82	SUMMER STORM, BUCKLAND	750	45.00	425.00
82	TESTING A SEAL SKIN FLOAT	750	28.00	325.00
83	CHASING MOULTING GEESE	750	32.00	645.00
83	ELFIN COVE	750	32.00	495.00
83	FISH BUYER, ELFIN COVE	750	40.00	440.00
83	IN THE PARK, FRANCE	500	15.00	550.00
83	PACKING FISH	500	28.00	220.00
83	POKER GAME	750	20.00	585.00
83	PRIEST, UNALASKA	750	36.00	595.00
83	ROOSTING BIRDS	200	85.00	530.00
83	SEAGULL STORY	750	32.00	355.00
83	SNOW BUNTINGS, GAMBELL	750	45.00	730.00
83	WHISTLING AT NORTHERN LIGHTS	500	36.00	650.00
83	WRANGELL WATER FRONT	750	40.00	465.00
84	BERRY PICKER	750	28.00	480.00
84	CHAPEL, ROCHE HARBOR	750	35.00	525.00
84	COMING HOME	750	45.00	695.00
84	CRABBER, UNALASKA	750	60.00	1175.00
84	DANCERS IN SEALGUT PARKAS	OP	20.00	20.00
84	FISH CAMP	750	48.00	395.00
84	GROCERIES NOME	750	38.00	475.00
84	IDITAROD, SHATOOLOK	750	64.00	600.00
84	ISTKA SUMMER FESTIVAL	OP	20.00	40.00
84	PACKING FISH	750	40.00	400.00
84	PAINT JOB THOMAS BASIN	750	36.00	335.00
84	POTLATCH BAR, KETCHIKAN	750	30.00	395.00
84	SANDHILL CRANES	750	50.00	695.00
84	ST. NICHOLAS, JUNEAU	750	38.00	695.00
84	STEAMBATH LAKE, ILIAMNA	750	30.00	650.00
84	STORY KNIFE	750	20.00	445.00
84	SWING, THE	750	20.00	430.00
84	TANGLED TRACES	750	20.00	385.00
84	WAITING FOR FERRY, TENAKEE	750	40.00	510.00
85	CLEANING FISH	750	40.00	245.00
85	CRAB POTS, SITKA	750	36.00	455.00
85	HALIBUT $1	750	60.00	970.00
85	JUNEAU CANNERY	750	45.00	525.00
85	NORTH STAR COMING	750	50.00	395.00
85	SPRING SUNDAY	750	38.00	395.00
85	WOMAN BEAR LEGEND	750	60.00	950.00
86	BLUEBERRIES	750	45.00	435.00
86	CACHE	750	36.00	230.00
86	CATHEDRAL, SITKA	750	48.00	395.00
86	CLEANING SALMON	750	48.00	235.00
86	DINNER, NOME	750	40.00	355.00
86	FALL MIGRATION	750	65.00	565.00
86	GREY POUPON	750	20.00	465.00
86	INNER HARBOR	750	45.00	390.00
86	JESSIE'S FLOWERS	750	45.00	450.00
86	LATE BOAT	750	48.00	425.00
86	LOOKING FOR HALLEY'S COMET	750	30.00	410.00
86	PACKING DUNGENESS	750	25.00	375.00
86	RASPBERRY PATCH	750	20.00	255.00
86	STORM AT FISH CAMP	750	50.00	190.00
86	UNLOADING WALRUS MEAT	750	50.00	295.00
86	WHALE	750	50.00	375.00
86	WHALE WATCH	750	40.00	395.00
87	ABANDONED CABIN	950	35.00	120.00
87	CASH BUYER, KOTZEBUE	750	40.00	165.00
87	DOWNHILL SKIERS, EAGLECREST	750	60.00	795.00
87	FIRST SNOW, STARR HILL	750	30.00	395.00
87	FIRST SNOW, TENAKEE	750	48.00	240.00
87	FISHERMAN'S FAMILY, EAGEGIK	750	35.00	165.00
87	GREENHOUSE	750	45.00	270.00
87	HAULING WATER, TENAKEE	750	28.00	28.00
87	MUG UP, METLAKATLA	750	45.00	105.00
87	PUNTING OVER TO THE MIDNIGHT SUN	750	42.00	220.00
87	RUSSIAN CHURCH, UNALASKA	750	30.00	180.00
87	SPRING FLOWERS	750	25.00	145.00
87	TEKAKEE CABIN	750	55.00	295.00
87	UNLOADING FREIGHT, GAMBRELL	750	65.00	725.00
88	CANNERY COOK, CRAIG	750	30.00	180.00
88	COMING INTO TENAKEE INLET	750	55.00	295.00

YR	NAME	LIMIT	ISSUE	QUOTE
88	FEEDING THE SWANS CORNWALL	750	55.00	365.00
88	FOLLOWING THE LEADER	750	45.00	370.00
88	GOING FISHING	750	32.00	380.00
88	LONDON PUB	750	25.00	170.00
88	NOATAK	750	48.00	320.00
88	RUNAWAY MITTENS	750	50.00	485.00
88	SELF PORTRAIT, 4TH ST. STAIRS	750	50.00	220.00
88	WINTER VILLAGE, NOATAK	750	55.00	315.00
89	BLUE MOON CAFE	750	55.00	175.00
89	EDDIE BAUER'S IDITAROD RACER	950	60.00	525.00
89	FALL COLORS	750	55.00	370.00
89	HOLY ASSUMPTION CHURCH	750	60.00	295.00
89	MUSHER	750	40.00	185.00
89	NIGHT SLEDING, JUNEAU	750	60.00	395.00
89	PTARMIGAN LIFT	750	60.00	495.00
89	SEABIRDS OF ALEUTIANS	750	65.00	215.00
89	WINTER, JUNEAU	750	65.00	295.00
90	ARK IN ALASKA	750	70.00	610.00
90	CREEK STREET, KETCHIKAN	750	72.00	585.00
90	EMBRACE, THE	750	35.00	650.00
90	LAUNDRY, EGEGIK	750	45.00	45.00
90	LOADING CRAB POTS	750	65.00	285.00
90	OFF TO THE BATH, TENAKEE	750	48.00	185.00
90	RUSSIAN CHURCH, JUNEAU	750	68.00	170.00
91	ANDY	950	45.00	135.00
91	MARRY ME, MY DEAR	950	40.00	85.00
91	NUMBER #27	950	45.00	95.00
91	SHADE TREE	950	65.00	65.00
91	SHARPENING AN ULU	950	68.00	68.00
91	SLIDING AT UNALAKLEET	950	90.00	235.00
91	SPRING MIGRATION	950	60.00	335.00
91	STAR PRINCESS	950	75.00	240.00
91	SWING, TENAKEE	750	55.00	215.00
91	TULIPS $2	950	50.00	125.00
91	WHALE LEGEND	950	60.00	60.00
91	WINTER CABIN, TENAKEE	950	55.00	215.00
91	WINTER GAMES	950	65.00	195.00
92	MOLLY-O	950	100.00	225.00
92	NORTHERN LIGHTS, JUNEAU	950	125.00	320.00

R. MUNOZ   **SERIGRAPH**

YR	NAME	LIMIT	ISSUE	QUOTE
74	CATS CRADLE	105	27.00	760.00
75	BELUGA WHALE & CALF	950	25.00	845.00
75	HONKERS	100	21.00	300.00
75	REINDEER HERD	*	27.00	325.00
75	SPLITTING WALRUS HIDE	100	27.00	215.00
76	CRESTED AUKLET	95	21.00	450.00
76	ICE FISHING	120	30.00	395.00
77	CANNERY WORKER	105	36.00	425.00
77	COMMERCIAL CRABBER	95	30.00	400.00
78	SEINER	350	25.00	1400.00
79	CARIBOU HUNTER	190	36.00	850.00
79	DANCER	250	50.00	795.00
79	NORTHERN LIGHTS, JUNEAU	250	75.00	775.00
79	RAVEN HAD TWO WIVES	90	50.00	1325.00
79	WOMAN BEAR LEGEND	183	36.00	1600.00
80	ADRIFT	250	60.00	1130.00
80	DRUMMER & DANCER	350	36.00	475.00
80	FISH GRADER	250	50.00	1500.00
80	SUMMER VOYAGE	250	75.00	900.00
81	INVITATION	250	65.00	856.00
81	RAVEN LEGEND	77	60.00	1295.00
82	SPRING ICE FISHING	200	85.00	1300.00
83	ESKIMO GAME	200	124.00	895.00
84	ARK IN ALASKA	200	125.00	1635.00
84	MERMAID	220	45.00	410.00
86	THROAT CHANTERS	750	110.00	1275.00

R. MUNOZ   **STONE LITHO**

YR	NAME	LIMIT	ISSUE	QUOTE
74	BUTCHERING AT GAMBELL	125	85.00	690.00
75	SEATED DANCER	125	50.00	175.00
81	WHALE DANCE	100	225.00	450.00
82	ESKIMO MOTHER	100	185.00	1700.00

ROMAN INC.

A. WILLIAMS   **ABBIE WILLIAMS**

YR	NAME	LIMIT	ISSUE	QUOTE
88	MARY, MOTHER OF THE CARPENTER	TL	100.00	100.00

F. HOOK   **HOOK**

YR	NAME	LIMIT	ISSUE	QUOTE
81	CARPENTER, THE	YR	100.00	1000.00

YR	NAME	LIMIT	ISSUE	QUOTE
81	CARPENTER, THE (REMARQUE)	YR	100.00	3000.00
82	BOUQUET	1200	70.00	350.00
82	FROLICKING	1200	60.00	350.00
82	GATHERING	1200	60.00	350.00
82	LITTLE CHILDREN, COME TO ME	1950	50.00	500.00
82	LITTLE CHILDREN, COME TO ME (REMARQUE)	50	100.00	500.00
82	POSING	1200	70.00	350.00
82	POULETS	1200	60.00	350.00
82	SURPRISE	1200	50.00	350.00

F. HOOK   **PORTRAITS OF LOVE**

YR	NAME	LIMIT	ISSUE	QUOTE
88	EXPECTATION	2500	25.00	25.00
88	IN MOTHER'S ARMS	2500	25.00	25.00
88	MY KITTY	2500	25.00	25.00
88	REMEMBER WHEN...	2500	25.00	25.00
88	SHARING	2500	25.00	25.00
88	SUNKISSED AFTERNOON	2500	25.00	25.00

SAN MARTIN FINE ART

ANNE-LAN

YR	NAME	LIMIT	ISSUE	QUOTE
88	LA NAISSANCE DU PRINTEMPS	175	250.00	1350.00
88	MATERNITE	225	250.00	1150.00
88	PERSEPHONE	385	600.00	800.00
88	SETTING SUN	495	950.00	1250.00
89	EYES OF THE NIGHT	385	350.00	750.00
89	FEMME FLEUR	385	250.00	500.00
89	REVE DE CHAT	262	250.00	800.00
90	HEURE BLEUE	262	500.00	500.00
90	L'AURORE	262	500.00	500.00
90	LA GRANDE CASCADE	230	200.00	240.00
90	PLUME	385	500.00	550.00
90	PUPUCE	230	200.00	240.00
91	EGLANTINE	450	60.00	60.00
91	INVITATION AU VOYAGE	262	500.00	500.00
91	LE CHATEAU FLEURI	300	450.00	450.00
91	LOVE STORY	450	60.00	60.00

SCHMID

J. FERRANDIZ   FERRANDIZ LITHOGRAPHS

YR	NAME	LIMIT	ISSUE	QUOTE
80	MOST PRECIOUS GIFT	425	125.00	1200.00
80	MOST PRECIOUS GIFT (REMARQUE)	50	225.00	2800.00
80	MY STAR	675	100.00	650.00
80	MY STAR (REMARQUE)	75	175.00	1800.00
81	HEART OF SEVEN COLORS	600	100.00	395.00
81	HEART OF SEVEN COLORS (REMARQUE)	75	175.00	1300.00
82	HE SEEMS TO SLEEP	450	150.00	700.00
82	HE SEEMS TO SLEEP (REMARQUE)	25	300.00	3200.00
82	MIRROR OF THE SOUL	225	150.00	425.00
82	MIRROR OF THE SOUL (REMARQUE)	35	250.00	2400.00
82	OH SMALL CHILD	450	125.00	495.00
82	OH SMALL CHILD (REMARQUE)	50	225.00	1450.00
82	ON THE THRESHOLD OF LIFE	425	150.00	450.00
82	ON THE THRESHOLD OF LIFE (REMARQUE)	50	275.00	1350.00
82	RIDING THROUGH THE RAIN	900	165.00	350.00
82	RIDING THROUGH THE RAIN (REMARQUE)	100	300.00	950.00
82	SPREADING THE WORD	675	125.00	250.00
82	SPREADING THE WORD (REMARQUE)	75	225.00	1075.00
83	FRIENDSHIP	460	165.00	450.00
83	FRIENDSHIP (REMARQUE)	15	1200.00	2300.00
84	STAR IN THE TEAPOT	410	165.00	165.00
84	STAR IN THE TEAPOT (REMARQUE)	15	1200.00	2100.00

L. DAVIS   LOWELL DAVIS LITHOGRAPHS

YR	NAME	LIMIT	ISSUE	QUOTE
81	DUKE'S MIXTURE	899	75.00	125.00
81	DUKE'S MIXTURE (REMARQUE)	101	150.00	350.00
81	PLUM TUCKERED OUT	899	75.00	390.00
81	PLUM TUCKERED OUT (REMARQUE)	101	100.00	350.00
81	SURPRISE IN THE CELLAR	899	75.00	553.00
81	SURPRISE IN THE CELLAR (REMARQUE)	101	100.00	400.00
82	BIRTH OF A BLOSSOM	400	125.00	325.00-520.00
82	BIRTH OF A BLOSSOM (REMARQUE)	50	200.00	450.00
82	BUSTIN' WITH PRIDE	899	75.00	125.00
82	BUSTIN' WITH PRIDE (REMARQUE)	101	150.00	250.00
82	FOXFIRE FARM	800	125.00	125.00
82	FOXFIRE FARM (REMARQUE)	100	200.00	250.00
82	SUPPERTIME	400	125.00	300.00
82	SUPPERTIME (REMARQUE)	50	200.00	450.00
85	SELF PORTRAIT	450	75.00	130.00-195.00
87	BLOSSOM'S GIFT	450	75.00	195.00

YR	NAME	LIMIT	ISSUE	QUOTE
89	SUN WORSHIPPERS	750	100.00	100.00
90	SUNDAY AFTERNOON TREAT	750	100.00	100.00
91	WARM MILK	750	100.00	100.00
91	WARM MILK	750	100.00	100.00
92	CAT AND JENNY WREN	750	100.00	100.00

M.I. HUMMEL

M.I. HUMMEL LITHOGRAPHS

YR	NAME	LIMIT	ISSUE	QUOTE
80	MOONLIGHT RETURN	900	150.00	850.00
81	A TIME TO REMEMBER	720	150.00	300.00
82	POPPIES	450	150.00	650.00
83	ANGELIC MESSENGER (75TH ANNIV. ED.)	195	375.00	700.00
83	ANGELIC MESSENGER, CHRISTMAS MESSENGER	400	275.00	450.00
85	BIRTHDAY BOUQUET I	195	450.00	550.00
85	BIRTHDAY BOUQUET II	225	375.00	375.00
85	BIRTHDAY BOUQUET III	100	195.00	395.00

SERENDIPITY TRADING CO.

B. RABBIT

YR	NAME	LIMIT	ISSUE	QUOTE
85	ELDERS, THE	950	65.00	200.00
87	FROM EARTH MAN CAME	950	65.00	200.00
88	FAITHFUL, THE	350	90.00	275.00
88	YESTERDAY, TODAY AND TOMORROW	1500	35.00	750.00
89	AFTER THE RAINS	650	65.00	200.00
89	PROMISES, DREAMS AND HOPE	650	65.00	200.00
90	ANCESTORS	350	126.00	375.00
90	COMING OF WINTER	200	250.00	750.00
90	FEAST DAY	350	75.00	375.00
90	PRICE OF PEPPERS, THE	650	75.00	75.00
90	PROPOSAL, THE	350	125.00	375.00
90	STRENGTH TOGETHER	350	125.00	375.00
90	WARMTH OF YOUR TOUCH	350	125.00	375.00

SIMON ART

C. BLACK

YR	NAME	LIMIT	ISSUE	QUOTE
84	BLUE LADY	290	100.00	120.00
85	SUMMER DAY/CHARLES STREET	350	70.00	80.00
86	CHRISTMAS MORNING	225	150.00	1500.00
86	HALTON HOMESTEAD	125	120.00	1000.00
86	MAITLAND HALL	125	100.00	600.00
86	NANA'S BACK DOOR	125	100.00	750.00
86	SILENT VISITOR	125	60.00	150.00
86	SNOW & THUNDER	125	150.00	300.00
86	WELCOME HOME	125	120.00	1200.00
87	CENTURY FARM	395	150.00	500.00
87	FIRST CHRISTMAS	395	150.00	200.00
87	HOME FOR CHRISTMAS	395	150.00	750.00
87	JOURNEY'S END	395	150.00	800.00
87	OLD APPLE TREE, THE	395	150.00	200.00
87	SNOWED IN	395	150.00	600.00
88	CAROLE'S GARDEN	395	200.00	240.00
88	DADDY'S GIRL	395	200.00	400.00
88	MORNING ON MAIN STREET	395	200.00	500.00
89	AUNT MARTHA'S	390	200.00	200.00
89	HIGH HOUSE	390	200.00	200.00
89	SILENT NIGHT	390	200.00	200.00
90	A NIGHT'S LODGING	390	250.00	250.00
90	HOME FOR THE HOLIDAYS	450	200.00	200.00
90	MARY'S KITCHEN	490	200.00	200.00
91	SATURDAY MORNING	*	160.00	160.00
91	SPRING PLANTING	*	160.00	160.00
86	BROKEN FENCE	390	50.00	50.00
86	LONER, THE	560	30.00	40.00
86	MAIL BOX, THE	450	120.00	200.00
86	OLD GOLD	560	30.00	60.00
86	OLD RED	390	50.00	50.00
86	ROUNDHOUSE, THE	200	120.00	150.00
86	SEA SCAVENGERS	450	120.00	120.00
86	SILENT MIST	390	80.00	80.00
86	SNOW TRACKS	450	120.00	120.00
86	WAITING OUT WINTER	560	30.00	30.00
86	WINTER BIRCH	560	30.00	60.00
87	CALM WATERS	450	150.00	150.00
87	COUNTRY FOLK	450	150.00	150.00
87	FISHING BOATS	450	150.00	150.00
87	GIANT, THE	200	180.00	225.00
87	HOMESTEAD & RURAL ROUTE, THE (SET OF 2)	450	250.00	250.00
87	OCTOBER	450	150.00	150.00
87	WINTER DRESS	450	150.00	150.00

YR	NAME	LIMIT	ISSUE	QUOTE
88	BOYS OF SUMMER	450	90.00	90.00
88	COUNTRY AUTUMN	450	150.00	150.00
88	HOME TEAM, THE	450	90.00	90.00
88	JUST A GAME	450	90.00	90.00
88	LASER FUN	450	150.00	150.00
88	SHINNY	450	150.00	400.00
88	SNOWBALLS	450	150.00	150.00
88	TADPOLES	450	150.00	150.00
89	CROSSING THE 16TH	200	180.00	180.00
89	MILL POND, THE	490	110.00	110.00
89	PLAYOFF, THE	450	180.00	270.00
89	SKATERS, THE	490	180.00	180.00
89	SNOWMAN, THE	450	180.00	180.00
89	TEMPESTUOUS SKY	450	180.00	180.00
90	A WINTER VISIT	490	200.00	200.00
90	COLLECTIBLES	490	110.00	110.00
90	MY HOME TOWN	490	180.00	180.00
90	SHADY LADY	490	190.00	190.00
90	SKI TRAIN	390	200.00	200.00
90	WHERE DREAMS BEGIN	490	190.00	250.00
91	CLEAR THE TRACK	*	180.00	180.00
91	DEDICATED	790	216.00	216.00
91	WINTER VIGIL	790	140.00	140.00
83	WATERS EDGE	350	115.00	230.00
85	COOL INTERLUDE	390	115.00	250.00
85	WATCHFUL GUARDIAN	390	115.00	170.00
86	AMBUSH!	690	140.00	900.00
86	MAY BRINGS FLOWERS	690	90.00	110.00
86	SILENT REFLECTIONS	350	115.00	800.00
87	MYSTICAL SHADOWS	790	190.00	300.00
87	SUMMER'S END-COYOTES	*	150.00	150.00
87	WINGING WESTWARD	790	160.00	800.00
88	MARCH FLURRIES	790	190.00	325.00
88	MORNING PATROL	790	190.00	300.00
89	GREAT ESCAPE, THE	590	225.00	425.00
89	THOSE EYES	590	150.00	150.00
90	DELICATE BALANCE	790	200.00	200.00
90	OLD TIRE SWING, THE	790	200.00	200.00
90	PHANTOM OF THE MARSH	950	225.00	225.00
90	SILENT WINGS	790	225.00	225.00
90	SPOOKING THE HERD	590	225.00	225.00
91	PLAYTIME	790	225.00	225.00
91	SIBLINGS	*	200.00	200.00
85	MR. EMMET'S FISHIN' HOLE	200	200.00	5200.00
85	SATURDAY MORNING	200	250.00	3000.00
86	ADRIFT	390	200.00	2600.00
86	BEYOND THE SHORE	390	200.00	1300.00
86	CHANGING SEASONS	390	200.00	375.00
86	COUNTRY KITCHEN	390	200.00	950.00
86	DEJA VU	390	200.00	575.00
86	DUNROWAN	450	160.00	2000.00
86	GONE FISHIN'	390	200.00	4400.00
86	JOY RIDE	390	200.00	400.00
86	KITE, THE	390	200.00	975.00
86	SECRET OF THE WELL	450	160.00	750.00
87	BIG CATCH, THE	390	250.00	1200.00
87	CATS	390	250.00	2800.00
87	INHERITANCE, THE	390	250.00	1200.00
87	MEMORIES FOR SALE	390	250.00	500.00
87	SUNSET MEMORIES	390	250.00	475.00
88	BILLY NINE FINGERS	590	250.00	400.00
88	CHERRY HILL ROAD COLLECTION (SET OF 4)	490	500.00	800.00
88	DOUBLE TROUBLE	490	250.00	495.00
88	FIRESIDE SHADOWS	590	250.00	1000.00
88	JUST FOR YOU	590	250.00	400.00
88	LUCKY STRIKE	790	250.00	1500.00
88	MISCHIEF	590	250.00	1500.00
88	OUT ON A LIMB	490	250.00	400.00
89	A WINTER'S GLOW	790	250.00	700.00
89	ABANDONED HERITAGE	790	280.00	280.00
89	LONE PINE	950	280.00	2000.00
89	MORNING REFLECTIONS	950	280.00	300.00
89	SHADES OF SUMMER	790	250.00	1300.00
89	SIDE BY SIDE	2183	350.00	1000.00
89	STIRRING MEMORIES	790	280.00	1400.00
89	SUMMERS PAST	790	280.00	360.00

YR	NAME	LIMIT	ISSUE	QUOTE
90	AN ENCHANTED EVENING	1500	280.00	250.00
90	CAT NAPPING	1500	280.00	580.00
90	DAYS GONE BY	950	280.00	575.00
90	DIFFERENT TIMES	1500	280.00	200.00
90	PLAYING THROUGH	950	280.00	800.00
90	SHOPPING	1500	280.00	200.00
91	A BOY AND HIS DREAM	*	275.00	400.00
91	A BOY AND HIS DREAM (CS)	*	1250.00	2750.00
91	MR. HOCKEY	*	275.00	150.00
91	MR. HOCKEY (CS)	*	1250.00	600.00
91	SUN NEVER SETS, THE	*	280.00	200.00
*	AT BAT	650	200.00	300.00
*	O.K., BLUE JAYS!	390	150.00	200.00
*	QUEEN & SPADINA	390	150.00	950.00
*	WHERE THE WORLD COMES TO PLAY	521	300.00	350.00
85	CAT TAILS	450	150.00	150.00
85	FLOWER HOUSE	450	150.00	600.00
85	NEAR ELORA	450	150.00	200.00
85	SNOW PODS	450	150.00	150.00
86	GEORGIAN BAY SKY	450	150.00	150.00
86	NORTHERN STREAM	450	150.00	150.00
87	RAIL FENCE	450	180.00	180.00
87	SNOW BANKS	450	180.00	180.00
87	SUGAR SHACK	450	180.00	180.00
88	BEDFORD MILLS	450	200.00	200.00
88	MORNING MAIL	450	150.00	150.00
88	MURPHY'S PLACE	450	150.00	150.00
88	SILENT STREAM AND STANDING BY (SET OF 2)	450	250.00	250.00
89	CHRISTMAS HOUSE	450	200.00	200.00
89	HURON COUNTRY	450	200.00	200.00
90	DAYBREAK	450	200.00	200.00
90	SHORELINE TRILOGY (SET OF 3)	450	150.00	150.00
88	A COUNTRY SCENE	590	250.00	250.00
88	A SUMMER PLACE	590	250.00	250.00
88	BACKYARD SETTING	590	250.00	250.00
88	FLOWER GIRL	590	250.00	250.00
88	LITTLE GARDENERS	450	250.00	650.00
89	CATHERINE	450	200.00	200.00
89	COUNTRY WALK	450	150.00	425.00
89	MARKET, THE	450	200.00	200.00
89	PLAYTIME	450	150.00	150.00
89	SUMMER RESORT	450	200.00	200.00
89	TEA TIME	450	250.00	250.00
90	FLOWER LOVER	590	175.00	175.00
90	GUARDIAN OF THE ROSES	590	250.00	250.00
90	SHARING	450	200.00	200.00
90	WINTER WARMTH	450	200.00	200.00

SOMERSET HOUSE PUBLISHING
G. HARVEY

74	POKER PALS	500	50.00	150.00
76	BOSS' NEW RIG	1500	60.00	160.00
76	CAREFREE COWHANDS	500	50.00	150.00
78	CROSSING THE CANYON	2000	50.00	800.00
78	DRIFTING COWHANDS	2000	60.00	350.00
78	LEAVIN' THE LINE SHACK	2000	50.00	350.00
79	CHANGING OF THE RANGELAND	250	150.00	2650.00
79	WHEN BANKERS WORE BOOTS	1000	75.00	790.00
80	COMING HOME, THE	1000	75.00	140.00
80	EARLY RUN	1000	75.00	350.00
80	GOOD LORD WILLIN/CREEK DON'T RISE	1000	90.00	190.00
80	IN THE LAND OF THE ROCKIES	1000	90.00	200.00
80	IN THE LAND OF THE WALKIN' RAIN	1000	75.00	190.00
80	RANCHING-PUMP JACK STYLE	1000	90.00	1225.00
80	RIDING THE SALT RIVER CANYON	1000	75.00	300.00
80	RIDING WITH GRANDPA	1000	90.00	190.00
80	SATURDAY NIGHT POKER PALACE	1000	75.00	175.00
80	SILENT HUNTER, THE	1000	75.00	180.00
80	SPRING PALETTE	1000	90.00	240.00
80	TEXAS FROM HIDE AND HORN	1000	90.00	310.00
80	TIMES REMEMBERED	2250	100.00	150.00
81	BOOMTOWN DRIFTERS	2250	150.00	390.00
81	OIL PATCH	1000	150.00	820.00
81	ON THE STREETS OF NEW ORLEANS	1000	150.00	350.00
81	WALL STREET	SO	150.00	400.00
81	WITH NO INTENTION OF CHARGING	1000	150.00	700.00
82	BOOT TOP DEEP	1000	150.00	2000.00

YR	NAME	LIMIT	ISSUE	QUOTE
82	COWBOYS' CHRISTMAS BALL	1000	150.00	150.00
82	COWTOWN 1880	1000	150.00	2100.00
82	DALLAS 1908	1200	150.00	1150.00
82	INDEPENDENT OILMEN	1000	150.00	550.00
82	LEAVING THE OIL PATCH	1000	150.00	480.00
82	PLAZA, NEW YORK, THE	1000	150.00	450.00
82	SUPPLIES FOR THE MISSION	1000	150.00	200.00
83	COUNTRY POST OFFICE	1000	150.00	320.00
83	FAMILY CHRISTMAS	1250	150.00	600.00
83	FRESH SNOW FIRST LIGHT	1250	150.00	230.00
83	STREETCARS ALONG THE AVENUE	2500	95.00	450.00
84	AMERICAN WEST	1250	150.00	300.00
84	EARLY DOWNTOWN HOUSTON	1250	150.00	310.00
84	GRAND OPENING	1250	150.00	170.00
84	ME, GRANDPA, AND LITTLE SIS	1250	150.00	165.00
84	TOO WET TO PLOW	1000	*	700.00
84	TRADING AT THE GENERAL STORE	1250	150.00	160.00
85	A NEW LEASE	1250	150.00	390.00
85	CHESTNUT VENDOR	1250	150.00	165.00
85	DALLAS REMEMBERED	1250	150.00	340.00
85	ONLY WORKING HORSEBACK	1250	150.00	440.00
85	SANTA FE PLAZA	1250	150.00	250.00
86	INDEPENDENT TEXANS	1250	150.00	470.00
86	REFLECTIONS OF YESTERDAY (W/BOOK)	1250	275.00	2200.00
86	ROYAL STREET	1250	160.00	180.00
86	TEXAS RANCHER	1250	150.00	170.00
86	TIES OF HOME, THE	1250	150.00	180.00
87	EVENING ALONG THE AVENUE	1250	150.00	300.00
87	FIFTH AVENUE	1250	150.00	340.00
88	FLOWER CART, THE	1250	150.00	550.00
88	MEN OF THE AMERICAN WEST	1250	150.00	900.00
88	PENNSYLVANIA AVENUE	2575	150.00	1350.00
88	SATURDAY NIGHT CONTRACT	1250	150.00	650.00
89	COWBOY'S PAYDAY	1250	165.00	790.00
89	EARLY RIDERS	*	150.00	230.00
89	JEB STUART'S RETURN	1800	165.00	700.00
89	WALL STREET-NEW YORK	4378	165.00	380.00
90	AN EVENING WITH THE PRESIDENT	*	165.00	800.00
90	CITY BY THE BAY	*	165.00	1000.00
90	HORSE TROLLEY ON PARK ROW	*	165.00	165.00
90	PICKET'S REPORT	1800	165.00	450.00
90	REMEMBERING THE GOOD TIMES	*	165.00	190.00
90	THINKING OF SPRING	*	165.00	240.00
90	THOUGHTS OF HOME	*	165.00	185.00
91	CATHEDRAL OF ST. BASIL, THE-RED SQUARE	*	165.00	330.00
91	GENTEEL NATION	*	165.00	200.00
91	WIND RIVER RANGE	*	165.00	185.00
86	BRIDGES AND BLOSSOMS	950	80.00	400.00
86	WHISPERING LIGHT	950	80.00	180.00
87	CASCADE OF COLOR	950	80.00	180.00
87	COURTYARD, THE	950	80.00	250.00
87	ENCHANTED POND, THE	950	80.00	155.00
87	QUIET VILLAGE, THE	950	80.00	800.00
88	MORNING LIGHT-DEVON	950	80.00	175.00
88	RIVERWALK	950	80.00	160.00
84	REFLECTIONS OF THE PAST	1000	40.00	350.00
84	TIMELESS ELEGANCE	1000	40.00	150.00
85	AUNT VERDI'S PORCH	1000	45.00	350.00
85	FRIENDSHIP QUILTS	1000	50.00	200.00
85	PRESERVED IN TIME	1000	50.00	75.00
85	SISTERS THREE	1000	50.00	150.00
85	SUMMERS REMEMBERED (PAIR)	5000	50.00	150.00
85	UPSTAIRS SEWING ROOM, THE	1000	45.00	185.00
85	YESTERDAY'S DREAMS	1000	45.00	160.00
86	A BOUQUET FOR ELIZABETH	1000	50.00	300.00
86	A CAMEO OF THE PAST	1000	50.00	90.00
86	FABRIC OF DREAMS, THE	1000	50.00	75.00
86	FOREVER YOURS (SET OF 3)	1500	90.00	110.00
86	IN THE GARRET	1000	50.00	70.00
86	VICTORIAN BOUQUET	1000	50.00	100.00
87	A BREATH OF SPRING	1000	50.00	60.00
87	COTILLION	1000	50.00	90.00
87	FIDDLER AND THE QUILT MAKER	1000	50.00	90.00
87	LITTLE WOMEN	1000	50.00	125.00
87	TEA, ROSES AND ROMANCE	1675	60.00	160.00
88	CHERISHED MOMENTS	1000	55.00	95.00

YR	NAME	LIMIT	ISSUE	QUOTE
88	LOVE SONGS	1000	55.00	150.00
88	ROSE OF SHARON	1000	55.00	125.00
88	SOMETHING OLD, SOMETHING NEW	1000	55.00	700.00

SPORTS COLLECTORS WAREHOUSE
C. PALUSO

YR	NAME	LIMIT	ISSUE	QUOTE
86	CARL YASTRZEMSKI	452	95.00	275.00
86	DON DRYSDALE	465	95.00	175.00
86	DON SUTTON	310	95.00	150.00
86	MICKEY MANTLE	250	175.00	2250.00
86	SPARKY ANDERSON	574	75.00	140.00
87	CARL HUBBELL	800	75.00	185.00
87	SANDY KOUFAX	950	100.00	400.00
88	BILL DICKEY	800	75.00	425.00
88	CHARLES GEHRINGER	800	75.00	185.00
88	LEFTY GOMEZ	800	75.00	185.00
88	MUHAMMAD ALI	300	250.00	1395.00
88	NOLAN RYAN	383	125.00	1795.00
88	TED WILLIAMS	406	185.00	950.00
89	BILLY HERMAN	800	110.00	140.00
89	BOB FELLER	500	125.00	140.00
89	JOE SEWELL	800	110.00	185.00
89	JOHNNY MIZE	500	125.00	140.00
89	LOU BOUDREAU	500	125.00	140.00
89	MONTE IRVIN	500	125.00	140.00
89	RALPH KINER	500	125.00	140.00
89	RICK FERRELL	800	110.00	125.00
89	ROY CAMPANELLA	250	600.00	1395.00
89	STAN MUSIAL	475	185.00	490.00
89	WILLIE MAYS	500	185.00	325.00
90	GORDIE HOWE	500	125.00	200.00
90	JOE MONTANA	400	400.00	750.00
90	JOHNNY UNITAS	500	150.00	250.00
90	MAURICE RICHARD	500	125.00	200.00
90	PEE WEE REESE	500	175.00	185.00
90	YOGI BERRA	500	185.00	225.00
*	BO JACKSON	1990	95.00	120.00
*	HUDDLE, THE	1000	50.00	1500.00
*	MONEY: M. JORDAN	1990	95.00	120.00
*	ROGER CRAIG	1060	65.00	120.00
87	SWEETNESS: WALTER PAYTON	1000	50.00	175.00
89	JERRY RICE	1060	65.00	120.00
89	JOE MONTANA	1060	80.00	500.00
89	NATURAL, THE: WILL CLARK	1060	65.00	175.00
90	MVP: JOE MONTANA	950	325.00	600.00
90	SPECIAL TEAMS	1000	120.00	120.00
90	STEVE LARGENT	1060	120.00	175.00
90	TOP GUN: DAN MARINO	950	240.00	240.00

SPORTS IMPRESSIONS
*

YR	NAME	LIMIT	ISSUE	QUOTE
*	ARTFUL DODGERS, THE	1000	95.00	395.00
*	MICK, THE: MANTLE	750	125.00	295.00
*	YANKEE GREATS	750	95.00	245.00
*	DON MATTINGLY H/S	950	125.00	200.00
*	BOYS OF SUMMER	500	125.00	350.00
*	DON MATTINGLY ROOKIE H/S	950	125.00	295.00
*	LIVING TRIPLE CROWN	950	195.00	450.00
*	MANTLE ALL STAR	750	125.00	375.00
*	MANTLE HALL OF FAME	750	125.00	375.00
*	MANTLE ROOKIE H/S	750	125.00	375.00
*	MANTLE TRIPLE CROWN	750	125.00	375.00
*	MICKEY AT NIGHT	750	125.00	450.00
*	STARS AND STRIPES	500	125.00	225.00
*	TED WILLIAMS G/E	950	125.00	250.00

JOHNSON
*

YR	NAME	LIMIT	ISSUE	QUOTE
*	DON MATTINGLY PLAYER OF THE YEAR H/S	950	125.00	350.00
*	DON MATTINGLY PLAYER OF THE YEAR U/S	950	95.00	200.00

STEINER PRINTS
R. STEINER

YR	NAME	LIMIT	ISSUE	QUOTE
81	1981 CALIFORNIA DUCK STAMP	1150	115.00	400.00
82	UNEXPECTED SPRIG	200	45.00	79.00
83	BULL SPRIG AT BUTTE SINK	450	85.00	295.00
83	FLUSHED WOODIES	450	45.00	79.00
83	STORMY MORNING MALLARDS	450	85.00	295.00
84	1984 NEVADA DUCK STAMP	1990	135.00	250.00
84	BLACK LAB WITH PINTAIL	950	25.00	150.00

YR	NAME	LIMIT	ISSUE	QUOTE
85	1985 MICHIGAN DUCK STAMP	980	135.00	200.00
85	EARLY LIGHT A/P	175	135.00	275.00
85	HONKERS AT DAWN	350	85.00	350.00
86	1986 FLORIDA DUCK STAMP	1000	135.00	250.00
86	CALIFORNIA PHESANT (CIRCLE)	100	189.00	399.00
86	REFLECTIVE SPRIG	350	45.00	99.00
86	SILENT PARTNER	780	65.00	295.00
87	1987 CALIFORNIA DUCK STAMP	750	135.00	400.00
87	1987 CALIFORNIA DUCK STAMP (MED.)	50	300.00	900.00
87	1987 NEW HAMPSHIRE DUCK STAMP	5507	135.00	500.00
87	1987 NEW HAMPSHIRE DUCK STAMP (GOV.)	50	850.00	3500.00
87	1987 NEW HAMPSHIRE DUCK STAMP (MED.)	50	300.00	1000.00
87	CALIFORNIA QUAIL W/POPPIES	450	65.00	99.00
87	EMPERORS OVER THE ALEUTIANS	350	85.00	139.00
87	OPENING DAY	350	65.00	99.00
87	PINTAILS AT THE COLORADO	450	85.00	139.00
88	1988 CALIFORNIA DUCK STAMP	750	135.00	300.00
88	1988 CALIFORNIA DUCK STAMP (MED.)	300	300.00	700.00
88	1988 NEW HAMPSHIRE DUCK STAMP	5507	135.00	300.00
88	1988 NEW HAMPSHIRE DUCK STAMP (GOV.)	100	500.00	300.00
88	1988 NEW HAMPSHIRE DUCK STAMP (MED.)	50	300.00	600.00
89	1989 ARIZONA DUCK STAMP	900	135.00	200.00
89	1989 ARIZONA DUCK STAMP (GOV.)	200	500.00	1200.00
89	1989 ARIZONA DUCK STAMP (MED.)	100	300.00	400.00
89	1989 CALIFORNIA DUCK STAMP	750	145.00	200.00
89	1989 CALIFORNIA DUCK STAMP (MED.)	300	300.00	500.00
89	1989 NEW HAMPSHIRE DUCK STAMP	5507	135.00	300.00
89	LATE SNOW WOOD DUCKS	100	79.00	99.00
90	1990 COLORADO GOVERNOR'S ED STAMP	4980	58.00	65.00
90	1990 COLORADO PRINT	14,500	169.00	250.00
90	1990 COLORADO PRINT (GOV)	400	619.00	1500.00
90	1990 COLORADO PRINT (MED)	2000	319.00	500.00
90	1990 NEW HAMPSHIRE GOVERNOR'S ED STAMP	1380	54.00	65.00
90	1990 NEW HAMPSHIRE PRINT	5507	140.00	300.00
90	1990 NEW HAMPSHIRE PRINT (GOV)	135	505.00	2000.00
90	1990 NEW HAMPSHIRE PRINT (MED)	50	305.00	600.00
90	1990 RHODE ISLAND GOVERNOR'S ED STAMP	1800	57.50	65.00
90	1990 RHODE ISLAND PRINT	3000	153.50	250.00
90	1990 RHODE ISLAND PRINT (GOV)	200	558.00	1500.00
90	1990 RHODE ISLAND PRINT (MED)	300	308.50	500.00
90	GRACEFUL ASCENT	1850	100.00	100.00
91	1991 COLORADO GOVERNOR'S ED STAMP	1380	55.00	65.00
91	1991 COLORADO PRINT	8000	169.00	200.00
91	1991 COLORADO PRINT (GOV)	200	619.00	1200.00
91	1991 COLORADO PRINT (MED)	1000	319.00	400.00
91	1991 NEW HAMPSHIRE GOVERNOR'S ED STAMP	990	54.00	65.00
91	1991 NEW HAMPSHIRE PRINT	5507	154.00	200.00
91	1991 NEW HAMPSHIRE PRINT (GOV)	130	519.00	1200.00
91	1991 NEW HAMPSHIRE PRINT (MED)	50	319.00	400.00
91	1991 NEW MEXICO GOVERNOR'S ED STAMP	3990	57.50	65.00
91	1991 NEW MEXICO PRINT	12,000	179.00	250.00
91	1991 NEW MEXICO PRINT (GOV)	500	649.00	1200.00
91	1991 NEW MEXICO PRINT (MED)	1000	339.00	500.00
91	1991 RHODE ISLAND GOVERNOR'S ED STAMP	1200	57.50	65.00
91	1991 RHODE ISLAND PRINT	8000	169.00	200.00
91	1991 RHODE ISLAND PRINT (GOV)	130	574.00	1200.00
91	1991 RHODE ISLAND PRINT (MED)	200	319.00	400.00
91	1991 UTAH PRINT	14,028	163.00	200.00
91	1991 UTAH PRINT (GOV)	75	618.00	1800.00
91	1991 UTAH PRINT (MED)	1600	318.00	400.00
92	1992 NEW MEXICO PRINT (GOV)	95	505.00	649.00
92	1992 NEW MEXICO PRINT (MED)	600	305.00	339.00

T.S.M. & COMPANY
A. MANOCCHIA

MANOCCHIA

YR	NAME	LIMIT	ISSUE	QUOTE
83	ROOM FOR ONLY ONE	600	65.00	95.00
83	SOARING	600	65.00	150.00
84	COYOTE	150	45.00	85.00
84	SKIRMISH IN THE TALL GRASS	500	60.00	150.00
87	ALONE AT HOME	500	85.00	250.00
87	EVENING HUNT	500	75.00	200.00
87	SAVE THE SOUND	OP	10.00	75.00
88	FALL FISHERMAN	350	40.00	60.00
88	FISHING THE EAST BRANCH	350	40.00	70.00
88	FROM HIGH ABOVE	OP	10.00	75.00
88	HARRIS HAWK	350	60.00	75.00
88	SPARROW	350	55.00	65.00

YR	NAME	LIMIT	ISSUE	QUOTE
89	EARLY MORNING AUSABLE	350	45.00	75.00
89	FALL FISHING	*	40.00	70.00
89	FALL WHITETAIL COUNTRY	*	35.00	80.00
89	FALL WHITETAIL COUNTRY	350	35.00	80.00
89	FIRST CATCH	150	40.00	80.00
89	FISHING THE EAST BRANCH	*	40.00	70.00
89	FROM HIGH ABOVE	*	25.00	75.00
89	MOUNT KATAHDIN-MOOSE	*	135.00	135.00
89	SPARROW	*	50.00	50.00
90	A WAITING GAME	*	85.00	85.00
90	BAY BRANT	*	200.00	350.00
90	IT DOESN'T GET BETTER THAN THIS...	*	75.00	75.00
90	JUSTIES SET	*	75.00	75.00
90	MOUNT KATAHDIN-WHITETAIL	*	135.00	135.00
90	TEAMWORK	*	80.00	80.00
91	AFTER THE LIMIT	*	200.00	200.00
91	EARLY MORNING WORKOUT	*	10.00	10.00
91	HONORS COURSE-9TH HOLE USGA	*	195.00	195.00
91	MOUNT KATAHDIN-BLACK BEAR	*	135.00	135.00
91	ROCK HOLE, THE	*	90.00	90.00
91	TODAY'S WATER TEMPERATURE IS...	*	45.00	45.00
91	TOO LATE FOR LUNCH	*	60.00	60.00
91	YELLOWSTONE MAGIC	*	75.00	75.00

V.F. FINE ARTS
S. KUCK

				KUCK
86	SILHOUETTE	250	80.00	220.00
86	SUMMER REFLECTIONS	900	60.00	250.00
86	TENDER MOMENTS	500	70.00	250.00
87	A QUIET TIME	900	40.00	150.00
87	DAISY, THE	900	30.00	185.00
87	FLOWER GIRL, THE	900	40.00	160.00
87	LE PAPILLION	350	90.00	150.00
87	LOVESEAT, THE	900	30.00	235.00
87	MOTHER'S LOVE	150	195.00	800.00
87	READING LESSON, THE	900	60.00	250.00
88	FIRST RECITAL	150	200.00	1100.00
88	KITTEN, THE	350	120.00	1950.00
88	LITTLE BALLERINA	150	110.00	300.00
88	MY DEAREST	350	160.00	660.00-775.00
88	WILD FLOWERS	350	160.00	270.00
89	BUNDLE OF JOY	1000	125.00	250.00
89	DAY DREAMING	900	150.00	250.00
89	INNOCENCE	900	150.00	250.00
89	PUPPY	500	120.00	600.00
89	ROSE GARDEN	500	95.00	290.00
89	SISTERS	900	95.00	350.00
89	SONATINA	900	150.00	290.00
90	CHOPSTICKS	1500	80.00	80.00
90	FIRST SNOW	500	95.00	240.00
90	LE BEAU	1500	80.00	160.00
90	LE BELLE	1500	80.00	165.00
90	LILLY POND	750	150.00	275.00
91	GOD'S GIFT	1500	95.00	170.00
91	MEMORIES	5000	195.00	235.00
92	JOYOUS DAY	1200	125.00	165.00

VOYAGEUR ART
K. DANIEL

*	ADORNMENT OF WINTER	*	85.00	150.00
*	CONSEQUENCE OF FIRE	*	225.00	260.00
*	FIRST RECITAL	*	125.00	175.00
*	LOST DECOY II	*	85.00	180.00
*	SEARCH FOR SURVIVAL	*	145.00	175.00
*	WINTER SILENCE	*	155.00	150.00
80	WETLAND AND WIKIS	*	120.00	175.00
81	BARNYARD TUSSLE	*	85.00	85.00
81	OUT ON A LIMB	*	85.00	175.00
81	PINE RIDGE	*	85.00	200.00
82	A TOUCH OF ORANGE	*	85.00	160.00
82	BEWILDERED	*	85.00	150.00
82	BLUE HERONS	*	85.00	150.00
82	CHICKADEE	*	50.00	50.00
82	SAFE AND SOUND	*	50.00	125.00
82	SILENT SENTINEL	*	85.00	170.00
83	PRIDE OF THE LAKES	*	85.00	390.00
84	BREAK IN THE STORM	*	85.00	150.00

YR	NAME	LIMIT	ISSUE	QUOTE
84	LOST DECOY	*	85.00	180.00
85	ON THE RUN	*	85.00	150.00
85	RUFFED GROUSE SPRING CREEK	*	85.00	175.00
85	SUMMER BLUE JAY	*	85.00	100.00
85	WINGS OF THE NORTH	*	85.00	185.00
86	BOUNDARY WATER SOLITUDE	*	85.00	140.00
86	MAJESTIC VIEW	*	85.00	190.00
90	CONSEQUENCE OF TIME	*	225.00	300.00
90	MISTY WATERS	*	155.00	300.00
90	STALKING THE BLUFFS	*	150.00	210.00
90	SWEET DREAMS	*	185.00	190.00
91	RHAPSODY IN BLOOM	*	185.00	175.00

WILDLIFE INTERNATIONALE
J. RUTHVEN
RUTHVEN

NAME	LIMIT	ISSUE	QUOTE
* ALGONQUIN	750	75.00	200.00
* ALLEN'S HUMMINGBIRD	750	75.00	125.00
* AMERICAN WIDGEON	950	65.00	100.00
* ANNA'S HUMMINGBIRD	750	75.00	125.00
* BALD EAGLE-INITIAL	1000	30.00	900.00
* BATELEUR EAGLE	750	110.00	250.00
* BENGAL TIGER-COMMISSION, IDAHO	1000	100.00	675.00
* BENGAL TIGER-REGAL	1000	80.00	2000.00
* BENGAL TIGER-SAFARI	5000	65.00	1000.00
* BLACK MANED LION	5000	65.00	165.00
* BLUE WINGED TEAL	500	75.00	190.00
* BLUEBIRDS-INITIAL	1000	30.00	700.00
* BLUEBIRDS-SPRING, COMMISSION	200	*	250.00
* BOBWHITE QUAIL-AMERICANA	1000	80.00	500.00
* BOBWHITE QUAIL-INITIAL	1000	30.00	600.00
* BOBWHITE QUAIL-KNOB CREEK	750	75.00	425.00
* BROADBILLED HUMMINGBIRD	500	75.00	125.00
* BROWN PELICAN	500	125.00	400.00
* CALIFORNIA VALLEY QUAIL	950	50.00	100.00
* CANADA GOOSE	1000	95.00	500.00
* CANVASBACKS-DU COMMISSION	150	425.00	750.00
* CANVASBACKS-NORTH AMERICAN	1000	50.00	650.00
* CARDINAL-INITIAL	1000	30.00	900.00
* CARDINAL-MARIEMONT	500	75.00	225.00
* CARDINAL-SONGBIRD	950	75.00	650.00
* CAROLINA PARAQUET	500	300.00	1200.00
* CAROLINA WREN	950	50.00	100.00
* CEDAR WAXWING	950	50.00	225.00
* CHICKADEES	950	50.00	150.00
* CHIPMUNK	750	50.00	450.00
* CHIPPEWA BRAVE	950	50.00	125.00
* CINNAMON TEAL	2000	30.00	285.00
* COMMON ELDERS-DU CANADA COMMISSION	100	125.00	200.00
* DECOY	750	125.00	1100.00
* DOUBLE TIME	750	85.00	200.00
* DOWNY WOODPECKER	600	55.00	425.00
* DUSTY	950	150.00	800.00
* EAGLE TO THE MOON	500	150.00	1590.00
* EASTERN WILD TURKEY-INITIAL	1000	30.00	600.00
* EASTERN WILD TURKEY-KNOB CREEK	750	75.00	500.00
* ELEPHANTS	5000	65.00	200.00
* FLICKERS	950	65.00	275.00
* FLYING SNOWY OWL	950	125.00	300.00
* FOX MASQUE I	1000	30.00	175.00
* FOX MASQUE II	1000	30.00	175.00
* FRIENDS-INDIAN CHILDREN	500	75.00	150.00
* GIANT PANDA	5000	65.00	700.00
* GOLDFINCH-COMMISSION	600	55.00	375.00
* GRANT'S ZEBRA	3500	75.00	170.00
* GRAY FOX FAMILY	950	150.00	1300.00
* GRAY FOX-MASTERPIECE	950	125.00	1280.00
* GRAY FOX-WOODLAND	1500	200.00	225.00
* GREAT HORNED OWL	1000	90.00	270.00
* GREEN WINGED TEAL	500	75.00	150.00
* GREY SQUIRREL	600	55.00	325.00
* HERRING GULL	1000	50.00	270.00
* HOODED MERGANSER	750	75.00	190.00
* HOODED MERGANSER (SM.)	1000	50.00	100.00
* INDIGO BUNTING	950	50.00	170.00
* IVORY BILLED WOODPECKERS	5000	350.00	800.00
* JAGUAR	950	65.00	600.00
* KIRTLAND WARBLER	1000	100.00	175.00

Beginning Friends *by Paul Calle reflects upon the days when the white man and the Indian were at peace with one another. Mill Pond Press is the publisher.*

At first glance, it seems as if a single wolf stands alone. A closer look at Arctic Cliff— White Wolves *reveals others in his pack. The image is by Robert Bateman; published by Mill Pond Press.*

Where do you turn When the Trail Grows Cold? *Paul Calle explores the plight in the limited edition print of the same name. Mill Pond Press.*

The sun is reflected in the icy waters, home to the Polar Bear *by wildlife artist Robert Bateman. The image is produced by Mill Pond Press.*

YR	NAME	LIMIT	ISSUE	QUOTE
*	KIT FOX	500	100.00	225.00
*	LABRADOR DUCK	500	350.00	850.00
*	LEOPARD	3500	75.00	200.00
*	MALLARD-INITIAL	1000	50.00	500.00
*	MALLARD/WOOD DUCK (PR.)	99	750.00	1850.00
*	MISTY-REDHEAD DUCKS	100	125.00	300.00
*	N.Y. STATE BLUEBIRD	1000	50.00	360.00
*	NATURE CENTER CARDINAL	1000	50.00	425.00
*	OAKGROVE PINTAIL (SM.)	3000	50.00	100.00
*	ON THE HUNT	1000	90.00	120.00
*	PASSENGER PIGEON-AQUATINT	500	350.00	1600.00
*	PASSENGER PIGEON-MARTHA	500	100.00	400.00
*	PEREGINE FALCON	600	65.00	65.00
*	PHEASANT (PAIR)	99	850.00	1750.00
*	PHEASANT-INITIAL	1000	30.00	650.00
*	RED FOX FAMILY	1000	90.00	1200.00
*	RED FOX-COMMISSION	1000	100.00	600.00
*	RED FOX-REGAL	1000	90.00	1700.00
*	RED FOX-WOODLAND	950	150.00	330.00
*	REDHEAD DUCKS	450	350.00	550.00
*	REDHEADED WOODPECKERS	1000	50.00	230.00
*	RIVOLI'S HUMMINGBIRD	750	75.00	125.00
*	ROADRUNNER	1000	50.00	125.00
*	ROBIN FAMILY	600	55.00	350.00
*	ROBINS	1000	50.00	360.00
*	RUBY-THROATED HUMMINGBIRD	750	75.00	125.00
*	RUDDY DUCKS-COMMISSION	650	55.00	500.00
*	RUDDY DUCKS-GEORGETOWN	1000	50.00	100.00
*	RUDDY DUCKS-NORTH AMERICAN	1000	50.00	650.00
*	RUFFED GROUSE (PAIR)	99	750.00	1200.00
*	RUFFED GROUSE-INITIAL	1000	40.00	600.00
*	RUFOUS HUMMINGBIRD	750	75.00	125.00
*	RUMMY	950	150.00	700.00
*	SAND HILL CRANE	950	150.00	150.00
*	SAW WHET OWL	950	50.00	80.00
*	SCARLET	950	150.00	150.00
*	SCREECH OWLS-HOMESTEAD	950	50.00	450.00
*	SCREECH OWLS-INITIAL	1000	30.00	800.00
*	SNOWY OWL	1000	50.00	135.00
*	TERNS	750	150.00	425.00
*	TIMBER WOLF	950	150.00	150.00
*	TOWHEES	950	75.00	250.00
*	WANDERING BRAVE	1000	90.00	900.00
*	WHITE TIGERS	1000	150.00	600.00
*	WHITE-TAILED DEER-KNOB CREEK	750	150.00	700.00
*	WHITE-TAILED DEER-OHIO DIV. WILDLIFE	500	125.00	300.00
*	WILD BOAR	200	100.00	200.00
*	WILSON'S PLOVER	500	75.00	175.00
*	WINSTON-SPRINGER SPANIEL	950	150.00	300.00
*	WOOD DUCKS-INITIAL	1000	40.00	215.00
*	WOOD DUCKS-NORTH AMERICAN	1000	90.00	650.00
*	WOOD DUCKS-OHIO DUCK STAMP (PRINT ONLY)	10,000	125.00	450.00
*	WOOD DUCKS-OHIO DUCK STAMP (STAMP ONLY)	10,000	5.75	60.00
76	BALD EAGLE-BICENTENNIAL	776	350.00	765.00
76	EASTERN WILD TURKEY-BICENTENNIAL	776	350.00	500.00
80	WINGS IN THE WIND	750	200.00	400.00
81	BLUEBIRDS-1981	950	75.00	500.00
81	CARDINAL-1981	950	75.00	500.00
81	MALLARD-1981	500	75.00	175.00
81	OSPREY	750	175.00	175.00
81	PHEASANT-1981	950	75.00	175.00
81	SWALLOW-TAILED KITES	500	100.00	175.00
82	KESTREL AND MOUSE	950	150.00	200.00
82	KINGLET	950	75.00	150.00
82	NUTHATCH	950	75.00	150.00
83	ARCTIC FOX	350	350.00	380.00
83	GOLDFINCH-1983	950	75.00	175.00
83	PAPAW BANDIT	600	125.00	190.00
83	PILEATED WOODPECKER	350	350.00	550.00
83	QUAIL WITH YOUNG	950	50.00	100.00
84	BENGAL TIGER	950	200.00	845.00
84	RIVER OTTERS	500	125.00	300.00
84	SPRING FLOWERS	600	125.00	250.00
85	BLACK DUCK FAMILY	600	125.00	225.00
85	EASTERN FOX SQUIRREL	600	75.00	150.00
85	RACCOONS (FAMILY)	1000	125.00	250.00

YR	NAME	LIMIT	ISSUE	QUOTE
85	WINTER REFLECTION	500	225.00	270.00
86	BLUEBIRDS-EASTERN	500	150.00	250.00
86	FROSTY MORNING	400	75.00	250.00
86	STONY RUN-RED FOX	750	225.00	400.00
87	WINTER QUARTET	400	75.00	200.00

WORLD ART EDITIONS

	MAGO			MAGO
82	DEPOSITION	300	325.00	325.00
82	SIPARIO	300	325.00	325.00
	F. MASSERIA			**MASSERIA**
80	EDUARDO	300	275.00	2700.00
80	FIRST KISS	300	375.00	2200.00
80	NINA	300	325.00	1950.00
80	ROSANNA	300	257.00	3200.00
81	ELEANOR	300	375.00	1900.00
81	ELISA WITH FLOWER	300	325.00	2200.00
81	FIRST FLOWER	300	325.00	2200.00
81	JESSICA	300	375.00	2300.00
81	JULIE	300	375.00	950.00
81	SELENE	300	325.00	2200.00
81	SOLANGE	300	325.00	2200.00
81	SUSAN SEWING	300	375.00	2500.00
82	AMY	300	425.00	720.00
82	JAMIE	300	425.00	750.00
82	JILL	300	425.00	750.00
82	JODIE	300	425.00	950.00
82	JUDITH	300	425.00	750.00
82	ROBIN	300	425.00	975.00
82	YASMIN	300	425.00	720.00
82	YVETTE	300	425.00	620.00
83	ANTONIO	300	450.00	1100.00
83	TARA	300	450.00	1100.00
84	BETTINA	250	550.00	700.00
84	CHRISTOPHER	300	450.00	700.00
84	MEMOIRS	300	450.00	700.00
84	PETER	950	395.00	495.00
84	REGINA	950	395.00	495.00
84	VINCENTE	360	550.00	1000.00
85	CHRISTINA	300	500.00	700.00
85	JORGITO	300	500.00	700.00
85	MARQUERITA	950	495.00	495.00
85	TO CATCH A BUTTERFLY	950	495.00	495.00

Steins

Ken Armke

Where contemporary steins are concerned, activity in the secondary market continues to center around the Anheuser-Busch issues. Rarities and steins from 1975-90 are actively and ardently sought after, along with special items. The *Bald Eagle* stein (CS 106), available for $24.95 when issued in 1989, now trades regularly in the $250 to $315 range. The 1988 *Classic I* (CS93), originally priced at $34.95, currently brings $135 to $170. The original *Bud Man* stein (CS1) first sold in 1975, enjoys strong demand at about $350 to $450— plus another $25 or so if found with the solid instead of hollow head.

The 1995 introduction of the Anheuser-Busch Collectors Club might lead to a new round of secondary market price increases once the club concept catches on with A-B collectors. This has been the trend in other collectible lines, including Swarovski and Armani, to name two of relatively recent vintage.

Look for the first Anheuser-Busch Collectors Club redemption stein, *Brew House Clock Tower*, to be a real sleeper in the secondary market of the future. Generally, this type of situation in a proven collectibles line is good news for those who get in on the ground floor. However, it's bad news for those who must later fork out big dollars to backtrack in succeeding years to fill a collection of club exclusives.

Within the United States, the demand for steins seems to center in three areas—the licensed, commissioned steins; the traditional German steins; and antique steins. M. Cornell Importers reports strong demand for its licensed products—especially steins depicting Coca-Cola—and steady demand for traditional German steins. Opa's Haus Inc. (OHI), which specializes in wildlife steins designed in the United States and produced in Germany, notes continued interest in these issues in both the primary *and* secondary markets.

KEN ARMKE SR. is president of Opa's Haus Inc. (OHI), a leading importer and producer of collectible steins. As a nationally recognized authority on beer steins, Armke oversees OHI retail and wholesale operations including secondary market sales.

YR NAME	LIMIT	ISSUE	QUOTE

STEINS

ANHEUSER-BUSCH INC.

* *

YR	NAME	LIMIT	ISSUE	QUOTE
		'92 OLYMPIC TEAM COLL. ED. SERIES		
92	1992 SUMMER OLYMPIC CS163	25,000	85.00	85.00
92	1992 U.S. OLYMPIC CS168	50,000	16.00	19.00
* *		**A & EAGLE HISTORICAL TRADEMARK SERIES**		
93	THE 1890 EDITION, CS218	RT	24.00	24.00
94	THE 1890 EDITION, CS219	RT	24.00	40.00
94	THE 1900 EDITION, CS238	20,000	28.00	28.00
93	THE 1872 EDITION, CS191	RT	22.00	45.00
93	THE 1872 EDITION, CS201	RT	31.00	45.00
94	A & EAGLE TRADEMARK III CS238	30,000	28.00	28.00
94	A & EAGLE TRADEMARK III CS240	20,000	25.00	25.00
* *		**ANHEUSER-BUSCH FOUNDER SERIES**		
93	ADOPHUS BUSCH CS216	10,000	180.00	180.00
94	AUGUST A. BUSCH, SR CS229	10,000	220.00	220.00
* *		**ARCHIVES COLLECTOR SERIES**		
92	1893 COLUMBIAN EXPOSITION CS169	75,000	35.00	35.00
92	GANYMEDE CS190	75,000	35.00	35.00
94	BUDWEISER'S GREATEST TRIUMPH CS222	75,000	35.00	35.00
* *		**BASEBALL MITT GIFTWARE**		
95	YOU'RE OUT CS244	OP	18.00	18.00
P. FORD		**BIRDS OF PREY SERIES**		
91	AMERICAN BALD EAGLE CS164	25,000	125.00	125.00
92	PEREGRINE FALCON CS183	25,000	125.00	125.00
94	OSPREY CS212	25,000	135.00	135.00
95	GREAT HORNED OWL CS264	25,000	137.00	137.00
* *		**BUD LABEL SERIES**		
89	BUDWEISER LABEL CS101	OP	14.00	14.00
90	ANTIQUE LABEL II CS127	RT	14.00	16.00
90	BOTTLED BEER III CS136	OP	15.00	15.00
H. DROOG		**BUDWEISER MILITARY SERIES**		
94	ARMY CS224	OP	19.00	19.00
94	AIR FORCE CS228	OP	19.00	19.00
95	BUDWEISER SALUTES THE NAVY CS243	OP	19.50	19.50
H. DROOG		**BUDWEISER RACING SERIES**		
93	BUDWEISER RACING TEAM CS194	OP	19.00	19.00
92	BUDWEISER RACING-ELLIOTT/JOHNSON CS3553	RT	19.00	19.00-45.00
D. LANGENECKERT		**CIVIL WAR SERIES**		
92	GENERAL GRANT CS181	25,000	150.00	150.00
93	GENERAL ROBERT E. LEE CS188	25,000	150.00	150.00
93	PRESIDENT ABRAHAM LINCOLN CS189	25,000	150.00	150.00
*		**CLASSIC SERIES**		
88	1ST EDITION CS93	RT	34.95	135.00-170.00
89	2ND EDITION CS104	RT	54.95	100.00-125.00
90	3RD EDITION CS113	RT	*	75.00-100.00
91	4TH EDITION CS130	25,000	75.00	60.00-75.00
88	1ST EDITION CS93	RT	34.95	135.00-170.00
89	2MD EDITION CS104	RT	54.95	95.00-110.00
90	3RD EDITION CS113	RT	65.00	60.00-75.00
91	4TH EDITION CS130	RT	75.00	40.00-75.00
*		**CLYDESDALES HOLIDAY SERIES**		
80	1ST HOLIDAY CS19	RT	9.95	70.00-90.00
81	2ND HOLIDAY CS50	RT	9.95	165.00-210.00
82	3RD HOLIDAY CS57 (50TH ANNIVERSARY)	RT	9.95	60.00-75.00
83	4TH HOLIDAY CS58	RT	9.95	25.00-32.00
84	5TH HOLIDAY CS62	RT	9.95	20.00-35.00
85	6TH HOLIDAY CS63	RT	9.95	20.00-35.00
86	7TH HOLIDAY CS66	RT	9.95	20.00-35.00
87	8TH HOLIDAY CS70	RT	9.95	20.00-35.00
88	9TH HOLIDAY CS88	RT	9.95	15.00-25.00
89	10TH HOLIDAY CS89	RT	12.95	15.00-25.00
76	BUDWEISER CHAMPION CLYDESDALES CS19A	RT	*	135.00-300.00
80	1ST HOLIDAY CS19	RT	9.95	95.00-125.00
81	2ND HOLIDAY CS50	RT	9.95	190.00-250.00
82	3RD HOLIDAY CS57 50TH ANNIVERSARY	RT	9.95	65.00-95.00
83	4TH HOLIDAY CS58	RT	9.95	40.00
84	5TH HOLIDAY CS62	RT	9.95	20.00
85	6TH HOLIDAY CS63	RT	9.95	20.00
86	7TH HOLIDAY CS66	RT	9.95	25.00-40.00
88	9TH HOLIDAY CS88	RT	9.95	13.00-20.00
89	10TH HOLIDAY CS89	RT	12.95	13.00-20.00
*		**CLYDESDALES SERIES**		
87	EIGHT HORSE HITCH CS74	RT	9.95	20.00-25.00

YR	NAME	LIMIT	ISSUE	QUOTE
88	MARE & FOAL CS90	RT	11.50	13.00-20.00
89	PARADE DRESS CS99	RT	11.50	13.00-20.00
91	TRAINING HITCH CS131	OP	13.00	20.00-25.00
92	CLYDESDALES ON PARADE CS161	OP	16.00	15.00-20.00
81	TRAINING HITCH CS131	RT	13.00	11.00-25.00
87	EIGHT HORSE HITCH CS74	RT	9.95	20.00-25.00
88	MARE & FOAL CS90	RT	11.50	20.00-25.00
89	PARADE DRESS CS99	RT	11.50	45.00
92	CLYDESDALES ON PARADE CS161	RT	16.00	16.00-25.00
94	PROUD AND FREE CS223	OP	17.00	17.00

J. TULL

COLLECTOR EDITION

| 94 | BUDWEISER WORLD CUP CS230 | 25,000 | 40.00 | 40.00 |

* *

CYYDESDALES HOLIDAY SERIES

| 87 | 8TH HOLIDAY CS70 | RT | 9.95 | 13.00-25.00 |

* *

DISCOVER AMERICA SERIES

90	NINA CS107	100,000	40.00	40.00
91	PINTA CS129	100,000	40.00	40.00
92	SANTA MARIA CS138	100,000	40.00	40.00

*

ENDANGERED SPECIES SERIES

89	BALD EAGLE CS106	RT	24.95	250.00-315.00
90	ASIAN TIGER CS126	100,000	27.50	45.00-57.00
91	AFRICAN ELEPHANT CS135	100,000	29.00	25.00-30.00
89	BALD EAGLE CS106	RT	24.95	250.00
90	ASIAN TIGER CS126	RT	27.50	35.00-60.00
91	AFRICAN ELEPHANT CS135	100,000	29.00	29.00
92	1992 RODEO CS184	OP	18.00	25.00
93	BUD MAN CHARACTER CS213	OP	45.00	45.00
94	BUDWEISER GOLF BAG CS225	OP	16.00	16.00
94	WALKING TALL BUDWEISER COWBOY BOOT CS251	OP	17.50	17.50
92	GIANT PANDA CS173	100,000	29.00	29.00
92	GRIZZLY CS199	100,000	29.50	29.50
94	GRAY WOLF CS226	100,000	29.50	29.50

* *

HERITAGE SERIES

91	AFTER THE HUNT CS155	25,000	100.00	100.00
90	BERNINGHAUS CS105	RT	75.00	40.00-75.00
92	CHERUB CS182	25,000	100.00	100.00

*

HISTORICAL LANDMARK SERIES

86	BREW HOUSE CS67	RT	19.95	25.00-125.00
87	STABLES CS73	100,000	19.95	25.00
88	GRANT CABIN CS83	RT	19.95	25.00
88	OLD SCHOOL HOUSE CS84	100,000	19.95	25.00
86	BREW HORSE CS67	RT	19.95	30.00-45.00
87	STABLES CS73	RT	19.95	25.00-35.00
88	GRANT CABIN CS83	RT	19.95	25.00-40.00
88	OLD SCHOOL HOUSE CS84	RT	19.95	25.00-35.00

*

HORSESHOE SERIES

86	HORSESHOE CS68	RT	14.95	35.00-44.00
86	HORSESHOE CS77	RT	16.00	35.00-44.00
87	HORSEHEAD CS76	RT	16.00	30.00-38.00
87	HORSEHEAD CS78	RT	14.95	50.00
88	HARNESS CS94	RT	16.00	50.00
86	HORSESHOE CS68	RT	14.95	40.00-75.00
86	HORSESHOE CS77	RT	16.00	40.00-75.00
87	HORSEHEAD CS76	RT	16.00	30.00-50.00
87	HORSEHEAD CS78	RT	14.95	60.00-75.00
88	HARNESS CS94	RT	16.00	50.00-80.00

L. FREEMAN

HUNTER'S COMPANION SERIES

93	LABRADOR RETRIEVER CS195	50,000	32.50	32.50
94	THE SETTER CS205	50,000	32.50	32.50
95	THE GOLDEN RETRIEVER CS248	50,000	34.00	34.00

*

LIMITED EDITION SERIES

85	BREWING & FERMENTING CS64	RT	29.95	125.00-175.00
86	AGING & COOPERAGE CS65	RT	29.95	40.00-50.00
87	TRANSPORTATION CS71	RT	29.95	40.00-50.00
88	TAVERNS & PUBLIC HOUSES CS75	100,000	29.95	30.00-40.00
89	FESTIVAL SCENE CS98	100,000	34.95	30.00-40.00

* *

LIMITED EDITION SERIES I

| 85 | BREWING & FERMENTING CS64 | RT | 29.95 | 175.00-200.00 |

* *

LIMITED EDITION SERIES II

| 86 | AGING & COOPERAGE CS65 | RT | 29.95 | 45.00-75.00 |

* *

LIMITED EDITION SERIES III

| 87 | TRANSPORTATION CS71 | RT | 29.95 | 30.00-50.00 |

* *

LIMITED EDITION SERIES IV

| 88 | TAVERNS & PUBLIC HOUSES CS75 | RT | 29.95 | 25.00-35.00 |

* *

LIMITED EDITION SERIES V

| 89 | FESTIVAL SCENE CS98 | RT | 34.95 | 25.00-35.00 |

The 1992 U.S. Olympic Team is honored in this stein by Anheuser-Busch.

The thrill of victory is celebrated in this 1992 Summer Olympics stein by Anheuser-Busch.

Anheuser-Busch reminds collectors that the Giant Panda is one of many endangered species.

Anheuser-Busch commemorates the 1893 Columbian Exposition.

YR	NAME	LIMIT	ISSUE	QUOTE
* *				**LOGO SERIES**
91	A & EAGLE CS148	OP	16.00	16.00
91	BUD DRY DRAFT CS156	OP	16.00	16.00
91	BUD LIGHT CS144	OP	16.00	16.00
91	BUDWEISER CS143	OP	16.00	16.00
91	BUSCH CS147	OP	16.00	16.00
91	MICHELOB CS145	RT	16.00	16.00
91	MICHELOB DRY CS146	OP	16.00	16.00
B. KEMPER		**MARINE CONSERVATION SERIES**		
94	MANATEE CS203	25,000	33.50	33.50
* *				**OCTOBERFEST SERIES**
92	1992 OCTOBERFEST CS185	35,000	16.00	16.00
93	1993 OCTOBERFEST CS202	35,000	18.00	18.00
H. DROOG		**PREMIER COLLECTION**		
93	BILL ELLIOTT CS196	25,000	150.00	150.00
93	BILL ELLIOTT, SIGNATURE ED. CS196SE	1,500	295.00	295.00
* *				**SEA WORLD SERIES**
92	DOLPHIN CS187	22,500	90.00	90.00
92	KILLER WHALE CS186	25,000	100.00	100.00
*				**SPECIALTY STEINS**
75	A&EAGLE CS2	RT	*	150.00-190.00
75	A&EAGLE LIFFED CSL2	RT	*	250.00-350.00
75	BUD MAN CS1	RT	*	350.00-450.00
75	GERMAN OLYMPIA CS4	RT	*	50.00-65.00
75	GERMAN OLYMPIA LIDDED CSL6	RT	*	150.00-300.00
75	GERMAN PILIQUE CS5	RT	*	375.00-500.00
75	GERMAN PILIQUE LIDDED CSL5	RT	*	320.00-400.00
75	KATAKOME CS3	RT	*	175.00-225.00
75	KATAKOME LIDDED CSL3	RT	*	275.00-345.00
75	MINIATURE BAVARIAN CS7	RT	*	225.00-300.00
75	SENIOR GRANDE CS6	RT	*	550.00-700.00
75	SENIOR GRANDE LIDDED CSL4	RT	*	475.00-650.00
76	A&EAGLE BARREL CS26	RT	*	120.00-150.00
76	A&EAGLE LIDDED CS28	RT	*	200.00-250.00
76	AMERICANA CS17	RT	*	415.00-520.00
76	BLUE DELFT CS11	RT	*	310.00-400.00
76	BUDWEISER CENTENNIAL CS13	RT	*	250.00-325.00
76	BUDWEISER CENTENNIAL CS22	RT	*	200.00-250.00
76	BUDWEISER CENTENNIAL LIDDED CSL7	RT	*	320.00-400.00
76	BUDWEISER LABEL CS18	RT	*	350.00-450.00
76	CLYDESDALES CS12	RT	*	290.00-375.00
76	CLYDESDALES DECANTER CS33	RT	*	1.00-1200.00
76	CLYDESDALES GRANTS FARM CS15	RT	*	250.00-300.00
76	CLYDESDALES HOFBRAU LIDDED CSL9	RT	*	225.00-325.00
76	CLYDESDALES LIDDED CS29	RT	*	160.00-200.00
76	CORACAO DECANTER SET CS31	RT	*	560.00-750.00
76	GERMAN CITIES CS16	RT	*	375.00-470.00
76	GERMAN WINE SET CS32	RT	*	400.00-500.00
76	MICHELOB CS27	RT	*	175.00-250.00
76	NATURAL LIGHT CS9	RT	*	550.00-700.00
76	ST. LOUIS DECANTER SET CS38	RT	*	1000.00-1250.00
76	U.S. BICENTENNIAL CS14	RT	*	250.00-325.00
76	U.S. BICENTENNIAL LIDDED CSL8	RT	*	490.00-600.00
77	A&EAGLE CS24	RT	*	450.00
77	BUDWEISER GIRL CS21	RT	*	500.00
78	BUSCH GARDENS CS41	RT	*	210.00-265.00
80	BUDWEISER CHICAGO SKYLINE CS40	RT	*	85.00-105.00
80	BUDWEISER LABEL CS46	RT	*	100.00-125.00
80	BUDWEISER LADIES CS20 (4 ASSORTED)	RT	*	2.00-2500.00
80	BUSCH LABEL CS44	RT	*	180.00-225.00
80	MICHELOB LABEL CS45	RT	*	60.00-75.00
80	NATURAL LIGHT LABEL CS43	RT	*	180.00-225.00
80	OKTOBERFEST-THE OLD COUNTRY CS42	RT	*	190.00-240.00
80	WURZBURGER HOFBRAU CS39	RT	*	350.00-450.00
81	BUDWEISER CALIFORNIA CS56	RT	*	45.00-57.00
81	BUDWEISER CHICAGOLAND CS51	RT	*	40.00-50.00
81	BUDWEISER TEXAS CS52	RT	*	50.00-63.00
83	BUD LIGHT BARON CS61	RT	*	35.00-45.00
83	BUDWEISER SAN FRANCISCO CS59	RT	*	150.00-190.00
84	BUDWEISER OLYMPIC GAMES CS60	RT	*	25.00-32.00
87	KING COBRA CS80	RT	*	150.00
87	SANTA CLAUS CS79	RT	*	60.00-75.00
87	WINTER OLYMPIC GAMES LIDDED CS81	RT	49.95	65.00-90.00
88	BUDWEISER SUMMER OLYMPIC GAMES CS92	RT	54.95	20.00
88	BUDWEISER WINTER OLYMPIC GAMES CS85	RT	24.95	20.00-27.00
88	BUDWEISER/FIELD & STREAM SET CS95	RT	69.95	200.00-300.00

YR	NAME	LIMIT	ISSUE	QUOTE
88	SUMMER OLYMPIC GAMES LIDDED CS91	RT	54.95	50.00-60.00
89	BUD MAN CS100	RT	29.95	40.00-50.00
90	BASEBALL CARDINAL STEIN CS125	RT	30.00	30.00-38.00
91	BEVO FOX STEIN CS160	RT	250.00	175.00-250.00
76	CANTEEN DECANTER SET CS36	RT	*	
76	HOLANDA BLUE DECANTER SET CS35	RT	*	750.00
76	HOLANDA BROWN DECANTER SET CS34	RT	*	275.00
76	ST. LOUIS DECANTER CS37	RT	*	400.00
* *			**SPORTS HISTORY SERIES**	
90	BASEBALL, AM.'S FAVORITE PASTIME CS124	RT	20.00	20.00-25.00
90	FOOTBALL,GRIDIRON LEGACY CS128	RT	20.00	20.00-22.00
91	AUTO RACING,CHASING/CHECKERED FLAG CS132	100,000	22.00	22.00
91	BASKETBALL,HEROES.HARDWOOD CS134	100,000	22.00	22.00
92	GOLF, PAR FOR THE COURSE CS165	100,000	22.00	22.00
93	HOCKEY,CENTER ICE CS209	100,000	22.00	22.00
* *			**SPORTS LEGEND SERIES**	
91	1992 WINTER OLYMPIC CS162	25,000	85.00	85.00
91	BABE RUTH CS142	50,000	85.00	85.00
92	JIM THORPE CS171	50,000	85.00	85.00
93	JOE LOUIS CS206	50,000	85.00	85.00
* *			**ST. PATRICK'S DAY SERIES**	
91	1991 ST. PATRICK'S DAY CS109	RT	15.00	40.00-45.00
92	1992 ST. PATRICK'S DAY CS166	100,000	15.00	15.00
93	1993 ST. PATRICK'S DAY CS193	RT	15.30	20.00-25.00
94	LUCK O' THE IRISH CS210	OP	18.00	18.00
95	1995 ST. PATRICK'S DAY CS242	OP	19.00	19.00
* *			**WHOLESALER HOLIDAY SERIES**	
90	AN AMERICAN TRADITION CS112	RT	13.50	14.50
90	AN AMERICAN TRADITION CS112-SE	RT	50.00	50.00-80.00
91	THE SEASON'S BEST CS133	RT	14.50	13.00-15.00
91	THE SEASON'S BEST CS133-SE	RT	50.00	25.00-50.00
92	THE PERFECT CHRISTMAS CS167	OP	14.50	14.50
92	THE PERFECT CHRISTMAS CS167-SE	OP	50.00	25.00
93	SPECIAL DELIVERY CS192	RT	15.00	20.00-25.00
93	SPECIAL DELIVERY CS192-SE	RT	60.00	100.00-125.00
94	HOMETOWN HOLIDAY CS211	OP	14.00	14.00
94	HOMETOWN HOLIDAY CS211-SE	10,000	65.00	65.00

M. CORNELL IMPORTERS

*			**CORNELL STEINS**	
86	JOIN US! GEMUETLICHKEIT 3766	10,000	30.00	40.00
87	A TOAST 3963	10,000	87.50	113.00
87	ALPINE FLOWER 4047	5000	90.00	100.00
87	BEERWAGON 6280	4000	110.00	133.00
87	BERLIN CITY 3788	5000	130.00	159.00
87	BERLIN CITY 3789	5000	87.50	113.00
87	CLUB HUNT 4402	8000	87.00	106.00
87	ELK 6340	5000	99.50	120.00
87	ELK UNLIDDED 6342	5000	30.00	37.50
87	FARMER & PLOW 3423	10,000	87.50	113.00
87	FARMER & PLOW UNLIDDED 3424	10,000	35.00	49.00
87	GOLDEN HOPS & MALT 6279	4000	159.00	219.00
87	GRIZZLY BEAR 6331	5000	99.50	120.00
87	GRIZZLY BEAR UNLIDDED 6333	5000	30.00	37.50
87	HAPPY DWARF 6282	4000	106.00	137.00
87	HEIDELBERG 6278	4000	100.00	125.00
87	HOT AIR BALLOON	5000	100.00	130.00
87	JOIN US! GEMUETLICHKEIT 3767	10,000	78.00	99.50
87	JOIN US! GEMUETLICHKEIT 3768	10,000	125.00	149.50
87	MAY STROLL 3770	10,000	79.00	99.50
87	MAY STROLL UNLIDDED 3769	10,000	30.00	40.00
87	MOOSE 6337	5000	99.50	120.00
87	MOOSE UNLIDDED 6339	5000	99.50	120.00
87	WEDDING PARADE 3776	10,000	85.00	104.00
87	WEDDING PARADE UNLIDDED 3775	10,000	35.00	48.00
87	WHITE TAIL DEER 6343	5000	99.50	120.00
87	WHITE TAIL DEER UNLIDDED 6345	5000	30.00	37.50
87	ZITHER PLAYER 3773	10,000	85.00	106.00
87	ZITHER PLAYER UNLIDDED 3772	10,000	35.00	48.00
88	BEER BARREL 6285	4000	130.00	137.00
88	FATHER & SON 6291	4000	115.00	135.00
88	PROLETARIAN 3970	5000	100.00	118.00
88	ROYAL KING LUDWIG 6287	4000	194.00	197.50
88	SUMMER 6286	4000	80.00	89.00
88	TYROLEAN 4413	9000	80.00	84.00
89	AHRENS-FOX FIRE ENGINE 3719	10,000	119.00	157.50
89	AHRENS-FOX FIRE ENGINE UNLIDDED 3720	10,000	35.00	44.00

YR	NAME	LIMIT	ISSUE	QUOTE
89	APOSTLE 6298	2000	239.00	290.00
89	BICYCLIST 4723	5000	68.00	86.00
89	CAROUSEL 6467	5000	159.00	190.00
89	CAROUSEL MUSICAL 6468	5000	184.00	220.00
89	COOPER (BARREL MAKER)	2000	110.00	135.00
89	FIREFIGHTER 4765	5000	68.00	86.00
89	GAMBRINUS 3792	10,000	125.00	130.00
89	GAMBRINUS UNLIDDED 3793	10,000	40.00	50.00
89	MUNICH 3790	10,000	115.00	190.00
89	PROLETARIAN UNLIDDED 3972	5000	45.00	60.00
89	RED BARON 6295	4000	100.00	130.00
89	SINGER 4768	5000	68.00	86.00
89	SINGER UNLIDDED 4767	5000	38.00	45.00
89	ST. GEORGE 4409	6000	150.00	165.00
89	VILLAGE BLACKSMITH 6308	2000	110.00	135.00
89	WEDDING DANCE JUG 4048	1500	239.00	299.00
89	WEIHNACHTEN 3716	10,000	150.00	185.00
89	WEIHNACHTEN 3717	10,000	110.00	139.00
90	BERLIN WALL 6320	2000	100.00	110.00
90	BICYCLIST 6325	4000	120.00	130.00
90	CLIPPER 3814	10,000	168.00	185.00
90	CLIPPER UNLIDDED 3811	10,000	47.00	50.00
90	FIREFIGHTER 6327	4000	120.00	135.00
90	FRIEDOLIN 3785	10,000	99.00	109.50
90	FRIEDOLIN UNLIDDED 3784	10,000	47.00	50.00
90	GOLFER 3820	10,000	168.00	185.00
90	GOLFER UNLIDDED 3816	10,000	47.00	50.00
90	GRENZAU CASTLE 4590	12,000	119.50	131.50
90	LORELEY 3782	10,000	95.00	104.00
90	LORELEY UNLIDDED 3781	10,000	42.50	47.00
90	MUNICH BIER-WAGON 6326	4000	150.00	165.00
90	NAS GRIZZLY BEAR 4451	20,000	175.00	193.00
90	NAS HUMPBACK WHALE	20,000	175.00	193.00
90	NAS PEREGRINE FALCON 4452	20,000	175.00	193.00
90	NAS WOOD DUCK 4453	20,000	175.00	193.00
90	NOAH'S ARK 6469	5000	129.00	150.00
90	SEPPL 3779	10,000	95.00	104.00
90	SEPPL UNLIDDED 3778	10,000	42.50	47.00
90	STONEWARE NUTCRACKER 6473	5000	139.00	150.00
90	TURNVATER JAHN 3797	10,000	137.50	150.00
90	TURNVATER JAHN UNLIDDED 3796	10,000	95.00	104.00
90	WIESBADEN 3794	2000	125.00	139.50
90	WIESBADEN 3795	2000	100.00	115.00
87	MALLARD 4041	4000	100.00	130.00
87	WILD BOAR 4044	4000	100.00	130.00
87	BIBLE 3870	10,000	80.00	99.00
87	BIBLE UNLIDDED 3869	10,000	30.00	42.00
87	CENTURIO 3861	10,000	73.50	88.00
87	CENTURIO UNLIDDED 3860	10,000	30.00	42.00
87	CHERUSKAN 3873	10,000	109.00	148.00
87	CHERUSKAN UNLIDDED 3872	10,000	40.00	55.00
87	DR. FAUST 3851	10,000	80.00	98.00
87	DR. FAUST 3852	10,000	30.00	40.00
87	MINUET 3876	10,000	79.00	108.00
87	MINUET UNLIDDED 3875	10,000	30.00	42.00
87	PATRIZIER 3864	10,000	75.00	88.00
87	PATRIZIER UNLIDDED 3863	10,000	30.00	42.00
87	THE BICYCLISTS 3858	10,000	80.00	100.00
87	THE BICYCLISTS UNLIDDED 3857	10,000	30.00	42.00
87	THE CARDPLAYER 3867	10,000	190.00	220.00
87	THE CARDPLAYER UNLIDDED 3868	10,000	35.00	47.00
88	DRAGON SLAYER 3980	10,000	165.00	197.50
88	DRAGON SLAYER BEER CHALICE 3982	10,000	79.00	105.00
88	ROYALTY 3878	10,000	79.50	88.00
88	ROYALTY 3880	10,000	110.00	130.00
89	CRUSADER 3883	10,000	145.00	179.50
89	GENERAL TILLY TANKARD 3715	5000	379.50	440.00
89	ROYALTY 3887	10,000	65.00	75.00
89	ROYALTY UNLIDDED 3888	10,000	35.00	47.00
90	BABA YAGA 4993	5000	238.00	249.00
89	BALD EAGLE 3721	10,000	150.00	175.00
89	BALD EAGLE 3722	10,000	110.00	139.00
89	BALD EAGLE UNLIDDED 3723	10,000	40.00	48.00
89	DRAGON REGIMENTAL 4992	5000	199.00	249.00

Index

ORNAMENTS

PLATES

PRINTS

STEINS

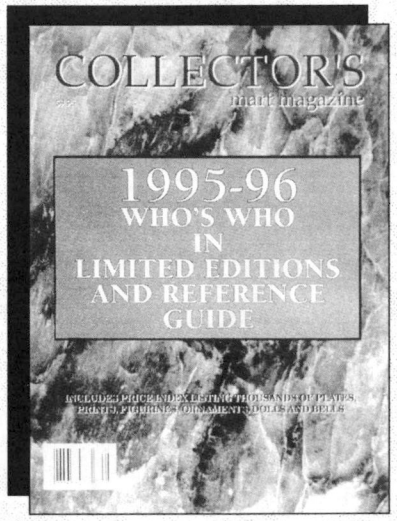

We are continually striving to bring you more accurate prices in our price guide. That's where you can help. If you have information on prices realized for limited edition collectibles, please send them to us so we can update our records.

Send prices to:

MARY SIEBER

700 E. State St.
Iola, WI 54990-0001

*Write For Our **Free** Catalog of Hobby and Collectibles Books and Periodicals.*